Pre-Calculus 12

Authors
Bruce McAskill, B.Sc., B.Ed., M.Ed., Ph.D.
Mathematics Consultant, Victoria, British Columbia

Wayne Watt, B.Sc., B.Ed., M.Ed.
Mathematics Consultant, Winnipeg, Manitoba

Eric Balzarini, B.Sc., B.Ed., M.Ed.
School District 35 (Langley), British Columbia

Blaise Johnson, B.Sc., B.Ed.
School District 45 (West Vancouver), British Columbia

Ron Kennedy, B.Ed.
Mathematics Consultant, Edmonton, Alberta

Terry Melnyk, B.Ed.
Edmonton Public Schools, Alberta

Chris Zarski, B.Ed., M.Ed.
Wetaskiwin Regional Division No. 11, Alberta

Contributing Author
Gail Poshtar, B.Ed.
Calgary Roman Catholic Separate School District, Alberta

Senior Program Consultants
Bruce McAskill, B.Sc., B.Ed., M.Ed., Ph.D.
Mathematics Consultant, Victoria, British Columbia

Wayne Watt, B.Sc., B.Ed., M.Ed.
Mathematics Consultant, Winnipeg, Manitoba

Assessment Consultant
Chris Zarski, B.Ed., M.Ed.
Wetaskiwin Regional Division No. 11, Alberta

Pedagogical Consultant
Scott Carlson, B.Ed., B. Sc.
Golden Hills School Division No. 75, Alberta

Aboriginal Consultant
Chun Ong, B.A., B.Ed.
Manitoba First Nations Education Resource Centre, Manitoba

Differentiated Instruction Consultant
Heather Granger
Prairie South School Division No. 210, Saskatchewan

Gifted and Career Consultant
Rick Wunderlich
School District 83 (North Okanagan/Shuswap), British Columbia

Math Processes Consultant
Reg Fogarty
School District 83 (North Okanagan/Shuswap), British Columbia

Technology Consultants
Ron Kennedy
Mathematics Consultant, Edmonton, Alberta

Ron Coleborn
School District 41 (Burnaby), British Columbia

Advisors
John Agnew, School District 63 (Saanich), British Columbia

Len Bonifacio, Edmonton Catholic Separate School District No. 7, Alberta

Katharine Borgen, School District 39 (Vancouver) and University of British Columbia, British Columbia

Renée Jackson, University of Alberta, Alberta

Gerald Krabbe, Calgary Board of Education, Alberta

Gail Poshtar, Calgary Roman Catholic Separate School District, Alberta

Harold Wardrop, Brentwood College School, Mill Bay (Independent), British Columbia

Francophone Advisors
Mario Chaput, Pembina Trails School Division, Manitoba

Luc Lerminiaux, Regina School Division No. 4, Saskatchewan

Inuit Advisor
Christine Purse, Mathematics Consultant, British Columbia

Métis Advisor
Greg King, Northern Lights School Division No. 69, Alberta

Technical Advisor
Darren Kuropatwa, Winnipeg School Division #1, Manitoba

McGraw-Hill Ryerson

Toronto   Montréal   Boston   Burr Ridge, IL   Dubuque, IA   Madison, WI   New York
San Francisco   St. Louis   Bangkok   Bogotá   Caracas   Kuala Lumpur   Lisbon   London
Madrid   Mexico City   Milan   New Delhi   Santiago   Seoul   Singapore   Sydney   Taipei

PROPERTY OF HARRY AINLAY HIGH SCHOOL

The McGraw·Hill Companies

COPIES OF THIS BOOK MAY BE OBTAINED BY CONTACTING:

McGraw-Hill Ryerson Ltd.

WEB SITE:
http://www.mcgrawhill.ca

E-MAIL:
orders@mcgrawhill.ca

TOLL-FREE FAX:
1-800-463-5885

TOLL-FREE CALL:
1-800-565-5758

OR BY MAILING YOUR ORDER TO:
McGraw-Hill Ryerson
Order Department
300 Water Street
Whitby, ON L1N 9B6

Please quote the ISBN and title when placing your order.

McGraw-Hill Ryerson
Pre-Calculus 12

Copyright © 2012, McGraw-Hill Ryerson Limited, a Subsidiary of The McGraw-Hill Companies. All rights reserved. No part of this publication may be reproduced or transmitted in any form or by any means, or stored in a data base or retrieval system, without the prior written permission of McGraw-Hill Ryerson Limited, or, in the case of photocopying or other reprographic copying, a licence from The Canadian Copyright Licensing Agency (Access Copyright). For an Access Copyright licence, visit *www.accesscopyright.ca* or call toll free to 1-800-893-5777.

ISBN-13: 978-0-07-073872-0
ISBN-10: 0-07-073872-6

http://www.mcgrawhill.ca

2 3 4 5 6 7 8 9 TCP 1 9 8 7 6 5 4 3 2

Printed and bound in Canada

Care has been taken to trace ownership of copyright material contained in this text. The publishers will gladly accept any information that will enable them to rectify any reference or credit in subsequent printings.

Microsoft® Excel is either a registered trademark or trademarks of Microsoft Corporation in the United States and/or other countries.

TI-84™ and TI-Nspire™ are registered trademarks of Texas Instruments.

The Geometer's Sketchpad®, Key Curriculum Press, 1150 65th Street, Emeryville, CA 94608, 1-800-995-MATH.

VICE-PRESIDENT, EDITORIAL: Beverley Buxton
MATHEMATICS PUBLISHER: Jean Ford
PROJECT MANAGER: Janice Dyer
DEVELOPMENTAL EDITORS: Maggie Cheverie, Jackie Lacoursiere, Jodi Rauch
MANAGER, EDITORIAL SERVICES: Crystal Shortt
SUPERVISING EDITOR: Jaime Smith
COPY EDITOR: Julie Cochrane
PHOTO RESEARCH & PERMISSIONS: Linda Tanaka
EDITORIAL ASSISTANT: Erin Hartley
EDITORIAL COORDINATION: Jennifer Keay
MANAGER, PRODUCTION SERVICES: Yolanda Pigden
PRODUCTION COORDINATOR: Scott Morrison
INDEXER: Belle Wong
INTERIOR DESIGN: Pronk & Associates
COVER DESIGN: Michelle Losier
ART DIRECTION: Tom Dart, First Folio Resource Group Inc.
ELECTRONIC PAGE MAKE-UP: Tom Dart, Kim Hutchinson, First Folio Resource Group Inc.
COVER IMAGE: Courtesy of Ocean/Corbis

Acknowledgements

There are many students, teachers, and administrators who the publisher, authors, and consultants of *Pre-Calculus 12* wish to thank for their thoughtful comments and creative suggestions about what would work best in their classrooms. Their input and assistance have been invaluable in making sure that the Student Resource and its related Teacher's Resource meet the needs of students and teachers who work within the Western and Northern Canadian Protocol Common Curriculum Framework.

Reviewers

Kristi Allen
Wetaskiwin Regional Public Schools
Alberta

Karen Bedard
School District 22 (Vernon)
British Columbia

Robert Burzminski
Medicine Hat Catholic Board of Education
Alberta

Tracy Connell
School District 57 (Prince George)
British Columbia

Janis Crighton
Lethbridge School District No. 51
Alberta

Cynthia L. Danyluk
Light of Christ Catholic School Division No. 16
Saskatchewan

Kelvin Dueck
School District 42 (Maple Ridge/Pitt Meadows)
British Columbia

Pat Forsyth
Elk Island Public Schools
Alberta

Barbara Gajdos
Calgary Catholic School District
Alberta

Murray D. Henry
Prince Albert Catholic School Board No. 6
Saskatchewan

Christopher Hunter
Curriculum and Instructional Services Centre
British Columbia

Jane Koleba
School District 61 (Greater Victoria)
British Columbia

R. Paul Ledet
School District 63 (Saanich)
British Columbia

Amos Lee
School District 41 (Burnaby)
British Columbia

Jay Lorenzen
Horizon School District No. 205
Saskatchewan

Deanna Matthews
Edmonton Public Schools
Alberta

Dick McDougall
Calgary Catholic School District
Alberta

Yasuko Nitta
School District 38 (Richmond)
British Columbia

Catherine Ramsay
River East Transcona School Division
Manitoba

Dixie Sillito
Prairie Rose School Division No. 8
Alberta

Jill Taylor
Fort McMurray Public School District
Alberta

John J. Verhagen
Livingstone Range School Division No. 68
Alberta

Jimmy Wu
School District 36 (Surrey)
British Columbia

Contents

A Tour of Your Textbook vii

Unit 1 Transformations and Functions 2

Chapter 1 Function Transformations 4
1.1 Horizontal and Vertical Translations 6
1.2 Reflections and Stretches 16
1.3 Combining Transformations 32
1.4 Inverse of a Relation 44
Chapter 1 Review 56
Chapter 1 Practice Test 58

Chapter 2 Radical Functions 60
2.1 Radical Functions and Transformations 62
2.2 Square Root of a Function 78
2.3 Solving Radical Equations Graphically 90
Chapter 2 Review 99
Chapter 2 Practice Test 102

Chapter 3 Polynomial Functions 104
3.1 Characteristics of Polynomial Functions 106
3.2 The Remainder Theorem 118
3.3 The Factor Theorem 126
3.4 Equations and Graphs of Polynomial Functions 136
Chapter 3 Review 153
Chapter 3 Practice Test 155

Unit 1 Project Wrap-Up 157

Cumulative Review, Chapters 1–3 .. 158

Unit 1 Test 160

Unit 2 Trigonometry 162

Chapter 4 Trigonometry and the Unit Circle 164
4.1 Angles and Angle Measure 166
4.2 The Unit Circle 180
4.3 Trigonometric Ratios 191
4.4 Introduction to Trigonometric Equations 206
Chapter 4 Review 215
Chapter 4 Practice Test 218

Chapter 5 Trigonometric Functions and Graphs 220
5.1 Graphing Sine and Cosine Functions 222
5.2 Transformations of Sinusoidal Functions 238
5.3 The Tangent Function 256
5.4 Equations and Graphs of Trigonometric Functions 266
Chapter 5 Review 282
Chapter 5 Practice Test 286

Chapter 6 Trigonometric Identities 288
6.1 Reciprocal, Quotient, and Pythagorean Identities 290
6.2 Sum, Difference, and Double-Angle Identities 299
6.3 Proving Identities 309
6.4 Solving Trigonometric Equations Using Identities 316
Chapter 6 Review 322
Chapter 6 Practice Test 324

Unit 2 Project Wrap-Up 325

Cumulative Review, Chapters 4–6 .. 326

Unit 2 Test 328

Unit 3 Exponential and Logarithmic Functions 330

Chapter 7 Exponential Functions 332
- 7.1 Characteristics of Exponential Functions 334
- 7.2 Transformations of Exponential Functions 346
- 7.3 Solving Exponential Equations 358
- Chapter 7 Review 366
- Chapter 7 Practice Test 368

Chapter 8 Logarithmic Functions 370
- 8.1 Understanding Logarithms 372
- 8.2 Transformations of Logarithmic Functions 383
- 8.3 Laws of Logarithms 392
- 8.4 Logarithmic and Exponential Equations 404
- Chapter 8 Review 416
- Chapter 8 Practice Test 419

Unit 3 Project Wrap-Up 421
Cumulative Review, Chapters 7–8 422
Unit 3 Test 424

Unit 4 Equations and Functions 426

Chapter 9 Rational Functions 428
- 9.1 Exploring Rational Functions Using Transformations 430
- 9.2 Analysing Rational Functions 446
- 9.3 Connecting Graphs and Rational Equations 457
- Chapter 9 Review 468
- Chapter 9 Practice Test 470

Chapter 10 Function Operations 472
- 10.1 Sums and Differences of Functions 474
- 10.2 Products and Quotients of Functions 488
- 10.3 Composite Functions 499
- Chapter 10 Review 510
- Chapter 10 Practice Test 512

Chapter 11 Permutations, Combinations, and the Binomial Theorem 514
- 11.1 Permutations 516
- 11.2 Combinations 528
- 11.3 Binomial Theorem 537
- Chapter 11 Review 546
- Chapter 11 Practice Test 548

Unit 4 Project Wrap-Up 549
Cumulative Review, Chapters 9–11 550
Unit 4 Test 552

Answers 554
Glossary 638
Index 643
Credits 646

A Tour of Your Textbook

Unit Opener

Each unit begins with a two-page spread. The first page of the **Unit Opener** introduces what you will learn in the unit. The **Unit Project** is introduced on the second page. Each Unit Project helps you connect the math in the unit to real life using experiences that may interest you.

Project Corner boxes throughout the chapters help you gather information for your project. Some **Project Corner** boxes include questions to help you to begin thinking about and discussing your project.

The **Unit Projects** in Units 1, 3, and 4 provide an opportunity for you to choose a single **Project Wrap-Up** at the end of the unit.

The **Unit Project** in Unit 2 is designed for you to complete in pieces, chapter by chapter, throughout the unit. At the end of the unit, a **Project Wrap-Up** allows you to consolidate your work in a meaningful presentation.

Chapter Opener

Each chapter begins with a two-page spread that introduces you to what you will learn in the chapter.

The opener includes information about a career that uses the skills covered in the chapter. A Web Link allows you to learn more about this career and how it involves the mathematics you are learning.

Visuals on the chapter opener spread show other ways the skills and concepts from the chapter are used in daily life.

Three-Part Lesson

Each numbered section is organized in a three-part lesson: Investigate, Link the Ideas, and Check Your Understanding.

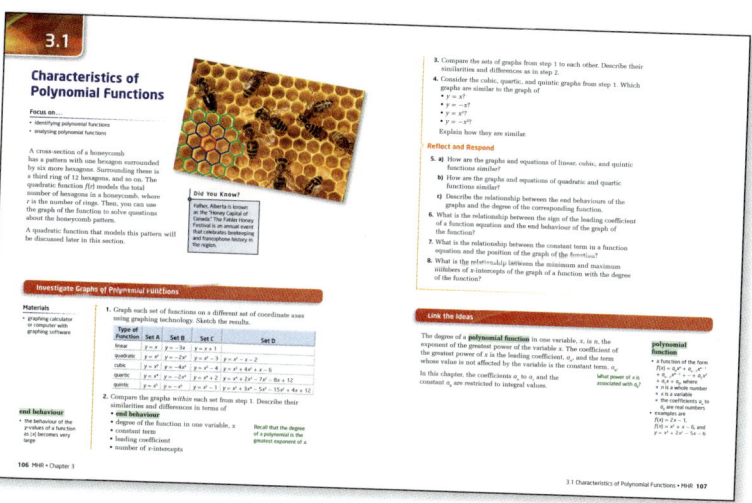

Investigate

- The **Investigate** consists of short steps often accompanied by illustrations. It is designed to help you build your own understanding of the new concept.

- The **Reflect and Respond** questions help you to analyse and communicate what you are learning and draw conclusions.

Link the Ideas

- The explanations in this section help you connect the concepts explored in the **Investigate** to the **Examples**.

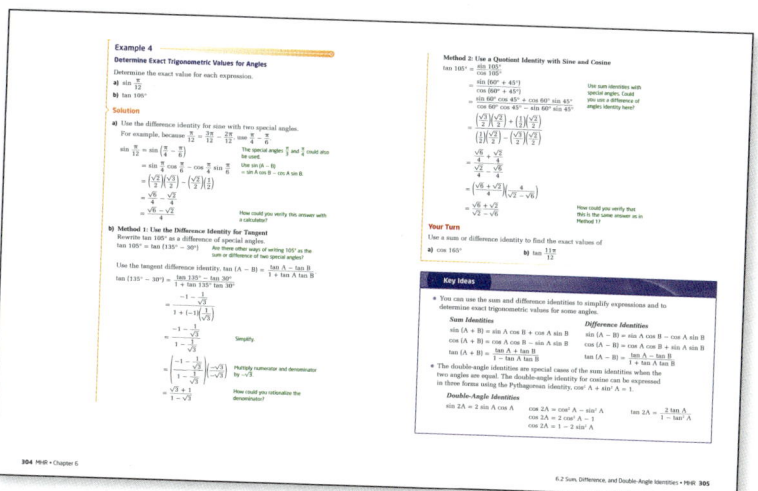

- The **Examples** and worked **Solutions** show how to use the concepts. The Examples include several tools to help you understand the work.
    - Words in green font help you think through the steps.
    - Different methods of solving the same problem are sometimes shown. One method may make more sense to you than the others. Or, you may develop another method that means more to you.

- Each Example is followed by a **Your Turn**. The Your Turn allows you to explore your understanding of the skills covered in the Example.

- After all the Examples are presented, the **Key Ideas** summarize the main new concepts.

A Tour of Your Textbook • MHR **vii**

Check Your Understanding

- **Practise:** These questions allow you to check your understanding of the concepts. You can often do the first few questions by checking the Link the Ideas notes or by following one of the worked Examples.

- **Apply:** These questions ask you to apply what you have learned to solve problems. You can choose your own methods of solving a variety of problem types.

- **Extend:** These questions may be more challenging. Many connect to other concepts or lessons. They also allow you to choose your own methods of solving a variety of problem types.

- **Create Connections:** These questions focus your thinking on the Key Ideas and also encourage communication. Many of these questions also connect to other subject areas or other topics within mathematics.

- **Mini-Labs**: These questions provide hands-on activities that encourage you to further explore the concept you are learning.

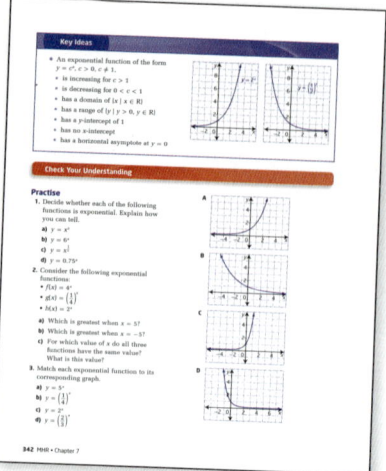

Other Features

Key Terms are listed on the Chapter Opener pages. You may already know the meaning of some of them. If not, watch for these terms the first time they are used in the chapter. The meaning is given in the margin. Many definitions include visuals that help clarify the term.

Some **Did You Know?** boxes provide additional information about the meaning of words that are not Key Terms. Other boxes contain interesting facts related to the math you are learning.

Opportunities are provided to use a variety of **Technology** tools. You can use technology to explore patterns and relationships, test predictions, and solve problems. A technology approach is usually provided as only one of a variety of approaches and tools to be used to help you develop your understanding.

Web Links provide Internet information related to some topics. Log on to www.mcgrawhill.ca/school/learningcentres and you will be able to link to recommended Web sites.

Key Terms
logarithmic function
logarithm
common logarithm
logarithmic equation

Did You Know?

The SI unit used to measure radioactivity is the becquerel (Bq), which is one particle emitted per second from a radioactive source. Commonly used multiples are kilobecquerel (kBq), for 10^3 Bq, and megabecquerel (MBq), for 10^6 Bq.

Web Link

To learn more about a career in radiology, go to www.mcgrawhill.ca/school/learningcentres and follow the links.

A **Chapter Review** and a **Practice Test** appear at the end of each chapter. The review is organized by section number so you can look back if you need help with a question. The test includes multiple choice, short answer, and extended response questions.

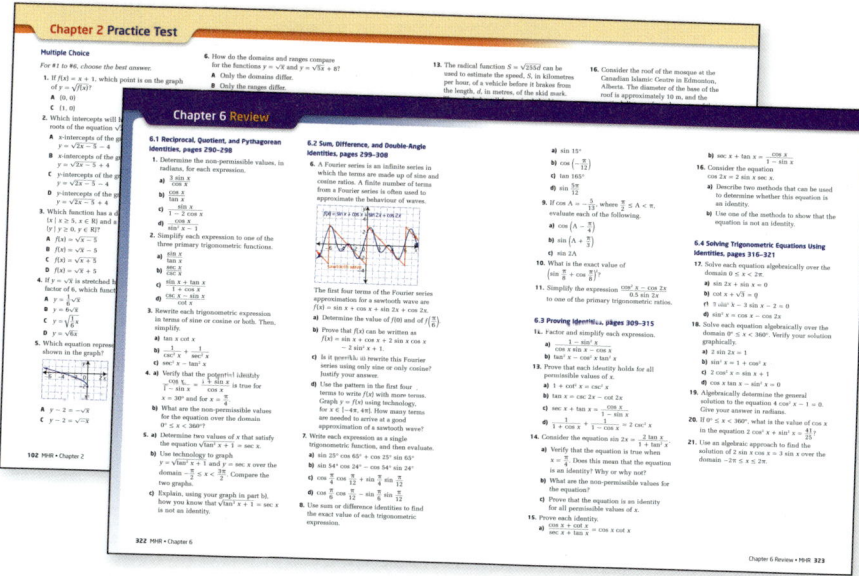

A **Cumulative Review** and a **Unit Test** appear at the end of each unit. The review is organized by chapter. The test includes multiple choice, numerical response, and written response questions.

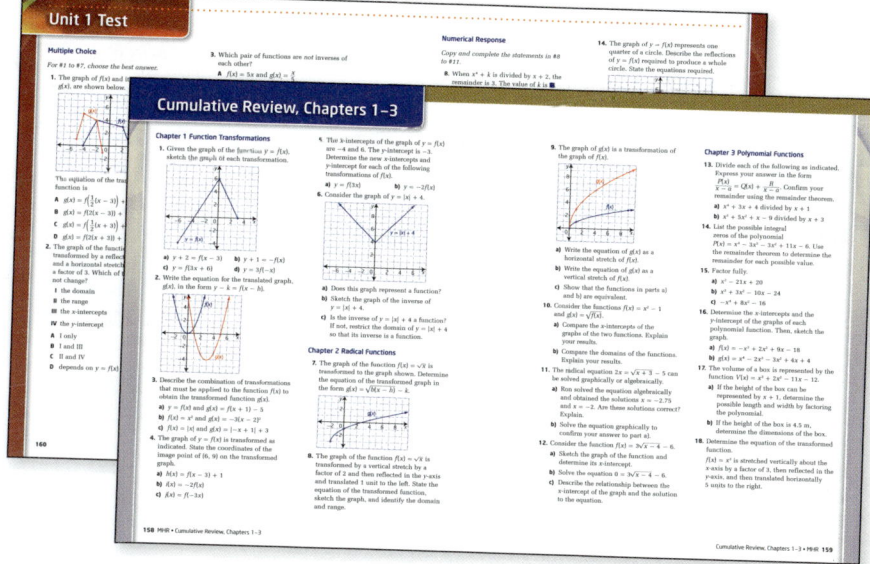

Answers are provided for the Practise, Apply, Extend, Create Connections, Chapter Review, Practice Test, Cumulative Review, and Unit Test questions. Sample answers are provided for questions that have a variety of possible answers or that involve communication. If you need help with a question like this, read the sample and then try to give an alternative response.

Refer to the illustrated **Glossary** at the back of the student resource if you need to check the exact meaning of mathematical terms.

If you want to find a particular math topic in *Pre-Calculus 12*, look it up in the **Index**, which is at the back of the student resource. The index provides page references that may help you review that topic.

Unit 1

Transformations and Functions

Functions help you make sense of the world around you. Many ordinary measuring devices are based on mathematical functions:

- Car odometer: The odometer reading is a function of the number of rotations of the car's transmission drive shaft.
- Display on a barcode reader: When the screen displays the data about the object, the reader performs an inverse function by decoding the barcode image.

Many natural occurrences can be modelled by mathematical functions:

- Ripples created by a water droplet in a pond: You can model the area spanned by the ripples by a polynomial function.
- Explosion of a supernova: You can model the time the explosion takes to affect a volume of space by a radical function.

In this unit, you will expand your knowledge of transformations while exploring radical and polynomial functions. These functions and associated transformations are useful in a variety of applications within mathematics.

Looking Ahead

In this unit, you will solve problems involving...
- transformations of functions
- inverses of functions
- radical functions and equations
- polynomial functions and equations

Unit 1 Project: The Art of Mathematics

Simone McLeod, a Cree-Ojibway originally from Winnipeg, Manitoba, now lives in Saskatchewan and is a member of the James Smith Cree Nation. Simone began painting later in life.

"I really believed that I had to wait until I could find something that had a lot of meaning to me. Each painting contains a piece of my soul. I have a strong faith in humankind and my paintings are silent prayers of hope for the future…."

"My Indian name is Earth Blanket (all that covers the earth such as grass, flowers, and trees). The sun, the blankets, and the flowers/rocks are all the same colours to show how all things are equal."

Simone's work is collected all over the world, including Europe, India, Asia, South Africa, and New Zealand.

In this project, you will search for mathematical functions in art, nature, and manufactured objects. You will determine equations for the functions or partial functions you find. You will justify your equations and display them superimposed on the image you have selected.

CHAPTER 1

Function Transformations

Mathematical shapes are found in architecture, bridges, containers, jewellery, games, decorations, art, and nature. Designs that are repeated, reflected, stretched, or transformed in some way are pleasing to the eye and capture our imagination.

In this chapter, you will explore the mathematical relationship between a function and its transformed graph. Throughout the chapter, you will explore how functions are transformed and develop strategies for relating complex functions to simpler functions.

Did You Know?

Albert Einstein (1879–1955) is often regarded as the father of modern physics. He won the Nobel Prize for Physics in 1921 for "his services to Theoretical Physics, and especially for his discovery of the law of the photoelectric effect." The Lorentz transformations are an important part of Einstein's theory of relativity.

Key Terms

transformation
mapping
translation
image point
reflection
invariant point
stretch
inverse of a function
horizontal line test

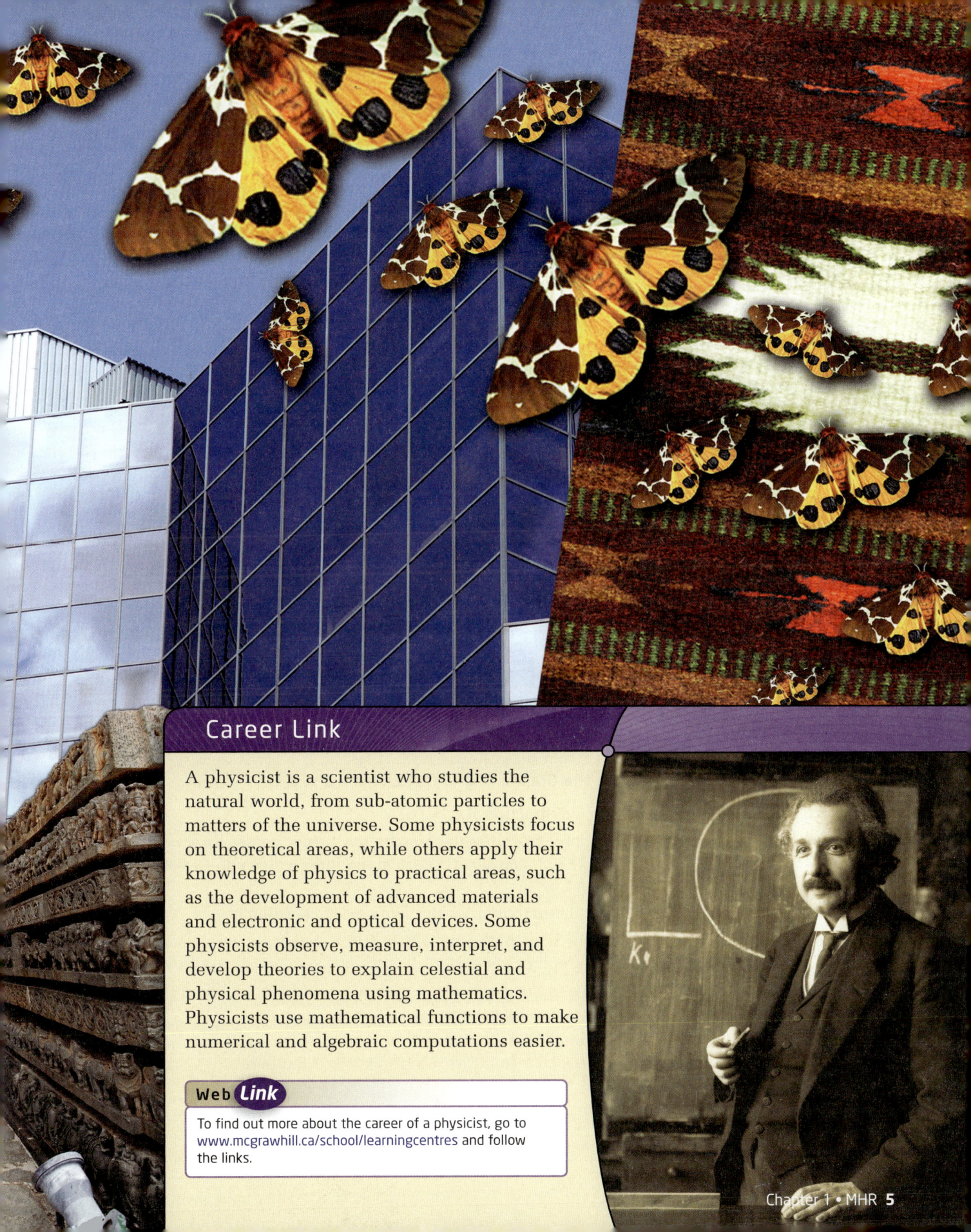

Career Link

A physicist is a scientist who studies the natural world, from sub-atomic particles to matters of the universe. Some physicists focus on theoretical areas, while others apply their knowledge of physics to practical areas, such as the development of advanced materials and electronic and optical devices. Some physicists observe, measure, interpret, and develop theories to explain celestial and physical phenomena using mathematics. Physicists use mathematical functions to make numerical and algebraic computations easier.

Web Link

To find out more about the career of a physicist, go to www.mcgrawhill.ca/school/learningcentres and follow the links.

1.1

Horizontal and Vertical Translations

Focus on...

- determining the effects of h and k in $y - k = f(x - h)$ on the graph of $y = f(x)$
- sketching the graph of $y - k = f(x - h)$ for given values of h and k, given the graph of $y = f(x)$
- writing the equation of a function whose graph is a vertical and/or horizontal translation of the graph of $y = f(x)$

A linear frieze pattern is a decorative pattern in which a section of the pattern repeats along a straight line. These patterns often occur in border decorations and textiles. Frieze patterns are also used by artists, craftspeople, musicians, choreographers, and mathematicians. Can you think of places where you have seen a frieze pattern?

Lantern Festival in China

Investigate Vertical and Horizontal Translations

Materials
- grid paper

A: Compare the Graphs of $y = f(x)$ and $y - k = f(x)$

1. Consider the function $f(x) = |x|$.
    a) Use a table of values to compare the output values for $y = f(x)$, $y = f(x) + 3$, and $y = f(x) - 3$ given input values of $-3, -2, -1, 0, 1, 2,$ and 3.
    b) Graph the functions on the same set of coordinate axes.
2. a) Describe how the graphs of $y = f(x) + 3$ and $y = f(x) - 3$ compare to the graph of $y = f(x)$.
   b) Relative to the graph of $y = f(x)$, what information about the graph of $y = f(x) + k$ does k provide?
3. Would the relationship between the graphs of $y = f(x)$ and $y = f(x) + k$ change if $f(x) = x$ or $f(x) = x^2$? Explain.

B: Compare the Graphs of $y = f(x)$ and $y = f(x - h)$

4. Consider the function $f(x) = |x|$.

   a) Use a table of values to compare the output values for $y = f(x)$, $y = f(x + 3)$, and $y = f(x - 3)$ given input values of -9, -6, -3, 0, 3, 6, and 9.

   b) Graph the functions on the same set of coordinate axes.

5. a) Describe how the graphs of $y = f(x + 3)$ and $y = f(x - 3)$ compare to the graph of $y = f(x)$.

   b) Relative to the graph of $y = f(x)$, what information about the graph of $y = f(x - h)$ does h provide?

6. Would the relationship between the graphs of $y = f(x)$ and $y = f(x - h)$ change if $f(x) = x$ or $f(x) = x^2$? Explain.

Reflect and Respond

7. How is the graph of a function $y = f(x)$ related to the graph of $y = f(x) + k$ when $k > 0$? when $k < 0$?

8. How is the graph of a function $y = f(x)$ related to the graph of $y = f(x - h)$ when $h > 0$? when $h < 0$?

9. Describe how the parameters h and k affect the properties of the graph of a function. Consider such things as shape, orientation, x-intercepts and y-intercept, domain, and range.

Link the Ideas

A **transformation** of a function alters the equation and any combination of the location, shape, and orientation of the graph.

Points on the original graph correspond to points on the transformed, or image, graph. The relationship between these sets of points can be called a **mapping**.

Mapping notation can be used to show a relationship between the coordinates of a set of points, (x, y), and the coordinates of a corresponding set of points, $(x, y + 3)$, for example, as $(x, y) \rightarrow (x, y + 3)$.

transformation
- a change made to a figure or a relation such that the figure or the graph of the relation is shifted or changed in shape

mapping
- the relating of one set of points to another set of points so that each point in the original set corresponds to exactly one point in the image set

> **Did You Know?**
>
> *Mapping notation* is an alternate notation for function notation. For example, $f(x) = 3x + 4$ can be written as $f: x \rightarrow 3x + 4$. This is read as "f is a function that maps x to $3x + 4$."

translation
- a slide transformation that results in a shift of a graph without changing its shape or orientation
- vertical and horizontal translations are types of transformations with equations of the forms $y - k = f(x)$ and $y = f(x - h)$, respectively
- a translated graph is congruent to the original graph

One type of transformation is a **translation**. A translation can move the graph of a function up, down, left, or right. A translation occurs when the location of a graph changes but not its shape or orientation.

Example 1

Graph Translations of the Form $y - k = f(x)$ and $y = f(x - h)$

a) Graph the functions $y = x^2$, $y - 2 = x^2$, and $y = (x - 5)^2$ on the same set of coordinate axes.

b) Describe how the graphs of $y - 2 = x^2$ and $y = (x - 5)^2$ compare to the graph of $y = x^2$.

Solution

a) The notation $y - k = f(x)$ is often used instead of $y = f(x) + k$ to emphasize that this is a transformation on y. In this case, the base function is $f(x) = x^2$ and the value of k is 2.

The notation $y = f(x - h)$ shows that this is a transformation on x. In this case, the base function is $f(x) = x^2$ and the value of h is 5.

Rearrange equations as needed and use tables of values to help you graph the functions.

x	$y = x^2$
−3	9
−2	4
−1	1
0	0
1	1
2	4
3	9

x	$y = x^2 + 2$
−3	11
−2	6
−1	3
0	2
1	3
2	6
3	11

x	$y = (x - 5)^2$
2	9
3	4
4	1
5	0
6	1
7	4
8	9

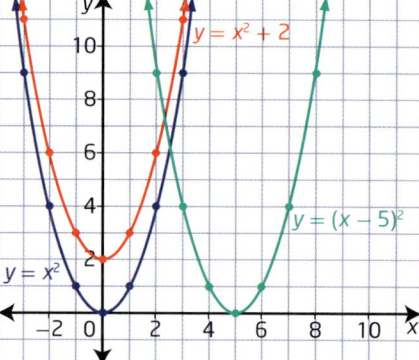

For $y = x^2 + 2$, the input values are the same but the output values change. Each point (x, y) on the graph of $y = x^2$ is transformed to $(x, y + 2)$.

For $y = (x - 5)^2$, to maintain the same output values as the base function table, the input values are different. Every point (x, y) on the graph of $y = x^2$ is transformed to $(x + 5, y)$. How do the input changes relate to the translation direction?

b) The transformed graphs are congruent to the graph of $y = x^2$.

Each point (x, y) on the graph of $y = x^2$ is transformed to become the point $(x, y + 2)$ on the graph of $y - 2 = x^2$. Using mapping notation, $(x, y) \rightarrow (x, y + 2)$.

Therefore, the graph of $y - 2 = x^2$ is the graph of $y = x^2$ translated vertically 2 units up.

Each point (x, y) on the graph of $y = x^2$ is transformed to become the point $(x + 5, y)$ on the graph of $y = (x - 5)^2$. In mapping notation, $(x, y) \rightarrow (x + 5, y)$.

Therefore, the graph of $y = (x - 5)^2$ is the graph of $y = x^2$ translated horizontally 5 units to the right.

Your Turn

How do the graphs of $y + 1 = x^2$ and $y = (x + 3)^2$ compare to the graph of $y = x^2$? Justify your reasoning.

Example 2

Horizontal and Vertical Translations

Sketch the graph of $y = |x - 4| + 3$.

Solution

For $y = |x - 4| + 3$, $h = 4$ and $k = -3$.
- Start with a sketch of the graph of the base function $y = |x|$, using key points.
- Apply the horizontal translation of 4 units to the right to obtain the graph of $y = |x - 4|$.

> To ensure an accurate sketch of a transformed function, translate key points on the base function first.

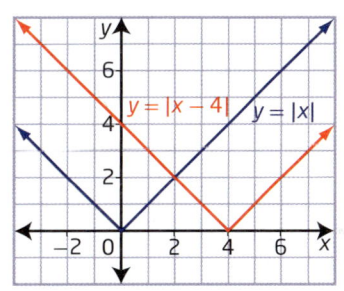

Did You Know?

Key points are points on a graph that give important information, such as the x-intercepts, the y-intercept, the maximum, and the minimum.

- Apply the vertical translation of 3 units up to $y = |x - 4|$ to obtain the graph of $y = |x - 4| + 3$.

> Would the graph be in the correct location if the order of the translations were reversed?

The point $(0, 0)$ on the function $y = |x|$ is transformed to become the point $(4, 3)$. In general, the transformation can be described as $(x, y) \rightarrow (x + 4, y + 3)$.

Your Turn

Sketch the graph of $y = (x + 5)^2 - 2$.

Example 3

Determine the Equation of a Translated Function

Describe the translation that has been applied to the graph of $f(x)$ to obtain the graph of $g(x)$. Determine the equation of the translated function in the form $y - k = f(x - h)$.

a)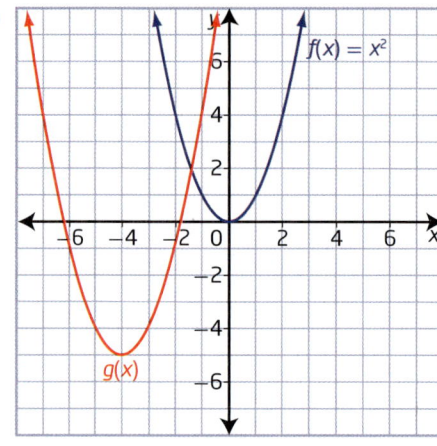

b)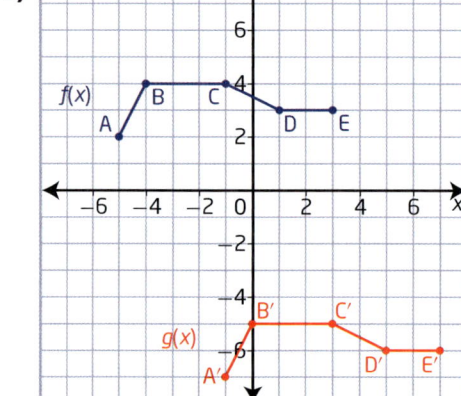

It is a common convention to use a prime (′) next to each letter representing an image point.

Solution

image point
- the point that is the result of a transformation of a point on the original graph

a) The base function is $f(x) = x^2$. Choose key points on the graph of $f(x) = x^2$ and locate the corresponding **image points** on the graph of $g(x)$.

$$
\begin{array}{ll}
f(x) & g(x) \\
(0, 0) & \to (-4, -5) \\
(-1, 1) & \to (-5, -4) \\
(1, 1) & \to (-3, -4) \\
(-2, 4) & \to (-6, -1) \\
(2, 4) & \to (-2, -1) \\
(x, y) & \to (x - 4, y - 5)
\end{array}
$$

For a horizontal translation and a vertical translation where every point (x, y) on the graph of $y = f(x)$ is transformed to $(x + h, y + k)$, the equation of the transformed graph is of the form $y - k = f(x - h)$.

To obtain the graph of g(x), the graph of $f(x) = x^2$ has been translated 4 units to the left and 5 units down. So, $h = -4$ and $k = -5$.

To write the equation in the form $y - k = f(x - h)$, substitute -4 for h and -5 for k.

$y + 5 = f(x + 4)$

b) Begin with key points on the graph of f(x). Locate the corresponding image points.

$\quad f(x) \quad\quad\quad g(x)$
$A(-5, 2) \to A'(-1, -7)$
$B(-4, 4) \to B'(0, -5)$
$C(-1, 4) \to C'(3, -5)$
$\quad D(1, 3) \to D'(5, -6)$
$\quad E(3, 3) \to E'(7, -6)$
$\quad (x, y) \to (x + 4, y - 9)$

To obtain the graph of g(x), the graph of f(x) has been translated 4 units to the right and 9 units down. Substitute $h = 4$ and $k = -9$ into the equation of the form $y - k = f(x - h)$:

$y + 9 = f(x - 4)$

Did You Know?

In Pre-Calculus 11, you graphed quadratic functions of the form $y = (x - p)^2 + q$ by considering transformations from the graph of $y = x^2$. In $y = (x - p)^2 + q$, the parameter p determines the horizontal translation and the parameter q determines the vertical translation of the graph. In this unit, the parameters for horizontal and vertical translations are represented by h and k, respectively.

Your Turn

Describe the translation that has been applied to the graph of f(x) to obtain the graph of g(x). Determine the equation of the translated function in the form $y - k = f(x - h)$.

 a)

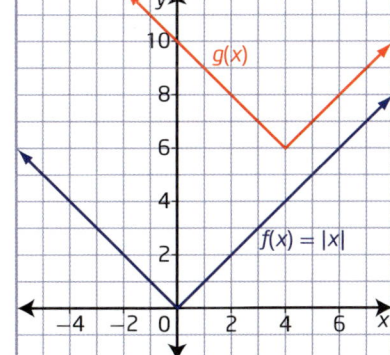

 b)

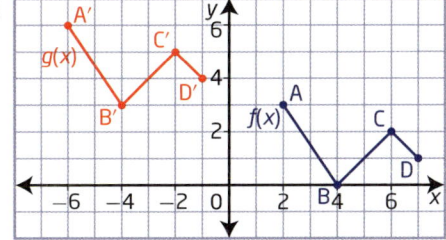

Key Ideas

- Translations are transformations that shift all points on the graph of a function up, down, left, and right without changing the shape or orientation of the graph.
- The table summarizes translations of the function $y = f(x)$.

Function	Transformation from $y = f(x)$	Mapping	Example
$y - k = f(x)$ or $y = f(x) + k$	A vertical translation. If $k > 0$, the translation is up. If $k < 0$, the translation is down.	$(x, y) \rightarrow (x, y + k)$	
$y = f(x - h)$	A horizontal translation. If $h > 0$, the translation is to the right. If $h < 0$, the translation is to the left.	$(x, y) \rightarrow (x + h, y)$	

- A sketch of the graph of $y - k = f(x - h)$, or $y = f(x - h) + k$, can be created by translating key points on the graph of the base function $y = f(x)$.

Check Your Understanding

Practise

1. For each function, state the values of h and k, the parameters that represent the horizontal and vertical translations applied to $y = f(x)$.

a) $y - 5 = f(x)$

b) $y = f(x) - 4$

c) $y = f(x + 1)$

d) $y + 3 = f(x - 7)$

e) $y = f(x + 2) + 4$

2. Given the graph of $y = f(x)$ and each of the following transformations,
- state the coordinates of the image points A′, B′, C′, D′ and E′
- sketch the graph of the transformed function

a) $g(x) = f(x) + 3$

b) $h(x) = f(x - 2)$

c) $s(x) = f(x + 4)$

d) $t(x) = f(x) - 2$

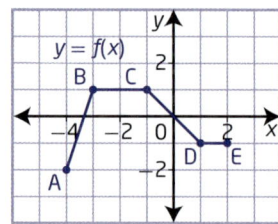

3. Describe, using mapping notation, how the graphs of the following functions can be obtained from the graph of $y = f(x)$.
   a) $y = f(x + 10)$
   b) $y + 6 = f(x)$
   c) $y = f(x - 7) + 4$
   d) $y - 3 = f(x - 1)$

4. Given the graph of $y = f(x)$, sketch the graph of the transformed function. Describe the transformation that can be applied to the graph of $f(x)$ to obtain the graph of the transformed function. Then, write the transformation using mapping notation.
   a) $r(x) = f(x + 4) - 3$
   b) $s(x) = f(x - 2) - 4$
   c) $t(x) = f(x - 2) + 5$
   d) $v(x) = f(x + 3) + 2$

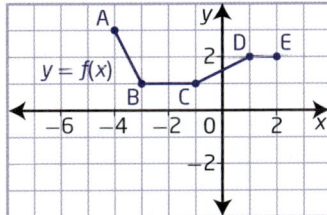

Apply

5. For each transformation, identify the values of h and k. Then, write the equation of the transformed function in the form $y - k = f(x - h)$.
   a) $f(x) = \frac{1}{x}$, translated 5 units to the left and 4 units up
   b) $f(x) = x^2$, translated 8 units to the right and 6 units up
   c) $f(x) = |x|$, translated 10 units to the right and 8 units down
   d) $y = f(x)$, translated 7 units to the left and 12 units down

6. What vertical translation is applied to $y = x^2$ if the transformed graph passes through the point (4, 19)?

7. What horizontal translation is applied to $y = x^2$ if the translation image graph passes through the point (5, 16)?

8. Copy and complete the table.

Translation	Transformed Function	Transformation of Points
vertical	$y = f(x) + 5$	$(x, y) \rightarrow (x, y + 5)$
	$y = f(x + 7)$	$(x, y) \rightarrow (x - 7, y)$
	$y = f(x - 3)$	
	$y = f(x) - 6$	
horizontal and vertical	$y + 9 = f(x + 4)$	
horizontal and vertical		$(x, y) \rightarrow (x + 4, y - 6)$
		$(x, y) \rightarrow (x - 2, y + 3)$
horizontal and vertical	$y = f(x - h) + k$	

9. The graph of the function $y = x^2$ is translated 4 units to the left and 5 units up to form the transformed function $y = g(x)$.
   a) Determine the equation of the function $y = g(x)$.
   b) What are the domain and range of the image function?
   c) How could you use the description of the translation of the function $y = x^2$ to determine the domain and range of the image function?

10. The graph of $f(x) = |x|$ is transformed to the graph of $g(x) = f(x - 9) + 5$.
    a) Determine the equation of the function $g(x)$.
    b) Compare the graph of $g(x)$ to the graph of the base function $f(x)$.
    c) Determine three points on the graph of $f(x)$. Write the coordinates of the image points if you perform the horizontal translation first and then the vertical translation.
    d) Using the same original points from part c), write the coordinates of the image points if you perform the vertical translation first and then the horizontal translation.
    e) What do you notice about the coordinates of the image points from parts c) and d)? Is the order of the translations important?

11. The graph of the function drawn in red is a translation of the original function drawn in blue. Write the equation of the translated function in the form $y - k = f(x - h)$.

   a)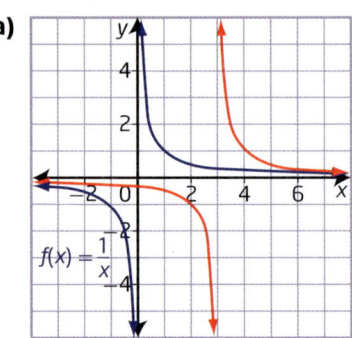

   b)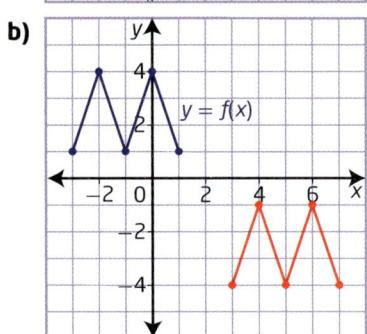

12. Janine is an avid cyclist. After cycling to a lake and back home, she graphs her distance versus time (graph A).

   a) If she left her house at 12 noon, briefly describe a possible scenario for Janine's trip.

   b) Describe the differences it would make to Janine's cycling trip if the graph of the function were translated, as shown in graph B.

   c) The equation for graph A could be written as $y = f(x)$. Write the equation for graph B.

   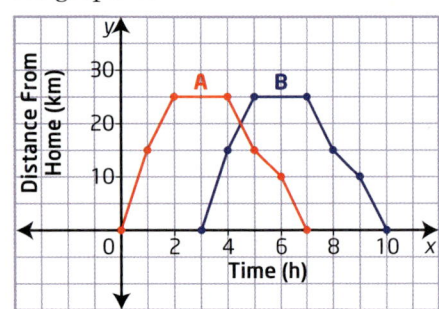

13. Architects and designers often use translations in their designs. The image shown is from an Italian roadway.

   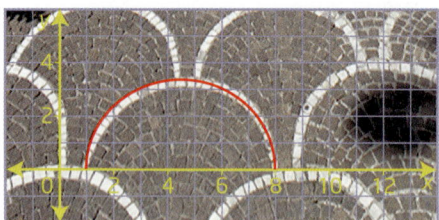

   a) Use the coordinate plane overlay with the base semicircle shown to describe the approximate transformations of the semicircles.

   b) If the semicircle at the bottom left of the image is defined by the function $y = f(x)$, state the approximate equations of three other semicircles.

14. This Pow Wow belt shows a frieze pattern where a particular image has been translated throughout the length of the belt.

   a) With or without technology, create a design using a pattern that is a function. Use a minimum of four horizontal translations of your function to create your own frieze pattern.

   b) Describe the translation of your design in words and in an equation of the form $y = f(x - h)$.

   > **Did You Know?**
   >
   > In First Nations communities today, Pow Wows have evolved into multi-tribal festivals. Traditional dances are performed by men, women, and children. The dancers wear traditional regalia specific to their dance style and nation of origin.

15. Michele Lake and Coral Lake, located near the Columbia Ice Fields, are the only two lakes in Alberta in which rare golden trout live.

Suppose the graph represents the number of golden trout in Michelle Lake in the years since 1970.

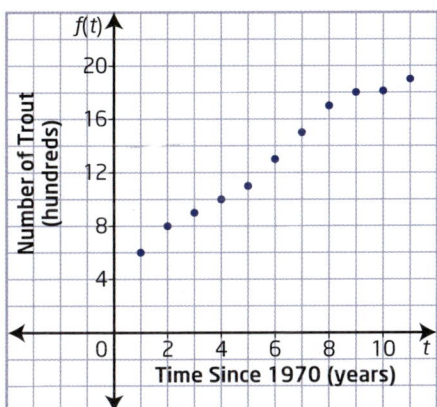

Let the function $f(t)$ represent the number of fish in Michelle Lake since 1970.

Describe an event or a situation for the fish population that would result in the following transformations of the graph. Then, use function notation to represent the transformation.

a) a vertical translation of 2 units up

b) a horizontal translation of 3 units to the right

16. Paul is an interior house painter. He determines that the function $n = f(A)$ gives the number of gallons, n, of paint needed to cover an area, A, in square metres. Interpret $n = f(A) + 10$ and $n = f(A + 10)$ in this context.

Extend

17. The graph of the function $y = x^2$ is translated to an image parabola with zeros 7 and 1.

    a) Determine the equation of the image function.

    b) Describe the translations on the graph of $y = x^2$.

    c) Determine the y-intercept of the translated function.

18. Use translations to describe how the graph of $y = \frac{1}{x}$ compares to the graph of each function.

    a) $y - 4 = \frac{1}{x}$ b) $y = \frac{1}{x + 2}$

    c) $y - 3 = \frac{1}{x - 5}$ d) $y = \frac{1}{x + 3} - 4$

19. a) Predict the relationship between the graph of $y = x^3 - x^2$ and the graph of $y + 3 = (x - 2)^3 - (x - 2)^2$.

    b) Graph each function to verify your prediction.

Create Connections

C1 The graph of the function $y = f(x)$ is transformed to the graph of $y = f(x - h) + k$.

   a) Show that the order in which you apply translations does not matter. Explain why this is true.

   b) How are the domain and range affected by the parameters h and k?

C2 Complete the square and explain how to transform the graph of $y = x^2$ to the graph of each function.

   a) $f(x) = x^2 + 2x + 1$

   b) $g(x) = x^2 - 4x + 3$

C3 The roots of the quadratic equation $x^2 - x - 12 = 0$ are -3 and 4. Determine the roots of the equation $(x - 5)^2 - (x - 5) - 12 = 0$.

C4 The function $f(x) = x + 4$ could be a vertical translation of 4 units up or a horizontal translation of 4 units to the left. Explain why.

1.2

Reflections and Stretches

Focus on...

- developing an understanding of the effects of reflections on the graphs of functions and their related equations
- developing an understanding of the effects of vertical and horizontal stretches on the graphs of functions and their related equations

Reflections, symmetry, as well as horizontal and vertical stretches, appear in architecture, textiles, science, and works of art. When something is symmetrical or stretched in the geometric sense, its parts have a one-to-one correspondence. How does this relate to the study of functions?

Ndebele artist, South Africa

Investigate Reflections and Stretches of Functions

Materials
- grid paper
- graphing technology

A: Graph Reflections in the *x*-Axis and the *y*-Axis

1. **a)** Draw a set of coordinate axes on grid paper. In quadrant I, plot a point A. Label point A with its coordinates.

   b) Use the *x*-axis as a mirror line, or line of reflection, and plot point A′, the mirror image of point A in the *x*-axis.

   c) How are the coordinates of points A and A′ related?

   d) If point A is initially located in any of the other quadrants, does the relationship in part c) still hold true?

2. Consider the graph of the function $y = f(x)$.

   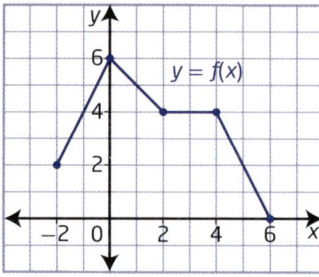

   a) Explain how you could graph the mirror image of the function in the *x*-axis.

   b) Make a conjecture about how the equation of $f(x)$ changes to graph the mirror image.

3. Use graphing technology to graph the function $y = x^2 + 2x$, $-5 \leq x \leq 5$, and its mirror image in the x-axis. What equation did you enter to graph the mirror image?

4. Repeat steps 1 to 3 for a mirror image in the y-axis.

Reflect and Respond

5. Copy and complete the table to record your observations. Write concluding statements summarizing the effects of reflections in the axes.

	Reflection in	Verbal Description	Mapping	Equation of Transformed Function
Function $y = f(x)$	x-axis		$(x, y) \rightarrow (\ , \ )$	
	y-axis		$(x, y) \rightarrow (\ , \ )$	

B: Graph Vertical and Horizontal Stretches

6. a) Plot a point A on a coordinate grid and label it with its coordinates.

   b) Plot and label a point A′ with the same x-coordinate as point A, but with the y-coordinate equal to 2 times the y-coordinate of point A.

   c) Plot and label a point A″ with the same x-coordinate as point A, but with the y-coordinate equal to $\frac{1}{2}$ the y-coordinate of point A.

   d) Compare the location of points A′ and A″ to the location of the original point A. Describe how multiplying the y-coordinate by a factor of 2 or a factor of $\frac{1}{2}$ affects the position of the image point.

   Has the distance to the x-axis or the y-axis changed?

7. Consider the graph of the function $y = f(x)$ in step 2. Sketch the graph of the function when the y-values have been

   a) multiplied by 2

   b) multiplied by $\frac{1}{2}$

8. What are the equations of the transformed functions in step 7 in the form $y = af(x)$?

9. For step 7a), the graph has been vertically stretched about the x-axis by a factor of 2. Explain the statement. How would you describe the graph in step 7b)?

10. Consider the graph of the function $y = f(x)$ in step 2.

    a) If the x-values were multiplied by 2 or multiplied by $\frac{1}{2}$, describe what would happen to the graph of the function $y = f(x)$.

    b) Determine the equations of the transformed functions in part a) in the form $y = f(bx)$.

Reflect and Respond

11. Copy and complete the table to record your observations. Write concluding statements summarizing the effects of stretches about the axes.

	Stretch About	Verbal Description	Mapping	Equation of Transformed Function
Function $y = f(x)$	x-axis		$(x, y) \rightarrow (\ , \ )$	
	y-axis		$(x, y) \rightarrow (\ , \ )$	

Link the Ideas

reflection
- a transformation where each point of the original graph has an image point resulting from a reflection in a line
- may result in a change of orientation of a graph while preserving its shape

A **reflection** of a graph creates a mirror image in a line called the line of reflection. Reflections, like translations, do not change the shape of the graph. However, unlike translations, reflections may change the orientation of the graph.

- When the output of a function $y = f(x)$ is multiplied by -1, the result, $y = -f(x)$, is a reflection of the graph in the x-axis.
- When the input of a function $y = f(x)$ is multiplied by -1, the result, $y = f(-x)$, is a reflection of the graph in the y-axis.

Example 1

Compare the Graphs of $y = f(x)$, $y = -f(x)$, and $y = f(-x)$

a) Given the graph of $y = f(x)$, graph the functions $y = -f(x)$ and $y = f(-x)$.

b) How are the graphs of $y = -f(x)$ and $y = f(-x)$ related to the graph of $y = f(x)$?

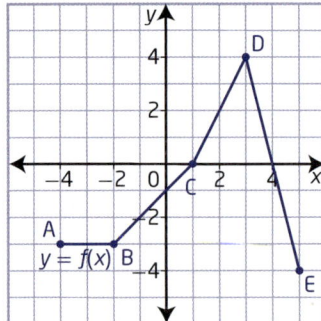

Solution

a) Use key points on the graph of $y = f(x)$ to create tables of values.

- The image points on the graph of $y = -f(x)$ have the same x-coordinates but different y-coordinates. Multiply the y-coordinates of points on the graph of $y = f(x)$ by -1.

The negative sign can be interpreted as a change in sign of one of the coordinates.

	x	$y = f(x)$
A	-4	-3
B	-2	-3
C	1	0
D	3	4
E	5	-4

	x	$y = -f(x)$
A′	-4	$-1(-3) = 3$
B′	-2	$-1(-3) = 3$
C′	1	$-1(0) = 0$
D′	3	$-1(4) = -4$
E′	5	$-1(-4) = 4$

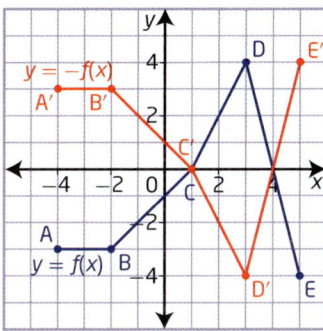

Each image point is the same distance from the line of reflection as the corresponding key point. A line drawn perpendicular to the line of reflection contains both the key point and its image point.

- The image points on the graph of $y = f(-x)$ have the same y-coordinates but different x-coordinates. Multiply the x-coordinates of points on the graph of $y = f(x)$ by -1.

	x	$y = f(x)$
A	-4	-3
B	-2	-3
C	1	0
D	3	4
E	5	-4

	x	$y = f(-x)$
A″	$-1(-4) = 4$	-3
B″	$-1(-2) = 2$	-3
C″	$-1(1) = -1$	0
D″	$-1(3) = -3$	4
E″	$-1(5) = -5$	-4

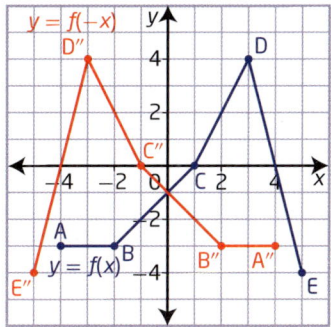

b) The transformed graphs are congruent to the graph of $y = f(x)$.

The points on the graph of $y = f(x)$ relate to the points on the graph of $y = -f(x)$ by the mapping $(x, y) \rightarrow (x, -y)$. The graph of $y = -f(x)$ is a reflection of the graph of $y = f(x)$ in the x-axis.

Notice that the point C(1, 0) maps to itself, C'(1, 0). This point is an **invariant point**.

What is another invariant point?

The points on the graph of $y = f(x)$ relate to the points on the graph of $y = f(-x)$ by the mapping $(x, y) \rightarrow (-x, y)$. The graph of $y = f(-x)$ is a reflection of the graph of $y = f(x)$ in the y-axis.

The point $(0, -1)$ is an invariant point.

invariant point
- a point on a graph that remains unchanged after a transformation is applied to it
- any point on a curve that lies on the line of reflection is an invariant point

Your Turn

a) Given the graph of $y = f(x)$, graph the functions $y = -f(x)$ and $y = f(-x)$.

b) Show the mapping of key points on the graph of $y = f(x)$ to image points on the graphs of $y = -f(x)$ and $y = f(-x)$.

c) Describe how the graphs of $y = -f(x)$ and $y = f(-x)$ are related to the graph of $y = f(x)$. State any invariant points.

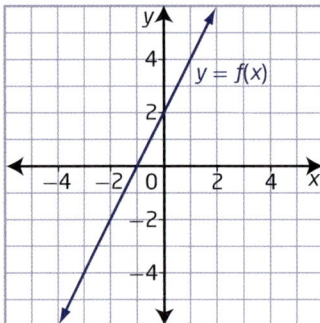

Vertical and Horizontal Stretches

stretch
- a transformation in which the distance of each *x*-coordinate or *y*-coordinate from the line of reflection is multiplied by some scale factor
- scale factors between 0 and 1 result in the point moving closer to the line of reflection; scale factors greater than 1 result in the point moving farther away from the line of reflection

A **stretch**, unlike a translation or a reflection, changes the shape of the graph. However, like translations, stretches do not change the orientation of the graph.

- When the output of a function $y = f(x)$ is multiplied by a non-zero constant a, the result, $y = af(x)$ or $\dfrac{y}{a} = f(x)$, is a vertical stretch of the graph about the x-axis by a factor of $|a|$. If $a < 0$, then the graph is also reflected in the x-axis.

- When the input of a function $y = f(x)$ is multiplied by a non-zero constant b, the result, $y = f(bx)$, is a horizontal stretch of the graph about the y-axis by a factor of $\dfrac{1}{|b|}$. If $b < 0$, then the graph is also reflected in the y-axis.

Example 2

Graph $y = af(x)$

Given the graph of $y = f(x)$,
- transform the graph of $f(x)$ to sketch the graph of $g(x)$
- describe the transformation
- state any invariant points
- state the domain and range of the functions

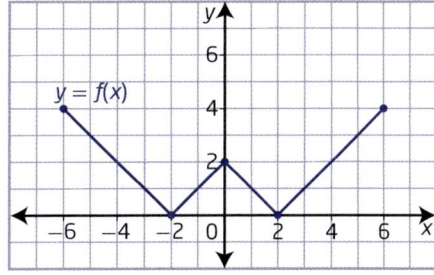

a) $g(x) = 2f(x)$

b) $g(x) = \frac{1}{2}f(x)$

Solution

a) Use key points on the graph of $y = f(x)$ to create a table of values.

The image points on the graph of $g(x) = 2f(x)$ have the same x-coordinates but different y-coordinates. Multiply the y-coordinates of points on the graph of $y = f(x)$ by 2.

x	$y = f(x)$	$y = g(x) = 2f(x)$
−6	4	8
−2	0	0
0	2	4
2	0	0
6	4	8

The vertical distances of the transformed graph have been changed by a factor of a, where $|a| > 1$. The points on the graph of $y = af(x)$ are farther away from the x-axis than the corresponding points of the graph of $y = f(x)$.

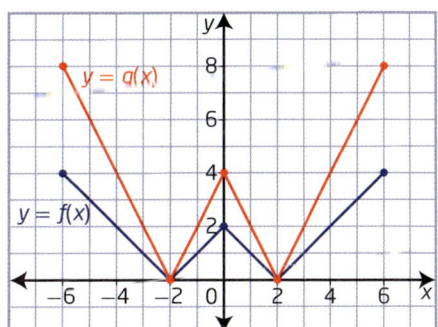

Since $a = 2$, the points on the graph of $y = g(x)$ relate to the points on the graph of $y = f(x)$ by the mapping $(x, y) \rightarrow (x, 2y)$. Therefore, each point on the graph of $g(x)$ is twice as far from the x-axis as the corresponding point on the graph of $f(x)$. The graph of $g(x) = 2f(x)$ is a vertical stretch of the graph of $y = f(x)$ about the x-axis by a factor of 2.

The invariant points are $(−2, 0)$ and $(2, 0)$.

For $f(x)$, the domain is $\{x \mid −6 \leq x \leq 6, x \in R\}$, or $[−6, 6]$, and the range is $\{y \mid 0 \leq y \leq 4, y \in R\}$, or $[0, 4]$.

For $g(x)$, the domain is $\{x \mid −6 \leq x \leq 6, x \in R\}$, or $[−6, 6]$, and the range is $\{y \mid 0 \leq y \leq 8, y \in R\}$, or $[0, 8]$.

What is unique about the invariant points?

How can you determine the range of the new function, $g(x)$, using the range of $f(x)$ and the parameter a?

Did You Know?

There are several ways to express the domain and range of a function. For example, you can use words, a number line, set notation, or interval notation.

b) The image points on the graph of $g(x) = \frac{1}{2}f(x)$ have the same x-coordinates but different y-coordinates. Multiply the y-coordinates of points on the graph of $y = f(x)$ by $\frac{1}{2}$.

x	y = f(x)	y = g(x) = $\frac{1}{2}$f(x)
−6	4	2
−2	0	0
0	2	1
2	0	0
6	4	2

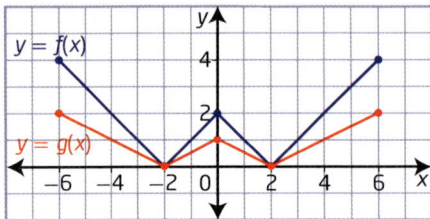

The vertical distances of the transformed graph have been changed by a factor a, where $0 < |a| < 1$. The points on the graph of $y = af(x)$ are closer to the x-axis than the corresponding points of the graph of $y = f(x)$.

Did You Know?

Translations and reflections are called *rigid* transformations because the shape of the graph does not change. Stretches are called *non-rigid* because the shape of the graph can change.

Since $a = \frac{1}{2}$, the points on the graph of $y = g(x)$ relate to the points on the graph of $y = f(x)$ by the mapping $(x, y) \rightarrow \left(x, \frac{1}{2}y\right)$. Therefore, each point on the graph of $g(x)$ is one half as far from the x-axis as the corresponding point on the graph of $f(x)$. The graph of $g(x) = \frac{1}{2}f(x)$ is a vertical stretch of the graph of $y = f(x)$ about the x-axis by a factor of $\frac{1}{2}$.

The invariant points are $(−2, 0)$ and $(2, 0)$.

What conclusion can you make about the invariant points after a vertical stretch?

For $f(x)$, the domain is $\{x \mid −6 \leq x \leq 6, x \in R\}$, or $[−6, 6]$, and the range is $\{y \mid 0 \leq y \leq 4, y \in R\}$, or $[0, 4]$.

For $g(x)$, the domain is $\{x \mid −6 \leq x \leq 6, x \in R\}$, or $[−6, 6]$, and the range is $\{y \mid 0 \leq y \leq 2, y \in R\}$, or $[0, 2]$.

Your Turn

Given the function $f(x) = x^2$,
- transform the graph of $f(x)$ to sketch the graph of $g(x)$
- describe the transformation
- state any invariant points
- state the domain and range of the functions

a) $g(x) = 4f(x)$

b) $g(x) = \frac{1}{3}f(x)$

Example 3

Graph y = f(bx)

Given the graph of $y = f(x)$,
- transform the graph of $f(x)$ to sketch the graph of $g(x)$
- describe the transformation
- state any invariant points
- state the domain and range of the functions

a) $g(x) = f(2x)$

b) $g(x) = f\left(\dfrac{1}{2}x\right)$

Solution

a) Use key points on the graph of $y = f(x)$ to create a table of values.

The image points on the graph of $g(x) = f(2x)$ have the same y-coordinates but different x-coordinates. Multiply the x-coordinates of points on the graph of $y = f(x)$ by $\dfrac{1}{2}$.

x	y = f(x)
−4	4
−2	0
0	2
2	0
4	4

x	y = g(x) = f(2x)
−2	4
−1	0
0	2
1	0
2	4

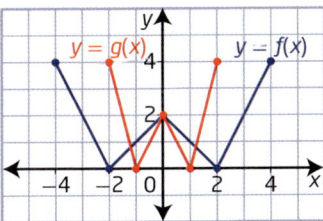

The horizontal distances of the transformed graph have been changed by a factor of $\dfrac{1}{b}$, where $|b| > 1$. The points on the graph of $y = f(bx)$ are closer to the y-axis than the corresponding points of the graph of $y = f(x)$.

Since $b = 2$, the points on the graph of $y = g(x)$ relate to the points on the graph of $y = f(x)$ by the mapping $(x, y) \rightarrow \left(\dfrac{1}{2}x, y\right)$. Therefore, each point on the graph of $g(x)$ is one half as far from the y-axis as the corresponding point on the graph of $f(x)$. The graph of $g(x) = f(2x)$ is a horizontal stretch about the y-axis by a factor of $\dfrac{1}{2}$ of the graph of $f(x)$.

The invariant point is $(0, 2)$.

For $f(x)$, the domain is $\{x \mid -4 \leq x \leq 4, x \in R\}$, or $[-4, 4]$, and the range is $\{y \mid 0 \leq y \leq 4, y \in R\}$, or $[0, 4]$.

How can you determine the domain of the new function, $g(x)$, using the domain of $f(x)$ and the parameter b?

For $g(x)$, the domain is $\{x \mid -2 \leq x \leq 2, x \in R\}$, or $[-2, 2]$, and the range is $\{y \mid 0 \leq y \leq 4, y \in R\}$, or $[0, 4]$.

b) The image points on the graph of $g(x) = f\left(\frac{1}{2}x\right)$ have the same y-coordinates but different x-coordinates. Multiply the x-coordinates of points on the graph of $y = f(x)$ by 2.

x	y = f(x)
−4	4
−2	0
0	2
2	0
4	4

x	$y = g(x) = f\left(\frac{1}{2}x\right)$
−8	4
−4	0
0	2
4	0
8	4

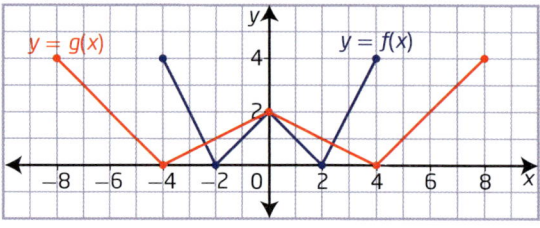

The horizontal distances of the transformed graph have been changed by a factor $\frac{1}{b}$, where $0 < |b| < 1$. The points on the graph of $y = f(bx)$ are farther away from the y-axis than the corresponding points of the graph of $y = f(x)$.

Since $b = \frac{1}{2}$, the points on the graph of $y = g(x)$ relate to the points on the graph of $y = f(x)$ by the mapping $(x, y) \rightarrow (2x, y)$. Therefore, each point on the graph of $g(x)$ is twice as far from the y-axis as the corresponding point on the graph of $f(x)$. The graph of $g(x) = f\left(\frac{1}{2}x\right)$ is a horizontal stretch about the y-axis by a factor of 2 of the graph of $f(x)$.

The invariant point is (0, 2).   How do you know which points will be invariant points after a horizontal stretch?

For $f(x)$, the domain is $\{x \mid -4 \leq x \leq 4, x \in R\}$, or $[-4, 4]$, and the range is $\{y \mid 0 \leq y \leq 4, y \in R\}$, or $[0, 4]$.

For $g(x)$, the domain is $\{x \mid -8 \leq x \leq 8, x \in R\}$, or $[-8, 8]$, and the range is $\{y \mid 0 \leq y \leq 4, y \in R\}$, or $[0, 4]$.

Your Turn

Given the function $f(x) = x^2$,
- transform the graph of $f(x)$ to sketch the graph of $g(x)$
- describe the transformation
- state any invariant points
- state the domain and range of the functions

a) $g(x) = f(3x)$

b) $g(x) = f\left(\frac{1}{4}x\right)$

Example 4

Write the Equation of a Transformed Function

The graph of the function $y = f(x)$ has been transformed by either a stretch or a reflection. Write the equation of the transformed graph, $g(x)$.

a)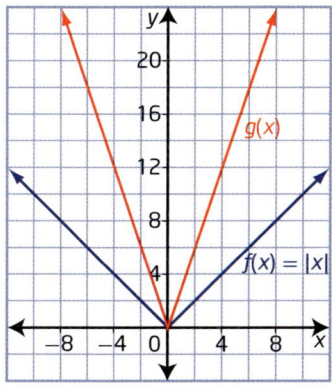

b)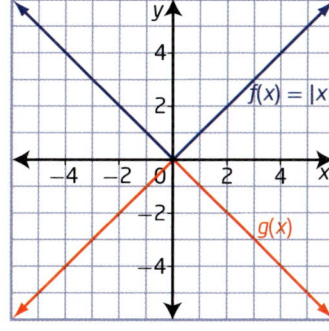

Solution

a) Notice that the V-shape has changed, so the graph has been transformed by a stretch.

Since the original function is $f(x) = |x|$, a stretch can be described in two ways.

Why is this the case?

Choose key points on the graph of $y = f(x)$ and determine their image points on the graph of the transformed function, $g(x)$.

Case 1
Check for a pattern in the y-coordinates.

x	y = f(x)	y = g(x)
−6	6	18
−4	4	12
−2	2	6
0	0	0
2	2	6
4	4	12
6	6	18

A vertical stretch results when the vertical distances of the transformed graph are a constant multiple of those of the original graph with respect to the x-axis.

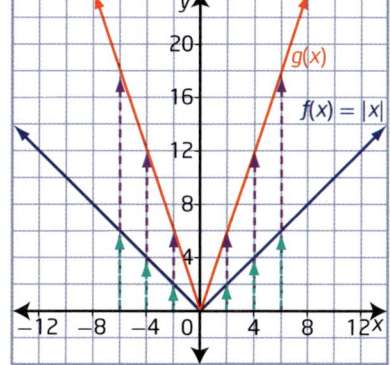

The transformation can be described by the mapping $(x, y) \rightarrow (x, 3y)$. This is of the form $y = af(x)$, indicating that there is a vertical stretch about the x-axis by a factor of 3. The equation of the transformed function is $g(x) = 3f(x)$ or $g(x) = 3|x|$.

Case 2

Check for a pattern in the x-coordinates.

x	y = f(x)
−12	12
−6	6
0	0
6	6
12	12

x	y = g(x)
−4	12
−2	6
0	0
2	6
4	12

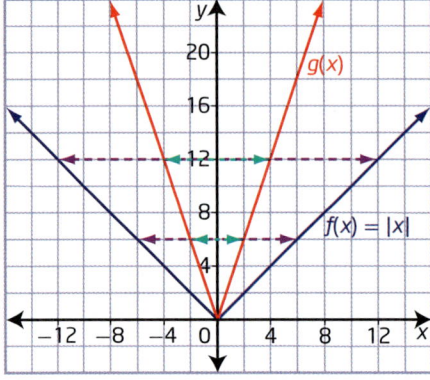

A horizontal stretch results when the horizontal distances of the transformed graph are a constant multiple of those of the original graph with respect to the y-axis.

The transformation can be described by the mapping $(x, y) \rightarrow \left(\frac{1}{3}x, y\right)$. This is of the form $y = f(bx)$, indicating that there is a horizontal stretch about the y-axis by a factor of $\frac{1}{3}$. The equation of the transformed function is $g(x) = f(3x)$ or $g(x) = |3x|$.

b) Notice that the shape of the graph has not changed, so the graph has been transformed by a reflection.

Choose key points on the graph of $f(x) = |x|$ and determine their image points on the graph of the transformed function, $g(x)$.

x	y = f(x)	y = g(x)
−4	4	−4
−2	2	−2
0	0	0
2	2	−2
4	4	−4

The transformation can be described by the mapping $(x, y) \rightarrow (x, -y)$. This is of the form $y = -f(x)$, indicating a reflection in the x-axis. The equation of the transformed function is $g(x) = -|x|$.

Your Turn

The graph of the function $y = f(x)$ has been transformed. Write the equation of the transformed graph, $g(x)$.

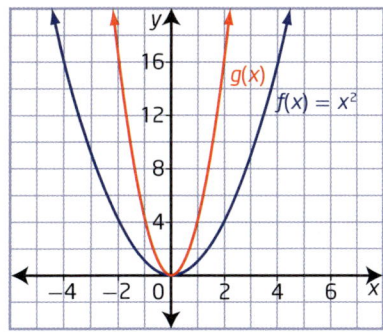

Key Ideas

- Any point on a line of reflection is an invariant point.

Function	Transformation from $y = f(x)$	Mapping	Example
$y = -f(x)$	A reflection in the x-axis	$(x, y) \rightarrow (x, -y)$	graph showing $y = f(x)$ and $y = -f(x)$
$y = f(-x)$	A reflection in the y-axis	$(x, y) \rightarrow (-x, y)$	graph showing $y = f(x)$ and $y = f(-x)$
$y = af(x)$	A vertical stretch about the x-axis by a factor of $\|a\|$; if $a < 0$, then the graph is also reflected in the x-axis	$(x, y) \rightarrow (x, ay)$	graph showing $y = f(x)$ and $y = af(x)$, $a > 1$
$y = f(bx)$	A horizontal stretch about the y-axis by a factor of $\frac{1}{\|b\|}$; if $b < 0$, then the graph is also reflected in the y-axis	$(x, y) \rightarrow \left(\frac{x}{b}, y\right)$	graph showing $y = f(x)$ and $y = f(bx)$, $b > 0$

Check Your Understanding

Practise

1. **a)** Copy and complete the table of values for the given functions.

x	$f(x) = 2x + 1$	$g(x) = -f(x)$	$h(x) = f(-x)$
−4			
−2			
0			
2			
4			

   b) Sketch the graphs of $f(x)$, $g(x)$, and $h(x)$ on the same set of coordinate axes.

   c) Explain how the points on the graphs of $g(x)$ and $h(x)$ relate to the transformation of the function $f(x) = 2x + 1$. List any invariant points.

   d) How is each function related to the graph of $f(x) = 2x + 1$?

2. **a)** Copy and complete the table of values for the given functions.

x	$f(x) = x^2$	$g(x) = 3f(x)$	$h(x) = \frac{1}{3}f(x)$
−6			
−3			
0			
3			
6			

   b) Sketch the graphs of $f(x)$, $g(x)$, and $h(x)$ on the same set of coordinate axes.

   c) Explain how the points on the graphs of $g(x)$ and $h(x)$ relate to the transformation of the function $f(x) = x^2$. List any invariant points.

   d) How is each function related to the graph of $f(x) = x^2$?

3. Consider each graph of a function.
   - Copy the graph of the function and sketch its reflection in the x-axis on the same set of axes.
   - State the equation of the reflected function in simplified form.
   - State the domain and range of each function.

   a)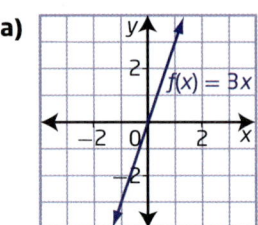

   b)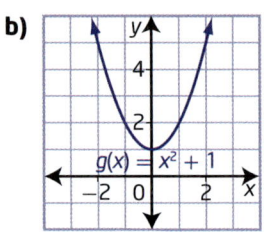

   c)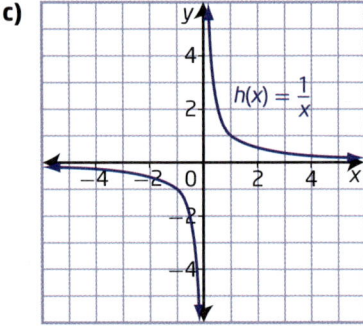

4. Consider each function in #3.
   - Copy the graph of the function and sketch its reflection in the y-axis on the same set of axes.
   - State the equation of the reflected function.
   - State the domain and range for each function.

5. Use words and mapping notation to describe how the graph of each function can be found from the graph of the function $y = f(x)$.

   a) $y = 4f(x)$
   b) $y = f(3x)$
   c) $y = -f(x)$
   d) $y = f(-x)$

6. The graph of the function $y = f(x)$ is vertically stretched about the x-axis by a factor of 2.

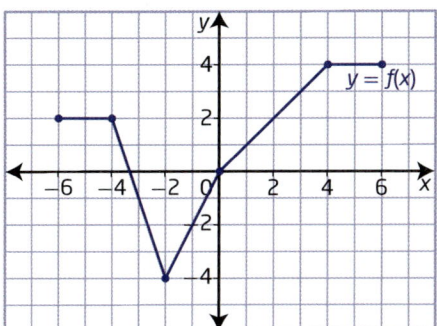

   a) Determine the domain and range of the transformed function.
   b) Explain the effect that a vertical stretch has on the domain and range of a function.

7. Describe the transformation that must be applied to the graph of $f(x)$ to obtain the graph of $g(x)$. Then, determine the equation of $g(x)$ in the form $y = af(bx)$.

   a)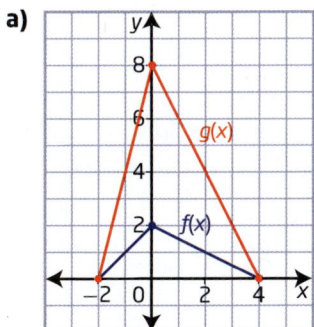

   b)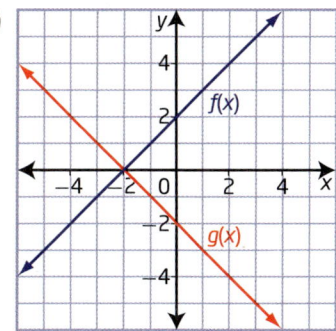

   c)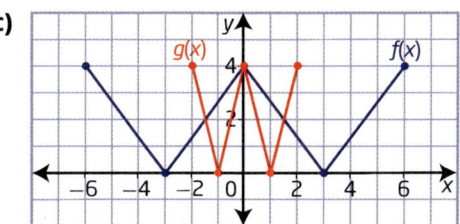

   d)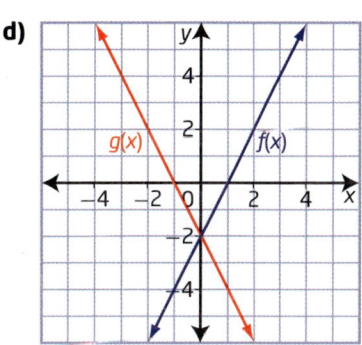

Apply

8. A weaver sets up a pattern on a computer using the graph shown. A new line of merchandise calls for the design to be altered to $y = f(0.5x)$. Sketch the graph of the new design.

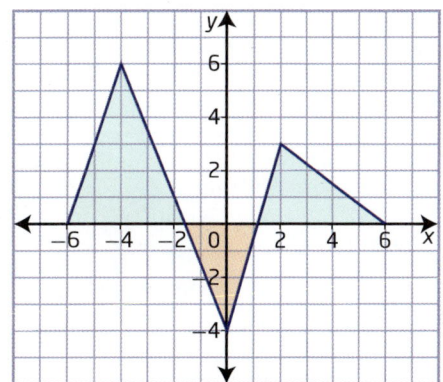

9. Describe what happens to the graph of a function $y = f(x)$ after the following changes are made to its equation.
   a) Replace x with $4x$.
   b) Replace x with $\frac{1}{4}x$.
   c) Replace y with $2y$.
   d) Replace y with $\frac{1}{4}y$.
   e) Replace x with $-3x$.
   f) Replace y with $-\frac{1}{3}y$.

10. Thomas and Sharyn discuss the order of the transformations of the graph of $y = -3|x|$ compared to the graph of $y = |x|$. Thomas states that the reflection must be applied first. Sharyn claims that the vertical stretch should be applied first.
    a) Sketch the graph of $y = -3|x|$ by applying the reflection first.
    b) Sketch the graph of $y = -3|x|$ by applying the stretch first.
    c) Explain your conclusions. Who is correct?

11. An object falling in a vacuum is affected only by the gravitational force. An equation that can model a free-falling object on Earth is $d = -4.9t^2$, where d is the distance travelled, in metres, and t is the time, in seconds. An object free falling on the moon can be modelled by the equation $d = -1.6t^2$.
    a) Sketch the graph of each function.
    b) Compare each function equation to the base function $d = t^2$.

    Did You Know?

    The actual strength of Earth's gravity varies depending on location.

    On March 17, 2009, the European Space Agency launched a gravity-mapping satellite called Gravity and Ocean Circulation Explorer (GOCE). The data transmitted from GOCE are being used to build a model of Earth's shape and a gravity map of the planet.

    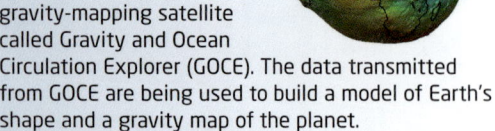

12. Explain the differences that occur in transforming the graph of the function $y = f(x)$ to the graph of the function $y = f(bx)$ as compared to transforming $y = f(x)$ to $y = af(x)$.

13. The speed of a vehicle the moment the brakes are applied can be determined by its skid marks. The length, D, in feet, of the skid mark is related to the speed, S, in miles per hour, of the vehicle before braking by the function $D = \frac{1}{30fn}S^2$, where f is the drag factor of the road surface and n is the braking efficiency as a decimal. Suppose the braking efficiency is 100% or 1.
    a) Sketch the graph of the length of the skid mark as a function of speed for a drag factor of 1, or $D = \frac{1}{30}S^2$.
    b) The drag factor for asphalt is 0.9, for gravel is 0.8, for snow is 0.55, and for ice is 0.25. Compare the graphs of the functions for these drag factors to the graph in part a).

Did You Know?

A technical accident investigator or reconstructionist is a specially trained police officer who investigates serious traffic accidents. These officers use photography, measurements of skid patterns, and other information to determine the cause of the collision and if any charges should be laid.

Extend

14. Consider the function $f(x) = (x + 4)(x - 3)$. Without graphing, determine the zeros of the function after each transformation.

 a) $y = 4f(x)$
 b) $y = f(-x)$
 c) $y = f\left(\frac{1}{2}x\right)$
 d) $y = f(2x)$

15. The graph of a function $y = f(x)$ is contained completely in the fourth quadrant. Copy and complete each statement.

 a) If $y = f(x)$ is transformed to $y = -f(x)$, it will be in quadrant ■.
 b) If $y = f(x)$ is transformed to $y = f(-x)$, it will be in quadrant ■.
 c) If $y = f(x)$ is transformed to $y = 4f(x)$, it will be in quadrant ■.
 d) If $y = f(x)$ is transformed to $y = f\left(\frac{1}{4}x\right)$, it will be in quadrant ■.

16. Sketch the graph of $f(x) = |x|$ reflected in each line.

 a) $x = 3$
 b) $y = -2$

Create Connections

C1 Explain why the graph of $g(x) = f(bx)$ is a horizontal stretch about the y-axis by a factor of $\frac{1}{b}$, for $b > 0$, rather than a factor of b.

C2 Describe a transformation that results in each situation. Is there more than one possibility?

 a) The x-intercepts are invariant points.
 b) The y-intercepts are invariant points.

C3 A point on the function $f(x)$ is mapped onto the image point on the function $g(x)$. Copy and complete the table by describing a possible transformation of $f(x)$ to obtain $g(x)$ for each mapping.

f(x)	g(x)	Transformation
(5, 6)	(5, −6)	
(4, 8)	(−4, 8)	
(2, 3)	(2, 12)	
(4, −12)	(2, −6)	

C4 Sound is a form of energy produced and transmitted by vibrating matter that travels in waves. Pitch is the measure of how high or how low a sound is. The graph of $f(x)$ demonstrates a normal pitch. Copy the graph, then sketch the graphs of $y = f(3x)$, indicating a higher pitch, and $y = f\left(\frac{1}{2}x\right)$, for a lower pitch.

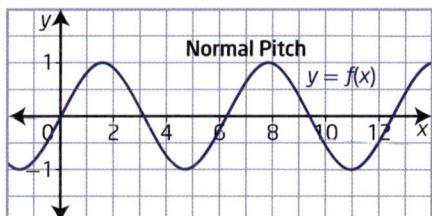

Did You Know?

The *pitch* of a sound wave is directly related to its *frequency*. A high-pitched sound has a high frequency (a mosquito). A low-pitched sound has a low frequency (a fog-horn).

A healthy human ear can hear frequencies in the range of 20 Hz to 20 000 Hz.

C5 a) Write the equation for the general term of the sequence −10, −6, −2, 2, 6,….

 b) Write the equation for the general term of the sequence 10, 6, 2, −2, −6,….

 c) How are the graphs of the two sequences related?

1.3

Combining Transformations

Focus on...

- sketching the graph of a transformed function by applying translations, reflections, and stretches
- writing the equation of a function that has been transformed from the function $y = f(x)$

Architects, artists, and craftspeople use transformations in their work. Towers that stretch the limits of architectural technologies, paintings that create futuristic landscapes from ordinary objects, and quilt designs that transform a single shape to create a more complex image are examples of these transformations.

In this section, you will apply a combination of transformations to base functions to create more complex functions.

National-Nederlanden Building in Prague, Czech Republic

Investigate the Order of Transformations

Materials

- grid paper

New graphs can be created by vertical or horizontal translations, vertical or horizontal stretches, or reflections in an axis. When vertical and horizontal translations are applied to the graph of a function, the order in which they occur does not affect the position of the final image.

Explore whether order matters when other combinations of transformations are applied. Consider the graph of $y = f(x)$.

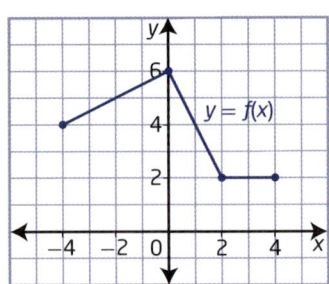

A: Stretches

1. **a)** Copy the graph of $y = f(x)$.

   b) Sketch the transformed graph after the following two stretches are performed in order. Write the resulting function equation after each transformation.
   - Stretch vertically about the *x*-axis by a factor of 2.
   - Stretch horizontally about the *y*-axis by a factor of 3.

c) Sketch the transformed graph after the same two stretches are performed in reverse order. Write the resulting function equation after each transformation.
   - Stretch horizontally about the y-axis by a factor of 3.
   - Stretch vertically about the x-axis by a factor of 2.

2. Compare the final graphs and equations from step 1b) and c). Did reversing the order of the stretches change the final result?

B: Combining Reflections and Translations

3. a) Copy the graph of $y = f(x)$.
   b) Sketch the transformed graph after the following two transformations are performed in order. Write the resulting function equation after each transformation.
   - Reflect in the x-axis.
   - Translate vertically 4 units up.
   c) Sketch the transformed graph after the same two transformations are performed in reverse order. Write the resulting function equation after each transformation.
   - Translate vertically 4 units up.
   - Reflect in the x-axis.

4. Compare the final graphs and equations from step 3b) and c). Did reversing the order of the transformations change the final result? Explain.

5. a) Copy the graph of $y = f(x)$.
   b) Sketch the transformed graph after the following two transformations are performed in order. Write the resulting function equation after each transformation.
   - Reflect in the y-axis.
   - Translate horizontally 4 units to the right.
   c) Sketch the transformed graph after the same two transformations are performed in reverse order. Write the resulting function equation after each transformation.
   - Translate horizontally 4 units to the right.
   - Reflect in the y-axis.

6. Compare the final graphs and equations from step 5b) and c). Did reversing the order of the transformations change the final result? Explain.

Reflect and Respond

7. a) What do you think would happen if the graph of a function were transformed by a vertical stretch about the x-axis and a vertical translation? Would the order of the transformations matter?
   b) Use the graph of $y = |x|$ to test your prediction.

8. In which order do you think transformations should be performed to produce the correct graph? Explain.

Link the Ideas

Multiple transformations can be applied to a function using the general transformation model $y - k = af(b(x - h))$ or $y = af(b(x - h)) + k$.

To accurately sketch the graph of a function of the form $y - k = af(b(x - h))$, the stretches and reflections (values of a and b) should occur before the translations (h-value and k-value). The diagram shows one recommended sequence for the order of transformations.

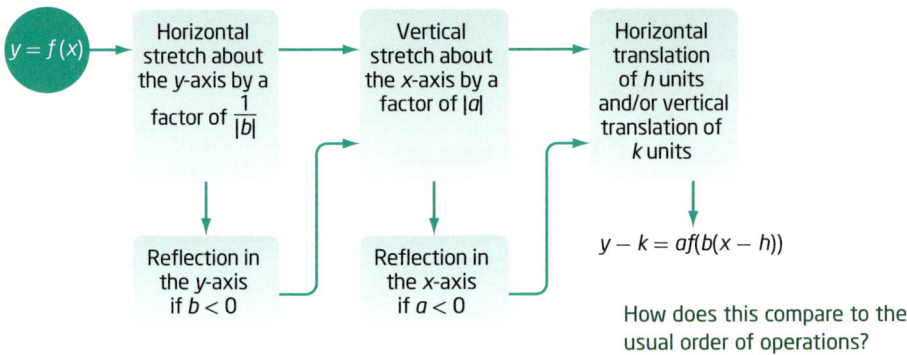

How does this compare to the usual order of operations?

Example 1

Graph a Transformed Function

Describe the combination of transformations that must be applied to the function $y = f(x)$ to obtain the transformed function. Sketch the graph, showing each step of the transformation.

a) $y = 3f(2x)$
b) $y = f(3x + 6)$

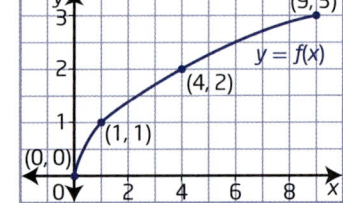

Solution

a) Compare the function to $y = af(b(x - h)) + k$. For $y = 3f(2x)$, $a = 3$, $b = 2$, $h = 0$, and $k = 0$.

The graph of $y = f(x)$ is horizontally stretched about the y-axis by a factor of $\frac{1}{2}$ and then vertically stretched about the x-axis by a factor of 3.

- Apply the horizontal stretch by a factor of $\frac{1}{2}$ to obtain the graph of $y = f(2x)$.

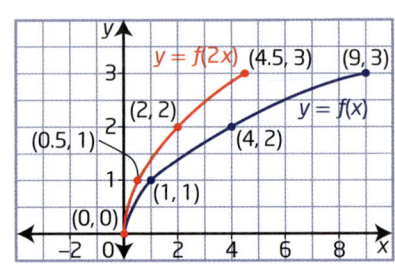

34 MHR • Chapter 1

- Apply the vertical stretch by a factor of 3 to $y = f(2x)$ to obtain the graph of $y = 3f(2x)$.

> Would performing the stretches in reverse order change the final result?

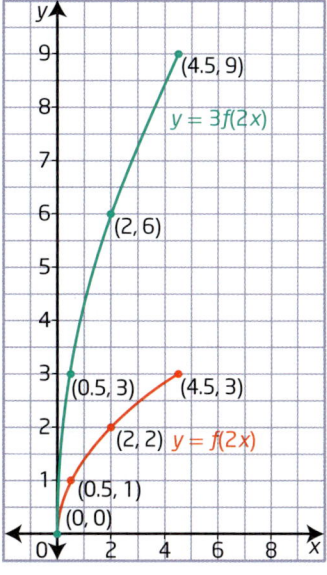

b) First, rewrite $y = f(3x + 6)$ in the form $y = af(b(x - h)) + k$. This makes it easier to identify specific transformations.

$y = f(3x + 6)$
$y = f(3(x + 2))$ Factor out the coefficient of x.
For $y = f(3(x + 2))$, $a = 1$, $b = 3$, $h = -2$, and $k = 0$.

The graph of $y = f(x)$ is horizontally stretched about the y-axis by a factor of $\frac{1}{3}$ and then horizontally translated 2 units to the left.

- Apply the horizontal stretch by a factor of $\frac{1}{3}$ to obtain the graph of $y = f(3x)$.

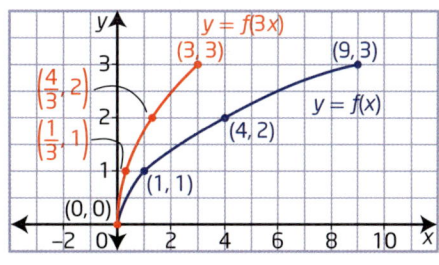

- Apply the horizontal translation of 2 units to the left to $y = f(3x)$ to obtain the graph of $y = f(3(x + 2))$.

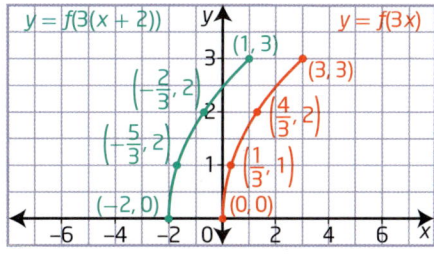

Your Turn

Describe the combination of transformations that must be applied to the function $y = f(x)$ to obtain the transformed function. Sketch the graph, showing each step of the transformation.

a) $y = 2f(x) - 3$ **b)** $y = f\left(\frac{1}{2}x - 2\right)$

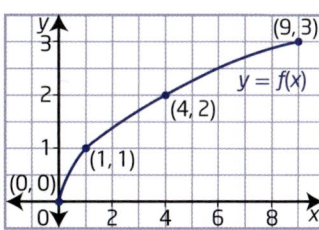

Example 2

Combination of Transformations

Show the combination of transformations that should be applied to the graph of the function $f(x) = x^2$ in order to obtain the graph of the transformed function $g(x) = -\frac{1}{2}f(2(x-4)) + 1$. Write the corresponding equation for $g(x)$.

Solution

For $g(x) = -\frac{1}{2}f(2(x-4)) + 1$, $a = -\frac{1}{2}$, $b = 2$, $h = 4$, and $k = 1$.

Description	Mapping	Graph
Horizontal stretch about the y-axis by a factor of $\frac{1}{2}$ $y = (2x)^2$	$(-2, 4) \to (-1, 4)$ $(0, 0) \to (0, 0)$ $(2, 4) \to (1, 4)$ $(x, y) \to \left(\frac{1}{2}x, y\right)$	
Vertical stretch about the x-axis by a factor of $\frac{1}{2}$ $y = \frac{1}{2}(2x)^2$	$(-1, 4) \to (-1, 2)$ $(0, 0) \to (0, 0)$ $(1, 4) \to (1, 2)$ $\left(\frac{1}{2}x, y\right) \to \left(\frac{1}{2}x, \frac{1}{2}y\right)$	
Reflection in the x-axis $y = -\frac{1}{2}(2x)^2$	$(-1, 2) \to (-1, -2)$ $(0, 0) \to (0, 0)$ $(1, 2) \to (1, -2)$ $\left(\frac{1}{2}x, \frac{1}{2}y\right) \to \left(\frac{1}{2}x, -\frac{1}{2}y\right)$	
Translation of 4 units to the right and 1 unit up $y = -\frac{1}{2}(2(x-4))^2 + 1$	$(-1, -2) \to (3, -1)$ $(0, 0) \to (4, 1)$ $(1, -2) \to (5, -1)$ $\left(\frac{1}{2}x, -\frac{1}{2}y\right) \to \left(\frac{1}{2}x + 4, -\frac{1}{2}y + 1\right)$	

The equation of the transformed function is $g(x) = -\frac{1}{2}(2(x-4))^2 + 1$.

Your Turn

Describe the combination of transformations that should be applied to the function $f(x) = x^2$ in order to obtain the transformed function $g(x) = -2f\left(\frac{1}{2}(x + 8)\right) - 3$. Write the corresponding equation and sketch the graph of $g(x)$.

Example 3

Write the Equation of a Transformed Function Graph

The graph of the function $y = g(x)$ represents a transformation of the graph of $y = f(x)$. Determine the equation of $g(x)$ in the form $y = af(b(x - h)) + k$. Explain your answer.

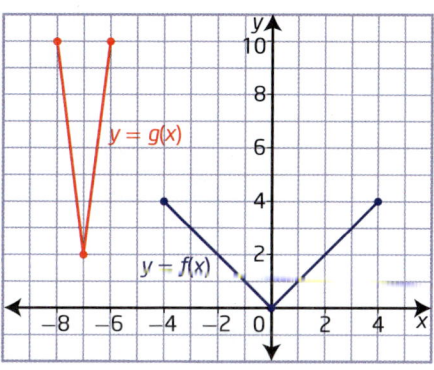

Solution

Locate key points on the graph of $f(x)$ and their image points on the graph of $g(x)$.

$(-4, 4) \rightarrow (-8, 10)$
$(0, 0) \rightarrow (-7, 2)$
$(4, 4) \rightarrow (-6, 10)$

The point $(0, 0)$ on the graph of $f(x)$ is not affected by any stretch, either horizontal or vertical, or any reflection so it can be used to determine the vertical and horizontal translations. The graph of $g(x)$ has been translated 7 units to the left and 2 units up.

$h = -7$ and $k = 2$
There is no reflection.

Compare the distances between key points. In the vertical direction, 4 units becomes 8 units. There is a vertical stretch by a factor of 2. In the horizontal direction, 8 units becomes 2 units. There is also a horizontal stretch by a factor of $\frac{1}{4}$.

$a = 2$ and $b = 4$

Substitute the values of a, b, h, and k into $y = af(b(x - h)) + k$.

The equation of the transformed function is $g(x) = 2f(4(x + 7)) + 2$.

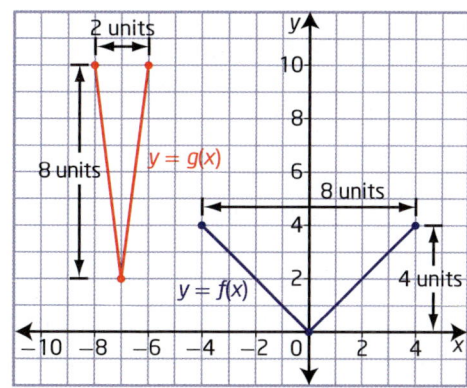

How could you use the mapping $(x, y) \rightarrow \left(\frac{1}{b}x + h, ay + k\right)$ to verify this equation?

Your Turn

The graph of the function $y = g(x)$ represents a transformation of the graph of $y = f(x)$. State the equation of the transformed function. Explain your answer.

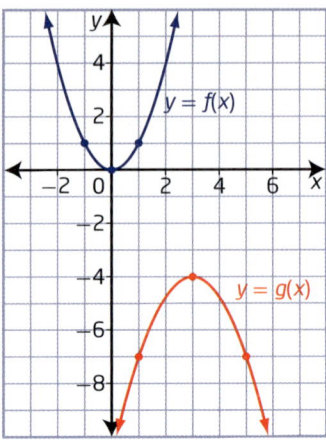

Key Ideas

- Write the function in the form $y = af(b(x - h)) + k$ to better identify the transformations.
- Stretches and reflections may be performed in any order before translations.
- The parameters a, b, h, and k in the function $y = af(b(x - h)) + k$ correspond to the following transformations:
  - a corresponds to a vertical stretch about the x-axis by a factor of $|a|$. If $a < 0$, then the function is reflected in the x-axis.
  - b corresponds to a horizontal stretch about the y-axis by a factor of $\frac{1}{|b|}$. If $b < 0$, then the function is reflected in the y-axis.
  - h corresponds to a horizontal translation.
  - k corresponds to a vertical translation.

Check Your Understanding

Practise

1. The function $y = x^2$ has been transformed to $y = af(bx)$. Determine the equation of each transformed function.

   a) Its graph is stretched horizontally about the y-axis by a factor of 2 and then reflected in the x-axis.

   b) Its graph is stretched horizontally about the y-axis by a factor of $\frac{1}{4}$, reflected in the y-axis, and then stretched vertically about the x-axis by a factor of $\frac{1}{4}$.

2. The function $y = f(x)$ is transformed to the function $g(x) = -3f(4x - 16) - 10$. Copy and complete the following statements by filling in the blanks.

   The function $f(x)$ is transformed to the function $g(x)$ by a horizontal stretch about the ■ by a factor of ■. It is vertically stretched about the ■ by a factor of ■. It is reflected in the ■, and then translated ■ units to the right and ■ units down.

3. Copy and complete the table by describing the transformations of the given functions, compared to the function $y = f(x)$.

Function	Reflections	Vertical Stretch Factor	Horizontal Stretch Factor	Vertical Translation	Horizontal Translation
$y - 4 = f(x - 5)$					
$y + 5 = 2f(3x)$					
$y = \frac{1}{2}f\left(\frac{1}{2}(x - 4)\right)$					
$y + 2 = -3f(2(x + 2))$					

4. Using the graph of $y = f(x)$, write the equation of each transformed graph in the form $y = af(b(x - h)) + k$.

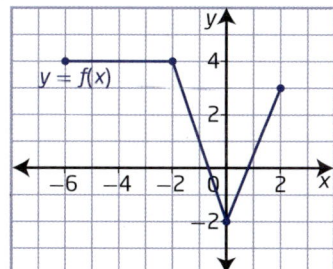

a)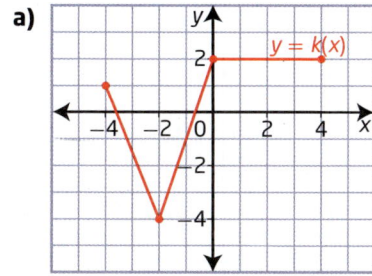

b)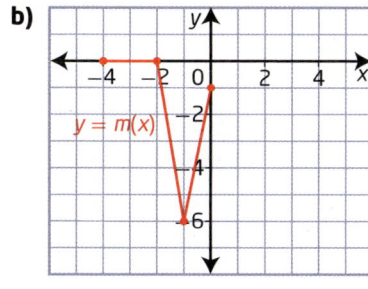

5. For each graph of $y = f(x)$, sketch the graph of the combined transformations. Show each transformation in the sequence.

a)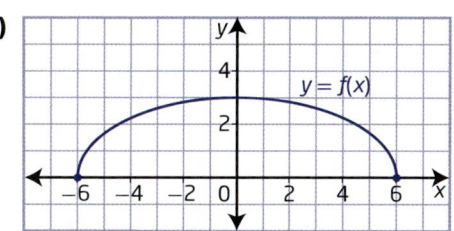

- vertical stretch about the x-axis by a factor of 2
- horizontal stretch about the y-axis by a factor of $\frac{1}{3}$
- translation of 5 units to the left and 3 units up

b)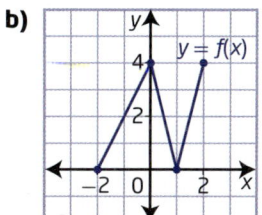

- vertical stretch about the x-axis by a factor of $\frac{3}{4}$
- horizontal stretch about the y-axis by a factor of 3
- translation of 3 units to the right and 4 units down

6. The key point $(-12, 18)$ is on the graph of $y = f(x)$. What is its image point under each transformation of the graph of $f(x)$?

a) $y + 6 = f(x - 4)$

b) $y = 4f(3x)$

c) $y = -2f(x - 6) + 4$

d) $y = -2f\left(-\frac{2}{3}x - 6\right) + 4$

e) $y + 3 = -\frac{1}{3}f(2(x + 6))$

Apply

7. Describe, using an appropriate order, how to obtain the graph of each function from the graph of $y = f(x)$. Then, give the mapping for the transformation.

a) $y = 2f(x - 3) + 4$

b) $y = -f(3x) - 2$

c) $y = -\frac{1}{4}f(-(x + 2))$

d) $y - 3 = -f(4(x - 2))$

e) $y = -\frac{2}{3}f\left(-\frac{3}{4}x\right)$

f) $3y - 6 = f(-2x + 12)$

8. Given the function $y = f(x)$, write the equation of the form $y - k = af(b(x - h))$ that would result from each combination of transformations.

a) a vertical stretch about the x-axis by a factor of 3, a reflection in the x-axis, a horizontal translation of 4 units to the left, and a vertical translation of 5 units down

b) a horizontal stretch about the y-axis by a factor of $\frac{1}{3}$, a vertical stretch about the x-axis by a factor of $\frac{3}{4}$, a reflection in both the x-axis and the y-axis, and a translation of 6 units to the right and 2 units up

9. The graph of $y = f(x)$ is given. Sketch the graph of each of the following functions.

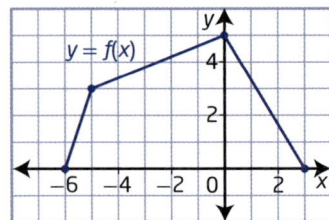

a) $y + 2 = f(x - 3)$

b) $y = -f(-x)$

c) $y = f(3(x - 2)) + 1$

d) $y = 3f\left(\frac{1}{3}x\right)$

e) $y + 2 = -3f(x + 4)$

f) $y = \frac{1}{2}f\left(-\frac{1}{2}(x + 2)\right) - 1$

10. The graph of the function $y = g(x)$ represents a transformation of the graph of $y = f(x)$. Determine the equation of $g(x)$ in the form $y = af(b(x - h)) + k$.

a)
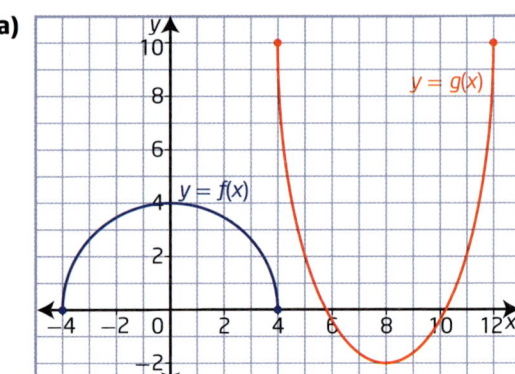

b)
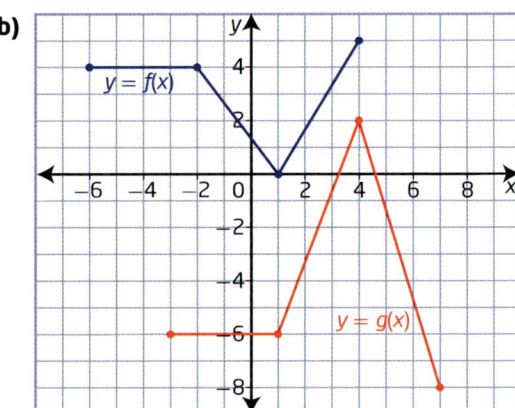

c)
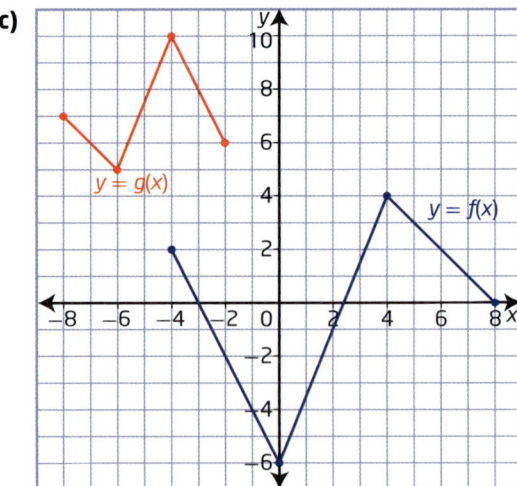

11. Given the function $f(x)$, sketch the graph of the transformed function $g(x)$.

a) $f(x) = x^2$, $g(x) = -2f(4(x + 2)) - 2$

b) $f(x) = |x|$, $g(x) = -2f(-3x + 6) + 4$

c) $f(x) = x$, $g(x) = -\frac{1}{3}f(-2(x + 3)) - 2$

12. Alison often sketches her quilt designs on a coordinate grid. The coordinates for a section of one her designs are A(−4, 6), B(−2, −2), C(0, 0), D(1, −1), and E(3, 6). She wants to transform the original design by a horizontal stretch about the y-axis by a factor of 2, a reflection in the x-axis, and a translation of 4 units up and 3 units to the left.

   a) Determine the coordinates of the image points, A′, B′, C′, D′, and E′.

   b) If the original design was defined by the function $y = f(x)$, determine the equation of the design resulting from the transformations.

13. Gil is asked to translate the graph of $y = |x|$ according to the equation $y = |2x − 6| + 2$. He decides to do the horizontal translation of 3 units to the right first, then the stretch about the y-axis by a factor of $\frac{1}{2}$, and lastly the translation of 2 units up. This gives him Graph 1. To check his work, he decides to apply the horizontal stretch about the y-axis by a factor of $\frac{1}{2}$ first, and then the horizontal translation of 6 units to the right and the vertical translation of 2 units up. This results in Graph 2.

   a) Explain why the two graphs are in different locations.

   b) How could Gil have rewritten the equation so that the order in which he did the transformations for Graph 2 resulted in the same position as Graph 1?

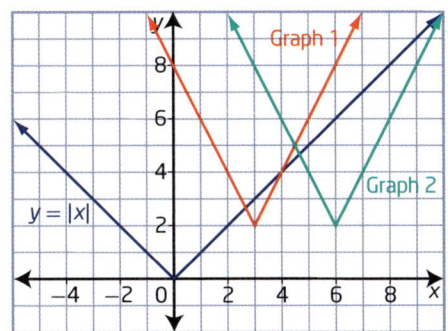

14. Two parabolic arches are being built. The first arch can be modelled by the function $y = -x^2 + 9$, with a range of $0 \le y \le 9$. The second arch must span twice the distance and be translated 6 units to the left and 3 units down.

   a) Sketch the graph of both arches.

   b) Determine the equation of the second arch.

Extend

15. If the x-intercept of the graph of $y = f(x)$ is located at $(a, 0)$ and the y-intercept is located at $(0, b)$, determine the x-intercept and y-intercept after the following transformations of the graph of $y = f(x)$.

   a) $y = -f(-x)$

   b) $y = 2f\left(\frac{1}{2}x\right)$

   c) $y + 3 = f(x - 4)$

   d) $y + 3 = \frac{1}{2}f\left(\frac{1}{4}(x - 4)\right)$

16. A rectangle is inscribed between the x-axis and the parabola $y = 9 - x^2$ with one side along the x-axis, as shown.

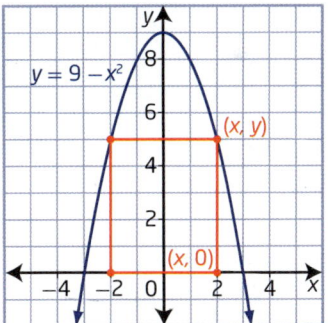

   a) Write the equation for the area of the rectangle as a function of x.

   b) Suppose a horizontal stretch by a factor of 4 is applied to the parabola. What is the equation for the area of the transformed rectangle?

   c) Suppose the point (2, 5) is the vertex of the rectangle on the original parabola. Use this point to verify your equations from parts a) and b).

17. The graph of the function $y = 2x^2 + x + 1$ is stretched vertically about the x-axis by a factor of 2, stretched horizontally about the y-axis by a factor of $\frac{1}{3}$, and translated 2 units to the right and 4 units down. Write the equation of the transformed function.

18. This section deals with transformations in a specific order. Give one or more examples of transformations in which the order does not matter. Show how you know that order does not matter.

Create Connections

C1 MINI LAB Many designs, such as this Moroccan carpet, are based on transformations.

Materials
- grid paper
- graphing calculator

Work with a partner. Use transformations of functions to create designs on a graphing calculator.

Step 1 The graph shows the function $f(x) = -x + 3$ and transformations 1, 2, and 3.

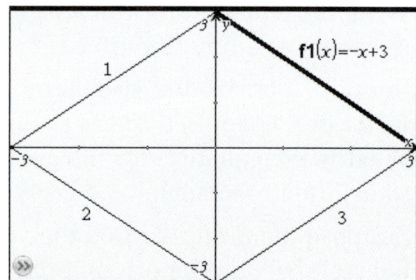

- Recreate the diagram on a graphing calculator. Use the window settings $x: [-3, 3, 1]$ $y: [-3, 3, 1]$.
- Describe the transformations necessary to create the image.
- Write the equations necessary to transform the original function.

Step 2 The graph shows the function $f(x) = x^2$ and transformations 1, 2, 3, and 4.

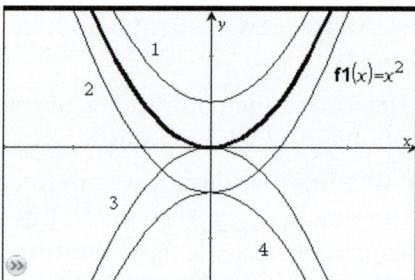

- Recreate the diagram on a graphing calculator. Use the window settings $x: [-3, 3, 1]$ $y: [-3, 3, 1]$.
- Describe the transformations necessary to create the image.
- Write the equations necessary to transform the original function.

C2 Kokitusi`aki (Diana Passmore) and Siksmissi (Kathy Anderson) make and sell beaded bracelets such as the one shown representing the bear and the wolf.

If they make b bracelets per week at a cost of $f(b)$, what do the following expressions represent? How do they relate to transformations?

a) $f(b + 12)$ b) $f(b) + 12$
c) $3f(b)$ d) $f(2b)$

> **Did You Know?**
>
> Sisters Diana Passmore and Kathy Anderson are descendants of the Little Dog Clan of the Piegan (Pikuni'l') Nation of the Blackfoot Confederacy.

C3 Express the function $y = 2x^2 - 12x + 19$ in the form $y = a(x - h)^2 + k$. Use that form to describe how the graph of $y = x^2$ can be transformed to the graph of $y = 2x^2 - 12x + 19$.

C4 Musical notes can be repeated (translated horizontally), transposed (translated vertically), inverted (horizontal mirror), in retrograde (vertical mirror), or in retrograde inversion (180° rotation). If the musical pattern being transformed is the pattern in red, describe a possible transformation to arrive at the patterns H, J, and K.

a)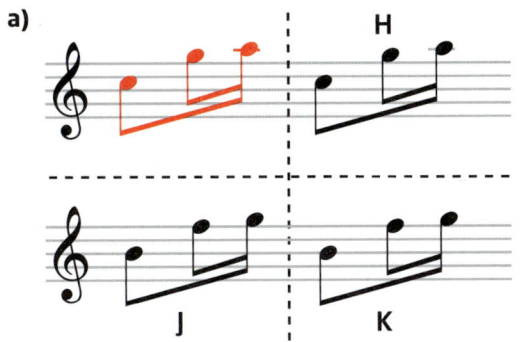

b)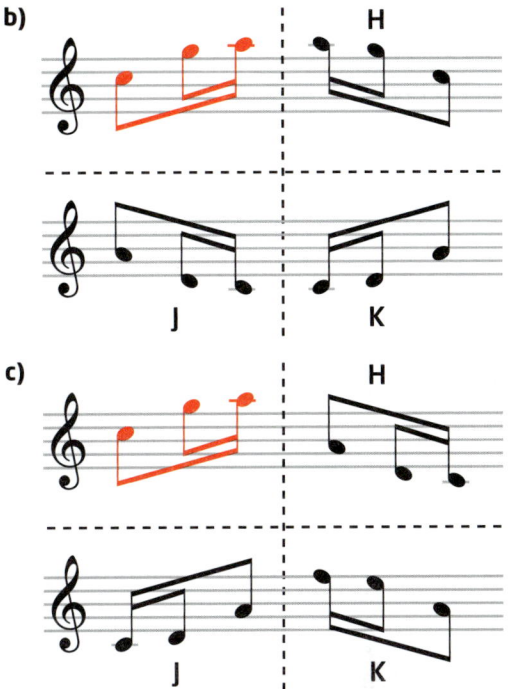

c)

Project Corner — Transformations Around You

- What type(s) of function(s) do you see in the image?
- Describe how each base function has been transformed.

$f(x) = -\dfrac{5}{4}\left(x - \dfrac{4}{5}\right)^2 + \dfrac{36}{5}$

$h(x) = -\dfrac{17}{40}\left|x - \dfrac{16}{3}\right| + \dfrac{9}{10}$

$g(x) = \dfrac{6}{5}x - 12$

1.4

Inverse of a Relation

Focus on...

- sketching the graph of the inverse of a relation
- determining if a relation and its inverse are functions
- determining the equation of an inverse

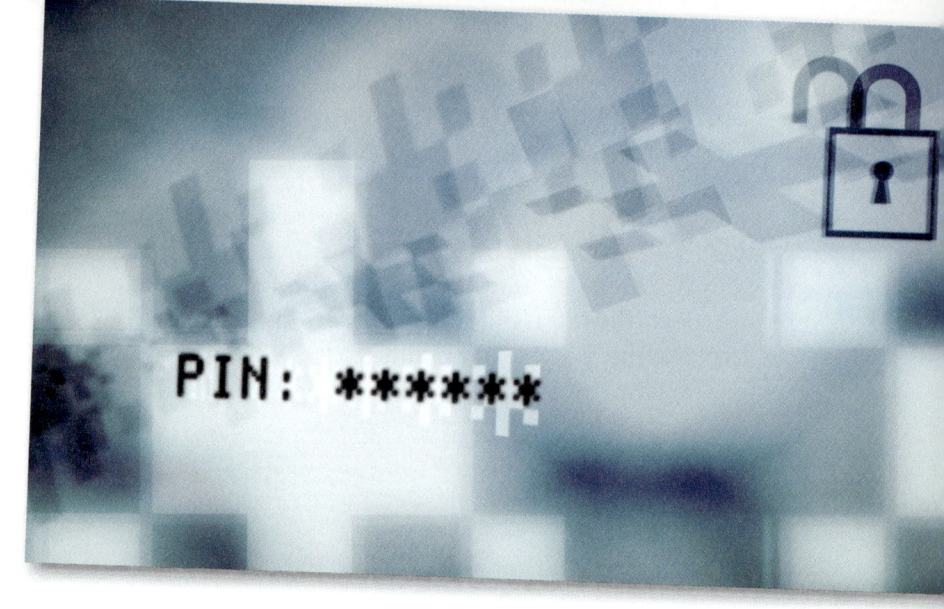

An inverse is often thought of as "undoing" or "reversing" a position, order, or effect. Whenever you undo something that you or someone else did, you are using an inverse, whether it is unwrapping a gift that someone else wrapped or closing a door that has just been opened, or deciphering a secret code.

For example, when sending a secret message, a key is used to encode the information. Then, the receiver uses the key to decode the information.

Let each letter in the alphabet be mapped to the numbers 0 to 25.

Plain Text	I	N	V	E	R	S	E
Numeric Values, x	8	13	21	4	17	18	4
Cipher, $x - 2$	6	11	19	2	15	16	2
Cipher Text	G	L	T	C	P	Q	C

Decrypting is the inverse of encrypting. What decryption function would you use on GLTCPQC? What other examples of inverses can you think of?

Investigate the Inverse of a Function

Materials

- grid paper

1. Consider the function $f(x) = \frac{1}{4}x - 5$.

   a) Copy the table. In the first column, enter the ordered pairs of five points on the graph of $f(x)$. To complete the second column of the table, interchange the x-coordinates and y-coordinates of the points in the first column.

Key Points on the Graph of $f(x)$	Image Points on the Graph of $g(x)$

b) Plot the points for the function $f(x)$ and draw a line through them.

  c) Plot the points for the relation $g(x)$ on the same set of axes and draw a line through them.

2. a) Draw the graph of $y = x$ on the same set of axes as in step 1.

  b) How do the distances from the line $y = x$ for key points and corresponding image points compare?

  c) What type of transformation occurs in order for $f(x)$ to become $g(x)$?

3. a) What observation can you make about the relationship of the coordinates of your ordered pairs between the graphs of $f(x)$ and $g(x)$?

  b) Determine the equation of $g(x)$. How is this equation related to $f(x) = \frac{1}{4}x - 5$?

  c) The relation $g(x)$ is considered to be the inverse of $f(x)$. Is the inverse of $f(x)$ a function? Explain.

Reflect and Respond

4. Describe a way to draw the graph of the **inverse of a function** using reflections.

5. Do you think all inverses of functions are functions? What factors did you base your decision on?

6. a) State a hypothesis for writing the equation of the inverse of a linear function.

  b) Test your hypothesis. Write the equation of the inverse of $y = 3x + 2$. Check by graphing.

7. Determine the equation of the inverse of $y = mx + b$, $m \neq 0$.

  a) Make a conjecture about the relationship between the slope of the inverse function and the slope of the original function.

  b) Make a conjecture about the relationship between the x-intercepts and the y-intercept of the original function and those of the inverse function.

8. Describe how you could determine if two relations are inverses of each other.

inverse of a function
- if f is a function with domain A and range B, the inverse function, if it exists, is denoted by f^{-1} and has domain B and range A
- f^{-1} maps y to x if and only if f maps x to y

Link the Ideas

The inverse of a relation is found by interchanging the *x*-coordinates and *y*-coordinates of the ordered pairs of the relation. In other words, for every ordered pair (x, y) of a relation, there is an ordered pair (y, x) on the inverse of the relation. This means that the graphs of a relation and its inverse are reflections of each other in the line $y = x$.

$(x, y) \rightarrow (y, x)$

Did You Know?

The −1 in $f^{-1}(x)$ does not represent an exponent; that is $f^{-1}(x) \neq \dfrac{1}{f(x)}$.

The inverse of a function $y = f(x)$ may be written in the form $x = f(y)$. The inverse of a function is not necessarily a function. When the inverse of *f* is itself a function, it is denoted as f^{-1} and read as "*f* inverse." When the inverse of a function is not a function, it may be possible to restrict the domain to obtain an inverse function for a portion of the original function.

The inverse of a function reverses the processes represented by that function. Functions $f(x)$ and $g(x)$ are inverses of each other if the operations of $f(x)$ reverse all the operations of $g(x)$ in the opposite order and the operations of $g(x)$ reverse all the operations of $f(x)$ in the opposite order.

For example, $f(x) = 2x + 1$ multiplies the input value by 2 and then adds 1. The inverse function subtracts 1 from the input value and then divides by 2. The inverse function is $f^{-1}(x) = \dfrac{x - 1}{2}$.

Example 1

Graph an Inverse

Consider the graph of the relation shown.

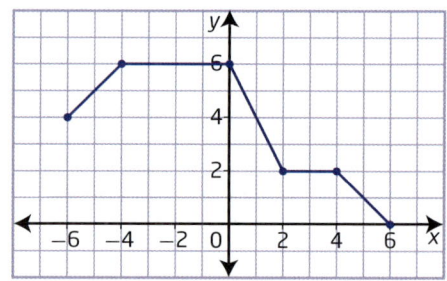

a) Sketch the graph of the inverse relation.
b) State the domain and range of the relation and its inverse.
c) Determine whether the relation and its inverse are functions.

Solution

a) To graph the inverse relation, interchange the *x*-coordinates and *y*-coordinates of key points on the graph of the relation.

Points on the Relation	Points on the Inverse Relation
(−6, 4)	(4, −6)
(−4, 6)	(6, −4)
(0, 6)	(6, 0)
(2, 2)	(2, 2)
(4, 2)	(2, 4)
(6, 0)	(0, 6)

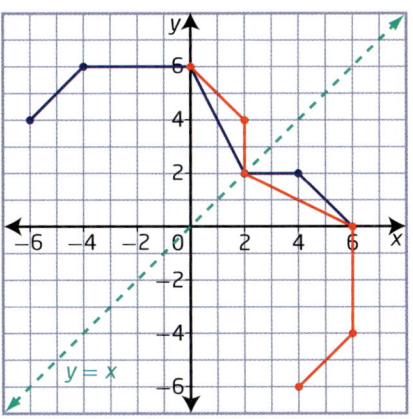

The graphs are reflections of each other in the line $y = x$. The points on the graph of the relation are related to the points on the graph of the inverse relation by the mapping $(x, y) \rightarrow (y, x)$.

What points are invariant after a reflection in the line $y = x$?

Did You Know?

A *one-to-one function* is a function for which every element in the range corresponds to exactly one element in the domain. The graph of a relation is a function if it passes the vertical line test. If, in addition, it passes the horizontal line test, it is a one-to-one function.

b) The domain of the relation becomes the range of the inverse relation and the range of the relation becomes the domain of the inverse relation.

	Domain	Range
Relation	$\{x \mid -6 \leq x \leq 6, x \in R\}$	$\{y \mid 0 \leq y \leq 6, y \in R\}$
Inverse Relation	$\{x \mid 0 \leq x \leq 6, x \in R\}$	$\{y \mid -6 \leq y \leq 6, y \in R\}$

c) The relation is a function of x because there is only one value of y in the range for each value of x in the domain. In other words, the graph of the relation passes the vertical line test.

The inverse relation is not a function of x because it fails the vertical line test. There is more than one value of y in the range for at least one value of x in the domain. You can confirm this by using the **horizontal line test** on the graph of the original relation.

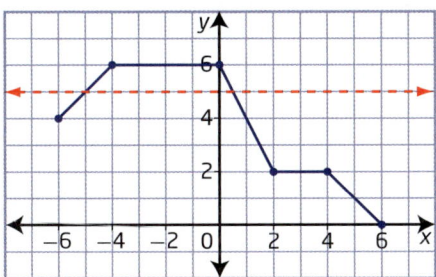

horizontal line test
- a test used to determine if the graph of an inverse relation will be a function
- if it is possible for a horizontal line to intersect the graph of a relation more than once, then the inverse of the relation is not a function

Your Turn

Consider the graph of the relation shown.
a) Determine whether the relation and its inverse are functions.
b) Sketch the graph of the inverse relation.
c) State the domain, range, and intercepts for the relation and the inverse relation.
d) State any invariant points.

1.4 Inverse of a Relation • MHR **47**

Example 2
Restrict the Domain

Consider the function $f(x) = x^2 - 2$.
a) Graph the function $f(x)$. Is the inverse of $f(x)$ a function?
b) Graph the inverse of $f(x)$ on the same set of coordinate axes.
c) Describe how the domain of $f(x)$ could be restricted so that the inverse of $f(x)$ is a function.

Solution

a) The graph of $f(x) = x^2 - 2$ is a translation of the graph of $y = x^2$ by 2 units down.

Since the graph of the function fails the horizontal line test, the inverse of $f(x)$ is not a function.

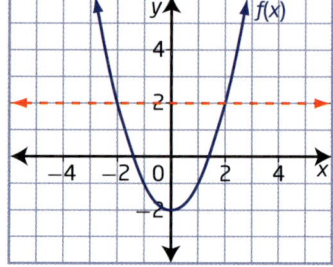

b) Use key points on the graph of $f(x)$ to help you sketch the graph of the inverse of $f(x)$.

> Notice that the graph of the inverse of $f(x)$ does not pass the vertical line test. The inverse of $f(x)$ is not a function.

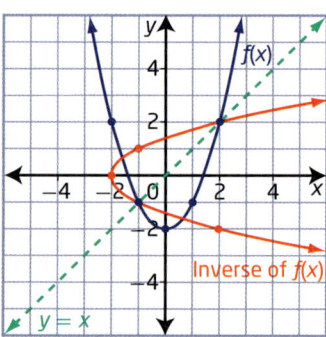

c) The inverse of $f(x)$ is a function if the graph of $f(x)$ passes the horizontal line test.

One possibility is to restrict the domain of $f(x)$ so that the resulting graph is only one half of the parabola. Since the equation of the axis of symmetry is $x = 0$, restrict the domain to $\{x \mid x \geq 0, x \in R\}$.

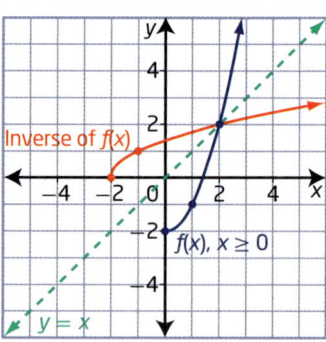

How else could the domain of $f(x)$ be restricted?

Your Turn

Consider the function $f(x) = (x + 2)^2$.
a) Graph the function $f(x)$. Is the inverse of $f(x)$ a function?
b) Graph the inverse of $f(x)$ on the same set of coordinate axes.
c) Describe how the domain of $f(x)$ could be restricted so that the inverse of $f(x)$ is a function.

Example 3

Determine the Equation of the Inverse

Algebraically determine the equation of the inverse of each function. Verify graphically that the relations are inverses of each other.
a) $f(x) = 3x + 6$
b) $f(x) = x^2 - 4$

Solution

a) Let $y = f(x)$. To find the equation of the inverse, $x = f(y)$, interchange x and y, and then solve for y.

$f(x) = 3x + 6$
$y = 3x + 6$ — Replace $f(x)$ with y.
$x = 3y + 6$ — Interchange x and y to determine the inverse.
$x - 6 = 3y$ — Solve for y.
$\dfrac{x - 6}{3} = y$
$f^{-1}(x) = \dfrac{x - 6}{3}$ — Replace y with $f^{-1}(x)$, since the inverse of a linear function is also a function.

Graph $y = 3x + 6$ and $y = \dfrac{x - 6}{3}$ on the same set of coordinate axes.

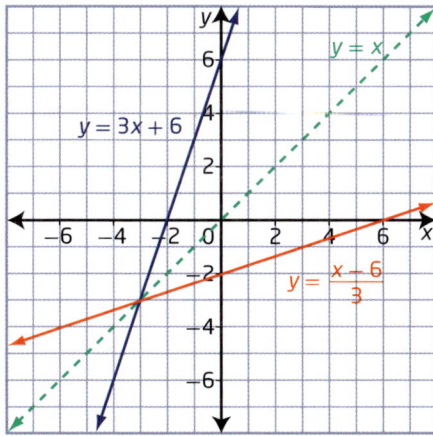

Notice that the x-intercept and y-intercept of $y = 3x + 6$ become the y-intercept and x-intercept, respectively, of $y = \dfrac{x - 6}{3}$. Since the functions are reflections of each other in the line $y = x$, the functions are inverses of each other.

b) The same method applies to quadratic functions.

$$f(x) = x^2 - 4$$
$$y = x^2 - 4 \quad \text{Replace } f(x) \text{ with } y.$$
$$x = y^2 - 4 \quad \text{Interchange } x \text{ and } y \text{ to determine the inverse.}$$
$$x + 4 = y^2 \quad \text{Solve for } y.$$
$$\pm\sqrt{x + 4} = y$$
$$y = \pm\sqrt{x + 4} \quad \text{Why is this } y \text{ not replaced with } f^{-1}(x)? \text{ What could be done so that } f^{-1}(x) \text{ could be used?}$$

Graph $y = x^2 - 4$ and $y = \pm\sqrt{x + 4}$ on the same set of coordinate axes.

x	$y = x^2 - 4$
−3	5
−2	0
−1	−3
0	−4
1	−3
2	0
3	5

x	$y = \pm\sqrt{x + 4}$
5	±3
0	±2
−3	±1
−4	0

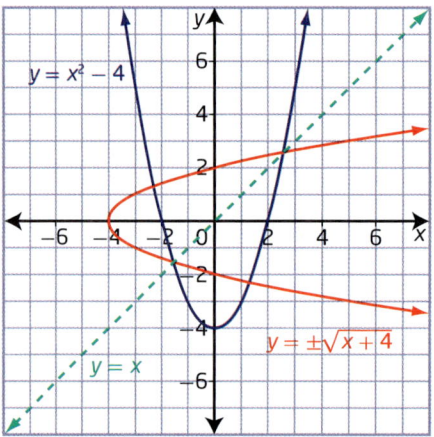

How could you use the tables of values to verify that the relations are inverses of each other?

Notice that the x-intercepts and y-intercept of $y = x^2 - 4$ become the y-intercepts and x-intercept, respectively, of $y = \pm\sqrt{x + 4}$. The relations are reflections of each other in the line $y = x$. While the relations are inverses of each other, $y = \pm\sqrt{x + 4}$ is not a function.

Your Turn

Write the equation for the inverse of the function $f(x) = \dfrac{x + 8}{3}$. Verify your answer graphically.

Key Ideas

- You can find the inverse of a relation by interchanging the x-coordinates and y-coordinates of the graph.
- The graph of the inverse of a relation is the graph of the relation reflected in the line $y = x$.
- The domain and range of a relation become the range and domain, respectively, of the inverse of the relation.
- Use the horizontal line test to determine if an inverse will be a function.
- You can create an inverse that is a function over a specified interval by restricting the domain of a function.
- When the inverse of a function $f(x)$ is itself a function, it is denoted by $f^{-1}(x)$.
- You can verify graphically whether two functions are inverses of each other.

Check Your Understanding

Practise

1. Copy each graph. Use the reflection line $y = x$ to sketch the graph of $x = f(y)$ on the same set of axes.

a)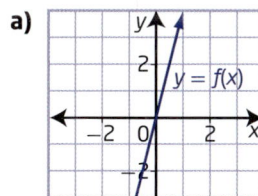

b)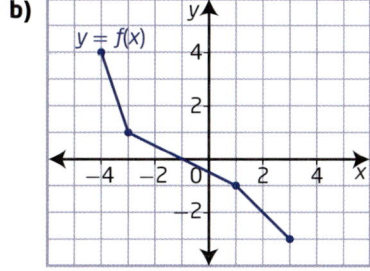

2. Copy the graph of each relation and sketch the graph of its inverse relation.

a)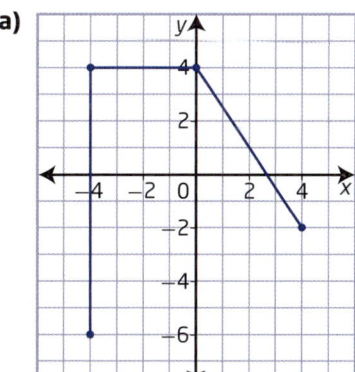

b)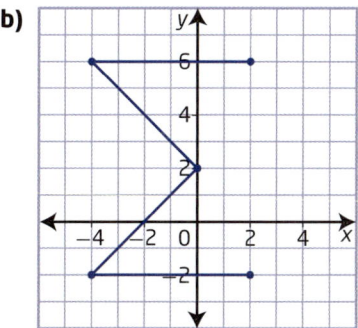

3. State whether or not the graph of the relation is a function. Then, use the horizontal line test to determine whether the inverse relation will be a function.

a)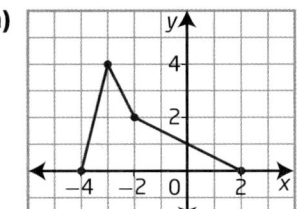

b)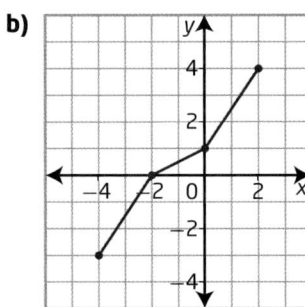

c)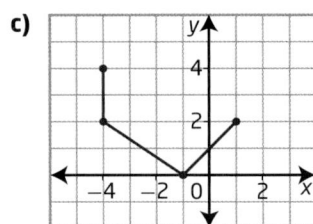

4. For each graph, identify a restricted domain for which the function has an inverse that is also a function.

a)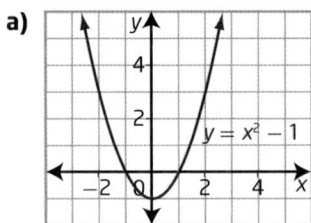

b)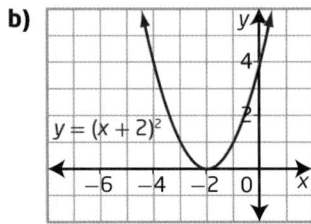

c)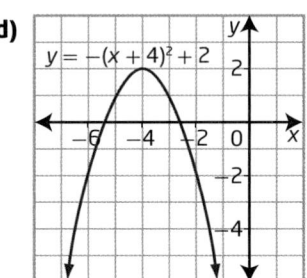

d)

5. Algebraically determine the equation of the inverse of each function.

a) $f(x) = 7x$

b) $f(x) = -3x + 4$

c) $f(x) = \dfrac{x+4}{3}$

d) $f(x) = \dfrac{x}{3} - 5$

e) $f(x) = 5 - 2x$

f) $f(x) = \dfrac{1}{2}(x+6)$

6. Match the function with its inverse.

Function

a) $y = 2x + 5$

b) $y = \dfrac{1}{2}x - 4$

c) $y = 6 - 3x$

d) $y = x^2 - 12, \ x \geq 0$

e) $y = \dfrac{1}{2}(x+1)^2, \ x \leq -1$

Inverse

A $y = \sqrt{x + 12}$

B $y = \dfrac{6-x}{3}$

C $y = 2x + 8$

D $y = -\sqrt{2x} - 1$

E $y = \dfrac{x-5}{2}$

Apply

7. For each table, plot the ordered pairs (x, y) and the ordered pairs (y, x). State the domain of the function and its inverse.

a)
x	y
−2	−2
−1	1
0	4
1	7
2	10

b)
x	y
−6	2
−4	4
−1	5
2	5
5	3

8. Copy each graph of $y = f(x)$ and then sketch the graph of its inverse. Determine if the inverse is a function. Give a reason for your answer.

a)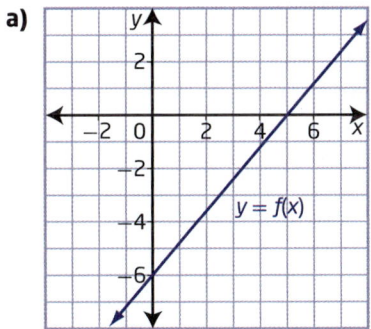

b)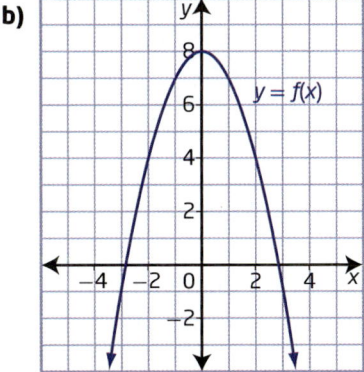

c)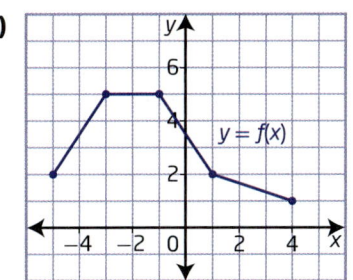

9. For each of the following functions,
- determine the equation for the inverse, $f^{-1}(x)$
- graph $f(x)$ and $f^{-1}(x)$
- determine the domain and range of $f(x)$ and $f^{-1}(x)$

a) $f(x) = 3x + 2$

b) $f(x) = 4 - 2x$

c) $f(x) = \frac{1}{2}x - 6$

d) $f(x) = x^2 + 2, x \leq 0$

e) $f(x) = 2 - x^2, x \geq 0$

10. For each function $f(x)$,
  i) determine the equation of the inverse of $f(x)$ by first rewriting the function in the form $y = a(x - h)^2 + k$
  ii) graph $f(x)$ and the inverse of $f(x)$

a) $f(x) = x^2 + 8x + 12$

b) $f(x) = x^2 - 4x + 2$

11. Jocelyn and Gerry determine that the inverse of the function $f(x) = x^2 - 5, x \geq 0$, is $f^{-1}(x) = \sqrt{x + 5}$. Does the graph verify that these functions are inverses of each other? Explain why.

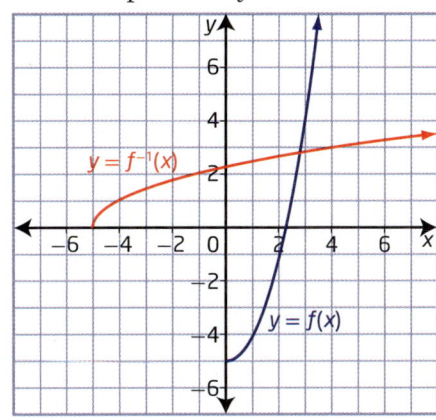

12. For each of the following functions,
- determine the equation of the inverse
- graph $f(x)$ and the inverse of $f(x)$
- restrict the domain of $f(x)$ so that the inverse of $f(x)$ is a function
- with the domain of $f(x)$ restricted, sketch the graphs of $f(x)$ and $f^{-1}(x)$

a) $f(x) = x^2 + 3$
b) $f(x) = \frac{1}{2}x^2$
c) $f(x) = -2x^2$
d) $f(x) = (x + 1)^2$
e) $f(x) = -(x - 3)^2$
f) $f(x) = (x - 1)^2 - 2$

13. Determine graphically whether the functions in each pair are inverses of each other.

a) $f(x) = x - 4$ and $g(x) = x + 4$
b) $f(x) = 3x + 5$ and $g(x) = \frac{x - 5}{3}$
c) $f(x) = x - 7$ and $g(x) = 7 - x$
d) $f(x) = \frac{x - 2}{2}$ and $g(x) = 2x + 2$
e) $f(x) = \frac{8}{x - 7}$ and $g(x) = \frac{8}{x + 7}$

14. For each function, state two ways to restrict the domain so that the inverse is a function.

a) $f(x) = x^2 + 4$
b) $f(x) = 2 - x^2$
c) $f(x) = (x - 3)^2$
d) $f(x) = (x + 2)^2 - 4$

15. Given the function $f(x) = 4x - 2$, determine each of the following.

a) $f^{-1}(4)$
b) $f^{-1}(-2)$
c) $f^{-1}(8)$
d) $f^{-1}(0)$

16. The function for converting the temperature from degrees Fahrenheit, x, to degrees Celsius, y, is $y = \frac{5}{9}(x - 32)$.

a) Determine the equivalent temperature in degrees Celsius for 90 °F.
b) Determine the inverse of this function. What does it represent? What do the variables represent?
c) Determine the equivalent temperature in degrees Fahrenheit for 32 °C.
d) Graph both functions. What does the invariant point represent in this situation?

17. A forensic specialist can estimate the height of a person from the lengths of their bones. One function relates the length, x, of the femur to the height, y, of the person, both in centimetres.

For a male: $y = 2.32x + 65.53$
For a female: $y = 2.47x + 54.13$

a) Determine the height of a male and of a female with a femur length of 45.47 cm.
b) Use inverse functions to determine the femur length of
  i) a male whose height is 187.9 cm
  ii) a female whose height is 175.26 cm

18. In Canada, ring sizes are specified using a numerical scale. The numerical ring size, y, is approximately related to finger circumference, x, in millimetres, by $y = \frac{x - 36.5}{2.55}$.

a) What whole-number ring size corresponds to a finger circumference of 49.3 mm?
b) Determine an equation for the inverse of the function. What do the variables represent?
c) What finger circumferences correspond to ring sizes of 6, 7, and 9?

Extend

19. When a function is constantly increasing or decreasing, its inverse is a function. For each graph of $f(x)$,

i) choose an interval over which the function is increasing and sketch the inverse of the function when it is restricted to that domain

ii) choose an interval over which the function is decreasing and sketch the inverse of the function when it is restricted to that domain

a)
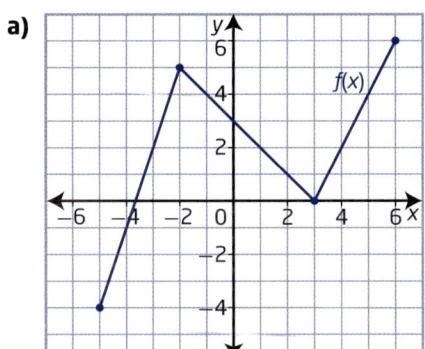

b)
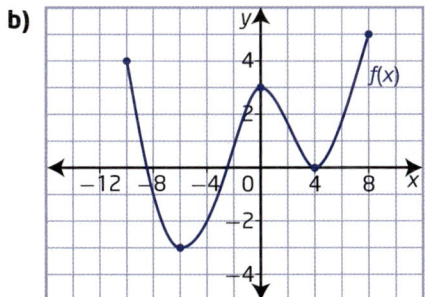

20. Suppose a function $f(x)$ has an inverse function, $f^{-1}(x)$.

a) Determine $f^{-1}(5)$ if $f(17) = 5$.

b) Determine $f(-2)$ if $f^{-1}(\sqrt{3}) = -2$.

c) Determine the value of a if $f^{-1}(a) = 1$ and $f(x) = 2x^2 + 5x + 3$, $x \geq -1.25$.

21. If the point $(10, 8)$ is on the graph of the function $y = f(x)$, what point must be on the graph of each of the following?

a) $y = f^{-1}(x + 2)$

b) $y = 2f^{-1}(x) + 3$

c) $y = -f^{-1}(-x) + 1$

Create Connections

C1 Describe the inverse sequence of operations for each of the following.

a) $f(x) = 6x + 12$

b) $f(x) = (x + 3)^2 - 1$

C2 a) Sketch the graphs of the function $f(x) = -x + 3$ and its inverse, $f^{-1}(x)$.

b) Explain why $f(x) = f^{-1}(x)$.

c) If a function and its inverse are the same, how are they related to the line $y = x$?

C3 Two students are arguing about whether or not a given relation and its inverse are functions. Explain how the students could verify who is correct.

C4 **MINI LAB** Two functions, $f(x) = \dfrac{x + 5}{3}$ and $g(x) = 3x - 5$, are inverses of each other.

Step 1 Evaluate output values for $f(x)$ for $x = 1$, $x = 4$, $x = -8$, and $x = a$. Use the results as input values for $g(x)$. What do you notice about the output values for $g(x)$? Explain why this happens. State a hypothesis that could be used to verify whether or not two functions are inverses of each other.

Step 2 Reverse the order in which you used the functions. Start with using the input values for $g(x)$, and then use the outputs in $f(x)$. What conclusion can you make about inverse functions?

Step 3 Test your conclusions and hypothesis by selecting two functions of your own.

Step 4 Explain how your results relate to the statement "if $f(a) = b$ and $f^{-1}(b) = a$, then the two functions are inverses of each other." Note that this must also be true when the function roles are switched.

Chapter 1 Review

1.1 Horizontal and Vertical Translations, pages 6–15

1. Given the graph of the function $y = f(x)$, sketch the graph of each transformed function.

   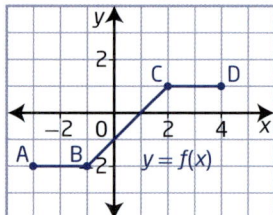

   a) $y - 3 = f(x)$
   b) $h(x) = f(x + 1)$
   c) $y + 1 = f(x - 2)$

2. Describe how to translate the graph of $y = |x|$ to obtain the graph of the function shown. Write the equation of the transformed function in the form $y - k = |x - h|$.

   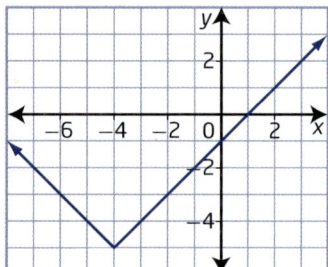

3. The range of the function $y = f(x)$ is $\{y \mid -2 \leq y \leq 5, y \in R\}$. What is the range of the function $y = f(x - 2) + 4$?

4. James wants to explain vertical and horizontal translations by describing the effect of the translation on the coordinates of a point on the graph of a function. He says, "If the point (a, b) is on the graph of $y = f(x)$, then the point $(a - 5, b + 4)$ is the image point on the graph of $y + 4 = f(x - 5)$." Do you agree with James? Explain your reasoning.

1.2 Reflections and Stretches, pages 16–31

5. Name the line of reflection when the graph of $y = f(x)$ is transformed as indicated. Then, state the coordinates of the image point of $(3, 5)$ on the graph of each reflection.

   a) $y = -f(x)$
   b) $y = f(-x)$

6. Copy each graph of $y = f(x)$. Then,
   - sketch the reflection indicated
   - state the domain and range of the transformed function
   - list any invariant points

   a) $y = f(-x)$ b) $y = -f(x)$

   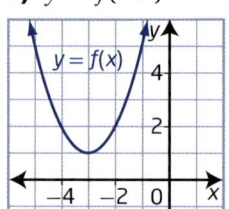 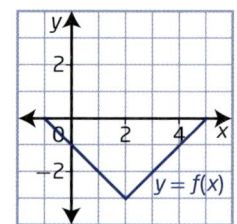

7. a) Sketch the graphs of the functions $f(x) = x^2$, $g(x) = f(2x)$, and $h(x) = f\left(\frac{1}{2}x\right)$ on the same set of coordinate axes.

   b) Describe how the value of the coefficient of x for $g(x)$ and $h(x)$ affects the graph of the function $f(x) = x^2$.

8. Consider the graphs of the functions $f(x)$ and $g(x)$.

   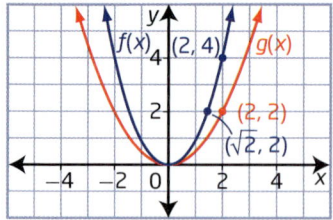

   a) Is the graph of $g(x)$ a horizontal or a vertical stretch of the graph of $f(x)$? Explain your reasoning.

   b) Write the equation that models the graph of $g(x)$ as a transformation of the graph of $f(x)$.

1.3 Combining Transformations, pages 32–43

9. Given the graph of $y = f(x)$, sketch the graph of each transformed function.

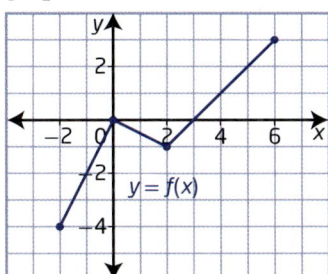

   a) $y = 2f\left(\dfrac{1}{2}x\right)$ b) $y = \dfrac{1}{2}f(3x)$

10. Explain how the transformations described by $y = f(4(x + 1))$ and $y = f(4x + 1)$ are similar and how they are different.

11. Write the equation for the graph of $g(x)$ as a transformation of the equation for the graph of $f(x)$.

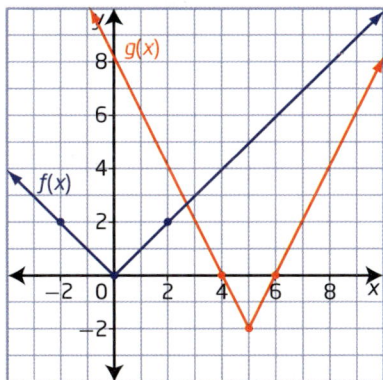

12. Consider the graph of $y = f(x)$. Sketch the graph of each transformation.

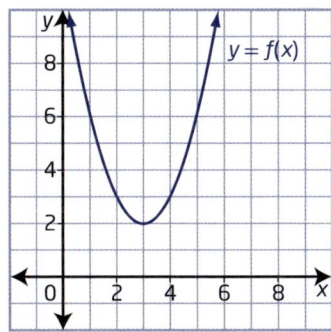

   a) $y = \dfrac{1}{2}f(-(x + 2))$
   b) $y - 2 = -f(2(x - 3))$
   c) $y - 1 = 3f(2x + 4)$

1.4 Inverse of a Relation, pages 44–55

13. a) Copy the graph of $y = f(x)$ and sketch the graph of $x = f(y)$.
    b) Name the line of reflection and list any invariant points.
    c) State the domain and range of the two functions.

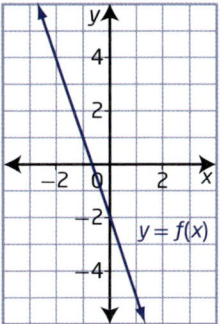

14. Copy and complete the table.

$y = f(x)$		$y = f^{-1}(x)$	
x	y	x	y
−3	7		
		4	2
10		−12	

15. Sketch the graph of the inverse relation for each graph. State whether the relation and its inverse are functions.

   a) 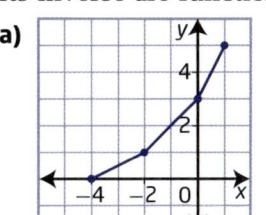   b)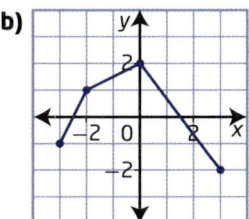

16. Algebraically determine the equation of the inverse of the function $y = (x - 3)^2 + 1$. Determine a restriction on the domain of the function in order for its inverse to be a function. Show your thinking.

17. Graphically determine if the functions are inverses of each other.

   a) $f(x) = -6x + 5$ and $g(x) = \dfrac{x + 5}{6}$
   b) $f(x) = \dfrac{x - 3}{8}$ and $g(x) = 8x + 3$

Chapter 1 Practice Test

Multiple Choice

For #1 to #7, choose the best answer.

1. What is the effect on the graph of the function $y = x^2$ when the equation is changed to $y = (x + 1)^2$?
   - **A** The graph is stretched vertically.
   - **B** The graph is stretched horizontally.
   - **C** The graph is the same shape but translated up.
   - **D** The graph is the same shape but translated to the left.

2. The graph shows a transformation of the graph of $y = |x|$. Which equation models the graph?

   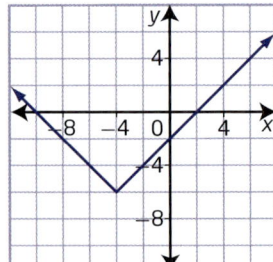

   - **A** $y + 4 = |x - 6|$
   - **B** $y - 6 = |x - 4|$
   - **C** $y - 4 = |x + 6|$
   - **D** $y + 6 = |x + 4|$

3. If (a, b) is a point on the graph of $y = f(x)$, which of the following points is on the graph of $y = f(x + 2)$?
   - **A** $(a + 2, b)$
   - **B** $(a - 2, b)$
   - **C** $(a, b + 2)$
   - **D** $(a, b - 2)$

4. Which equation represents the image of $y = x^2 + 2$ after a reflection in the y-axis?
   - **A** $y = -x^2 - 2$
   - **B** $y = x^2 + 2$
   - **C** $y = -x^2 + 2$
   - **D** $y = x^2 - 2$

5. The effect on the graph of $y = f(x)$ if it is transformed to $y = \frac{1}{4}f(3x)$ is
   - **A** a vertical stretch by a factor of $\frac{1}{4}$ and a horizontal stretch by a factor of 3
   - **B** a vertical stretch by a factor of $\frac{1}{4}$ and a horizontal stretch by a factor of $\frac{1}{3}$
   - **C** a vertical stretch by a factor of 4 and a horizontal stretch by a factor of 3
   - **D** a vertical stretch by a factor of 4 and a horizontal stretch by a factor of $\frac{1}{3}$

6. Which of the following transformations of $f(x)$ produces a graph that has the same y-intercept as $f(x)$? Assume that $(0, 0)$ is not a point on $f(x)$.
   - **A** $-9f(x)$
   - **B** $f(x) - 9$
   - **C** $f(-9x)$
   - **D** $f(x - 9)$

7. Given the graphs of $y = f(x)$ and $y = g(x)$, what is the equation for $g(x)$ in terms of $f(x)$?

   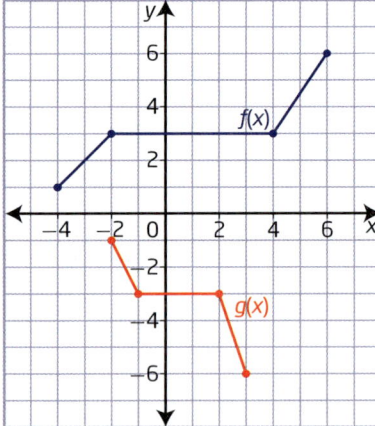

   - **A** $g(x) = f\left(-\frac{1}{2}x\right)$
   - **B** $g(x) = f(-2x)$
   - **C** $g(x) = -f(2x)$
   - **D** $g(x) = -f\left(\frac{1}{2}x\right)$

Short Answer

8. The domain of the function $y = f(x)$ is $\{x \mid -3 \leq x \leq 4, x \in R\}$. What is the domain of the function $y = f(x + 2) - 1$?

9. Given the graph of $y = f(x)$, sketch the graph of $y - 4 = -\dfrac{1}{4} f\left(\dfrac{1}{2}(x + 3)\right)$.

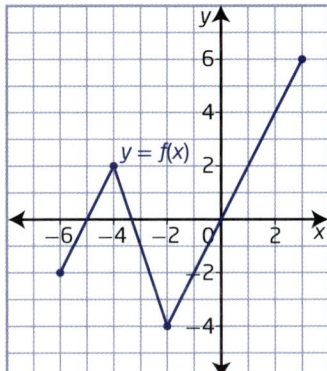

10. Consider the graph of the function $y = f(x)$.

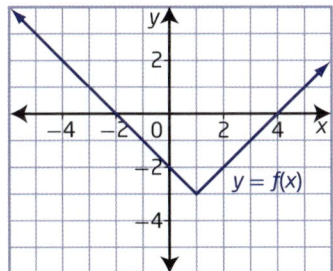

   a) Sketch the graph of the inverse.
   b) Explain how the coordinates of key points are transformed.
   c) State any invariant points.

11. Write the equation of the inverse function of $y = 5x + 2$. Verify graphically that the functions are inverses of each other.

12. A transformation of the graph of $y = f(x)$ results in a horizontal stretch about the y-axis by a factor of 2, a horizontal reflection in the y-axis, a vertical stretch about the x-axis by a factor of 3, and a horizontal translation of 2 units to the right. Write the equation for the transformed function.

Extended Response

13. The graph of the function $f(x) = |x|$ is transformed to the graph of $g(x) = f(x + 2) - 7$.
    a) Describe the transformation.
    b) Write the equation of the function $g(x)$.
    c) Determine the minimum value of $g(x)$.
    d) The domain of the function $f(x)$ is the set of real numbers. The domain of the function $g(x)$ is also the set of real numbers. Does this imply that all of the points are invariant? Explain your answer.

14. The function $g(x)$ is a transformation of the function $f(x)$.

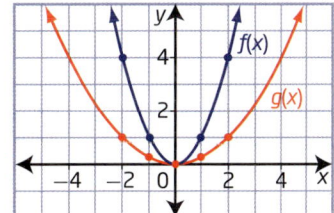

   a) Write the equation of the function $f(x)$.
   b) Write the equation of the function $g(x)$ in the form $g(x) = af(x)$, and describe the transformation.
   c) Write the equation of the function $g(x)$ in the form $g(x) = f(bx)$, and describe the transformation.
   d) Algebraically prove that the two equations from parts b) and c) are equivalent.

15. Consider the function $h(x) = -(x + 3)^2 - 5$.
    a) Explain how you can determine whether or not the inverse of $h(x)$ is a function.
    b) Write the equation of the inverse relation in simplified form.
    c) What restrictions could be placed on the domain of the function so that the inverse is also a function?

CHAPTER 2

Radical Functions

How far can you see from the top of a hill? What range of vision does a submarine's periscope have? How much fertilizer is required for a particular crop? How much of Earth's surface can a satellite "see"? You can model each of these situations using a radical function. The functions can range from simple square root functions to more complex radical functions of higher orders.

In this chapter, you will explore a variety of square root functions and work with radical functions used by an aerospace engineer when relating the distance to the horizon for a satellite above Earth. Would you expect this to be a simple or a complex radical function?

Did You Know?

Some satellites are put into *polar orbits*, where they follow paths perpendicular to the equator. Other satellites are put into *geostationary orbits* that are parallel to the equator.

Polar orbiting satellites are useful for taking high-resolution photographs. Geostationary satellites allow for weather monitoring and communications for a specific country or continent.

Geostationary Satellite, approximate altitude of 36 000-km

Polar Orbiting Satellite, approximate altitude of 800-km

Key Terms
radical function   square root of a function

Career Link

Scientists and engineers use remote sensing to create satellite images. They use instruments and satellites to produce information that is used to manage resources, investigate environmental issues, and produce sophisticated maps.

Web Link

To learn more about a career or educational opportunities involving remote sensing, go to www.mcgrawhill.ca/school/learningcentres and follow the links.

Yellowknife Wetlands

2.1

Radical Functions and Transformations

Focus on...

- investigating the function $y = \sqrt{x}$ using a table of values and a graph
- graphing radical functions using transformations
- identifying the domain and range of radical functions

Does a feather fall more slowly than a rock? Galileo Galilei, a mathematician and scientist, pondered this question more than 400 years ago. He theorized that the rate of falling objects depends on air resistance, not on mass. It is believed that he tested his idea by dropping spheres of different masses but the same diameter from the top of the Leaning Tower of Pisa in what is now Italy. The result was exactly as he predicted—they fell at the same rate.

In 1971, during the Apollo 15 lunar landing, Commander David Scott performed a similar demonstration on live television. Because the surface of the moon is essentially a vacuum, a hammer and a feather fell at the same rate.

Web Link

For more information about Galileo or the Apollo 15 mission, go to www.mcgrawhill.ca/school/learningcentres and follow the links.

Investigate a Radical Function

Materials
- grid paper
- graphing technology (optional)

For objects falling near the surface of Earth, the function $d = 5t^2$ approximately models the time, t, in seconds, for an object to fall a distance, d, in metres, if the resistance caused by air can be ignored.

1. **a)** Identify any restrictions on the domain of this function. Why are these restrictions necessary? What is the range of the function?

   b) Create a table of values and a graph showing the distance fallen as a function of time.

2. Express time in terms of distance for the distance-time function from step 1. Represent the new function graphically and using a table of values.

3. For each representation, how is the equation of the new function from step 2 related to the original function?

Reflect and Respond

4. a) The original function is a distance-time function. What would you call the new function? Under what circumstances would you use each function?

b) What is the shape of the graph of the original function? Describe the shape of the graph of the new function.

Link the Ideas

The function that gives the predicted fall time for an object under the influence of gravity is an example of a **radical function**. Radical functions have restricted domains if the index of the radical is an even number. Like many types of functions, you can represent radical functions in a variety of ways, including tables, graphs, and equations. You can create graphs of radical functions using tables of values or technology, or by transforming the base radical function, $y = \sqrt{x}$.

radical function
- a function that involves a radical with a variable in the radicand
- $y = \sqrt{3x}$ and $y = 4\sqrt[3]{5 + x}$ are radical functions.

Example 1

Graph Radical Functions Using Tables of Values

Use a table of values to sketch the graph of each function. Then, state the domain and range of each function.

a) $y = \sqrt{x}$ **b)** $y = \sqrt{x-2}$ **c)** $y = \sqrt{x} - 3$

Solution

a) For the function $y = \sqrt{x}$, the radicand x must be greater than or equal to zero, $x \geq 0$.

x	y
0	0
1	1
4	2
9	3
16	4
25	5

How can you choose values of x that allow you to complete the table without using a calculator?

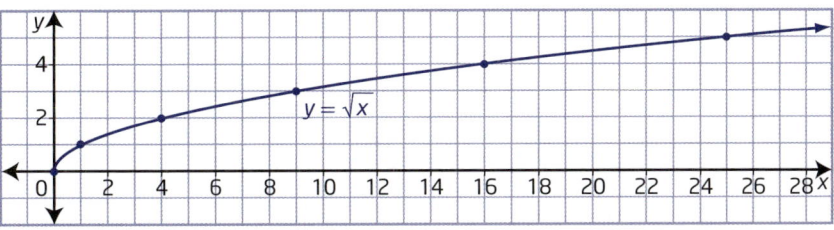

The graph has an endpoint at (0, 0) and continues up and to the right. The domain is $\{x \mid x \geq 0, x \in R\}$. The range is $\{y \mid y \geq 0, y \in R\}$.

b) For the function $y = \sqrt{x - 2}$, the value of the radicand must be greater than or equal to zero.

$x - 2 \geq 0$
$x \geq 2$

x	y
2	0
3	1
6	2
11	3
18	4
27	5

How is this table related to the table for $y = \sqrt{x}$ in part a)?

How does the graph of $y = \sqrt{x - 2}$ compare to the graph of $y = \sqrt{x}$?

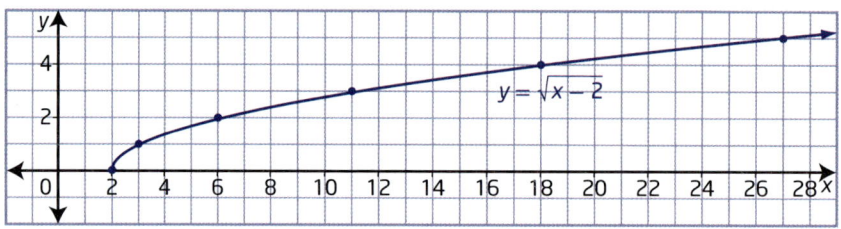

The domain is $\{x \mid x \geq 2, x \in R\}$. The range is $\{y \mid y \geq 0, y \in R\}$.

c) The radicand of $y = \sqrt{x} - 3$ must be non-negative.

$x \geq 0$

x	y
0	−3
1	−2
4	−1
9	0
16	1
25	2

How does the graph of $y = \sqrt{x} - 3$ compare to the graph of $y = \sqrt{x}$?

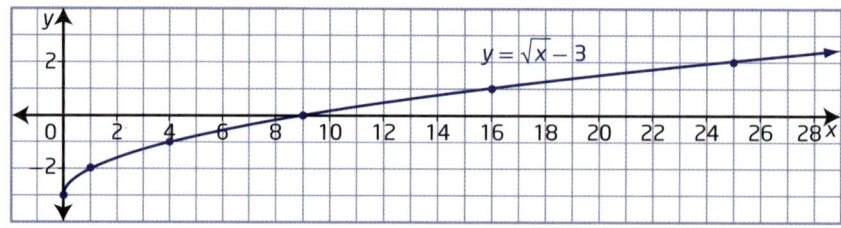

The domain is $\{x \mid x \geq 0, x \in R\}$ and the range is $\{y \mid y \geq -3, y \in R\}$.

Your Turn

Sketch the graph of the function $y = \sqrt{x + 5}$ using a table of values. State the domain and the range.

Graphing Radical Functions Using Transformations

You can graph a radical function of the form $y = a\sqrt{b(x - h)} + k$ by transforming the graph of $y = \sqrt{x}$ based on the values of a, b, h, and k. The effects of changing parameters in radical functions are the same as the effects of changing parameters in other types of functions.

- Parameter a results in a vertical stretch of the graph of $y = \sqrt{x}$ by a factor of $|a|$. If $a < 0$, the graph of $y = \sqrt{x}$ is reflected in the x-axis.
- Parameter b results in a horizontal stretch of the graph of $y = \sqrt{x}$ by a factor of $\frac{1}{|b|}$. If $b < 0$, the graph of $y = \sqrt{x}$ is reflected in the y-axis.
- Parameter h determines the horizontal translation. If $h > 0$, the graph of $y = \sqrt{x}$ is translated to the right h units. If $h < 0$, the graph is translated to the left $|h|$ units.
- Parameter k determines the vertical translation. If $k > 0$, the graph of $y = \sqrt{x}$ is translated up k units. If $k < 0$, the graph is translated down $|k|$ units.

Example 2

Graph Radical Functions Using Transformations

Sketch the graph of each function using transformations. Compare the domain and range to those of $y = \sqrt{x}$ and identify any changes.

a) $y = 3\sqrt{-(x - 1)}$ **b)** $y - 3 = -\sqrt{2x}$

Solution

a) The function $y = 3\sqrt{-(x - 1)}$ is expressed in the form $y = a\sqrt{b(x - h)} + k$. Identify the value of each parameter and how it will transform the graph of $y = \sqrt{x}$.

Why is it acceptable to have a negative sign under a square root sign?

- $a = 3$ results in a vertical stretch by a factor of 3 (step 1).
- $b = -1$ results in a reflection in the y-axis (step 2).
- $h = 1$ results in a horizontal translation of 1 unit to the right (step 3).
- $k = 0$, so the graph has no vertical translation.

Method 1: Transform the Graph Directly
Start with a sketch of $y = \sqrt{x}$ and apply the transformations one at a time.

In what order do transformations need to be performed?

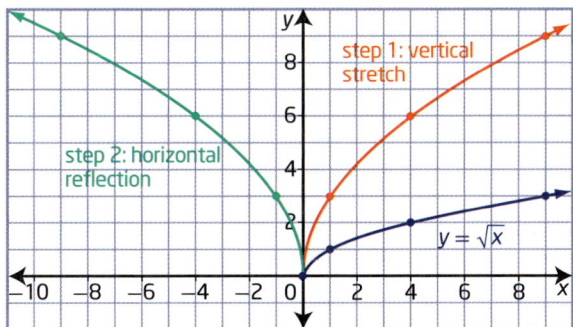
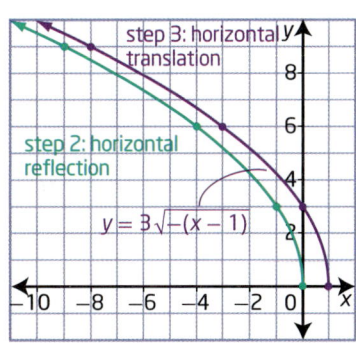

Method 2: Map Individual Points

Choose key points on the graph of $y = \sqrt{x}$ and map them for each transformation.

> How can you use mapping notation to express each transformation step?

Transformation of $y = \sqrt{x}$	Mapping
Vertical stretch by a factor of 3	$(0, 0) \to (0, 0)$ $(1, 1) \to (1, 3)$ $(4, 2) \to (4, 6)$ $(9, 3) \to (9, 9)$
Horizontal reflection in the y-axis	$(0, 0) \to (0, 0)$ $(1, 3) \to (-1, 3)$ $(4, 6) \to (-4, 6)$ $(9, 9) \to (-9, 9)$
Horizontal translation of 1 unit to the right	$(0, 0) \to (1, 0)$ $(-1, 3) \to (0, 3)$ $(-4, 6) \to (-3, 6)$ $(-9, 9) \to (-8, 9)$

Plot the image points to create the transformed graph.

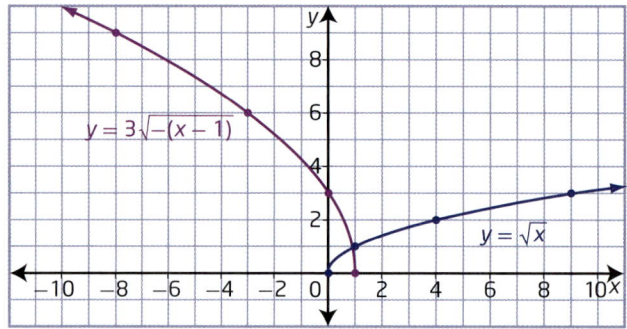

The function $y = \sqrt{x}$ is reflected horizontally, stretched vertically by a factor of 3, and then translated 1 unit right. So, the graph of $y = 3\sqrt{-(x-1)}$ extends to the left from $x = 1$ and its domain is $\{x \mid x \leq 1, x \in R\}$.

Since the function is not reflected vertically or translated vertically, the graph of $y = 3\sqrt{-(x-1)}$ extends up from $y = 0$, similar to the graph of $y = \sqrt{x}$. The range, $\{y \mid y \geq 0, y \in R\}$, is unchanged by the transformations.

b) Express the function $y - 3 = -\sqrt{2x}$ in the form $y = a\sqrt{b(x-h)} + k$ to identify the value of each parameter.
$$y - 3 = -\sqrt{2x}$$
$$y = -\sqrt{2x} + 3$$

- $b = 2$ results in horizontal stretch by a factor of $\frac{1}{2}$ (step 1).
- $a = -1$ results in a reflection in the x-axis (step 2).
- $h = 0$, so the graph is not translated horizontally.
- $k = 3$ results in a vertical translation of 3 units up (step 3).

Apply these transformations either directly to the graph of $y = \sqrt{x}$ or to key points, and then sketch the transformed graph.

Method 1: Transform the Graph Directly
Use a sketch of $y = \sqrt{x}$ and apply the transformations to the curve one at a time.

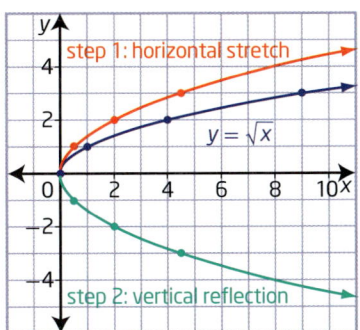
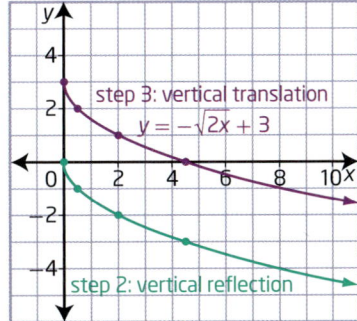

Method 2: Use Mapping Notation
Apply each transformation to the point (x, y) to determine a general mapping notation for the transformed function.

Transformation of $y = \sqrt{x}$	Mapping
Horizontal stretch by a factor of $\frac{1}{2}$	$(x, y) \to \left(\frac{1}{2}x, y\right)$
Reflection in the x-axis	$\left(\frac{1}{2}x, y\right) \to \left(\frac{1}{2}x, -y\right)$
Vertical translation of 3 units up	$\left(\frac{1}{2}x, -y\right) \to \left(\frac{1}{2}x, -y + 3\right)$

Choose key points on the graph of $y = \sqrt{x}$ and use the general mapping notation $(x, y) \to \left(\frac{1}{2}x, -y + 3\right)$ to determine their image points on the function $y - 3 = -\sqrt{2x}$.

$(0, 0) \to (0, 3)$
$(1, 1) \to (0.5, 2)$
$(4, 2) \to (2, 1)$
$(9, 3) \to (4.5, 0)$

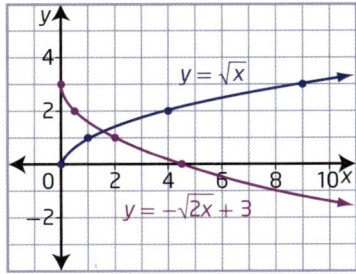

Since there are no horizontal reflections or translations, the graph still extends to the right from $x = 0$. The domain, $\{x \mid x \geq 0, x \in R\}$, is unchanged by the transformations as compared with $y = \sqrt{x}$.

The function is reflected vertically and then translated 3 units up, so the graph extends down from $y = 3$. The range is $\{y \mid y \leq 3, y \in R\}$, which has changed as compared to $y = \sqrt{x}$.

Your Turn

a) Sketch the graph of the function $y = -2\sqrt{x+3} - 1$ by transforming the graph of $y = \sqrt{x}$.

b) Identify the domain and range of $y = \sqrt{x}$ and describe how they are affected by the transformations.

Example 3

Determine a Radical Function From a Graph

Mayleen is designing a symmetrical pattern. She sketches the curve shown and wants to determine its equation and the equation of its reflection in each quadrant. The graph is a transformation of the graph of $y = \sqrt{x}$. What are the equations of the four functions Mayleen needs to work with?

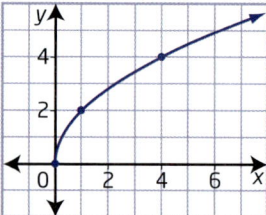

Solution

The base function $y = \sqrt{x}$ is not reflected or translated, but it is stretched. A radical function that involves a stretch can be obtained from either a vertical stretch or a horizontal stretch. Use an equation of the form $y = a\sqrt{x}$ or $y = \sqrt{bx}$ to represent the image function for each type of stretch.

Method 1: Compare Vertical or Horizontal Distances
Superimpose the graph of $y = \sqrt{x}$ and compare corresponding distances to determine the factor by which the function has been stretched.

View as a Vertical Stretch ($y = a\sqrt{x}$)	View as a Horizontal Stretch ($y = \sqrt{bx}$)
Each vertical distance is 2 times the corresponding distance for $y = \sqrt{x}$.	Each horizontal distance is $\frac{1}{4}$ the corresponding distance for $y = \sqrt{x}$.
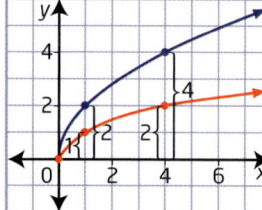	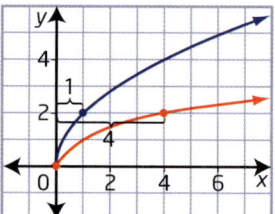
This represents a vertical stretch by a factor of 2, which means $a = 2$. The equation $y = 2\sqrt{x}$ represents the function.	This represents a horizontal stretch by a factor of $\frac{1}{4}$, which means $b = 4$. The equation $y = \sqrt{4x}$ represents the function.

Express the equation of the function as either $y = 2\sqrt{x}$ or $y = \sqrt{4x}$.

Method 2: Substitute Coordinates of a Point

Use the coordinates of one point on the function, such as (1, 2), to determine the stretch factor.

View as a Vertical Stretch	**View as a Horizontal Stretch**
Substitute 1 for x and 2 for y in the equation $y = a\sqrt{x}$. Then, solve for a. $y = a\sqrt{x}$ $2 = a\sqrt{1}$ $2 = a(1)$ $2 = a$ The equation of the function is $y = 2\sqrt{x}$.	Substitute the coordinates (1, 2) in the equation $y = \sqrt{bx}$ and solve for b. $y = \sqrt{bx}$ $2 = \sqrt{b(1)}$ $2 = \sqrt{b}$ $2^2 = (\sqrt{b})^2$ $4 = b$ The equation can also be expressed as $y = \sqrt{4x}$.

Represent the function in simplest form by $y = 2\sqrt{x}$ or by $y = \sqrt{4x}$.

Determine the equations of the reflected curves using $y = 2\sqrt{x}$.
- A reflection in the y-axis results in the function $y = 2\sqrt{-x}$, since $b = -1$.
- A reflection in the x-axis results in $y = -2\sqrt{x}$, since $a = -1$.

Reflecting these graphs into the third quadrant results in the function $y = -2\sqrt{-x}$.

Are the restrictions on the domain in each function consistent with the quadrant in which the curve lies?

Mayleen needs to use the equations $y = 2\sqrt{x}$, $y = 2\sqrt{-x}$, $y = -2\sqrt{x}$, and $y = -2\sqrt{-x}$. Similarly, she could use the equations $y = \sqrt{4x}$, $y = \sqrt{-4x}$, $y = -\sqrt{4x}$, and $y = -\sqrt{-4x}$.

Your Turn

a) Determine two forms of the equation for the function shown. The function is a transformation of the function $y = \sqrt{x}$.
b) Show algebraically that the two equations are equivalent.
c) What is the equation of the curve reflected in each quadrant?

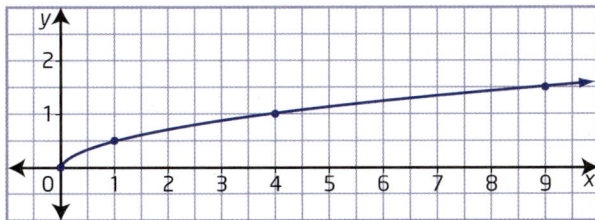

Example 4

Model the Speed of Sound

Justin's physics textbook states that the speed, s, in metres per second, of sound in dry air is related to the air temperature, T, in degrees Celsius, by the function $s = 331.3\sqrt{1 + \dfrac{T}{273.15}}$.

a) Determine the domain and range in this context.

b) On the Internet, Justin finds another formula for the speed of sound, $s = 20\sqrt{T + 273}$. Use algebra to show that the two functions are approximately equivalent.

c) How is the graph of this function related to the graph of the base square root function? Which transformation do you predict will be the most noticeable on a graph?

d) Graph the function $s = 331.3\sqrt{1 + \dfrac{T}{273.15}}$ using technology.

e) Determine the speed of sound, to the nearest metre per second, at each of the following temperatures.
  i) 20 °C (normal room temperature)
  ii) 0 °C (freezing point of water)
  iii) −63 °C (coldest temperature ever recorded in Canada)
  iv) −89 °C (coldest temperature ever recorded on Earth)

Solution

a) Use the following inequality to determine the domain:
$$\text{radicand} \geq 0$$
$$1 + \dfrac{T}{273.15} \geq 0$$
$$\dfrac{T}{273.15} \geq -1$$
$$T \geq -273.15$$

The domain is $\{T \mid T \geq -273.15, T \in \mathbb{R}\}$. This means that the temperature must be greater than or equal to −273.15 °C, which is the lowest temperature possible and is referred to as absolute zero.

The range is $\{s \mid s \geq 0, s \in \mathbb{R}\}$, which means that the speed of sound is a non-negative value.

b) Rewrite the function from the textbook in simplest form.

$$s = 331.3\sqrt{1 + \dfrac{T}{273.15}}$$
$$s = 331.3\sqrt{\dfrac{273.15}{273.15} + \dfrac{T}{273.15}}$$
$$s = 331.3\sqrt{\dfrac{273.15 + T}{273.15}}$$
$$s = 331.3\dfrac{\sqrt{273.15 + T}}{\sqrt{273.15}}$$
$$s \approx 20\sqrt{T + 273}$$

How could you verify that these expressions are approximately equivalent?

The function found on the Internet, $s = 20\sqrt{T + 273}$, is the approximate simplest form of the function in the textbook.

c) Analyse the transformations and determine the order in which they must be performed.

The graph of $s = \sqrt{T}$ is stretched vertically by a factor of about 20 and then translated about 273 units to the left. Translating 273 units to the left will be most noticeable on the graph of the function.

Are these transformations consistent with the domain and range?

d)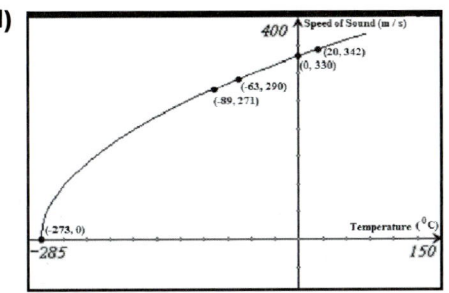

Are your answers to part c) confirmed by the graph?

e)

	Temperature (°C)	Approximate Speed of Sound (m/s)
i)	20	343
ii)	0	331
iii)	−63	291
iv)	−89	272

Your Turn

A company estimates its cost of production using the function $C(n) = 20\sqrt{n} + 1000$, where C represents the cost, in dollars, to produce n items.

a) Describe the transformations represented by this function as compared to $C = \sqrt{n}$.
b) Graph the function using technology. What does the shape of the graph imply about the situation?
c) Interpret the domain and range in this context.
d) Use the graph to determine the expected cost to produce 12 000 items.

Did You Know?

Eureka, on Ellesmere Island, Nunavut, holds the North American record for the lowest-ever average monthly temperature, −47.9 °C in February 1979. For 18 days, the temperature stayed below −45 °C.

Key Ideas

- The base radical function is $y = \sqrt{x}$. Its graph has the following characteristics:
  - a left endpoint at (0, 0)
  - no right endpoint
  - the shape of half of a parabola
  - a domain of $\{x \mid x \geq 0, x \in R\}$ and a range of $\{y \mid y \geq 0, y \in R\}$

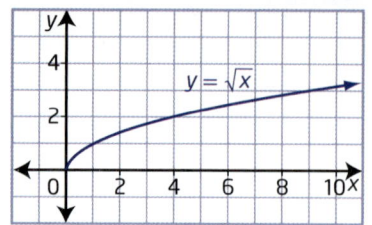

- You can graph radical functions of the form $y = a\sqrt{b(x - h)} + k$ by transforming the base function $y = \sqrt{x}$.

How does each parameter affect the graph of $y = \sqrt{x}$?

- You can analyse transformations to identify the domain and range of a radical function of the form $y = a\sqrt{b(x - h)} + k$.

Check Your Understanding

Practise

1. Graph each function using a table of values. Then, identify the domain and range.
   a) $y = \sqrt{x - 1}$
   b) $y = \sqrt{x + 6}$
   c) $y = \sqrt{3 - x}$
   d) $y = \sqrt{-2x - 5}$

2. Explain how to transform the graph of $y = \sqrt{x}$ to obtain the graph of each function. State the domain and range in each case.
   a) $y = 7\sqrt{x - 9}$
   b) $y = \sqrt{-x} + 8$
   c) $y = -\sqrt{0.2x}$
   d) $4 + y = \frac{1}{3}\sqrt{x + 6}$

3. Match each function with its graph.
   a) $y = \sqrt{x} - 2$
   b) $y = \sqrt{-x} + 2$
   c) $y = -\sqrt{x + 2}$
   d) $y = -\sqrt{-(x - 2)}$

A 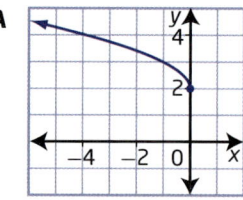 B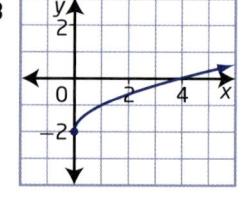

C 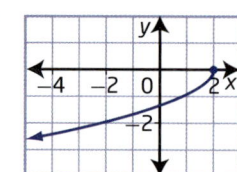 D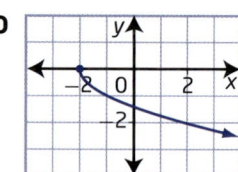

4. Write the equation of the radical function that results by applying each set of transformations to the graph of $y = \sqrt{x}$.

   a) vertical stretch by a factor of 4, then horizontal translation of 6 units left

   b) horizontal stretch by a factor of $\frac{1}{8}$, then vertical translation of 5 units down

   c) horizontal reflection in the *y*-axis, then horizontal translation of 4 units right and vertical translation of 11 units up

   d) vertical stretch by a factor of 0.25, vertical reflection in the *x*-axis, and horizontal stretch by a factor of 10

5. Sketch the graph of each function using transformations. State the domain and range of each function.

   a) $f(x) = \sqrt{-x} - 3$

   b) $r(x) = 3\sqrt{x+1}$

   c) $p(x) = -\sqrt{x-2}$

   d) $y - 1 = -\sqrt{-4(x-2)}$

   e) $m(x) = \sqrt{\frac{1}{2}x} + 4$

   f) $y + 1 = \frac{1}{3}\sqrt{-(x+2)}$

Apply

6. Consider the function $f(x) = \frac{1}{4}\sqrt{5x}$.

   a) Identify the transformations represented by $f(x)$ as compared to $y = \sqrt{x}$.

   b) Write two functions equivalent to $f(x)$: one of the form $y = a\sqrt{x}$ and the other of the form $y = \sqrt{bx}$

   c) Identify the transformation(s) represented by each function you wrote in part b).

   d) Use transformations to graph all three functions. How do the graphs compare?

7. a) Express the radius of a circle as a function of its area.

   b) Create a table of values and a graph to illustrate the relationship that this radical function represents.

8. For an observer at a height of h feet above the surface of Earth, the approximate distance, d, in miles, to the horizon can be modelled using the radical function $d = \sqrt{1.50h}$.

   a) Use the language of transformations to describe how to obtain the graph from the base square root graph.

   b) Determine an approximate equivalent function of the form $d = a\sqrt{h}$ for the function. Which form of the function do you prefer, and why?

   c) A lifeguard on a tower is looking out over the water with binoculars. How far can she see if her eyes are 20 ft above the level of the water? Express your answer to the nearest tenth of a mile.

9. The function $4 - y = \sqrt{3x}$ is translated 9 units up and reflected in the *x*-axis.

   a) Without graphing, determine the domain and range of the image function.

   b) Compared to the base function, $y = \sqrt{x}$, by how many units and in which direction has the given function been translated horizontally? vertically?

10. For each graph, write the equation of a radical function of the form $y = a\sqrt{b(x - h)} + k$.

   a)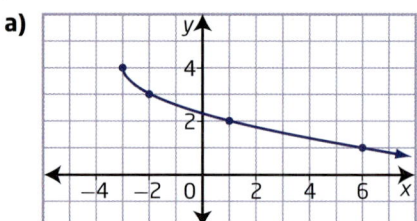

   b)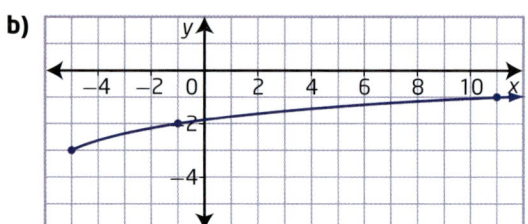

   c)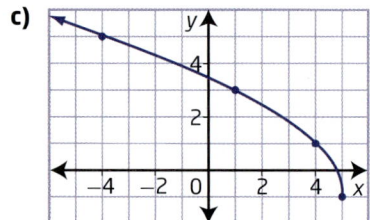

   d)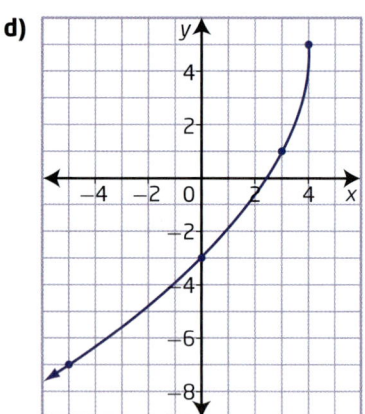

11. Write the equation of a radical function with each domain and range.

   a) $\{x \mid x \geq 6, x \in R\}, \{y \mid y \geq 1, y \in R\}$
   b) $\{x \mid x \geq -7, x \in R\}, \{y \mid y \leq -9, y \in R\}$
   c) $\{x \mid x \leq 4, x \in R\}, \{y \mid y \geq -3, y \in R\}$
   d) $\{x \mid x \leq -5, x \in R\}, \{y \mid y \leq 8, y \in R\}$

12. Agronomists use radical functions to model and optimize corn production. One factor they analyse is how the amount of nitrogen fertilizer applied affects the crop yield. Suppose the function $Y(n) = 760\sqrt{n} + 2000$ is used to predict the yield, Y, in kilograms per hectare, of corn as a function of the amount, n, in kilograms per hectare, of nitrogen applied to the crop.

   a) Use the language of transformations to compare the graph of this function to the graph of $y = \sqrt{n}$.
   b) Graph the function using transformations.
   c) Identify the domain and range.
   d) What do the shape of the graph, the domain, and the range tell you about this situation? Are the domain and range realistic in this context? Explain.

Did You Know?

Over 6300 years ago, the Indigenous people in the area of what is now Mexico domesticated and cultivated several varieties of corn. The cultivation of corn is now global.

13. A manufacturer wants to predict the consumer interest in a new smart phone. The company uses the function $P(d) = -2\sqrt{-d} + 20$ to model the number, P, in millions, of pre-orders for the phone as a function of the number, d, of days before the phone's release date.

   a) What are the domain and range and what do they mean in this situation?

   b) Identify the transformations represented by the function as compared to $y = \sqrt{d}$.

   c) Graph the function and explain what the shape of the graph indicates about the situation.

   d) Determine the number of pre-orders the manufacturer can expect to have 30 days before the release date.

14. During election campaigns, campaign managers use surveys and polls to make projections about the election results. One campaign manager uses a radical function to model the possible error in polling predictions as a function of the number of days until the election, as shown in the graph.

   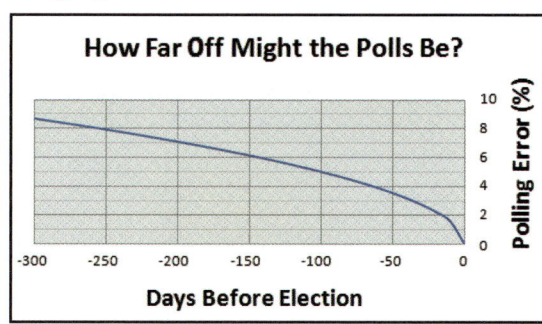

   a) Explain what the graph shows about the accuracy of polls before elections.

   b) Determine an equation to represent the function. Show how you developed your answer.

   c) Describe the transformations that the function represents as compared to $y = \sqrt{x}$.

15. While meeting with a client, a manufacturer of custom greenhouses sketches a greenhouse in the shape of the graph of a radical function. What equation could the manufacturer use to represent the shape of the greenhouse roof?

    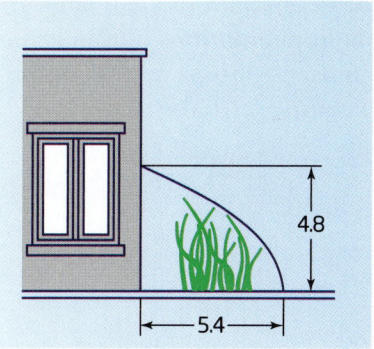

    Did You Know?

    People living in the Arctic are starting to use greenhouses to grow some of their food. There are greenhouse societies in both Iqaluit, Nunavut and Inuvik, Northwest Territories that grow beans, lettuce, carrots, tomatoes, and herbs.

    Web Link

    To learn more about greenhouse communities in the Arctic, go to www.mcgrawhill.ca/school/learningcentres and follow the links.

16. Determine the equation of a radical function with

    a) endpoint at (2, 5) and passing through the point (6, 1)

    b) endpoint at (3, −2) and an *x*-intercept with a value of −6

17. The Penrose method is a system for giving voting powers to members of assemblies or legislatures based on the square root of the number of people that each member represents, divided by 1000. Consider a parliament that represents the people of the world and how voting power might be given to different nations. The table shows the estimated populations of Canada and the three most populous and the three least populous countries in the world.

Country	Population
China	1 361 513 000
India	1 251 696 000
United States	325 540 000
Canada	35 100 000
Tuvalu	11 000
Nauru	10 000
Vatican City	1 000

   a) Share your answers to the following two questions with a classmate and explain your thinking:
   - Which countries might feel that a "one nation, one vote" system is an unfair way to allocate voting power?
   - Which countries might feel that a "one person, one vote" system is unfair?

   b) What percent of the voting power would each nation listed above have under a "one person, one vote" system, assuming a world population of approximately 7.302 billion?

   c) If x represents the population of a country and $V(x)$ represents its voting power, what function could be written to represent the Penrose method?

   d) Under the Penrose method, the sum of the world voting power using the given data is approximately 765. What percent of the voting power would this system give each nation in the table?

   e) Why might the Penrose method be viewed as a compromise for allocating voting power?

18. **MINI LAB** The period of a pendulum is the time for one complete swing back and forth. As long as the initial swing angle is kept relatively small, the period of a pendulum is related to its length by a radical function.

    Materials
    - thread
    - washer or other suitable mass
    - tape
    - ruler
    - stopwatch or timer

    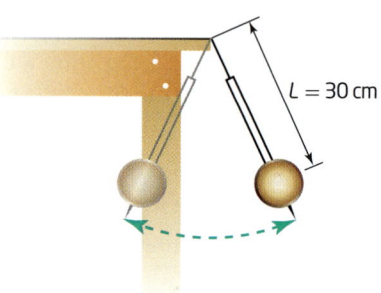

    Step 1 Tie a length of thread to a washer or other mass. Tape the thread to the edge of a table or desk top so that the length between the pivot point and the centre of the washer is 30 cm.

    Step 2 Pull the mass to one side and allow it to swing freely. Measure the total time for 10 complete swings back and forth and then divide by 10 to determine the period for this length. Record the length and period in a table.

    Step 3 Repeat steps 1 and 2 using lengths of 25 cm, 20 cm, 15 cm, 10 cm, 5 cm, and 3 cm (and shorter distances if possible).

    Step 4 Create a scatter plot showing period as a function of length. Draw a smooth curve through or near the points. Does it appear to be a radical function? Justify your answer.

    Step 5 What approximate transformation(s) to the graph of $y = \sqrt{x}$ would produce your result? Write a radical function that approximates the graph, where T represents the period and L represents the length of the pendulum.

Extend

19. The inverse of $f(x) = \sqrt{x}$ is $f^{-1}(x) = x^2, x \geq 0$.

a) Graph both functions, and use them to explain why the restriction is necessary on the domain of the inverse function.

b) Determine the equation, including any restrictions, of the inverse of each of the following functions.

   i) $g(x) = -\sqrt{x-5}$
   ii) $h(x) = \sqrt{-x} + 3$
   iii) $j(x) = \sqrt{2x-7} - 6$

20. If $f(x) = \dfrac{5}{8}\sqrt{-\dfrac{7}{12}x}$ and $g(x) = -\dfrac{2}{5}\sqrt{6(x+3)} - 4$, what transformations could you apply to the graph of $f(x)$ to create the graph of $g(x)$?

Create Connections

C1 Which parameters in $y = a\sqrt{b(x-h)} + k$ affect the domain of $y = \sqrt{x}$? Which parameters affect the range? Explain, using examples.

C2 Sarah claims that any given radical function can be simplified so that there is no value of b, only a value of a. Is she correct? Explain, using examples.

C3 Compare and contrast the process of graphing a radical function using transformations with graphing a quadratic function using transformations.

C4 MINI LAB The Wheel of Theodorus, or Square Root Spiral, is a geometric construction that contains line segments with length equal to the square root of any whole number.

Materials
- ruler, drafting square, or other object with a right angle
- millimetre ruler

Step 1 Create an isosceles right triangle with legs that are each 1 cm long. Mark one end of the hypotenuse as point C. What is the length of the hypotenuse, expressed as a radical?

Step 2 Use the hypotenuse of the first triangle as one leg of a new right triangle. Draw a length of 1 cm as the other leg, opposite point C. What is the length of the hypotenuse of this second triangle, expressed as a radical?

Step 3 Continue to create right triangles, each time using the hypotenuse of the previous triangle as a leg of the next triangle, and a length of 1 cm as the other leg (drawn so that the 1-cm leg is opposite point C). Continue the spiral until you would overlap the initial base.

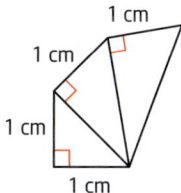

Step 4 Create a table to represent the length of the hypotenuse as a function of the triangle number (first, second, third triangle in the pattern, etc.). Express lengths both in exact radical form and in approximate decimal form.

Step 5 Write an equation to represent this function, where L represents the hypotenuse length and n represents the triangle number. Does the equation involve any transformations on the base square root function? Explain.

2.2

Square Root of a Function

Focus on...

- sketching the graph of $y = \sqrt{f(x)}$ given the graph of $y = f(x)$
- explaining strategies for graphing $y = \sqrt{f(x)}$ given the graph of $y = f(x)$
- comparing the domains and ranges of the functions $y = f(x)$ and $y = \sqrt{f(x)}$, and explaining any differences

The Pythagorean theorem is often applied by engineers. They use right triangles in the design of large domes, bridges, and other structures because the triangle is a strong support unit. For example, a truss bridge consists of triangular units of steel beams connected together to support the bridge deck.

You are already familiar with the square root operation (and its effect on given values) in the Pythagorean theorem. How does the square root operation affect the graph of the function? If you are given the graph of a function, what does the graph of the square root of that function look like?

Web Link

For more information about how triangles are fundamental to the design of domes, go to www.mcgrawhill.ca/school/learningcentres and follow the links.

Truss bridge over the Bow River in Morley, Alberta located on Chiniki First Nation territory.

Investigate Related Functions: $y = f(x)$ and $y = \sqrt{f(x)}$

Materials

- grid paper and ruler, or graphing calculator
- dynamic geometry or graphing software (optional)

A: Right Triangles, Area, and Length

1. Draw several right triangles with a hypotenuse of 5 cm and legs of various lengths. For each triangle, label the legs as v and h.

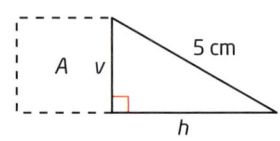

78 MHR • Chapter 2

2. a) Write an equation for the length of v as a function of h. Graph the function using an appropriate domain for the situation.

b) Compare the measured values for side v in the triangles you drew to the calculated values of v from your graph.

3. a) Draw a square on side v of each triangle. Let the area of this square be A, and write an equation for A as a function of h.

b) Graph the area function.

Reflect and Respond

4. a) How are the equations of the two functions related?

b) How do the domains of the two functions compare?

c) What is the relationship between the ranges of the two functions?

B: Compare a Function and Its Square Root

5. Consider the functions $y = 2x + 4$ and $y = \sqrt{2x + 4}$.

a) Describe the relationship between the equations for these two functions.

b) Graph the two functions, and note any connections between the two graphs.

c) Compare the values of y for the same values of x. How are they related?

6. a) Create at least two more pairs of functions that share the same relationship as those in step 5.

b) Compare the tables and graphs of each pair of functions.

Reflect and Respond

7. Consider pairs of functions where one function is the square root of the other function.

a) How do the domains compare? Explain why you think there are differences.

b) How are the values of y related for pairs of functions like these?

c) What differences occur in the ranges, and why do you think they occur?

8. How might you use the connections you have identified in this investigation as a method of graphing $y = \sqrt{f(x)}$ if you are given the graph of $y = f(x)$?

Link the Ideas

You can determine how two functions, $y = f(x)$ and $y = \sqrt{f(x)}$, are related by comparing how the values of y are calculated:

- For $y = 2x + 1$, multiply x by 2 and add 1.
- For $y = \sqrt{2x + 1}$, multiply x by 2, add 1, and take the square root.

The two functions start with the same two operations, but the function $y = \sqrt{2x + 1}$ has the additional step of taking the square root. For any value of x, the resulting value of y for $y = \sqrt{2x + 1}$ is the square root of the value of y for $y = 2x + 1$, as shown in the table.

x	y = 2x + 1	y = √(2x + 1)
0	1	1
4	9	3
12	25	5
24	49	7
⋮	⋮	⋮

The function $y = \sqrt{2x + 1}$ represents the **square root of the function** $y = 2x + 1$.

square root of a function
- the function $y = \sqrt{f(x)}$ is the square root of the function $y = f(x)$
- $y = \sqrt{f(x)}$ is only defined for $f(x) \geq 0$

Example 1

Compare Graphs of a Linear Function and the Square Root of the Function

a) Given $f(x) = 3 - 2x$, graph the functions $y = f(x)$ and $y = \sqrt{f(x)}$.
b) Compare the two functions.

Solution

a) Use a table of values to graph $y = 3 - 2x$ and $y = \sqrt{3 - 2x}$.

x	y = 3 − 2x	y = √(3 − 2x)
−2	7	√7
−1	5	√5
0	3	√3
1	1	1
1.5	0	0

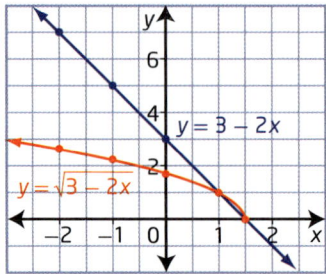

80 MHR • Chapter 2

b) Compare the graphs.

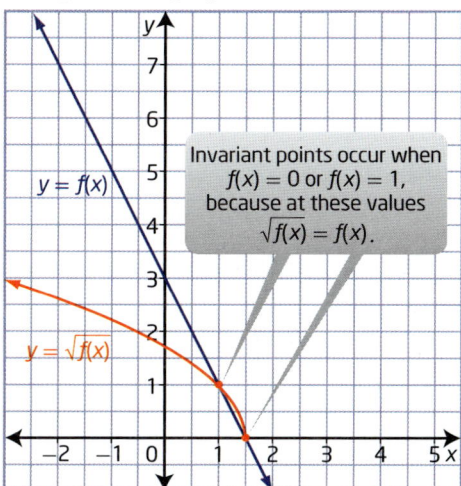

Why is the graph of $y = \sqrt{f(x)}$ above the graph of $y = f(x)$ for values of y between 0 and 1? Will this always be true?

Invariant points occur when $f(x) = 0$ or $f(x) = 1$, because at these values $\sqrt{f(x)} = f(x)$.

For $y = f(x)$, the domain is $\{x \mid x \in R\}$ and the range is $\{y \mid y \in R\}$.
For $y = \sqrt{f(x)}$, the domain is $\{x \mid x \leq 1.5, x \in R\}$ and the range is $\{y \mid y \geq 0, y \in R\}$.

Invariant points occur at (1, 1) and (1.5, 0).

How does the domain of the graph of $y = \sqrt{f(x)}$ relate to the restrictions on the variable in the radicand? How could you determine the domain algebraically?

Your Turn

a) Given $g(x) = 3x + 6$, graph the functions $y = g(x)$ and $y = \sqrt{g(x)}$.
b) Identify the domain and range of each function and any invariant points.

Relative Locations of $y = f(x)$ and $y = \sqrt{f(x)}$

The domain of $y = \sqrt{f(x)}$ consists only of the values in the domain of $f(x)$ for which $f(x) \geq 0$.

The range of $y = \sqrt{f(x)}$ consists of the square roots of the values in the range of $y = f(x)$ for which $\sqrt{f(x)}$ is defined.

The graph of $y = \sqrt{f(x)}$ exists only where $f(x) \geq 0$. You can predict the location of $y = \sqrt{f(x)}$ relative to $y = f(x)$ using the values of $f(x)$.

Value of $f(x)$	$f(x) < 0$	$f(x) = 0$	$0 < f(x) < 1$	$f(x) = 1$	$f(x) > 1$
Relative Location of Graph of $y = \sqrt{f(x)}$	The graph of $y = \sqrt{f(x)}$ is undefined.	The graphs of $y = \sqrt{f(x)}$ and $y = f(x)$ intersect on the x-axis.	The graph of $y = \sqrt{f(x)}$ is above the graph of $y = f(x)$.	The graph of $y = \sqrt{f(x)}$ intersects the graph of $y = f(x)$.	The graph of $y = \sqrt{f(x)}$ is below the graph of $y = f(x)$.

Example 2

Compare the Domains and Ranges of $y = f(x)$ and $y = \sqrt{f(x)}$

Identify and compare the domains and ranges of the functions in each pair.

a) $y = 2 - 0.5x^2$ and $y = \sqrt{2 - 0.5x^2}$
b) $y = x^2 + 5$ and $y = \sqrt{x^2 + 5}$

Solution

a) Method 1: Analyse Graphically

Since the function $y = 2 - 0.5x^2$ is a quadratic function, its square root, $y = \sqrt{2 - 0.5x^2}$, cannot be expressed in the form $y = a\sqrt{b(x - h)} + k$. It cannot be graphed by transforming $y = \sqrt{x}$.

Both graphs can be created using technology. Use the *maximum* and *minimum* or equivalent features to find the coordinates of points necessary to determine the domain and range.

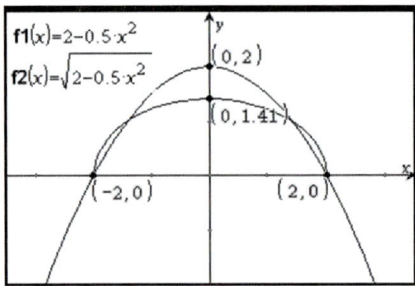

The graph of $y = 2 - 0.5x^2$ extends from (0, 2) down and to the left and right infinitely. Its domain is $\{x \mid x \in \mathbb{R}\}$, and its range is $\{y \mid y \leq 2, y \in \mathbb{R}\}$.

The graph of $y = \sqrt{2 - 0.5x^2}$ includes values of x from -2 to 2 inclusive, so its domain is $\{x \mid -2 \leq x \leq 2, x \in \mathbb{R}\}$. The graph covers values of y from 0 to approximately 1.41 inclusive, so its approximate range is $\{y \mid 0 \leq y \leq 1.41, y \in \mathbb{R}\}$.

To determine the exact value that 1.41 represents, you need to analyse the function algebraically.

The domain and range of $y = \sqrt{2 - 0.5x^2}$ are subsets of the domain and range of $y = 2 - 0.5x^2$.

Method 2: Analyse Key Points

Use the locations of any intercepts and the maximum value or minimum value to determine the domain and range of each function.

Function	$y = 2 - 0.5x^2$	$y = \sqrt{2 - 0.5x^2}$
x-Intercepts	−2 and 2	−2 and 2
y-Intercept	2	$\sqrt{2}$
Maximum Value	2	$\sqrt{2}$
Minimum Value	none	0

How can you justify this information algebraically?

Quadratic functions are defined for all real numbers. So, the domain of $y = 2 - 0.5x^2$ is $\{x \mid x \in R\}$. Since the maximum value is 2, the range of $y = 2 - 0.5x^2$ is $\{y \mid y \leq 2, y \in R\}$.

The locations of the x-intercepts of $y = \sqrt{2 - 0.5x^2}$ mean that the function is defined for $-2 \leq x \leq 2$. So, the domain is $\{x \mid -2 \leq x \leq 2, x \in R\}$. Since $y = \sqrt{2 - 0.5x^2}$ has a minimum value of 0 and a maximum value of $\sqrt{2}$, the range is $\{y \mid 0 \leq y \leq \sqrt{2}, y \in R\}$.

b) Method 1: Analyse Graphically
Graph the functions $y = x^2 + 5$ and $y = \sqrt{x^2 + 5}$ using technology.

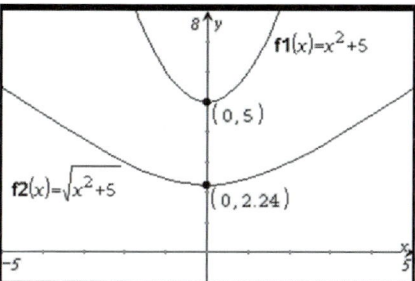

Both functions extend infinitely to the left and the right, so the domain of each function is $\{x \mid x \in R\}$.

The range of $y = x^2 + 5$ is $\{y \mid y \geq 5, y \in R\}$.

The range of $y = \sqrt{x^2 + 5}$ is approximately $\{y \mid y \geq 2.24, y \in R\}$.

Method 2: Analyse Key Points
Use the locations of any intercepts and the maximum value or minimum value to determine the domain and range of each function.

Function	$y = x^2 + 5$	$y = \sqrt{x^2 + 5}$
x-Intercepts	none	none
y-Intercept	5	$\sqrt{5}$
Maximum Value	none	none
Minimum Value	5	$\sqrt{5}$

Quadratic functions are defined for all real numbers. So, the domain of $y = x^2 + 5$ is $\{x \mid x \in R\}$. Since the minimum value is 5, the range of $y = x^2 + 5$ is $\{y \mid y \geq 5, y \in R\}$.

Since $y = \sqrt{x^2 + 5}$ has no x-intercepts, the function is defined for all real numbers. So, the domain is $\{x \mid x \in R\}$. Since $y = \sqrt{x^2 + 5}$ has a minimum value of $\sqrt{5}$ and no maximum value, the range is $\{y \mid y \geq \sqrt{5}, y \in R\}$.

Your Turn

Identify and compare the domains and ranges of the functions $y = x^2 - 1$ and $y = \sqrt{x^2 - 1}$. Verify your answers.

Example 3

Graph the Square Root of a Function From the Graph of the Function

Using the graphs of $y = f(x)$ and $y = g(x)$, sketch the graphs of $y = \sqrt{f(x)}$ and $y = \sqrt{g(x)}$.

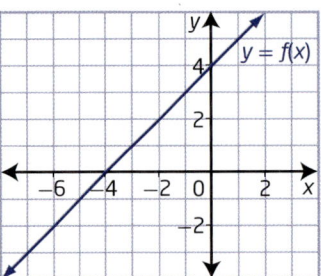
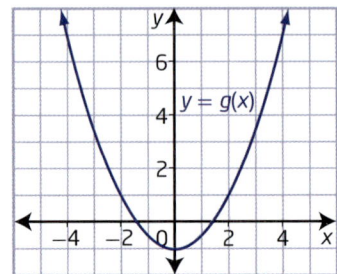

Solution

Sketch each graph by locating key points, including invariant points, and determining the image points on the graph of the square root of the function.

Step 1: Locate invariant points on $y = f(x)$ and $y = g(x)$. When graphing the square root of a function, invariant points occur at $y = 0$ and $y = 1$.

What is significant about $y = 0$ and $y = 1$? Does this apply to all graphs of functions and their square roots? Why?

Step 2: Draw the portion of each graph between the invariant points for values of $y = f(x)$ and $y = g(x)$ that are positive but less than 1. Sketch a smooth curve *above* those of $y = f(x)$ and $y = g(x)$ in these intervals.

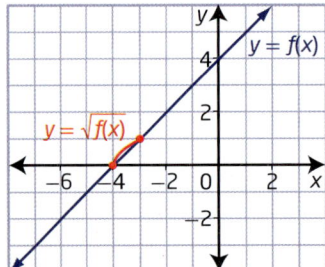
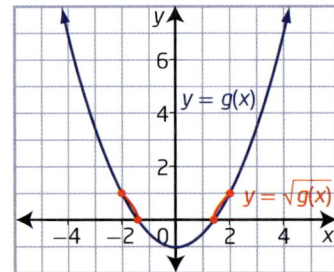

Step 3: Locate other key points on $y = f(x)$ and $y = g(x)$ where the values are greater than 1. Transform these points to locate image points on the graphs of $y = \sqrt{f(x)}$ and $y = \sqrt{g(x)}$.

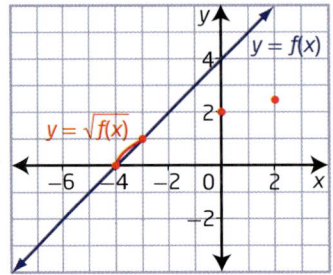
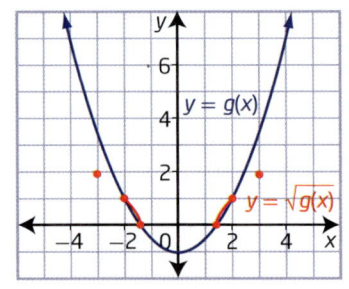

How can a value of y be mapped to a point on the square root of the function?

Step 4: Sketch smooth curves between the image points; they will be below those of $y = f(x)$ and $y = g(x)$ in the remaining intervals. Recall that graphs of $y = \sqrt{f(x)}$ and $y = \sqrt{g(x)}$ do not exist in intervals where $y = f(x)$ and $y = g(x)$ are negative (below the x-axis).

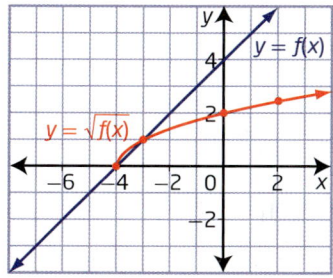
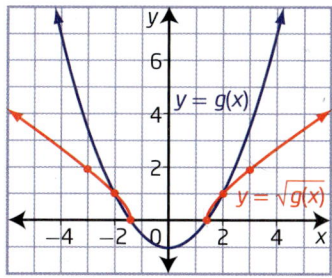

Where is the square root of a function above the original function? Where is it below? Where are they equal? Where are the endpoints on a graph of the square root of a function? Why?

Your Turn

Using the graph of $y = h(x)$, sketch the graph of $y = \sqrt{h(x)}$.

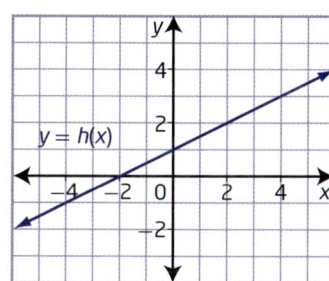

Key Ideas

- You can use values of $f(x)$ to predict values of $\sqrt{f(x)}$ and to sketch the graph of $y = \sqrt{f(x)}$.

- The key values to consider are $f(x) = 0$ and $f(x) = 1$.

- The domain of $y = \sqrt{f(x)}$ consists of all values in the domain of $f(x)$ for which $f(x) \geq 0$.

- The range of $y = \sqrt{f(x)}$ consists of the square roots of all values in the range of $f(x)$ for which $f(x)$ is defined.

- The y-coordinates of the points on the graph of $y = \sqrt{f(x)}$ are the square roots of the y-coordinates of the corresponding points on the original function $y = f(x)$.

What do you know about the graph of $y = \sqrt{f(x)}$ at $f(x) = 0$ and $f(x) = 1$? How do the graphs of $y = f(x)$ and $y = \sqrt{f(x)}$ compare on either side of these locations?

Check Your Understanding

Practise

1. Copy and complete the table.

f(x)	√f(x)
36	
	0.03
1	
−9	
	1.6
0	

2. For each point on the graph of $y = f(x)$, does a corresponding point on the graph of $y = \sqrt{f(x)}$ exist? If so, state the coordinates (rounded to two decimal places, if necessary).

   a) (4, 12) b) (−2, 0.4)
   c) (10, −2) d) (0.09, 1)
   e) (−5, 0) f) (m, n)

3. Match each graph of $y = f(x)$ to the corresponding graph of $y = \sqrt{f(x)}$.

   a)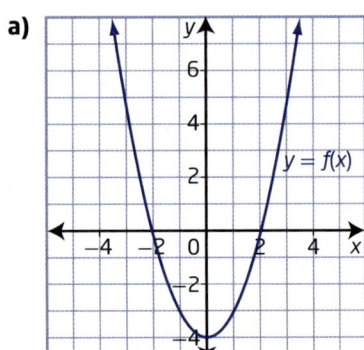

   b)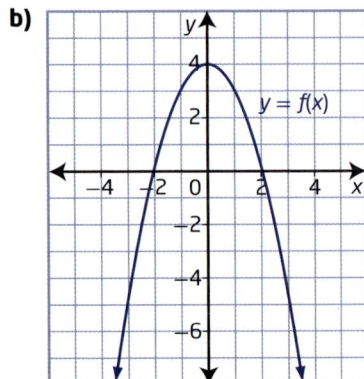

   c)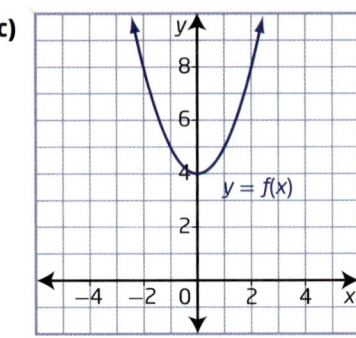

   d)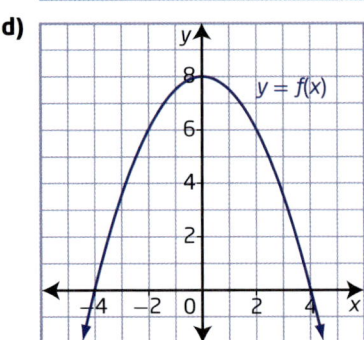

   A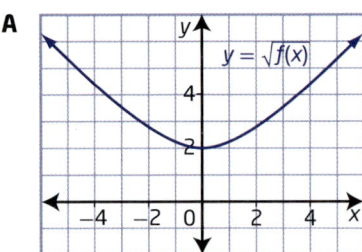

   B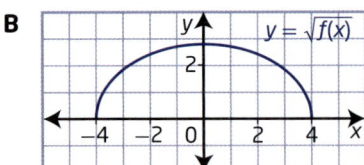

   C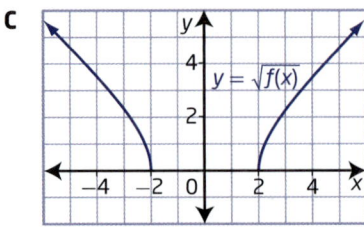

   D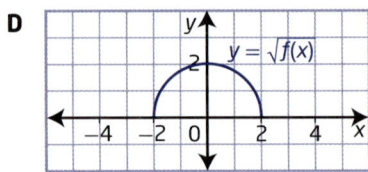

4. a) Given $f(x) = 4 - x$, graph the functions $y = f(x)$ and $y = \sqrt{f(x)}$.

b) Compare the two functions and explain how their values are related.

c) Identify the domain and range of each function, and explain any differences.

5. Determine the domains and ranges of the functions in each pair graphically and algebraically. Explain why the domains and ranges differ.

a) $y = x - 2$, $y = \sqrt{x - 2}$

b) $y = 2x + 6$, $y = \sqrt{2x + 6}$

c) $y = -x + 9$, $y = \sqrt{-x + 9}$

d) $y = -0.1x - 5$, $y = \sqrt{-0.1x - 5}$

6. Identify and compare the domains and ranges of the functions in each pair.

a) $y = x^2 - 9$ and $y = \sqrt{x^2 - 9}$

b) $y = 2 - x^2$ and $y = \sqrt{2 - x^2}$

c) $y = x^2 + 6$ and $y = \sqrt{x^2 + 6}$

d) $y = 0.5x^2 + 3$ and $y = \sqrt{0.5x^2 + 3}$

7. For each function, identify and explain any differences in the domains and ranges of $y = f(x)$ and $y = \sqrt{f(x)}$.

a) $f(x) = x^2 - 25$

b) $f(x) = x^2 + 3$

c) $f(x) = 32 - 2x^2$

d) $f(x) = 5x^2 + 50$

8. Using each graph of $y = f(x)$, sketch the graph of $y = \sqrt{f(x)}$.

a)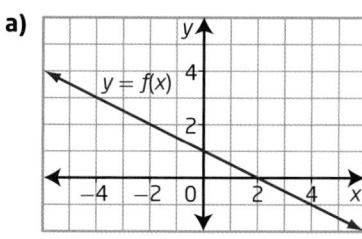

b)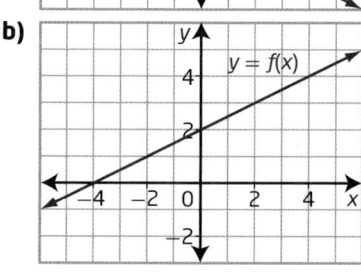

c)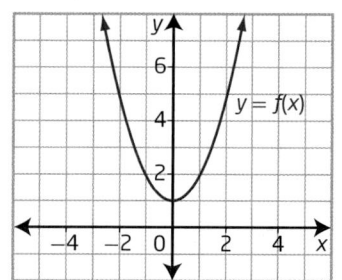

Apply

9. a) Use technology to graph each function and identify the domain and range.

i) $f(x) = x^2 + 4$

ii) $g(x) = x^2 - 4$

iii) $h(x) = -x^2 + 4$

iv) $j(x) = -x^2 - 4$

b) Graph the square root of each function in part a) using technology.

c) What do you notice about the graph of $y = \sqrt{j(x)}$? Explain this observation based on the graph of $y = j(x)$. Then, explain this observation algebraically.

d) In general, how are the domains of the functions in part a) related to the domains of the functions in part b)? How are the ranges related?

10. a) Identify the domains and ranges of $y = x^2 - 4$ and $y = \sqrt{x^2 - 4}$.

b) Why is $y = \sqrt{x^2 - 4}$ undefined over an interval? How does this affect the domain of the function?

11. The graph of $y = f(x)$ is shown.

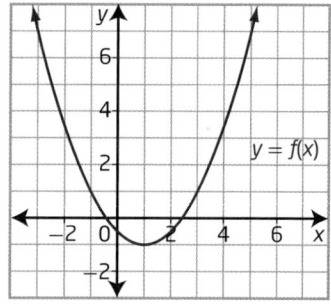

a) Sketch the graph of $y = \sqrt{f(x)}$, and explain the strategy you used.

b) State the domain and range of each function, and explain how the domains and the ranges are related.

12. For relatively small heights above Earth, a simple radical function can be used to approximate the distance to the horizon.

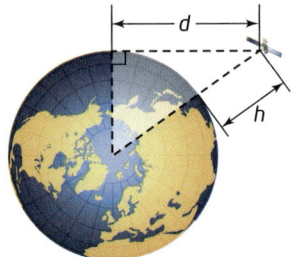

   a) If Earth's radius is assumed to be 6378 km, determine the equation for the distance, d, in kilometres, to the horizon for an object that is at a height of h kilometres above Earth's surface.
   b) Identify the domain and range of the function.
   c) How can you use a graph of the function to find the distance to the horizon for a satellite that is 800 km above Earth's surface?
   d) If the function from part a) were just an arbitrary mathematical function rather than in this context, would the domain or range be any different? Explain.

13. a) When determining whether the graph shown represents a function or the square root of the function, Chris states, "it must be the function $y = f(x)$ because the domain consists of negative values, and the square root of a function $y = \sqrt{f(x)}$ is not defined for negative values."

   Do you agree with Chris's answer? Why?

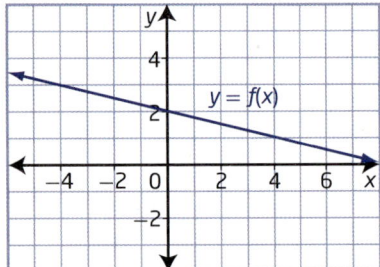

   b) Describe how you would determine whether a graph shows the function or the square root of the function.

14. The main portion of an iglu (Inuit spelling of the English word igloo) is approximately hemispherical in shape.

   a) For an iglu with diameter 3.6 m, determine a function that gives the vertical height, v, in metres, in terms of the horizontal distance, h, in metres, from the centre.
   b) What are the domain and range of this function, and how are they related to the situation?
   c) What is the height of this iglu at a point 1 m in from the bottom edge of the wall?

   Did You Know?

   An iglu is actually built in a spiral from blocks cut from inside the iglu floor space. Half the floor space is left as a bed platform in large iglus. This traps cold air below the sleeping area.

15. **MINI LAB** Investigate how the constants in radical functions affect their graphs, domains, and ranges.

   Step 1 Graph the function $y = \sqrt{a^2 - x^2}$ for various values of a. If you use graphing software, you may be able to create sliders that allow you to vary the value of a and dynamically see the resulting changes in the graph.

   Step 2 Describe how the value of a affects the graph of the function and its domain and range.

   Step 3 Choose one value of a and write an equation for the reflection of this function in the x-axis. Graph both functions and describe the graph.

   Step 4 Repeat steps 1 to 3 for the function $y = \sqrt{a^2 + x^2}$ as well as another square root of a function involving x^2.

Extend

16. If $(-24, 12)$ is a point on the graph of the function $y = f(x)$, identify one point on the graph of each of the following functions.
  a) $y = \sqrt{4f(x + 3)}$
  b) $y = -\sqrt{f(4x)} + 12$
  c) $y = -2\sqrt{f(-(x - 2)) - 4} + 6$

17. Given the graph of the function $y = f(x)$, sketch the graph of each function.

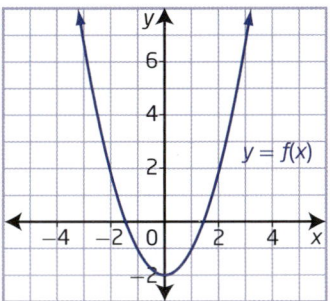

  a) $y = 2\sqrt{f(x)} - 3$
  b) $y = -\sqrt{2f(x - 3)}$
  c) $y = \sqrt{-f(2x) + 3}$
  d) $y = \sqrt{2f(-x) - 3}$

18. Explain your strategy for completing #17b).

19. Develop a formula for radius as a function of surface area for
  a) a cylinder with equal diameter and height
  b) a cone with height three times its diameter

Create Connections

C1 Write a summary of your strategy for graphing the function $y = \sqrt{f(x)}$ if you are given only the graph of $y = f(x)$.

C2 Explain how the relationship between the two equations $y = 16 - 4x$ and $y = \sqrt{16 - 4x}$ is connected to the relationship between their graphs.

C3 Is it possible to completely graph the function $y = f(x)$ given only the graph of $y = \sqrt{f(x)}$? Discuss this with a classmate and share several examples that you create. Write a summary of your conclusions.

C4 a) Given $f(x) = (x - 1)^2 - 4$, graph the functions $y = f(x)$ and $y = \sqrt{f(x)}$.
  b) Compare the two functions and explain how their values are related using several points on each graph.

Project Corner **Form Follows Function**

- What radical functions are represented by the curves drawn on each image?

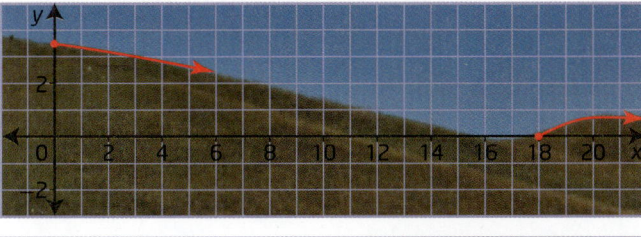

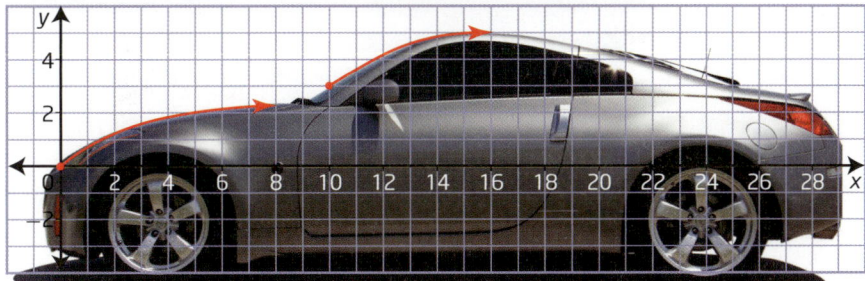

2.3

Solving Radical Equations Graphically

Focus on...

- relating the roots of radical equations and the *x*-intercepts of the graphs of radical functions
- determining approximate solutions of radical equations graphically

Parachutes slow the speed of falling objects by greatly increasing the drag force of the air. Manufacturers must make careful calculations to ensure that their parachutes are large enough to create enough drag force to allow parachutists to descend at a safe speed, but not so large that they are impractical. Radical equations can be used to relate the area of a parachute to the descent speed and mass of the object it carries, allowing parachute designers to ensure that their designs are reliable.

Did You Know?

French inventor Louis Sébastien-Lenormand introduced the first practical parachute in 1783.

Investigate Solving Radical Equations Graphically

Materials

- graphing calculator or graphing software

The radical equation $\sqrt{x-4} = 5$ can be solved in several ways.

1. **a)** Discuss with a classmate how you might solve the equation graphically. Could you use more than one graphical method?

   b) Write step-by-step instructions that explain how to use your method(s) to determine the solution to the radical equation.

   c) Use your graphical method(s) to solve the equation.

2. **a)** Describe one method of solving the equation algebraically.

   b) Use this method to determine the solution.

   c) How might you verify your solution algebraically?

   d) Share your method and solution with those of another pair and discuss any similarities and differences.

Reflect and Respond

3. **a)** How does the solution you found graphically compare with the one you found algebraically?

   b) Will a graphical solution always match an algebraic solution? Discuss your answer with a classmate and explain your thoughts.

4. Do you prefer an algebraic or a graphical method for solving a radical equation like this one? Explain why.

Link the Ideas

You can solve many types of equations algebraically and graphically. Algebraic solutions sometimes produce extraneous roots, whereas graphical solutions do not produce extraneous roots. However, algebraic solutions are generally exact while graphical solutions are often approximate. You can solve equations, including radical equations, graphically by identifying the x-intercepts of the graph of the corresponding function.

Example 1
Relate Roots and x-Intercepts

a) Determine the root(s) of $\sqrt{x+5} - 3 = 0$ algebraically.
b) Using a graph, determine the x-intercept(s) of the graph of $y = \sqrt{x+5} - 3$.
c) Describe the connection between the root(s) of the equation and the x-intercept(s) of the graph of the function.

Solution

a) Identify any restrictions on the variable in the radical.
$$x + 5 \geq 0$$
$$x \geq -5$$
To solve a radical equation algebraically, first isolate the radical.
$$\sqrt{x+5} - 3 = 0$$
$$\sqrt{x+5} = 3$$
$$(\sqrt{x+5})^2 = 3^2$$
$$x + 5 = 9$$
$$x = 4$$

Why do you need to square both sides?

Is this an extraneous root? Does it meet the restrictions on the variable in the square root?

The value $x = 4$ is the root or solution to the equation.

b) To find the x-intercepts of the graph of $y = \sqrt{x+5} - 3$, graph the function using technology and determine the x-intercepts.

The function has a single x-intercept at (4, 0).

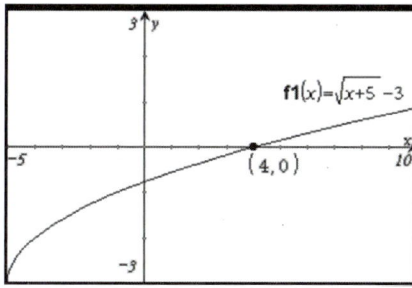

c) The value $x = 4$ is the zero of the function because the value of the function is 0 when $x = 4$. The roots to a radical equation are equal to the x-intercepts of the graph of the corresponding radical function.

Your Turn

a) Use a graph to locate the x-intercept(s) of the graph of $y = \sqrt{x+2} - 4$.
b) Algebraically determine the root(s) of the equation $\sqrt{x+2} - 4 = 0$.
c) Describe the relationship between your findings in parts a) and b).

Example 2

Solve a Radical Equation Involving an Extraneous Solution

Solve the equation $\sqrt{x + 5} = x + 3$ algebraically and graphically.

Solution

$$\sqrt{x + 5} = x + 3$$
$$(\sqrt{x + 5})^2 = (x + 3)^2$$
$$x + 5 = x^2 + 6x + 9$$
$$0 = x^2 + 5x + 4$$
$$0 = (x + 4)(x + 1)$$
$$x + 4 = 0 \quad \text{or} \quad x + 1 = 0$$
$$x = -4 \qquad\qquad x = -1$$

Check:
Substitute $x = -4$ and $x = -1$ into the original equation to identify any extraneous roots.

Why do extraneous roots occur?

Left Side	Right Side	Left Side	Right Side
$\sqrt{x + 5}$	$x + 3$	$\sqrt{x + 5}$	$x + 3$
$= \sqrt{-4 + 5}$	$= -4 + 3$	$= \sqrt{-1 + 5}$	$= -1 + 3$
$= \sqrt{1}$	$= -1$	$= \sqrt{4}$	$= 2$
$= 1$		$= 2$	
Left Side $\neq$ Right Side		Left Side $=$ Right Side	

The solution is $x = -1$.

Solve the equation graphically using functions to represent the two sides of the equation.
$y_1 = \sqrt{x + 5}$
$y_2 = x + 3$

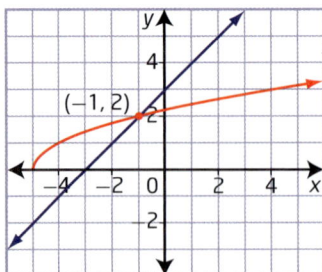

The two functions intersect at the point $(-1, 2)$. The value of x at this point, $x = -1$, is the solution to the equation.

Your Turn

Solve the equation $4 - x = \sqrt{6 - x}$ graphically and algebraically.

Example 3

Approximate Solutions to Radical Equations

a) Solve the equation $\sqrt{3x^2 - 5} = x + 4$ graphically. Express your answer to the nearest tenth.

b) Verify your solution algebraically.

Solution

a) To determine the roots or solutions to an equation of the form $f(x) = g(x)$, identify the x-intercepts of the graph of the corresponding function, $y = f(x) - g(x)$.

Method 1: Use a Single Function

Rearrange the radical equation so that one side is equal to zero:

$$\sqrt{3x^2 - 5} = x + 4$$
$$\sqrt{3x^2 - 5} - x - 4 = 0$$

Graph the corresponding function, $y = \sqrt{3x^2 - 5} - x - 4$, and determine the x-intercepts of the graph.

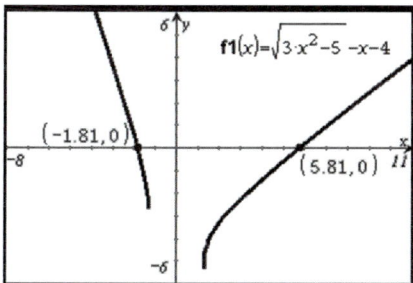

The values of the x-intercepts of the graph are the same as the solutions to the original equation. Therefore, the solution is $x \approx -1.8$ and $x \approx 5.8$.

Method 2: Use a System of Two Functions

Express each side of the equation as a function:
$y_1 = \sqrt{3x^2 - 5}$
$y_2 = x + 4$

Graph these functions and determine the value of x at the point(s) of intersection, i.e., where $y_1 = y_2$.

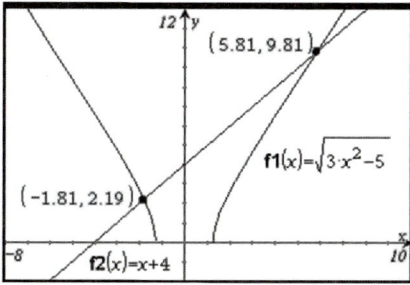

The solution to the equation $\sqrt{3x^2 - 5} = x + 4$ is $x \approx -1.8$ and $x \approx 5.8$.

b) Identify the values of x for which the radical is defined.
$$3x^2 - 5 \geq 0$$
$$3x^2 \geq 5$$
$$x^2 \geq \frac{5}{3}$$
$$|x| \geq \sqrt{\frac{5}{3}}$$

Case 1

If $x \geq 0$, $x \geq \sqrt{\frac{5}{3}}$.

Case 2

If $x < 0$, $x < -\sqrt{\frac{5}{3}}$.

Solve for x:
$$\sqrt{3x^2 - 5} = x + 4$$
$$(\sqrt{3x^2 - 5})^2 = (x + 4)^2 \quad \textcolor{green}{\text{Why do you need to square both sides?}}$$
$$3x^2 - 5 = x^2 + 8x + 16$$
$$2x^2 - 8x - 21 = 0$$
$$x = \frac{-(-8) \pm \sqrt{(-8)^2 - 4(2)(-21)}}{2(2)} \quad \textcolor{green}{\text{Why does the quadratic formula need to be used here?}}$$
$$x = \frac{8 \pm \sqrt{232}}{4}$$
$$x = \frac{8 \pm 2\sqrt{58}}{4}$$
$$x = \frac{4 \pm \sqrt{58}}{2}$$

$x = \frac{4 + \sqrt{58}}{2}$ or $x = \frac{4 - \sqrt{58}}{2}$

$x \approx 5.8$ $\qquad\qquad x \approx -1.8$

\textcolor{green}{Do these solutions meet the restrictions on x? How can you determine whether either of the roots is extraneous?}

The algebraic method gives an exact solution. The approximate solution obtained algebraically, $x \approx -1.8$ and $x \approx 5.8$, is the same as the approximate solution obtained graphically.

Your Turn

Solve the equation $x + 3 = \sqrt{12 - 2x^2}$ using two different methods.

Example 4

Solve a Problem Involving a Radical Equation

An engineer designs a roller coaster that involves a vertical drop section just below the top of the ride. She uses the equation $v = \sqrt{(v_0)^2 + 2ad}$ to model the velocity, v, in feet per second, of the ride's cars after dropping a distance, d, in feet, with an initial velocity, v_0, in feet per second, at the top of the drop, and constant acceleration, a, in feet per second squared. The design specifies that the speed of the ride's cars be 120 ft/s at the bottom of the vertical drop section. If the initial velocity of the coaster at the top of the drop is 10 ft/s and the only acceleration is due to gravity, 32 ft/s², what vertical drop distance should be used, to the nearest foot?

Did You Know?

Top Thrill Dragster is a vertical drop-launched roller coaster in Cedar Point amusement park, in Sandusky, Ohio. When it opened in 2003, it set three new records for roller coasters: tallest, fastest top speed, and steepest drop. It stands almost 130 m tall, and on a clear day riders at the top can see Canada's Pelee Island across Lake Erie.

> **Solution**

Substitute the known values into the formula. Then, graph the functions that correspond to both sides of the equation and determine the point of intersection.

$$v = \sqrt{(v_0)^2 + 2ad}$$
$$120 = \sqrt{(10)^2 + 2(32)d}$$
$$120 = \sqrt{100 + 64d}$$

What two functions do you need to graph?

Web Link

To see a computer animation of *Top Thrill Dragster*, go to www.mcgrawhill.ca/school/learningcentres and follow the links.

The intersection point indicates that the drop distance should be approximately 223 ft to result in a velocity of 120 ft/s at the bottom of the drop.

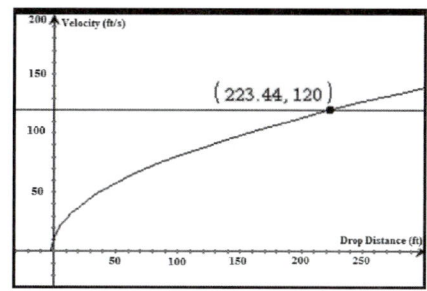

Your Turn

Determine the initial velocity required in a roller coaster design if the velocity will be 26 m/s at the bottom of a vertical drop of 34 m. (Acceleration due to gravity in SI units is 9.8 m/s².)

Key Ideas

- You can solve radical equations algebraically and graphically.
- The solutions or roots of a radical equation are equivalent to the x-intercepts of the graph of the corresponding radical function. You can use either of the following methods to solve radical equations graphically:
  - Graph the corresponding function and identify the value(s) of the x-intercept(s).
  - Graph the system of functions that corresponds to the expression on each side of the equal sign, and then identify the value(s) of x at the point(s) of intersection.

Check Your Understanding

Practise

1. Match each equation to the single function that can be used to solve it graphically. For all equations, $x \geq -4$.

   a) $2 + \sqrt{x + 4} = 4$
   b) $x - 4 = \sqrt{x + 4}$
   c) $2 = \sqrt{x + 4} - 4$
   d) $\sqrt{x + 4} + 2 = x + 6$

   A $y = x - 4 - \sqrt{x + 4}$
   B $y = \sqrt{x + 4} - 2$
   C $y = \sqrt{x + 4} - x - 4$
   D $y = \sqrt{x + 4} - 6$

2. a) Determine the root(s) of the equation $\sqrt{x + 7} - 4 = 0$ algebraically.
   b) Determine the x-intercept(s) of the graph of the function $y = \sqrt{x + 7} - 4$ graphically.
   c) Explain the connection between the root(s) of the equation and the x-intercept(s) of the graph of the function.

3. Determine the approximate solution to each equation graphically. Express your answers to three decimal places.

   a) $\sqrt{7x - 4} = 13$
   b) $9 + \sqrt{6 - 11x} = 45$
   c) $\sqrt{x^2 + 2} - 5 = 0$
   d) $45 - \sqrt{10 - 2x^2} = 25$

4. a) Solve the equation $2\sqrt{3x + 5} + 7 = 16, x \geq -\dfrac{5}{3}$, algebraically.
   b) Show how you can use the graph of the function $y = 2\sqrt{3x + 5} - 9, x \geq -\dfrac{5}{3}$, to find the solution to the equation in part a).

5. Solve each equation graphically. Identify any restrictions on the variable.

   a) $\sqrt{2x - 9} = 11$
   b) $7 = \sqrt{12 - x} + 4$
   c) $5 + 2\sqrt{5x + 32} = 12$
   d) $5 = 13 - \sqrt{25 - 2x}$

6. Solve each equation algebraically. What are the restrictions on the variables?
   a) $\sqrt{5x^2 + 11} = x + 5$
   b) $x + 3 = \sqrt{2x^2 - 7}$
   c) $\sqrt{13 - 4x^2} = 2 - x$
   d) $x + \sqrt{-2x^2 + 9} = 3$

7. Solve each equation algebraically and graphically. Identify any restrictions on the variables.
   a) $\sqrt{8 - x} = x + 6$
   b) $4 = x + 2\sqrt{x - 7}$
   c) $\sqrt{3x^2 - 11} = x + 1$
   d) $x = \sqrt{2x^2 - 8} + 2$

Apply

8. Determine, graphically, the approximate value(s) of a in each formula if $b = 6.2$, $c = 9.7$, and $d = -12.9$. Express answers to the nearest hundredth.
   a) $c = \sqrt{ab - d}$
   b) $d + 7\sqrt{a + c} = b$
   c) $c = b - \sqrt{a^2 + d}$
   d) $\sqrt{2a^2 + c} + d = a - b$

9. Naomi says that the equation $6 + \sqrt{x + 4} = 2$ has no solutions.
   a) Show that Naomi is correct, using both a graphical and an algebraic approach.
   b) Is it possible to tell that this equation has no solutions just by examining the equation? Explain.

10. Two researchers, Greg and Yolanda, use the function $N(t) = 1.3\sqrt{t} + 4.2$ to model the number of people that might be affected by a certain medical condition in a region of 7.4 million people. In the function, N represents the number of people, in millions, affected after t years. Greg predicts that the entire population would be affected after 6 years. Yolanda believes that it would take only 1.5 years. Who is correct? Justify your answer.

11. The period, T, in seconds, of a pendulum depends on the distance, L, in metres, between the pivot and the pendulum's centre of mass. If the initial swing angle is relatively small, the period is given by the radical function $T = 2\pi\sqrt{\dfrac{L}{g}}$, where g represents acceleration due to gravity (approximately 9.8 m/s² on Earth). Jeremy is building a machine and needs it to have a pendulum that takes 1 s to swing from one side to the other. How long should the pendulum be, in centimetres?

12. Cables and ropes are made of several strands that contain individual wires or threads. The term "7 × 19 cable" refers to a cable with 7 strands, each containing 19 wires.

    Suppose a manufacturer uses the function $d = \sqrt{\dfrac{b}{30}}$ to relate the diameter, d, in millimetres, of its 7 × 19 stainless steel aircraft cable to the safe working load, b, in kilograms.

    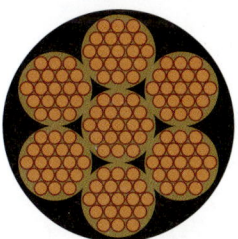

    a) Is a cable with a diameter of 6.4 mm large enough to support a mass of 1000 kg?
    b) What is the safe working load for a cable that is 10 mm in diameter?

    Did You Know?

    The safe working load for a cable or rope is related to its breaking strength, or minimum mass required for it to break. To ensure safety, manufacturers rate a cable's safe working load to be much less than its actual breaking strength.

13. Hazeem states that the equations $\sqrt{x^2} = 9$ and $(\sqrt{x})^2 = 9$ have the same solution. Is he correct? Justify your answer.

14. What real number is exactly one greater than its square root?

15. A parachute-manufacturing company uses the formula $d = 3.69\sqrt{\dfrac{m}{v^2}}$ to model the diameter, d, in metres, of its dome-shaped circular parachutes so that an object with mass, m, in kilograms, has a descent velocity, v, in metres per second, under the parachute.

  a) What is the landing velocity for a 20-kg object using a parachute that is 3.2 m in diameter? Express your answer to the nearest metre per second.

  b) A velocity of 2 m/s is considered safe for a parachutist to land. If the parachute has a diameter of 16 m, what is the maximum mass of the parachutist, in kilograms?

Extend

16. If the function $y = \sqrt{-3(x + c)} + c$ passes through the point $(-1, 1)$, what is the value of c? Confirm your answer graphically, and use the graph to create a similar question for the same function.

17. Heron's formula, $A = \sqrt{s(s - a)(s - b)(s - c)}$, relates the area, A, of a triangle to the lengths of the three sides, a, b, and c, and its semi-perimeter (half its perimeter), $s = \dfrac{a + b + c}{2}$. A triangle has an area of 900 cm² and one side that measures 60 cm. The other two side lengths are unknown, but one is twice the length of the other. What are the lengths of the three sides of the triangle?

Create Connections

C1 How can the graph of a function be used to find the solutions to an equation? Create an example to support your answer.

C2 The speed, in metres per second, of a tsunami travelling across the ocean is equal to the square root of the product of the depth of the water, in metres, and the acceleration due to gravity, 9.8 m/s².

  a) Write a function for the speed of a tsunami. Define the variables you used.

  b) Calculate the speed of a wave at a depth of 2500 m, and use unit analysis to show that the resulting speed has the correct units.

  c) What depth of water would produce a speed of 200 m/s? Solve graphically and algebraically.

  d) Which method of solving do you prefer in this case: algebraic or graphical? Do you always prefer one method over the other, or does it depend? Explain.

C3 Does every radical equation have at least one solution? How can using a graphical approach to solving equations help you answer this question? Support your answer with at least two examples.

C4 Describe two methods of identifying extraneous roots in a solution to a radical equation. Explain why extraneous roots may occur.

Chapter 2 Review

2.1 Radical Functions and Transformations, pages 62–77

1. Graph each function. Identify the domain and range, and explain how they connect to the values in a table of values and the shape of the graph.

   a) $y = \sqrt{x}$
   b) $y = \sqrt{3 - x}$
   c) $y = \sqrt{2x + 7}$

2. What transformations can you apply to $y = \sqrt{x}$ to obtain the graph of each function? State the domain and range in each case.

   a) $y = 5\sqrt{x + 20}$
   b) $y = \sqrt{-2x} - 8$
   c) $y = -\sqrt{\frac{1}{6}(x - 11)}$

3. Write the equation and state the domain and range of the radical function that results from each set of transformations on the graph of $y = \sqrt{x}$.

   a) a horizontal stretch by a factor of 10 and a vertical translation of 12 units up
   b) a vertical stretch by a factor of 2.5, a reflection in the x-axis, and a horizontal translation of 9 units left
   c) a horizontal stretch by a factor of $\frac{5}{2}$, a vertical stretch by a factor of $\frac{1}{20}$, a reflection in the y-axis, and a translation of 7 units right and 3 units down

4. Sketch the graph of each function by transforming the graph of $y = \sqrt{x}$. State the domain and range of each.

   a) $y = -\sqrt{x - 1} + 2$
   b) $y = 3\sqrt{-x} - 4$
   c) $y = \sqrt{2(x + 3)} + 1$

5. How can you use transformations to identify the domain and range of the function $y = -2\sqrt{3(x - 4)} + 9$?

6. The sales, S, in units, of a new product can be modelled as a function of the time, t, in days, since it first appears in stores using the function $S(t) = 500 + 100\sqrt{t}$.

   a) Describe how to graph the function by transforming the graph of $y = \sqrt{t}$.
   b) Graph the function and explain what the shape of the graph indicates about the situation.
   c) What are the domain and range? What do they mean in this situation?
   d) Predict the number of items sold after 60 days.

7. Write an equation of the form $y = a\sqrt{b(x - h)} + k$ for each graph.

   a)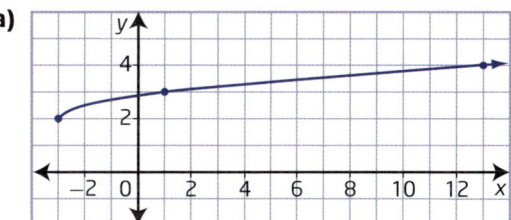

   b)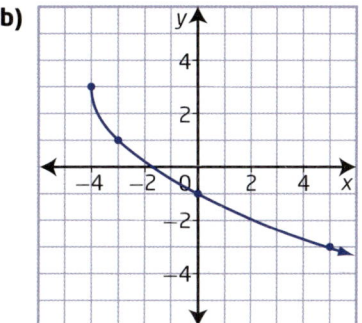

   c)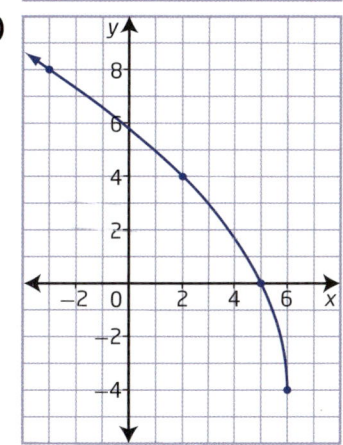

2.2 Square Root of a Function, pages 78–89

8. Identify the domains and ranges of the functions in each pair and explain any differences.
   a) $y = x - 2$ and $y = \sqrt{x - 2}$
   b) $y = 10 - x$ and $y = \sqrt{10 - x}$
   c) $y = 4x + 11$ and $y = \sqrt{4x + 11}$

9. The graph of $y = f(x)$ is shown.

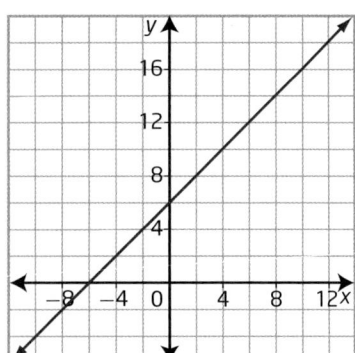

   a) Graph the function $y = \sqrt{f(x)}$ and describe your strategy.
   b) Explain how the graphs are related.
   c) Identify the domain and range of each function and explain any differences.

10. Identify and compare the domains and ranges of the functions in each pair, and explain why they differ.
    a) $y = 4 - x^2$ and $y = \sqrt{4 - x^2}$
    b) $y = 2x^2 + 24$ and $y = \sqrt{2x^2 + 24}$
    c) $y = x^2 - 6x$ and $y = \sqrt{x^2 - 6x}$

11. A 25-ft-long ladder leans against a wall. The height, h, in feet, of the top of the ladder above the ground is related to its distance, d, in feet, from the base of the wall.
    a) Write an equation to represent h as a function of d.
    b) Graph the function and identify the domain and range.
    c) Explain how the shape of the graph, the domain, and the range relate to the situation.

12. Using each graph of $y = f(x)$, sketch the graph of $y = \sqrt{f(x)}$.

   a)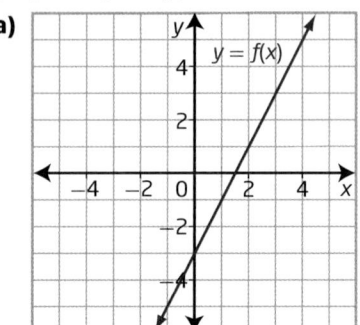

   b)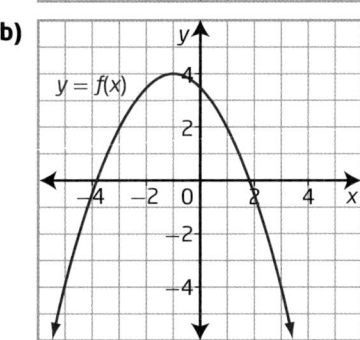

   c)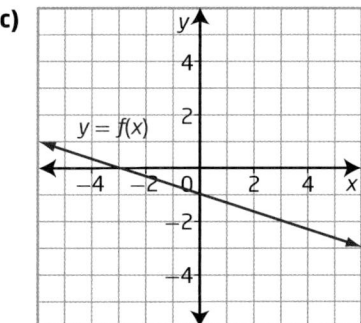

2.3 Solving Radical Equations Graphically, pages 90–98

13. a) Determine the root(s) of the equation $\sqrt{x + 3} - 7 = 0$ algebraically.
    b) Use a graph to locate the x-intercept(s) of the function $f(x) = \sqrt{x + 3} - 7$.
    c) Use your answers to describe the connection between the x-intercepts of the graph of a function and the roots of the corresponding equation.

14. Determine the approximate solution to each equation graphically. Express answers to three decimal places.

a) $\sqrt{7x - 9} - 4 = 0$

b) $50 = 12 + \sqrt{8 - 12x}$

c) $\sqrt{2x^2 + 5} = 11$

15. The speed, s, in metres per second, of water flowing out of a hole near the bottom of a tank relates to the height, h, in metres, of the water above the hole by the formula $s = \sqrt{2gh}$. In the formula, g represents the acceleration due to gravity, 9.8 m/s². At what height is the water flowing out a speed of 9 m/s?

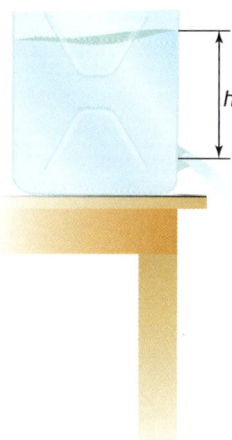

Did You Know?

The speed of fluid flowing out of a hole near the bottom of a tank filled to a depth, h, is the same as the speed an object acquires in falling freely from the height h. This relationship was discovered by Italian scientist Evangelista Torricelli in 1643 and is referred to as Torricelli's law.

16. Solve each equation graphically and algebraically.

a) $\sqrt{5x + 14} = 9$

b) $7 + \sqrt{8 - x} = 12$

c) $23 - 4\sqrt{2x - 10} = 12$

d) $x + 3 = \sqrt{18 - 2x^2}$

17. Atid, Carly, and Jaime use different methods to solve the radical equation $3 + \sqrt{x - 1} = x$.

Their solutions are as follows:
- Atid: $x = 2$
- Carly: $x = 5$
- Jaime: $x = 2, 5$

a) Who used an algebraic approach? Justify your answer.

b) Who used a graphical method? How do you know?

c) Who made an error in solving the equation? Justify your answer.

18. Assume that the shape of a tipi approximates a cone. The surface area, S, in square metres, of the walls of a tipi can be modelled by the function $S(r) = \pi r\sqrt{36 + r^2}$, where r represents the radius of the base, in metres.

Blackfoot Crossing, Alberta

a) If a tipi has a radius of 5.2 m, what is the minimum area of canvas required for the walls, to the nearest square metre?

b) If you use 160 m² of canvas to make the walls for this tipi, what radius will you use?

Chapter 2 Practice Test

Multiple Choice

For #1 to #6, choose the best answer.

1. If $f(x) = x + 1$, which point is on the graph of $y = \sqrt{f(x)}$?
   - **A** (0, 0)
   - **B** (0, 1)
   - **C** (1, 0)
   - **D** (1, 1)

2. Which intercepts will help you find the roots of the equation $\sqrt{2x - 5} = 4$?
   - **A** x-intercepts of the graph of the function $y = \sqrt{2x - 5} - 4$
   - **B** x-intercepts of the graph of the function $y = \sqrt{2x - 5} + 4$
   - **C** y-intercepts of the graph of the function $y = \sqrt{2x - 5} - 4$
   - **D** y-intercepts of the graph of the function $y = \sqrt{2x - 5} + 4$

3. Which function has a domain of $\{x \mid x \geq 5, x \in R\}$ and a range of $\{y \mid y \geq 0, y \in R\}$?
   - **A** $f(x) = \sqrt{x - 5}$
   - **B** $f(x) = \sqrt{x} - 5$
   - **C** $f(x) = \sqrt{x + 5}$
   - **D** $f(x) = \sqrt{x} + 5$

4. If $y = \sqrt{x}$ is stretched horizontally by a factor of 6, which function results?
   - **A** $y = \dfrac{1}{6}\sqrt{x}$
   - **B** $y = 6\sqrt{x}$
   - **C** $y = \sqrt{\dfrac{1}{6}x}$
   - **D** $y = \sqrt{6x}$

5. Which equation represents the function shown in the graph?

   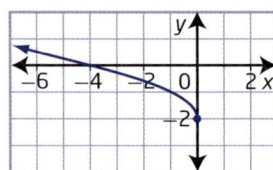

   - **A** $y - 2 = -\sqrt{x}$
   - **B** $y + 2 = -\sqrt{x}$
   - **C** $y - 2 = \sqrt{-x}$
   - **D** $y + 2 = \sqrt{-x}$

6. How do the domains and ranges compare for the functions $y = \sqrt{x}$ and $y = \sqrt{5x} + 8$?
   - **A** Only the domains differ.
   - **B** Only the ranges differ.
   - **C** Both the domains and ranges differ.
   - **D** Neither the domains nor the ranges differ.

Short Answer

7. Solve the equation $5 + \sqrt{9 - 13x} = 20$ graphically. Express your answer to the nearest hundredth.

8. Determine two forms of the equation that represents the function shown in the graph.

   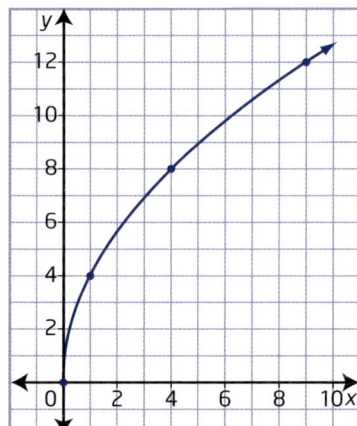

9. How are the domains and ranges of the functions $y = 7 - x$ and $y = \sqrt{7 - x}$ related? Explain why they differ.

10. If $f(x) = 8 - 2x^2$, what are the domains and ranges of $y = f(x)$ and $y = \sqrt{f(x)}$?

11. Solve the equation $\sqrt{12 - 3x^2} = x + 2$ using two different graphical methods. Show your graphs.

12. Solve the equation $4 + \sqrt{x + 1} = x$ graphically and algebraically. Express your answer to the nearest tenth.

13. The radical function $S = \sqrt{255d}$ can be used to estimate the speed, S, in kilometres per hour, of a vehicle before it brakes from the length, d, in metres, of the skid mark. The vehicle has all four wheels braking and skids to a complete stop on a dry road.

a) Use the language of transformations to describe how to create a graph of this function from a graph of the base square root function.

b) Sketch the graph of the function and use it to determine the approximate length of skid mark expected from a vehicle travelling at 100 km/h on this road.

Extended Response

14. a) How can you use transformations to graph the function $y = -\sqrt{2x} + 3$?

b) Sketch the graph.

c) Identify the domain and range of the function.

d) Describe how the domain and range connect to your answer to part a).

e) How can the graph be used to solve the equation $5 + \sqrt{2x} = 8$?

15. Using the graph of $y = f(x)$, sketch the graph of $y = \sqrt{f(x)}$ and explain your strategy.

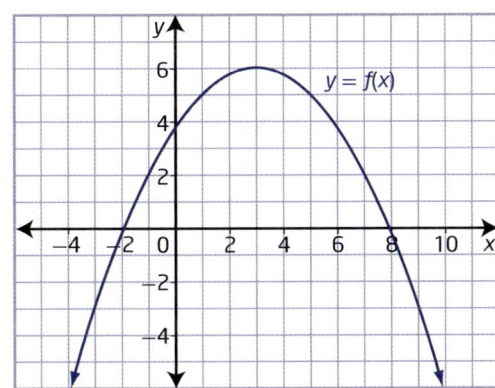

16. Consider the roof of the mosque at the Canadian Islamic Centre in Edmonton, Alberta. The diameter of the base of the roof is approximately 10 m, and the vertical distance from the centre of the roof to the base is approximately 5 m.

Canadian Islamic Centre (Al-Rashid), Edmonton, Alberta

a) Determine a function of the form $y = a\sqrt{b(x - h)} + k$, where y represents the distance from the base to the roof and x represents the horizontal distance from the centre.

b) What are the domain and range of this function? How do they relate to the situation?

c) Use the function you wrote in part a) to determine, graphically, the approximate height of the roof at a point 2 m horizontally from the centre of the roof.

CHAPTER 3

Polynomial Functions

Polynomial functions can be used to model different real-world applications, from business profit and demand to construction and fabrication design. Many calculators use polynomial approximations to compute function key calculations. For example, the first four terms of the Taylor polynomial approximation for the square root function are
$$\sqrt{x} \approx 1 + \frac{1}{2}(x - 1) - \frac{1}{8}(x - 1)^2 + \frac{1}{16}(x - 1)^3.$$

Try calculating $\sqrt{1.2}$ using this expression. How close is your answer to the one the square root key on a calculator gives you?

In this chapter, you will study polynomial functions and use them to solve a variety of problems.

Did You Know?

A Taylor polynomial is a partial sum of the Taylor series. Developed by British mathematician Brook Taylor (1685–1731), the Taylor series representation of a function has an infinite number of terms. The more terms included in the Taylor polynomial computation, the more accurate the answer.

Key Terms
polynomial function
end behaviour
synthetic division
remainder theorem
factor theorem
integral zero theorem
multiplicity (of a zero)

Career Link

Computer engineers apply their knowledge of mathematics and science to solve practical and technical problems in a wide variety of industries. As computer technology is integrated into an increasing range of products and services, more and more designers, service workers, and technical specialists will be needed.

Web Link

To learn more about a career in the field of computer engineering, go to www.mcgrawhill.ca/school/learningcentres and follow the links.

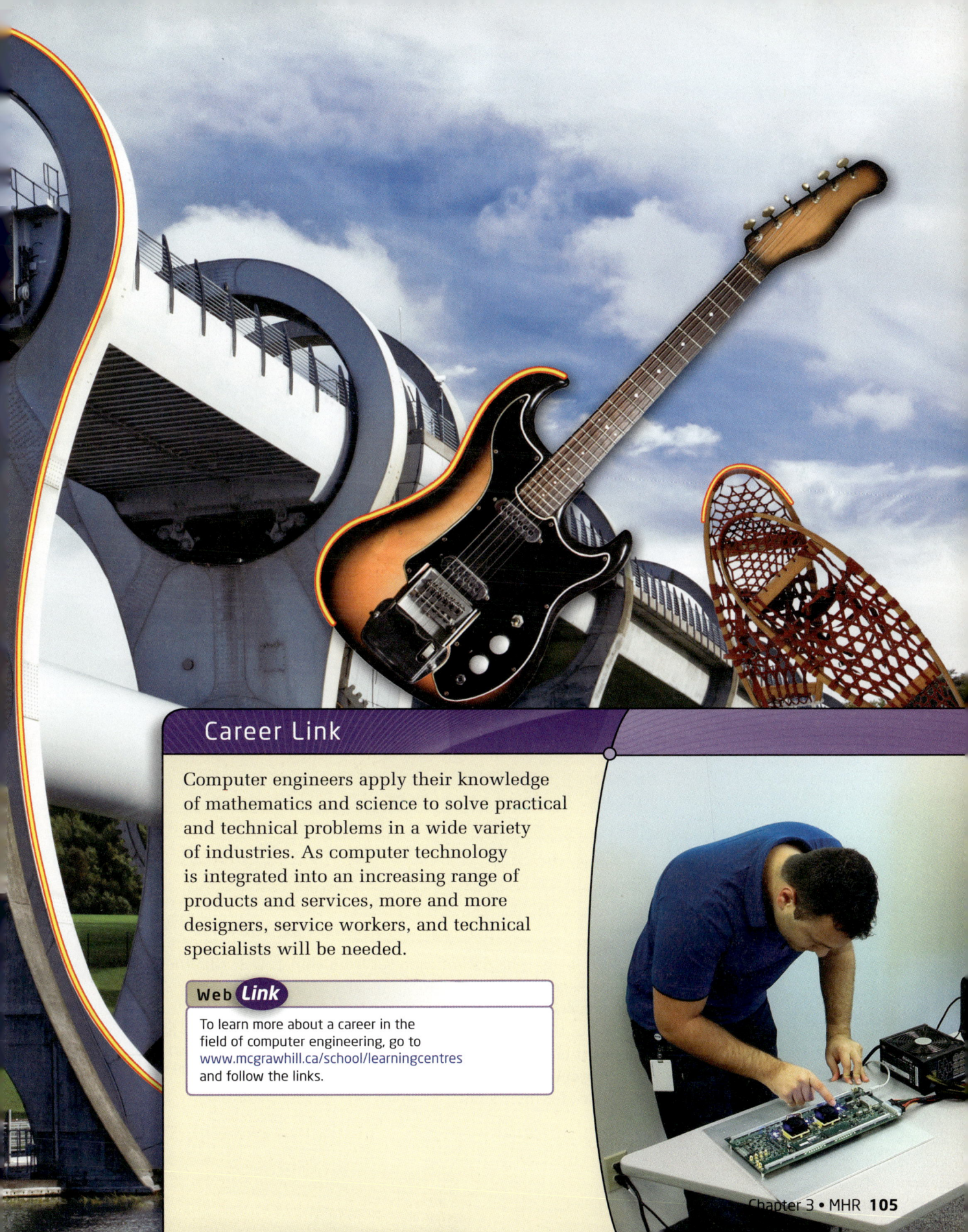

3.1 Characteristics of Polynomial Functions

Focus on...
- identifying polynomial functions
- analysing polynomial functions

A cross-section of a honeycomb has a pattern with one hexagon surrounded by six more hexagons. Surrounding these is a third ring of 12 hexagons, and so on. The quadratic function $f(r)$ models the total number of hexagons in a honeycomb, where r is the number of rings. Then, you can use the graph of the function to solve questions about the honeycomb pattern.

A quadratic function that models this pattern will be discussed later in this section.

Did You Know?

Falher, Alberta is known as the "Honey Capital of Canada." The Falher Honey Festival is an annual event that celebrates beekeeping and francophone history in the region.

Investigate Graphs of Polynomial Functions

Materials
- graphing calculator or computer with graphing software

1. Graph each set of functions on a different set of coordinate axes using graphing technology. Sketch the results.

Type of Function	Set A	Set B	Set C	Set D
linear	$y = x$	$y = -3x$	$y = x + 1$	
quadratic	$y = x^2$	$y = -2x^2$	$y = x^2 - 3$	$y = x^2 - x - 2$
cubic	$y = x^3$	$y = -4x^3$	$y = x^3 - 4$	$y = x^3 + 4x^2 + x - 6$
quartic	$y = x^4$	$y = -2x^4$	$y = x^4 + 2$	$y = x^4 + 2x^3 - 7x^2 - 8x + 12$
quintic	$y = x^5$	$y = -x^5$	$y = x^5 - 1$	$y = x^5 + 3x^4 - 5x^3 - 15x^2 + 4x + 12$

2. Compare the graphs *within* each set from step 1. Describe their similarities and differences in terms of
   - **end behaviour**
   - degree of the function in one variable, x
   - constant term
   - leading coefficient
   - number of x-intercepts

Recall that the degree of a polynomial is the greatest exponent of x.

end behaviour
- the behaviour of the y-values of a function as $|x|$ becomes very large

3. Compare the sets of graphs from step 1 to each other. Describe their similarities and differences as in step 2.

4. Consider the cubic, quartic, and quintic graphs from step 1. Which graphs are similar to the graph of
   - $y = x$?
   - $y = -x$?
   - $y = x^2$?
   - $y = -x^2$?

   Explain how they are similar.

Reflect and Respond

5. **a)** How are the graphs and equations of linear, cubic, and quintic functions similar?

   b) How are the graphs and equations of quadratic and quartic functions similar?

   c) Describe the relationship between the end behaviours of the graphs and the degree of the corresponding function.

6. What is the relationship between the sign of the leading coefficient of a function equation and the end behaviour of the graph of the function?

7. What is the relationship between the constant term in a function equation and the position of the graph of the function?

8. What is the minimum and maximum numbers of x-intercepts of the graph of a function with the degree of the function?

Link the Ideas

The degree of a **polynomial function** in one variable, x, is n, the exponent of the greatest power of the variable x. The coefficient of the greatest power of x is the leading coefficient, a_n, and the term whose value is not affected by the variable is the constant term, a_0.

In this chapter, the coefficients a_n to a_1 and the constant a_0 are restricted to integral values.

What power of x is associated with a_0?

polynomial function
- a function of the form $f(x) = a_n x^n + a_{n-1} x^{n-1} + a_{n-2} x^{n-2} + \dots + a_2 x^2 + a_1 x + a_0$, where
  - n is a whole number
  - x is a variable
  - the coefficients a_n to a_0 are real numbers
- examples are
  $f(x) = 2x - 1$,
  $f(x) = x^2 + x - 6$, and
  $y = x^3 + 2x^2 - 5x - 6$

Example 1

Identify Polynomial Functions

Which functions are polynomials? Justify your answer. State the degree, the leading coefficient, and the constant term of each polynomial function.

a) $g(x) = \sqrt{x} + 5$
b) $f(x) = 3x^4$
c) $y = |x|$
d) $y = 2x^3 + 3x^2 - 4x - 1$

Solution

a) The function $g(x) = \sqrt{x} + 5$ is a radical function, not a polynomial function.
$\sqrt{x}$ is the same as $x^{\frac{1}{2}}$, which has an exponent that is not a whole number.

b) The function $f(x) = 3x^4$ is a polynomial function of degree 4. The leading coefficient is 3 and the constant term is 0.

c) The function $y = |x|$ is an absolute value function, not a polynomial function.
$|x|$ cannot be written directly as x^n.

d) $y = 2x^3 + 3x^2 - 4x - 1$ is a polynomial of degree 3. The leading coefficient is 2 and the constant term is -1.

Your Turn

Identify whether each function is a polynomial function. Justify your answer. State the degree, the leading coefficient, and the constant term of each polynomial function.

a) $h(x) = \frac{1}{x}$
b) $y = 3x^2 - 2x^5 + 4$
c) $y = -4x^4 - 4x + 3$
d) $y = x^{\frac{1}{2}} - 7$

Characteristics of Polynomial Functions

Polynomial functions and their graphs can be analysed by identifying the degree, end behaviour, domain and range, and the number of x-intercepts.

The chart shows the characteristics of polynomial functions with positive leading coefficients up to degree 5.

How would the characteristics of polynomial functions change if the leading coefficient were negative?

Degree 0: Constant Function

Even degree
Number of x-intercepts: 0 (for $f(x) \neq 0$)

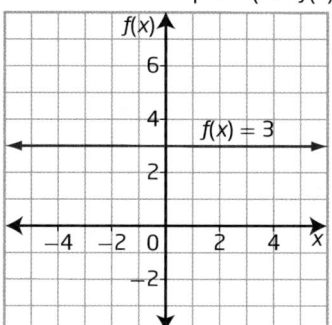

Example: $f(x) = 3$
End behaviour: extends horizontally
Domain: $\{x \mid x \in R\}$
Range: $\{3\}$
Number of x-intercepts: 0

Degree 1: Linear Function

Odd degree
Number of x-intercepts: 1

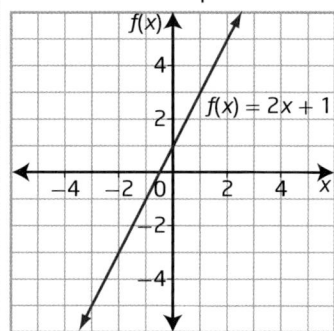

Example: $f(x) = 2x + 1$
End behaviour: line extends down into quadrant III and up into quadrant I
Domain: $\{x \mid x \in R\}$
Range: $\{y \mid y \in R\}$
Number of x-intercepts: 1

Degree 2: Quadratic Function

Even degree
Number of x-intercepts: 0, 1, or 2

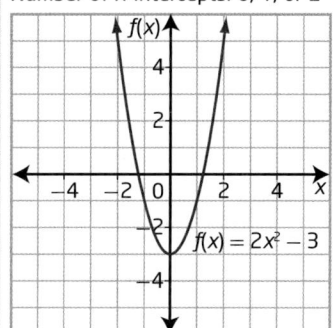

Example: $f(x) = 2x^2 - 3$
End behaviour: curve extends up into quadrant II and up into quadrant I
Domain: $\{x \mid x \in R\}$
Range: $\{y \mid y \geq -2, y \in R\}$
Number of x-intercepts: 2

Degree 3: Cubic Function

Odd degree
Number of x-intercepts: 1, 2, or 3

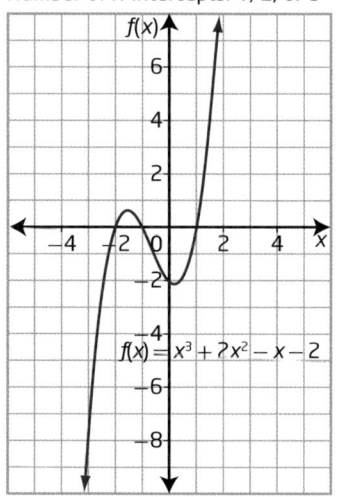

Example:
$f(x) = x^3 + 2x^2 - x - 2$
End behaviour: curve extends down into quadrant III and up into quadrant I
Domain: $\{x \mid x \in R\}$
Range: $\{y \mid y \in R\}$
Number of x-intercepts: 3

Degree 4: Quartic Function

Even degree
Number of x-intercepts: 0, 1, 2, 3, or 4

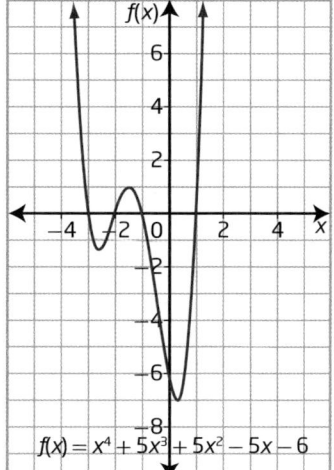

Example:
$f(x) = x^4 + 5x^3 + 5x^2 - 5x - 6$
End behaviour: curve extends up into quadrant II and up into quadrant I
Domain: $\{x \mid x \in R\}$
Range: $\{y \mid y \geq -6.91, y \in R\}$
Number of x-intercepts: 4

Degree 5: Quintic Function

Odd degree
Number of x-intercepts: 1, 2, 3, 4, or 5

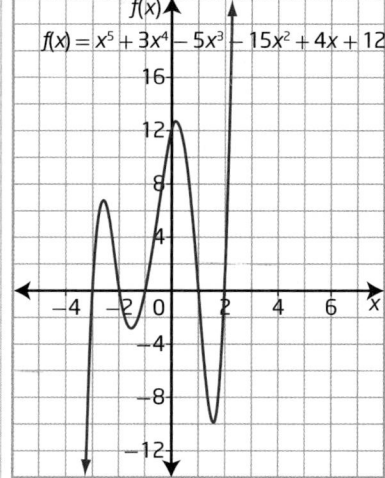

Example:
$f(x) = x^5 + 3x^4 - 5x^3 - 15x^2 + 4x + 12$
End behaviour: curve extends down into quadrant III and up into quadrant I
Domain: $\{x \mid x \in R\}$
Range: $\{y \mid y \in R\}$
Number of x-intercepts: 5

Example 2

Match a Polynomial Function With Its Graph

Identify the following characteristics of the graph of each polynomial function:
- the type of function and whether it is of even or odd degree
- the end behaviour of the graph of the function
- the number of possible x-intercepts
- whether the graph will have a maximum or minimum value
- the y-intercept

Then, match each function to its corresponding graph.

a) $g(x) = -x^4 + 10x^2 + 5x - 4$
b) $f(x) = x^3 + x^2 - 5x + 3$
c) $p(x) = -2x^5 + 5x^3 - x$
d) $h(x) = x^4 + 4x^3 - x^2 - 16x - 12$

A
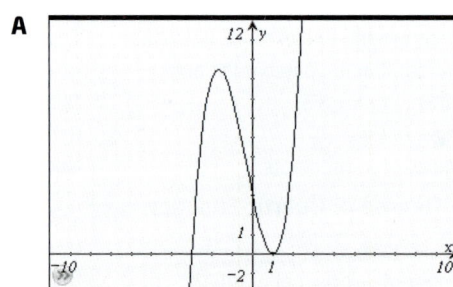

B
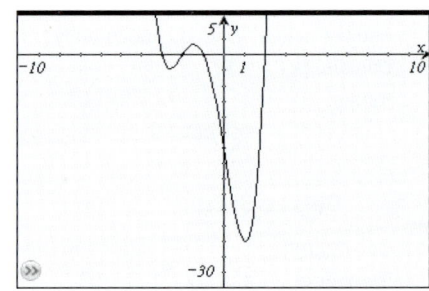

C
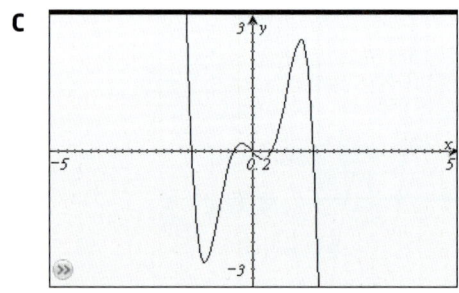

D
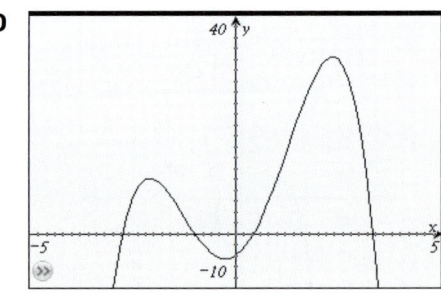

Solution

a) The function $g(x) = -x^4 + 10x^2 + 5x - 4$ is a quartic (degree 4), which is an even-degree polynomial function. Its graph has a maximum of four x-intercepts. Since the leading coefficient is negative, the graph of the function opens downward, extending down into quadrant III and down into quadrant IV (similar to $y = -x^2$), and has a maximum value. The graph has a y-intercept of $a_0 = -4$. This function corresponds to graph D.

b) The function $f(x) = x^3 + x^2 - 5x + 3$ is a cubic (degree 3), which is an odd-degree polynomial function. Its graph has at least one x-intercept and at most three x-intercepts. Since the leading coefficient is positive, the graph of the function extends down into quadrant III and up into quadrant I (similar to the line $y = x$). The graph has no maximum or minimum values. The graph has a y-intercept of $a_0 = 3$. This function corresponds to graph A.

c) The function $p(x) = -2x^5 + 5x^3 - x$ is a quintic (degree 5), which is an odd-degree polynomial function. Its graph has at least one x-intercept and at most five x-intercepts. Since the leading coefficient is negative, the graph of the function extends up into quadrant II and down into quadrant IV (similar to the line $y = -x$). The graph has no maximum or minimum values. The graph has a y-intercept of $a_0 = 0$. This function corresponds to graph C.

d) The function $h(x) = x^4 + 4x^3 - x^2 - 16x - 12$ is a quartic (degree 4), which is an even-degree polynomial function. Its graph has a maximum of four x-intercepts. Since the leading coefficient is positive, the graph of the function opens upward, extending up into quadrant II and up into quadrant I (similar to $y = x^2$), and has a minimum value. The graph has a y-intercept of $a_0 = -12$. This function corresponds to graph B.

Your Turn

a) Describe the end behaviour of the graph of the function $f(x) = -x^3 - 3x^2 + 2x + 1$. State the possible number of x-intercepts, the y-intercept, and whether the graph has a maximum or minimum value.

b) Which of the following is the graph of the function?

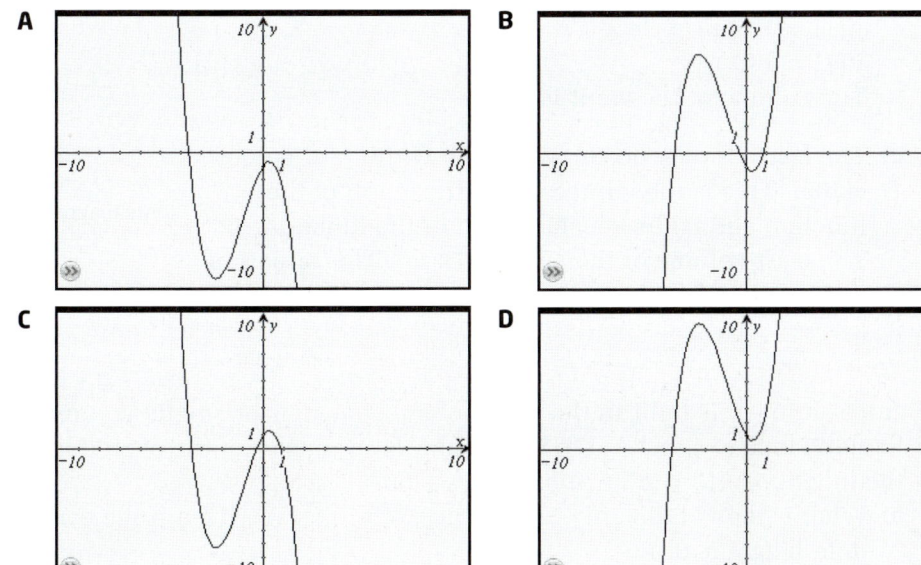

Example 3

Application of a Polynomial Function

A bank vault is built in the shape of a rectangular prism. Its volume, V, is related to the width, w, in metres, of the vault doorway by the function $V(w) = w^3 + 13w^2 + 54w + 72$.

a) What is the volume, in cubic metres, of the vault if the door is 1 m wide?

b) What is the least volume of the vault? What is the width of the door for this volume? Why is this situation not realistic?

Solution

a) Method 1: Graph the Polynomial Function

Use a graphing calculator or computer with graphing software to graph the polynomial function. Then, use the trace feature to determine the value of V that corresponds to $w = 1$.

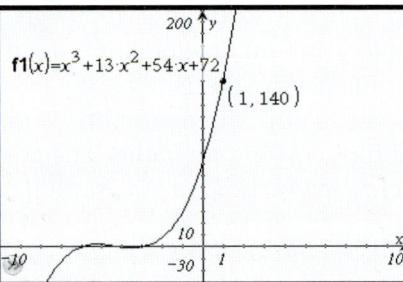

The volume of the vault is 140 m³.

Method 2: Substitute Into the Polynomial Function

Substitute $w = 1$ into the function and evaluate the result.
$V(w) = w^3 + 13w^2 + 54w + 72$
$V(1) = 1^3 + 13(1)^2 + 54(1) + 72$
$V(1) = 1 + 13 + 54 + 72$
$V(1) = 140$
The volume of the vault is 140 m³.

b) The least volume occurs when the width of the door is 0 m. This is the y-intercept of the graph of the function and is the constant term of the function, 72. The least volume of the vault is 72 m³. This situation is not realistic because the vault would not have a door.

What is the domain of the function in this situation?

Your Turn

A toaster oven is built in the shape of a rectangular prism. Its volume, V, in cubic inches, is related to the height, h, in inches, of the oven door by the function $V(h) = h^3 + 10h^2 + 31h + 30$.

a) What is the volume, in cubic inches, of the toaster oven if the oven door height is 8 in.?

b) What is the height of the oven door for the least toaster oven volume? Explain.

Key Ideas

- A polynomial function has the form $f(x) = a_n x^n + a_{n-1} x^{n-1} + a_{n-2} x^{n-2} + \cdots + a_2 x^2 + a_1 x + a_0$, where a_n is the leading coefficient; a_0 is the constant; and the degree of the polynomial, n, is the exponent of the greatest power of the variable, x.

- Graphs of odd-degree polynomial functions have the following characteristics:
  - a graph that extends down into quadrant III and up into quadrant I (similar to the graph of $y = x$) when the leading coefficient is positive
  - a graph that extends up into quadrant II and down into quadrant IV (similar to the graph of $y = -x$) when the leading coefficient is negative

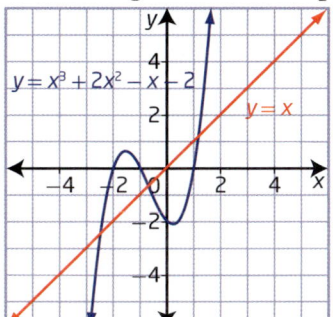 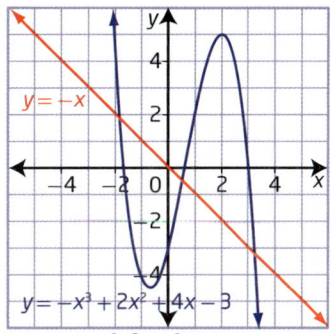

  - a y-intercept that corresponds to the constant term of the function
  - at least one x-intercept and up to a maximum of n x-intercepts, where n is the degree of the function
  - a domain of $\{x \mid x \in \mathbb{R}\}$ and a range of $\{y \mid y \in \mathbb{R}\}$
  - no maximum or minimum points

- Graphs of even-degree polynomial functions have the following characteristics:
  - a graph that extends up into quadrant II and up into quadrant I (similar to the graph of $y = x^2$) when the leading coefficient is positive
  - a graph that extends down into quadrant III and down into quadrant IV (similar to the graph of $y = -x^2$) when the leading coefficient is negative

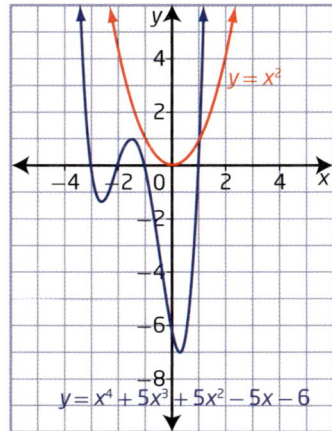 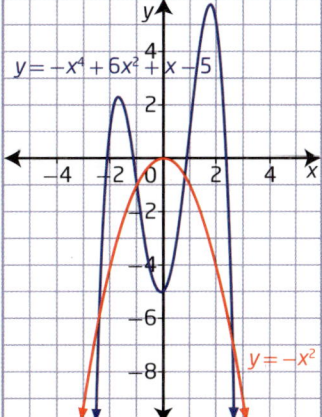

  - a y-intercept that corresponds to the constant term of the function
  - from zero to a maximum of n x-intercepts, where n is the degree of the function
  - a domain of $\{x \mid x \in \mathbb{R}\}$ and a range that depends on the maximum or minimum value of the function

Check Your Understanding

Practise

1. Identify whether each of the following is a polynomial function. Justify your answers.
   a) $h(x) = 2 - \sqrt{x}$
   b) $y = 3x + 1$
   c) $f(x) = 3^x$
   d) $g(x) = 3x^4 - 7$
   e) $p(x) = x^{-3} + x^2 + 3x$
   f) $y = -4x^3 + 2x + 5$

2. What are the degree, type, leading coefficient, and constant term of each polynomial function?
   a) $f(x) = -x + 3$
   b) $y = 9x^2$
   c) $g(x) = 3x^4 + 3x^2 - 2x + 1$
   d) $k(x) = 4 - 3x^3$
   e) $y = -2x^5 - 2x^3 + 9$
   f) $h(x) = -6$

3. For each of the following:
   - determine whether the graph represents an odd-degree or an even-degree polynomial function
   - determine whether the leading coefficient of the corresponding function is positive or negative
   - state the number of x-intercepts
   - state the domain and range

   a)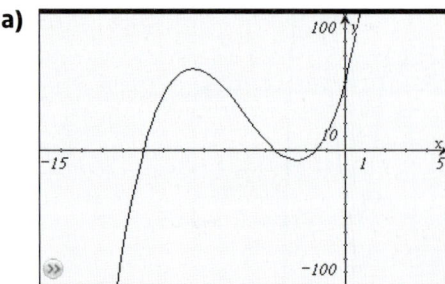

   b)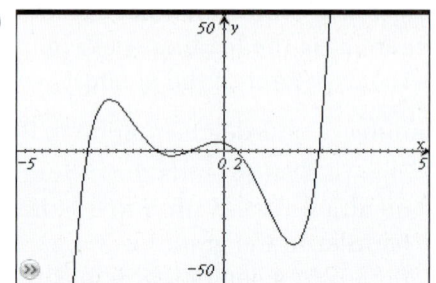

   c)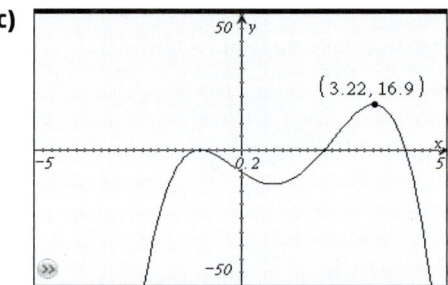

   d)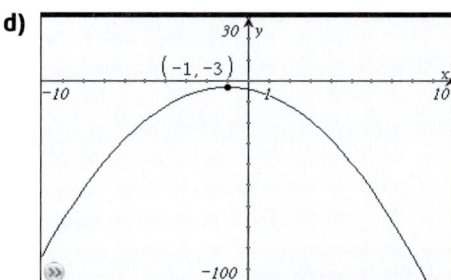

4. Use the degree and the sign of the leading coefficient of each function to describe the end behaviour of the corresponding graph. State the possible number of x-intercepts and the value of the y-intercept.
   a) $f(x) = x^2 + 3x - 1$
   b) $g(x) = -4x^3 + 2x^2 - x + 5$
   c) $h(x) = -7x^4 + 2x^3 - 3x^2 + 6x + 4$
   d) $q(x) = x^5 - 3x^2 + 9x$
   e) $p(x) = 4 - 2x$
   f) $v(x) = -x^3 + 2x^4 - 4x^2$

Apply

5. Jake claims that all graphs of polynomial functions of the form $y = ax^n + x + b$, where a, b, and n are even integers, extend from quadrant II to quadrant I. Do you agree? Use examples to explain your answer.

6. A snowboard manufacturer determines that its profit, P, in dollars, can be modelled by the function $P(x) = 1000x + x^4 - 3000$, where x represents the number, in hundreds, of snowboards sold.

   a) What is the degree of the function $P(x)$?

   b) What are the leading coefficient and constant of this function? What does the constant represent?

   c) Describe the end behaviour of the graph of this function.

   d) What are the restrictions on the domain of this function? Explain why you selected those restrictions.

   e) What do the x-intercepts of the graph represent for this situation?

   f) What is the profit from the sale of 1500 snowboards?

7. A medical researcher establishes that a patient's reaction time, r, in minutes, to a dose of a particular drug is $r(d) = -3d^3 + 3d^2$, where d is the amount of the drug, in millilitres, that is absorbed into the patient's blood.

   a) What type of polynomial function is $r(d)$?

   b) What are the leading coefficient and constant of this function?

   c) Make a sketch of what you think the function will look like. Then, graph the function using technology. How does it compare to your sketch?

   d) What are the restrictions on the domain of this function? Explain why you selected those restrictions.

8. Refer to the honeycomb example at the beginning of this section (page 106).

   a) Show that the polynomial function $f(r) = 3r^2 - 3r + 1$ gives the correct total number of hexagons when $r = 1, 2,$ and 3.

   b) Determine the total number of hexagons in a honeycomb with 12 rings.

Did You Know?

Approximately 80% of Canadian honey production is concentrated in the three prairie provinces of Alberta, Saskatchewan, and Manitoba.

9. Populations in rural communities have declined in Western Canada, while populations in larger urban centres have increased. This is partly due to expanding agricultural operations and fewer traditional family farms. A demographer uses a polynomial function to predict the population, P, of a town t years from now. The function is $P(t) = t^4 - 20t^3 - 20t^2 + 1500t + 15\,000$. Assume this model can be used for the next 20 years.

a) What are the key features of the graph of this function?

b) What is the current population of this town?

c) What will the population of the town be 10 years from now?

d) When will the population of the town be approximately 24 000?

> **Did You Know?**
>
> A demographer uses statistics to study human populations. Demographers study the size, structure, and distribution of populations in response to birth, migration, aging, and death.

Extend

10. The volume, V, in cubic centimetres, of a collection of open-topped boxes can be modelled by $V(x) = 4x^3 - 220x^2 + 2800x$, where x is the height, in centimetres, of each box.

a) Use technology to graph $V(x)$. State the restrictions.

b) Fully factor $V(x)$. State the relationship between the factored form of the equation and the graph.

11. a) Graph each pair of even-degree functions. What do you notice? Provide an algebraic explanation for what you observe.
- $y = (-x)^2$ and $y = x^2$
- $y = (-x)^4$ and $y = x^4$
- $y = (-x)^6$ and $y = x^6$

b) Repeat part a) for each pair of odd-degree functions.
- $y = (-x)^3$ and $y = x^3$
- $y = (-x)^5$ and $y = x^5$
- $y = (-x)^7$ and $y = x^7$

c) Describe what you have learned about functions of the form $y = (-x)^n$, where n is a whole number. Support your answer with examples.

12. a) Describe the relationship between the graphs of $y = x^2$ and $y = 3(x - 4)^2 + 2$.

b) Predict the relationship between the graphs of $y = x^4$ and $y = 3(x - 4)^4 + 2$.

c) Verify the accuracy of your prediction in part b) by graphing using technology.

13. If a polynomial equation of degree n has exactly one real root, what can you conclude about the form of the corresponding polynomial function? Explain.

Create Connections

C1 Prepare a brief summary of the relationship between the degree of a polynomial function and the following features of the corresponding graph:
- the number of x-intercepts
- the maximum or minimum point
- the domain and range

C2 a) State a possible equation for a polynomial function whose graph extends

i) from quadrant III to quadrant I

ii) from quadrant II to quadrant I

iii) from quadrant II to quadrant IV

iv) from quadrant III to quadrant IV

b) Compare your answers to those of a classmate. Discuss what is similar and different between your answers.

C3 Describe to another student the similarities and differences between the line $y = x$ and polynomial functions with odd degree greater than one. Use graphs to support your answer.

C4 MINI LAB

Step 1 Graph each of the functions using technology. Copy and complete the table.

Step 2 For two functions with the same degree, how does the sign of the leading coefficient affect the end behaviour of the graph?

Step 3 How do the end behaviours of even-degree functions compare?

Step 4 How do the end behaviours of odd-degree functions compare?

Function	Degree	End Behaviour
$y = x + 2$		
$y = -3x + 1$		
$y = x^2 - 4$		
$y = -2x^2 - 2x + 4$		
$y = x^3 - 4x$		
$y = -x^3 + 3x - 2$		
$y = 2x^3 + 16$		
$y = -x^3 - 4x$		
$y = x^4 - 4x^2 + 5$		
$y = -x^4 + x^3 + 4x^2 - 4x$		
$y = x^4 + 2x^2 + 1$		
$y = x^5 - 2x^4 - 3x^3 + 5x^2 + 4x - 1$		
$y = x^5 - 1$		
$y = -x^5 + x^4 + 8x^3 + 8x^2 - 16x - 16$		
$y = x(x + 1)^2(x + 4)^2$		

Project Corner — Polynomials Abound

- Each image shows a portion of an object that can be modelled by a polynomial function. Describe the polynomial function that models each object.

3.1 Characteristics of Polynomial Functions • MHR **117**

3.2

The Remainder Theorem

Focus on...

- describing the relationship between polynomial long division and synthetic division
- dividing polynomials by binomials of the form $x - a$ using long division or synthetic division
- explaining the relationship between the remainder when a polynomial is divided by a binomial of the form $x - a$ and the value of the polynomial at $x = a$

Nested boxes or pots are featured in the teaching stories of many nations in many lands. A manufacturer of gift boxes receives an order for different-sized boxes that can be nested within each other. The box heights range from 6 cm to 16 cm. Based on cost calculations, the volume, V, in cubic centimetres, of each box can be modelled by the polynomial $V(x) = x^3 + 7x^2 + 14x + 8$, where x is a positive integer such that $5 \leq x \leq 15$. The height, h, of each box, in centimetres, is a linear function of x such that $h(x) = x + 1$. How can the box manufacturer use this information to determine the dimensions of the boxes in terms of polynomials?

Did You Know?

In Haida Gwaii, off the northwest coast of British Columbia, legends such as "Raven Steals the Light" are used to teach mathematical problem solving. This legend is about the trickster Raven who steals the light from three nested boxes to create the sun and stars. It is used to help students learn about surface area, perimeter, and volume.

Investigate Polynomial Division

A: Polynomial Long Division

1. Examine the two long-division statements.

a)
$$\begin{array}{r} 27 \\ 12\overline{)327} \\ \underline{24} \\ 87 \\ \underline{84} \\ 3 \end{array}$$

b)
$$\begin{array}{r} x + 4 \\ x + 3\overline{)x^2 + 7x + 17} \\ \underline{x^2 + 3x} \\ 4x + 17 \\ \underline{4x + 12} \\ 5 \end{array}$$

For statements a) and b), identify the value or expression that corresponds to
- the divisor
- the dividend
- the quotient
- the remainder

118 MHR • Chapter 3

Reflect and Respond

2. **a)** Describe the long-division process used to divide the numbers in part a) of step 1.
   b) Describe the long-division process used to divide the polynomial by the binomial in part b) of step 1.
   c) What similarities and differences do you observe in the two processes?

3. Describe how you would check that the result of each long-division statement is correct.

B: Determine a Remainder

4. Copy the table. Identify the value of a in each binomial divisor of the form $x - a$. Then, substitute the value $x = a$ into the polynomial dividend and evaluate the result. Record these values in the last column of the table.

Polynomial Dividend	Binomial Divisor $x - a$	Value of a	Quotient	Remainder	Result of Substituting $x = a$ Into the Polynomial
	$x - 3$		$x^2 + 5x + 10$	24	
	$x - 2$		$x^2 + 4x + 3$	0	
$x^3 + 2x^2 - 5x - 6$	$x - 1$		$x^2 + 3x - 2$	-8	
	$x + 1$		$x^2 + x - 6$	0	
	$x + 2$		$x^2 - 5$	4	

5. Compare the values of each remainder from the long division to the value from substituting $x = a$ into the dividend. What do you notice?

Reflect and Respond

6. Make a conjecture about how to determine a remainder without using division.

7. **a)** Use your conjecture to predict the remainder when the polynomial $2x^3 - 4x^2 + 3x - 6$ is divided by each binomial.
   i) $x + 1$
   ii) $x + 3$
   iii) $x - 2$
   b) Verify your predictions using long division.

8. Describe the relationship between the remainder when a polynomial in x, $P(x)$, is divided by a binomial $x - a$, and the value of $P(a)$.

Did You Know?

The ancient Greeks called the practical use of computing (adding, subtracting, multiplying, and dividing numbers) *logistic*. They considered arithmetic to be the study of abstract relationships connecting numbers—what we call number theory today.

Link the Ideas

You can divide polynomials by other polynomials using the same long division process that you use to divide numbers.

> The result of the division of a polynomial in x, $P(x)$, by a binomial of the form $x - a$, $a \in I$, is $\frac{P(x)}{x - a} = Q(x) + \frac{R}{x - a}$, where $Q(x)$ is the quotient and R is the remainder.

Check the division of a polynomial by multiplying the quotient, $Q(x)$, by the binomial divisor, $x - a$, and adding the remainder, R. The result should be equivalent to the polynomial dividend, $P(x)$:
$P(x) = (x - a)Q(x) + R$

Example 1

Divide a Polynomial by a Binomial of the Form $x - a$

a) Divide the polynomial $P(x) = 5x^3 + 10x - 13x^2 - 9$ by $x - 2$. Express the result in the form $\frac{P(x)}{x - a} = Q(x) + \frac{R}{x - a}$.

b) Identify any restrictions on the variable.

c) Write the corresponding statement that can be used to check the division.

d) Verify your answer.

Solution

a) Write the polynomial in order of descending powers:
$5x^3 - 13x^2 + 10x - 9$

$$\begin{array}{r} 5x^2 - 3x + 4 \\ x - 2 \overline{\smash{\big)}\, 5x^3 - 13x^2 + 10x - 9} \\ \underline{5x^3 - 10x^2 } \\ -3x^2 + 10x \\ \underline{-3x^2 + 6x } \\ 4x - 9 \\ \underline{4x - 8} \\ -1 \end{array}$$

Divide $5x^3$ by x to get $5x^2$.
Multiply $x - 2$ by $5x^2$ to get $5x^3 - 10x^2$.
Subtract. Bring down the next term, $10x$.
Then, divide $-3x^2$ by x to get $-3x$.
Multiply $x - 2$ by $-3x$ to get $-3x^2 + 6x$.
Subtract. Bring down the next term, -9.
Then, divide $4x$ by x to get 4.
Multiply $x - 2$ by 4 to get $4x - 8$.
Subtract. The remainder is -1.

$$\frac{5x^3 + 10x - 13x^2 - 9}{x - 2} = 5x^2 - 3x + 4 + \left(\frac{-1}{x - 2}\right)$$

b) Since division by zero is not defined, the divisor cannot be zero: $x - 2 \neq 0$ or $x \neq 2$.

c) The corresponding statement that can be used to check the division is
$5x^3 + 10x - 13x^2 - 9 = (x - 2)(5x^2 - 3x + 4) - 1$.

d) To check, multiply the divisor by the quotient and add the remainder.
$(x - 2)(5x^2 - 3x + 4) - 1 = 5x^3 - 3x^2 + 4x - 10x^2 + 6x - 8 - 1$
$= 5x^3 - 13x^2 + 10x - 9$
$= 5x^3 + 10x - 13x^2 - 9$

Your Turn

a) Divide the polynomial $P(x) = x^4 - 2x^3 + x^2 - 3x + 4$ by $x - 1$. Express the result in the form $\frac{P(x)}{x - a} = Q(x) + \frac{R}{x - a}$.

b) Identify any restrictions on the variable.

c) Verify your answer.

Example 2

Apply Polynomial Long Division to Solve a Problem

The volume, V, of the nested boxes in the introduction to this section, in cubic centimetres, is given by $V(x) = x^3 + 7x^2 + 14x + 8$. What are the possible dimensions of the boxes in terms of x if the height, h, in centimetres, is $x + 1$?

Solution

Divide the volume of the box by the height to obtain an expression for the area of the base of the box: $\frac{V(x)}{h} = lw$, where lw is the area of the base.

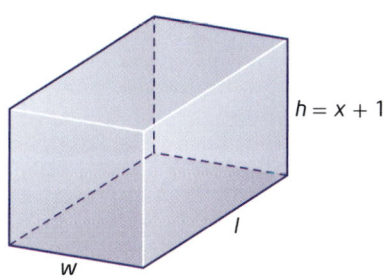

$$\begin{array}{r} x^2 + 6x + 8 \\ x + 1 \overline{) x^3 + 7x^2 + 14x + 8} \\ \underline{x^3 + x^2} \\ 6x^2 + 14x \\ \underline{6x^2 + 6x} \\ 8x + 8 \\ \underline{8x + 8} \\ 0 \end{array}$$

Since the remainder is zero, the volume $x^3 + 7x^2 + 14x + 8$ can be expressed as $(x + 1)(x^2 + 6x + 8)$. The quotient $x^2 + 6x + 8$ represents the area of the base. This expression can be factored as $(x + 2)(x + 4)$. The factors represent the possible width and length of the base of the box.

Expressions for the possible dimensions, in centimetres, are $x + 1$, $x + 2$, and $x + 4$.

Your Turn

The volume of a rectangular prism is given by $V(x) = x^3 + 3x^2 - 36x + 32$. Determine possible measures for w and h in terms of x if the length, l, is $x - 4$.

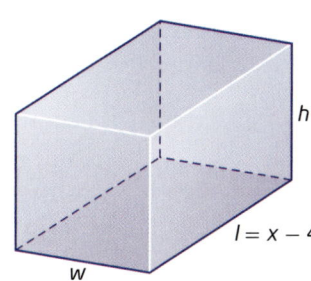

synthetic division
- a method of performing polynomial long division involving a binomial divisor that uses only the coefficients of the terms and fewer calculations

Synthetic division is an alternate process for dividing a polynomial by a binomial of the form $x - a$. It allows you to calculate without writing variables and requires fewer calculations.

Example 3
Divide a Polynomial Using Synthetic Division

a) Use synthetic division to divide $2x^3 + 3x^2 - 4x + 15$ by $x + 3$.
b) Check the results using long division.

Did You Know?

Paolo Ruffini, an Italian mathematician, first described synthetic division in 1809.

Solution

a) Write the terms of the dividend in order of descending power. Use zero for the coefficient of any missing powers.
Write just the coefficients of the dividend. To the left, write the value of $+3$ from the factor $x + 3$. Below $+3$, place a "$-$" symbol to represent subtraction. Use the "$\times$" sign below the horizontal line to indicate multiplication of the divisor and the terms of the quotient.

$$\begin{array}{c|cccc} & 2x^3 & 3x^2 & -4x & 15 \\ & \downarrow & \downarrow & \downarrow & \downarrow \\ +3 & 2 & 3 & -4 & 15 \\ - & & & & \\ \hline \times & & & & \end{array}$$

To perform the synthetic division, bring down the first coefficient, 2, to the right of the $\times$ sign.

$$\begin{array}{c|cccc} +3 & 2 & 3 & -4 & 15 \\ - & \downarrow & 6 & -9 & 15 \\ \hline \times & 2 & -3 & 5 & 0 \end{array}$$
remainder

Multiply $+3$ (top left) by 2 (right of $\times$ sign) to get 6. Write 6 below 3 in the second column.
Subtract 6 from 3 to get -3.
Multiply $+3$ by -3 to get -9. Continue with $-4 - (-9) = 5$, $+3 \times 5 = 15$, and $15 - 15 = 0$.
2, -3, and 5 are the coefficients of the quotient, $2x^2 - 3x + 5$.

$(2x^3 + 3x^2 - 4x + 15) \div (x + 3) = 2x^2 - 3x + 5$
Restriction: $x + 3 \neq 0$ or $x \neq -3$

b) Long division check:

$$\begin{array}{r} 2x^2 - 3x + 5 \\ x + 3 \overline{\smash{)}2x^3 + 3x^2 - 4x + 15} \\ \underline{2x^3 + 6x^2 } \\ -3x^2 - 4x \\ \underline{-3x^2 - 9x } \\ 5x + 15 \\ \underline{5x + 15} \\ 0 \end{array}$$

The result of the long division is the same as that using synthetic division.

Your Turn

Use synthetic division to determine $\dfrac{x^3 + 7x^2 - 3x + 4}{x - 2}$.

The **remainder theorem** states that when a polynomial in x, $P(x)$, is divided by a binomial of the form $x - a$, the remainder is $P(a)$.

remainder theorem
- when a polynomial in x, $P(x)$, is divided by $x - a$, the remainder is $P(a)$

Example 4
Apply the Remainder Theorem

a) Use the remainder theorem to determine the remainder when $P(x) = x^3 - 10x + 6$ is divided by $x + 4$.

b) Verify your answer using synthetic division.

Solution

a) Since the binomial is $x + 4 = x - (-4)$, determine the remainder by evaluating $P(x)$ at $x = -4$, or $P(-4)$.
$P(x) = x^3 - 10x + 6$
$P(-4) = (-4)^3 - 10(-4) + 6$
$P(-4) = -64 + 40 + 6$
$P(-4) = -18$

The remainder when $x^3 - 10x + 6$ is divided by $x + 4$ is -18.

b) To use synthetic division, first rewrite $P(x)$ as $P(x) = x^3 + 0x^2 - 10x + 6$.

Why is it important to rewrite the polynomial in this way?

```
+4 | 1    0   -10    6
 - |      4   -16   24
 × | 1   -4     6  -18
                     ↑
                 remainder
```

The remainder when using synthetic division is -18.

Your Turn

What is the remainder when $11x - 4x^4 - 7$ is divided by $x - 3$? Verify your answer using either long or synthetic division.

Key Ideas

- Use long division to divide a polynomial by a binomial.
- Synthetic division is an alternate form of long division.
- The result of the division of a polynomial in x, $P(x)$, by a binomial of the form $x - a$ can be written as $\frac{P(x)}{x - a} = Q(x) + \frac{R}{x - a}$ or $P(x) = (x - a)Q(x) + R$, where $Q(x)$ is the quotient and R is the remainder.
- To check the result of a division, multiply the quotient, $Q(x)$, by the divisor, $x - a$, and add the remainder, R, to the product. The result should be the dividend, $P(x)$.
- The remainder theorem states that when a polynomial in x, $P(x)$, is divided by a binomial, $x - a$, the remainder is $P(a)$. A non-zero remainder means that the binomial is not a factor of $P(x)$.

Check Your Understanding

Practise

1. **a)** Use long division to divide $x^2 + 10x - 24$ by $x - 2$. Express the result in the form $\frac{P(x)}{x - a} = Q(x) + \frac{R}{x - a}$.
   b) Identify any restrictions on the variable.
   c) Write the corresponding statement that can be used to check the division.
   d) Verify your answer.

2. **a)** Divide the polynomial $3x^4 - 4x^3 - 6x^2 + 17x - 8$ by $x + 1$ using long division. Express the result in the form $\frac{P(x)}{x - a} = Q(x) + \frac{R}{x - a}$.
   b) Identify any restrictions on the variable.
   c) Write the corresponding statement that can be used to check the division.
   d) Verify your answer.

3. Determine each quotient, Q, using long division.
   a) $(x^3 + 3x^2 - 3x - 2) \div (x - 1)$
   b) $\frac{x^3 + 2x^2 - 7x - 2}{x - 2}$
   c) $(2w^3 + 3w^2 - 5w + 2) \div (w + 3)$
   d) $(9m^3 - 6m^2 + 3m + 2) \div (m - 1)$
   e) $\frac{t^4 + 6t^3 - 3t^2 - t + 8}{t + 1}$
   f) $(2y^4 - 3y^2 + 1) \div (y - 3)$

4. Determine each quotient, Q, using synthetic division.
   a) $(x^3 + x^2 + 3) \div (x + 4)$
   b) $\frac{m^4 - 2m^3 + m^2 + 12m - 6}{m - 2}$
   c) $(2 - x + x^2 - x^3 - x^4) \div (x + 2)$
   d) $(2s^3 + 3s^2 - 9s - 10) \div (s - 2)$
   e) $\frac{h^3 + 2h^2 - 3h + 9}{h + 3}$
   f) $(2x^3 + 7x^2 - x + 1) \div (x + 2)$

5. Perform each division. Express the result in the form $\frac{P(x)}{x - a} = Q(x) + \frac{R}{x - a}$. Identify any restrictions on the variable.
   a) $(x^3 + 7x^2 - 3x + 4) \div (x + 2)$
   b) $\frac{11t - 4t^4 - 7}{t - 3}$
   c) $(x^3 + 3x^2 - 2x + 5) \div (x + 1)$
   d) $(4n^2 + 7n - 5) \div (n + 3)$
   e) $\frac{4n^3 - 15n + 2}{n - 3}$
   f) $(x^3 + 6x^2 - 4x + 1) \div (x + 2)$

6. Use the remainder theorem to determine the remainder when each polynomial is divided by $x + 2$.
   a) $x^3 + 3x^2 - 5x + 2$
   b) $2x^4 - 2x^3 + 5x$
   c) $x^4 + x^3 - 5x^2 + 2x - 7$
   d) $8x^3 + 4x^2 - 19$
   e) $3x^3 - 12x - 2$
   f) $2x^3 + 3x^2 - 5x + 2$

7. Determine the remainder resulting from each division.
   a) $(x^3 + 2x^2 - 3x + 9) \div (x + 3)$
   b) $\frac{2t - 4t^3 - 3t^2}{t - 2}$
   c) $(x^3 + 2x^2 - 3x + 5) \div (x - 3)$
   d) $\frac{n^4 - 3n^2 - 5n + 2}{n - 2}$

Apply

8. For each dividend, determine the value of k if the remainder is 3.
   a) $(x^3 + 4x^2 - x + k) \div (x - 1)$
   b) $(x^3 + x^2 + kx - 15) \div (x - 2)$
   c) $(x^3 + kx^2 + x + 5) \div (x + 2)$
   d) $(kx^3 + 3x + 1) \div (x + 2)$

9. For what value of c will the polynomial $P(x) = -2x^3 + cx^2 - 5x + 2$ have the same remainder when it is divided by $x - 2$ and by $x + 1$?

10. When $3x^2 + 6x - 10$ is divided by $x + k$, the remainder is 14. Determine the value(s) of k.

11. The area, $A(x)$, of a rectangle is represented by the polynomial $2x^2 - x - 6$.
    a) If the height of the rectangle is $x - 2$, what is the width in terms of x?
    b) If the height of the rectangle were changed to $x - 3$, what would the remainder of the quotient be? What does this remainder represent?

12. The product, $P(n)$, of two numbers is represented by the expression $2n^2 - 4n + 3$, where n is a real number.
    a) If one of the numbers is represented by $n - 3$, what expression represents the other number?
    b) What are the two numbers if $n = 1$?

13. A design team determines that a cost-efficient way of manufacturing cylindrical containers for their products is to have the volume, V, in cubic centimetres, modelled by $V(x) = 9\pi x^3 + 51\pi x^2 + 88\pi x + 48\pi$, where x is an integer such that $2 \leq x \leq 8$. The height, h, in centimetres, of each cylinder is a linear function given by $h(x) = x + 3$.
    a) Determine the quotient $\dfrac{V(x)}{h(x)}$ and interpret this result.
    b) Use your answer in part a) to express the volume of a container in the form $\pi r^2 h$.
    c) What are the possible dimensions of the containers for the given values of x?

Extend

14. When the polynomial $mx^3 - 3x^2 + nx + 2$ is divided by $x + 3$, the remainder is -1. When it is divided by $x - 2$, the remainder is -4. What are the values of m and n?

15. When the polynomial $3x^3 + ax^2 + bx - 9$ is divided by $x - 2$, the remainder is -5. When it is divided by $x + 1$, the remainder is -16. What are the values of a and b?

16. Explain how to determine the remainder when $10x^4 - 11x^3 - 8x^2 + 7x + 9$ is divided by $2x - 3$ using synthetic division.

17. Write a polynomial that satisfies each set of conditions.
    a) a quadratic polynomial that gives a remainder of -4 when it is divided by $x - 3$
    b) a cubic polynomial that gives a remainder of 4 when it is divided by $x + 2$
    c) a quartic polynomial that gives a remainder of 1 when it is divided by $2x - 1$

Create Connections

C1 How are numerical long division and polynomial long division similar, and how are they different?

C2 When the polynomial $bx^2 + cx + d$ is divided by $x - a$, the remainder is zero.
a) What can you conclude from this result?
b) Write an expression for the remainder in terms of a, b, c, and d.

C3 The support cable for a suspension bridge can be modelled by the function $h(d) = 0.0003d^2 + 2$, where $h(d)$ is the height, in metres, of the cable above the road, and d is the horizontal distance, in metres, from the lowest point on the cable.

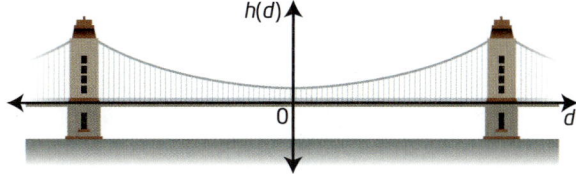

a) What is the remainder when $0.0003d^2 + 2$ is divided by $d - 500$?
b) What is the remainder when $0.0003d^2 + 2$ is divided by $d + 500$?
c) Compare your results from parts a) and b). Use the graph of the function $h(d) = 0.0003d^2 + 2$ to explain your findings.

3.3

The Factor Theorem

Focus on...

- factoring polynomials
- explaining the relationship between the linear factors of a polynomial expression and the zeros of the corresponding function
- modelling and solving problems involving polynomial functions

Port of Vancouver

Each year, more than 1 million intermodal containers pass through the Port of Vancouver. The total volume of these containers is over 2 million twenty-foot equivalent units (TEU). Suppose the volume, in cubic feet, of a 1-TEU container can be approximated by the polynomial function $V(x) = x^3 + 7x^2 - 28x + 20$, where x is a positive real number. What dimensions, in terms of x, could the container have?

Did You Know?

An intermodal container is a standard-sized metal box that can be easily transferred between different modes of transportation, such as ships, trains, and trucks. A TEU represents the volume of a 20-ft intermodal container. Although container heights vary, the equivalent of 1 TEU is accepted as 1360 ft³.

Investigate Determining the Factors of a Polynomial

A: Remainder for a Factor of a Polynomial

1. **a)** Determine the remainder when $x^3 + 2x^2 - 5x - 6$ is divided by $x + 1$.
   b) Determine the quotient $\dfrac{x^3 + 2x^2 - 5x - 6}{x + 1}$. Write the corresponding statement that can be used to check the division.
   c) Factor the quadratic portion of the statement written in part b).
   d) Write $x^3 + 2x^2 - 5x - 6$ as the product of its three factors.
   e) What do you notice about the remainder when you divide $x^3 + 2x^2 - 5x - 6$ by any one of its three factors?

Reflect and Respond

2. What is the relationship between the remainder and the factors of a polynomial?

B: Determine Factors

3. Which of the following are factors of $P(x) = x^3 - 7x + 6$? Justify your reasoning.

   a) $x + 1$ **b)** $x - 1$ **c)** $x + 2$
   d) $x - 2$ **e)** $x + 3$ **f)** $x - 3$

   Why would a factor such as $x - 5$ not be considered as a possible factor?

126 MHR • Chapter 3

Reflect and Respond

4. Write a statement that describes the condition when a divisor $x - a$ is a factor of a polynomial $P(x)$.

5. What are the relationships between the factors of a polynomial expression, the zeros of the corresponding polynomial function, the x-intercepts of the graph of the corresponding polynomial function, and the remainder theorem?

6. a) Describe a method you could use to determine the factors of a polynomial.

   b) Use your method to determine the factors of $f(x) = x^3 + 2x^2 - x - 2$.

   c) Verify your answer.

Link the Ideas

The **factor theorem** states that $x - a$ is a factor of a polynomial in x, $P(x)$, if and only if $P(a) = 0$.

factor theorem
- a polynomial in x, $P(x)$, has a factor $x - a$ if and only if $P(a) = 0$

For example, given the polynomial $P(x) = x^3 - x^2 - 5x + 2$, determine if $x - 1$ and $x + 2$ are factors by calculating $P(1)$ and $P(-2)$, respectively.

$P(x) = x^3 - x^2 - 5x + 2$ $P(x) = x^3 - x^2 - 5x + 2$
$P(1) = 1^3 - 1^2 - 5(1) + 2$ $P(-2) = (-2)^3 - (-2)^2 - 5(-2) + 2$
$P(1) = 1 - 1 - 5 + 2$ $P(-2) = -8 - 4 + 10 + 2$
$P(1) = -3$ $P(-2) = 0$

Did You Know?

"If and only if" is a term used in logic to say that the result works both ways.

So, the factor theorem means
- if $x - a$ is a factor of $P(x)$, then $P(a) = 0$
- if $P(a) = 0$, then $x - a$ is a factor of $P(x)$

Since $P(1) = -3$, $P(x)$ is not divisible by $x - 1$. Therefore, $x - 1$ is not a factor of $P(x)$.

Since $P(-2) = 0$, $P(x)$ is divisible by $x + 2$. Therefore, $x + 2$ is a factor of $P(x)$.

The zeros of a polynomial function are related to the factors of the polynomial. The graph of $P(x) = x^3 - x^2 - 4x + 4$ shows that the zeros of the function, or the x-intercepts of the graph, are at $x = -2$, $x = 1$, and $x = 2$. The corresponding factors of the polynomial are $x + 2$, $x - 1$, and $x - 2$.

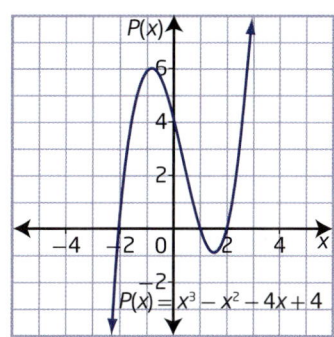

Example 1

Use the Factor Theorem to Test for Factors of a Polynomial

Which binomials are factors of the polynomial $P(x) = x^3 - 3x^2 - x + 3$? Justify your answers.

a) $x - 1$
b) $x + 1$
c) $x + 3$
d) $x - 3$

Solution

a) Use the factor theorem to evaluate $P(a)$ given $x - a$.
For $x - 1$, substitute $x = 1$ into the polynomial expression.
$P(x) = x^3 - 3x^2 - x + 3$
$P(1) = 1^3 - 3(1)^2 - 1 + 3$
$P(1) = 1 - 3 - 1 + 3$
$P(1) = 0$
Since the remainder is zero, $x - 1$ is a factor of $P(x)$.

b) For $x + 1$, substitute $x = -1$ into the polynomial expression.
$P(x) = x^3 - 3x^2 - x + 3$
$P(-1) = (-1)^3 - 3(-1)^2 - (-1) + 3$
$P(-1) = -1 - 3 + 1 + 3$
$P(-1) = 0$
Since the remainder is zero, $x + 1$ is a factor of $P(x)$.

c) For $x + 3$, substitute $x = -3$ into the polynomial expression.
$P(x) = x^3 - 3x^2 - x + 3$
$P(-3) = (-3)^3 - 3(-3)^2 - (-3) + 3$
$P(-3) = -27 - 27 + 3 + 3$
$P(-3) = -48$
Since the remainder is not zero, $x + 3$ is not a factor of $P(x)$.

d) For $x - 3$, substitute $x = 3$ into the polynomial expression.
$P(x) = x^3 - 3x^2 - x + 3$
$P(3) = 3^3 - 3(3)^2 - 3 + 3$
$P(3) = 27 - 27 - 3 + 3$
$P(3) = 0$
Since the remainder is zero, $x - 3$ is a factor of $P(x)$.

Your Turn

Determine which of the following binomials are factors of the polynomial $P(x) = x^3 + 2x^2 - 5x - 6$.
$x - 1, x + 1, x - 2, x + 2, x - 3, x + 3, x - 6, x + 6$

Possible Factors of a Polynomial

When factoring a polynomial, $P(x)$, it is helpful to know which integer values of a to try when determining if $P(a) = 0$.

Consider the polynomial $P(x) = x^3 - 7x^2 + 14x - 8$. If $x = a$ satisfies $P(a) = 0$, then $a^3 - 7a^2 + 14a - 8 = 0$, or $a^3 - 7a^2 + 14a = 8$. Factoring out the common factor on the left side of the equation gives the product $a(a^2 - 7a + 14) = 8$. Then, the possible integer values for the factors in the product on the left side are the factors of 8. They are ±1, ±2, ±4, and ±8.

> The relationship between the factors of a polynomial and the constant term of the polynomial is stated in the **integral zero theorem**.
>
> The integral zero theorem states that if $x - a$ is a factor of a polynomial function $P(x)$ with integral coefficients, then a is a factor of the constant term of $P(x)$.

integral zero theorem
- if $x = a$ is an integral zero of a polynomial, $P(x)$, with integral coefficients, then a is a factor of the constant term of $P(x)$

Example 2
Factor Using the Integral Zero Theorem

a) Factor $2x^3 - 5x^2 - 4x + 3$ fully.
b) Describe how to use the factors of the polynomial expression to determine the zeros of the corresponding polynomial function.

Solution

a) Let $P(x) = 2x^3 - 5x^2 - 4x + 3$. Find a factor by evaluating $P(x)$ for values of x that are factors of 3: ±1 and ±3.
Test the values.
$P(x) = 2x^3 - 5x^2 - 4x + 3$
$P(1) = 2(1)^3 - 5(1)^2 - 4(1) + 3$
$P(1) = 2 - 5 - 4 + 3$
$P(1) = -4$
Since $P(1) \neq 0$, $x - 1$ is not a factor of $2x^3 - 5x^2 - 4x + 3$.

$P(x) = 2x^3 - 5x^2 - 4x + 3$
$P(-1) = 2(-1)^3 - 5(-1)^2 - 4(-1) + 3$
$P(-1) = -2 - 5 + 4 + 3$
$P(-1) = 0$
Since $P(-1) = 0$, $x + 1$ is a factor of $2x^3 - 5x^2 - 4x + 3$.

Use synthetic or long division to find the other factors.

```
+1 |  2   -5   -4   3
 - |       2   -7   3
 × |  2   -7    3   0
```

The remaining factor is $2x^2 - 7x + 3$.
So, $2x^3 - 5x^2 - 4x + 3 = (x + 1)(2x^2 - 7x + 3)$.
Factoring $2x^2 - 7x + 3$ gives $(2x - 1)(x - 3)$.
Therefore, $2x^3 - 5x^2 - 4x + 3 = (x + 1)(2x - 1)(x - 3)$.

b) Since the factors of $2x^3 - 5x^2 - 4x + 3$ are $x + 1$, $2x - 1$, and $x - 3$, the corresponding zeros of the function are -1, $\frac{1}{2}$, and 3. Confirm the zeros by graphing $P(x)$ and using the trace or zero feature of a graphing calculator.

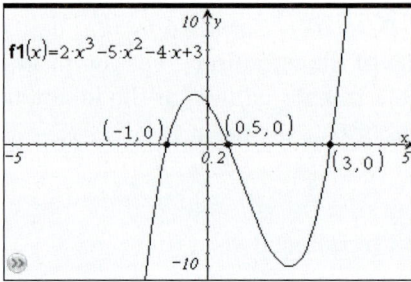

Your Turn

What is the factored form of $x^3 - 4x^2 - 11x + 30$? How can you use the graph of the corresponding polynomial function to simplify your search for integral roots?

Example 3

Factor Higher-Degree Polynomials

Fully factor $x^4 - 5x^3 + 2x^2 + 20x - 24$.

Solution

Let $P(x) = x^4 - 5x^3 + 2x^2 + 20x - 24$.
Find a factor by testing factors of -24: ± 1, ± 2, ± 3, ± 4, ± 6, ± 8, ± 12, and ± 24

$P(x) = x^4 - 5x^3 + 2x^2 + 20x - 24$
$P(1) = 1^4 - 5(1)^3 + 2(1)^2 + 20(1) - 24$
$P(1) = 1 - 5 + 2 + 20 - 24$
$P(1) = -6$

When should you stop testing possible factors?

$P(x) = x^4 - 5x^3 + 2x^2 + 20x - 24$
$P(-1) = (-1)^4 - 5(-1)^3 + 2(-1)^2 + 20(-1) - 24$
$P(-1) = 1 + 5 + 2 - 20 - 24$
$P(-1) = -36$

$P(x) = x^4 - 5x^3 + 2x^2 + 20x - 24$
$P(2) = 2^4 - 5(2)^3 + 2(2)^2 + 20(2) - 24$
$P(2) = 16 - 40 + 8 + 40 - 24$
$P(2) = 0$

Since $P(2) = 0$, $x - 2$ is a factor of $x^4 - 5x^3 + 2x^2 + 20x - 24$.

Use division to find the other factors.

-2	1	-5	2	20	-24
$-$		-2	6	8	-24
$\times$	1	-3	-4	12	0

The remaining factor is $x^3 - 3x^2 - 4x + 12$.

Method 1: Apply the Factor Theorem Again

Let $f(x) = x^3 - 3x^2 - 4x + 12$.

Since $f(2) = 0$, $x - 2$ is a second factor.

Use division to determine that the other factor is $x^2 - x - 6$.

```
-2 | 1  -3  -4  12
   |    -2   2  12
 × | 1  -1  -6   0
```

Factoring $x^2 - x - 6$ gives $(x + 2)(x - 3)$.

Therefore,
$x^4 - 5x^3 + 2x^2 + 20x - 24 = (x - 2)(x - 2)(x + 2)(x - 3)$
$\qquad\qquad\qquad\qquad\qquad\quad = (x - 2)^2(x + 2)(x - 3)$

Method 2: Factor by Grouping

$x^3 - 3x^2 - 4x + 12 = x^2(x - 3) - 4(x - 3)$ Group the first two terms and factor out x^2. Then, group the second two terms and factor out -4.

$\qquad\qquad\qquad\qquad\quad = (x - 3)(x^2 - 4)$ Factor out $x - 3$.
$\qquad\qquad\qquad\qquad\quad = (x - 3)(x - 2)(x + 2)$ Factor the difference of squares $x^2 - 4$.

Therefore,
$\quad x^4 - 5x^3 + 2x^2 + 20x - 24$
$= (x - 2)(x - 3)(x - 2)(x + 2)$
$= (x - 2)^2(x + 2)(x - 3)$

Your Turn

What is the fully factored form of $x^4 - 3x^3 - 7x^2 + 15x + 18$?

Example 4

Solve Problems Involving Polynomial Expressions

An intermodal container that has the shape of a rectangular prism has a volume, in cubic feet, represented by the polynomial function $V(x) = x^3 + 7x^2 - 28x + 20$, where x is a positive real number.

What are the factors that represent possible dimensions, in terms of x, of the container?

Dockside at Port of Vancouver

Solution

Method 1: Use Factoring

The possible integral factors correspond to the factors of the constant term of the polynomial, 20: ±1, ±2, ±4, ±5, ±10, and ±20. Use the factor theorem to determine which of these values correspond to the factors of the polynomial. Use a graphing calculator or spreadsheet to help with the multiple calculations.

Define poly(x)=x³+7·x²−28·x+20	Done
poly(1)	0
poly(−1)	54
poly(2)	0
poly(−2)	96
poly(4)	84
poly(5)	180
	12/12

x	P(x)
1	0
-1	54
2	0
-2	96
4	84
-4	180
5	180
-5	210
10	1440
-10	0
20	10260
-20	-4620

The values of x that result in a remainder of zero are -10, 1, and 2. The factors that correspond to these values are $x + 10$, $x - 1$, and $x - 2$. The factors represent the possible dimensions, in terms of x, of the container.

Method 2: Use Graphing

Since the zeros of the polynomial function correspond to the factors of the polynomial expression, use the graph of the function to determine the factors.

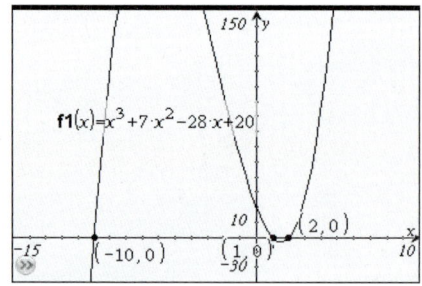

For this example, what are the restrictions on the domain?

The trace or zero feature of a graphing calculator shows that the zeros of the function are $x = -10$, $x = 1$, and $x = 2$. These correspond to the factors $x + 10$, $x - 1$, and $x - 2$. The factors represent the possible dimensions, in terms of x, of the container.

Your Turn

A form that is used to make large rectangular blocks of ice comes in different dimensions such that the volume, V, in cubic centimetres, of each block can be modelled by $V(x) = x^3 + 7x^2 + 16x + 12$, where x is in centimetres. Determine the possible dimensions, in terms of x, that result in this volume.

Key Ideas

- The factor theorem states that $x - a$ is a factor of a polynomial $P(x)$ if and only if $P(a) = 0$.
- The integral zero theorem states that if $x - a$ is a factor of a polynomial function $P(x)$ with integral coefficients, then a is a factor of the constant term of $P(x)$.
- You can use the factor theorem and the integral zero theorem to factor some polynomial functions.
  - Use the integral zero theorem to list possible integer values for the zeros.
  - Next, apply the factor theorem to determine one factor.
  - Then, use division to determine the remaining factor.
  - Repeat the above steps until all factors are found or the remaining factor is a trinomial which can be factored.

Check Your Understanding

Practise

1. What is the corresponding binomial factor of a polynomial, $P(x)$, given the value of the zero?
   a) $P(1) = 0$
   b) $P(-3) = 0$
   c) $P(4) = 0$
   d) $P(a) = 0$

2. Determine whether $x - 1$ is a factor of each polynomial.
   a) $x^3 - 3x^2 + 4x - 2$
   b) $2x^3 - x^2 - 3x - 2$
   c) $3x^3 - x - 3$
   d) $2x^3 + 4x^2 - 5x - 1$
   e) $x^4 - 3x^3 + 2x^2 - x + 1$
   f) $4x^4 - 2x^3 + 3x^2 - 2x + 1$

3. State whether each polynomial has $x + 2$ as a factor.
   a) $5x^2 + 2x + 6$
   b) $2x^3 - x^2 - 5x - 8$
   c) $2x^3 + 2x^2 - x - 6$
   d) $x^4 - 2x^2 + 3x - 4$
   e) $x^4 + 3x^3 - x^2 - 3x + 6$
   f) $3x^4 + 5x^3 + x - 2$

4. What are the possible integral zeros of each polynomial?
   a) $P(x) = x^3 + 3x^2 - 6x - 8$
   b) $P(s) = s^3 + 4s^2 - 15s - 18$
   c) $P(n) = n^3 - 3n^2 - 10n + 24$
   d) $P(p) = p^4 - 2p^3 - 8p^2 + 3p - 4$
   e) $P(z) = z^4 + 5z^3 + 2z^2 + 7z - 15$
   f) $P(y) = y^4 - 5y^3 - 7y^2 + 21y + 4$

5. Factor fully.
   a) $P(x) = x^3 - 6x^2 + 11x - 6$
   b) $P(x) = x^3 + 2x^2 - x - 2$
   c) $P(v) = v^3 + v^2 - 16v - 16$
   d) $P(x) = x^4 + 4x^3 - 7x^2 - 34x - 24$
   e) $P(k) = k^5 + 3k^4 - 5k^3 - 15k^2 + 4k + 12$

6. Factor fully.
   a) $x^3 - 2x^2 - 9x + 18$
   b) $t^3 + t^2 - 22t - 40$
   c) $h^3 - 27h + 10$
   d) $x^5 + 8x^3 + 2x - 15$
   e) $q^4 + 2q^3 + 2q^2 - 2q - 3$

Apply

7. Determine the value(s) of k so that the binomial is a factor of the polynomial.
   a) $x^2 - x + k$, $x - 2$
   b) $x^2 - 6x - 7$, $x + k$
   c) $x^3 + 4x^2 + x + k$, $x + 2$
   d) $x^2 + kx - 16$, $x - 2$

8. The volume, $V(h)$, of a bookcase can be represented by the expression $h^3 - 2h^2 + h$, where h is the height of the bookcase. What are the possible dimensions of the bookcase in terms of h?

9. A racquetball court has a volume that can be represented by the polynomial $V(l) = l^3 - 2l^2 - 15l$, where l is the length of the side walls. Factor the expression to determine the possible width and height of the court in terms of l.

10. Mikisiti Saila (1939–2008), an Inuit artist from Cape Dorset, Nunavut, was the son of famous soapstone carver Pauta Saila. Mikisita's preferred theme was wildlife presented in a minimal but graceful and elegant style. Suppose a carving is created from a rectangular block of soapstone whose volume, V, in cubic centimetres, can be modelled by $V(x) = x^3 + 5x^2 - 2x - 24$. What are the possible dimensions of the block, in centimetres, in terms of binomials of x?

Walrus created in 1996 by Mikisiti Saila

11. The volume of water in a rectangular fish tank can be modelled by the polynomial $V(x) = x^3 + 14x^2 + 63x + 90$. If the depth of the tank is given by the polynomial $x + 6$, what polynomials represent the possible length and width of the fish tank?

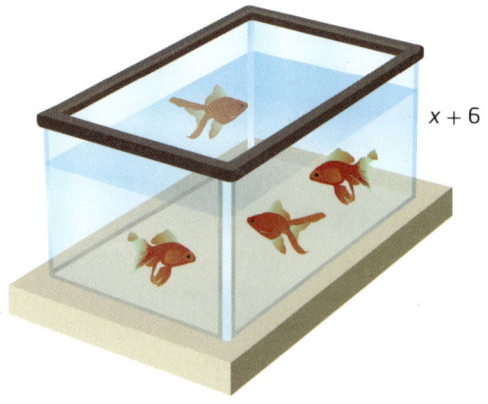

12. When a certain type of plastic is cut into sections, the length of each section determines its relative strength. The function $f(x) = x^4 - 14x^3 + 69x^2 - 140x + 100$ describes the relative strength of a section of length x feet. After testing the plastic, engineers discovered that 5-ft sections were extremely weak.

    a) Why is $x - 5$ a possible factor when $x = 5$ is the length of the pipe? Show that $x - 5$ is a factor of the polynomial function.

    b) Are there other lengths of plastic that are extremely weak? Explain your reasoning.

    Did You Know?

    The strength of a material can be affected by its mechanical resonance. Mechanical resonance is the tendency of a mechanical system to absorb more energy when it oscillates at the system's natural frequency of vibration. It may cause intense swaying motions and even catastrophic failure in improperly constructed structures including bridges, buildings, and airplanes. The collapse of the Tacoma Narrows Bridge into Puget Sound on November 7, 1940, was due in part to the effects of mechanical resonance.

13. The product of four integers is $x^4 + 6x^3 + 11x^2 + 6x$, where x is one of the integers. What are possible expressions for the other three integers?

Extend

14. Consider the polynomial $f(x) = ax^4 + bx^3 + cx^2 + dx + e$, where $a + b + c + d + e = 0$. Show that this polynomial is divisible by $x - 1$.

15. Determine the values of m and n so that the polynomials $2x^3 + mx^2 + nx - 3$ and $x^3 - 3mx^2 + 2nx + 4$ are both divisible by $x - 2$.

16. a) Factor each polynomial.
    i) $x^3 - 1$
    ii) $x^3 - 27$
    iii) $x^3 + 1$
    iv) $x^3 + 64$

    b) Use the results from part a) to decide whether $x + y$ or $x - y$ is a factor of $x^3 + y^3$. State the other factor(s).

    c) Use the results from part a) to decide whether $x + y$ or $x - y$ is a factor of $x^3 - y^3$. State the other factor(s).

    d) Use your findings to factor $x^6 + y^6$.

Create Connections

C1 Explain to a classmate how to use the graph of $f(x) = x^4 - 3x^2 - 4$ to determine at least one binomial factor of the polynomial. What are all of the factors of the polynomial?

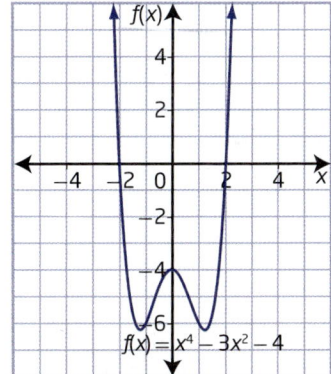

C2 Identify the possible factors of the expression $x^4 - x^3 + 2x^2 - 5$. Explain your reasoning in more than one way.

C3 How can the factor theorem, the integral zero theorem, the quadratic formula, and synthetic division be used together to factor a polynomial of degree greater than or equal to three?

3.4

Equations and Graphs of Polynomial Functions

Focus on...

- describing the relationship between zeros, roots, and x-intercepts of polynomial functions and equations
- sketching the graph of a polynomial function without technology
- modelling and solving problems involving polynomial functions

On an airplane, carry-on baggage must fit into the overhead compartment or under the seat in front of you. As a result, the dimensions of carry-on baggage for some airlines are restricted so that the width of the carry-on is 17 cm less than the height, and the length is no more than 15 cm greater than the height. The maximum volume, V, in cubic centimetres, of carry-on bags can be represented by the polynomial function $V(h) = h^3 - 2h^2 - 255h$, where h is the height, in centimetres, of the bag. If the maximum volume of the overhead compartment is 50 600 cm³, how could you determine the maximum dimensions of the carry-on bags?

In this section, you will use polynomial functions to model real-life situations such as this one. You will also sketch graphs of polynomial functions to help you solve problems.

Did You Know?

In 1973, Rosella Bjornson became the first female pilot in Canada to be hired by an airline. In 1990, she became the first female captain.

Investigate Sketching the Graph of a Polynomial Function

Materials
- graphing calculator or computer with graphing software

A: The Relationship Among the Roots, x-Intercepts, and Zeros of a Function

1. **a)** Graph the function $f(x) = x^4 + x^3 - 10x^2 - 4x + 24$ using graphing technology.
   b) Determine the x-intercepts from the graph.
   c) Factor $f(x)$. Then, use the factors to determine the zeros of $f(x)$.

   What are the possible integral factors of this polynomial?

2. **a)** Set the polynomial function $f(x) = x^4 + x^3 - 10x^2 - 4x + 24$ equal to 0. Solve the equation $x^4 + x^3 - 10x^2 - 4x + 24 = 0$ to determine the roots.
   b) What do you notice about the roots of the equation and the x-intercepts of the graph of the function?

Reflect and Respond

3. What is the relationship between the zeros of a function, the *x*-intercepts of the corresponding graph, and the roots of the polynomial equation?

B: Determine When a Function Is Positive and When It Is Negative

4. Refer to the graph you made in step 1. The *x*-intercepts divide the *x*-axis into four intervals. Copy and complete the table by writing in the intervals and indicating whether the function is positive (above the *x*-axis) or negative (below the *x*-axis) for each interval.

Interval	$x < -3$			
Sign of $f(x)$	positive			

Reflect and Respond

5. a) What happens to the sign of $f(x)$ if the graph crosses from one side of the *x*-axis to the other?

b) How does the graph behave if there are two identical zeros?

C: Sketch the Graph of a Polynomial Function

Materials
- grid paper

6. Without using a graphing calculator, determine the following characteristics of the function $f(x) = -x^3 - 5x^2 - 3x + 9$:
- the degree of the polynomial
- the sign of the leading coefficient
- the zeros of the function
- the *y*-intercept
- the interval(s) where the function is positive
- the interval(s) where the function is negative

7. Use the characteristics you determined in step 6 to sketch the graph of the function. Graph the function using technology and compare the result to your hand-drawn sketch.

Reflect and Respond

8. Describe how to sketch the graph of a polynomial using the *x*-intercepts, the *y*-intercept, the sign of the leading coefficient, and the degree of the function.

Did You Know?

Polynomiography is a fusion of art, mathematics, and computer science. It creates a visualization of the approximation of zeros of polynomial functions.

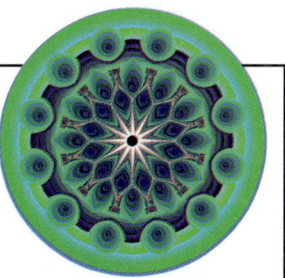

Link the Ideas

As is the case with quadratic functions, the zeros of any polynomial function $y = f(x)$ correspond to the x-intercepts of the graph and to the roots of the corresponding equation, $f(x) = 0$. For example, the function $f(x) = (x - 1)(x - 1)(x + 2)$ has two identical zeros at $x = 1$ and a third zero at $x = -2$. These are the roots of the equation $(x - 1)(x - 1)(x + 2) = 0$.

multiplicity (of a zero)
- the number of times a zero of a polynomial function occurs
- the shape of the graph of a function close to a zero depends on its multiplicity

If a polynomial has a factor $x - a$ that is repeated n times, then $x = a$ is a zero of **multiplicity**, n. The function $f(x) = (x - 1)^2(x + 2)$ has a zero of multiplicity 2 at $x = 1$ and the equation $(x - 1)^2(x + 2) = 0$ has a root of multiplicity 2 at $x = 1$.

Consider the graph of the function $f(x) = (x - 1)(x - 1)(x + 2)$.

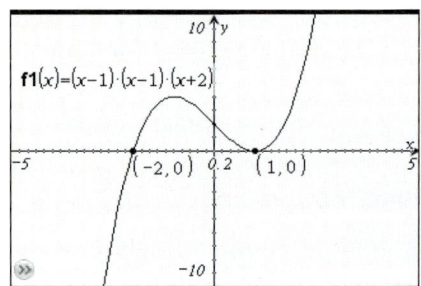

At $x = -2$ (zero of odd multiplicity), the sign of the function changes.

At $x = 1$ (zero of even multiplicity), the sign of the function does not change.

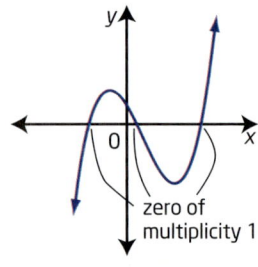
zero of multiplicity 1

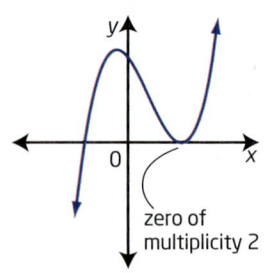
zero of multiplicity 2

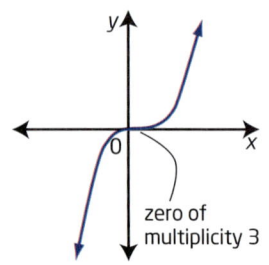
zero of multiplicity 3

Example 1

Analyse Graphs of Polynomial Functions

For each graph of a polynomial function, determine
- the least possible degree
- the sign of the leading coefficient
- the x-intercepts and the factors of the function with least possible degree
- the intervals where the function is positive and the intervals where it is negative

a)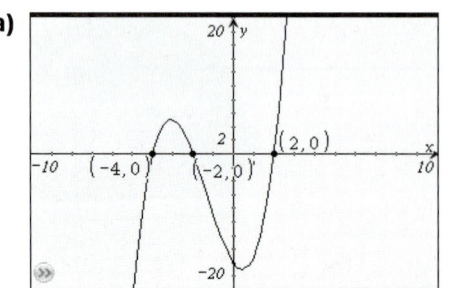

b)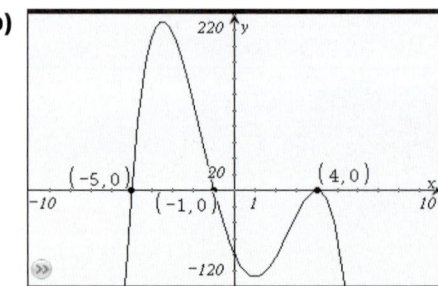

Did You Know?

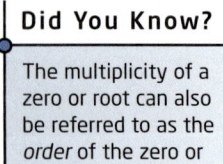

The multiplicity of a zero or root can also be referred to as the *order* of the zero or root.

138 MHR • Chapter 3

Solution

a) • The graph of the polynomial function crosses the x-axis (negative to positive or positive to negative) at all three x-intercepts. The three x-intercepts are of odd multiplicity. The least possible multiplicity of each x-intercept is 1, so the least possible degree is 3.

Could the multiplicity of each x-intercept be something other than 1?

• The graph extends down into quadrant III and up into quadrant I, so the leading coefficient is positive.

• The x-intercepts are -4, -2, and 2. The factors are $x + 4$, $x + 2$, and $x - 2$.

• The function is positive for values of x in the intervals $-4 < x < -2$ and $x > 2$. The function is negative for values of x in the intervals $x < -4$ and $-2 < x < 2$.

b) • The graph of the polynomial function crosses the x-axis at two of the x-intercepts and touches the x-axis at one of the x-intercepts. The least possible multiplicities of these x-intercepts are, respectively, 1 and 2, so the least possible degree is 4.

Could the multiplicities of the x-intercepts be something other than 1 or 2?

• The graph extends down into quadrant III and down into quadrant IV, so the leading coefficient is negative.

• The x-intercepts are -5, -1, and 4 (multiplicity 2). The factors are $x + 5$, $x + 1$, and $(x - 4)^2$.

• The function is positive for values of x in the interval $-5 < x < -1$. The function is negative for values of x in the intervals $x < -5$, $-1 < x < 4$, and $x > 4$.

Your Turn

For the graph of the polynomial function shown, determine
• the least possible degree
• the sign of the leading coefficient
• the x-intercepts and the factors of the function of least possible degree
• the intervals where the function is positive and the intervals where it is negative

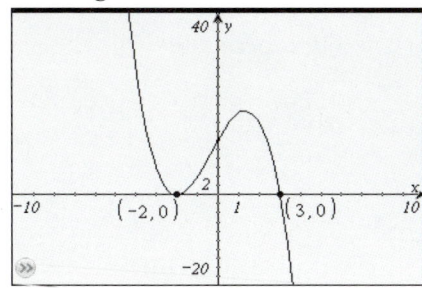

Example 2

Analyse Equations to Sketch Graphs of Polynomial Functions

Sketch the graph of each polynomial function.
a) $y = (x - 1)(x + 2)(x + 3)$
b) $f(x) = -(x + 2)^3(x - 4)$
c) $y = -2x^3 + 6x - 4$

Solution

a) The function $y = (x - 1)(x + 2)(x + 3)$ is in factored form.

Use a table to organize information about the function. Then, use the information to sketch the graph.

Degree	3
Leading Coefficient	1
End Behaviour	extends down into quadrant III and up into quadrant I
Zeros/x-Intercepts	−3, −2, and 1
y-Intercept	$(0 - 1)(0 + 2)(0 + 3) = -6$
Interval(s) Where the Function is Positive or Negative	positive values of $f(x)$ in the intervals $-3 < x < -2$ and $x > 1$ negative values of $f(x)$ in the intervals $x < -3$ and $-2 < x < 1$

To check whether the function is positive or negative, test values within the interval, rather than close to either side of the interval.

Mark the intercepts. Since the multiplicity of each zero is 1, the graph crosses the x-axis at each x-intercept. Beginning in quadrant III, sketch the graph so that it passes through $x = -3$ to above the x-axis, back down through $x = -2$ to below the x-axis, through the y-intercept −6, up through $x = 1$, and upward in quadrant I.

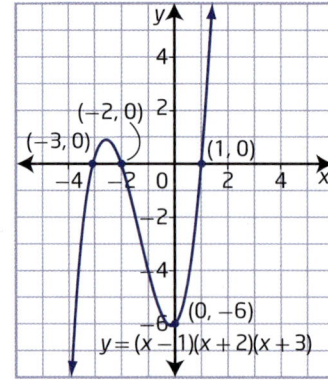

b) The function $f(x) = -(x + 2)^3(x - 4)$ is in factored form.

Degree	When the function is expanded, the exponent of the highest-degree term is 4. The function is of degree 4.
Leading Coefficient	When the function is expanded, the leading coefficient is $(-1)(1^3)(1)$ or -1.
End Behaviour	extends down into quadrant III and down into quadrant IV
Zeros/x-Intercepts	-2 (multiplicity 3) and 4
y-Intercept	$-(0 + 2)^3(0 - 4) = 32$
Interval(s) Where the Function Is Positive or Negative	positive values of $f(x)$ in the interval $-2 < x < 4$ negative values of $f(x)$ in the intervals $x < -2$ and $x > 4$

Mark the intercepts. Since the multiplicity of each zero is odd, the graph crosses the x-axis at both x-intercepts. Beginning in quadrant III, sketch the graph so that it passes through $x = -2$ to above the x-axis through the y-intercept 32, continuing upward, and then back down to pass through $x = 4$, and then downward in quadrant IV. In the neighbourhood of $x = -2$, the graph behaves like the cubic curve $y = (x + 2)^3$.

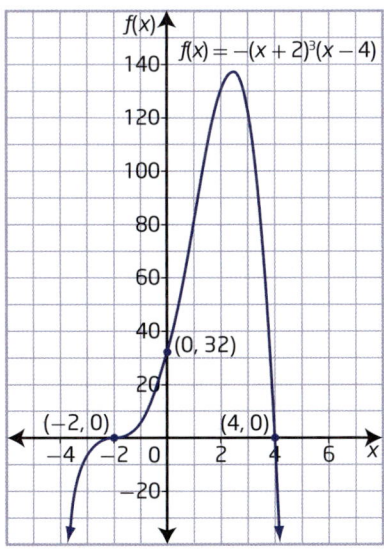

Why is it useful to evaluate the function for values such as $x = 2$ and $x = 3$?

How are the multiplicity of the zero of -2 and the shape of the graph at this x-intercept related?

c) First factor out the common factor.
$y = -2x^3 + 6x - 4$
$y = -2(x^3 - 3x + 2)$

How does factoring out the common factor help?

Next, use the integral zero theorem and the factor theorem to determine the factors of the polynomial expression $x^3 - 3x + 2$. Test possible factors of 2, that is, ± 1 and ± 2.

Substitute $x = 1$.
$\quad x^3 - 3x + 2$
$= 1^3 - 3(1) + 2$
$= 1 - 3 + 2$
$= 0$

Therefore, $x - 1$ is a factor.

Divide the polynomial expression $x^3 - 3x + 2$ by $x - 1$ to get the factor $x^2 + x - 2$.

```
−1 | 1   0  −3   2
   |    −1  −1   2
 × | 1   1  −2   0
```

Why is one of the coefficients 0?

Then, factor $x^2 + x - 2$ to give $(x + 2)(x - 1)$. So, the factored form of $y = -2x^3 + 6x - 4$ is $y = -2(x - 1)^2(x + 2)$.

How can you check that the factored form is equivalent to the original polynomial?

Degree	3
Leading Coefficient	−2
End Behaviour	extends up into quadrant II and down into quadrant IV
Zeros/x-Intercepts	−2 and 1 (multiplicity 2)
y-Intercept	−4
Interval(s) Where the Function Is Positive or Negative	positive values of $f(x)$ in the interval $x < -2$ negative values of $f(x)$ in the intervals $-2 < x < 1$ and $x > 1$

Mark the intercepts. The graph crosses the x-axis at $x = -2$ (multiplicity 1) and touches the x-axis at $x = 1$ (multiplicity 2). Beginning in quadrant II, sketch the graph so that it passes through $x = -2$ to below the x-axis, up through the y-intercept −4 to touch the x-axis at $x = 1$, and then downward in quadrant IV.

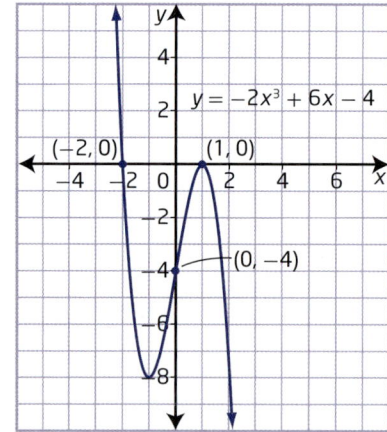

Your Turn

Sketch a graph of each polynomial function by hand. State the characteristics of the polynomial functions that you used to sketch the graphs.

a) $g(x) = (x - 2)^3(x + 1)$
b) $f(x) = -x^3 + 13x + 12$

Graphing Polynomial Functions using Transformations

The graph of a function of the form $y = a(b(x - h))^n + k$ is obtained by applying transformations to the graph of the general polynomial function $y = x^n$, where $n \in \mathbb{N}$. The effects of changing parameters in polynomial functions are the same as the effects of changing parameters in other types of functions.

Parameter	Transformation
k	• Vertical translation up or down • $(x, y) \rightarrow (x, y + k)$
h	• Horizontal translation left or right • $(x, y) \rightarrow (x + h, y)$
a	• Vertical stretch about the x-axis by a factor of $|a|$ • For $a < 0$, the graph is also reflected in the x-axis. • $(x, y) \rightarrow (x, ay)$
b	• Horizontal stretch about the y-axis by a factor of $\frac{1}{|b|}$ • For $b < 0$, the graph is also reflected in the y-axis. • $(x, y) \rightarrow \left(\frac{x}{b}, y\right)$

To obtain an accurate sketch of a transformed graph, apply the transformations represented by a and b (reflections and stretches) before the transformations represented by h and k (translations).

Example 3

Apply Transformations to Sketch a Graph

The graph of $y = x^3$ is transformed to obtain the graph of $y = -2(4(x - 1))^3 + 3$.

a) State the parameters and describe the corresponding transformations.

b) Copy and complete the table to show what happens to the given points under each transformation.

$y = x^3$	$y = (4x)^3$	$y = -2(4x)^3$	$y = -2(4(x - 1))^3 + 3$
$(-2, -8)$			
$(-1, -1)$			
$(0, 0)$			
$(1, 1)$			
$(2, 8)$			

c) Sketch the graph of $y = -2(4(x - 1))^3 + 3$.

Solution

a) Compare the functions $y = -2(4(x-1))^3 + 3$ and $y = a(b(x-h))^n + k$ to determine the values of the parameters.
- $b = 4$ corresponds to a horizontal stretch of factor $\frac{1}{4}$. Multiply the x-coordinates of the points in column 1 by $\frac{1}{4}$.
- $a = -2$ corresponds to a vertical stretch of factor 2 and a reflection in the x-axis. Multiply the y-coordinates of the points in column 2 by -2.
- $h = 1$ corresponds to a translation of 1 unit to the right and $k = 3$ corresponds to a translation of 3 units up. Add 1 to the x-coordinates and 3 to the y-coordinates of the points in column 3.

b)

$y = x^3$	$y = (4x)^3$	$y = -2(4x)^3$	$y = -2(4(x-1))^3 + 3$
(−2, −8)	(−0.5, −8)	(−0.5, 16)	(0.5, 19)
(−1, −1)	(−0.25, −1)	(−0.25, 2)	(0.75, 5)
(0, 0)	(0, 0)	(0, 0)	(1, 3)
(1, 1)	(0.25, 1)	(0.25, −2)	(1.25, 1)
(2, 8)	(0.5, 8)	(0.5, −16)	(1.5, −13)

c) To sketch the graph, plot the points from column 4 and draw a smooth curve through them.

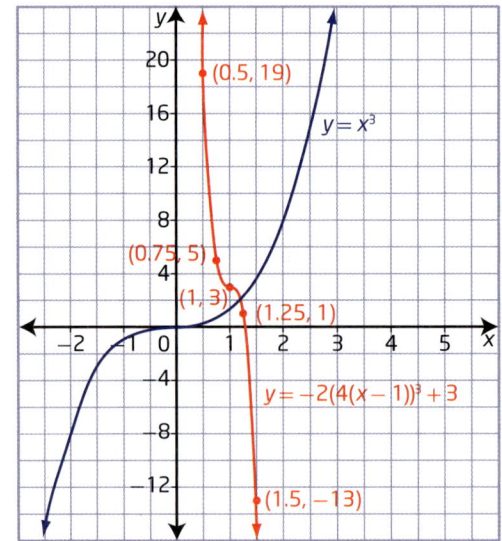

Your Turn

Transform the graph of $y = x^3$ to sketch the graph of $y = -4(2(x+2))^3 - 5$.

Example 4

Model and Solve Problems Involving Polynomial Functions

Bill is preparing to make an ice sculpture. He has a block of ice that is 3 ft wide, 4 ft high, and 5 ft long. Bill wants to reduce the size of the block of ice by removing the same amount from each of the three dimensions. He wants to reduce the volume of the ice block to 24 ft³.

a) Write a polynomial function to model this situation.
b) How much should he remove from each dimension?

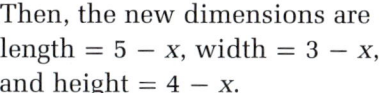

Solution

a) Let x represent the amount to be removed from each dimension.

Then, the new dimensions are length $= 5 - x$, width $= 3 - x$, and height $= 4 - x$.

The volume of the ice block is
$V(x) = lwh$
$V(x) = (5 - x)(3 - x)(4 - x)$

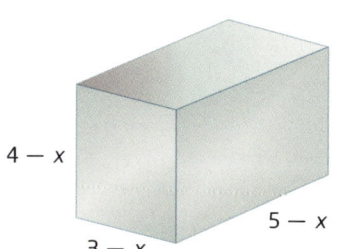

b) **Method 1: Intersecting Graphs**

Sketch the graphs of $V(x) = (5 - x)(3 - x)(4 - x)$ and $V(x) = 24$ on the same set of coordinate axes. The point of intersection of the two graphs gives the value of x that will result in a volume of 24 ft³.

Degree	3
Leading Coefficient	−1
End Behaviour	extends up into quadrant II and down into quadrant IV
Zeros/x-Intercepts	3, 4, and 5
y-Intercept	60
Interval(s) Where the Function Is Positive or Negative	positive values of $V(x)$ in the intervals $x < 3$ and $4 < x < 5$ negative values of $V(x)$ in the intervals $3 < x < 4$ and $x > 5$

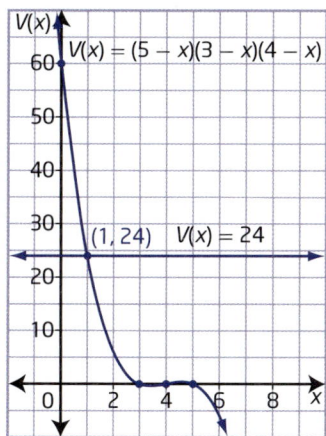

Since the point of intersection is (1, 24), 1 ft should be removed from each dimension.

Method 2: Factoring

Since the volume of the reduced block of ice is 24 ft³, substitute this value into the function.

$V(x) = (5 - x)(3 - x)(4 - x)$
$24 = (5 - x)(3 - x)(4 - x)$
$24 = -x^3 + 12x^2 - 47x + 60$ Expand the right side.
$0 = -x^3 + 12x^2 - 47x + 36$ Collect like terms.
$0 = -(x^3 - 12x^2 + 47x - 36)$

The possible integral factors of the constant term of the polynomial expression $x^3 - 12x^2 + 47x - 36$ are $\pm 1, \pm 2, \pm 3, \pm 4, \pm 6, \pm 9, \pm 12, \pm 18,$ and ± 36.

Test $x = 1$.
$x^3 - 12x^2 + 47x - 36$
$= 1^3 - 12(1)^2 + 47(1) - 36$
$= 1 - 12 + 47 - 36$
$= 0$
Therefore, $x - 1$ is a factor.

Divide the polynomial expression $x^3 - 12x^2 + 47x - 36$ by this factor.

$$\frac{x^3 - 12x^2 + 47x - 36}{x - 1} = x^2 - 11x + 36$$

The remaining factor, $x^2 - 11x + 36$, cannot be factored further.

Then, the roots of the equation are the solutions to $x - 1 = 0$ and $x^2 - 11x + 36 = 0$.

Use the quadratic formula with $a = 1$, $b = -11$, and $c = 36$ to check for other real roots.

$x = \dfrac{-b \pm \sqrt{b^2 - 4ac}}{2a}$

$x = \dfrac{-(-11) \pm \sqrt{(-11)^2 - 4(1)(36)}}{2(1)}$

$x = \dfrac{11 \pm \sqrt{121 - 144}}{2}$

$x = \dfrac{11 \pm \sqrt{-23}}{2}$ Since the square root of a negative number is not a real number, there are no real roots.

So, the only real root of $0 = -(x^3 - 12x^2 + 47x - 36)$ is $x = 1$. Bill needs to remove 1 ft from each dimension to get a volume of 24 ft³.

Your Turn

Three consecutive integers have a product of −210.
a) Write a polynomial function to model this situation.
b) What are the three integers?

Key Ideas

- You can sketch the graph of a polynomial function using the x-intercepts, the y-intercept, the degree of the function, and the sign of the leading coefficient.
- The x-intercepts of the graph of a polynomial function are the roots of the corresponding polynomial equation.
- When a polynomial function is in factored form, you can determine the zeros from the factors. When it is not in factored form, you can use the factor theorem and the integral zero theorem to determine the factors.
- When a factor is repeated n times, the corresponding zero has multiplicity, n.
- The shape of a graph close to a zero of $x = a$ (multiplicity n) is similar to the shape of the graph of a function with degree equal to n of the form $y = (x - a)^n$. For example, the graph of a function with a zero of $x = 1$ (multiplicity 3) will look like the graph of the cubic function (degree 3) $y = (x - 1)^3$ in the region close to $x = 1$.

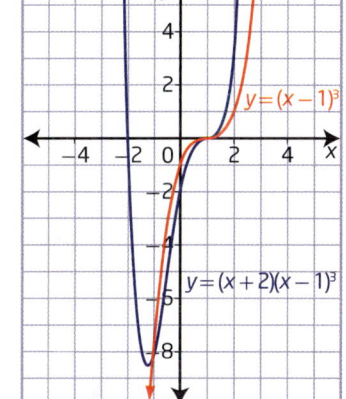

- Polynomial functions change sign at x-intercepts that correspond to zeros of odd multiplicity. The graph crosses over the x-axis at these intercepts.
- Polynomial functions do not change sign at x-intercepts that correspond to zeros of even multiplicity. The graph touches, but does not cross, the x-axis at these intercepts.
- The graph of a polynomial function of the form $y = a(b(x - h))^n + k$ [or $y - k = a(b(x - h))^n$] can be sketched by applying transformations to the graph of $y = x^n$, where $n \in \mathbb{N}$. The transformations represented by a and b may be applied in any order before the transformations represented by h and k.

Check Your Understanding

Practise

1. Solve.
   a) $x(x + 3)(x - 4) = 0$
   b) $(x - 3)(x - 5)(x + 1) = 0$
   c) $(2x + 4)(x - 3) = 0$

2. Solve.
   a) $(x + 1)^2(x + 2) = 0$
   b) $x^3 - 1 = 0$
   c) $(x + 4)^3(x + 2)^2 = 0$

3. Use the graph of the given function to write the corresponding polynomial possible equation. State the roots of the equation. The roots are all integral values.

a)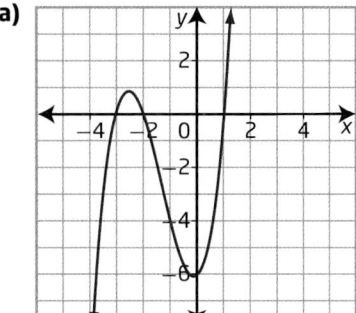

b)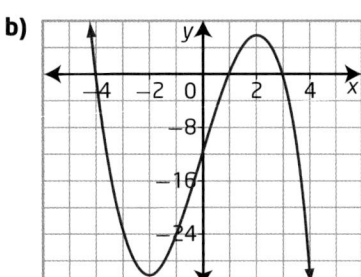

c)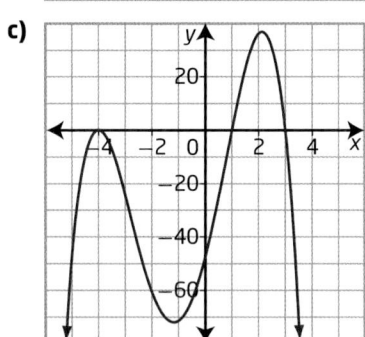

b)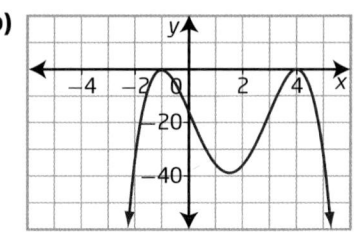

c)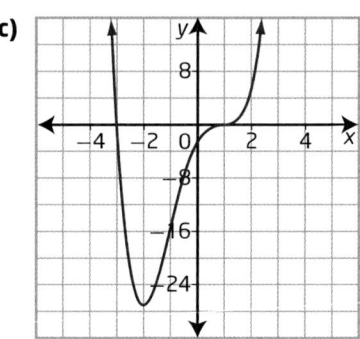

d)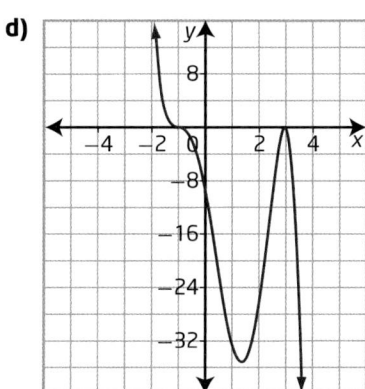

4. For each graph,
   i) state the x-intercepts
   ii) state the intervals where the function is positive and the intervals where it is negative
   iii) explain whether the graph might represent a polynomial that has zero(s) of multiplicity 1, 2, or 3

a)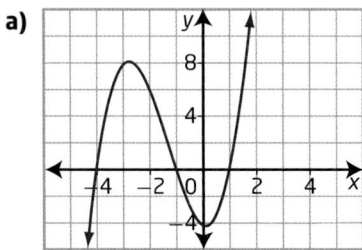

5. Without using technology, match each graph with the corresponding function. Justify your choice.

a) 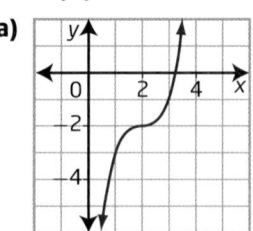 b)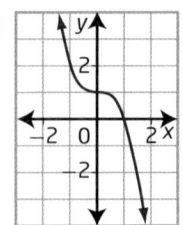

c) 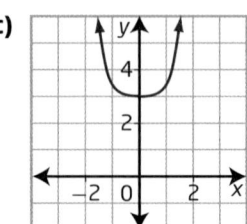 d)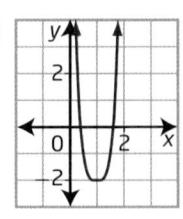

A $y = (2(x-1))^4 - 2$ **B** $y = (x-2)^3 - 2$
C $y = 0.5x^4 + 3$ **D** $y = (-x)^3 + 1$

148 MHR • Chapter 3

6. The graph of $y = x^3$ is transformed to obtain the graph of
$y = 0.5(-3(x - 1))^3 + 4$.

   a) What are the parameters and corresponding transformations?

   b) Copy and complete the table. Use the headings $y = (-3x)^3$, $y = 0.5(-3x)^3$, and $y = 0.5(-3(x - 1))^3 + 4$ for columns two, three, and four, respectively.

$y = x^3$			
(−2, −8)			
(−1, −1)			
(0, 0)			
(1, 1)			
(2, 8)			

   c) Sketch the graph of $y = 0.5(-3(x - 1))^3 + 4$.

7. For each function, determine

   i) the x-intercepts of the graph

   ii) the degree and end behaviour of the graph

   iii) the zeros and their multiplicity

   iv) the y-intercept of the graph

   v) the intervals where the function is positive and the intervals where it is negative

   a) $y = x^3 - 4x^2 - 45x$

   b) $f(x) = x^4 - 81x^2$

   c) $h(x) = x^3 + 3x^2 - x - 3$

   d) $k(x) = -x^4 - 2x^3 + 7x^2 + 8x - 12$

8. Sketch the graph of each function in #7.

9. Without using technology, sketch the graph of each function. Label all intercepts.

   a) $f(x) = x^4 - 4x^3 + x^2 + 6x$

   b) $y = x^3 + 3x^2 - 6x - 8$

   c) $y = x^3 - 4x^2 + x + 6$

   d) $h(x) = -x^3 + 5x^2 - 7x + 3$

   e) $g(x) = (x - 1)(x + 2)^2(x + 3)^2$

   f) $f(x) = -x^4 - 2x^3 + 3x^2 + 4x - 4$

Apply

10. For each graph of a polynomial function shown, determine
    - the sign of the leading coefficient
    - the x-intercepts
    - the intervals where the function is positive and the intervals where it is negative
    - the equation for the polynomial function

    a)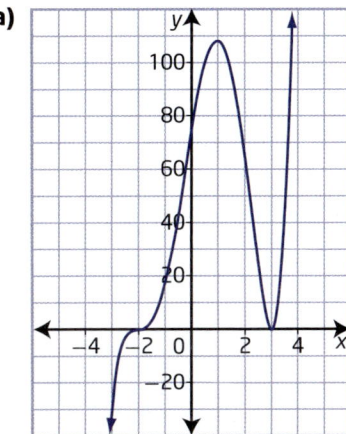

    b)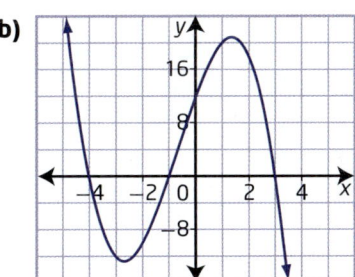

    c)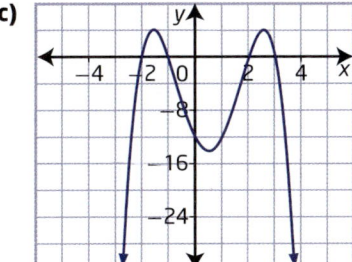

    d)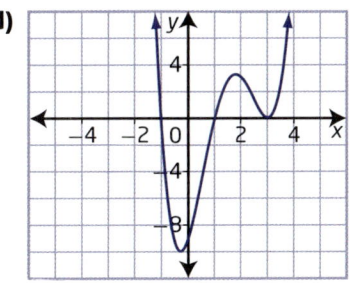

11. a) Given the function $y = x^3$, list the parameters of the transformed polynomial function $y = \left(\frac{1}{2}(x-2)\right)^3 - 3$.

b) Describe how each parameter in part a) transforms the graph of the function $y = x^3$.

c) Determine the domain and range for the transformed function.

12. The competition swimming pool at Saanich Commonwealth Place is in the shape of a rectangular prism and has a volume of 2100 m³. The dimensions of the pool are x metres deep by $25x$ metres long by $10x + 1$ metres wide. What are the actual dimensions of the pool?

Did You Know?

Forty-four aquatic events in diving and swimming were held at the Saanich Commonwealth Pool during the 1994 Commonwealth Games held in Victoria, British Columbia. Canada won 32 medals in aquatics.

13. A boardwalk that is x feet wide is built around a rectangular pond. The pond is 30 ft wide and 40 ft long. The combined surface area of the pond and the boardwalk is 2000 ft². What is the width of the boardwalk?

14. Determine the equation with least degree for each polynomial function. Sketch a graph of each.

a) a cubic function with zeros −3 (multiplicity 2) and 2 and y-intercept −18

b) a quintic function with zeros −1 (multiplicity 3) and 2 (multiplicity 2) and y-intercept 4

c) a quartic function with a negative leading coefficient, zeros −2 (multiplicity 2) and 3 (multiplicity 2), and a constant term of −6

15. The width of a rectangular prism is w centimetres. The height is 2 cm less than the width. The length is 4 cm more than the width. If the magnitude of the volume of the prism is 8 times the measure of the length, what are the dimensions of the prism?

16. Three consecutive odd integers have a product of −105. What are the three integers?

17. A monument consists of two cubical blocks of limestone. The smaller block rests on the larger. The total height of the monument is 5 m and the area of exposed surface is 61 m². Determine the dimensions of the blocks.

Did You Know?

A type of limestone called Tyndall stone has been quarried in Garson, Manitoba, since the 1890s. You can see this stone in structures such as the Parliament Buildings in Ottawa, Ontario, the Saskatchewan Legislative Building in Regina, Saskatchewan, and the Manitoba Legislative Building in Winnipeg, Manitoba.

18. Olutie is learning from her grandmother how to make traditional Inuit wall hangings from stroud and felt. She plans to make a square border for her square wall hanging. The dimensions of the wall hanging with its border are shown. Olutie needs 144 in.² of felt for the border.

   a) Write a polynomial expression to model the area of the border.
   b) What are the dimensions of her wall hanging, in inches?
   c) What are the dimensions of the border, in inches?

Did You Know?

Stroud is a coarse woollen cloth traditionally used to make wall hangings.

Inuit wall hanging, artist unknown.

19. Four consecutive integers have a product of 840. What are the four integers?

Extend

20. Write a cubic function with x-intercepts of $\sqrt{3}$, $-\sqrt{3}$, and 1 and a y-intercept of -1.

21. The roots of the equation $2x^3 + 3x^2 - 23x - 12 = 0$ are represented by a, b, and c (from least to greatest). Determine the equation with roots $a + b$, $\dfrac{a}{b}$, and ab.

22. a) Predict the relationship between the graphs of $y = x^3 - x^2$ and $y = (x - 2)^3 - (x - 2)^2$.
   b) Graph each function using technology to verify your prediction.
   c) Factor each function in part a) to determine the x-intercepts.

23. Suppose a spherical floating buoy has radius 1 m and density $\dfrac{1}{4}$ that of sea water. Given that the formula for the volume of a spherical cap is $V_{cap} = \dfrac{\pi x}{6}(3a^2 + x^2)$, to what depth does the buoy sink in sea water?

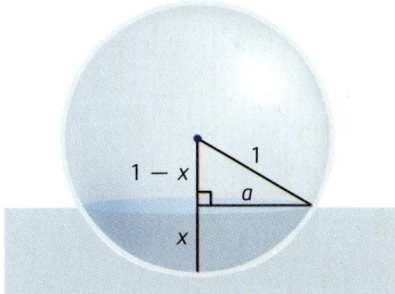

Did You Know?

Archimedes of Syracuse (287–212 B.C.E.) was a Greek mathematician, physicist, engineer, inventor, and astronomer. He developed what is now known as Archimedes' principle: Any floating object displaces its own weight of fluid.

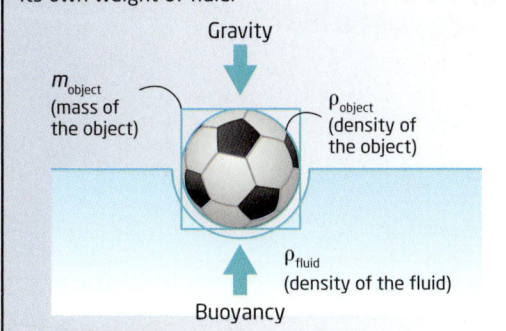

Create Connections

C1 Why is it useful to express a polynomial in factored form? Explain with examples.

C2 Describe what is meant by a root, a zero, and an x-intercept. How are they related?

C3 How can you tell from a graph if the multiplicity of a zero is 1, an even number, or an odd number greater than 1?

C4 MINI LAB

Materials
- graphing calculator or computer with graphing software

Apply your prior knowledge of transformations to predict the effects of translations, stretches, and reflections on polynomial functions of the form $y = a(b(x - h))^n + k$ and the associated graphs.

Step 1 Graph each set of functions on one set of coordinate axes. Sketch the graphs in your notebook.

Set A
i) $y = x^3$
ii) $y = x^3 + 2$
iii) $y = x^3 - 2$

Set B
i) $y = x^4$
ii) $y = (x + 2)^4$
iii) $y = (x - 2)^4$

a) Compare the graphs in set A. For any constant k, describe the relationship between the graphs of $y = x^3$ and $y = x^3 + k$.

b) Compare the graphs in set B. For any constant h, describe the relationship between the graphs of $y = x^4$ and $y = (x - h)^4$.

Step 2 Describe the roles of the parameters h and k in functions of the form $y = a(b(x - h))^n + k$.

Step 3 Graph each set of functions on one set of coordinate axes. Sketch the graphs in your notebook.

Set C
i) $y = x^3$
ii) $y = 3x^3$
iii) $y = -3x^3$

Set D
i) $y = x^4$
ii) $y = \frac{1}{3}x^4$
iii) $y = -\frac{1}{3}x^4$

a) Compare the graphs in set C. For any integer value a, describe the relationship between the graphs of $y = x^3$ and $y = ax^3$.

b) Compare the graphs in set D. For any rational value a such that $-1 < a < 0$ or $0 < a < 1$, describe the relationship between the graphs of $y = x^4$ and $y = ax^4$.

Step 4 Graph each set of functions on one set of coordinate axes. Sketch the graphs in your notebook.

Set E
i) $y = x^3$
ii) $y = (3x)^3$
iii) $y = (-3x)^3$

Set F
i) $y = x^4$
ii) $y = \left(\frac{1}{3}x\right)^4$
iii) $y = \left(-\frac{1}{3}x\right)^4$

a) Compare the graphs in set E. For any integer value b, describe the relationship between the graphs of $y = x^3$ and $y = (bx)^3$.

b) Compare the graphs in set F. For any rational value b such that $-1 < b < 0$ or $0 < b < 1$, describe the relationship between the graphs of $y = x^4$ and $y = (bx)^4$.

Step 5 Describe the roles of the parameters a and b in functions of the form $y = a(b(x - h))^n + k$.

Chapter 3 Review

3.1 Characteristics of Polynomial Functions, pages 106–117

1. Which of the following are polynomial functions? Justify your answer.
   a) $y = \sqrt{x + 1}$
   b) $f(x) = 3x^4$
   c) $g(x) = -3x^3 - 2x^2 + x$
   d) $y = \frac{1}{2}x + 7$

2. Use the degree and the sign of the leading coefficient of each function to describe the end behaviour of its corresponding graph. State the possible number of x-intercepts and the value of the y-intercept.
   a) $s(x) = x^4 - 3x^2 + 5x$
   b) $p(x) = -x^3 + 5x^2 - x + 4$
   c) $y = 3x - 2$
   d) $y = 2x^2 - 4$
   e) $y = 2x^5 - 3x^3 + 1$

3. A parachutist jumps from a plane 11 500 ft above the ground. The height, h, in feet, of the parachutist above the ground t seconds after the jump can be modelled by the function $h(t) = 11\,500 - 16t^2$.
   a) What type of function is $h(t)$?
   b) What will the parachutist's height above the ground be after 12 s?
   c) When will the parachutist be 1500 ft above the ground?
   d) Approximately how long will it take the parachutist to reach the ground?

3.2 The Remainder Theorem, pages 118–125

4. Use the remainder theorem to determine the remainder for each division. Then, perform each division using the indicated method. Express the result in the form $\frac{P(x)}{x - a} = Q(x) + \frac{R}{x - a}$ and identify any restrictions on the variable.
   a) $x^3 + 9x^2 - 5x + 3$ divided by $x - 2$ using long division
   b) $2x^3 + x^2 - 2x + 1$ divided by $x + 1$ using long division
   c) $12x^3 + 13x^2 - 23x + 7$ divided by $x - 1$ using synthetic division
   d) $-8x^4 - 4x + 10x^3 + 15$ divided by $x + 1$ using synthetic division

5. a) Determine the value of k such that when $f(x) = x^4 + kx^3 - 3x - 5$ is divided by $x - 3$, the remainder is -14.
   b) Using your value from part a), determine the remainder when $f(x)$ is divided by $x + 3$.

6. For what value of b will the polynomial $P(x) = 4x^3 - 3x^2 + bx + 6$ have the same remainder when it is divided by both $x - 1$ and $x + 3$?

3.3 The Factor Theorem, pages 126–135

7. Which binomials are factors of the polynomial $P(x) = x^3 - x^2 - 16x + 16$? Justify your answers.
   a) $x - 1$
   b) $x + 1$
   c) $x + 4$
   d) $x - 4$

8. Factor fully.
   a) $x^3 - 4x^2 + x + 6$
   b) $-4x^3 - 4x^2 + 16x + 16$
   c) $x^4 - 4x^3 - x^2 + 16x - 12$
   d) $x^5 - 3x^4 - 5x^3 + 27x^2 - 32x + 12$

9. Rectangular blocks of granite are to be cut and used to build the front entrance of a new hotel. The volume, V, in cubic metres, of each block can be modelled by the function $V(x) = 2x^3 + 7x^2 + 2x - 3$, where x is in metres.

  a) What are the possible dimensions of the blocks in terms of x?

  b) What are the possible dimensions of the blocks when $x = 1$?

10. Determine the value of k so that $x + 3$ is a factor of $x^3 + 4x^2 - 2kx + 3$.

3.4 Equations and Graphs of Polynomial Functions, pages 136–152

11. For each function, determine
  - the x-intercepts of the graph
  - the degree and end behaviour of the graph
  - the zeros and their multiplicity
  - the y-intercept of the graph
  - the interval(s) where the function is positive and the interval(s) where it is negative

Then, sketch the graph.

  a) $y = (x + 1)(x - 2)(x + 3)$
  b) $y = (x - 3)(x + 2)^2$
  c) $g(x) = x^4 - 16x^2$
  d) $g(x) = -x^5 + 16x$

12. The graph of $y = x^3$ is transformed to obtain the graph of $y = 2(-4(x - 1))^3 + 3$.

  a) What are the parameters and corresponding transformations?

  b) Copy and complete the table.

Transformation	Parameter Value	Equation
horizontal stretch/ reflection in y-axis		$y =$
vertical stretch/ reflection in x-axis		$y =$
translation left/right		$y =$
translation up/down		$y =$

  c) Sketch the graph of $y = 2(-4(x - 1))^3 + 3$.

13. Determine the equation of the polynomial function that corresponds to each graph.

  a)
  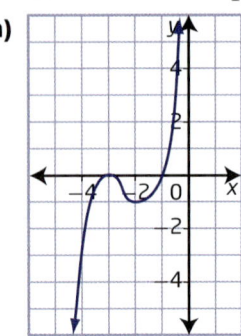

  b)
  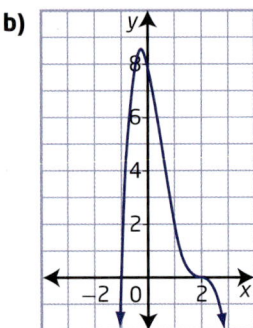

14. The zeros of a quartic function are $-2, -1$, and 3 (multiplicity 2).

  a) Determine equations for two functions that satisfy this condition.

  b) Determine the equation of the function that satisfies this condition and passes through the point $(2, 24)$.

15. The specifications for a cardboard box state that the width must be 5 cm less than the length, and the height must be double the length.

  a) Write the equation for the volume of the box.

  b) What are the dimensions of a box with a volume of 384 cm³?

Chapter 3 Practice Test

Multiple Choice

For #1 to #5, choose the best answer.

1. Which statement is true?
   - **A** Some odd-degree polynomial functions have no x-intercepts.
   - **B** Even-degree polynomial functions always have an even number of x-intercepts.
   - **C** All odd-degree polynomial functions have at least one x-intercept.
   - **D** All even-degree polynomial functions have at least one x-intercept.

2. Which statement is true for $P(x) = 3x^3 + 4x^2 + 2x - 9$?
   - **A** When $P(x)$ is divided by $x + 1$, the remainder is 6.
   - **B** $x - 1$ is a factor of $P(x)$.
   - **C** $P(3) = 36$
   - **D** $P(x) = (x + 3)(3x^2 - 5x + 17) + 42$

3. Which set of values for x should be tested to determine the possible zeros of $x^4 - 2x^3 - 7x^2 - 8x + 12$?
   - **A** $\pm 1, \pm 2, \pm 4, \pm 12$
   - **B** $\pm 1, \pm 2, \pm 3, \pm 4, \pm 6$
   - **C** $\pm 1, \pm 2, \pm 3, \pm 4, \pm 6, \pm 8$
   - **D** $\pm 1, \pm 2, \pm 3, \pm 4, \pm 6, \pm 12$

4. Which of the following is a factor of $2x^3 - 5x^2 - 9x + 18$?
   - **A** $x - 1$
   - **B** $x + 2$
   - **C** $x + 3$
   - **D** $x - 6$

5. Which statement describes how to transform the function $y = x^3$ into $y = 3\left(\frac{1}{4}(x - 5)\right)^3 - 2$?
   - **A** stretch horizontally by a factor of 3, stretch vertically by a factor of $\frac{1}{4}$, and translate 5 units to the left and 2 units up
   - **B** stretch horizontally by a factor of 3, stretch vertically by a factor of $\frac{1}{4}$, and translate 2 units to the right and 5 units down
   - **C** stretch horizontally by a factor of 4, stretch vertically by a factor of 3, and translate 5 units to the right and 2 units down
   - **D** stretch horizontally by a factor of 4, stretch vertically by a factor of 3, and translate 2 units to the left and 5 units up

Short Answer

6. Determine the real roots of each equation.
   - **a)** $(x + 4)^2(x - 3) = 0$
   - **b)** $(x - 3)^2(x + 1)^2 = 0$
   - **c)** $(4x^2 - 16)(x^2 - 3x - 10) = 0$
   - **d)** $(9x^2 - 81)(x^2 - 9) = 0$

7. Factor each polynomial in x.
   - **a)** $P(x) = x^3 + 4x^2 + 5x + 2$
   - **b)** $P(x) = x^3 - 13x^2 + 12$
   - **c)** $P(x) = -x^3 + 6x^2 - 9x$
   - **d)** $P(x) = x^3 - 3x^2 + x + 5$

8. Match each equation with the corresponding graph of a polynomial function. Justify your choices.
   a) $y = x^4 + 3x^3 - 3x^2 - 7x + 6$
   b) $y = x^3 - 4x^2 + 4x$
   c) $y = -2x^3 + 6x^2 + 2x - 6$

A
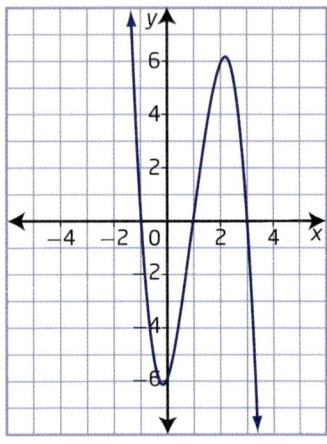

B
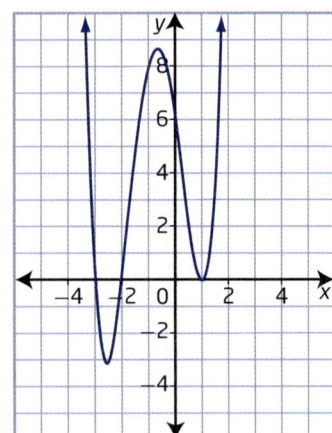

C
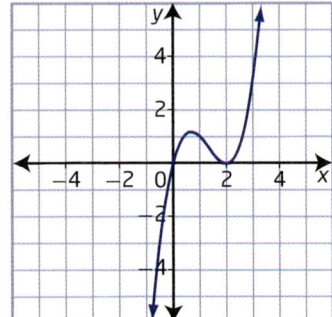

Extended Response

9. Boxes for candies are to be constructed from cardboard sheets that measure 36 cm by 20 cm. Each box is formed by folding a sheet along the dotted lines, as shown.

   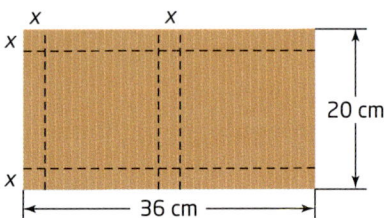

   a) What is the volume of the box as a function of x?
   b) What are the possible whole-number dimensions of the box if the volume is to be 512 cm³?

10. a) Identify the parameters a, b, h, and k in the polynomial $y = \frac{1}{3}(x + 3)^3 - 2$. Describe how each parameter transforms the base function $y = x^3$.
    b) State the domain and range of the transformed function.
    c) Sketch graphs of the base function and the transformed function on the same set of axes.

Unit 1 Project Wrap-Up

The Art of Mathematics

- Select a piece of artwork, a photo, or an image that clearly illustrates at least two different types of functions you have encountered in this unit, such as linear, absolute value, quadratic, radical, and polynomial.
- Determine function equations that model at least two aspects or portions of the image.
- Justify your choice of equations by superimposing them on the image.
- Display your piece of art. You may wish to use a poster, a PowerPoint presentation, a brochure, or some other format of your choice.

You may wish to create a class bulletin board to display your artwork.

Cumulative Review, Chapters 1–3

Chapter 1 Function Transformations

1. Given the graph of the function $y = f(x)$, sketch the graph of each transformation.

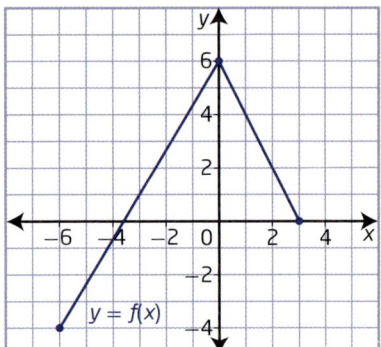

   a) $y + 2 = f(x - 3)$
   b) $y + 1 = -f(x)$
   c) $y = f(3x + 6)$
   d) $y = 3f(-x)$

2. Write the equation for the translated graph, $g(x)$, in the form $y - k = f(x - h)$.

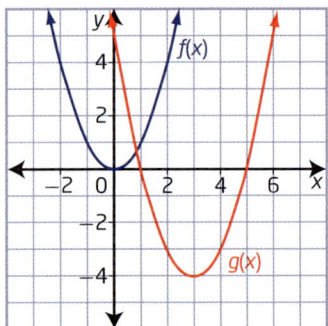

3. Describe the combination of transformations that must be applied to the function $f(x)$ to obtain the transformed function $g(x)$.

   a) $y = f(x)$ and $g(x) = f(x + 1) - 5$
   b) $f(x) = x^2$ and $g(x) = -3(x - 2)^2$
   c) $f(x) = |x|$ and $g(x) = |-x + 1| + 3$

4. The graph of $y = f(x)$ is transformed as indicated. State the coordinates of the image point of $(6, 9)$ on the transformed graph.

   a) $h(x) = f(x - 3) + 1$
   b) $i(x) = -2f(x)$
   c) $j(x) = f(-3x)$

5. The x-intercepts of the graph of $y = f(x)$ are -4 and 6. The y-intercept is -3. Determine the new x-intercepts and y-intercept for each of the following transformations of $f(x)$.

   a) $y = f(3x)$
   b) $y = -2f(x)$

6. Consider the graph of $y = |x| + 4$.

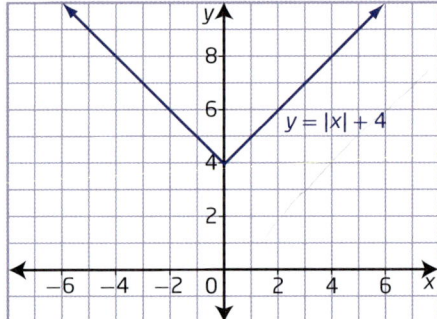

   a) Does this graph represent a function?
   b) Sketch the graph of the inverse of $y = |x| + 4$.
   c) Is the inverse of $y = |x| + 4$ a function? If not, restrict the domain of $y = |x| + 4$ so that its inverse is a function.

Chapter 2 Radical Functions

7. The graph of the function $f(x) = \sqrt{x}$ is transformed to the graph shown. Determine the equation of the transformed graph in the form $g(x) = \sqrt{b(x - h)} - k$.

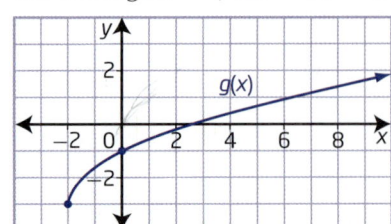

8. The graph of the function $f(x) = \sqrt{x}$ is transformed by a vertical stretch by a factor of 2 and then reflected in the y-axis and translated 1 unit to the left. State the equation of the transformed function, sketch the graph, and identify the domain and range.

9. The graph of $g(x)$ is a transformation of the graph of $f(x)$.

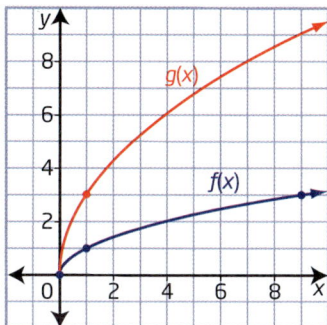

a) Write the equation of $g(x)$ as a horizontal stretch of $f(x)$.

b) Write the equation of $g(x)$ as a vertical stretch of $f(x)$.

c) Show that the functions in parts a) and b) are equivalent.

10. Consider the functions $f(x) = x^2 - 1$ and $g(x) = \sqrt{f(x)}$.

a) Compare the x-intercepts of the graphs of the two functions. Explain your results.

b) Compare the domains of the functions. Explain your results.

11. The radical equation $2x = \sqrt{x + 3} - 5$ can be solved graphically or algebraically.

a) Ron solved the equation algebraically and obtained the solutions $x = -2.75$ and $x = -2$. Are these solutions correct? Explain.

b) Solve the equation graphically to confirm your answer to part a).

12. Consider the function $f(x) = 3\sqrt{x - 4} - 6$.

a) Sketch the graph of the function and determine its x-intercept.

b) Solve the equation $0 = 3\sqrt{x - 4} - 6$.

c) Describe the relationship between the x-intercept of the graph and the solution to the equation.

Chapter 3 Polynomial Functions

13. Divide each of the following as indicated. Express your answer in the form $\frac{P(x)}{x - a} = Q(x) + \frac{R}{x - a}$. Confirm your remainder using the remainder theorem.

a) $x^4 + 3x + 4$ divided by $x + 1$

b) $x^3 + 5x^2 + x - 9$ divided by $x + 3$

14. List the possible integral zeros of the polynomial $P(x) = x^4 - 3x^3 - 3x^2 + 11x - 6$. Use the remainder theorem to determine the remainder for each possible value.

15. Factor fully.

a) $x^3 - 21x + 20$

b) $x^3 + 3x^2 - 10x - 24$

c) $-x^4 + 8x^2 - 16$

16. Determine the x-intercepts and the y-intercept of the graphs of each polynomial function. Then, sketch the graph.

a) $f(x) = -x^3 + 2x^2 + 9x - 18$

b) $g(x) = x^4 - 2x^3 - 3x^2 + 4x + 4$

17. The volume of a box is represented by the function $V(x) = x^3 + 2x^2 - 11x - 12$.

a) If the height of the box can be represented by $x + 1$, determine the possible length and width by factoring the polynomial.

b) If the height of the box is 4.5 m, determine the dimensions of the box.

18. Determine the equation of the transformed function.

$f(x) = x^3$ is stretched vertically about the x-axis by a factor of 3, then reflected in the y-axis, and then translated horizontally 5 units to the right.

Unit 1 Test

Multiple Choice

For #1 to #7, choose the best answer.

1. The graph of $f(x)$ and its transformation, $g(x)$, are shown below.

   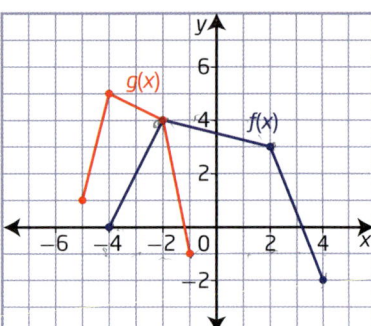

   The equation of the transformed function is

   A $g(x) = f\left(\frac{1}{2}(x - 3)\right) + 1$

   B $g(x) = f(2(x - 3)) + 1$

   C $g(x) = f\left(\frac{1}{2}(x + 3)\right) + 1$

   D $g(x) = f(2(x + 3)) + 1$

2. The graph of the function $y = f(x)$ is transformed by a reflection in the y-axis and a horizontal stretch about the y-axis by a factor of 3. Which of the following will not change?

   I   the domain
   II the range
   III the x-intercepts
   IV the y-intercept

   A I only
   B I and III
   C II and IV
   D depends on $y = f(x)$

3. Which pair of functions are *not* inverses of each other?

   A $f(x) = 5x$ and $g(x) = \frac{x}{5}$
   B $f(x) = x + 3$ and $g(x) = x - 3$
   C $f(x) = 4x - 1$ and $g(x) = \frac{1}{4}x + \frac{1}{4}$
   D $f(x) = \frac{x}{2} + 5$ and $g(x) = 2x - 5$

4. Which function has a domain of $\{x \mid x \in R\}$ and a range of $\{y \mid y \geq -3, y \in R\}$?

   A $y = |x + 4| - 3$
   B $y = \sqrt{x + 4} - 3$
   C $y = \sqrt{x^2 - 4} - 3$
   D $y = (x - 4)^3 - 3$

5. If the graph of $y = \sqrt{x + 3}$ is reflected in the line $y = x$, then which statement is true?

   A All invariant points lie on the y-axis.
   B The new graph is not a function.
   C The point $(6, 3)$ will become $(-3, 6)$.
   D The domain of the new graph is $\{x \mid x \geq 0, x \in R\}$.

6. If the graph of a polynomial function of degree 3 passes through $(2, 4)$ and has x-intercepts of -2 and 3 only, the function could be

   A $f(x) = x^3 + x^2 - 8x - 12$
   B $f(x) = x^3 - x^2 - 8x + 12$
   C $f(x) = x^3 - 4x^2 - 3x + 18$
   D $f(x) = x^3 + 4x^2 - 3x - 18$

7. If $P(x) = -x^3 - 4x^2 + x + 4$, then

   A $x + 1$ is a factor
   B $P(0) = -1$
   C the y-intercept is -4
   D $x - 1$ is not a factor

Numerical Response

Copy and complete the statements in #8 to #11.

8. When $x^4 + k$ is divided by $x + 2$, the remainder is 3. The value of k is ■.

9. If the range of the function $y = f(x)$ is $\{y \mid y \geq 11, y \in R\}$, then the range of the new function $g(x) = f(x + 2) - 3$ is ■.

10. The graph of the function $f(x) = |x|$ is transformed so that the point (x, y) becomes $(x - 2, y + 3)$. The equation of the transformed function is $g(x) = $ ■.

11. The root of the equation $x = \sqrt{2x - 1} + 2$ is ■.

Written Response

12. a) The graph of $y = x^2$ is stretched horizontally about the y-axis by a factor of $\frac{1}{2}$ and then translated horizontally 6 units to the right. Sketch the graph.

    b) The graph of $y = x^2$ is translated horizontally 6 units to the right and then stretched horizontally about the y-axis by a factor of $\frac{1}{2}$. Sketch the graph.

    c) How are the two images related? Explain.

13. Consider $f(x) = x^2 - 9$.

    a) Sketch the graph of $f(x)$.

    b) Determine the equation of the inverse of $f(x)$ and sketch its graph.

    c) State the equation of $y = \sqrt{f(x)}$ and sketch its graph.

    d) Identify and compare the domain and range of the three relations.

14. The graph of $y = f(x)$ represents one quarter of a circle. Describe the reflections of $y = f(x)$ required to produce a whole circle. State the equations required.

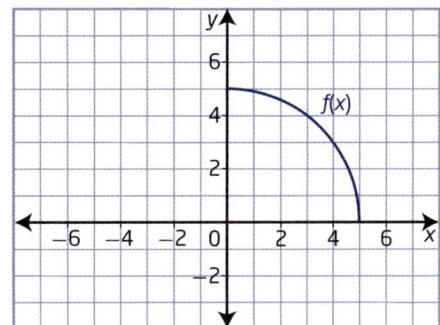

15. Mary and John were asked to solve the equation $2x = \sqrt{x + 1} + 4$.

    a) Mary chose to solve the equation algebraically. Her first steps are shown. Identify any errors in her work, and complete the correct solution.

    $$2x = \sqrt{x + 1} + 4$$
    Step 1: $(2x)^2 = (\sqrt{x + 1} + 4)^2$
    Step 2: $4x^2 = x + 1 + 16$

    b) John decided to find the solution graphically. He entered the following equations in his calculator. Could his method lead to a correct answer? Explain.

    $$y = \sqrt{x + 1} + 4$$
    $$y = 2x$$

16. Given that $x + 3$ is a factor of the polynomial $P(x) = x^4 + 3x^3 + cx^2 - 7x + 6$, determine the value of c. Then, factor the polynomial fully.

17. Consider $P(x) = x^3 - 7x - 6$.

    a) List the possible integral zeros of $P(x)$.

    b) Factor $P(x)$ fully.

    c) State the x-intercepts and y-intercept of the graph of the function $P(x)$.

    d) Determine the intervals where $P(x) \geq 0$.

Unit 2

Trigonometry

Trigonometry is used extensively in our daily lives. For example, will you listen to music today? Most songs are recorded digitally and are compressed into MP3 format. These processes all involve trigonometry.

Your phone may have a built-in Global Positioning System (GPS) that uses trigonometry to tell where you are on Earth's surface. GPS satellites send a signal to receivers such as the one in your phone. The signal from each satellite can be represented using trigonometric functions. The receiver uses these signals to determine the location of the satellite and then uses trigonometry to calculate your position.

Looking Ahead

In this unit, you will solve problems involving…

- angle measures and the unit circle
- trigonometric functions and their graphs
- the proofs of trigonometric identities
- the solutions of trigonometric equations

Unit 2 Project — Applications of Trigonometry

In this project, you will explore angle measurement, trigonometric equations, and trigonometric functions, and you will explore how they relate to past and present applications.

In Chapter 4, you will research the history of units of angle measure such as radians. In Chapter 5, you will gather information about the application of periodic functions to the field of communications. Finally, in Chapter 6, you will explore the use of trigonometric identities in Mach numbers.

At the end of the unit, you will choose at least one of the following options:
- Research the history, usage, and relationship of types of units for angle measure.
- Examine an application of periodic functions in electronic communications and investigate why it is an appropriate model.
- Apply the skills you have learned about trigonometric identities to supersonic travel.
- Explore the science of forensics through its applications of trigonometry.

CHAPTER 4

Trigonometry and the Unit Circle

Have you ever wondered about the repeating patterns that occur around us? Repeating patterns occur in sound, light, tides, time, and molecular motion. To analyse these repeating, cyclical patterns, you need to move from using ratios in triangles to using circular functions to approach trigonometry.

In this chapter, you will learn how to model and solve trigonometric problems using the unit circle and circular functions of radian measures.

Did You Know?

The flower in the photograph is called the Trigonometry daffodil. Why do you think this name was chosen?

Key Terms
radian
coterminal angles
general form
unit circle
cosecant
secant
cotangent
trigonometric equation

164 MHR • Chapter 4

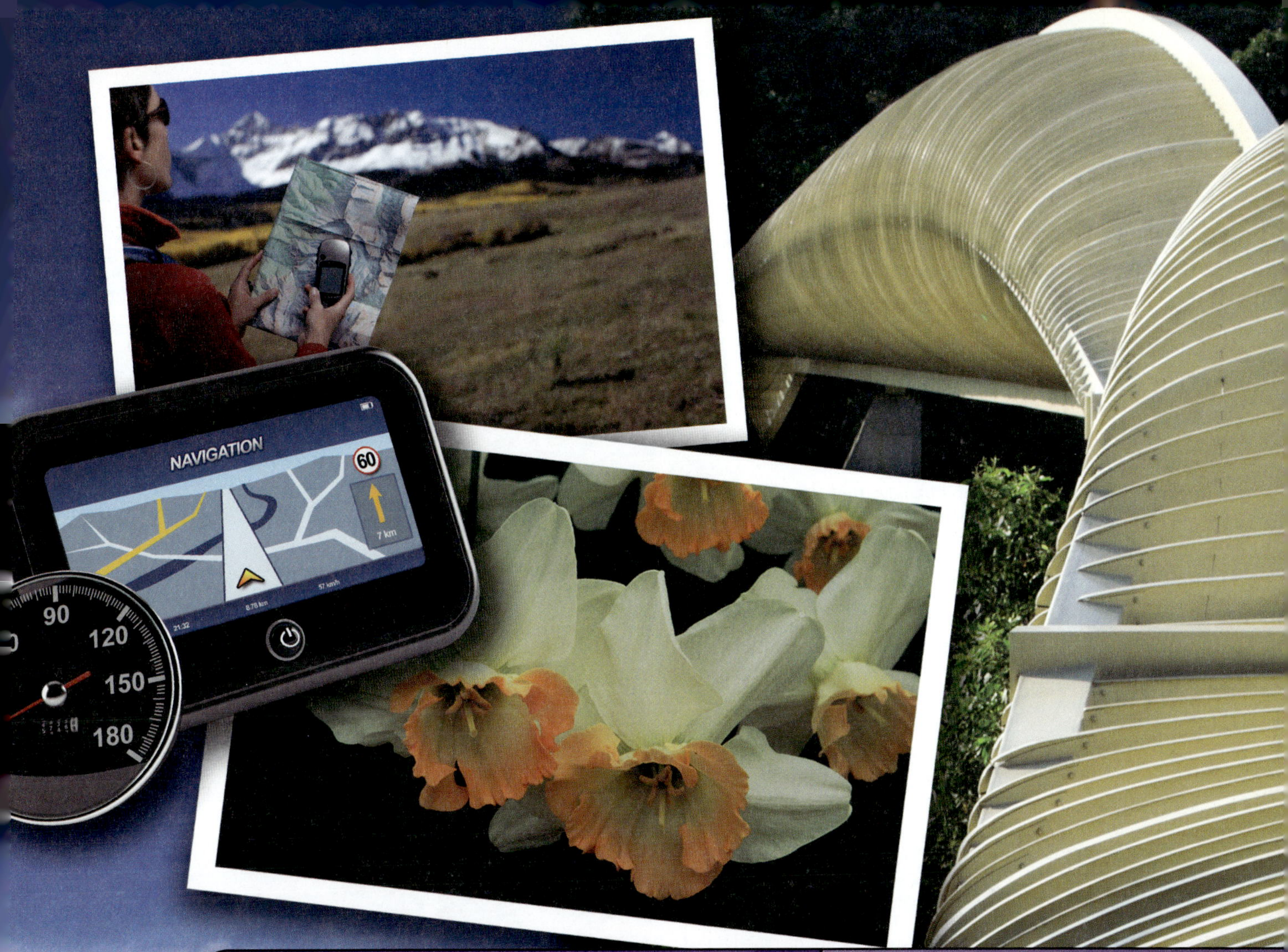

Career Link

Engineers, police investigators, and legal experts all play key roles following a serious collision. Investigating and analysing a motor vehicle collision can provide valuable evidence for police and insurance reports. You can be trained in this fascinating and important field at police schools, engineering departments, and technical institutes.

Web Link

To learn more about accident reconstruction and training to become a forensic analysis investigator, go to www.mcgrawhill.ca/school/learningcentres and follow the links.

4.1

Angles and Angle Measure

Focus on...

- sketching angles in standard position measured in degrees and radians
- converting angles in degree measure to radian measure and vice versa
- determining the measures of angles that are coterminal with a given angle
- solving problems involving arc lengths, central angles, and the radius in a circle

Angles can be measured using different units, such as revolutions, degrees, radians, and gradians. Which of these units are you familiar with? Check how many of these units are on your calculator.

Angles are everywhere and can be found in unexpected places. How many different angles can you see in the structure of the racing car?

Did You Know?

Sound (undamaged) hooves of all horses share certain angle aspects determined by anatomy and the laws of physics. A front hoof normally exhibits a 30° hairline and a 49° toe angle, while a hind hoof has a 30° hairline and a 55° toe angle.

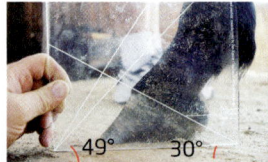
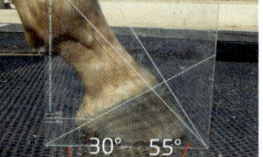

Investigate Angle Measure

Materials
- masking tape
- sidewalk chalk
- string
- measuring tape

Work in small groups.

1. Mark the centre of a circle on the floor with sidewalk chalk. Then, using a piece of string greater than 1 m long for the radius, outline the circle with chalk or pieces of masking tape.

2. Label the centre of the circle O. Choose any point A on the circumference of the circle. OA is the radius of the circle. Have one member of your group walk heel-to-toe along the radius, counting foot lengths. Then, have the same person count the same number of foot lengths moving counterclockwise from A along the circumference. Label the endpoint B. Use tape to make the radii AO and BO. Have another member of the group confirm that the radius AO is the same length as arc AB.

3. Determine, by walking round the circle from B, approximately how many times the length of the radius fits onto the circumference.

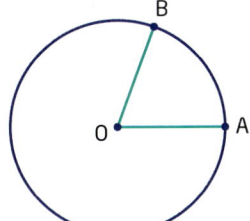

Reflect and Respond

4. Use your knowledge of circumference to show that your answer in step 3 is reasonable.

5. Is ∠AOB in step 3 greater than, equal to, or less than 60°? Discuss this with your group.

6. Determine the degree measure of ∠AOB, to the nearest tenth of a degree.

7. Compare your results with those of other groups. Does the central angle AOB maintain its size if you use a larger circle? a smaller circle?

Link the Ideas

In the investigation, you encountered several key points associated with angle measure.

By convention, angles measured in a counterclockwise direction are said to be positive. Those measured in a clockwise direction are negative.

The angle AOB that you created measures 1 **radian**.

One full rotation is 360° or 2π radians.

One half rotation is 180° or π radians.

One quarter rotation is 90° or $\frac{\pi}{2}$ radians.

One eighth rotation is 45° or $\frac{\pi}{4}$ radians.

Many mathematicians omit units for radian measures. For example, $\frac{2\pi}{3}$ radians may be written as $\frac{2\pi}{3}$. Angle measures without units are considered to be in radians.

radian
- one radian is the measure of the central angle subtended in a circle by an arc equal in length to the radius of the circle
- $2\pi = 360°$ = 1 full rotation (or revolution)

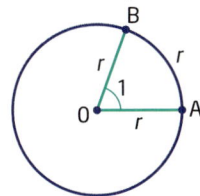

Example 1

Convert Between Degree and Radian Measure

Draw each angle in standard position. Change each degree measure to radian measure and each radian measure to degree measure. Give answers as both exact and approximate measures (if necessary) to the nearest hundredth of a unit.

a) 30° **b)** −120°
c) $\dfrac{5\pi}{4}$ **d)** 2.57

Solution

a)

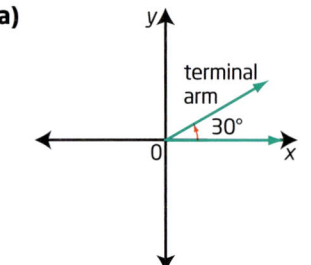

Unitary Method

$360° = 2\pi$

$1° = \dfrac{2\pi}{360}$

$= \dfrac{\pi}{180}$

$30° = 30\left(\dfrac{\pi}{180}\right)$

$= \dfrac{\pi}{6}$

≈ 0.52

An angle in standard position has its centre at the origin and its initial arm along the positive *x*-axis.

In which direction are positive angles measured?

$\dfrac{\pi}{6}$ is an exact value.

b)

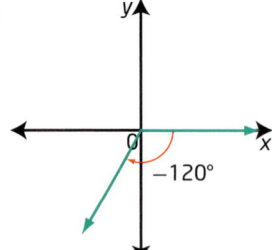

Proportion Method

$180° = \pi$

$\dfrac{-120°}{180°} = \dfrac{x}{\pi}$

$x = \dfrac{-120\pi}{180}$

$= -\dfrac{2\pi}{3}$

≈ -2.09

Why is the angle drawn using a clockwise rotation?

So, −120° is equivalent to $-\dfrac{2\pi}{3}$ or approximately −2.09.

168 MHR • Chapter 4

c) π is $\frac{1}{2}$ rotation.

$\frac{\pi}{4}$ is $\frac{1}{8}$ rotation.

So $\frac{5\pi}{4}$ terminates in the third quadrant.

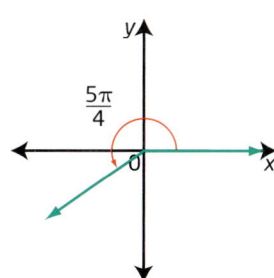

Unit Analysis

$\frac{5\pi}{4} = \left(\frac{5\pi}{4}\right)\left(\frac{180°}{\pi}\right)$

$= \frac{5(180°)}{4}$

$= 225°$

Why does $\left(\frac{180°}{\pi}\right)$ have value 1?

$\frac{5\pi}{4}$ is equivalent to 225°.

d) π (approximately 3.14) is $\frac{1}{2}$ rotation.

$\frac{\pi}{2}$ (approximately 1.57) is $\frac{1}{4}$ rotation.

2.57 is between 1.57 and 3.14, so it terminates in the second quadrant.

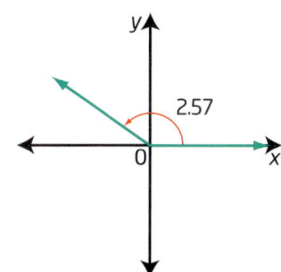

Unitary Method

$\pi = 180°$

$1 = \frac{180°}{\pi}$

2.57

$= 2.57\left(\frac{180°}{\pi}\right)$

$= \frac{462.6°}{\pi}$

$\approx 147.25°$

Proportion Method

$\frac{x}{2.57} = \frac{180°}{\pi}$

$x = 2.57\left(\frac{180°}{\pi}\right)$

$x = \frac{462.6°}{\pi}$

$x \approx 147.25°$

Unit Analysis

2.57

$= 2.57\left(\frac{180°}{\pi}\right)$

$= \frac{462.6°}{\pi}$

$\approx 147.25°$

2.57 is equivalent to $\frac{462.6°}{\pi}$ or approximately 147.25°.

Your Turn

Draw each angle in standard position. Change each degree measure to radians and each radian measure to degrees. Give answers as both exact and approximate measures (if necessary) to the nearest hundredth of a unit.

a) $-270°$

b) $150°$

c) $\frac{7\pi}{6}$

d) -1.2

Did You Know?

Most scientific and graphing calculators can calculate using angle measures in both degrees and radians. Find out how to change the mode on your calculator.

Coterminal Angles

When you sketch an angle of 60° and an angle of 420° in standard position, the terminal arms coincide. These are **coterminal angles**.

coterminal angles
- angles in standard position with the same terminal arms
- may be measured in degrees or radians
- $\frac{\pi}{4}$ and $\frac{9\pi}{4}$ are coterminal angles, as are 40° and −320°

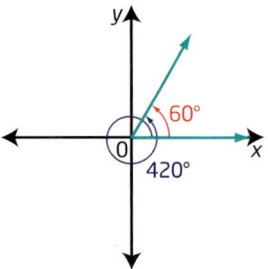

Example 2
Identify Coterminal Angles

Determine one positive and one negative angle measure that is coterminal with each angle. In which quadrant does the terminal arm lie?

a) 40° b) −430° c) $\frac{8\pi}{3}$

Solution

a) The terminal arm is in quadrant I.
To locate coterminal angles, begin on the terminal arm of the given angle and rotate in a positive or negative direction until the new terminal arm coincides with that of the original angle.

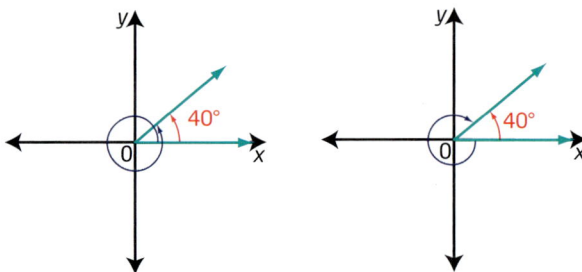

40° + 360° = 400°   40° + (−360°) = −320°

Two angles coterminal with 40° are 400° and −320°.

What other answers are possible?

b) The terminal arm of −430° is in quadrant IV.

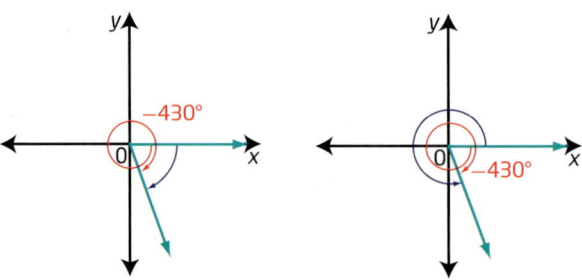

−430° + 360° = −70°   −430° + 720° = 290°

Two angles coterminal with −430° are 290° and −70°.

The reference angle is 70°.

c)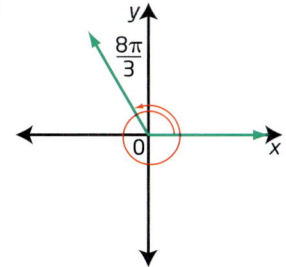

$$\frac{8\pi}{3} = \frac{6\pi}{3} + \frac{2\pi}{3}$$

So, the angle is one full rotation (2π) plus $\frac{2\pi}{3}$.

The terminal arm is in quadrant II.

There are 2π or $\frac{6\pi}{3}$ in one full rotation.

Counterclockwise one full rotation: $\frac{8\pi}{3} + \frac{6\pi}{3} = \frac{14\pi}{3}$

Clockwise one full rotation: $\frac{8\pi}{3} - \frac{6\pi}{3} = \frac{2\pi}{3}$

Clockwise two full rotations: $\frac{8\pi}{3} - \frac{12\pi}{3} = -\frac{4\pi}{3}$

Two angles coterminal with $\frac{8\pi}{3}$ are $\frac{2\pi}{3}$ and $-\frac{4\pi}{3}$.

Your Turn

For each angle in standard position, determine one positive and one negative angle measure that is coterminal with it.

a) 270°   **b)** $-\frac{5\pi}{4}$ **c)** 740°

Coterminal Angles in General Form

By adding or subtracting multiples of one full rotation, you can write an infinite number of angles that are coterminal with any given angle.

For example, some angles that are coterminal with 40° are
40° + (360°)(1) = 400°   40° − (360°)(1) = −320°
40° + (360°)(2) = 760°   40° − (360°)(2) = −680°

In general, the angles coterminal with 40° are 40° ± (360°)n, where n is any natural number.

Some angles coterminal with $\frac{2\pi}{3}$ are

$$\frac{2\pi}{3} + 2\pi(1) = \frac{2\pi}{3} + \frac{6\pi}{3} \qquad \frac{2\pi}{3} - 2\pi(1) = \frac{2\pi}{3} - \frac{6\pi}{3}$$
$$= \frac{8\pi}{3} \qquad\qquad\qquad\qquad = -\frac{4\pi}{3}$$
$$\frac{2\pi}{3} + 2\pi(2) = \frac{2\pi}{3} + \frac{12\pi}{3} \qquad \frac{2\pi}{3} - 2\pi(2) = \frac{2\pi}{3} - \frac{12\pi}{3}$$
$$= \frac{14\pi}{3} \qquad\qquad\qquad\qquad = -\frac{10\pi}{3}$$

In general, the angles coterminal with $\frac{2\pi}{3}$ are $\frac{2\pi}{3} \pm 2\pi n$, where n is any natural number.

> Any given angle has an infinite number of angles coterminal with it, since each time you make one full rotation from the terminal arm, you arrive back at the same terminal arm. Angles coterminal with any angle θ can be described using the expression
>
> θ ± (360°)n or θ ± 2πn,
>
> where n is a natural number. This way of expressing an answer is called the **general form**.

general form
- an expression containing parameters that can be given specific values to generate any answer that satisfies the given information or situation
- represents all possible cases

Example 3

Express Coterminal Angles in General Form

a) Express the angles coterminal with 110° in general form. Identify the angles coterminal with 110° that satisfy the domain −720° ≤ θ < 720°.

b) Express the angles coterminal with $\frac{8\pi}{3}$ in general form. Identify the angles coterminal with $\frac{8\pi}{3}$ in the domain −4π ≤ θ < 4π.

Solution

a) Angles coterminal with 110° occur at 110° ± (360°)n, n ∈ N.

Substitute values for n to determine these angles.

n	1	2	3
110° − (360°)n	−250°	−610°	−970°
110° + (360°)n	470°	830°	1190°

From the table, the values that satisfy the domain −720° ≤ θ < 720° are −610°, −250°, and 470°. These angles are coterminal.

b) $\frac{8\pi}{3} \pm 2\pi n$, n ∈ N, represents all angles coterminal with $\frac{8\pi}{3}$.

Substitute values for n to determine these angles.

n	1	2	3	4
$\frac{8\pi}{3} - 2\pi n$	$\frac{2\pi}{3}$	$-\frac{4\pi}{3}$	$-\frac{10\pi}{3}$	$-\frac{16\pi}{3}$
$\frac{8\pi}{3} + 2\pi n$	$\frac{14\pi}{3}$	$\frac{20\pi}{3}$	$\frac{26\pi}{3}$	$\frac{32\pi}{3}$

The angles in the domain −4π ≤ θ < 4π that are coterminal are $-\frac{10\pi}{3}, -\frac{4\pi}{3},$ and $\frac{2\pi}{3}$.

Why is $-\frac{16\pi}{3}$ not an acceptable answer?

Your Turn

Write an expression for all possible angles coterminal with each given angle. Identify the angles that are coterminal that satisfy −360° ≤ θ < 360° or −2π ≤ θ < 2π.

a) −500° **b)** 650° **c)** $\frac{9\pi}{4}$

Arc Length of a Circle

All arcs that subtend a right angle $\left(\dfrac{\pi}{2}\right)$ have the same central angle, but they have different arc lengths depending on the radius of the circle. The arc length is proportional to the radius. This is true for any central angle and related arc length.

Consider two concentric circles with centre O. The radius of the smaller circle is 1, and the radius of the larger circle is r. A central angle of θ radians is subtended by arc AB on the smaller circle and arc CD on the larger one. You can write the following proportion, where x represents the arc length of the smaller circle and a is the arc length of the larger circle.

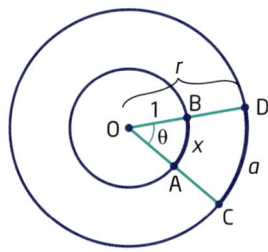

$$\dfrac{a}{x} = \dfrac{r}{1}$$
$$a = xr \qquad \text{①}$$

Consider the circle with radius 1 and the sector with central angle θ. The ratio of the arc length to the circumference is equal to the ratio of the central angle to one full rotation.

$$\dfrac{x}{2\pi r} = \dfrac{\theta}{2\pi} \qquad \text{Why is } r = 1?$$
$$x = \left(\dfrac{\theta}{2\pi}\right) 2\pi (1)$$
$$x = \theta$$

Substitute $x = \theta$ in ①.
$$a = \theta r$$

This formula, $a = \theta r$, works for any circle, provided that θ is measured in radians and both a and r are measured in the same units.

Example 4

Determine Arc Length in a Circle

Rosemarie is taking a course in industrial engineering. For an assignment, she is designing the interface of a DVD player. In her plan, she includes a decorative arc below the on/off button. The arc has central angle 130° in a circle with radius 6.7 mm. Determine the length of the arc, to the nearest tenth of a millimetre.

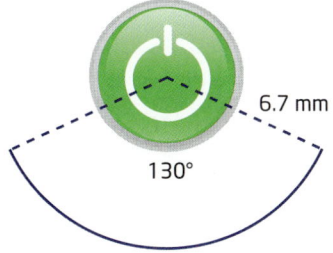

4.1 Angles and Angle Measure • MHR **173**

Solution

Method 1: Convert to Radians and Use the Formula $a = \theta r$

Convert the measure of the central angle to radians before using the formula $a = \theta r$, where a is the arc length; θ is the central angle, in radians; and r is the length of the radius.

$180° = \pi$

$1° = \dfrac{\pi}{180}$

$130° = 130\left(\dfrac{\pi}{180}\right)$

$ = \dfrac{13\pi}{18}$

$a = \theta r$

$ = \left(\dfrac{13\pi}{18}\right)(6.7)$

$ = \dfrac{87.1\pi}{18}$

$ = 15.201\ldots$

Why is it important to use exact values throughout the calculation and only convert to decimal fractions at the end?

The arc length is 15.2 mm, to the nearest tenth of a millimetre.

Method 2: Use a Proportion

Let a represent the arc length.

$\dfrac{\text{arc length}}{\text{circumference}} = \dfrac{\text{central angle}}{\text{full rotation}}$

$\dfrac{a}{2\pi(6.7)} = \dfrac{130°}{360°}$

$a = \dfrac{2\pi(6.7)130°}{360°}$

$ = 15.201\ldots$

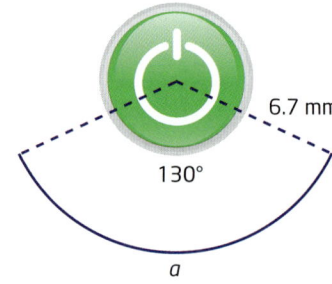

The arc length is 15.2 mm, to the nearest tenth of a millimetre.

Your Turn

If a represents the length of an arc of a circle with radius r, subtended by a central angle of θ, determine the missing quantity. Give your answers to the nearest tenth of a unit.

a) $r = 8.7$ cm, $\theta = 75°$, $a = \blacksquare$ cm
b) $r = \blacksquare$ mm, $\theta = 1.8$, $a = 4.7$ mm
c) $r = 5$ m, $a = 13$ m, $\theta = \blacksquare$

Key Ideas

- Angles can be measured using different units, including degrees and radians.
- An angle measured in one unit can be converted to the other unit using the relationships 1 full rotation = 360° = 2π.
- An angle in standard position has its vertex at the origin and its initial arm along the positive *x*-axis.
- Angles that are coterminal have the same initial arm and the same terminal arm.
- An angle θ has an infinite number of angles that are coterminal expressed by θ ± (360°)*n*, *n* ∈ N, in degrees, or θ ± 2π*n*, *n* ∈ N, in radians.
- The formula $a = \theta r$, where a is the arc length; θ is the central angle, in radians; and r is the length of the radius, can be used to determine any of the variables given the other two, as long as a and r are in the same units.

Check Your Understanding

Practise

1. For each angle, indicate whether the direction of rotation is clockwise or counterclockwise.
   - **a)** −4π
   - **b)** 750°
   - **c)** −38.7°
   - **d)** 1

2. Convert each degree measure to radians. Write your answers as exact values. Sketch the angle and label it in degrees and in radians.
   - **a)** 30°
   - **b)** 45°
   - **c)** −330°
   - **d)** 520°
   - **e)** 90°
   - **f)** 21°

3. Convert each degree measure to radians. Express your answers as exact values and as approximate measures, to the nearest hundredth of a radian.
   - **a)** 60°
   - **b)** 150°
   - **c)** −270°
   - **d)** 72°
   - **e)** −14.8°
   - **f)** 540°

4. Convert each radian measure to degrees. Express your answers as exact values and as approximate measures, to the nearest tenth of a degree, if necessary.
   - **a)** $\dfrac{\pi}{6}$
   - **b)** $\dfrac{2\pi}{3}$
   - **c)** $-\dfrac{3\pi}{8}$
   - **d)** $-\dfrac{5\pi}{2}$
   - **e)** 1
   - **f)** 2.75

5. Convert each radian measure to degrees. Express your answers as exact values and as approximate measures, to the nearest thousandth.
   - **a)** $\dfrac{2\pi}{7}$
   - **b)** $\dfrac{7\pi}{13}$
   - **c)** $\dfrac{2}{3}$
   - **d)** 3.66
   - **e)** −6.14
   - **f)** −20

6. Sketch each angle in standard position. In which quadrant does each angle terminate?
   - **a)** 1
   - **b)** −225°
   - **c)** $\dfrac{17\pi}{6}$
   - **d)** 650°
   - **e)** $-\dfrac{2\pi}{3}$
   - **f)** −42°

7. Determine one positive and one negative angle coterminal with each angle.
   a) 72°
   b) $\frac{3\pi}{4}$
   c) −120°
   d) $\frac{11\pi}{2}$
   e) −205°
   f) 7.8

8. Determine whether the angles in each pair are coterminal. For one pair of angles, explain how you know.
   a) $\frac{5\pi}{6}, \frac{17\pi}{6}$
   b) $\frac{5\pi}{2}, -\frac{9\pi}{2}$
   c) 410°, −410°
   d) 227°, −493°

9. Write an expression for all of the angles coterminal with each angle. Indicate what your variable represents.
   a) 135°
   b) $-\frac{\pi}{2}$
   c) −200°
   d) 10

10. Draw and label an angle in standard position with negative measure. Then, determine an angle with positive measure that is coterminal with your original angle. Show how to use a general expression for coterminal angles to find the second angle.

11. For each angle, determine all angles that are coterminal in the given domain.
    a) 65°, 0° ≤ θ < 720°
    b) −40°, −180° ≤ θ < 360°
    c) −40°, −720° ≤ θ < 720°
    d) $\frac{3\pi}{4}$, −2π ≤ θ < 2π
    e) $-\frac{11\pi}{6}$, −4π ≤ θ < 4π
    f) $\frac{7\pi}{3}$, −2π ≤ θ < 4π
    g) 2.4, −2π ≤ θ < 2π
    h) −7.2, −4π ≤ θ < 2π

12. Determine the arc length subtended by each central angle. Give answers to the nearest hundredth of a unit.
    a) radius 9.5 cm, central angle 1.4
    b) radius 1.37 m, central angle 3.5
    c) radius 7 cm, central angle 130°
    d) radius 6.25 in., central angle 282°

13. Use the information in each diagram to determine the value of the variable. Give your answers to the nearest hundredth of a unit.
    a)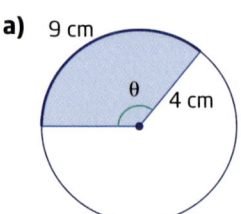
    b)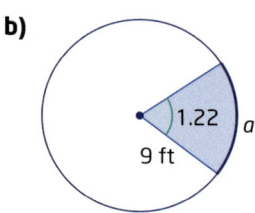
    c)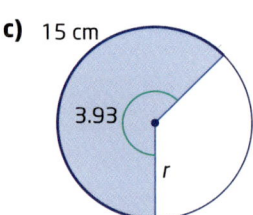
    d)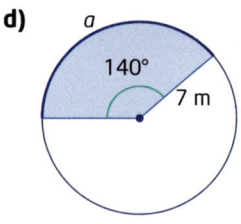

Apply

14. A rotating water sprinkler makes one revolution every 15 s. The water reaches a distance of 5 m from the sprinkler.
    a) What is the arc length of the sector watered when the sprinkler rotates through $\frac{5\pi}{3}$? Give your answer as both an exact value and an approximate measure, to the nearest hundredth.
    b) Show how you could find the area of the sector watered in part a).
    c) What angle does the sprinkler rotate through in 2 min? Express your answer in radians and degrees.

15. Angular velocity describes the rate of change in a central angle over time. For example, the change could be expressed in revolutions per minute (rpm), radians per second, degrees per hour, and so on. All that is required is an angle measurement expressed over a unit of time.

a) Earth makes one revolution every 24 h. Express the angular velocity of Earth in three other ways.

b) An electric motor rotates at 1000 rpm. What is this angular velocity expressed in radians per second?

c) A bicycle wheel completes 10 revolutions every 4 s. Express this angular velocity in degrees per minute.

16. Skytrek Adventure Park in Revelstoke, British Columbia, has a sky swing. Can you imagine a 170-ft flight that takes riders through a scary pendulum swing? At one point you are soaring less than 10 ft from the ground at speeds exceeding 60 mph.

a) The length of the cable is 72 ft and you travel on an arc of length 170 ft on one particular swing. What is the measure of the central angle? Give your answer in radians, to the nearest hundredth.

b) What is the measure of the central angle from part a), to the nearest tenth of a degree?

17. Copy and complete the table by converting each angle measure to its equivalent in the other systems. Round your answers to the nearest tenth where necessary.

	Revolutions	Degrees	Radians
a)	1 rev		
b)		270°	
c)			$\frac{5\pi}{6}$
d)			−1.7
e)		−40°	
f)	0.7 rev		
g)	−3.25 rev		
h)		460°	
i)			$-\frac{3\pi}{8}$

18. Joran and Jasmine are discussing expressions for the general form of coterminal angles of 78°. Joran claims the answer must be expressed as 78° + (360°)n, $n \in$ I. Jasmine indicates that although Joran's expression is correct, another answer is possible. She prefers 78° ± k(360°), $k \in$ N, where N represents positive integers. Who is correct? Why?

19. The gradian (grad) is another unit of angle measure. It is defined as $\frac{1}{400}$ of a revolution, so one full rotation contains 400 grads.

a) Determine the number of gradians in 50°.

b) Describe a process for converting from degree measure to gradians and vice versa.

c) Identify a possible reason that the gradian was created.

> **Did You Know?**
>
> Gradians originated in France in the 1800s. They are still used in some engineering work.

20. Yellowknife, Northwest Territories, and Crowsnest Pass, Alberta, lie along the 114° W line of longitude. The latitude of Yellowknife is 62.45° N and the latitude of Crowsnest Pass is 49.63° N. Consider Earth to be a sphere with radius 6400 km.

   a) Sketch the information given above using a circle. Label the centre of Earth, its radius to the equator, and the locations of Yellowknife and Crowsnest Pass.

   b) Determine the distance between Yellowknife and Crowsnest Pass. Give your answer to the nearest hundredth of a kilometre.

   c) Choose a town or city either where you live or nearby. Determine the latitude and longitude of this location. Find another town or city with the same longitude. What is the distance between the two places?

   Did You Know?

   Lines of latitude and longitude locate places on Earth. Lines of latitude are parallel to the equator and are labelled from 0° at the equator to 90° at the North Pole. Lines of longitude converge at the poles and are widest apart at the equator. 0° passes through Greenwich, England, and the lines are numbered up to 180° E and 180° W, meeting at the International Date Line.

   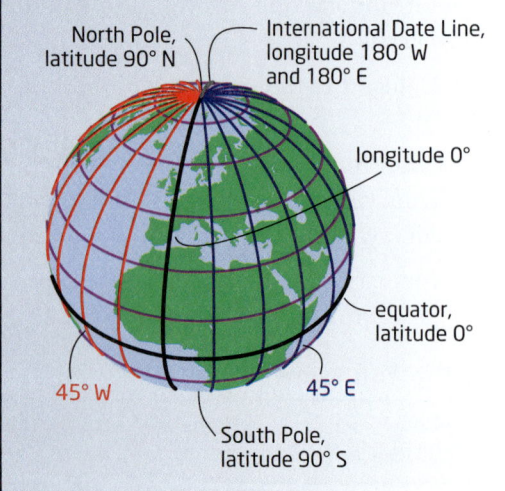

21. Sam Whittingham from Quadra Island, British Columbia, holds five 2009 world human-powered speed records on his recumbent bicycle. In the 200-m flying start, he achieved a speed of 133.284 km/h.

   a) Express the speed in metres per minute.

   b) The diameter of his bicycle wheel is 60 cm. Through how many radians per minute must the wheels turn to achieve his world record in the 200-m flying start?

22. A water wheel with diameter 3 m is used to measure the approximate speed of the water in a river. If the angular velocity of the wheel is 15 rpm, what is the speed of the river, in kilometres per hour?

23. Earth is approximately 93 000 000 mi from the sun. It revolves around the sun, in an almost circular orbit, in about 365 days. Calculate the linear speed, in miles per hour, of Earth in its orbit. Give your answer to the nearest hundredth.

Extend

24. Refer to the Did You Know? below.

   a) With a partner, show how to convert 69.375° to 69° 22′ 30″.

   b) Change the following angles into degrees-minutes-seconds.

   i) 40.875°   ii) 100.126°

   iii) 14.565°   iv) 80.385°

   Did You Know?

   You have expressed degree measures as decimal numbers, for example, 69.375°. Another way subdivides 1° into 60 parts called minutes. Each minute can be subdivided into 60 parts called seconds. Then, an angle such as 69.375° can be written as 69° 22 min 30 s or 69° 22′ 30″.

25. a) Reverse the process of question 24 and show how to convert 69° 22′ 30″ to 69.375°. Hint: Convert 30″ into a decimal fraction part of a minute. Combine this part of a minute with the 22′ and then convert the minutes to part of a degree.

b) Change each angle measure into degrees, rounded to the nearest thousandth.

   i) 45° 30′ 30″

   ii) 72° 15′ 45″

   iii) 105° 40′ 15″

   iv) 28° 10′

26. A segment of a circle is the region between a chord and the arc subtended by that chord. Consider chord AB subtended by central angle θ in a circle with radius r. Derive a formula using r and θ for the area of the segment subtended by θ.

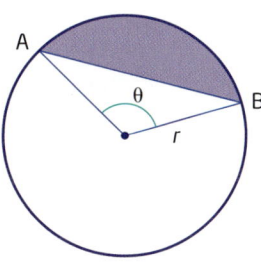

27. The hour hand of an analog clock moves in proportion to the movement of the minute hand. This means that at 4:05, the hour hand will have moved beyond the 4 by $\frac{5}{60}$ of the distance it would move in an hour.

a) What is the measure of the obtuse angle between the hands of a clock at 4:00? Give your answer in degrees.

b) What is the measure, in degrees, of the acute angle between the hands of a clock at 4:10?

c) At certain times, the hands of a clock are at right angles to each other. What are two of these times?

d) At how many different times does the angle between the hands of a clock measure 90° between 4:00 and 5:00?

e) Does one of the times occur before, at, or shortly after 4:05? Explain.

Create Connections

C1 Draw a diagram and use it to help explain whether 6 radians is greater than, equal to, or less than 360°.

C2 In mathematics, angle measures are commonly defined in degrees or radians. Describe the difference between 1° and 1 radian. Use drawings to support your answer.

C3 The following angles are in standard position. What is the measure of the reference angle for each? Write an expression for all coterminal angles associated with each given angle.

a) 860°

b) −7 (give the reference angle to the nearest hundredth)

C4 a) Make a circle diagram similar to the one shown. On the outside of the circle, label all multiples of 45° in the domain 0° ≤ θ < 360°. Show the radian equivalent as an exact value inside the circle.

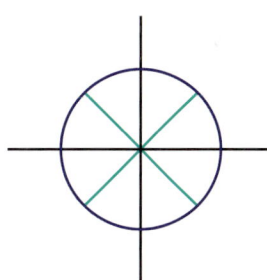

b) Make another circle diagram. This time, mark and label all the multiples of 30° in the domain 0° ≤ θ < 360°. Again, show the degree values outside the circle and the exact radian equivalents inside the circle.

C5 A line passes through the point (3, 0). Find the equation of the line if the angle formed between the line and the positive x-axis is

a) $\frac{\pi}{2}$ **b)** 45°

4.2

The Unit Circle

Focus on...

- developing and applying the equation of the unit circle
- generalizing the equation of a circle with centre (0, 0) and radius r
- using symmetry and patterns to locate the coordinates of points on the unit circle

A gauge is a measuring tool that is used in many different situations. There are two basic types of gauges—radial (circular) and linear. What gauges can you think of that are linear? What gauges are you familiar with that are circular? How are linear and circular gauges similar, and how do they differ?

Have you ever wondered why some phenomena, such as tides and hours of daylight, are so predictable? It is because they have repetitive or cyclical patterns. Why is sin 30° the same as sin 150°? Why is cos 60° = sin 150°? How do the coordinates of a point on a circle of radius 1 unit change every quarter-rotation?

Investigate Circular Number Lines

Materials
- paper
- scissors
- tape
- can or other cylinder
- straight edge
- compass

1. Select a can or other cylinder. Cut a strip of paper about 1.5 cm wide and the same length as the circumference of the cylinder.

2. Create a number line by drawing a line along the centre of the strip. Label the left end of the line 0 and the right end 2π. According to this labelling, how long is the number line?

3. Divide the number line into eight equal subdivisions. What value would you use to label the point midway between 0 and 2π? What value would you use to label halfway between 0 and the middle of the number line? Continue until all seven points that subdivide the number line are labelled. Write all values in terms of π. Express fractional values in lowest terms.

4. Tape the number line around the bottom of the can, so that the labels read in a counterclockwise direction.

5. Use the can to draw a circle on a sheet of paper. Locate the centre of the circle and label it O. Draw coordinate axes through O that extend beyond the circle. Place the can over the circle diagram so that the zero of the number line lies above where the circle intersects the positive x-axis.

6. Mark the coordinates of all points where the circle crosses the axes on your diagram. Label these points as P(θ) = (x, y), where P(θ) represents a point on the circle that has a central angle θ in standard position. For example, label the point where the circle crosses the positive y-axis as $P\left(\frac{\pi}{2}\right) = (0, 1)$.

7. Now, create a second number line. Label the ends as 0 and 2π. Divide this number line into 12 equal segments. Label divisions in terms of π. Express fractional values in lowest terms.

Reflect and Respond

8. Since each number line shows the circumference of the can and the circle to be 2π units, what assumption is being made about the length of the radius?

9. **a)** Two students indicate that the points in step 6 are simply multiples of $\frac{\pi}{2}$. Do you agree? Explain.
   b) In fact, they argue that the values on the original number line are all multiples of $\frac{\pi}{4}$. Is this true? Explain.

10. Show how to determine the coordinates for $P\left(\frac{\pi}{4}\right)$. Hint: Use your knowledge of the ratios of the side lengths of a 45°-45°-90° triangle. Mark the coordinates for all the points on the circle that are midway between the axes. What is the only difference in the coordinates for these four points? What negative values for θ would generate the same points on the circle midway between the axes?

Link the Ideas

Unit Circle

The circle you drew in the investigation is a **unit circle**.

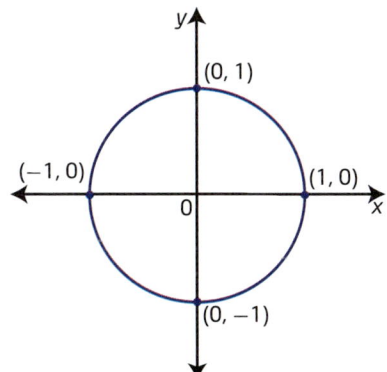

unit circle
- a circle with radius 1 unit
- a circle of radius 1 unit with centre at the origin on the Cartesian plane is known as *the* unit circle

You can find the equation of the unit circle using the Pythagorean theorem.

Consider a point P on the unit circle. Let P have coordinates (x, y).
Draw right triangle OPA as shown.

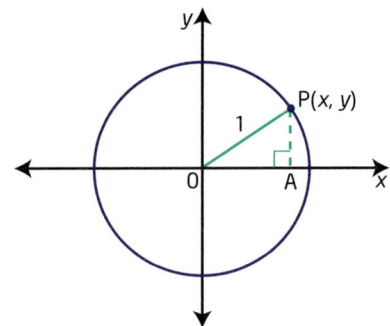

$OP = 1$ The radius of the unit circle is 1.

$PA = |y|$ The absolute value of the y-coordinate represents the distance from a point to the x-axis. Why is this true?

$OA = |x|$

$(OP)^2 = (OA)^2 + (PA)^2$ Pythagorean theorem

$1^2 = |x|^2 + |y|^2$ How would the equation for a circle with centre $O(0, 0)$ differ if the radius were r rather than 1?

$1 = x^2 + y^2$

The equation of the unit circle is $x^2 + y^2 = 1$.

Example 1

Equation of a Circle Centred at the Origin

Determine the equation of the circle with centre at the origin and radius 2.

Solution

Choose a point, P, on the circle with coordinates (x, y).

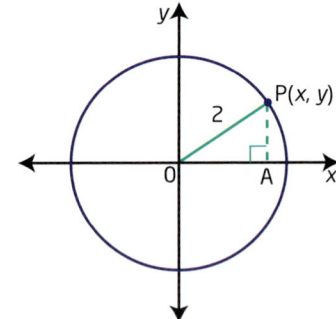

The radius of the circle is 2, and a vertical line from the y-coordinate to the x-axis forms a right angle with the axis. This means you can use the Pythagorean theorem.

$|x|^2 + |y|^2 = 2^2$
$x^2 + y^2 = 4$

Since this is true for every point P on the circle, the equation of the circle is $x^2 + y^2 = 4$.

Your Turn

Determine the equation of a circle with centre at the origin and radius 6.

Example 2

Determine Coordinates for Points of the Unit Circle

Determine the coordinates for all points on the unit circle that satisfy the conditions given. Draw a diagram in each case.

a) the x-coordinate is $\frac{2}{3}$

b) the y-coordinate is $-\frac{1}{\sqrt{2}}$ and the point is in quadrant III

Solution

a) Coordinates on the unit circle satisfy the equation $x^2 + y^2 = 1$.

$$\left(\frac{2}{3}\right)^2 + y^2 = 1 \quad \text{Since } x \text{ is positive, which quadrants could the points be in?}$$

$$\frac{4}{9} + y^2 = 1$$

$$y^2 = \frac{5}{9}$$

$$y = \pm\frac{\sqrt{5}}{3} \quad \text{Why are there two answers?}$$

Two points satisfy the given conditions: $\left(\frac{2}{3}, \frac{\sqrt{5}}{3}\right)$ in quadrant I and $\left(\frac{2}{3}, -\frac{\sqrt{5}}{3}\right)$ in quadrant IV.

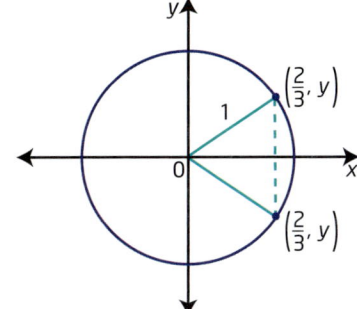

b) $y = -\frac{1}{\sqrt{2}}$

y is negative in quadrants III and IV. But the point is in quadrant III, so x is also negative.

$$x^2 + y^2 = 1$$

$$x^2 + \left(-\frac{1}{\sqrt{2}}\right)^2 = 1$$

$$x^2 + \frac{1}{2} = 1$$

$$x^2 = \frac{1}{2}$$

$$x = -\frac{1}{\sqrt{2}} \quad \text{Why is there only one answer?}$$

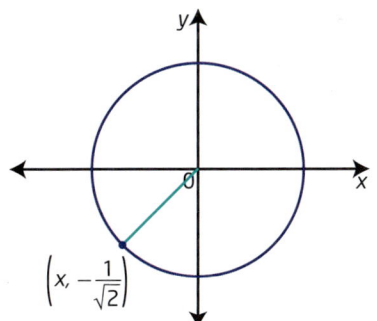

The point is $\left(-\frac{1}{\sqrt{2}}, -\frac{1}{\sqrt{2}}\right)$, or $\left(-\frac{\sqrt{2}}{2}, -\frac{\sqrt{2}}{2}\right)$.

Your Turn

Determine the missing coordinate(s) for all points on the unit circle satisfying the given conditions. Draw a diagram and tell which quadrant(s) the points lie in.

a) $\left(-\frac{5}{8}, y\right)$ **b)** $\left(x, \frac{5}{13}\right)$, where the point is in quadrant II

Relating Arc Length and Angle Measure in Radians

The formula $a = \theta r$, where a is the arc length; θ is the central angle, in radians; and r is the radius, applies to any circle, as long as a and r are measured in the same units. In the unit circle, the formula becomes $a = \theta(1)$ or $a = \theta$. This means that a central angle and its subtended arc on the unit circle have the same numerical value.

You can use the function $P(\theta) = (x, y)$ to link the arc length, θ, of a central angle in the unit circle to the coordinates, (x, y), of the point of intersection of the terminal arm and the unit circle.

If you join $P(\theta)$ to the origin, you create an angle θ in standard position. Now, θ radians is the central angle and the arc length is θ units.

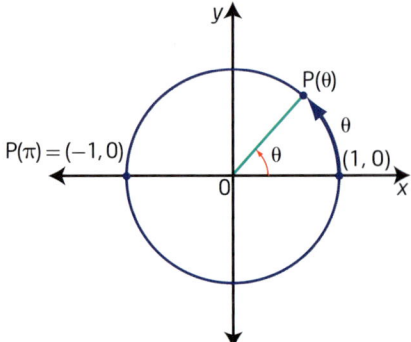

Function P takes real-number values for the central angle or the arc length on the unit circle and matches them with specific points. For example, if $\theta = \pi$, the point is $(-1, 0)$. Thus, you can write $P(\pi) = (-1, 0)$.

Example 3
Multiples of $\frac{\pi}{3}$ on the Unit Circle

a) On a diagram of the unit circle, show the integral multiples of $\frac{\pi}{3}$ in the interval $0 \leq \theta \leq 2\pi$.
b) What are the coordinates for each point $P(\theta)$ in part a)?
c) Identify any patterns you see in the coordinates of the points.

Solution

a) This is essentially a counting problem using $\frac{\pi}{3}$.

Multiples of $\frac{\pi}{3}$ in the interval $0 \leq \theta \leq 2\pi$ are

$0\left(\frac{\pi}{3}\right) = 0$, $1\left(\frac{\pi}{3}\right) = \frac{\pi}{3}$, $2\left(\frac{\pi}{3}\right) = \frac{2\pi}{3}$, $3\left(\frac{\pi}{3}\right) = \pi$, $4\left(\frac{\pi}{3}\right) = \frac{4\pi}{3}$, $5\left(\frac{\pi}{3}\right) = \frac{5\pi}{3}$, and $6\left(\frac{\pi}{3}\right) = 2\pi$.

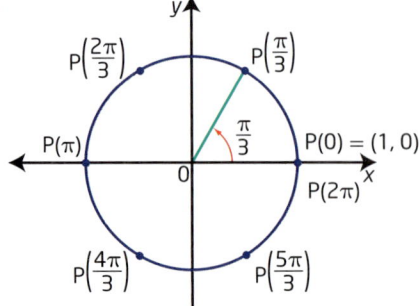

Why must you show only the multiples in one positive rotation in the unit circle?

b) Recall that a 30°-60°-90° triangle has sides in the ratio $1:\sqrt{3}:2$ or $\frac{1}{2}:\frac{\sqrt{3}}{2}:1$.

Place △POA in the unit circle as shown.

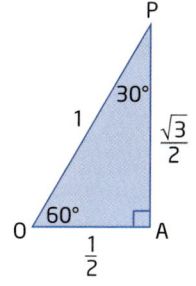

Why is the 30°-60°-90° triangle used?

Why are $\left(\frac{1}{2}, \frac{\sqrt{3}}{2}\right)$ the coordinates of $P\left(\frac{\pi}{3}\right)$?

△POA could be placed in the second quadrant with O at the origin and OA along the x-axis as shown. This gives $P\left(\frac{2\pi}{3}\right) = \left(-\frac{1}{2}, \frac{\sqrt{3}}{2}\right)$.

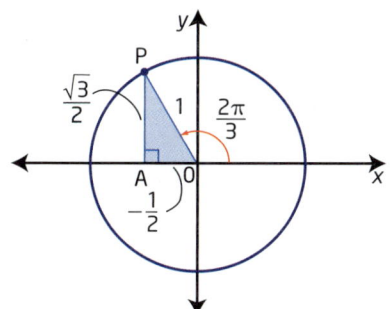

Why is the x-coordinate negative?

What transformation could be used to move △POA from quadrant I to quadrant II?

Continue, placing △POA in quadrants III and IV to find the coordinates of $P\left(\frac{4\pi}{3}\right)$ and $P\left(\frac{5\pi}{3}\right)$. Then, the coordinates of point P corresponding to angles that are multiples of $\frac{\pi}{3}$ are

$P(0) = P(2\pi) = (1, 0)$ $P(\pi) = (-1, 0)$ $P\left(\frac{\pi}{3}\right) = \left(\frac{1}{2}, \frac{\sqrt{3}}{2}\right)$

$P\left(\frac{2\pi}{3}\right) = \left(-\frac{1}{2}, \frac{\sqrt{3}}{2}\right)$ $P\left(\frac{4\pi}{3}\right) = \left(-\frac{1}{2}, -\frac{\sqrt{3}}{2}\right)$ $P\left(\frac{5\pi}{3}\right) = \left(\frac{1}{2}, -\frac{\sqrt{3}}{2}\right)$

c) Some patterns are:
- The points corresponding to angles that are multiples of $\frac{\pi}{3}$ that cannot be simplified, for example, $P\left(\frac{\pi}{3}\right)$, $P\left(\frac{2\pi}{3}\right)$, $P\left(\frac{4\pi}{3}\right)$, and $P\left(\frac{5\pi}{3}\right)$, have the same coordinates except for their signs.
- Any points where θ reduces to a multiple of π, for example, P(0), $P\left(\frac{3\pi}{3}\right) = P(\pi)$, and $P\left(\frac{6\pi}{3}\right) = P(2\pi)$, fall on an axis.

Your Turn

a) On a diagram of the unit circle, show all the integral multiples of $\frac{\pi}{6}$ in the interval $0 \leq \theta < 2\pi$.

b) Label the coordinates for each point P(θ) on your diagram.

c) Describe any patterns you see in the coordinates of the points.

Key Ideas

- The equation for the unit circle is $x^2 + y^2 = 1$. It can be used to determine whether a point is on the unit circle or to determine the value of one coordinate given the other. The equation for a circle with centre at (0, 0) and radius r is $x^2 + y^2 = r^2$.
- On the unit circle, the measure in radians of the central angle and the arc subtended by that central angle are numerically equivalent.
- Some of the points on the unit circle correspond to exact values of the special angles learned previously.
- You can use patterns to determine coordinates of points. For example, the numerical value of the coordinates of points on the unit circle change to their opposite sign every $\frac{1}{2}$ rotation.

  If $P(\theta) = (a, b)$ is in quadrant I, then both a and b are positive. $P(\theta + \pi)$ is in quadrant III. Its coordinates are $(-a, -b)$, where $a > 0$ and $b > 0$.

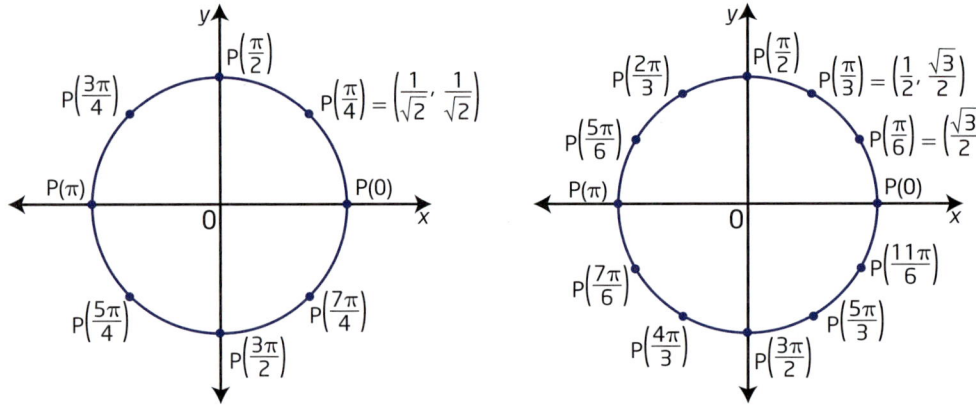

Check Your Understanding

Practise

1. Determine the equation of a circle with centre at the origin and radius
   a) 4 units
   b) 3 units
   c) 12 units
   d) 2.6 units

2. Is each point on the unit circle? How do you know?
   a) $\left(-\frac{3}{4}, \frac{1}{4}\right)$
   b) $\left(\frac{\sqrt{5}}{8}, \frac{7}{8}\right)$
   c) $\left(-\frac{5}{13}, \frac{12}{13}\right)$
   d) $\left(\frac{4}{5}, -\frac{3}{5}\right)$
   e) $\left(-\frac{\sqrt{3}}{2}, -\frac{1}{2}\right)$
   f) $\left(\frac{\sqrt{7}}{4}, \frac{3}{4}\right)$

3. Determine the missing coordinate(s) for all points on the unit circle satisfying the given conditions. Draw a diagram to support your answer.

   a) $\left(\frac{1}{4}, y\right)$ in quadrant I
   b) $\left(x, \frac{2}{3}\right)$ in quadrant II
   c) $\left(-\frac{7}{8}, y\right)$ in quadrant III
   d) $\left(x, -\frac{5}{7}\right)$ in quadrant IV
   e) $\left(x, \frac{1}{3}\right)$, where $x < 0$
   f) $\left(\frac{12}{13}, y\right)$, not in quadrant I

4. If $P(\theta)$ is the point at the intersection of the terminal arm of angle θ and the unit circle, determine the exact coordinates of each of the following.

   a) $P(\pi)$
   b) $P\left(-\frac{\pi}{2}\right)$
   c) $P\left(\frac{\pi}{3}\right)$
   d) $P\left(-\frac{\pi}{6}\right)$
   e) $P\left(\frac{3\pi}{4}\right)$
   f) $P\left(-\frac{7\pi}{4}\right)$
   g) $P(4\pi)$
   h) $P\left(\frac{5\pi}{2}\right)$
   i) $P\left(\frac{5\pi}{6}\right)$
   j) $P\left(-\frac{4\pi}{3}\right)$

5. Identify a measure for the central angle θ in the interval $0 \leq \theta < 2\pi$ such that $P(\theta)$ is the given point.

   a) $(0, -1)$
   b) $(1, 0)$
   c) $\left(\frac{\sqrt{2}}{2}, \frac{\sqrt{2}}{2}\right)$
   d) $\left(-\frac{1}{\sqrt{2}}, \frac{1}{\sqrt{2}}\right)$
   e) $\left(\frac{1}{2}, \frac{\sqrt{3}}{2}\right)$
   f) $\left(\frac{1}{2}, -\frac{\sqrt{3}}{2}\right)$
   g) $\left(-\frac{\sqrt{3}}{2}, \frac{1}{2}\right)$
   h) $\left(-\frac{\sqrt{3}}{2}, -\frac{1}{2}\right)$
   i) $\left(-\frac{\sqrt{2}}{2}, -\frac{\sqrt{2}}{2}\right)$
   j) $(-1, 0)$

6. Determine one positive and one negative measure for θ if $P(\theta) = \left(-\frac{\sqrt{3}}{2}, \frac{1}{2}\right)$.

Apply

7. Draw a diagram of the unit circle.

   a) Mark two points, $P(\theta)$ and $P(\theta + \pi)$, on your diagram. Use measurements to show that these points have the same coordinates except for their signs.
   b) Choose a different quadrant for the original point, $P(\theta)$. Mark it and $P(\theta + \pi)$ on your diagram. Is the result from part a) still true?

8. **MINI LAB** Determine the pattern in the coordinates of points that are $\frac{1}{4}$ rotation apart on the unit circle.

   Step 1 Start with the points $P(0) = (1, 0)$, $P\left(\frac{\pi}{3}\right) = \left(\frac{1}{2}, \frac{\sqrt{3}}{2}\right)$, and $P\left(\frac{5\pi}{3}\right) = \left(\frac{1}{2}, -\frac{\sqrt{3}}{2}\right)$.
   Show these points on a diagram.

   Step 2 Move $+\frac{1}{4}$ rotation from each point. Determine each new point and its coordinates. Show these points on your diagram from step 1.

   Step 3 Move $-\frac{1}{4}$ rotation from each original point. Determine each new point and its coordinates. Mark these points on your diagram.

   Step 4 How do the values of the x-coordinates and y-coordinates of points change with each quarter-rotation? Make a copy of the diagram and complete the coordinates to summarize your findings.

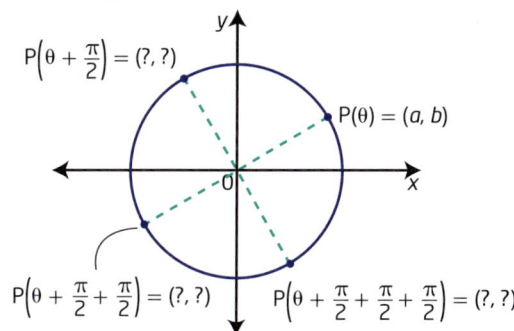

4.2 The Unit Circle • MHR **187**

9. Use the diagram below to help answer these questions.

   a) What is the equation of this circle?

   b) If the coordinates of C are $\left(-\dfrac{2}{3}, \dfrac{\sqrt{5}}{3}\right)$, what are the coordinates of B?

   c) If the measure of $\overset{\frown}{AB}$ is θ, what is an expression for the measure of $\overset{\frown}{AC}$?

   Note: $\overset{\frown}{AB}$ means the arc length from A to B.

   d) Let P(θ) = B. In which quadrant is $P\left(\theta - \dfrac{\pi}{2}\right)$?

   e) What are the maximum and minimum values for either the x-coordinates or y-coordinates of points on the unit circle?

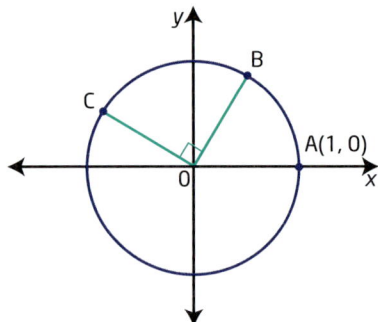

10. Mya claims that every value of x between 0 and 1 can be used to find the coordinates of a point on the unit circle in quadrant I.

    a) Do you agree with Mya? Explain.

    b) Mya showed the following work to find the y-coordinate when x = 0.807.

    $y = 1 - (0.807)^2$
    $= 0.348\ 751$

    The point on the unit circle is (0.807, 0.348 751).

    How can you check Mya's answer? Is she correct? If not, what is the correct answer?

    c) If y = 0.2571, determine x so the point is on the unit circle and in the first quadrant.

11. Wesley enjoys tricks and puzzles. One of his favourite tricks involves remembering the coordinates for $P\left(\dfrac{\pi}{3}\right)$, $P\left(\dfrac{\pi}{4}\right)$, and $P\left(\dfrac{\pi}{6}\right)$. He will not tell you his trick. However, you can discover it for yourself.

    a) Examine the coordinates shown on the diagram.

    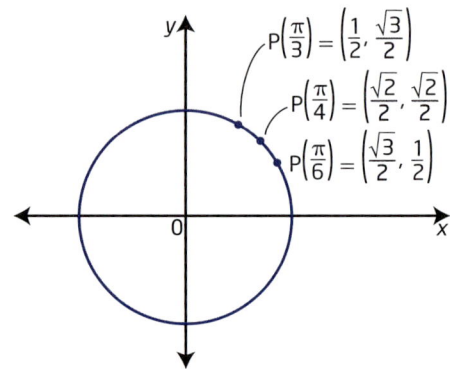

    b) What do you notice about the denominators?

    c) What do you notice about the numerators of the x-coordinates? Compare them with the numerators of the y-coordinates. Why do these patterns make sense?

    d) Why are square roots involved?

    e) Explain this memory trick to a partner.

12. a) Explain, with reference to the unit circle, what the interval $-2\pi \leq \theta < 4\pi$ represents.

    b) Use your explanation to determine all values for θ in the interval $-2\pi \leq \theta < 4\pi$ such that $P(\theta) = \left(-\dfrac{1}{2}, \dfrac{\sqrt{3}}{2}\right)$.

    c) How do your answers relate to the word "coterminal"?

13. If $P(\theta) = \left(-\dfrac{1}{3}, -\dfrac{2\sqrt{2}}{3}\right)$, determine the following.

    a) What does P(θ) represent? Explain using a diagram.

    b) In which quadrant does θ terminate?

    c) Determine the coordinates of $P\left(\theta + \dfrac{\pi}{2}\right)$.

    d) Determine the coordinates of $P\left(\theta - \dfrac{\pi}{2}\right)$.

14. In ancient times, determining the perimeter and area of a circle were considered major mathematical challenges. One of Archimedes' greatest contributions to mathematics was his method for approximating π. Now, it is your turn to be a mathematician. Using a unit circle diagram, show the difference between π units and π square units.

> **Did You Know?**
>
> Archimedes was a Greek mathematician, physicist, inventor, and astronomer who lived from 287 BCE– 212 BCE. He died in the Roman siege of Syracuse. He is considered one of the greatest mathematicians of all time. He correctly determined the value of π as being between $\frac{22}{7}$ and $\frac{223}{71}$ and proved the area of a circle to be πr^2, where r is the radius.

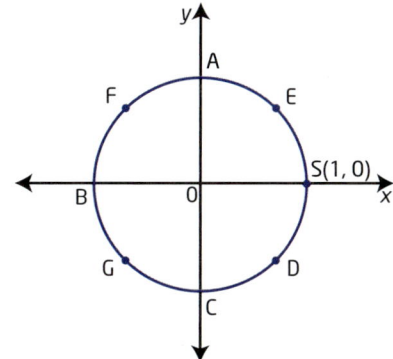

15. a) In the diagram, A has coordinates (a, b). ABCD is a rectangle with sides parallel to the axes. What are the coordinates of B, C, and D?

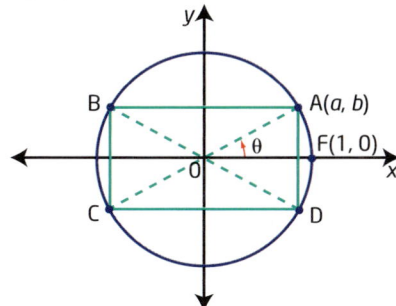

b) ∠FOA = θ, and A, B, C, and D lie on the unit circle. Through which point will the terminal arm pass for each angle? Assume all angles are in standard position.

   i) θ + π   **ii)** θ − π
   iii) −θ + π   **iv)** −θ − π

c) How are the answers in part b) different if θ is given as the measure of arc FA?

16. Use the unit circle diagram to answer the following questions. Points E, F, G, and D are midway between the axes.

a) What angle of rotation creates arc SG? What is the arc length of SG?

b) Which letter on the diagram corresponds to $P\left(\frac{13\pi}{2}\right)$? Explain your answer fully so someone not taking this course would understand. Use a diagram and a written explanation.

c) Between which two points would you find P(5)? Explain.

Extend

17. a) Determine the coordinates of all points where the line represented by $y = -3x$ intersects the unit circle. Give your answers as exact values in simplest form.

b) If one of the points is labelled P(θ + π), draw a diagram and show at least two values for θ. Explain what θ represents.

18. a) P(θ) lies at the intersection of the unit circle and the line joining A(5, 2) to the origin. Use your knowledge of similar triangles and the unit circle to determine the exact coordinates of P(θ).

b) Determine the radius of a larger circle with centre at the origin and passing through point A.

c) Write the equation for this larger circle.

19. In previous grades, you used sine and cosine as trigonometric ratios of sides of right triangles. Show how that use of trigonometry relates to the unit circle. Specifically, show that the coordinates of P(θ) can be represented by (cos θ, sin θ) for any θ in the unit circle.

20. You can locate a point in a plane using Cartesian coordinates (x, y), where $|x|$ is the distance from the y-axis and $|y|$ is the distance from the x-axis. You can also locate a point in a plane using $(r, θ)$, where r, $r \geq 0$, is the distance from the origin and θ is the angle of rotation from the positive x-axis. These are known as polar coordinates. Determine the polar coordinates for each point.

a) $\left(\frac{\sqrt{2}}{2}, \frac{\sqrt{2}}{2}\right)$ **b)** $\left(-\frac{\sqrt{3}}{2}, -\frac{1}{3}\right)$

c) $(2, 2)$ **d)** $(4, -3)$

Create Connections

C1 The diagram represents the unit circle with some positive arc lengths shown.

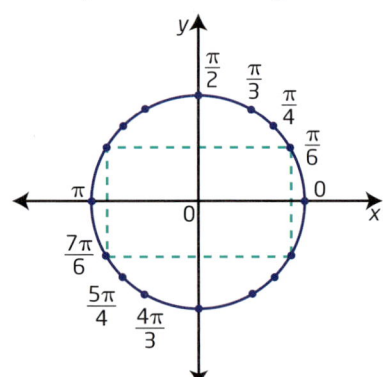

a) Draw a similar diagram in your notebook. Complete the labelling for positive measures.

b) Write the corresponding negative value beside each positive value. Complete this process over the interval $-2π \leq θ < 0$.

c) Give the exact coordinates for the vertices of the dashed rectangle.

d) Identify several patterns from your unit circle diagrams. Patterns can relate to arc lengths, coordinates of points, and symmetry.

C2 Consider the isosceles △AOB drawn in the unit circle.

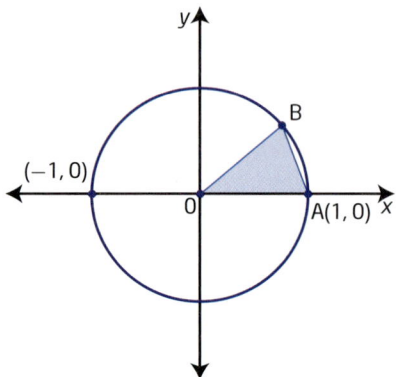

a) If the measure of one of the equal angles is twice the measure of the third angle, determine the exact measure of arc AB.

b) Draw a new △COA in which $P(C) = P\left(B + \frac{π}{2}\right)$. What is the exact measure of ∠CAO, in radians?

C3 a) Draw a diagram of a circle with centre at the origin and radius r units. What is the equation of this circle?

b) Show that the equation of any circle with centre (h, k) and radius r can be expressed as $(x - h)^2 + (y - k)^2 = r^2$. Hint: Use transformations to help with your explanation.

C4 The largest possible unit circle is cut from a square piece of paper as shown.

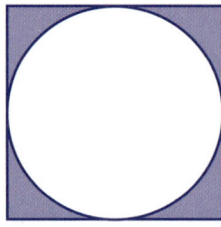

a) What percent of the paper is cut off? Give your answer to one decimal place.

b) What is the ratio of the circumference of the circle to the perimeter of the original piece of paper?

4.3

Trigonometric Ratios

Focus on...

- relating the trigonometric ratios to the coordinates of points on the unit circle
- determining exact and approximate values for trigonometric ratios
- identifying the measures of angles that generate specific trigonometric values
- solving problems using trigonometric ratios

What do a software designer, a civil engineer, an airline pilot, and a long-distance swimmer's support team have in common? All of them use angles and trigonometric ratios to help solve problems. The software designer uses trigonometry to present a 3-D world on a 2-D screen. The engineer uses trigonometric ratios in designs of on-ramps and off-ramps at highway interchanges. A pilot uses an approach angle that is determined based on the tangent ratio. The support team for a long-distance swimmer uses trigonometry to compensate for the effect of wind and currents and to guide the swimmer's direction.

Investigate Trigonometric Ratios and the Unit Circle

1. Draw a unit circle as shown, with a positive angle θ in standard position. Work with a partner to describe the location of points P and Q. Be specific.

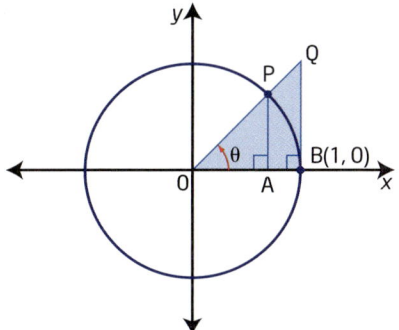

Materials
- grid paper
- straight edge
- compass

2. From your drawing, identify a single line segment whose length is equivalent to sin θ. Hint: Use the ratio definition of sin θ and the unit circle to help you.

3. Identify a line segment whose length is equivalent to cos θ and a line segment whose length is equivalent to tan θ in your diagram.

4. From your answers in steps 2 and 3, what could you use to represent the coordinates of point P?

Reflect and Respond

5. Present an argument or proof that the line segment you selected in step 3 for cos θ is correct.

6. What equation relates the coordinates of point P? Does this apply to any point P that lies at the intersection of the terminal arm for an angle θ and the unit circle? Why?

7. What are the maximum and minimum values for cos θ and sin θ? Express your answer in words and using an inequality. Confirm your answer using a calculator.

8. The value of tan θ changes from 0 to undefined for positive values of θ less than or equal to 90°. Explain how this change occurs with reference to angle θ in quadrant I of the unit circle. What happens on a calculator when tan θ is undefined?

Link the Ideas

Coordinates in Terms of Primary Trigonometric Ratios

If $P(\theta) = (x, y)$ is the point on the terminal arm of angle θ that intersects the unit circle, notice that

- $\cos \theta = \dfrac{x}{1} = x$, which
  is the first coordinate of $P(\theta)$
- $\sin \theta = \dfrac{y}{1} = y$, which
  is the second coordinate of $P(\theta)$

How do these ratios connect to the right-triangle definition for cosine and sine?

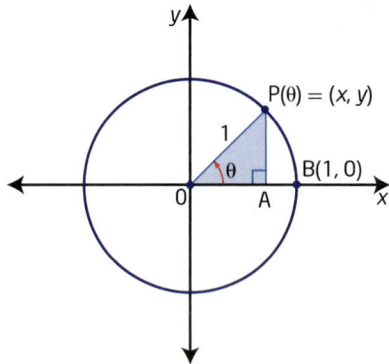

You can describe the coordinates of any point $P(\theta)$ as (cos θ, sin θ). This is true for any point $P(\theta)$ at the intersection of the terminal arm of an angle θ and the unit circle.

Also, you know that $\tan \theta = \dfrac{y}{x}$.

Explain how this statement is consistent with the right-triangle definition of the tangent ratio.

Reciprocal Trigonometric Ratios

Three other trigonometric ratios are defined: they are the reciprocals of sine, cosine, and tangent. These are **cosecant**, **secant**, and **cotangent**.

By definition, $\csc \theta = \dfrac{1}{\sin \theta}$, $\sec \theta = \dfrac{1}{\cos \theta}$, and $\cot \theta = \dfrac{1}{\tan \theta}$.

Example 1
Determine the Trigonometric Ratios for Angles in the Unit Circle

The point $A\left(-\dfrac{3}{5}, -\dfrac{4}{5}\right)$ lies at the intersection of the unit circle and the terminal arm of an angle θ in standard position.

a) Draw a diagram to model the situation.
b) Determine the values of the six trigonometric ratios for θ. Express answers in lowest terms.

Solution

a)

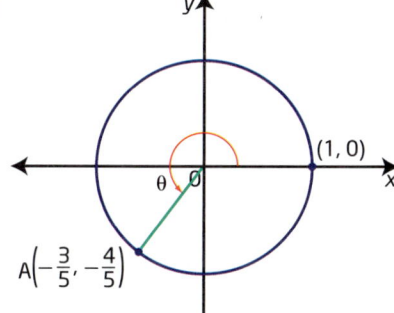

b) $\sin \theta = -\dfrac{4}{5}$ The y-coordinate of $P(\theta)$ is defined as $\sin \theta$.

$\cos \theta = -\dfrac{3}{5}$ Why is this true?

$\tan \theta = \dfrac{y}{x}$

$= \dfrac{-\dfrac{4}{5}}{-\dfrac{3}{5}}$ Explain the arithmetic used to simplify this double fraction.

$= \dfrac{4}{3}$ Why does it make sense for $\tan \theta$ to be positive?

$\csc \theta = \dfrac{1}{\sin \theta}$

$= -\dfrac{5}{4}$ Explain how this answer was determined.

$\sec \theta = \dfrac{1}{\cos \theta}$ Read as "sec θ equals the reciprocal of cos θ."

$= -\dfrac{5}{3}$

$\cot \theta = \dfrac{1}{\tan \theta}$

$= \dfrac{3}{4}$

---

cosecant ratio
- the reciprocal of the sine ratio
- abbreviated csc
- for $P(\theta) = (x, y)$ on the unit circle, $\csc \theta = \dfrac{1}{y}$
- if $\sin \theta = -\dfrac{\sqrt{3}}{2}$, then $\csc \theta = -\dfrac{2}{\sqrt{3}}$ or $-\dfrac{2\sqrt{3}}{3}$

secant ratio
- the reciprocal of the cosine ratio
- abbreviated sec
- for $P(\theta) = (x, y)$ on the unit circle, $\sec \theta = \dfrac{1}{x}$
- if $\cos \theta = \dfrac{1}{2}$, then $\sec \theta = \dfrac{2}{1}$ or 2

cotangent ratio
- the reciprocal of the tangent ratio
- abbreviated cot
- for $P(\theta) = (x, y)$ on the unit circle, $\cot \theta = \dfrac{x}{y}$
- if $\tan \theta = 0$, then $\cot \theta$ is undefined

Your Turn

The point $B\left(-\frac{1}{3}, \frac{2\sqrt{2}}{3}\right)$ lies at the intersection of the unit circle and the terminal arm of an angle θ in standard position.
a) Draw a diagram to model the situation.
b) Determine the values of the six trigonometric ratios for θ. Express your answers in lowest terms.

Exact Values of Trigonometric Ratios

Exact values for the trigonometric ratios can be determined using special triangles (30°-60°-90° or 45°-45°-90°) and multiples of $\theta = 0, \frac{\pi}{6}, \frac{\pi}{4}, \frac{\pi}{3},$ and $\frac{\pi}{2}$ or θ = 0°, 30°, 45°, 60°, and 90° for points P(θ) on the unit circle.

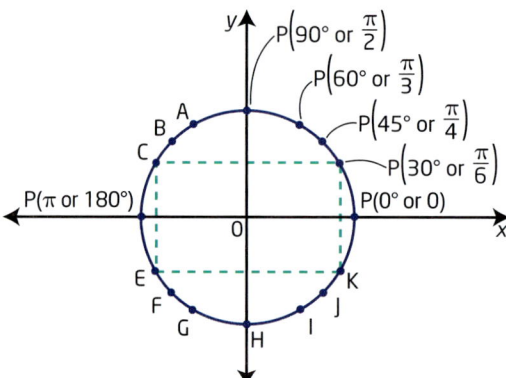

How are P(30°), C, E, and K related?

What points have the same coordinates as $P\left(\frac{\pi}{3}\right)$ except for their signs?

For P(45°), what are the coordinates and in which quadrant is θ?

Which special triangle would you use and where would it be placed for θ = 135°?

Example 2
Exact Values for Trigonometric Ratios

Determine the exact value for each. Draw diagrams to illustrate your answers.

a) $\cos \frac{5\pi}{6}$

b) $\sin \left(-\frac{4\pi}{3}\right)$

c) sec 315°

d) cot 270°

Solution

a) The point $P\left(\frac{5\pi}{6}\right)$ lies in quadrant II.

The reference angle for $\frac{5\pi}{6}$ is
$\theta_R = \pi - \frac{5\pi}{6} = \frac{\pi}{6}$.

Its x-coordinate is negative and its y-coordinate is positive.

$P(\theta) = \left(-\frac{\sqrt{3}}{2}, \frac{1}{2}\right)$

$\cos \frac{5\pi}{6} = -\frac{\sqrt{3}}{2}$ $P\left(\frac{5\pi}{6}\right)$ has the same coordinates as $P\left(\frac{\pi}{6}\right)$, except the x-coordinates have different signs.

Recall that the reference angle, θ_R, is the acute angle formed between the terminal arm and the x-axis.

b) $-\dfrac{4\pi}{3}$ is a clockwise rotation from the positive x-axis.

$P\left(-\dfrac{4\pi}{3}\right)$ lies in quadrant II.

The reference angle for $-\dfrac{4\pi}{3}$ is $\theta_R = \pi - \dfrac{2\pi}{3} = \dfrac{\pi}{3}$.

$$P(\theta) = \left(-\dfrac{1}{2}, \dfrac{\sqrt{3}}{2}\right)$$

$$\sin\left(-\dfrac{4\pi}{3}\right) = \dfrac{\sqrt{3}}{2}$$

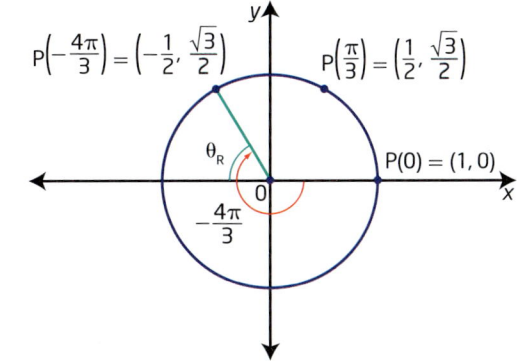

What is a positive coterminal angle for $-\dfrac{4\pi}{3}$?

c) An angle of 315° is a counterclockwise rotation that terminates in quadrant IV.

The reference angle for 315° is $\theta_R = 360° - 315° = 45°$.

$$P(\theta) = \left(\dfrac{1}{\sqrt{2}}, -\dfrac{1}{\sqrt{2}}\right)$$

$$\sec 315° = \dfrac{1}{\cos 315°}$$
$$= \dfrac{\sqrt{2}}{1} \text{ or } \sqrt{2}$$

Explain how to get the coordinates for $P(\theta)$.

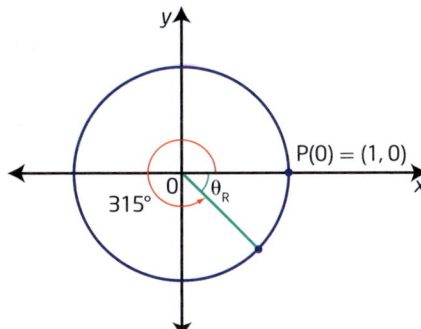

d) An angle of 270° terminates on the negative y-axis.
$P(270°) = (0, -1)$

Since $\tan \theta = \dfrac{y}{x}$, $\cot \theta = \dfrac{x}{y}$.

Therefore,
$$\cot 270° = \dfrac{0}{-1}$$
$$= 0$$

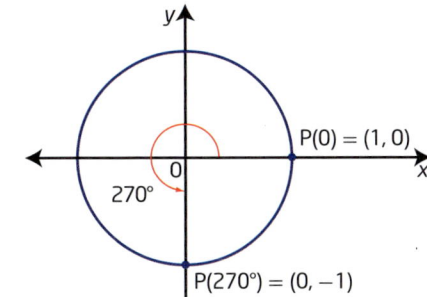

Your Turn

Draw diagrams to help you determine the exact value of each trigonometric ratio.

a) $\tan \dfrac{\pi}{2}$

b) $\csc \dfrac{7\pi}{6}$

c) $\sin(-300°)$

d) $\sec 60°$

Approximate Values of Trigonometric Ratios

You can determine approximate values for sine, cosine, and tangent using a scientific or graphing calculator. Most calculators can determine trigonometric values for angles measured in degrees or radians. You will need to set the mode to the correct angle measure. Check using

$\cos 60° = 0.5$ (degree mode)
$\cos 60 = -0.952\,412\,980...$ (radian mode)

In which quadrant does an angle of 60 terminate?

Most calculators can compute trigonometric ratios for negative angles. However, you should use your knowledge of reference angles and the signs of trigonometric ratios for the quadrant to check that your calculator display is reasonable.

$\cos(-200°) = -0.939\,692\,620...$

Is the negative value appropriate? What is the reference angle for $-200°$? What other trigonometric ratio could you compute as a check?

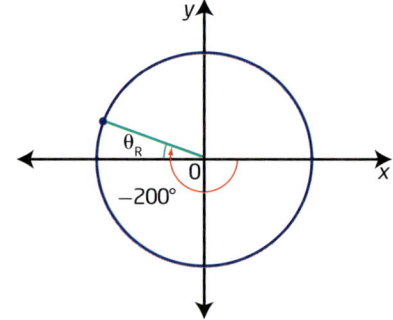

You can find the value of a trigonometric ratio for cosecant, secant, or cotangent using the correct reciprocal relationship.

$\sec 3.3 = \dfrac{1}{\cos 3.3}$
$ = -1.012\,678\,973...$
$ \approx -1.0127$

Example 3

Approximate Values for Trigonometric Ratios

Determine the approximate value for each trigonometric ratio. Give your answers to four decimal places.

a) $\tan \dfrac{7\pi}{5}$
b) $\cos 260°$
c) $\sin 4.2$
d) $\csc(-70°)$

Solution

a) $\dfrac{7\pi}{5}$ is measured in radians.

$\tan \dfrac{7\pi}{5} = 3.077\,683\,537...$
$\phantom{\tan \dfrac{7\pi}{5}} \approx 3.0777$

In which quadrant does an angle of $\dfrac{7\pi}{5}$ terminate?
Make sure your calculator is in radian mode. Why is the answer positive?

b) $\cos 260° = -0.173\,648\,177...$
$ \approx -0.1736$

In which quadrant does $260°$ terminate?

c) sin 4.2 = −0.871 575 772…
       ≈ −0.8716

Which angle mode do you need here?
Why is the answer negative?

d) An angle of −70° terminates in quadrant IV.
The *y*-coordinate for points in quadrant IV is negative.

$$\csc(-70°) = \frac{1}{\sin(-70°)}$$
$$= -1.064\ 177\ 772\ldots$$
$$\approx -1.0642$$

What steps are needed to evaluate $\frac{1}{\sin(-70°)}$ on your calculator?

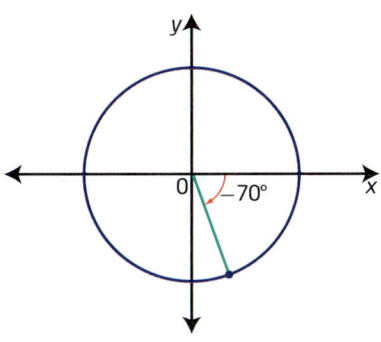

Your Turn

What is the approximate value for each trigonometric ratio? Round answers to four decimal places. Justify the sign of each answer.

a) sin 1.92
b) tan (−500°)
c) sec 85.4°
d) cot 3

Approximate Values of Angles

How can you find the measure of an angle when the value of the trigonometric ratio is given? To reverse the process (for example, to determine θ if you know sin θ), use the inverse trigonometric function keys on a calculator.

sin 30° = 0.5 ⟹ sin⁻¹ 0.5 = 30°

Note that sin⁻¹ is an abbreviation for "the inverse of sine." Do not confuse this with (sin 30°)⁻¹, which means $\frac{1}{\sin 30°}$, or the reciprocal of sin 30°.

The calculator keys sin⁻¹, cos⁻¹, and tan⁻¹ return one answer only, when there are often two angles with the same trigonometric function value in any full rotation. In general, it is best to use the reference angle applied to the appropriate quadrants containing the terminal arm of the angle.

Example 4

Find Angles Given Their Trigonometric Ratios

Determine the measures of all angles that satisfy the following. Use diagrams in your explanation.

a) $\sin \theta = 0.879$ in the domain $0 \leq \theta < 2\pi$. Give answers to the nearest tenth of a radian.

b) $\cos \theta = -0.366$ in the domain $0° \leq \theta < 360°$. Give answers to the nearest tenth of a degree.

c) $\tan \theta = \sqrt{3}$ in the domain $-180° \leq \theta < 180°$. Give exact answers.

d) $\sec \theta = \dfrac{2}{\sqrt{3}}$ in the domain $-2\pi \leq \theta < 2\pi$. Give exact answers.

Solution

Did You Know?

By convention, if the domain is given in radian measure, express answers in radians. If the domain is expressed using degrees, give the answers in degrees.

a) $\sin \theta > 0$ in quadrants I and II.
The domain consists of one positive rotation.
Therefore, two answers need to be identified.

$\sin^{-1} 0.879 = 1.073\,760\,909\ldots$ Use a calculator in radian mode.
≈ 1.1

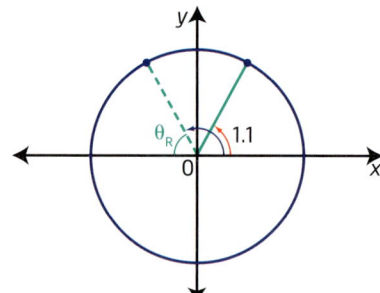

In quadrant I, $\theta \approx 1.1$, to the nearest tenth. This is the reference angle.
In quadrant II, $\theta \approx \pi - 1.1$ or 2.0, to the nearest tenth.
The answers, to the nearest tenth of a radian, are 1.1 and 2.0.

b) $\cos \theta < 0$ in quadrants II and III.

Why will the answer be measured in degrees?

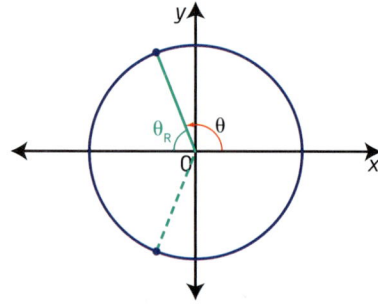

$\cos^{-1}(-0.366) \approx 111.5°$, to the nearest tenth.
This answer is in quadrant II.
The reference angle for other answers is $68.5°$.
In quadrant III, $\theta \approx 180° + 68.5°$ or $248.5°$.

Did you check that your calculator is in degree mode?

How do you determine this reference angle from 111.5°?

The answers, to the nearest tenth of a degree, are $111.5°$ and $248.5°$.

c) tan θ > 0 in quadrants I and III.

The domain includes both quadrants. In the positive direction an answer will be in quadrant I, and in the negative direction an answer will be in quadrant III.

To answer with exact values, work with the special coordinates on a unit circle.

tan 60° = √3

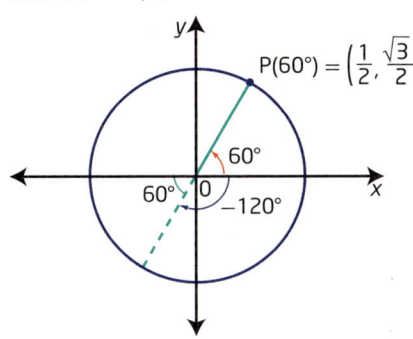

How do you know that tan 60° = √3? Could you use a calculator here?

In quadrant I, from the domain 0° ≤ θ < 180°, θ = 60°. This is the reference angle. In quadrant III, from the domain −180° ≤ θ < 0°, θ = −180° + 60° or −120°.

The exact answers are 60° and −120°.

d) sec θ > 0 in quadrants I and IV since sec θ = $\frac{1}{\cos \theta}$ and cos θ > 0 in quadrants I and IV.

The domain includes four quadrants in both the positive and negative directions. Thus, there are two positive answers and two negative answers.

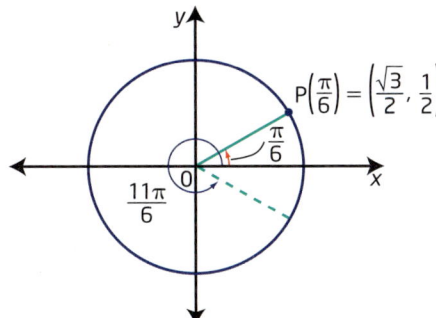

$\cos \theta = \frac{1}{\sec \theta} = \frac{\sqrt{3}}{2}$

$\cos \frac{\pi}{6} = \frac{\sqrt{3}}{2}$

θ = $\frac{\pi}{6}$ and θ = $\frac{11\pi}{6}$ in the domain 0 ≤ θ < 2π.

θ = $-\frac{\pi}{6}$ and θ = $-\frac{11\pi}{6}$ in the domain −2π ≤ θ < 0.

How do coterminal angles help?

The exact answers in radians are $\frac{\pi}{6}$, $\frac{11\pi}{6}$, $-\frac{\pi}{6}$, and $-\frac{11\pi}{6}$.

Your Turn

Determine the measures of all angles that satisfy each of the following. Use diagrams to show the possible answers.

a) $\cos \theta = 0.843$ in the domain $-360° < \theta < 180°$. Give approximate answers to the nearest tenth.

b) $\sin \theta = 0$ in the domain $0° \leq \theta \leq 180°$. Give exact answers.

c) $\cot \theta = -2.777$ in the domain $-\pi \leq \theta \leq \pi$. Give approximate answers to the nearest tenth.

d) $\csc \theta = -\dfrac{2}{\sqrt{2}}$ in the domain $-2\pi \leq \theta \leq \pi$. Give exact answers.

Example 5

Calculating Trigonometric Values for Points Not on the Unit Circle

The point A(−4, 3) lies on the terminal arm of an angle θ in standard position. What is the exact value of each trigonometric ratio for θ?

Solution

△ABO is a right triangle.

Identify trigonometric values for θ using the lengths of the sides of △ABO.

△ABO has sides of lengths 3, 4, and 5.

Recall that OA is a length and the segments OB and BA are considered as directed lengths.

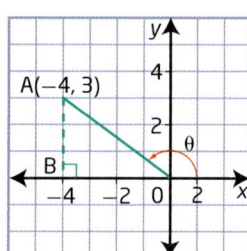

Confirm this using the Pythagorean theorem.

$\sin \theta = \dfrac{y}{r}$ $\qquad$ $\csc \theta = \dfrac{1}{\sin \theta}$

$\quad\;\; = \dfrac{3}{5}$ $\qquad\qquad\;\; = \dfrac{5}{3}$

$\cos \theta = \dfrac{x}{r}$ $\qquad$ $\sec \theta = \dfrac{1}{\cos \theta}$

$\quad\;\; = \dfrac{-4}{5}$ $\qquad\qquad\;\; = -\dfrac{5}{4}$

$\quad\;\; = -\dfrac{4}{5}$

$\tan \theta = \dfrac{y}{x}$ $\qquad$ $\cot \theta = \dfrac{1}{\tan \theta}$

$\quad\;\; = \dfrac{3}{-4}$ $\qquad\qquad\;\; = -\dfrac{4}{3}$

$\quad\;\; = -\dfrac{3}{4}$

Your Turn

The point D(−5, −12) lies on the terminal arm of an angle θ in standard position. What is the exact value of each trigonometric ratio for θ?

Key Ideas

- Points that are on the intersection of the terminal arm of an angle θ in standard position and the unit circle can be defined using trigonometric ratios.

  P(θ) = (cos θ, sin θ)

- Each primary trigonometric ratio—sine, cosine, and tangent—has a reciprocal trigonometric ratio. The reciprocals are cosecant, secant, and cotangent, respectively.

  $\csc \theta = \dfrac{1}{\sin \theta}$ $\sec \theta = \dfrac{1}{\cos \theta}$ $\cot \theta = \dfrac{1}{\tan \theta}$ If sin θ = $\dfrac{2}{3}$, then csc θ = $\dfrac{3}{2}$, and vice versa.

- You can determine the trigonometric ratios for any angle in standard position using the coordinates of the point where the terminal arm intersects the unit circle.

- Exact values of trigonometric rations for special angles such as 0, $\dfrac{\pi}{6}$, $\dfrac{\pi}{4}$, $\dfrac{\pi}{3}$, and $\dfrac{\pi}{2}$ and their multiples may be determined using the coordinates of points on the unit circle.

- You can determine approximate values for trigonometric ratios using a calculator in the appropriate mode: radians or degrees.

- You can use a scientific or graphing calculator to determine an angle measure given the value of a trigonometric ratio. Then, use your knowledge of reference angles, coterminal angles, and signs of ratios in each quadrant to determine other possible angle measures. Unless the domain is restricted, there are an infinite number of answers.

- Determine the trigonometric ratios for an angle θ in standard position from the coordinates of a point on the terminal arm of θ and right triangle definitions of the trigonometric ratios.

Check Your Understanding

Practise

1. What is the exact value for each trigonometric ratio?
   a) sin 45°
   b) tan 30°
   c) cos $\dfrac{3\pi}{4}$
   d) cot $\dfrac{7\pi}{6}$
   e) csc 210°
   f) sec (−240°)
   g) tan $\dfrac{3\pi}{2}$
   h) sec π
   i) cot (−120°)
   j) cos 390°
   k) sin $\dfrac{5\pi}{3}$
   l) csc 495°

2. Determine the approximate value for each trigonometric ratio. Give answers to two decimal places.
   a) cos 47°
   b) cot 160°
   c) sec 15°
   d) csc 4.71
   e) sin 5
   f) tan 0.94
   g) sin $\dfrac{5\pi}{7}$
   h) tan 6.9
   i) cos 302°
   j) sin $\left(-\dfrac{11\pi}{19}\right)$
   k) cot 6
   l) sec (−270°)

3. If θ is an angle in standard position with the following conditions, in which quadrants may θ terminate?
   a) cos θ > 0
   b) tan θ < 0
   c) sin θ < 0
   d) sin θ > 0 and cot θ < 0
   e) cos θ < 0 and csc θ > 0
   f) sec θ > 0 and tan θ > 0

4. Express the given quantity using the same trigonometric ratio and its reference angle. For example, cos 110° = −cos 70°. For angle measures in radians, give exact answers. For example, cos 3 = −cos (π − 3).
   a) sin 250°
   b) tan 290°
   c) sec 135°
   d) cos 4
   e) csc 3
   f) cot 4.95

5. For each point, sketch two coterminal angles in standard position whose terminal arm contains the point. Give one positive and one negative angle, in radians, where neither angle exceeds one full rotation.
   a) (3, 5)
   b) (−2, −1)
   c) (−3, 2)
   d) (5, −2)

6. Indicate whether each trigonometric ratio is positive or negative. Do not use a calculator.
   a) cos 300°
   b) sin 4
   c) cot 156°
   d) csc (−235°)
   e) $\tan \frac{13\pi}{6}$
   f) $\sec \frac{17\pi}{3}$

7. Determine each value. Explain what the answer means.
   a) $\sin^{-1} 0.2$
   b) $\tan^{-1} 7$
   c) sec 450°
   d) cot (−180°)

8. The point $P(\theta) = \left(\frac{3}{5}, y\right)$ lies on the terminal arm of an angle θ in standard position and on the unit circle. P(θ) is in quadrant IV.
   a) Determine y.
   b) What is the value of tan θ?
   c) What is the value of csc θ?

Apply

9. Determine the exact value of each expression.
   a) cos 60° + sin 30°
   b) (sec 45°)²
   c) $\left(\cos \frac{5\pi}{3}\right)\left(\sec \frac{5\pi}{3}\right)$
   d) (tan 60°)² − (sec 60°)²
   e) $\left(\cos \frac{7\pi}{4}\right)^2 + \left(\sin \frac{7\pi}{4}\right)^2$
   f) $\left(\cot \frac{5\pi}{6}\right)^2$

10. Determine the exact measure of all angles that satisfy the following. Draw a diagram for each.
    a) $\sin \theta = -\frac{1}{2}$ in the domain $0 \leq \theta < 2\pi$
    b) cot θ = 1 in the domain $-\pi \leq \theta < 2\pi$
    c) sec θ = 2 in the domain $-180° \leq \theta < 90°$
    d) (cos θ)² = 1 in the domain $-360° \leq \theta < 360°$

11. Determine the approximate measure of all angles that satisfy the following. Give answers to two decimal places. Use diagrams to show the possible answers.
    a) cos θ = 0.42 in the domain $-\pi \leq \theta \leq \pi$
    b) tan θ = −4.87 in the domain $-\frac{\pi}{2} \leq \theta \leq \pi$
    c) csc θ = 4.87 in the domain $-360° \leq \theta < 180°$
    d) cot θ = 1.5 in the domain $-180° \leq \theta < 360°$

12. Determine the exact values of the other five trigonometric ratios under the given conditions.
    a) $\sin \theta = \frac{3}{5}, \frac{\pi}{2} < \theta < \pi$
    b) $\cos \theta = \frac{-2\sqrt{2}}{3}, -\pi \leq \theta \leq \frac{3\pi}{2}$
    c) $\tan \theta = \frac{2}{3}, -360° < \theta < 180°$
    d) $\sec \theta = \frac{4\sqrt{3}}{3}, -180° \leq \theta \leq 180°$

13. Using the point B(−2, −3), explain how to determine the exact value of cos θ given that B is a point on the terminal arm of an angle θ in standard position.

14. The measure of angle θ in standard position is 4900°.
    a) Describe θ in terms of revolutions. Be specific.
    b) In which quadrant does 4900° terminate?
    c) What is the measure of the reference angle?
    d) Give the value of each trigonometric ratio for 4900°.

15. a) Determine the positive value of sin (cos^{-1} 0.6). Use your knowledge of the unit circle to explain why the answer is a rational number.
    b) Without calculating, what is the positive value of cos (sin^{-1} 0.6)? Explain.

16. a) Jason got an answer of 1.051 176 209 when he used a calculator to determine the value of sec $\frac{40\pi}{7}$. Is he correct? If not, where did he make his mistake?
    b) Describe the steps you would use to determine an approximate value for sec $\frac{40\pi}{7}$ on your calculator.

17. a) Arrange the following values of sine in increasing order.
    sin 1, sin 2, sin 3, sin 4
    b) Show what the four values represent on a diagram of the unit circle. Use your diagram to justify the order from part a).
    c) Predict the correct increasing order for cos 1, cos 2, cos 3, and cos 4. Check with a calculator. Was your prediction correct?

18. Examine the diagram. A piston rod, PQ, is connected to a wheel at P and to a piston at Q. As P moves around the wheel in a counterclockwise direction, Q slides back and forth.

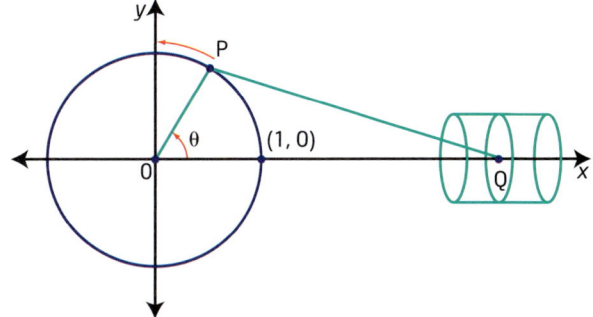

   a) What is the maximum distance that Q can move?
   b) If the wheel starts with P at (1, 0) and rotates at 1 radian/s, draw a sketch to show where P will be located after 1 min.
   c) What distance will Q have moved 1 s after start-up? Give your answer to the nearest hundredth of a unit.

19. Each point lies on the terminal arm of an angle θ in standard position. Determine θ in the specified domain. Round answers to the nearest hundredth of a unit.
    a) A(−3, 4), 0 < θ ≤ 4π
    b) B(5, −1), −360° ≤ θ < 360°
    c) C(−2, −3), $-\frac{3\pi}{2} < \theta < \frac{7\pi}{2}$

Extend

20. Draw △ABC with ∠A = 15° and ∠C = 90°. Let BC = 1. D is a point on AC such that ∠DBC = 60°. Use your diagram to help you show that tan 15° = $\frac{1}{\sqrt{3} + 2}$.

21. The diagram shows a quarter-circle of radius 5 units. Consider the point on the curve where $x = 2.5$. Show that this point is one-third the distance between (0, 5) and (5, 0) on the arc of the circle.

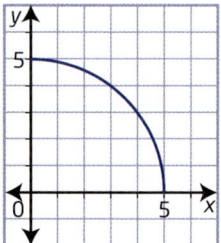

22. *Alice Through the Looking Glass* by Lewis Carroll introduced strange new worlds where time ran backwards. Your challenge is to imagine a unit circle in which a positive rotation is defined to be clockwise. Assume the coordinate system remains as we know it.

  a) Draw a unit circle in which positive angles are measured clockwise from (0, 1). Label where $R\left(\dfrac{\pi}{6}\right)$, $R\left(\dfrac{5\pi}{6}\right)$, $R\left(\dfrac{7\pi}{6}\right)$, and $R\left(\dfrac{11\pi}{6}\right)$ are on your new unit circle.

  b) What are the coordinates for the new $R\left(\dfrac{\pi}{6}\right)$ and $R\left(\dfrac{5\pi}{6}\right)$?

  c) How do angles in this new system relate to conventional angles in standard position?

  d) How does your new system of angle measure relate to bearings in navigation? Explain.

23. In the investigation at the beginning of this section, you identified line segments whose lengths are equivalent to cos θ, sin θ, and tan θ using the diagram shown.

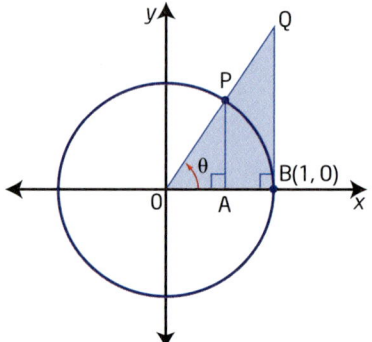

  a) Determine a line segment from the diagram whose length is equivalent to sec θ. Explain your reasoning

  b) Make a copy of the diagram. Draw a horizontal line tangent to the circle that intersects the positive y-axis at C and OQ at D. Now identify segments whose lengths are equivalent to csc θ and cot θ. Explain your reasoning.

Create Connections

C1 a) Paula sees that sine ratios increase from 0 to 1 in quadrant 1. She concludes that the sine relation is increasing in quadrant I. Show whether Paula is correct using specific values for sine.

  b) Is sine increasing in quadrant II? Explain why or why not.

  c) Does the sine ratio increase in any other quadrant, and if so, which? Explain.

C2 A regular hexagon is inscribed in the unit circle as shown. If one vertex is at (1, 0), what are the exact coordinates of the other vertices? Explain your reasoning.

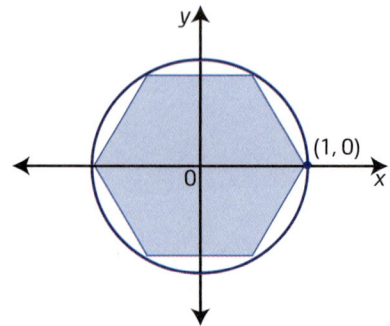

C3 Let P be the point of intersection of the unit circle and the terminal arm of an angle θ in standard position.

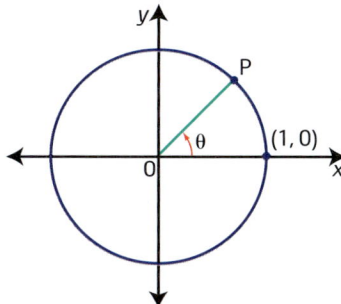

a) What is a formula for the slope of OP? Write your formula in terms of trigonometric ratios.
b) Does your formula apply in every quadrant? Explain.
c) Write an equation for any line OP. Use your trigonometric value for the slope.
d) Use transformations to show that your equation from part c) applies to any line where the slope is defined.

C4 Use the diagram to help find the value of each expression.

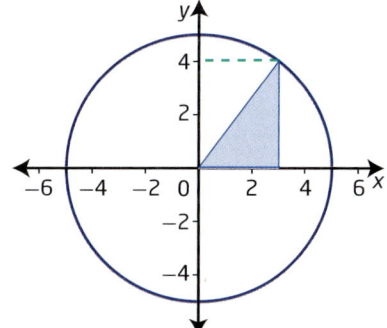

a) $\sin\left(\sin^{-1}\left(\frac{4}{5}\right)\right)$
b) $\cos\left(\tan^{-1}\left(\frac{4}{3}\right)\right)$
c) $\csc\left(\cos^{-1}\left(-\frac{3}{5}\right)\right)$, where the angle is in quadrant II
d) $\sin\left(\tan^{-1}\left(-\frac{4}{3}\right)\right)$, where the angle is in quadrant IV

Project Corner — History of Angle Measurement

- The use of the angular measurement unit "degree" is believed to have originated with the Babylonians. One theory is that their division of a circle into 360 parts is approximately the number of days in a year.

- Degree measures can also be subdivided into minutes (′) and seconds (″), where one degree is divided into 60 min, and one minute is divided into 60 s. For example, 30.1875° = 30° 11′ 15″.

- The earliest textual evidence of π dates from about 2000 B.C.E., with recorded approximations by the Babylonians $\left(\frac{25}{8}\right)$ and the Egyptians $\left(\frac{256}{81}\right)$. Roger Cotes (1682–1716) is credited with the concept of radian measure of angles, although he did not name the unit.

Rhind Papyrus, ancient Egypt c1650 B.C.E.

- The radian is widely accepted as the standard unit of angular measure in many fields of mathematics and in physics. The use of radians allows for the simplification of formulas and provides better approximations.

- What are some alternative units for measuring angles? What are some advantages and disadvantages of these units? What are some contexts in which these units are used?

4.4

Introduction to Trigonometric Equations

Focus on...

- algebraically solving first-degree and second-degree trigonometric equations in radians and in degrees
- verifying that a specific value is a solution to a trigonometric equation
- identifying exact and approximate solutions of a trigonometric equation in a restricted domain
- determining the general solution of a trigonometric equation

This old silver-gelatin photograph of traditional Kwakiutl spear fishing was taken in 1914 by Edward S. Curtis. The Kwakiutl First Nation's people have lived on the north-eastern shores of Vancouver Island for thousands of years. Today, the band council is based in Fort Rupert and owns 295 hectares of land in the area.

Many situations in nature involve cyclical patterns, such as average daily temperature at a specific location. Other applications of trigonometry relate to electricity or the way light passes from air into water. When you look at a fish in the water, it is not precisely where it appears to be, due to the refraction of light. The Kwakiutl peoples from Northwest British Columbia figured this out centuries ago. They became expert spear fishermen.

In this section, you will explore how to use algebraic techniques, similar to those used in solving linear and quadratic equations, to solve **trigonometric equations**. Your knowledge of coterminal angles, points on the unit circle, and inverse trigonometric functions will be important for understanding the solution of trigonometric equations.

trigonometric equation
- an equation involving trigonometric ratios

Investigate Trigonometric Equations

Did You Know?

In equations, mathematicians often use the notation $\cos^2 \theta$. This means the same as $(\cos \theta)^2$.

1. What are the exact measures of θ if $\cos \theta = -\frac{1}{2}$, $0 \leq \theta < 2\pi$? How is the equation related to $2 \cos \theta + 1 = 0$?

2. What is the answer for step 1 if the domain is given as $0° \leq \theta < 360°$?

3. What are the approximate measures for θ if $3 \cos \theta + 1 = 0$ and the domain is $0 \leq \theta < 2\pi$?

4. Set up a T-chart like the one below. In the left column, show the steps you would use to solve the quadratic equation $x^2 - x = 0$. In the right column, show similar steps that will lead to the solution of the trigonometric equation $\cos^2 \theta - \cos \theta = 0$, $0 \leq \theta < 2\pi$.

Quadratic Equation	Trigonometric Equation

Reflect and Respond

5. How is solving the equations in steps 1 to 3 similar to solving a linear equation? How is it different? Use examples.
6. When solving a trigonometric equation, how do you know whether to give your answers in degrees or radians?
7. Identify similarities and differences between solving a quadratic equation and solving a trigonometric equation that is quadratic.

Link the Ideas

In the investigation, you explored solving trigonometric equations. Did you realize that in Section 4.3 you were already solving simple trigonometric equations? The same processes will be used each time you solve a trigonometric equation, and these processes are the same as those used in solving linear and quadratic equations.

The notation $[0, \pi]$ represents the interval from 0 to π inclusive and is another way of writing $0 \leq \theta \leq \pi$.

- $\theta \in (0, \pi)$ means the same as $0 < \theta < \pi$.
- $\theta \in [0, \pi)$ means the same as $0 \leq \theta < \pi$.

How would you show $-\pi < \theta \leq 2\pi$ using interval notation?

Example 1
Solve Trigonometric Equations

Solve each trigonometric equation in the specified domain.
a) $5 \sin \theta + 2 = 1 + 3 \sin \theta$, $0 \leq \theta < 2\pi$
b) $3 \csc x - 6 = 0$, $0° \leq x < 360°$

Solution

a)
$$5 \sin \theta + 2 = 1 + 3 \sin \theta$$
$$5 \sin \theta + 2 - 3 \sin \theta = 1 + 3 \sin \theta - 3 \sin \theta$$
$$2 \sin \theta + 2 = 1$$
$$2 \sin \theta + 2 - 2 = 1 - 2$$
$$2 \sin \theta = -1$$
$$\sin \theta = -\frac{1}{2}$$

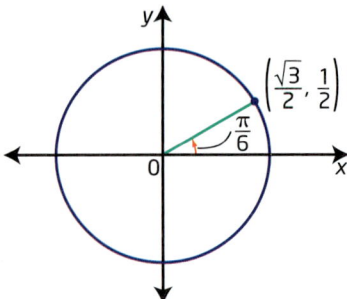

The reference angle is $\theta_R = \dfrac{\pi}{6}$.

In which quadrants must θ terminate if $\sin \theta = -\dfrac{1}{2}$?

$\theta = \pi + \dfrac{\pi}{6} = \dfrac{7\pi}{6}$ (quadrant III)

$\theta = 2\pi - \dfrac{\pi}{6} = \dfrac{11\pi}{6}$ (quadrant IV)

The solutions are $\theta = \dfrac{7\pi}{6}$ and $\theta = \dfrac{11\pi}{6}$ in the domain $0 \leq \theta < 2\pi$.

b) $3 \csc x - 6 = 0$

$3 \csc x = 6$

$\csc x = 2$ *What operations were performed to arrive at this equation?*

If $\csc x = 2$, then $\sin x = \dfrac{1}{2}$

$x = 30°$ and $150°$ *Explain how to arrive at these answers.*

The solutions are $x = 30°$ and $x = 150°$ in the domain $0° \leq x < 360°$.

Your Turn

Solve each trigonometric equation in the specified domain.
a) $3 \cos \theta - 1 = \cos \theta + 1$, $-2\pi \leq \theta \leq 2\pi$
b) $4 \sec x + 8 = 0$, $0° \leq x < 360°$

Example 2

Factor to Solve a Trigonometric Equation

Solve for θ.

$\tan^2 \theta - 5 \tan \theta + 4 = 0$, $0 \leq \theta < 2\pi$

Give solutions as exact values where possible. Otherwise, give approximate angle measures, to the nearest thousandth of a radian.

Solution

$\tan^2 \theta - 5 \tan \theta + 4 = 0$

$(\tan \theta - 1)(\tan \theta - 4) = 0$

$\tan \theta - 1 = 0$ or $\tan \theta - 4 = 0$

$\tan \theta = 1$ $\quad\quad\quad$ $\tan \theta = 4$

$\theta = \dfrac{\pi}{4}, \dfrac{5\pi}{4}$ $\quad\quad$ $\tan^{-1} 4 = \theta$

$\theta = 1.3258\ldots$

$\theta \approx 1.326$ is a measure in quadrant I.

How is this similar to solving $x^2 - 5x + 4 = 0$?

In which quadrants is $\tan \theta > 0$?

What angle mode must your calculator be in to find $\tan^{-1} 4$?

How do you know that 1.326 is in quadrant I?

In quadrant III,

$\theta = \pi + \theta_R$
$= \pi + \tan^{-1} 4$
$= \pi + 1.3258\ldots$
$= 4.467\,410\,317\ldots$
≈ 4.467

Why is $\tan^{-1} 4$ used as the reference angle here?

The solutions are $\theta = \frac{\pi}{4}$, $\theta = \frac{5\pi}{4}$ (exact), $\theta \approx 1.326$, and $\theta \approx 4.467$ (to the nearest thousandth).

Your Turn

Solve for θ.

$\cos^2 \theta - \cos \theta - 2 = 0$, $0° \leq \theta < 360°$

Give solutions as exact values where possible. Otherwise, give approximate measures to the nearest thousandth of a degree.

Example 3

General Solution of a Trigonometric Equation

a) Solve for x in the interval $0 \leq x < 2\pi$ if $\sin^2 x - 1 = 0$. Give answers as exact values.

b) Determine the general solution for $\sin^2 x - 1 = 0$ over the real numbers if x is measured in radians.

Solution

a) Method 1: Use Square Root Principles

$\sin^2 x - 1 = 0$
$\quad \sin^2 x = 1$
$\quad\; \sin x = \pm 1$
$\quad\; \sin x = 1$ or $\sin x = -1$

Why are there two values for $\sin x$?

If $\sin x = 1$, then $x = \frac{\pi}{2}$.

If $\sin x = -1$, then $x = \frac{3\pi}{2}$.

Where did $\frac{\pi}{2}$ and $\frac{3\pi}{2}$ come from? Why is $\frac{5\pi}{2}$ not an acceptable answer?

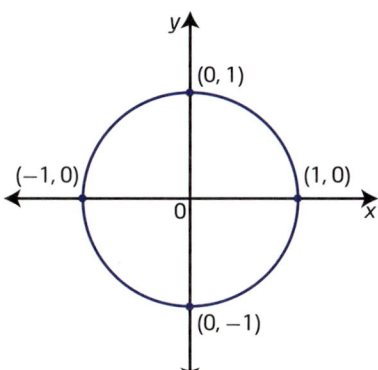

Method 2: Use Factoring
$$\sin^2 x - 1 = 0$$
$$(\sin x - 1)(\sin x + 1) = 0$$
$$\sin x - 1 = 0 \quad \text{or} \quad \sin x + 1 = 0$$

Continue as in Method 1.

Check: $x = \dfrac{\pi}{2}$ $\qquad\qquad\qquad x = \dfrac{3\pi}{2}$

Left Side	Right Side	Left Side	Right Side
$\sin^2 x - 1$	0	$\sin^2 x - 1$	0
$= \left(\sin \dfrac{\pi}{2}\right)^2 - 1$		$= \left(\sin \dfrac{3\pi}{2}\right)^2 - 1$	
$= 1^2 - 1$		$= (-1)^2 - 1$	
$= 0$		$= 0$	

Both answers are verified.
The solution is $x = \dfrac{\pi}{2}, \dfrac{3\pi}{2}$.

b) If the domain is real numbers, you can make an infinite number of rotations on the unit circle in both a positive and a negative direction.

Values corresponding to $x = \dfrac{\pi}{2}$ are $\ldots -\dfrac{7\pi}{2}, -\dfrac{3\pi}{2}, \dfrac{\pi}{2}, \dfrac{5\pi}{2}, \dfrac{9\pi}{2}, \ldots$

What patterns do you see in these values for θ?

Values corresponding to $x = \dfrac{3\pi}{2}$ are $\ldots -\dfrac{5\pi}{2}, -\dfrac{\pi}{2}, \dfrac{3\pi}{2}, \dfrac{7\pi}{2}, \dfrac{11\pi}{2}, \ldots$

Do you see that the terminal arm is at the point (0, 1) or (0, −1) with any of the angles above?

An expression for the values corresponding to $x = \dfrac{\pi}{2}$ is $x = \dfrac{\pi}{2} + 2\pi n$, where $n \in I$.

An expression for the values corresponding to $x = \dfrac{3\pi}{2}$ is $x = \dfrac{3\pi}{2} + 2\pi n$, where $n \in I$.

The two expressions above can be combined to form the general solution $x = \dfrac{\pi}{2} + \pi n$, where $n \in I$.

The solution can also be described as "odd integral multiples of $\dfrac{\pi}{2}$." In symbols, this is written as $(2n + 1)\left(\dfrac{\pi}{2}\right)$, $n \in I$.

How can you show algebraically that $(2n + 1)\left(\dfrac{\pi}{2}\right)$, $n \in I$, and $\dfrac{\pi}{2} + \pi n$, $n \in I$, are equivalent?

Did You Know?

$2n$, where $n \in I$, represents all even integers.

$2n + 1$, where $n \in I$, is an expression for all odd integers.

Your Turn

a) If $\cos^2 x - 1 = 0$, solve for x in the domain $0° \leq x < 360°$. Give solutions as exact values.

b) Determine the general solution for $\cos^2 x - 1 = 0$, where the domain is real numbers measured in degrees.

Key Ideas

- To solve a trigonometric equation algebraically, you can use the same techniques as used in solving linear and quadratic equations.
- When you arrive at $\sin \theta = a$ or $\cos \theta = a$ or $\tan \theta = a$, where $a \in R$, then use the unit circle for exact values of θ and inverse trigonometric function keys on a calculator for approximate measures. Use reference angles to find solutions in other quadrants.
- To solve a trigonometric equation involving $\csc \theta$, $\sec \theta$, or $\cot \theta$, you may need to work with the related reciprocal value(s).
- To determine a general solution or if the domain is real numbers, find the solutions in one positive rotation (2π or $360°$). Then, use the concept of coterminal angles to write an expression that identifies all possible measures.

Check Your Understanding

Practise

1. Without solving, determine the number of solutions for each trigonometric equation in the specified domain. Explain your reasoning.
   a) $\sin \theta = \frac{\sqrt{3}}{2}$, $0 \leq \theta < 2\pi$
   b) $\cos \theta = \frac{1}{\sqrt{2}}$, $-2\pi \leq \theta < 2\pi$
   c) $\tan \theta = -1$, $-360° \leq \theta \leq 180°$
   d) $\sec \theta = \frac{2\sqrt{3}}{3}$, $-180° \leq \theta < 180°$

2. The equation $\cos \theta = \frac{1}{2}$, $0 \leq \theta < 2\pi$, has solutions $\frac{\pi}{3}$ and $\frac{5\pi}{3}$. Suppose the domain is not restricted.
   a) What is the general solution corresponding to $\theta = \frac{\pi}{3}$?
   b) What is the general solution corresponding to $\theta = \frac{5\pi}{3}$?

3. Determine the exact roots for each trigonometric equation or statement in the specified domain.
   a) $2 \cos \theta - \sqrt{3} = 0$, $0 \leq \theta < 2\pi$
   b) $\csc \theta$ is undefined, $0° \leq \theta < 360°$
   c) $5 - \tan^2 \theta = 4$, $-180° \leq \theta \leq 360°$
   d) $\sec \theta + \sqrt{2} = 0$, $-\pi \leq \theta \leq \frac{3\pi}{2}$

4. Solve each equation for $0 \leq \theta < 2\pi$. Give solutions to the nearest hundredth of a radian.
   a) $\tan \theta = 4.36$
   b) $\cos \theta = -0.19$
   c) $\sin \theta = 0.91$
   d) $\cot \theta = 12.3$
   e) $\sec \theta = 2.77$
   f) $\csc \theta = -1.57$

5. Solve each equation in the specified domain.
   a) $3 \cos \theta - 1 = 4 \cos \theta$, $0 \leq \theta < 2\pi$
   b) $\sqrt{3} \tan \theta + 1 = 0$, $-\pi \leq \theta \leq 2\pi$
   c) $\sqrt{2} \sin x - 1 = 0$, $-360° < x \leq 360°$
   d) $3 \sin x - 5 = 5 \sin x - 4$, $-360° \leq x < 180°$
   e) $3 \cot x + 1 = 2 + 4 \cot x$, $-180° < x < 360°$
   f) $\sqrt{3} \sec \theta + 2 = 0$, $-\pi \leq \theta \leq 3\pi$

6. Copy and complete the table to express each domain or interval using the other notation.

	Domain	Interval Notation
a)	$-2\pi \leq \theta \leq 2\pi$	
b)	$-\frac{\pi}{3} \leq \theta \leq \frac{7\pi}{3}$	
c)	$0° \leq \theta \leq 270°$	
d)		$\theta \in [0, \pi)$
e)		$\theta \in (0°, 450°)$
f)		$\theta \in (-2\pi, 4\pi]$

7. Solve for θ in the specified domain. Give solutions as exact values where possible. Otherwise, give approximate measures to the nearest thousandth.

  a) $2\cos^2 \theta - 3\cos \theta + 1 = 0, 0 \leq \theta < 2\pi$
  b) $\tan^2 \theta - \tan \theta - 2 = 0, 0° \leq \theta < 360°$
  c) $\sin^2 \theta - \sin \theta = 0, \theta \in [0, 2\pi)$
  d) $\sec^2 \theta - 2\sec \theta - 3 = 0, \theta \in [-180°, 180°)$

8. Todd believes that 180° and 270° are solutions to the equation $5\cos^2 \theta = -4\cos \theta$. Show how you would check to determine whether Todd's solutions are correct.

Apply

9. Aslan and Shelley are finding the solution for $2\sin^2 \theta = \sin \theta, 0 < \theta \leq \pi$. Here is their work.

$2\sin^2 \theta = \sin \theta$
$\dfrac{2\sin^2 \theta}{\sin \theta} = \dfrac{\sin \theta}{\sin \theta}$ Step 1
$2\sin \theta = 1$ Step 2
$\sin \theta = \dfrac{1}{2}$ Step 3
$\theta = \dfrac{\pi}{6}, \dfrac{5\pi}{6}$ Step 4

  a) Identify the error that Aslan and Shelley made and explain why their solution is incorrect.
  b) Show a correct method to determine the solution for $2\sin^2 \theta = \sin \theta, 0 < \theta \leq \pi$.

10. Explain why the equation $\sin \theta = 0$ has no solution in the interval $(\pi, 2\pi)$.

11. What is the solution for $\sin \theta = 2$? Show how you know. Does the interval matter?

12. Jaycee says that the trigonometric equation $\cos \theta = \dfrac{1}{2}$ has an infinite number of solutions. Do you agree? Explain.

13. a) Helene is asked to solve the equation $3\sin^2 \theta - 2\sin \theta = 0, 0 \leq \theta \leq \pi$. She finds that $\theta = \pi$. Show how she could check whether this is a correct root for the equation.

  b) Find all the roots of the equation $3\sin^2 \theta - 2\sin \theta = 0, \theta \in [0, \pi]$.

14. Refer to the Did You Know? below. Use Snell's law of refraction to determine the angle of refraction of a ray of light passing from air into water if the angle of incidence is 35°. The refractive index is 1.000 29 for air and 1.33 for water.

Did You Know?

Willebrord Snell, a Dutch physicist, discovered that light is bent (refracted) as it passes from one medium into another. Snell's law is shown in the diagram.

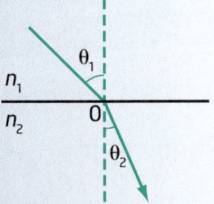

$n_1 \sin \theta_1 = n_2 \sin \theta_2$,
where θ_1 is the angle of incidence,
θ_2 is the angle of refraction, and
n_1 and n_2 are the refractive indices of the mediums.

15. The average number of air conditioners sold in western Canada varies seasonally and depends on the month of the year. The formula $y = 5.9 + 2.4 \sin\left(\frac{\pi}{6}(t - 3)\right)$ gives the expected sales, y, in thousands, according to the month, t, where $t = 1$ represents January, $t = 2$ is February, and so on.
   a) In what month are sales of 8300 air conditioners expected?
   b) In what month are sales expected to be least?
   c) Does this formula seem reasonable? Explain.

16. Nora is required to solve the following trigonometric equation.
$9 \sin^2 \theta + 12 \sin \theta + 4 = 0, \theta \in [0°, 360°)$
Nora did the work shown below. Examine her work carefully. Identify any errors. Rewrite the solution, making any changes necessary for it to be correct.

$9 \sin^2 \theta + 12 \sin \theta + 4 = 0$
$(3 \sin \theta + 2)^2 = 0$
$3 \sin \theta + 2 = 0$
Therefore, $\sin \theta = -\frac{2}{3}$
Use a calculator.
$\sin^{-1}\left(-\frac{2}{3}\right) = -41.810\,314\,9$
So, the reference angle is 41.8°, to the nearest tenth of a degree.
Sine is negative in quadrants II and III.
The solution in quadrant II is 180° − 41.8° = 138.2°.
The solution in quadrant III is 180° + 41.8° = 221.8°.
Therefore, $\theta = 138.2°$ and $\theta = 221.8°$, to the nearest tenth of a degree.

17. Identify two different cases when a trigonometric equation would have no solution. Give an example to support each case.

18. Find the value of $\sec \theta$ if $\cot \theta = \frac{3}{4}$, $180° \leq \theta \leq 270°$.

Extend

19. A beach ball is riding the waves near Tofino, British Columbia. The ball goes up and down with the waves according to the formula $h = 1.4 \sin\left(\frac{\pi t}{3}\right)$, where h is the height, in metres, above sea level, and t is the time, in seconds.
   a) In the first 10 s, when is the ball at sea level?
   b) When does the ball reach its greatest height above sea level? Give the first time this occurs and then write an expression for every time the maximum occurs.
   c) According to the formula, what is the most the ball goes below sea level?

20. The current, I, in amperes, for an electric circuit is given by the formula $I = 4.3 \sin 120\pi t$, where t is time, in seconds.
   a) The alternating current used in western Canada cycles 60 times per second. Demonstrate this using the given formula.
   b) At what times is the current at its maximum value? How does your understanding of coterminal angles help in your solution?
   c) At what times is the current at its minimum value?
   d) What is the maximum current?

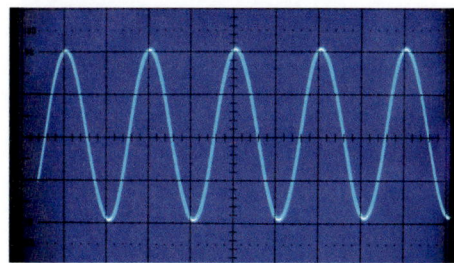

Oscilloscopes can measure wave functions of varying voltages.

21. Solve the trigonometric equation $\cos\left(x - \dfrac{\pi}{2}\right) = \dfrac{\sqrt{3}}{2}$, $-\pi < x < \pi$.

22. Consider the trigonometric equation $\sin^2 \theta + \sin \theta - 1 = 0$.
    a) Can you solve the equation by factoring?
    b) Use the quadratic formula to solve for $\sin \theta$.
    c) Determine all solutions for θ in the interval $0 < \theta \le 2\pi$. Give answers to the nearest hundredth of a radian, if necessary.

23. Jaime plans to build a new deck behind her house. It is to be an isosceles trapezoid shape, as shown. She would like each outer edge of the deck to measure 4 m.

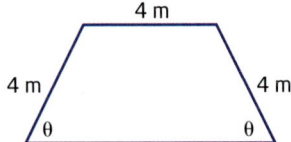

   a) Show that the area, A, of the deck is given by $A = 16 \sin \theta(1 + \cos \theta)$.
   b) Determine the exact value of θ in radians if the area of the deck is $12\sqrt{3}$ m².
   c) The angle in part b) gives the maximum area for the deck. How can you prove this? Compare your method with that of another student.

Create Connections

C1 Compare and contrast solving linear and quadratic equations with solving linear and quadratic trigonometric equations.

C2 A computer determines that a point on the unit circle has coordinates $A(0.384\,615\,384\,6,\ 0.923\,076\,923\,1)$.
   a) How can you check whether a point is on the unit circle? Use your method to see if A is on the unit circle.
   b) If A is the point where the terminal arm of an angle θ intersects the unit circle, determine the values of $\cos \theta$, $\tan \theta$, and $\csc \theta$. Give your answers to three decimal places.
   c) Determine the measure of angle θ, to the nearest tenth of a degree. Does this approximate measure for θ seem reasonable for point A? Explain using a diagram.

C3 Use your knowledge of non-permissible values for rational expressions to answer the following.
   a) What is meant by the expression "non-permissible values"? Give an example.
   b) Use the fact that any point on the unit circle has coordinates $P(\theta) = (\cos \theta, \sin \theta)$ to identify a trigonometric relation that could have non-permissible values.
   c) For the trigonometric relation that you identified in part b), list all the values of θ in the interval $0 \le \theta < 4\pi$ that are non-permissible.
   d) Create a general statement for all the non-permissible values of θ for your trigonometric relation over the real numbers.

C4 a) Determine all solutions for the equation $2 \sin^2 \theta = 1 - \sin \theta$ in the domain $0° \le \theta < 360°$.
   b) Are your solutions exact or approximate? Why?
   c) Show how you can check one of your solutions to verify its correctness.

Chapter 4 Review

4.1 Angles and Angle Measure, pages 166–179

1. If each angle is in standard position, in which quadrant does it terminate?
   a) 100°
   b) 500°
   c) 10
   d) $\dfrac{29\pi}{6}$

2. Draw each angle in standard position. Convert each degree measure to radian measure and each radian measure to degree measure. Give answers as exact values.
   a) $\dfrac{5\pi}{2}$
   b) 240°
   c) −405°
   d) −3.5

3. Convert each degree measure to radian measure and each radian measure to degree measure. Give answers as approximate values to the nearest hundredth, where necessary.
   a) 20°
   b) −185°
   c) −1.75
   d) $\dfrac{5\pi}{12}$

4. Determine the measure of an angle coterminal with each angle in the domain $0° \leq \theta < 360°$ or $0 \leq \theta < 2\pi$. Draw a diagram showing the quadrant in which each angle terminates.
   a) 6.75
   b) 400°
   c) −3
   d) −105°

5. Write an expression for all of the angles coterminal with each angle. Indicate what your variable represents.
   a) 250°
   b) $\dfrac{5\pi}{2}$
   c) −300°
   d) 6

6. A jet engine motor cycle is tested at 80 000 rpm. What is this angular velocity in
   a) radians per minute?
   b) degrees per second?

4.2 The Unit Circle, pages 180–190

7. $P(\theta) = (x, y)$ is the point where the terminal arm of an angle θ intersects the unit circle. What are the coordinates for each point?
   a) $P\left(\dfrac{5\pi}{6}\right)$
   b) $P(-150°)$
   c) $P\left(-\dfrac{11\pi}{2}\right)$
   d) $P(45°)$
   e) $P(120°)$
   f) $P\left(\dfrac{11\pi}{3}\right)$

8. a) If the coordinates for $P\left(\dfrac{\pi}{3}\right)$ are $\left(\dfrac{1}{2}, \dfrac{\sqrt{3}}{2}\right)$, explain how you can determine the coordinates for $P\left(\dfrac{2\pi}{3}\right)$, $P\left(\dfrac{4\pi}{3}\right)$, and $P\left(\dfrac{5\pi}{3}\right)$.

b) If the coordinates for $P(\theta)$ are $\left(-\dfrac{2\sqrt{2}}{3}, \dfrac{1}{3}\right)$, what are the coordinates for $P\left(\theta + \dfrac{\pi}{2}\right)$?

c) In which quadrant does $P\left(\dfrac{5\pi}{6} + \pi\right)$ lie? Explain how you know. If $P\left(\dfrac{5\pi}{6} + \pi\right)$ represents $P(\theta)$, what is the measure of θ and what are the coordinates of $P(\theta)$?

9. Identify all measures for θ in the interval $-2\pi \le \theta < 2\pi$ such that $P(\theta)$ is the given point.

  a) $(0, 1)$

  b) $\left(\dfrac{\sqrt{3}}{2}, -\dfrac{1}{2}\right)$

  c) $\left(-\dfrac{1}{\sqrt{2}}, \dfrac{1}{\sqrt{2}}\right)$

  d) $\left(-\dfrac{1}{2}, \dfrac{\sqrt{3}}{2}\right)$

10. Identify all measures for θ in the domain $-180° < \theta \le 360°$ such that $P(\theta)$ is the given point.

  a) $\left(-\dfrac{\sqrt{3}}{2}, -\dfrac{1}{2}\right)$

  b) $(-1, 0)$

  c) $\left(-\dfrac{\sqrt{2}}{2}, \dfrac{\sqrt{2}}{2}\right)$

  d) $\left(\dfrac{1}{2}, -\dfrac{\sqrt{3}}{2}\right)$

11. If $P(\theta) = \left(\dfrac{\sqrt{5}}{3}, -\dfrac{2}{3}\right)$, answer the following questions.

  a) What is the measure of θ? Explain using a diagram.

  b) In which quadrant does θ terminate?

  c) What are the coordinates of $P(\theta + \pi)$?

  d) What are the coordinates of $P\left(\theta + \dfrac{\pi}{2}\right)$?

  e) What are the coordinates of $P\left(\theta - \dfrac{\pi}{2}\right)$?

4.3 Trigonometric Ratios, pages 191–205

12. If $\cos\theta = \dfrac{1}{3}$, $0° \le \theta \le 270°$, what is the value of each of the other trigonometric ratios of θ? When radicals occur, leave your answer in exact form.

13. Without using a calculator, determine the exact value of each trigonometric ratio.

  a) $\sin\left(-\dfrac{3\pi}{2}\right)$

  b) $\cos\dfrac{3\pi}{4}$

  c) $\cot\dfrac{7\pi}{6}$

  d) $\sec(-210°)$

  e) $\tan 720°$

  f) $\csc 300°$

14. Determine the approximate measure of all angles that satisfy the following. Give answers to the nearest hundredth of a unit. Draw a sketch to show the quadrant(s) involved.

  a) $\sin\theta = 0.54$, $-2\pi < \theta \le 2\pi$

  b) $\tan\theta = 9.3$, $-180° \le \theta < 360°$

  c) $\cos\theta = -0.77$, $-\pi \le \theta < \pi$

  d) $\csc\theta = 9.5$, $-270° < \theta \le 90°$

15. Determine each trigonometric ratio, to three decimal places.
    a) sin 285°
    b) cot 130°
    c) cos 4.5
    d) sec 7.38

16. The terminal arm of an angle θ in standard position passes through the point A(−3, 4).
    a) Draw the angle and use a protractor to determine its measure, to the nearest degree.
    b) Show how to determine the exact value of cos θ.
    c) What is the exact value of csc θ + tan θ?
    d) From the value of cos θ, determine the measure of θ in degrees and in radians, to the nearest tenth.

4.4 Introduction to Trigonometric Equations, pages 206–214

17. Factor each trigonometric expression.
    a) $\cos^2 \theta + \cos \theta$
    b) $\sin^2 \theta - 3 \sin \theta - 4$
    c) $\cot^2 \theta - 9$
    d) $2 \tan^2 \theta - 9 \tan \theta + 10$

18. Explain why it is impossible to find each of the following values.
    a) $\sin^{-1} 2$
    b) tan 90°

19. Without solving, determine the number of solutions for each trigonometric equation or statement in the specified domain.
    a) 4 cos θ − 3 = 0, 0° < θ ≤ 360°
    b) sin θ + 0.9 = 0, −π ≤ θ ≤ π
    c) 0.5 tan θ − 1.5 = 0, −180° ≤ θ ≤ 0°
    d) csc θ is undefined, θ ∈ [−2π, 4π)

20. Determine the exact roots for each trigonometric equation.
    a) csc θ = √2, θ ∈ [0°, 360°]
    b) 2 cos θ + 1 = 0, 0 ≤ θ < 2π
    c) 3 tan θ − √3 = 0, −180° ≤ θ < 360°
    d) cot θ + 1 = 0, −π ≤ θ < π

21. Solve for θ. Give solutions as exact values where possible. Otherwise, give approximate measures, to the nearest thousandth.
    a) $\sin^2 \theta + \sin \theta - 2 = 0$, 0 ≤ θ < 2π
    b) $\tan^2 \theta + 3 \tan \theta = 0$, 0° < θ ≤ 360°
    c) $6 \cos^2 \theta + \cos \theta = 1$, θ ∈ (0°, 360°)
    d) $\sec^2 \theta - 4 = 0$, θ ∈ [−π, π]

22. Determine a domain for which the equation $\sin \theta = \dfrac{\sqrt{3}}{2}$ would have the following solution.
    a) $\theta = \dfrac{\pi}{3}, \dfrac{2\pi}{3}$
    b) $\theta = -\dfrac{5\pi}{3}, -\dfrac{4\pi}{3}, \dfrac{\pi}{3}$
    c) θ = −660°, −600°, −300°, −240°
    d) θ = −240°, 60°, 120°, 420°

23. Determine each general solution using the angle measure specified.
    a) $\sin x = -\dfrac{1}{2}$, in radians
    b) $\sin x = \sin^2 x$, in degrees
    c) sec x + 2 = 0, in degrees
    d) $(\tan x - 1)(\tan x - \sqrt{3}) = 0$, in radians

Chapter 4 Practice Test

Multiple Choice

For #1 to #5, choose the best answer.

1. If $\cos \theta = \dfrac{\sqrt{3}}{2}$, which could be the measure of θ?

   A $\dfrac{2\pi}{3}$ **B** $\dfrac{5\pi}{6}$ **C** $\dfrac{5\pi}{3}$ **D** $\dfrac{11\pi}{6}$

2. Which exact measures of θ satisfy $\sin \theta = -\dfrac{\sqrt{3}}{2}$, $0° \leq \theta < 360°$?

   A $60°, 120°$
   B $-60°, -120°$
   C $240°, 300°$
   D $-240°, -300°$

3. If $\cot \theta = 1.4$, what is one approximate measure in radians for θ?

   A 0.620
   B 0.951
   C 1.052
   D 0.018

4. The coordinates of point P on the unit circle are $\left(-\dfrac{3}{4}, \dfrac{\sqrt{7}}{4}\right)$. What are the coordinates of Q if Q is a 90° counterclockwise rotation from P?

   A $\left(\dfrac{\sqrt{7}}{4}, -\dfrac{3}{4}\right)$
   B $\left(-\dfrac{\sqrt{7}}{4}, -\dfrac{3}{4}\right)$
   C $\left(\dfrac{3}{4}, \dfrac{\sqrt{7}}{4}\right)$
   D $\left(-\dfrac{3}{4}, -\dfrac{\sqrt{7}}{4}\right)$

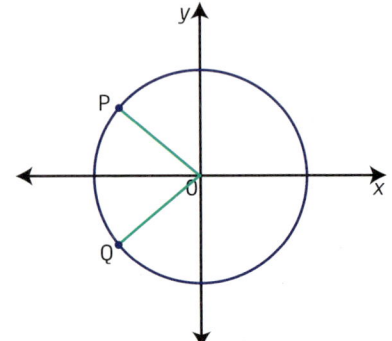

5. Determine the number of solutions for the trigonometric equation $\sin \theta (\sin \theta + 1) = 0$, $-180° < \theta < 360°$.

   A 3
   B 4
   C 5
   D 6

Short Answer

6. A vehicle has tires that are 75 cm in diameter. A point is marked on the edge of the tire.

   a) Determine the measure of the angle through which the point turns every second if the vehicle is travelling at 110 km/h. Give your answer in degrees and in radians, to the nearest tenth.

   b) What is the answer in radians if the diameter of the tire is 66 cm? Do you think that tire diameter affects tire life? Explain.

7. a) What is the equation for any circle with centre at the origin and radius 1 unit?

   b) Determine the value(s) for the missing coordinate for all points on the unit circle satisfying the given conditions. Draw diagrams.

   i) $\left(\dfrac{2\sqrt{3}}{5}, y\right)$

   ii) $\left(x, \dfrac{\sqrt{7}}{4}\right)$, $x < 0$

   c) Explain how to use the equation for the unit circle to find the value of $\cos \theta$ if you know the y-coordinate of the point where the terminal arm of an angle θ in standard position intersects the unit circle.

8. Suppose that the cosine of an angle is negative and that you found one solution in quadrant III.
   a) Explain how to find the other solution between 0 and 2π.
   b) Describe how to write the general solution.

9. Solve the equation $2 \cos \theta + \sqrt{2} = 0$, where $\theta \in R$.

10. Explain the difference between an angle measuring 3° and one measuring 3 radians.

11. An angle in standard position measures −500°.
    a) In which quadrant does −500° terminate?
    b) What is the measure of the reference angle?
    c) What is the approximate value, to one decimal place, of each trigonometric ratio for −500°?

12. Identify one positive and one negative angle measure that is coterminal with each angle. Then, write a general expression for all the coterminal angles in each case.
    a) $\dfrac{13\pi}{4}$
    b) −575°

Extended Response

13. The diagram shows a stretch of road from A to E. The curves are arcs of circles. Determine the length of the road from A to E. Give your answer to the nearest tenth of a kilometre.

14. Draw any △ABC with A at the origin, side AB along the positive x-axis, and C in quadrant I. Show that the area of your triangle can be expressed as $\dfrac{1}{2}bc \sin A$ or $\dfrac{1}{2}ac \sin B$.

15. Solve for θ. Give solutions as exact values where possible. Otherwise, give approximate measures to the nearest hundredth.
    a) $3 \tan^2 \theta - \tan \theta - 4 = 0, -\pi < \theta < 2\pi$
    b) $\sin^2 \theta + \sin \theta - 1 = 0, 0 \leq \theta < 2\pi$
    c) $\tan^2 \theta = 4 \tan \theta, \theta \in [0, 2\pi]$

16. Jack chooses a horse to ride on the West Edmonton Mall carousel. The horse is located 8 m from the centre of the carousel. If the carousel turns through an angle of 210° before stopping to let a crying child get off, how far did Jack travel? Give your answer as both an exact value and an approximate measure to the nearest hundredth of a metre.

CHAPTER 5

Trigonometric Functions and Graphs

You have seen different types of functions and how these functions can mathematically model the real world. Many sinusoidal and periodic patterns occur within nature. Movement on the surface of Earth, such as earthquakes, and stresses within Earth can cause rocks to fold into a sinusoidal pattern. Geologists and structural engineers study models of trigonometric functions to help them understand these formations. In this chapter, you will study trigonometric functions for which the function values repeat at regular intervals.

Key Terms
periodic function
period
sinusoidal curve
amplitude
vertical displacement
phase shift

Career Link

A geologist studies the composition, structure, and history of Earth's surface to determine the processes affecting the development of Earth. Geologists apply their knowledge of physics, chemistry, biology, and mathematics to explain these phenomena. Geological engineers apply geological knowledge to projects such as dam, tunnel, and building construction.

Web Link

To learn more about a career as a geologist, go to www.mcgrawhill.ca/school/learningcentres and follow the links.

5.1

Graphing Sine and Cosine Functions

Focus on...

- sketching the graphs of $y = \sin x$ and $y = \cos x$
- determining the characteristics of the graphs of $y = \sin x$ and $y = \cos x$
- demonstrating an understanding of the effects of vertical and horizontal stretches on the graphs of sinusoidal functions
- solving a problem by analysing the graph of a trigonometric function

The Hopewell Rocks on the Bay of Fundy coastline are sculpted by the cyclic tides.

Many natural phenomena are cyclic, such as the tides of the ocean, the orbit of Earth around the Sun, and the growth and decline in animal populations. What other examples of cyclic natural phenomena can you describe?

You can model these types of natural behaviour with periodic functions such as sine and cosine functions.

> **Did You Know?**
>
> The Bay of Fundy, between New Brunswick and Nova Scotia, has the highest tides in the world. The highest recorded tidal range is 17 m at Burntcoat Head, Nova Scotia.

Investigate the Sine and Cosine Functions

Materials

- grid paper
- ruler

1. a) Copy and complete the table. Use your knowledge of special angles to determine exact values for each trigonometric ratio. Then, determine the approximate values, to two decimal places. One row has been completed for you.

Angle, θ	$y = \sin θ$	$y = \cos θ$
0		
$\frac{\pi}{6}$	$\frac{1}{2} = 0.50$	$\frac{\sqrt{3}}{2} \approx 0.87$
$\frac{\pi}{4}$		
$\frac{\pi}{3}$		
$\frac{\pi}{2}$		

b) Extend the table to include multiples of the special angles in the other three quadrants.

2. **a)** Graph $y = \sin \theta$ on the interval $\theta \in [0, 2\pi]$

   b) Summarize the following characteristics of the function $y = \sin \theta$.
   - the maximum value and the minimum value
   - the interval over which the pattern of the function repeats
   - the zeros of the function in the interval $\theta \in [0, 2\pi]$
   - the y-intercept
   - the domain and range

3. Graph $y = \cos \theta$ on the interval $\theta \in [0, 2\pi]$ and create a summary similar to the one you developed in step 2b).

Reflect and Respond

4. **a)** Suppose that you extended the graph of $y = \sin \theta$ to the right of 2π. Predict the shape of the graph. Use a calculator to investigate a few points to the right of 2π. At what value of θ will the next cycle end?

   b) Suppose that you extended the graph of $y = \sin \theta$ to the left of 0. Predict the shape of the graph. Use a calculator to investigate a few points to the left of 0. At what value of θ will the next cycle end?

5. Repeat step 4 for $y = \cos \theta$.

Did You Know?

The sine function is based upon one of the trigonometric ratios originally calculated by the astronomer Hipparchus of Nicaea in the second century b.c.e. He was trying to make sense of the movement of the stars and the moon in the night sky.

Link the Ideas

Sine and cosine functions are **periodic functions**. The values of these functions repeat over a specified **period**.

A sine graph is a graph of the function $y = \sin \theta$. You can also describe a sine graph as a **sinusoidal curve**.

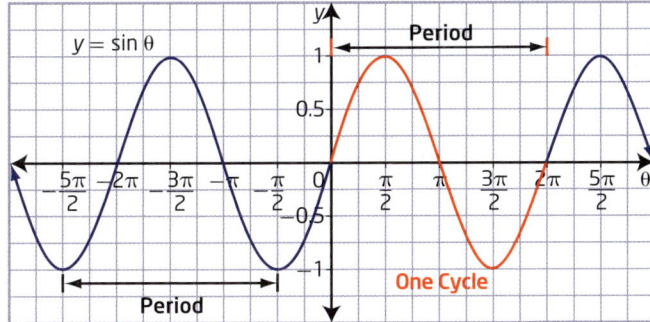

Trigonometric functions are sometimes called circular because they are based on the unit circle.

periodic function
- a function that repeats itself over regular intervals (cycles) of its domain

period
- the length of the interval of the domain over which a graph repeats itself
- the horizontal length of one cycle on a periodic graph

sinusoidal curve
- the name given to a curve that fluctuates back and forth like a sine graph
- a curve that oscillates repeatedly up and down from a centre line

The sine function, $y = \sin \theta$, relates the measure of angle θ in standard position to the *y*-coordinate of the point P where the terminal arm of the angle intersects the unit circle.

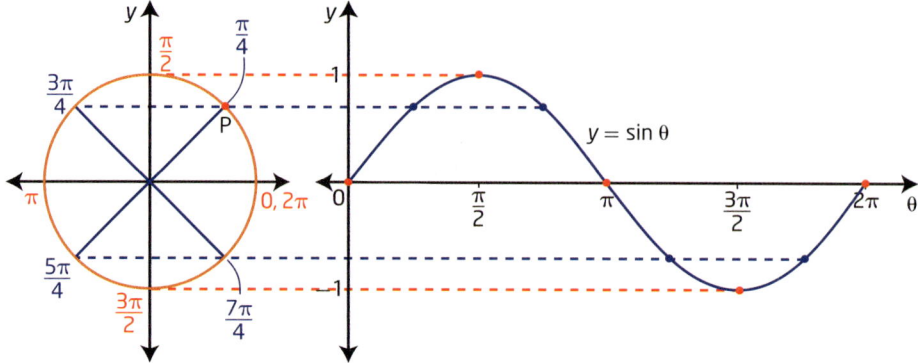

The cosine function, $y = \cos \theta$, relates the measure of angle θ in standard position to the *x*-coordinate of the point P where the terminal arm of the angle intersects the unit circle.

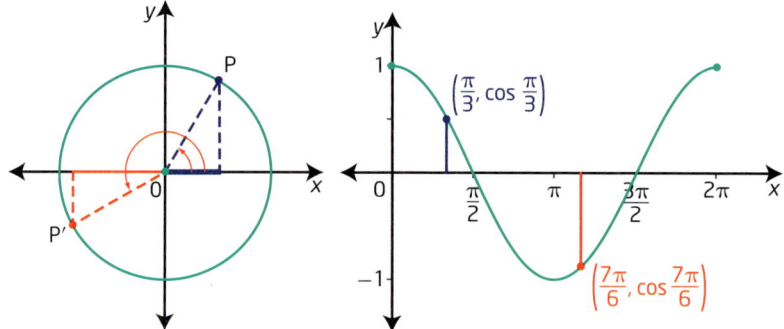

The coordinates of point P repeat after point P travels completely around the unit circle. The unit circle has a circumference of 2π. Therefore, the smallest distance before the cycle of values for the functions $y = \sin \theta$ or $y = \cos \theta$ begins to repeat is 2π. This distance is the period of $\sin \theta$ and $\cos \theta$.

Example 1

Graph a Periodic Function

Sketch the graph of $y = \sin \theta$ for $0° \leq \theta \leq 360°$ or $0 \leq \theta \leq 2\pi$. Describe its characteristics.

Solution

To sketch the graph of the sine function for $0° \leq \theta \leq 360°$ or $0 \leq \theta \leq 2\pi$, select values of θ and determine the corresponding values of $\sin \theta$. Plot the points and join them with a smooth curve.

θ	Degrees	0°	30°	45°	60°	90°	120°	135°	150°	180°	210°	225°	240°	270°	300°	315°	330°	360°
	Radians	0	$\frac{\pi}{6}$	$\frac{\pi}{4}$	$\frac{\pi}{3}$	$\frac{\pi}{2}$	$\frac{2\pi}{3}$	$\frac{3\pi}{4}$	$\frac{5\pi}{6}$	π	$\frac{7\pi}{6}$	$\frac{5\pi}{4}$	$\frac{4\pi}{3}$	$\frac{3\pi}{2}$	$\frac{5\pi}{3}$	$\frac{7\pi}{4}$	$\frac{11\pi}{6}$	2π
	sin θ	0	$\frac{1}{2}$	$\frac{\sqrt{2}}{2}$	$\frac{\sqrt{3}}{2}$	1	$\frac{\sqrt{3}}{2}$	$\frac{\sqrt{2}}{2}$	$\frac{1}{2}$	0	$-\frac{1}{2}$	$-\frac{\sqrt{2}}{2}$	$-\frac{\sqrt{3}}{2}$	-1	$-\frac{\sqrt{3}}{2}$	$-\frac{\sqrt{2}}{2}$	$-\frac{1}{2}$	0

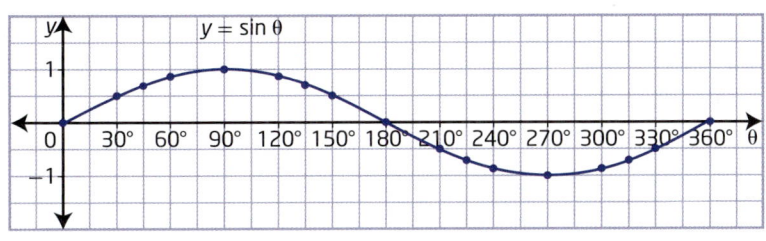

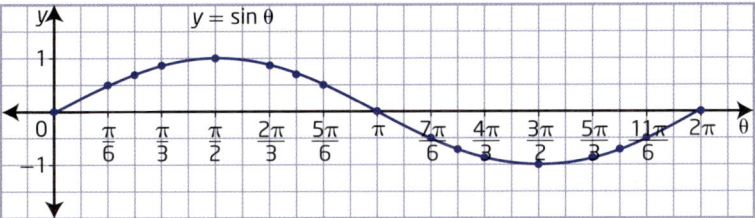

From the graph of the sine function, you can make general observations about the characteristics of the sine curve:

- The curve is periodic.
- The curve is continuous.
- The domain is {θ | θ ∈ R}.
- The range is {y | −1 ≤ y ≤ 1, y ∈ R}.
- The maximum value is +1.
- The minimum value is −1.
- The **amplitude** of the curve is 1.
- The period is 360° or 2π.
- The y-intercept is 0.
- In degrees, the θ-intercepts are
  …, −540°, −360°, −180°, 0°, 180°, 360°, …, or 180°n,
  where n ∈ I.
  The θ-intercepts, in radians, are
  …, −3π, −2π, −π, 0, π, 2π, …, or nπ,
  where n ∈ I.

Which points would you determine to be the key points for sketching a graph of the sine function?

Look for a pattern in the values.

Did You Know?

The Indo-Asian mathematician Aryabhata (476–550) made tables of half-chords that are now known as sine and cosine tables.

amplitude (of a sinusoidal function)
- the maximum vertical distance the graph of a sinusoidal function varies above and below the horizontal central axis of the curve

Your Turn

Sketch the graph of y = cos θ for 0° ≤ θ ≤ 360°. Describe its characteristics.

Example 2

Determine the Amplitude of a Sine Function

Any function of the form $y = af(x)$ is related to $y = f(x)$ by a vertical stretch of a factor $|a|$ about the x-axis, including the sine and cosine functions. If $a < 0$, the function is also reflected in the x-axis.

a) On the same set of axes, graph $y = 3 \sin x$, $y = 0.5 \sin x$, and $y = -2 \sin x$ for $0 \leq x \leq 2\pi$.
b) State the amplitude for each function.
c) Compare each graph to the graph of $y = \sin x$. Consider the period, amplitude, domain, and range.

Solution

a) **Method 1: Graph Using Transformations**

Sketch the graph of $y = \sin x$.

For the graph of $y = 3 \sin x$, apply a vertical stretch by a factor of 3.

For the graph of $y = 0.5 \sin x$, apply a vertical stretch by a factor of 0.5.

For the graph of $y = -2 \sin x$, reflect in the x-axis and apply a vertical stretch by a factor of 2.

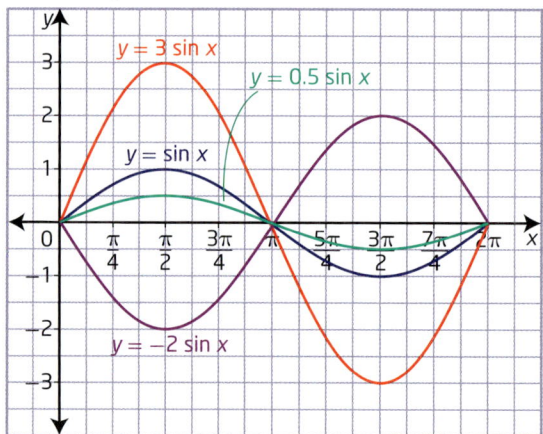

Method 2: Use a Graphing Calculator
Select radian mode.

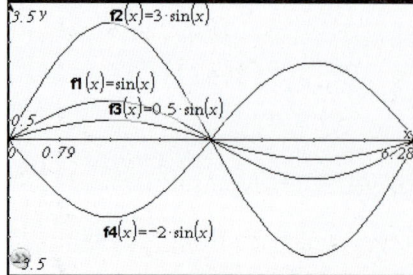

Use the following window settings:
$x: \left[0, 2\pi, \dfrac{\pi}{4}\right]$
$y: [-3.5, 3.5, 0.5]$

b) Determine the amplitude of a sine function using the formula

Amplitude = $\dfrac{\text{maximum value} - \text{minimum value}}{2}$.

The amplitude of $y = \sin x$ is $\dfrac{1 - (-1)}{2}$, or 1.

The amplitude of $y = 3 \sin x$ is $\dfrac{3 - (-3)}{2}$, or 3.

The amplitude of $y = 0.5 \sin x$ is $\dfrac{0.5 - (-0.5)}{2}$, or 0.5.

The amplitude of $y = -2 \sin x$ is $\dfrac{2 - (-2)}{2}$, or 2.

How is the amplitude related to the range of the function?

c)

Function	Period	Amplitude	Specified Domain	Range
$y = \sin x$	2π	1	$\{x \mid 0 \leq x \leq 2\pi, x \in R\}$	$\{y \mid -1 \leq y \leq 1, y \in R\}$
$y = 3 \sin x$	2π	3	$\{x \mid 0 \leq x \leq 2\pi, x \in R\}$	$\{y \mid -3 \leq y \leq 3, y \in R\}$
$y = 0.5 \sin x$	2π	0.5	$\{x \mid 0 \leq x \leq 2\pi, x \in R\}$	$\{y \mid -0.5 \leq y \leq 0.5, y \in R\}$
$y = -2 \sin x$	2π	2	$\{x \mid 0 \leq x \leq 2\pi, x \in R\}$	$\{y \mid -2 \leq y \leq 2, y \in R\}$

Changing the value of a affects the amplitude of a sinusoidal function. For the function $y = a \sin x$, the amplitude is $|a|$.

Your Turn

a) On the same set of axes, graph $y = 6 \cos x$ and $y = -4 \cos x$ for $0 \leq x \leq 2\pi$.
b) State the amplitude for each graph.
c) Compare your graphs to the graph of $y = \cos x$. Consider the period, amplitude, domain, and range.
d) What is the amplitude of the function $y = 1.5 \cos x$?

Period of $y = \sin bx$ or $y = \cos bx$

The graph of a function of the form $y = \sin bx$ or $y = \cos bx$ for $b \neq 0$ has a period different from 2π when $|b| \neq 1$. To show this, remember that $\sin bx$ or $\cos bx$ will take on all possible values as bx ranges from 0 to 2π. Therefore, to determine the period of either of these functions, solve the compound inequality as follows.

$0 \leq x \leq 2\pi$ Begin with the interval of one cycle of $y = \sin x$ or $y = \cos x$.

$0 \leq |b|x \leq 2\pi$ Replace x with $|b|x$ for the interval of one cycle of $y = \sin bx$ or $y = \cos bx$.

$0 \leq x \leq \dfrac{2\pi}{|b|}$ Divide by $|b|$.

Solving this inequality determines the length of a cycle for the sinusoidal curve, where the start of a cycle of $y = \sin bx$ is 0 and the end is $\dfrac{2\pi}{|b|}$.

Determine the period, or length of the cycle, by finding the distance from 0 to $\dfrac{2\pi}{|b|}$. Thus, the period for $y = \sin bx$ or $y = \cos bx$ is $\dfrac{2\pi}{|b|}$, in radians, or $\dfrac{360°}{|b|}$, in degrees.

Why do you use $|b|$ to determine the period?

Example 3

Determine the Period of a Sine Function

Any function of the form $y = f(bx)$ is related to $y = f(x)$ by a horizontal stretch by a factor of $\frac{1}{|b|}$ about the y-axis, including the sine and cosine functions. If $b < 0$, then the function is also reflected in the y-axis.

a) Sketch the graph of the function $y = \sin 4x$ for $0 \leq x \leq 360°$. State the period of the function and compare the graph to the graph of $y = \sin x$.

b) Sketch the graph of the function $y = \sin \frac{1}{2}x$ for $0 \leq x \leq 4\pi$. State the period of the function and compare the graph to the graph of $y = \sin x$.

Solution

a) Sketch the graph of $y = \sin x$.

For the graph of $y = \sin 4x$, apply a horizontal stretch by a factor of $\frac{1}{4}$.

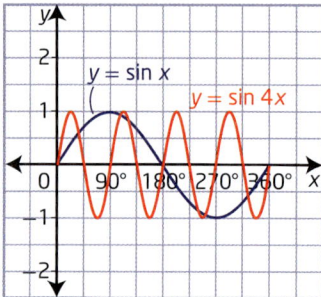

To find the period of a function, start from any point on the graph (for example, the y-intercept) and determine the length of the interval until one cycle is complete.

From the graph of $y = \sin 4x$, the period is 90°.

You can also determine this using the formula Period $= \frac{360°}{|b|}$.

Period $= \frac{360°}{|b|}$

Period $= \frac{360°}{|4|}$ Substitute 4 for b.

Period $= \frac{360°}{4}$

Period $= 90°$

Compared to the graph of $y = \sin x$, the graph of $y = \sin 4x$ has the same amplitude, domain, and range, but a different period.

b) Sketch the graph of $y = \sin x$.

For the graph of $y = \sin \frac{1}{2}x$, apply a horizontal stretch by a factor of 2.

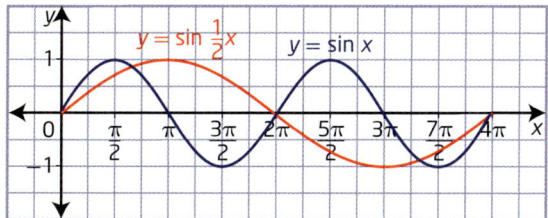

From the graph, the period for $y = \sin \frac{1}{2}x$ is 4π.
Using the formula,

Period $= \dfrac{2\pi}{|b|}$

Period $= \dfrac{2\pi}{\left|\frac{1}{2}\right|}$ Substitute $\frac{1}{2}$ for b.

Period $= \dfrac{2\pi}{\frac{1}{2}}$

Period $= 4\pi$

Compared to the graph of $y = \sin x$, the graph of $y = \sin \frac{1}{2}x$ has the same amplitude, domain, and range, but a different period.

Changing the value of b affects the period of a sinusoidal function.

Your Turn

a) Sketch the graph of the function $y = \cos 3x$ for $0 \leq x \leq 360°$. State the period of the function and compare the graph to the graph of $y = \cos x$.

b) Sketch the graph of the function $y = \cos \frac{1}{3}x$ for $0 \leq x \leq 6\pi$. State the period of the function and compare the graph to the graph of $y = \cos x$.

c) What is the period of the graph of $y = \cos(-3x)$?

Example 4

Sketch the Graph of $y = a \cos bx$

a) Sketch the graph of $y = -3\cos 2x$ for at least one cycle.

b) Determine
- the amplitude
- the period
- the maximum and minimum values
- the x-intercepts and the y-intercept
- the domain and range

Solution

a) Method 1: Graph Using Transformations

Compared to the graph of $y = \cos x$, the graph of $y = -3 \cos 2x$ is stretched horizontally by a factor of $\frac{1}{2}$ about the y-axis, stretched vertically by a factor of 3 about the x-axis, and reflected in the x-axis.

Begin with the graph of $y = \cos x$. Apply a horizontal stretch of $\frac{1}{2}$ about the y-axis.

Why is the horizontal stretch by a factor of $\frac{1}{2}$?

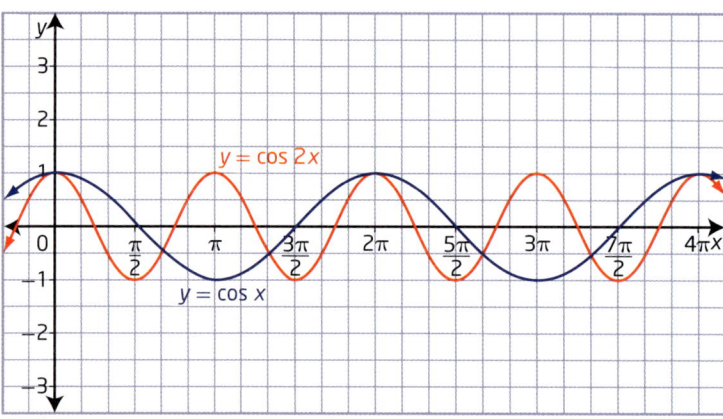

Then, apply a vertical stretch by a factor of 3.

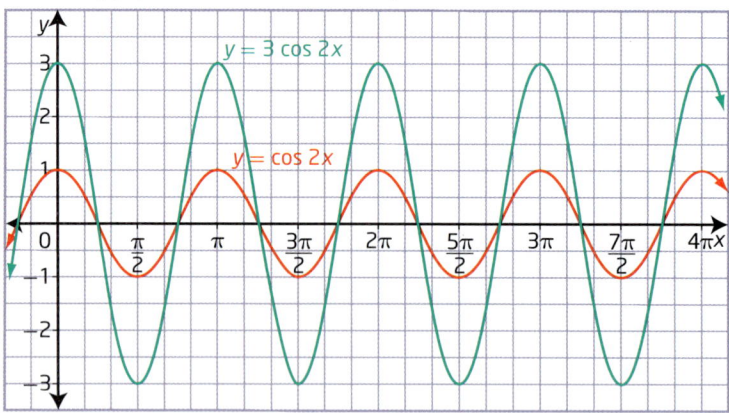

Finally, reflect the graph of $y = 3 \cos 2x$ in the x-axis.

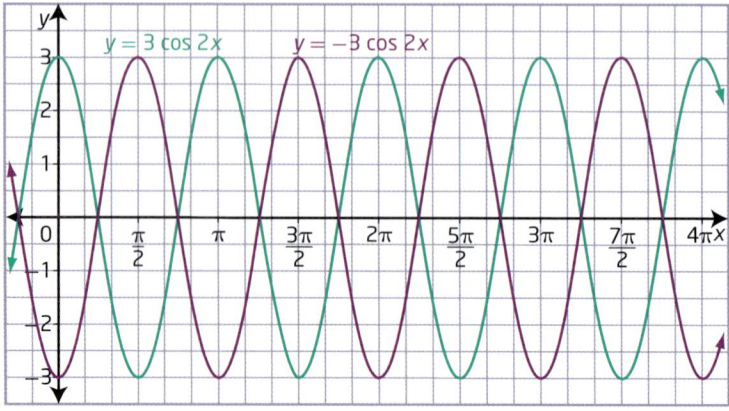

Method 2: Graph Using Key Points
This method is based on the fact that one cycle of a cosine function $y = \cos bx$, from 0 to $\frac{2\pi}{|b|}$, includes two x-intercepts, two maximums, and a minimum. These five points divide the period into quarters.

Compare $y = -3\cos 2x$ to $y = a\cos bx$.

Since $a = -3$, the amplitude is $|-3|$, or 3. Thus, the maximum value is 3 and the minimum value is -3.

Since $b = 2$, the period is $\frac{2\pi}{|2|}$, or π. One cycle will start at $x = 0$ and end at $x = \pi$. Divide this cycle into four equal segments using the values $0, \frac{\pi}{4}, \frac{\pi}{2}, \frac{3\pi}{4}$, and π for x.

How do you know where the maximums or minimums will occur?

The key points are $(0, -3)$, $\left(\frac{\pi}{4}, 0\right)$, $\left(\frac{\pi}{2}, 3\right)$, $\left(\frac{3\pi}{4}, 0\right)$, and $(\pi, -3)$.

Why are there two minimums instead of two maximums?

Connect the points in a smooth curve and sketch the graph through one cycle. The graph of $y = -3\cos 2x$ repeats every π units in either direction.

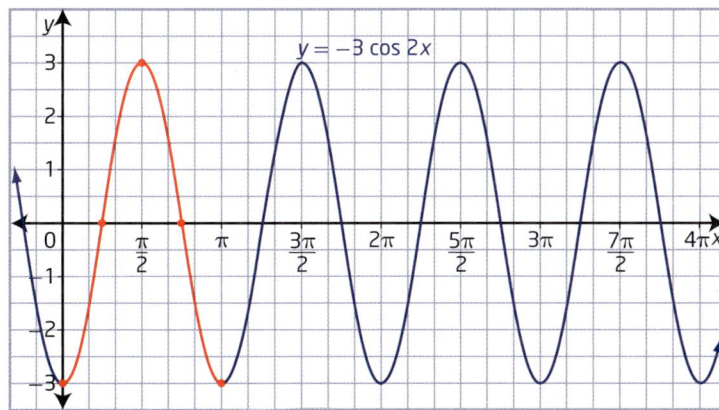

b) The amplitude of $y = -3\cos 2x$ is 3.
The period is π.
The maximum value is 3.
The minimum value is -3
The y-intercept is -3.
The x-intercepts are $\frac{\pi}{4}, \frac{3\pi}{4}, \frac{5\pi}{4}, \frac{7\pi}{4}$ or $\frac{\pi}{4} + \frac{\pi}{2}n, n \in I$.
The domain of the function is $\{x \mid x \in R\}$.
The range of the function is $\{y \mid -3 \leq y \leq 3, y \in R\}$.

Your Turn

a) Graph $y = 3 \sin 4x$, showing at least two cycles.

b) Determine
- the amplitude
- the period
- the maximum and minimum values
- the x-intercepts and the y-intercept
- the domain and range

Key Ideas

- To sketch the graphs of $y = \sin \theta$ and $y = \cos \theta$ for $0° \leq \theta \leq 360°$ or $0 \leq \theta \leq 2\pi$, determine the coordinates of the key points representing the θ-intercepts, maximum(s), and minimum(s).

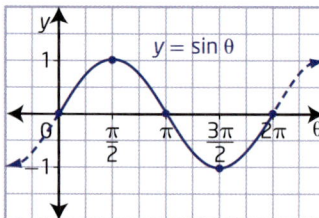

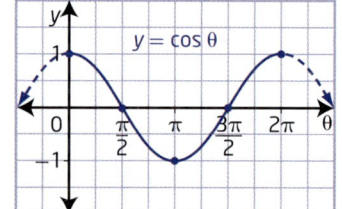

How are the characteristics different for $y = \cos \theta$?

The maximum value is $+1$.
The minimum value is -1.
The amplitude is 1.
The period is 2π.
The y-intercept is 0.
The θ-intercepts for the cycle shown are 0, π, and 2π.
The domain of $y = \sin \theta$ is $\{\theta \mid \theta \in R\}$.
The range of $y = \sin \theta$ is $\{y \mid -1 \leq y \leq 1, y \in R\}$.

- Determine the amplitude and period of a sinusoidal function of the form $y = a \sin bx$ or $y = a \cos bx$ by inspecting graphs or directly from the sinusoidal function.

  - You can determine the amplitude using the formula
    $$\text{Amplitude} = \frac{\text{maximum value} - \text{minimum value}}{2}.$$
    The amplitude is given by $|a|$.
    You can change the amplitude of a function by varying the value of a.

    How can you determine the amplitude from the graph of the sine function? cosine function?

  - The period is the horizontal length of one cycle on the graph of a function. It is given by $\frac{2\pi}{|b|}$ or $\frac{360°}{|b|}$.
    You can change the period of a function by varying the value of b.

    How can you identify the period on the graph of a sine function? cosine function?

Check Your Understanding

Practise

1. **a)** State the five key points for $y = \sin x$ that occur in one complete cycle from 0 to 2π.
   b) Use the key points to sketch the graph of $y = \sin x$ for $-2\pi \leq x \leq 2\pi$. Indicate the key points on your graph.
   c) What are the x-intercepts of the graph?
   d) What is the y-intercept of the graph?
   e) What is the maximum value of the graph? the minimum value?

2. **a)** State the five key points for $y = \cos x$ that occur in one complete cycle from 0 to 2π.
   b) Use the key points to sketch a graph of $y = \cos x$ for $-2\pi \leq x \leq 2\pi$. Indicate the key points on your graph.
   c) What are the x-intercepts of the graph?
   d) What is the y-intercept of the graph?
   e) What is the maximum value of the graph? the minimum value?

3. Copy and complete the table of properties for $y = \sin x$ and $y = \cos x$ for all real numbers.

Property	$y = \sin x$	$y = \cos x$
maximum		
minimum		
amplitude		
period		
domain		
range		
y-intercept		
x-intercepts		

4. State the amplitude of each periodic function. Sketch the graph of each function.
   a) $y = 2 \sin \theta$
   b) $y = \dfrac{1}{2} \cos \theta$
   c) $y = -\dfrac{1}{3} \sin x$
   d) $y = -6 \cos x$

5. State the period for each periodic function, in degrees and in radians. Sketch the graph of each function.
   a) $y = \sin 4\theta$
   b) $y = \cos \dfrac{1}{3}\theta$
   c) $y = \sin \dfrac{2}{3}x$
   d) $y = \cos 6x$

Apply

6. Match each function with its graph.
   a) $y = 3 \cos x$
   b) $y = \cos 3x$
   c) $y = -\sin x$
   d) $y = -\cos x$

A
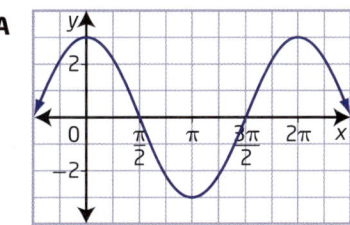

B
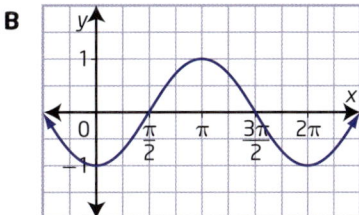

C
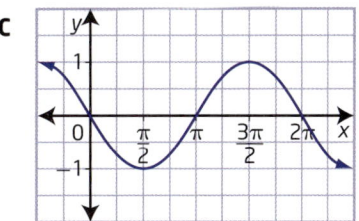

D
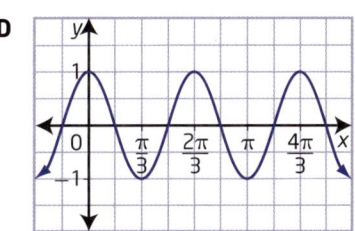

7. Determine the amplitude of each function. Then, use the language of transformations to describe how each graph is related to the graph of $y = \sin x$.

   a) $y = 3 \sin x$
   b) $y = -5 \sin x$
   c) $y = 0.15 \sin x$
   d) $y = -\dfrac{2}{3} \sin x$

8. Determine the period (in degrees) of each function. Then, use the language of transformations to describe how each graph is related to the graph of $y = \cos x$.

   a) $y = \cos 2x$
   b) $y = \cos(-3x)$
   c) $y = \cos \dfrac{1}{4}x$
   d) $y = \cos \dfrac{2}{3}x$

9. Without graphing, determine the amplitude and period of each function. State the period in degrees and in radians.

   a) $y = 2 \sin x$
   b) $y = -4 \cos 2x$
   c) $y = \dfrac{5}{3} \sin\left(-\dfrac{2}{3}x\right)$
   d) $y = 3 \cos \dfrac{1}{2}x$

10. a) Determine the period and the amplitude of each function in the graph.

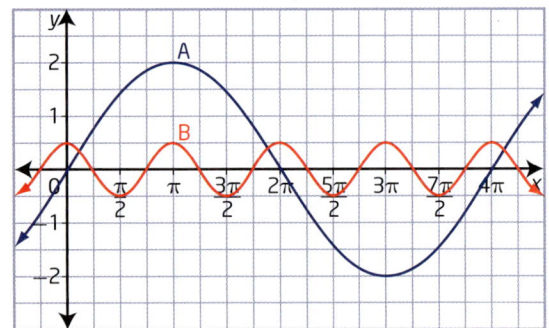

   b) Write an equation in the form $y = a \sin bx$ or $y = a \cos bx$ for each function.

   c) Explain your choice of either sine or cosine for each function.

11. Sketch the graph of each function over the interval $[-360°, 360°]$. For each function, clearly label the maximum and minimum values, the x-intercepts, the y-intercept, the period, and the range.

   a) $y = 2 \cos x$
   b) $y = -3 \sin x$
   c) $y = \dfrac{1}{2} \sin x$
   d) $y = -\dfrac{3}{4} \cos x$

12. The points indicated on the graph shown represent the x-intercepts and the maximum and minimum values.

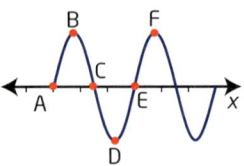

   a) Determine the coordinates of points B, C, D, and E if $y = 3 \sin 2x$ and A has coordinates $(0, 0)$.

   b) Determine the coordinates of points C, D, E, and F if $y = 2 \cos x$ and B has coordinates $(0, 2)$.

   c) Determine the coordinates of points B, C, D, and E if $y = \sin \dfrac{1}{2}x$ and A has coordinates $(-4\pi, 0)$.

13. The second harmonic in sound is given by $f(x) = \sin 2x$, while the third harmonic is given by $f(x) = \sin 3x$. Sketch the curves and compare the graphs of the second and third harmonics for $-2\pi \leq x \leq 2\pi$.

   Did You Know?

   A harmonic is a wave whose frequency is an integral multiple of the fundamental frequency. The fundamental frequency of a periodic wave is the inverse of the period length.

14. Sounds heard by the human ear are vibrations created by different air pressures. Musical sounds are regular or periodic vibrations. Pure tones will produce single sine waves on an oscilloscope. Determine the amplitude and period of each single sine wave shown.

   a)

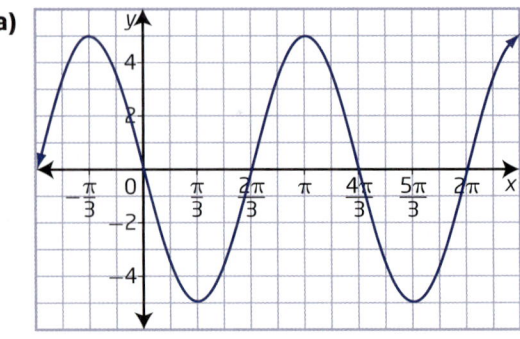

b)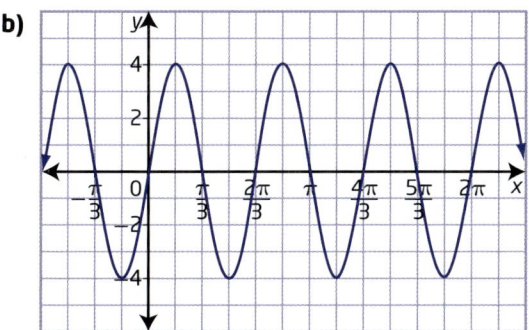

Did You Know?

Pure tone audiometry is a hearing test used to measure the hearing threshold levels of a patient. This test determines if there is hearing loss. Pure tone audiometry relies on a patient's response to pure tone stimuli.

15. Systolic and diastolic pressures mark the upper and lower limits in the changes in blood pressure that produce a pulse. The length of time between the peaks relates to the period of the pulse.

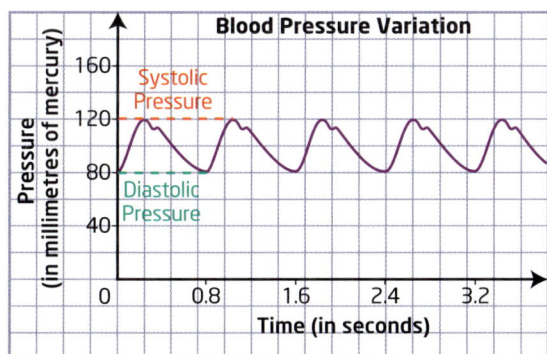

a) Determine the period and amplitude of the graph.

b) Determine the pulse rate (number of beats per minute) for this person.

16. **MINI LAB** Follow these steps to draw a sine curve.

Materials
- paper
- protractor
- compass
- ruler
- grid paper

Step 1 Draw a large circle.
   a) Mark the centre of the circle.
   b) Use a protractor and mark every 15° from 0° to 180° along the circumference of the circle.
   c) Draw a line radiating from the centre of the circle to each mark.
   d) Draw a vertical line to complete a right triangle for each of the angles that you measured.

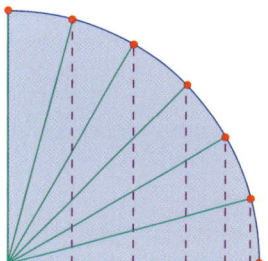

Step 2 Recall that the sine ratio is the length of the opposite side divided by the length of the hypotenuse. The hypotenuse of each triangle is the radius of the circle. Measure the length of the opposite side for each triangle and complete a table similar to the one shown.

Angle, x	Opposite	Hypotenuse	$\sin x = \dfrac{\text{opposite}}{\text{hypotenuse}}$
0°			
15°			
30°			
45°			

Step 3 Draw a coordinate grid on a sheet of grid paper.
   a) Label the x-axis from 0° to 360° in increments of 15°.
   b) Label the y-axis from -1 to $+1$.
   c) Create a scatter plot of points from your table. Join the dots with a smooth curve.

Step 4 Use one of the following methods to complete one cycle of the sine graph:
- complete the diagram from 180° to 360°
- extend the table by measuring the lengths of the sides of the triangle
- use the symmetry of the sine curve to complete the cycle

17. Sketch one cycle of a sinusoidal curve with the given amplitude and period and passing through the given point.

   a) amplitude 2, period 180°, point (0, 0)

   b) amplitude 1.5, period 540°, point (0, 0)

18. The graphs of $y = \sin \theta$ and $y = \cos \theta$ show the coordinates of one point. Determine the coordinates of four other points on the graph with the same y-coordinate as the point shown. Explain how you determined the θ-coordinates.

   a)
   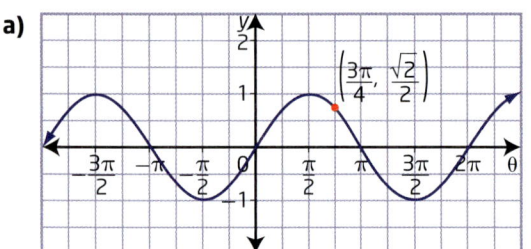

   b)
   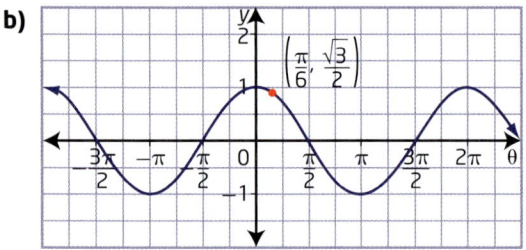

19. Graph $y = \sin \theta$ and $y = \cos \theta$ on the same set of axes for $-2\pi \leq \theta \leq 2\pi$.

   a) How are the two graphs similar?

   b) How are they different?

   c) What transformation could you apply to make them the same graph?

Extend

20. If $y = f(x)$ has a period of 6, determine the period of $y = f\left(\dfrac{1}{2}x\right)$.

21. Determine the period, in radians, of each function using two different methods.

   a) $y = -2 \sin 3x$

   b) $y = -\dfrac{2}{3} \cos \dfrac{\pi}{6} x$

22. If $\sin \theta = 0.3$, determine the value of $\sin \theta + \sin (\theta + 2\pi) + \sin (\theta + 4\pi)$.

23. Consider the function $y = \sqrt{\sin x}$.

   a) Use the graph of $y = \sin x$ to sketch a prediction for the shape of the graph of $y = \sqrt{\sin x}$.

   b) Use graphing technology or grid paper and a table of values to check your prediction. Resolve any differences.

   c) How do you think the graph of $y = \sqrt{\sin x + 1}$ will differ from the graph of $y = \sqrt{\sin x}$?

   d) Graph $y = \sqrt{\sin x + 1}$ and compare it to your prediction.

24. Is the function $f(x) = 5 \cos x + 3 \sin x$ sinusoidal? If it is sinusoidal, state the period of the function.

> **Did You Know?**
>
> In 1822, French mathematician Joseph Fourier discovered that any wave could be modelled as a combination of different types of sine waves. This model applies even to unusual waves such as square waves and highly irregular waves such as human speech. The discipline of reducing a complex wave to a combination of sine waves is called Fourier analysis and is fundamental to many of the sciences.

Create Connections

C1 MINI LAB Explore the relationship between the unit circle and the sine and cosine graphs with a graphing calculator.

Step 1 In the first list, enter the angle values from 0 to 2π by increments of $\dfrac{\pi}{12}$. In the second and third lists, calculate the cosine and sine of the angles in the first list, respectively.

Step 2 Graph the second and third lists for the unit circle.

Step 3 Graph the first and third lists for the sine curve.

Step 4 Graph the first and second lists for the cosine curve.

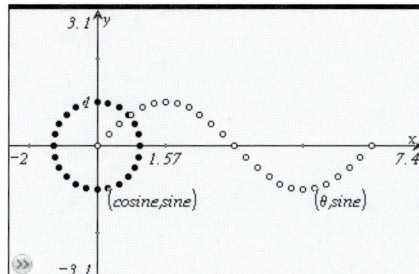

Step 5 a) Use the trace feature on the graphing calculator and trace around the unit circle. What do you notice about the points that you trace? What do they represent?

b) Move the cursor to trace the sine or cosine curve. How do the points on the graph of the sine or cosine curve relate to the points on the unit circle? Explain.

C2 The value of $(\cos \theta)^2 + (\sin \theta)^2$ appears to be constant no matter the value of θ. What is the value of the constant? Why is the value constant? (Hint: Use the unit circle and the Pythagorean theorem in your explanation.)

C3 The graph of $y = f(x)$ is sinusoidal with a period of 40° passing through the point (4, 0). Decide whether each of the following can be determined from this information, and justify your answer.

a) $f(0)$
b) $f(4)$
c) $f(84)$

C4 Identify the regions that each of the following characteristics fall into.

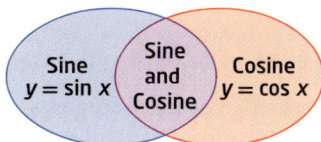

a) domain $\{x \mid x \in R\}$
b) range $\{y \mid -1 \leq y \leq 1, y \in R\}$
c) period is 2π
d) amplitude is 1
e) x-intercepts are $n(180°)$, $n \in I$
f) x-intercepts are $90° + n(180°)$, $n \in I$
g) y-intercept is 1
h) y-intercept is 0
i) passes through point (0, 1)
j) passes through point (0, 0)
k) a maximum value occurs at (360°, 1)
l) a maximum value occurs at (90°, 1)

m)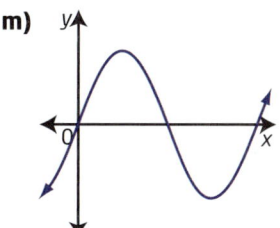

n)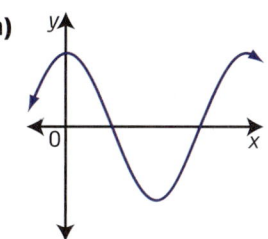

C5 a) Sketch the graph of $y = |\cos x|$ for $-2\pi \leq x \leq 2\pi$. How does the graph compare to the graph of $y = \cos x$?

b) Sketch the graph of $y = |\sin x|$ for $-2\pi \leq x \leq 2\pi$. How does the graph compare to the graph of $y = \sin x$?

5.2

Transformations of Sinusoidal Functions

Focus on...

- graphing and transforming sinusoidal functions
- identifying the domain, range, phase shift, period, amplitude, and vertical displacement of sinusoidal functions
- developing equations of sinusoidal functions, expressed in radian and degree measure, from graphs and descriptions
- solving problems graphically that can be modelled using sinusoidal functions
- recognizing that more than one equation can be used to represent the graph of a sinusoidal function

Electric power and the light waves it generates are sinusoidal waveforms.

The pistons and connecting rods of a steam train drive the wheels with a motion that is sinusoidal.

Ocean waves created by the winds may be modelled by sinusoidal curves.

The motion of a body attached to a suspended spring, the motion of the plucked string of a musical instrument, and the pendulum of a clock produce oscillatory motion that you can model with sinusoidal functions. To use the functions $y = \sin x$ and $y = \cos x$ in applied situations, such as these and the ones in the images shown, you need to be able to transform the functions.

Investigate Transformations of Sinusoidal Functions

Materials

- grid paper
- graphing technology

A: Graph $y = \sin \theta + d$ or $y = \cos \theta + d$

1. On the same set of axes, sketch the graphs of the following functions for $0° \leq \theta \leq 360°$.

   $y = \sin \theta$
   $y = \sin \theta + 1$
   $y = \sin \theta - 2$

2. Using the language of transformations, compare the graphs of $y = \sin \theta + 1$ and $y = \sin \theta - 2$ to the graph of $y = \sin \theta$.

3. Predict what the graphs of $y = \sin \theta + 3$ and $y = \sin \theta - 4$ will look like. Justify your predictions.

Reflect and Respond

4. a) What effect does the parameter d in the function $y = \sin \theta + d$ have on the graph of $y = \sin \theta$ when $d > 0$?

b) What effect does the parameter d in the function $y = \sin \theta + d$ have on the graph of $y = \sin \theta$ when $d < 0$?

5. a) Predict the effect varying the parameter d in the function $y = \cos \theta + d$ has on the graph of $y = \cos \theta$.

b) Use a graph to verify your prediction.

B: Graph $y = \cos(\theta - c)$ or $y = \sin(\theta - c)$ Using Technology

6. On the same set of axes, sketch the graphs of the following functions for $-\pi \leq \theta \leq 2\pi$.

$y = \cos \theta$

$y = \cos\left(\theta + \dfrac{\pi}{2}\right)$

$y = \cos(\theta - \pi)$

7. Using the language of transformations, compare the graphs of $y = \cos\left(\theta + \dfrac{\pi}{2}\right)$ and $y = \cos(\theta - \pi)$ to the graph of $y = \cos \theta$.

8. Predict what the graphs of $y = \cos\left(\theta - \dfrac{\pi}{2}\right)$ and $y = \cos\left(\theta + \dfrac{3\pi}{2}\right)$ will look like. Justify your predictions.

Reflect and Respond

9. a) What effect does the parameter c in the function $y = \cos(\theta - c)$ have on the graph of $y = \cos \theta$ when $c > 0$?

b) What effect does the parameter c in the function $y = \cos(\theta - c)$ have on the graph of $y = \cos \theta$ when $c < 0$?

10. a) Predict the effect varying the parameter c in the function $y = \sin(\theta - c)$ has on the graph of $y = \sin \theta$.

b) Use a graph to verify your prediction.

Link the Ideas

You can translate graphs of functions up or down or left or right and stretch them vertically and/or horizontally. The rules that you have applied to the transformations of functions also apply to transformations of sinusoidal curves.

Example 1

Graph $y = \sin(x - c) + d$

a) Sketch the graph of the function $y = \sin(x - 30°) + 3$.
b) What are the domain and range of the function?
c) Use the language of transformations to compare your graph to the graph of $y = \sin x$.

Solution

a)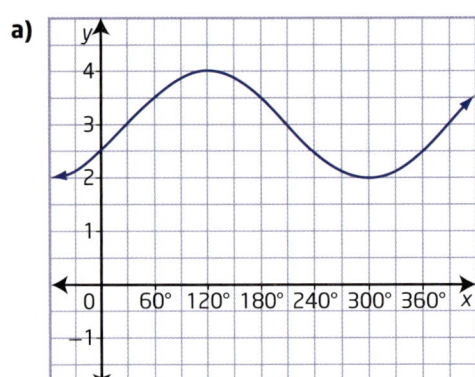

b) Domain: $\{x \mid x \in \mathrm{R}\}$
Range: $\{y \mid 2 \leq y \leq 4, y \in \mathrm{R}\}$

c) The graph has been translated 3 units up. This is the **vertical displacement**. The graph has also been translated 30° to the right. This is called the **phase shift**.

Your Turn

a) Sketch the graph of the function $y = \cos(x + 45°) - 2$.
b) What are the domain and range of the function?
c) Use the language of transformations to compare your graph to the graph of $y = \cos x$.

vertical displacement
- the vertical translation of the graph of a periodic function

phase shift
- the horizontal translation of the graph of a periodic function

Example 2

Graph $y = a \cos(\theta - c) + d$

a) Sketch the graph of the function $y = -2\cos(\theta + \pi) - 1$ over two cycles.
b) Use the language of transformations to compare your graph to the graph of $y = \cos \theta$. Indicate which parameter is related to each transformation.

Solution

a)

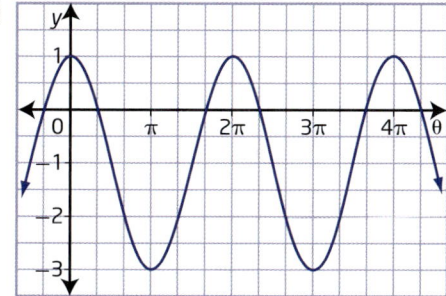

b) Since a is -2, the graph has been reflected about the θ-axis and then stretched vertically by a factor of two. The d-value is -1, so the graph is translated 1 unit down. The sinusoidal axis is defined as $y = -1$. Finally, the c-value is $-\pi$. Therefore, the graph is translated π units to the left.

Your Turn

a) Sketch the graph of the function $y = 2 \sin\left(\theta - \frac{\pi}{2}\right) + 2$ over two cycles.
b) Compare your graph to the graph of $y = \sin \theta$.

Did You Know?

In this chapter, the parameters for horizontal and vertical translations are represented by c and d, respectively.

Example 3

Graph $y = a \sin b(x - c) + d$

Sketch the graph of the function $y = 3 \sin\left(2x - \frac{2\pi}{3}\right) + 2$ over two cycles. What are the vertical displacement, amplitude, period, phase shift, domain, and range for the function?

Solution

First, rewrite the function in the standard form $y = a \sin b(x - c) + d$.

$y = 3 \sin 2\left(x - \frac{\pi}{3}\right) + 2$

Method 1: Graph Using Transformations
Step 1: Sketch the graph of $y = \sin x$ for one cycle. Apply the horizontal and vertical stretches to obtain the graph of $y = 3 \sin 2x$.

Compared to the graph of $y = \sin x$, the graph of $y = 3 \sin 2x$ is a horizontal stretch by a factor of $\frac{1}{2}$ and a vertical stretch by a factor of 3.

For the function $y = 3 \sin 2x$, $b = 2$.

Period $= \frac{2\pi}{|b|}$
$= \frac{2\pi}{2}$
$= \pi$

So, the period is π.

For the function $y = 3 \sin 2x$, $|a| = 3$.
So, the amplitude is 3.

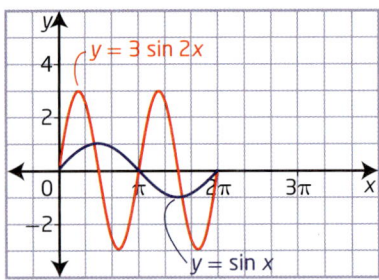

Step 2: Apply the horizontal translation to obtain the graph of $y = 3 \sin 2\left(x - \dfrac{\pi}{3}\right)$.

The phase shift is determined by the value of parameter c for a function in the standard form $y = a \sin b(x - c) + d$.

Compared to the graph of $y = 3 \sin 2x$, the graph of $y = 3 \sin 2\left(x - \dfrac{\pi}{3}\right)$ is translated horizontally $\dfrac{\pi}{3}$ units to the right.

The phase shift is $\dfrac{\pi}{3}$ units to the right.

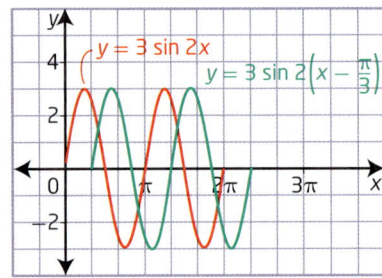

Step 3: Apply the vertical translation to obtain the graph of $y = 3 \sin 2\left(x - \dfrac{\pi}{3}\right) + 2$.

The vertical displacement is determined by the value of parameter d for a function in the standard form $y = a \sin b(x - c) + d$.

Compared to the graph of $y = 3 \sin 2\left(x - \dfrac{\pi}{3}\right)$, the graph of $y = 3 \sin 2\left(x - \dfrac{\pi}{3}\right) + 2$ is translated up 2 units.

The vertical displacement is 2 units up.

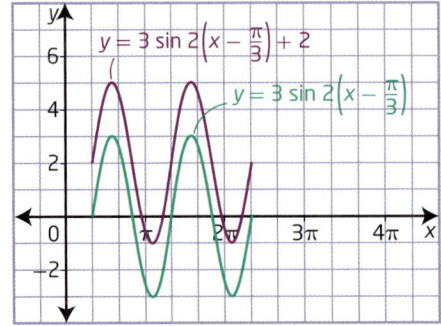

Would it matter if the order of the transformations were changed? Try a different order for the transformations.

Compared to the graph of $y = \sin x$, the graph of $y = 3 \sin 2\left(x - \frac{\pi}{3}\right) + 2$ is

- horizontally stretched by a factor of $\frac{1}{2}$
- vertically stretched by a factor of 3
- horizontally translated $\frac{\pi}{3}$ units to the right
- vertically translated 2 units up

The vertical displacement is 2 units up.
The amplitude is 3.
The phase shift is $\frac{\pi}{3}$ units to the right.
The domain is $\{x \mid x \in R\}$.
The range is $\{y \mid -1 \leq y \leq 5, y \in R\}$.

Method 2: Graph Using Key Points
You can identify five key points to graph one cycle of the sine function. The first, third, and fifth points indicate the start, the middle, and the end of the cycle. The second and fourth points indicate the maximum and minimum points.

Comparing $y = 3 \sin 2\left(x - \frac{\pi}{3}\right) + 2$ to $y = a \sin b(x - c) + d$ gives $a = 3$, $b = 2$, $c = \frac{\pi}{3}$, and $d = 2$.

The amplitude is $|a|$, or 3.

The period is $\frac{2\pi}{|b|}$, or π.

The vertical displacement is d, or 2. Therefore, the equation of the sinusoidal axis or mid-line is $y = 2$.

You can use the amplitude and vertical displacement to determine the maximum and minimum values.

The maximum value is
$d + |a| = 2 + 3$
$ = 5$

The minimum value is
$d - |a| = 2 - 3$
$ = -1$

Determine the values of x for the start and end of one cycle from the function $y = a \sin b(x - c) + d$ by solving the compound inequality $0 \leq b(x - c) \leq 2\pi$.

$0 \leq 2\left(x - \frac{\pi}{3}\right) \leq 2\pi$

How does this inequality relate to the period of the function?

$0 \leq x - \frac{\pi}{3} \leq \pi$

$\frac{\pi}{3} \leq x \leq \frac{4\pi}{3}$

Divide the interval $\frac{\pi}{3} \leq x \leq \frac{4\pi}{3}$ into four equal segments. By doing this, you can locate five key values of x along the sinusoidal axis.

$\frac{\pi}{3}, \frac{7\pi}{12}, \frac{5\pi}{6}, \frac{13\pi}{12}, \frac{4\pi}{3}$

Use the above information to sketch one cycle of the graph, and then a second cycle.

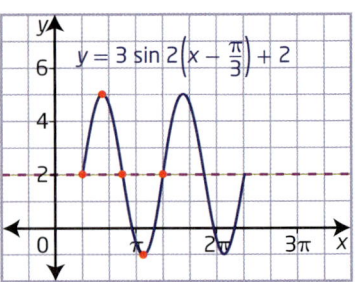

Note the five key points and how you can use them to sketch one cycle of the graph of the function.

For the graph of the function $y = 3 \sin 2\left(x - \frac{\pi}{3}\right) + 2$,
- the vertical displacement is 2 units up
- the amplitude is 3
- the phase shift is $\frac{\pi}{3}$ units to the right
- the domain is $\{x \mid x \in R\}$
- the range is $\{y \mid -1 \leq y \leq 5, y \in R\}$

Your Turn

Sketch the graph of the function $y = 2 \cos 4(x + \pi) - 1$ over two cycles. What are the vertical displacement, amplitude, period, phase shift, domain, and range for the function?

Example 4

Determine an Equation From a Graph

The graph shows the function $y = f(x)$.
a) Write the equation of the function in the form $y = a \sin b(x - c) + d, a > 0$.
b) Write the equation of the function in the form $y = a \cos b(x - c) + d, a > 0$.
c) Use technology to verify your solutions.

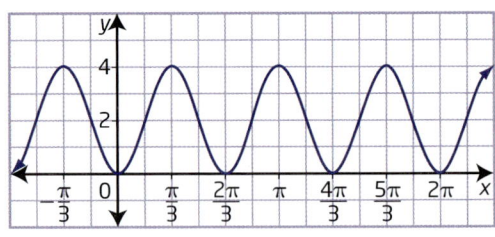

Solution

a) Determine the values of the parameters a, b, c, and d.

Locate the sinusoidal axis or mid-line. Its position determines the value of d. Thus, $d = 2$.

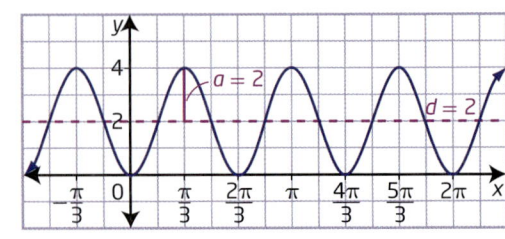

Use the sinusoidal axis from the graph or use the formula to determine the amplitude.

How can you use the maximum and minimum values of the graph to find the value of d?

$$\text{Amplitude} = \frac{\text{maximum value} - \text{minimum value}}{2}$$

$$a = \frac{4 - 0}{2}$$

$$a = 2$$

The amplitude is 2.

Determine the period and the value of b.

Method 1: Count the Number of Cycles in 2π

Determine the number of cycles in a distance of 2π.

In this function, there are three cycles. Therefore, the value of b is 3 and the period is $\frac{2\pi}{3}$.

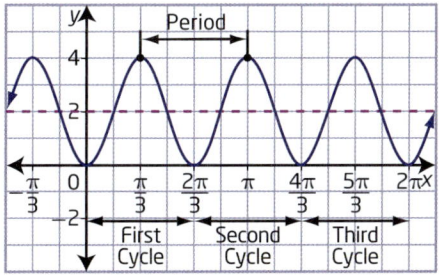

Method 2: Determine the Period First

Locate the start and end of one cycle of the sine curve.

Recall that one cycle of $y = \sin x$ starts at (0, 0). How is that point transformed? How could this information help you determine the start for one cycle of this sine curve?

The start of the first cycle of the sine curve that is closest to the y-axis is at $x = \frac{\pi}{6}$ and the end is at $x = \frac{5\pi}{6}$.

The period is $\frac{5\pi}{6} - \frac{\pi}{6}$, or $\frac{2\pi}{3}$.

Solve the equation for b.

$$\text{Period} = \frac{2\pi}{|b|}$$

$$\frac{2\pi}{3} = \frac{2\pi}{|b|}$$

$$b = 3 \quad \text{Choose b to be positive.}$$

Determine the phase shift, c.

Locate the start of the first cycle of the sine curve to the right of the y-axis. Thus, $c = \frac{\pi}{6}$.

Substitute the values of the parameters $a = 2$, $b = 3$, $c = \frac{\pi}{6}$, and $d = 2$ into the equation $y = a \sin b(x - c) + d$.

The equation of the function in the form $y = a \sin b(x - c) + d$ is $y = 2 \sin 3\left(x - \frac{\pi}{6}\right) + 2$.

b) To write an equation in the form $y = a \cos b(x - c) + d$, determine the values of the parameters a, b, c, and d using steps similar to what you did for the sine function in part a).

$a = 2$
$b = 3$
$c = \dfrac{\pi}{3}$ Why is $c = \dfrac{\pi}{3}$? Are there other possible values for c?
$d = 2$

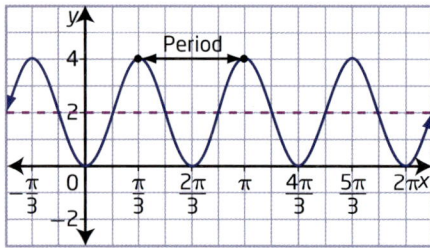

The equation of the function in the form $y = a \cos b(x - c) + d$ is
$y = 2 \cos 3\left(x - \dfrac{\pi}{3}\right) + 2.$

How do the two equations compare?

Could other equations define the function $y = f(x)$?

c) Enter the functions on a graphing calculator. Compare the graphs to the original and to each other.

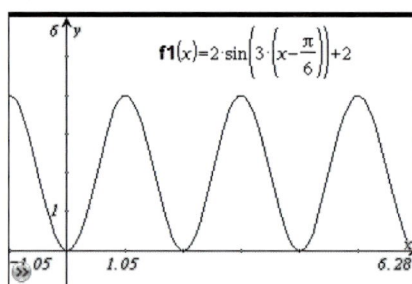
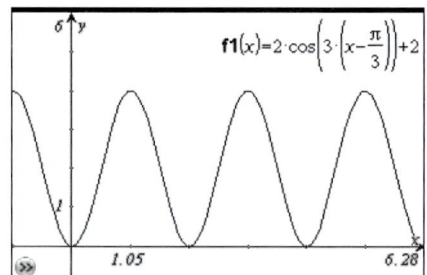

The graphs confirm that the equations for the function are correct.

Your Turn

The graph shows the function $y = f(x)$.

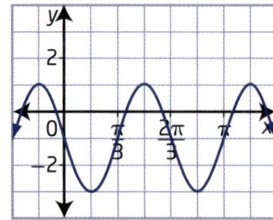

a) Write the equation of the function in the form $y = a \sin b(x - c) + d$, $a > 0$.
b) Write the equation of the function in the form $y = a \cos b(x - c) + d$, $a > 0$.
c) Use technology to verify your solutions.

Example 5

Interpret Graphs of Sinusoidal Functions

Prince Rupert, British Columbia, has the deepest natural harbour in North America. The depth, d, in metres, of the berths for the ships can be approximated by the equation $d(t) = 8 \cos \frac{\pi}{6} t + 12$, where t is the time, in hours, after the first high tide.

a) Graph the function for two cycles.
b) What is the period of the tide?
c) An ocean liner requires a minimum of 13 m of water to dock safely. From the graph, determine the number of hours per cycle the ocean liner can safely dock.
d) If the minimum depth of the berth occurs at 6 h, determine the depth of the water. At what other times is the water level at a minimum? Explain your solution.

Solution

a)

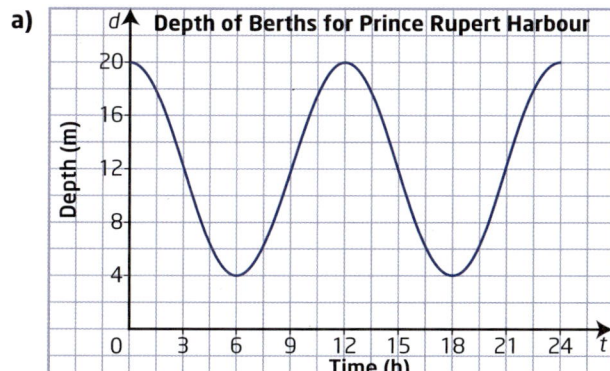

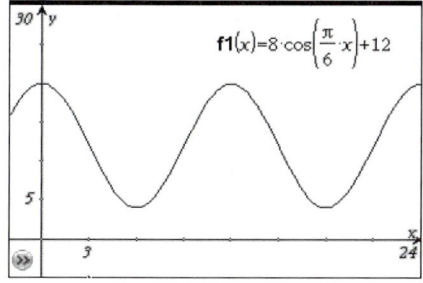

Why should you set the calculator to radian mode when graphing sinusoidal functions that represent real-world situations?

b) Use $b = \frac{\pi}{6}$ to determine the period.

Period $= \frac{2\pi}{|b|}$

Period $= \frac{2\pi}{\left|\frac{\pi}{6}\right|}$

Period $= 12$

The period for the tides is 12 h.

What does the period of 12 h represent?

c) To determine the number of hours an ocean liner can dock safely, draw the line $y = 13$ to represent the minimum depth of the berth. Determine the points of intersection of the graphs of $y = 13$ and $d(t) = 8 \cos \frac{\pi}{6} t + 12$.

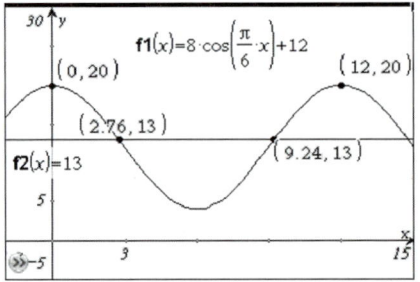

More precise answers can be obtained using technology.

The points of intersection for the first cycle are approximately (2.76, 13) and (9.26, 13).

The depth is greater than 13 m from 0 h to approximately 2.76 h and from approximately 9.24 h to 12 h. The total time when the depth is greater than 13 m is 2.76 + 2.76, or 5.52 h, or about 5 h 30 min per cycle.

d) To determine the berth depth at 6 h, substitute the value of $t = 6$ into the equation.

$d(t) = 8 \cos \frac{\pi}{6} t + 12$

$d(6) = 8 \cos \frac{\pi}{6}(6) + 12$

$d(6) = 8 \cos \pi + 12$

$d(6) = 8(-1) + 12$

$d(6) = 4$

You can use the graph to verify the solution.

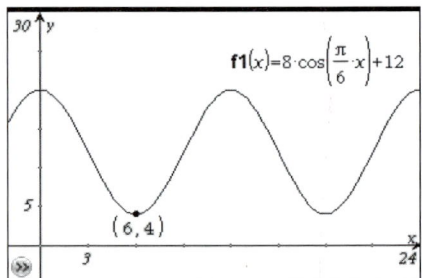

The berth depth at 6 h is 4 m. Add 12 h (the period) to 6 h to determine the next time the berth depth is 4 m. Therefore, the berth depth of 4 m occurs again at 18 h.

Your Turn

The depth, d, in metres, of the water in the harbour at New Westminster, British Columbia, is approximated by the equation $d(t) = 0.6 \cos \frac{2\pi}{13} t + 3.7$, where t is the time, in hours, after the first high tide.

a) Graph the function for two cycles starting at $t = 0$.
b) What is the period of the tide?
c) If a boat requires a minimum of 3.5 m of water to launch safely, for how many hours per cycle can the boat safely launch?
d) What is the depth of the water at 7 h? At what other times is the water level at this depth? Explain your solution.

Key Ideas

- You can determine the amplitude, period, phase shift, and vertical displacement of sinusoidal functions when the equation of the function is given in the form $y = a \sin b(x - c) + d$ or $y = a \cos b(x - c) + d$.

  For: $y = a \sin b(x - c) + d$
  $y = a \cos b(x - c) + d$

  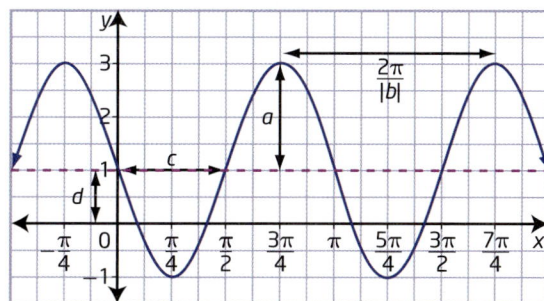

  How does changing each parameter affect the graph of a function?

  Vertical stretch by a factor of $|a|$
  - changes the amplitude to $|a|$
  - reflected in the x-axis if $a < 0$

  Horizontal stretch by a factor of $\dfrac{1}{|b|}$
  - changes the period to $\dfrac{360°}{|b|}$ (in degrees) or $\dfrac{2\pi}{|b|}$ (in radians)
  - reflected in the y-axis if $b < 0$

  Horizontal phase shift represented by c
  - to right if $c > 0$
  - to left if $c < 0$

  Vertical displacement represented by d
  - up if $d > 0$
  - down if $d < 0$

  $$d = \dfrac{\text{maximum value} + \text{minimum value}}{2}$$

- You can determine the equation of a sinusoidal function given its properties or its graph.

Check Your Understanding

Practise

1. Determine the phase shift and the vertical displacement with respect to $y = \sin x$ for each function. Sketch a graph of each function.
   a) $y = \sin(x - 50°) + 3$
   b) $y = \sin(x + \pi)$
   c) $y = \sin\left(x + \frac{2\pi}{3}\right) + 5$
   d) $y = 2\sin(x + 50°) - 10$
   e) $y = -3\sin(6x + 30°) - 3$
   f) $y = 3\sin\frac{1}{2}\left(x - \frac{\pi}{4}\right) - 10$

2. Determine the phase shift and the vertical displacement with respect to $y = \cos x$ for each function. Sketch a graph of each function.
   a) $y = \cos(x - 30°) + 12$
   b) $y = \cos\left(x - \frac{\pi}{3}\right)$
   c) $y = \cos\left(x + \frac{5\pi}{6}\right) + 16$
   d) $y = 4\cos(x + 15°) + 3$
   e) $y = 4\cos(x - \pi) + 4$
   f) $y = 3\cos\left(2x - \frac{\pi}{6}\right) + 7$

3. a) Determine the range of each function.
   i) $y = 3\cos\left(x - \frac{\pi}{2}\right) + 5$
   ii) $y = -2\sin(x + \pi) - 3$
   iii) $y = 1.5\sin x + 4$
   iv) $y = \frac{2}{3}\cos(x + 50°) + \frac{3}{4}$
   b) Describe how to determine the range when given a function of the form $y = a\cos b(x - c) + d$ or $y = a\sin b(x - c) + d$.

4. Match each function with its description in the table.
   a) $y = -2\cos 2(x + 4) - 1$
   b) $y = 2\sin 2(x - 4) - 1$
   c) $y = 2\sin(2x - 4) - 1$
   d) $y = 3\sin(3x - 9) - 1$
   e) $y = 3\sin(3x + \pi) - 1$

	Amplitude	Period	Phase Shift	Vertical Displacement
A	3	$\frac{2\pi}{3}$	3 right	1 down
B	2	π	2 right	1 down
C	2	π	4 right	1 down
D	2	π	4 left	1 down
E	3	$\frac{2\pi}{3}$	$\frac{\pi}{3}$ left	1 down

5. Match each function with its graph.
   a) $y = \sin\left(x - \frac{\pi}{4}\right)$
   b) $y = \sin\left(x + \frac{\pi}{4}\right)$
   c) $y = \sin x - 1$
   d) $y = \sin x + 1$

   A

   B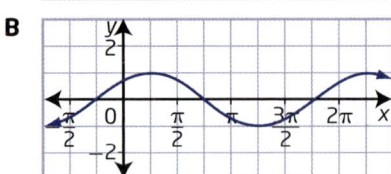

   C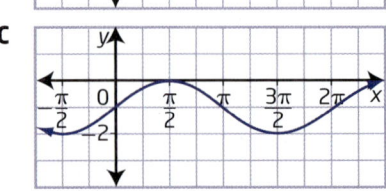

   D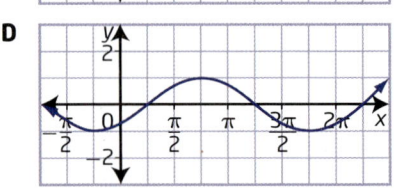

Apply

6. Write the equation of the sine function in the form $y = a \sin b(x - c) + d$ given its characteristics.

   a) amplitude 4, period π, phase shift $\frac{\pi}{2}$ to the right, vertical displacement 6 units down

   b) amplitude 0.5, period 4π, phase shift $\frac{\pi}{6}$ to the left, vertical displacement 1 unit up

   c) amplitude $\frac{3}{4}$, period $720°$, no phase shift, vertical displacement 5 units down

7. The graph of $y = \cos x$ is transformed as described. Determine the values of the parameters a, b, c, and d for the transformed function. Write the equation for the transformed function in the form $y = a \cos b(x - c) + d$.

   a) vertical stretch by a factor of 3 about the x-axis, horizontal stretch by a factor of 2 about the y-axis, translated 2 units to the left and 3 units up

   b) vertical stretch by a factor of $\frac{1}{2}$ about the x-axis, horizontal stretch by a factor of $\frac{1}{4}$ about the y-axis, translated 3 units to the right and 5 units down

   c) vertical stretch by a factor of $\frac{3}{2}$ about the x-axis, horizontal stretch by a factor of 3 about the y-axis, reflected in the x-axis, translated $\frac{\pi}{4}$ units to the right and 1 unit down

8. When white light shines through a prism, the white light is broken into the colours of the visible light spectrum. Each colour corresponds to a different wavelength of the electromagnetic spectrum. Arrange the colours, in order from greatest to smallest period.

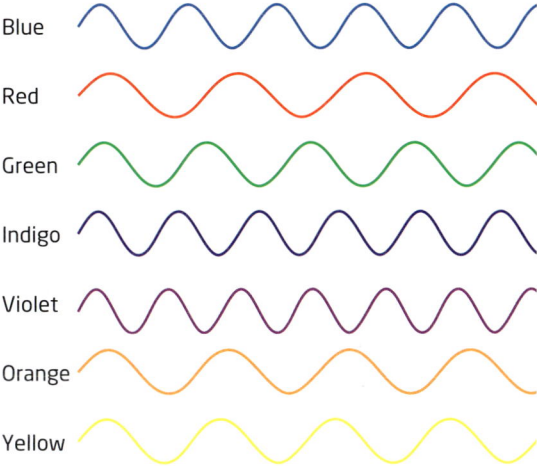

9. The piston engine is the most commonly used engine in the world. The height of the piston over time can be modelled by a sine curve. Given the equation for a sine curve, $y = a \sin b(x - c) + d$, which parameter(s) would be affected as the piston moves faster?

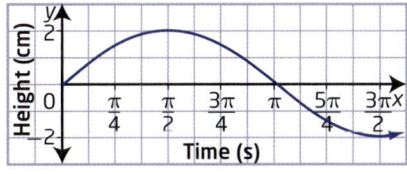

10. Victor and Stewart determined the phase shift for the function $f(x) = 4 \sin (2x - 6) + 12$. Victor said that the phase shift was 6 units to the right, while Stewart claimed it was 3 units to the right.

  a) Which student was correct? Explain your reasoning.

  b) Graph the function to verify your answer from part a).

11. A family of sinusoidal graphs with equations of the form $y = a \sin b(x - c) + d$ is created by changing only the vertical displacement of the function. If the range of the original function is $\{y \mid -3 \leq y \leq 3, y \in R\}$, determine the range of the function with each given value of d.

  a) $d = 2$

  b) $d = -3$

  c) $d = -10$

  d) $d = 8$

12. Sketch the graph of the curve that results after applying each transformation to the graph of the function $f(x) = \sin x$.

  a) $f\left(x - \dfrac{\pi}{3}\right)$

  b) $f\left(x + \dfrac{\pi}{4}\right)$

  c) $f(x) + 3$

  d) $f(x) - 4$

13. The range of a trigonometric function in the form $y = a \sin b(x - c) + d$ is $\{y \mid -13 \leq y \leq 5, y \in R\}$. State the values of a and d.

14. For each graph of a sinusoidal function, state

  i) the amplitude

  ii) the period

  iii) the phase shift

  iv) the vertical displacement

  v) the domain and range

  vi) the maximum value of y and the values of x for which it occurs over the interval $0 \leq x \leq 2\pi$

  vii) the minimum value of y and the values of x for which it occurs over the interval $0 \leq x \leq 2\pi$

  a) a sine function

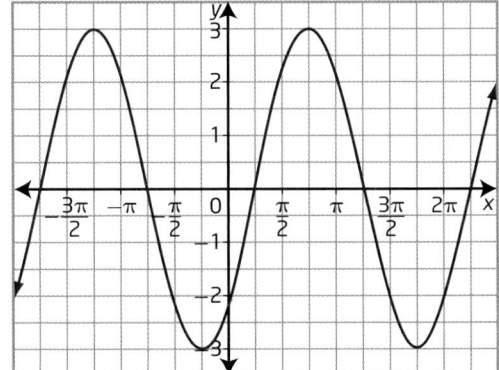

  b) a cosine function

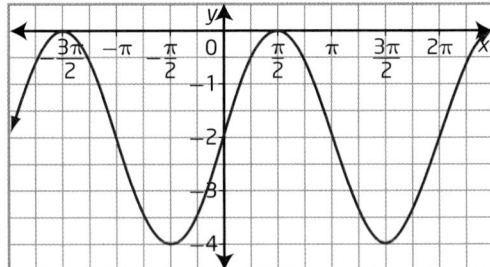

  c) a sine function

15. Determine an equation in the form $y = a \sin b(x - c) + d$ for each graph.

a)
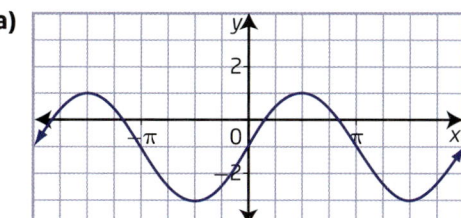

b)
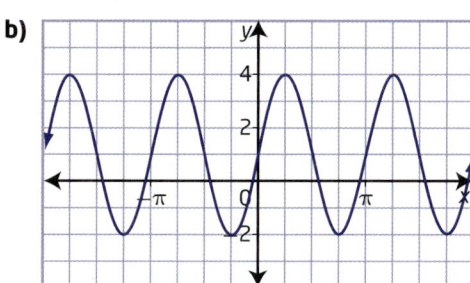

c)
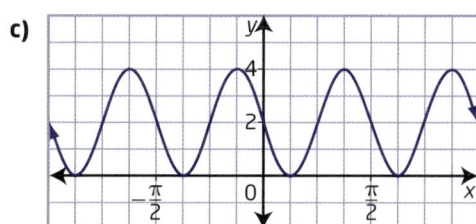

16. For each graph, write an equation in the form $y = a \cos b(x - c) + d$.

a)
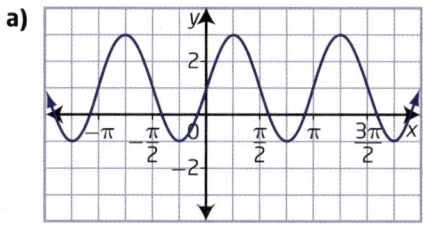

b)
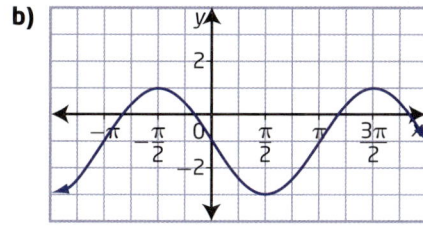

c)
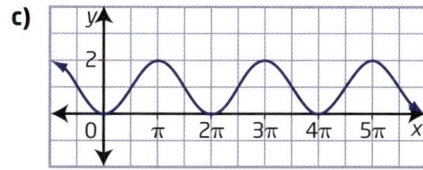

17. a) Graph the function $f(x) = \cos\left(x - \frac{\pi}{2}\right)$.

b) Consider the graph. Write an equation of the function in the form $y = a \sin b(x - c) + d$.

c) What conclusions can you make about the relationship between the two equations of the function?

18. Given the graph of the function $f(x) = \sin x$, what transformation is required so that the function $g(x) = \cos x$ describes the graph of the image function?

19. For each start and end of one cycle of a cosine function in the form $y = 3 \cos b(x - c)$,

   i) state the phase shift, period, and x-intercepts

   ii) state the coordinates of the minimum and maximum values

   a) $30° \leq x \leq 390°$

   b) $\frac{\pi}{4} \leq x \leq \frac{5\pi}{4}$

20. The Wave is a spectacular sandstone formation on the slopes of the Coyote Buttes of the Paria Canyon in Northern Arizona. The Wave is made from 190 million-year-old sand dunes that have turned to red rock. Assume that a cycle of the Wave may be approximated using a cosine curve. The maximum height above sea level is 5100 ft and the minimum height is 5000 ft. The beginning of the cycle is at the 1.75 mile mark of the canyon and the end of this cycle is at the 2.75 mile mark. Write an equation that approximates the pattern of the Wave.

21. Compare the graphs of the functions
 $y = 3 \sin \frac{\pi}{3}(x - 2) - 1$ and
 $y = 3 \cos \frac{\pi}{3}\left(x - \frac{7}{2}\right) - 1$. Are the
 graphs equivalent? Support your answer graphically.

22. Noise-cancelling headphones are designed to give you maximum listening pleasure by cancelling ambient noise and actively creating their own sound waves. These waves mimic the incoming noise in every way, except that they are out of sync with the intruding noise by 180°.

 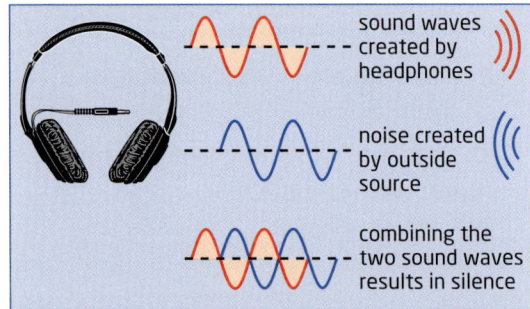

 Suppose that the amplitude and period for the sine waves created by the outside noise are 4 and $\frac{\pi}{2}$, respectively. Determine the equation of the sound waves the headphones produce to effectively cancel the ambient noise.

23. The overhang of the roof of a house is designed to shade the windows for cooling in the summer and allow the Sun's rays to enter the house for heating in the winter. The Sun's angle of elevation, A, in degrees, at noon in Estevan, Saskatchewan, can be modelled by the formula $A = -23.5 \sin \frac{360}{365}(x + 102) + 41$, where x is the number of days elapsed beginning with January 1.
 a) Use technology to sketch the graph showing the changes in the Sun's angle of elevation throughout the year.
 b) Determine the Sun's angle of elevation at noon on February 12.
 c) On what date is the angle of elevation the greatest in Estevan?

24. After exercising for 5 min, a person has a respiratory cycle for which the rate of air flow, r, in litres per second, in the lungs is approximated by $r = 1.75 \sin \frac{\pi}{2}t$, where t is the time, in seconds.
 a) Determine the time for one full respiratory cycle.
 b) Determine the number of cycles per minute.
 c) Sketch the graph of the rate of air flow function.
 d) Determine the rate of air flow at a time of 30 s. Interpret this answer in the context of the respiratory cycle.
 e) Determine the rate of air flow at a time of 7.5 s. Interpret this answer in the context of the respiratory cycle.

Extend

25. The frequency of a wave is the number of cycles that occur in 1 s. Adding two sinusoidal functions with similar, but unequal, frequencies results in a function that pulsates, or exhibits beats. Piano tuners often use this phenomenon to help them tune a piano.
 a) Graph the function $y = \cos x + \cos 0.9x$.
 b) Determine the amplitude and the period of the resulting wave.

26. a) Copy each equation. Fill in the missing values to make the equation true.
  i) $4 \sin (x - 30°) = 4 \cos (x - \blacksquare)$
  ii) $2 \sin \left(x - \frac{\pi}{4}\right) = 2 \cos (x - \blacksquare)$
  iii) $-3 \cos \left(x - \frac{\pi}{2}\right) = 3 \sin (x + \blacksquare)$
  iv) $\cos (-2x + 6\pi) = \sin 2(x + \blacksquare)$
 b) Choose one of the equations in part a) and explain how you got your answer.

27. Determine the equation of the sine function with

a) amplitude 3, maximum $\left(-\frac{\pi}{2}, 5\right)$, and nearest maximum to the right at $\left(\frac{3\pi}{2}, 5\right)$

b) amplitude 3, minimum $\left(\frac{\pi}{4}, -2\right)$, and nearest maximum to the right at $\left(\frac{3\pi}{4}, 4\right)$

c) minimum $(-\pi, 3)$ and nearest maximum to the right at $(0, 7)$

d) minimum $(90°, -6)$ and nearest maximum to the right at $(150°, 4)$

28. The angle, P, in radians, between a pendulum and the vertical may be modelled by the equation $P = a \cos bt$, where a represents the maximum angle that the pendulum swings from the vertical; b is the horizontal stretch factor; and t is time, in seconds. The period of a pendulum may be approximated by the formula Period $= 2\pi\sqrt{\frac{L}{g}}$, where L is the pendulum length and g is the acceleration due to gravity (9.8 m/s²).

a) Sketch the graph that models the position of the pendulum in the diagram from $0 \leq t \leq 5$.

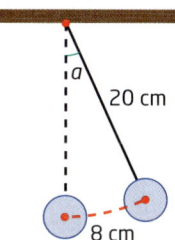

b) Determine the position of the pendulum after 6 s. Express your answer to the nearest tenth of a centimetre.

Create Connections

C1 Consider a sinusoidal function of the form $y = a \sin b(x - c) + d$. Describe the effect that each of the parameters a, b, c, and d has on the graph of the function. Compare this to what you learned in Chapter 1 Function Transformations.

C2 Sketch the graphs of $y = -\sin x$ and $y = \sin(-x)$.

a) Compare the two graphs. How are they alike? different?

b) Explain why this happens.

c) How would you expect the graphs of $y = -\cos x$ and $y = \cos(-x)$ to compare?

d) Check your hypothesis from part c). If it is incorrect, write a correct statement about the cosine function.

> **Did You Know?**
>
> An *even function* satisfies the property $f(-x) = f(x)$ for all x in the domain of $f(x)$.
>
> An *odd function* satisfies the property $f(-x) = -f(x)$ for all x in the domain of $f(x)$.

C3 Triangle ABC is inscribed between the graphs of $f(x) = 5 \sin x$ and $g(x) = 5 \cos x$. Determine the area of $\triangle ABC$.

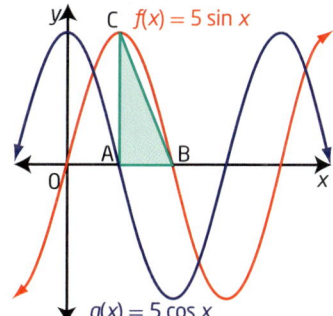

C4 The equation of a sine function can be expressed in the form $y = a \sin b(x - c) + d$. Determine the values of the parameters a, b, c, and/or d, where $a > 0$ and $b > 0$, for each of the following to be true.

a) The period is greater than 2π.

b) The amplitude is greater than 1 unit.

c) The graph passes through the origin.

d) The graph has no x-intercepts.

e) The graph has a y-intercept of a.

f) The length of one cycle is $120°$.

5.3

The Tangent Function

Focus on...
- sketching the graph of $y = \tan x$
- determining the amplitude, domain, range, and period of $y = \tan x$
- determining the asymptotes and *x*-intercepts for the graph of $y = \tan x$
- solving a problem by analysing the graph of the tangent function

You can derive the tangent of an angle from the coordinates of a point on a line tangent to the unit circle at point (1, 0). These values have been tabulated and programmed into scientific calculators and computers. This allows you to apply trigonometry to surveying, engineering, and navigation problems.

> ### Did You Know?
> Tangent comes from the Latin word *tangere*, "to touch."
>
> Tangent was first mentioned in 1583 by T. Fincke, who introduced the word *tangens* in Latin. E. Gunter (1624) used the notation *tan*, and J.H. Lambert (1770) discovered the fractional representation of this function.

Investigate the Tangent Function

Materials
- grid paper
- ruler
- protractor
- compass
- graphing technology

A: Graph the Tangent Function

A tangent line to a curve is a line that touches a curve, or a graph of a function, at a single point.

1. On a piece of grid paper, draw and label the *x*-axis and *y*-axis. Draw a circle of radius 1 so that its centre is at the origin. Draw a tangent to the circle at the point where the *x*-axis intersects the circle on the right side.

2. To sketch the graph of the tangent function over the interval $0° \leq \theta \leq 360°$, you can draw angles in standard position on the unit circle and extend the terminal arm to the right so that it intersects the tangent line, as shown in the diagram. The *y*-coordinate of the point of intersection represents the value of the tangent function. Plot points represented by the coordinates (angle measure, *y*-coordinate of point of intersection).

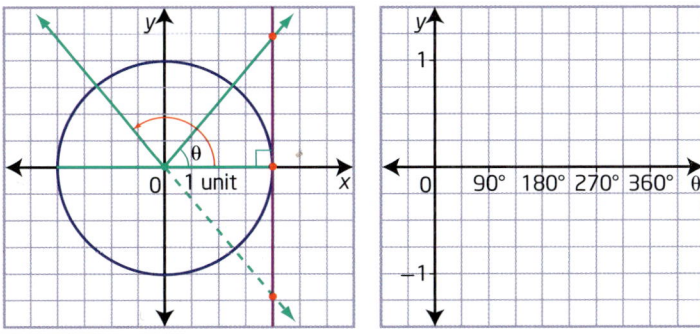

a) Begin with an angle of 0°. Where does the extension of the terminal arm intersect the tangent line?

b) Draw the terminal arm for an angle of 45°. Where does the extension of the terminal arm intersect the tangent line?

c) If the angle is 90°, where does the extension of the terminal arm intersect the tangent line?

d) Use a protractor to measure various angles for the terminal arm. Determine the y-coordinate of the point where the terminal arm intersects the tangent line. Plot the ordered pair (angle measure, y-coordinate on tangent line) on a graph like the one shown above on the right.

Angle Measure	0°	45°	90°	135°	180°	225°	270°	315°	360°
y-coordinate on Tangent Line									

What can you conclude about the value of tan 90°? How do you show this on a graph?

3. Use graphing technology to verify the shape of your graph.

Reflect and Respond

4. When θ = 90° and θ = 270°, the tangent function is undefined. How does this relate to the graph of the tangent function?

5. What is the period of the tangent function?

6. What is the amplitude of the tangent function? What does this mean?

7. Explain how a point P(x, y) on the unit circle relates to the sine, cosine, and tangent ratios.

B: Connect the Tangent Function to the Slope of the Terminal Arm

8. The diagram shows an angle θ in standard position whose terminal arm intersects the tangent AB at point B. Express the ratio of tan θ in terms of the sides of △AOB.

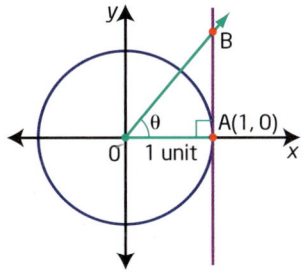

9. Using your knowledge of special triangles, state the exact value of tan 60°. If θ = 60° in the diagram, what is the length of line segment AB?

10. Using the measurement of the length of line segment AB from step 9, determine the slope of line segment OB.

11. How does the slope of line segment OB relate to the tangent of an angle in standard position?

Reflect and Respond

12. How could you use the concept of slope to determine the tangent ratio when θ = 0°? when θ = 90°?

13. Using a calculator, determine the values of tan θ as θ approaches 90°. What is tan 90°?

14. Explain the relationship between the terminal arm of an angle θ and the tangent of the line passing through the point (1, 0) when θ = 90°. (Hint: Can the terminal arm intersect the tangent line?)

Link the Ideas

The value of the tangent of an angle θ is the slope of the line passing through the origin and the point on the unit circle (cos θ, sin θ). You can think of it as the slope of the terminal arm of angle θ in standard position.

$$\tan \theta = \frac{\sin \theta}{\cos \theta}$$

When sin θ = 0, what is tan θ? Explain.
When cos θ = 0, what is tan θ? Explain.

The tangent ratio is the length of the line segment tangent to the unit circle at the point A(1, 0) from the x-axis to the terminal arm of angle θ at point Q.

From the diagram, the distance AQ is equal to the y-coordinate of point Q. Therefore, point Q has coordinates (1, tan θ).

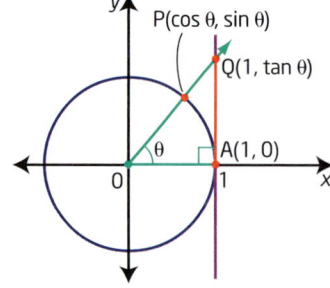

How could you show that the coordinates of Q are (1, tan θ)?

Example 1

Graph the Tangent Function

Graph the function $y = \tan \theta$ for $-2\pi \leq \theta \leq 2\pi$. Describe its characteristics.

Solution

The function $y = \tan \theta$ is known as the tangent function. Using the unit circle, you can plot values of y against the corresponding values of θ.

Between asymptotes, the graph of $y = \tan \theta$ passes through a point with y-coordinate -1, a θ-intercept, and a point with y-coordinate 1.

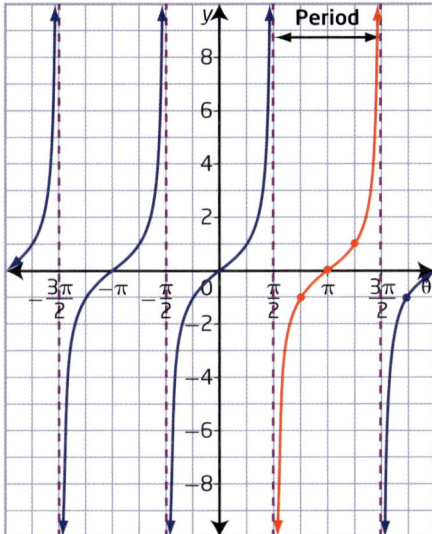

You can observe the properties of the tangent function from the graph.

- The curve is not continuous. It breaks at $\theta = -\dfrac{3\pi}{2}$, $\theta = -\dfrac{\pi}{2}$, $\theta = \dfrac{\pi}{2}$, and $\theta = \dfrac{3\pi}{2}$, where the function is undefined.
- $\tan \theta = 0$ when $\theta = -2\pi$, $\theta = -\pi$, $\theta = 0$, $\theta = \pi$, and $\theta = 2\pi$.
- $\tan \theta = 1$ when $\theta = -\dfrac{7\pi}{4}$, $\theta = -\dfrac{3\pi}{4}$, $\theta = \dfrac{\pi}{4}$, and $\theta = \dfrac{5\pi}{4}$.
- $\tan \theta = -1$ when $\theta = -\dfrac{5\pi}{4}$, $\theta = -\dfrac{\pi}{4}$, $\theta = \dfrac{3\pi}{4}$, and $\theta = \dfrac{7\pi}{4}$.
- The graph of $y = \tan \theta$ has no amplitude because it has no maximum or minimum values.
- The range of $y = \tan \theta$ is $\{y \mid y \in \mathbb{R}\}$.

- As point P moves around the unit circle in either a clockwise or a counterclockwise direction, the tangent curve repeats for every interval of π. The period for $y = \tan \theta$ is π.

  For tangent graphs, the distance between any two consecutive vertical asymptotes represents one complete period.

- The tangent is undefined whenever $\cos \theta = 0$. This occurs when $\theta = \dfrac{\pi}{2} + n\pi, n \in I$. At these points, the value of the tangent approaches infinity and is undefined. When graphing the tangent, use dashed lines to show where the value of the tangent is undefined. These vertical lines are called asymptotes.

  Why is tan θ undefined for cos θ = 0?

- The domain of $y = \tan \theta$ is $\left\{\theta \mid \theta \neq \dfrac{\pi}{2} + n\pi, \theta \in R, n \in I\right\}$.

Your Turn

Graph the function $y = \tan \theta, 0° \leq \theta \leq 360°$. Describe how the characteristics are different from those in Example 1.

Example 2

Model a Problem Using the Tangent Function

A small plane is flying at a constant altitude of 6000 m directly toward an observer. Assume that the ground is flat in the region close to the observer.

Why is this assumption made?

a) Determine the relation between the horizontal distance, in metres, from the observer to the plane and the angle, in degrees, formed from the vertical to the plane.
b) Sketch the graph of the function.
c) Where are the asymptotes located in this graph? What do they represent?
d) Explain what happens when the angle is equal to 0°.

Solution

a) Draw a diagram to model the situation.

Let d represent the horizontal distance from the observer to the plane. Let θ represent the angle formed by the vertical and the line of sight to the plane.

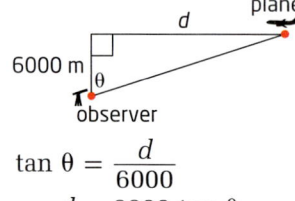

$\tan \theta = \dfrac{d}{6000}$

$d = 6000 \tan \theta$

b) The graph represents the horizontal distance between the plane and the observer. As the plane flies toward the observer, that distance decreases. As the plane moves from directly overhead to the observer's left, the distance values become negative. The domain of the function is $\{\theta \mid -90° < \theta < 90°, \theta \in R\}$.

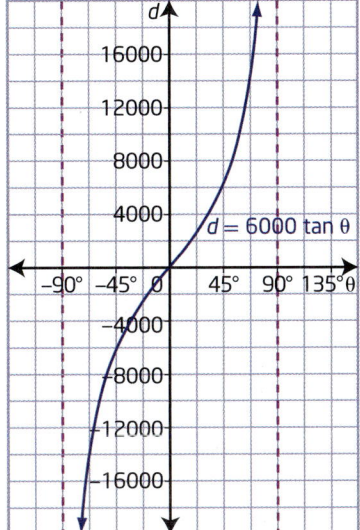

c) The asymptotes are located at $\theta = 90°$ and $\theta = -90°$. They represent when the plane is on the ground to the right or left of the observer, which is impossible, because the plane is flying in a straight line at a constant altitude of 6000 m.

d) When the angle is equal to 0°, the plane is directly over the head of the observer. The horizontal distance is 0 m.

Your Turn

A small plane is flying at a constant altitude of 5000 m directly toward an observer. Assume the ground is flat in the region close to the observer.

a) Sketch the graph of the function that represents the relation between the horizontal distance, in metres, from the observer to the plane and the angle, in degrees, formed by the vertical and the line of sight to the plane.

b) Use the characteristics of the tangent function to describe what happens to the graph as the plane flies from the right of the observer to the left of the observer.

Key Ideas

- You can use asymptotes and three points to sketch one cycle of a tangent function. To graph $y = \tan x$, draw one asymptote; draw the points where $y = -1$, $y = 0$, and $y = 1$; and then draw another asymptote.

  How can you determine the location of the asymptotes for the function $y = \tan x$?

  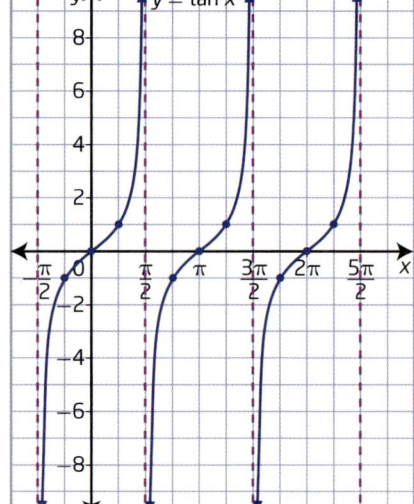

- The tangent function $y = \tan x$ has the following characteristics:
  - The period is π.
  - The graph has no maximum or minimum values.
  - The range is $\{y \mid y \in R\}$.
  - Vertical asymptotes occur at $x = \frac{\pi}{2} + n\pi$, $n \in I$.
  - The domain is $\left\{x \mid x \neq \frac{\pi}{2} + n\pi, x \in R, n \in I\right\}$.
  - The x-intercepts occur at $x = n\pi$, $n \in I$.
  - The y-intercept is 0.

Check Your Understanding

Practise

1. For each diagram, determine $\tan \theta$ and the value of θ, in degrees. Express your answer to the nearest tenth, when necessary.

   a)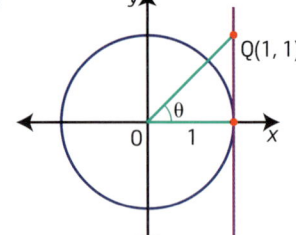

   b)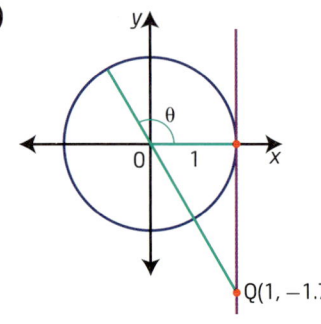

   c)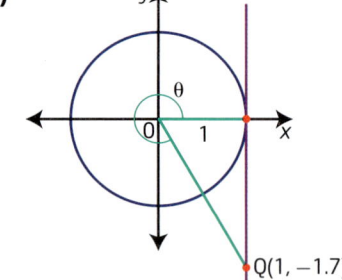

   d)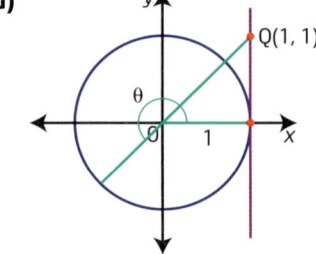

2. Use the graph of the function $y = \tan \theta$ to determine each value.

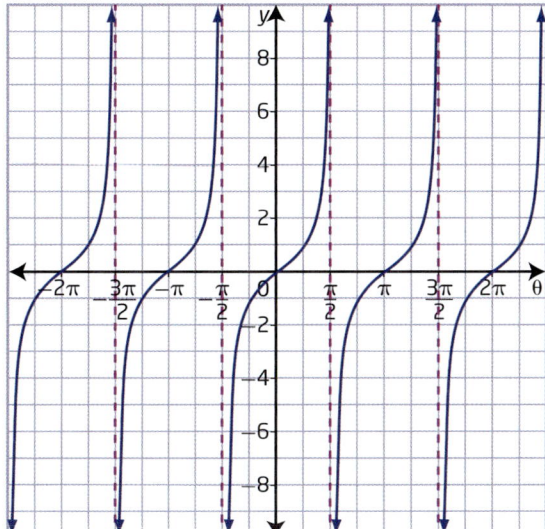

a) $\tan \dfrac{\pi}{2}$

b) $\tan \dfrac{3\pi}{4}$

c) $\tan \left(-\dfrac{7\pi}{4}\right)$

d) $\tan 0$

e) $\tan \pi$

f) $\tan \dfrac{5\pi}{4}$

3. Does $y = \tan x$ have an amplitude? Explain.

4. Use graphing technology to graph $y = \tan x$ using the following window settings: $x: [-360°, 360°, 30°]$ and $y: [-3, 3, 1]$. Trace along the graph to locate the value of $\tan x$ when $x = 60°$. Predict the other values of x that will produce the same value for $\tan x$ within the given domain. Verify your predictions.

Apply

5. In the diagram, $\triangle PON$ and $\triangle QOA$ are similar triangles. Use the diagram to justify the statement $\tan \theta = \dfrac{\sin \theta}{\cos \theta}$.

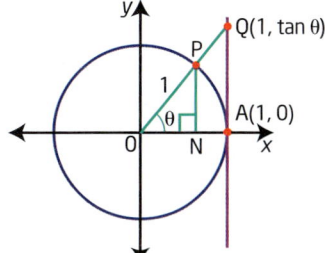

6. Point $P(x, y)$ is plotted where the terminal arm of angle θ intersects the unit circle.

a) Use $P(x, y)$ to determine the slope of the terminal arm.

b) Explain how your result from part a) is related to $\tan \theta$.

c) Write your results for the slope from part a) in terms of sine and cosine.

d) From your answer in part c), explain how you could determine $\tan \theta$ when the coordinates of point P are known.

7. Consider the unit circle shown.

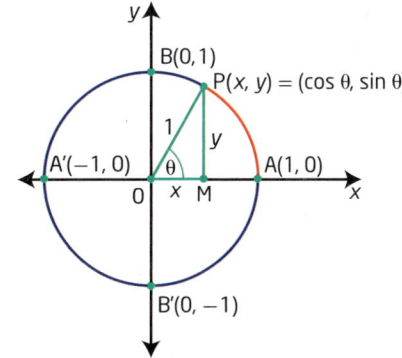

a) From $\triangle POM$, write the ratio for $\tan \theta$.

b) Use $\cos \theta$ and $\sin \theta$ to write the ratio for $\tan \theta$.

c) Explain how your answers from parts a) and b) are related.

8. The graph of $y = \tan \theta$ appears to be vertical as θ approaches 90°.

   a) Copy and complete the table. Use a calculator to record the tangent values as θ approaches 90°.

θ	$\tan \theta$
89.5°	
89.9°	
89.999°	
89.999 999°	

   b) What happens to the value of $\tan \theta$ as θ approaches 90°?

   c) Predict what will happen as θ approaches 90° from the other direction.

θ	$\tan \theta$
90.5°	
90.01°	
90.001°	
90.000 001°	

9. A security camera scans a long straight fence that encloses a section of a military base. The camera is mounted on a post that is located 5 m from the midpoint of the fence. The camera makes one complete rotation in 60 s.

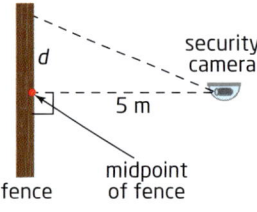

   a) Determine the tangent function that represents the distance, d, in metres, along the fence from its midpoint as a function of time, t, in seconds, if the camera is aimed at the midpoint of the fence at $t = 0$.

   b) Graph the function in the interval $-15 \leq t \leq 15$.

   c) What is the distance from the midpoint of the fence at $t = 10$ s, to the nearest tenth of a metre?

   d) Describe what happens when $t = 15$ s.

10. A rotating light on top of a lighthouse sends out rays of light in opposite directions. As the beacon rotates, the ray at angle θ makes a spot of light that moves along the shore. The lighthouse is located 500 m from the shoreline and makes one complete rotation every 2 min.

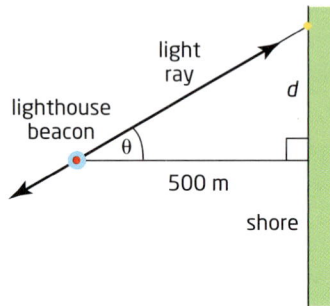

   a) Determine the equation that expresses the distance, d, in metres, as a function of time, t, in minutes.

   b) Graph the function in part a).

   c) Explain the significance of the asymptote in the graph at $\theta = 90°$.

Did You Know?

The Fisgard Lighthouse was the first lighthouse built on Canada's west coast. It was built in 1860 before Vancouver Island became part of Canada and is located at the entrance to Esquimalt harbour.

11. A plane flying at an altitude of 10 km over level ground will pass directly over a radar station. Let d be the ground distance from the antenna to a point directly under the plane. Let x represent the angle formed from the vertical at the radar station to the plane. Write d as a function of x and graph the function over the interval $0 \leq x \leq \frac{\pi}{2}$.

12. Andrea uses a pole of known height, a piece of string, a measuring tape, and a calculator for an assignment. She places the pole in a vertical position in the school field and runs the string from the top of the pole to the tip of the shadow formed by the pole. Every 15 min, Andrea measures the length of the shadow and then calculates the slope of the string and the measure of the angle. She records the data and graphs the slope as a function of the angle.

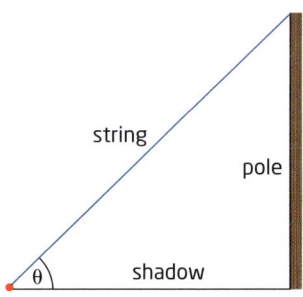

   a) What type of graph would you expect Andrea to graph to represent her data?

   b) When the Sun is directly overhead and no shadow results, state the slope of the string. How does Andrea's graph represent this situation?

Extend

13. a) Graph the line $y = \frac{3}{4}x$, where $x > 0$. Mark an angle θ that represents the angle formed by the line and the positive x-axis. Plot a point with integral coordinates on the line $y = \frac{3}{4}x$.

   b) Use these coordinates to determine $\tan \theta$.

   c) Compare the equation of the line with your results in part b). Make a conjecture based on your findings.

14. Have you ever wondered how a calculator or computer program evaluates the sine, cosine, or tangent of a given angle? The calculator or computer program approximates these values using a power series. The terms of a power series contain ascending positive integral powers of a variable. The more terms in the series, the more accurate the approximation. With a calculator in radian mode, verify the following for small values of x, for example, $x = 0.5$.

   a) $\tan x = x + \frac{x^3}{3} + \frac{2x^5}{15} + \frac{17x^7}{315}$

   b) $\sin x = x - \frac{x^3}{6} + \frac{x^5}{120} - \frac{x^7}{5040}$

   c) $\cos x = 1 - \frac{x^2}{2} + \frac{x^4}{24} - \frac{x^6}{720}$

Create Connections

C1 How does the domain of $y = \tan x$ differ from that of $y = \sin x$ and $y = \cos x$? Explain why.

C2 a) On the same set of axes, graph the functions $f(x) = \cos x$ and $g(x) = \tan x$. Describe how the two functions are related.

   b) On the same set of axes, graph the functions $f(x) = \sin x$ and $g(x) = \tan x$. Describe how the two functions are related.

C3 Explain how the equation $\tan (x + \pi) = \tan x$ relates to circular functions.

5.4

Equations and Graphs of Trigonometric Functions

Focus on...

- using the graphs of trigonometric functions to solve equations
- analysing a trigonometric function to solve a problem
- determining a trigonometric function that models a problem
- using a model of a trigonometric function for a real-world situation

One of the most useful characteristics of trigonometric functions is their periodicity. For example, the times of sunsets, sunrises, and comet appearances; seasonal temperature changes; the movement of waves in the ocean; and even the quality of a musical sound can be described using trigonometric functions. Mathematicians and scientists use the periodic nature of trigonometric functions to develop mathematical models to predict many natural phenomena.

Investigate Trigonometric Equations

Materials

- marker
- ruler
- compass
- stop watch
- centimetre grid paper

Work with a partner.

1. On a sheet of centimetre grid paper, draw a circle of radius 8 cm. Draw a line tangent to the bottom of the circle.

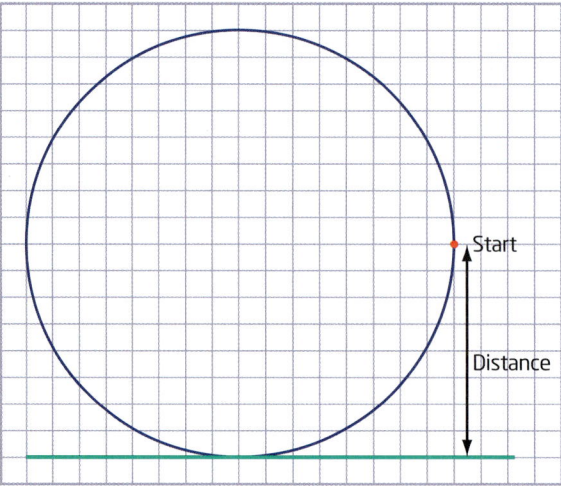

266 MHR • Chapter 5

2. Place a marker at the three o'clock position on the circle. Move the marker around the circle in a counterclockwise direction, measuring the time it takes to make one complete trip around the circle.

3. Move the marker around the circle a second time stopping at time intervals of 2 s. Measure the vertical distance from the marker to the tangent line. Complete a table of times and distances.

Time (s)	0	2	4	6	8	10	12	14	16	18	20
Distance (cm)	8										

Aim to complete one revolution in 20 s. You may have to practice this several times to maintain a consistent speed.

4. Create a scatterplot of distance versus time. Draw a smooth curve connecting the points.

5. Write a function for the resulting curve.

6. a) From your initial starting position, move the marker around the circle in a counterclockwise direction for 3 s. Measure the vertical distance of the marker from the tangent line. Label this point on your graph.

   b) Continue to move the marker around the circle to a point that is the same distance as the distance you recorded in part a). Label this point on your graph.

   c) How do these two points relate to your function in step 5?

   d) How do the measured and calculated distances compare?

7. Repeat step 6 for other positions on the circle.

Did You Know?

A scatter plot is the result of plotting data that can be represented as ordered pairs on a graph.

Reflect and Respond

8. What is the connection between the circular pattern followed by your marker and the graph of distance versus time?

9. Describe how the circle, the graph, and the function are related.

Link the Ideas

You can represent phenomena with periodic behaviour or wave characteristics by trigonometric functions or model them approximately with sinusoidal functions. You can identify a trend or pattern, determine an appropriate mathematical model to describe the process, and use it to make predictions (interpolate or extrapolate).

You can use graphs of trigonometric functions to solve trigonometric equations that model periodic phenomena, such as the swing of a pendulum, the motion of a piston in an engine, the motion of a Ferris wheel, variations in blood pressure, the hours of daylight throughout a year, and vibrations that create sounds.

Example 1

Solve a Trigonometric Equation in Degrees

Determine the solutions for the trigonometric equation $2\cos^2 x - 1 = 0$ for the interval $0° \leq x \leq 360°$.

Solution

Method 1: Solve Graphically

Graph the related function $f(x) = 2\cos^2 x - 1$.

Use the graphing window [0, 360, 30] by [−2, 2, 1].

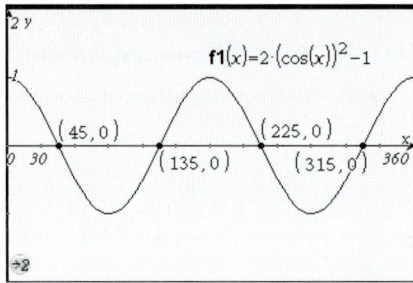

The solutions to the equation $2\cos^2 x - 1 = 0$ for the interval $0° \leq x \leq 360°$ are the x-intercepts of the graph of the related function.

The solutions for the interval $0° \leq x \leq 360°$ are $x = 45°, 135°, 225°,$ and $315°$.

Method 2: Solve Algebraically

$$2\cos^2 x - 1 = 0$$
$$2\cos^2 x = 1$$
$$\cos^2 x = \frac{1}{2}$$
$$\cos x = \pm\sqrt{\frac{1}{2}}$$

Why is the ± symbol used?

For $\cos x = \frac{1}{\sqrt{2}}$ or $\frac{\sqrt{2}}{2}$, the angles in the interval $0° \leq x \leq 360°$ that satisfy the equation are $45°$ and $315°$.

For $\cos x = -\sqrt{\frac{1}{2}}$, the angles in the interval $0° \leq x \leq 360°$ that satisfy the equation are $135°$ and $225°$.

The solutions for the interval $0° \leq x \leq 360°$ are $x = 45°, 135°, 225°,$ and $315°$.

Your Turn

Determine the solutions for the trigonometric equation $4\sin^2 x - 3 = 0$ for the interval $0° \leq x \leq 360°$.

Example 2

Solve a Trigonometric Equation in Radians

Determine the general solutions for the trigonometric equation $16 = 6\cos\frac{\pi}{6}x + 14$. Express your answers to the nearest hundredth.

Solution

Method 1: Determine the Zeros of the Function

Rearrange the equation $16 = 6\cos\frac{\pi}{6}x + 14$ so that one side is equal to 0.

$6\cos\frac{\pi}{6}x - 2 = 0$

Graph the related function $y = 6\cos\frac{\pi}{6}x - 2$. Use the window $[-1, 12, 1]$ by $[-10, 10, 1]$.

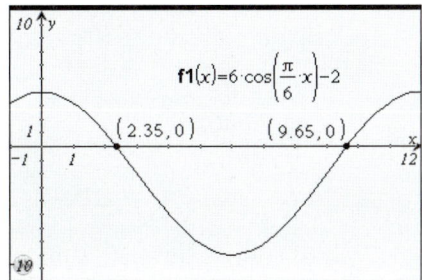

Why should you set the calculator to radian mode?

The solutions to the equation $6\cos\frac{\pi}{6}x - 2 = 0$ are the x-intercepts.

The x-intercepts are approximately $x = 2.35$ and $x = 9.65$. The period of the function is 12 radians. So, the x-intercepts repeat in multiples of 12 radians from each of the original intercepts.

The general solutions to the equation $16 = 6\cos\frac{\pi}{6}x + 14$ are $x \approx 2.35 + 12n$ radians and $x \approx 9.65 + 12n$ radians, where n is an integer.

Method 2: Determine the Points of Intersection

Graph the functions $y = 6\cos\frac{\pi}{6}x + 14$ and $y = 16$ using a window $[-1, 12, 1]$ by $[-2, 22, 2]$.

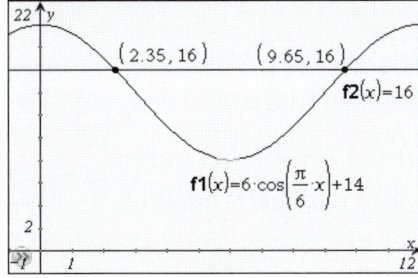

The solution to the equation $16 = 6 \cos \frac{\pi}{6}x + 14$ is given by the points of intersection of the curve $y = 6 \cos \frac{\pi}{6}x + 14$ and the line $y = 16$. In the interval $0 \le x \le 12$, the points of intersection occur at $x \approx 2.35$ and $x \approx 9.65$.

The period of the function is 12 radians. The points of intersection repeat in multiples of 12 radians from each of the original intercepts.

The general solutions to the equation $16 = 6 \cos \frac{\pi}{6}x + 14$ are $x \approx 2.35 + 12n$ radians and $x \approx 9.65 + 12n$ radians, where n is an integer.

Method 3: Solve Algebraically

$$16 = 6 \cos \frac{\pi}{6}x + 14$$
$$2 = 6 \cos \frac{\pi}{6}x$$
$$\frac{2}{6} = \cos \frac{\pi}{6}x$$
$$\frac{1}{3} = \cos \frac{\pi}{6}x$$
$$\cos^{-1}\left(\frac{1}{3}\right) = \frac{\pi}{6}x$$
$$1.2309... = \frac{\pi}{6}x$$
$$x = 2.3509...$$

Since the cosine function is positive in quadrants I and IV, a second possible value of x can be determined. In quadrant IV, the angle is $2\pi - \frac{\pi}{6}x$.

$$\frac{1}{3} = \cos\left(2\pi - \frac{\pi}{6}x\right)$$
$$\cos^{-1}\left(\frac{1}{3}\right) = 2\pi - \frac{\pi}{6}x$$
$$\frac{\pi}{6}x = 2\pi - \cos^{-1}\left(\frac{1}{3}\right)$$
$$x = 12 - \frac{6}{\pi} \cos^{-1}\left(\frac{1}{3}\right)$$
$$x = 9.6490...$$

Two solutions to the equation $16 = 6 \cos \frac{\pi}{6}x + 14$ are $x \approx 2.35$ and $x \approx 9.65$.

The period of the function is 12 radians, then the solutions repeat in multiples of 12 radians from each original solution.

The general solutions to the equation $16 = 6 \cos \frac{\pi}{6}x + 14$ are $x \approx 2.35 + 12n$ radians and $x \approx 9.65 + 12n$ radians, where n is an integer.

Your Turn

Determine the general solutions for the trigonometric equation $10 = 6 \sin \frac{\pi}{4}x + 8$.

Did You Know?

No matter in which quadrant θ falls, $-\theta$ has the same reference angle and both θ and $-\theta$ are located on the same side of the y-axis. Since $\cos \theta$ is positive on the right side of the y-axis and negative on the left side of the y-axis, $\cos \theta = \cos(-\theta)$.

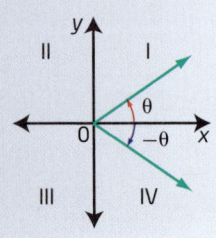

Example 3

Model Electric Power

The electricity coming from power plants into your house is alternating current (AC). This means that the direction of current flowing in a circuit is constantly switching back and forth. In Canada, the current makes 60 complete cycles each second.

The voltage can be modelled as a function of time using the sine function $V = 170 \sin 120\pi t$.

a) What is the period of the current in Canada?

b) Graph the voltage function over two cycles. Explain what the scales on the axes represent.

c) Suppose you want to switch on a heat lamp for an outdoor patio. If the heat lamp requires 110 V to start up, determine the time required for the voltage to first reach 110 V.

Did You Know?

Tidal power is a form of hydroelectric power that converts the energy of tides into electricity. Estimates of Canada's tidal energy potential off the Canadian Pacific coast are equivalent to approximately half of the country's current electricity demands.

Solution

a) Since there are 60 complete cycles in each second, each cycle takes $\frac{1}{60}$ s. So, the period is $\frac{1}{60}$.

b) To graph the voltage function over two cycles on a graphing calculator, use the following window settings:
x: [−0.001, 0.035, 0.01]
y: [−200, 200, 50]

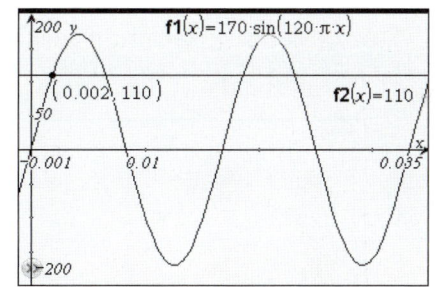

The y-axis represents the number of volts. Each tick mark on the y-axis represents 50 V.

The x-axis represents the time passed. Each tick mark on the x-axis represents 0.01 s.

c) Graph the line $y = 110$ and determine the first point of intersection with the voltage function. It will take approximately 0.002 s for the voltage to first reach 110 V.

Did You Know?

The number of cycles per second of a periodic phenomenon is called the frequency. The hertz (Hz) is the SI unit of frequency. In Canada, the frequency standard for AC is 60 Hz.

Voltages are expressed as root mean square (RMS) voltage. RMS is the square root of the mean of the squares of the values. The RMS voltage is given by $\frac{\text{peak voltage}}{\sqrt{2}}$. What is the RMS voltage for Canada?

Your Turn

In some Caribbean countries, the current makes 50 complete cycles each second and the voltage is modelled by $V = 170 \sin 100\pi t$.

a) Graph the voltage function over two cycles. Explain what the scales on the axes represent.

b) What is the period of the current in these countries?

c) How many times does the voltage reach 110 V in the first second?

Example 4
Model Hours of Daylight

Iqaluit is the territorial capital and the largest community of Nunavut. Iqaluit is located at latitude 63° N. The table shows the number of hours of daylight on the 21st day of each month as the day of the year on which it occurs for the capital (based on a 365-day year).

Why is the 21st day of each month chosen for the data in the table?

Hours of Daylight by Day of the Year for Iqaluit, Nunavut											
Jan 21	Feb 21	Mar 21	Apr 21	May 21	June 21	July 21	Aug 21	Sept 21	Oct 21	Nov 21	Dec 21
21	52	80	111	141	172	202	233	264	294	325	355
6.12	9.36	12.36	15.69	18.88	20.83	18.95	15.69	12.41	9.24	6.05	4.34

a) Draw a scatter plot for the number of hours of daylight, h, in Iqaluit on the day of the year, t.
b) Which sinusoidal function will best fit the data without requiring a phase shift: $h(t) = \sin t$, $h(t) = -\sin t$, $h(t) = \cos t$, or $h(t) = -\cos t$? Explain.
c) Write the sinusoidal function that models the number of hours of daylight.
d) Graph the function from part c).
e) Estimate the number of hours of daylight on each date.
  i) March 15 (day 74)   **ii)** July 10 (day 191)   **iii)** December 5 (day 339)

Solution

a) Graph the data as a scatter plot.

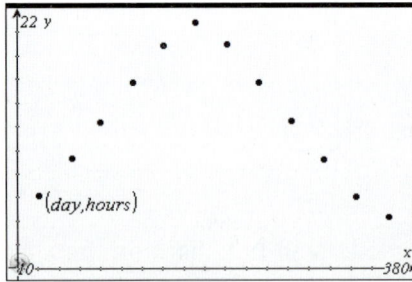

b) Note that the data starts at a minimum value, climb to a maximum value, and then decrease to the minimum value. The function $h(t) = -\cos t$ exhibits this same behaviour.

c) The maximum value is 20.83, and the minimum value is 4.34. Use these values to find the amplitude and the equation of the sinusoidal axis.

$$\text{Amplitude} = \frac{\text{maximum value} - \text{minimum value}}{2}$$
$$|a| = \frac{20.83 - 4.34}{2}$$
$$|a| = 8.245$$

The sinusoidal axis lies halfway between the maximum and minimum values. Its position will determine the value of d.

$d = \dfrac{\text{maximum value} + \text{minimum value}}{2}$

$d = \dfrac{20.83 + 4.34}{2}$

$d = 12.585$

Determine the value of b. You know that the period is 365 days.

Period $= \dfrac{2\pi}{|b|}$

$365 = \dfrac{2\pi}{|b|}$

$b = \dfrac{2\pi}{365}$ Choose b to be positive.

Why is the period 365 days?

Determine the phase shift, the value of c. For $h(t) = -\cos t$ the minimum value occurs at $t = 0$. For the daylight hours curve, the actual minimum occurs at day 355, which represents a 10-day shift to the left. Therefore, $c = -10$.

The number of hours of daylight, h, on the day of the year, t, is given by the function $h(t) = -8.245 \cos\left(\dfrac{2\pi}{365}(t + 10)\right) + 12.585$.

d) Graph the function in the same window as your scatter plot.

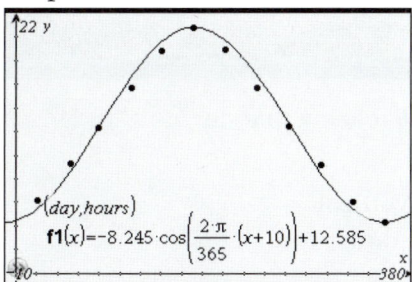

e) Use the value feature of the calculator or substitute the values into the equation of the function.

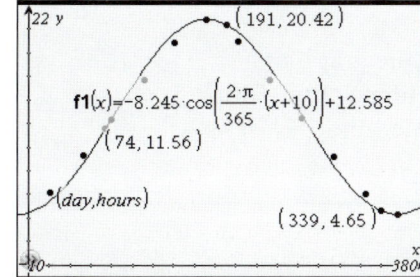

  i) The number of hours of daylight on March 15 (day 74) is approximately 11.56 h.

  ii) The number of hours of daylight on July 10 (day 191) is approximately 20.42 h.

  iii) The number of hours of daylight on December 5 (day 339) is approximately 4.65 h.

Your Turn

Windsor, Ontario, is located at latitude 42° N. The table shows the number of hours of daylight on the 21st day of each month as the day of the year on which it occurs for this city.

Hours of Daylight by Day of the Year for Windsor, Ontario											
21	52	80	111	141	172	202	233	264	294	325	355
9.62	10.87	12.20	13.64	14.79	15.28	14.81	13.64	12.22	10.82	9.59	9.08

a) Draw a scatter plot for the number of hours of daylight, h, in Windsor, Ontario on the day of the year, t.
b) Write the sinusoidal function that models the number of hours of daylight.
c) Graph the function from part b).
d) Estimate the number of hours of daylight on each date.
   i) March 10
   ii) July 24
   iii) December 3
e) Compare the graphs for Iqaluit and Windsor. What conclusions can you draw about the number of hours of daylight for the two locations?

Key Ideas

- You can use sinusoidal functions to model periodic phenomena that do not involve angles as the independent variable.

- You can adjust the amplitude, phase shift, period, and vertical displacement of the basic trigonometric functions to fit the characteristics of the real-world application being modelled.

- You can use technology to create the graph modelling the application. Use this graph to interpolate or extrapolate information required to solve the problem.

- You can solve trigonometric equations graphically. Use the graph of a function to determine the x-intercepts or the points of intersection with a given line. You can express your solutions over a specified interval or as a general solution.

Check Your Understanding

Practise

1. **a)** Use the graph of $y = \sin x$ to determine the solutions to the equation $\sin x = 0$ for the interval $0 \leq x \leq 2\pi$.

   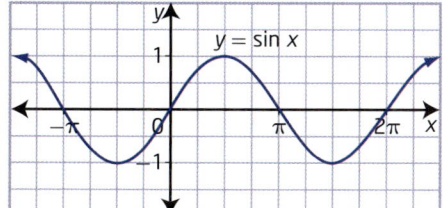

   b) Determine the general solution for $\sin x = 0$.

   c) Determine the solutions for $\sin 3x = 0$ in the interval $0 \leq x \leq 2\pi$.

2. The partial sinusoidal graphs shown below are intersected by the line $y = 6$. Each point of intersection corresponds to a value of x where $y = 6$. For each graph shown determine the approximate value of x where $y = 6$.

   a)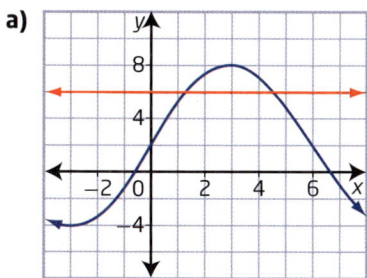

   b)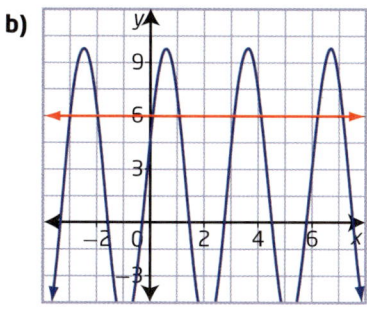

3. The partial graph of a sinusoidal function $y = 4 \cos (2(x - 60°)) + 6$ and the line $y = 3$ are shown below. From the graph determine the approximate solutions to the equation $4 \cos (2(x - 60°)) + 6 = 3$.

   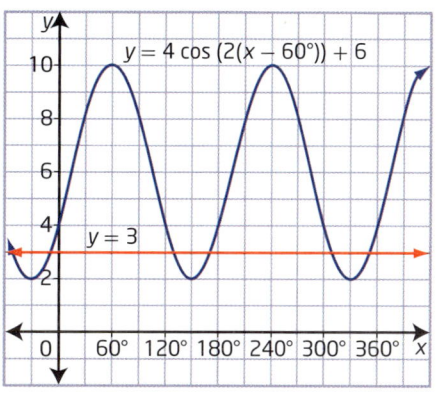

4. Solve each of the following equations graphically.

   a) $-2.8 \sin \left(\frac{\pi}{6}(x - 12)\right) + 16 = 16$, $0 \leq x \leq 2\pi$

   b) $12 \cos (2(x - 45°)) + 8 = 10$, $0° \leq x \leq 360°$

   c) $7 \cos (3x - 18) = 4$, $0 \leq x \leq 2\pi$

   d) $6.2 \sin (4(x + 8°)) - 1 = 4$, $0° \leq x \leq 360°$

5. Solve each of the following equations.

   a) $\sin \left(\frac{\pi}{4}(x - 6)\right) = 0.5$, $0 \leq x \leq 2\pi$

   b) $4 \cos (x - 45°) + 7 = 10$, $0° \leq x \leq 360°$

   c) $8 \cos (2x - 5) = 3$, general solution in radians

   d) $5.2 \sin (45(x + 8°)) - 1 = -3$, general solution in degrees

6. State a possible domain and range for the given functions, which represent real-world applications.

  a) The population of a lakeside town with large numbers of seasonal residents is modelled by the function $P(t) = 6000 \sin(t - 8) + 8000$.

  b) The height of the tide on a given day can be modelled using the function $h(t) = 6 \sin(t - 5) + 7$.

  c) The height above the ground of a rider on a Ferris wheel can be modelled by $h(t) = 6 \sin 3(t - 30) + 12$.

  d) The average daily temperature may be modelled by the function $h(t) = 9 \cos \frac{2\pi}{365}(t - 200) + 14$.

7. A trick from Victorian times was to listen to the pitch of a fly's buzz, reproduce the musical note on the piano, and say how many times the fly's wings had flapped in 1 s. If the fly's wings flap 200 times in one second, determine the period of the musical note.

8. Determine the period, the sinusoidal axis, and the amplitude for each of the following.

  a) The first maximum of a sine function occurs at the point (30°, 24), and the first minimum to the right of the maximum occurs at the point (80°, 6).

  b) The first maximum of a cosine function occurs at (0, 4), and the first minimum to the right of the maximum occurs at $\left(\frac{2\pi}{3}, -16\right)$.

  c) An electron oscillates back and forth 50 times per second, and the maximum and minimum values occur at +10 and −10, respectively.

Apply

9. A point on an industrial flywheel experiences a motion described by the function $h(t) = 13 \cos\left(\frac{2\pi}{0.7}t\right) + 15$, where h is the height, in metres, and t is the time, in minutes.

  a) What is the maximum height of the point?

  b) After how many minutes is the maximum height reached?

  c) What is the minimum height of the point?

  d) After how many minutes is the minimum height reached?

  e) For how long, within one cycle, is the point less than 6 m above the ground?

  f) Determine the height of the point if the wheel is allowed to turn for 1 h 12 min.

10. Michelle is balancing the wheel on her bicycle. She has marked a point on the tire that when rotated can be modelled by the function $h(t) = 59 + 24 \sin 125t$, where h is the height, in centimetres, and t is the time, in seconds. Determine the height of the mark, to the nearest tenth of a centimetre, when $t = 17.5$ s.

11. The typical voltage, V, in volts (V), supplied by an electrical outlet in Cuba is a sinusoidal function that oscillates between −155 V and +155 V and makes 60 complete cycles each second. Determine an equation for the voltage as a function of time, t.

12. The University of Calgary's Institute for Space Research is leading a project to launch Cassiope, a hybrid space satellite. Cassiope will follow a path that may be modelled by the function $h(t) = 350 \sin 28\pi(t - 25) + 400$, where h is the height, in kilometres, of the satellite above Earth and t is the time, in days.

    a) Determine the period of the satellite.

    b) How many minutes will it take the satellite to orbit Earth?

    c) How many orbits per day will the satellite make?

13. The Arctic fox is common throughout the Arctic tundra. Suppose the population, F, of foxes in a region of northern Manitoba is modelled by the function $F(t) = 500 \sin \frac{\pi}{12}t + 1000$, where t is the time, in months.

    a) How many months would it take for the fox population to drop to 650? Round your answer to the nearest month.

    b) One of the main food sources for the Arctic fox is the lemming. Suppose the population, L, of lemmings in the region is modelled by the function $L(t) = 5000 \sin \frac{\pi}{12}(t - 12) + 10\,000$.

    Graph the function $L(t)$ using the same set of axes as for $F(t)$.

    c) From the graph, determine the maximum and minimum numbers of foxes and lemmings and the months in which these occur.

    d) Describe the relationships between the maximum, minimum, and mean points of the two curves in terms of the lifestyles of the foxes and lemmings. List possible causes for the fluctuation in populations.

14. Office towers are designed to sway with the wind blowing from a particular direction. In one situation, the horizontal sway, h, in centimetres, from vertical can be approximated by the function $h = 40 \sin 0.526t$, where t is the time, in seconds.

    a) Graph the function using graphing technology. Use the following window settings: x: [0, 12, 1], y: [−40, 40, 5].

    b) If a guest arrives on the top floor at $t = 0$, how far will the guest have swayed from the vertical after 2.034 s?

    c) If a guest arrives on the top floor at $t = 0$, how many seconds will have elapsed before the guest has swayed 20 cm from the vertical?

15. In Inuvik, Northwest Territories (latitude 68.3° N), the Sun does not set for 56 days during the summer. The midnight Sun sequence below illustrates the rise and fall of the polar Sun during a day in the summer.

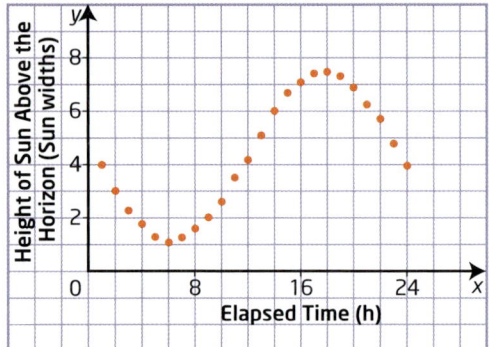

a) Determine the maximum and minimum heights of the Sun above the horizon in terms of Sun widths.

b) What is the period?

c) Determine the sinusoidal equation that models the midnight Sun.

Did You Know?

In 2010, a study showed that the Sun's width, or diameter, is a steady 1 500 000 km. The researchers discovered over a 12-year period that the diameter changed by less than 1 km.

16. The table shows the average monthly temperature in Winnipeg, Manitoba, in degrees Celsius.

Average Monthly Temperatures for Winnipeg, Manitoba (°C)					
Jan	Feb	Mar	Apr	May	Jun
−16.5	−12.7	−5.6	3	11.3	17.3

Average Monthly Temperatures for Winnipeg, Manitoba (°C)					
Jul	Aug	Sep	Oct	Nov	Dec
19.7	18	12.5	4.5	−4.3	−11.7

a) Plot the data on a scatter plot.

b) Determine the temperature that is halfway between the maximum average monthly temperature and the minimum average monthly temperature for Winnipeg.

c) Determine a sinusoidal function to model the temperature for Winnipeg.

d) Graph your model. How well does your model fit the data?

e) For how long in a 12-month period does Winnipeg have a temperature greater than or equal to 16 °C?

17. An electric heater turns on and off on a cyclic basis as it heats the water in a hot tub. The water temperature, T, in degrees Celsius, varies sinusoidally with time, t, in minutes. The heater turns on when the temperature of the water reaches 34 °C and turns off when the water temperature is 43 °C. Suppose the water temperature drops to 34 °C and the heater turns on. After another 30 min the heater turns off, and then after another 30 min the heater starts again.

a) Write the equation that expresses temperature as a function of time.

b) Determine the temperature 10 min after the heater first turns on.

18. A mass attached to the end of a long spring is bouncing up and down. As it bounces, its distance from the floor varies sinusoidally with time. When the mass is released, it takes 0.3 s to reach a high point of 60 cm above the floor. It takes 1.8 s for the mass to reach the first low point of 40 cm above the floor.

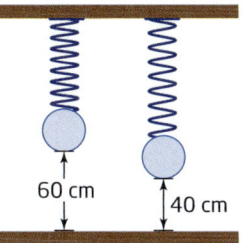

a) Sketch the graph of this sinusoidal function.

b) Determine the equation for the distance from the floor as a function of time.

c) What is the distance from the floor when the stopwatch reads 17.2 s?

d) What is the first positive value of time when the mass is 59 cm above the floor?

19. A Ferris wheel with a radius of 10 m rotates once every 60 s. Passengers get on board at a point 2 m above the ground at the bottom of the Ferris wheel. A sketch for the first 150 s is shown.

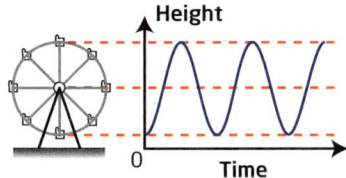

a) Write an equation to model the path of a passenger on the Ferris wheel, where the height is a function of time.

b) If Emily is at the bottom of the Ferris wheel when it begins to move, determine her height above the ground, to the nearest tenth of a metre, when the wheel has been in motion for 2.3 min.

c) Determine the amount of time that passes before a rider reaches a height of 18 m for the first time. Determine one other time the rider will be at that height within the first cycle.

20. The Canadian National Historic Windpower Centre, at Etzikom, Alberta, has various styles of windmills on display. The tip of the blade of one windmill reaches its minimum height of 8 m above the ground at a time of 2 s. Its maximum height is 22 m above the ground. The tip of the blade rotates 12 times per minute.

a) Write a sine or a cosine function to model the rotation of the tip of the blade.

b) What is the height of the tip of the blade after 4 s?

c) For how long is the tip of the blade above a height of 17 m in the first 10 s?

21. In a 366-day year, the average daily maximum temperature in Vancouver, British Columbia, follows a sinusoidal pattern with the highest value of 23.6 °C on day 208, July 26, and the lowest value of 4.2 °C on day 26, January 26.

  a) Use a sine or a cosine function to model the temperatures as a function of time, in days.

  b) From your model, determine the temperature for day 147, May 26.

  c) How many days will have an expected maximum temperature of 21.0 °C or higher?

Extend

22. An investment company invests the money it receives from investors on a collective basis, and each investor shares in the profits and losses. One company has an annual cash flow that has fluctuated in cycles of approximately 40 years since 1920, when it was at a high point. The highs were approximately +20% of the total assets, while the lows were approximately −10% of the total assets.

  a) Model this cash flow as a cosine function of the time, in years, with $t = 0$ representing 1920.

  b) Graph the function from part a).

  c) Determine the cash flow for the company in 2008.

  d) Based on your model, do you feel that this is a company you would invest with? Explain.

23. Golden, British Columbia, is one of the many locations for heliskiing in Western Canada. When skiing the open powder, the skier leaves behind a trail, with two turns creating one cycle of the sinusoidal curve. On one section of the slope, a skier makes a total of 10 turns over a 20-s interval.

  a) If the distance for a turn, to the left or to the right, from the midline is 1.2 m, determine the function that models the path of the skier.

  b) How would the function change if the skier made only eight turns in the same 20-s interval?

Create Connections

C1 a) When is it best to use a sine function as a model?

  b) When is it best to use a cosine function as a model?

C2 a) Which of the parameters in $y = a \sin b(x - c) + d$ has the greatest influence on the graph of the function? Explain your reasoning.

  b) Which of the parameters in $y = a \cos b(x - c) + d$ has the greatest influence on the graph of the function? Explain your reasoning.

C3 The sinusoidal door by the architectural firm Matharoo Associates is in the home of a diamond merchant in Surat, India. The door measures 5.2 m high and 1.7 m wide. It is constructed from 40 sections of 254-mm-thick Burma teak. Each section is carved so that the door integrates 160 pulleys, 80 ball bearings, a wire rope, and a counterweight hidden within the single pivot. When the door is in an open position, the shape of it may be modelled by a sinusoidal function.

a) Assuming the amplitude is half the width of the door and there is one cycle created within the height of the door, determine a sinusoidal function that could model the shape of the open door.

b) Sketch the graph of your model over one period.

Project Corner — Broadcasting

- Radio broadcasts, television productions, and cell phone calls are examples of electronic communication.

- A carrier waveform is used in broadcasting the music and voices we hear on the radio. The wave form, which is typically sinusoidal, carries another electrical waveform or message. In the case of AM radio, the sounds (messages) are broadcast through amplitude modulation.

- An NTSC (National Television System Committee) television transmission is comprised of video and sound signals broadcast using carrier waveforms. The video signal is amplitude modulated, while the sound signal is frequency modulated.

- Explain the difference between amplitude modulation and frequency modulation with respect to transformations of functions.

- How are periodic functions involved in satellite radio broadcasting, satellite television broadcasting, or cell phone transmissions?

Chapter 5 Review

5.1 Graphing Sine and Cosine Functions, pages 222–237

1. Sketch the graph of $y = \sin x$ for $-360° \leq x \leq 360°$.
   a) What are the x-intercepts?
   b) What is the y-intercept?
   c) State the domain, range, and period of the function.
   d) What is the greatest value of $y = \sin x$?

2. Sketch the graph of $y = \cos x$ for $-360° \leq x \leq 360°$.
   a) What are the x-intercepts?
   b) What is the y-intercept?
   c) State the domain, range, and period of the function.
   d) What is the greatest value of $y = \cos x$?

3. Match each function with its correct graph.
   a) $y = \sin x$
   b) $y = \sin 2x$
   c) $y = -\sin x$
   d) $y = \frac{1}{2} \sin x$

   A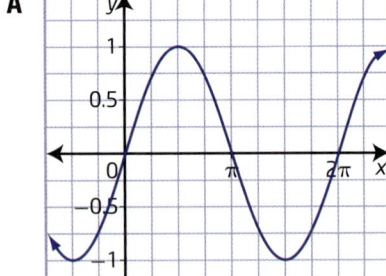

   B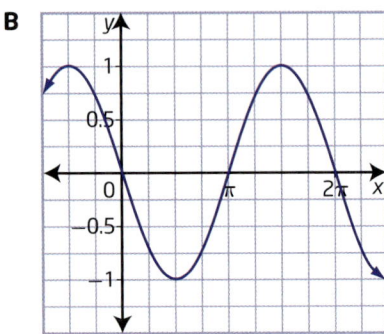

   C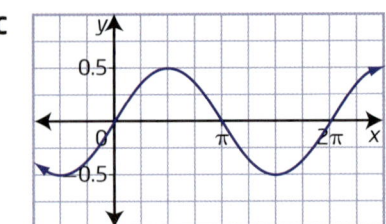

   D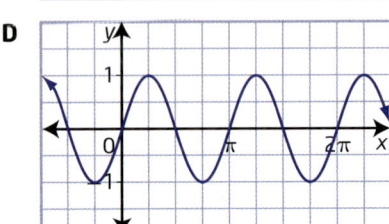

4. Without graphing, determine the amplitude and period, in radians and degrees, of each function.
   a) $y = -3 \sin 2x$
   b) $y = 4 \cos 0.5x$
   c) $y = \frac{1}{3} \sin \frac{5}{6}x$
   d) $y = -5 \cos \frac{3}{2}x$

5. a) Describe how you could distinguish between the graphs of $y = \sin x$, $y = \sin 2x$, and $y = 2 \sin x$. Graph each function to check your predictions.
   b) Describe how you could distinguish between the graphs of $y = \sin x$, $y = -\sin x$, and $y = \sin(-x)$. Graph each function to check your predictions.
   c) Describe how you could distinguish between the graphs of $y = \cos x$, $y = -\cos x$, and $y = \cos(-x)$. Graph each function to check your predictions.

6. Write the equation of the cosine function in the form $y = a \cos bx$ with the given characteristics.
   a) amplitude 3, period π
   b) amplitude 4, period 150°
   c) amplitude $\frac{1}{2}$, period 720°
   d) amplitude $\frac{3}{4}$, period $\frac{\pi}{6}$

7. Write the equation of the sine function in the form $y = a \sin bx$ with the given characteristics.

   a) amplitude 8, period 180°
   b) amplitude 0.4, period 60°
   c) amplitude $\frac{3}{2}$, period 4π
   d) amplitude 2, period $\frac{2\pi}{3}$

5.2 Transformations of Sinusoidal Functions, pages 238–255

8. Determine the amplitude, period, phase shift, and vertical displacement with respect to $y = \sin x$ or $y = \cos x$ for each function. Sketch the graph of each function for two cycles.

   a) $y = 2 \cos 3\left(x - \frac{\pi}{2}\right) - 8$
   b) $y = \sin \frac{1}{2}\left(x - \frac{\pi}{4}\right) + 3$
   c) $y = -4 \cos 2(x - 30°) + 7$
   d) $y = \frac{1}{3} \sin \frac{1}{4}(x - 60°) - 1$

9. Sketch graphs of the functions $f(x) = \cos 2\left(x - \frac{\pi}{2}\right)$ and $g(x) = \cos\left(2x - \frac{\pi}{2}\right)$ on the same set of axes for $0 \le x \le 2\pi$.

   a) State the period of each function.
   b) State the phase shift for each function.
   c) State the phase shift of the function $y = \cos b(x - \pi)$.
   d) State the phase shift of the function $y = \cos (bx - \pi)$.

10. Write the equation for each graph in the form $y = a \sin b(x - c) + d$ and in the form $y = a \cos b(x - c) + d$.

    a)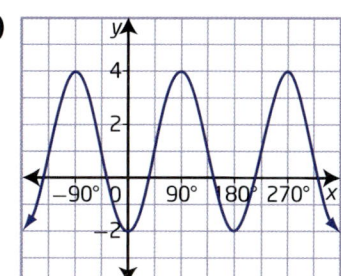

    b)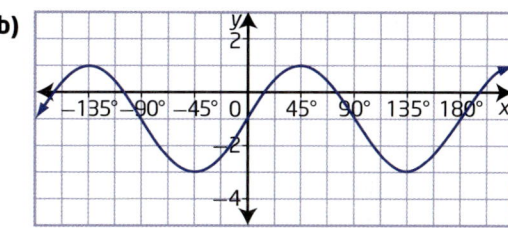

    c)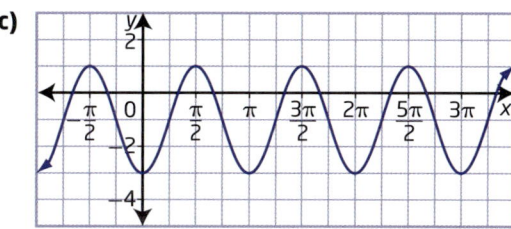

    d)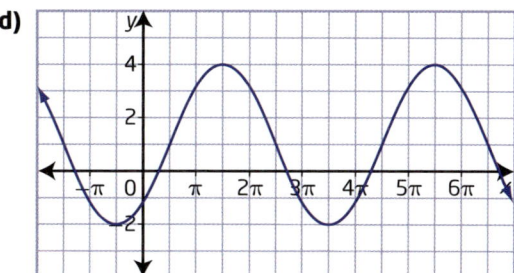

11. a) Write the equation of the sine function with amplitude 4, period π, phase shift $\frac{\pi}{3}$ units to the right, and vertical displacement 5 units down.

    b) Write the equation of the cosine function with amplitude 0.5, period 4π, phase shift $\frac{\pi}{6}$ units to the left, and vertical displacement 1 unit up.

    c) Write the equation of the sine function with amplitude $\frac{2}{3}$, period 540°, no phase shift, and vertical displacement 5 units down.

12. Graph each function. State the domain, the range, the maximum and minimum values, and the x-intercepts and y-intercept.
    a) $y = 2 \cos (x - 45°) + 3$
    b) $y = 4 \sin 2\left(x - \frac{\pi}{3}\right) + 1$

13. Using the language of transformations, describe how to obtain the graph of each function from the graph of $y = \sin x$ or $y = \cos x$.
    a) $y = 3 \sin 2\left(x - \frac{\pi}{3}\right) + 6$
    b) $y = -2 \cos \frac{1}{2}\left(x + \frac{\pi}{4}\right) - 3$
    c) $y = \frac{3}{4} \cos 2(x - 30°) + 10$
    d) $y = -\sin 2(x + 45°) - 8$

14. The sound that the horn of a cruise ship makes as it approaches the dock is different from the sound it makes when it departs. The equation of the sound wave as the ship approaches is $y = 2 \sin 2\theta$, while the equation of the sound wave as it departs is $y = 2 \sin \frac{1}{2}\theta$.
    a) Compare the two sounds by sketching the graphs of the sound waves as the ship approaches and departs for the interval $0 \leq \theta \leq 2\pi$.
    b) How do the two graphs compare to the graph of $y = \sin \theta$?

5.3 The Tangent Function, pages 256–265

15. a) Graph $y = \tan \theta$ for $-2\pi \leq \theta \leq 2\pi$ and for $-360° \leq \theta \leq 360°$.
    b) Determine the following characteristics.
       i) domain
       ii) range
       iii) y-intercept
       iv) x-intercepts
       v) equations of the asymptotes

16. A point on the unit circle has coordinates $P\left(\frac{\sqrt{3}}{2}, \frac{1}{2}\right)$.
    a) Determine the exact coordinates of point Q.
    b) Describe the relationship between $\sin \theta$, $\cos \theta$, and $\tan \theta$.
    c) Using the diagram, explain what happens to $\tan \theta$ as θ approaches 90°.

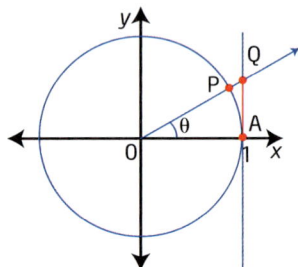

    d) What happens to $\tan \theta$ when $\theta = 90°$?

17. a) Explain how $\cos \theta$ relates to the asymptotes of the graph of $y = \tan \theta$.
    b) Explain how $\sin \theta$ relates to the x-intercepts of the graph of $y = \tan \theta$.

18. Tan θ is sometimes used to measure the lengths of shadows given the angle of elevation of the Sun and the height of a tree. Explain what happens to the shadow of the tree when the Sun is directly overhead. How does this relate to the graph of $y = \tan \theta$?

19. What is a vertical asymptote? How can you tell when a trigonometric function will have a vertical asymptote?

5.4 Equations and Graphs of Trigonometric Functions, pages 266–281

20. Solve each of the following equations graphically.
    a) $2 \sin x - 1 = 0,\ 0 \leq x \leq 2\pi$
    b) $0 = 2 \cos (x - 30°) + 5,\ 0° \leq x \leq 360°$
    c) $\sin \left(\frac{\pi}{4}(x - 6)\right) = 0.5$, general solution in radians
    d) $4 \cos (x - 45°) + 7 = 10$, general solution in degrees

21. The Royal British Columbia Museum, home to the First Peoples Exhibit, located in Victoria, British Columbia, was founded in 1886. To preserve the many artifacts, the air-conditioning system in the building operates when the temperature in the building is greater than 22 °C. In the summer, the building's temperature varies with the time of day and is modelled by the function $T = 12 \cos t + 19$, where T represents the temperature in degrees Celsius and t represents the time, in hours.

a) Graph the function.
b) Determine, to the nearest tenth of an hour, the amount of time in one day that the air conditioning will operate.
c) Why is a model for temperature variance important in this situation?

22. The height, h, in metres, above the ground of a rider on a Ferris wheel after t seconds can be modelled by the sine function $h(t) = 12 \sin \frac{\pi}{45}(t - 30) + 15$.

a) Graph the function using graphing technology.
b) Determine the maximum and minimum heights of the rider above the ground.
c) Determine the time required for the Ferris wheel to complete one revolution.
d) Determine the height of the rider above the ground after 45 s.

23. The number of hours of daylight, L, in Lethbridge, Alberta, may be modelled by a sinusoidal function of time, t. The longest day of the year is June 21, with 15.7 h of daylight, and the shortest day is December 21, with 8.3 h of daylight.

a) Determine a sinusoidal function to model this situation.
b) How many hours of daylight are there on April 3?

24. For several hundred years, astronomers have kept track of the number of solar flares, or sunspots, that occur on the surface of the Sun. The number of sunspots counted in a given year varies periodically from a minimum of 10 per year to a maximum of 110 per year. There have been 18 complete cycles between the years 1750 and 1948. Assume that a maximum number of sunspots occurred in the year 1750.

a) How many sunspots would you expect there were in the year 2000?
b) What is the first year after 2000 in which the number of sunspots will be about 35?
c) What is the first year after 2000 in which the number of sunspots will be a maximum?

Chapter 5 Practice Test

Multiple Choice

For #1 to #7, choose the best answer.

1. The range of the function $y = 2 \sin x + 1$ is
   - **A** $\{y \mid -1 \leq y \leq 3, y \in R\}$
   - **B** $\{y \mid -1 \leq y \leq 1, y \in R\}$
   - **C** $\{y \mid 1 \leq y \leq 3, y \in R\}$
   - **D** $\{y \mid 0 \leq y \leq 2, y \in R\}$

2. What are the phase shift, period, and amplitude, respectively, for the function $f(x) = 3 \sin 2\left(x - \dfrac{\pi}{3}\right) + 1$?
   - **A** $\dfrac{\pi}{3}, 3, \pi$
   - **B** $\pi, \dfrac{\pi}{3}, 3$
   - **C** $3, \dfrac{\pi}{3}, \pi$
   - **D** $\dfrac{\pi}{3}, \pi, 3$

3. Two functions are given as $f(x) = \sin\left(x - \dfrac{\pi}{4}\right)$ and $g(x) = \cos(x - a)$. Determine the smallest positive value for a so that the graphs are identical.
   - **A** $\dfrac{\pi}{4}$
   - **B** $\dfrac{\pi}{2}$
   - **C** $\dfrac{3\pi}{4}$
   - **D** $\dfrac{5\pi}{4}$

4. A cosine curve has a maximum point at (3, 14). The nearest minimum point to the right of this maximum point is (8, 2). Which of the following is a possible equation for this curve?
   - **A** $y = 6 \cos \dfrac{2\pi}{5}(x + 3) + 8$
   - **B** $y = 6 \cos \dfrac{2\pi}{5}(x - 3) + 8$
   - **C** $y = 6 \cos \dfrac{\pi}{5}(x + 3) + 8$
   - **D** $y = 6 \cos \dfrac{\pi}{5}(x - 3) + 8$

5. The graph of a sinusoidal function is shown. A possible equation for the function is

   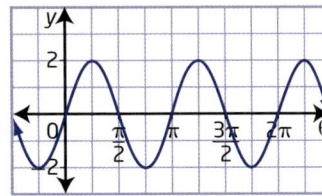

   - **A** $y = 2 \cos \dfrac{1}{2}\theta$
   - **B** $y = 2 \sin 2\theta$
   - **C** $y = 2 \cos 2\theta$
   - **D** $y = 2 \sin \dfrac{1}{2}\theta$

6. Monique makes the following statements about a sine function of the form $y = a \sin b(x - c) + d$:

   I The values of a and d affect the range of the function.

   II The values of c and d determine the horizontal and vertical translations, respectively.

   III The value of b determines the number of cycles within the distance of 2π.

   IV The values of a and b are vertical and horizontal stretches.

   Monique's correct statements are
   - **A** I, II, III, and IV
   - **B** I only
   - **C** I, II, and III only
   - **D** I, II, and IV only

7. The graph shows how the height of a bicycle pedal changes as the bike is pedalled at a constant speed. How would the graph change if the bicycle were pedalled at a greater constant speed?

   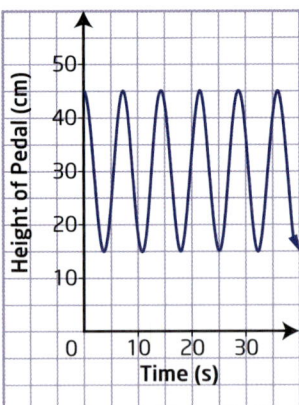

   - **A** The height of the function would increase.
   - **B** The height of the function would decrease.
   - **C** The period of the function would decrease.
   - **D** The period of the function would increase.

Short Answer

8. What is the horizontal distance between two consecutive zeros of the function $f(x) = \sin 2x$?

9. For the function $y = \tan \theta$, state the asymptotes, domain, range, and period.

10. What do the functions $f(x) = -4 \sin x$ and $g(x) = -4 \cos \frac{1}{2}x$ have in common?

11. An airplane's electrical generator produces a time-varying output voltage described by the equation $V(t) = 120 \sin 2513t$, where t is the time, in seconds, and V is in volts. What are the amplitude and period of this function?

12. Suppose the depth, d, in metres, of the tide in a certain harbour can be modelled by $d(t) = -3 \cos \frac{\pi}{6} t + 5$, where t is the time, in hours. Consider a day in which $t = 0$ represents the time 00:00. Determine the time for the high and low tides and the depths of each.

13. Solve each of the following equations graphically.

    a) $\sin \left(\frac{\pi}{3}(x - 1) \right) = 0.5$, general solution in radians

    b) $4 \cos (15(x + 30°)) + 1 = -2$, general solution in degrees

Extended Response

14. Compare and contrast the two graphs of sinusoidal functions.

    I
    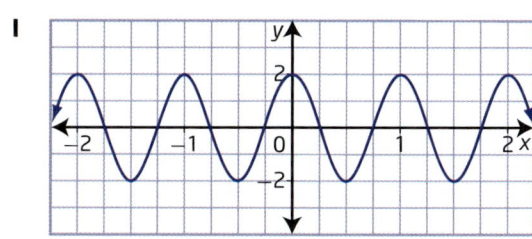

    II
    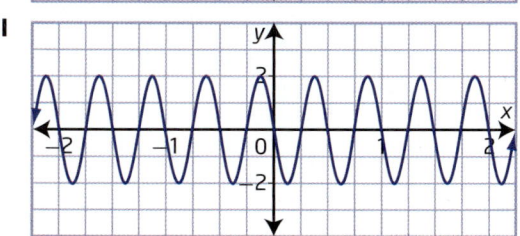

15. Suppose a mass suspended on a spring is bouncing up and down. The mass's distance from the floor when it is at rest is 1 m. The maximum displacement is 10 cm as it bounces. It takes 2 s to complete one bounce or cycle. Suppose the mass is at rest at $t = 0$ and that the spring bounces up first.

    a) Write a function to model the displacement as a function of time.

    b) Graph the function to determine the approximate times when the mass is 1.05 m above the floor in the first cycle.

    c) Verify your solutions to part b) algebraically.

16. The graph of a sinusoidal function is shown.

    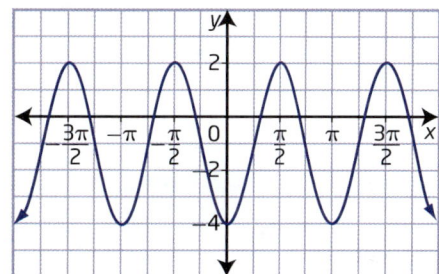

    a) Determine a function for the graph in the form $y = a \sin b(x - c) + d$.

    b) Determine a function for the graph in the form $y = a \cos b(x - c) + d$.

17. A student is investigating the effects of changing the values of the parameters a, b, c, and d in the function $y = a \sin b(x - c) + d$. The student graphs the following functions:

    A $f(x) = \sin x$

    B $g(x) = 2 \sin x$

    C $h(x) = \sin 2x$

    D $k(x) = \sin (2x + 2)$

    E $m(x) = \sin 2x + 2$

    a) Which graphs have the same x-intercepts?

    b) Which graphs have the same period?

    c) Which graph has a different amplitude than the others?

CHAPTER 6

Trigonometric Identities

Trigonometric functions are used to model behaviour in the physical world. You can model projectile motion, such as the path of a thrown javelin or a lobbed tennis ball with trigonometry. Sometimes equivalent expressions for trigonometric functions can be substituted to allow scientists to analyse data or solve a problem more efficiently. In this chapter, you will explore equivalent trigonometric expressions.

Did You Know?

Elizabeth Gleadle, of Vancouver, British Columbia, holds the Canadian women's javelin record, with a distance of 58.21 m thrown in July 2009.

Key Terms
trigonometric identity

288 MHR • Chapter 6

Career Link

An athletic therapist works with athletes to prevent, assess, and rehabilitate sports-related injuries, and facilitate a return to competitive sport after injury. Athletic therapists can begin their careers by obtaining a Bachelor of Kinesiology from an institution such as the University of Calgary. This degree can provide entrance to medical schools and eventually sports medicine as a specialty.

Web Link

To learn more about kinesiology and a career as an athletic therapist, go to www.mcgrawhill.ca/school/learningcentres and follow the links.

6.1

Reciprocal, Quotient, and Pythagorean Identities

Focus on...

- verifying a trigonometric identity numerically and graphically using technology
- exploring reciprocal, quotient, and Pythagorean identities
- determining non-permissible values of trigonometric identities
- explaining the difference between a trigonometric identity and a trigonometric equation

Digital music players store large sound files by using trigonometry to compress (store) and then decompress (play) the file when needed. A large sound file can be stored in a much smaller space using this technique. Electronics engineers have learned how to use the periodic nature of music to compress the audio file into a smaller space.

Engineer using an electronic spin resonance spectroscope

Investigate Comparing Two Trigonometric Expressions

Materials
- graphing technology

1. Graph the curves $y = \sin x$ and $y = \cos x \tan x$ over the domain $-360° \leq x < 360°$. Graph the curves on separate grids using the same range and scale. What do you notice?

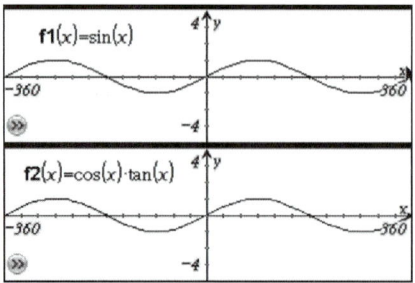

2. Make and analyse a table of values for these functions in multiples of 30° over the domain $-360° \leq x < 360°$. Describe your findings.

3. Use your knowledge of $\tan x$ to simplify the expression $\cos x \tan x$.

Reflect and Respond

4. a) Are the curves $y = \sin x$ and $y = \cos x \tan x$ identical? Explain your reasoning.

   b) Why was it important to look at the graphs *and* at the table of values?

5. What are the non-permissible values of x in the equation $\sin x = \cos x \tan x$? Explain.

6. Are there any permissible values for x outside the domain in step 2 for which the expressions $\sin x$ and $\cos x \tan x$ are not equal? Share your response with a classmate.

Link the Ideas

The equation $\sin x = \cos x \tan x$ that you explored in the investigation is an example of a **trigonometric identity**. Both sides of the equation have the same value for all permissible values of x. In other words, when the expressions on either side of the equal sign are evaluated for any permissible value, the resulting values are equal. Trigonometric identities can be verified both numerically and graphically.

trigonometric identity
- a trigonometric equation that is true for all permissible values of the variable in the expressions on both sides of the equation

You are familiar with two groups of identities from your earlier work with trigonometry: the reciprocal identities and the quotient identity.

Reciprocal Identities
$$\csc x = \frac{1}{\sin x} \qquad \sec x = \frac{1}{\cos x} \qquad \cot x = \frac{1}{\tan x}$$

Quotient Identities
$$\tan x = \frac{\sin x}{\cos x} \qquad \cot x = \frac{\cos x}{\sin x}$$

Example 1

Verify a Potential Identity Numerically and Graphically

a) Determine the non-permissible values, in degrees, for the equation $\sec \theta = \dfrac{\tan \theta}{\sin \theta}$.

b) Numerically verify that $\theta = 60°$ and $\theta = \dfrac{\pi}{4}$ are solutions of the equation.

c) Use technology to graphically decide whether the equation could be an identity over the domain $-360° < \theta \leq 360°$.

Solution

a) To determine the non-permissible values, assess each trigonometric function in the equation individually and examine expressions that may have non-permissible values. Visualize the graphs of $y = \sin x$, $y = \cos x$ and $y = \tan x$ to help you determine the non-permissible values.

First consider the left side, sec θ:

$\sec \theta = \dfrac{1}{\cos \theta}$, and $\cos \theta = 0$ when $\theta = 90°, 270°, \ldots$.

So, the non-permissible values for sec θ are $\theta \neq 90° + 180°n$, where $n \in I$.

Now consider the right side, $\dfrac{\tan \theta}{\sin \theta}$:

tan θ is not defined when $\theta = 90°, 270°, \ldots$.

Why must these values be excluded?

So, the non-permissible values for tan θ are $\theta \neq 90° + 180°n$, where $n \in I$.

How do these non-permissible values compare to the ones found for the left side?

Also, the expression $\dfrac{\tan \theta}{\sin \theta}$ is undefined when $\sin \theta = 0$.

$\sin \theta = 0$ when $\theta = 0°, 180°, \ldots$.

So, further non-permissible values for $\dfrac{\tan \theta}{\sin \theta}$ are $\theta \neq 180°n$, where $n \in I$.

Are these non-permissible values included in the ones already found?

The three sets of non-permissible values for the equation $\sec \theta = \dfrac{\tan \theta}{\sin \theta}$ can be expressed as a single restriction, $\theta \neq 90°n$, where $n \in I$.

b) Substitute $\theta = 60°$.

Left Side $= \sec \theta$
$= \sec 60°$
$= \dfrac{1}{\cos 60°}$
$= \dfrac{1}{0.5}$
$= 2$

Right Side $= \dfrac{\tan \theta}{\sin \theta}$
$= \dfrac{\tan 60°}{\sin 60°}$
$= \dfrac{\sqrt{3}}{\frac{\sqrt{3}}{2}}$
$= 2$

Why does substituting 60° in both sides of the equation not prove that the identity is true?

Left Side = Right Side

The equation $\sec \theta = \dfrac{\tan \theta}{\sin \theta}$ is true for $\theta = 60°$.

Substitute $\theta = \dfrac{\pi}{4}$.

Left Side $= \sec \theta$
$= \sec \dfrac{\pi}{4}$
$= \dfrac{1}{\cos \dfrac{\pi}{4}}$
$= \dfrac{1}{\frac{1}{\sqrt{2}}}$
$= \sqrt{2}$

Right Side $= \dfrac{\tan \theta}{\sin \theta}$
$= \dfrac{\tan \dfrac{\pi}{4}}{\sin \dfrac{\pi}{4}}$
$= \dfrac{1}{\frac{1}{\sqrt{2}}}$
$= \sqrt{2}$

Left Side = Right Side

The equation $\sec \theta = \dfrac{\tan \theta}{\sin \theta}$ is true for $\theta = \dfrac{\pi}{4}$.

c) Use technology, with domain $-360° < x \leq 360°$, to graph $y = \sec \theta$ and $y = \dfrac{\tan \theta}{\sin \theta}$. The graphs look identical, so $\sec \theta = \dfrac{\tan \theta}{\sin \theta}$ could be an identity.

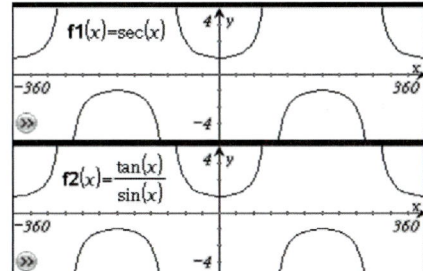

How do these graphs show that there are non-permissible values for this identity?

Does graphing the related functions on each side of the equation prove that the identity is true? Explain.

Your Turn

a) Determine the non-permissible values, in degrees, for the equation $\cot x = \dfrac{\cos x}{\sin x}$.

b) Verify that $x = 45°$ and $x = \dfrac{\pi}{6}$ are solutions to the equation.

c) Use technology to graphically decide whether the equation could be an identity over the domain $-360° < x \leq 360°$.

Example 2

Use Identities to Simplify Expressions

a) Determine the non-permissible values, in radians, of the variable in the expression $\dfrac{\cot x}{\csc x \cos x}$.

b) Simplify the expression.

Solution

a) The trigonometric functions $\cot x$ and $\csc x$ both have non-permissible values in their domains.

For $\cot x$, $x \neq \pi n$, where $n \in I$.
For $\csc x$, $x \neq \pi n$, where $n \in I$.

Why are these the non-permissible values for both reciprocal functions?

Also, the denominator of $\dfrac{\cot x}{\csc x \cos x}$ cannot equal zero. In other words, $\csc x \cos x \neq 0$.

There are no values of x that result in $\csc x = 0$.
However, for $\cos x$, $x \neq \dfrac{\pi}{2} + \pi n$, where $n \in I$.

Combined, the non-permissible values for $\dfrac{\cot x}{\csc x \cos x}$ are $x \neq \dfrac{\pi}{2}n$, where $n \in I$.

Why can you write this single general restriction?

b) To simplify the expression, use reciprocal and quotient identities to write trigonometric functions in terms of cosine and sine.

$$\frac{\cot x}{\csc x \cos x} = \frac{\dfrac{\cos x}{\sin x}}{\dfrac{1}{\sin x} \cos x}$$

$$= \frac{\dfrac{\cos x}{\sin x}}{\dfrac{\cos x}{\sin x}} \qquad \text{Simplify the fraction.}$$

$$= 1$$

Your Turn

a) Determine the non-permissible values, in radians, of the variable in the expression $\dfrac{\sec x}{\tan x}$.

b) Simplify the expression.

Pythagorean Identity

Recall that point P on the terminal arm of an angle θ in standard position has coordinates $(\cos \theta, \sin \theta)$. Consider a right triangle with a hypotenuse of 1 and legs of $\cos \theta$ and $\sin \theta$.

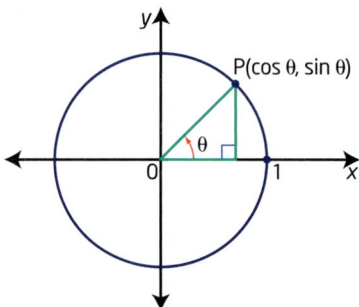

The hypotenuse is 1 because it is the radius of the unit circle. Apply the Pythagorean theorem in the right triangle to establish the Pythagorean identity:

$$x^2 + y^2 = 1^2$$
$$\cos^2 \theta + \sin^2 \theta = 1$$

Example 3

Use the Pythagorean Identity

a) Verify that the equation $\cot^2 x + 1 = \csc^2 x$ is true when $x = \dfrac{\pi}{6}$.

b) Use quotient identities to express the Pythagorean identity $\cos^2 x + \sin^2 x = 1$ as the equivalent identity $\cot^2 x + 1 = \csc^2 x$.

Solution

a) Substitute $x = \dfrac{\pi}{6}$.

$$\begin{aligned}\text{Left Side} &= \cot^2 x + 1 \\ &= \cot^2 \dfrac{\pi}{6} + 1 \\ &= \dfrac{1}{\tan^2 \dfrac{\pi}{6} + 1} \\ &= \dfrac{1}{\dfrac{1}{(\sqrt{3})^2}} + 1 \\ &= (\sqrt{3})^2 + 1 \\ &= 4 \end{aligned}$$

$$\begin{aligned}\text{Right Side} &= \csc^2 x \\ &= \csc^2 \dfrac{\pi}{6} \\ &= \dfrac{1}{\sin^2 \dfrac{\pi}{6}} \\ &= \dfrac{1}{\left(\dfrac{1}{2}\right)^2} \\ &= 2^2 \\ &= 4 \end{aligned}$$

Left Side = Right Side

The equation $\cot^2 x + 1 = \csc^2 x$ is true when $x = \dfrac{\pi}{6}$.

b) $\cos^2 x + \sin^2 x = 1$

Since this identity is true for all permissible values of x, you can multiply both sides by $\dfrac{1}{\sin^2 x}$, $x \neq \pi n$, where $n \in I$.

$$\left(\dfrac{1}{\sin^2 x}\right)\cos^2 x + \left(\dfrac{1}{\sin^2 x}\right)\sin^2 x = \left(\dfrac{1}{\sin^2 x}\right)1$$

$$\dfrac{\cos^2 x}{\sin^2 x} + 1 = \dfrac{1}{\sin^2 x}$$

$$\cot^2 x + 1 = \csc^2 x$$

Why multiply both sides by $\dfrac{1}{\sin^2 x}$? How else could you simplify this equation?

Your Turn

a) Verify the equation $1 + \tan^2 x = \sec^2 x$ numerically for $x = \dfrac{3\pi}{4}$.

b) Express the Pythagorean identity $\cos^2 x + \sin^2 x = 1$ as the equivalent identity $1 + \tan^2 x = \sec^2 x$.

The three forms of the Pythagorean identity are

$\cos^2 \theta + \sin^2 \theta = 1 \qquad \cot^2 \theta + 1 = \csc^2 \theta \qquad 1 + \tan^2 \theta = \sec^2 \theta$

Key Ideas

- A trigonometric identity is an equation involving trigonometric functions that is true for all permissible values of the variable.
- You can verify trigonometric identities
  - numerically by substituting specific values for the variable
  - graphically, using technology
- Verifying that two sides of an equation are equal for given values, or that they appear equal when graphed, is not sufficient to conclude that the equation is an identity.
- You can use trigonometric identities to simplify more complicated trigonometric expressions.
- The reciprocal identities are

  $$\csc x = \frac{1}{\sin x} \qquad \sec x = \frac{1}{\cos x} \qquad \cot x = \frac{1}{\tan x}$$

- The quotient identities are

  $$\tan x = \frac{\sin x}{\cos x} \qquad \cot x = \frac{\cos x}{\sin x}$$

- The Pythagorean identities are

  $$\cos^2 x + \sin^2 x = 1 \qquad 1 + \tan^2 x = \sec^2 x \qquad \cot^2 x + 1 = \csc^2 x$$

Check Your Understanding

Practise

1. Determine the non-permissible values of x, in radians, for each expression.

   a) $\dfrac{\cos x}{\sin x}$
   b) $\dfrac{\sin x}{\tan x}$
   c) $\dfrac{\cot x}{1 - \sin x}$
   d) $\dfrac{\tan x}{\cos x + 1}$

2. Why do some identities have non-permissible values?

3. Simplify each expression to one of the three primary trigonometric functions, $\sin x$, $\cos x$ or $\tan x$. For part a), verify graphically, using technology, that the given expression is equivalent to its simplified form.

   a) $\sec x \sin x$
   b) $\sec x \cot x \sin^2 x$
   c) $\dfrac{\cos x}{\cot x}$

4. Simplify, and then rewrite each expression as one of the three reciprocal trigonometric functions, $\csc x$, $\sec x$, or $\cot x$.

   a) $\left(\dfrac{\cos x}{\tan x}\right)\left(\dfrac{\tan x}{\sin x}\right)$
   b) $\csc x \cot x \sec x \sin x$
   c) $\dfrac{\cos x}{1 - \sin^2 x}$

5. a) Verify that the equation
   $$\dfrac{\sec x}{\tan x + \cot x} = \sin x$$
   is true for $x = 30°$ and for $x = \dfrac{\pi}{4}$.

   b) What are the non-permissible values of the equation in the domain $0° \leq x < 360°$?

6. Consider the equation
$\dfrac{\sin x \cos x}{1 + \cos x} = \dfrac{1 - \cos x}{\tan x}$.

   a) What are the non-permissible values, in radians, for this equation?

   b) Graph the two sides of the equation using technology, over the domain $0 \leq x < 2\pi$. Could it be an identity?

   c) Verify that the equation is true when $x = \dfrac{\pi}{4}$. Use exact values for each expression in the equation.

Apply

7. When a polarizing lens is rotated through an angle θ over a second lens, the amount of light passing through both lenses decreases by $1 - \sin^2 \theta$.

   a) Determine an equivalent expression for this decrease using only cosine.

   b) What fraction of light is lost when $\theta = \dfrac{\pi}{6}$?

   c) What percent of light is lost when $\theta = 60°$?

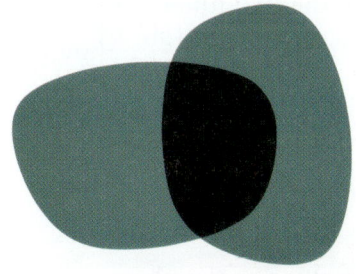

8. Compare $y = \sin x$ and $y = \sqrt{1 - \cos^2 x}$ by completing the following.

   a) Verify that $\sin x = \sqrt{1 - \cos^2 x}$ for $x = \dfrac{\pi}{3}$, $x = \dfrac{5\pi}{6}$, and $x = \pi$.

   b) Graph $y = \sin x$ and $y = \sqrt{1 - \cos^2 x}$ in the same window.

   c) Determine whether $\sin x = \sqrt{1 - \cos^2 x}$ is an identity. Explain your answer.

9. Illuminance (E) is a measure of the amount of light coming from a light source and falling onto a surface. If the light is projected onto the surface at an angle θ, measured from the perpendicular, then a formula relating these values is $\sec \theta = \dfrac{I}{ER^2}$, where I is a measure of the luminous intensity and R is the distance between the light source and the surface.

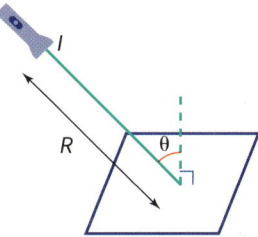

   a) Rewrite the formula so that E is isolated and written in terms of cos θ.

   b) Show that $E = \dfrac{I \cot \theta}{R^2 \csc \theta}$ is equivalent to your equation from part a).

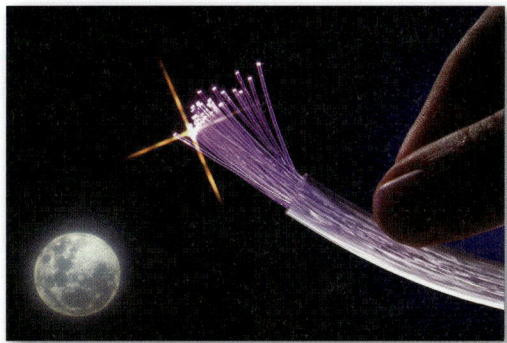

Fibre optic cable

10. Simplify $\dfrac{\csc x}{\tan x + \cot x}$ to one of the three primary trigonometric ratios. What are the non-permissible values of the original expression in the domain $0 \leq x < 2\pi$?

11. a) Determine graphically, using technology, whether the expression $\dfrac{\csc^2 x - \cot^2 x}{\cos x}$ appears to be equivalent to $\csc x$ or $\sec x$.

b) What are the non-permissible values, in radians, for the identity from part a)?

c) Express $\dfrac{\csc^2 x - \cot^2 x}{\cos x}$ as the single reciprocal trigonometric ratio that you identified in part a).

12. a) Substitute $x = \dfrac{\pi}{4}$ into the equation $\dfrac{\cot x}{\sec x} + \sin x = \csc x$ to determine whether it could be an identity. Use exact values.

b) Algebraically confirm that the expression on the left side simplifies to $\csc x$.

13. Stan, Lina, and Giselle are working together to try to determine whether the equation $\sin x + \cos x = \tan x + 1$ is an identity.

a) Stan substitutes $x = 0$ into each side of the equation. What is the result?

b) Lina substitutes $x = \dfrac{\pi}{2}$ into each side of the equation. What does she observe?

c) Stan points out that Lina's choice is not permissible for this equation. Explain why.

d) Giselle substitutes $x = \dfrac{\pi}{4}$ into each side of the equation. What does she find?

e) Do the three students have enough information to conclude whether or not the given equation is an identity? Explain.

14. Simplify $(\sin x + \cos x)^2 + (\sin x - \cos x)^2$.

Extend

15. Given $\csc^2 x + \sin^2 x = 7.89$, find the value of $\dfrac{1}{\csc^2 x} + \dfrac{1}{\sin^2 x}$.

16. Show algebraically that $\dfrac{1}{1 + \sin \theta} + \dfrac{1}{1 - \sin \theta} = 2 \sec^2 \theta$ is an identity.

17. Determine an expression for m that makes $\dfrac{2 - \cos^2 x}{\sin x} = m + \sin x$ an identity.

Create Connections

C1 Explain how a student who does not know the $\cot^2 x + 1 = \csc^2 x$ form of the Pythagorean identity could simplify an expression that contained the expression $\cot^2 x + 1$ using the fact that $1 = \dfrac{\sin^2 x}{\sin^2 x}$.

C2 For some trigonometric expressions, multiplying by a conjugate helps to simplify the expression. Simplify $\dfrac{\sin \theta}{1 + \cos \theta}$ by multiplying the numerator and the denominator by the conjugate of the denominator, $1 - \cos \theta$. Describe how this process helps to simplify the expression.

C3 MINI LAB Explore the effect of different domains on apparent identities.

Materials
- graphing calculator

Step 1 Graph the two functions $y = \tan x$ and $y = \left|\dfrac{\sin x}{\cos x}\right|$ on the same grid, using a domain of $0 \leq x < \dfrac{\pi}{2}$. Is there graphical evidence that $\tan x = \left|\dfrac{\sin x}{\cos x}\right|$ is an identity? Explain.

Step 2 Graph the two functions $y = \tan x$ and $y = \left|\dfrac{\sin x}{\cos x}\right|$ again, using the expanded domain $-2\pi < x \leq 2\pi$. Is the equation $\tan x = \left|\dfrac{\sin x}{\cos x}\right|$ an identity? Explain.

Step 3 Find and record a different trigonometric equation that is true over a restricted domain but is not an identity when all permissible values are checked. Compare your answer with that of a classmate.

Step 4 How does this activity show the weakness of using graphical and numerical methods for verifying potential identities?

6.2

Sum, Difference, and Double-Angle Identities

Focus on...

- applying sum, difference, and double-angle identities to verify the equivalence of trigonometric expressions
- verifying a trigonometric identity numerically and graphically using technology

Paris gold box

In addition to holograms and security threads, paper money often includes special Guilloché patterns in the design to prevent counterfeiting. The sum and product of nested sinusoidal functions are used to form the blueprint of some of these patterns. Guilloché patterns have been created since the sixteenth century, but their origin is uncertain. They can be found carved in wooden door frames and etched on the metallic surfaces of objects such as vases.

Web

To learn more about Guilloché patterns, go to www.mcgrawhill.ca/school/learningcentres and follow the links.

Investigate Expressions for sin ($\alpha + \beta$) and cos ($\alpha + \beta$)

1. **a)** Draw a large rectangle and label its vertices A, B, C, and D, where BC < 2AB. Mark a point E on BC. Join AE and use a protractor to draw EF perpendicular to AE. Label all right angles on your diagram. Label ∠BAE as α and ∠EAF as β.

   b) Measure the angles α and β. Use the angle sum of a triangle to determine the measures of all the remaining acute angles in your diagram. Record their measures on the diagram.

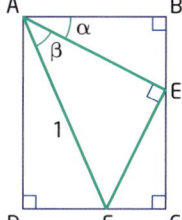

Materials
- ruler
- protractor

2. **a)** Explain how you know that ∠CEF = α.

   b) Determine an expression for each of the other acute angles in the diagram in terms of α and β. Label each angle on your diagram.

3. Suppose the hypotenuse AF of the inscribed right triangle has a length of 1 unit. Explain why the length of AE can be represented as cos β. Label AE as cos β.

4. Determine expressions for line segments AB, BE, EF, CE, CF, AD, and DF in terms of sin α, cos α, sin β, and cos β. Label each side length on your diagram using these sines and cosines. Note that AD equals the sum of segments BE and EC, and DF equals AB minus CF.

5. Which angle in the diagram is equivalent to α + β? Determine possible identities for sin (α + β) and cos (α + β) from △ADF using the sum or difference of lengths. Compare your results with those of a classmate.

Reflect and Respond

6. a) Verify your possible identities numerically using the measures of α and β from step 1. Compare your results with those of a classmate.

   b) Does each identity apply to angles that are obtuse? Are there any restrictions on the domain? Describe your findings.

7. Consider the special case where α = β. Write simplified equivalent expressions for sin 2α and cos 2α.

Link the Ideas

In the investigation, you discovered the angle sum identities for sine and cosine. These identities can be used to determine the angle sum identity for tangent.

> The sum identities are
> $$\sin (A + B) = \sin A \cos B + \cos A \sin B$$
> $$\cos (A + B) = \cos A \cos B - \sin A \sin B$$
> $$\tan (A + B) = \frac{\tan A + \tan B}{1 - \tan A \tan B}$$

The angle sum identities for sine, cosine, and tangent can be used to determine angle difference identities for sine, cosine, and tangent.

For sine,
$$\sin (A - B) = \sin (A + (-B))$$
$$= \sin A \cos (-B) + \cos A \sin (-B)$$
$$= \sin A \cos B + \cos A (-\sin B) \quad \text{Why is } \cos (-B) = \cos B?$$
$$= \sin A \cos B - \cos A \sin B \quad \text{Why is } \sin (-B) = -\sin B?$$

Web Link

To see a derivation of the difference cos (A − B), go to www.mcgrawhill.ca/school/learningcentres and follow the links.

> The three angle difference identities are
> $$\sin (A - B) = \sin A \cos B - \cos A \sin B$$
> $$\cos (A - B) = \cos A \cos B + \sin A \sin B$$
> $$\tan (A - B) = \frac{\tan A - \tan B}{1 + \tan A \tan B}$$

A special case occurs in the angle sum identities when A = B. Substituting B = A results in the double-angle identities.

For example, sin 2A = sin (A + A)
$$= \sin A \cos A + \cos A \sin A$$
$$= 2 \sin A \cos A$$

Similarly, it can be shown that
$$\cos 2A = \cos^2 A - \sin^2 A$$
$$\tan 2A = \frac{2 \tan A}{1 - \tan^2 A}$$

> The double-angle identities are
> $$\sin 2A = 2 \sin A \cos A$$
> $$\cos 2A = \cos^2 A - \sin^2 A$$
> $$\tan 2A = \frac{2 \tan A}{1 - \tan^2 A}$$

Example 1

Simplify Expressions Using Sum, Difference, and Double-Angle Identities

Write each expression as a single trigonometric function.

a) sin 48° cos 17° − cos 48° sin 17°

b) $\cos^2 \frac{\pi}{3} - \sin^2 \frac{\pi}{3}$

Solution

a) The expression sin 48° cos 17° − cos 48° sin 17° has the same form as the right side of the difference identity for sine, sin (A − B) = sin A cos B − cos A sin B.

Thus,
sin 48° cos 17° − cos 48° sin 17° = sin (48° − 17°)
$$= \sin 31°$$

b) The expression $\cos^2 \frac{\pi}{3} - \sin^2 \frac{\pi}{3}$ has the same form as the right side of the double-angle identity for cosine, cos 2A = cos² A − sin² A.

Therefore,
$$\cos^2 \frac{\pi}{3} - \sin^2 \frac{\pi}{3} = \cos\left(2\left(\frac{\pi}{3}\right)\right)$$
$$= \cos \frac{2\pi}{3}$$

How could you use technology to verify these solutions?

Your Turn

Write each expression as a single trigonometric function.

a) cos 88° cos 35° + sin 88° sin 35°

b) $2 \sin \frac{\pi}{12} \cos \frac{\pi}{12}$

Example 2

Determine Alternative Forms of the Double-Angle Identity for Cosine

Determine an identity for cos 2A that contains only the cosine ratio.

Solution

An identity for cos 2A is $\cos 2A = \cos^2 A - \sin^2 A$.

Write an equivalent expression for the term containing sin A.

Use the Pythagorean identity, $\cos^2 A + \sin^2 A = 1$.

Substitute $\sin^2 A = 1 - \cos^2 A$ to obtain another form of the double-angle identity for cosine.

$$\begin{aligned}\cos 2A &= \cos^2 A - \sin^2 A \\ &= \cos^2 A - (1 - \cos^2 A) \\ &= \cos^2 A - 1 + \cos^2 A \\ &= 2\cos^2 A - 1\end{aligned}$$

Your Turn

Determine an identity for cos 2A that contains only the sine ratio.

Example 3

Simplify Expressions Using Identities

Consider the expression $\dfrac{1 - \cos 2x}{\sin 2x}$.

a) What are the permissible values for the expression?
b) Simplify the expression to one of the three primary trigonometric functions.
c) Verify your answer from part b), in the interval $[0, 2\pi)$, using technology.

Solution

a) Identify any non-permissible values. The expression is undefined when $\sin 2x = 0$.

   Method 1: Simplify the Double Angle
   Use the double-angle identity for sine to simplify sin 2x first.

   $\sin 2x = 2 \sin x \cos x$
   $2 \sin x \cos x \neq 0$
   So, $\sin x \neq 0$ and $\cos x \neq 0$.
   $\sin x = 0$ when $x = \pi n$, where $n \in I$.
   $\cos x = 0$ when $x = \dfrac{\pi}{2} + \pi n$, where $n \in I$.
   When these two sets of non-permissible values are combined, the permissible values for the expression are all real numbers except $x \neq \dfrac{\pi n}{2}$, where $n \in I$.

Method 2: Horizontal Transformation of sin x

First determine when sin $x = 0$. Then, stretch the domain horizontally by a factor of $\frac{1}{2}$.

sin $x = 0$ when $x = \pi n$, where $n \in I$.

Therefore, sin $2x = 0$ when $x = \frac{\pi n}{2}$, where $n \in I$.

The permissible values of the expression $\frac{1 - \cos 2x}{\sin 2x}$ are all real numbers except $x \neq \frac{\pi n}{2}$, where $n \in I$.

b) $\frac{1 - \cos 2x}{\sin 2x} = \frac{1 - (1 - 2\sin^2 x)}{2 \sin x \cos x}$ Replace sin 2x in the denominator. Replace cos 2x with the form of the identity from Example 2 that will simplify most fully.

$= \frac{2 \sin^2 x}{2 \sin x \cos x}$

$= \frac{\sin x}{\cos x}$

$= \tan x$

The expression $\frac{1 - \cos 2x}{\sin 2x}$ is equivalent to tan x.

c) Use technology, with domain $0 \leq x < 2\pi$, to graph $y = \frac{1 - \cos 2x}{\sin 2x}$ and $y = \tan x$. The graphs look identical, which verifies, but does not prove, the answer in part b).

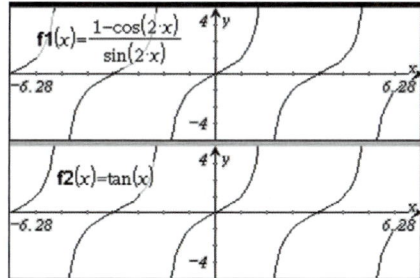

Your Turn

Consider the expression $\frac{\sin 2x}{\cos 2x + 1}$.

a) What are the permissible values for the expression?
b) Simplify the expression to one of the three primary trigonometric functions.
c) Verify your answer from part b), in the interval [0, 2π), using technology.

6.2 Sum, Difference, and Double-Angle Identities • MHR **303**

Example 4

Determine Exact Trigonometric Values for Angles

Determine the exact value for each expression.

a) $\sin \frac{\pi}{12}$

b) $\tan 105°$

Solution

a) Use the difference identity for sine with two special angles.
For example, because $\frac{\pi}{12} = \frac{3\pi}{12} - \frac{2\pi}{12}$, use $\frac{\pi}{4} - \frac{\pi}{6}$.

$$\sin \frac{\pi}{12} = \sin\left(\frac{\pi}{4} - \frac{\pi}{6}\right)$$
The special angles $\frac{\pi}{3}$ and $\frac{\pi}{4}$ could also be used.

$$= \sin \frac{\pi}{4} \cos \frac{\pi}{6} - \cos \frac{\pi}{4} \sin \frac{\pi}{6}$$
Use $\sin(A - B) = \sin A \cos B - \cos A \sin B$.

$$= \left(\frac{\sqrt{2}}{2}\right)\left(\frac{\sqrt{3}}{2}\right) - \left(\frac{\sqrt{2}}{2}\right)\left(\frac{1}{2}\right)$$

$$= \frac{\sqrt{6}}{4} - \frac{\sqrt{2}}{4}$$

$$= \frac{\sqrt{6} - \sqrt{2}}{4}$$
How could you verify this answer with a calculator?

b) Method 1: Use the Difference Identity for Tangent

Rewrite $\tan 105°$ as a difference of special angles.

$\tan 105° = \tan(135° - 30°)$ Are there other ways of writing 105° as the sum or difference of two special angles?

Use the tangent difference identity, $\tan(A - B) = \dfrac{\tan A - \tan B}{1 + \tan A \tan B}$.

$$\tan(135° - 30°) = \frac{\tan 135° - \tan 30°}{1 + \tan 135° \tan 30°}$$

$$= \frac{-1 - \frac{1}{\sqrt{3}}}{1 + (-1)\left(\frac{1}{\sqrt{3}}\right)}$$

$$= \frac{-1 - \frac{1}{\sqrt{3}}}{1 - \frac{1}{\sqrt{3}}} \quad \text{Simplify.}$$

$$= \left(\frac{-1 - \frac{1}{\sqrt{3}}}{1 - \frac{1}{\sqrt{3}}}\right)\left(\frac{-\sqrt{3}}{-\sqrt{3}}\right) \quad \text{Multiply numerator and denominator by } -\sqrt{3}.$$

$$= \frac{\sqrt{3} + 1}{1 - \sqrt{3}} \quad \text{How could you rationalize the denominator?}$$

Method 2: Use a Quotient Identity with Sine and Cosine

$$\tan 105° = \frac{\sin 105°}{\cos 105°}$$

$$= \frac{\sin(60° + 45°)}{\cos(60° + 45°)}$$

$$= \frac{\sin 60° \cos 45° + \cos 60° \sin 45°}{\cos 60° \cos 45° - \sin 60° \sin 45°}$$

$$= \frac{\left(\frac{\sqrt{3}}{2}\right)\left(\frac{\sqrt{2}}{2}\right) + \left(\frac{1}{2}\right)\left(\frac{\sqrt{2}}{2}\right)}{\left(\frac{1}{2}\right)\left(\frac{\sqrt{2}}{2}\right) - \left(\frac{\sqrt{3}}{2}\right)\left(\frac{\sqrt{2}}{2}\right)}$$

$$= \frac{\frac{\sqrt{6}}{4} + \frac{\sqrt{2}}{4}}{\frac{\sqrt{2}}{4} - \frac{\sqrt{6}}{4}}$$

$$= \left(\frac{\sqrt{6} + \sqrt{2}}{4}\right)\left(\frac{4}{\sqrt{2} - \sqrt{6}}\right)$$

$$= \frac{\sqrt{6} + \sqrt{2}}{\sqrt{2} - \sqrt{6}}$$

Use sum identities with special angles. Could you use a difference of angles identity here?

How could you verify that this is the same answer as in Method 1?

Your Turn

Use a sum or difference identity to find the exact values of

a) $\cos 165°$ **b)** $\tan \frac{11\pi}{12}$

Key Ideas

- You can use the sum and difference identities to simplify expressions and to determine exact trigonometric values for some angles.

  Sum Identities

  $\sin(A + B) = \sin A \cos B + \cos A \sin B$

  $\cos(A + B) = \cos A \cos B - \sin A \sin B$

  $\tan(A + B) = \dfrac{\tan A + \tan B}{1 - \tan A \tan B}$

  Difference Identities

  $\sin(A - B) = \sin A \cos B - \cos A \sin B$

  $\cos(A - B) = \cos A \cos B + \sin A \sin B$

  $\tan(A - B) = \dfrac{\tan A - \tan B}{1 + \tan A \tan B}$

- The double-angle identities are special cases of the sum identities when the two angles are equal. The double-angle identity for cosine can be expressed in three forms using the Pythagorean identity, $\cos^2 A + \sin^2 A = 1$.

  Double-Angle Identities

  $\sin 2A = 2 \sin A \cos A$ $\qquad$ $\cos 2A = \cos^2 A - \sin^2 A$ $\qquad$ $\tan 2A = \dfrac{2 \tan A}{1 - \tan^2 A}$

  $\cos 2A = 2\cos^2 A - 1$

  $\cos 2A = 1 - 2\sin^2 A$

Check Your Understanding

Practise

1. Write each expression as a single trigonometric function.
   a) $\cos 43° \cos 27° - \sin 43° \sin 27°$
   b) $\sin 15° \cos 20° + \cos 15° \sin 20°$
   c) $\cos^2 19° - \sin^2 19°$
   d) $\sin \frac{3\pi}{2} \cos \frac{5\pi}{4} - \cos \frac{3\pi}{2} \sin \frac{5\pi}{4}$
   e) $8 \sin \frac{\pi}{3} \cos \frac{\pi}{3}$

2. Simplify and then give an exact value for each expression.
   a) $\cos 40° \cos 20° - \sin 40° \sin 20°$
   b) $\sin 20° \cos 25° + \cos 20° \sin 25°$
   c) $\cos^2 \frac{\pi}{6} - \sin^2 \frac{\pi}{6}$
   d) $\cos \frac{\pi}{2} \cos \frac{\pi}{3} - \sin \frac{\pi}{2} \sin \frac{\pi}{3}$

3. Using only one substitution, which form of the double-angle identity for cosine will simplify the expression $1 - \cos 2x$ to one term? Show how this happens.

4. Write each expression as a single trigonometric function.
   a) $2 \sin \frac{\pi}{4} \cos \frac{\pi}{4}$
   b) $(6 \cos^2 24° - 6 \sin^2 24°) \tan 48°$
   c) $\frac{2 \tan 76°}{1 - \tan^2 76°}$
   d) $2 \cos^2 \frac{\pi}{6} - 1$
   e) $1 - 2 \cos^2 \frac{\pi}{12}$

5. Simplify each expression to a single primary trigonometric function.
   a) $\frac{\sin 2\theta}{2 \cos \theta}$
   b) $\cos 2x \cos x + \sin 2x \sin x$
   c) $\frac{\cos 2\theta + 1}{2 \cos \theta}$
   d) $\frac{\cos^3 x}{\cos 2x + \sin^2 x}$

6. Show using a counterexample that the following is not an identity: $\sin (x - y) = \sin x - \sin y$.

7. Simplify $\cos (90° - x)$ using a difference identity.

8. Determine the exact value of each trigonometric expression.
   a) $\cos 75°$
   b) $\tan 165°$
   c) $\sin \frac{7\pi}{12}$
   d) $\cos 195°$
   e) $\csc \frac{\pi}{12}$
   f) $\sin \left(-\frac{\pi}{12}\right)$

Apply

Yukon River at Whitehorse

9. On the winter solstice, December 21 or 22, the power, P, in watts, received from the sun on each square metre of Earth can be determined using the equation $P = 1000 (\sin x \cos 113.5° + \cos x \sin 113.5°)$, where x is the latitude of the location in the northern hemisphere.
   a) Use an identity to write the equation in a more useful form.
   b) Determine the amount of power received at each location.
      i) Whitehorse, Yukon, at 60.7° N
      ii) Victoria, British Columbia, at 48.4° N
      iii) Igloolik, Nunavut, at 69.4° N
   c) Explain the answer for part iii) above. At what latitude is the power received from the sun zero?

10. Simplify $\cos(\pi + x) + \cos(\pi - x)$.

11. Angle θ is in quadrant II and $\sin\theta = \frac{5}{13}$. Determine an exact value for each of the following.
    a) $\cos 2\theta$
    b) $\sin 2\theta$
    c) $\sin\left(\theta + \frac{\pi}{2}\right)$

12. The double-angle identity for tangent in terms of the tangent function is $\tan 2x = \frac{2\tan x}{1 - \tan^2 x}$.
    a) Verify numerically that this equation is true for $x = \frac{\pi}{6}$.
    b) The expression $\tan 2x$ can also be written using the quotient identity for tangent: $\tan 2x = \frac{\sin 2x}{\cos 2x}$. Verify this equation numerically when $x = \frac{\pi}{6}$.
    c) The expression $\frac{\sin 2x}{\cos 2x}$ from part b) can be expressed as $\frac{2\sin x \cos x}{\cos^2 x - \sin^2 x}$ using double-angle identities. Show how the expression for $\tan 2x$ used in part a) can also be rewritten in the form $\frac{2\sin x \cos x}{\cos^2 x - \sin^2 x}$.

13. The horizontal distance, d, in metres, travelled by a ball that is kicked at an angle, θ, with the ground is modelled by the formula $d = \frac{2(v_0)^2 \sin\theta \cos\theta}{g}$, where v_0 is the initial velocity of the ball, in metres per second, and g is the force of gravity (9.8 m/s²).
    a) Rewrite the formula using a double-angle identity.
    b) Determine the angle $\theta \in (0°, 90°)$ that would result in a maximum distance for an initial velocity v_0.
    c) Explain why it might be easier to answer part b) with the double-angle version of the formula that you determined in part a).

14. If $(\sin x + \cos x)^2 = k$, then what is the value of $\sin 2x$ in terms of k?

15. Show that each expression can be simplified to $\cos 2x$.
    a) $\cos^4 x - \sin^4 x$
    b) $\frac{\csc^2 x - 2}{\csc^2 x}$

16. Simplify each expression to the equivalent expression shown.
    a) $\frac{1 - \cos 2x}{2}$ $\sin^2 x$
    b) $\frac{4 - 8\sin^2 x}{2\sin x \cos x}$ $\frac{4}{\tan 2x}$

17. If the point (2, 5) lies on the terminal arm of angle x in standard position, what is the value of $\cos(\pi + x)$?

18. What value of k makes the equation $\sin 5x \cos x + \cos 5x \sin x = 2\sin kx \cos kx$ true?

19. a) If $\cos\theta = \frac{3}{5}$ and $0 < \theta < 2\pi$, determine the value(s) of $\sin\left(\theta + \frac{\pi}{6}\right)$.
    b) If $\sin\theta = -\frac{2}{3}$ and $\frac{3\pi}{2} < \theta < 2\pi$, determine the value(s) of $\cos\left(\theta + \frac{\pi}{3}\right)$.

20. If $\angle A$ and $\angle B$ are both in quadrant I, and $\sin A = \frac{4}{5}$ and $\cos B = \frac{12}{13}$, evaluate each of the following.
    a) $\cos(A - B)$
    b) $\sin(A + B)$
    c) $\cos 2A$
    d) $\sin 2A$

Extend

21. Determine the missing primary trigonometric ratio that is required for the expression $\frac{\blacksquare \sin 2x}{2 - 2\cos^2 x}$ to simplify to
    a) $\cos x$
    b) 1

22. Use a double-angle identity for cosine to determine the half-angle formula for cosine, $\cos\frac{x}{2} = \pm\sqrt{\frac{1 + \cos x}{2}}$.

23. a) Graph the curve $y = 4 \sin x - 3 \cos x$. Notice that it resembles a sine function.

b) What are the approximate values of a and c for the curve in the form $y = a \sin (x - c)$, where $0 < c < 90°$?

c) Use the difference identity for sine to rewrite the curve for $y = 4 \sin x - 3 \cos x$ in the form $y = a \sin (x - c)$.

24. Write the following equation in the form $y = A \sin Bx + D$, where A, B, and D are constants:
$y = 6 \sin x \cos^3 x + 6 \sin^3 x \cos x - 3$

Create Connections

C1 a) Determine the value of $\sin 2x$ if $\cos x = -\dfrac{5}{13}$ and $\pi < x < \dfrac{3\pi}{2}$ using

  i) transformations

  ii) a double-angle identity

b) Which method do you prefer? Explain.

C2 a) Graph the function $f(x) = 6 \sin x \cos x$ over the interval $0° \le x \le 360°$.

b) The function can be written as a sine function in the form $f(x) = a \sin bx$. Compare how to determine this sine function from the graph versus using the double-angle identity for sine.

C3 a) Over the domain $0° \le x \le 360°$, sketch the graphs of $y_1 = \sin^2 x$ and $y_2 = \cos^2 x$. How do these graphs compare?

b) Predict what the graph of $y_1 + y_2$ looks like. Explain your prediction. Graph to test your prediction.

c) Graph the difference of the two functions: $y_1 - y_2$. Describe how the two functions interact with each other in the new function.

d) The new function from part c) is sinusoidal. Determine the function in the form $f(x) = a \cos bx$. Explain how you determined the expression.

Project Corner — Mach Numbers

- In aeronautics, the Mach number, M, of an aircraft is the ratio of its speed as it moves through air to the speed of sound in air. An aircraft breaks the sound barrier when its speed is greater than the speed of sound in dry air at 20 °C.

- When an aircraft exceeds Mach 1, $M > 1$, a shock wave forms a cone that spreads backward and outward from the aircraft. The angle at the vertex of a cross-section of the cone is related to the Mach number by $\dfrac{1}{M} = \sin \dfrac{\theta}{2}$.

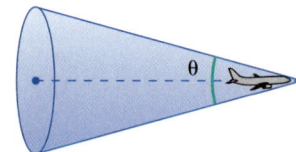

- How could you use the half-angle identity, $\sin \dfrac{\theta}{2} = \pm\sqrt{\dfrac{1 - \cos \theta}{2}}$, to express the Mach number, M, as a function of θ?

- If plane A is travelling twice as fast as plane B, how are the angles of the cones formed by the planes related?

6.3

Proving Identities

Focus on...

- proving trigonometric identities algebraically
- understanding the difference between verifying and proving an identity
- showing that verifying that the two sides of a potential identity are equal for a given value is insufficient to prove the identity

Many formulas in science contain trigonometric functions. In physics, torque (τ), work (W), and magnetic forces (F_B) can be calculated using the following formulas:

$$\tau = rF \sin \theta \qquad W = F\delta r \cos \theta \qquad F_B = qvB \sin \theta$$

In dynamics, which is the branch of mechanics that deals with motion, trigonometric functions may be required to calculate horizontal and vertical components. Skills with identities reduce the time it takes to work with formulas involving trigonometric functions.

Investigate the Equivalence of Two Trigonometric Expressions

Two physics students are investigating the horizontal distance, d, travelled by a model rocket. The rocket is launched with an angle of elevation θ. Katie has found a formula to model this situation: $d = \dfrac{(v_0)^2 \sin 2\theta}{g}$, where g represents the force of gravity and v_0 represents the initial velocity. Sergey has found a different formula: $d = \dfrac{2(v_0)^2}{g} (\tan \theta - \tan \theta \sin^2 \theta)$.

Materials
- graphing calculator

1. Are the two expressions, $\dfrac{(v_0)^2 \sin 2\theta}{g}$ and $\dfrac{2(v_0)^2}{g} (\tan \theta - \tan \theta \sin^2 \theta)$, equivalent? Use graphical and numerical methods to explain your answer. The initial velocity, v_0, of the rocket is 14 m/s and g is 9.8 m/s², so first substitute these values and simplify each expression.

2. Which parts are common to both formulas?

3. Write an identity with the parts of the formulas that are not common. Use your knowledge of identities to rewrite each side and show that they are equivalent.

4. Compare your reasoning with that of a classmate.

Reflect and Respond

5. How does this algebraic method for verifying an identity compare to verifying an identity graphically or numerically? Why do numerical and graphical verification fail to prove that an identity is true?

Link the Ideas

To prove that an identity is true for all permissible values, it is necessary to express both sides of the identity in equivalent forms. One or both sides of the identity must be algebraically manipulated into an equivalent form to match the other side.

You cannot perform operations across the equal sign when proving a potential identity. Simplify the expressions on each side of the identity independently.

Example 1

Verify Versus Prove That an Equation Is an Identity

a) Verify that $1 - \sin^2 x = \sin x \cos x \cot x$ for some values of x. Determine the non-permissible values for x. Work in degrees.

b) Prove that $1 - \sin^2 x = \sin x \cos x \cot x$ for all permissible values of x.

Solution

a) First, determine the non-permissible values.

The only function in the equation that has non-permissible values in its domain is $\cot x$.

Recall that $\cot x$ is undefined when $\sin x = 0$.

Therefore, $x \neq 180°n$, where $n \in I$.

Verify the identity graphically and numerically.

Method 1: Verify Graphically

Use technology to graph $y = 1 - \sin^2 x$ and $y = \sin x \cos x \cot x$ over the domain $-360° \leq x \leq 360°$. The graphs appear to be the same. So, graphically, it seems that $1 - \sin^2 x = \sin x \cos x \cot x$ is an identity.

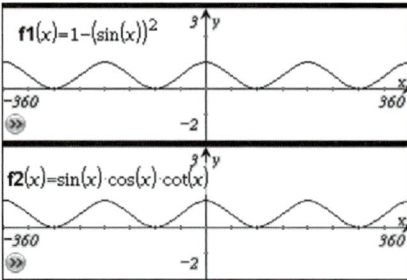

Why are the non-permissible values not apparent from these graphs?

Method 2: Verify Numerically

Use $x = 30°$.

Why is 30° a good choice?

Left Side $= 1 - \sin^2 x$
$= 1 - \sin^2 30°$
$= 1 - \left(\dfrac{1}{2}\right)^2$
$= 1 - \dfrac{1}{4}$
$= \dfrac{3}{4}$

Right Side $= \sin x \cos x \cot x$
$= \sin 30° \cos 30° \cot 30°$
$= \left(\dfrac{1}{2}\right)\left(\dfrac{\sqrt{3}}{2}\right)\left(\dfrac{\sqrt{3}}{1}\right)$
$= \dfrac{3}{4}$

Left Side = Right Side

The equation $1 - \sin^2 x = \sin x \cos x \cot x$ is verified for $x = 30°$.

b) To prove the identity algebraically, examine both sides of the equation and simplify each side to a common expression.

Left Side $= 1 - \sin^2 x$
$= \cos^2 x$ *Why is this true?*

Right Side $= \sin x \cos x \cot x$
$= \sin x \cos x \left(\dfrac{\cos x}{\sin x}\right)$
$= \cos^2 x$

Left Side = Right Side

Therefore, $1 - \sin^2 x = \sin x \cos x \cot x$ is an identity for $x \neq 180°n$, where $n \in I$.

Your Turn

a) Determine the non-permissible values for the equation $\dfrac{\tan x \cos x}{\csc x} = 1 - \cos^2 x$.

b) Verify that the equation may be an identity, either graphically using technology or by choosing one value for x.

c) Prove that the identity is true for all permissible values of x.

Example 2

Prove an Identity Using Double-Angle Identities

Prove that $\tan x = \dfrac{1 - \cos 2x}{\sin 2x}$ is an identity for all permissible values of x.

Solution

Left Side $= \tan x$

Right Side $= \dfrac{1 - \cos 2x}{\sin 2x}$
$= \dfrac{1 - (1 - 2\sin^2 x)}{2 \sin x \cos x}$ *Recall the double-angle identities.*
$= \dfrac{2 \sin^2 x}{2 \sin x \cos x}$
$= \dfrac{\sin x}{\cos x}$ *Remove common factors.*
$= \tan x$

Left Side = Right Side

Therefore, $\tan x = \dfrac{1 - \cos 2x}{\sin 2x}$ is an identity for all permissible values of x.

Your Turn

Prove that $\dfrac{\sin 2x}{\cos 2x + 1} = \tan x$ is an identity for all permissible values of x.

In the previous example, you did not need to simplify the left side of the identity. However, tan x could have been expressed as $\frac{\sin x}{\cos x}$ using the quotient identity for tangent. In this case, the right side of the proof would have ended one step earlier, at $\frac{\sin x}{\cos x}$. Sometimes it is advisable to convert all trigonometric functions to expressions of sine or cosine.

Example 3

Prove More Complicated Identities

Prove that $\dfrac{1 - \cos x}{\sin x} = \dfrac{\sin x}{1 + \cos x}$ is an identity for all permissible values of x.

Solution

Left Side $= \dfrac{1 - \cos x}{\sin x}$

Right Side $= \dfrac{\sin x}{1 + \cos x}$

$= \dfrac{\sin x}{1 + \cos x} \times \dfrac{1 - \cos x}{1 - \cos x}$

$= \dfrac{\sin x (1 - \cos x)}{1 - \cos^2 x}$

$= \dfrac{\sin x (1 - \cos x)}{\sin^2 x}$

$= \dfrac{1 - \cos x}{\sin x}$

Left Side = Right Side

How does multiplying by 1 − cos x, which is the conjugate of 1 + cos x, let you express the denominator in terms of sin x?

Therefore, $\dfrac{1 - \cos x}{\sin x} = \dfrac{\sin x}{1 + \cos x}$ is an identity for all permissible values of x.

Your Turn

Prove that $\dfrac{1}{1 + \sin x} = \dfrac{\sec x - \sin x \sec x}{\cos x}$ is an identity for all permissible values of x.

Example 4

Prove an Identity That Requires Factoring

Prove the identity $\cot x - \csc x = \dfrac{\cos 2x - \cos x}{\sin 2x + \sin x}$ for all permissible values of x.

Solution

Left Side $= \cot x - \csc x$
$= \dfrac{\cos x}{\sin x} - \dfrac{1}{\sin x}$
$= \dfrac{\cos x - 1}{\sin x}$

Right Side $= \dfrac{\cos 2x - \cos x}{\sin 2x + \sin x}$
$= \dfrac{(2\cos^2 x - 1) - \cos x}{2 \sin x \cos x + \sin x}$
$= \dfrac{2\cos^2 x - \cos x - 1}{\sin x (2\cos x + 1)}$
$= \dfrac{(2\cos x + 1)(\cos x - 1)}{\sin x (2\cos x + 1)}$
$= \dfrac{\cos x - 1}{\sin x}$

Why is $2\cos^2 x - 1$ substituted for $\cos 2x$?

Left Side $=$ Right Side

Therefore, $\cot x - \csc x = \dfrac{\cos 2x - \cos x}{\sin 2x + \sin x}$ is an identity for all permissible values of x.

Your Turn

Prove the identity $\dfrac{\sin 2x - \cos x}{4\sin^2 x - 1} = \dfrac{\sin^2 x \cos x + \cos^3 x}{2\sin x + 1}$ for all permissible values of x.

Key Ideas

- Verifying an identity using a specific value validates that it is true for that value only. Proving an identity is done algebraically and validates the identity for all permissible values of the variable.
- To prove a trigonometric identity algebraically, separately simplify both sides of the identity into identical expressions.
- It is usually easier to make a complicated expression simpler than it is to make a simple expression more complicated.
- Some strategies that may help you prove identities include:
  - Use known identities to make substitutions.
  - If quadratics are present, the Pythagorean identity or one of its alternate forms can often be used.
  - Rewrite the expression using sine and cosine only.
  - Multiply the numerator and the denominator by the conjugate of an expression.
  - Factor to simplify expressions.

Check Your Understanding

Practise

1. Factor and simplify each rational trigonometric expression.

   a) $\dfrac{\sin x - \sin x \cos^2 x}{\sin^2 x}$

   b) $\dfrac{\cos^2 x - \cos x - 2}{6 \cos x - 12}$

   c) $\dfrac{\sin x \cos x - \sin x}{\cos^2 x - 1}$

   d) $\dfrac{\tan^2 x - 3 \tan x - 4}{\sin x \tan x + \sin x}$

2. Use factoring to help to prove each identity for all permissible values of x.

   a) $\cos x + \cos x \tan^2 x = \sec x$

   b) $\dfrac{\sin^2 x - \cos^2 x}{\sin x + \cos x} = \sin x - \cos x$

   c) $\dfrac{\sin x \cos x - \sin x}{\cos^2 x - 1} = \dfrac{1 - \cos x}{\sin x}$

   d) $\dfrac{1 - \sin^2 x}{1 + 2 \sin x - 3 \sin^2 x} = \dfrac{1 + \sin x}{1 + 3 \sin x}$

3. Use a common denominator to express the rational expressions as a single term.

   a) $\dfrac{\sin x}{\cos x} + \sec x$

   b) $\dfrac{1}{\sin x - 1} + \dfrac{1}{\sin x + 1}$

   c) $\dfrac{\sin x}{1 + \cos x} + \dfrac{\cos x}{\sin x}$

   d) $\dfrac{\cos x}{\sec x - 1} + \dfrac{\cos x}{\sec x + 1}$

4. a) Rewrite the expression $\dfrac{\sec x - \cos x}{\tan x}$ in terms of sine and cosine functions only.

   b) Simplify the expression to one of the primary trigonometric functions.

5. Verify graphically that $\cos x = \dfrac{\sin 2x}{2 \sin x}$ could be an identity. Then, prove the identity. Determine any non-permissible values.

6. Expand and simplify the expression $(\sec x - \tan x)(\sin x + 1)$ to a primary trigonometric function.

7. Prove each identity.

   a) $\dfrac{\csc x}{2 \cos x} = \csc 2x$

   b) $\sin x + \cos x \cot x = \csc x$

Apply

8. As the first step of proving the identity $\dfrac{\cos 2x - 1}{\sin 2x} = -\tan x$, Hanna chose to substitute $\cos 2x = 1 - 2 \sin^2 x$, while Chloe chose $\cos 2x = 2 \cos^2 x - 1$. Which choice leads to a shorter proof? Explain. Prove the identity.

9. The distance, d, in metres, that a golf ball travels when struck by a golf club is given by the formula $d = \dfrac{(v_0)^2 \sin 2\theta}{g}$, where v_0 is the initial velocity of the ball, θ is the angle between the ground and the initial path of the ball, and g is the acceleration due to gravity (9.8 m/s²).

   a) What distance, in metres, does the ball travel if its initial velocity is 21 m/s and the angle θ is 55°?

   b) Prove the identity $\dfrac{(v_0)^2 \sin 2\theta}{g} = \dfrac{2(v_0)^2(1 - \cos^2 \theta)}{g \tan \theta}$.

10. Verify each potential identity by graphing, and then prove the identity.

    a) $\dfrac{\csc x}{2 \cos x} = \csc 2x$

    b) $\dfrac{\sin x \cos x}{1 + \cos x} = \dfrac{1 - \cos x}{\tan x}$

    c) $\dfrac{\sin x + \tan x}{1 + \cos x} = \dfrac{\sin 2x}{2 \cos^2 x}$

11. Prove each identity.

    a) $\dfrac{\sin 2x}{\cos x} + \dfrac{\cos 2x}{\sin x} = \csc x$

    b) $\csc^2 x + \sec^2 x = \csc^2 x \sec^2 x$

    c) $\dfrac{\cot x - 1}{1 - \tan x} = \dfrac{\csc x}{\sec x}$

12. Prove each identity.
   a) $\sin(90° + \theta) = \sin(90° - \theta)$
   b) $\sin(2\pi - \theta) = -\sin\theta$

13. Prove that
$2\cos x \cos y = \cos(x + y) + \cos(x - y)$.

14. Consider the equation
$\cos 2x = 2\sin x \cos x$.
   a) Graph each side of the equation. Could the equation be an identity?
   b) Either prove that the equation is an identity or find a counterexample to show that it is not an identity.

15. Consider the equation $\dfrac{\sin 2x}{1 - \cos 2x} = \cot x$.
   a) Determine the non-permissible values for x.
   b) Prove that the equation is an identity for all permissible values of x.

Extend

16. Use double-angle identities to prove the identity $\tan x = \dfrac{\sin 4x - \sin 2x}{\cos 4x + \cos 2x}$.

17. Verify graphically and then prove the identity $\dfrac{\sin 2x}{1 - \cos 2x} = 2\csc 2x - \tan x$.

18. Prove the identity
$\dfrac{1 - \sin^2 x - 2\cos x}{\cos^2 x - \cos x - 2} = \dfrac{1}{1 + \sec x}$.

19. When a ray of light hits a lens at angle of incidence θ_i, some of the light is refracted (bent) as it passes through the lens, and some is reflected by the lens. In the diagram, θ_r is the angle of reflection and θ_t is the angle of refraction. Fresnel equations describe the behaviour of light in this situation.

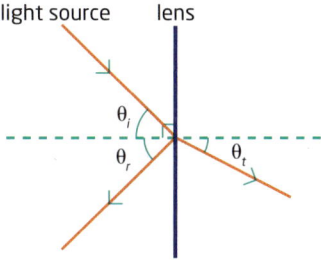

   a) Snells's law states that $n_1 \sin\theta_i = n_2 \sin\theta_t$, where n_1 and n_2 are the refractive indices of the mediums. Isolate $\sin\theta_t$ in this equation.

   b) Under certain conditions, a Fresnel equation to find the fraction, R, of light reflected is
$$R = \left(\dfrac{n_1 \cos\theta_i - n_2 \cos\theta_t}{n_1 \cos\theta_i + n_2 \cos\theta_t}\right)^2.$$
   Use identities to prove that this can be written as
$$R = \left(\dfrac{n_1 \cos\theta_i - n_2 \sqrt{1 - \sin^2\theta_t}}{n_1 \cos\theta_i + n_2 \sqrt{1 - \sin^2\theta_t}}\right)^2.$$

   c) Use your work from part a) to prove that
$$\left(\dfrac{n_1 \cos\theta_i - n_2 \sqrt{1 - \sin^2\theta_t}}{n_1 \cos\theta_i + n_2 \sqrt{1 - \sin^2\theta_t}}\right)^2 = \left(\dfrac{n_1 \cos\theta_i - n_2 \sqrt{1 - \left(\dfrac{n_1}{n_2}\right)^2 \sin^2\theta_i}}{n_1 \cos\theta_i + n_2 \sqrt{1 - \left(\dfrac{n_1}{n_2}\right)^2 \sin^2\theta_i}}\right)^2$$

Did You Know?

Fresnel equations were developed by French physicist Augustin-Jean Fresnel (1788–1827). A Fresnel lens is also named for him, and is a common lens in lights used for movies, TV, and live theatre. A new use for Fresnel lenses is to focus light in a solar array to allow for much more efficient collection of solar energy.

Create Connections

C1 Why is verifying, either numerically or graphically, that both sides of an equation seem to be equal not sufficient to prove that the equation is an identity?

C2 Use the difference identity for cosine to prove the identity $\cos\left(\dfrac{\pi}{2} - x\right) = \sin x$.

C3 Consider the equation $\cos x = \sqrt{1 - \sin^2 x}$.
   a) What are the non-permissible values for x in this equation?
   b) What is a value for x that makes this equation true?
   c) What is a value for x that does not work in this equation and provides evidence that this equation is not an identity?
   d) Explain the difference between an identity and an equation.

6.4 Solving Trigonometric Equations Using Identities

Focus on...

- solving trigonometric equations algebraically using known identities
- determining exact solutions for trigonometric equations where possible
- determining the general solution for trigonometric equations
- identifying and correcting errors in a solution for a trigonometric equation

Sound from a musical instrument is composed of sine waves. Technicians often fade the sound near the end of a song. To create this effect, the sound equipment is programmed to use mathematical damping techniques. The technicians have three choices: a linear fade, a logarithmic fade, or an inverse logarithmic fade. You will explore logarithmic functions in Chapter 8.

Knowledge of trigonometric identities can help to simplify the expressions involved in the trigonometric equations of sound waves in music.

Did You Know?

The musical instrument with the purest sound wave is the flute. The most complex musical sound wave can be created with a cymbal.

Investigate Solving Trigonometric Equations

Materials

- graphing technology

1. Graph the function $y = \sin 2x - \sin x$ over the domain $-720° < x \leq 720°$. Make a sketch of the graph and describe it in words.

2. From the graph, determine an expression for the zeros of the function $y = \sin 2x - \sin x$ over the domain of all real numbers.

3. Algebraically solve the equation $\sin 2x - \sin x = 0$ over the domain of all real numbers. Compare your answer and method with those of a classmate.

Reflect and Respond

4. Which method, graphic or algebraic, do you prefer to solve the equation $\sin 2x - \sin x = 0$? Explain.

Link the Ideas

To solve some trigonometric equations, you need to make substitutions using the trigonometric identities that you have studied in this chapter. This often involves ensuring that the equation is expressed in terms of one trigonometric function.

Example 1
Solve by Substituting Trigonometric Identities and Factoring

Solve each equation algebraically over the domain $0 \leq x < 2\pi$.
a) $\cos 2x + 1 - \cos x = 0$
b) $1 - \cos^2 x = 3 \sin x - 2$

Solution

a)
$$\cos 2x + 1 - \cos x = 0$$
$$(2 \cos^2 x - 1) + 1 - \cos x = 0 \quad \text{Why is this version of the identity for } \cos 2x \text{ chosen?}$$
$$2 \cos^2 x - \cos x = 0 \quad \text{Simplify.}$$
$$\cos x (2 \cos x - 1) = 0 \quad \text{Factor.}$$

$\cos x = 0$ or $2 \cos x - 1 = 0$ Use the zero product property.
$x = \dfrac{\pi}{2}$ or $x = \dfrac{3\pi}{2}$ or $\cos x = \dfrac{1}{2}$
$ x = \dfrac{\pi}{3}$ or $x = \dfrac{5\pi}{3}$

There are no non-permissible values for the original equation, so the solutions over the domain $0 \leq x < 2\pi$ are $x = \dfrac{\pi}{3}$, $x = \dfrac{\pi}{2}$, $x = \dfrac{3\pi}{2}$, and $x = \dfrac{5\pi}{3}$.

b)
$$1 - \cos^2 x = 3 \sin x - 2$$
$$\sin^2 x = 3 \sin x - 2 \quad \text{Use the Pythagorean identity.}$$
$$\sin^2 x - 3 \sin x + 2 = 0$$
$$(\sin x - 1)(\sin x - 2) = 0 \quad \text{Use the zero product property.}$$

$\sin x - 1 = 0$ or $\sin x - 2 = 0$
$\sin x = 1$ $\sin x = 2$
$x = \dfrac{\pi}{2}$ $\sin x = 2$ has no solution.

Why is there no solution for $\sin x = 2$?

There are no non-permissible values for the original equation, so the solution over the domain $0 \leq x < 2\pi$ is $x = \dfrac{\pi}{2}$.

Your Turn

Solve each equation algebraically over the domain $0 \leq x < 2\pi$.
a) $\sin 2x - \cos x = 0$
b) $2 \cos x + 1 - \sin^2 x = 3$

Example 2

Solve an Equation With a Quotient Identity Substitution

a) Solve the equation $\cos^2 x = \cot x \sin x$ algebraically in the domain $0° \leq x < 360°$.

b) Verify your answer graphically.

Solution

a)
$$\cos^2 x = \cot x \sin x$$ *What is the quotient identity for cot x?*
$$\cos^2 x = \left(\frac{\cos x}{\sin x}\right) \sin x$$
$$\cos^2 x = \cos x$$ *Why is it incorrect to divide by cos x here?*
$$\cos^2 x - \cos x = 0$$
$$\cos x (\cos x - 1) = 0$$ *Factor.*
$$\cos x = 0 \text{ or } \cos x = 1$$ *Apply the zero product property.*

For $\cos x = 0$, $x = 90°$ and $x = 270°$.
For $\cos x = 1$, $x = 0°$.

Check whether there are any non-permissible values for the initial equation.

For cot x, the domain has the restriction $\sin x \neq 0$, which gives the non-permissible values $x \neq 0°$ and $x \neq 180°$.

Therefore, the solution for $\cos^2 x = \cot x \sin x$ is limited to $x = 90°$ and $x = 270°$.

b) Graph $y = \cos^2 x$ and $y = \cot x \sin x$ over the domain $0° \leq x < 360°$. Determine the points of intersection of the two functions.

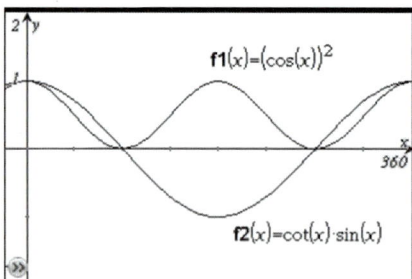

It appears from the graph that a solution is $x = 0$. Note that $y = \cot x \sin x$ is not defined at $x = 0$ because it is a non-permissible value for cot x.

What solutions are confirmed by the graph?

Your Turn

a) Solve the equation $\sin^2 x = \frac{1}{2} \tan x \cos x$ algebraically over the domain $0° \leq x < 360°$.

b) Verify your answer graphically.

Example 3

Determine the General Solution for a Trigonometric Equation

Solve the equation $\sin 2x = \sqrt{2} \cos x$ algebraically. Give the general solution expressed in radians.

Solution

$$\sin 2x = \sqrt{2} \cos x$$
$$2 \sin x \cos x = \sqrt{2} \cos x \quad \text{Use the double-angle identity for sin 2x.}$$
$$2 \sin x \cos x - \sqrt{2} \cos x = 0$$
$$\cos x (2 \sin x - \sqrt{2}) = 0 \quad \text{Why is it incorrect to divide by cos x here?}$$

Then, $\cos x = 0$ or $2 \sin x - \sqrt{2} = 0$
$$\sin x = \frac{\sqrt{2}}{2}$$

For $\cos x = 0$, $x = \frac{\pi}{2} + \pi n$, where $n \in I$.

For $\sin x = \frac{\sqrt{2}}{2}$, $x = \frac{\pi}{4} + 2\pi n$ and $x = \frac{3\pi}{4} + 2\pi n$, where $n \in I$.

Since there are no non-permissible values for the original equation, the solution is $x = \frac{\pi}{2} + \pi n$, $x = \frac{\pi}{4} + 2\pi n$, and $x = \frac{3\pi}{4} + 2\pi n$, where $n \in I$.

Your Turn

Algebraically solve $\cos 2x = \cos x$. Give general solutions expressed in radians.

Example 4

Determine the General Solution Using Reciprocal Identities

Algebraically solve $2 \sin x = 7 - 3 \csc x$. Give general solutions expressed in radians.

Solution

$$2 \sin x = 7 - 3 \csc x$$
$$2 \sin x = 7 - \frac{3}{\sin x} \quad \text{Use the reciprocal identity for cosecant.}$$
$$\sin x (2 \sin x) = \sin x \left(7 - \frac{3}{\sin x}\right) \quad \text{Why multiply both sides by sin x?}$$
$$2 \sin^2 x = 7 \sin x - 3$$
$$2 \sin^2 x - 7 \sin x + 3 = 0$$
$$(2 \sin x - 1)(\sin x - 3) = 0 \quad \text{Factor.}$$

For $2 \sin x - 1 = 0$, $\quad$ Use the zero product property.
$$\sin x = \frac{1}{2}$$
$$x = \frac{\pi}{6} + 2\pi n \text{ and } x = \frac{5\pi}{6} + 2\pi n$$

For $\sin x - 3 = 0$,
$$\sin x = 3 \quad \text{Why is there no solution for sin x = 3?}$$
There is no solution for $\sin x = 3$.

The restriction on the original equation is sin $x \neq 0$ because of the presence of csc x.

Since sin $x = 0$ does not occur in the solution, all determined solutions are permissible.

The solution is $x = \frac{\pi}{6} + 2\pi n$ and $x = \frac{5\pi}{6} + 2\pi n$, where $n \in I$.

Your Turn

Algebraically solve $3 \cos x + 2 = 5 \sec x$. Give general solutions expressed in radians.

Key Ideas

- Reciprocal, quotient, Pythagorean, and double-angle identities can be used to help solve a trigonometric equation algebraically.
- The algebraic solution for a trigonometric equation can be verified graphically.
- Check that solutions for an equation do not include non-permissible values from the original equation.
- Unless the domain is restricted, give general solutions. For example, for $2 \cos x = 1$, the general solution is $x = \frac{\pi}{3} + 2\pi n$ and $x = \frac{5\pi}{3} + 2\pi n$, where $n \in I$. If the domain is specified as $0° \leq x < 360°$, then the solutions are 60° and 300°.

Check Your Understanding

Practise

1. Solve each equation algebraically over the domain $0 \leq x < 2\pi$.
   a) $\tan^2 x - \tan x = 0$
   b) $\sin 2x - \sin x = 0$
   c) $\sin^2 x - 4 \sin x = 5$
   d) $\cos 2x = \sin x$

2. Solve each equation algebraically over the domain $0° \leq x < 360°$. Verify your solution graphically.
   a) $\cos x - \cos 2x = 0$
   b) $\sin^2 x - 3 \sin x = 4$
   c) $\tan x \cos x \sin x - 1 = 0$
   d) $\tan^2 x + \sqrt{3} \tan x = 0$

3. Rewrite each equation in terms of sine only. Then, solve algebraically for $0 \leq x < 2\pi$.
   a) $\cos 2x - 3 \sin x = 2$
   b) $2 \cos^2 x - 3 \sin x - 3 = 0$
   c) $3 \csc x - \sin x = 2$
   d) $\tan^2 x + 2 = 0$

4. Solve $4 \sin^2 x = 1$ algebraically over the domain $-180° \leq x < 180°$.

5. Solve $2 \tan^2 x + 3 \tan x - 2 = 0$ algebraically over the domain $0 \leq x < 2\pi$.

Apply

6. Determine the mistake that Sanesh made in the following work. Then, complete a correct solution.

Solve $2 \cos^2 x = \sqrt{3} \cos x$. Express your answer(s) in degrees.

Solution:
$$\frac{1}{\cos x}(2 \cos^2 x) = (\sqrt{3} \cos x)\frac{1}{\cos x}$$
$$2 \cos x = \sqrt{3}$$
$$\cos x = \frac{\sqrt{3}}{2}$$
$$x = 30° + 360°n \text{ and } x = 330° + 360°n$$

7. a) Solve algebraically $\sin 2x = 0.5$, $0 \leq x < 2\pi$.

b) Solve the equation from part a) using a different method.

8. Solve $\sin^2 x = \cos^2 x + 1$ algebraically for all values of x. Give your answer(s) in radians.

9. Solve $\cos x \sin 2x - 2 \sin x = -2$ algebraically over the domain of real numbers. Give your answer(s) in radians.

10. How many solutions does the equation $(7 \sin x + 2)(3 \cos x + 3)(\tan^2 x - 2) = 0$ have over the interval $0° < x \leq 360°$? Explain your reasoning.

11. Solve $\sqrt{3} \cos x \csc x = -2 \cos x$ for x over the domain $0 \leq x < 2\pi$.

12. If $\cos x = \frac{2}{3}$ and $\cos x = -\frac{1}{3}$ are the solutions for a trigonometric equation, what are the values of B and C if the equation is of the form $9 \cos^2 x + B \cos x + C = 0$?

13. Create a trigonometric equation that includes $\sin 2x$ and that can be solved by factoring. Then, solve it.

14. Solve $\sin 2x = 2 \cos x \cos 2x$ algebraically. Give the general solution expressed in radians.

15. Algebraically determine the number of solutions for the equation $\cos 2x \cos x - \sin 2x \sin x = 0$ over the domain $-360° < x \leq 360°$.

16. Solve $\sec x + \tan^2 x - 3 \cos x = 2$ algebraically. Give the general solution expressed in radians.

Extend

17. Solve $4 \sin^2 x = 3 \tan^2 x - 1$ algebraically. Give the general solution expressed in radians.

18. Solve $\dfrac{1 - \sin^2 x - 2 \cos x}{\cos^2 x - \cos x - 2} = -\dfrac{1}{3}$ algebraically over the domain $-\pi \leq x \leq \pi$.

19. Find the general solution for the equation $4(16^{\cos^2 x}) = 2^{6 \cos x}$. Give your answer in radians.

20. For some angles α and β, $\sin^2 \alpha + \cos^2 \beta = m^2$ and $\cos^2 \alpha + \sin^2 \beta = m$. Find the possible value(s) for m.

Create Connections

C1 Refer to the equation $\sin x - \cos 2x = 0$ to answer the following.

a) Which identity would you use to express the equation in terms of one trigonometric function?

b) How can you solve the resulting equation by factoring?

c) What is the solution for the domain $0° \leq x < 360°$?

d) Verify your solution by graphing.

C2 Refer to the equation $3 \cos^2 x + \cos x - 1 = 0$ to answer the following.

a) Why is not possible to factor the left side of the equation?

b) Solve the equation using the quadratic formula.

c) What is the solution over the domain $0° \leq x < 720°$?

C3 Use the double-angle identity for sine to create an equation that is not an identity. Solve the equation and explain why it is not an identity.

Chapter 6 Review

6.1 Reciprocal, Quotient, and Pythagorean Identities, pages 290–298

1. Determine the non-permissible values, in radians, for each expression.
   a) $\dfrac{3 \sin x}{\cos x}$
   b) $\dfrac{\cos x}{\tan x}$
   c) $\dfrac{\sin x}{1 - 2 \cos x}$
   d) $\dfrac{\cos x}{\sin^2 x - 1}$

2. Simplify each expression to one of the three primary trigonometric functions.
   a) $\dfrac{\sin x}{\tan x}$
   b) $\dfrac{\sec x}{\csc x}$
   c) $\dfrac{\sin x + \tan x}{1 + \cos x}$
   d) $\dfrac{\csc x - \sin x}{\cot x}$

3. Rewrite each trigonometric expression in terms of sine or cosine or both. Then, simplify.
   a) $\tan x \cot x$
   b) $\dfrac{1}{\csc^2 x} + \dfrac{1}{\sec^2 x}$
   c) $\sec^2 x - \tan^2 x$

4. a) Verify that the potential identity $\dfrac{\cos x}{1 - \sin x} = \dfrac{1 + \sin x}{\cos x}$ is true for $x = 30°$ and for $x = \dfrac{\pi}{4}$.
   b) What are the non-permissible values for the equation over the domain $0° \leq x < 360°$?

5. a) Determine two values of x that satisfy the equation $\sqrt{\tan^2 x + 1} = \sec x$.
   b) Use technology to graph $y = \sqrt{\tan^2 x + 1}$ and $y = \sec x$ over the domain $-\dfrac{\pi}{2} \leq x < \dfrac{3\pi}{2}$. Compare the two graphs.
   c) Explain, using your graph in part b), how you know that $\sqrt{\tan^2 x + 1} = \sec x$ is not an identity.

6.2 Sum, Difference, and Double-Angle Identities, pages 299–308

6. A Fourier series is an infinite series in which the terms are made up of sine and cosine ratios. A finite number of terms from a Fourier series is often used to approximate the behaviour of waves.

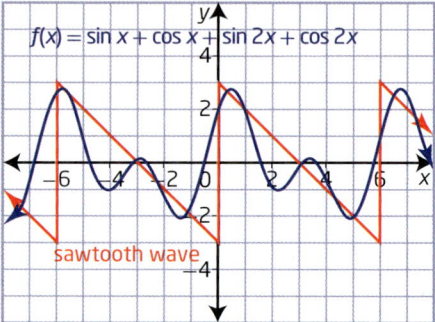

sawtooth wave

The first four terms of the Fourier series approximation for a sawtooth wave are $f(x) = \sin x + \cos x + \sin 2x + \cos 2x$.

a) Determine the value of $f(0)$ and of $f\left(\dfrac{\pi}{6}\right)$.

b) Prove that $f(x)$ can be written as
$f(x) = \sin x + \cos x + 2 \sin x \cos x - 2 \sin^2 x + 1$.

c) Is it possible to rewrite this Fourier series using only sine or only cosine? Justify your answer.

d) Use the pattern in the first four terms to write $f(x)$ with more terms. Graph $y = f(x)$ using technology, for $x \in [-4\pi, 4\pi]$. How many terms are needed to arrive at a good approximation of a sawtooth wave?

7. Write each expression as a single trigonometric function, and then evaluate.
   a) $\sin 25° \cos 65° + \cos 25° \sin 65°$
   b) $\sin 54° \cos 24° - \cos 54° \sin 24°$
   c) $\cos \dfrac{\pi}{4} \cos \dfrac{\pi}{12} + \sin \dfrac{\pi}{4} \sin \dfrac{\pi}{12}$
   d) $\cos \dfrac{\pi}{6} \cos \dfrac{\pi}{12} - \sin \dfrac{\pi}{6} \sin \dfrac{\pi}{12}$

8. Use sum or difference identities to find the exact value of each trigonometric expression.
   a) $\sin 15°$
   b) $\cos\left(-\dfrac{\pi}{12}\right)$
   c) $\tan 165°$
   d) $\sin \dfrac{5\pi}{12}$

9. If $\cos A = -\dfrac{5}{13}$, where $\dfrac{\pi}{2} \leq A < \pi$, evaluate each of the following.
   a) $\cos\left(A - \dfrac{\pi}{4}\right)$
   b) $\sin\left(A + \dfrac{\pi}{3}\right)$
   c) $\sin 2A$

10. What is the exact value of $\left(\sin \dfrac{\pi}{8} + \cos \dfrac{\pi}{8}\right)^2$?

11. Simplify the expression $\dfrac{\cos^2 x - \cos 2x}{0.5 \sin 2x}$ to one of the primary trigonometric ratios.

6.3 Proving Identities, pages 309–315

12. Factor and simplify each expression.
    a) $\dfrac{1 - \sin^2 x}{\cos x \sin x - \cos x}$
    b) $\tan^2 x - \cos^2 x \tan^2 x$

13. Prove that each identity holds for all permissible values of x.
    a) $1 + \cot^2 x = \csc^2 x$
    b) $\tan x = \csc 2x - \cot 2x$
    c) $\sec x + \tan x = \dfrac{\cos x}{1 - \sin x}$
    d) $\dfrac{1}{1 + \cos x} + \dfrac{1}{1 - \cos x} = 2 \csc^2 x$

14. Consider the equation $\sin 2x = \dfrac{2 \tan x}{1 + \tan^2 x}$.
    a) Verify that the equation is true when $x = \dfrac{\pi}{4}$. Does this mean that the equation is an identity? Why or why not?
    b) What are the non-permissible values for the equation?
    c) Prove that the equation is an identity for all permissible values of x.

15. Prove each identity.
    a) $\dfrac{\cos x + \cot x}{\sec x + \tan x} = \cos x \cot x$
    b) $\sec x + \tan x = \dfrac{\cos x}{1 - \sin x}$

16. Consider the equation $\cos 2x = 2 \sin x \sec x$.
    a) Describe two methods that can be used to determine whether this equation could be an identity.
    b) Use one of the methods to show that the equation is not an identity.

6.4 Solving Trigonometric Equations Using Identities, pages 316–321

17. Solve each equation algebraically over the domain $0 \leq x < 2\pi$.
    a) $\sin 2x + \sin x = 0$
    b) $\cot x + \sqrt{3} = 0$
    c) $2 \sin^2 x - 3 \sin x - 2 = 0$
    d) $\sin^2 x = \cos x - \cos 2x$

18. Solve each equation algebraically over the domain $0° \leq x < 360°$. Verify your solution graphically.
    a) $2 \sin 2x = 1$
    b) $\sin^2 x = 1 + \cos^2 x$
    c) $2 \cos^2 x = \sin x + 1$
    d) $\cos x \tan x - \sin^2 x = 0$

19. Algebraically determine the general solution to the equation $4 \cos^2 x - 1 = 0$. Give your answer in radians.

20. If $0° \leq x < 360°$, what is the value of $\cos x$ in the equation $2 \cos^2 x + \sin^2 x = \dfrac{41}{25}$?

21. Use an algebraic approach to find the solution of $2 \sin x \cos x = 3 \sin x$ over the domain $-2\pi \leq x \leq 2\pi$.

Chapter 6 Practice Test

Multiple Choice

For #1 to #6, choose the best answer.

1. Which expression is equivalent to $\dfrac{\cos 2x - 1}{\sin 2x}$?

   A $-\tan x$ **B** $-\cot x$

   C $\tan x$ **D** $\cot x$

2. Which expression is equivalent to $\cot \theta + \tan \theta$?

   A $\dfrac{1}{\sin \theta \cos \theta}$ **B** $\dfrac{\cos \theta + \sin \theta}{\sin \theta \cos \theta}$

   C 1 **D** 2

3. Which expression is equivalent to $\tan^2 \theta \csc \theta + \dfrac{1}{\sin \theta}$?

   A $\sec^3 \theta$ **B** $\csc^3 \theta$

   C $\csc^2 \theta \sec \theta$ **D** $\sec^2 \theta \csc \theta$

4. Which single trigonometric function is equivalent to $\cos \dfrac{\pi}{5} \cos \dfrac{\pi}{6} - \sin \dfrac{\pi}{5} \sin \dfrac{\pi}{6}$?

   A $\cos \dfrac{\pi}{30}$ **B** $\sin \dfrac{\pi}{30}$

   C $\sin \dfrac{11\pi}{30}$ **D** $\cos \dfrac{11\pi}{30}$

5. Simplified, $4 \cos^2 x - 2$ is equivalent to

   A $2 \cos 2x$ **B** $4 \cos 2x$

   C $2 \cos 4x$ **D** $4 \cos x$

6. If $\sin \theta = c$ and $0 \leq \theta < \dfrac{\pi}{2}$, which expression is equivalent to $\cos (\pi + \theta)$?

   A $1 - c$ **B** $c - 1$

   C $\sqrt{1 - c^2}$ **D** $-\sqrt{1 - c^2}$

Short Answer

7. Determine the exact value of each trigonometric ratio.

   a) $\cos 105°$ b) $\sin \dfrac{5\pi}{12}$

8. Prove the identity $\cot \theta - \tan \theta = 2 \cot 2\theta$. Determine the non-permissible value(s), if any.

9. In physics, two students are doing a report on the intensity of light passing through a filter. After some research, they each find a different formula for the situation. In each formula, I is the intensity of light passing through the filter, I_0 is the initial light shining on the filter, θ is the angle between the axes of polarization.

   Theo's formula: $I = I_0 \cos^2 \theta$

   Sany's formula: $I = I_0 - \dfrac{I_0}{\csc^2 \theta}$

   Prove that the two formulas are equivalent.

10. Determine the general solution, in radians, for each equation.

    a) $\sec A + 2 = 0$

    b) $2 \sin B = 3 \tan^2 B$

    c) $\sin 2\theta \sin \theta + \cos^2 \theta = 1$

11. Solve the equation $\sin 2x + 2 \cos x = 0$ algebraically. Give the general solution in radians.

12. If $\sin \theta = -\dfrac{4}{5}$ and θ is in quadrant III, determine the exact value(s) of $\cos \left(\theta - \dfrac{\pi}{6}\right)$.

13. Solve $2 \tan x \cos^2 x = 1$ algebraically over the domain $0 \leq x < 2\pi$.

Extended Response

14. Solve $\sin^2 x + \cos 2x - \cos x = 0$ over the domain $0° \leq x < 360°$. Verify your solution graphically.

15. Prove each identity.

    a) $\dfrac{\cot x}{\csc x - 1} = \dfrac{\csc x + 1}{\cot x}$

    b) $\sin (x + y) \sin (x - y) = \sin^2 x - \sin^2 y$

16. Algebraically find the general solution for $2 \cos^2 x + 3 \sin x - 3 = 0$. Give your answer in radians.

Unit 2 Project Wrap-Up

Applications of Trigonometry

You can describe the relationships between angles, trigonometric ratios, and the unit circle. You can graph and analyse trigonometric functions and transformations of sinusoidal functions. You can identify and prove trigonometric identities. This knowledge will help you solve problems using trigonometric ratios and equations.

Complete at least one of the following options:

Option 1 Angle Measure

Research the types of units for angle measure and their history.

- Search for when, why, who, where, and what, relating to degrees, radians, and other types of units for angular measure.
- Prepare a presentation or report discussing the following:
  - Why was radian measure invented?
  - Why is π used for radian measure?
  - Which unit of measure do you prefer? Explain.
  - Why do other types of units for angle measure exist? In which situations are they used?

Option 2 Broadcasting

Research periodic functions as they relate to broadcasting.

- Search the Internet for carrier waveforms—what they are, how they work, and their connection to periodic functions.
- Prepare a presentation or report including the following:
  - a brief description of carrier waveforms and their significance
  - an example of carrier waveforms in use, including a diagram
  - an explanation of the mathematics involved and how it helps to model a broadcast

Option 3 Mach Numbers

Search for information relating supersonic travel and trigonometry.

- Prepare a presentation or report including the following:
  - a brief description of Mach numbers and an explanation of the mathematics involved in expressing a Mach number as a function of θ
  - examples of Mach numbers and resulting shock wave cones
  - an explanation of the effects of increasing Mach numbers on the cone angle, θ

Option 4 Crime Scene Investigation

Research how trigonometry and trigonometric functions are used to analyse crime scenes.

- Prepare a report that addresses at least two areas that are used by forensic scientists to solve and piece together the events of a crime scene.
  - Some choices are trajectory determination, blood pattern identification, and background sound analysis from videotapes or cell phones.
- Identify and explain the trigonometric functions used, one of which must be a sine function, and what the variables represent.
- Show the application to a problem by providing the calculations and interpreting the results.

Cumulative Review, Chapters 4–6

Chapter 4 Trigonometry and the Unit Circle

1. Draw each angle in standard position. Write an expression for all angles that are coterminal with each given angle.

   a) $\dfrac{7\pi}{3}$ b) $-100°$

2. Convert each radian measure to degrees. Express your answers to the nearest degree.

   a) 4   b) $\dfrac{-5\pi}{3}$

3. Convert each degree measure to radians. Express your answers as exact values.

   a) $210°$ b) $-500°$

4. A Ferris wheel that is 175 ft in diameter has 42 gondolas.

   a) Determine the arc length, to the nearest tenth of a foot, between each gondola.
   b) When the first gondola rotates through $70°$, determine the distance it travels, to the nearest tenth of a foot.

5. Determine the equation of a circle centred at the origin

   a) with a radius of 5
   b) if the point $P(3, \sqrt{7})$ is on the circle

6. $P(\theta)$ is the point where the terminal arm of an angle θ intersects the unit circle. If $P(\theta) = \left(-\dfrac{1}{2}, -\dfrac{\sqrt{3}}{2}\right)$, complete the following.

   a) In which quadrant does θ terminate?
   b) Determine all measures for θ in the interval $-2\pi \leq \theta \leq 2\pi$.
   c) What are the coordinates of $P\left(\theta + \dfrac{\pi}{2}\right)$? Explain how you know.
   d) What are the coordinates of $P(\theta - \pi)$? Explain how you know.

7. $P(\theta)$ is the point where the terminal arm of an angle θ intersects the unit circle.

   a) Determine the coordinates of $P(-45°)$ and $P(45°)$. How are the answers related?
   b) Determine the coordinates of $P(675°)$ and $P(765°)$. How are the answers related?

8. Determine the exact value of each trigonometric ratio.

   a) $\sin \dfrac{4\pi}{3}$ b) $\cos 300°$
   c) $\tan(-570°)$ d) $\csc 135°$
   e) $\sec\left(-\dfrac{3\pi}{2}\right)$ f) $\cot \dfrac{23\pi}{6}$

9. The terminal arm of an angle θ in standard position passes through the point $P(-9, 12)$.

   a) Draw the angle in standard position.
   b) Determine the exact values of the six trigonometric ratios.
   c) Determine the approximate measure of all possible values of θ, to the nearest hundredth of a degree.

10. Determine the exact roots for each equation.

    a) $\sin \theta = -\dfrac{1}{2}$, $-2\pi \leq \theta \leq 2\pi$
    b) $\sec \theta = \dfrac{2\sqrt{3}}{3}$, $-180° \leq \theta \leq 180°$
    c) $\tan \theta = -1$, $0 \leq \theta \leq 2\pi$

11. Determine the general solution, in radians, for each equation.

    a) $\cos \theta = -\dfrac{\sqrt{2}}{2}$ b) $\csc \theta = 1$
    c) $\cot \theta = 0$

12. Solve each equation over the domain $0 \leq \theta \leq 2\pi$. Express your answers as exact values.

    a) $\sin \theta = \sin \theta \tan \theta$
    b) $2\cos^2 \theta + 5\cos \theta + 2 = 0$

13. Solve for θ, where $0° \leq \theta \leq 360°$. Give your answers as approximate measures, to the nearest degree.

    a) $4\tan^2 \theta - 1 = 0$
    b) $3\sin^2 \theta - 2\sin \theta = 1$

Chapter 5 Trigonometric Functions and Graphs

14. Write the equation of the sine function with amplitude 3, period 4π, and phase shift $\dfrac{\pi}{4}$ units to the left.

15. Determine the amplitude, period, phase shift, and vertical displacement with respect to $y = \sin \theta$ or $y = \cos \theta$ for each function. Sketch the graph of each function for two cycles.

a) $y = 3 \cos 2\theta$

b) $y = -2 \sin (3\theta + 60°)$

c) $y = \dfrac{1}{2} \cos (\theta + \pi) - 4$

d) $y = \sin \left(\dfrac{1}{2}\left(\theta - \dfrac{\pi}{4} \right) \right) + 1$

16. Write an equation for each graph in the form $y = a \sin b(x - c) + d$ and in the form $y = a \cos b(x - c) + d$.

a)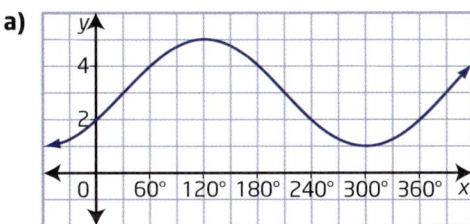

b)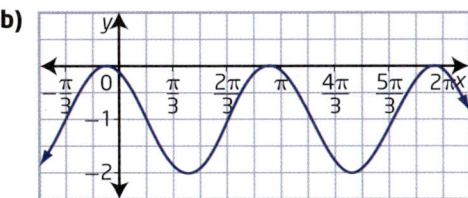

17. Write the equation of the cosine function with amplitude 4, period 300°, phase shift of 30° to the left, and vertical displacement 3 units down.

18. a) Graph $y = \tan \theta$ for $-2\pi \leq \theta \leq 0$.

b) State the equations of the asymptotes for the graph in part a).

19. A Ferris wheel has a radius of 25 m. The centre of the wheel is 26 m above the ground. The wheel rotates twice in 22 min.

a) Determine the equation of the sinusoidal function, $h(x)$, that models the height of a passenger on the ride as a function of time.

b) If a passenger gets on at the bottom of the wheel, when is the passenger 30 m above the ground? Express the answer to the nearest tenth of a minute.

Chapter 6 Trigonometric Identities

20. Determine the non-permissible values for each expression. Then, simplify the expression.

a) $\dfrac{1 - \cos^2 \theta}{\cos^2 \theta}$

b) $\sec x \csc x \tan x$

21. Use a sum or difference identity to determine the exact values of each trigonometric expression.

a) $\sin 195°$

b) $\cos \left(-\dfrac{5\pi}{12} \right)$

22. Write each expression as a single trigonometric ratio and then evaluate.

a) $2 \cos^2 \dfrac{3\pi}{8} - 1$

b) $\sin 10° \cos 80° + \cos 10° \sin 80°$

c) $\dfrac{\tan \dfrac{5\pi}{12} + \tan \dfrac{23\pi}{12}}{1 - \tan \dfrac{5\pi}{12} \tan \dfrac{23\pi}{12}}$

23. a) Verify the equation
$\sin^2 A + \cos^2 A + \tan^2 A = \sec^2 A$
for $A = 30°$.

b) Prove that the equation in part a) is an identity.

24. Consider the equation
$\dfrac{1 + \tan x}{\sec x} = \sin x + \cos x$.

a) Verify graphically that the equation could be an identity.

b) Prove that the equation is an identity for all permissible values of x.

25. Prove the identity
$\dfrac{\cos \theta - \sin \theta}{\cos \theta + \sin \theta} = \dfrac{\cos 2\theta}{1 + \sin 2\theta}$ algebraically.

26. Solve each equation. Give the general solution in radians.

a) $\sec^2 x = 4 \tan^2 x$

b) $\sin 2x + \cos x = 0$

27. a) Solve $(\sin \theta + \cos \theta)^2 - \sin 2\theta = 1$. Give the general solution in degrees.

b) Is the equation $(\sin \theta + \cos \theta)^2 - \sin 2\theta = 1$ an identity? Explain.

Unit 2 Test

Multiple Choice

For #1 to #8, choose the best answer.

1. If $\tan \theta = \dfrac{3}{2}$ and $\cos \theta < 0$, then the value of $\cos 2\theta$ is

   A $\dfrac{1}{13}$ B $-\dfrac{5}{13}$

   C $\dfrac{5}{13}$ D 1

2. If the point (3, −5) lies on the terminal arm of an angle θ in standard position, the value of $\sin(\pi - \theta)$ is

   A $\dfrac{3}{\sqrt{34}}$ B $-\dfrac{3}{\sqrt{34}}$

   C $\dfrac{5}{\sqrt{34}}$ D $-\dfrac{5}{\sqrt{34}}$

3. The function $y = a \sin b(x - c) + d$ has a range of $\{y \mid -2 \leq y \leq 6, y \in \mathbb{R}\}$. What are the values of the parameters a and d?

   A $a = -2$ and $d = 8$

   B $a = 2$ and $d = 4$

   C $a = 4$ and $d = 2$

   D $a = 8$ and $d = -2$

4. What are the period and phase shift for the function $f(x) = 3 \cos\left(4x + \dfrac{\pi}{2}\right)$?

   A period = $\dfrac{\pi}{2}$, phase shift = $\dfrac{\pi}{2}$ units to the left

   B period = 4, phase shift = $\dfrac{\pi}{8}$ units to the left

   C period = $\dfrac{\pi}{2}$, phase shift = $\dfrac{\pi}{8}$ units to the left

   D period = 4, phase shift = $\dfrac{\pi}{2}$ units to the left

5. Which sinusoidal function has a graph equivalent to the graph of $y = 3 \sin x$?

   A $y = 3 \cos\left(x + \dfrac{\pi}{2}\right)$

   B $y = 3 \cos\left(x - \dfrac{\pi}{2}\right)$

   C $y = 3 \cos\left(x - \dfrac{\pi}{4}\right)$

   D $y = 3 \cos\left(x + \dfrac{\pi}{4}\right)$

6. The function $y = \tan x$, where x is in degrees, is

   A defined for all values of x

   B undefined when $x = \pm 1°$

   C undefined when $x = 180°n, n \in I$

   D undefined when $x = 90° + 180°n, n \in I$

7. The expression $\dfrac{\sin \theta + \tan \theta}{1 + \cos \theta}$ is equivalent to

   A $\sin \theta$

   B $\cos \theta$

   C $\tan \theta$

   D $\cot \theta$

8. Which of the following is not an identity?

   A $\dfrac{\sec \theta \csc \theta}{\cot \theta} = \sec \theta$

   B $\tan^2 \theta - \sin^2 \theta = \sin^2 \theta \tan^2 \theta$

   C $\dfrac{1 - \cos 2\theta}{2} = \sin^2 \theta$

   D $\dfrac{\tan^2 \theta}{1 + \tan^2 \theta} = \sin^2 \theta$

Numerical Response

Copy and complete the statements in #9 to #13.

9. The exact value of $\sin \dfrac{17\pi}{3}$ is ■.

10. Point $P\left(x, \dfrac{\sqrt{5}}{3}\right)$ is on the unit circle. The possible values of x are ■ and ■.

11. If $\cos \theta = \dfrac{-5}{13}$ and $\dfrac{\pi}{2} \leq \theta \leq \pi$, then the exact value of $\sin\left(\theta + \dfrac{\pi}{4}\right)$ is ■.

12. An arc of a circle subtends a central angle θ. The length of the arc is 6 cm and the radius is 4 cm. The measures of θ in radians and in degrees, to the nearest tenth of a unit, are ■ and ■.

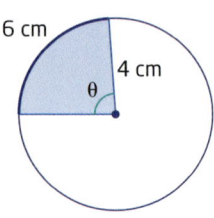

328 MHR • Unit 2 Test

13. The solutions to $\sqrt{3}\sec\theta - 2 = 0$ for $-2\pi \leq \theta \leq 2\pi$, as exact values, are ■, ■, ■, and ■.

Written Response

14. Consider the angle $\theta = -\dfrac{5\pi}{3}$.

   a) Draw the angle in standard position.

   b) Convert the angle measure to degrees.

   c) Write an expression for all angles that are coterminal with θ, in radians.

   d) Is $\dfrac{10\pi}{3}$ coterminal with θ? Justify your answer.

15. Solve $5\sin^2\theta + 3\sin\theta - 2 = 0$, $0 \leq \theta \leq 2\pi$, algebraically. Give your answers to the nearest thousandth of a radian.

16. Pat solved the equation $4\sin^2 x = 3$, $0 \leq x \leq 2\pi$, as follows:

$4\sin^2 x = 3$
$2\sin x = \sqrt{3}$
$\sin x = \dfrac{\sqrt{3}}{2}$
$x = \dfrac{\pi}{3}, \dfrac{2\pi}{3}$

Sam checks the answer graphically and says that there are four zeros in the given domain. Who is correct? Identify the error that the other person made.

17. a) Sketch the graph of the function $f(x) = 3\sin\dfrac{1}{2}(x + 60°) - 1$ for $-360° \leq x \leq 360°$.

   b) State the range of the function.

   c) Identify the amplitude, period, phase shift, and vertical displacement for the function.

   d) Determine the roots of the equation $3\sin\dfrac{1}{2}(x + 60°) - 1 = 0$. Give your answers to the nearest degree.

18. a) Use technology to graph $f(\theta) = 2\cot\theta \sin^2\theta$ over the domain $0 \leq \theta \leq 2\pi$.

   b) Determine an equation equivalent to $f(\theta)$ in the form $g(\theta) = a\sin[b(\theta - c)] + d$, where a, b, c, and d are constants.

   c) Prove algebraically that $f(\theta) = g(\theta)$.

19. Consider the equation $\tan x + \dfrac{1}{\tan x} = \dfrac{\sec x}{\sin x}$.

   a) Verify that the equation is true for $x = \dfrac{2\pi}{3}$.

   b) What are the non-permissible values for the equation?

   c) Prove that the equation is an identity for all permissible values of x.

20. The predicted height, h, in metres, of the tides at Prince Rupert, British Columbia, for one day in February is approximated by the function $h(t) = 2.962\sin(0.508t - 0.107) + 3.876$, where t is the time, in hours, since midnight.

   a) Predict the maximum height of the tide on this day.

   b) Determine the period of the sinusoidal function.

   c) Predict the height of the tide at 12 noon on this day.

> **Web Link**
>
> To search for data on predicted heights and times of tides at various locations across Canada, go to www.mcgrawhill.ca/school/learningcentres and follow the links.

Marina at Prince Rupert

Unit 3

Exponential and Logarithmic Functions

Exponential and logarithmic functions can be used to describe and solve a wide range of problems. Some of the questions that can be answered using these two types of functions include:
- How much will your bank deposit be worth in five years, if it is compounded monthly?
- How will your car loan payment change if you pay it off in three years instead of four?
- How acidic is a water sample with a pH of 8.2?
- How long will a medication stay in your bloodstream with a concentration that allows it to be effective?
- How thick should the walls of a spacecraft be in order to protect the crew from harmful radiation?

In this unit, you will explore a variety of situations that can modelled with an exponential function or its inverse, the logarithmic function. You will learn techniques for solving various problems, such as those posed above.

Looking Ahead

In this unit, you will solve problems involving...
- exponential functions and equations
- logarithmic functions and equations

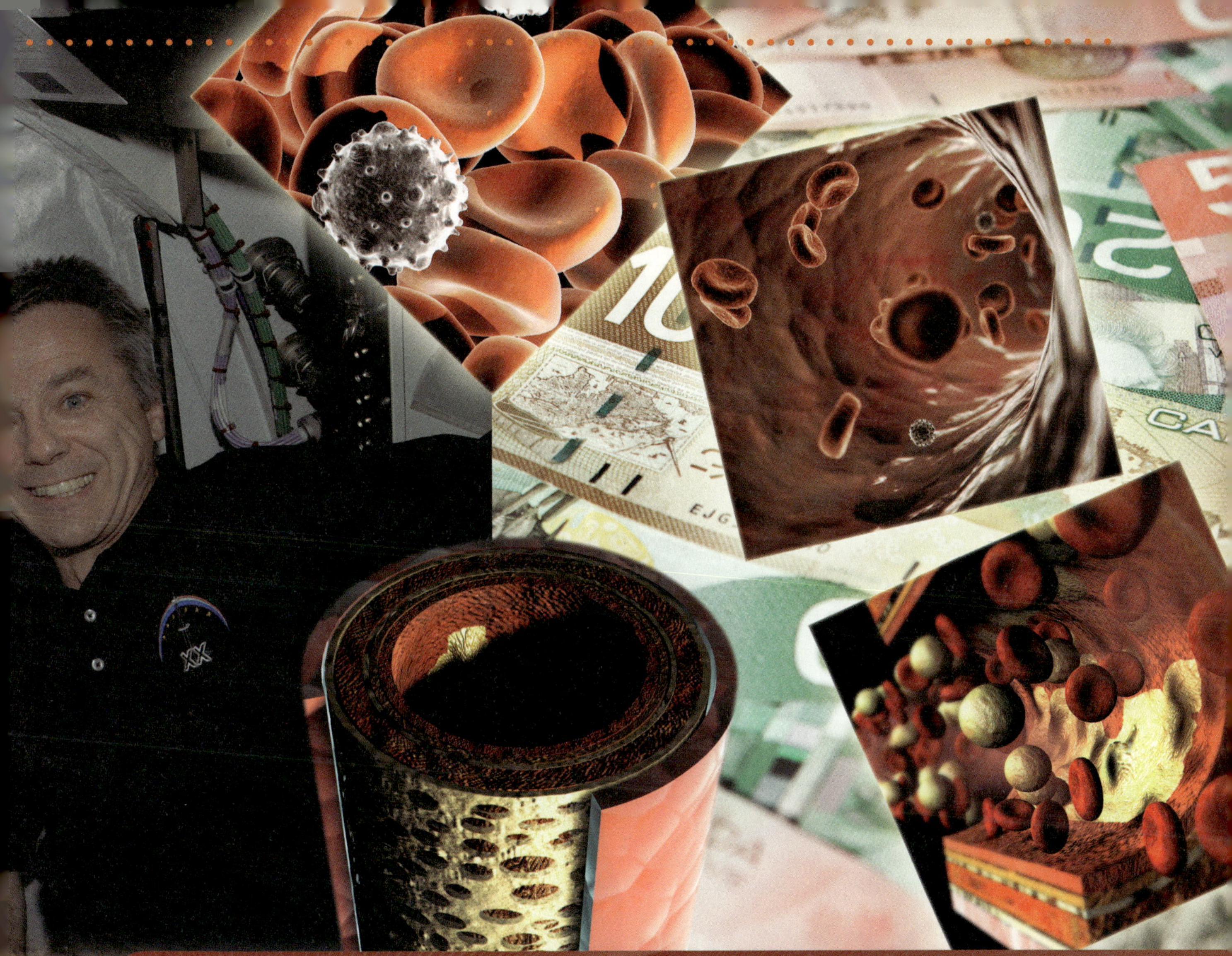

Unit 3 Project   At the Movies

In 2010, Canadian and American movie-goers spent $10.6 billion on tickets, or 33% of the worldwide box office ticket sales. Of the films released in 2010, only 25 were in 3D, but they brought in $2.2 billion of the ticket sales!

You will examine box office revenues for newly released movies, investigate graphs of the revenue over time, determine the function that best represents the data and graph, and use this function to make predictions.

In this project, you will explore the use of mathematics to model box office revenues for a movie of your choice.

Unit 3 Exponential and Logarithmic Functions • MHR 331

CHAPTER 7

Exponential Functions

In the 1920s, watch companies produced glow-in-the-dark dials by using radioluminescent paint, which was made of zinc sulphide mixed with radioactive radium salts. Today, a material called tritium is used in wristwatches and other equipment such as aircraft instruments. In commercial use, the tritium gas is put into tiny vials of borosilicate glass that are placed on the hands and hour markers of a watch dial.

Both radium and tritium are radioactive materials that decay into other elements by emitting different types of radiation. The rate at which radioactive materials decay can be modelled using exponential functions. Exponential functions can also be used to model situations where there is geometric growth, such as in bacterial colonies and financial investments.

In this chapter, you will study exponential functions and use them to solve a variety of problems.

Did You Know?

Radium was once an additive in toothpaste, hair creams, and even food items due to its supposed curative powers. Once it was discovered that radium is over one million times as radioactive as the same mass of uranium, these products were prohibited because of their serious adverse health effects.

Key Terms
exponential function
exponential growth
exponential decay
half-life
exponential equation

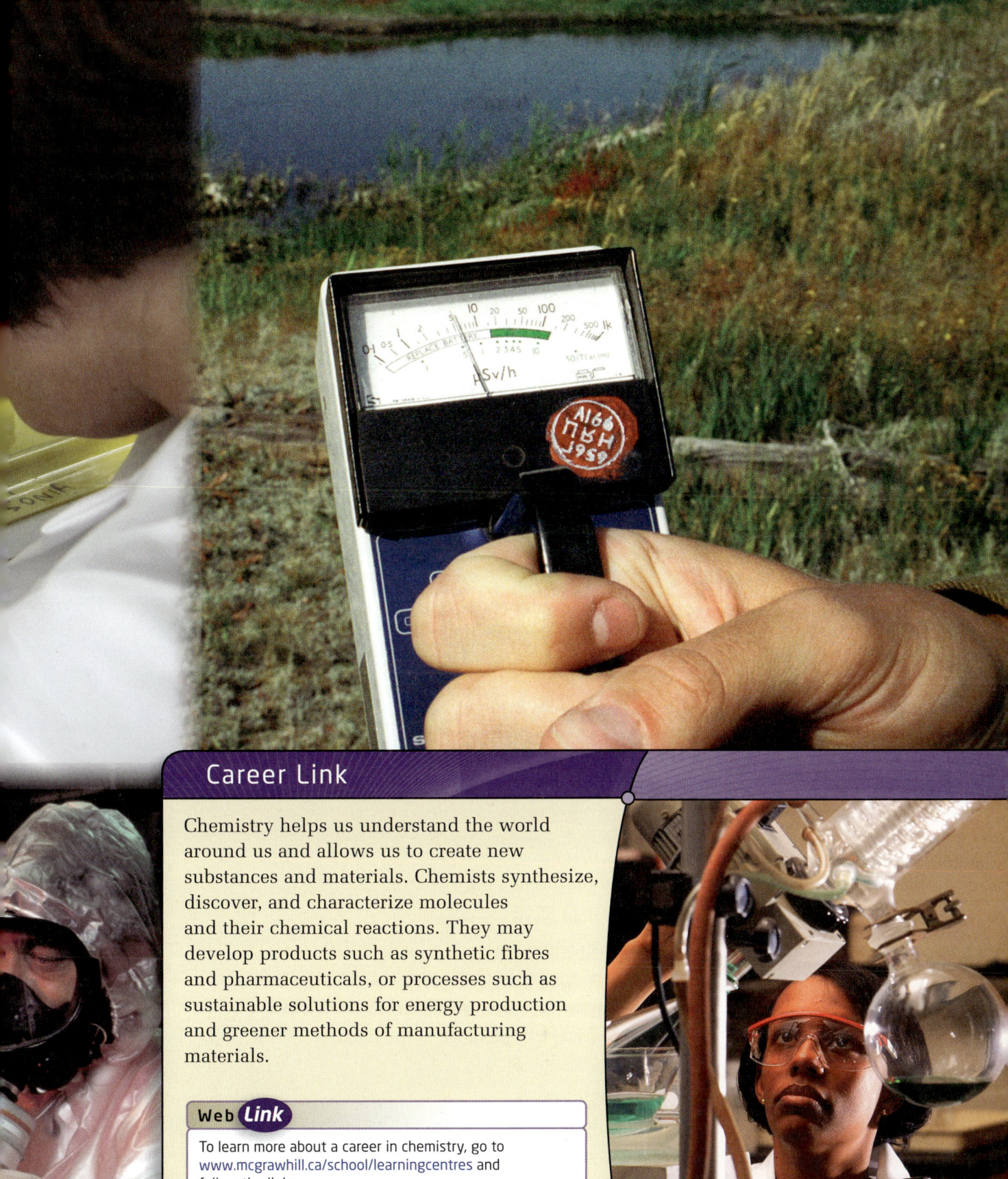

Career Link

Chemistry helps us understand the world around us and allows us to create new substances and materials. Chemists synthesize, discover, and characterize molecules and their chemical reactions. They may develop products such as synthetic fibres and pharmaceuticals, or processes such as sustainable solutions for energy production and greener methods of manufacturing materials.

Web Link

To learn more about a career in chemistry, go to www.mcgrawhill.ca/school/learningcentres and follow the links.

7.1

Characteristics of Exponential Functions

Focus on...
- analysing graphs of exponential functions
- solving problems that involve exponential growth or decay

The following ancient fable from India has several variations, but each makes the same point.

> When the creator of the game of chess showed his invention to the ruler of the country, the ruler was so pleased that he gave the inventor the right to name his prize for the invention. The man, who was very wise, asked the king that he be given one grain of rice for the first square of the chessboard, two for the second one, four for the third one, and so on. The ruler quickly accepted the inventor's offer, believing the man had made a mistake in not asking for more.
>
> By the time he was compensated for half the chessboard, the man owned all of the rice in the country, and, by the sixty-fourth square, the ruler owed him almost 20 000 000 000 000 000 000 grains of rice.

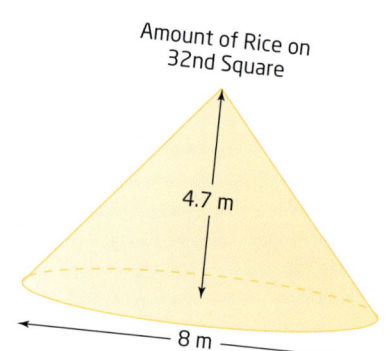

Amount of Rice on 32nd Square

The final amount of rice is approximately equal to the volume of a mountain 140 times as tall as Mount Everest. This is an example of how things grow exponentially. What exponential function can be used to model this situation?

Investigate Characteristics of Exponential Functions

Materials
- graphing technology

Explore functions of the form $y = c^x$.

1. Consider the function $y = 2^x$.
   a) Graph the function.
   b) Describe the shape of the graph.
2. Determine the following and justify your reasoning.
   a) the domain and the range of the function $y = 2^x$
   b) the y-intercept
   c) the x-intercept
   d) the equation of the horizontal line (asymptote) that the graph approaches as the values of x get very small

3. Select at least two different values for c in $y = c^x$ that are greater than 2. Graph your functions. Compare each graph to the graph of $y = 2^x$. Describe how the graphs are similar and how they are different.

4. Select at least two different values for c in $y = c^x$ that are between 0 and 1. Graph your functions. How have the graphs changed compared to those from steps 2 and 3?

5. Predict what the graph will look like if $c < 0$. Confirm your prediction using a table of values and a graph.

Reflect and Respond

6. **a)** Summarize how the value of c affects the shape and characteristics of the graph of $y = c^x$.

   b) Predict what will happen when $c = 1$. Explain.

Link the Ideas

The graph of an **exponential function**, such as $y = c^x$, is increasing for $c > 1$, decreasing for $0 < c < 1$, and neither increasing nor decreasing for $c = 1$. From the graph, you can determine characteristics such as domain and range, any intercepts, and any asymptotes.

exponential function
- a function of the form $y = c^x$, where c is a constant ($c > 0$) and x is a variable

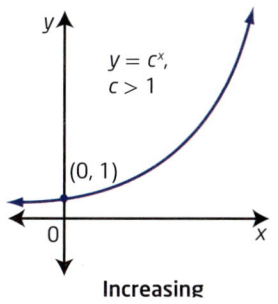
Increasing

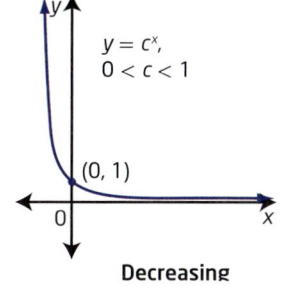
Decreasing

Why is the definition of an exponential function restricted to positive values of c?

Did You Know?

Any letter can be used to represent the base in an exponential function. Some other common forms are $y = a^x$ and $y = b^x$. In this chapter, you will use the letter c. This is to avoid any confusion with the transformation parameters, a, b, h, and k, that you will apply in Section 7.2.

Example 1

Analyse the Graph of an Exponential Function

Graph each exponential function. Then identify the following:
- the domain and range
- the x-intercept and y-intercept, if they exist
- whether the graph represents an increasing or a decreasing function
- the equation of the horizontal asymptote

a) $y = 4^x$

b) $f(x) = \left(\dfrac{1}{2}\right)^x$

Solution

a) Method 1: Use Paper and Pencil

Use a table of values to graph the function.
Select integral values of x that make it easy to calculate the corresponding values of y for $y = 4^x$.

x	y
−2	$\dfrac{1}{16}$
−1	$\dfrac{1}{4}$
0	1
1	4
2	16

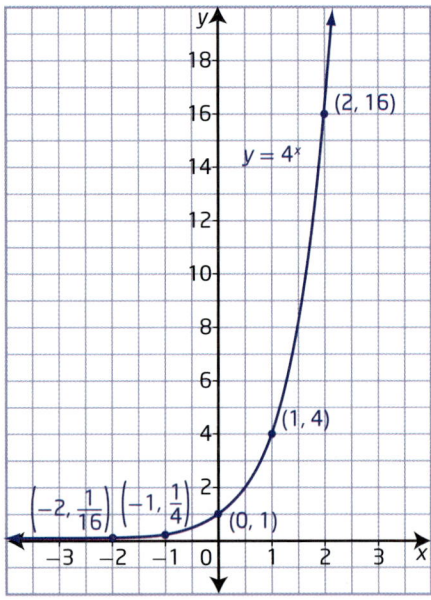

Method 2: Use a Graphing Calculator

Use a graphing calculator to graph $y = 4^x$.

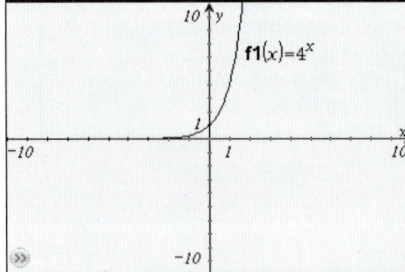

The function is defined for all values of x. Therefore, the domain is $\{x \mid x \in R\}$.

The function has only positive values for y. Therefore, the range is $\{y \mid y > 0, y \in R\}$.

The graph never intersects the x-axis, so there is no x-intercept.

The graph crosses the y-axis at $y = 1$, so the y-intercept is 1.

The graph rises to the right throughout its domain, indicating that the values of y increase as the values of x increase. Therefore, the function is increasing over its domain.

Since the graph approaches the line $y = 0$ as the values of x get very small, $y = 0$ is the equation of the horizontal asymptote.

b) Method 1: Use Paper and Pencil

Use a table of values to graph the function.
Select integral values of x that make it easy to calculate the corresponding values of y for $f(x) = \left(\frac{1}{2}\right)^x$.

x	f(x)
−3	8
−2	4
−1	2
0	1
1	$\frac{1}{2}$
2	$\frac{1}{4}$

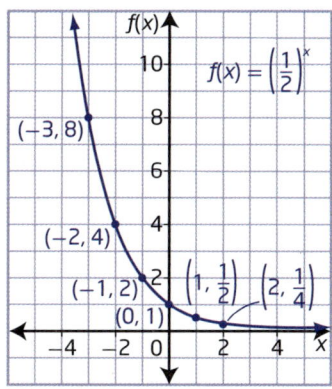

Method 2: Use a Graphing Calculator

Use a graphing calculator to graph $f(x) = \left(\frac{1}{2}\right)^x$.

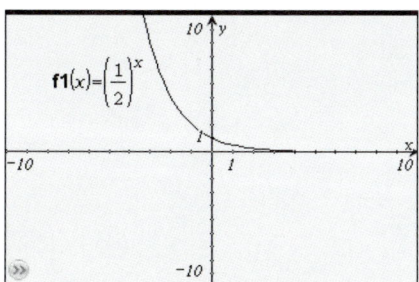

The function is defined for all values of x. Therefore, the domain is $\{x \mid x \in \mathbb{R}\}$.

The function has only positive values for y. Therefore, the range is $\{y \mid y > 0, y \in \mathbb{R}\}$.

The graph never intersects the x-axis, so there is no x-intercept.

The graph crosses the y-axis at $y = 1$, so the y-intercept is 1.

Why do the graphs of these exponential functions have a y-intercept of 1?

The graph falls to the right throughout its domain, indicating that the values of y decrease as the values of x increase. Therefore, the function is decreasing over its domain.

Since the graph approaches the line $y = 0$ as the values of x get very large, $y = 0$ is the equation of the horizontal asymptote.

Your Turn

Graph the exponential function $y = 3^x$ without technology. Identify the following:
- the domain and range
- the x-intercept and the y-intercept, if they exist
- whether the graph represents an increasing or a decreasing function
- the equation of the horizontal asymptote

Verify your results using graphing technology.

Example 2

Write the Exponential Function Given Its Graph

What function of the form $y = c^x$ can be used to describe the graph shown?

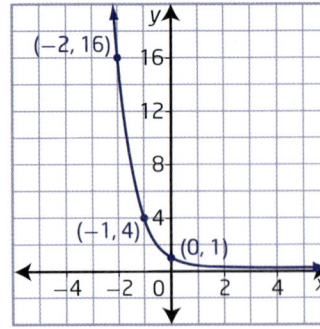

Solution

Look for a pattern in the ordered pairs from the graph.

x	y
−2	16
−1	4
0	1

As the value of x increases by 1 unit, the value of y decreases by a factor of $\frac{1}{4}$. Therefore, for this function, $c = \frac{1}{4}$.

Choose a point other than (0, 1) to substitute into the function $y = \left(\frac{1}{4}\right)^x$ to verify that the function is correct. Try the point (−2, 16).

Why should you not use the point (0, 1) to verify that the function is correct?

Check:

Left Side Right Side

y $\quad\quad\left(\frac{1}{4}\right)^x$

$= 16 \quad = \left(\frac{1}{4}\right)^{-2}$

$\quad\quad\quad = \dfrac{1}{\left(\frac{1}{4}\right)^2}$

Why is the power with a negative exponent, $\left(\frac{1}{4}\right)^{-2}$, equivalent to the reciprocal of the power with a positive exponent, $\dfrac{1}{\left(\frac{1}{4}\right)^2}$?

$\quad\quad\quad = \left(\frac{4}{1}\right)^2$

$\quad\quad\quad = 16$

The right side equals the left side, so the function that describes the graph is $y = \left(\frac{1}{4}\right)^x$.

What is another way of expressing this exponential function?

Your Turn

What function of the form $y = c^x$ can be used to describe the graph shown?

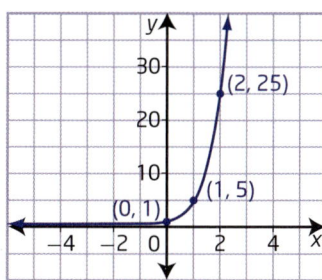

exponential growth
- an increasing pattern of values that can be modelled by a function of the form $y = c^x$, where $c > 1$

exponential decay
- a decreasing pattern of values that can be modelled by a function of the form $y = c^x$, where $0 < c < 1$

half-life
- the length of time for an unstable element to spontaneously decay to one half its original mass

Exponential functions of the form $y = c^x$, where $c > 1$, can be used to model **exponential growth**. Exponential functions with $0 < c < 1$ can be used to model **exponential decay**.

Example 3
Application of an Exponential Function

A radioactive sample of radium (Ra-225) has a **half-life** of 15 days. The mass, m, in grams, of Ra-225 remaining over time, t, in 15-day intervals, can be modelled using the exponential graph shown.

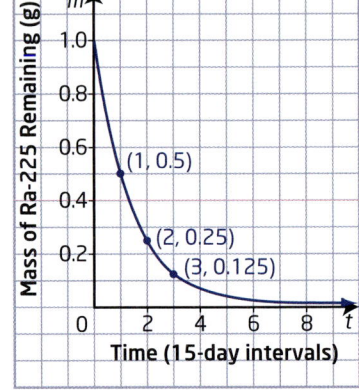

a) What is the initial mass of Ra-225 in the sample? What value does the mass of Ra-225 remaining approach as time passes?

b) What are the domain and range of this function?

c) Write the exponential decay model that relates the mass of Ra-225 remaining to time, in 15-day intervals.

d) Estimate how many days it would take for Ra-225 to decay to $\frac{1}{30}$ of its original mass.

Solution

a) From the graph, the m-intercept is 1. So, the initial mass of Ra-225 in the sample is 1 g.

   The graph is decreasing by a constant factor over time, representing exponential decay. It appears to approach $m = 0$ or 0 g of Ra-225 remaining in the sample.

b) From the graph, the domain of the function is $\{t \mid t \geq 0, t \in \mathbb{R}\}$, and the range of the function is $\{m \mid 0 < m \leq 1, m \in \mathbb{R}\}$.

c) The exponential decay model that relates the mass of Ra-225 remaining to time, in 15-day intervals, is the function $m(t) = \left(\frac{1}{2}\right)^t$.

Why is the base of the exponential function $\frac{1}{2}$?

d) Method 1: Use the Graph of the Function

$\frac{1}{30}$ of 1 g is equivalent to 0.0333... or approximately 0.03 g. Locate this approximate value on the vertical axis of the graph and draw a horizontal line until it intersects the graph of the exponential function.

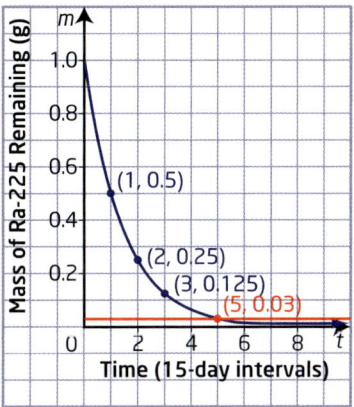

The horizontal line appears to intersect the graph at the point (5, 0.03). Therefore, it takes approximately five 15-day intervals, or 75 days, for Ra-225 to decay to $\frac{1}{30}$ of its original mass.

Method 2: Use a Table of Values

$\frac{1}{30}$ of 1 g is equivalent to $\frac{1}{30}$ g or approximately 0.0333 g.

Create a table of values for $m(t) = \left(\frac{1}{2}\right)^t$.

The table shows that the number of 15-day intervals is between 4 and 5. You can determine a better estimate by looking at values between these numbers.

Since 0.0333 is much closer to 0.031 25, try 4.8: $\left(\frac{1}{2}\right)^{4.8} \approx 0.0359$. This is greater than 0.0333.

Try 4.9: $\left(\frac{1}{2}\right)^{4.9} \approx 0.0335$.

t	m
1	0.5
2	0.25
3	0.125
4	0.0625
5	0.031 25
6	0.015 625

Therefore, it will take approximately 4.9 15-day intervals, or 73.5 days, for Ra-225 to decay to $\frac{1}{30}$ of its original mass.

Your Turn

Under ideal circumstances, a certain bacteria population triples every week. This is modelled by the following exponential graph.

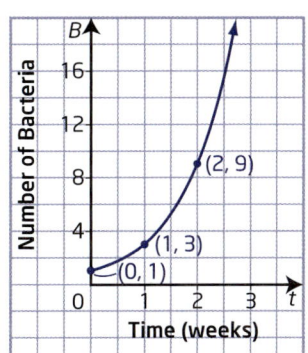

a) What are the domain and range of this function?
b) Write the exponential growth model that relates the number, B, of bacteria to the time, t, in weeks.
c) Determine approximately how many days it would take for the number of bacteria to increase to eight times the quantity on day 1.

Did You Know?

Exponential functions can be used to model situations involving continuous or discrete data. For example, problems involving radioactive decay are based on continuous data, while those involving populations are based on discrete data. In the case of discrete data, the continuous model will only be valid for a restricted domain.

Key Ideas

- An exponential function of the form $y = c^x$, $c > 0$,
  - is increasing for $c > 1$
  - is decreasing for $0 < c < 1$
  - is neither increasing nor decreasing for $c = 1$
  - has a domain of $\{x \mid x \in \mathbb{R}\}$
  - has a range of $\{y \mid y > 0, y \in \mathbb{R}\}$
  - has a y-intercept of 1
  - has no x-intercept
  - has a horizontal asymptote at $y = 0$

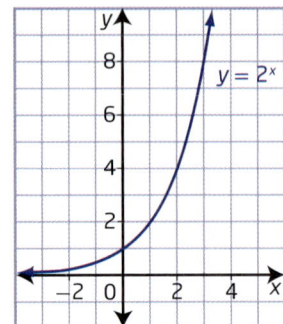
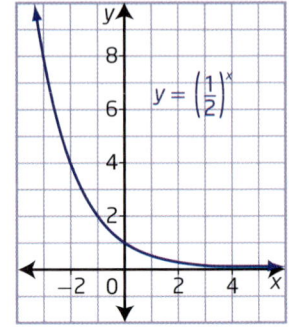

Check Your Understanding

Practise

1. Decide whether each of the following functions is exponential. Explain how you can tell.
   a) $y = x^3$
   b) $y = 6^x$
   c) $y = x^{\frac{1}{2}}$
   d) $y = 0.75^x$

2. Consider the following exponential functions:
   - $f(x) = 4^x$
   - $g(x) = \left(\dfrac{1}{4}\right)^x$
   - $h(x) = 2^x$

   a) Which is greatest when $x = 5$?
   b) Which is greatest when $x = -5$?
   c) For which value of x do all three functions have the same value? What is this value?

3. Match each exponential function to its corresponding graph.
   a) $y = 5^x$
   b) $y = \left(\dfrac{1}{4}\right)^x$
   c) $y = \left(\dfrac{2}{3}\right)^x$

   A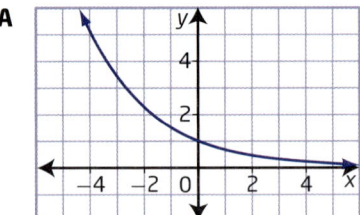

   B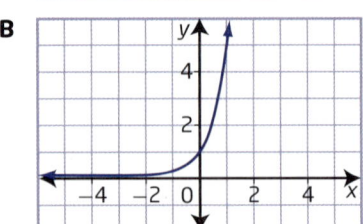

   C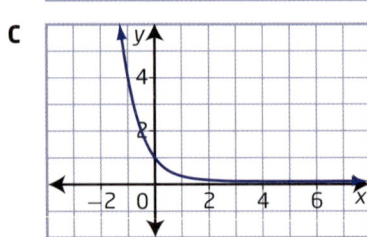

4. Write the function equation for each graph of an exponential function.

a)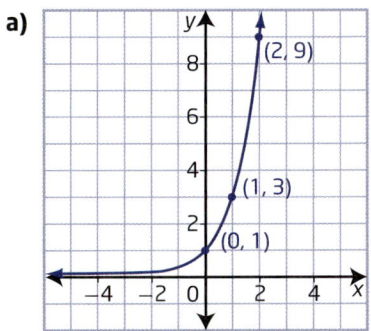

b)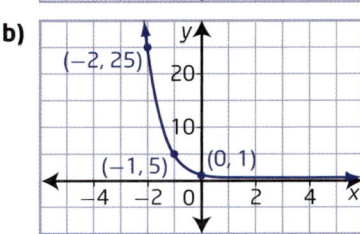

5. Sketch the graph of each exponential function. Identify the domain and range, the y-intercept, whether the function is increasing or decreasing, and the equation of the horizontal asymptote.

   a) $g(x) = 6^x$
   b) $h(x) = 3.2^x$
   c) $f(x) = \left(\dfrac{1}{10}\right)^x$
   d) $k(x) = \left(\dfrac{3}{4}\right)^x$

Apply

6. Each of the following situations can be modelled using an exponential function. Indicate which situations require a value of $c > 1$ (growth) and which require a value of $0 < c < 1$ (decay). Explain your choices.

   a) Bacteria in a Petri dish double their number every hour.
   b) The half-life of the radioactive isotope actinium-225 is 10 days.
   c) As light passes through every 1-m depth of water in a pond, the amount of light available decreases by 20%.
   d) The population of an insect colony triples every day.

7. A flu virus is spreading through the student population of a school according to the function $N = 2^t$, where N is the number of people infected and t is the time, in days.

   a) Graph the function. Explain why the function is exponential.
   b) How many people have the virus at each time?
      i) at the start when $t = 0$
      ii) after 1 day
      iii) after 4 days
      iv) after 10 days

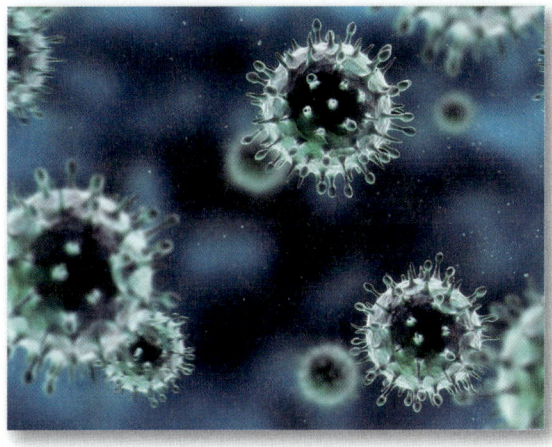

8. If a given population has a constant growth rate over time and is never limited by food or disease, it exhibits exponential growth. In this situation, the growth rate alone controls how quickly (or slowly) the population grows. If a population, P, of fish, in hundreds, experiences exponential growth at a rate of 10% per year, it can be modelled by the exponential function $P(t) = 1.1^t$, where t is time, in years.

   a) Why is the base for the exponential function that models this situation 1.1?
   b) Graph the function $P(t) = 1.1^t$. What are the domain and range of the function?
   c) If the same population of fish decreased at a rate of 5% per year, how would the base of the exponential model change?
   d) Graph the new function from part c). What are the domain and range of this function?

9. Scuba divers know that the deeper they dive, the more light is absorbed by the water above them. On a dive, Petra's light meter shows that the amount of light available decreases by 10% for every 10 m that she descends.

   a) Write the exponential function that relates the amount, L, as a percent expressed as a decimal, of light available to the depth, d, in 10-m increments.
   b) Graph the function.
   c) What are the domain and range of the function for this situation?
   d) What percent of light will reach Petra if she dives to a depth of 25 m?

10. The CANDU (CANada Deuterium Uranium) reactor is a Canadian-invented pressurized heavy-water reactor that uses uranium-235 (U-235) fuel with a half-life of approximately 700 million years.

   a) What exponential function can be used to represent the radioactive decay of 1 kg of U-235? Define the variables you use.
   b) Graph the function.
   c) How long will it take for 1 kg of U-235 to decay to 0.125 kg?
   d) Will the sample in part c) decay to 0 kg? Explain.

   Did You Know?

   Canada is one of the world's leading uranium producers, accounting for 18% of world primary production. All of the uranium produced in Canada comes from Saskatchewan mines. The energy potential of Saskatchewan's uranium reserves is approximately equivalent to 4.5 billion tonnes of coal or 17.5 billion barrels of oil.

11. Money in a savings account earns compound interest at a rate of 1.75% per year. The amount, A, of money in an account can be modelled by the exponential function $A = P(1.0175)^n$, where P is the amount of money first deposited into the savings account and n is the number of years the money remains in the account.

   a) Graph this function using a value of $P = \$1$ as the initial deposit.
   b) Approximately how long will it take for the deposit to triple in value?
   c) Does the amount of time it takes for a deposit to triple depend on the value of the initial deposit? Explain.
   d) In finance, the *rule of 72* is a method of estimating an investment's doubling time when interest is compounded annually. The number 72 is divided by the annual interest rate to obtain the approximate number of years required for doubling. Use your graph and the rule of 72 to approximate the doubling time for this investment.

12. Statistics indicate that the world population since 1995 has been growing at a rate of about 1.27% per year. United Nations records estimate that the world population in 2011 was approximately 7 billion. Assuming the same exponential growth rate, when will the population of the world be 9 billion?

Extend

13. a) On the same set of axes, sketch the graph of the function $y = 5^x$, and then sketch the graph of the inverse of the function by reflecting its graph in the line $y = x$.
   b) How do the characteristics of the graph of the inverse of the function relate to the characteristics of the graph of the original exponential function?
   c) Express the equation of the inverse of the exponential function in terms of y. That is, write $x = F(y)$.

14. The Krumbein phi scale is used in geology to classify sediments such as silt, sand, and gravel by particle size. The scale is modelled by the function $D(\varphi) = 2^{-\varphi}$, where D is the diameter of the particle, in millimetres, and φ is the Krumbein scale value. Fine sand has a Krumbein scale value of approximately 3. Coarse gravel has a Krumbein scale value of approximately -5.

A sampler showing grains sorted from silt to very coarse sand.

   a) Why would a coarse material have a negative scale value?

   b) How does the diameter of fine sand compare with the diameter of coarse gravel?

15. Typically, compound interest for a savings account is calculated every month and deposited into the account at that time. The interest could also be calculated daily, or hourly, or even by the second. When the period of time is infinitesimally small, the interest calculation is called continuous compounding. The exponential function that models this situation is $A(t) = Pe^{rt}$, where P is the amount of the initial deposit, r is the annual rate of interest as a decimal value, t is the number of years, and e is the base (approximately equal to 2.7183).

   a) Use graphing technology to estimate the doubling period, assuming an annual interest rate of 2% and continuous compounding.

   b) Use graphing technology to estimate the doubling period using the compound interest formula $A = P(1 + i)^n$.

   c) How do the results in parts a) and b) compare? Which method results in a shorter doubling period?

   Did You Know?

   The number e is irrational because it cannot be expressed as a ratio of integers. It is sometimes called *Euler's number* after the Swiss mathematician Leonhard Euler (pronounced "oiler").

Create Connections

C1 Consider the functions $f(x) = 3x$, $g(x) = x^3$, and $h(x) = 3^x$.

   a) Graph each function.

   b) List the key features for each function: domain and range, intercepts, and equations of any asymptotes.

   c) Identify key features that are common to each function.

   d) Identify key features that are different for each function.

C2 Consider the function $f(x) = (-2)^x$.

   a) Copy and complete the table of values.

x	f(x)
0	
1	
2	
3	
4	
5	

   b) Plot the ordered pairs.

   c) Do the points form a smooth curve? Explain.

   d) Use technology to try to evaluate $f\left(\dfrac{1}{2}\right)$ and $f\left(\dfrac{5}{2}\right)$. Use numerical reasoning to explain why these values are undefined.

   e) Use these results to explain why exponential functions are defined to only include positive bases.

7.2

Transformations of Exponential Functions

Focus on...

- applying translations, stretches, and reflections to the graphs of exponential functions
- representing these transformations in the equations of exponential functions
- solving problems that involve exponential growth or decay

Transformations of exponential functions are used to model situations such as population growth, carbon dating of samples found at archaeological digs, the physics of nuclear chain reactions, and the processing power of computers.

In this section, you will examine transformations of exponential functions and the impact the transformations have on the corresponding graph.

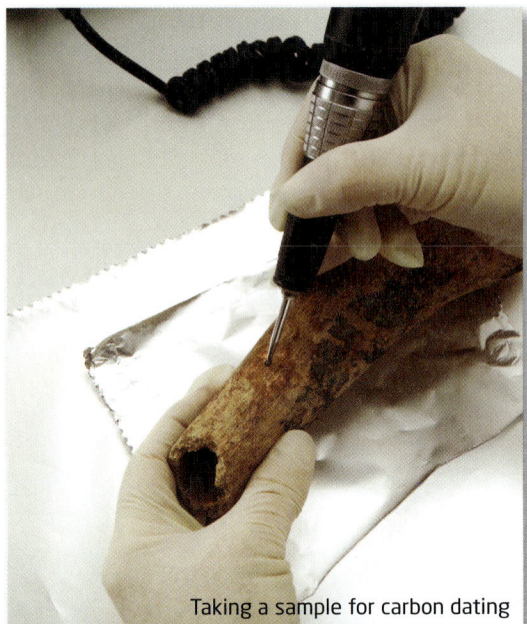

Taking a sample for carbon dating

D-wave wafer processor

> **Did You Know?**
>
> Moore's law describes a trend in the history of computing hardware. It states that the number of transistors that can be placed on an integrated circuit will double approximately every 2 years. The trend has continued for over half a century.

Investigate Transforming an Exponential Function

Materials
- graphing technology

Apply your prior knowledge of transformations to predict the effects of translations, stretches, and reflections on exponential functions of the form $f(x) = a(c)^{b(x-h)} + k$ and their associated graphs.

A: The Effects of Parameters h and k on the Function $f(x) = a(c)^{b(x-h)} + k$

1. a) Graph each set of functions on one set of coordinate axes. Sketch the graphs in your notebook.

   Set A
   i) $f(x) = 3^x$
   ii) $f(x) = 3^x + 2$
   iii) $f(x) = 3^x - 4$

   Set B
   i) $f(x) = 2^x$
   ii) $f(x) = 2^{x-3}$
   iii) $f(x) = 2^{x+1}$

b) Compare the graphs in set A. For any constant k, describe the relationship between the graphs of $f(x) = 3^x$ and $f(x) = 3^x + k$.

c) Compare the graphs in set B. For any constant h, describe the relationship between the graphs of $f(x) = 2^x$ and $f(x) = 2^{x-h}$.

Reflect and Respond

2. Describe the roles of the parameters h and k in functions of the form $f(x) = a(c)^{b(x-h)} + k$.

B: The Effects of Parameters *a* and *b* on the Function $f(x) = a(c)^{b(x-h)} + k$

3. a) Graph each set of functions on one set of coordinate axes. Sketch the graphs in your notebook.

Set C

 i) $f(x) = \left(\dfrac{1}{2}\right)^x$

 ii) $f(x) = 3\left(\dfrac{1}{2}\right)^x$

 iii) $f(x) = \dfrac{3}{4}\left(\dfrac{1}{2}\right)^x$

 iv) $f(x) = -4\left(\dfrac{1}{2}\right)^x$

 v) $f(x) = -\dfrac{1}{3}\left(\dfrac{1}{2}\right)^x$

Set D

 i) $f(x) = 2^x$

 ii) $f(x) = 2^{3x}$

 iii) $f(x) = 2^{\frac{1}{3}x}$

 iv) $f(x) = 2^{-2x}$

 v) $f(x) = 2^{-\frac{2}{3}x}$

What effect does the negative sign have on the graph?

b) Compare the graphs in set C. For any real value a, describe the relationship between the graphs of $f(x) = \left(\dfrac{1}{2}\right)^x$ and $f(x) = a\left(\dfrac{1}{2}\right)^x$.

c) Compare the graphs in set D. For any real value b, describe the relationship between the graphs of $f(x) = 2^x$ and $f(x) = 2^{bx}$.

Reflect and Respond

4. Describe the roles of the parameters a and b in functions of the form $f(x) = a(c)^{b(x-h)} + k$.

Link the Ideas

The graph of a function of the form $f(x) = a(c)^{b(x-h)} + k$ is obtained by applying transformations to the graph of the base function $y = c^x$, where $c > 0$.

Parameter	Transformation	Example
a	• Vertical stretch about the x-axis by a factor of $|a|$ • For $a < 0$, reflection in the x-axis • $(x, y) \rightarrow (x, ay)$	Graph showing $y = 3^x$, $y = 4(3)^x$, and $y = -2(3)^x$
b	• Horizontal stretch about the y-axis by a factor of $\frac{1}{|b|}$ • For $b < 0$, reflection in the y-axis • $(x, y) \rightarrow \left(\frac{x}{b}, y\right)$	Graph showing $y = 2^x$, $y = 2^{3x}$, and $y = 2^{-0.5x}$
k	• Vertical translation up or down • $(x, y) \rightarrow (x, y + k)$	Graph showing $y = 4^x$, $y = 4^x + 2$, and $y = 4^x - 3$
h	• Horizontal translation left or right • $(x, y) \rightarrow (x + h, y)$	Graph showing $y = 6^x$, $y = 6^{x+2}$, and $y = 6^{x-3}$

An accurate sketch of a transformed graph is obtained by applying the transformations represented by a and b before the transformations represented by h and k.

How does this compare to your past experience with transformations?

Example 1

Apply Transformations to Sketch a Graph

Consider the base function $y = 3^x$. For each transformed function,
i) state the parameters and describe the corresponding transformations
ii) create a table to show what happens to the given points under each transformation

$y = 3^x$
$\left(-1, \frac{1}{3}\right)$
(0, 1)
(1, 3)
(2, 9)
(3, 27)

iii) sketch the graph of the base function and the transformed function
iv) describe the effects on the domain, range, equation of the horizontal asymptote, and intercepts

a) $y = 2(3)^{x-4}$

b) $y = -\frac{1}{2}(3)^{\frac{1}{5}x} - 5$

Solution

a) i) Compare the function $y = 2(3)^{x-4}$ to $y = a(c)^{b(x-h)} + k$ to determine the values of the parameters.
 • $b = 1$ corresponds to no horizontal stretch.
 • $a = 2$ corresponds to a vertical stretch of factor 2. Multiply the y-coordinates of the points in column 1 by 2.
 • $h = 4$ corresponds to a translation of 4 units to the right. Add 4 to the x-coordinates of the points in column 2.
 • $k = 0$ corresponds to no vertical translation.
ii) Add columns to the table representing the transformations.

$y = 3^x$	$y = 2(3)^x$	$y = 2(3)^{x-4}$
$\left(-1, \frac{1}{3}\right)$	$\left(-1, \frac{2}{3}\right)$	$\left(3, \frac{2}{3}\right)$
(0, 1)	(0, 2)	(4, 2)
(1, 3)	(1, 6)	(5, 6)
(2, 9)	(2, 18)	(6, 18)
(3, 27)	(3, 54)	(7, 54)

7.2 Transformations of Exponential Functions • MHR **349**

iii) To sketch the graph, plot the points from column 3 and draw a smooth curve through them.

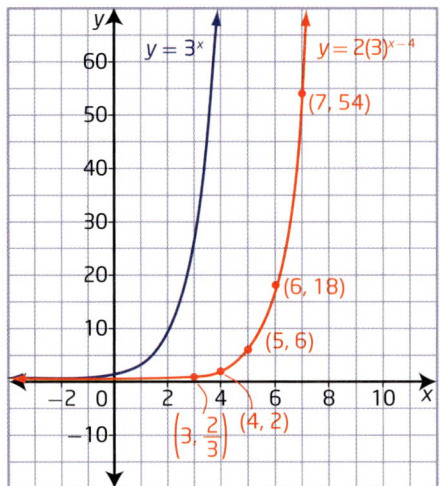

iv) The domain remains the same: $\{x \mid x \in \mathbb{R}\}$.

The range also remains unchanged: $\{y \mid y > 0, y \in \mathbb{R}\}$.

The equation of the asymptote remains as $y = 0$.

There is still no x-intercept, but the y-intercept changes to $\dfrac{2}{81}$ or approximately 0.025.

b) i) Compare the function $y = -\dfrac{1}{2}(3)^{\frac{1}{5}x} - 5$ to $y = a(c)^{b(x-h)} + k$ to determine the values of the parameters.

- $b = \dfrac{1}{5}$ corresponds to a horizontal stretch of factor 5. Multiply the x-coordinates of the points in column 1 by 5.
- $a = -\dfrac{1}{2}$ corresponds to a vertical stretch of factor $\dfrac{1}{2}$ and a reflection in the x-axis. Multiply the y-coordinates of the points in column 2 by $-\dfrac{1}{2}$.
- $h = 0$ corresponds to no horizontal translation.
- $k = -5$ corresponds to a translation of 5 units down. Subtract 5 from the y-coordinates of the points in column 3.

ii) Add columns to the table representing the transformations.

$y = 3^x$	$y = 3^{\frac{1}{5}x}$	$y = -\frac{1}{2}(3)^{\frac{1}{5}x}$	$y = -\frac{1}{2}(3)^{\frac{1}{5}x} - 5$
$\left(-1, \frac{1}{3}\right)$	$\left(-5, \frac{1}{3}\right)$	$\left(-5, -\frac{1}{6}\right)$	$\left(-5, -\frac{31}{6}\right)$
$(0, 1)$	$(0, 1)$	$\left(0, -\frac{1}{2}\right)$	$\left(0, -\frac{11}{2}\right)$
$(1, 3)$	$(5, 3)$	$\left(5, -\frac{3}{2}\right)$	$\left(5, -\frac{13}{2}\right)$
$(2, 9)$	$(10, 9)$	$\left(10, -\frac{9}{2}\right)$	$\left(10, -\frac{19}{2}\right)$
$(3, 27)$	$(15, 27)$	$\left(15, -\frac{27}{2}\right)$	$\left(15, -\frac{37}{2}\right)$

iii) To sketch the graph, plot the points from column 4 and draw a smooth curve through them.

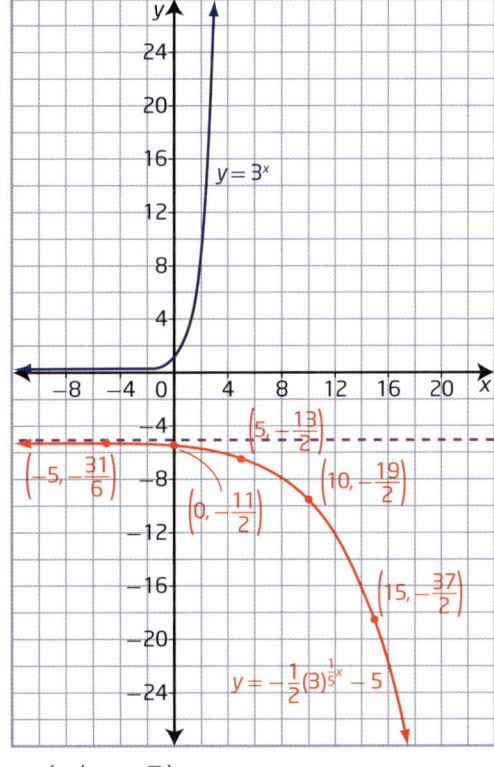

Why do the exponential curves have different horizontal asymptotes?

iv) The domain remains the same: $\{x \mid x \in \mathbb{R}\}$.

The range changes to $\{y \mid y < -5, y \in \mathbb{R}\}$ because the graph of the transformed function only exists below the line $y = -5$.

The equation of the asymptote changes to $y = -5$.

There is still no x-intercept, but the y-intercept changes to $-\frac{11}{2}$ or -5.5.

Your Turn

Transform the graph of $y = 4^x$ to sketch the graph of $y = 4^{-2(x+5)} - 3$. Describe the effects on the domain, range, equation of the horizontal asymptote, and intercepts.

Example 2

Use Transformations of an Exponential Function to Model a Situation

A cup of water is heated to 100 °C and then allowed to cool in a room with an air temperature of 20 °C. The temperature, T, in degrees Celsius, is measured every minute as a function of time, m, in minutes, and these points are plotted on a coordinate grid. It is found that the temperature of the water decreases exponentially at a rate of 25% every 5 min. A smooth curve is drawn through the points, resulting in the graph shown.

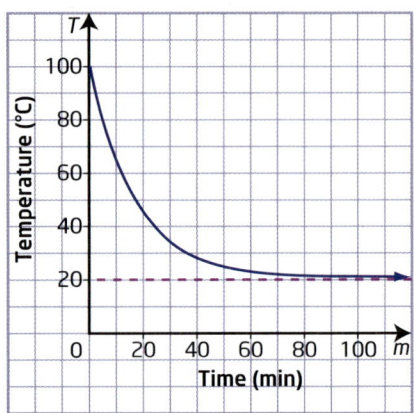

a) What is the transformed exponential function in the form $y = a(c)^{b(x-h)} + k$ that can be used to represent this situation?

b) Describe how each of the parameters in the transformed function relates to the information provided.

Solution

a) Since the water temperature decreases by 25% for each 5-min time interval, the base function must be $T(t) = \left(\frac{3}{4}\right)^t$, where T is the temperature and t is the time, in 5-min intervals.

Why is the base of the exponential function $\frac{3}{4}$ when the temperature is reduced by 25%?

The exponent t can be replaced by the rational exponent $\frac{m}{5}$, where m represents the number of minutes: $T(m) = \left(\frac{3}{4}\right)^{\frac{m}{5}}$.

What is the value of the exponent $\frac{m}{5}$ when $m = 5$? How does this relate to the exponent t in the first version of the function?

The asymptote at $T = 20$ means that the function has been translated vertically upward 20 units. This is represented in the function as $T(m) = \left(\frac{3}{4}\right)^{\frac{m}{5}} + 20$.

The T-intercept of the graph occurs at $(0, 100)$. So, there must be a vertical stretch factor, a. Use the coordinates of the T-intercept to determine a.

$$T(m) = a\left(\frac{3}{4}\right)^{\frac{m}{5}} + 20$$
$$100 = a\left(\frac{3}{4}\right)^{\frac{0}{5}} + 20$$
$$100 = a(1) + 20$$
$$80 = a$$

Substitute $a = 80$ into the function: $T(m) = 80\left(\frac{3}{4}\right)^{\frac{m}{5}} + 20$.

Check: Substitute $m = 20$ into the function. Compare the result to the graph.

$$T(m) = 80\left(\frac{3}{4}\right)^{\frac{m}{5}} + 20$$

$$T(20) = 80\left(\frac{3}{4}\right)^{\frac{20}{5}} + 20$$

$$= 80\left(\frac{3}{4}\right)^{4} + 20$$

$$= 80\left(\frac{81}{256}\right) + 20$$

$$= 45.3125$$

From the graph, the value of T when $m = 20$ is approximately 45. This matches the calculated value. Therefore, the transformed function that models the water temperature as it cools is $T(m) = 80\left(\frac{3}{4}\right)^{\frac{m}{5}} + 20$.

b) Based on the function $y = a(c)^{b(x-h)} + k$, the parameters of the transformed function are
- $b = \frac{1}{5}$, representing the interval of time, 5 min, over which a 25% decrease in temperature of the water occurs
- $a = 80$, representing the difference between the initial temperature of the heated cup of water and the air temperature of the room
- $h = 0$, representing the start time of the cooling process
- $k = 20$, representing the air temperature of the room

Your Turn

The radioactive element americium (Am) is used in household smoke detectors. Am-241 has a half-life of approximately 432 years. The average smoke detector contains 200 μg of Am-241.

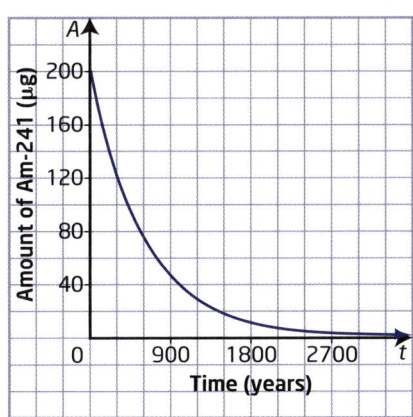

Did You Know?

In SI units, the symbol "μg" represents a microgram, or one millionth of a gram. In the medical field, the symbol "mcg" is used to avoid any confusion with milligrams (mg) in written prescriptions.

a) What is the transformed exponential function that models the graph showing the radioactive decay of 200 μg of Am-241?

b) Identify how each of the parameters of the function relates to the transformed graph.

Key Ideas

- To sketch the graph of an exponential function of the form $y = a(c)^{b(x-h)} + k$, apply transformations to the graph of $y = c^x$, where $c > 0$. The transformations represented by a and b may be applied in any order before the transformations represented by h and k.

- The parameters a, b, h, and k in exponential functions of the form $y = a(c)^{b(x-h)} + k$ correspond to the following transformations:
  - a corresponds to a vertical stretch about the x-axis by a factor of $|a|$ and, if $a < 0$, a reflection in the x-axis.
  - b corresponds to a horizontal stretch about the y-axis by a factor of $\frac{1}{|b|}$ and, if $b < 0$, a reflection in the y-axis.
  - h corresponds to a horizontal translation left or right.
  - k corresponds to a vertical translation up or down.

- Transformed exponential functions can be used to model real-world applications of exponential growth or decay.

Check Your Understanding

Practise

1. Match each function with the corresponding transformation of $y = 3^x$.
   a) $y = 2(3)^x$
   b) $y = 3^{x-2}$
   c) $y = 3^x + 4$
   d) $y = 3^{\frac{x}{5}}$

   A translation up
   B horizontal stretch
   C vertical stretch
   D translation right

2. Match each function with the corresponding transformation of $y = \left(\frac{3}{5}\right)^x$.
   a) $y = \left(\frac{3}{5}\right)^{x+1}$
   b) $y = -\left(\frac{3}{5}\right)^x$
   c) $y = \left(\frac{3}{5}\right)^{-x}$
   d) $y = \left(\frac{3}{5}\right)^x - 2$

   A reflection in the x-axis
   B reflection in the y-axis
   C translation down
   D translation left

3. For each function, identify the parameters a, b, h, and k and the type of transformation that corresponds to each parameter.
   a) $f(x) = 2(3)^x - 4$
   b) $g(x) = 6^{x-2} + 3$
   c) $m(x) = -4(3)^{x+5}$
   d) $y = \left(\frac{1}{2}\right)^{3(x-1)}$
   e) $n(x) = -\frac{1}{2}(5)^{2(x-4)} + 3$
   f) $y = -\left(\frac{2}{3}\right)^{2x-2}$
   g) $y = 1.5(0.75)^{\frac{x-4}{2}} - \frac{5}{2}$

4. Without using technology, match each graph with the corresponding function. Justify your choice.

a)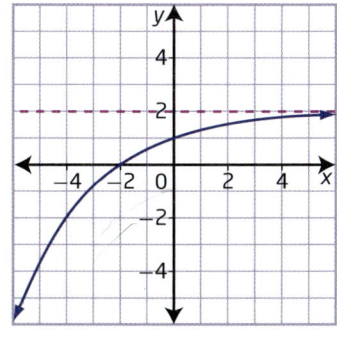

b)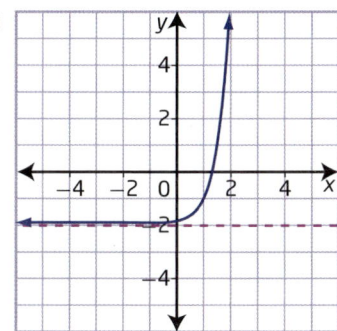

c)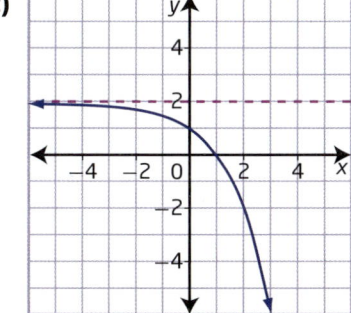

d)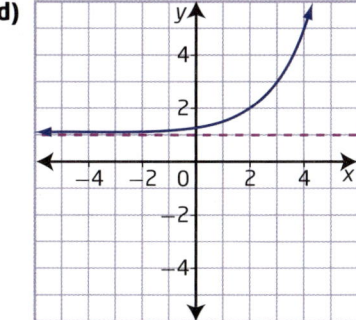

A $y = 3^{2(x-1)} - 2$

B $y = 2^{x-2} + 1$

C $y = -\left(\frac{1}{2}\right)^{\frac{1}{2}x} + 2$

D $y = -\frac{1}{2}(4)^{\frac{1}{2}(x+1)} + 2$

5. The graph of $y = 4^x$ is transformed to obtain the graph of $y = \frac{1}{2}(4)^{-(x-3)} + 2$.

a) What are the parameters and corresponding transformations?

b) Copy and complete the table.

$y = 4^x$	$y = 4^{-x}$	$y = \frac{1}{2}(4)^{-x}$	$y = \frac{1}{2}(4)^{-(x-3)} + 2$
$\left(-2, \frac{1}{16}\right)$			
$\left(-1, \frac{1}{4}\right)$			
(0, 1)			
(1, 4)			
(2, 16)			

c) Sketch the graph of $y = \frac{1}{2}(4)^{-(x-3)} + 2$.

d) Identify the domain, range, equation of the horizontal asymptote, and any intercepts for the function $y = \frac{1}{2}(4)^{-(x-3)} + 2$.

6. For each function,

i) state the parameters a, b, h, and k

ii) describe the transformation that corresponds to each parameter

iii) sketch the graph of the function

iv) identify the domain, range, equation of the horizontal asymptote, and any intercepts

a) $y = 2(3)^x + 4$

b) $m(r) = -(2)^{r-3} + 2$

c) $y = \frac{1}{3}(4)^{x+1} + 1$

d) $n(s) = -\frac{1}{2}\left(\frac{1}{3}\right)^{\frac{1}{4}s} - 3$

Apply

7. Describe the transformations that must be applied to the graph of each exponential function $f(x)$ to obtain the transformed function. Write each transformed function in the form $y = a(c)^{b(x-h)} + k$.

a) $f(x) = \left(\frac{1}{2}\right)^x$, $y = f(x-2) + 1$

b) $f(x) = 5^x$, $y = -0.5f(x-3)$

c) $f(x) = \left(\frac{1}{4}\right)^x$, $y = -f(3x) + 1$

d) $f(x) = 4^x$, $y = 2f\left(-\frac{1}{3}(x-1)\right) - 5$

8. For each pair of exponential functions in #7, sketch the original and transformed functions on the same set of coordinate axes. Explain your procedure.

9. The persistence of drugs in the human body can be modelled using an exponential function. Suppose a new drug follows the model $M(h) = M_0(0.79)^{\frac{h}{3}}$, where M is the mass, in milligrams, of drug remaining in the body; M_0 is the mass, in milligrams, of the dose taken; and h is the time, in hours, since the dose was taken.

   a) Explain the roles of the numbers 0.79 and $\frac{1}{3}$.

   b) A standard dose is 100 mg. Sketch the graph showing the mass of the drug remaining in the body for the first 48 h.

   c) What does the M-intercept represent in this situation?

   d) What are the domain and range of this function?

10. The rate at which liquids cool can be modelled by an approximation of Newton's law of cooling, $T(t) = (T_i - T_f)(0.9)^{\frac{t}{5}} + T_f$, where T_f represents the final temperature, in degrees Celsius; T_i represents the initial temperature, in degrees Celsius; and t represents the elapsed time, in minutes. Suppose a cup of coffee is at an initial temperature of 95 °C and cools to a temperature of 20 °C.

    a) State the parameters a, b, h, and k for this situation. Describe the transformation that corresponds to each parameter.

    b) Sketch a graph showing the temperature of the coffee over a period of 200 min.

    c) What is the approximate temperature of the coffee after 100 min?

    d) What does the horizontal asymptote of the graph represent?

11. A biologist places agar, a gel made from seaweed, in a Petri dish and infects it with bacteria. She uses the measurement of the growth ring to estimate the number of bacteria present. The biologist finds that the bacteria increase in population at an exponential rate of 20% every 2 days.

    a) If the culture starts with a population of 5000 bacteria, what is the transformed exponential function in the form $P = a(c)^{bx}$ that represents the population, P, of the bacteria over time, x, in days?

    b) Describe the parameters used to create the transformed exponential function.

    c) Graph the transformed function and use it to predict the bacteria population after 9 days.

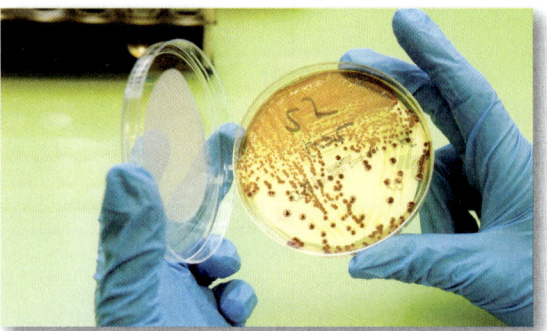

12. Living organisms contain carbon-12 (C-12), which does not decay, and carbon-14 (C-14), which does. When an organism dies, the amount of C-14 in its tissues decreases exponentially with a half-life of about 5730 years.

    a) What is the transformed exponential function that represents the percent, P, of C-14 remaining after t years?

    b) Graph the function and use it to determine the approximate age of a dead organism that has 20% of the original C-14 present in its tissues.

> **Did You Know?**
>
> Carbon dating can only be used to date organic material, or material from once-living things. It is only effective in dating organisms that lived up to about 60 000 years ago.

Extend

13. On Monday morning, Julia found that a colony of bacteria covered an area of 100 cm² on the agar. After 10 h, she found that the area had increased to 200 cm². Assume that the growth is exponential.

  a) By Tuesday morning (24 h later), what area do the bacteria cover?

  b) Consider Earth to be a sphere with radius 6378 km. How long would these bacteria take to cover the surface of Earth?

14. Fifteen years ago, the fox population of a national park was 325 foxes. Today, it is 650 foxes. Assume that the population has experienced exponential growth.

  a) Project the fox population in 20 years.

  b) What is one factor that might slow the growth rate to less than exponential? Is exponential growth healthy for a population? Why or why not?

Create Connections

C1 The graph of an exponential function of the form $y = c^x$ does not have an x-intercept. Explain why this occurs using an example of your own.

C2 a) Which parameters of an exponential function affect the x-intercept of the graph of the function? Explain.

  b) Which parameters of an exponential function affect the y-intercept of the graph of the function? Explain.

Project Corner — Modelling a Curve

It is not easy to determine the best mathematical model for real data. In many situations, one model works best for a limited period of time, and then another model is better. Work with a partner. Let x represent the time, in weeks, and let y represent the cumulative box office revenue, in millions of dollars.

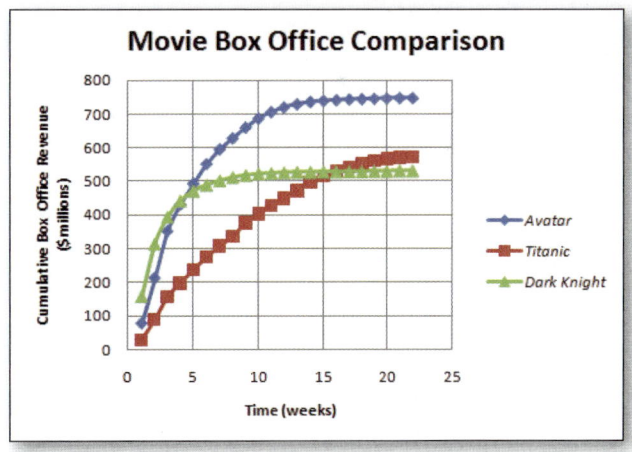

- The curves for *Avatar* and *Dark Knight* appear to have a horizontal asymptote. What do you think this represents in this context? Do you think the curve for *Titanic* will eventually exhibit this characteristic as well? Explain.

- Consider the curve for *Titanic*.
  - If the vertex is located at (22, 573), determine a quadratic function of the form $y = a(x - h)^2 + k$ that might model this portion of the curve.
  - Suppose that the curve has a horizontal asymptote with equation $y = 600$. Determine an exponential function of the form $y = -35(0.65)^{0.3(x-h)} + k$ that might model the curve.
  - Which type of function do you think better models this curve? Explain.

7.3

Solving Exponential Equations

Focus on...

- determining the solution of an exponential equation in which the bases are powers of one another
- solving problems that involve exponential growth or decay
- solving problems that involve the application of exponential equations to loans, mortgages, and investments

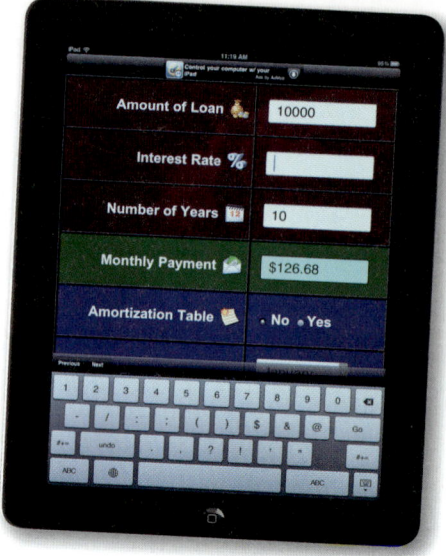

Banks, credit unions, and investment firms often have financial calculators on their Web sites. These calculators use a variety of formulas, some based on exponential functions, to help users calculate amounts such as annuity values or compound interest in savings accounts. For compound interest calculators, users must input the dollar amount of the initial deposit; the amount of time the money is deposited, called the term; and the interest rate the financial institution offers.

Did You Know?

In 1935, the first Franco-Albertan credit union was established in Calgary.

Investigate the Different Ways to Express Exponential Expressions

Materials

- graphing technology

1. a) Copy the table into your notebook and complete it by
- substituting the value of n into each exponential expression
- using your knowledge of exponent laws to rewrite each expression as an equivalent expression with base 2

n	$\left(\frac{1}{2}\right)^n$	2^n	4^n
-2	$\left(\frac{1}{2}\right)^{-2} = (2^{-1})^{-2}$ $= 2^2$		
-1			
0			
1			
2			$4^2 = (2^2)^2$ $= 2^4$

b) What patterns do you observe in the equivalent expressions? Discuss your findings with a partner.

358 MHR • Chapter 7

2. For each exponential expression in the column for 2^n, identify the equivalent exponential expressions with different bases in the other expression columns.

Reflect and Respond

3. a) Explain how to rewrite the **exponential equation** $2^x = 8^{x-1}$ so that the bases are the same.

b) Describe how you could use this information to solve for x. Then, solve for x.

c) Graph the exponential functions on both sides of the equation in part a) on the same set of axes. Explain how the point of intersection of the two graphs relates to the solution you determined in part b).

4. a) Consider the exponential equation $3^x = 4^{2x-1}$. Can this equation be solved in the same way as the one in step 3a)? Explain.

b) What are the limitations when solving exponential equations that have terms with different bases?

exponential equation
- an equation that has a variable in an exponent

Link the Ideas

Exponential expressions can be written in different ways. It is often useful to rewrite an exponential expression using a different base than the one that is given. This is helpful when solving exponential equations because the exponents of exponential expressions with the same base can be equated to each other. For example,

$4^{2x} = 8^{x+1}$
$(2^2)^{2x} = (2^3)^{x+1}$ Express the base on each side as a power of 2.
$2^{4x} = 2^{3x+3}$

Since the bases on both sides of the equation are now the same, the exponents must be equal.

Is this statement true for all bases? Explain.

$4x = 3x + 3$ Equate exponents.
$x = 3$

This method of solving an exponential equation is based on the property that if $c^x = c^y$, then $x = y$, for $c \neq -1, 0, 1$.

Example 1

Change the Base of Powers

Rewrite each expression as a power with a base of 3.

a) 27   **b)** 9^2 **c)** $27^{\frac{1}{3}}\left(\sqrt[3]{81}\right)^2$

Solution

a) $27 = 3^3$ 27 is the third power of 3.

b) $9^2 = (3^2)^2$ Write 9 as 3^2.
$\quad\;\; = 3^4$ Apply the power of a power law.

c) $27^{\frac{1}{3}}\left(\sqrt[3]{81}\right)^2 = 27^{\frac{1}{3}}\left(81^{\frac{2}{3}}\right)$ Write the radical in exponential form.
$\qquad\qquad\quad = (3^3)^{\frac{1}{3}}(3^4)^{\frac{2}{3}}$ Express the bases as powers of 3.
$\qquad\qquad\quad = 3^1\left(3^{\frac{8}{3}}\right)$ Apply the power of a power law.
$\qquad\qquad\quad = 3^{1 + \frac{8}{3}}$ Apply the product of powers law.
$\qquad\qquad\quad = 3^{\frac{11}{3}}$ Simplify.

Your Turn

Write each expression as a power with base 2.

a) 4^3 **b)** $\dfrac{1}{8}$ **c)** $8^{\frac{2}{3}}\left(\sqrt{16}\right)^3$

Example 2

Solve an Equation by Changing the Base

Solve each equation.

a) $4^{x+2} = 64^x$ **b)** $4^{2x} = 8^{2x-3}$

Solution

a) Method 1: Apply a Change of Base
$4^{x+2} = 64^x$
$4^{x+2} = (4^3)^x$ Express the base on the right side as a power with base 4.
$4^{x+2} = 4^{3x}$ Apply the power of a power law.

Since both sides are single powers of the same base, the exponents must be equal.

Equate the exponents.
$x + 2 = 3x$
$\quad\;\; 2 = 2x$ Isolate the term containing x.
$\quad\;\; x = 1$

Check:

Left Side	Right Side
4^{x+2}	64^x
$= 4^{1+2}$	$= 64^1$
$= 4^3$	$= 64$
$= 64$	

Left Side = Right Side

The solution is $x = 1$.

Method 2: Use a Graphing Calculator

Enter the left side of the equation as one function and the right side as another function. Identify where the graphs intersect using the intersection feature.

You may have to adjust the window settings to view the point of intersection.

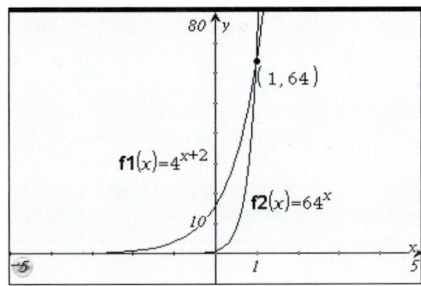

The graphs intersect at the point (1, 64).
The solution is $x = 1$.

b)
$$4^{2x} = 8^{2x-3}$$
$$(2^2)^{2x} = (2^3)^{2x-3} \quad \text{Express the bases on both sides as powers of 2.}$$
$$2^{4x} = 2^{6x-9} \quad \text{Apply the power of a power law.}$$
$$4x = 6x - 9 \quad \text{Equate the exponents.}$$
$$-2x = -9 \quad \text{Isolate the term containing } x.$$
$$x = \frac{9}{2} \quad \text{Solve for } x.$$

Check:

Left Side	Right Side
4^{2x}	8^{2x-3}
$= 4^{2\left(\frac{9}{2}\right)}$	$= 8^{2\left(\frac{9}{2}\right)-3}$
$= 4^9$	$= 8^{9-3}$
$= 262\ 144$	$= 8^6$
	$= 262\ 144$

Left Side = Right Side

The solution is $x = \frac{9}{2}$.

Your Turn

Solve. Check your answers using graphing technology.

a) $2^{4x} = 4^{x+3}$

b) $9^{4x} = 27^{x-1}$

Example 3

Solve Problems Involving Exponential Equations With Different Bases

Christina plans to buy a car. She has saved $5000. The car she wants costs $5900. How long will Christina have to invest her money in a term deposit that pays 6.12% per year, compounded quarterly, before she has enough to buy the car?

Solution

The formula for compound interest is $A = P(1 + i)^n$, where A is the amount of money at the end of the investment; P is the principal amount deposited; i is the interest rate per compounding period, expressed as a decimal; and n is the number of compounding periods. In this problem:
$A = 5900$
$P = 5000$
$i = 0.0612 \div 4$ or 0.0153 *Divide the interest rate by 4 because interest is paid quarterly or four times a year.*

Substitute the known values into the formula.
$A = P(1 + r)^n$
$5900 = 5000(1 + 0.0153)^n$
$1.18 = 1.0153^n$

You will learn how to solve equations like this algebraically when you study logarithms in Chapter 8.

The exponential equation consists of bases that cannot be changed into the same form without using more advanced mathematics.

Method 1: Use Systematic Trial
Use systematic trial to find the approximate value of n that satisfies this equation.

Substitute an initial guess into the equation and evaluate the result. Adjust the estimated solution according to whether the result is too high or too low.

Try $n = 10$.   *Why choose whole numbers for n?*
$1.0153^{10} = 1.1639...$, which is less than 1.18.

The result is less than the left side of the equation, so try a value of $n = 14$.
$1.0153^{14} = 1.2368...$, which is greater than 1.18.

The result is more than the left side of the equation, so try a value of $n = 11$.
$1.0153^{11} = 1.1817...$, which is approximately equal to 1.18.

The number of compounding periods is approximately 11.

Since interest is paid quarterly, there are four compounding periods in each year. Therefore, it will take approximately $\frac{11}{4}$ or 2.75 years for Christina's investment to reach a value of $5900.

Method 2: Use a Graphing Calculator

Enter the single function
$y = 1.0153^x - 1.18$ and identify where
the graph intersects the x-axis.

How is this similar to graphing the left side and right side of the equation and determining where the two graphs intersect?

You may have to adjust the window settings to view the point of intersection.

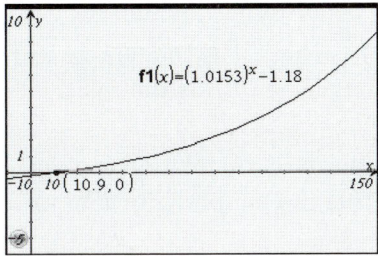

Use the features of the graphing calculator to show that the zero of the function is approximately 11.

Since interest is paid quarterly, there are four compounding periods in each year. Therefore, it will take approximately $\frac{11}{4}$ or 2.75 years for Christina's investment to reach a value of $5900.

Your Turn

Determine how long $1000 needs to be invested in an account that earns 8.3% compounded semi-annually before it increases in value to $1490.

Key Ideas

- Some exponential equations can be solved directly if the terms on either side of the equal sign have the same base or can be rewritten so that they have the same base.
  - If the bases are the same, then equate the exponents and solve for the variable.
  - If the bases are different but can be rewritten with the same base, use the exponent laws, and then equate the exponents and solve for the variable.
- Exponential equations that have terms with bases that you cannot rewrite using a common base can be solved approximately. You can use either of the following methods:
  - Use systematic trial. First substitute a reasonable estimate for the solution into the equation, evaluate the result, and adjust the next estimate according to whether the result is too high or too low. Repeat this process until the sides of the equation are approximately equal.
  - Graph the functions that correspond to the expressions on each side of the equal sign, and then identify the value of x at the point of intersection, or graph as a single function and find the x-intercept.

Check Your Understanding

Practise

1. Write each expression with base 2.
   a) 4^6
   b) 8^3
   c) $\left(\dfrac{1}{8}\right)^2$
   d) 16

2. Rewrite the expressions in each pair so that they have the same base.
   a) 2^3 and 4^2
   b) 9^x and 27
   c) $\left(\dfrac{1}{2}\right)^{2x}$ and $\left(\dfrac{1}{4}\right)^{x-1}$
   d) $\left(\dfrac{1}{8}\right)^{x-2}$ and 16^x

3. Write each expression as a single power of 4.
   a) $\left(\sqrt{16}\right)^2$
   b) $\sqrt[3]{16}$
   c) $\sqrt{16}\left(\sqrt[3]{64}\right)^2$
   d) $\left(\sqrt{2}\right)^8\left(\sqrt[4]{4}\right)^4$

4. Solve. Check your answers using substitution.
   a) $2^{4x} = 4^{x+3}$
   b) $25^{x-1} = 5^{3x}$
   c) $3^{w+1} = 9^{w-1}$
   d) $36^{3m-1} = 6^{2m+5}$

5. Solve. Check your answers using graphing technology.
   a) $4^{3x} = 8^{x-3}$
   b) $27^x = 9^{x-2}$
   c) $125^{2y-1} = 25^{y+4}$
   d) $16^{2k-3} = 32^{k+3}$

6. Solve for x using systematic trial. Check your answers using graphing technology. Round answers to one decimal place.
   a) $2 = 1.07^x$
   b) $3 = 1.1^x$
   c) $0.5 = 1.2^{x-1}$
   d) $5 = 1.08^{x+2}$

7. Solve for t graphically. Round answers to two decimal places, if necessary.
   a) $100 = 10(1.04)^t$
   b) $10 = \left(\dfrac{1}{2}\right)^{2t}$
   c) $12 = \left(\dfrac{1}{4}\right)^{\frac{t}{3}}$
   d) $100 = 25\left(\dfrac{1}{2}\right)^{\frac{t}{4}}$
   e) $2^t = 3^{t-1}$
   f) $5^{t-2} = 4^t$
   g) $8^{t+1} = 3^{t-1}$
   h) $7^{2t+1} = 4^{t-2}$

Apply

8. If seafood is not kept frozen (below 0 °C), it will spoil due to bacterial growth. The relative rate of spoilage increases with temperature according to the model $R = 100(2.7)^{\frac{T}{8}}$, where T is the temperature, in degrees Celsius, and R is the relative spoilage rate.
   a) Sketch a graph of the relative spoilage rate R versus the temperature T from 0 °C to 25 °C.
   b) Use your graph to predict the temperature at which the relative spoilage rate doubles to 200.
   c) What is the relative spoilage rate at 15 °C?
   d) If the maximum acceptable relative spoilage rate is 500, what is the maximum storage temperature?

   Did You Know?

   The relative rate of spoilage for seafood is defined as the shelf life at 0° C divided by the shelf life at temperature T, in degrees Celsius.

9. A bacterial culture starts with 2000 bacteria and doubles every 0.75 h. After how many hours will the bacteria count be 32 000?

10. Simionie needs $7000 to buy a snowmobile, but only has $6000. His bank offers a GIC that pays an annual interest rate of 3.93%, compounded annually. How long would Simionie have to invest his money in the GIC to have enough money to buy the snowmobile?

    Did You Know?

    A Guaranteed Investment Certificate (GIC) is a secure investment that guarantees 100% of the original amount that is invested. The investment earns interest, at either a fixed or a variable rate, based on a predetermined formula.

11. A $1000 investment earns interest at a rate of 8% per year, compounded quarterly.
    a) Write an equation for the value of the investment as a function of time, in years.
    b) Determine the value of the investment after 4 years.
    c) How long will it take for the investment to double in value?

12. Cobalt-60 (Co-60) has a half-life of approximately 5.3 years.
    a) Write an exponential function to model this situation.
    b) What fraction of a sample of Co-60 will remain after 26.5 years?
    c) How long will it take for a sample of Co-60 to decay to $\frac{1}{512}$ of its original mass?

13. A savings bond offers interest at a rate of 6.6% per year, compounded semi-annually. Suppose that you buy a $500 bond.
    a) Write an equation for the value of the investment as a function of time, in years.
    b) Determine the value of the investment after 5 years.
    c) How long will it take for the bond to triple in value?

14. Glenn and Arlene plan to invest money for their newborn grandson so that he has $20 000 available for his education on his 18th birthday. Assuming a growth rate of 7% per year, compounded semi-annually, how much will Glenn and Arlene need to invest today?

> **Did You Know?**
>
> When the principal, P, needed to generate a future amount is unknown, you can rearrange the compound interest formula to isolate P: $P = A(1 + i)^{-n}$. In this form, the principal is referred to as the present value and the amount is referred to as the future value. Then, you can calculate the present value, PV, the amount that must be invested or borrowed today to result in a specific future value, FV, using the formula $PV = FV(1 + i)^{-n}$, where i is the interest rate per compounding period, expressed as a decimal value, and n is the number of compounding periods.

Extend

15. a) Solve each inequality.
       i) $2^{3x} > 4^{x+1}$ ii) $81^x < 27^{2x+1}$
    b) Use a sketch to help you explain how you can use graphing technology to check your answers.
    c) Create an inequality involving an exponential expression. Solve the inequality graphically.

16. Does the equation $4^{2x} + 2(4^x) - 3 = 0$ have any real solutions? Explain your answer.

17. If $4^x - 4^{x-1} = 24$, what is the value of $(2^x)^x$?

18. The formula for calculating the monthly mortgage payment, PMT, for a property is $PMT = PV\left[\dfrac{i}{1 - (1 + i)^{-n}}\right]$, where PV is the present value of the mortgage; i is the interest rate per compounding period, as a decimal; and n is the number of payment periods. To buy a house, Tyseer takes out a mortgage worth $150 000 at an equivalent monthly interest rate of 0.25%. He can afford monthly mortgage payments of $831.90. Assuming the interest rate and monthly payments stay the same, how long will it take Tyseer to pay off the mortgage?

Create Connections

C1 a) Explain how you can write 16^2 with base 4.
   b) Explain how you can write 16^2 with two other, different, bases.

C2 The steps for solving the equation $16^{2x} = 8^{x-3}$ are shown below, but in a jumbled order.

$$2^{8x} = 2^{3x-9}$$
$$16^{2x} = 8^{x-3}$$
$$x = -\frac{9}{5}$$
$$8x = 3x - 9$$
$$(2^4)^{2x} = (2^3)^{x-3}$$
$$5x = -9$$

   a) Copy the steps into your notebook, rearranged in the correct order.
   b) Write a brief explanation beside each step.

Chapter 7 Review

7.1 Characteristics of Exponential Functions, pages 334–345

1. Match each item in set A with its graph from set B.

   Set A
   a) The population of a country, in millions, grows at a rate of 1.5% per year.
   b) $y = 10^x$
   c) Tungsten-187 is a radioactive isotope that has a half-life of 1 day.
   d) $y = 0.2^x$

   Set B

   A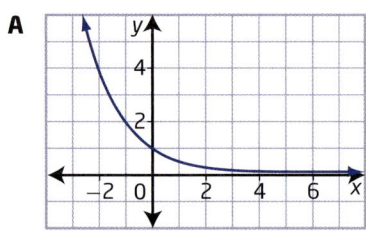

   B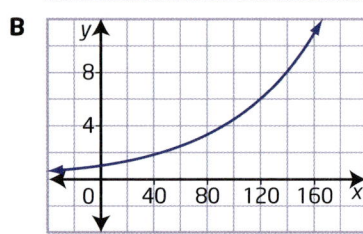

   C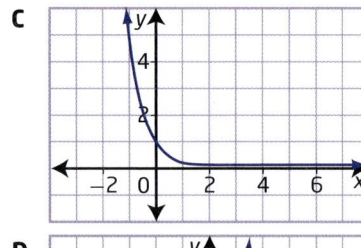

   D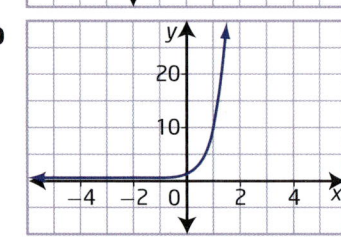

2. Consider the exponential function $y = 0.3^x$.
   a) Make a table of values and sketch the graph of the function.
   b) Identify the domain, range, intercepts, and intervals of increase or decrease, as well as any asymptotes.

3. What exponential function in the form $y = c^x$ is represented by the graph shown?

   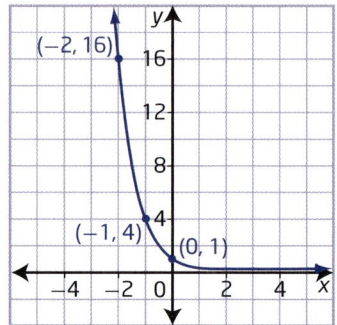

4. The value, v, of a dollar invested for t years at an annual interest rate of 3.25% is given by $v = 1.0325^t$.
   a) Explain why the base of the exponential function is 1.0325.
   b) What will be the value of $1 if it is invested for 10 years?
   c) How long will it take for the value of the dollar invested to reach $2?

7.2 Transformations of Exponential Functions, page 346–357

5. The graph of $y = 4^x$ is transformed to obtain the graph of $y = -2(4)^{3(x-1)} + 2$.
   a) What are the parameters and corresponding transformations?
   b) Copy and complete the table.

Transformation	Parameter Value	Function Equation
horizontal stretch		
vertical stretch		
translation left/right		
translation up/down		

   c) Sketch the graph of $y = -2(4)^{3(x-1)} + 2$.
   d) Identify the domain, range, equation of the horizontal asymptote, and any intercepts for the function $y = -2(4)^{3(x-1)} + 2$.

6. Identify the transformation(s) used in each case to transform the base function $y = 3^x$.

a)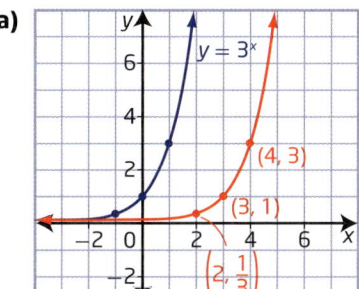

b)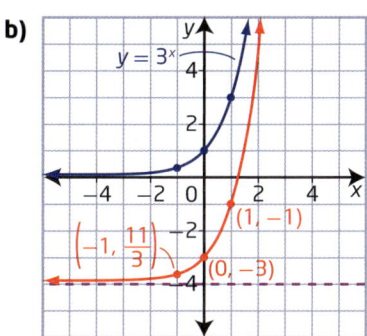

c)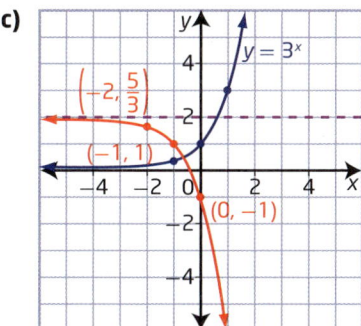

7. Write the equation of the function that results from each set of transformations, and then sketch the graph of the function.

   a) $f(x) = 5^x$ is stretched vertically by a factor of 4, stretched horizontally by a factor of $\frac{1}{2}$, reflected in the y-axis, and translated 1 unit up and 4 units to the left.

   b) $g(x) = \left(\frac{1}{2}\right)^x$ is stretched horizontally by a factor of $\frac{1}{4}$, stretched vertically by a factor of 3, reflected in the x-axis, and translated 2 units to the right and 1 unit down.

8. The function $T = 190\left(\frac{1}{2}\right)^{\frac{1}{10}t}$ can be used to determine the length of time, t, in hours, that milk of a certain fat content will remain fresh. T is the storage temperature, in degrees Celsius.

   a) Describe how each of the parameters in the function transforms the base function $T = \left(\frac{1}{2}\right)^t$.

   b) Graph the transformed function.

   c) What are the domain and range for this situation?

   d) How long will milk keep fresh at 22 °C?

7.3 Solving Exponential Equations, pages 358–365

9. Write each as a power of 6.

   a) 36

   b) $\frac{1}{36}$

   c) $\left(\sqrt[3]{216}\right)^5$

10. Solve each equation. Check your answers using graphing technology.

    a) $3^{5x} = 27^{x-1}$

    b) $\left(\frac{1}{8}\right)^{2x+1} = 32^{x-3}$

11. Solve for x. Round answers to two decimal places.

    a) $3^{x-2} = 5^x$

    b) $2^{x-2} = 3^{x+1}$

12. Nickel-65 (Ni-65) has a half-life of 2.5 h.

    a) Write an exponential function to model this situation.

    b) What fraction of a sample of Ni-65 will remain after 10 h?

    c) How long will it take for a sample of Ni-65 to decay to $\frac{1}{1024}$ of its original mass?

Chapter 7 Practice Test

Multiple Choice

For #1 to #5, choose the best answer.

1. Consider the exponential functions $y = 2^x$, $y = \left(\dfrac{2}{3}\right)^x$, and $y = 7^x$. Which value of x results in the same y-value for each?

   A -1

   B 0

   C 1

   D There is no such value of x.

2. Which statement describes how to transform the function $y = 3^x$ into $y = 3^{\frac{1}{4}(x-5)} - 2$?

   A stretch vertically by a factor of $\dfrac{1}{4}$ and translate 5 units to the left and 2 units up

   B stretch horizontally by a factor of $\dfrac{1}{4}$ and translate 2 units to the right and 5 units down

   C stretch horizontally by a factor of 4 and translate 5 units to the right and 2 units down

   D stretch horizontally by a factor of 4 and translate 2 units to the left and 5 units up

3. An antique automobile was found to double in value every 10 years. If the current value is $100 000, what was the value of the vehicle 20 years ago?

   A $50 000   B $25 000

   C $12 500   D $5000

4. What is $\dfrac{2^9}{(4^3)^2}$ expressed as a power of 2?

   A 2^{-3}

   B 2^3

   C 2^1

   D 2^{-1}

5. The intensity, I, in lumens, of light passing through the glass of a pair of sunglasses is given by the function $I(x) = I_0(0.8)^x$, where x is the thickness of the glass, in millimetres, and I_0 is the intensity of light entering the glasses. Approximately how thick should the glass be so that it will block 25% of the light entering the sunglasses?

   A 0.7 mm

   B 0.8 mm

   C 1.1 mm

   D 1.3 mm

Short Answer

6. Determine the function that represents each transformed graph.

   a)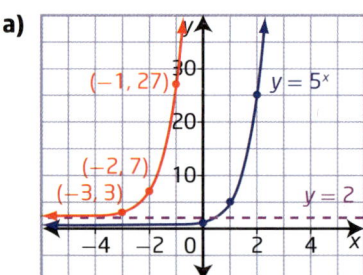

   b)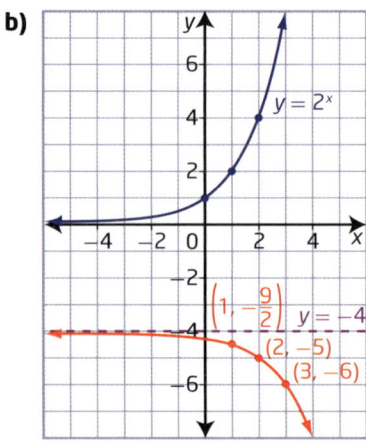

7. Sketch and label the graph of each exponential function.
   a) $y = \frac{1}{2}(3)^x + 2$
   b) $y = -2\left(\frac{3}{2}\right)^{x-1} - 2$
   c) $y = 3^{2(x+3)} - 4$

8. Consider the function $g(x) = 2(3)^{x+3} - 4$.
   a) Determine the base function for $g(x)$ and describe the transformations needed to transform the base function to $g(x)$.
   b) Graph the function $g(x)$.
   c) Identify the domain, the range, and the equation of the horizontal asymptote for $g(x)$.

9. Solve for x.
   a) $3^{2x} = 9^{\frac{1}{2}(x-4)}$
   b) $27^{x-4} = 9^{x+3}$
   c) $1024^{2x-1} = 16^{x+4}$

10. Solve each equation using graphing technology. Round answers to one decimal place.
    a) $3 = 1.12^x$
    b) $2.7 = 0.3^{2x-1}$

Extended Response

11. According to a Statistics Canada report released in 2010, Saskatoon had the fastest-growing population in Canada, with an annual growth rate of 2.77%.
    a) If the growth rate remained constant, by what factor would the population have been multiplied after 1 year?
    b) What function could be used to model this situation?
    c) What are the domain and range of the function for this situation?
    d) At this rate, approximately how long would it take for Saskatoon's population to grow by 25%?

12. The measure of the acidity of a solution is called its pH. The pH of swimming pools needs to be checked regularly. This is done by measuring the concentration of hydrogen ions (H⁺) in the water. The relationship between the hydrogen ion concentration, H, in moles per litre (mol/L), is $H(P) = \left(\frac{1}{10}\right)^P$, where P is the pH.

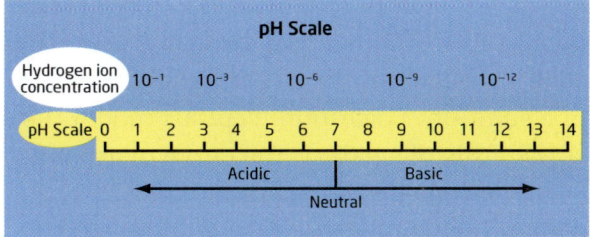

   a) Sketch the graph of this function.
   b) Water with a pH of less than 7.0 is acidic. What is the hydrogen ion concentration for a pH of 7.0?
   c) Water in a swimming pool should have a pH of between 7.0 and 7.6. What is the equivalent range of hydrogen ion concentration?

13. Lucas is hoping to take a vacation after he finishes university. To do this, he estimates he needs $5000. Lucas is able to finish his last year of university with $3500 in an investment that pays 8.4% per year, compounded quarterly. How long will Lucas have to wait before he has enough money to take the vacation he wants?

14. A computer, originally purchased for $3000, depreciates in value according to the function $V(t) = 3000\left(\frac{1}{2}\right)^{\frac{t}{3}}$, where V is the value, in dollars, of the computer at any time, t, in years. Approximately how long will it take for the computer to be worth 10% of its purchase price?

CHAPTER 8

Logarithmic Functions

Logarithms were developed over 400 years ago, and they still have numerous applications in the modern world. Logarithms allow you to solve any exponential equation. Logarithmic scales use manageable numbers to represent quantities in science that vary over vast ranges, such as the energy of an earthquake or the pH of a solution. Logarithmic spirals model the spiral arms of a galaxy, the curve of animal horns, the shape of a snail, the growth of certain plants, the arms of a hurricane, and the approach of a hawk to its prey.

In this chapter, you will learn what logarithms are, how to represent them, and how to use them to model situations and solve problems.

Did You Know?

Logarithms were developed independently by John Napier (1550–1617), from Scotland, and Jobst Bürgi (1552–1632), from Switzerland. Since Napier published his work first, he is given the credit. Napier was also the first to use the decimal point in its modern context.

Logarithms were developed before exponents were used. It was not until the end of the seventeenth century that mathematicians recognized that logarithms are exponents.

Key Terms
logarithmic function
logarithm
common logarithm
logarithmic equation

Career Link

A radiologist is a physician trained in diagnosing and treating disease and injury using medical-imaging techniques. Radiologists use X-rays, computerized tomography (CT), magnetic resonance imaging (MRI), positron emission tomography (PET), fusion imaging, and ultrasound. Since some of these imaging techniques involve the use of radioactive isotopes, radiologists have special training in radiation physics, the effects of radiation on the body, and radiation safety and protection.

Web Link

To learn more about a career in radiology, go to www.mcgrawhill.ca/school/learningcentres and follow the links.

8.1

Understanding Logarithms

Focus on…

- demonstrating that a logarithmic function is the inverse of an exponential function
- sketching the graph of $y = \log_c x$, $c > 0$, $c \neq 1$
- determining the characteristics of the graph of $y = \log_c x$, $c > 0$, $c \neq 1$
- explaining the relationship between logarithms and exponents
- expressing a logarithmic function as an exponential function and vice versa
- evaluating logarithms using a variety of methods

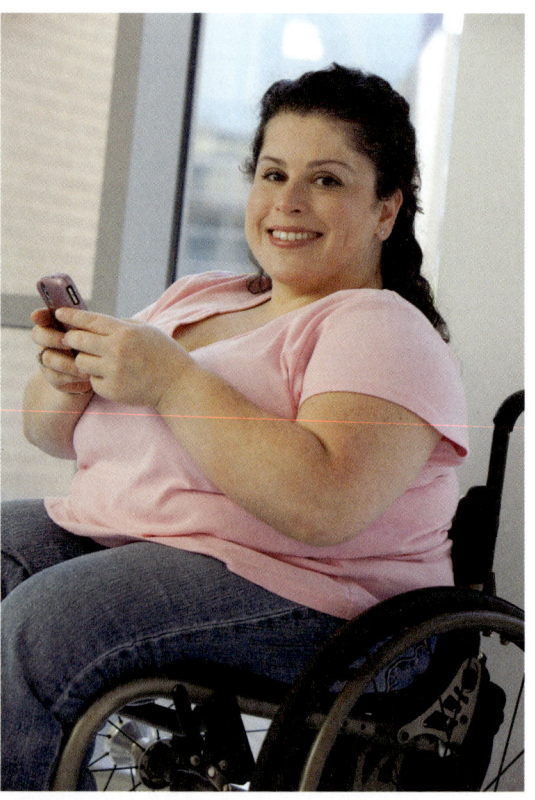

Do you have a favourite social networking site? Some social networking sites can be modelled by an exponential function, where the number of users is a function of time. You can use the exponential function to predict the number of users accessing the site at a certain time.

What if you wanted to predict the length of time required for a social networking site to be accessed by a certain number of users? In this type of relationship, the length of time is a function of the number of users. This situation can be modelled by using the inverse of an exponential function.

Investigate Logarithms

Materials
- grid paper

1. Use a calculator to determine the decimal approximation of the exponent, x, in each equation, to one decimal place.

 a) $10^x = 0.5$ **b)** $10^x = 4$ **c)** $10^x = 8$

2. a) Copy and complete the table of values for the exponential function $y = 10^x$ and then draw the graph of the function.

x	−1		0			1
y		0.5		4	8	

  b) Identify the following characteristics of the graph.

   i) the domain

   ii) the range

   iii) the x-intercept, if it exists

   iv) the y-intercept, if it exists

   v) the equation of any asymptotes

3. a) Copy and complete the table of values for $x = 10^y$, which is the inverse of $y = 10^x$. Then, draw the graph of the inverse function.

x		0.5		4	8	
y	−1		0			1

b) Identify the following characteristics of the inverse graph.
  i) the domain
  ii) the range
  iii) the x-intercept, if it exists
  iv) the y-intercept, if it exists
  v) the equation of the asymptote

4. Use the log function on a calculator to find the decimal approximation of each expression, to three decimal places. What do you notice about these values?
  a) log 0.5
  b) log 4
  c) log 8

Reflect and Respond

5. Explain how the graph of the exponential function $y = 10^x$ and its inverse graph are related.

6. Does the inverse graph represent a function? Explain.

7. Points on the inverse graph are of the form $(x, \log x)$. Explain the meaning of $\log x$.

Link the Ideas

For the exponential function $y = c^x$, the inverse is $x = c^y$. This inverse is also a function and is called a **logarithmic function**. It is written as $y = \log_c x$, where c is a positive number other than 1.

Logarithmic Form   **Exponential Form**

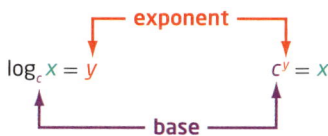

Since our number system is based on powers of 10, **logarithms** with base 10 are widely used and are called **common logarithms**. When you write a common logarithm, you do not need to write the base. For example, log 3 means $\log_{10} 3$.

logarithmic function
- a function of the form $y = \log_c x$, where $c > 0$ and $c \neq 1$, that is the inverse of the exponential function $y = c^x$

logarithm
- an exponent
- in $x = c^y$, y is called the logarithm to base c of x

common logarithm
- a logarithm with base 10

Example 1

Evaluating a Logarithm

Evaluate.

a) $\log_7 49$ **b)** $\log_6 1$ **c)** $\log 0.001$ **d)** $\log_2 \sqrt{8}$

Solution

a) The logarithm is the exponent that must be applied to base 7 to obtain 49. Determine the value by inspection.
Since $7^2 = 49$, the value of the logarithm is 2.
Therefore, $\log_7 49 = 2$.

b) The logarithm is the exponent that must be applied to base 6 to obtain 1.
Since, $6^0 = 1$, the value of the logarithm is 0.
Therefore, $\log_6 1 = 0$.

What is the value of any logarithm with an argument of 1? Why?

c) This is a common logarithm. You need to find the exponent that must be applied to base 10 to obtain 0.001.
Let $\log_{10} 0.001 = x$. Express in exponential form.
$10^x = 0.001$
$10^x = \dfrac{1}{1000}$
$10^x = \dfrac{1}{10^3}$
$10^x = 10^{-3}$
$x = -3$
Therefore, $\log 0.001 = -3$.

d) The logarithm is the exponent that must be applied to base 2 to obtain $\sqrt{8}$. Let $\log_2 \sqrt{8} = x$. Express in exponential form.
$2^x = \sqrt{8}$
$2^x = \sqrt{2^3}$
$2^x = (2^3)^{\frac{1}{2}}$ *Express the radical as a power with a rational exponent.*
$2^x = 2^{\frac{3}{2}}$
$x = \dfrac{3}{2}$
Therefore, $\log_2 \sqrt{8} = \dfrac{3}{2}$.

Your Turn

Evaluate.

a) $\log_2 32$ **b)** $\log_9 \sqrt[5]{81}$
c) $\log 1\,000\,000$ **d)** $\log_3 9\sqrt{3}$

> **Did You Know?**
>
> The input value for a logarithm is called an argument. For example, in the expression $\log_6 1$, the argument is 1.

If $c > 0$ and $c \neq 1$, then   *Why does c have these restrictions?*
- $\log_c 1 = 0$ since in exponential form $c^0 = 1$
- $\log_c c = 1$ since in exponential form $c^1 = c$
- $\log_c c^x = x$ since in exponential form $c^x = c^x$
- $c^{\log_c x} = x$, $x > 0$, since in logarithmic form $\log_c x = \log_c x$

The last two results are sometimes called the inverse properties, since logarithms and powers are inverse mathematical operations that undo each other. In $\log_c c^x = x$, the logarithm of a power with the same base equals the exponent, x. In $c^{\log_c x} = x$, a power raised to the logarithm of a number with the same base equals that number, x.

Example 2

Determine an Unknown in an Expression in Logarithmic Form

Determine the value of x.
a) $\log_5 x = -3$
b) $\log_x 36 = 2$
c) $\log_{64} x = \dfrac{2}{3}$

Solution

a) $\log_5 x = -3$
$\quad 5^{-3} = x$ *Express in exponential form.*
$\quad \dfrac{1}{125} = x$

b) $\log_x 36 = 2$
$\quad x^2 = 36$ *Express in exponential form.*
$\quad x = \pm\sqrt{36}$
Since the base of a logarithm must be greater than zero, $x = -6$ is not an acceptable answer. So, $x = 6$.

c) $\log_{64} x = \dfrac{2}{3}$
$\quad 64^{\frac{2}{3}} = x$ *Express in exponential form.*
$\quad (\sqrt[3]{64})^2 = x$
$\quad 4^2 = x$
$\quad 16 = x$

Your Turn

Determine the value of x.
a) $\log_4 x = -2$
b) $\log_{16} x = -\dfrac{1}{4}$
c) $\log_x 9 = \dfrac{2}{3}$

Example 3

Graph the Inverse of an Exponential Function

a) State the inverse of $f(x) = 3^x$.

b) Sketch the graph of the inverse. Identify the following characteristics of the inverse graph:
- the domain and range
- the x-intercept, if it exists
- the y-intercept, if it exists
- the equations of any asymptotes

Solution

a) The inverse of $y = f(x) = 3^x$ is $x = 3^y$ or, expressed in logarithmic form, $y = \log_3 x$. Since the inverse is a function, it can be written in function notation as $f^{-1}(x) = \log_3 x$.

How do you know that $y = \log_3 x$ is a function?

b) Set up tables of values for both the exponential function, $f(x)$, and its inverse, $f^{-1}(x)$. Plot the points and join them with a smooth curve.

$f(x) = 3^x$	
x	y
−3	$\frac{1}{27}$
−2	$\frac{1}{9}$
−1	$\frac{1}{3}$
0	1
1	3
2	9
3	27

$f^{-1}(x) = \log_3 x$	
x	y
$\frac{1}{27}$	−3
$\frac{1}{9}$	−2
$\frac{1}{3}$	−1
1	0
3	1
9	2
27	3

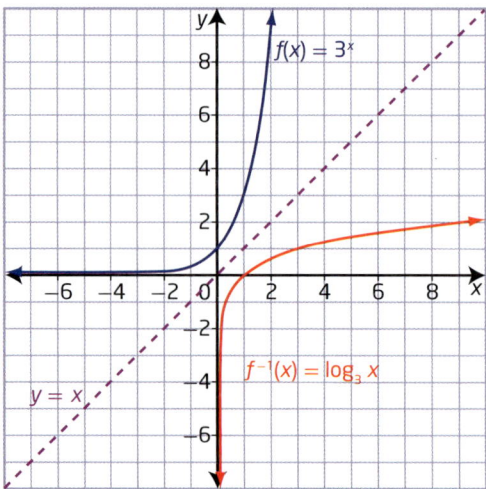

How are the values of x and y related in these two functions? Explain.

The graph of the inverse, $f^{-1}(x) = \log_3 x$, is a reflection of the graph of $f(x) = 3^x$ about the line $y = x$. For $f^{-1}(x) = \log_3 x$,

- the domain is $\{x \mid x > 0, x \in R\}$ and the range is $\{y \mid y \in R\}$
- the x-intercept is 1
- there is no y-intercept
- the vertical asymptote, the y-axis, has equation $x = 0$; there is no horizontal asymptote

How do the characteristics of $f^{-1}(x) = \log_3 x$ compare to the characteristics of $f(x) = 3^x$?

Your Turn

a) Write the inverse of $f(x) = \left(\dfrac{1}{2}\right)^x$.

b) Sketch the graphs of $f(x)$ and its inverse. Identify the following characteristics of the inverse graph:
- the domain and range
- the x-intercept, if it exists
- the y-intercept, if it exists
- the equations of any asymptotes

Example 4

Estimate the Value of a Logarithm

Without using technology, estimate the value of $\log_2 14$, to one decimal place.

Solution

The logarithm is the exponent that must be applied to base 2 to obtain 14.

Since $2^3 = 8$, $\log_2 8 = 3$.
Also, $2^4 = 16$, so $\log_2 16 = 4$.
Since 14 is closer to 16 than to 8, try an estimate of 3.7.

Then, $2^{3.7} \approx 13$, so $\log_2 13 \approx 3.7$. This is less than $\log_2 14$.

Try 3.8. Then, $2^{3.8} \approx 14$, so $\log_2 14 \approx 3.8$.

Your Turn

Without using technology, estimate the value of $\log_3 50$, to one decimal place.

Example 5

An Application of Logarithms

Naikoon Provincial Park, Haida Gwaii

In 1935, American seismologist Charles R. Richter developed a scale formula for measuring the magnitude of earthquakes. The Richter magnitude, M, of an earthquake is defined as $M = \log \dfrac{A}{A_0}$, where A is the amplitude of the ground motion, usually in microns, measured by a sensitive seismometer, and A_0 is the amplitude, corrected for the distance to the actual earthquake, that would be expected for a "standard" earthquake.

a) In 1946, an earthquake struck Vancouver Island off the coast of British Columbia. It had an amplitude that was $10^{7.3}$ times A_0. What was the earthquake's magnitude on the Richter scale?

b) The strongest recorded earthquake in Canada struck Haida Gwaii, off the coast of British Columbia, in 1949. It had a Richter reading of 8.1. How many times as great as A_0 was its amplitude?

c) Compare the seismic shaking of the 1949 Haida Gwaii earthquake with that of the earthquake that struck Vancouver Island in 1946.

Did You Know?

A "standard" earthquake has amplitude of 1 micron, or 0.0001 cm, and magnitude 0. Each increase of 1 unit on the Richter scale is equivalent to a tenfold increase in the intensity of an earthquake.

Solution

a) Since the amplitude of the Vancouver Island earthquake was $10^{7.3}$ times A_0, substitute $10^{7.3} A_0$ for A in the formula $M = \log \dfrac{A}{A_0}$.

$$M = \log \left(\dfrac{10^{7.3} A_0}{A_0} \right)$$

$M = \log 10^{7.3}$

$M = 7.3$ $\log_c c^x = x$, since in exponential form $c^x = c^x$.

The Vancouver Island earthquake had magnitude of 7.3 on the Richter scale.

b) Substitute 8.1 for M in the formula $M = \log \dfrac{A}{A_0}$ and express A in terms of A_0.

$$8.1 = \log \dfrac{A}{A_0}$$

$$10^{8.1} = \dfrac{A}{A_0} \quad \text{Write in exponential form.}$$

$$10^{8.1} A_0 = A$$

$$125\,892\,541 A_0 \approx A$$

The amplitude of the Haida Gwaii earthquake was approximately 126 million times the amplitude of a standard earthquake.

c) Compare the amplitudes of the two earthquakes.

$$\frac{\text{amplitude of Haida Gwaii earthquake}}{\text{amplitude of Vancouver Island earthquake}} = \frac{10^{8.1} \cancel{A_0}^{1}}{10^{7.3} \cancel{A_0}^{1}}$$

$$= \frac{10^{8.1}}{10^{7.3}}$$

$$\approx 6.3$$

The Haida Gwaii earthquake created shaking 6.3 times as great in amplitude as the Vancouver Island earthquake.

Your Turn

The largest measured earthquake struck Chile in 1960. It measured 9.5 on the Richter scale. How many times as great was the seismic shaking of the Chilean earthquake than the 1949 Haida Gwaii earthquake, which measured 8.1 on the Richter scale?

Key Ideas

- A logarithm is an exponent.
- Equations in exponential form can be written in logarithmic form and vice versa.

  Exponential Form **Logarithmic Form**
  $x = c^y$ $y = \log_c x$

- The inverse of the exponential function $y = c^x$, $c > 0$, $c \neq 1$, is $x = c^y$ or, in logarithmic form, $y = \log_c x$. Conversely, the inverse of the logarithmic function $y = \log_c x$, $c > 0$, $c \neq 1$, is $x = \log_c y$ or, in exponential form, $y = c^x$.

- The graphs of an exponential function and its inverse logarithmic function are reflections of each other in the line $y = x$, as shown.

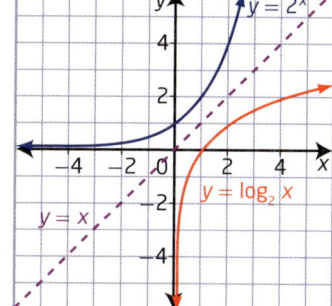

- For the logarithmic function $y = \log_c x$, $c > 0$, $c \neq 1$,
  - the domain is $\{x \mid x > 0, x \in R\}$
  - the range is $\{y \mid y \in R\}$
  - the x-intercept is 1
  - the vertical asymptote is $x = 0$, or the y-axis

- A common logarithm has base 10. It is not necessary to write the base for common logarithms:

  $\log_{10} x = \log x$

Check Your Understanding

Practise

1. For each exponential graph,
   i) copy the graph on grid paper, and then sketch the graph of the inverse on the same grid
   ii) write the equation of the inverse
   iii) determine the following characteristics of the inverse graph:
      - the domain and range
      - the x-intercept, if it exists
      - the y-intercept, if it exists
      - the equation of the asymptote

   a)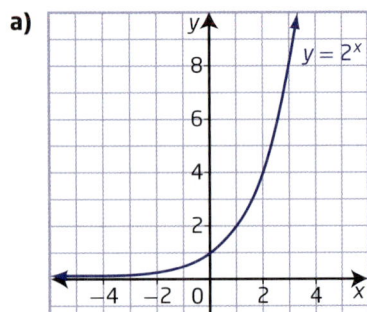

   b)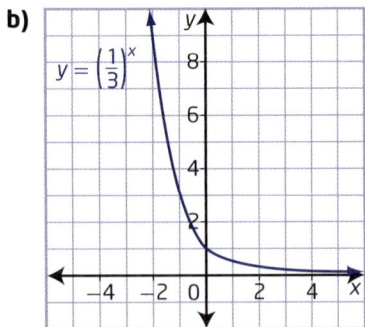

2. Express in logarithmic form.
   a) $12^2 = 144$
   b) $8^{\frac{1}{3}} = 2$
   c) $10^{-5} = 0.00001$
   d) $7^{2x} = y + 3$

3. Express in exponential form.
   a) $\log_5 25 = 2$
   b) $\log_8 4 = \frac{2}{3}$
   c) $\log 1\,000\,000 = 6$
   d) $\log_{11}(x + 3) = y$

4. Use the definition of a logarithm to evaluate.
   a) $\log_5 125$
   b) $\log 1$
   c) $\log_4 \sqrt[3]{4}$
   d) $\log_{\frac{1}{3}} 27$

5. Without using technology, find two consecutive whole numbers, a and b, such that $a < \log_2 28 < b$.

6. State a value of x so that $\log_3 x$ is
   a) a positive integer
   b) a negative integer
   c) zero
   d) a rational number

7. The base of a logarithm can be any positive real number except 1. Use examples to illustrate why the base of a logarithm cannot be
   a) 0
   b) 1
   c) negative

8. a) If $f(x) = 5^x$, state the equation of the inverse, $f^{-1}(x)$.
   b) Sketch the graph of $f(x)$ and its inverse. Identify the following characteristics of the inverse graph:
      - the domain and range
      - the x-intercept, if it exists
      - the y-intercept, if it exists
      - the equations of any asymptotes

9. a) If $g(x) = \log_{\frac{1}{4}} x$, state the equation of the inverse, $g^{-1}(x)$.
   b) Sketch the graph of $g(x)$ and its inverse. Identify the following characteristics of the inverse graph:
      - the domain and range
      - the x-intercept, if it exists
      - the y-intercept, if it exists
      - the equations of any asymptotes

Apply

10. Explain the relationship between the characteristics of the functions $y = 7^x$ and $y = \log_7 x$.

11. Graph $y = \log_2 x$ and $y = \log_{\frac{1}{2}} x$ on the same coordinate grid. Describe the ways the graphs are
  a) alike
  b) different

12. Determine the value of x in each.
  a) $\log_6 x = 3$
  b) $\log_x 9 = \dfrac{1}{2}$
  c) $\log_{\frac{1}{4}} x = -3$
  d) $\log_x 16 = \dfrac{4}{3}$

13. Evaluate each expression.
  a) 5^m, where $m = \log_5 7$
  b) 8^n, where $n = \log_8 6$

14. Evaluate.
  a) $\log_2 (\log_3 (\log_4 64))$
  b) $\log_4 (\log_2 (\log 10^{16}))$

15. Determine the x-intercept of $y = \log_7 (x + 2)$.

16. The point $\left(\dfrac{1}{8}, -3\right)$ is on the graph of the logarithmic function $f(x) = \log_c x$, and the point $(4, k)$ is on the graph of the inverse, $y = f^{-1}(x)$. Determine the value of k.

17. The growth of a new social networking site can be modelled by the exponential function $N(t) = 1.1^t$, where N is the number of users after t days.
  a) Write the equation of the inverse.
  b) How long will it take, to the nearest day, for the number of users to exceed 1 000 000?

18. The Palermo Technical Impact Hazard scale was developed to rate the potential hazard impact of a near-Earth object. The Palermo scale, P, is defined as $P = \log R$, where R is the relative risk. Compare the relative risks of two asteroids, one with a Palermo scale value of -1.66 and the other with a Palermo scale value of -4.83.

19. The formula for the Richter magnitude, M, of an earthquake is $M = \log \dfrac{A}{A_0}$, where A is the amplitude of the ground motion and A_0 is the amplitude of a standard earthquake. In 1985, an earthquake with magnitude 6.9 on the Richter scale was recorded in the Nahanni region of the Northwest Territories. The largest recorded earthquake in Saskatchewan occurred in 1982 near the town of Big Beaver. It had a magnitude of 3.9 on the Richter scale. How many times as great as the seismic shaking of the Saskatchewan earthquake was that of the Nahanni earthquake?

> **Did You Know?**
>
> Scientists at the Geological Survey of Canada office, near Sidney, British Columbia, record and locate earthquakes every day. Of the approximately 1000 earthquakes each year in Western Canada, fewer than 50 are strong enough to be felt by humans. In Canada, there have been no casualties directly related to earthquakes. A tsunami triggered by a major earthquake off the coast of California could be hazardous to the British Columbia coast.

20. If $\log_5 x = 2$, then determine $\log_5 125x$.

Extend

21. If $\log_3 (m - n) = 0$ and $\log_3 (m + n) = 3$, determine the values of m and n.

22. If $\log_3 m = n$, then determine $\log_3 m^4$, in terms of n.

23. Determine the equation of the inverse of $y = \log_2 (\log_3 x)$.

24. If $m = \log_2 n$ and $2m + 1 = \log_2 16n$, determine the values of m and n.

Create Connections

C1 Graph $y = |\log_2 x|$. Describe how the graph of $y = |\log_2 x|$ is related to the graph of $y = \log_2 x$.

C2 Create a mind map to summarize everything you know about the graph of the logarithmic function $y = \log_c x$, where $c > 0$ and $c \neq 1$. Enhance your mind map by sharing ideas with classmates.

C3 MINI LAB Recall that an irrational number cannot be expressed in the form $\frac{a}{b}$, where a and b are integers and $b \neq 0$. Irrational numbers cannot be expressed as a terminating or a repeating decimal. The number π is irrational. Another special irrational number is represented by the letter e. Its existence was implied by John Napier, the inventor of logarithms, but it was later studied by the Swiss mathematician Leonhard Euler. Euler was the first to use the letter e to represent it, and, as a result, e is sometimes called Euler's number.

Step 1 The number e can be approximated in a variety of ways.

  a) Use the e or e^x key on a calculator to find the decimal approximation of e to nine decimal places.

  b) You can obtain a better approximation of the number e by substituting larger values for x in the expression $\left(1 + \frac{1}{x}\right)^x$.

x	$\left(1 + \frac{1}{x}\right)^x$
10	2.593 742 460
100	2.704 813 829
1 000	2.716 923 932
10 000	2.718 145 927

As a power of 10, what is the minimum value of x needed to approximate e correctly to nine decimal places?

Step 2 **a)** Graph the inverse of the exponential function $y = e^x$. Identify the following characteristics of the inverse graph:
  • the domain and range
  • the x-intercept, if it exists
  • the y-intercept, if it exists
  • the equation of the asymptote

  b) A logarithm to base e is called a *natural logarithm*. The natural logarithm of any positive real number x is denoted by $\log_e x$ or $\ln x$. What is the inverse of the exponential function $y = e^x$?

Step 3 The shell of the chambered nautilus is a logarithmic spiral. Other real-world examples of logarithmic spirals are the horns of wild sheep, the curve of elephant tusks, the approach of a hawk to its prey, and the arms of spiral galaxies.

A logarithmic spiral can be formed by starting at point P(1, 0) and then rotating point P counterclockwise an angle of θ, in radians, such that the distance, r, from point P to the origin is always $r = e^{0.14\theta}$.

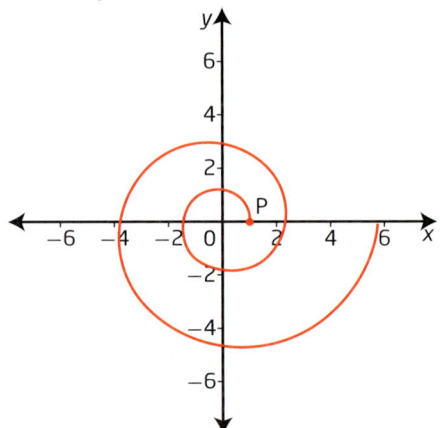

  a) Determine the distance, r, from point P to the origin after the point has rotated 2π. Round your answer to two decimal places.

  b) The spiral is logarithmic because the relationship between r and θ may be expressed using logarithms.

  i) Express $r = e^{0.14\theta}$ in logarithmic form.

  ii) Determine the angle, θ, of rotation that corresponds to a value for r of 12. Give your answer in radians to two decimal places.

8.2

Transformations of Logarithmic Functions

Focus on...

- explaining the effects of the parameters a, b, h, and k in $y = a \log_c (b(x - h)) + k$ on the graph of $y = \log_c x$, where $c > 1$
- sketching the graph of a logarithmic function by applying a set of transformations to the graph of $y = \log_c x$, where $c > 1$, and stating the characteristics of the graph

In some situations people are less sensitive to differences in the magnitude of a stimulus as the intensity of the stimulus increases. For example, if you compare a 50-W light bulb to a 100-W light bulb, the 100-W light bulb seems much brighter. However, if you compare a 150-W light bulb to a 200-W light bulb, they appear almost the same. In 1860, Gustav Fechner, the founder of psychophysics, proposed a logarithmic curve to describe this relationship.

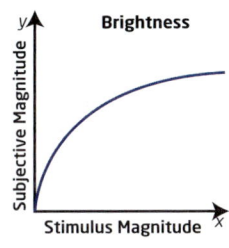

Describe another situation that might be modelled by a logarithmic curve.

Investigate Transformations of Logarithmic Functions

1. The graphs show how $y = \log x$ is transformed into $y = a \log (b(x - h)) + k$ by changing one parameter at a time. Graph 1 shows $y = \log x$ and the effect of changing one parameter. The effect on one key point is shown at each step. For graphs 1 to 4, describe the effect of the parameter introduced and write the equation of the transformed function.

2. Suppose that before the first transformation, $y = \log x$ is reflected in an axis. Describe the effect on the equation if the reflection is in

   a) the x-axis

   b) the y-axis

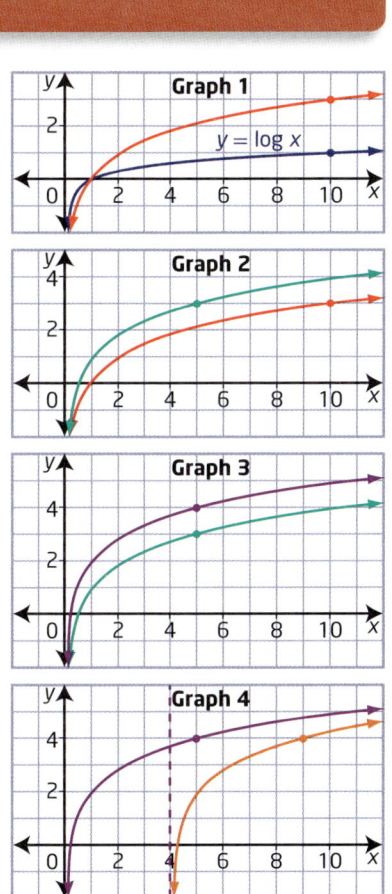

Reflect and Respond

3. In general, describe how the parameters a, b, h, and k in the logarithmic function $y = a \log_c (b(x - h)) + k$ affect the following characteristics of $y = \log_c x$.

   a) the domain

   b) the range

   c) the vertical asymptote

Link the Ideas

The graph of the logarithmic function $y = a \log_c (b(x - h)) + k$ can be obtained by transforming the graph of $y = \log_c x$. The table below uses mapping notation to show how each parameter affects the point (x, y) on the graph of $y = \log_c x$.

Parameter	Transformation
a	$(x, y) \rightarrow (x, ay)$
b	$(x, y) \rightarrow \left(\dfrac{x}{b}, y\right)$
h	$(x, y) \rightarrow (x + h, y)$
k	$(x, y) \rightarrow (x, y + k)$

How would you describe the effects of each parameter?

Example 1

Translations of a Logarithmic Function

a) Use transformations to sketch the graph of the function $y = \log_3 (x + 9) + 2$.

b) Identify the following characteristics of the graph of the function.
  i) the equation of the asymptote **ii)** the domain and range
  iii) the y-intercept, if it exists **iv)** the x-intercept, if it exists

Solution

a) To sketch the graph of $y = \log_3 (x + 9) + 2$, translate the graph of $y = \log_3 x$ to the left 9 units and up 2 units.

Choose some key points to sketch the base function, $y = \log_3 x$. Examine how the coordinates of key points and the position of the asymptote change. Each point (x, y) on the graph of $y = \log_3 x$ is translated to become the point $(x - 9, y + 2)$ on the graph of $y = \log_3 (x + 9) + 2$.

In mapping notation, $(x, y) \rightarrow (x - 9, y + 2)$.

$y = \log_3 x$	$y = \log_3 (x + 9) + 2$
$(1, 0)$	$(-8, 2)$
$(3, 1)$	$(-6, 3)$
$(9, 2)$	$(0, 4)$

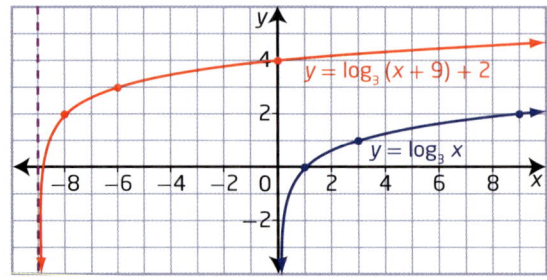

b) i) For $y = \log_3 x$, the asymptote is the y-axis, that is, the equation $x = 0$. For $y = \log_3 (x + 9) + 2$, the equation of the asymptote occurs when $x + 9 = 0$. Therefore, the equation of the vertical asymptote is $x = -9$.

ii) The domain is $\{x \mid x > -9, x \in R\}$ and the range is $\{y \mid y \in R\}$.

iii) To determine the y-intercept, substitute $x = 0$. Then, solve for y.
$y = \log_3 (0 + 9) + 2$
$y = \log_3 9 + 2$
$y = 2 + 2$
$y = 4$
The y-intercept is 4.

iv) To determine the x-intercept, substitute $y = 0$. Then, solve for x.
$$0 = \log_3 (x + 9) + 2$$
$$-2 = \log_3 (x + 9)$$
$$3^{-2} = x + 9$$
$$\frac{1}{9} = x + 9$$
$$-\frac{80}{9} = x$$

The x-intercept is $-\frac{80}{9}$ or approximately -8.9.

Your Turn

a) Use transformations to sketch the graph of the function $y = \log (x - 10) - 1$.

b) Identify the following characteristics of the graph of the function.
   i) the equation of the asymptote
   ii) the domain and range
   iii) the y-intercept, if it exists
   iv) the x-intercept, if it exists

Example 2

Reflections, Stretches, and Translations of a Logarithmic Function

a) Use transformations to sketch the graph of the function $y = -\log_2 (2x + 6)$.

b) Identify the following characteristics of the graph of the function.
   i) the equation of the asymptote
   ii) the domain and range
   iii) the y-intercept, if it exists
   iv) the x-intercept, if it exists

Solution

a) Factor the expression $2x + 6$ to identify the horizontal translation.
$y = -\log_2 (2x + 6)$
$y = -\log_2 (2(x + 3))$

To sketch the graph of $y = -\log_2(2(x + 3))$ from the graph of $y = \log_2 x$,

- horizontally stretch about the y-axis by a factor of $\frac{1}{2}$
- reflect in the x-axis
- horizontally translate 3 units to the left

Start by horizontally stretching about the y-axis by a factor of $\frac{1}{2}$. Key points on the graph of $y = \log_2 x$ change as shown.

In mapping notation, $(x, y) \rightarrow \left(\frac{1}{2}x, y\right)$.

$y = \log_2 x$	$y = \log_2 2x$
(1, 0)	(0.5, 0)
(2, 1)	(1, 1)
(4, 2)	(2, 2)
(8, 3)	(4, 3)

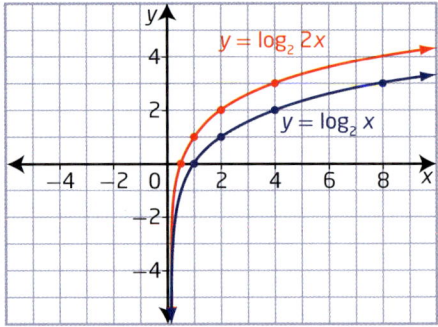

At this stage, the asymptote remains unchanged: it is the vertical line $x = 0$.

Next, reflect in the x-axis. The key points change as shown.

In mapping notation, $(x, y) \rightarrow (x, -y)$.

$y = \log_2 2x$	$y = -\log_2 2x$
(0.5, 0)	(0.5, 0)
(1, 1)	(1, −1)
(2, 2)	(2, −2)
(4, 3)	(4, −3)

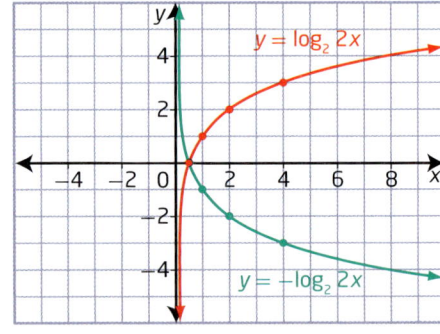

The asymptote is still $x = 0$ at this stage.

Lastly, translate horizontally 3 units to the left. The key points change as shown.

In mapping notation, $(x, y) \rightarrow (x - 3, y)$.

$y = -\log_2 2x$	$y = -\log_2(2(x + 3))$
(0.5, 0)	(−2.5, 0)
(1, −1)	(−2, −1)
(2, −2)	(−1, −2)
(4, −3)	(1, −3)

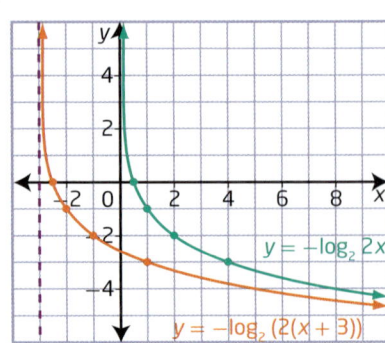

The asymptote is now shifted 3 units to the left to become the vertical line $x = -3$.

b) i) From the equation of the function, $y = -\log_2(2x + 6)$, the equation of the vertical asymptote occurs when $2x + 6 = 0$. Therefore, the equation of the vertical asymptote is $x = -3$.

ii) The domain is $\{x \mid x > -3, x \in R\}$ and the range is $\{y \mid y \in R\}$.

iii) To determine the y-intercept from the equation of the function, substitute $x = 0$. Then, solve for y.
$y = -\log_2(2(0) + 6)$
$y = -\log_2 6$ *Use a calculator to determine the approximate value.*
$y \approx -2.6$
The y-intercept is approximately -2.6.

iv) To determine the x-intercept from the equation of the function, substitute $y = 0$. Then, solve for x.
$0 = -\log_2(2x + 6)$
$0 = \log_2(2x + 6)$
$2^0 = 2x + 6$
$1 = 2x + 6$
$-5 = 2x$
$-\dfrac{5}{2} = x$
The x-intercept is $-\dfrac{5}{2}$ or -2.5.

Your Turn

a) Use transformations to sketch the graph of the function $y = 2\log_3(-x + 1)$.

b) Identify the following characteristics.
   i) the equation of the asymptote   **ii)** the domain and range
   iii) the y-intercept, if it exists   **iv)** the x-intercept, if it exists

Example 3

Determine the Equation of a Logarithmic Function Given Its Graph

The red graph can be generated by stretching the blue graph of $y = \log_4 x$. Write the equation that describes the red graph.

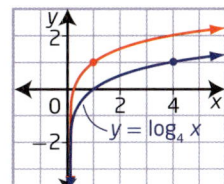

Solution

The red graph has been horizontally stretched since a vertical stretch does not change the x-intercept.

Method 1: Compare With the Graph of $y = \log_4 x$

The key point $(4, 1)$ on the graph of $y = \log_4 x$ has become the image point $(1, 1)$ on the red graph. Thus, the red graph can be generated by horizontally stretching the graph of $y = \log_4 x$ about the y-axis by a factor of $\dfrac{1}{4}$. The red graph can be described by the equation $y = \log_4 4x$.

Method 2: Use Points and Substitution

The equation of the red graph is of the form $y = \log_4 bx$. Substitute the coordinates of a point on the red graph, such as (4, 2), into the equation. Solve for b.

$y = \log_4 bx$
$2 = \log_4 4b$ Which other point could you have used?
$4^2 = 4b$
$4 = b$

The red graph can be described by the equation $y = \log_4 4x$.

Your Turn

The red graph can be generated by stretching and reflecting the graph of $y = \log_4 x$. Write the equation that describes the red graph.

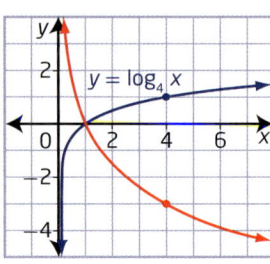

Example 4

An Application Involving a Logarithmic Function

Welding is the most common way to permanently join metal parts together. Welders wear helmets fitted with a filter shade to protect their eyes from the intense light and radiation produced by a welding light. The filter shade number, N, is defined by the function $N = \dfrac{7(-\log T)}{3} + 1$, where T is the fraction of visible light that passes through the filter. Shade numbers range from 2 to 14, with a lens shade number of 14 allowing the least amount of light to pass through.

The correct filter shade depends on the type of welding. A shade number 12 is suggested for arc welding. What fraction of visible light is passed through the filter to the welder, as a percent to the nearest ten thousandth?

Solution

Substitute 12 for N and solve for T.

$$12 = -\frac{7}{3} \log_{10} T + 1$$
$$11 = -\frac{7}{3} \log_{10} T$$
$$11\left(-\frac{3}{7}\right) = \log_{10} T$$
$$-\frac{33}{7} = \log_{10} T$$
$$10^{-\frac{33}{7}} = T$$
$$0.000\,019 \approx T$$

A filter shade number 12 allows approximately 0.000 019, or 0.0019%, of the visible light to pass through the filter.

Your Turn

There is a logarithmic relationship between butterflies and flowers. In one study, scientists found that the relationship between the number, F, of flower species that a butterfly feeds on and the number, B, of butterflies observed can be modelled by the function $F = -2.641 + 8.958 \log B$.

Predict the number of butterfly observations in a region with 25 flower species.

Arctic butterfly, oeneis chryxus

Did You Know?

Eighty-seven different species of butterfly have been seen in Nunavut. Northern butterflies survive the winters in a larval stage and manufacture their own antifreeze to keep from freezing. They manage the cool summer temperatures by angling their wings to catch the sun's rays.

Key Ideas

- To represent real-life situations, you may need to transform the basic logarithmic function $y = \log_b x$ by applying reflections, stretches, and translations. These transformations should be performed in the same manner as those applied to any other function.

- The effects of the parameters a, b, h, and k in $y = a \log_c (b(x - h)) + k$ on the graph of the logarithmic function $y = \log_c x$ are shown below.

    Vertically stretch by a factor of $|a|$ about the x-axis. Reflect in the x-axis if $a < 0$.

    Vertically translate k units.

    $$y = a \log_c (b(x - h)) + k$$

    Horizontally stretch by a factor of $\left|\frac{1}{b}\right|$ about the y-axis. Reflect in the y-axis if $b < 0$.

    Horizontally translate h units.

- Only parameter h changes the vertical asymptote and the domain. None of the parameters change the range.

Check Your Understanding

Practise

1. Describe how the graph of each logarithmic function can be obtained from the graph of $y = \log_5 x$.

   a) $y = \log_5 (x - 1) + 6$

   b) $y = -4 \log_5 3x$

   c) $y = \frac{1}{2} \log_5 (-x) + 7$

2. a) Sketch the graph of $y = \log_3 x$, and then apply, in order, each of the following transformations.
   - Stretch vertically by a factor of 2 about the x-axis.
   - Translate 3 units to the left.

   b) Write the equation of the final transformed image.

3. a) Sketch the graph of $y = \log_2 x$, and then apply, in order, each of the following transformations.
  - Reflect in the y-axis.
  - Translate vertically 5 units up.

b) Write the equation of the final transformed image.

4. Sketch the graph of each function.
  a) $y = \log_2 (x + 4) - 3$
  b) $y = -\log_3 (x + 1) + 2$
  c) $y = \log_4 (-2(x - 8))$

5. Identify the following characteristics of the graph of each function.
  i) the equation of the asymptote
  ii) the domain and range
  iii) the y-intercept, to one decimal place if necessary
  iv) the x-intercept, to one decimal place if necessary

  a) $y = -5 \log_3 (x + 3)$
  b) $y = \log_6 (4(x + 9))$
  c) $y = \log_5 (x + 3) - 2$
  d) $y = -3 \log_2 (x + 1) - 6$

6. In each, the red graph is a stretch of the blue graph. Write the equation of each red graph.

a)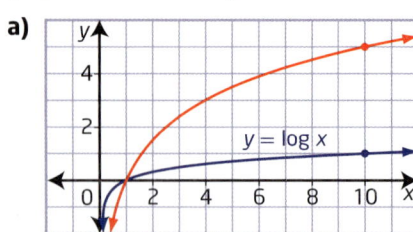

b)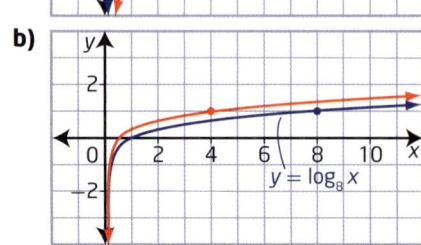

c)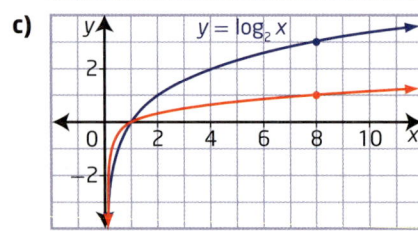

d)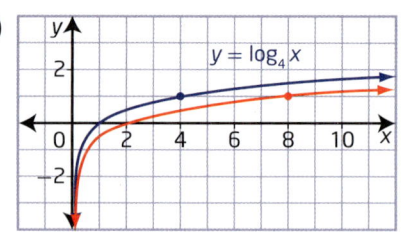

7. Describe, in order, a series of transformations that could be applied to the graph of $y = \log_7 x$ to obtain the graph of each function.
  a) $y = \log_7 (4(x + 5)) + 6$
  b) $y = 2 \log_7 \left(-\frac{1}{3}(x - 1)\right) - 4$

Apply

8. The graph of $y = \log_3 x$ has been transformed to $y = a \log_3 (b(x - h)) + k$. Find the values of a, b, h, and k for each set of transformations. Write the equation of the transformed function.

  a) a reflection in the x-axis and a translation of 6 units left and 3 units up

  b) a vertical stretch by a factor of 5 about the x-axis and a horizontal stretch about the y-axis by a factor of $\frac{1}{3}$

  c) a vertical stretch about the x-axis by a factor of $\frac{3}{4}$, a horizontal stretch about the y-axis by a factor of 4, a reflection in the y-axis, and a translation of 2 units right and 5 units down

9. Describe how the graph of each logarithmic function could be obtained from the graph of $y = \log_3 x$.
  a) $y = 5 \log_3 (-4x + 12) - 2$
  b) $y = -\frac{1}{4} \log_3 (6 - x) + 1$

10. a) Only a vertical translation has been applied to the graph of $y = \log_3 x$ so that the graph of the transformed image passes through the point $(9, -4)$. Determine the equation of the transformed image.

  b) Only a horizontal stretch has been applied to the graph of $y = \log_2 x$ so that the graph of the transformed image passes through the point $(8, 1)$. Determine the equation of the transformed image.

11. Explain how the graph of $\frac{1}{3}(y + 2) = \log_6 (x - 4)$ can be generated by transforming the graph of $y = \log_6 x$.

12. The equivalent amount of energy, E, in kilowatt-hours (kWh), released for an earthquake with a Richter magnitude of R is determined by the function $R = 0.67 \log 0.36E + 1.46$.

    a) Describe how the function is transformed from $R = \log E$.

    b) The strongest earthquake in Eastern Canada occurred in 1963 at Charlevoix, Québec. It had a Richter magnitude of 7.0. What was the equivalent amount of energy released, to the nearest kilowatt-hour?

13. In a study, doctors found that in young people the arterial blood pressure, P, in millimetres of mercury (mmHg), is related to the vessel volume, V, in microlitres (µL), of the radial artery by the logarithmic function $V = 0.23 + 0.35 \log (P - 56.1)$, $P > 56.1$.

    a) To the nearest tenth of a microlitre, predict the vessel volume when the arterial blood pressure is 110 mmHg.

    b) To the nearest millimetre of mercury, predict the arterial blood pressure when the vessel volume is 0.7 µL.

14. According to the Ehrenberg relation, the average measurements of heights, h, in centimetres, and masses, m, in kilograms, of children between the ages of 5 and 13 are related by the function $\log m = 0.008h + 0.4$.

    a) Predict the height of a 10-year-old child with a mass of 60 kg, to the nearest centimetre.

    b) Predict the mass of a 12-year-old child with a height of 150 cm, to the nearest kilogram.

Extend

15. The graph of $f(x) = \log_8 x$ can also be described by the equation $g(x) = a \log_2 x$. Find the value of a.

16. Determine the equation of the transformed image after the transformations described are applied to the given graph.

    a) The graph of $y = 2 \log_5 x - 7$ is reflected in the x-axis and translated 6 units up.

    b) The graph of $y = \log (6(x - 3))$ is stretched horizontally about the y-axis by a factor of 3 and translated 9 units left.

17. The graph of $f(x) = \log_2 x$ has been transformed to $g(x) = a \log_2 x + k$. The transformed image passes through the points $\left(\frac{1}{4}, -9\right)$ and $(16, -6)$. Determine the values of a and k.

Create Connections

C1 The graph of $f(x) = 5^x$ is
- reflected in the line $y = x$
- vertically stretched about the x-axis by a factor of $\frac{1}{4}$
- horizontally stretched about the y-axis by a factor of 3
- translated 4 units right and 1 unit down

If the equation of the transformed image is written in the form $g(x) = a \log_c (b(x - h)) + k$, determine the values of a, b, h, and k. Write the equation of the function $g(x)$.

C2 a) Given $f(x) = \log_2 x$, write the equations for the functions $y = -f(x)$, $y = f(-x)$, and $y = f^{-1}(x)$.

b) Sketch the graphs of the four functions in part a). Describe how each transformed graph can be obtained from the graph of $f(x) = \log_2 x$.

C3 a) The graph of $y = 3(7^{2x-1}) + 5$ is reflected in the line $y = x$. What is the equation of the transformed image?

b) If $f(x) = 2 \log_3 (x - 1) + 8$, find the equation of $f^{-1}(x)$.

C4 Create a poster, digital presentation, or video to illustrate the different transformations you studied in this section.

8.3

Laws of Logarithms

Focus on...
- developing the laws of logarithms
- determining an equivalent form of a logarithmic expression using the laws of logarithms
- applying the laws of logarithms to logarithmic scales

Today you probably take hand-held calculators for granted. But John Napier, the inventor of logarithms, lived in a time when scientists, especially astronomers, spent much time performing tedious arithmetic calculations on paper. Logarithms revolutionized mathematics and science by simplifying these calculations. Using the laws of logarithms, you can convert multiplication to addition and division to subtraction. The French mathematician and astronomer Pierre-Simon Laplace claimed that logarithms, "by shortening the labours, doubled the life of the astronomer." This allowed scientists to be more productive. Many of the advances in science would not have been possible without the invention of logarithms.

The laws that made logarithms so useful as a calculation tool are still important. They can be used to simplify logarithmic functions and expressions and in solving both exponential and logarithmic equations.

> **Did You Know?**
>
> The world's first hand-held scientific calculator was the Hewlett-Packard HP-35, so called because it had 35 keys. Introduced in 1972, it retailed for approximately U.S. $395. Market research at the time warned that the demand for a pocket-sized calculator was too small. Hewlett-Packard estimated that they needed to sell 10 000 calculators in the first year to break even. They ended up selling 10 times that. By the time it was discontinued in 1975, sales of the HP-35 exceeded 300 000.

Investigate the Laws of Logarithms

1. a) Show that $\log (1000 \times 100) \neq (\log 1000)(\log 100)$.

  b) Use a calculator to find the approximate value of each expression, to four decimal places.

  i) $\log 6 + \log 5$ **ii)** $\log 21$

  iii) $\log 11 + \log 9$ **iv)** $\log 99$

  v) $\log 7 + \log 3$ **vi)** $\log 30$

c) Based on the results in part b), suggest a possible law for
log M + log N, where M and N are positive real numbers.

d) Use your conjecture from part c) to express log 1000 + log 100 as a single logarithm.

2. a) Show that $\log \dfrac{1000}{100} \neq \dfrac{\log 1000}{\log 100}$.

b) Use a calculator to find the approximate value of each expression, to four decimal places.

  i) log 12
  ii) log 35 − log 5
  iii) log 36
  iv) log 72 − log 2
  v) log 48 − log 4
  vi) log 7

c) Based on the results in part b), suggest a possible law for
log M − log N, where M and N are positive real numbers.

d) Use your conjecture from part c) to express log 1000 − log 100 as a single logarithm.

3. a) Show that $\log 1000^2 \neq (\log 1000)^2$.

b) Use a calculator to find the approximate value of each expression, to four decimal places.

  i) 3 log 5
  ii) log 49
  iii) log 125
  iv) log 16
  v) 4 log 2
  vi) 2 log 7

c) Based on the results in part b), suggest a possible law for P log M, where M is a positive real number and P is any real number.

d) Use your conjecture from part c) to express 2 log 1000 as a logarithm without a coefficient.

Reflect and Respond

4. The laws of common logarithms are also true for any logarithm with a base that is a positive real number other than 1. Without using technology, evaluate each of the following.

   a) $\log_6 18 + \log_6 2$

   b) $\log_2 40 - \log_2 5$

   c) $4 \log_9 3$

5. Each of the three laws of logarithms corresponds to one of the three laws of powers:

   • product law of powers: $(c^x)(c^y) = c^{x+y}$

   • quotient law of powers: $\dfrac{c^x}{c^y} = c^{x-y}, c \neq 0$

   • power of a power law: $(c^x)^y = c^{xy}$

   Explain how the laws of logarithms are related to the laws of powers.

Link the Ideas

Since logarithms are exponents, the laws of logarithms are related to the laws of powers.

Product Law of Logarithms

The logarithm of a product of numbers can be expressed as the sum of the logarithms of the numbers.

$$\log_c MN = \log_c M + \log_c N$$

Proof

Let $\log_c M = x$ and $\log_c N = y$, where M, N, and c are positive real numbers with $c \neq 1$.

Write the equations in exponential form as $M = c^x$ and $N = c^y$:

$$MN = (c^x)(c^y)$$
$$MN = c^{x+y} \quad \text{Apply the product law of powers.}$$
$$\log_c MN = x + y \quad \text{Write in logarithmic form.}$$
$$\log_c MN = \log_c M + \log_c N \quad \text{Substitute for } x \text{ and } y.$$

Quotient Law of Logarithms

The logarithm of a quotient of numbers can be expressed as the difference of the logarithms of the dividend and the divisor.

$$\log_c \frac{M}{N} = \log_c M - \log_c N$$

Proof

Let $\log_c M = x$ and $\log_c N = y$, where M, N, and c are positive real numbers with $c \neq 1$.

Write the equations in exponential form as $M = c^x$ and $N = c^y$:

$$\frac{M}{N} = \frac{c^x}{c^y}$$
$$\frac{M}{N} = c^{x-y} \quad \text{Apply the quotient law of powers.}$$
$$\log_c \frac{M}{N} = x - y \quad \text{Write in logarithmic form.}$$
$$\log_c \frac{M}{N} = \log_c M - \log_c N \quad \text{Substitute for } x \text{ and } y.$$

Power Law of Logarithms

The logarithm of a power of a number can be expressed as the exponent times the logarithm of the number.

$$\log_c M^P = P \log_c M$$

How could you prove the quotient law using the product law and the power law?

Proof

Let $\log_c M = x$, where M and c are positive real numbers with $c \neq 1$.

Write the equation in exponential form as $M = c^x$.

Let P be a real number.

$$M = c^x$$
$$M^P = (c^x)^P$$
$$M^P = c^{xP} \quad \text{Simplify the exponents.}$$
$$\log_c M^P = xP \quad \text{Write in logarithmic form.}$$
$$\log_c M^P = (\log_c M)P \quad \text{Substitute for } x.$$
$$\log_c M^P = P \log_c M$$

The laws of logarithms can be applied to logarithmic functions, expressions, and equations.

Example 1

Use the Laws of Logarithms to Expand Expressions

Write each expression in terms of individual logarithms of x, y, and z.

a) $\log_5 \dfrac{xy}{z}$

b) $\log_7 \sqrt[3]{x}$

c) $\log_6 \dfrac{1}{x^2}$

d) $\log \dfrac{x^3}{y\sqrt{z}}$

Solution

a) $\log_5 \dfrac{xy}{z} = \log_5 xy - \log_5 z$
$\phantom{\log_5 \dfrac{xy}{z}} = \log_5 x + \log_5 y - \log_5 z$

b) $\log_7 \sqrt[3]{x} = \log_7 x^{\frac{1}{3}}$
$\phantom{\log_7 \sqrt[3]{x}} = \dfrac{1}{3} \log_7 x$

c) $\log_6 \dfrac{1}{x^2} = \log_6 x^{-2}$ You could also start by applying the quotient law to
$\phantom{\log_6 \dfrac{1}{x^2}} = -2 \log_6 x$ the original expression. Try this. You should arrive at the same answer.

d) $\log \dfrac{x^3}{y\sqrt{z}} = \log x^3 - \log y\sqrt{z}$
$\phantom{\log \dfrac{x^3}{y\sqrt{z}}} = \log x^3 - \left(\log y + \log z^{\frac{1}{2}}\right)$
$\phantom{\log \dfrac{x^3}{y\sqrt{z}}} = 3 \log x - \log y - \dfrac{1}{2} \log z$

Your Turn

Write each expression in terms of individual logarithms of x, y, and z.

a) $\log_6 \dfrac{x}{y}$

b) $\log_5 \sqrt{xy}$

c) $\log_3 \dfrac{9}{\sqrt[3]{x^2}}$

d) $\log_7 \dfrac{x^5 y}{\sqrt{z}}$

Example 2
Use the Laws of Logarithms to Evaluate Expressions

Use the laws of logarithms to simplify and evaluate each expression.
a) $\log_6 8 + \log_6 9 - \log_6 2$
b) $\log_7 7\sqrt{7}$
c) $2 \log_2 12 - \left(\log_2 6 + \frac{1}{3} \log_2 27\right)$

Solution

a) $\quad \log_6 8 + \log_6 9 - \log_6 2$
$= \log_6 \frac{8 \times 9}{2}$
$= \log_6 36$
$= \log_6 6^2$
$= 2$

b) $\quad \log_7 7\sqrt{7}$
$= \log_7 \left(7 \times 7^{\frac{1}{2}}\right)$
$= \log_7 7 + \log_7 7^{\frac{1}{2}}$
$= \log_7 7 + \frac{1}{2} \log_7 7$
$= 1 + \frac{1}{2}(1)$
$= \frac{3}{2}$

How can you use your knowledge of exponents to evaluate this expression using only the power law for logarithms?

c) $\quad 2 \log_2 12 - \left(\log_2 6 + \frac{1}{3} \log_2 27\right)$
$= \log_2 12^2 - \left(\log_2 6 + \log_2 27^{\frac{1}{3}}\right)$
$= \log_2 144 - \left(\log_2 6 + \log_2 \sqrt[3]{27}\right)$
$= \log_2 144 - (\log_2 6 + \log_2 3)$
$= \log_2 144 - \log_2 (6 \times 3)$
$= \log_2 \frac{144}{18}$
$= \log_2 8$
$= 3$

Your Turn

Use the laws of logarithms to simplify and evaluate each expression.
a) $\log_3 9\sqrt{3}$
b) $\log_5 1000 - \log_5 4 - \log_5 2$
c) $2 \log_3 6 - \frac{1}{2} \log_3 64 + \log_3 2$

Example 3

Use the Laws of Logarithms to Simplify Expressions

Write each expression as a single logarithm in simplest form. State the restrictions on the variable.

a) $\log_7 x^2 + \log_7 x - \dfrac{5 \log_7 x}{2}$

b) $\log_5 (2x - 2) - \log_5 (x^2 + 2x - 3)$

Solution

a)
$$\log_7 x^2 + \log_7 x - \dfrac{5 \log_7 x}{2}$$
$$= \log_7 x^2 + \log_7 x - \dfrac{5}{2} \log_7 x$$
$$= \log_7 x^2 + \log_7 x - \log_7 x^{\frac{5}{2}}$$
$$= \log_7 \dfrac{(x^2)(x)}{x^{\frac{5}{2}}}$$
$$= \log_7 x^{2 + 1 - \frac{5}{2}}$$
$$= \log_7 x^{\frac{1}{2}}$$
$$= \dfrac{1}{2} \log_7 x, \ x > 0$$

The logarithmic expression is written as a single logarithm that cannot be further simplified by the laws of logarithms.

b)
$$\log_5 (2x - 2) - \log_5 (x^2 + 2x - 3)$$
$$= \log_5 \dfrac{2x - 2}{x^2 + 2x - 3}$$
$$= \log_5 \dfrac{2(x - 1)}{(x + 3)(x - 1)}$$
$$= \log_5 \dfrac{2}{x + 3}$$

For the original expression to be defined, both logarithmic terms must be defined.

$2x - 2 > 0$	$x^2 + 2x - 3 > 0$
$2x > 2$	$(x + 3)(x - 1) > 0$
$x > 1$ and	$x < -3$ or $x > 1$

What other methods could you have used to solve this quadratic inequality?

The conditions $x > 1$ and $x < -3$ or $x > 1$ are both satisfied when $x > 1$.

Hence, the variable x needs to be restricted to $x > 1$ for the original expression to be defined and then written as a single logarithm.

Therefore, $\log_5 (2x - 2) - \log_5 (x^2 + 2x - 3) = \log_5 \dfrac{2}{x + 3}$, $x > 1$.

Your Turn

Write each expression as a single logarithm in simplest form. State the restrictions on the variable.

a) $4 \log_3 x - \dfrac{1}{2}(\log_3 x + 5 \log_3 x)$

b) $\log_2 (x^2 - 9) - \log_2 (x^2 - x - 6)$

Did You Know?

The unit used to measure the intensity of sound is the decibel (dB), named after Alexander Graham Bell, the inventor of the telephone. Bell was born in Scotland but lived most of his life in Canada.

Example 4

Solve a Problem Involving a Logarithmic Scale

The human ear is sensitive to a large range of sound intensities. Scientists have found that the sensation of loudness can be described using a logarithmic scale. The intensity level, β, in decibels, of a sound is defined as $\beta = 10 \log \dfrac{I}{I_0}$, where I is the intensity of the sound, in watts per square metre (W/m²), and I_0 is 10^{-12} W/m², corresponding to the faintest sound that can be heard by a person of normal hearing.

a) Audiologists recommend that people should wear hearing protection if the sound level exceeds 85 dB. The sound level of a chainsaw is about 85 dB. The maximum volume setting of a portable media player with headphones is about 110 dB. How many times as intense as the sound of the chainsaw is the maximum volume setting of the portable media player?

b) Sounds that are at most 100 000 times as intense as a whisper are considered safe, no matter how long or how often you hear them. The sound level of a whisper is about 20 dB. What sound level, in decibels, is considered safe no matter how long it lasts?

Solution

a) Let the decibel levels of two sounds be $\beta_1 = 10 \log \dfrac{I_1}{I_0}$ and $\beta_2 = 10 \log \dfrac{I_2}{I_0}$.

Then, compare the two intensities.

$\beta_2 - \beta_1 = 10 \log \dfrac{I_2}{I_0} - 10 \log \dfrac{I_1}{I_0}$

$\beta_2 - \beta_1 = 10 \left(\log \dfrac{I_2}{I_0} - \log \dfrac{I_1}{I_0} \right)$

$\beta_2 - \beta_1 = 10 \left(\log \left(\dfrac{I_2}{I_0} \div \dfrac{I_1}{I_0} \right) \right)$ **Apply the quotient law of logarithms.**

$\beta_2 - \beta_1 = 10 \left(\log \left(\dfrac{I_2}{I_0} \times \dfrac{I_0}{I_1} \right) \right)$

$\beta_2 - \beta_1 = 10 \left(\log \dfrac{I_2}{I_1} \right)$

Decibel Scale

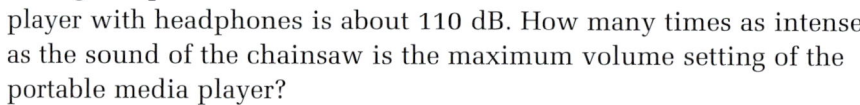

0 dB	Threshold for human hearing
10 dB	
20 dB	Whisper
30 dB	Quiet library
40 dB	Quiet conversation
50 dB	
60 dB	Normal conversation
70 dB	Hair dryer
80 dB	
90 dB	Lawnmower
100 dB	
110 dB	Car horn
120 dB	Rock concert
150 dB	Jet engine up close

For each increase of 10 on the decibel scale, there is a tenfold increase in the intensity of sound.

Substitute $\beta_2 = 110$ and $\beta_1 = 85$ into the equation $\beta_2 - \beta_1 = 10 \log \frac{I_2}{I_1}$.

$$110 - 85 = 10 \log \frac{I_2}{I_1}$$
$$25 = 10 \log \frac{I_2}{I_1}$$
$$2.5 = \log \frac{I_2}{I_1}$$
$$10^{2.5} = \frac{I_2}{I_1} \quad \text{Write in exponential form.}$$
$$316 \approx \frac{I_2}{I_1} \quad \text{What is another approach you could have used to find the ratio } \frac{I_2}{I_1}?$$

The ratio of these two intensities is approximately 316. Hence, the maximum volume level of the portable media player is approximately 316 times as intense as the sound of a chainsaw.

b) The ratio of the intensity of sounds considered safe to the intensity of a whisper is 100 000 to 1. In the equation $\beta_2 - \beta_1 = 10 \log \frac{I_2}{I_1}$, substitute $\beta_1 = 20$ and $\frac{I_2}{I_1} = 100\,000$.

$$\beta_2 - 20 = 10 \log 100\,000$$
$$\beta_2 = 10 \log 100\,000 + 20$$
$$\beta_2 = 10 \log 10^5 + 20$$
$$\beta_2 = 10(5) + 20$$
$$\beta_2 = 70$$

Sounds that are 70 dB or less pose no known risk of hearing loss, no matter how long they last.

Web Link

Some studies suggest that people exposed to excessive noise from leisure activities tend to develop hearing loss. The risk of noise-induced hearing loss depends on the sound level and the duration of the exposure. For more information, go to www.mcgrawhill.ca/school/learningcentres and follow the links.

Your Turn

The pH scale is used to measure the acidity or alkalinity of a solution. The pH of a solution is defined as $pH = -\log [H^+]$, where $[H^+]$ is the hydrogen ion concentration in moles per litre (mol/L). A neutral solution, such as pure water, has a pH of 7. Solutions with a pH of less than 7 are acidic and solutions with a pH of greater than 7 are basic or alkaline. The closer the pH is to 0, the more acidic the solution is.

a) A common ingredient in cola drinks is phosphoric acid, the same ingredient found in many rust removers. A cola drink has a pH of 2.5. Milk has a pH of 6.6. How many times as acidic as milk is a cola drink?

b) An apple is 5 times as acidic as a pear. If a pear has a pH of 3.8, then what is the pH of an apple?

Key Ideas

- Let P be any real number, and M, N, and c be positive real numbers with $c \neq 1$. Then, the following laws of logarithms are valid.

Name	Law	Description
Product	$\log_c MN = \log_c M + \log_c N$	The logarithm of a product of numbers is the sum of the logarithms of the numbers.
Quotient	$\log_c \dfrac{M}{N} = \log_c M - \log_c N$	The logarithm of a quotient of numbers is the difference of the logarithms of the dividend and divisor.
Power	$\log_c M^P = P \log_c M$	The logarithm of a power of a number is the exponent times the logarithm of the number.

- Many quantities in science are measured using a logarithmic scale. Two commonly used logarithmic scales are the decibel scale and the pH scale.

Check Your Understanding

Practise

1. Write each expression in terms of individual logarithms of x, y, and z.
   a) $\log_7 xy^3 \sqrt{z}$
   b) $\log_5 (xyz)^8$
   c) $\log \dfrac{x^2}{y\sqrt[3]{z}}$
   d) $\log_3 x\sqrt{\dfrac{y}{z}}$

2. Use the laws of logarithms to simplify and evaluate each expression.
   a) $\log_{12} 24 - \log_{12} 6 + \log_{12} 36$
   b) $3 \log_5 10 - \dfrac{1}{2} \log_5 64$
   c) $\log_3 27\sqrt{3}$
   d) $\log_2 72 - \dfrac{1}{2}(\log_2 3 + \log_2 27)$

3. Write each expression as a single logarithm in simplest form.
   a) $\log_9 x - \log_9 y + 4 \log_9 z$
   b) $\dfrac{\log_3 x}{2} - 2 \log_3 y$
   c) $\log_6 x - \dfrac{1}{5}(\log_6 x + 2 \log_6 y)$
   d) $\dfrac{\log x}{3} + \dfrac{\log y}{3}$

4. The original use of logarithms was to simplify calculations. Use the approximations shown on the right and the laws of logarithms to perform each calculation using only paper and pencil.
   a) 1.44×1.2 $\quad \log 1.44 \approx 0.158\,36$
   b) $1.728 \div 1.2$ $\quad \log 1.2 \approx 0.079\,18$
   c) $\sqrt{1.44}$ $\quad \log 1.728 \approx 0.237\,54$

5. Evaluate.
   a) 3^k, where $k = \log_2 40 - \log_2 5$
   b) 7^n, where $n = 3 \log_8 4$

Apply

6. To obtain the graph of $y = \log_2 8x$, you can either stretch or translate the graph of $y = \log_2 x$.
   a) Describe the stretch you need to apply to the graph of $y = \log_2 x$ to result in the graph of $y = \log_2 8x$.
   b) Describe the translation you need to apply to the graph of $y = \log_2 x$ to result in the graph of $y = \log_2 8x$.

7. Decide whether each equation is true or false. Justify your answer. Assume c, x, and y are positive real numbers and $c \neq 1$.
   a) $\dfrac{\log_c x}{\log_c y} = \log_c x - \log_c y$
   b) $\log_c (x + y) = \log_c x + \log_c y$
   c) $\log_c c^n = n$
   d) $(\log_c x)^n = n \log_c x$
   e) $-\log_c \left(\dfrac{1}{x}\right) = \log_c x$

8. If $\log 3 = P$ and $\log 5 = Q$, write an algebraic expression in terms of P and Q for each of the following.
   a) $\log \dfrac{3}{5}$
   b) $\log 15$
   c) $\log 3\sqrt{5}$
   d) $\log \dfrac{25}{9}$

9. If $\log_2 7 = K$, write an algebraic expression in terms of K for each of the following.
   a) $\log_2 7^6$
   b) $\log_2 14$
   c) $\log_2 (49 \times 4)$
   d) $\log_2 \dfrac{\sqrt[5]{7}}{8}$

10. Write each expression as a single logarithm in simplest form. State any restrictions on the variable.
    a) $\log_5 x + \log_5 \sqrt{x^3} - 2 \log_5 x$
    b) $\log_{11} \dfrac{x}{\sqrt{x}} + \log_{11} \sqrt{x^5} - \dfrac{7}{3} \log_{11} x$

11. Write each expression as a single logarithm in simplest form. State any restrictions on the variable.
    a) $\log_2 (x^2 - 25) - \log_2 (3x - 15)$
    b) $\log_7 (x^2 - 16) - \log_7 (x^2 - 2x - 8)$
    c) $2 \log_8 (x + 3) - \log_8 (x^2 + x - 6)$

12. Show that each equation is true for $c > 0$ and $c \neq 1$.
    a) $\log_c 48 - (\log_c 3 + \log_c 2) = \log_c 8$
    b) $7 \log_c 4 = 14 \log_c 2$
    c) $\dfrac{1}{2}(\log_c 2 + \log_c 6) = \log_c 2 + \log_c \sqrt{3}$
    d) $\log_c (5c)^2 = 2(\log_c 5 + 1)$

13. Sound intensity, β, in decibels is defined as $\beta = 10 \log \left(\dfrac{I}{I_0}\right)$, where I is the intensity of the sound measured in watts per square metre (W/m²) and I_0 is 10^{-12} W/m², the threshold of hearing.
    a) The sound intensity of a hairdryer is 0.000 01 W/m². Find its decibel level.
    b) A fire truck siren has a decibel level of 118 dB. City traffic has a decibel level of 85 dB. How many times as loud as city traffic is the fire truck siren?

   c) The sound of Elly's farm tractor is 63 times as intense as the sound of her car. If the decibel level of the car is 80 dB, what is the decibel level of the farm tractor?

14. Abdi incorrectly states, "A noise of 20 dB is twice as loud as a noise of 10 dB." Explain the error in Abdi's reasoning.

15. The term *decibel* is also used in electronics for current and voltage ratios. Gain is defined as the ratio between the signal coming in and the signal going out. The gain, G, in decibels, of an amplifier is defined as $G = 20 \log \dfrac{V}{V_i}$, where V is the voltage output and V_i is the voltage input. If the gain of an amplifier is 24 dB when the voltage input is 0.2 V, find the voltage output, V. Answer to the nearest tenth of a volt.

16. The logarithmic scale used to express the pH of a solution is pH = −log [H⁺], where [H⁺] is the hydrogen ion concentration, in moles per litre (mol/L).

   a) Lactic acidosis is medical condition characterized by elevated lactates and a blood pH of less than 7.35. A patient is severely ill when his or her blood pH is 7.0. Find the hydrogen ion concentration in a patient with a blood pH of 7.0.

   b) Acid rain is caused when compounds from combustion react with water in the atmosphere to produce acids. It is generally accepted that rain is acidic if its pH is less than 5.3. The average pH of rain in some regions of Ontario is about 4.5. How many times as acidic as normal rain with a pH of 5.6 is acid rain with a pH of 4.5?

   c) The hair conditioner that Alana uses is 500 times as acidic as the shampoo she uses. If the shampoo has a pH of 6.1, find the pH of the conditioner.

17. The change in velocity, Δv, in kilometres per second, of a rocket with an exhaust velocity of 3.1 km/s can be found using the Tsiolkovsky rocket equation $\Delta v = \dfrac{3.1}{0.434}(\log m_0 - \log m_f)$, where m_0 is the initial total mass and m_f is the final total mass, in kilograms, after a fuel burn. Find the change in the velocity of the rocket if the mass ratio, $\dfrac{m_0}{m_f}$, is 1.06.

   Answer to the nearest hundredth of a kilometre per second.

Extend

18. Graph the functions $y = \log x^2$ and $y = 2 \log x$ on the same coordinate grid.

   a) How are the graphs alike? How are they different?

   b) Explain why the graphs are not identical.

   c) Although the functions $y = \log x^2$ and $y = 2 \log x$ are not the same, the equation $\log x^2 = 2 \log x$ is true. This is because the variable x in the equation is restricted to values for which both logarithms are defined. What is the restriction on x in the equation?

19. a) Prove the change of base formula, $\log_c x = \dfrac{\log_d x}{\log_d c}$, where c and d are positive real numbers other than 1.

   b) Apply the change of base formula for base $d = 10$ to find the approximate value of $\log_2 9.5$ using common logarithms. Answer to four decimal places.

   c) The Krumbein phi (φ) scale is used in geology to classify the particle size of natural sediments such as sand and gravel. The formula for the φ-value may be expressed as $\varphi = -\log_2 D$, where D is the diameter of the particle, in millimetres. The φ-value can also be defined using a common logarithm. Express the formula for the φ-value as a common logarithm.

   d) How many times the diameter of medium sand with a φ-value of 2 is the diameter of a pebble with a φ-value of −5.7? Determine the answer using both versions of the φ-value formula from part c).

20. Prove each identity.

   a) $\log_{q^3} p^3 = \log_q p$

   b) $\dfrac{1}{\log_p 2} - \dfrac{1}{\log_q 2} = \log_2 \dfrac{p}{q}$

   c) $\dfrac{1}{\log_q p} + \dfrac{1}{\log_q p} = \dfrac{1}{\log_{q^2} p}$

   d) $\log_{\frac{1}{q}} p = \log_q \dfrac{1}{p}$

Create Connections

C1 Describe how you could obtain the graph of each function from the graph of $y = \log x$.
  a) $y = \log x^3$
  b) $y = \log(x+2)^5$
  c) $y = \log \frac{1}{x}$
  d) $y = \log \frac{1}{\sqrt{x-6}}$

C2 Evaluate $\log_2 \left(\sin \frac{\pi}{4}\right) + \log_2 \left(\sin \frac{3\pi}{4}\right)$.

C3 a) What is the common difference, d, in the arithmetic series $\log 2 + \log 4 + \log 8 + \log 16 + \log 32$?

  b) Express the sum of the series as a multiple of the common difference.

C4 Copy the Frayer Model template shown for each law of logarithms. In the appropriate space, give the name of the law, an algebraic representation, a written description, an example, and common errors.

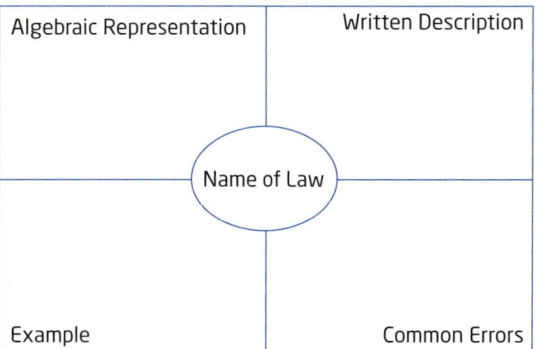

Project Corner — Modelling Data

The table shows box office receipts for a popular new movie.

- Determine the equation of a logarithmic function of the form $y = 20 \log_{1.3}(x - h) + k$ that fits the data.

- Determine the equation of an exponential function of the form $y = -104(0.74)^{x-h} + k$ that fits the data.

- Compare the logarithmic function to the exponential function. Is one model better than the other? Explain.

Week	Cumulative Box Office Revenue (millions of dollars)
1	70
2	144
3	191
4	229
5	256
6	275
7	291
8	304
9	313
10	320
11	325
12	328
13	330
14	332
15	334
16	335
17	335
18	336
19	337

8.4

Logarithmic and Exponential Equations

Focus on...

- solving a logarithmic equation and verifying the solution
- explaining why a value obtained in solving a logarithmic equation may be extraneous
- solving an exponential equation in which the bases are not powers of one another
- solving a problem that involves exponential growth or decay
- solving a problem that involves the application of exponential equations to loans, mortgages, and investments
- solving a problem by modelling a situation with an exponential or logarithmic equation

Change is taking place in our world at a pace that is unprecedented in human history. Think of situations in your life that show exponential growth.

Imagine you purchase a computer with 1 TB (terabyte) of available disk space. One terabyte equals 1 048 576 MB (megabytes). On the first day you store 1 MB (megabyte) of data on the disk space. On each successive day you store twice the data stored on the previous day. Predict on what day you will run out of disk space.

The table below shows how the disk space fills up.

Computer Disk Space					
Day	Data Stored (MB)	Space Used (MB)	Space Unused (MB)	Percent Used	Percent Unused
1	1	1	1048575	0.0	100.0
2	2	3	1048573	0.0	100.0
3	4	7	1048569	0.0	100.0
4	8	15	1048561	0.0	100.0
5	16	31	1048545	0.0	100.0
6	32	63	1048513	0.0	100.0
7	64	127	1048449	0.0	100.0
8	128	255	1048321	0.0	100.0
9	256	511	1048065	0.0	100.0
10	512	1023	1047553	0.1	99.9
11	1024	2047	1046529	0.2	99.8
12	2048	4095	1044481	0.4	99.6
13	4096	8191	1040385	0.8	99.2
14	8192	16383	1032193	1.6	98.4
15	16384	32767	1015809	3.1	96.9
16	32768	65535	983041	6.2	93.8
17	65536	131071	917505	12.5	87.5
18	131072	262143	786433	25.0	75.0
19	262144	524287	524289	50.0	50.0
20	524288	1048575	1	100.0	0.0

On what day will you realise that you are running out of disk space?

Notice that the amount stored on any given day, after the first day, exceeds the total amount stored on all the previous days.

Suppose you purchase an external hard drive with an additional 15 TB of disk storage space. For how long can you continue doubling the amount stored?

You can find the amount of data stored on a certain day by using logarithms to solve an exponential equation. Solving problems involving exponential and logarithmic equations helps us to understand and shape our ever-changing world.

Investigate Logarithmic and Exponential Equations

Part A: Explore Logarithmic Equations

Consider the **logarithmic equation** $2 \log x = \log 36$.

1. Use the following steps to solve the equation.
   a) Apply one of the laws of logarithms to the left side of the equation.
   b) Describe how you might solve the resulting equation.
   c) Determine two values of x that satisfy the rewritten equation in part a).
2. a) Describe how you could solve the original equation graphically.
   b) Use your description to solve the original equation graphically.

logarithmic equation
- an equation containing the logarithm of a variable

Reflect and Respond

3. What value or values of x satisfy the original equation? Explain.

Part B: Explore Exponential Equations

Adam and Sarah are asked to solve the exponential equation $2(25^{x+1}) = 250$. Each person uses a different method.

	Adam's Method	Sarah's Method
	$2(25^{x+1}) = 250$	$2(25^{x+1}) = 250$
Step 1	$25^{x+1} = 125$	$25^{x+1} = 125$
Step 2	$(5^2)^{x+1} = 5^3$	$\log 25^{x+1} = \log 125$
Step 3	$5^{2(x+1)} = 5^3$	$(x+1) \log 25 = \log 125$
Step 4	$2(x+1) = 3$ $2x + 2 = 3$ $2x = 1$ $x = 0.5$	$x \log 25 + \log 25 = \log 125$ $x \log 25 = \log 125 - \log 25$ $x = \dfrac{\log\left(\dfrac{125}{25}\right)}{\log 25}$ $= \dfrac{\log 5}{\log 5^2}$ $= \dfrac{\cancel{\log 5}^{\,1}}{2\,\cancel{\log 5}_{\,1}}$ $= \dfrac{1}{2}$

4. Explain each step in each student's work.
5. What is another way that Adam could have completed step 4 of his work? Show another way Sarah could have completed step 4 of her work.

Reflect and Respond

6. Which person's method do you prefer? Explain why.

7. What types of exponential equations could be solved using Adam's method? What types of exponential equations could not be solved using Adam's method and must be solved using Sarah's method? Explain.

8. Sarah used common logarithms in step 2 of her work. Could she instead have used logarithms to another base? Justify your answer.

Link the Ideas

The following equality statements are useful when solving an exponential equation or a logarithmic equation.

Given $c, L, R > 0$ and $c \neq 1$,
- if $\log_c L = \log_c R$, then $L = R$
- if $L = R$, then $\log_c L = \log_c R$

Proof
Let $\log_c L = \log_c R$.
$$c^{\log_c R} = L \quad \text{Write in exponential form.}$$
$$R = L \quad \text{Apply the inverse property of logarithms, } c^{\log_c x} = x, \text{ where } x > 0.$$

When solving a logarithmic equation, identify whether any roots are extraneous by substituting into the original equation and determining whether all the logarithms are defined. The logarithm of zero or a negative number is undefined.

Example 1

Solve Logarithmic Equations

Solve.
a) $\log_6 (2x - 1) = \log_6 11$ **b)** $\log (8x + 4) = 1 + \log (x + 1)$
c) $\log_2 (x + 3)^2 = 4$

Solution

a) Method 1: Solve Algebraically
The following statement is true for $c, L, R > 0$ and $c \neq 1$.
If $\log_c L = \log_c R$, then $L = R$.
Hence,
$$\log_6 (2x - 1) = \log_6 11$$
$$2x - 1 = 11$$
$$2x = 12$$
$$x = 6$$

The equation $\log_6 (2x - 1) = \log_6 11$ is defined when $2x - 1 > 0$. This occurs when $x > \frac{1}{2}$. Since the value of x satisfies this restriction, the solution is $x = 6$.

Check $x = 6$ in the original equation, $\log_6 (2x - 1) = \log_6 11$.

Left Side | Right Side
$\log_6 (2x - 1)$ | $\log_6 11$
$= \log_6 (2(6) - 1)$
$= \log_6 11$
Left Side = Right Side

Method 2: Solve Graphically
Find the graphical solution to the system of equations:
$y = \log_6 (2x - 1)$
$y = \log_6 11$
The x-coordinate at the point of intersection of the graphs of the functions is the solution, $x = 6$.

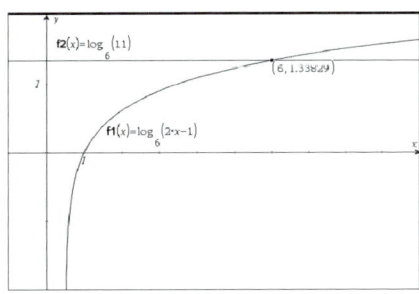

How could you have used the graph of $y = \log_6 (2x - 1) - \log_6 11$ to solve the equation?

b)
$$\log (8x + 4) = 1 + \log (x + 1)$$
$$\log_{10} (8x + 4) = 1 + \log_{10} (x + 1)$$
$$\log_{10} (8x + 4) - \log_{10} (x + 1) = 1 \quad \text{Isolate the logarithmic terms on one side of the equation.}$$
$$\log_{10} \frac{8x + 4}{x + 1} = 1 \quad \text{Apply the quotient law for logarithms.}$$

Select a strategy to solve for x.

Method 1: Express Both Sides of the Equation as Logarithms

$\log_{10} \frac{8x + 4}{x + 1} = 1$

$\log_{10} \frac{8x + 4}{x + 1} = \log_{10} 10^1$ Use the property $\log_b b^n = n$ to substitute $\log_{10} 10^1$ for 1.

$\frac{8x + 4}{x + 1} = 10$ Use the property that if $\log_c L = \log_c R$, then $L = R$.

$8x + 4 = 10(x + 1)$ Multiply both sides of the equation by $x + 1$, the lowest common denominator (LCD).

$8x + 4 = 10x + 10$

$-6 = 2x$ Solve the linear equation.

$-3 = x$

Method 2: Convert to Exponential Form

$\log_{10} \frac{8x + 4}{x + 1} = 1$

$\frac{8x + 4}{x + 1} = 10^1$ Write in exponential form.

$8x + 4 = 10(x + 1)$ Multiply both sides of the equation by the LCD, $x + 1$.

$8x + 4 = 10x + 10$

$-6 = 2x$ Solve the linear equation.

$-3 = x$

The solution $x = -3$ is extraneous. When -3 is substituted for x in the original equation, both $\log (8x + 4)$ and $\log (x + 1)$ are undefined. Hence, there is no solution to the equation.

Why is the logarithm of a negative number undefined?

c) $\log_2 (x + 3)^2 = 4$
$(x + 3)^2 = 2^4$

If the power law of logarithms was used, how would this affect the solution?

$x^2 + 6x + 9 = 16$
$x^2 + 6x - 7 = 0$
$(x + 7)(x - 1) = 0$
$x = -7 \quad \text{or} \quad x = 1$

When either -7 or 1 is substituted for x in the original equation, $\log_2 (x + 3)^2$ is defined.

Check:
Substitute $x = -7$ and $x = 1$ in the original equation, $\log_2 (x + 3)^2 = 4$.

When $x = -7$:
Left Side   Right Side
$\log_2 (x + 3)^2$ 4
$= \log_2 (-7 + 3)^2$
$= \log_2 (-4)^2$
$= \log_2 16$
$= 4$
   Left Side = Right Side

When $x = 1$:
Left Side   Right Side
$\log_2 (x + 3)^2$ 4
$= \log_2 (1 + 3)^2$
$= \log_2 (4)^2$
$= \log_2 16$
$= 4$
   Left Side = Right Side

Your Turn

Solve.
a) $\log_7 x + \log_7 4 = \log_7 12$
b) $\log_2 (x - 6) = 3 - \log_2 (x - 4)$
c) $\log_3 (x^2 - 8x)^5 = 10$

Example 2

Solve Exponential Equations Using Logarithms

Solve. Round your answers to two decimal places.
a) $4^x = 605$
b) $8(3^{2x}) = 568$
c) $4^{2x-1} = 3^{x+2}$

Solution

a) Method 1: Take Common Logarithms of Both Sides
$4^x = 605$
$\log 4^x = \log 605$
$x \log 4 = \log 605$
$x = \dfrac{\log 605}{\log 4}$
$x \approx 4.62$

Method 2: Convert to Logarithmic Form

$$4^x = 605$$
$$\log_4 605 = x$$
$$4.62 \approx x$$

Which method do you prefer? Explain why.

Check $x \approx 4.62$ in the original equation, $4^x = 605$.

Left Side	Right Side
$4^{4.62}$	605
≈ 605	

Left Side $\approx$ Right Side

b)
$$8(3^{2x}) = 568$$
$$3^{2x} = 71$$
$$\log 3^{2x} = \log 71$$
$$2x(\log 3) = \log 71$$
$$x = \frac{\log 71}{2 \log 3}$$
$$x \approx 1.94$$

Explain why $8(3^{2x})$ cannot be expressed as 24^{2x}.

Explain the steps in this solution. How else could you have used logarithms to solve for x?

Check $x \approx 1.94$ in the original equation, $8(3^{2x}) = 568$.

Left Side	Right Side
$8(3^{2(1.94)})$	568
≈ 568	

Left Side $\approx$ Right Side

c)
$$4^{2x-1} = 3^{x+2}$$
$$\log 4^{2x-1} = \log 3^{x+2}$$
$$(2x - 1) \log 4 = (x + 2) \log 3$$
$$2x \log 4 - \log 4 = x \log 3 + 2 \log 3$$
$$2x \log 4 - x \log 3 = 2 \log 3 + \log 4$$
$$x(2 \log 4 - \log 3) = 2 \log 3 + \log 4$$
$$x = \frac{2 \log 3 + \log 4}{2 \log 4 - \log 3}$$
$$x \approx 2.14$$

Check $x \approx 2.14$ in the original equation, $4^{2x-1} = 3^{x+2}$.

Left Side	Right Side
$4^{2(2.14)-1}$	$3^{2.14+2}$
≈ 94	≈ 94

Left Side $\approx$ Right Side

What is another way you can verify the solution?

Your Turn

Solve. Round answers to two decimal places.

a) $2^x = 2500$ **b)** $5^{x-3} = 1700$ **c)** $6^{3x+1} = 8^{x+3}$

Example 3

Model a Situation Using a Logarithmic Equation

Palaeontologists can estimate the size of a dinosaur from incomplete skeletal remains. For a carnivorous dinosaur, the relationship between the length, s, in metres, of the skull and the body mass, m, in kilograms, can be expressed using the logarithmic equation $3.6022 \log s = \log m - 3.4444$. Determine the body mass, to the nearest kilogram, of an Albertosaurus with a skull length of 0.78 m.

Albertosaurus display, Royal Tyrrell Museum, Drumheller, Alberta

Did You Know?

Albertosaurus was the top predator in the semi-tropical Cretaceous ecosystem, more than 70 million years ago. It was smaller than its close relative Tyrannosaurus rex, which lived a few million years later. The first Albertosaurus was discovered by Joseph B. Tyrrell, a geologist searching for coal deposits in the Red Deer River valley, in 1884. Since then, more than 30 Albertosauruses have been discovered in western North America.

Solution

Substitute $s = 0.78$ into the equation $3.6022 \log s = \log m - 3.4444$.

$$3.6022 \log_{10} 0.78 = \log_{10} m - 3.4444$$
$$3.6022 \log_{10} 0.78 + 3.4444 = \log_{10} m$$
$$3.0557 \approx \log_{10} m$$
$$10^{3.0557} \approx m$$
$$1137 \approx m$$

The mass of the Albertosaurus was approximately 1137 kg.

Your Turn

To the nearest hundredth of a metre, what was the skull length of a Tyrannosaurus rex with an estimated body mass of 5500 kg?

Example 4

Solve a Problem Involving Exponential Growth and Decay

When an animal dies, the amount of radioactive carbon-14 (C-14) in its bones decreases. Archaeologists use this fact to determine the age of a fossil based on the amount of C-14 remaining.
The half-life of C-14 is 5730 years.

Head-Smashed-In Buffalo Jump in southwestern Alberta is recognized as the best example of a buffalo jump in North America. The oldest bones unearthed at the site had 49.5% of the C-14 left. How old were the bones when they were found?

Buffalo skull display, Head-Smashed-In buffalo Jump Visitor Centre, near Fort McLeod, Alberta

Did You Know?

First Nations hunters used a variety of strategies to harvest the largest land mammal in North America, the buffalo. The most effective method for securing large quantities of food was the buffalo jump. The extraordinary amount of work required to plan, coordinate, and implement a successful harvest demonstrates First Nations Peoples' ingenuity, communal cooperation, and organizational skills that enabled them to utilize this primary resource in a sustainable manner for millennia.

Solution

Carbon-14 decays by one half for each 5730-year interval. The mass, m, remaining at time t can be found using the relationship $m(t) = m_0 \left(\dfrac{1}{2}\right)^{\frac{t}{5730}}$, where m_0 is the original mass.

Since 49.5% of the C-14 remains after t years, substitute $0.495 m_0$ for $m(t)$ in the formula $m(t) = m_0 \left(\dfrac{1}{2}\right)^{\frac{t}{5730}}$.

$$0.495 m_0 = m_0 \left(\dfrac{1}{2}\right)^{\frac{t}{5730}}$$
$$0.495 = 0.5^{\frac{t}{5730}}$$
$$\log 0.495 = \log 0.5^{\frac{t}{5730}}$$
$$\log 0.495 = \dfrac{t}{5730} \log 0.5$$
$$\dfrac{5730 \log 0.495}{\log 0.5} = t$$
$$5813 \approx t$$

Instead of taking the common logarithm of both sides, you could have converted from exponential form to logarithmic form. Try this. Which approach do you prefer? Why?

The oldest buffalo bones found at Head-Smashed-In Buffalo Jump date to about 5813 years ago. The site has been used for at least 6000 years.

Your Turn

The rate at which an organism duplicates is called its doubling period. The general equation is $N(t) = N_0 (2)^{\frac{t}{d}}$, where N is the number present after time t, N_0 is the original number, and d is the doubling period. *E. coli* is a rod-shaped bacterium commonly found in the intestinal tract of warm-blooded animals. Some strains of *E. coli* can cause serious food poisoning in humans. Suppose a biologist originally estimates the number of *E. coli* bacteria in a culture to be 1000. After 90 min, the estimated count is 19 500 bacteria. What is the doubling period of the *E. coli* bacteria, to the nearest minute?

Key Ideas

- When solving a logarithmic equation algebraically, start by applying the laws of logarithms to express one side or both sides of the equation as a single logarithm.
- Some useful properties are listed below, where $c, L, R > 0$ and $c \neq 1$.
  - If $\log_c L = \log_c R$, then $L = R$.
  - The equation $\log_c L = R$ can be written with logarithms on both sides of the equation as $\log_c L = \log_c c^R$.
  - The equation $\log_c L = R$ can be written in exponential form as $L = c^R$.
  - The logarithm of zero or a negative number is undefined. To identify whether a root is extraneous, substitute the root into the original equation and check whether all of the logarithms are defined.
- You can solve an exponential equation algebraically by taking logarithms of both sides of the equation. If $L = R$, then $\log_c L = \log_c R$, where $c, L, R > 0$ and $c \neq 1$. Then, apply the power law for logarithms to solve for an unknown.
- You can solve an exponential equation or a logarithmic equation using graphical methods.
- Many real-world situations can be modelled with an exponential or a logarithmic equation. A general model for many problems involving exponential growth or decay is

  $$\text{final quantity} = \text{initial quantity} \times (\text{change factor})^{\text{number of changes}}$$

Check Your Understanding

Practise

1. Solve. Give exact answers.
   a) $15 = 12 + \log x$
   b) $\log_5 (2x - 3) = 2$
   c) $4 \log_3 x = \log_3 81$
   d) $2 = \log (x - 8)$

2. Solve for x. Give your answers to two decimal places.
   a) $4(7^x) = 92$
   b) $2^{\frac{x}{3}} = 11$
   c) $6^{x-1} = 271$
   d) $4^{2x+1} = 54$

3. Hamdi algebraically solved the equation $\log_3 (x - 8) - \log_3 (x - 6) = 1$ and found $x = 5$ as a possible solution. The following shows Hamdi's check for $x = 5$.

   Left Side
   $\log_3 \dfrac{x - 8}{x - 6}$
   $= \log_3 \dfrac{5 - 8}{5 - 6}$
   $= \log_3 3$
   $= 1$

   Right Side
   1

   Left Side = Right Side

   Do you agree with Hamdi's check? Explain why or why not.

4. Determine whether the possible roots listed are extraneous to the logarithmic equation given.
   a) $\log_7 x + \log_7 (x - 1) = \log_7 4x$
      possible roots: $x = 0$, $x = 5$
   b) $\log_6 (x^2 - 24) - \log_6 x = \log_6 5$
      possible roots: $x = 3$, $x = -8$
   c) $\log_3 (x + 3) + \log_3 (x + 5) = 1$
      possible roots: $x = -2$, $x = -6$
   d) $\log_2 (x - 2) = 2 - \log_2 (x - 5)$
      possible roots: $x = 1$, $x = 6$

5. Solve for x.
   a) $2 \log_3 x = \log_3 32 + \log_3 2$
   b) $\frac{3}{2} \log_7 x = \log_7 125$
   c) $\log_2 x - \log_2 3 = 5$
   d) $\log_6 x = 2 - \log_6 4$

Apply

6. Three students each attempted to solve a different logarithmic equation. Identify and describe any error in each person's work, and then correctly solve the equation.
   a) *Rubina's work:*
      $\log_6 (2x + 1) - \log_6 (x - 1) = \log_6 5$
      $\log_6 (x + 2) = \log_6 5$
      $x + 2 = 5$
      $x = 3$
      The solution is $x = 3$.
   b) *Ahmed's work:*
      $2 \log_5 (x + 3) = \log_5 9$
      $\log_5 (x + 3)^2 = \log_5 9$
      $(x + 3)^2 = 9$
      $x^2 + 6x + 9 = 9$
      $x(x + 6) = 0$
      $x = 0$ or $x = -6$
      There is no solution.
   c) *Jennifer's work:*
      $\log_2 x + \log_2 (x + 2) = 3$
      $\log_2 (x(x + 2)) = 3$
      $x(x + 2) = 3$
      $x^2 + 2x - 3 = 0$
      $(x + 3)(x - 1) = 0$
      $x = -3$ or $x = 1$
      The solution is $x = 1$.

7. Determine the value of x. Round your answers to two decimal places.
   a) $7^{2x} = 2^{x+3}$
   b) $1.6^{x-4} = 5^{3x}$
   c) $9^{2x-1} = 71^{x+2}$
   d) $4(7^{x+2}) = 9^{2x-3}$

8. Solve for x.
   a) $\log_5 (x - 18) - \log_5 x = \log_5 7$
   b) $\log_2 (x - 6) + \log_2 (x - 8) = 3$
   c) $2 \log_4 (x + 4) - \log_4 (x + 12) = 1$
   d) $\log_3 (2x - 1) = 2 - \log_3 (x + 1)$
   e) $\log_2 \sqrt{x^2 + 4x} = \frac{5}{2}$

9. The apparent magnitude of a celestial object is how bright it appears from Earth. The absolute magnitude is its brightness as it would seem from a reference distance of 10 parsecs (pc). The difference between the apparent magnitude, m, and the absolute magnitude, M, of a celestial object can be found using the equation $m - M = 5 \log d - 5$, where d is the distance to the celestial object, in parsecs. Sirius, the brightest star visible at night, has an apparent magnitude of -1.44 and an absolute magnitude of 1.45.
   a) How far is Sirius from Earth in parsecs?
   b) Given that 1 pc is approximately 3.26 light years, what is the distance in part a) in light years?

10. Small animal characters in animated features are often portrayed with big endearing eyes. In reality, the eye size of many vertebrates is related to body mass by the logarithmic equation $\log E = \log 10.61 + 0.1964 \log m$, where E is the eye axial length, in millimetres, and m is the body mass, in kilograms. To the nearest kilogram, predict the mass of a mountain goat with an eye axial length of 24 mm.

11. A remote lake that previously contained no northern pike is stocked with these fish. The population, P, of northern pike after t years can be determined by the equation $P = 10\,000(1.035)^t$.
    a) How many northern pike were put into the lake when it was stocked?
    b) What is the annual growth rate, as a percent?
    c) How long will it take for the number of northern pike in the lake to double?

12. The German astronomer Johannes Kepler developed three major laws of planetary motion. His third law can be expressed by the equation $\log T = \frac{3}{2} \log d - 3.263$, where T is the time, in Earth years, for the planet to revolve around the sun and d is the average distance, in millions of kilometres, from the sun.
    a) Pluto is on average 5906 million kilometres from the sun. To the nearest Earth year, how long does it take Pluto to revolve around the sun?
    b) Mars revolves around the sun in 1.88 Earth years. How far is Mars from the sun, to the nearest million kilometres?

13. The compound interest formula is $A = P(1 + i)^n$, where A is the future amount, P is the present amount or principal, i is the interest rate per compounding period expressed as a decimal, and n is the number of compounding periods. All interest rates are annual percentage rates (APR).
    a) David inherits $10 000 and invests in a guaranteed investment certificate (GIC) that earns 6%, compounded semi-annually. How long will it take for the GIC to be worth $11 000?
    b) Linda used a credit card to purchase a $1200 laptop computer. The rate of interest charged on the overdue balance is 28% per year, compounded daily. How many days is Linda's payment overdue if the amount shown on her credit card statement is $1241.18?
    c) How long will it take for money invested at 5.5%, compounded semi-annually, to triple in value?

14. A mortgage is a long-term loan secured by property. A mortgage with a present value of $250 000 at a 7.4% annual percentage rate requires semi-annual payments of $10 429.01 at the end of every 6 months. The formula for the present value, PV, of the mortgage is $PV = \dfrac{R[1 - (1 + i)^{-n}]}{i}$, where n is the number of equal periodic payments of R dollars and i is the interest rate per compounding period, as a decimal. After how many years will the mortgage be completely paid off?

15. Swedish researchers report that they have discovered the world's oldest living tree. The spruce tree's roots were radiocarbon dated and found to have 31.5% of their carbon-14 (C-14) left. The half-life of C-14 is 5730 years. How old was the tree when it was discovered?

Norway spruce, Dalarna, Sweden

16. Radioisotopes are used to diagnose various illnesses. Iodine-131 (I-131) is administered to a patient to diagnose thyroid gland activity. The original dosage contains 280 MBq of I-131. If none is lost from the body, then after 6 h there are 274 MBq of I-131 in the patient's thyroid. What is the half-life of I-131, to the nearest day?

> **Did You Know?**
>
> The SI unit used to measure radioactivity is the becquerel (Bq), which is one particle emitted per second from a radioactive source. Commonly used multiples are kilobecquerel (kBq), for 10^3 Bq, and megabecquerel (MBq), for 10^6 Bq.

17. The largest lake lying entirely within Canada is Great Bear Lake, in the Northwest Territories. On a summer day, divers find that the light intensity is reduced by 4% for every metre below the water surface. To the nearest tenth of a metre, at what depth is the light intensity 25% of the intensity at the surface?

18. If $\log_3 81 = x - y$ and $\log_2 32 = x + y$, determine the values of x and y.

Extend

19. Find the error in each.

a) $\log 0.1 < 3 \log 0.1$
Since $3 \log 0.1 = \log 0.1^3$,
$\log 0.1 < \log 0.1^3$
$\log 0.1 < \log 0.001$
Therefore, $0.1 < 0.001$.

b) $\frac{1}{5} > \frac{1}{25}$
$\log \frac{1}{5} > \log \frac{1}{25}$
$\log \frac{1}{5} > \log \left(\frac{1}{5}\right)^2$
$\log \frac{1}{5} > 2 \log \frac{1}{5}$
Therefore, $1 > 2$.

20. Solve for x.

a) $x^{\frac{2}{\log x}} = x$

b) $\log x^{\log x} = 4$

c) $(\log x)^2 = \log x^2$

21. Solve for x.

a) $\log_4 x + \log_2 x = 6$

b) $\log_3 x - \log_{27} x = \frac{4}{3}$

22. Determine the values of x that satisfy the equation $(x^2 + 3x - 9)^{2x-8} = 1$.

Create Connections

C1 Fatima started to solve the equation $8(2^x) = 512$, as shown.

$8(2^x) = 512$
$\log 8(2^x) = \log 512$
$\log 8 + \log 2^x = \log 512$

a) Copy and complete the solution using Fatima's approach.

b) Suggest another approach Fatima could have used to solve the equation. Compare the different approaches among classmates.

c) Which approach do you prefer? Explain why.

C2 The general term, t_n, of a geometric sequence is $t_n = t_1 r^{n-1}$, where t_1 is the first term of the sequence, n is the number of terms, and r is the common ratio. Determine the number of terms in the geometric sequence 4, 12, 36, ..., 708 588.

C3 The sum, S_n, of the first n terms of a geometric series can be found using the formula $S_n = \dfrac{t_1(r^n - 1)}{r - 1}, r \neq 1$, where t_1 is the first term and r is the common ratio. The sum of the first n terms in the geometric series $8192 + 4096 + 2048 + \cdots$ is 16 383. Determine the value of n.

C4 Solve for x, $0 \leq x \leq 2\pi$.

a) $2 \log_2 (\cos x) + 1 = 0$

b) $\log (\sin x) + \log (2 \sin x - 1) = 0$

C5 Copy the concept chart. Provide worked examples in the last row.

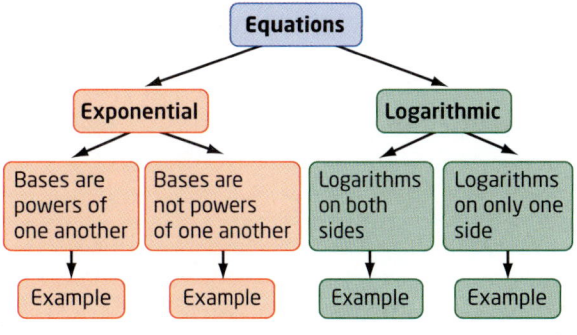

Chapter 8 Review

8.1 Understanding Logarithms, pages 372–382

1. A graph of $f(x) = 0.2^x$ is shown.

   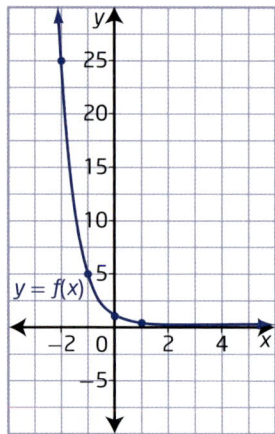

   a) Make a copy of the graph and on the same grid sketch the graph of $y = f^{-1}(x)$.

   b) Determine the following characteristics of $y = f^{-1}(x)$.
      i) the domain and range
      ii) the x-intercept, if it exists
      iii) the y-intercept, if it exists
      iv) the equation of the asymptote

   c) State the equation of $f^{-1}(x)$.

2. The point $(2, 16)$ is on the graph of the inverse of $y = \log_c x$. What is the value of c?

3. Explain why the value of $\log_2 24$ must be between 4 and 5.

4. Determine the value of x.

   a) $\log_{125} x = \dfrac{2}{3}$

   b) $\log_9 \dfrac{1}{81} = x$

   c) $\log_3 27\sqrt{3} = x$

   d) $\log_x 8 = \dfrac{3}{4}$

   e) $6^{\log x} = \dfrac{1}{36}$

5. The formula for the Richter magnitude, M, of an earthquake is $M = \log \dfrac{A}{A_0}$, where A is the amplitude of the ground motion and A_0 is the amplitude of a standard earthquake. In 2011, an earthquake with a Richter magnitude of 9.0 struck off the east coast of Japan. In the aftermath of the earthquake, a 10-m-tall tsunami swept across the country. Hundreds of aftershocks came in the days that followed, some with magnitudes as great as 7.4 on the Richter scale. How many times as great as the seismic shaking of the large aftershock was the shaking of the initial earthquake?

8.2 Transformations of Logarithmic Functions, pages 383–391

6. The graph of $y = \log_4 x$ is
   - stretched horizontally about the y-axis by a factor of $\dfrac{1}{2}$
   - reflected in the x-axis
   - translated 5 units down

   a) Sketch the graph of the transformed image.

   b) If the equation of the transformed image is written in the form $y = a \log_c (b(x - h)) + k$, determine the values of a, b, c, h, and k.

7. The red graph is a stretch of the blue graph. Determine the equation of the red graph.

   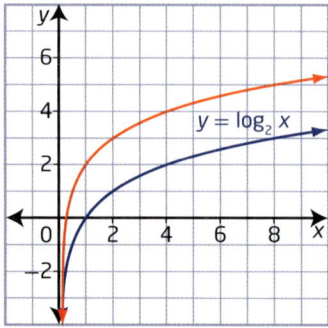

8. Describe, in order, a series of transformations that could be applied to the graph of $y = \log_5 x$ to draw the graph of each function.

   a) $y = -\log_5 (3(x - 12)) + 2$

   b) $y + 7 = \dfrac{\log_5 (6 - x)}{4}$

9. Identify the following characteristics of the graph of the function $y = 3 \log_2 (x + 8) + 6$.

   a) the equation of the asymptote
   b) the domain and range
   c) the y-intercept
   d) the x-intercept

10. Starting at the music note A, with a frequency of 440 Hz, the frequency of the other musical notes can be determined using the function $n = 12 \log_2 \dfrac{f}{440}$, where n is the number of notes away from A.

    a) Describe how the function is transformed from $n = \log_2 f$.
    b) How many notes above A is the note D, if D has a frequency of 587.36 Hz?
    c) Find the frequency of F, located eight notes above A. Answer to the nearest hundredth of a hertz.

8.3 Laws of Logarithms, pages 392–403

11. Write each expression in terms of the individual logarithms of x, y, and z.

    a) $\log_5 \dfrac{x^5}{y\sqrt[3]{z}}$

    b) $\log \sqrt{\dfrac{xy^2}{z}}$

12. Write each expression as a single logarithm in simplest form.

    a) $\log x - 3 \log y + \dfrac{2}{3} \log z$

    b) $\log x - \dfrac{1}{2}(\log y + 3 \log z)$

13. Write each expression as a single logarithm in simplest form. State any restrictions.

    a) $2 \log x + 3 \log \sqrt{x} - \log x^3$

    b) $\log (x^2 - 25) - 2 \log (x + 5)$

14. Use the laws of logarithms to simplify and then evaluate each expression.

    a) $\log_6 18 - \log_6 2 + \log_6 4$

    b) $\log_4 \sqrt{12} + \log_4 \sqrt{9} - \log_4 \sqrt{27}$

15. The pH of a solution is defined as pH = $-\log$ [H$^+$], where [H$^+$] is the hydrogen ion concentration, in moles per litre (mol/L). How many times as acidic is the blueberry, with a pH of 3.2, as a saskatoon berry, with a pH of 4.0?

Saskatoon berries

Did You Know?

The saskatoon berry is a shrub native to Western Canada and the northern plains of the United States. It produces a dark purple, berry-like fruit. The Plains Cree called the berry "misaskwatomin," meaning "fruit of the tree of many branches." This berry is called "okonok" by the Blackfoot and "k'injíe" by the Dene tha'.

16. The apparent magnitude, m, of a celestial object is a measure of how bright it appears to an observer on Earth. The brighter the object, the lower the value of its magnitude. The difference between the apparent magnitudes, m_2 and m_1, of two celestial objects can be found using the equation $m_2 - m_1 = -2.5 \log \left(\dfrac{F_2}{F_1}\right)$, where F_1 and F_2 are measures of the brightness of the two celestial objects, in watts per square metre, and $m_2 < m_1$. The apparent magnitude of the Sun is -26.74 and the average apparent magnitude of the full moon is -12.74. How many times brighter does the sun appear than the full moon, to an observer on Earth?

17. The sound intensity, β, in decibels, is defined as $\beta = 10 \log \dfrac{I}{I_0}$, where I is the intensity of the sound, in watts per square metre (W/m²), and I_0, the threshold of hearing, is 10^{-12} W/m². In some cities, police can issue a fine to the operator of a motorcycle when the sound while idling is 20 times as intense as the sound of an automobile. If the decibel level of an automobile is 80 dB, at what decibel level can police issue a fine to a motorcycle operator?

Device used to measure motorcycle noise levels

8.4 Logarithmic and Exponential Equations, pages 404–415

18. Determine the value of x, to two decimal places.
  a) $3^{2x+1} = 75$
  b) $7^{x+1} = 4^{2x-1}$

19. Determine x.
  a) $2 \log_5 (x - 3) = \log_5 (4)$
  b) $\log_4 (x + 2) - \log_4 (x - 4) = \dfrac{1}{2}$
  c) $\log_2 (3x + 1) = 2 - \log_2 (x - 1)$
  d) $\log \sqrt{x^2 - 21x} = 1$

20. A computer depreciates 32% per year. After how many years will a computer bought for $1200 be worth less than $100?

21. According to Kleiber's law, a mammal's resting metabolic rate, R, in kilocalories per day, is related to its mass, m, in kilograms, by the equation $\log R = \log 73.3 + 0.75 \log m$. Predict the mass of a wolf with a resting metabolic rate of 1050 kCal/day. Answer to the nearest kilogram.

22. Technetium-99m (Tc-99m) is the most widely used radioactive isotope for radiographic scanning. It is used to evaluate the medical condition of internal organs. It has a short half-life of only 6 h. A patient is administered an 800-MBq dose of Tc-99m. If none is lost from the body, when will the radioactivity of the Tc-99m in the patient's body be 600 MBq? Answer to the nearest tenth of an hour.

23. a) Mahal invests $500 in an account with an annual percentage rate (APR) of 5%, compounded quarterly. How long will it take for Mahal's single investment to double in value?

b) Mahal invests $500 at the end of every 3 months in an account with an APR of 4.8%, compounded quarterly. How long will it take for Mahal's investment to be worth $100 000? Use the formula $FV = \dfrac{R[(1 + i)^n - 1]}{i}$, where FV is the future value, n is the number of equal periodic payments of R dollars, and i is the interest rate per compounding period expressed as a decimal.

Chapter 8 Practice Test

Multiple Choice

For #1 to #6, choose the best answer.

1. Which graph represents the inverse of $y = \left(\dfrac{1}{4}\right)^x$?

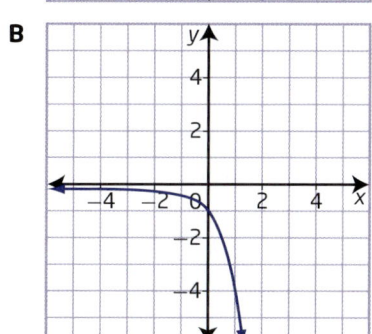

2. The exponential form of $k = -\log_h 5$ is

   A $h^k = \dfrac{1}{5}$ **B** $h^k = -5$

   C $k^h = \dfrac{1}{5}$ **D** $k^h = -5$

3. The effect on the graph of $y = \log_3 x$ if it is transformed to $y = \log_3 \sqrt{x + 7}$ can be described as

   A a vertical stretch about the x-axis by a factor of $\dfrac{1}{2}$ and a vertical translation of 7 units up

   B a vertical stretch about the x-axis by a factor of $\dfrac{1}{2}$ and a horizontal translation of 7 units left

   C a horizontal stretch about the y-axis by a factor of $\dfrac{1}{2}$ and a vertical translation of 7 units up

   D a horizontal stretch about the y-axis by a factor of $\dfrac{1}{2}$ and a horizontal translation of 7 units left

4. The logarithm $\log_3 \dfrac{x^p}{x^q}$ is equal to

   A $(p - q) \log_3 x$ **B** $\dfrac{p}{q}$

   C $p - q$ **D** $\dfrac{p}{q} \log_3 x$

5. If $x = \log_2 3$, then $\log_2 8\sqrt{3}$ can be represented as an algebraic expression, in terms of x, as

   A $\dfrac{1}{2}x + 8$ **B** $2x + 8$

   C $\dfrac{1}{2}x + 3$ **D** $2x + 3$

6. The pH of a solution is defined as pH $= -\log [\text{H}^+]$, where $[\text{H}^+]$ is the hydrogen ion concentration, in moles per litre (mol/L). Acetic acid has a pH of 2.9. Formic acid is 4 times as concentrated as acetic acid. What is the pH of formic acid?

   A 1.1   **B** 2.3

   C 3.5   **D** 6.9

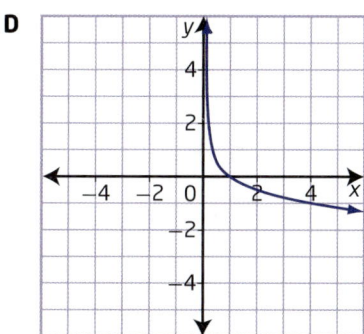

Short Answer

7. Determine the value of x.

   a) $\log_9 x = -2$
   b) $\log_x 125 = \dfrac{3}{2}$
   c) $\log_3 (\log_x 125) = 1$
   d) $7^{\log_7 3} = x$
   e) $\log_2 8^{x-3} = 4$

8. If $5^{m+n} = 125$ and $\log_{m-n} 8 = 3$, determine the values of m and n.

9. Describe a series of transformations that could be applied to the graph of $y = \log_2 x$ to obtain the graph of $y = -5 \log_2 8(x - 1)$. What other series of transformations could be used?

10. Identify the following characteristics of the graph of the function $y = 2 \log_5 (x + 5) + 6$.

    a) the equation of the asymptote
    b) the domain and range
    c) the y-intercept
    d) the x-intercept

11. Determine the value of x.

    a) $\log_2 (x - 4) - \log_2 (x + 2) = 4$
    b) $\log_2 (x - 4) = 4 - \log_2 (x + 2)$
    c) $\log_2 (x^2 - 2x)^7 = 21$

12. Solve for x. Express answers to two decimal places.

    a) $3^{2x+1} = 75$
    b) $12^{x-2} = 3^{2x+1}$

Extended Response

13. Holly wins $1 000 000 in a lottery and invests the entire amount in an annuity with an annual interest rate of 6%, compounded semi-annually. Holly plans to make a withdrawal of $35 000 at the end of every 6 months. For how many years can she make the semi-annual withdrawals? Use the formula $PV = \dfrac{R[1 - (1 + i)^{-n}]}{i}$, where PV is the present value, n is the number of equal periodic payments of R dollars, and i is the interest rate per compounding period expressed as a decimal.

14. The exchange of free energy, ΔG, in calories (Cal), to transport a mole of a substance across a human cell wall is described as $\Delta G = 1427.6(\log C_2 - \log C_1)$, where C_1 is the concentration inside the cell and C_2 is the concentration outside the cell. If the exchange of free energy to transport a mole of glucose is 4200 Cal, how many times as great is the glucose concentration outside the cell as inside the cell?

15. The sound intensity, β, in decibels is defined as $\beta = 10 \log \dfrac{I}{I_0}$, where I is the intensity of the sound, in watts per square metre (W/m²), and I_0, the threshold of hearing, is 10^{-12} W/m². A refrigerator in the kitchen of a restaurant has a decibel level of 45 dB. The owner would like to install a second such refrigerator so that the two run side by side. She is concerned that the noise of the two refrigerators will be too loud. Should she be concerned? Justify your answer.

16. Ethanol is a high-octane renewable fuel derived from crops such as corn and wheat. Through the process of fermentation, yeast cells duplicate in a bioreactor and convert carbohydrates into ethanol. Researchers start with a yeast-cell concentration of 4.0 g/L in a bioreactor. Eight hours later, the yeast-cell concentration is 12.8 g/L. What is the doubling time of the yeast cells, to the nearest tenth of an hour?

17. The Consumer Price Index (CPI) measures changes in consumer prices by comparing, through time, the cost of a fixed basket of commodities. The CPI compares prices in a given year to prices in 1992. The 1992 price of the basket is 100%. The 2006 price of the basket was 129.9%, that is, 129.9% of the 1992 price. If the CPI continues to grow at the same rate, in what year will the price of the basket be twice the 1992 price?

Unit 3 Project Wrap-Up

At the Movies

- Investigate one of your favourite movies. Find and record the box office revenues for the first 10 weeks. You may wish to change the time period depending on the availability of data, but try to get about ten successive data points.
- Graph the data.
- Which type of function do you think would best describe the graph? Is one function appropriate or do you think it is more appropriate to use different functions for different parts of the domain?
- Develop a function (or functions) to model the movie's cumulative box office revenue.
- Use your function to predict the cumulative revenue after week 15.
- Discuss whether this model will work for all movies.

Be prepared to present your findings to your classmates.

Cumulative Review, Chapters 7–8

Chapter 7 Exponential Functions

1. Consider the exponential functions $y = 4^x$ and $y = \frac{1}{4}^x$.
   a) Sketch the graph of each function.
   b) Compare the domain, range, intercepts, and equations of the asymptotes.
   c) Is each function increasing or decreasing? Explain.

2. Match each equation with its graph.
   a) $y = 5(2^x) + 1$
   b) $y = \left(\frac{1}{2}\right)^{x+5}$
   c) $y + 1 = 2^{5-x}$
   d) $y = 5\left(\frac{1}{2}\right)^{-x}$

   A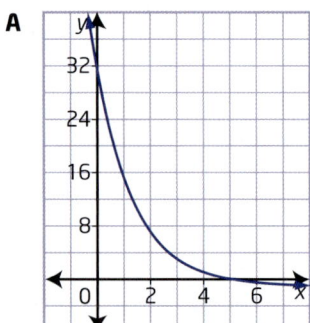

   B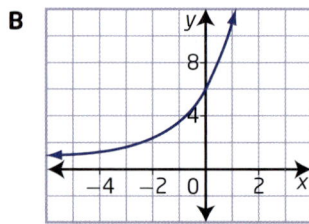

   C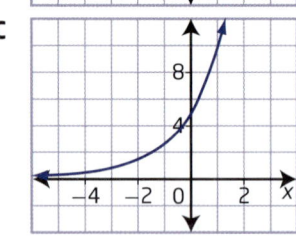

   D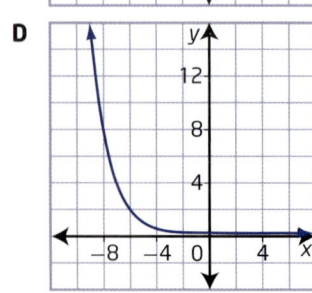

3. The number, B, of bacteria in a culture after t hours is given by $B(t) = 1000\left(2^{\frac{t}{3}}\right)$.
   a) How many bacteria were there initially?
   b) What is the doubling period, in hours?
   c) How many bacteria are present after 24 h?
   d) When will there be 128 000 bacteria?

4. The graph of $f(x) = 3^x$ is transformed to obtain the graph of $g(x) = 2(3^{x+4}) + 1$.
   a) Describe the transformations.
   b) Sketch the graph of $g(x)$.
   c) Identify the changes in the domain, range, equations of the asymptotes, and any intercepts due to the transformations.

5. Write the expressions in each pair so that they have the same base.
   a) 2^{3x+6} and 8^{x-5}
   b) 27^{4-x} and $\left(\frac{1}{9}\right)^{2x}$

6. Solve for x algebraically.
   a) $5 = 2^{x+4} - 3$
   b) $\dfrac{25^{x+3}}{625^{x-4}} = 125^{2x+7}$

7. Solve for x graphically. Round your answers to two decimal places.
   a) $3(2^{x+1}) = 6^{-x}$
   b) $4^{2x} = 3^{x-1} + 5$

8. A pump reduces the air pressure in a tank by 17% each second. Thus, the percent air pressure, p, is given by $p = 100(0.83^t)$, where t is the time, in seconds.
   a) Determine the percent air pressure in the tank after 5 s.
   b) When will the air pressure be 50% of the starting pressure?

Chapter 8 Logarithmic Functions

9. Express in logarithmic form.
   a) $y = 3^x$
   b) $m = 2^{a+1}$

10. Express in exponential form.
    a) $\log_x 3 = 4$
    b) $\log_a (x + 5) = b$

11. Evaluate.

a) $\log_3 \dfrac{1}{81}$

b) $\log_2 \sqrt{8} + \dfrac{1}{3} \log_2 512$

c) $\log_2 (\log_5 \sqrt{5})$

d) 7^k, where $k = \log_7 49$

12. Solve for x.

a) $\log_x 16 = 4$

b) $\log_2 x = 5$

c) $5^{\log_5 x} = \dfrac{1}{125}$

d) $\log_x (\log_3 \sqrt{27}) = \dfrac{1}{5}$

13. Describe how the graph of
$y = \dfrac{\log_6 (2x - 8)}{3} + 5$ can be obtained by transforming the graph of $y = \log_6 x$.

14. Determine the equation of the transformed image of the logarithmic function $y = \log x$ after each set of transformations is applied.

a) a vertical stretch about the x-axis by a factor of 3 and a horizontal translation of 5 units left

b) a horizontal stretch about the y-axis by a factor of $\dfrac{1}{2}$, a reflection in the x-axis, and a vertical translation of 2 units down

15. The pH of a solution is defined as pH = $-\log [H^+]$, where $[H^+]$ is the hydrogen ion concentration, in moles per litre. The pH of a soil solution indicates the nutrients, such as nitrogen and potassium, that plants need in specific amounts to grow.

a) Alfalfa grows best in soils with a pH of 6.2 to 7.8. Determine the range of the concentration of hydrogen ions that is best for alfalfa.

b) When the pH of the soil solution is above 5.5, nitrogen is made available to plants. If the concentration of hydrogen ions is 3.0×10^{-6} mol/L, is nitrogen available?

16. Write each expression as a single logarithm in simplest form. State any restrictions on the variables.

a) $2 \log m - (\log \sqrt{n} + 3 \log p)$

b) $\dfrac{1}{3}(\log_a x - \log_a \sqrt{x}) + \log_a 3x^2$

c) $2 \log (x + 1) + \log (x - 1) - \log (x^2 - 1)$

d) $\log_2 27^x - \log_2 3^x$

17. Zack attempts to solve a logarithmic equation as shown. Identify and describe any errors, and then correctly solve the equation.

$\log_3 (x - 4)^2 = 4$
$3^4 = (x - 4)^2$
$81 = x^2 - 8x + 16$
$0 = x^2 - 8x - 65$
$x = -13$ or $x = 5$

18. Determine the value of x. Round your answers to two decimal places if necessary.

a) $4^{2x+1} = 9(4^{1-x})$

b) $\log_3 x + 3 \log_3 x^2 = 14$

c) $\log (2x - 3) = \log (4x - 3) - \log x$

d) $\log_2 x + \log_2 (x + 6) = 4$

19. The Richter magnitude, M, of an earthquake is related to the energy, E, in joules, released by the earthquake according to the equation $\log E = 4.4 + 1.4M$.

a) Determine the energy for earthquakes with magnitudes 4 and 5.

b) For each increase in M of 1, by what factor does E change?

20. At the end of each quarter year, Aaron makes a $625 payment into a mutual fund that earns an annual percentage rate of 6%, compounded quarterly. The future value, FV, of Aaron's investment is $FV = \dfrac{R[(1 + i)^n - 1]}{i}$, where n is the number of equal periodic payments of R dollars, and i is the interest rate per compounding period expressed as a decimal. After how long will Aaron's investment be worth $1 000 000?

Unit 3 Test

Multiple Choice

For #1 to #7, select the best answer.

1. The graph of the function $y = a(2^{bx})$ is shown.

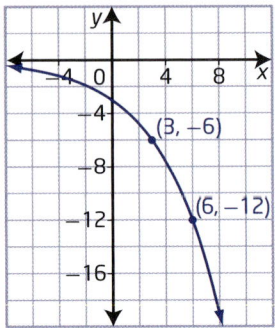

   The value of a is

   A 3

   B $\dfrac{1}{3}$

   C $-\dfrac{1}{3}$

   D -3

2. The graph of the function $y = b^x$, $b > 1$, is transformed to $y = 3(b^{x+1}) - 2$. The characteristics of the function that change are

   A the domain and the range

   B the range, the x-intercept, and the y-intercept

   C the domain, the x-intercept, and the y-intercept

   D the domain, the range, the x-intercept, and the y-intercept

3. The half-life of carbon-14 is 5730 years. If a bone has lost 40% of its carbon-14, then an equation that can be used to determine its age is

   A $60 = 100\left(\dfrac{1}{2}\right)^{\frac{t}{5730}}$

   B $60 = 100\left(\dfrac{1}{2}\right)^{\frac{5730}{t}}$

   C $40 = 100\left(\dfrac{1}{2}\right)^{\frac{t}{5730}}$

   D $40 = 100\left(\dfrac{1}{2}\right)^{\frac{5730}{t}}$

4. Which of the following is an equivalent form for $2x = \log_3 (y - 1)$?

   A $y = 3^{2x} - 1$

   B $y = 3^{2x+1}$

   C $y = 9^x + 1$

   D $y = 9^{x+1}$

5. The domain of $f(x) = -\log_2 (x + 3)$ is

   A $\{x \mid x > -3, x \in R\}$

   B $\{x \mid x \geq -3, x \in R\}$

   C $\{x \mid x < 3, x \in R\}$

   D $\{x \mid x \in R\}$

6. If $\log_2 5 = x$, then $\log_2 \sqrt[4]{25^3}$ is equivalent to

   A $\dfrac{3x}{2}$

   B $\dfrac{3x}{8}$

   C $x^{\frac{3}{2}}$

   D $x^{\frac{3}{8}}$

7. If $\log_4 16 = x + 2y$ and $\log 0.0001 = x - y$, then the value of y is

   A -2

   B $-\dfrac{1}{2}$

   C $\dfrac{1}{2}$

   D 2

Numerical Response

Copy and complete the statements in #8 to #12.

8. The graph of the function $f(x) = \left(\dfrac{1}{4}\right)^x$ is transformed by a vertical stretch about the x-axis by a factor of 2, a reflection about the x-axis, and a horizontal translation of 3 units right. The equation of the transformed function is ■.

9. The quotient $\dfrac{9^{\frac{1}{2}}}{27^{\frac{2}{3}}}$ expressed as a single power of 3 is ■.

10. The point P(2, 1) is on the graph of the logarithmic function $y = \log_2 x$. When the function is reflected in the x-axis and translated 1 unit down, the coordinates of the image of P are ■.

11. The solution to the equation $\log 10^x = 0.001$ is ■.

12. Evaluating $\log_5 40 - 3 \log_5 10$ results in ■.

Written Response

13. Consider $f(x) = 3^{-x} - 2$.
    a) Sketch the graph of the function.
    b) State the domain and the range.
    c) Determine the zeros of $f(x)$, to one decimal place.

14. Solve for x and verify your solution.
    a) $9^{\frac{1}{4}} \left(\dfrac{1}{3}\right)^{\frac{x}{2}} = \sqrt[3]{27^4}$
    b) $5(2^{x-1}) = 10^{2x-3}$

15. Let $f(x) = 1 - \log(x - 2)$.
    a) Determine the domain, range, and equations of the asymptotes of $f(x)$.
    b) Determine the equation of $f^{-1}(x)$.
    c) Determine the y-intercepts of $f^{-1}(x)$.

16. Solve for x algebraically.
    a) $\log 4 = \log x + \log(13 - 3x)$
    b) $\log_3(3x + 6) - \log_3(x - 4) = 2$

17. The following shows how Giovanni attempted to solve the equation $2(3^x) = 8$. Identify, describe, and correct his errors.

    $2(3^x) = 8$
    $6^x = 8$
    $\log 6^x = \log 8$
    $x \log 6 = \log 8$
    $x = \dfrac{\log 8}{\log 6}$
    $x = \log 8 - \log 6$
    $x \approx 0.12$

    The solution is $x \approx 0.12$.

18. The Richter magnitude, M, of an earthquake is defined as $M = \log\left(\dfrac{A}{A_0}\right)$, where A is the amplitude of the ground motion and A_0 is the amplitude, corrected for the distance to the actual earthquake, that would be expected for a standard earthquake. An earthquake near Tofino, British Columbia, measures 5.6 on the Richter scale. An aftershock is $\dfrac{1}{4}$ the amplitude of the original earthquake. Determine the magnitude of the aftershock on the Richter scale, to the nearest tenth.

19. The world population was approximately 6 billion in 2000. Assume that the population grows at a rate of 1.3% per year.
    a) Write an equation to represent the population of the world.
    b) When will the population reach at least 10 billion?

20. To save for a new highway tractor, a truck company deposits $11 500 at the end of every 6 months into an account with an annual percentage rate of 5%, compounded semi-annually. Determine the number of deposits needed so that the account has at least $150 000. Use the formula $FV = \dfrac{R[(1 + i)^n - 1]}{i}$, where FV is the future value, n is the number of equal periodic payments of R dollars, and i is the interest rate per compounding period expressed as a decimal.

Unit 4

Equations and Functions

Functions and equations can be used to model many real-world situations. Some situations involve functions with less complicated equations:
- The density, d, of a 10-kg rock sample with volume V is given by the function $d = \dfrac{10}{V}$.
- The illuminance or brightness, I, of one type of light at a distance d from the light is given by $I = \dfrac{100}{d^2}$.

Equations for more complicated functions can be created by adding, subtracting, multiplying, or dividing two simpler functions:
- The function $h(x) = 3x^2 + 2 + \sqrt{x + 4}$ is the sum of the functions $f(x) = 3x^2 + 2$ and $g(x) = \sqrt{x + 4}$.
- The rational function $h(x) = \dfrac{x^2}{x - 1}$ is the quotient of the functions $f(x) = x^2$ and $g(x) = x - 1$.

Some real-world situations involve counting selections or arrangements of objects or items:
- the number of ways genetic codes can be combined
- the number of licence plates possible in a province

In this unit, you will explore rational functions before moving on to work with operations on functions in general. You will also learn about permutations, combinations, and the binomial theorem and apply them to solve problems.

Looking Ahead

In this unit, you will solve problems involving...
- rational functions
- operations on functions, including sums, differences, products, quotients, and compositions
- permutations, combinations, and the binomial theorem

Unit 4 Project

Representing Equations and Functions

For this project, you will choose a topic in Unit 4. Then, you will create a video or slide show, a song, or a piece of artwork to communicate and/or demonstrate your understanding of the concept you have chosen.

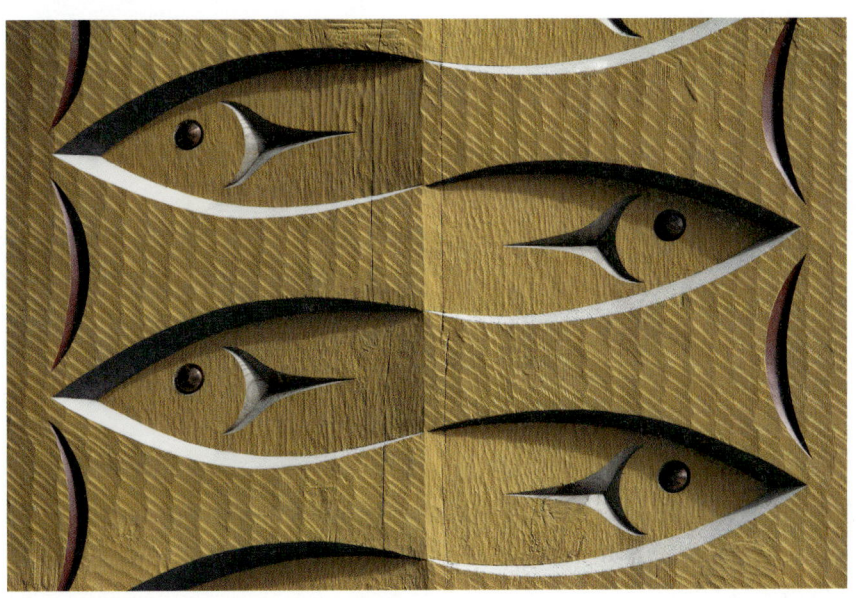

A detail from The Gateways at Brockton Point in Stanley Park, Vancouver, by Coast Salish artist Susan A. Point.

Unit 4 Equations and Functions • MHR 427

CHAPTER 9

Rational Functions

Why does the lens on a camera need to move to focus on objects that are nearer or farther away? What is the relationship between the travel time for a plane and the velocity of the wind in which it is flying? How can you relate the amount of light from a source to the distance from the source? The mathematics behind all of these situations involves rational functions.

A simple rational function is used to relate distance, time, and speed. More complicated rational functions may be used in a business to model average costs of production or by a doctor to predict the amount of medication remaining in a patient's bloodstream.

In this chapter, you will explore a variety of rational functions. You have used the term *rational* before, with rational numbers and rational expressions, so what is a rational *function*?

Key Terms
rational function   point of discontinuity

Career Link

To become a chartered accountant (CA), you need education, experience, and evaluation. A CA student first completes a bachelor's degree including several accounting courses. Then, the CA student works for a chartered firm while taking courses that lead to a final series of examinations that determine whether he or she meets the requirements of a CA.

Why should you do all this work? CAs are business, tax, and personal accounting specialists. Many CAs go on to careers in senior management because their skills are so valued.

Web Link

To learn more about a career as a chartered accountant, go to www.mcgrawhill.ca/school/learningcentres and follow the links.

9.1

Exploring Rational Functions Using Transformations

Focus on...
- graphing, analysing, and comparing rational functions using transformations and using technology
- examining the behaviour of the graphs of rational functions near non-permissible values

The Trans Canada Trail is a system of 22 000 km of linked trails that passes through every province and territory and connects the Pacific, Arctic, and Atlantic Oceans. When completely developed, it will be the world's longest network of trails. Millions of people walk, run, cycle, hike, canoe, horseback ride, snowmobile, and more on the trail.

If you cycle a 120-km section of the Trans Canada Trail, the time it takes is related to your average speed. Cycling more quickly means it takes less time; cycling more slowly means it takes more time. The relationship between the time and the average speed can be expressed mathematically with a **rational function**. What does the graph of this function look like?

Trans Canada Trail at Kettle Valley, British Columbia

rational function
- a function that can be written in the form $f(x) = \dfrac{p(x)}{q(x)}$, where $p(x)$ and $q(x)$ are polynomial expressions and $q(x) \neq 0$
- some examples are $y = \dfrac{20}{x}$, $C(n) = \dfrac{100 + 2n}{n}$, and $f(x) = \dfrac{3x^2 + 4}{x - 5}$

Did You Know?

Some sections of the Trans Canada Trail are based on long-established routes of travel, such as the Dempster Highway in Northern Canada. This narrow gravel road is over 500 km long and connects Dawson City, Yukon Territory, with Inuvik, Norhwest Territories on the Mackenzie River delta. The route is based on an old First Nations trading route dating back to the last ice age. This corridor was ice-free during that period and is believed by many to be a route used by the first people in North America.

Web Link

To learn more about the Trans Canada Trail, go to www.mcgrawhill.ca/school/learningcentres and follow the links.

Investigate Rational Functions

A: Relate Time and Speed

Materials
- graphing technology

1. **a)** Copy and complete the table of values giving the time to cycle a 120-km stretch of the Trans Canada Trail for a variety of average speeds.

Average Speed (km/h)	1	2	3	4	5	6	8	10	12	15	20	24	30	40
Time (h)														

   b) What happens to the time as the average speed gets smaller and smaller in value? larger and larger in value?

2. **a)** Write an equation to express the time, t, in hours, as a function of the average speed, v, in kilometres per hour.

   b) Is the value zero a part of the domain or the range in this situation? Explain.

3. **a)** Graph the function.

   b) How does the shape of the graph relate to your answer to step 2b)?

   c) What does the graph show about the time to cycle a 120-km stretch of the Trans Canada Trail as the average speed gets closer to zero?

Reflect and Respond

4. **a)** How is the relationship between average speed and time connected to the shape of the graph?

   b) Does the graph of this function have endpoints? Explain.

B: The Effect of the Parameters a, h, and k on the Function $y = \dfrac{a}{x - h} + k$

5. **a)** Graph the functions $y = \dfrac{1}{x}$, $y = \dfrac{4}{x}$, and $y = \dfrac{12}{x}$ using technology.

   b) Describe the behaviour of these functions as x approaches zero.

   c) What happens to the values of these functions as $|x|$ becomes larger and larger?

   d) Compare the graphs. For any real value a, describe the relationship between the graphs of $y = \dfrac{1}{x}$ and $y = \dfrac{a}{x}$.

6. **a)** Graph the functions $y = \dfrac{1}{x}$ and $y = \dfrac{4}{x - 3} + 2$.

   b) Compare the graphs. How do the numbers in the transformed function equation affect the shape and position of its graph relative to the graph of the base function $y = \dfrac{1}{x}$?

   c) What function from step 5 has a graph that is congruent to the graph of $y = \dfrac{4}{x - 3} + 2$? Why do you think this is?

7. a) Predict the effects of the parameters in the function $y = -\dfrac{12}{x+1} - 5$. Graph the function to check your predictions.

 b) Which function from step 5 has a graph that is congruent to the graph of this function? How are the equations and graphs connected?

Reflect and Respond

8. Are the locations of the asymptotes of the function $y = \dfrac{1}{x}$ affected if a vertical stretch by a factor of a is applied to the function? Explain your thinking.

9. a) Can you tell from the equation of the transformed rational function $y = \dfrac{a}{x-h} + k$ where its graph has a vertical asymptote? Explain.

 b) Describe how the values of a function change as x approaches a non-permissible value.

 c) What non-translated function has a graph that is congruent to the graph of $y = \dfrac{8}{x-7} + 6$? How might you graph $y = \dfrac{8}{x-7} + 6$ without technology using this relationship?

Link the Ideas

> **Did You Know?**
>
> The equation of the function $y = \dfrac{a}{x}$ is equivalent to $xy = a$. The equation $xy = a$ shows that for any point on the graph, the product of the x- and y-coordinates is always equal to a.

The rational function that relates speed to time for a given distance is related to the base function $y = \dfrac{1}{x}$ by a vertical stretch.

The graph of a rational function of the form $y = \dfrac{a}{x}$ represents a vertical stretch by a factor of a of the graph of $y = \dfrac{1}{x}$, because $y = \dfrac{a}{x}$ can be written as $y = a\left(\dfrac{1}{x}\right)$.

Graphs of rational functions of the form $y = \dfrac{a}{x}$ have two separate branches that approach the asymptotes at $x = 0$ and $y = 0$.

Example 1

Graph a Rational Function Using a Table of Values

Analyse the function $y = \dfrac{10}{x}$ using a table of values and a graph. Identify characteristics of the graph, including the behaviour of the function for its non-permissible value.

Solution

Select values of x that make it easy to calculate the corresponding values of y for $y = \frac{10}{x}$.

Why is the function undefined when x is zero?

The equation of the function can be rearranged to give $xy = 10$. How might this form be used to generate ordered pairs for the table and points on the graph?

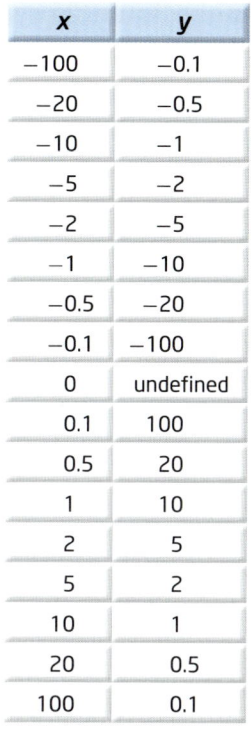

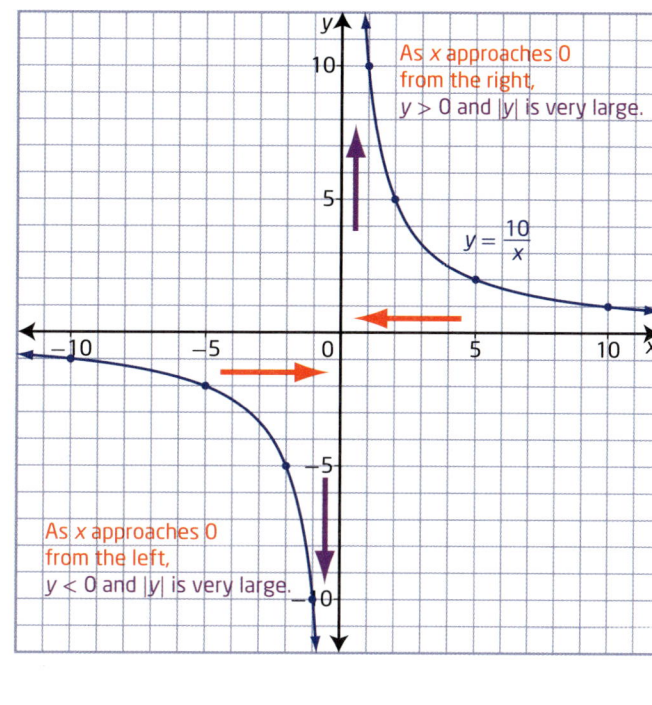

Why does $|y|$ get larger as the values of x approach zero?

What happens to the values of y as $|x|$ becomes very large?

For this function, when 0 is substituted for the value of x, the denominator has a value of 0. Since division by 0 is undefined, 0 is a non-permissible value. This corresponds to the vertical asymptote in the graph at $x = 0$. As the values of x approach zero, the absolute value of y gets very large.

Summarize the characteristics of the function using a table.

Characteristic	$y = \frac{10}{x}$
Non-permissible value	$x = 0$
Behaviour near non-permissible value	As x approaches 0, $|y|$ becomes very large.
End behaviour	As $|x|$ becomes very large, y approaches 0.
Domain	$\{x \mid x \neq 0, x \in R\}$
Range	$\{y \mid y \neq 0, y \in R\}$
Equation of vertical asymptote	$x = 0$
Equation of horizontal asymptote	$y = 0$

Your Turn

Analyse the function $y = \frac{6}{x}$ using a table of values and a graph. Identify characteristics of the graph, including the behaviour of the function for its non-permissible value.

Did You Know?

In Pre-Calculus 11, you graphed and analysed rational functions that are reciprocals of linear or quadratic functions: $y = \frac{1}{f(x)}$, where $f(x) \neq 0$. In this chapter, you will explore rational functions with numerators and denominators that are monomials, binomials, or trinomials.

9.1 Exploring Rational Functions Using Transformations • MHR 433

You can sometimes graph and analyse more complicated rational functions by considering how they are related by transformations to base rational functions.

To obtain the graph of a rational function of the form $y = \dfrac{a}{x - h} + k$ from the graph of $y = \dfrac{1}{x}$, apply a vertical stretch by a factor of a, followed by translations of h units horizontally and k units vertically.

- The graph has a vertical asymptote at $x = h$.
- The graph has a horizontal asymptote at $y = k$.
- Knowing the location of the asymptotes and drawing them first can help you graph and analyse the function.

Example 2

Graph a Rational Function Using Transformations

Sketch the graph of the function $y = \dfrac{6}{x - 2} - 3$ using transformations, and identify any important characteristics of the graph.

Solution

Compare the function $y = \dfrac{6}{x - 2} - 3$ to the form $y = \dfrac{a}{x - h} + k$ to determine the values of the parameters: $a = 6$, $h = 2$, and $k = -3$.

To obtain the graph of $y = \dfrac{6}{x - 2} - 3$ from the graph of $y = \dfrac{1}{x}$, apply a vertical stretch by a factor of 6, and then a translation of 2 units to the right and 3 units down.

The asymptotes of the graph of $y = \dfrac{6}{x - 2} - 3$ translate in the same way from their original locations of $x = 0$ and $y = 0$. Therefore, the vertical asymptote is located 2 units to the right at $x = 2$, and the horizontal asymptote is located 3 units down at $y = -3$.

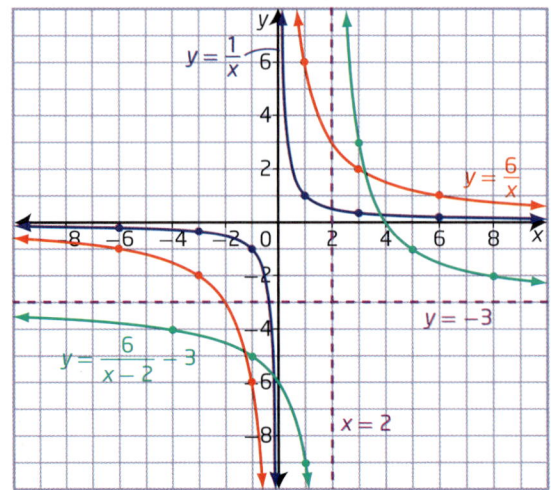

How can you use the asymptotes to help you sketch the graph?

How might considering ordered pairs for $y = \dfrac{6}{x}$ help you graph $y = \dfrac{6}{x - 2} - 3$?

What happens to $|y|$ as the values of x approach 2?

What happens to the values of y as $|x|$ becomes very large?

Summarize the characteristics of the graph using a table:

Characteristic	$y = \dfrac{6}{x-2} - 3$
Non-permissible value	$x = 2$
Behaviour near non-permissible value	As x approaches 2, $|y|$ becomes very large.
End behaviour	As $|x|$ becomes very large, y approaches -3.
Domain	$\{x \mid x \neq 2,\ x \in R\}$
Range	$\{y \mid y \neq -3,\ y \in R\}$
Equation of vertical asymptote	$x = 2$
Equation of horizontal asymptote	$y = -3$

Which of the characteristics listed are related to each other?

How is each of the function's characteristics related to the equation of the function?

Your Turn
Sketch the graph of the function $y = \dfrac{4}{x+1} + 5$ using transformations, and identify the important characteristics of the graph.

Example 3

Graph a Rational Function With Linear Expressions in the Numerator and the Denominator

Graph the function $y = \dfrac{4x - 5}{x - 2}$. Identify any asymptotes and intercepts.

Solution

Method 1: Use Paper and Pencil
Determine the locations of the intercepts and asymptotes first, and then use them as a guide to sketch the graph.

Find the y-intercept of the function by substituting 0 for x.
$$y = \frac{4x - 5}{x - 2}$$
$$y = \frac{4(0) - 5}{0 - 2}$$
$$y = 2.5$$
The y-intercept occurs at $(0, 2.5)$.

Find the x-intercept of the function by solving for x when $y = 0$.
$$y = \frac{4x - 5}{x - 2}$$
$$0 = \frac{4x - 5}{x - 2}$$
$$(x - 2)(0) = (x - 2)\left(\frac{4x - 5}{x - 2}\right)$$
$$0 = 4x - 5$$
$$x = 1.25$$
The x-intercept occurs at $(1.25, 0)$.

Manipulate the equation of this function algebraically to obtain the form $y = \dfrac{a}{x-h} + k$, which reveals the location of both the vertical asymptote and the horizontal asymptote.

$y = \dfrac{4x - 5}{x - 2}$

$y = \dfrac{4x - 8 + 8 - 5}{x - 2}$

$y = \dfrac{4(x - 2) + 3}{x - 2}$

Why is it necessary to change the numerator so that it involves the expression $(x - 2)$?

$y = \dfrac{4(x - 2)}{x - 2} + \dfrac{3}{x - 2}$

$y = 4 + \dfrac{3}{x - 2}$

How is this form related to polynomial division?

$y = \dfrac{3}{x - 2} + 4$

To obtain the graph of the function $y = \dfrac{3}{x - 2} + 4$ from the graph of $y = \dfrac{1}{x}$, apply a vertical stretch by a factor of 3, and then a translation of 2 units to the right and 4 units up.

Translate the asymptotes in the same way, to $x = 2$ and $y = 4$.

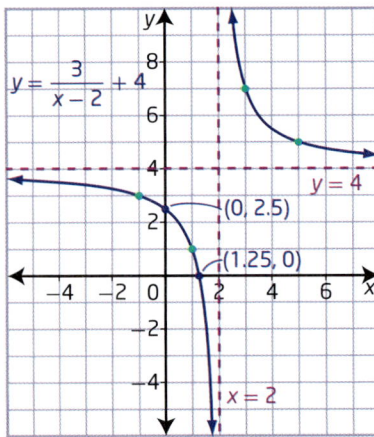

How can considering the pattern of ordered pairs for $y = \dfrac{3}{x}$ help you locate the points shown in green?

How are these four green points related to the symmetry in the graph?

Method 2: Use a Graphing Calculator

Graph the function $y = \dfrac{4x - 5}{x - 2}$ using a graphing calculator. Adjust the dimensions of the window so that all of the important features of the graph are visible.

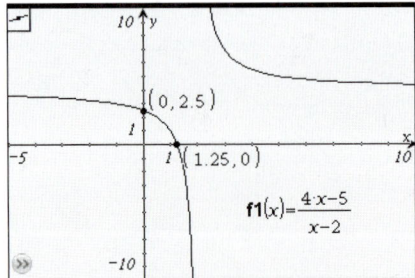

Use the zero, value, trace and table features to verify the locations of the intercepts and asymptotes. The graph of the function has
- a y-intercept of 2.5
- an x-intercept of 1.25
- a vertical asymptote at $x = 2$
- a horizontal asymptote at $y = 4$

Your Turn

Graph the function $y = \dfrac{2x + 2}{x - 4}$. Identify any asymptotes and intercepts.

Example 4

Compare Rational Functions

Consider the functions $f(x) = \dfrac{1}{x^2}$, $g(x) = \dfrac{3}{x^2 - 10x + 25}$, and $h(x) = 6 - \dfrac{1}{(x + 4)^2}$.

Graph each pair of functions.
- $f(x)$ and $g(x)$
- $f(x)$ and $h(x)$

Compare the characteristics of the graphs of the functions.

Solution

Graph the functions using a graphing calculator. Set the window dimensions so that important features are visible.

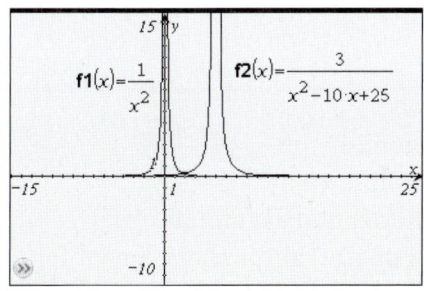 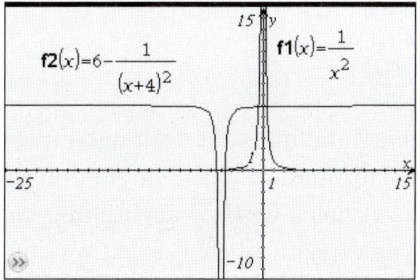

Rewrite the functions $g(x)$ and $h(x)$ algebraically to reveal how they are related to the base function $f(x) = \dfrac{1}{x^2}$. Then, use transformations to explain some of the similarities in the graphs.

$$g(x) = \frac{3}{x^2 - 10x + 25}$$

$$g(x) = \frac{3}{(x-5)^2}$$

$$g(x) = 3\left(\frac{1}{(x-5)^2}\right)$$

$$g(x) = 3f(x-5)$$

To obtain the graph of $g(x)$ from the graph of $f(x)$, apply a vertical stretch by a factor of 3 and a translation of 5 units to the right.

$$h(x) = 6 - \frac{1}{(x+4)^2}$$

$$h(x) = -\frac{1}{(x+4)^2} + 6$$

$$h(x) = -f(x+4) + 6$$

To obtain the graph of $h(x)$ from the graph of $f(x)$, apply a reflection in the x-axis and a translation of 4 units to the left and 6 units up.

Use the appropriate graphing technology features to verify the locations of the asymptotes.

Characteristic	$f(x) = \frac{1}{x^2}$	$g(x) = \frac{3}{x^2 - 10x + 25}$	$h(x) = 6 - \frac{1}{(x+4)^2}$
Non-permissible value	$x = 0$	$x = 5$	$x = -4$
Behaviour near non-permissible value	As x approaches 0, $|y|$ becomes very large.	As x approaches 5, $|y|$ becomes very large.	As x approaches -4, $|y|$ becomes very large.
End behaviour	As $|x|$ becomes very large, y approaches 0.	As $|x|$ becomes very large, y approaches 0.	As $|x|$ becomes very large, y approaches 6.
Domain	$\{x \mid x \neq 0, x \in R\}$	$\{x \mid x \neq 5, x \in R\}$	$\{x \mid x \neq -4, x \in R\}$
Range	$\{y \mid y > 0, y \in R\}$	$\{y \mid y > 0, y \in R\}$	$\{y \mid y < 6, y \in R\}$
Equation of vertical asymptote	$x = 0$	$x = 5$	$x = -4$
Equation of horizontal asymptote	$y = 0$	$y = 0$	$y = 6$

The graphs have the following in common:
- Each function has a single non-permissible value.
- Each has a vertical asymptote and a horizontal asymptote.
- The domain of each function consists of all real numbers except for a single value. The range of each function consists of a restricted set of the real numbers.
- $|y|$ becomes very large for each function when the values of x approach the non-permissible value for the function.

Your Turn

Graph the functions $f(x) = \frac{1}{x^2}$, $g(x) = \frac{-1}{(x-3)^2}$, and $h(x) = 2 + \frac{5}{x^2 + 2x + 1}$. Compare the characteristics of the graphs.

Example 5

Apply Rational Functions

A mobile phone service provider offers several different prepaid plans. One of the plans has a $10 monthly fee and a rate of 10¢ per text message sent or minute of talk time. Another plan has a monthly fee of $5 and a rate of 15¢ per text message sent or minute of talk time. Talk time is billed per whole minute.

a) Represent the average cost per text or minute of each plan with a rational function.
b) Graph the functions.
c) What do the graphs show about the average cost per text or minute for these two plans as the number of texts and minutes changes?
d) Which plan is the better choice?

Solution

a) Write a function to represent each plan.
Let f_1 and f_2 represent the average cost per text sent or minute used for the first and second plans, respectively.
Let x be the combined number of texts sent and minutes used. x is a whole number.

Calculate the average cost per text or minute of each plan as the quotient of the total cost and the combined number of texts and minutes.

Determine expressions for the total cost of each plan.

Total cost = monthly fee + (rate per text or minute)(combined number of texts and minutes)

Total cost = $10 + 0.1x$ for the first plan

or

Total cost = $5 + 0.15x$ for the second plan

Substitute each expression into the following formula:

$$\text{Average cost} = \frac{\text{total cost}}{\text{combined number of texts and minutes}}$$

$f_1(x) = \dfrac{10 + 0.1x}{x}$ and $f_2(x) = \dfrac{5 + 0.15x}{x}$

Since $x \neq 0$, the domain becomes the set of natural numbers.

b) Graph the two functions using technology.

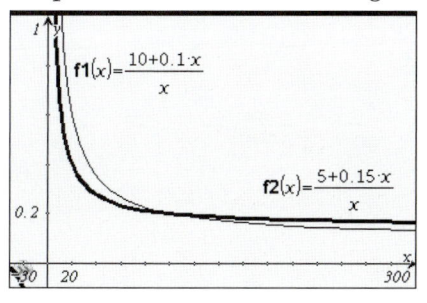

Why does the graph show only quadrant I?

c) Both functions have a vertical asymptote at $x = 0$, corresponding to the non-permissible value of each function.

Although the data is discrete, the function that models it is continuous. Therefore, the average cost function is only valid in the domain $\{x \mid x \in N\}$. The average cost per text or minute is undefined when x is exactly zero, but the average cost gets higher and higher as the combined number of texts and minutes approaches the non-permissible value of zero.

Both functions also appear to have a horizontal asymptote. The average cost for each plan decreases as the combined number of texts and minutes increases.

Rewrite the equations of the two functions in the form $y = \dfrac{a}{x - h} + k$ so you can analyse them using the locations of the asymptotes:

$f_1(x) = \dfrac{10 + 0.1x}{x}$ $\qquad$ $f_2(x) = \dfrac{5 + 0.15x}{x}$

$f_1(x) = \dfrac{10}{x} + \dfrac{0.1x}{x}$ $\qquad$ $f_2(x) = \dfrac{5}{x} + \dfrac{0.15x}{x}$

$f_1(x) = \dfrac{10}{x} + 0.1$ $\qquad$ $f_2(x) = \dfrac{5}{x} + 0.15$

The horizontal asymptote of the function $f_1(x)$ is $y = 0.1$, and the horizontal asymptote of the function $f_2(x)$ is $y = 0.15$. The monthly fee is spread out over the combined number of texts and minutes used. The greater the combined number of texts and minutes becomes, the closer the average cost gets to the value of $0.10 or $0.15.

d) To decide how to make a choice between the two plans, determine when they have the same cost. The two functions intersect when $x = 100$. The plans have the same average cost for 100 combined texts and minutes. The first plan is better for more than 100 combined texts and minutes, while the second plan is better for fewer than 100 combined texts and minutes.

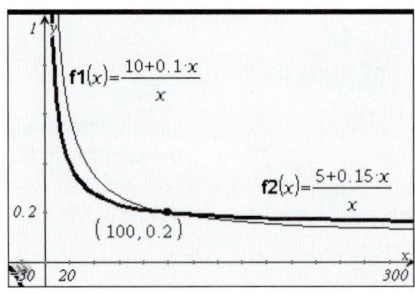

440 MHR • Chapter 9

Your Turn

Marlysse is producing a tourism booklet for the town of Atlin, British Columbia, and its surrounding area. She is comparing the cost of printing from two different companies. The first company charges a $50 setup fee and $2.50 per booklet. The second charges $80 for setup and $2.10 per booklet.

a) Represent the average cost per booklet for each company as a function of the number of booklets printed.
b) Graph the two functions.
c) Explain how the characteristics of the graphs are related to the situation.
d) Give Marlysse advice about how she should choose a printing company.

Atlin, British Columbia

> **Did You Know?**
>
> Atlin is a remote but spectacularly beautiful community in the northwest corner of British Columbia on the eastern shore of Atlin Lake. The surrounding area has been used by the Taku River Tlingit First Nations people for many years, and the name *Atlin* comes from the Tlingit word *Aa Tlein*, meaning *big water*.

Key Ideas

- Rational functions are functions of the form $f(x) = \dfrac{p(x)}{q(x)}$, where $p(x)$ and $q(x)$ are polynomial expressions and $q(x) \neq 0$.

- Rational functions where $p(x)$ and $q(x)$ have no common factor other than one have vertical asymptotes that correspond to the non-permissible values of the function, if there are any.

- You can sometimes use transformations to graph rational functions and explain common characteristics and differences between them.

- You can express the equations of some rational functions in an equivalent form and use it to analyse and graph functions without using technology.

Check Your Understanding

Practise

1. The equations and graphs of four rational functions are shown. Which graph matches which function? Give reason(s) for each choice.

   $A(x) = \dfrac{2}{x} - 1$ $\quad B(x) = \dfrac{2}{x+1}$

   $C(x) = \dfrac{2}{x-1}$ $\quad D(x) = \dfrac{2}{x} + 1$

   a)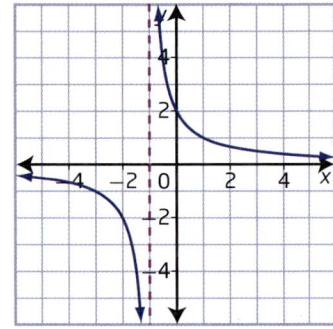

   b)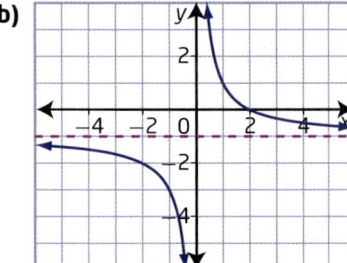

   c)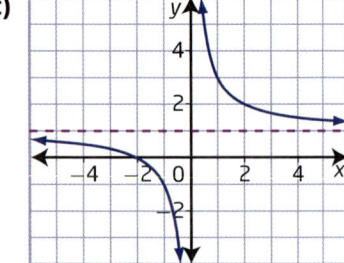

   d)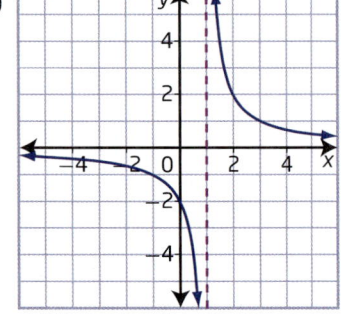

2. Identify the appropriate base rational function, $y = \dfrac{1}{x}$ or $y = \dfrac{1}{x^2}$, and then use transformations of its graph to sketch the graph of each of the following functions. Identify the asymptotes.

   a) $y = \dfrac{1}{x+2}$ b) $y = \dfrac{1}{x-3}$

   c) $y = \dfrac{1}{(x+1)^2}$ d) $y = \dfrac{1}{(x-4)^2}$

3. Sketch the graph of each function using transformations. Identify the domain and range, intercepts, and asymptotes.

   a) $y = \dfrac{6}{x+1}$

   b) $y = \dfrac{4}{x} + 1$

   c) $y = \dfrac{2}{x-4} - 5$

   d) $y = -\dfrac{8}{x-2} + 3$

4. Graph each function using technology and identify any asymptotes and intercepts.

   a) $y = \dfrac{2x+1}{x-4}$

   b) $y = \dfrac{3x-2}{x+1}$

   c) $y = \dfrac{-4x+3}{x+2}$

   d) $y = \dfrac{2-6x}{x-5}$

5. Write each function in the form $y = \dfrac{a}{x-h} + k$. Determine the location of any asymptotes and intercepts. Then, confirm your answers by graphing with technology.

   a) $y = \dfrac{11x+12}{x}$

   b) $y = \dfrac{x}{x+8}$

   c) $y = \dfrac{-x-2}{x+6}$

6. Graph the functions $f(x) = \dfrac{1}{x^2}$, $g(x) = \dfrac{-8}{(x+6)^2}$, and $h(x) = \dfrac{4}{x^2-4x+4} - 3$. Discuss the characteristics of the graphs and identify any common features.

Apply

7. Write the equation of each function in the form $y = \dfrac{a}{x-h} + k$.

a)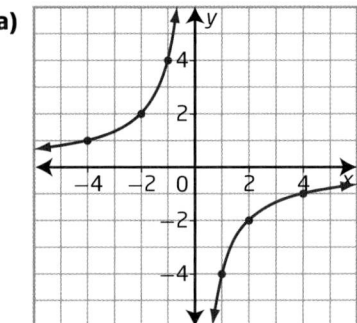

b)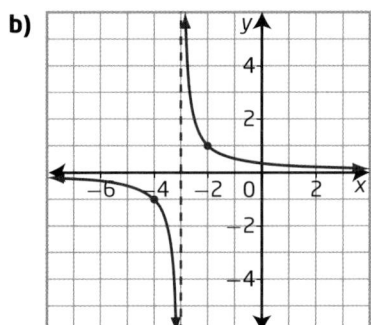

c)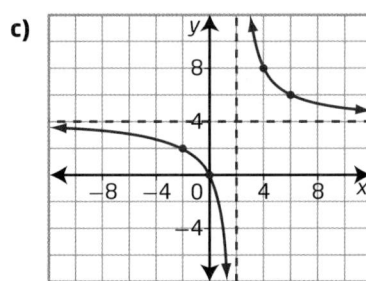

d)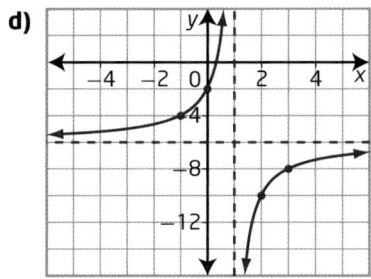

8. The rational function $y = \dfrac{a}{x-5} + k$ passes through the points (10, 1) and (2, 9).

  a) Determine the values of a and k.

  b) Graph the function.

9. a) Write a possible equation in the form $y = \dfrac{p(x)}{q(x)}$ that has asymptotes at $x = 2$ and $y = -3$.

  b) Sketch its graph and identify its domain and range.

  c) Is there only one possible function that meets these criteria? Explain.

10. Mira uses algebra to rewrite the function $y = \dfrac{2-3x}{x-7}$ in an equivalent form that she can graph by hand.

$y = \dfrac{2-3x}{x-7}$

$y = \dfrac{-3x+2}{x-7}$

$y = \dfrac{-3x-21+21+2}{x-7}$

$y = \dfrac{-3(x-7)+23}{x-7}$

$y = \dfrac{-3(x-7)}{x-7} + \dfrac{23}{x-7}$

$y = -3 + \dfrac{23}{x-7}$

$y = \dfrac{23}{x-7} - 3$

  a) Identify and correct any errors in Mira's work.

  b) How might Mira have discovered that she had made an error without using technology? How might she have done so with technology?

11. a) Write the function $y = \dfrac{x-2}{2x+4}$ in the form $y = \dfrac{a}{x-h} + k$.

  b) Sketch the graph of the function using transformations.

12. Determine the locations of the intercepts of the function $y = \dfrac{3x-5}{2x+3}$. Use a graph of the function to help you determine the asymptotes.

13. The number, N, of buyers looking to buy a home in a particular city is related to the average price, p, of a home in that city by the function $N(p) = \dfrac{500\,000}{p}$. Explain how the values of the function behave as the value of p changes and what the behaviour means in this situation.

9.1 Exploring Rational Functions Using Transformations • MHR **443**

14. A rectangle has a constant area of 24 cm².

  a) Write an equation to represent the length, *l*, as a function of the width, *w*, for this rectangle. Graph the function.

  b) Describe how the length changes as the width varies.

15. The student council at a large high school is having a fundraiser for a local charity. The council president suggests that they set a goal of raising $4000.

  a) Let *x* represent the number of students who contribute. Let *y* represent the average amount required per student to meet the goal. What function *y* in terms of *x* represents this situation?

  b) Graph the function.

  c) Explain what the behaviour of the function for various values of *x* means in this context.

  d) How would the equation and graph of the function change if the student council also received a $1000 donation from a local business?

16. Hanna is shopping for a new deep freezer and is deciding between two models. One model costs $500 and has an estimated electricity cost of $100/year. A second model that is more energy efficient costs $800 but has an estimated electricity cost of $60/year.

  a) For each freezer, write an equation for the average cost per year as a function of the time, in years.

  b) Graph the functions for a reasonable domain.

  c) Identify important characteristics of each graph and explain what they show about the situation.

  d) How can the graph help Hanna decide which model to choose?

17. Ohm's law relates the current, *I*, in amperes (A); the voltage, *V*, in volts (V); and the resistance, *R*, in ohms (Ω), in electrical circuits with the formula $I = \dfrac{V}{R}$. Consider the electrical circuit in the diagram.

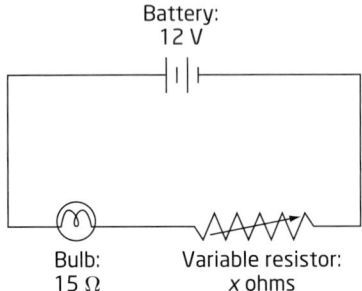

A variable resistor is used to control the brightness of a small light bulb and can be set anywhere from 0 Ω to 100 Ω. The total resistance in the circuit is the sum of the resistances of the variable resistor and the bulb.

  a) Write an equation for the current, *I*, in the circuit as a function of the resistance of the variable resistor, *x*.

  b) What domain is appropriate for this situation? Does the graph of the function have a vertical asymptote? Explain.

  c) Graph the function. What setting is needed on the variable resistor to produce a current of exactly 0.2 A?

  d) How would the function change if the circuit consisted of only the battery and the variable resistor? Explain the significance of the vertical asymptote in this case.

18. Two stores rent bikes. One charges a fixed fee of $20 plus $4/h, and the other charges a fixed fee of $10 plus $5/h.

  a) Write equations for the average cost per hour for each store as a function of the rental time, in hours. Graph the functions.

  b) Identify key features of the graphs. What do the graphs show about how the average cost changes for different rental times?

  c) Is one store always the better choice? Explain.

Extend

19. A truck leaves Regina and drives eastbound. Due to road construction, the truck takes 2 h to travel the first 80 km. Once it leaves the construction zone, the truck travels at 100 km/h for the rest of the trip.

  a) Let v represent the average speed, in kilometres per hour, over the entire trip and t represent the time, in hours, since leaving the construction zone. Write an equation for v as a function of t.

  b) Graph the function for an appropriate domain.

  c) What are the equations of the asymptotes in this situation? Do they have meaning in this situation? Explain.

  d) How long will the truck have to drive before its average speed is 80 km/h?

  e) Suppose your job is to develop GPS technology. How could you use these types of calculations to help travellers save fuel?

20. Determine the equation of a rational function of the form $y = \dfrac{ax + b}{cx + d}$ that has a vertical asymptote at $x = 6$, a horizontal asymptote at $y = -4$, and an x-intercept of -1.

21. For each rational function given, determine the inverse function, $f^{-1}(x)$.

  a) $f(x) = \dfrac{x - 3}{x + 1}$

  b) $f(x) = \dfrac{2x}{x - 5} + 4$

22. State the characteristics of the graph of the function $y = \dfrac{x}{x + 2} + \dfrac{x - 4}{x - 2}$.

Create Connections

C1 Would you say that using transformations with rational functions is more difficult, easier, or no different than using transformations with other functions that you have studied? Give reasons for your answer using specific examples.

C2 The owners of a manufacturing plant are trying to eliminate harmful emissions. They use the function $C(p) = \dfrac{200\,000p}{100 - p}$ to estimate the cost, C, in dollars, to eliminate p percent of the emissions from the plant.

  a) What domain is appropriate in this situation? Why?

  b) Graph the function. How is its shape related to the manufacturing context?

  c) Does it cost twice as much to eliminate 80% as it does to eliminate 40%? Explain.

  d) Is it possible to completely eliminate all of the emissions according to this model? Justify your answer in terms of the characteristics of the graph.

C3 What are the similarities and differences between graphing the functions $y = \dfrac{2}{x - 3} + 4$ and $y = 2\sqrt{x - 3} + 4$ without using technology?

9.2

Analysing Rational Functions

Focus on...

- graphing, analysing, and comparing rational functions
- determining whether graphs of rational functions have an asymptote or a point of discontinuity for a non-permissible value

The speed at which an airplane travels depends on the speed of the wind in which it is flying. A plane's *airspeed* is how fast it travels in relation to the air around it, but its *ground speed* is how fast it travels relative to the ground. A plane's ground speed is greater if it flies with a tailwind and less if it flies with a headwind.

Near McClusky Lake, Wind River, Yukon

Investigate Analysing Rational Functions

Materials

- graphing technology

1. Consider the function $y = \dfrac{x^2 - x - 2}{x - 2}$.

  a) What value of x is important to consider when analysing this function? Predict the nature of the graph for this value of x.

  b) Graph the function and display a table of values.

  c) Are the pattern in the table and the shape of the graph what you expected? Explain.

2. a) What are the restrictions on the domain of this function?

  b) How can you simplify the function? What function is it equivalent to?

  c) Graph the simplified function and display a table of values. How do these compare to those of the original function?

  d) How could you sketch the graphs of these two functions so that the difference between them is clear?

Reflect and Respond

3. a) How does the behaviour of the function $y = \dfrac{x^2 - x - 2}{x - 2}$ near its non-permissible value differ from the rational functions you have looked at previously?

  b) What aspect of the equation of the original function do you think is the reason for this difference?

Link the Ideas

Graphs of rational functions can have a variety of shapes and different features—vertical asymptotes are one such feature. A vertical asymptote of the graph of a rational function corresponds to a non-permissible value in the equation of the function, but not all non-permissible values result in vertical asymptotes. Sometimes a non-permissible value instead results in a **point of discontinuity** in the graph.

point of discontinuity
- a point, described by an ordered pair, at which the graph of a function is not continuous
- occurs in a graph of a rational function when its function can be simplified by dividing the numerator and denominator by a common factor that includes a variable
- results in a single point missing from the graph, which is represented using an open circle
- sometimes referred to as a "hole in the graph"

Example 1

Graph a Rational Function With a Point of Discontinuity

Sketch the graph of the function $f(x) = \dfrac{x^2 - 5x + 6}{x - 3}$. Analyse its behaviour near its non-permissible value.

Solution

You can sometimes analyse and graph rational functions more easily by simplifying the equation of the function algebraically. To simplify the equation of $f(x)$, factor the numerator and the denominator:

$f(x) = \dfrac{x^2 - 5x + 6}{x - 3}$

$f(x) = \dfrac{(x - 2)(x - 3)}{(x - 3)}$

$f(x) = x - 2, \; x \neq 3$

As long as the restriction is included, this simplified equation represents the same function.

The graph of $f(x)$ is the same as the graph of $y = x - 2$, except that $f(x)$ has a point of discontinuity at $(3, y)$. To determine the y-coordinate of the point of discontinuity, substitute $x = 3$ into the simplified function equation.

$y = x - 2$
$y = 3 - 2$
$y = 1$

What happens when $x = 3$ is substituted into the original function?

The point of discontinuity occurs at $(3, 1)$.

Graph a line with a y-intercept of -2 and a slope of 1. Plot an open circle on the graph at $(3, 1)$ to indicate that the function does not exist at that point.

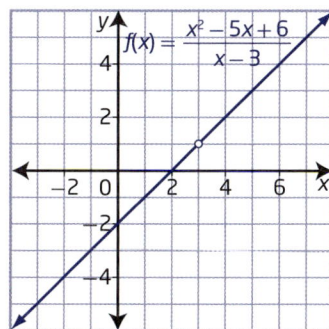

Why is the graph a straight line when its equation looks quite complex?

The function $f(x)$ has a point of discontinuity at (3, 1) because the numerator and the denominator have a common factor of $x - 3$. The common factor does not affect the values of the function except at $x = 3$, where $f(x)$ does not exist.

A table of values for the function shows the behaviour of the function near its non-permissible value $x = 3$:

x	2.5	2.8	2.9	2.99	2.999	3	3.001	3.01	3.1	3.2	3.5
f(x)	0.5	0.8	0.9	0.99	0.999	does not exist	1.001	1.01	1.1	1.2	1.5

From the table, it appears that the value of $f(x)$ gets closer and closer to 1 as x gets closer to 3 from either side even though the function does not exist when x is exactly 3.

Your Turn

Sketch the graph of the function $f(x) = \dfrac{x^2 + 2x - 3}{x - 1}$. Analyse its behaviour near its non-permissible value.

Example 2

Rational Functions: Points of Discontinuity Versus Asymptotes

a) Compare the behaviour of the functions $f(x) = \dfrac{x^2 - 2x}{4 - 2x}$ and $g(x) = \dfrac{x^2 + 2x}{4 - 2x}$ near any non-permissible values.

b) Explain any differences.

Solution

a) Use a graphing calculator to graph the functions.

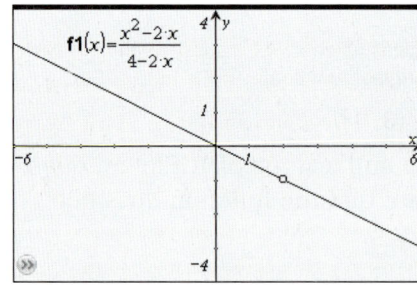
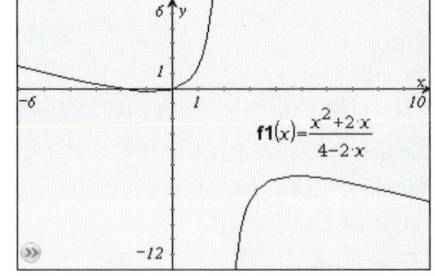

Why are the graphs so different when the equations look so similar?

Did You Know?

In calculus, the term "undefined" is used for an asymptote, while the term "indeterminate" is used for a point of discontinuity.
- $\dfrac{n}{0}$ is undefined.
- $\dfrac{0}{0}$ is indeterminate.

The non-permissible value for both functions is 2. However, the graph on the left does not exist at (2, −1), whereas the the graph on the right is undefined at $x = 2$.

Characteristic	$f(x) = \dfrac{x^2 - 2x}{4 - 2x}$	$g(x) = \dfrac{x^2 + 2x}{4 - 2x}$
Non-permissible value	$x = 2$	$x = 2$
Feature at non-permissible value	point of discontinuity	vertical asymptote
Behaviour near non-permissible value	As x approaches 2, y approaches -1.	As x approaches 2, $|y|$ becomes very large.

b) To explain the differences in the behaviour of the two functions near $x = 2$, factor the numerator and denominator of each function.

$f(x) = \dfrac{x^2 - 2x}{4 - 2x}$

$f(x) = \dfrac{x(x - 2)}{-2(x - 2)}$

$f(x) = -\dfrac{1}{2}x, \; x \neq 2$

$f(x)$ has a point of discontinuity at $(2, -1)$ because the numerator and denominator have a common factor of $x - 2$.

$g(x) = \dfrac{x^2 + 2x}{4 - 2x}$

$g(x) = \dfrac{x(x + 2)}{-2(x - 2)}, \; x \neq 2$

$g(x)$ has a vertical asymptote at $x = 2$ because $x - 2$ is a factor of the denominator but not the numerator.

Your Turn

Compare the functions $f(x) = \dfrac{x^2 - 3x}{2x + 6}$ and $g(x) = \dfrac{x^2 + 3x}{2x + 6}$ and explain any differences.

Example 3

Match Graphs and Equations for Rational Functions

Match the equation of each rational function with the most appropriate graph. Give reasons for each choice.

$A(x) = \dfrac{x^2 + 2x}{x^2 - 4}$ $B(x) = \dfrac{2x + 4}{x^2 + 1}$ $C(x) = \dfrac{2x}{x^2 - 4}$

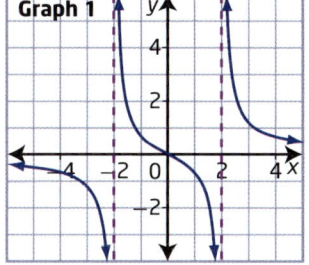
Graph 1

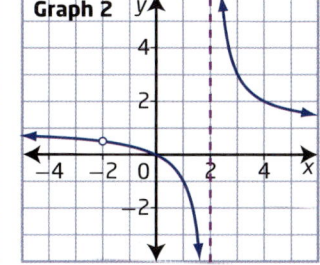
Graph 2

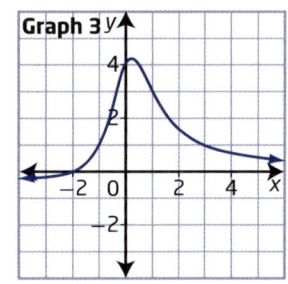
Graph 3

Solution

To match the equations of the functions with their graphs, use the locations of points of discontinuity, asymptotes, and intercepts. Write each function in factored form to determine the factors of the numerator and denominator and use them to predict the characteristics of each graph.

$A(x) = \dfrac{x^2 + 2x}{x^2 - 4}$

$A(x) = \dfrac{x(x + 2)}{(x - 2)(x + 2)}$

The graph of $A(x)$ has
- a vertical asymptote at $x = 2$
- a point of discontinuity at $\left(-2, \dfrac{1}{2}\right)$
- an x-intercept of 0

Therefore, graph 2 represents $A(x)$.

How do the factors in the equation reveal the features of the graph?

$B(x) = \dfrac{2x + 4}{x^2 + 1}$

$B(x) = \dfrac{2(x + 2)}{x^2 + 1}$

The graph of $B(x)$ has
- no vertical asymptotes or points of discontinuity
- an x-intercept of -2

Therefore, graph 3 represents $B(x)$.

How can you tell that the graph of $B(x)$ will have no points of discontinuity or vertical asymptotes?

$C(x) = \dfrac{2x}{x^2 - 4}$

$C(x) = \dfrac{2x}{(x - 2)(x + 2)}$

The graph of $C(x)$ has
- vertical asymptotes at $x = -2$ and $x = 2$
- no points of discontinuity
- an x-intercept of 0

Therefore, graph 1 represents $C(x)$.

How can you tell that the graph of $C(x)$ will have two vertical asymptotes and one x-intercept, but no points of discontinuity?

Your Turn

Match the equation of each rational function with the most appropriate graph. Explain your reasoning.

$K(x) = \dfrac{x^2 + 2}{x^2 - x - 2}$

$L(x) = \dfrac{x - 1}{x^2 - 1}$

$M(x) = \dfrac{x^2 - 5x + 6}{3 - x}$

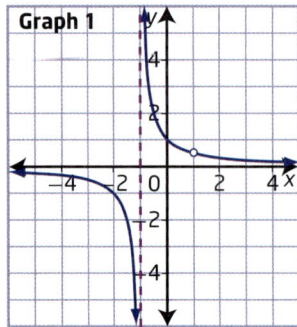
Graph 1

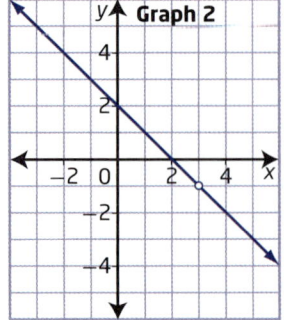
Graph 2

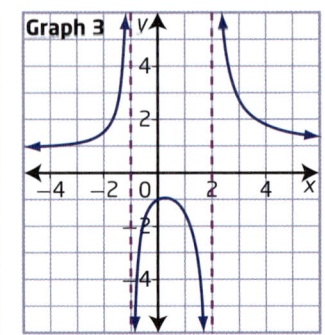
Graph 3

Key Ideas

- The graph of a rational function
  - has either a vertical asymptote or a point of discontinuity corresponding to each of its non-permissible values
  - has no vertical asymptotes or points of discontinuity
- To find any x-intercepts, points of discontinuity, and vertical asymptotes of a rational function, analyse the numerator and denominator.
  - A factor of only the numerator corresponds to an x-intercept.
  - A factor of only the denominator corresponds to a vertical asymptote.
  - A factor of both the numerator and the denominator corresponds to a point of discontinuity.
- To analyse the behaviour of a function near a non-permissible value, use a table of values or the graph, even though the function is undefined or does not exist at the non-permissible value itself.

Check Your Understanding

Practise

1. The graph of the rational function $y = \dfrac{x-4}{x^2 - 6x + 8}$ is shown.

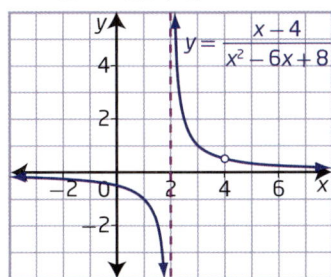

a) Copy and complete the table to summarize the characteristics of the function.

Characteristic	$y = \dfrac{x-4}{x^2 - 6x + 8}$
Non-permissible value(s)	
Feature exhibited at each non-permissible value	
Behaviour near each non-permissible value	
Domain	
Range	

b) Explain the behaviour at each non-permissible value.

2. Create a table of values for each function for values near its non-permissible value. Explain how your table shows whether a point of discontinuity or an asymptote occurs in each case.

a) $y = \dfrac{x^2 - 3x}{x}$

b) $y = \dfrac{x^2 - 3x - 10}{x - 2}$

c) $y = \dfrac{3x^2 + 4x - 4}{x + 4}$

d) $y = \dfrac{5x^2 + 4x - 1}{5x - 1}$

3. a) Graph the functions $f(x) = \dfrac{x^2 - 2x - 3}{x + 3}$ and $g(x) = \dfrac{x^2 + 2x - 3}{x + 3}$ and analyse their characteristics.

b) Explain any differences in their behaviour near non-permissible values.

9.2 Analysing Rational Functions • MHR 451

4. For each function, predict the locations of any vertical asymptotes, points of discontinuity, and intercepts. Then, graph the function to verify your predictions.

a) $y = \dfrac{x^2 + 4x}{x^2 + 9x + 20}$

b) $y = \dfrac{2x^2 - 5x - 3}{x^2 - 1}$

c) $y = \dfrac{x^2 + 2x - 8}{x^2 - 2x - 8}$

d) $y = \dfrac{2x^2 + 7x - 15}{9 - 4x^2}$

5. Which graph matches each rational function? Explain your choices.

a) $A(x) = \dfrac{x^2 + 2x}{x^2 + 4}$ b) $B(x) = \dfrac{x - 2}{x^2 - 2x}$

c) $C(x) = \dfrac{x + 2}{x^2 - 4}$ d) $D(x) = \dfrac{2x}{x^2 + 2x}$

A
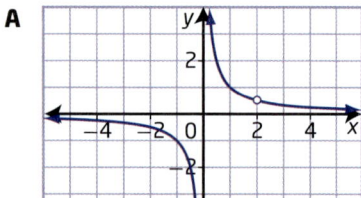

B
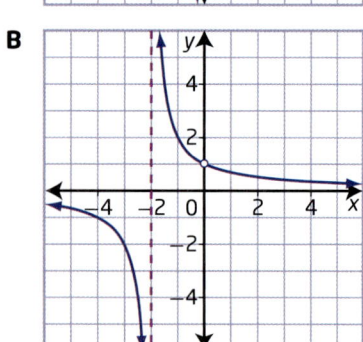

C
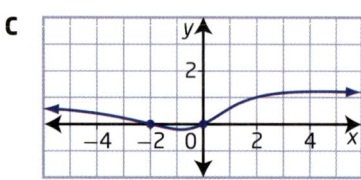

D
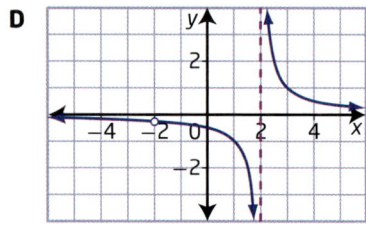

6. Match the graph of each rational function with the most appropriate equation. Give reasons for each choice.

a)
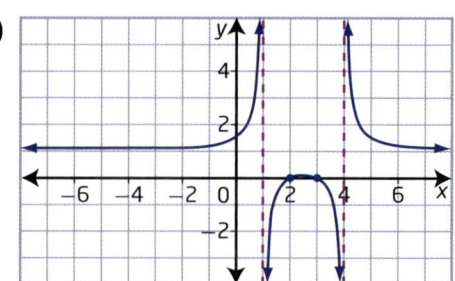

b)
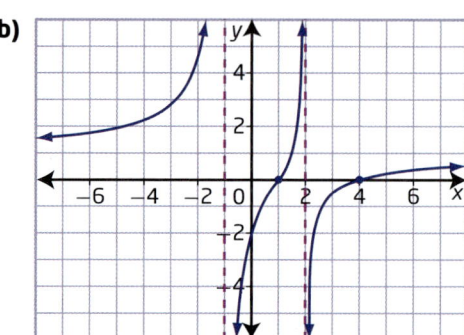

c)
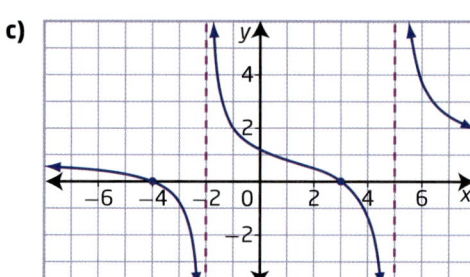

d)
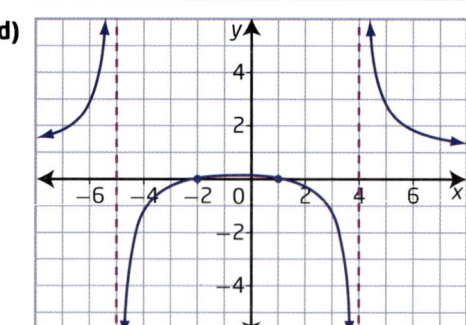

A $f(x) = \dfrac{x^2 + x - 2}{x^2 + x - 20}$

B $g(x) = \dfrac{x^2 - 5x + 4}{x^2 - x - 2}$

C $h(x) = \dfrac{x^2 - 5x + 6}{x^2 - 5x + 4}$

D $j(x) = \dfrac{x^2 + x - 12}{x^2 - 3x - 10}$

Apply

7. Write the equation for each rational function graphed below.

a)

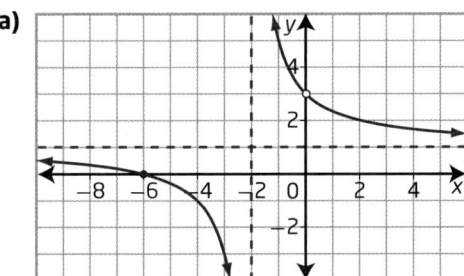

b)

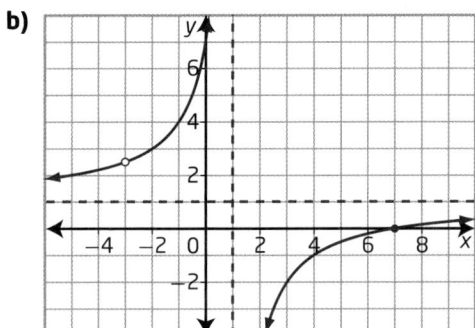

8. Write the equation of a possible rational function with each set of characteristics.

a) vertical asymptotes at $x = \pm 5$ and x-intercepts of -10 and 4

b) a vertical asymptote at $x = -4$, a point of discontinuity at $\left(-\frac{11}{2}, 9\right)$, and an x-intercept of 8

c) a point of discontinuity at $\left(-2, \frac{1}{5}\right)$, a vertical asymptote at $x = 3$, and an x-intercept of -1

d) vertical asymptotes at $x = 3$ and $x = \frac{6}{7}$, and x-intercepts of $-\frac{1}{4}$ and 0

9. Sydney noticed that the functions $f(x) = \dfrac{x - 3}{x^2 - 5x - 6}$ and $g(x) = \dfrac{x - 3}{x^2 - 5x + 6}$ have equations that are very similar. She assumed that their graphs would also be very similar.

a) Predict whether or not Sydney is correct. Give reasons for your answer.

b) Graph the functions. Explain why your predictions were or were not accurate.

10. What rational function is shown in the graph?

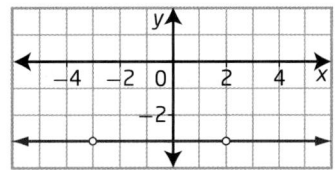

11. a) Predict the shape of the graph of $y = \dfrac{2x^2 + 2}{x^2 - 1}$ and explain your reasoning.

b) Use graphing technology to confirm your prediction.

c) How would the graph of each of the following functions compare to the one in part a)? Check using graphing technology.

i) $y = \dfrac{2x^2 - 2}{x^2 - 1}$ **ii)** $y = \dfrac{2x^2 + 2}{x^2 + 1}$

12. A de Havilland Beaver is a small plane that is capable of an airspeed of about 250 km/h in still air. Consider a situation where this plane is flying 500 km from Lake Athabasca, Saskatchewan, to Great Slave Lake, Northwest Territories.

a) Let w represent the speed of the wind, in kilometres per hour, where w is positive for a tailwind and negative for a headwind, and t represent the time, in hours, it takes to fly. What equation represents t as a function of w? What is the non-permissible value for the function?

b) Graph the function for a domain that includes its non-permissible value.

c) Explain what the behaviour of the function for various values of w means in this context, including near its non-permissible value.

d) Which part(s) of your graph are actually realistic in this situation? Discuss this with a partner, and explain your thoughts.

> **Did You Know?**
>
> Bush planes like the de Havilland Beaver have been and still are critical to exploration and transportation in remote areas of Northern Canada where roads do not exist.

13. Ryan and Kandra are kayaking near Lowe Inlet Marine Provincial Park on Grenville Channel, British Columbia. The current can flow in either direction at up to 4 km/h depending on tidal conditions. Ryan and Kandra are capable of kayaking steadily at 4 km/h without the current.

   a) What function relates the time, t, in hours, it will take them to travel 4 km along the channel as a function of the speed, w, in kilometres per hour, of the current? What domain is possible for w in this context?

   b) Graph the function for an appropriate domain.

   c) Explain the behaviour of the graph for values at and near its non-permissible value and what the behaviour means in this situation.

   Did You Know?

   The fastest navigable tidal currents in the world, which can have speeds of up to 30 km/h at their peak, occur in the Nakwakto Rapids, another narrow channel on British Columbia's coast. The name originates from the kwakwaka'wakw language meaning "trembling rock."

14. Paul is a humanitarian aid worker. He uses the function $C(p) = \dfrac{500p}{100 - p}$ to estimate the cost, C, in thousands of dollars, of vaccinating p percent of the population of the country in which he is working.

   a) Predict the nature of the graph for its non-permissible value. Give a reason for your answer.

   b) Graph the function for an appropriate domain. Explain what the graph shows about the situation.

   c) Do you think this is a good model for the estimated cost of vaccinating the population? Explain.

15. The function $h(v) = \dfrac{6378v^2}{125 - v^2}$ gives the maximum height, h, in kilometres, as a function of the initial velocity, v, in kilometres per second, for an object launched upward from Earth's surface, if the object gets no additional propulsion and air resistance is ignored.

   a) Graph the function. What parts of the graph are applicable to this situation?

   b) Explain what the graph indicates about how the maximum height is affected by the initial velocity.

   c) The term *escape velocity* refers to the initial speed required to break free of a gravitational field. Describe the nature of the graph for its non-permissible value, and explain why it represents the escape velocity for the object.

16. Determine the equation of the rational function shown without using technology.

   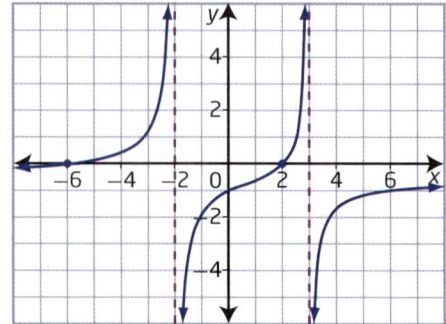

17. A convex lens focuses light rays from an object to create an image, as shown in the diagram. The image distance, I, is related to the object distance, b, by the function $I = \dfrac{fb}{b-f}$, where the focal length, f, is a constant for the particular lens used based on its specific curvature. When the object is placed closer to the lens than the focal length of the lens, an image is perceived to be behind the lens and is called a virtual image.

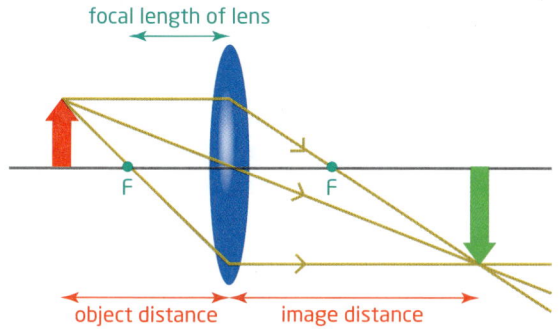

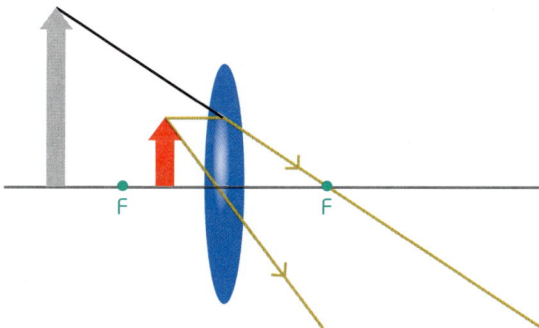

a) Graph I as a function of b for a lens with a focal length of 4 cm.

b) How does the location of the image change as the values of b change?

c) What type of behaviour does the graph exhibit for its non-permissible value? How is this connected to the situation?

Did You Know?

The image in your bathroom mirror is a virtual image—you perceive the image to be behind the mirror, even though the light rays do not actually travel or focus behind the mirror. You cannot project a virtual image on a screen. The study of images of objects using lenses and mirrors is part of a branch of physics called optics.

18. Consider the functions $f(x) = \dfrac{x+a}{x+b}$, $g(x) = \dfrac{x+a}{(x+b)(x+c)}$, and $h(x) = \dfrac{(x+a)(x+c)}{(x+b)(x+c)}$, where a, b, and c are different real numbers.

a) Which pair of functions do you think will have graphs that appear to be most similar to each other? Explain your choice.

b) What common characteristics will all three graphs have? Give reasons for your answer.

19. If the function $y = \dfrac{x^2 + bx + c}{4x^2 + 29x + c}$, where b and c are real numbers, has a point of discontinuity at $\left(-8, \dfrac{11}{35}\right)$, where does it have x-intercept(s) and vertical asymptote(s), if any?

Extend

20. Given $f(x) = \dfrac{2x^2 - 4x}{x^2 + 3x - 28}$, what is the equation of $y = \dfrac{1}{4}f[-(x-3)]$ in simplest form?

21. Write the equation of the rational function shown in each graph. Leave your answers in factored form.

a)
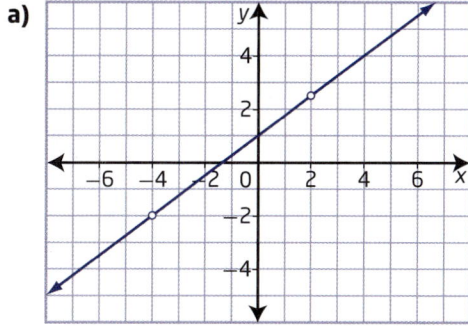

b)
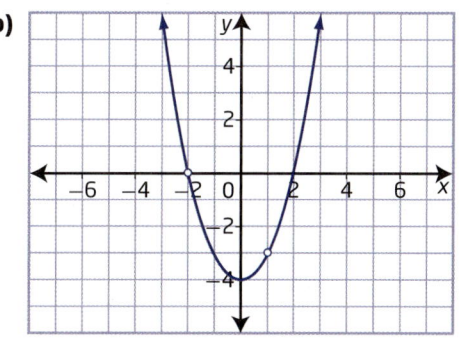

22. The functions $f(x) = \dfrac{x^2 + 4}{x^2 - 4}$ and $g(x) = \dfrac{x^2 - 4}{x^2 + 4}$ are reciprocals of each other. That is, $f(x) = \dfrac{1}{g(x)}$ and vice versa. Graph the two functions on the same set of axes and explain how the shapes of the graphs support this fact.

23. Predict the location of any asymptotes and points of discontinuity for each function. Then, use technology to check your predictions.

   a) $y = \dfrac{x + 2}{x^2 - 4} + \dfrac{5}{x + 2}$

   b) $y = \dfrac{2x^3 - 7x^2 - 15x}{x^2 - x - 20}$

Create Connections

C1 Jeremy was absent the day his math class started learning about rational functions. His friend Rohan tells him that rational functions are functions that have asymptotes and points of discontinuity, but Jeremy is not sure what he means.

   a) Jeremy takes Rohan's statement to mean that all rational functions have asymptotes and points of discontinuity. Is this statement true? Explain using several examples.

   b) How would you elaborate on Rohan's explanation about what rational functions are to make it more clear for Jeremy?

C2 Consider the statement, "All polynomial functions are rational functions." Is this statement true? Explain your thinking.

C3 **MINI LAB** Graphs of rational functions can take on many shapes with a variety of features. Work with a partner to create your own classification system for rational functions.

Step 1 Use technology to create graphs for rational functions. Try creating graphs with as many different general shapes as you can by starting with a variety of types of equations. How many different general shapes can you create?

Step 2 Group the rational functions you have created into categories or classes. Consider the types of features, aspects, and symmetries that the various graphs exhibit.

Step 3 Create a descriptive name for each of your categories.

Step 4 For each category, describe an example function, including its equation and graph.

Project Corner — Visual Presentation

Create a video or slide presentation that demonstrates your understanding of a topic in Unit 4.
- Once you have chosen a topic, write a script for your movie or outline for your slide presentation.
- If you are making a video, choose your presenter and/or cast and the location. Prepare any materials needed and rehearse your presentation. Film your movie, edit it, add sound, and create the title and credits.
- If you are making a slide presentation, collect or make any digital images that you need; create title, contents, and credits slides; add sound or music; and test the presentation.

9.3

Connecting Graphs and Rational Equations

Focus on...
- relating the roots of rational equations to the *x*-intercepts of the graphs of rational functions
- determining approximate solutions to rational equations graphically

A wide range of illnesses and medical conditions can be effectively treated with various medications. Pharmacists, doctors, and other medical professionals need to understand how the level of medication in a patient's bloodstream changes after its administration. For example, they may need to know when the level will drop to a certain point. How might they predict when this will occur?

> **Did You Know?**
>
> Only a small fraction of the amount of many medications taken orally actually makes it into the bloodstream. The ratio of the amount of a medication in a patient's bloodstream to the amount given to the patient is called its *bioavailability*.

Investigate Solving Rational Equations

Work with a partner.

Materials
- graphing technology

A: Determine Medication Levels

1. The function $C(t) = \dfrac{40t}{1.1t^2 + 0.3}$ models the bloodstream concentration, C, in milligrams per decilitre (mg/dL), of a certain medication as a function of the time, t, in hours, since it was taken orally.

   a) Graph the function for a reasonable domain.

   b) What does the graph show about the situation?

2. A doctor needs to know when a patient's bloodstream concentration drops to 10 mg/dL.

   a) Why might a doctor need to know this?

   b) Brainstorm a list of possible methods you could use to determine the length of time it will take.

   c) Use at least two of the methods you came up with to determine the length of time. Explain the steps required in each of your methods.

   d) Share your solution methods with other pairs in your class. Are your methods similar? Explain.

Reflect and Respond

3. What are the strengths of each method you used? Which one do you prefer? Why?

B: Solve a Rational Equation Graphically and Algebraically

Consider the rational equation $\dfrac{x+2}{x-3} = x - 6$.

4. How can you solve the equation algebraically? Write a step-by-step algebraic solution, including an explanation of each step. Is there a restriction on the value of *x*?

5. How can you solve the equation graphically? Discuss possible methods with your partner, and then choose one and use it to solve the equation. Explain your process.

Reflect and Respond

6. Which method of solving this equation do you prefer, the algebraic approach or the graphical one? Give reasons for your choice.

Link the Ideas

Just as with many other types of equations, rational equations can be solved algebraically or graphically. Solving rational equations using an algebraic approach will sometimes result in extraneous roots. For example, an algebraic solution to the equation $\dfrac{8}{x^2 - 16} + 1 = \dfrac{1}{x - 4}$ results in *x*-values of −3 and 4. *Why is x = 4 not a valid solution?*

Solving a rational equation graphically involves using technology to graph the corresponding rational function and identify the *x*-intercepts of the graph. The *x*-intercepts of the graph of the corresponding function give the roots of the equation.

For example, a graphical solution to the equation $\dfrac{8}{x^2 - 16} + 1 = \dfrac{1}{x - 4}$ shows one solution, $x = -3$.

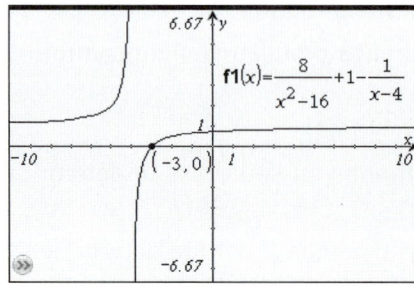

Note that the extraneous solution of $x = 4$, which was determined algebraically, is not observed when solving the equation graphically.

Example 1

Relate Roots and x-Intercepts

a) Determine the roots of the rational equation $x + \dfrac{6}{x+2} - 5 = 0$ algebraically.

b) Graph the rational function $y = x + \dfrac{6}{x+2} - 5$ and determine the x-intercepts.

c) What is the connection between the roots of the equation and the x-intercepts of the graph of the function?

Solution

a) Identify any restrictions on the variable before solving. The solution cannot be a non-permissible value. This equation has a single non-permissible value of -2.

To solve the rational equation algebraically, multiply each term in the equation by the lowest common denominator and then solve for x.

$$x + \frac{6}{x+2} - 5 = 0$$

$$(x+2)\left(x + \frac{6}{x+2} - 5\right) = (x+2)(0)$$

$$(x+2)(x) + (x+2)\left(\frac{6}{x+2}\right) - (x+2)(5) = 0$$

$$x^2 + 2x + 6 - 5x - 10 = 0$$

$$x^2 - 3x - 4 = 0$$

$$(x+1)(x-4) = 0$$

$x + 1 = 0$ or $x - 4 = 0$
$x = -1$ $x = 4$

Neither -1 nor 4 is a non-permissible value of the original equation.

Check:

For $x = -1$,
Left Side   Right Side
$x + \dfrac{6}{x+2} - 5$ 0
$= -1 + \dfrac{6}{-1+2} - 5$
$= -1 + 6 - 5$
$= 0$
  Left Side = Right Side

For $x = 4$,
Left Side   Right Side
$x + \dfrac{6}{x+2} - 5$ 0
$= 4 + \dfrac{6}{4+2} - 5$
$= 4 + 1 - 5$
$= 0$
  Left Side = Right Side

The equation has two roots or solutions, $x = -1$ and $x = 4$.

b) Use a graphing calculator to graph the function $y = x + \dfrac{6}{x + 2} - 5$ and determine the x-intercepts.

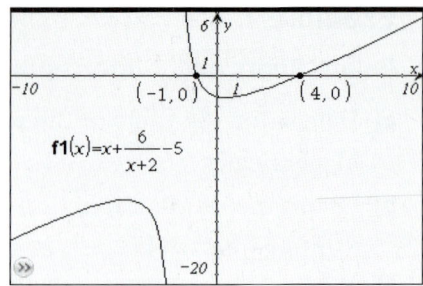

The function has x-intercepts at $(-1, 0)$ and $(4, 0)$.

c) The value of the function is 0 when the value of x is -1 or 4. The x-intercepts of the graph of the corresponding function are the roots of the equation.

Your Turn

a) Determine the roots of the equation $\dfrac{14}{x} - x + 5 = 0$ algebraically.

b) Determine the x-intercepts of the graph of the corresponding function $y = \dfrac{14}{x} - x + 5$.

c) Explain the connection between the roots of the equation and the x-intercepts of the graph of the corresponding function.

Example 2

Determine Approximate Solutions for Rational Equations

a) Solve the equation $\dfrac{x^2 - 3x - 7}{3 - 2x} = x - 1$ graphically. Express your answer to the nearest hundredth.

b) Verify your solution algebraically.

Solution

a) Method 1: Use a Single Function

Rearrange the rational equation so that one side is equal to zero:

$$\dfrac{x^2 - 3x - 7}{3 - 2x} = x - 1$$

$$\dfrac{x^2 - 3x - 7}{3 - 2x} - x + 1 = 0$$

Graph the corresponding function, $y = \dfrac{x^2 - 3x - 7}{3 - 2x} - x + 1$, and determine the x-intercept(s) of the graph.

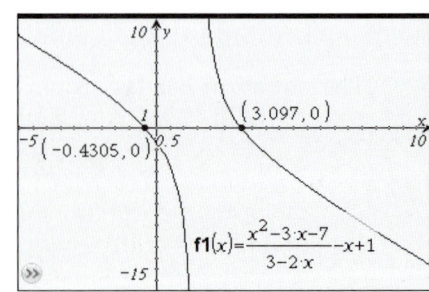

The solution to the equation is $x \approx -0.43$ and $x \approx 3.10$.

Method 2: Use a System of Two Functions
Write a function that corresponds to each side of the equation.
$$y_1 = \frac{x^2 - 3x - 7}{3 - 2x}$$
$$y_2 = x - 1$$

Use graphing technology to graph these functions and determine the value(s) of x at the point(s) of intersection, or where $y_1 = y_2$.

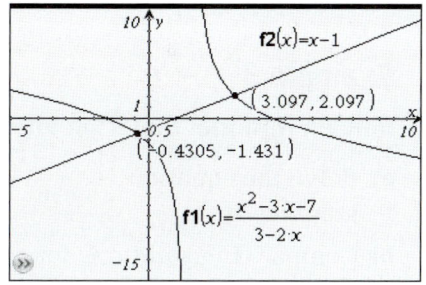

The solution to the equation is $x \approx -0.43$ and $x \approx 3.10$.

b) Determine any restrictions on the variable in this equation. To determine non-permissible values, set the denominator equal to zero and solve.
$$3 - 2x = 0$$
$$x = 1.5$$
The non-permissible value is $x = 1.5$.

Solve the equation by multiplying both sides by $3 - 2x$:
$$\frac{x^2 - 3x - 7}{3 - 2x} = x - 1$$
$$(3 - 2x)\frac{x^2 - 3x - 7}{3 - 2x} = (3 - 2x)(x - 1)$$
$$x^2 - 3x - 7 = 3x - 3 - 2x^2 + 2x$$
$$3x^2 - 8x - 4 = 0$$

$$x = \frac{-b \pm \sqrt{b^2 - 4ac}}{2a}$$
$$x = \frac{-(-8) \pm \sqrt{(-8)^2 - 4(3)(-4)}}{2(3)}$$
$$x = \frac{8 \pm \sqrt{112}}{6}$$
$$x = \frac{8 \pm 4\sqrt{7}}{6}$$
$$x = \frac{4 \pm 2\sqrt{7}}{3}$$

Why is the quadratic formula required here?

$x = \frac{4 - 2\sqrt{7}}{3}$ or $x = \frac{4 + 2\sqrt{7}}{3}$

$x = -0.4305...$ $x = 3.0971...$

$x \approx -0.43$ $x \approx 3.10$

How can you tell if either of these roots is extraneous?

The algebraic method gives an exact solution. The approximate values obtained algebraically, $x \approx -0.43$ and $x \approx 3.10$, are the same as the values obtained graphically.

Your Turn

a) Solve the equation $2 - \dfrac{3x}{2} = \dfrac{1 + 4x - x^2}{4x + 10}$ graphically. Express your answer to the nearest hundredth.

b) Verify your solution algebraically.

Example 3

Solve a Rational Equation With an Extraneous Root

a) Solve the equation $\dfrac{x}{2x + 5} + 2x = \dfrac{8x + 15}{4x + 10}$ algebraically and graphically.

b) Compare the solutions found using each method.

Solution

a) Factor the denominators to determine the non-permissible values.

$$\dfrac{x}{2x + 5} + 2x = \dfrac{8x + 15}{2(2x + 5)}$$

The equation has one non-permissible value of $-\dfrac{5}{2}$.

Multiply both sides of the equation by the lowest common denominator, $2(2x + 5)$.

$$2(2x + 5)\left(\dfrac{x}{2x + 5} + 2x\right) = 2(2x + 5)\left(\dfrac{8x + 15}{2(2x + 5)}\right)$$

$$2(2x + 5)\left(\dfrac{x}{2x + 5}\right) + 2(2x + 5)(2x) = 2(2x + 5)\left(\dfrac{8x + 15}{2(2x + 5)}\right)$$

$$2x + 8x^2 + 20x = 8x + 15$$
$$8x^2 + 14x - 15 = 0$$
$$(2x + 5)(4x - 3) = 0$$

$2x + 5 = 0$ or $4x - 3 = 0$
$x = -\dfrac{5}{2}$ $x = \dfrac{3}{4}$

However, $-\dfrac{5}{2}$ is a non-permissible value for the original equation. It is an extraneous root and must be rejected.

Therefore, the solution is $x = \dfrac{3}{4}$.

To solve the equation graphically, use two functions to represent the two sides of the equation.

$y_1 = \dfrac{x}{2x + 5} + 2x$

$y_2 = \dfrac{8x + 15}{4x + 10}$

The graphs of the two functions intersect when x is 0.75.

The solution to the equation is $x = 0.75$, or $\dfrac{3}{4}$.

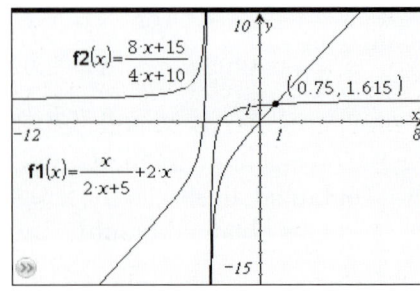

The curves appear to meet at the top and bottom of the graphing calculator screen. Do these represent points of intersection? Explain.

b) The solutions obtained by both methods are the same. For this equation, the algebraic solution produced two values, one of which was rejected because it was extraneous. The graphical solution did not produce the extraneous root. There is only one point of intersection on the graph of the two functions.

Your Turn

a) Solve the equation $\frac{x+3}{2x-6} = 2x - \frac{x}{3-x}$ algebraically and graphically.

b) Compare the solutions found using each method.

Example 4

Solve a Problem Using a Rational Equation

In basketball, a player's free-throw percentage is given by dividing the total number of successful free-throw baskets by the total number of attempts. So far this year, Larry has attempted 19 free-throws and has been successful on 12 of them. If he is successful on every attempt from now on, how many more free-throws does he need to attempt before his free-throw percentage is 80%?

Did You Know?

Basketball is one of the sports competitions included in the Canadian Francophone Games. The Canadian Francophone Games gives French speaking youth from across Canada a chance to demonstrate their talents in the areas of art, leadership, and sports.

Solution

Let x represent the number of free-throws Larry takes from now on.

Let P represent Larry's new free-throw percentage, as a decimal.

$P = \frac{\text{successes}}{\text{attempts}}$

$P = \frac{12 + x}{19 + x}$

Why is x used in both the numerator and the denominator?

Since the number of free-throws is discrete data, the continuous model is only valid in the domain $\{x \mid x \in W\}$.

Determine the value of x when P is 80%, or 0.8. Substitute 0.8 for P and solve the resulting equation.

$$P = \frac{12 + x}{19 + x}$$

$$0.8 = \frac{12 + x}{19 + x}$$

Method 1: Solve Graphically

Graph two functions and determine the point of intersection.

$$y_1 = \frac{12 + x}{19 + x}$$

$$y_2 = 0.8$$

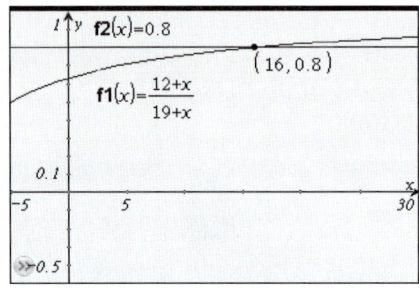

What domain is appropriate for this situation?

Larry will have a free-throw percentage of 80% after 16 more free-throw attempts if he is successful on all of them.

Method 2: Solve Algebraically

Multiply both sides of the equation by $19 + x$:

$$0.8 = \frac{12 + x}{19 + x}$$

$$0.8(19 + x) = \frac{12 + x}{19 + x}(19 + x)$$

$$15.2 + 0.8x = 12 + x$$

$$3.2 = 0.2x$$

$$x = 16$$

Is there a non-permissible value of x for this situation? Explain.

Larry will have a free-throw percentage of 80% after 16 more free-throw attempts if he is successful on all of them.

Your Turn

Megan and her friends are organizing a fundraiser for the local children's hospital. They are asking local businesses to each donate a door prize. So far, they have asked nine businesses, but only one has donated a prize. Their goal was to have three quarters of the businesses donate. If they succeed in getting every business to donate a prize from now on, how many more businesses do they need to ask to reach their goal?

Key Ideas

- You can solve rational equations algebraically or graphically.
- The solutions or roots of a rational equation are equivalent to the *x*-intercepts of the graph of the corresponding rational function. You can use either of the following methods to solve rational equations graphically:
  - Manipulate the equation so that one side is equal to zero; then, graph the corresponding function and identify the value(s) of the *x*-intercept(s).
  - Graph a system of functions that corresponds to the expressions on both sides of the equal sign; then, identify the value(s) of *x* at the point(s) of intersection.
- When solving rational equations algebraically, remember to check for extraneous roots and to verify that the solution does not include any non-permissible values.

Check Your Understanding

Practise

1. Match each equation to the single function that can be used to solve it graphically.

a) $\dfrac{x}{x-2} + 6 = x$

b) $6 - x = \dfrac{x}{x-2} + 2$

c) $6 - \dfrac{x}{x-2} = x - 2$

d) $x + 6 = \dfrac{x}{x-2}$

A $y = \dfrac{x}{x-2} + x - 8$

B $y = \dfrac{x}{x-2} - x + 6$

C $y = \dfrac{x}{x-2} - x - 6$

D $y = \dfrac{x}{x-2} + x - 4$

2. a) Determine the roots of the rational equation $-\dfrac{2}{x} + x + 1 = 0$ algebraically.

b) Graph the rational function $y = -\dfrac{2}{x} + x + 1$ and determine the *x*-intercepts.

c) Explain the connection between the roots of the equation and the *x*-intercepts of the graph of the function.

3. Solve each equation algebraically.

a) $\dfrac{5x}{3x+4} = 7$

b) $2 = \dfrac{20 - 3x}{x}$

c) $\dfrac{x^2}{x-2} = x - 6$

d) $1 + \dfrac{2}{x} = \dfrac{x}{x+3}$

4. Use a graphical method to solve each equation. Then, use another method to verify your solution.

a) $\dfrac{8}{x} - 4 = x + 3$

b) $2x = \dfrac{10x}{2x-1}$

c) $\dfrac{3x^2 + 4x - 15}{x+3} = 2x - 1$

d) $\dfrac{3}{5x-7} + x = 1 + \dfrac{x^2 - 4x}{7 - 5x}$

5. Determine the approximate solution to each rational equation graphically, to the nearest hundredth. Then, solve the equation algebraically.

a) $\dfrac{x+1}{2x} = x - 3$

b) $\dfrac{x^2 - 4x - 5}{2 - 5x} = x + 3$

c) $\dfrac{2}{x} = 3 - \dfrac{7x}{x - 2}$

d) $2 + \dfrac{5}{x + 3} = 1 - \dfrac{x + 1}{x}$

6. Solve each equation algebraically and graphically. Compare the solutions found using each method.

a) $\dfrac{3x}{x - 2} + 5x = \dfrac{x + 4}{x - 2}$

b) $2x + 3 = \dfrac{3x^2 + 14x + 8}{x + 4}$

c) $\dfrac{6x}{x - 3} + 3x = \dfrac{2x^2}{x - 3} - 5$

d) $\dfrac{2x - 1}{x^2 - x} + 4 = \dfrac{x}{x - 1}$

Apply

7. Yunah is solving the equation $2 + \dfrac{x^2}{x - 1} = \dfrac{1}{x - 1}$ graphically. She uses the following steps and then enters the resulting function into her graphing calculator.

$$2 + \dfrac{x^2}{x - 1} = \dfrac{1}{x - 1}$$
$$2(x - 1) + x^2 = 1$$
$$2(x - 1) + x^2 - 1 = 0$$

Enter $Y_1 = 2(x - 1) + x^2 - 1$ and find the x-intercepts.

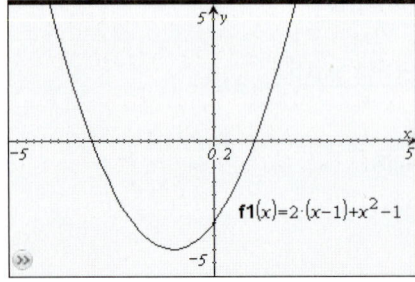

Is her approach correct? Explain.

8. Determine the solution to the equation $\dfrac{2x + 1}{x - 1} = \dfrac{2}{x + 2} - \dfrac{3}{2}$ using two different methods.

9. Solve the equation $2 - \dfrac{1}{x + 2} = \dfrac{x}{x + 2} + 1$ algebraically and graphically, and explain how the results of both methods verify each other.

10. The intensity, I, of light, in watts per square metre (W/m²), at a distance, d, in metres, from the point source is given by the formula $I = \dfrac{P}{4\pi d^2}$, where P is the average power of the source, in watts. How far away from a 500-W light source is intensity 5 W/m²?

11. A researcher is studying the effects of caffeine on the body. As part of her research, she monitors the levels of caffeine in a person's bloodstream over time after drinking coffee. The function $C(t) = \dfrac{50t}{1.2t^2 + 5}$ models the level of caffeine in one particular person's bloodstream, where t is the time, in hours, since drinking the coffee and $C(t)$ is the person's bloodstream concentration of caffeine, in milligrams per litre. How long after drinking coffee has the person's level dropped to 2 mg/L?

12. The time it takes for two people working together to complete a job is given by the formula $T = \dfrac{ab}{a+b}$, where a and b are the times it takes for the two people to complete the same job individually. Sarah can set up the auditorium for an assembly in 30 min, but when she works with James they can set it up in 10 min. How long would it take James to set it up by himself?

13. In hockey, a player's shooting percentage is given by dividing the player's total goals scored by the player's total shots taken on goal. So far this season, Rachel has taken 28 shots on net but scored only 2 goals. She has set a target of achieving a 30% shooting percentage this season.

  a) Write a function for Rachel's shooting percentage if x represents the number of shots she takes from now on and she scores on half of them.

  b) How many more shots will it take for her to bring her shooting percentage up to her target?

14. The coefficient, C, in parts per million per kelvin, of thermal expansion for copper at a temperature, T, in kelvins, can be modelled with the function
$C(T) = \dfrac{21.2T^2 - 877T + 9150}{T^2 + 23.6T + 760}$.

  a) For what temperature is $C(T) = 15$ according to this model?

  b) By how many kelvins does the temperature have to increase for copper's coefficient of thermal expansion to increase from 10 to 17?

> **Did You Know?**
>
> Most materials expand as the temperature increases, but not all in the same way. The *coefficient of thermal expansion* (CTE) for a given material is a measure of how much it will expand for each degree of temperature change as it is heated up. The higher the CTE, the more the material will expand per unit of temperature. A material's CTE value does not remain constant, but varies based on temperature. It is a ratio per unit of temperature, with units such as parts per million per kelvin or percent per degree Celsius. One part per million is equivalent to 0.0001%.

Extend

15. Solution A has a concentration of 0.05 g/mL and solution B has a concentration of 0.01 g/mL. You start with 200 mL of solution A, and pour in x millilitres of solution B.

  a) Write an equation for the concentration, $C(x)$, of the solution after x millilitres have been added.

  b) You need to make a solution with a concentration of 0.023 g/mL. How can you use your function equation to determine how many millilitres need to be added?

16. Solve the equation $\dfrac{x}{x+2} - 3 = \dfrac{5x}{x^2-4} + x$ graphically and algebraically.

17. Solve each inequality.

  a) $\dfrac{x-18}{x-1} \leq 5$

  b) $\dfrac{5}{x-2} \geq \dfrac{2x+17}{x+6}$

Create Connections

C1 Connor tells Brian that rational equations will always have at least one solution. Is this correct? Use a graphical approach and support your answer with examples.

C2 The rational equation $\dfrac{3x}{x+2} = x - \dfrac{6}{x+2}$ and the radical equation $x = \sqrt{x+6}$ both have an extraneous root. Compare and contrast why they occur in each of these equations and how they can be identified when solving.

C3 Which method for solving a rational equation do you prefer to use: graphical, algebraic, or a combination of both? Discuss with a partner, and give reasons for your choice.

Chapter 9 Review

9.1 Exploring Rational Functions Using Transformations, pages 430–445

1. Sketch the graph of each function using transformations. Identify the domain and range, intercepts, and asymptotes.

   a) $y = \dfrac{8}{x-1}$

   b) $y = \dfrac{3}{x} + 2$

   c) $y = -\dfrac{12}{x+4} - 5$

2. Graph each function, and identify any asymptotes and intercepts.

   a) $y = \dfrac{x}{x+2}$

   b) $y = \dfrac{2x+5}{x-1}$

   c) $y = \dfrac{-5x-3}{x-6}$

3. Graph the functions $f(x) = \dfrac{1}{x^2}$, $g(x) = \dfrac{6}{(x-3)^2} + 2$, and $h(x) = \dfrac{-4}{x^2 + 12x + 36}$. Compare the characteristics of the graphs and identify any common features.

4. A baseball league is planning to order new uniforms from a company that will charge $500 plus $35 per uniform.

   a) Represent the average cost per uniform for the company as a function of the number of uniforms ordered using an equation and a graph.

   b) Identify key features of the graph and explain what the graph shows about how the average cost changes for different numbers of uniforms ordered.

   c) The league needs to keep the cost per uniform at $40. How many uniforms does it have to order?

9.2 Analysing Rational Functions, pages 446–456

5. Graph and analyse each function, including the behaviour near any non-permissible values.

   a) $y = \dfrac{x^2 + 2x}{x}$

   b) $y = \dfrac{x^2 - 16}{x - 4}$

   c) $y = \dfrac{2x^2 - 3x - 5}{2x - 5}$

6. Which rational function matches each graph? Give reasons for your choices.

   $A(x) = \dfrac{x - 4}{x^2 - 5x + 4}$

   $B(x) = \dfrac{x^2 + 5x + 4}{x^2 + 1}$

   $C(x) = \dfrac{x - 1}{x^2 - 4}$

Graph 1
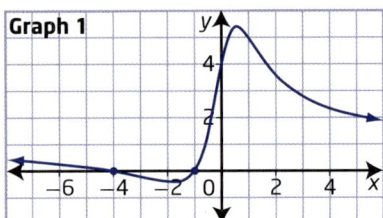

Graph 2
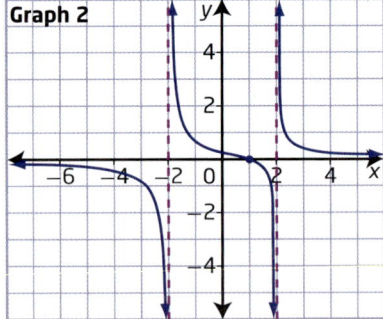

Graph 3
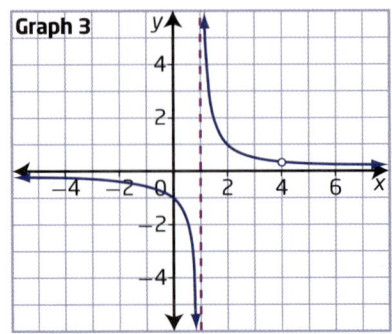

7. A company uses the function $C(p) = \dfrac{40\,000p}{100 - p}$ to estimate the cost of cleaning up a hazardous spill, where C is the cost, in dollars, and p is the percent of the spill that is cleaned up.

   a) Graph the function for a domain applicable to the situation.

   b) What does the shape of the graph show about the situation?

   c) According to this model, is it possible to clean up the spill entirely? Justify your answer in terms of the features of the graph.

   Did You Know?

   Environment Canada responds to approximately 1000 hazardous spills each year. Given the location and quantity and type of substance spilled, the scientists from Environment Canada's National Spill Modelling Team run spill models. Spill modelling helps to minimize the environmental impact of spills involving hazardous substances and provides emergency teams with critical information.

9.3 Connecting Graphs and Rational Equations, pages 457–467

8. a) Determine the roots of the rational equation $x + \dfrac{4}{x - 2} - 7 = 0$ algebraically.

   b) Graph the rational function $y = x + \dfrac{4}{x - 2} - 7$ and determine the x-intercepts.

   c) Explain the connection between the roots of the equation and the x-intercepts of the graph of the function.

9. Determine the solution to each equation graphically, and then verify algebraically.

   a) $x - 8 = \dfrac{33}{x}$

   b) $\dfrac{x - 10}{x - 7} = x - 2$

   c) $x = \dfrac{3x - 1}{x + 2} + 3$

   d) $2x + 1 = \dfrac{13 - 4x}{x - 5}$

10. Solve each equation graphically, to the nearest hundredth.

    a) $\dfrac{x - 4}{5 - 2x} = 3$

    b) $1.2x = \dfrac{x}{x + 6.7} + 3.9$

    c) $3x + 2 = \dfrac{5x + 4}{x + 1}$

    d) $\dfrac{x^2 - 2x - 8}{x + 2} = \dfrac{1}{4}x - 2$

11. The lever system shown is used to lift a mass of m kilograms on a cable with a constant force applied 0.4 m from the fulcrum. The maximum mass that can be lifted depends on the position, d, in metres, of the mass along the lever and is given by the formula $m = \dfrac{20}{d + 0.4}$.

    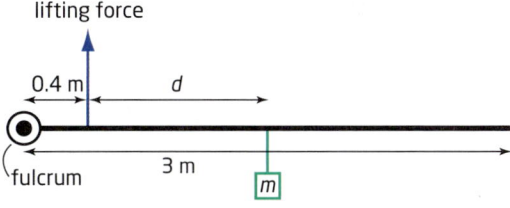

    a) What is the domain in this situation if the mass can be positioned at any point along the 3-m-long lever?

    b) Graph the function. What does it show about this context?

    c) Describe the behaviour of the function for its non-permissible value, and explain what the behaviour means in this situation.

    d) How far from the fulcrum can the lever support a maximum possible mass of 17.5 kg?

Chapter 9 Practice Test

Multiple Choice

For #1 to #6, choose the best answer.

1. Which function has a vertical asymptote at $x = 2$?
   - **A** $y = \dfrac{x-2}{x}$
   - **B** $y = \dfrac{x+2}{x}$
   - **C** $y = \dfrac{x}{x-2}$
   - **D** $y = \dfrac{x}{x+2}$

2. Which graph represents $y = \dfrac{x^2 - 2x}{x^2 - 5x + 6}$?

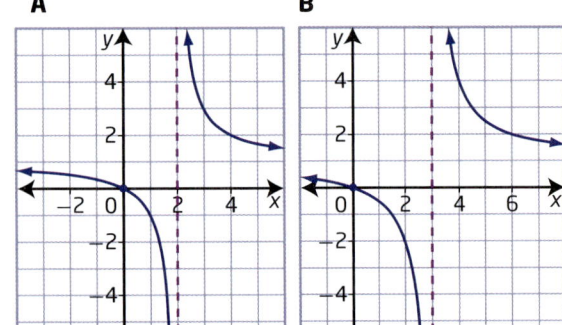

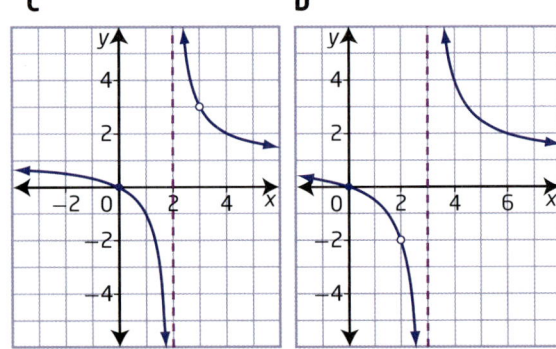

3. Which statement is true about the function $y = -\dfrac{4}{x-2}$?
   - **A** As x approaches -2, $|y|$ becomes very large.
   - **B** As $|x|$ becomes very large, y approaches -4.
   - **C** As x approaches 2, $|y|$ becomes very large.
   - **D** As $|x|$ becomes very large, y approaches 4.

4. The roots of $5 - x = \dfrac{x+2}{2x-3}$ can be determined using which of the following?
   - **A** the x-coordinates of the points of intersection of $y = \dfrac{x+2}{2x-3}$ and $y = x - 5$
   - **B** the x-intercepts of the function $y = \dfrac{x+2}{2x-3} + x - 5$
   - **C** the x-coordinates of the points of intersection of $y = \dfrac{x+2}{2x-3}$ and $y = x + 5$
   - **D** the x-intercepts of the function $y = \dfrac{x+2}{2x-3} - x + 5$

5. Which function is equivalent to $y = \dfrac{6x - 5}{x + 7}$?
   - **A** $y = \dfrac{37}{x+7} + 6$
   - **B** $y = -\dfrac{37}{x+7} + 6$
   - **C** $y = \dfrac{47}{x+7} + 6$
   - **D** $y = -\dfrac{47}{x+7} + 6$

6. Which statement about the function $y = \dfrac{x}{x^2 - x}$ is true?
   - **A** It has an x-intercept of 0.
   - **B** It has a y-intercept of 0.
   - **C** It has a point of discontinuity at $(0, -1)$.
   - **D** It has a vertical asymptote at $x = 0$.

Short Answer

7. Solve the equation $x - 6 = \dfrac{x^2}{x+1}$ graphically and algebraically.

8. a) Sketch the graph of the function $y = -\dfrac{6}{x+4} - 3$.
   b) Identify the domain and range, and state the locations of any asymptotes and intercepts.

9. Determine the approximate solution(s) to $\dfrac{3}{x} + 4 = \dfrac{2}{x+3} - 1$ graphically. Give your answer(s) to two decimal places.

10. a) Sketch the graph of the function $y = \dfrac{x^2 - 2x - 8}{x - 4}$.
    b) Explain the behaviour of the function for values of x near its non-permissible value.

11. Predict the locations of any vertical asymptotes, points of discontinuity, and intercepts for the function $y = \dfrac{2x^2 + 7x - 4}{x^2 + x - 12}$. Give a reason for each prediction.

12. Match each rational function to its graph. Give reasons for each choice.

a) $A(x) = \dfrac{x^2 - 9x}{x}$ b) $B(x) = \dfrac{x^2}{x^2 - 9}$

c) $C(x) = \dfrac{x^2 - 9}{x^2}$ d) $D(x) = \dfrac{x^2}{x^2 - 9x}$

A
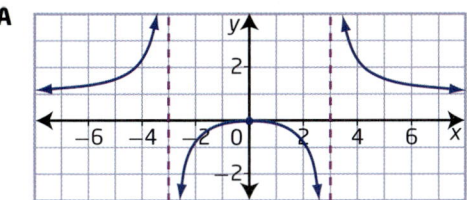

B
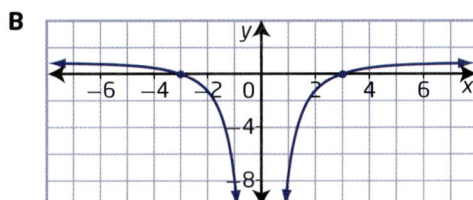

C
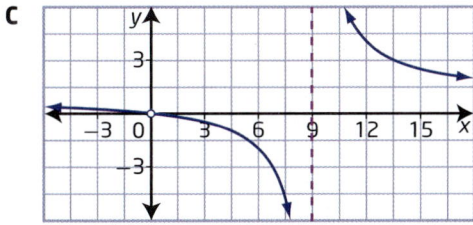

D
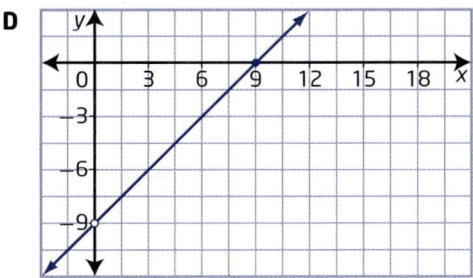

Extended Response

13. Compare the graphs of the functions $f(x) = \dfrac{2x - 3}{4x^2 - 9}$ and $g(x) = \dfrac{2x - 3}{4x^2 + 9}$. Explain any significant differences in the graphs by comparing the function equations.

14. Alex solved the equation $\dfrac{x^2}{x - 2} - 2 = \dfrac{3x - 2}{x - 2}$ algebraically and found a solution that consisted of two different values of x.

a) Solve the equation algebraically and explain what is incorrect about Alex's result.

b) Use a graphical approach to solve the problem. Explain how this method can help you avoid the error that Alex made.

15. Jennifer is preparing for a golf tournament by practising her putting. So far she has been successful on 10 out of 31 putts.

a) If she tries x putts from now on and she is successful on half of them, what equation represents A, her overall average putting success rate as a function of x?

b) Use a graphical approach to determine how many putts it will take before her average is up to 40%.

16. Jarek lives 20 km upstream from his friend Edward on a river in which the water flows at 4 km/h. If Jarek travels by boat to Edward's house and back again, the total time, t, in hours, for the round trip is given by the function $t = \dfrac{40v}{v^2 - 16}$, where v is the boat's speed, in kilometres per hour.

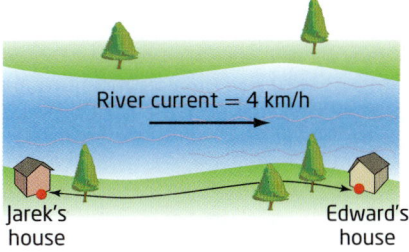

a) What is the domain if Jarek makes the complete round trip? Explain.

b) Graph the function and explain what it shows about the situation.

c) Explain what the behaviour of the function near its non-permissible value represents in this context.

d) What boat speed does Jarek need to keep the trip to 45 min each way?

CHAPTER 10
Function Operations

Throughout your mathematics courses, you have learned methods of interpreting a variety of functions. It is important to understand functional relationships between variables since they apply to the fields of engineering, business, physical sciences, and social sciences, to name a few.

The relationships that exist between variables can be complex and can involve combining two or more functions. In this chapter, you will learn how to use various combinations of functions to model real-world phenomena.

Did You Know?

Wave interference occurs when two or more waves travel through the same medium at the same time. The net amplitude at each point of the resulting wave is the sum of the amplitudes of the individual waves. For example, waves interfere in wave pools and in noise-cancelling headphones.

Key Terms
composite function

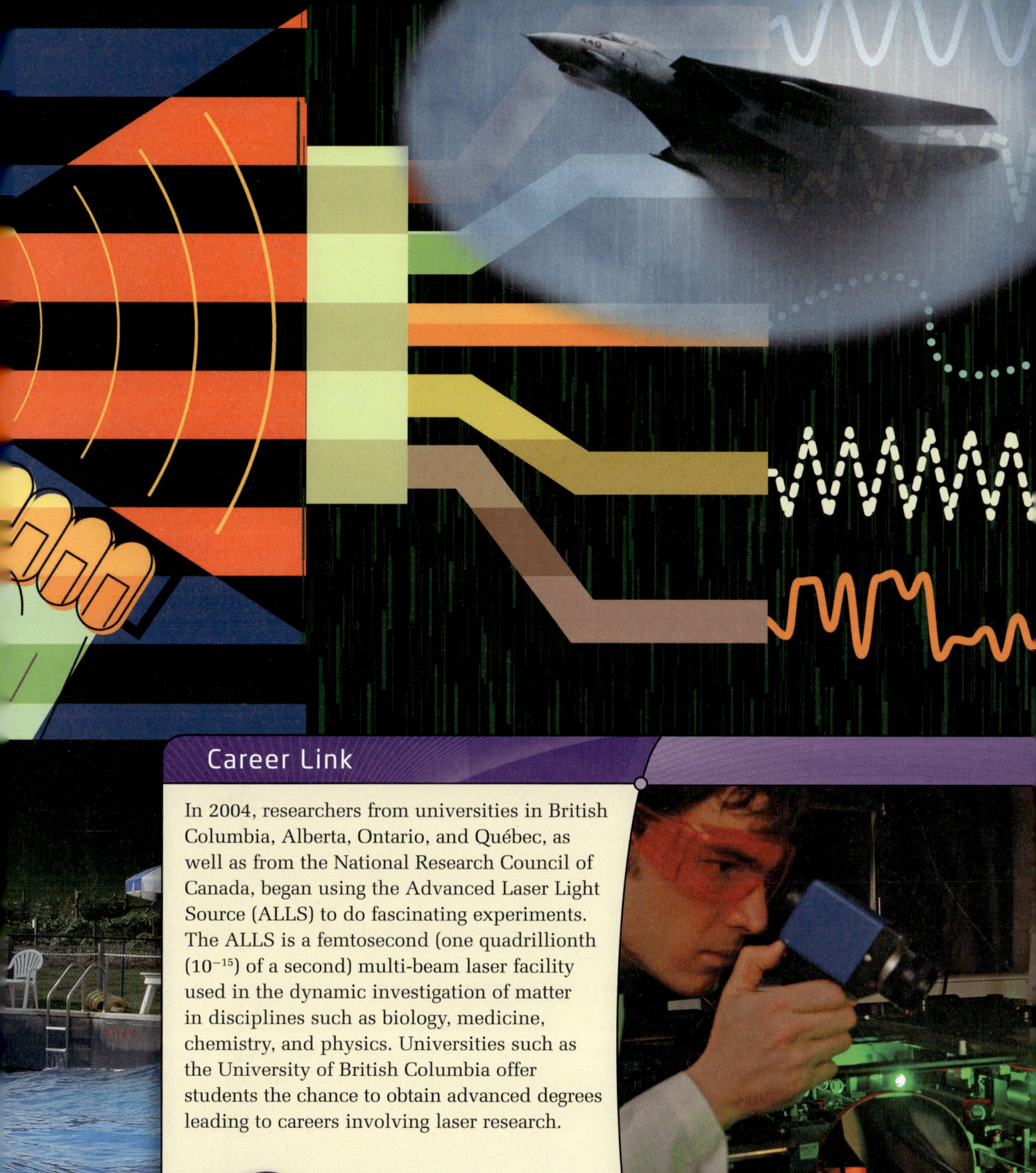

Career Link

In 2004, researchers from universities in British Columbia, Alberta, Ontario, and Québec, as well as from the National Research Council of Canada, began using the Advanced Laser Light Source (ALLS) to do fascinating experiments. The ALLS is a femtosecond (one quadrillionth (10^{-15}) of a second) multi-beam laser facility used in the dynamic investigation of matter in disciplines such as biology, medicine, chemistry, and physics. Universities such as the University of British Columbia offer students the chance to obtain advanced degrees leading to careers involving laser research.

Web Link

To learn more about a career involving laser research, go to www.mcgrawhill.ca/school/learningcentres and follow the links.

10.1

Sums and Differences of Functions

Focus on...
- sketching the graph of a function that is the sum or difference of two functions
- determining the domain and range of a function that is the sum or difference of two functions
- writing the equation of a function that is the sum or difference of two functions

Physicists use ripple tanks to model wave motion. You know from previous work that sinusoidal functions can be used to model single wave functions. Waves are said to interfere with one another when they collide. Their collision can be modelled by the addition or subtraction of two sine waves.

Investigate Sums and Differences of Functions

Materials
- grid paper
- computer with spreadsheet software (optional)

1. Consider the graphs of the functions $f(x)$, $g(x)$, and $h(x)$.

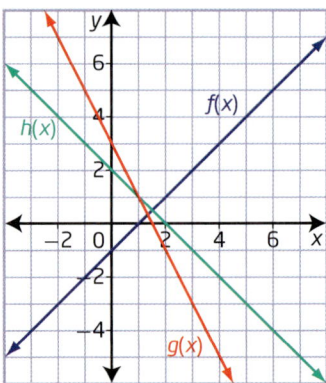

a) Copy the table and use the graph of each function to complete the columns.

x	f(x)	g(x)	h(x)
−2			
−1			
0			
1			
2			
3			
4			

b) What do you notice about the relationship between each value of $h(x)$ and the corresponding values of $f(x)$ and $g(x)$?

2. a) Determine the equation, in slope-intercept form, of each function graphed in step 1.

   b) Using your equations, write the equation of a new function, $s(x)$, that represents the sum of the functions $f(x)$ and $g(x)$. Is this new function related to $h(x)$? Explain.

3. a) What are the domain and range of the functions $f(x)$ and $g(x)$?

   b) State the domain and range of $h(x)$. How do they relate to the domains and ranges of $f(x)$ and $g(x)$?

4. Add a fifth column to your table from step 1 using the heading $k(x) = f(x) - g(x)$, and fill in the values for the column.

5. a) Sketch the graphs of $f(x)$, $g(x)$, and $k(x)$ on the same set of coordinate axes.

   b) State the domain and range of $k(x)$. How do they relate to the domains and ranges of $f(x)$ and $g(x)$?

6. Using your equations from step 2, write the equation of a new function, $d(x)$, that represents the difference $g(x) - f(x)$. Is this new function related to $k(x)$? Explain.

Reflect and Respond

7. a) Choose two functions, $f(x)$ and $g(x)$, of your own. Sketch the graphs of $f(x)$ and $g(x)$ on the same set of coordinate axes.

   b) Explain how you can write the equation and produce the graph of the sum of $f(x)$ and $g(x)$.

   c) Explain how you can write the equation and produce the graph of the difference function, $g(x) - f(x)$.

8. Will your results of adding functions and subtracting functions apply to every type of function? Explain your reasoning.

Link the Ideas

You can form new functions by performing operations with functions.

To combine two functions, $f(x)$ and $g(x)$, add or subtract as follows:

Sum of Functions
$h(x) = f(x) + g(x)$
$h(x) = (f + g)(x)$

Difference of Functions
$h(x) = f(x) - g(x)$
$h(x) = (f - g)(x)$

Example 1

Determine the Sum of Two Functions

Consider the functions $f(x) = 2x + 1$ and $g(x) = x^2$.
a) Determine the equation of the function $h(x) = (f + g)(x)$.
b) Sketch the graphs of $f(x)$, $g(x)$, and $h(x)$ on the same set of coordinate axes.
c) State the domain and range of $h(x)$.
d) Determine the values of $f(x)$, $g(x)$, and $h(x)$ when $x = 4$.

Solution

a) Add $f(x)$ and $g(x)$ to determine the equation of the function $h(x) = (f + g)(x)$.

$h(x) = (f + g)(x)$
$h(x) = f(x) + g(x)$
$h(x) = 2x + 1 + x^2$
$h(x) = x^2 + 2x + 1$

Is the function $(f + g)(x)$ the same as $(g + f)(x)$? Will this always be true?

b) **Method 1: Use Paper and Pencil**

x	$f(x) = 2x + 1$	$g(x) = x^2$	$h(x) = x^2 + 2x + 1$
−2	−3	4	1
−1	−1	1	0
0	1	0	1
1	3	1	4
2	5	4	9

How could you use the values in the columns for $f(x)$ and $g(x)$ to determine the values in the column for $h(x)$?

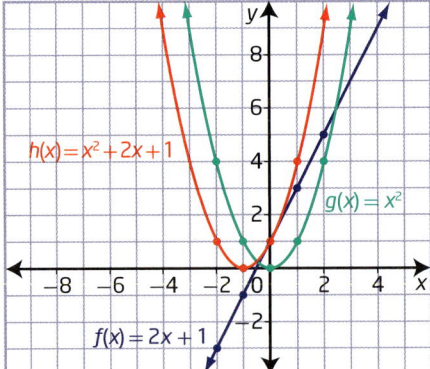

How are the y-coordinates of points on the graph of $h(x)$ related to those on the graphs of $f(x)$ and $g(x)$?

476 MHR • Chapter 10

Method 2: Use a Spreadsheet
You can generate a table of values using a spreadsheet. From these values, you can create a graph.

x	f(x)	g(x)	h(x)
-4	-7	16	9
-3	-5	9	4
-2	-3	4	1
-1	-1	1	0
0	1	0	1
1	3	1	4
2	5	4	9
3	7	9	16

c) The function $f(x) = 2x + 1$ has domain $\{x \mid x \in \mathbb{R}\}$.
The function $g(x) = x^2$ has domain $\{x \mid x \in \mathbb{R}\}$.
The function $h(x) = (f + g)(x)$ has domain $\{x \mid x \in \mathbb{R}\}$, which consists of all values that are in both the domain of $f(x)$ and the domain of $g(x)$.
The range of $h(x)$ is $\{y \mid y \geq 0, y \in \mathbb{R}\}$.

d) Substitute $x = 4$ into $f(x)$, $g(x)$, and $h(x)$.

$f(x) = 2x + 1$ $g(x) = x^2$ $h(x) = x^2 + 2x + 1$
$f(4) = 2(4) + 1$ $g(4) = 4^2$ $h(4) = 4^2 + 2(4) + 1$
$f(4) = 8 + 1$ $g(4) = 16$ $h(4) = 16 + 8 + 1$
$f(4) = 9$ $h(4) = 25$

Your Turn

Consider the functions $f(x) = -4x - 3$ and $g(x) = 2x^2$.
a) Determine the equation of the function $h(x) = (f + g)(x)$.
b) Sketch the graphs of $f(x)$, $g(x)$, and $h(x)$ on the same set of coordinate axes.
c) State the domain and range of $h(x)$.

Example 2

Determine the Difference of Two Functions

Consider the functions $f(x) = \sqrt{x - 1}$ and $g(x) = x - 2$.

a) Determine the equation of the function $h(x) = (f - g)(x)$.
b) Sketch the graphs of $f(x)$, $g(x)$, and $h(x)$ on the same set of coordinate axes.
c) State the domain of $h(x)$.
d) Use the graph to approximate the range of $h(x)$.

Solution

a) Subtract $g(x)$ from $f(x)$ to determine the equation of the function $h(x) = (f - g)(x)$.
$h(x) = (f - g)(x)$
$h(x) = f(x) - g(x)$
$h(x) = \sqrt{x - 1} - (x - 2)$
$h(x) = \sqrt{x - 1} - x + 2$

b) **Method 1: Use Paper and Pencil**

For the function $f(x) = \sqrt{x - 1}$, the value of the radicand must be greater than or equal to zero: $x - 1 \geq 0$ or $x \geq 1$.

x	$f(x) = \sqrt{x - 1}$	$g(x) = x - 2$	$h(x) = \sqrt{x - 1} - x + 2$
−2	undefined	−4	undefined
−1	undefined	−3	undefined
0	undefined	−2	undefined
1	0	−1	1
2	1	0	1
5	2	3	−1
10	3	8	−5

Why is the function $h(x)$ undefined when $x < 1$?

How could you use the values in the columns for $f(x)$ and $g(x)$ to determine the values in the column for $h(x)$?

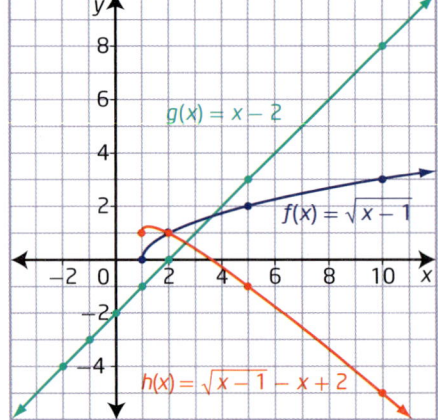

How could you use the y-coordinates of points on the graphs of $f(x)$ and $g(x)$ to create the graph of $h(x)$?

Method 2: Use a Spreadsheet

You can generate a table of values using a spreadsheet. From these values, you can create a graph.

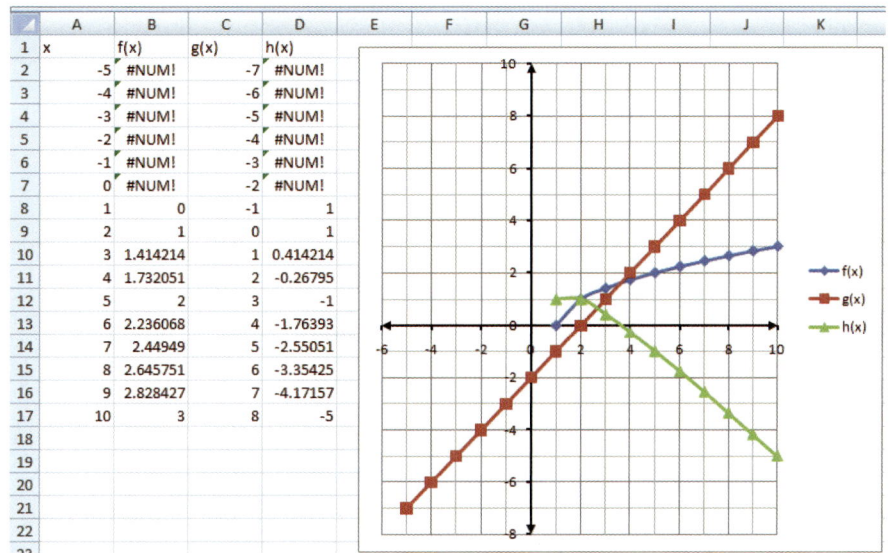

c) The function $f(x) = \sqrt{x-1}$ has domain $\{x \mid x \geq 1, x \in R\}$.
The function $g(x) = x - 2$ has domain $\{x \mid x \in R\}$.
The function $h(x) = (f - g)(x)$ has domain $\{x \mid x \geq 1, x \in R\}$, which consists of all values that are in both the domain of $f(x)$ and the domain of $g(x)$.

What values of x belong to the domains of both $f(x)$ and $g(x)$?

d) From the graph, the range of $h(x)$ appears to be approximately $\{y \mid y \leq 1.2, y \in R\}$.

How can you use a graphing calculator to verify the range?

Your Turn

Consider the functions $f(x) = |x|$ and $g(x) = x - 5$.
a) Determine the equation of the function $h(x) = (f - g)(x)$.
b) Sketch the graphs of $f(x)$, $g(x)$, and $h(x)$ on the same set of coordinate axes.
c) State the domain and range of $h(x)$.
d) Is $(f - g)(x)$ equal to $(g - f)(x)$? If not, what are the similarities and differences?

Example 3

Determine a Combined Function From Graphs

Sketch the graph of $h(x) = (f + g)(x)$ given the graphs of $f(x)$ and $g(x)$.

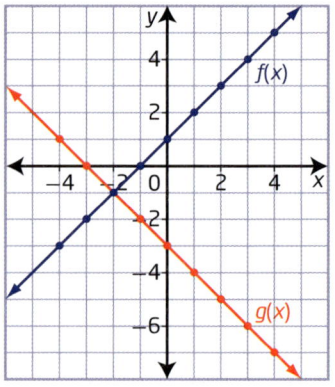

Solution

Method 1: Add the y-Coordinates of Corresponding Points
Create a table of values from the graphs of $f(x)$ and $g(x)$.

Add the y-coordinates at each point to determine points on the graph of $h(x) = (f + g)(x)$. Plot these points and draw the graph of $h(x) = (f + g)(x)$.

x	f(x)	g(x)	h(x) = (f + g)(x)
−4	−3	1	−3 + 1 = −2
−3	−2	0	−2 + 0 = −2
−2	−1	−1	−1 + (−1) = −2
−1	0	−2	0 + (−2) = −2
0	1	−3	1 + (−3) = −2
1	2	−4	2 + (−4) = −2
2	3	−5	3 + (−5) = −2
3	4	−6	4 + (−6) = −2
4	5	−7	5 + (−7) = −2

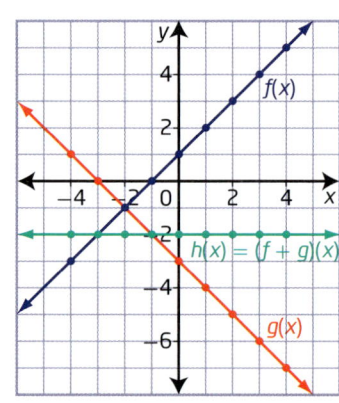

The result is a line with a slope of 0 and a y-intercept of −2. Therefore, $h(x) = -2$.

Method 2: Determine the Equations
To determine $h(x)$, you could first determine the equations of $f(x)$ and $g(x)$.

For the graph of $f(x)$, the y-intercept is 1 and the slope is 1. So, the equation is $f(x) = x + 1$.

For $g(x)$, the equation is $g(x) = -x - 3$.

What are the slope and y-intercept of this line?

Determine the equation of $h(x)$ algebraically.
$h(x) = (f + g)(x)$
$h(x) = x + 1 + (-x - 3)$
$h(x) = -2$

The graph of $h(x) = -2$ is a horizontal line.

Did You Know?

When the order of operands can be reversed and still produce the same result, the operation is said to be commutative. For example, $(f + g)(x) = (g + f)(x)$

You can verify your answer by graphing $f(x) = x + 1$, $g(x) = -x - 3$, and $h(x) = f(x) + g(x)$ using a graphing calculator.

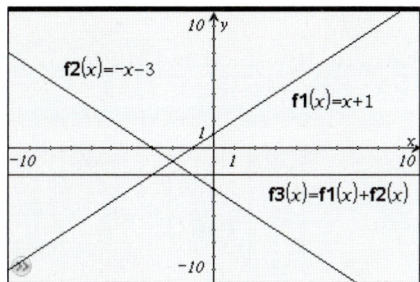

Your Turn

Sketch the graph of $m(x) = (f - g)(x)$ given the graphs of $f(x)$ and $g(x)$.

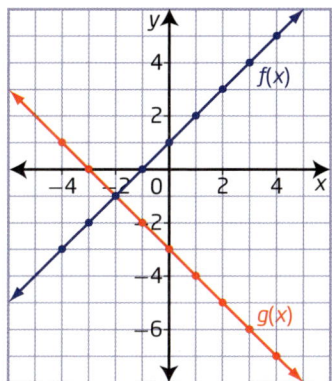

Example 4

Application of the Difference of Two Functions

Reach for the Top is an academic challenge program offered to students across Canada. Suppose the cost of T-shirts for the program includes $125 in fixed costs and $7.50 per T-shirt. The shirts are sold for $12.00 each.

a) Write an equation to represent
  • the total cost, C, as a function of the number, n, of T-shirts produced
  • the revenue, R, as a function of the number, n, of T-shirts sold
b) Graph the total cost and revenue functions on the same set of axes. What does the point of intersection represent?
c) Profit, P, is the difference between revenue and cost. Write a function representing P in terms of n.
d) Identify the domain of the total cost, revenue, and profit functions in the context of this problem.

Solution

a) The total cost of producing the T-shirts can be represented by the function $C(n) = 7.5n + 125$.
The revenue can be represented by the function $R(n) = 12n$.

b) Graph the functions.

The point of intersection represents the point at which the total cost equals the revenue, or the break-even point. Any further sales of T-shirts will result in profit.

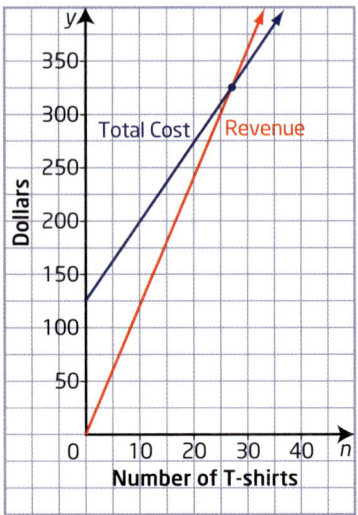

c) Profit can be represented by a combined function:
$P(n) = R(n) - C(n)$
$P(n) = 12n - (7.5n + 125)$
$P(n) = 4.5n - 125$

d) The domain of $C(n) = 7.5n + 125$ is $\{n \mid n \geq 0, n \in W\}$.

The domain of $R(n) = 12n$ is $\{n \mid n \geq 0, n \in W\}$.

The domain of $P(n) = 4.5n - 125$ is $\{n \mid n \geq 0, n \in W\}$.

Your Turn

Math Kangaroo is an international mathematics competition that is held in over 40 countries, including Canada. Suppose the cost of preparing booklets for the Canadian version of the contest includes $675 in fixed costs and $3.50 per booklet. The booklets are sold for $30 each.

a) Write an equation to represent
  • the total cost, C, as a function of the number, n, of booklets produced
  • the revenue, R, as a function of the number, n, of booklets sold
  • the profit, P, the difference between revenue and total cost
b) Graph the total cost, revenue, and profit functions on the same set of axes. How many booklets must be sold to make a profit?
c) Identify the domain of the total cost, revenue, and profit functions in the context of this problem.

> **Did You Know?**
>
> *Math Kangaroo* or *Kangourou sans frontières* originated in France in 1991. The first Canadian edition of the competition was held in 2001.

Key Ideas

- You can add two functions, $f(x)$ and $g(x)$, to form the combined function $h(x) = (f + g)(x)$.
- You can subtract two functions, $f(x)$ and $g(x)$, to form the combined function $h(x) = (f - g)(x)$.
- The domain of the combined function formed by the sum or difference of two functions is the domain common to the individual functions. For example,

    Domain of $f(x)$: $\{x \mid x \leq 3, x \in R\}$
    Domain of $g(x)$: $\{x \mid x \geq -5, x \in R\}$
    Domain of $h(x)$: $\{x \mid -5 \leq x \leq 3, x \in R\}$

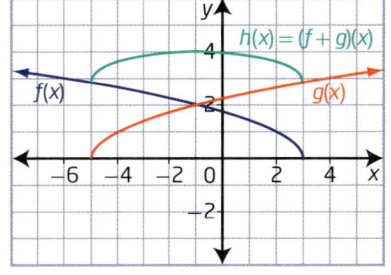

- The range of a combined function can be determined using its graph.
- To sketch the graph of a sum or difference of two functions given their graphs, add or subtract the y-coordinates at each point.

Check Your Understanding

Practise

1. For each pair of functions, determine $h(x) = f(x) + g(x)$.
   a) $f(x) = |x - 3|$ and $g(x) = 4$
   b) $f(x) = 3x - 5$ and $g(x) = -x + 2$
   c) $f(x) = x^2 + 2x$ and $g(x) = x^2 + x + 2$
   d) $f(x) = -x - 5$ and $g(x) = (x + 3)^2$

2. For each pair of functions, determine $h(x) = f(x) - g(x)$.
   a) $f(x) = 6x$ and $g(x) = x - 2$
   b) $f(x) = -3x + 7$ and $g(x) = 3x^2 + x - 2$
   c) $f(x) = 6 - x$ and $g(x) = (x + 1)^2 - 7$
   d) $f(x) = \cos x$ and $g(x) = 4$

3. Consider $f(x) = -6x + 1$ and $g(x) = x^2$.
   a) Determine $h(x) = f(x) + g(x)$ and find $h(2)$.
   b) Determine $m(x) = f(x) - g(x)$ and find $m(1)$.
   c) Determine $p(x) = g(x) - f(x)$ and find $p(1)$.

4. Given $f(x) = 3x^2 + 2$, $g(x) = \sqrt{x + 4}$, and $h(x) = 4x - 2$, determine each combined function and state its domain.
   a) $y = (f + g)(x)$
   b) $y = (h - g)(x)$
   c) $y = (g - h)(x)$
   d) $y = (f + h)(x)$

5. Let $f(x) = 2^x$ and $g(x) = 1$. Graph each of the following, stating its domain and range.
   a) $y = (f + g)(x)$
   b) $y = (f - g)(x)$
   c) $y = (g - f)(x)$

6. Use the graphs of $f(x)$ and $g(x)$ to evaluate the following.
   a) $(f + g)(4)$
   b) $(f + g)(-4)$
   c) $(f + g)(-5)$
   d) $(f + g)(-6)$

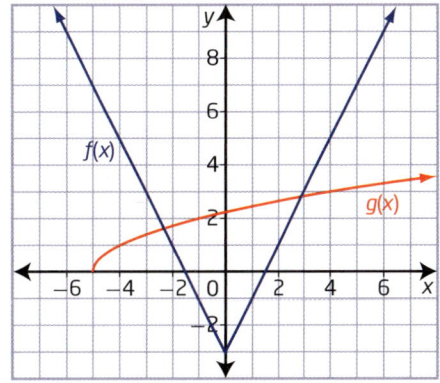

7. Use the graphs of $f(x)$ and $g(x)$ to determine which graph matches each combined function.

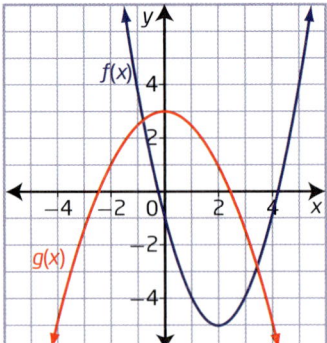

a) $y = (f + g)(x)$
b) $y = (f - g)(x)$
c) $y = (g - f)(x)$

A
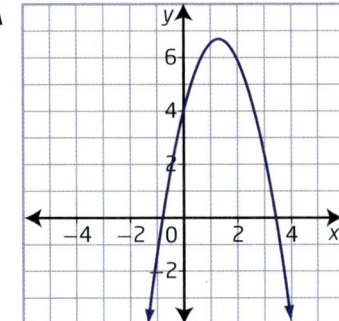

B
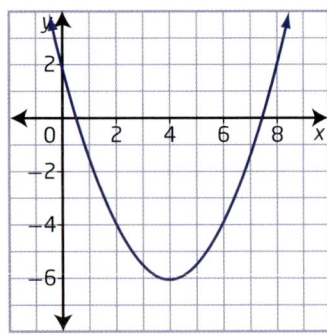

C
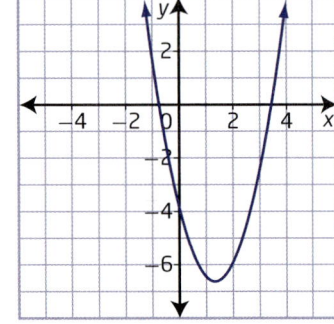

8. Copy each graph. Add the sketch of the graph of each combined function to the same set of axes.

a)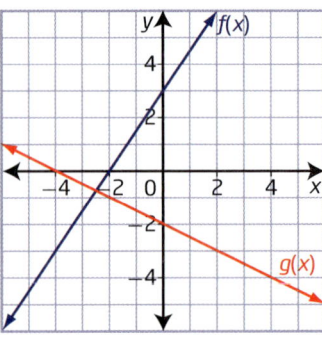

b)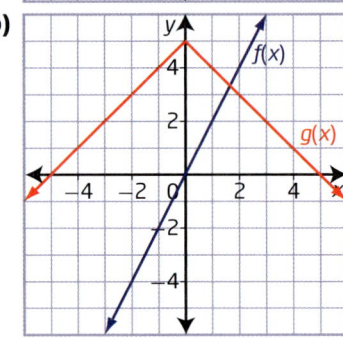

i) $y = (f + g)(x)$
ii) $y = (f - g)(x)$
iii) $y = (g - f)(x)$

Apply

9. Given $f(x) = 3x^2 + 2$, $g(x) = 4x$, and $h(x) = 7x - 1$, determine each combined function.

a) $y = f(x) + g(x) + h(x)$
b) $y = f(x) + g(x) - h(x)$
c) $y = f(x) - g(x) + h(x)$
d) $y = f(x) - g(x) - h(x)$

10. If $h(x) = (f + g)(x)$ and $f(x) = 5x + 2$, determine $g(x)$.

a) $h(x) = x^2 + 5x + 2$
b) $h(x) = \sqrt{x + 7} + 5x + 2$
c) $h(x) = 2x + 3$
d) $h(x) = 3x^2 + 4x - 2$

11. If $h(x) = (f - g)(x)$ and $f(x) = 5x + 2$, determine $g(x)$.

a) $h(x) = -x^2 + 5x + 3$
b) $h(x) = \sqrt{x - 4} + 5x + 2$
c) $h(x) = -3x + 11$
d) $h(x) = -2x^2 + 16x + 8$

12. An eco-friendly company produces a water bottle waist pack from recycled plastic. The supply, S, in hundreds of waist packs, is a function of the price, p, in dollars, and is modelled by the function $S(p) = p + 4$. The demand, D, for the waist packs is modelled by $D(p) = -0.1(p + 8)(p - 10)$.

   a) Graph these functions on the same set of axes. What do the points of intersection represent? Should both points be considered? Explain.

   b) Graph the function $y = S(p) - D(p)$. Explain what it models.

13. The daily costs for a hamburger vendor are $135 per day plus $1.25 per hamburger sold. He sells each burger for $3.50, and the maximum number of hamburgers he can sell in a day is 300.

   a) Write equations to represent the total cost, C, and the total revenue, R, as functions of the number, n, of hamburgers sold.

   b) Graph $C(n)$ and $R(n)$ on the same set of axes.

   c) The break-even point is where $C(n) = R(n)$. Identify this point.

   d) Develop an algebraic and a graphical model for the profit function.

   e) What is the maximum daily profit the vendor can earn?

14. Two waves are generated in a ripple tank. Suppose the height, in centimetres, above the surface of the water, of the waves can be modelled by $f(x) = \sin x$ and $g(x) = 3 \sin x$, where x is in radians.

   a) Graph $f(x)$ and $g(x)$ on the same set of coordinate axes.

   b) Use your graph to sketch the graph of $h(x) = (f + g)(x)$.

   c) What is the maximum height of the resultant wave?

15. Automobile mufflers are designed to reduce exhaust noise in part by applying wave interference. The resonating chamber of a muffler contains a specific volume of air and has a specific length that is calculated to produce a wave that cancels out a certain frequency of sound. Suppose the engine noise can be modelled by $E(t) = 10 \sin 480\pi t$ and the resonating chamber produces a wave modelled by $R(t) = 8 \sin 480\pi(t - 0.002)$, where t is the time, in seconds.

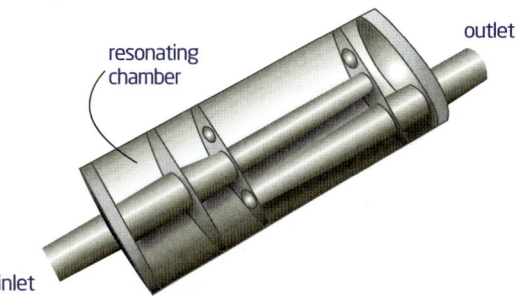

   a) Graph $E(t)$ and $R(t)$ using technology for a time period of 0.02 s.

   b) Describe the general relationship between the locations of the maximum and minimum values of the two functions. Will this result in destructive interference or constructive interference?

   c) Graph $E(t) + R(t)$.

   Did You Know?

   Destructive interference occurs when the sum of two waves has a lesser amplitude than the component waves.

   Constructive interference occurs when the sum of two waves has a greater amplitude than the component waves.

   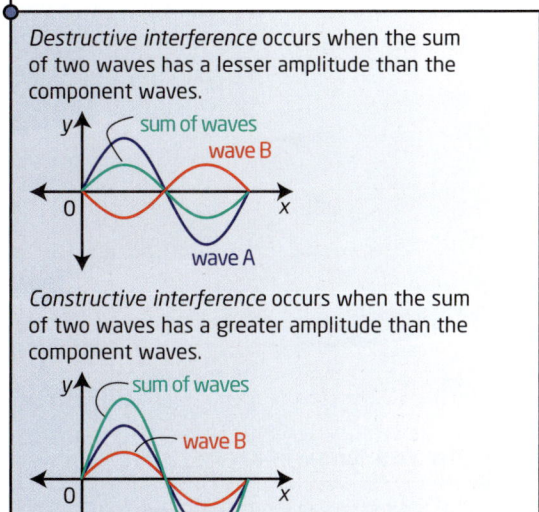

16. An alternating current–direct current (AC-DC) voltage signal is made up of the following two components, each measured in volts (V): $V_{AC}(t) = 10 \sin t$ and $V_{DC}(t) = 15$.
   a) Sketch the graphs of these two functions on the same set of axes. Work in radians.
   b) Graph the combined function $V_{AC}(t) + V_{DC}(t)$.
   c) Identify the domain and range of $V_{AC}(t) + V_{DC}(t)$.
   d) Use the range of the combined function to determine the following values of this voltage signal.
      i) minimum
      ii) maximum

17. During a race in the Sportsman category of drag racing, it is common for cars with different performance potentials to race against each other while using a handicap system. Suppose the distance, d_1, in metres, that the faster car travels is given by $d_1(t) = 10t^2$, where t is the time, in seconds, after the driver starts. The distance, d_2, in metres, that the slower car travels is given by $d_2(t) = 5(t + 2)^2$, where t is the time, in seconds, after the driver of the faster car starts. Write a function, $h(t)$, that gives the relative distance between the cars over time.

Did You Know?

The Saskatchewan International Raceway is the oldest drag strip in Western Canada. It was built in 1966 and is located outside of Saskatoon.

18. a) Use technology to graph $f(x) = \sin x$ and $g(x) = x$, where x is in radians, on the same graph.
    b) Predict the shape of $h(x) = f(x) + g(x)$. Verify your prediction using graphing technology.

Extend

19. A skier is skiing through a series of moguls down a course that is 200 m in length at a constant speed of 1 m/s. The constant slope of the hill is -1.

   a) Write a function representing the skier's distance, d, from the base of the hill versus time, t, in seconds (neglecting the effects of the moguls).
   b) If the height, m, of the skier through the moguls, ignoring the slope of the hill, is $m(t) = 0.75 \sin 1.26t$, write a function that represents the skier's actual path of height versus time.
   c) Graph the function in part a) and the two functions in part b) on the same set of axes.

Did You Know?

Moguls are representative wave models. The crests are the high points of a mogul and the troughs are the low points.

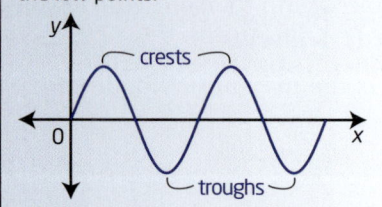

20. An *even function* satisfies the property $f(-x) = f(x)$ for all x in the domain of $f(x)$. An *odd function* satisfies the property $f(-x) = -f(x)$ for all x in the domain of $f(x)$.

    Devise and test an algebraic method to determine if the sum of two functions is even, odd, or neither. Show by example how your method works. Use at least three of the functions you have studied: absolute value, radical, polynomial, trigonometric, exponential, logarithmic, and rational.

21. The graph shows either the sum or the difference of two functions. Identify the types of functions that were combined. Verify your thinking using technology.

    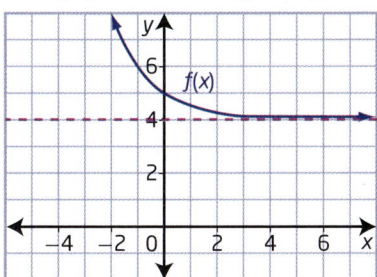

22. Consider $f(x) = x^2 - 9$ and $g(x) = \frac{1}{x}$.

    a) State the domain and range of each function.

    b) Determine $h(x) = f(x) + g(x)$.

    c) How do the domain and range of each function compare to the domain and range of $h(x)$?

Create Connections

C1 a) Is $f(x) + g(x) = g(x) + f(x)$ true for all functions? Justify your answer.

  b) Is $(f - g)(x) = (g - f)(x)$ true for all functions? Justify your answer.

C2 Let $y_1 = x^3$ and $y_2 = 4$. Use graphs, numbers, and words to determine

  a) the function $y_3 = y_1 + y_2$

  b) the domain and range of y_3

C3 MINI LAB

Model the path of a bungee jumper. The table gives the height versus time data of a bungee jumper. Heights are referenced to the rest position of the bungee jumper, which is well above ground level.

Materials
- grid paper or graphing technology

Time (s)	Height (m)	Time (s)	Height (m)	Time (s)	Height (m)
0	100	13	−11	26	−39
1	90	14	11	27	−39
2	72	15	30	28	−35
3	45	16	44	29	−27
4	14	17	53	30	−16
5	−15	18	54	31	−4
6	−41	19	48	32	6
7	−61	20	37	33	17
8	−71	21	23	34	24
9	−73	22	6	35	28
10	−66	23	−8	36	29
11	−52	24	−23	37	26
12	−32	25	−33		

Step 1 Create a graph of height versus time. How does the graph exhibit sinusoidal features?

Step 2 Describe how the graph exhibits exponential features.

Step 3 Construct a cosine function that has the same period (wavelength) as the graph in step 1.

Step 4 Construct an exponential function to model the decay in amplitude of the graph in step 1.

Step 5 Construct a combined function to model the height-time relationship of the bungee jumper.

Step 6 How far will the bungee jumper be above the rest position at his fourth crest?

10.2

Products and Quotients of Functions

Focus on...

- sketching the graph of a function that is the product or quotient of two functions
- determining the domain and range of a function that is the product or quotient of two functions
- writing the equation of a function that is the product or quotient of two functions

You have explored how functions can be combined through addition and subtraction. When combining functions using products or quotients, you will use techniques similar to those you learned when multiplying and dividing rational expressions, including the identification of non-permissible values.

You can use products and quotients of functions to solve problems related to populations, revenues at a sports venue, and the movement of a pendulum on a clock, to name a few examples.

Winnipeg Jets celebrate scoring in game against Montreal at MTS Centre Winnipeg on October 9, 2011

Investigate Products and Quotients of Functions

Materials

- grid paper

1. Consider the graphs of the functions $f(x)$ and $g(x)$.

   a) Copy the table and use the graph of each function to complete the columns for $f(x)$ and $g(x)$. In the last column, enter the product of the values of $f(x)$ and $g(x)$.

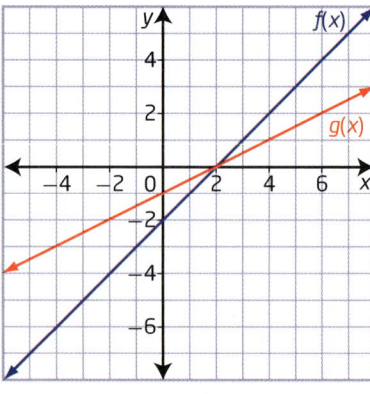

x	f(x)	g(x)	p(x)
−4			
−2			
0			
2			
4			
6			

488 MHR • Chapter 10

b) Predict the shape of the graph of $p(x)$. Then, copy the graphs of $f(x)$ and $g(x)$ and sketch the graph of $p(x)$ on the same set of axes.

c) How are the x-intercepts of the graph of $p(x)$ related to those of the graphs of $f(x)$ and $g(x)$?

2. a) Determine the equations of the functions $f(x)$ and $g(x)$.

b) How can you use the equations of $f(x)$ and $g(x)$ to write the equation of the function $p(x)$? Write the equation of $p(x)$ and verify that it matches the graph.

3. a) What are the domain and range of the functions $f(x)$, $g(x)$, and $p(x)$?

b) Is the relationship between the domains of $f(x)$, $g(x)$, and $p(x)$ the same as it was for addition and subtraction of functions? Explain.

4. a) Add a fifth column to your table from step 1 using the heading $q(x)$. Fill in the column with the quotient of the values of $f(x)$ and $g(x)$.

b) Predict the shape of the graph of $q(x)$. Then, copy the graphs of $f(x)$ and $g(x)$ and sketch the graph of $q(x)$ on the same set of axes.

c) How are the x-intercepts of the graphs of $f(x)$ and $g(x)$ related to the values of $q(x)$?

5. a) How can you use the equations from step 2a) to write the equation of the function $q(x)$? Write the equation of $q(x)$ and verify that it matches the graph.

b) State the domain and range of $q(x)$. Is the relationship between the domains of $f(x)$, $g(x)$, and $q(x)$ the same as it was for addition and subtraction of functions? Explain.

Reflect and Respond

6. Consider the graphs of $f(x) = x$ and $g(x) = -2x + 2$.

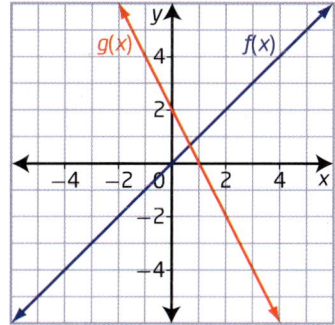

a) Explain how you can write the equation and produce the graph of the product of $f(x)$ and $g(x)$.

b) Explain how you can write the equation and produce the graph of the quotient of $f(x)$ and $g(x)$.

c) What must you consider when determining the domain of a product of functions or the domain of a quotient of functions?

Link the Ideas

Did You Know?

Multiplication can be shown using a centred dot. For example, $2 \times 5 = 2 \cdot 5$

To combine two functions, $f(x)$ and $g(x)$, multiply or divide as follows:

Product of Functions

$h(x) = f(x)g(x)$

$h(x) = (f \cdot g)(x)$

Quotient of Functions

$h(x) = \dfrac{f(x)}{g(x)}$

$h(x) = \left(\dfrac{f}{g}\right)(x)$

The domain of a product of functions is the domain common to the original functions. However, the domain of a quotient of functions must take into consideration that division by zero is undefined. The domain of a quotient, $h(x) = \dfrac{f(x)}{g(x)}$, is further restricted for values of x where $g(x) = 0$.

Consider $f(x) = \sqrt{x - 1}$ and $g(x) = x - 2$.

The domain of $f(x)$ is $\{x \mid x \geq 1, x \in R\}$, and the domain of $g(x)$ is $\{x \mid x \in R\}$. So, the domain of $(f \cdot g)(x)$ is $\{x \mid x \geq 1, x \in R\}$, while the domain of $\left(\dfrac{f}{g}\right)(x)$ is $\{x \mid x \geq 1, x \neq 2, x \in R\}$

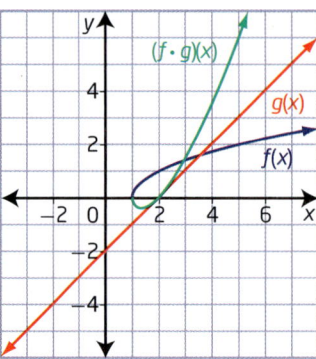 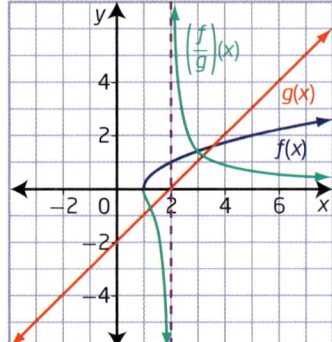

Example 1

Determine the Product of Functions

Given $f(x) = (x + 2)^2 - 5$ and $g(x) = 3x - 4$, determine $h(x) = (f \cdot g)(x)$. State the domain and range of $h(x)$.

Solution

To determine $h(x) = (f \cdot g)(x)$, multiply the two functions.
$h(x) = (f \cdot g)(x)$
$h(x) = f(x)g(x)$
$h(x) = ((x + 2)^2 - 5)(3x - 4)$
$h(x) = (x^2 + 4x - 1)(3x - 4)$
$h(x) = 3x^3 - 4x^2 + 12x^2 - 16x - 3x + 4$
$h(x) = 3x^3 + 8x^2 - 19x + 4$

How can you tell from the original functions that the product is a cubic function?

The function $f(x) = (x + 2)^2 - 5$ is quadratic with domain $\{x \mid x \in R\}$.

The function $g(x) = 3x - 4$ is linear with domain $\{x \mid x \in R\}$.

The domain of $h(x) = (f \cdot g)(x)$ consists of all values that are in both the domain of $f(x)$ and the domain of $g(x)$.

Therefore, the cubic function $h(x) = 3x^3 + 8x^2 - 19x + 4$ has domain $\{x \mid x \in R\}$ and range $\{y \mid y \in R\}$.

Your Turn

Given $f(x) = x^2$ and $g(x) = \sqrt{4x - 5}$, determine $h(x) = f(x)g(x)$. State the domain and range of $h(x)$.

Example 2

Determine the Quotient of Functions

Consider the functions $f(x) = x^2 + x - 6$ and $g(x) = 2x + 6$.

a) Determine the equation of the function $h(x) = \left(\dfrac{g}{f}\right)(x)$.

b) Sketch the graphs of $f(x)$, $g(x)$, and $h(x)$ on the same set of coordinate axes.

c) State the domain and range of $h(x)$.

Solution

a) To determine $h(x) = \left(\dfrac{g}{f}\right)(x)$, divide the two functions.

$h(x) = \left(\dfrac{g}{f}\right)(x)$

$h(x) = \dfrac{g(x)}{f(x)}$

$h(x) = \dfrac{2x + 6}{x^2 + x - 6}$

$h(x) = \dfrac{2(x + 3)}{(x + 3)(x - 2)}$ Factor.

$h(x) = \dfrac{2(x + 3)}{(x + 3)(x - 2)}$

$h(x) = \dfrac{2}{x - 2}, x \neq -3, 2$ Identify any non-permissible values.

b) Method 1: Use Paper and Pencil

How could you use the values in the columns for $f(x)$ and $g(x)$ to determine the values in the column for $h(x)$?

x	$f(x) = x^2 + x - 6$	$g(x) = 2x + 6$	$h(x) = \dfrac{2}{x-2}, x \neq -3, 2$
−3	0	0	does not exist
−2	−4	2	$-\dfrac{1}{2}$
−1	−6	4	$-\dfrac{2}{3}$
0	−6	6	−1
1	−4	8	−2
2	0	10	undefined
3	6	12	2
4	14	14	1

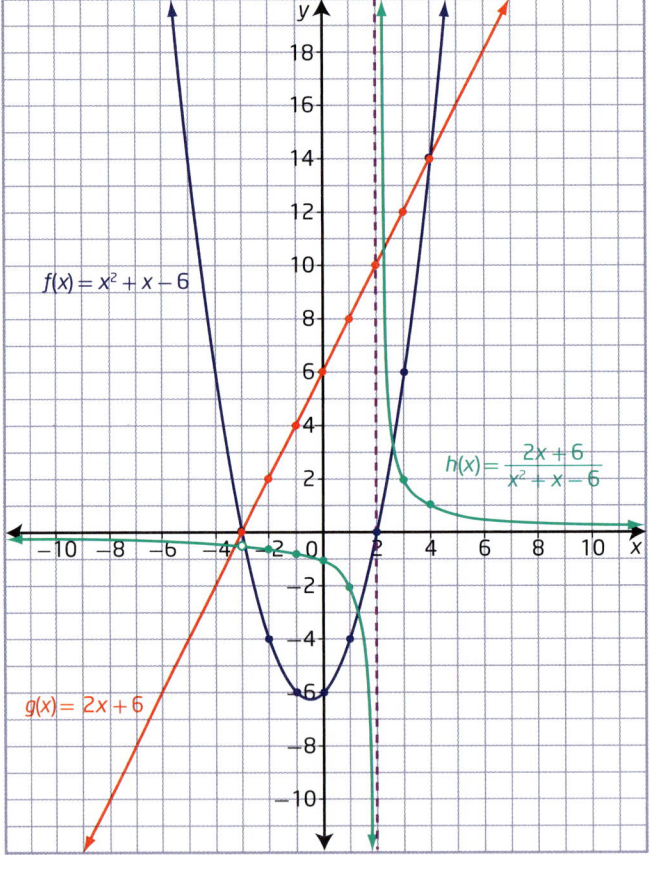

How are the y-coordinates of points on the graph of $h(x)$ related to those on the graphs of $f(x)$ and $g(x)$?

Method 2: Use a Graphing Calculator

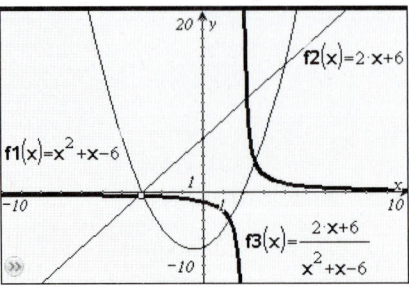

c) The function $f(x) = x^2 + x - 6$ is quadratic with domain $\{x \mid x \in \mathbb{R}\}$.
The function $g(x) = 2x + 6$ is linear with domain $\{x \mid x \in \mathbb{R}\}$.
The domain of $h(x) = \left(\dfrac{g}{f}\right)(x)$ consists of all values that are in both the domain of $f(x)$ and the domain of $g(x)$, excluding values of x where $f(x) = 0$.

Since the function $h(x)$ does not exist at $\left(-3, -\dfrac{2}{5}\right)$ and is undefined at $x = 2$, the domain is $\{x \mid x \neq -3, x \neq 2, x \in \mathbb{R}\}$. This is shown in the graph by the point of discontinuity at $\left(-3, -\dfrac{2}{5}\right)$ and the vertical asymptote that appears at $x = 2$.

How do you know there is a point of discontinuity and an asymptote?

Domain of
$f(x) = x^2 + x - 6$

Domain of
$g(x) = 2x + 6$

Domain of
$h(x) = \left(\dfrac{g}{f}\right)(x)$

The range of $h(x)$ is $\left\{y \mid y \neq 0, -\dfrac{2}{5}, y \in \mathbb{R}\right\}$.

Your Turn

Let $f(x) = x + 2$ and $g(x) = x^2 + 9x + 14$.

a) Determine the equation of the function $h(x) = \left(\dfrac{f}{g}\right)(x)$.
b) Sketch the graphs of $f(x)$, $g(x)$, and $h(x)$ on the same set of coordinate axes.
c) State the domain and range of $h(x)$.

Example 3

Application of Products and Quotients of Functions

A local hockey team owner would like to boost fan support at the games. He decides to reduce the ticket prices, T, in dollars, according to the function $T(g) = 10 - 0.1g$, where g represents the game number.

To further increase fan support, he decides to randomly give away noisemakers. The number, N, in hundreds, of noisemakers can be modelled by the function $N(g) = 2 - 0.05g$. The community fan base is small but the owner notices that since the incentives were put in place, attendance, A, in hundreds, can be modelled by $A(g) = 8 + 0.2g$.

a) Determine $r(g) = T(g)A(g)$ algebraically and explain what it represents.
b) Use the graph of $r(g) = T(g)A(g)$ to determine whether the owner increases or decreases revenue from the ticket sales with the changes made to draw in new fans.
c) Develop an algebraic and a graphical model for $p(g) = \dfrac{N(g)}{A(g)}$. Explain what it means. What is the chance of receiving a free noisemaker for a fan attending game 4?

Solution

a) Multiply $T(g)$ by $A(g)$ to produce $r(g) = T(g)A(g)$.
$r(g) = T(g)A(g)$
$r(g) = (10 - 0.1g)(8 + 0.2g)$
$r(g) = 80 + 2g - 0.8g - 0.02g^2$
$r(g) = 80 + 1.2g - 0.02g^2$

This new function multiplies the ticket price by the attendance. Therefore, $r(g) = T(g)A(g)$ represents the revenue from ticket sales, in hundreds of dollars.

b) Enter $r(g) = 80 + 1.2g - 0.02g^2$ on a graphing calculator. Then, use the trace feature or the table feature to view increasing and decreasing values.

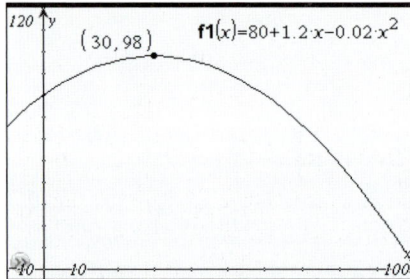

The graph of $r(g) = 80 + 1.2g - 0.02g^2$ is a parabola that continues to increase until game 30, at which time it begins to decrease.

The owner will increase revenue up to a maximum at 30 games, after which revenue will decrease.

c) To determine the quotient, divide $N(g)$ by $A(g)$.

$p(g) = \dfrac{N(g)}{A(g)}$

$p(g) = \dfrac{2 - 0.05g}{8 + 0.2g}$ What is the non-permissible value of g? How does it affect this situation?

Use graphing technology to graph the new function.

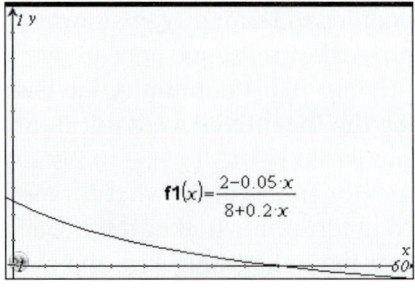

Which window settings would you use in this situation?

This combined function represents the number of free noisemakers that will be randomly handed out divided by the number of fans attending. This function represents the probability that a fan will receive a free noisemaker as a function of the game number.

To determine the probability of receiving a free noisemaker at game 4, evaluate $p(g) = \dfrac{2 - 0.05g}{8 + 0.2g}$ for $g = 4$.

$p(g) = \dfrac{2 - 0.05g}{8 + 0.2g}$

$p(4) = \dfrac{2 - 0.05(4)}{8 + 0.2(4)}$

$p(4) = \dfrac{1.8}{8.8}$

$p(4) = 0.2045...$

There is approximately a 0.20 or 20% chance of receiving a free noisemaker.

Did You Know?

The probability that an event will occur is the total number of favourable outcomes divided by the total number of possible outcomes.

Your Turn

A pendulum is released and allowed to swing back and forth. The periodic nature of the motion is described as $p(t) = 10 \cos 2t$, where p is the horizontal displacement, in centimetres, from the pendulum's resting position as a function of time, t, in seconds. The decay of the amplitude is given by $q(t) = 0.95^t$.

a) Write the combined function that is the product of the two components. Explain what the product represents.

b) Graph the combined function. Describe its characteristics and explain how the graph models the motion of the pendulum.

Did You Know?

In 1851, Jean Foucault demonstrated that the Earth rotates by using a long pendulum that swung in the same plane while the Earth rotated beneath it.

Key Ideas

- The combined function $h(x) = (f \cdot g)(x)$ represents the product of two functions, $f(x)$ and $g(x)$.
- The combined function $h(x) = \left(\dfrac{f}{g}\right)(x)$ represents the quotient of two functions, $f(x)$ and $g(x)$, where $g(x) \neq 0$.
- The domain of a product or quotient of functions is the domain common to both $f(x)$ and $g(x)$. The domain of the quotient $\left(\dfrac{f}{g}\right)(x)$ is further restricted by excluding values where $g(x) = 0$.
- The range of a combined function can be determined using its graph.

Check Your Understanding

Practise

1. Determine $h(x) = f(x)g(x)$ and $k(x) = \dfrac{f(x)}{g(x)}$ for each pair of functions.
   a) $f(x) = x + 7$ and $g(x) = x - 7$
   b) $f(x) = 2x - 1$ and $g(x) = 3x + 4$
   c) $f(x) = \sqrt{x + 5}$ and $g(x) = x + 2$
   d) $f(x) = \sqrt{x - 1}$ and $g(x) = \sqrt{6 - x}$

2. Use the graphs of $f(x)$ and $g(x)$ to evaluate the following.

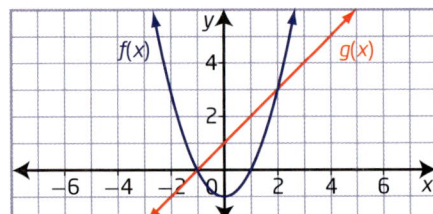

   a) $(f \cdot g)(-2)$
   b) $(f \cdot g)(1)$
   c) $\left(\dfrac{f}{g}\right)(0)$
   d) $\left(\dfrac{f}{g}\right)(1)$

3. Copy the graph. Add the sketch of the graph of each combined function to the same set of axes.

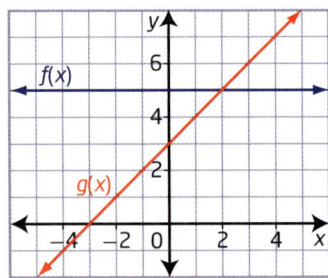

   a) $h(x) = f(x)g(x)$
   b) $h(x) = \dfrac{f(x)}{g(x)}$

4. For each pair of functions, $f(x)$ and $g(x)$,
   - determine $h(x) = (f \cdot g)(x)$
   - sketch the graphs of $f(x)$, $g(x)$, and $h(x)$ on the same set of coordinate axes
   - state the domain and range of the combined function $h(x)$

   a) $f(x) = x^2 + 5x + 6$ and $g(x) = x + 2$
   b) $f(x) = x - 3$ and $g(x) = x^2 - 9$
   c) $f(x) = \dfrac{1}{x + 1}$ and $g(x) = \dfrac{1}{x}$

5. Repeat #4 using $h(x) = \left(\dfrac{f}{g}\right)(x)$.

Apply

6. Given $f(x) = x + 2$, $g(x) = x - 3$, and $h(x) = x + 4$, determine each combined function.
   a) $y = f(x)g(x)h(x)$
   b) $y = \dfrac{f(x)g(x)}{h(x)}$
   c) $y = \dfrac{f(x) + g(x)}{h(x)}$
   d) $y = \dfrac{f(x)}{h(x)} \times \dfrac{g(x)}{h(x)}$

7. If $h(x) = f(x)g(x)$ and $f(x) = 2x + 5$, determine $g(x)$.
   a) $h(x) = 6x + 15$
   b) $h(x) = -2x^2 - 5x$
   c) $h(x) = 2x\sqrt{x} + 5\sqrt{x}$
   d) $h(x) = 10x^2 + 13x - 30$

8. If $h(x) = \dfrac{f(x)}{g(x)}$ and $f(x) = 3x - 1$, determine $g(x)$.
   a) $h(x) = \dfrac{3x - 1}{x + 7}$
   b) $h(x) = \dfrac{3x - 1}{\sqrt{x + 6}}$
   c) $h(x) = 1.5x - 0.5$
   d) $h(x) = \dfrac{1}{x + 9}$

9. Consider $f(x) = 2x + 5$ and $g(x) = \cos x$.
   a) Graph $f(x)$ and $g(x)$ on the same set of axes and state the domain and range of each function.
   b) Graph $y = f(x)g(x)$ and state the domain and range for the combined function.

10. Given $f(x)$ and $g(x)$, graph $y = \left(\dfrac{f}{g}\right)(x)$. State the domain and range of the combined function and any restrictions.
    a) $f(x) = \tan x$ and $g(x) = \cos x$
    b) $f(x) = \cos x$ and $g(x) = 0.8^x$

11. Let $f(x) = \sin x$ and $g(x) = \cos x$.
    a) Write an expression as a quotient of functions that is equivalent to $\tan x$.
    b) Write an expression as a product of functions that is equivalent to $1 - \cos^2 x$.
    c) Use graphing technology to verify your answers to parts a) and b).

12. A fish farm plans to expand. The fish population, P, in hundreds of thousands, as a function of time, t, in years, can be modelled by the function $P(t) = 6(1.03)^t$. The farm biologists use the function $F(t) = 8 + 0.04t$, where F is the amount of food, in units, that can sustain the fish population for 1 year. One unit can sustain one fish for 1 year.

Fish farm at Sonora Island, British Columbia

   a) Graph $P(t)$ and $F(t)$ on the same set of axes and describe the trends.
   b) The amount of food per fish is calculated using $y = \dfrac{F(t)}{P(t)}$. Graph $y = \dfrac{F(t)}{P(t)}$ on a different set of axes. Identify a suitable window setting for your graph. Are there values that should not be considered?
   c) At what time is the amount of food per fish a maximum?
   d) The fish farm will no longer be viable when there is not enough food to sustain the population. When will this occur? Explain how you determined your result.

13. Let $f(x) = \sqrt{36 - x^2}$ and $g(x) = \sin x$.
    a) Graph $f(x)$, $g(x)$, and $y = (f \cdot g)(x)$ on the same set of axes.
    b) State the domain and range of the combined function.
    c) Graph $y = \left(\dfrac{f}{g}\right)(x)$ and state its domain and range.
    d) Explain how the domain and range for $y = \left(\dfrac{g}{f}\right)(x)$ differs from the domain and range in part c).

14. The motion of a damped harmonic oscillator can be modelled by a function of the form $d(t) = (A \sin kt) \times 0.4^{ct}$, where d represents the distance as a function of time, t, and A, k, and c are constants.
    a) If $d(t) = f(t)g(t)$, identify the equations of the functions $f(t)$ and $g(t)$ and graph them on the same set of axes.
    b) Graph $d(t)$ on the same set of axes.

> **Did You Know?**
>
> A damped harmonic oscillator is an object whose motion is cyclic with decreasing amplitude over time. Examples include a child on a swing after the initial push and a freely swinging pendulum.

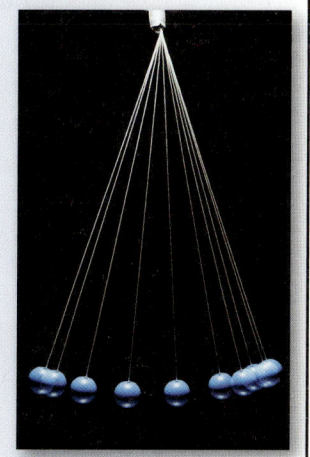

Extend

15. The graph of $y = f(x)g(x)$, where $g(x)$ is a sinusoidal function, will oscillate between the graphs of $f(x)$ and $-f(x)$. When the amplitude of the wave is reduced, this is referred to as damping.

  a) Given the functions $f(x) = \dfrac{2}{x^2 + 1}$ and $g(x) = \sin(6x - 1)$, show that the above scenario occurs.

  b) Does the above scenario occur for $f(x) = \cos x$ and $g(x) = \sin(6x - 1)$?

16. The price, p, in dollars, set by a manufacturer for x tonnes of steel is $p(x) = 12x\left(\dfrac{x + 2}{x + 1}\right)$. Using the quotient of functions, determine whether the price per tonne decreases as the number of tonnes increases, algebraically and graphically.

17. A rectangle is inscribed in a circle of radius r. If the rectangle has length $2x$, write the area of the rectangle as the product of two functions.

Create Connections

C1 Is the product of functions commutative? Choose functions to represent $f(x)$ and $g(x)$ to explain whether $f(x)g(x) = g(x)f(x)$.

C2 Compare and contrast the properties of the domains of products of functions and quotients of functions.

C3 The volume, V, in cubic centimetres, of a square-based box is given by $V(x) = 4x^3 + 4x^2 - 39x + 36$.

  a) Write a combined function to represent the area, $A(x)$, of the base, if the side length of the base is $2x - 3$.

  b) Graph $A(x)$ and state its domain and range in this context.

  c) Determine the combined function $h(x) = \dfrac{V(x)}{A(x)}$. What does this represent in this context?

  d) Graph $h(x)$ and state its domain and range in this context.

Project Corner — Musical Presentation

Write lyrics to a song that demonstrate your understanding of a topic in Unit 4.

- You might examine the lyrics of a popular song to understand the structure (chorus and verse), line length, and rhymes.
- Choose a title for your song. Then, think of questions and answers that your title might suggest. Use a list of related words and phrases to help you write the lyrics.
- Finally, write your own melody or choose an existing melody to fit your lyrics to.

10.3

Composite Functions

Focus on...
- determining values of a composite function
- writing the equation of a composite function and explaining any restrictions
- sketching the graph of a composite function

Approaching downtown Saskatoon, Saskatchewan

You have learned four ways of combining functions—adding, subtracting, multiplying, and dividing. Another type of combined function occurs any time a change in one quantity produces a change in another, which, in turn, produces a change in a third quantity. For example,

- the cost of travelling by car depends on the amount of gasoline consumed, and the amount of gasoline consumed depends on the number of kilometres driven
- the cost of an item on sale after taxes depends on the sale price, and the sale price of an item depends on the original price

Investigate Composition of Functions

1. Consider the functions $f(x) = 2x$ and $g(x) = x^2 + 2$. The output values of a function can become the input values for another function. Copy and complete the mapping diagram below.

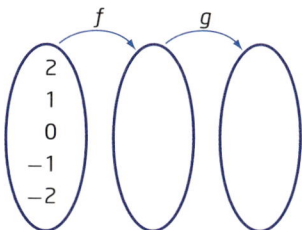

2. Which of the following functions can be used to obtain the results from step 1 directly?

   A $h(x) = 2x^3 + 4x$ **B** $h(x) = x^2 + 2x + 2$
   C $h(x) = 2x^2 + 4$ **D** $h(x) = 4x^2 + 2$

3. Show, algebraically, how to create the equation you chose in step 2 from the original equations for f and g.
4. Suppose the output values of g become the input values for f.
   a) Create a mapping diagram to show this process.
   b) Write an equation that would give your results in one step.

Reflect and Respond

5. When working with two functions where one function is used as the input for the other function, does it make a difference which of the two functions is the input function? Explain.
6. Given the functions $f(x) = 4x + 2$ and $g(x) = -3x$ and using f as the input for g, list the steps you would use to determine a single equation to represent this situation.
7. Identify a real-life situation, different from the ones in the introduction to this section, where one function is used as the input for another function.

Link the Ideas

composite function
- the composition of $f(x)$ and $g(x)$ is defined as $f(g(x))$ and is formed when the equation of $g(x)$ is substituted into the equation of $f(x)$
- $f(g(x))$ exists only for those x in the domain of g for which $g(x)$ is in the domain of f
- $f(g(x))$ is read as "f of g of x" or "f at g of x" or "f composed with g"
- $(f \circ g)(x)$ is another way to write $f(g(x))$
- composition of functions must not be confused with multiplication, that is, $(f \circ g)(x)$ does not mean $(fg)(x)$

To compute $\sqrt{2(7) - 3}$ on many graphing calculators, the entire expression can be entered in one step. However, on some scientific calculators the expression must be entered in sequential steps. In this example, enter the expression $2(7) - 3$ and press the $=$ button, which evaluates the calculation as 11. Then, press the $\sqrt{M}$ button, which results in the square root of 11 or 3.3166…. The output of the expression $2(7) - 3$ is used as the input for the square root operation.

Composite functions are functions that are formed from two functions, $f(x)$ and $g(x)$, in which the output or result of one of the functions is used as the input for the other function. For example, if $f(x) = \sqrt{x}$ and $g(x) = 2x - 3$, then the composition of $f(x)$ and $g(x)$ is $f(g(x)) = \sqrt{2x - 3}$, as shown in the mapping diagram.

When composing functions, the order is important. $f(g(x))$ is not necessarily the same as $g(f(x))$. $f(g(x))$ means first substitute into g, and then substitute the result into f. On the other hand, $g(f(x))$ means first substitute into f, and then substitute the result into g.

Example 1

Evaluate a Composite Function

If $f(x) = 4x$, $g(x) = x + 6$, and $h(x) = x^2$, determine each value.

a) $f(g(3))$
b) $g(h(-2))$
c) $h(h(2))$

Solution

a) Method 1: Determine the Value of the Inner Function and Then Substitute

Evaluate the function inside the brackets for the indicated value of x. Then, substitute this value into the outer function.

Determine $g(3)$.
$g(x) = x + 6$
$g(3) = 3 + 6$
$g(3) = 9$

Substitute $g(3) = 9$ into $f(x)$.
$f(g(3)) = f(9)$ Substitute 9 for $g(3)$.
$f(g(3)) = 4(9)$ Evaluate $f(x) = 4x$ when x is 9.
$f(g(3)) = 36$

Method 2: Determine the Composite Function and Then Substitute

Determine the composite function first and then substitute.
$f(g(x)) = f(x + 6)$ Substitute $x + 6$ for $g(x)$.
$f(g(x)) = 4(x + 6)$ Substitute $x + 6$ into $f(x) = 4x$.
$f(g(x)) = 4x + 24$

Substitute $x = 3$ into $f(g(x))$.
$f(g(3)) = 4(3) + 24$
$f(g(3)) = 36$

When you evaluate composite functions, the result will not change if you compose first and then evaluate or evaluate first and then compose.

b) Determine $h(-2)$ and then $g(h(-2))$.
$h(x) = x^2$
$h(-2) = (-2)^2$
$h(-2) = 4$

Substitute $h(-2) = 4$ into $g(x)$.
$g(h(-2)) = g(4)$ Substitute 4 for $h(-2)$.
$g(h(-2)) = 4 + 6$ Evaluate $g(x) = x + 6$ when x is 4.
$g(h(-2)) = 10$

c) Determine $h(h(x))$ and then evaluate.
$h(h(x)) = h(x^2)$ Substitute x^2 for $h(x)$.
$h(h(x)) = (x^2)^2$ Substitute x^2 into $h(x) = x^2$.
$h(h(x)) = x^4$

Substitute $x = 2$ into $h(h(x))$.
$h(h(2)) = (2)^4$
$h(h(2)) = 16$

Your Turn

If $f(x) = |x|$ and $g(x) = x + 1$, determine $f(g(-11))$ using two methods.

Which method do you prefer? Why?

Example 2

Compose Functions With Restrictions

Consider $f(x) = \sqrt{x - 1}$ and $g(x) = x^2$.
a) Determine $(f \circ g)(x)$ and $(g \circ f)(x)$.
b) State the domain of $f(x)$, $g(x)$, $(f \circ g)(x)$, and $(g \circ f)(x)$.

Solution

a) Determine $(f \circ g)(x) = f(g(x))$.
$(f \circ g)(x) = f(x^2)$ Substitute x^2 for $g(x)$.
$(f \circ g)(x) = \sqrt{(x^2) - 1}$ Substitute x^2 into $f(x) = \sqrt{x - 1}$.
$(f \circ g)(x) = \sqrt{x^2 - 1}$

Determine $(g \circ f)(x) = g(f(x))$.
$(g \circ f)(x) = g(\sqrt{x - 1})$ Substitute $\sqrt{x - 1}$ for $f(x)$.
$(g \circ f)(x) = (\sqrt{x - 1})^2$ Substitute $\sqrt{x - 1}$ into $g(x) = x^2$.
$(g \circ f)(x) = x - 1$

Order does matter when composing functions. In this case, $(f \circ g)(x) \neq (g \circ f)(x)$.

b) The domain of $f(x)$ is $\{x \mid x \geq 1, x \in R\}$.
The domain of $g(x)$ is $\{x \mid x \in R\}$.

The domain of $(f \circ g)(x)$ is the set of all values of x in the domain of g for which $g(x)$ is in the domain of f. So, any restrictions on the inner function as well as the composite function must be taken into consideration.
• There are no restrictions on the domain of $g(x)$.
• The restriction on the domain of $(f \circ g)(x)$ is $x \leq -1$ or $x \geq 1$.

Combining these restrictions gives the domain of $(f \circ g)(x)$ as $\{x \mid x \leq -1 \text{ or } x \geq 1, x \in R\}$.

The domain of $(g \circ f)(x)$ is the set of all values of x in the domain of f for which $f(x)$ is in the domain of g. So, any restrictions on the inner function and the composite function must be taken into consideration.
- The restriction on the domain of $f(x)$ is $x \geq 1$.
- There are no restrictions on the domain of $(g \circ f)(x)$.

Combining these restrictions gives the domain of $(g \circ f)(x)$ as $\{x \mid x \geq 1, x \in \mathbb{R}\}$.

Your Turn

Given the functions $f(x) = \sqrt{x - 1}$ and $g(x) = -x^2$, determine $(g \circ f)(x)$. Then, state the domain of $f(x)$, $g(x)$, and $(g \circ f)(x)$.

Example 3
Determine the Composition of Two Functions

Let $f(x) = x + 1$ and $g(x) = x^2$. Determine the equation of each composite function, graph it, and state its domain and range.
a) $y = f(g(x))$
b) $y = g(f(x))$
c) $y = f(f(x))$
d) $y = g(g(x))$

Solution

a) Determine $f(g(x))$.
$f(g(x)) = f(x^2)$
$f(g(x)) = (x^2) + 1$
$f(g(x)) = x^2 + 1$

The graph of the composite function $y = f(g(x))$ is a parabola that opens upward with vertex at $(0, 1)$, domain of $\{x \mid x \in \mathbb{R}\}$, and range of $\{y \mid y \geq 1, y \in \mathbb{R}\}$.

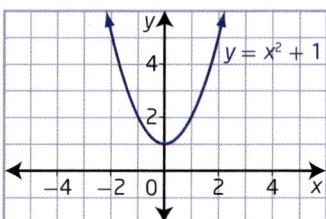

b) Determine $g(f(x))$.
$g(f(x)) = g(x + 1)$
$g(f(x)) = (x + 1)^2$
$g(f(x)) = x^2 + 2x + 1$

The graph of the composite function $y = g(f(x))$ is a parabola that opens upward with vertex at $(-1, 0)$, domain of $\{x \mid x \in \mathbb{R}\}$, and range of $\{y \mid y \geq 0, y \in \mathbb{R}\}$.

How do you know the coordinates of the vertex?

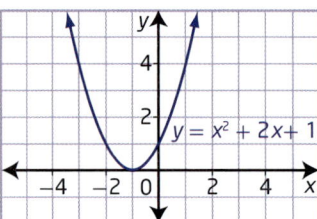

c) Determine $f(f(x))$.
$f(f(x)) = f(x + 1)$
$f(f(x)) = (x + 1) + 1$
$f(f(x)) = x + 2$

The graph of the composite function $y = f(f(x))$ represents a linear function. The domain and range of the function are both the set of real numbers.

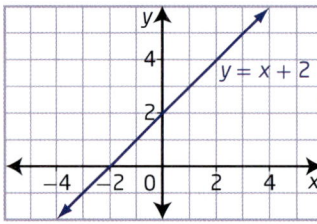

What are the slope and y-intercept of this line?

d) Determine $g(g(x))$.
$g(g(x)) = g(x^2)$
$g(g(x)) = (x^2)^2$
$g(g(x)) = x^4$

The graph of the composite function $y = g(g(x))$ is a quartic function that opens upward with domain of $\{x \mid x \in \mathbb{R}\}$ and range of $\{y \mid y \geq 0, y \in \mathbb{R}\}$.

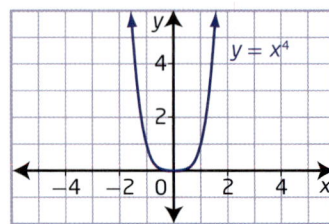

Your Turn

Given $f(x) = |x|$ and $g(x) = x + 1$, determine the equations of $y = f(g(x))$ and $y = f(f(x))$, graph each composite function, and state the domain and range.

Example 4

Determine the Original Functions From a Composition

If $h(x) = f(g(x))$, determine $f(x)$ and $g(x)$.
a) $h(x) = (x - 2)^2 + (x - 2) + 1$
b) $h(x) = \sqrt{x^3 + 1}$

Solution

In this case, the inner function is $g(x)$ and the outer function is $f(x)$.

a) Look for a function that may be common to more than one term in $h(x)$. The same expression, $x - 2$, occurs in two terms.
Let $g(x) = x - 2$. Then, work backward to determine $f(x)$.
$$h(x) = (x - 2)^2 + (x - 2) + 1$$
$$f(g(x)) = (g(x))^2 + (g(x)) + 1$$
$$f(x) = (x)^2 + (x) + 1$$

The two functions are $f(x) = x^2 + x + 1$ and $g(x) = x - 2$.

b) Let $g(x) = x^3 + 1$. Then, work backward to determine $f(x)$.
$$h(x) = \sqrt{x^3 + 1}$$
$$f(g(x)) = \sqrt{g(x)}$$
$$f(x) = \sqrt{x}$$

The two functions are $f(x) = \sqrt{x}$ and $g(x) = x^3 + 1$.

Is this the only solution? Explain.

Your Turn

If $h(x) = f(g(x))$, determine $f(x)$ and $g(x)$.
$$h(x) = \sqrt[3]{x} + \frac{3}{3 + \sqrt[3]{x}}$$

Example 5

Application of Composite Functions

A spherical weather balloon is being inflated. The balloon's radius, r, in feet, after t minutes is given by $r = \sqrt{t}$.
a) Express the volume of the balloon as a function of time, t.
b) After how many minutes will the volume be 4000 ft³?

Cambridge Bay Upper Air, Nunavut

Did You Know?

The Global Climate Observing System (GCOS) Upper Air Network is a worldwide network of almost 170 stations that collect data for climate monitoring and research. Five of these stations are located in Canada, including Alert Upper Air Station, Nunavut; Cambridge Bay Upper Air Station, Nunavut; and Fort Smith Upper Air Station, Northwest Territories.

Solution

a) The formula for the volume of a sphere is $V(r) = \frac{4}{3}\pi r^3$. Since r is a function of t, you can compose the two functions.

$$V(r) = \frac{4}{3}\pi r^3$$
$$V(r(t)) = \frac{4}{3}\pi(\sqrt{t})^3$$
$$V(r(t)) = \frac{4}{3}\pi\left(t^{\frac{1}{2}}\right)^3$$
$$V(r(t)) = \frac{4}{3}\pi t^{\frac{3}{2}}$$

b) To determine when the volume reaches 4000 ft³, substitute 4000 for V and solve for t.

$$V(r(t)) = \frac{4}{3}\pi t^{\frac{3}{2}}$$
$$4000 = \frac{4}{3}\pi t^{\frac{3}{2}}$$
$$\frac{3(4000)}{4\pi} = t^{\frac{3}{2}}$$
$$\left(\frac{3000}{\pi}\right)^{\frac{2}{3}} = \left(t^{\frac{3}{2}}\right)^{\frac{2}{3}}$$
$$t = \left(\frac{3000}{\pi}\right)^{\frac{2}{3}}$$
$$t = 96.972\ldots$$

After approximately 97 min, the volume will be 4000 ft³.

Your Turn

A spherical weather balloon is being blown up. The balloon's radius, r, in feet, after t minutes have elapsed is given by $r = \sqrt{t}$.
a) Express the surface area of the balloon as a function of time, t.
b) After how many minutes will the surface area be 180 ft²?

Key Ideas

- Two functions, $f(x)$ and $g(x)$, can be combined using composition to produce two new functions, $f(g(x))$ and $g(f(x))$.

- To evaluate a composite function, $f(g(x))$, at a specific value, substitute the value into the equation for $g(x)$ and then substitute the result into $f(x)$ and evaluate, or determine the composite function first and then evaluate for the value of x.

- To determine the equation of a composite function, substitute the second function into the first as read from left to right. To compose $f(g(x))$, substitute the equation of $g(x)$ into the equation of $f(x)$.

- The domain of $f(g(x))$ is the set of all values of x in the domain of g for which $g(x)$ is in the domain of f. Restrictions on the inner function as well as the composite function must be considered.

Check Your Understanding

Practise

1. Given $f(2) = 3$, $f(3) = 4$, $f(5) = 0$, $g(2) = 5$, $g(3) = 2$, and $g(4) = -1$, evaluate the following.
   a) $f(g(3))$
   b) $f(g(2))$
   c) $g(f(2))$
   d) $g(f(3))$

2. Use the graphs of $f(x)$ and $g(x)$ to evaluate the following.

   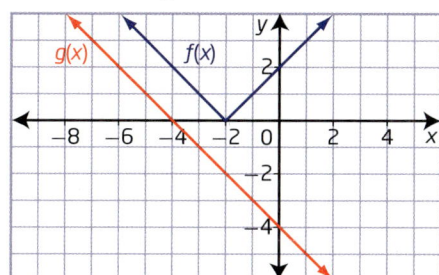

   a) $f(g(-4))$
   b) $f(g(0))$
   c) $g(f(-2))$
   d) $g(f(-3))$

3. If $f(x) = 2x + 8$ and $g(x) = 3x - 2$, determine each of the following.
   a) $f(g(1))$
   b) $f(g(-2))$
   c) $g(f(-4))$
   d) $g(f(1))$

4. If $f(x) = 3x + 4$ and $g(x) = x^2 - 1$, determine each of the following.
   a) $f(g(a))$
   b) $g(f(a))$
   c) $f(g(x))$
   d) $g(f(x))$
   e) $f(f(x))$
   f) $g(g(x))$

5. For each pair of functions, $f(x)$ and $g(x)$, determine $f(g(x))$ and $g(f(x))$.
   a) $f(x) = x^2 + x$ and $g(x) = x^2 + x$
   b) $f(x) = \sqrt{x^2 + 2}$ and $g(x) = x^2$
   c) $f(x) = |x|$ and $g(x) = x^2$

6. Given $f(x) = \sqrt{x}$ and $g(x) = x - 1$, sketch the graph of each composite function. Then, determine the domain and range of each composite function.
   a) $y = f(g(x))$
   b) $y = g(f(x))$

7. If $h(x) = (f \circ g)(x)$, determine $g(x)$.
   a) $h(x) = (2x - 5)^2$ and $f(x) = x^2$
   b) $h(x) = (5x + 1)^2 - (5x + 1)$ and $f(x) = x^2 - x$

Apply

8. Ron and Christine are determining the composite function $(f \circ g)(x)$, where $f(x) = x^2 + x - 6$ and $g(x) = x^2 + 2$. Who is correct? Explain your reasoning.

   Ron's Work
   $(f \circ g)(x) = f(g(x))$
   $= (x^2 + 2)^2 + x - 6$
   $= x^4 + 4x^2 + 4 + x - 6$
   $= x^4 + 4x^2 + x - 2$

   Christine's Work
   $(f \circ g)(x) = f(g(x))$
   $= (x^2 + 2)^2 + (x^2 + 2) - 6$
   $= x^4 + 4x^2 + 4 + x^2 + 2 - 6$
   $= x^4 + 5x^2$

9. Let $j(x) = x^2$ and $k(x) = x^3$. Does $k(j(x)) = j(k(x))$ for all values of x? Explain.

10. If $s(x) = x^2 + 1$ and $t(x) = x - 3$, does $s(t(x)) = t(s(x))$ for all values of x? Explain.

11. A manufacturer of lawn chairs models the weekly production of chairs since 2009 by the function $C(t) = 100 + 35t$, where t is the time, in years, since 2009 and C is the number of chairs. The size of the workforce at the manufacturer's site is modelled by $W(C) = 3\sqrt{C}$.
    a) Write the size of the workforce as a function of time.
    b) State the domain and range of the new function in this context.

12. Tobias is shopping at a local sports store that is having a 25%-off sale on apparel. Where he lives, the federal tax adds 5% to the selling price.

   a) Write the function, $s(p)$, that relates the regular price, p, to the sale price, s, both in dollars.

   b) Write the function, $t(s)$, that relates the sale price, s, to the total cost including taxes, t, both in dollars.

   c) Write a composite function that expresses the total cost in terms of the regular price. How much did Tobias pay for a jacket with a regular price of $89.99?

13. Jordan is examining her car expenses. Her car uses gasoline at a rate of 6 L/100 km, and the average cost of a litre of gasoline where she lives is $1.23.

   a) Write the function, $g(d)$, that relates the distance, d, in kilometres, driven to the quantity, g, in litres, of gasoline used.

   b) Write the function, $c(g)$, that relates the quantity, g, in litres, of gasoline used to the average cost, c, in dollars, of a litre of gasoline.

   c) Write the composite function that expresses the cost of gasoline in terms of the distance driven. How much would it cost Jordan to drive 200 km in her car?

   d) Write the composite function that expresses the distance driven in terms of the cost of gasoline. How far could Jordan drive her car on $40?

14. Use the functions $f(x) = 3x$, $g(x) = x - 7$, and $h(x) = x^2$ to determine each of the following.

   a) $(f \circ g \circ h)(x)$

   b) $g(f(h(x)))$

   c) $f(h(g(x)))$

   d) $(h \circ g \circ f)(x)$

15. A Ferris wheel rotates such that the angle, θ, of rotation is given by $\theta = \dfrac{\pi t}{15}$, where t is the time, in seconds. A rider's height, h, in metres, above the ground can be modelled by $h(\theta) = 20 \sin \theta + 22$.

   a) Write the equation of the rider's height in terms of time.

   b) Graph $h(\theta)$ and $h(t)$ on separate sets of axes. Compare the periods of the graphs.

> **Did You Know?**
>
> The first Ferris wheel was designed for the 1893 World's Columbian Exposition in Chicago, Illinois, with a height of 80.4 m. It was built to rival the 324-m Eiffel Tower built for the 1889 Paris Exposition.

16. Environmental biologists measure the pollutants in a lake. The concentration, C, in parts per million (ppm), of pollutant can be modelled as a function of the population, P, of a nearby city, as $C(P) = 1.15P + 53.12$. The city's population, in ten thousands, can be modelled by the function $P(t) = 12.5(2)^{\frac{t}{10}}$, where t is time, in years.

   a) Determine the equation of the concentration of pollutant as a function of time.

   b) How long will it take for the concentration to be over 100 ppm? Show two different methods to solve this.

17. If $h(x) = f(g(x))$, determine $f(x)$ and $g(x)$.
    a) $h(x) = 2x^2 - 1$
    b) $h(x) = \dfrac{2}{3 - x^2}$
    c) $h(x) = |x^2 - 4x + 5|$

18. Consider $f(x) = 1 - x$ and $g(x) = \dfrac{x}{1 - x}$, $x \neq 1$.
    a) Show that $g(f(x)) = \dfrac{1}{g(x)}$.
    b) Does $f(g(x)) = \dfrac{1}{f(x)}$?

19. According to Einstein's special theory of relativity, the mass, m, of a particle moving at velocity v is given by $m = \dfrac{m_0}{\sqrt{1 - \dfrac{v^2}{c^2}}}$, where m_0 is the particle's mass at rest and c is the velocity of light. Suppose that velocity, v, in miles per hour, is given as $v = t^3$.
    a) Express the mass as a function of time.
    b) Determine the particle's mass at time $t = \sqrt[3]{\dfrac{c}{2}}$ hours.

Extend

20. In general, two functions $f(x)$ and $g(x)$ are inverses of each other if and only if $f(g(x)) = x$ and $g(f(x)) = x$. Verify that the pairs of functions are inverses of each other.
    a) $f(x) = 5x + 10$ and $g(x) = \dfrac{1}{5}x - 2$
    b) $f(x) = \dfrac{x - 1}{2}$ and $g(x) = 2x + 1$
    c) $f(x) = \sqrt[3]{x + 1}$ and $g(x) = x^3 - 1$
    d) $f(x) = 5^x$ and $g(x) = \log_5 x$

21. Consider $f(x) = \log x$ and $g(x) = \sin x$.
    a) What is the domain of $f(x)$?
    b) Determine $f(g(x))$.
    c) Use a graphing calculator to graph $y = f(g(x))$. Work in radians.
    d) State the domain and range of $y = f(g(x))$.

22. If $f(x) = \dfrac{1}{1 + x}$ and $g(x) = \dfrac{1}{2 + x}$, determine $f(g(x))$.

23. Let $f_1(x) = x$, $f_2(x) = \dfrac{1}{x}$, $f_3(x) = 1 - x$, $f_4(x) = \dfrac{x}{x - 1}$, $f_5(x) = \dfrac{1}{1 - x}$, and $f_6(x) = \dfrac{x - 1}{x}$.
    a) Determine the following.
        i) $f_2(f_3(x))$
        ii) $(f_3 \circ f_5)(x)$
        iii) $f_1(f_2(x))$
        iv) $f_2(f_1(x))$
    b) $f_6^{-1}(x)$ is the same as which function listed in part a)?

Create Connections

C1 Does $f(g(x))$ mean the same as $(f \cdot g)(x)$? Explain using examples.

C2 Let $f = \{(1, 5), (2, 6), (3, 7)\}$ and $g = \{(5, 10), (6, 11), (7, 0)\}$. Explain how each equation is true.
   a) $g(f(1)) = 10$
   b) $g(f(3)) = 0$

C3 Suppose that $f(x) = 4 - 3x$ and $g(x) = \dfrac{4 - x}{3}$. Does $g(f(x)) = f(g(x))$ for all x? Explain.

C4 MINI LAB
Step 1 Consider $f(x) = 2x + 3$.
   a) Determine $f(x + h)$.
   b) Determine $\dfrac{f(x + h) - f(x)}{h}$.

Step 2 Repeat step 1 with $f(x) = -3x - 5$.

Step 3 Predict what $\dfrac{f(x + h) - f(x)}{h}$ will be for $f(x) = \dfrac{3}{4}x - 5$. How are each of the values you found related to the functions?

Chapter 10 Review

10.1 Sums and Differences of Functions, pages 474–487

1. Given $f(x) = 3x - 1$ and $g(x) = 2x + 7$, determine
   a) $(f + g)(4)$
   b) $(f + g)(-1)$
   c) $(f - g)(3)$
   d) $(g - f)(-5)$

2. Consider the functions $g(x) = x + 2$ and $h(x) = x^2 - 4$.
   a) Determine the equation and sketch the graph of each combined function. Then, state the domain and range.
      i) $f(x) = g(x) + h(x)$
      ii) $f(x) = h(x) - g(x)$
      iii) $f(x) = g(x) - h(x)$
   b) What is the value of $f(2)$ for each combined function in part a)?

3. For each graph of $f(x)$ and $g(x)$,
   - determine the equation and graph of $y = (f + g)(x)$ and state its domain and range
   - determine the equation and graph of $y = (f - g)(x)$ and state its domain and range

   a)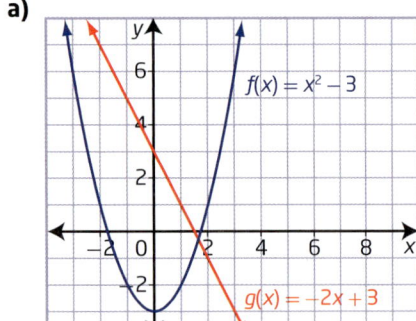

   b)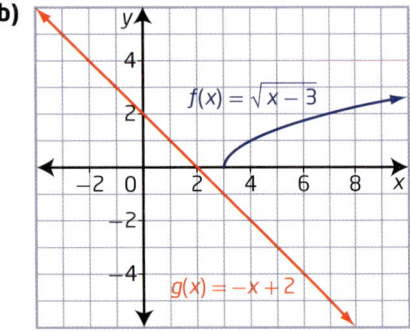

4. Let $f(x) = \dfrac{1}{x - 1}$ and $g(x) = \sqrt{x}$. Determine the equation of each combined function and state its domain and range.
   a) $(f + g)(x)$
   b) $(f - g)(x)$

5. A biologist has been recording the births and deaths of a rodent population on several sections of farmland for the past 5 years. Suppose the function $b(x) = -4x + 78$ models the number of births and the function $d(x) = -6x + 84$ models the number of deaths, where x is the time, in years. The net change in population, P, is equal to the number of births minus the number of deaths.
   a) Write an expression that reflects the net change in population at any given time.
   b) Assuming that the rates continue, predict how the population of rodents will behave over the next 5 years.
   c) At what point in time does the population start to increase? Explain.

10.2 Products and Quotients of Functions, pages 488–498

6. Consider the functions $g(x) = x + 2$ and $h(x) = x^2 - 4$. Determine the equation and sketch the graph of each combined function $f(x)$. Then, state the domain and range and identify any asymptotes.
   a) $f(x) = g(x)h(x)$
   b) $f(x) = \dfrac{h(x)}{g(x)}$
   c) $f(x) = \dfrac{g(x)}{h(x)}$

7. Determine the value of $f(-2)$ for each combined function in #6.

8. Given $g(x) = \dfrac{1}{x+4}$ and $h(x) = \dfrac{1}{x^2-16}$, determine the equation of each combined function and state its domain and range.
   a) $f(x) = g(x)h(x)$
   b) $f(x) = \dfrac{g(x)}{h(x)}$
   c) $f(x) = \dfrac{h(x)}{g(x)}$

9. For each graph of $f(x)$ and $g(x)$,
   - determine the equation and graph of $y = (f \cdot g)(x)$ and state its domain and range
   - determine the equation and graph of $y = \left(\dfrac{f}{g}\right)(x)$ and state its domain and range

   a)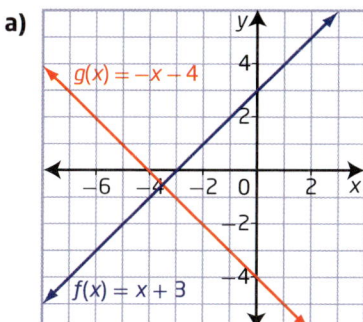

   b)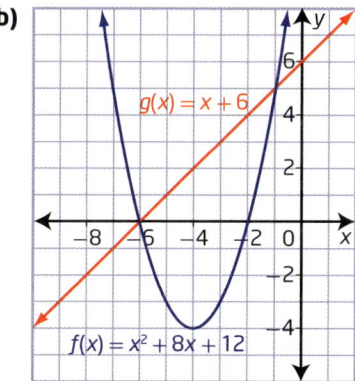

10.3 Composite Functions, pages 499–509

10. Given $f(x) = x^2$ and $g(x) = x + 1$, determine the following.
    a) $f(g(-2))$
    b) $g(f(-2))$

11. For $f(x) = 2x^2$ and $g(x) = \dfrac{4}{x}$, determine the following and state any restrictions.
    a) $f(g(x))$
    b) $g(f(x))$
    c) $g(f(-2))$

12. Consider $f(x) = -\dfrac{2}{x}$ and $g(x) = \sqrt{x}$.
    a) Determine $y = f(g(x))$.
    b) State the domain and range of $y = f(g(x))$.

13. If $f(x) = 2x - 5$ and $g(x) = x + 6$, determine $y = (f \circ g)(x)$. Then, sketch the graphs of the three functions.

14. The temperature of Earth's crust is a linear function of the depth below the surface. An equation expressing this relationship is $T = 0.01d + 20$, where T is the temperature, in degrees Celsius, and d is the depth, in metres. If you go down a vertical shaft below ground in an elevator at a rate of 5 m/s, express the temperature as a function of time, t, in seconds, of travel.

15. While shopping for a tablet computer, Jolene learns of a 1-day sale of 25% off. In addition, she has a coupon for $10 off.
    a) Let x represent the current price of the tablet. Express the price, d, of the tablet after the discount and the price, c, of the tablet after the coupon as functions of the current price.
    b) Determine $c(d(x))$ and explain what this function represents.
    c) Determine $d(c(x))$ and explain what this function represents.
    d) If the tablet costs $400, which method results in the lower sale price? Explain your thinking.

Chapter 10 Practice Test

Multiple Choice

For #1 to #5, choose the best answer.

1. Let $f(x) = (x + 3)^2$ and $g(x) = x + 4$. Which function represents the combined function $h(x) = f(x) + g(x)$?
   - **A** $h(x) = x^2 + 7x + 7$
   - **B** $h(x) = x^2 + 7x + 13$
   - **C** $h(x) = x^2 + x + 13$
   - **D** $h(x) = x^2 + 2x + 7$

2. If $f(x) = x + 8$ and $g(x) = 2x^2 - 128$, what is the domain of $y = \dfrac{g(x)}{f(x)}$?
   - **A** $\{x \mid x \in R\}$
   - **B** $\{x \mid x \in I\}$
   - **C** $\{x \mid x \neq 8, x \in R\}$
   - **D** $\{x \mid x \neq -8, x \in R\}$

3. The graphs of two functions are shown.

   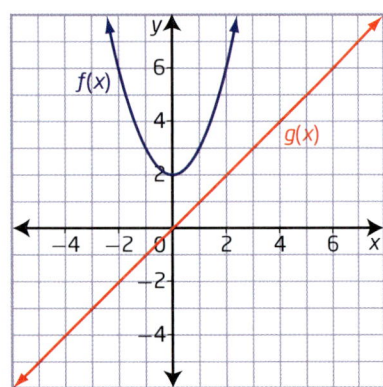

   Which is true for $x \in R$?
   - **A** $g(x) - f(x) < 0$
   - **B** $\dfrac{f(x)}{g(x)} > 1, x \neq 0$
   - **C** $f(x) < g(x)$
   - **D** $g(x) + f(x) < 0$

4. Given $f(x) = 5 - x$ and $g(x) = 2\sqrt{3x}$, what is the value of $f(g(3))$?
   - **A** $5 - 2\sqrt{6}$
   - **B** $2\sqrt{15 - 3x^2}$
   - **C** -1
   - **D** 1

5. Which function represents $y = f(g(x))$, if $f(x) = x + 5$ and $g(x) = x^2$?
   - **A** $y = x^2 + 5$
   - **B** $y = x^2 + 25$
   - **C** $y = x^2 + x + 5$
   - **D** $y = x^2 + 10x + 25$

Short Answer

6. Given $f(x) = \sin x$ and $g(x) = 2x^2$, determine each combined function.
   a) $h(x) = (f + g)(x)$
   b) $h(x) = (f - g)(x)$
   c) $h(x) = (f \cdot g)(x)$
   d) $h(x) = \left(\dfrac{f}{g}\right)(x)$

7. Copy and complete the table by determining the missing terms.

	$g(x)$	$f(x)$	$(f + g)(x)$	$(f \circ g)(x)$
a)	$x - 8$	$\sqrt{x}$		
b)	$x + 3$	$4x$		
c)		$\sqrt{x - 4}$		$\sqrt{x^2 - 4}$
d)	$\dfrac{1}{x}$			x

8. Determine the product of $g(x) = \dfrac{1}{1 + x}$ and $h(x) = \dfrac{1}{3 + 2x}$. Then, state the domain of the combined function.

9. Use the graphs of $f(x)$ and $g(x)$ to sketch the graph of each combined function.

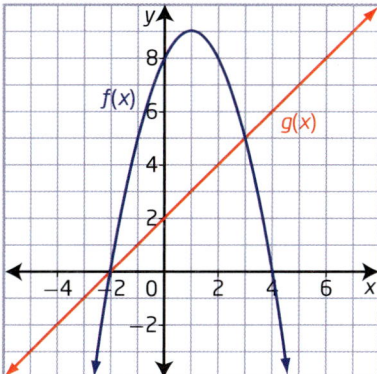

   a) $y = (f - g)(x)$
   b) $y = \left(\dfrac{f}{g}\right)(x)$

10. For each of the following pairs of functions, determine $g(f(x))$ and state its domain and range.

   a) $f(x) = 3 - x$ and $g(x) = |x + 3|$
   b) $f(x) = 4^x$ and $g(x) = x + 1$
   c) $f(x) = x^4$ and $g(x) = \sqrt{x}$

11. Becky has $200 deducted from every paycheque for her retirement. This can be done before or after federal income tax is assessed. Suppose her federal income tax rate is 28%.

   a) Let x represent Becky's earnings per pay period. Represent her income, r, after the retirement deduction and her income, t, after federal taxes as functions of her earnings per pay period.
   b) Determine $t(r(x))$. What does this represent?
   c) If Becky earns $2700 every pay period, calculate her net income using the composite function from part b).
   d) Calculate Becky's net income using $r(t(x))$.
   e) Explain the differences in net income.

12. A pendulum is released and allowed to swing back and forth according to the equation $x(t) = (10 \cos 2t)(0.95^t)$, where x is the horizontal displacement from the resting position, in centimetres, as a function of time, t, in seconds.

   a) Graph the function.
   b) The equation is the product of two functions. Identify each function and explain which is responsible for
      • the periodic motion
      • the exponential decay of the amplitude

Extended Response

13. Given $f(x) = 2x^2 + 11x - 21$ and $g(x) = 2x - 3$, determine the equation and sketch the graph of each combined function.

   a) $y = f(x) - g(x)$
   b) $y = f(x) + g(x)$
   c) $y = \dfrac{f(x)}{g(x)}$
   d) $y = f(g(x))$

14. A stone is dropped into a lake, creating a circular ripple that travels outward at a speed of 50 cm/s.

   a) Write an equation that represents the area of the circle as a function of time. State the type of combined function you wrote.
   b) Graph the function.
   c) What is the area of the circle after 5 s?
   d) Is it reasonable to calculate the area of the circle after 30 s? Explain.

CHAPTER 11

Permutations, Combinations, and the Binomial Theorem

Combinatorics, a branch of discrete mathematics, can be defined as the art of counting. Famous links to combinatorics include Pascal's triangle, the magic square, the Königsberg bridge problem, Kirkman's schoolgirl problem, and myriorama cards. Are you familiar with any of these?

Myriorama cards were invented in France around 1823 by Jean-Pierre Brès and further developed in England by John Clark. Early myrioramas were decorated with people, buildings, and scenery that could be laid out in any order to create a variety of landscapes. One 24-card set is sold as "The Endless Landscape."

How long do you think it would take to generate the 6.2×10^{23} possible different arrangements from a 24-card myriorama set?

Key Terms
fundamental counting principle
factorial
permutation
combination
binomial theorem

Career Link

Actuaries are business professionals who calculate the likelihood of events, especially those involving risk to a business or government. They use their mathematical skills to devise ways of reducing the chance of negative events occurring and lessening their impact should they occur. This information is used by insurance companies to set rates and by corporations to minimize the negative effects of risk-taking. The work is as challenging as correctly predicting the future!

Web Link

To find out more about the career of an actuary, go to www.mcgrawhill.ca/school/learningcentres and follow the links.

11.1

Permutations

Focus on...

- solving counting problems using the fundamental counting principle
- determining, using a variety of strategies, the number of permutations of *n* elements taken *r* at a time
- solving counting problems when two or more elements are identical
- solving an equation that involves $_nP_r$ notation

How safe is your password? It has been suggested that a four-character letters-only password can be hacked in under 10 s. However, an eight-character password with at least one number could take up to 7 years to crack. Why is there such a big difference?

In how many possible ways can you walk from A to B in a four by six "rectangular city" if you must walk on the grid lines and move only up or to the right?

The diagram shows one successful path from A to B. What strategies might help you solve this problem?

You will learn how to solve problems like these in this section.

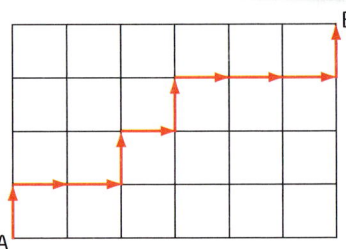

Investigate Possible Arrangements

You are packing clothing to go on a trip. You decide to take three different tops and two pairs of pants.

1. If all of the items go together, how many different outfits can you make? Show how to get the answer using different strategies. Discuss your strategies with a partner.

2. You also take two pairs of shoes. How many different outfits consisting of a top, a pair of pants, and a pair of shoes are possible?

3. **a)** Determine the number of different outfits you can make when you take four pairs of pants, two shirts, and two hats, if an outfit consists of a pair of pants, a shirt, and a hat.

   b) Check your answer using a tree diagram.

Reflect and Respond

4. Make a conjecture about how you can use multiplication only to arrive at the number of different outfits possible in steps 1 to 3.

5. A friend claims he can make 1000 different outfits using only tops, pants, and shoes. Show how your friend could be correct.

Link the Ideas

Counting methods are used to determine the number of members of a specific set as well as the outcomes of an event. You can display all of the possible choices using tables, lists, or tree diagrams and then count the number of outcomes. Another method of determining the number of possible outcomes is to use the **fundamental counting principle**.

fundamental counting principle
- if one task can be performed in a ways and a second task can be performed in b ways, then the two tasks can be performed in $a \times b$ ways
- for example, a restaurant meal consists of one of two salad options, one of three entrees, and one of four desserts, so there are (2)(3)(4) or 24 possible meals

Example 1

Arrangements With or Without Restrictions

a) A store manager has selected four possible applicants for two different positions at a department store. In how many ways can the manager fill the positions?

b) In how many ways can a teacher seat four girls and three boys in a row of seven seats if a boy must be seated at each end of the row?

Solution

a) Method 1: List Outcomes and Count the Total

Use a tree diagram and count the outcomes, or list all of the hiring choices in a table. Let A represent applicant 1, B represent applicant 2, C represent applicant 3, and D represent applicant 4.

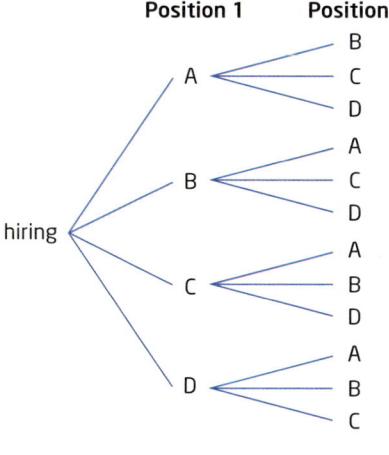

Position 1	Position 2
A	B
A	C
A	D
B	A
B	C
B	D
C	A
C	B
C	D
D	A
D	B
D	C

Total pathways = 12   12 possibilities

There are 12 possible ways to fill the 2 positions.

Method 2: Use the Fundamental Counting Principle

■   ■
(number of choices for position 1)   (number of choices for position 2)

If the manager chooses a person for position 1, then there are four choices. Once position 1 is filled, there are only three choices left for position 2.

      4   3
(number of choices for position 1)   (number of choices for position 2)

According to the fundamental counting principle, there are (4)(3) or 12 ways to fill the positions.

b) Use seven blanks to represent the seven seats in the row.

■   ■   ■   ■   ■   ■   ■
(Seat 1) (Seat 2) (Seat 3) (Seat 4) (Seat 5) (Seat 6) (Seat 7)

There is a restriction: a boy must be in each end seat. Fill seats 1 and 7 first.

> Why do you fill these two seats first?

If the teacher starts with seat 1, there are three boys to choose. Once the teacher fills seat 1, there are two choices for seat 7.

3   ■   ■   ■   ■   ■   2
(Seat 1) (Seat 2) (Seat 3) (Seat 4) (Seat 5) (Seat 6) (Seat 7)
Boy   Boy

Once the end seats are filled, there are five people (four girls and one boy) to arrange in the seats as shown.

> Why do you not need to distinguish between boys and girls for the second through sixth seats?

3   5   4   3   2   1   2
(Seat 1) (Seat 2) (Seat 3) (Seat 4) (Seat 5) (Seat 6) (Seat 7)

By the fundamental counting principle, the teacher can arrange the girls and boys in $(3)(5)(4)(3)(2)(1)(2) = 720$ ways.

Your Turn

Use any method to solve each problem.
a) How many three-digit numbers can you make using the digits 1, 2, 3, 4, and 5? Repetition of digits is not allowed.
b) How does the application of the fundamental counting principle in part a) change if repetition of the digits is allowed? Determine how many three-digit numbers can be formed that include repetitions.

---

factorial
- for any positive integer n, the product of all of the positive integers up to and including n
- $4! = (4)(3)(2)(1)$
- $0!$ is defined as 1

In Example 1b), the remaining five people (four girls and one boy) can be arranged in $(5)(4)(3)(2)(1)$ ways. This product can be abbreviated as $5!$ and is read as "five **factorial**."

Therefore, $5! = (5)(4)(3)(2)(1)$.
In general, $n! = (n)(n-1)(n-2)\ldots(3)(2)(1)$, where $n \in \mathbb{N}$.

The arrangement of objects or people in a line is called a linear **permutation**. In a permutation, the order of the objects is important. When the objects are distinguishable from one another, a new order of objects creates a new permutation.

Seven different objects can be arranged in 7! ways.

$7! = (7)(6)(5)(4)(3)(2)(1)$ Explain why 7! is equivalent to 7(6!) or to 7(6)(5)(4!).

If there are seven members on the student council, in how many ways can the council select three students to be the chair, the secretary, and the treasurer of the council?

Using the fundamental counting principle, there are (7)(6)(5) possible ways to fill the three positions. Using the factorial notation,

$$\frac{7!}{4!} = \frac{(7)(6)(5)(4)(3)(2)(1)}{(4)(3)(2)(1)}$$
$$= (7)(6)(5)$$
$$= 210$$

> The notation $_nP_r$ is used to represent the number of permutations, or arrangements in a definite order, of r items taken from a set of n distinct items. A formula for $_nP_r$ is $_nP_r = \frac{n!}{(n-r)!}$, $n \in \mathbb{N}$.

Using permutation notation, $_7P_3$ represents the number of arrangements of three objects taken from a set of seven objects.

$$_7P_3 = \frac{7!}{(7-3)!}$$
$$= \frac{7!}{4!}$$
$$= 210$$

So, there are 210 ways that the 3 positions can be filled from the 7-member council.

Example 2

Using Factorial Notation

a) Evaluate $_9P_4$ using factorial notation.
b) Show that $100! + 99! = 101(99!)$ without using technology.
c) Solve for n if $_nP_3 = 60$, where n is a natural number.

> **Solution**

a) $_9P_4 = \frac{9!}{(9-4)!}$
$= \frac{9!}{5!}$
$= \frac{(9)(8)(7)(6)5!}{5!}$ Why is 9! the same as (9)(8)(7)(6)5!?
$= (9)(8)(7)(6)$
$= 3024$

permutation
- an ordered arrangement or sequence of all or part of a set
- for example, the possible permutations of the letters A, B, and C are ABC, ACB, BAC, BCA, CAB, and CBA

Did You Know?

The notation n! was introduced in 1808 by Christian Kramp (1760–1826) as a convenience to the printer. Until then, n⌋ had been used.

Did You Know?

Most scientific and graphing calculators can evaluate factorials and calculate the number of permutations for n distinct objects taken r at a time. Learn to use these features on the calculator you use.

b) $100! + 99! = 100(99!) + 99!$
$= 99!(100 + 1)$
$= 99!(101)$
$= 101(99!)$

What math technique was used in going from step 1 to step 2?

c) $$_nP_3 = 60$$
$$\frac{n!}{(n-3)!} = 60$$
$$\frac{n(n-1)(n-2)(n-3)!}{(n-3)!} = 60$$
$$n(n-1)(n-2) = 60$$

Why must $n \geq 3$?

Method 1: Use Reasoning

$n(n-1)(n-2) = 60$
$n(n-1)(n-2) = 5(4)(3)$
$n = 5$

Why is 60 rewritten as the product of three consecutive natural numbers?
Will any other values work for n? Why or why not?

The solution to $_nP_3 = 60$ is $n = 5$.

Method 2: Use Algebra

$n(n-1)(n-2) = 60$
$n^3 - 3n^2 + 2n - 60 = 0$

Since n must be a natural number, only factors of 60 that are natural numbers must be considered: 1, 2, 3, 4, 5, 6, 10, 12, 15, 20, 30, 60.

Test these factors using the factor theorem.
$P(n) = n^3 - 3n^2 + 2n - 60$
$P(5) = 5^3 - 3(5)^2 + 2(5) - 60$
$= 0$

Therefore, $n = 5$ is a solution.

Test $n = 5$ in the original equation.
Left Side $= n(n-1)(n-2)$ Right Side $= 60$
$= 5(5-1)(5-2)$
$= 60$

Do you need to test any other values for n? Why or why not?

The solution to $_nP_3 = 60$ is $n = 5$.

Which of the three methods do you prefer?

Method 3: Use Graphing

Graph to solve the equation $n(n-1)(n-2) = 60$.
Graph $y = n(n-1)(n-2)$ and $y = 60$ and find the point of intersection.

Where does the solution for the original equation occur on your graph?

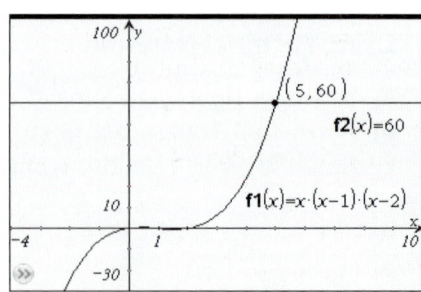

The solution to $_nP_3 = 60$ is $n = 5$.

Your Turn

a) Evaluate $_7P_2$ using factorial notation.
b) Show that $5! - 3! = 19(3!)$.
c) Solve for n if $_nP_2 = 56$.

Permutations With Repeating Objects

Consider the number of four-letter arrangements possible using the letters from the word *pool*.

p*oo*l   *o*p*o*l   *oo*pl   *oo*lp   p*o*l*o*   *o*pl*o*   *o*lp*o*   *o*l*o*p   pl*oo*   lp*oo*   l*o*p*o*   l*oo*p
p*oo*l   *o*p*o*l   *oo*pl   *oo*lp   p*o*l*o*   *o*pl*o*   *o*lp*o*   *o*l*o*p   pl*oo*   lp*oo*   l*o*p*o*   l*oo*p

If all of the letters were different, the number of possible four-letter arrangements would be 4! = 24.

There are two identical letters (*o*), which, if they were different, could be arranged in 2! = 2 ways.

The number of four-letter arrangements possible when two of the letters are the same is $\frac{4!}{2!} = \frac{24}{2}$ or 12.   **Why do you divide by 2!?**

> A set of *n* objects with *a* of one kind that are identical, *b* of a second kind that are identical, and *c* of a third kind that are identical, and so on, can be arranged in $\frac{n!}{a!b!c!...}$ different ways.

Example 3
Repeating Objects

a) How many different eight-letter arrangements can you make using the letters of *aardvark*?

b) How many paths can you follow from A to B in a four by six rectangular grid if you move only up or to the right?

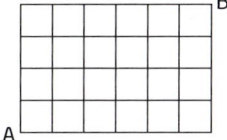

Solution

a) There are eight letters in *aardvark*. There are 8! ways to arrange eight letters. But of the eight letters, three are the letter *a* and two are the letter *r*. There are 3! ways to arrange the *a*'s and 2! ways to arrange the *r*'s. The number of different eight-letter arrangements is $\frac{8!}{3!2!} = 3360$.

b) Each time you travel 1 unit up, it is the same distance no matter where you are on the grid. Similarly, each horizontal movement is the same distance to the right. So, using U to represent 1 unit up and R to represent 1 unit to the right, one possible path is UUUURRRRRR. The problem is to find the number of arrangements of UUUURRRRRR.

The number of different paths is $\frac{10!}{4!6!} = 210$.   **Where did the numbers 10, 4, and 6 come from?**

For every path from A to B, how many units of distance must you travel?

How many vertical units must you travel?

How many horizontal units must you travel?

Your Turn

a) How many different 5-digit numbers can you make by arranging all of the digits of 17 171?

b) In how many different ways can you walk from A to B in a three by five rectangular grid if you must move only down or to the right?

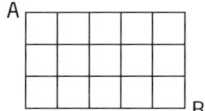

11.1 Permutations • MHR **521**

Example 4
Permutations with Constraints

Five people (A, B, C, D, and E) are seated on a bench. In how many ways can they be arranged if
a) E is seated in the middle? **b)** A and B must be seated together?
c) A and B cannot be together?

Solution

a) Since E must be in the middle, there is only 1 choice for that position. This leaves four people to be arranged in (4)(3)(2)(1) ways.

$$\underset{\text{(Seat 1)}}{4} \quad \underset{\text{(Seat 2)}}{3} \quad \underset{\substack{\text{(Seat 3)}\\ \text{Middle}}}{1} \quad \underset{\text{(Seat 4)}}{2} \quad \underset{\text{(Seat 5)}}{1}$$

What is the restriction?

There are $(4)(3)(1)(2)(1) = 24$ ways to arrange the five people with E seated in the middle.

b) There are 2! ways to arrange A and B together, AB or BA.
Consider A and B together as 1 object. This means that there are 4 objects (C, D, E, and AB) to arrange in $4! = 24$ ways.
Then, there are $2!4! = 48$ ways to arrange five people if A and B must be seated together.

c) Method 1: Use Positions When A and B Are Not Together
There are five positions on the bench. A and B are not together when they are in the following positions:

1st and 3rd   1st and 4th   1st and 5th
2nd and 4th   2nd and 5th   3rd and 5th   (6 ways)

For any one of these six arrangements, A and B can be interchanged.   (2 ways)

The remaining 3 people can always be arranged 3! or 6 ways. (6 ways)
There are $(6)(2)(6) = 72$ ways where A and B are not seated together.

Why is it necessary to multiply to get the final answer?

Method 2: Use Positions When A and B Are Together
The total number of arrangements for five people in a row with no restrictions is $5! = 120$. Arrangements with A and B together is 48 from part b).
Therefore, the number of arrangements with A and B not together is
Total number of arrangements − Number of arrangements together
$= 5! − 2!4!$
$= 120 − 48$
$= 72$

Your Turn

How many ways can one French poster, two mathematics posters, and three science posters be arranged in a row on a wall if
a) the two mathematics posters must be together on an end?
b) the three science posters must be together?
c) the three science posters cannot all be together?

Arrangements Requiring Cases

To solve some problems, you must count the different arrangements in cases. For example, you might need to determine the number of arrangements of four girls and three boys in a row of seven seats if the ends of the rows must be either both female or both male.

Case 1: Girls on Ends of Rows   Arrangements

     Girl   (2 Girls and 3 Boys)   Girl
     4   5!   3   (4)(5!)(3) = 1440

Case 2: Boys on Ends of Rows

     Boy   (4 Girls and 1 Boy)   Boy
     3   5!   2   (3)(5!)(2) = 720

                Total number of arrangements: 1440 + 720 = 2160

Example 5

Using Cases to Determine Permutations

How many different 3-digit even numbers greater than 300 can you make using the digits 1, 2, 3, 4, 5, and 6? No digits are repeated.

Solution

When determining the number of permutations for a situation in which there are restrictions, you must first address the choices with the restrictions.

Case 1: Numbers That Are Even and Start With 3 or 5

Numbers start with 3 or 5, so there are two choices for the first digit.

Numbers are even, so there are three choices for the third digit.

Number of choices for first digit	Number of choices for second digit	Number of choices for third digit
2	4	3

Number of possibilities = 2(4)(3)
                          = 24

Why does the solution to this example require the identification of cases?

How do you know there are four possible choices for the middle digit?

Case 2: Numbers That Are Even and Start With 4 or 6

Numbers start with 4 or 6, so there are two choices for the first digit.

Numbers are even, so two choices remain for the third digit.

Number of choices for first digit	Number of choices for second digit	Number of choices for third digit
2	4	2

Number of possibilities = 2(4)(2)
                          = 16

Why are there only two choices for the third digit?

The final answer is the sum of the possibilities from the two cases.

There are 24 + 16, or 40, 3-digit even numbers greater than 300.

Your Turn

How many 4-digit odd numbers can you make using the digits 1 to 7 if the numbers must be less than 6000? No digits are repeated.

Key Ideas

- The fundamental counting principle can be used to determine the number of different arrangements. If one task can be performed in a ways, a second task in b ways, and a third task in c ways, then all three tasks can be arranged in $a \times b \times c$ ways.

- Factorial notation is an abbreviation for products of successive positive integers.
  $$5! = (5)(4)(3)(2)(1)$$
  $$(n+1)! = (n+1)(n)(n-1)(n-2)\cdots(3)(2)(1)$$

- A permutation is an arrangement of objects in a definite order. The number of permutations of n different objects taken r at a time is given by $_nP_r = \dfrac{n!}{(n-r)!}$.

- A set of n objects containing a identical objects of one kind, b identical objects of another kind, and so on, can be arranged in $\dfrac{n!}{a!b!\ldots}$ ways.

- Some problems have more than one case. One way to solve such problems is to establish cases that together cover all of the possibilities. Calculate the number of arrangements for each case and then add the values for all cases to obtain the total number of arrangements.

Check Your Understanding

Practise

1. Use an organized list or a tree diagram to identify the possible arrangements for
   a) the ways that three friends, Jo, Amy, and Mike, can arrange themselves in a row.
   b) the ways that you can arrange the digits 2, 5, 8, and 9 to form two-digit numbers.
   c) the ways that a customer can choose a starter, a main course, and a dessert from the following menu.

   LUNCH SPECIAL MENU
   Starter: soup or salad
   Main: chili or hamburger or chicken or fish
   Dessert: ice cream or fruit salad

2. Evaluate each expression.
   a) $_8P_2$
   b) $_7P_5$
   c) $_6P_6$
   d) $_4P_1$

3. Show that $4! + 3! \neq (4+3)!$.

4. What is the value of each expression?
   a) $9!$
   b) $\dfrac{9!}{5!4!}$
   c) $(5!)(3!)$
   d) $6(4!)$
   e) $\dfrac{102!}{100!2!}$
   f) $7! - 5!$

5. In how many different ways can you arrange all of the letters of each word?
   a) hoodie
   b) decided
   c) aqilluqqaaq
   d) deeded
   e) puppy
   f) baguette

   Did You Know?
   The Inuit have many words to describe snow. The word *aqilluqqaaq* means fresh and soggy snow in one dialect of Inuktitut.

6. Four students are running in an election for class representative on the student council. In how many different ways can the four names be listed on the ballot?

7. Solve for the variable.
   a) $_nP_2 = 30$
   b) $_nP_3 = 990$
   c) $_6P_r = 30$
   d) $2(_nP_2) = 60$

8. Determine the number of pathways from A to B.
   a) Move only down or to the right.
   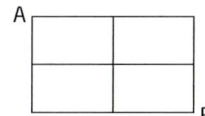
   b) Move only up or to the right.
   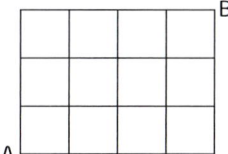
   c) Move only up or to the left.
   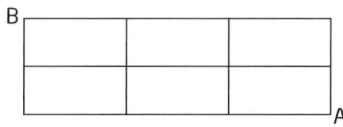

9. Describe the cases you could use to solve each problem. Do not solve.
   a) How many 3-digit even numbers greater than 200 can you make using the digits 1, 2, 3, 4, and 5?
   b) How many four-letter arrangements beginning with either B or E and ending with a vowel can you make using the letters A, B, C, E, U, and G?

10. In how many ways can four girls and two boys be arranged in a row if
    a) the boys are on each end of the row?
    b) the boys must be together?
    c) the boys must be together in the middle of the row?

11. In how many ways can seven books be arranged on a shelf if
    a) the books are all different?
    b) two of the books are identical?
    c) the books are different and the mathematics book must be on an end?
    d) the books are different and four particular books must be together?

Apply

12. How many six-letter arrangements can you make using all of the letters A, B, C, D, E, and F, without repetition? Of these, how many begin and end with a consonant?

13. A national organization plans to issue its members a 4-character ID code. The first character can be any letter other than O. The last 3 characters are to be 3 different digits. If the organization has 25 300 members, will they be able to assign each member a different ID code? Explain.

14. Iblauk lives in Baker Lake, Nunavut. She makes oven mitts to sell. She has wool duffel in red, dark blue, green, light blue, and yellow for the body of each mitt. She has material for the wrist edge in dark green, pink, royal blue, and red. How many different colour combinations of mitts can Iblauk make?

15. You have forgotten the number sequence to your lock. You know that the correct code is made up of three numbers (right-left-right). The numbers can be from 0 to 39 and repetitions are allowed. If you can test one number sequence every 15 s, how long will it take to test all possible number sequences? Express your answer in hours.

16. Jodi is parking seven different types of vehicles side by side facing the display window at the dealership where she works.

   a) In how many ways can she park the vehicles?

   b) In how many ways can she park them so that the pickup truck is next to the hybrid car?

   c) In how many ways can she park them so that the convertible is not next to the subcompact?

17. a) How many arrangements using all of the letters of the word *parallel* are possible?

   b) How many of these arrangements have all of the *l*'s together?

18. The number of different permutations using all of the letters in a particular set is given by $\frac{5!}{2!2!}$.

   a) Create a set of letters for which this is true.

   b) What English word could have this number of arrangements of its letters?

19. How many integers from 3000 to 8999, inclusive, contain no 7s?

20. Postal codes in Canada consist of three letters and three digits. Letters and digits alternate, as in the code R7B 5K1.

   a) How many different postal codes are possible with this format?

   b) Do you think Canada will run out of postal codes? Why or why not?

> **Did You Know?**
>
> The Canadian postal code system was established in 1971. The first letters of the codes are assigned to provinces and territories from east to west:
>
> A = Newfoundland and Labrador
>
> ...
>
> Y = Yukon Territory
>
> Some provinces have more than one letter, such as H and J for Québec. Some letters, such as I, are not currently used.

21. *Cent mille milliards de poèmes* (*One Hundred Million Million Poems*) was written in 1961 by Raymond Queneau, a French poet, novelist, and publisher. The book is 10 pages long, with 1 sonnet per page. A sonnet is a poem with 14 lines. Each line of every sonnet can be replaced by a line at the same position on a different page. Regardless of which lines are used, the poem makes sense.

   a) How many arrangements of the lines are possible for one sonnet?

   b) Is the title of the book of poems reasonable? Explain.

22. Use your understanding of factorial notation and the symbol $_nP_r$ to solve each equation.

   a) $_3P_r = 3!$

   b) $_7P_r = 7!$

   c) $_nP_3 = 4(_{n-1}P_2)$

   d) $n(_5P_3) = {_7P_5}$

23. Use $_nP_n$ to show that $0! = 1$.

24. Explain why $_3P_5$ gives an error message when evaluated on a calculator.

25. How many odd numbers of at most three digits can be formed using the digits 0, 1, 2, 3, 4, and 5 without repetitions?

26. How many even numbers of at least four digits can be formed using the digits 0, 1, 2, 3, and 5 without repetitions?

27. How many integers between 1 and 1000 do not contain repeated digits?

28. A box with a lid has inside dimensions of 3 cm by 2 cm by 1 cm. You have four identical blue cubes and two identical yellow cubes, each 1 cm by 1 cm by 1 cm.

How many different six-cube arrangements of blue and yellow cubes are possible? You must be able to close the lid after any arrangement. The diagram below shows one possible arrangement. Show two different ways to solve the problem.

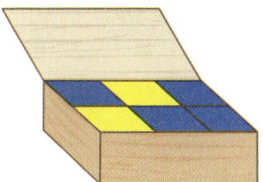

Extend

29. You have two colours of paint. In how many different ways can you paint the faces of a cube if each face is painted? Painted cubes are considered to be the same if you can rotate one cube so that it matches the other one exactly.

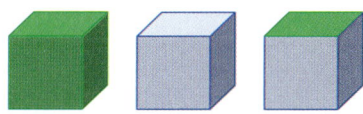

30. Nine students take a walk on four consecutive days. They always walk in rows of three across. Show how to arrange the students so that each student walks only once in a row with any two other students during the four-day time frame. In other words, no three-across triplets are repeated.

> **Did You Know?**
>
> Thomas Kirkman (1806–1895) was born in England and studied mathematics in Dublin. He first presented a version of the problem in #30 in 1847 in the *Cambridge and Dublin Mathematical Journal*. Subsequently, it was published as the "fifteen schoolgirl problem" in the 1850 *Ladies' and Gentlemen's Diary*. There are many solutions and generalizations of the problem.

31. If 100! is evaluated, how many zeros are at the end of the number? Explain how you know.

32. There are five people: A, B, C, D, and E. The following pairs know each other: A and C, B and C, A and D, D and E, and C and D.

a) Arrange the five people in a row so that nobody is next to a stranger.

b) How many different arrangements are possible such that nobody is next to a stranger?

c) The five people are joined by a sixth person, F, who knows only A. In how many ways can the six people stand in a row if nobody can be next to a stranger? Explain your answer.

Create Connections

C1 a) Explain what the notation $_aP_b$ represents. Use examples to support your explanation.

b) Which statement best describes the relationship between b and a? Explain.

$b > a \quad b = a \quad b < a \quad b \leq a \quad b \geq a$

C2 Explain why a set of n objects, a of which are of one type and b of which are of a second type, can be arranged in $\dfrac{n!}{a!b!}$ different ways and not in $n!$ ways.

C3 Simplify.

a) $\dfrac{3!(n+2)!}{4!(n-1)!}$

b) $\dfrac{7!(r-1)!}{6!(r+1)!} + \dfrac{5!r!}{3!(r+1)!}$

C4 Create a mathematics career file for this chapter. Identify one occupation or career requiring the use of, or connections to, the mathematics in this section. Write at least two problems that might be used by someone working in the chosen occupation or career. Briefly describe how your problems relate to the occupation or career.

C5 a) What is the value of 9!?

b) Determine the value of log (9!).

c) Determine the value of log (10!).

d) How are the answers to parts b) and c) related? Explain why.

11.2

Combinations

Focus on...

- explaining the differences between a permutation and a combination
- determining the number of ways to select *r* elements from *n* different elements
- solving problems using the number of combinations of *n* different elements taken *r* at a time
- solving an equation that involves $_nC_r$ notation

Sorting by hand mail that has been rejected by the machine sort due to unrecognizable hand-written or missing postal codes

Sometimes you must consider the order in which the elements of a set are arranged. In other situations, the order is not important. For example, when addressing an envelope, it is important to write the six-character postal code in the correct order. In contrast, addressing an envelope, affixing a stamp, and inserting the contents can be completed in any order.

In this section, you will learn about counting outcomes when order does not matter.

Did You Know?

In the six-character postal code used in Canada, the first three characters define a geographical region and the last three characters specify a local delivery unit.

Investigate Making Selections When Order Is Not Important

Problem solving, reasoning, and decision-making are highly prized skills in today's workforce. Here is your opportunity to demonstrate those skills.

1. From a group of four students, three are to be elected to an executive committee with a specific position. The positions are as follows:
   1st position   President
   2nd position   Vice President
   3rd position   Treasurer

   a) Does the order in which the students are elected matter? Why?

   b) In how many ways can the positions be filled from this group?

2. Now suppose that the three students are to be selected to serve on a committee.
   a) Is the order in which the three students are selected still important? Why or why not?
   b) How many committees from the group of four students are now possible?
   c) How does your answer in part b) relate to the answer in step 1b)?
3. You are part of a group of 6 students.
   a) How many handshakes are possible if each student shakes every other student's hand once?
   b) What strategies could you use to solve this problem? Discuss with a partner and try to solve the problem in more than one way.

Reflect and Respond

4. What formula could you create to solve a handshake problem involving n students?
5. In step 1, you worked with permutations, but in step 2, you worked with **combinations**. Identify all of the possible three-letter permutations and three-letter combinations of the letters A, B, and C. What are the similarities between permutations and combinations? What are the differences?

combination
- a selection of objects without regard to order
- all of the three-letter combinations of P, Q, R, and S are PQR, PQS, PRS, and QRS (arrangements such as PQR and RPQ are the same combination)

Link the Ideas

A combination is a selection of a group of objects, taken from a larger group, for which the kinds of objects selected is important, but not the order in which they are selected.

There are several ways to find the number of possible combinations. One is to use reasoning. Use the fundamental counting principle and divide by the number of ways that the objects can be arranged among themselves. For example, calculate the number of combinations of three digits made from the digits 1, 2, 3, 4, and 5 without repetitions:

Number of choices for the first digit	Number of choices for the second digit	Number of choices for the third digit
5	4	3

There are $5 \times 4 \times 3$ or 60 ways to arrange 3 items from 5. However, 3 digits can be arranged in 3! ways among themselves, and in a combination these are considered to be the same selection.

So,
$$\text{number of combinations} = \frac{\text{number of permutations}}{3!}$$

What does 3! represent?

$$= \frac{60}{3!}$$
$$= \frac{60}{6}$$
$$= 10$$

The notation $_nC_r$, or $\binom{n}{r}$, represents the number of combinations of n items taken r at a time, where $n \geq r$ and $r \geq 0$.

$$_nC_r = \frac{_nP_r}{r!}$$

$$= \frac{\frac{n!}{(n-r)!}}{r!}$$

$$= \frac{n!}{(n-r)!r!}$$

Why must $n \geq r \geq 0$?

Did You Know?

The number of combinations of n items taken r at a time is equivalent to the number of combinations of n items taken $n - r$ at a time.

$_nC_r = \,_nC_{n-r}$

The number of ways of choosing three digits from five digits is

$$_5C_3 = \frac{5!}{(5-3)!3!}$$

$$= \frac{5!}{2!3!}$$

$$= \frac{(5)(4)}{(2)(1)}$$

$$= 10$$

Explain how to simplify the expression in step 2 to get the expression shown in step 3.

How many ways are there to choose two digits from five digits? What do you notice?

There are ten ways to select three items from a set of five.

Example 1

Combinations and the Fundamental Counting Principle

There are 12 females and 18 males in a grade 12 class. The principal wishes to meet with a group of 5 students to discuss graduation.
a) How many selections are possible?
b) How many selections are possible if the group consists of two females and three males?
c) One of the female students is named Brooklyn. How many five-member selections consisting of Brooklyn, one other female, and three males are possible?

Solution

Ask yourself if the order of selection is important in these questions.

a) The question involves choosing 5 students out of 30. In this group, the order of selection is unimportant. So, this is a combinations problem. Use the combinations formula.

Substitute $n = 30$ and $r = 5$ into $_nC_r = \dfrac{n!}{(n-r)!r!}$:

$$_{30}C_5 = \dfrac{30!}{(30-5)!5!}$$

$$= \dfrac{30!}{25!5!}$$

$$= \dfrac{(30)(29)(28)(27)(26)(25!)}{25!(5)(4)(3)(2)(1)}$$

$$= 142\ 506$$

There are 142 506 possible ways of selecting the group of 5 students.

b) There are $_{12}C_2$ ways of selecting two female students.

There are $_{18}C_3$ ways of selecting three male students.

Using the fundamental counting principle, the number of ways of selecting two females and three males is

$$_{12}C_2 \times {_{18}C_3} = \dfrac{12!}{(12-2)!2!} \times \dfrac{18!}{(18-3)!3!}$$

$$= \dfrac{(12)(11)(10!)}{(10!)(2)(1)} \times \dfrac{(18)(17)(16)(15!)}{(15!)(3)(2)(1)}$$

$$= 66 \times 816$$

$$= 53\ 856$$

Why are the elements $_{12}C_2$ and $_{18}C_3$ multiplied together?

There are 53 856 ways to select a group consisting of 2 females and 3 males.

c) There is one way to select Brooklyn.

There are 11 females remaining, so there are $_{11}C_1$ or 11 choices for the second female.

Why is $_{11}C_1 = 11$?

There are $_{18}C_3$ ways to select the three males.

There are $1 \times 11 \times {_{18}C_3}$ or 8976 ways to select this five-member group.

Your Turn

In how many ways can the debating club coach select a team from six grade 11 students and seven grade 12 students if the team has
a) four members?
b) four members, only one of whom is in grade 11?

Example 2
Combinations With Cases

Rianna is writing a geography exam. The instructions say that she must answer a specified number of questions from each section. How many different selections of questions are possible if
a) she must answer two of the four questions in part A and three of the five questions in part B?
b) she must answer two of the four questions in part A and at least four of the five questions in part B?

Solution

Why should you use combinations rather than permutations to solve this problem?

a) The number of ways of selecting two questions in part A is $_4C_2$.

The number of ways of selecting three questions in part B is $_5C_3$.

According to the fundamental counting principle, the number of possible question selections is $_4C_2 \times {_5C_3} = 6 \times 10$ or 60.

There are 60 different ways in which Rianna can choose 2 of the 4 questions in part A and 3 of the 5 questions in part B.

b) "At least four" means that Rianna can answer either four questions or five questions in part B. Solve the problem using two cases.

Case 1: Answering Four Questions in Part B

Part A Choices	Part B Choices
$_4C_2$	$_5C_4$

The number of ways of choosing these questions is $_4C_2 \times {_5C_4} = 6 \times 5$ or 30.

Why do you multiply the possibilities for parts A and B?

Case 2: Answering Five Questions in Part B

Part A Choices	Part B Choices
$_4C_2$	$_5C_5$

The number of ways of choosing these questions is $_4C_2 \times {_5C_5} = 6 \times 1$ or 6.

Each case represents an exclusive or separate event. The final answer is the sum of both cases.

The number of possible ways of choosing either 4 questions or 5 questions in part B is 30 + 6 or 36.

Why do you add the two cases?

Your Turn

A bag contains seven black balls and six red balls. In how many ways can you draw groups of five balls if at least three must be red?

Example 3

Simplifying Expressions and Solving Equations With Combinations

a) Express as factorials and simplify $\dfrac{{}_nC_5}{{}_{n-1}C_3}$.

b) Solve for n if $2({}_nC_2) = {}_{n+1}C_3$.

Solution

a)
$$\dfrac{{}_nC_5}{{}_{n-1}C_3} = \dfrac{\dfrac{n!}{(n-5)!5!}}{\dfrac{(n-1)!}{(n-4)!3!}}$$

What is the formula for ${}_nC_r$?

Why is $(n-4)!$ in the lower denominator?

$$= \left(\dfrac{n!}{(n-5)!5!}\right)\left(\dfrac{(n-4)!3!}{(n-1)!}\right)$$

$$= \dfrac{n(n-1)!}{(n-5)!(5)(4)(3!)} \times \dfrac{(n-4)(n-5)!3!}{(n-1)!}$$

Explain why $n!$ can be written as $n(n-1)!$.

$$= \dfrac{n(n-4)}{20}$$

b)
$$2({}_nC_2) = {}_{n+1}C_3$$

$$2\left(\dfrac{n!}{(n-2)!2!}\right) = \dfrac{(n+1)!}{(n-2)!3!}$$

$$n! = \dfrac{(n+1)!}{3!}$$

$$3! = \dfrac{(n+1)!}{n!}$$

$$6 = \dfrac{(n+1)(n!)}{n!}$$

$$6 = n+1$$

$$5 = n$$

Your Turn

a) Express in factorial notation and simplify $({}_{n-1}C_3)\left(\dfrac{1}{{}_{n-2}C_3}\right)$.

b) Solve for n if $720({}_nC_5) = {}_{n+1}P_5$.

Key Ideas

- A selection of objects in which order is not important is a combination.
- When determining the number of possibilities in a situation, if order matters, it is a permutation. If order does not matter, it is a combination.
- The number of combinations of n objects taken r at a time can be represented by ${}_nC_r$, where $n \geq r$ and $r \geq 0$. A formula for ${}_nC_r$ is ${}_nC_r = \dfrac{{}_nP_r}{r!}$ or ${}_nC_r = \dfrac{n!}{(n-r)!r!}$.

Check Your Understanding

The questions in this section involve permutations or combinations. Always determine whether order is important.

Practise

1. Decide whether each of the following is a combination or a permutation problem. Briefly describe why. You do not need to solve the problem.

   a) In a traditional Aboriginal welcome circle, each member shakes hands with each other member twice. If there are eight people in a welcome circle, how many handshakes occur?

   b) How many numbers less than 300 can you make using the digits 1, 2, 3, 4, and 5?

   c) A car dealer has 15 mid-sized cars. In how many ways can a rental agency purchase 10 of the cars?

   d) A hockey team has 18 players. In how many ways can the driver select six of the players to ride in the team van?

2. Describe the differences between $_5P_3$ and $_5C_3$, and then evaluate each one.

3. Evaluate.

   a) $_6P_4$
   b) $_7C_3$
   c) $_5C_2$
   d) $_{10}C_7$

4. From ten employees, in how many ways can you

   a) select a group of four?
   b) assign four different jobs?

5. a) List all of the combinations of A, B, C, and D taken two at a time.

   b) List all of the permutations of A, B, C, and D taken two at a time.

   c) How is the number of combinations related to the number of permutations?

6. Solve for n.

   a) $_nC_1 = 10$
   b) $_nC_2 = 21$
   c) $_nC_{n-2} = 6$
   d) $_{n+1}C_{n-1} = 15$

7. Identify the cases you could use to solve each problem. Do not solve.

   a) How many numbers less than 1000 can you make using any number of the digits 1, 2, 3, 4, and 5?

   b) In how many ways can a team be selected from six grade 11 students and five grade 12 students if the five-person team has four members from either grade and a spare from grade 11?

8. Show that $_{11}C_3 = {_{11}C_8}$.

9. a) Evaluate $_5C_5$ to determine the number of ways you can select five objects from a group of five.

   b) Evaluate $_5C_0$ to determine the number of ways you can select no objects from a group of five. Explain why the answer makes sense.

Apply

10. From a penny, a nickel, a dime, and a quarter, how many different sums of money can be formed consisting of

    a) three coins?
    b) at most two coins?

11. From six females, in how many ways can you select

    a) a group of four females?
    b) a group of at least four females?

12. Verify the identity $_nC_{r-1} + {_nC_r} = {_{n+1}C_r}$.

13. At the local drive-in, you can order a burger with tomato, lettuce, pickle, hot peppers, onion, or cheese. How many different burgers with any three different choices for the extras can you order? Does this question involve permutations or combinations? Explain.

534 MHR • Chapter 11

14. A pizzeria offers ten different toppings.

   a) How many different four-topping pizzas are possible?

   b) Is this a permutation or a combination question? Explain.

15. Consider five points, no three of which are collinear.

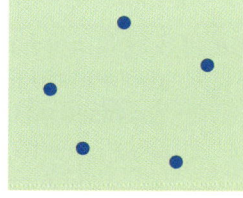

   a) How many line segments can you draw connecting any two of the points? Complete this question using two different methods.

   b) How many triangles, with vertices selected from the given points, can you draw?

   c) Write an expression using factorials for the number of triangles if there are ten non-collinear points. How does this answer compare to the number of line segments for the same ten points?

16. Verify that $_nC_r = {_nC_{n-r}}$.

17. A jury pool consists of 12 women and 8 men.

   a) How many 12-person juries can be selected?

   b) How many juries containing seven women and five men can be selected?

   c) How many juries containing at least ten women can be selected?

18. Consider a standard deck of 52 well-shuffled cards.

   a) In how many ways can you select five cards?

   b) In how many ways can you select five cards if three of them are hearts?

   c) In how many ways can you select five cards if only one of them is black?

> **Did You Know?**
>
> A standard deck of playing cards contains 52 cards in four suits: clubs, diamonds, hearts, and spades. Each suit contains 13 cards labelled 2 to 10, jack, queen, king, and ace. Playing cards are thought to have originated in India. They were introduced into Europe around 1275.

19. a) In how many ways can you select a set of four science books and three geography books from six different science books and seven different geography books?

   b) In how many ways can you place the four science books and the three geography books in a row on a shelf if the science books must remain together?

20. A Manitoba gallery wishes to display 20 paintings to showcase the work of artist George Fagnan.

   a) How many selections are possible if the artist allows the gallery to choose from 40 of his works? Leave your answer in factorial form.

   b) The gallery curator wants to set 4 of the paintings from the 20 selected in a row near the entrance. In how many ways can this be accomplished?

> **Did You Know?**
>
> George Fagnan grew up in Swan River, Manitoba. He is a proud member of the Sapotaweyak Cree Nation, and he currently lives in Brandon, Manitoba. He began his art career around the age of 5. He enjoys traditional native art and other creative activities.

Blue Garden, 2009

21. The cards from a standard deck of playing cards are dealt to 4 people, 13 cards at a time. This means that the first person receives the first 13 cards, the second person gets the next 13 cards, and so on.
    a) How many such sets of four 13-card hands can be dealt? Leave your answer as a product of factorials.
    b) Without using a calculator, show that the answer in part a) simplifies to $\frac{52!}{(13!)^4}$.
    c) Evaluate the answer to part a).

Extend

22. How many parallelograms are formed if four parallel lines intersect another set of six parallel lines? The lines in the first set are not parallel to the lines in the second set.

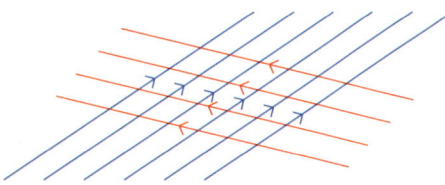

23. In a bowl of ice cream, the order of the scoops does not matter.
    a) Suppose you can make 630 two-scoop bowls of ice cream, each containing two different flavours, at the shop where you work. How many flavours of ice cream are available in this shop?
    b) How many two-scoop bowls could you make if you can duplicate flavours?

24. Consider the following conjecture. If p is a prime number, $_aC_b$ and $_{pa}C_{pb}$ have the same remainder when you divide by p.
    a) Show that the statement is true for $_5C_2$ when $p = 3$.
    b) Is this statement true for $_5C_2$ when $p = 7$? What is the remainder?
    c) How many remainders are possible when dividing by 7? What are they?
    d) Describe what you could do to prove the initial conjecture.

Create Connections

C1 Does a combination lock involve combinations in a mathematical sense? Explain.

C2 a) Explain what the notation $_aC_b$ represents. Use examples to support your explanation.
   b) Write an inequality that describes the relationship between all possible values for a and b.
   c) What can you say for sure about the value of b?

C3 A teacher asks her students to calculate the number of ways in which a hospital administrator could assign four patients to six private rooms. Beth says that the answer is $_6C_4$. Bryan disagrees. He claims the answer is $_6P_4$. Who is correct? Why?

C4 MINI LAB Eight points lie on the circumference of a circle. Explore how many different inscribed quadrilaterals can be drawn using the points as vertices.

Step 1 Suppose the eight points are on the unit circle at P(0°), P(45°), P(90°), P(135°), P(180°), P(225°), P(270°), and P(315°). Draw a diagram. Show a quadrilateral that is an isosceles trapezoid with four of the given points as vertices.

Step 2 Create a table in which you identify the number of possible quadrilaterals that are squares, rectangles, parallelograms, and isosceles trapezoids that can be created using four of the eight points from Step 1.

Step 3 Make a conclusion. How many different inscribed quadrilaterals can be drawn using four of the eight points that lie on the circumference of a circle as vertices?

11.3

The Binomial Theorem

Focus on...

- relating the coefficients in the expansion of $(x + y)^n$, $n \in N$, to Pascal's triangle and to combinations
- expanding $(x + y)^n$, $n \in N$, in a variety of ways, including the binomial theorem
- determining a specific term in the expansion of $(x + y)^n$

In 1653, Blaise Pascal, a French mathematician, described a triangular array of numbers corresponding to the number of ways to choose r elements from a set of n objects. Some interesting number patterns occur in Pascal's triangle. Have you encountered Pascal's triangle before? Have you explored its many patterns? Did you realize it can give you the number of combinations in certain situations?

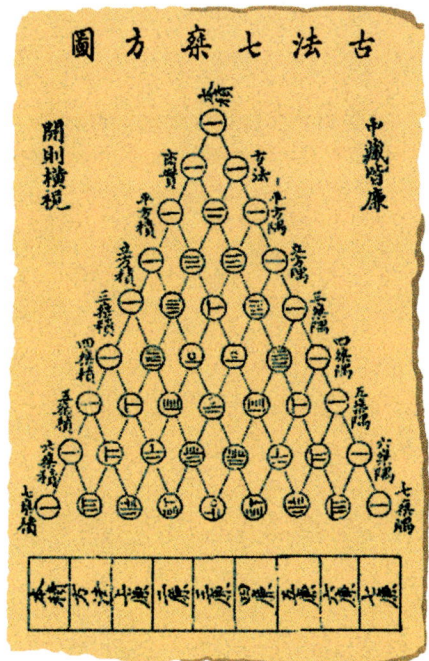

Yang Hui's triangle, 13th century China

Investigate Patterns in Pascal's Triangle

1. Examine Pascal's triangle and identify at least three patterns. Compare and discuss your patterns with a partner.

    ```
            1
          1   1
        1   2   1
      1   3   3   1
    1   4   6   4   1
    ```

2. Write the next row for the Pascal's triangle shown.

3. Some of the patterns in Pascal's triangle are spatial and relate to whole sections in the chart. Create a large Pascal's triangle with at least 20 rows. Mark or use counters to cover all of the multiples of 7 in your 20-row triangle. Then, cover all of the multiples of 5 and multiples of 3. What do you conclude? What happens for multiples of even numbers?

4. Other patterns may appear unexpectedly. Determine the sum of the numbers in each horizontal row. What pattern did you find?

5. Each number in Pascal's triangle can be written as a combination using the notation $_nC_r$, where n is the number of objects in the set and r is the number selected. For example, you can express the third row as

    $_2C_0 \quad _2C_1 \quad _2C_2$

    Express the fifth row using combination notation. Check whether your combinations have the same values as the numbers in the fifth row of Pascal's triangle.

Materials

- counters
- copy of Pascal's triangle

Did You Know?

Pascal was not the first person to discover the triangle of numbers that bears his name. It was known in India, Persia, and China centuries before. The Chinese called it "Yang Hui's triangle" in honour of Yang Hui, who lived from 1238 to 1298.

6. Expand the following binomials by multiplying.
   $(x + y)^2$
   $(x + y)^3$
   $(x + y)^4$

Reflect and Respond

7. Explain how to get the numbers in the next row from the numbers in the previous row of Pascal's triangle. Use examples.

8. How are the values you obtained in steps 4 and 5 related? Explain using values from specific rows.

9. How do the coefficients of the simplified terms in your binomial expansions in step 6 relate to Pascal's triangle?

Link the Ideas

If you expand a power of a binomial expression, you get a series of terms.

$(x + y)^4 = 1x^4 + 4x^3y + 6x^2y^2 + 4xy^3 + 1y^4$

How could you get this expansion by multiplying?

What patterns do you observe?

There are many patterns in the binomial expansion of $(x + y)^4$.

The coefficients in a binomial expansion can be determined from Pascal's triangle. In the expansion of $(x + y)^n$, where $n \in \mathbb{N}$, the coefficients of the terms are identical to the numbers in the $(n + 1)$th row of Pascal's triangle.

Binomial	Pascal's Triangle in Binomial Expansion	Row
$(x + y)^0$	1	1
$(x + y)^1$	$1x$ + $1y$	2
$(x + y)^2$	$1x^2$ + $2xy$ + $1y^2$	3
$(x + y)^3$	$1x^3$ + $3x^2y$ + $3xy^2$ + $1y^3$	4
$(x + y)^4$	$1x^4$ + $4x^3y$ + $6x^2y^2$ + $4xy^3$ + $1y^4$	5

The coefficients in a binomial expansion can also be determined using combinations.

Pascal's Triangle	Combinations
1	$_0C_0$
1 1	$_1C_0$ $_1C_1$
1 2 1	$_2C_0$ $_2C_1$ $_2C_2$
1 3 3 1	$_3C_0$ $_3C_1$ $_3C_2$ $_3C_3$
1 4 6 4 1	$_4C_0$ $_4C_1$ $_4C_2$ $_4C_3$ $_4C_4$
1 5 10 10 5 1	$_5C_0$ $_5C_1$ $_5C_2$ $_5C_3$ $_5C_4$ $_5C_5$

$$_5C_2 = \frac{5!}{3!2!}$$
$$= \frac{(5)(4)}{2}$$
$$= 10$$

Note that $_5C_2$ represents the number of combinations of five items taken two at a time. In the expansion of $(x + y)^5$, it represents the coefficient of the term containing x^3y^2 and shows the number of selections possible for three x's and two y's.

Example 1

Expand Binomials

a) Expand $(p + q)^6$.
b) Identify patterns in the expansion of $(p + q)^6$.

Solution

a) Method 1: Use Patterns and Pascal's Triangle

The coefficients for the terms of the expansion of $(p + q)^6$ occur in the $(6 + 1)$th or seventh row of Pascal's triangle.

Why is the row number different by one from the exponent on the binomial?

The seventh row of Pascal's triangle is
1 6 15 20 15 6 1

How are the numbers obtained?

$$(p + q)^6 = 1(p)^6(q)^0 + 6(p)^5(q)^1 + 15(p)^4(q)^2 + 20(p)^3(q)^3 + 15(p)^2(q)^4 \\ + 6(p)^1(q)^5 + 1(p)^0(q)^6$$
$$= p^6 + 6p^5q + 15p^4q^2 + 20p^3q^3 + 15p^2q^4 + 6pq^5 + q^6$$

Method 2: Use Combinations to Determine Coefficients in the Expansion

$$(p + q)^6 = {}_6C_0(p)^6(q)^0 + {}_6C_1(p)^5(q)^1 + {}_6C_2(p)^4(q)^2 + {}_6C_3(p)^3(q)^3 + {}_6C_4(p)^2(q)^4 \\ + {}_6C_5(p)^1(q)^5 + {}_6C_6(p)^0(q)^6$$
$$= p^6 + 6p^5q + 15p^4q^2 + 20p^3q^3 + 15p^2q^4 + 6pq^5 + q^6$$

Show that ${}_6C_4 = 15$. How does symmetry help you find the terms?

b) Some patterns are as follows:
- There are $6 + 1$, or 7, terms in the expansion of $(p + q)^6$.
- The powers of p decrease from 6 to 0 in successive terms of the expansion.
- The powers of q increase from 0 to 6.
- Each term is of degree 6 (the sum of the exponents for p and q is 6 for each term)
- The coefficients are symmetrical, 1 6 15 20 15 6 1, and begin and end with 1.

Your Turn

a) What are the coefficients in the expansion of $(c + d)^5$?
b) Do you prefer to use Pascal's triangle or combinations to determine the coefficients in a binomial expansion? Why?
c) How many terms are in the expansion of $(c + d)^5$?
d) What is the simplified expression for the second term in the expansion of $(c + d)^5$ if the terms are written with descending powers of c?

binomial theorem

- used to expand $(x + y)^n$, $n \in \mathbb{N}$
- each term has the form ${}_nC_k(x)^{n-k}(y)^k$, where $k + 1$ is the term number

You can use the **binomial theorem** to expand any power of a binomial expression.

$$(x + y)^n = {}_nC_0(x)^n(y)^0 + {}_nC_1(x)^{n-1}(y)^1 + {}_nC_2(x)^{n-2}(y)^2 + \cdots + {}_nC_{n-1}(x)^1(y)^{n-1} + {}_nC_n(x)^0(y)^n$$

In this chapter, all binomial expansions will be written in descending order of the exponent of the first term in the binomial.

The following are some important observations about the expansion of $(x + y)^n$, where x and y represent the terms of the binomial and $n \in \mathbb{N}$:

- the expansion contains $n + 1$ terms
- the number of objects, k, selected in the combination ${}_nC_k$ can be taken to match the number of factors of the second variable selected; that is, it is the same as the exponent on the second variable
- the general term, t_{k+1}, has the form

$${}_nC_k(x)^{n-k}(y)^k$$

the same

- the sum of the exponents in any term of the expansion is n

Did You Know?

In French, the binomial theorem is referred to as Newton's binomial formula (binôme de Newton). While Newton was not the first to describe binomial expansion, he did develop a formula that can be used to expand the general case $(x + y)^n$, $n \in \mathbb{R}$.

Example 2

Use the Binomial Theorem

a) Use the binomial theorem to expand $(2a - 3b)^4$.
b) What is the third term in the expansion of $(4b - 5)^6$?
c) In the expansion of $\left(a^2 - \dfrac{1}{a}\right)^5$, which term, in simplified form, contains a? Determine the value of the term.

Solution

a) Use the binomial theorem to expand $(x + y)^n$, $n \in \mathbb{N}$.

$$(x + y)^n = {}_nC_0(x)^n(y)^0 + {}_nC_1(x)^{n-1}(y)^1 + {}_nC_2(x)^{n-2}(y)^2 + \cdots + {}_nC_{n-1}(x)^1(y)^{n-1} + {}_nC_n(x)^0(y)^n$$

In this case, $(2a - 3b)^4 = [2a + (-3b)]^4$, so, in the binomial expansion, substitute $x = 2a$, $y = -3b$, and $n = 4$.

$(2a - 3b)^4$
$= {}_4C_0(2a)^4(-3b)^0 + {}_4C_1(2a)^3(-3b)^1 + {}_4C_2(2a)^2(-3b)^2 + {}_4C_3(2a)^1(-3b)^3 + {}_4C_4(2a)^0(-3b)^4$
$= 1(16a^4)(1) + 4(8a^3)(-3b) + 6(4a^2)(9b^2) + 4(2a)(-27b^3) + 1(1)(81b^4)$
$= 16a^4 - 96a^3b + 216a^2b^2 - 216ab^3 + 81b^4$

What pattern occurs in the signs of the terms?

b) The coefficients in the expansion of $(4b - 5)^6$ involve the pattern $_6C_0, {}_6C_1, {}_6C_2, {}_6C_3, \ldots$

The coefficient of the third term involves $_6C_2$.

Why does the coefficient of the third term not involve $_6C_3$?

In the general term $t_{k+1} = {}_nC_k(x)^{n-k}(y)^k$, substitute $x = 4b$, $y = -5$, $n = 6$, and $k = 2$.

$$t_3 = {}_6C_2(4b)^{6-2}(-5)^2$$
$$= \frac{6!}{4!2!}(4b)^4(-5)^2$$
$$= (15)(256b^4)(25)$$
$$= 96\,000b^4$$

The third term in the expansion of $(4b - 5)^6$ is $96\,000b^4$.

c) Determine the first few terms of the expanded binomial. Simplify the variable part of each term to find the pattern.

In the binomial expansion, substitute $x = a^2$, $y = -\frac{1}{a}$, and $n = 5$.

$$\left(a^2 - \frac{1}{a}\right)^5 = {}_5C_0(a^2)^5\left(-\frac{1}{a}\right)^0 + {}_5C_1(a^2)^4\left(-\frac{1}{a}\right)^1 + {}_5C_2(a^2)^3\left(-\frac{1}{a}\right)^2 + \cdots$$
$$= {}_5C_0 a^{10} + {}_5C_1(a^8)\left(-\frac{1}{a}\right) + {}_5C_2 a^6\left(\frac{1}{a^2}\right) + \cdots$$
$$= {}_5C_0 a^{10} - {}_5C_1 a^7 + {}_5C_2 a^4 + \cdots$$

The pattern shows that the exponents for a are decreasing by 3 in each successive term. The next term will contain a^{4-3} or a^1, the term after that will contain a^{1-3} or a^{-2}, and the last term will contain a^{-5}.

The fourth term contains a^1, or a, in its simplest form.

Its value is $_5C_3(a^2)^2\left(-\frac{1}{a}\right)^3 = 10(a^4)\left(-\frac{1}{a^3}\right)$
$$= -10a$$

Your Turn

a) How many terms are in the expansion of $(2a - 7)^8$?

b) What is the value of the fourth term in the expansion of $(2a - 7)^8$?

c) Use the binomial theorem to find the first four terms of the expansion of $(3a + 2b)^7$.

Key Ideas

- Pascal's triangle has many patterns. For example, each row begins and ends with 1. Each number in the interior of any row is the sum of the two numbers to its left and right in the row above.

- You can use Pascal's triangle or combinations to determine the coefficients in the expansion of $(x + y)^n$, where n is a natural number.

- You can use the binomial theorem to expand any binomial of the form $(x + y)^n$, $n \in \mathbb{N}$.

- You can determine any term in the expansion of $(x + y)^n$ using patterns without having to perform the entire expansion. The general term, t_{k+1}, has the form $_nC_k(x)^{n-k}(y)^k$.

Check Your Understanding

Practise

1. Some rows from Pascal's triangle are shown. What is the next row in each case?
   a) 1 3 3 1
   b) 1 7 21 35 35 21 7 1
   c) 1 10 45 120 210 252 210 120 45 10 1

2. Express each row of Pascal's triangle using combinations. Leave each term in the form $_nC_r$.
   a) 1 2 1
   b) 1 4 6 4 1
   c) 1 7 21 35 35 21 7 1

3. Express each circled term in the given row of Pascal's triangle as a combination.
   a) 1 3 ③ 1
   b) 1 6 15 ⑳ 15 6 1
   c) ① 1

4. How many terms are in the expansion of each expression?
   a) $(x - 3y)^4$
   b) $(1 + 3t^2)^7$
   c) $(a + 6)^q$

5. Use the binomial theorem to expand.
   a) $(x + y)^2$
   b) $(a + 1)^3$
   c) $(1 - p)^4$

6. Expand and simplify using the binomial theorem.
   a) $(a + 3b)^3$
   b) $(3a - 2b)^5$
   c) $(2x - 5)^4$

7. Determine the simplified value of the specified term.
   a) the sixth term of $(a + b)^9$
   b) the fourth term of $(x - 3y)^6$
   c) the seventh term of $(1 - 2t)^{14}$
   d) the middle term of $(4x + y)^4$
   e) the second-last term of $(3w^2 + 2)^8$

Apply

8. Explain how Pascal's triangle is constructed.

```
                    1                      Row 1
                 1     1                   Row 2
              1     2     1                Row 3
           1     3     3     1             Row 4
        1     4     6     4     1
     1     5    10    10     5     1
```

9. a) Determine the sum of the numbers in each of the first five rows in Pascal's triangle.
   b) What is an expression for the sum of the numbers in the ninth row of Pascal's triangle?
   c) What is a formula for the sum of the numbers in the nth row?

10. Examine the numbers in each "hockey stick" pattern within Pascal's triangle.

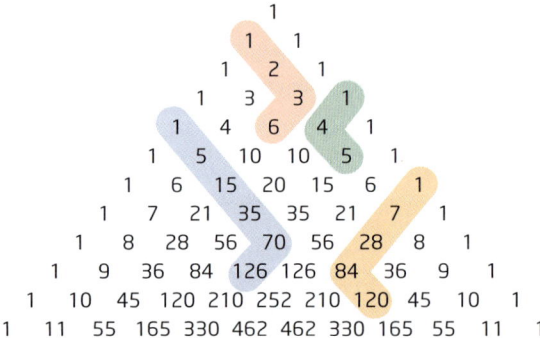

   a) Describe one pattern for the numbers within each hockey stick.
   b) Does your pattern work for all possible hockey sticks? Explain.

11. Answer the following questions for $(x + y)^{12}$ without expanding or computing all of its coefficients.
   a) How many terms are in the expansion?
   b) What is the simplified fourth term in the expansion?
   c) For what value of r does $_{12}C_r$ give the maximum coefficient? What is that coefficient?

12. Express each expansion in the form $(a + b)^n$, $n \in \mathbb{N}$.

  a) $_4C_0 x^4 + {_4C_1} x^3 y + {_4C_2} x^2 y^2 + {_4C_3} xy^3 + {_4C_4} y^4$

  b) $_5C_0 - {_5C_1} y + {_5C_2} y^2 - {_5C_3} y^3 + {_5C_4} y^4 - {_5C_5} y^5$

13. a) Penelope claims that if you read any row in Pascal's triangle as a single number, it can be expressed in the form 11^m, where m is a whole number. Do you agree? Explain.

  b) What could m represent?

14. a) Expand $(x + y)^3$ and $(x - y)^3$. How are the expansions different?

  b) Show that $(x + y)^3 + (x - y)^3 = 2x(x^2 + 3y^2)$.

  c) What is the result for $(x + y)^3 - (x - y)^3$? How do the answers in parts b) and c) compare?

15. You invite five friends for dinner but forget to ask for a reply.

  a) What are the possible cases for the number of dinner guests?

  b) How many combinations of your friends could come for dinner?

  c) How does your answer in part b) relate to Pascal's triangle?

16. a) Draw a tree diagram that depicts tossing a coin three times. Use H to represent a head and T to represent a tail landing face up. List the arrangements of heads (H) and tails (T) by the branches of your tree diagram.

  b) Expand $(H + T)^3$ by multiplying the factors. In the first step write the factors in full. For example, the first term will be HHH. You should have eight different terms. Simplify this arrangement of terms by writing HHH as H^3, and so on. Combine like terms.

  c) What does HHH or H^3 represent in both part a) and part b)? Explain what 3HHT or $3H^2T$ represents in parts a) and b).

17. Expand and simplify. Use the binomial theorem.

  a) $\left(\dfrac{a}{b} + 2\right)^3$

  b) $\left(\dfrac{a}{b} - a\right)^4$

  c) $\left(1 - \dfrac{x}{2}\right)^6$

  d) $\left(2x^2 - \dfrac{1}{x}\right)^4$

18. a) Determine the middle term in the expansion of $(a - 3b^3)^8$.

  b) Determine the term containing x^{11} in the expansion of $\left(x^2 - \dfrac{1}{x}\right)^{10}$.

19. a) Determine the constant term in the expansion $\left(x^2 - \dfrac{2}{x}\right)^{12}$.

  b) What is the constant term in the expansion of $\left(y - \dfrac{1}{y^2}\right)^{12}$?

20. One term in the expansion of $(2x - m)^7$ is $-15\,120 x^4 y^3$. Determine m.

21. MINI LAB Some students argue that using Pascal's triangle to find the coefficients in a binomial expansion is only helpful for small powers. What if you could find a pattern that allowed you to write any row in Pascal's triangle?

Work with a partner. Consider the fifth row in Pascal's triangle. Each number is related to the previous number as shown.

$$1 \quad \xrightarrow{\times \frac{4}{1}} \quad 4 \quad \xrightarrow{\times \frac{3}{2}} \quad 6 \quad \xrightarrow{\times \frac{2}{3}} \quad 4 \quad \xrightarrow{\times \frac{1}{4}} \quad 1$$

Step 1 What pattern do you see in the multipliers? Check whether your pattern works for the sixth row: 1 5 10 10 5 1

Step 2 What pattern exists between the row number and the second element in the row?

Step 3 What are the first 2 terms in the 21st row of Pascal's triangle? What are the multipliers for successive terms in row 21?

Extend

22. Five rows of the Leibniz triangle are shown.

$$\begin{array}{ccccccccc}
 & & & & 1 & & & & \\
 & & & \frac{1}{2} & & \frac{1}{2} & & & \\
 & & \frac{1}{3} & & \frac{1}{6} & & \frac{1}{3} & & \\
 & \frac{1}{4} & & \frac{1}{12} & & \frac{1}{12} & & \frac{1}{4} & \\
\frac{1}{5} & & \frac{1}{20} & & \frac{1}{30} & & \frac{1}{20} & & \frac{1}{5}
\end{array}$$

a) In the Leibniz triangle, each entry is the sum of two numbers. However, it is not the same pattern of sums as in Pascal's triangle. Which two numbers are added to get each entry?

b) Write the next two rows in the Leibniz triangle.

c) Describe at least two patterns in the Leibniz triangle.

> **Did You Know?**
>
> Gottfried Wilhelm Leibniz lived in Germany from 1646 to 1716. He was a great mathematician and philosopher. He has been described as the last universal genius. He developed calculus independently of Sir Isaac Newton and was very involved in the invention of mechanical calculators.

23. Show how to expand a trinomial using the binomial theorem. Expand and simplify $(a + b + c)^3$.

24. a) Complete a table in your notebook similar to the one shown, for one to six points.

The table relates the number of points on the circumference of a circle, the number of possible line segments you can make by joining any two of the points, and the number of triangles, quadrilaterals, pentagons, or hexagons formed. Make your own diagrams 3, 4, 5, and 6. Do not include values of zero in your table.

Diagram	Points	Line Segments	Triangles	Quadrilaterals	Pentagons	Hexagons
	1					
	2	1				
	3					
	4					
	5					
	6					

b) Show how the numbers in any row of the table relate to Pascal's triangle.

c) What values would you expect for eight points on a circle?

25. The real number e is the base of natural logarithms. It appears in certain mathematics problems involving growth or decay and is part of Stirling's formula for approximating factorials. One way to calculate e is shown below.

$$e = \frac{1}{0!} + \frac{1}{1!} + \frac{1}{2!} + \frac{1}{3!} + \frac{1}{4!} + \cdots$$

a) Determine the approximate value of e using the first five terms of the series shown.

b) How does the approximate value of e change if you use seven terms? eight terms? What do you conclude?

c) What is the value of e on your calculator?

d) Stirling's approximation can be expressed as
$$n! \approx \left(\frac{n}{e}\right)^n \sqrt{2\pi n}$$
Use Stirling's approximation to estimate 15!, and compare this result with the true value.

e) A more accurate approximation uses the following variation of Stirling's formula:
$$n! \approx \left(\frac{n}{e}\right)^n \sqrt{2\pi n}\left(1 + \frac{1}{12n}\right)$$
Use the formula from part d) and the variation to compare estimates for 50!.

Create Connections

C1 Relate the coefficients of the terms of the expansion of $(x + y)^n$, $n \in \mathbb{N}$, to Pascal's triangle. Use at least two examples.

C2 a) Create three problems for which $\frac{4!}{2!2!}$ either is an expression for the answer or is part of the answer. One of your problems must be a permutation, one must be a combination, and one must involve the expansion of a power of the binomial $a + b$.

 b) Show how your three problems are similar and how they are different.

C3 a) Which method, Pascal's triangle or combinations, do you prefer to use to express the coefficients in the expansion of $(a + b)^n$, $n \in \mathbb{N}$?

 b) Identify the strengths and the weaknesses of each method.

C4 Add to your mathematics career file for this chapter. Identify an occupation or career requiring the use of the binomial theorem. Create at least two problems that could apply to someone working in the chosen occupation or career. Explain how your problems relate to the occupation or career.

Project Corner — Art Presentation

Create a piece of art, by hand or using technology, that demonstrates a topic from this mathematics course.
- Decide whether to use mathematics either to model a real-world object or to create something using your imagination.
- Use any medium you like for your creation.

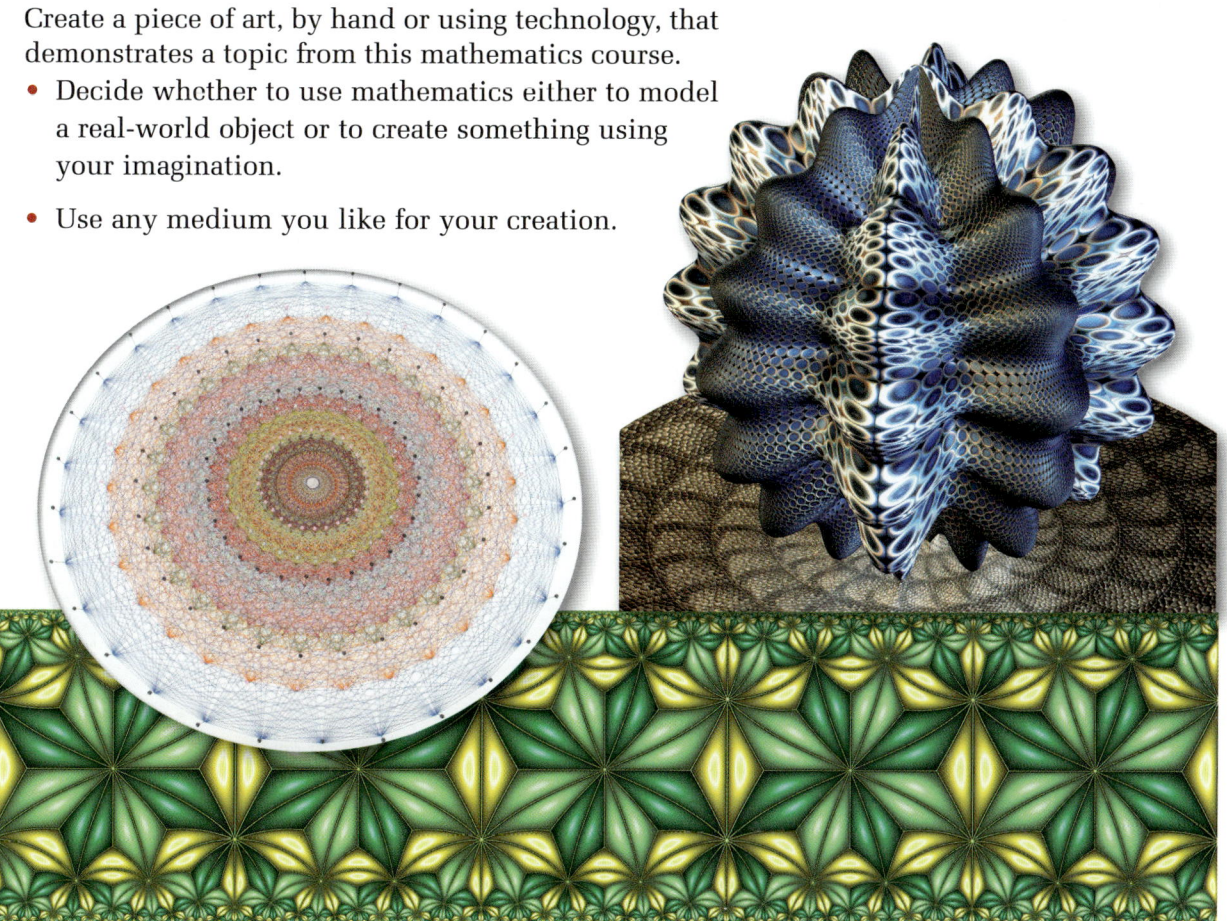

Chapter 11 Review

11.1 Permutations, pages 516–527

1. A young couple plans to have three children.
   a) Draw a tree diagram to show the possible genders for three children.
   b) Use your tree diagram to determine the number of outcomes that give them one boy and two girls.

2. A football stadium has nine gates: four on the north side and five on the south side.
   a) In how many ways can you enter and leave the stadium?
   b) In how many ways can you enter through a north gate and leave by any other gate?

3. How many different arrangements can you make using all of the letters of each word?
   a) bite
   b) bitten
   c) mammal
   d) mathematical (leave this answer in factorial form)

4. Five people, Anna, Bob, Cleo, Dina, and Eric, are seated in a row. In how many ways can they be seated if
   a) Anna and Cleo must sit together?
   b) Anna and Cleo must sit together and so must Dina and Eric?
   c) Anna and Cleo must not sit together?

5. In how many ways can the letters of *olympic* be arranged if
   a) there are no restrictions?
   b) consonants and vowels (o, i, and y) alternate?
   c) all vowels are in the middle of each arrangement?

6. Passwords on a certain Web site can have from four to eight characters. A character can be any digit or letter. Any password can have at most one digit on this Web site. Repetitions are allowed.
   a) How many four-character passwords are possible?
   b) How many eight-character passwords are possible?
   c) If a hacker can check one combination every 10 s, how much longer does it take to check all of the eight-character passwords than to check all of the four-character passwords?

7. Simplify each expression.
   a) $\dfrac{n! + (n-1)!}{n! - (n-1)!}$
   b) $\dfrac{(x+1)! + (x-1)!}{x!}$

11.2 Combinations, pages 528–536

8. Imagine that you have ten small, coloured-light bulbs, of which three are burned out.
   a) In how many ways can you randomly select four of the light bulbs?
   b) In how many ways can you select two good light bulbs and two burned out light bulbs?

9. Calculate the value of each expression.
   a) $_{10}C_3$
   b) $_{10}P_4$
   c) $_5C_3 \times {_5P_2}$
   d) $\left(\dfrac{15!}{4!11!}\right)(_6P_3)$

10. a) How many different sums of money can you form using one penny, one nickel, one dime, and one quarter?
    b) List all possible sums to confirm your answer from part a).

11. Solve for *n*. Show that each answer is correct.
    a) $_nC_2 = 28$
    b) $_nC_3 = 4(_nP_2)$

12. Ten students are instructed to break into a group of two, a group of three, and a group of five. In how many ways can this be done?

13. a) Create two problems where the answer to each is represented by $\left(\dfrac{5!}{2!3!}\right)$. One problem must involve a permutation and the other a combination. Explain which is which.

b) Five colours of paint are on sale. Is the number of ways of choosing two colours from the five options the same as the number of ways of choosing three colours from the five? Explain your answer.

11.3 The Binomial Theorem, pages 537–545

14. For each row from Pascal's triangle, write the next row.

  a) 1   2   1
  b) 1   8   28   56   70   56   28   8   1

15. Explain how to determine the coefficients of the terms in the expansion of $(x + y)^n$, $n \in \mathbb{N}$, using multiplication, Pascal's triangle, or combinations. Use examples to support your explanations.

16. Expand using the binomial theorem. Simplify.

  a) $(a + b)^5$ **b)** $(x - 3)^3$
  c) $\left(2x^2 - \dfrac{1}{x^2}\right)^4$

17. Determine the indicated term in each binomial expansion. Simplify each answer.

  a) third term of $(a + b)^9$
  b) sixth term of $(x - 2y)^6$
  c) middle term of $\left(\dfrac{1}{x} - 2x^2\right)^6$

18. You can determine the number of possible routes from A to each intersection in the diagram. Assume you can move only up or to the right.

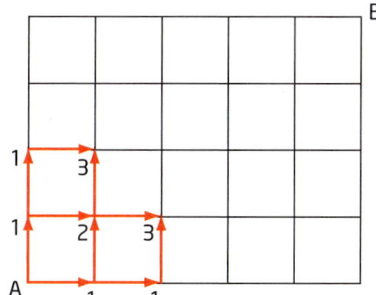

a) Draw a diagram like the one shown. Mark the number of possible routes or pathways from A to each intersection in your diagram. A few have been done for you. Use counting and patterns.

b) Show how you can superimpose Pascal's triangle to get the number of pathways from A to any point on the grid.

c) How many pathways are possible to go from A to B?

d) Use a different method to determine the number of possible pathways going from A to B.

19. Ten green and ten yellow counters are placed alternately in a row.

On each move, a counter can only jump one of its opposite colour. The task is to arrange all of the counters in two groups so that all of the green counters are at one end and all of the yellow counters are at the other end.

a) How many moves are necessary if you have ten green and ten yellow counters?

b) Establish a pattern for 2 to 12 counters of each colour. Use 2 different colours of counters.

c) How many moves are necessary for 25 of each colour?

Chapter 11 Practice Test

Multiple Choice

For #1 to #6, choose the best answer.

1. How many three-digit numbers with no repeating digits can be formed using the digits 0, 1, 2, 8, and 9?

   A 100 **B** 60 **C** 48 **D** 125

2. In how many ways can the letters of the word SWEEPERS be arranged in a row?

   A 40 320 **B** 20 160
   C 6720   **D** 3360

3. How many five-member committees containing two Conservatives, two New Democrats, and one Liberal can be formed from seven Conservatives, six New Democrats, and five Liberals?

   A 6300 **B** 3150 **C** 1575 **D** 8568

4. How many terms are in the expansion of $(2x - 5y^2)^{11}$?

   A 13 **B** 12 **C** 11 **D** 10

5. What is a simplified expression for the third term in the expansion of $(2x^2 + 3y)^7$?

   A $6048x^{10}y^2$ **B** $9072x^8y^3$
   C $12\,096x^{10}y^2$ **D** $15\,120x^8y^3$

6. The numbers 1 6 15 20 15 6 1 represent the seventh row in Pascal's triangle. What is the sixth number in the next row?

   A 1 **B** 7 **C** 21 **D** 35

Short Answer

7. For six multiple choice questions, two answers are A, two answers are B, one answer is C, and one answer is D.

   a) How many answer keys are possible?

   b) List the possible answer keys if you know that the answers to questions 3 and 5 are C and D, respectively.

8. Carla claims that when you solve $_nP_2 = 72$, there are two possible answers, and that one of the answers is -8. Do you agree with her? Explain.

9. Consider the diagram.

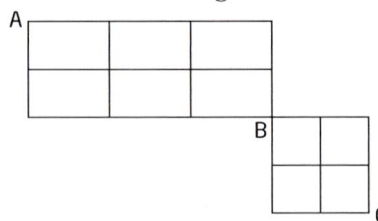

   a) How many pathways from A to B are possible, moving only down or to the right?

   b) How many pathways from A to C are possible, moving only down or to the right? Explain using permutations and the fundamental counting principle.

10. How many numbers of at most three digits can be created from the digits 0, 1, 2, 3, and 4?

11. Explain, using examples, the difference between a permutation and a combination.

12. Determine the simplified term that contains x^9 in the expansion of $\left(x^2 + \dfrac{2}{x}\right)^9$.

Extended Response

13. a) How many 4-digit even numbers greater than 5000 can you form using the digits 0, 1, 2, 3, 5, 6, 8, and 9 without repetitions?

    b) How many of these numbers end in 0?

14. Solve for n.

    a) $_nP_3 = 120$

    b) $3(_nC_2) = 12(_nC_1)$

15. Expand $\left(y - \dfrac{2}{y^2}\right)^5$ using the binomial theorem. Simplify your answer.

16. How many ways can all the letters of *aloha* be arranged if

    a) the a's must be together?

    b) the a's cannot be together?

    c) each arrangement must begin with a vowel and the consonants cannot be together?

Unit 4 Project Wrap-Up

Representing Equations and Functions

For the topic of your choice, finalize one of the representations: a video or slide show, a song, or a piece of artwork. Be prepared to demonstrate your creation to the class.

Your presentation should include the following:

- the important details of the concept you have chosen and why you chose it
- information about how the concept may be applied in real-world or problem situations
- an opportunity for feedback from your classmates

Cumulative Review, Chapters 9–11

Chapter 9 Rational Functions

1. The rational function $f(x) = \frac{1}{x}$ is transformed to $g(x) = \frac{2}{x-1} + 3$.
   a) Describe the transformations.
   b) Sketch the graph of $g(x)$.
   c) State the domain, range, any intercepts, and the equations of any asymptotes of $g(x)$.

2. Consider the rational function $y = \frac{3x - 4}{x + 1}$.
   a) Graph the function.
   b) State the domain, range, any intercepts, and the equations of any asymptotes.

3. Match each equation with the graph of its function. Justify your choices.
   a) $y = \frac{x^2 - 3x}{x^2 - 9}$
   b) $y = \frac{x^2 - 1}{x + 1}$
   c) $y = \frac{x^2 + 4x + 3}{x^2 + 1}$

   A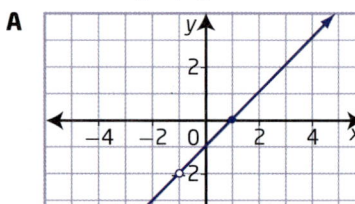

   B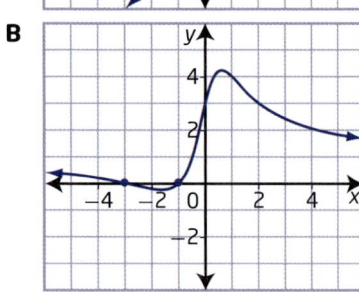

   C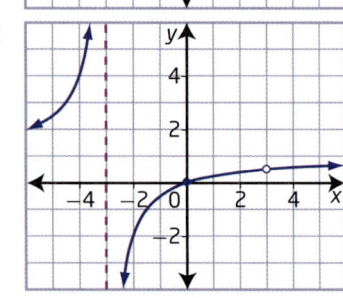

4. Solve each equation algebraically.
   a) $\frac{1}{x^2 - 9} + \frac{1}{x + 3} = 0$
   b) $\frac{8x}{x - 3} = x + 3$
   c) $\frac{x + 4}{4} = \frac{x + 5}{x^2 + 6x + 5}$

5. Determine the roots of each equation graphically. Give your answers to two decimal places.
   a) $\frac{1}{x + 1} - \frac{1}{x - 1} = \frac{2}{x^2}$
   b) $1 + \frac{3x}{3x - 1} = \frac{1}{6 - x}$

Chapter 10 Function Operations

6. Consider the functions $f(x) = \sqrt{x + 2}$ and $g(x) = x - 2$.
   a) Determine the equations of $h(x) = (f + g)(x)$ and $k(x) = (f - g)(x)$.
   b) Sketch the graphs of all four functions on the same set of coordinate axes.
   c) Determine the domain and range of $f(x)$, $g(x)$, $h(x)$, and $k(x)$.

7. Consider the functions $f(x) = x$ and $g(x) = \sqrt{100 - x^2}$.
   a) Graph $f(x)$ and $g(x)$ on the same set of axes and state the domain and range of each function.
   b) Determine the equation of $h(x) = (f \cdot g)(x)$.
   c) Graph $h(x)$ and state its domain and range.

8. Consider $f(x) = x^2 + 3x + 2$ and $g(x) = x^2 - 4$.
   a) Determine an algebraic and a graphical model for $h(x) = \frac{f(x)}{g(x)}$ and $k(x) = \frac{g(x)}{f(x)}$.
   b) Compare the domains and ranges of the combined functions.

9. Copy the graph. Add the sketch of the combined function $y = (f + g)(x)$.

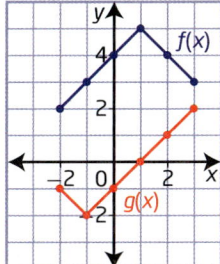

10. Consider the functions $f(x) = x - 3$, $g(x) = \frac{1}{x}$, and $h(x) = x^2 - 9$. Evaluate
    a) $f(h(3))$
    b) $g(f(5))$

11. Let $f(x) = x^3$ and $g(x) = x - 3$.
    a) Determine the equations of the composite functions $(f \circ g)(x)$ and $(g \circ f)(x)$.
    b) Graph the composite functions.
    c) Compare the composite functions. Describe $(f \circ g)(x)$ and $(g \circ f)(x)$ as transformations of $f(x)$.

12. Given each pair of functions, determine the indicated composite function. State the domain of the composite function.
    a) $f(x) = \log x$ and $g(x) = 10^x$; $f(g(x))$
    b) $f(x) = \sin x$ and $g(x) = \frac{1}{x}$; $g(f(x))$
    c) $f(x) = \frac{1}{x-1}$ and $g(x) = x^2$; $f(g(x))$

Chapter 11 Permutations, Combinations, and the Binomial Theorem

13. For the graduation banquet, the menu consists of two main courses, three vegetable options, two potato options, two salad choices, and four dessert options. How many different meals are possible?

14. Determine the number of ways to arrange the letters of the word NUMBER if the vowels cannot be together.

15. Evaluate $_7C_3 + {}_5P_2$ without using technology.

16. A committee of five is selected from six women and seven men. If there are exactly two women on the committee, determine the number of ways to select the committee.

17. a) How many ways are there of arranging three different mathematics books, five different history books, and four different French books side by side on a shelf if books of the same subject must be together?
    b) How many arrangements of these books are possible if a mathematics book must be on each end and the French books are together?

18. Solve for n.
    a) $\dfrac{(n+4)!}{(n+2)!} = 42$
    b) $_nP_3 = 20n$
    c) $_{n+2}C_n = 21$

19. Relate the coefficients of the terms in the expansion of $(x + y)^n$, $n \in \mathbb{N}$, to Pascal's triangle and to combinations. Use two examples where $n \geq 4$.

20. Expand and simplify.
    a) $(3x - 5)^4$
    b) $\left(\dfrac{1}{x} - 2x\right)^5$

21. Determine the numerical coefficient of the fourth term of each expansion.
    a) $(5x + y)^5$
    b) $\left(\dfrac{1}{x^2} - x^3\right)^8$

22. One row of Pascal's triangle starts with the following four terms: 1, 25, 300, 2300, ….
    a) Determine the next term, in combination notation.
    b) Determine the number of terms in this row.
    c) Write the term 2300 as the sum of two terms using combination notation.

Unit 4 Test

Multiple Choice

For #1 to #7, choose the best answer.

1. If $y = \dfrac{x+2}{x^2 - 3x - 10}$, which statement is true?

   A The equations of the vertical asymptotes are $x = -2$ and $x = 5$.

   B There is a point of discontinuity in the graph of the function at $\left(-2, -\dfrac{1}{7}\right)$ and at $(5, 1)$.

   C The range is $\{x \mid x \neq -2, 5, x \in R\}$.

   D The non-permissible values are $x = -2$ and $x = 5$.

2. The graph of a rational function has a horizontal asymptote at $y = 3$, a vertical asymptote at $x = -2$, and a y-intercept of 1. What is the equation of the function?

   A $y = \dfrac{4}{x+2} + 3$

   B $y = \dfrac{-4}{x+2} + 3$

   C $y = \dfrac{-9}{x-3} - 2$

   D $y = \dfrac{9}{x-3} - 2$

3. Consider the revenue function $R(x) = 10x - 0.001x^2$ and the cost function $C(x) = 2x + 5000$, where x is the number of items. The profit function is $P(x) = R(x) - C(x)$. The profit is zero when the number of items is approximately

   A 683

   B 2500

   C 8582

   D no solution

4. Consider the functions $f(x) = \dfrac{1}{x}$ and $g(x) = (x+1)^2$. What is the domain of the combined function $h(x) = (f \cdot g)(x)$?

   A $\{x \mid x \neq 1, x \in R\}$

   B $\{x \mid x \neq 0, x \in R\}$

   C $\{x \mid x \neq -1, x \in R\}$

   D $\{x \mid x \in R\}$

5. Let $f(x) = \sqrt{x+1}$ and $g(x) = x^2 - 2$. What is the equation of the composite function $m(x) = f(g(x))$?

   A $m(x) = x - 1$

   B $m(x) = \sqrt{x^2 - 1}$

   C $m(x) = \sqrt{x^2 - 2}$

   D $m(x) = \sqrt{x+1} - 2$

6. There are five empty desks in a row in a classroom. In how many ways can two students be assigned to these seats?

   A $5!$ B $2!$

   C $_5C_2$ D $_5P_2$

7. What is the value of $_6C_2 + {}_4P_3$?

   A 15   B 24

   C 39   D 43

Numerical Response

Copy and complete the statements in #8 to #11.

8. The graph of the function $y = \dfrac{x-3}{2x^2 - 5x - 3}$ has a point of discontinuity at ■.

9. The roots of the equation $\dfrac{x^2}{x^2+1} = \dfrac{x}{4}$ are $x = $ ■, $x \approx$ ■, and $x \approx$ ■, to the nearest hundredth.

10. The third term in the expansion of $(2x + 5y^2)^4$ is ■.

11. If $(x-2)^5 = a_0x^5 + a_1x^4 + a_2x^3 + a_3x^2 + a_4x + a_5$, then the value of $a_0 + a_1 + a_2 + a_3 + a_4 + a_5$ is ■.

Written Response

12. The graph of $f(x) = \dfrac{1}{x}$ is transformed to the graph of $g(x) = \dfrac{2}{x+1} - 3$.

    a) Describe the transformations.

    b) State the equations of any asymptotes.

    c) Explain the behaviour of the graph of $g(x)$ for values of x near the non-permissible value.

13. Consider the rational function $y = \dfrac{3x - 1}{x + 2}$.

  a) Graph the function.

  b) State the domain, range, and any intercepts of the graph of the function.

  c) Determine the root(s) of the equation $0 = \dfrac{3x - 1}{x + 2}$.

  d) How are the answer(s) to part c) related to part of the answer to part b)?

14. Predict the locations of any vertical asymptotes, points of discontinuity, and intercepts for each function, giving a reason for each feature. Then, graph the function to verify your predictions.

  a) $f(x) = \dfrac{x - 4}{x^2 - 2x - 8}$

  b) $f(x) = \dfrac{x^2 + x - 6}{x^2 + 2x - 3}$

  c) $f(x) = \dfrac{x^2 - 5x}{x^2 - 2x - 3}$

15. For the graphs of $f(x)$ and $g(x)$, determine the equation and graph of each combined function. Then, state its domain and range.

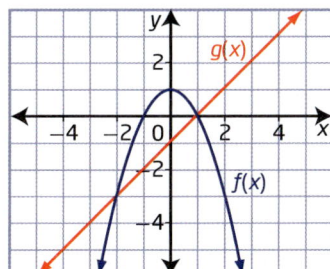

  a) $y = (f + g)(x)$ **b)** $y = (f - g)(x)$

  c) $y = \left(\dfrac{f}{g}\right)(x)$ **d)** $y = (f \cdot g)(x)$

16. If $f(x) = x - 3$ and $g(x) = \sqrt{x - 1}$, determine each combined function, $h(x)$, and state its domain.

  a) $h(x) = f(x) + g(x)$

  b) $h(x) = f(x) - g(x)$

  c) $h(x) = \left(\dfrac{f}{g}\right)(x)$

  d) $h(x) = (f \cdot g)(x)$

17. For $f(x) = x^2 - 3$ and $g(x) = |x|$, determine the following.

  a) $f(g(2))$

  b) $(f \circ g)(-2)$

  c) $f(g(x))$

  d) $(g \circ f)(x)$

18. If $h(x) = f(g(x))$, determine $f(x)$ and $g(x)$ for each of the following to be true.

  a) $h(x) = 2^{3x+2}$

  b) $h(x) = \sqrt{\sin x + 2}$

19. Solve for n.

  a) $\dfrac{n!}{(n - 2)!} = 420$

  b) $_nC_2 = 78$

  c) $_nC_{n-2} = 45$

20. Liz arranged the letters ABCD without repeating the letters.

  a) How many arrangements are possible?

  b) If the letters may be repeated, how many more four-letter arrangements are possible?

  c) Compared to your answer in part a), are there more ways to arrange four letters if two are the same, for example, ABCC? Explain.

21. A student council decides to form a sub-committee of five council members. There are four boys and five girls on council.

  a) How many different ways can the sub-committee be selected with exactly three girls?

  b) How many different ways can the sub-committee be selected with at least three girls?

22. One term of $(3x + a)^7$ is $81\,648x^5$. Determine the possible value(s) of a.

Answers

Chapter 1 Function Transformations

1.1 Horizontal and Vertical Translations, pages 12 to 15

1. **a)** $h = 0, k = 5$ **b)** $h = 0, k = -4$ **c)** $h = -1, k = 0$
   d) $h = 7, k = -3$ **e)** $h = -2, k = 4$
2. **a)** A′(−4, 1), B′(−3, 4), C′(−1, 4), D′(1, 2), E′(2, 2)
   b) A′(−2, −2), B′(−1, 1), C′(1, 1), D′(3, −1), E′(4, −1)

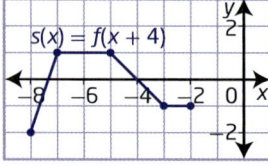

   c) A′(−8, −2), B′(−7, 1), C′(−5, 1), D′(−3, −1), E′(−2, −1)
   d) A′(−4, −4), B′(−3, −1), C′(−1, −1), D′(1, −3), E′(2, −3)

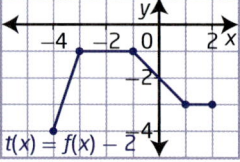

3. **a)** $(x, y) \rightarrow (x - 10, y)$ **b)** $(x, y) \rightarrow (x, y - 6)$
   c) $(x, y) \rightarrow (x + 7, y + 4)$ **d)** $(x, y) \rightarrow (x + 1, y + 3)$
4. **a)** 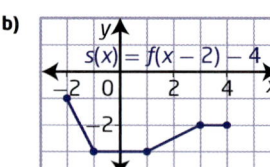 a vertical translation of 3 units down and a horizontal translation of 4 units left; $(x, y) \rightarrow (x - 4, y - 3)$
   b) a vertical translation of 4 units down and a horizontal translation of 2 units right; $(x, y) \rightarrow (x + 2, y - 4)$
   c) a vertical translation of 5 units up and a horizontal translation of 2 units right; $(x, y) \rightarrow (x + 2, y + 5)$
   d) 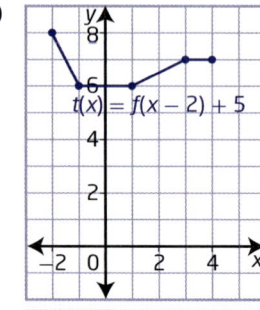 a vertical translation of 2 units up and a horizontal translation of 3 units left; $(x, y) \rightarrow (x - 3, y + 2)$

5. **a)** $h = -5, k = 4; y - 4 = f(x + 5)$
   b) $h = 8, k = 6; y - 6 = f(x - 8)$
   c) $h = 10, k = -8; y + 8 = f(x - 10)$
   d) $h = -7, k = -12; y + 12 = f(x + 7)$
6. It has been translated 3 units up.
7. It has been translated 1 unit right.
8.

Translation	Transformed Function	Transformation of Points
vertical	$y = f(x) + 5$	$(x, y) \rightarrow (x, y + 5)$
horizontal	$y = f(x + 7)$	$(x, y) \rightarrow (x - 7, y)$
horizontal	$y = f(x - 3)$	$(x, y) \rightarrow (x + 3, y)$
vertical	$y = f(x) - 6$	$(x, y) \rightarrow (x, y - 6)$
horizontal and vertical	$y + 9 = f(x + 4)$	$(x, y) \rightarrow (x - 4, y - 9)$
horizontal and vertical	$y = f(x - 4) - 6$	$(x, y) \rightarrow (x + 4, y - 6)$
horizontal and vertical	$y = f(x + 2) + 3$	$(x, y) \rightarrow (x - 2, y + 3)$
horizontal and vertical	$y = f(x - h) + k$	$(x, y) \rightarrow (x + h, y + k)$

9. **a)** $y = (x + 4)^2 + 5$ **b)** $\{x \mid x \in R\}, \{y \mid y \geq 5, y \in R\}$
   c) To determine the image function's domain and range, add the horizontal and vertical translations to the domain and range of the base function. Since the domain is the set of real numbers, nothing changes, but the range does change.
10. **a)** $g(x) = |x - 9| + 5$
    b) The new graph is a vertical and horizontal translation of the original by 5 units up and 9 units right.
    c) Example: (0, 0), (1, 1), (2, 2) → (9, 5), (10, 6), (11, 7)
    d) Example: (0, 0), (1, 1), (2, 2) → (9, 5), (10, 6), (11, 7)
    e) The coordinates of the image points from parts c) and d) are the same. The order that the translations are made does not matter.
11. **a)** $y = f(x - 3)$ **b)** $y + 5 = f(x - 6)$
12. **a)** Example: It takes her 2 h to cycle to the lake, 25 km away. She rests at the lake for 2 h and then returns home in 3 h.
    b) This translation shows what would happen if she left the house at a later time.
    c) $y = f(x - 3)$
13. **a)** Example: Translated 8 units right.
    b) Example: $y = f(x - 8), y = f(x - 4) + 3.5, y = f(x + 4) + 3.5$
14. **a)** Example: A repeating X by using two linear equations $y = \pm x$.
    b) Example: $y = f(x - 3)$. The translation is horizontal by 3 units right.
15. **a)** The transformed function starts with a higher number of trout in 1970. $y = f(t) + 2$
    b) The transformed function starts in 1974 instead of 1971. $y = f(t - 3)$
16. The first case, $n = f(A) + 10$, represents the number of gallons he needs for a given area plus 10 more gallons. The second case, $n = f(A + 10)$, represents how many gallons he needs to cover an area A less 10 units of area.
17. **a)** $y = (x - 7)(x - 1)$ or $y = (x - 4)^2 - 9$
    b) Horizontal translation of 4 units right and vertical translation of 9 units down.
    c) y-intercept 7

18. a) The original function is 4 units lower.
b) The original function is 2 units to the right.
c) The original function is 3 units lower and 5 units left.
d) The original function is 4 units higher and 3 units right.

19. a) The new graph will be translated 2 units right and 3 units down.
b)

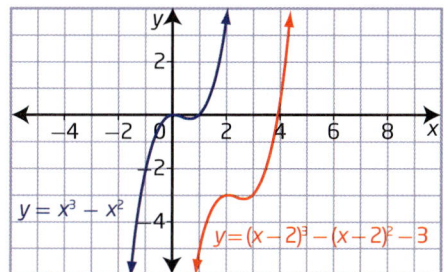

C1 a) $y = f(x) \rightarrow y = f(x - h) \rightarrow y = f(x - h) + k$. Looking at the problem in small steps, it is easy to see that it does not matter which way the translations are done since they do not affect the other translation.
b) The domain is shifted by h and the range is shifted by k.

C2 a) $f(x) = (x + 1)^2$; horizontal translation of 1 unit left
b) $g(x) = (x - 2)^2 - 1$; horizontal translation of 2 units right and 1 unit down

C3 The roots are 2 and 9.

C4 The 4 can be taken as h or k in this problem. If it is h then it is -4, which makes it in the left direction.

1.2 Reflections and Stretches, pages 28 to 31

1. a)

x	$f(x) = 2x + 1$	$g(x) = -f(x)$	$h(x) = f(-x)$
-4	-7	7	9
-2	-3	3	5
0	1	-1	1
2	5	-5	-3
4	9	-9	-7

b)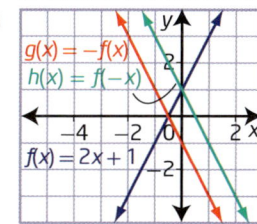

c) The y-coordinates of $g(x)$ have changed sign. The invariant point is $(-0.5, 0)$. The x-coordinates of $h(x)$ have changed sign. The invariant point is $(0, 1)$.

d) The graph of $g(x)$ is the reflection of the graph of $f(x)$ in the x-axis, while the graph of $h(x)$ is the reflection of the graph of $f(x)$ in the y-axis.

2. a)

x	$f(x) = x^2$	$g(x) = 3f(x)$	$h(x) = \frac{1}{3}f(x)$
-6	36	108	12
-3	9	27	3
0	0	0	0
3	9	27	3
6	36	108	12

b)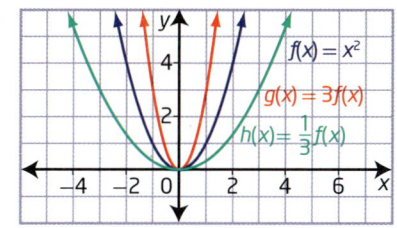

c) The y-coordinates of $g(x)$ are three times larger. The invariant point is $(0, 0)$. The y-coordinates of $h(x)$ are three times smaller. The invariant point is $(0, 0)$.

d) The graph of $g(x)$ is a vertical stretch by a factor of 3 of the graph of $f(x)$, while the graph of $h(x)$ is a vertical stretch by a factor of $\frac{1}{3}$ of the graph of $f(x)$.

3. a)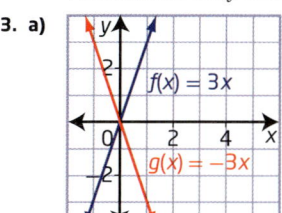
$g(x) = -3x$
$f(x)$: domain $\{x \mid x \in R\}$, range $\{y \mid y \in R\}$
$g(x)$: domain $\{x \mid x \in R\}$, range $\{y \mid y \in R\}$

b)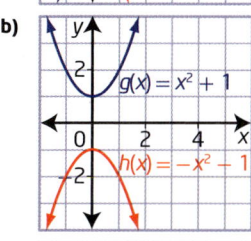
$h(x) = -x^2 - 1$
$g(x)$: domain $\{x \mid x \in R\}$, range $\{y \mid y \geq 1, y \in R\}$
$h(x)$: domain $\{x \mid x \in R\}$, range $\{y \mid y \leq -1, y \in R\}$

c)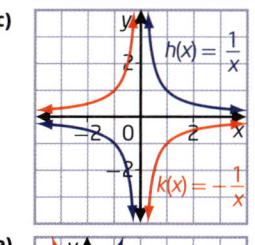
$k(x) = -\frac{1}{x}$
$h(x)$: domain $\{x \mid x \neq 0, x \in R\}$, range $\{y \mid y \neq 0, y \in R\}$
$k(x)$: domain $\{x \mid x \neq 0, x \in R\}$, range $\{y \mid y \neq 0, y \in R\}$

4. a)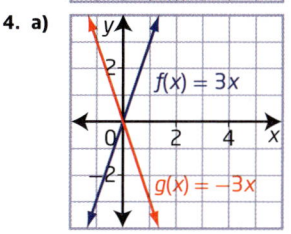
$g(x) = -3x$
$f(x)$: domain $\{x \mid x \in R\}$, range $\{y \mid y \in R\}$
$g(x)$: domain $\{x \mid x \in R\}$, range $\{y \mid y \in R\}$

b)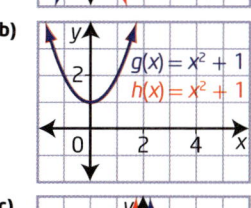
$h(x) = x^2 + 1$
$g(x)$: domain $\{x \mid x \in R\}$, range $\{y \mid y \geq 1, y \in R\}$
$h(x)$: domain $\{x \mid x \in R\}$, range $\{y \mid y \geq 1, y \in R\}$

c)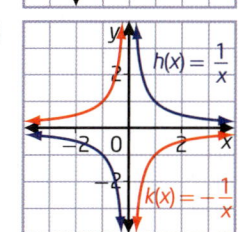
$k(x) = -\frac{1}{x}$
$h(x)$: domain $\{x \mid x \neq 0, x \in R\}$, range $\{y \mid y \neq 0, y \in R\}$
$k(x)$: domain $\{x \mid x \neq 0, x \in R\}$, range $\{y \mid y \neq 0, y \in R\}$

5. a) The graph of $y = 4f(x)$ is a vertical stretch by a factor of 4 of the graph of $y = f(x)$. $(x, y) \rightarrow (x, 4y)$
  b) The graph of $y = f(3x)$ is a horizontal stretch by a factor of $\frac{1}{3}$ of the graph of $y = f(x)$. $(x, y) \rightarrow \left(\frac{x}{3}, y\right)$
  c) The graph of $y = -f(x)$ is a reflection in the x-axis of the graph of $y = f(x)$. $(x, y) \rightarrow (x, -y)$
  d) The graph of $y = f(-x)$ is a reflection in the y-axis of the graph of $y = f(x)$. $(x, y) \rightarrow (-x, y)$

6. a) domain $\{x \mid -6 \leq x \leq 6, x \in R\}$, range $\{y \mid -8 \leq y \leq 8, y \in R\}$
  b) The vertical stretch affects the range by increasing it by the stretch factor of 2.

7. a) The graph of $g(x)$ is a vertical stretch by a factor of 4 of the graph of $f(x)$. $y = 4f(x)$
  b) The graph of $g(x)$ is a reflection in the x-axis of the graph of $f(x)$. $y = -f(x)$
  c) The graph of $g(x)$ is a horizontal stretch by a factor of $\frac{1}{3}$ of the graph of $f(x)$. $y = f(3x)$
  d) The graph of $g(x)$ is a reflection in the y-axis of the graph of $f(x)$. $y = f(-x)$

8.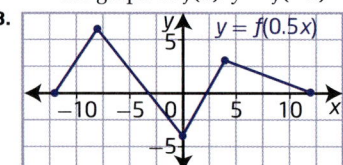

9. a) horizontally stretched by a factor of $\frac{1}{4}$
  b) horizontally stretched by a factor of 4
  c) vertically stretched by a factor of $\frac{1}{2}$
  d) vertically stretched by a factor of 4
  e) horizontally stretched by a factor of $\frac{1}{3}$ and reflected in the y-axis
  f) vertically stretched by a factor of 3 and reflected in the x-axis

10. a) 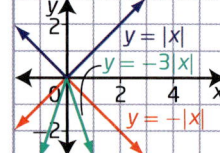   **b)**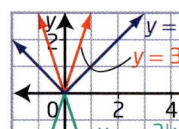
  c) They are both incorrect. It does not matter in which order you proceed.

11. a)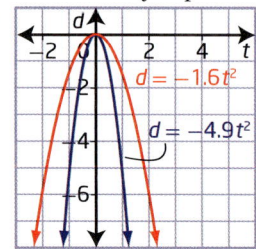
  b) Both the functions are reflections of the base function in the t-axis. The object falling on Earth is stretched vertically more than the object falling on the moon.

12. Example: When the graph of $y = f(x)$ is transformed to the graph of $y = f(bx)$, it undergoes a horizontal stretch about the y-axis by a factor of $\frac{1}{|b|}$ and only the x-coordinates are affected. When the graph of $y = f(x)$ is transformed to the graph of $y = af(x)$, it undergoes a vertical stretch about the x-axis by a factor of $|a|$ and only the y-coordinates are affected.

13. a)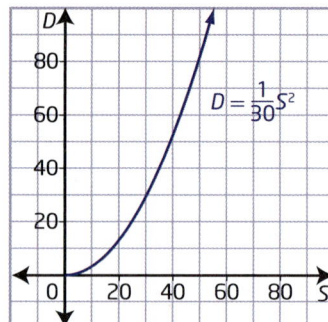
  b) As the drag factor decreases, the length of the skid mark increases for the same speed.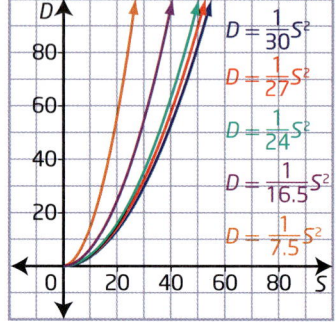

14. a) $x = -4, x = 3$ **b)** $x = 4, x = -3$
  c) $x = -8, x = 6$ **d)** $x = -2, x = 1.5$

15. a) I **b)** III **c)** IV **d)** IV

16. a)
  b)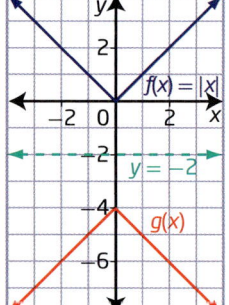

C1 Example: When the input values for $g(x)$ are b times the input values for $f(x)$, the scale factor must be $\frac{1}{b}$ for the same output values. $g(x) = f\left(\frac{1}{b}(bx)\right) = f(x)$

C2 Examples:
  a) a vertical stretch or a reflection in the x-axis
  b) a horizontal stretch or a reflection in the y-axis

C3

f(x)	g(x)	Transformation
(5, 6)	(5, −6)	reflection in the x-axis
(4, 8)	(−4, 8)	reflection in the y-axis
(2, 3)	(2, 12)	vertical stretch by a factor of 4
(4, −12)	(2, −6)	horizontal stretch by a factor of $\frac{1}{2}$ and vertical stretch by a factor of $\frac{1}{2}$

C4

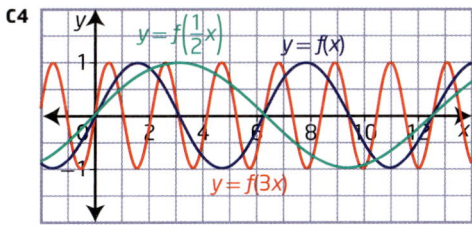

C5 a) $t_n = 4n - 14$ b) $t_n = -4n + 14$
c) They are reflections of each other in the x-axis.

1.3 Combining Transformations, pages 38 to 43

1. a) $y = -f\left(\frac{1}{2}x\right)$ or $y = -\frac{1}{4}x^2$
   b) $y = \frac{1}{4}f(-4x)$ or $y = 4x^2$

2. The function $f(x)$ is transformed to the function $g(x)$ by a horizontal stretch about the y-axis by a factor of $\frac{1}{4}$. It is vertically stretched about the x-axis by a factor of 3. It is reflected in the x-axis, and then translated 4 units right and 10 units down.

3.

Function	Reflections	Vertical Stretch Factor	Horizontal Stretch Factor	Vertical Translation	Horizontal Translation
$y - 4 = f(x - 5)$	none	none	none	4	5
$y + 5 = 2f(3x)$	none	2	$\frac{1}{3}$	-5	none
$y = \frac{1}{2}f\left(\frac{1}{2}(x - 4)\right)$	none	$\frac{1}{2}$	2	none	4
$y + 2 = -3f(2(x + 2))$	x-axis	3	$\frac{1}{2}$	-2	-2

4. a) $y = f(-(x + 2)) - 2$ b) $y = f(2(x + 1)) - 4$

5. a)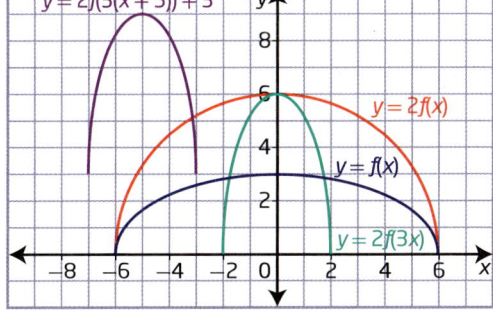

   b)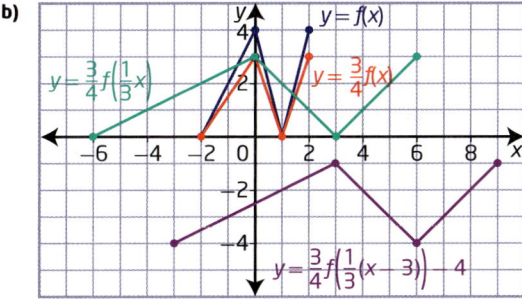

6. a) $(-8, 12)$ b) $(-4, 72)$ c) $(-6, -32)$
   d) $(9, -32)$ e) $(-12, -9)$

7. a) vertical stretch by a factor of 2 and translation of 3 units right and 4 units up;
   $(x, y) \to (x + 3, 2y + 4)$
   b) horizontal stretch by a factor of $\frac{1}{3}$, reflection in the x-axis, and translation of 2 units down;
   $(x, y) \to \left(\frac{1}{3}x, -y - 2\right)$
   c) reflection in the y-axis, reflection in the x-axis, vertical stretch by a factor of $\frac{1}{4}$, and translation of 2 units left; $(x, y) \to \left(-x - 2, -\frac{1}{4}y\right)$
   d) horizontal stretch by a factor of $\frac{1}{4}$, reflection in the x-axis, and translation of 2 units right and 3 units up; $(x, y) \to \left(\frac{1}{4}x + 2, -y + 3\right)$
   e) reflection in the y-axis, horizontal stretch by a factor of $\frac{4}{3}$, reflection in the x-axis, and vertical stretch by a factor of $\frac{2}{3}$; $(x, y) \to \left(-\frac{4}{3}x, -\frac{2}{3}y\right)$
   f) reflection in the y-axis, horizontal stretch by a factor of $\frac{1}{2}$, vertical stretch by a factor of $\frac{1}{3}$, and translation of 6 units right and 2 units up;
   $(x, y) \to \left(-\frac{1}{2}x + 6, \frac{1}{3}y + 2\right)$

8. a) $y + 5 = -3f(x + 4)$ b) $y - 2 = -\frac{3}{4}f(-3(x - 6))$

9. a)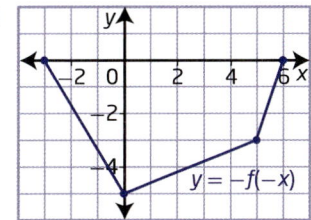

   b)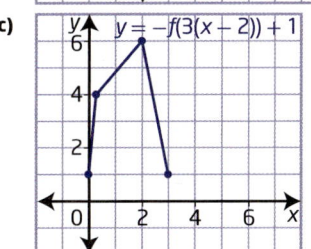

   c)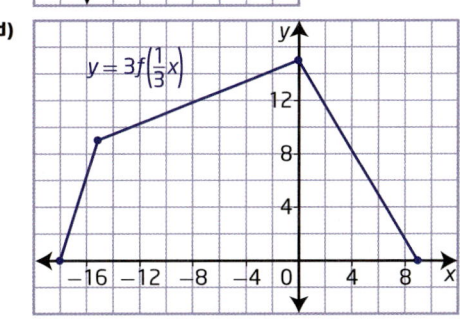

   d)

e)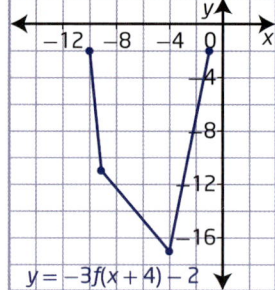

f)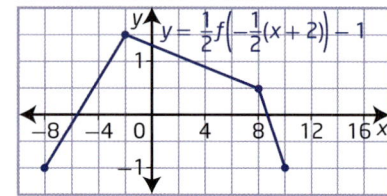

10. a) $y = -3f(x - 8) + 10$ b) $y = -2f(x - 3) + 2$
    c) $y = -\frac{1}{2}f(-2(x + 4)) + 7$

11. a)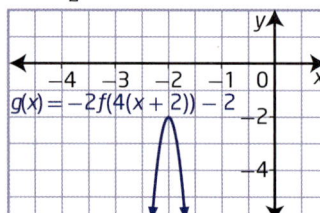

b)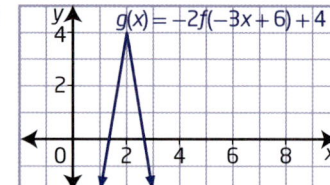

c)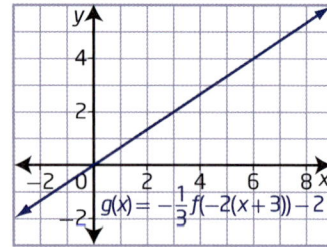

12. a) A′(−11, −2), B′(−7, 6), C′(−3, 4), D′(−1, 5), E′(3, −2)
    b) $y = -f\left(\frac{1}{2}(x + 3)\right) + 4$

13. a) The graphs are in two locations because the transformations performed to obtain Graph 2 do not match those in $y = |2x - 6| + 2$. Gil forgot to factor out the coefficient of the x-term, 2, from −6. The horizontal translation should have been 3 units right, not 6 units.
    b) He should have rewritten the function as $y = |2(x - 3)| + 2$.

14. a)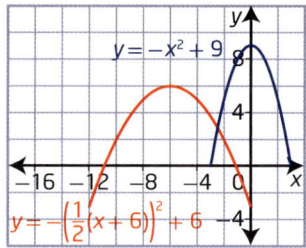
    b) $y = -\left(\frac{1}{2}(x + 6)\right)^2 + 6$

15. a) $(-a, 0), (0, -b)$ b) $(2a, 0), (0, 2b)$
    c) and d) There is not enough information to determine the locations of the new intercepts. When a transformation involves translations, the locations of the new intercepts will vary with different base functions.

16. a) $A = -2x^3 + 18x$ b) $A = -\frac{1}{8}x^3 + 18x$
    c) For (2, 5), the area of the rectangle in part a) is 20 square units.
    $A = -2x^3 + 18x$
    $A = -2(2)^3 + 18(2)$
    $A = 20$
    For (8, 5), the area of the rectangle in part b) is 80 square units.
    $A = -\frac{1}{8}x^3 + 18x$
    $A = -\frac{1}{8}(8)^3 + 18(8)$
    $A = 80$

17. $y = 36(x - 2)^2 + 6(x - 2) - 2$

18. Example: vertical stretches and horizontal stretches followed by reflections

C1 **Step 1** They are reflections in the axes.
    1: $y = x + 3$, 2: $y = -x - 3$, 3: $y = x - 3$
    Step 2 They are vertical translations coupled with reflections. 1: $y = x^2 + 1$, 2: $y = x^2 - 1$, 3: $y = -x^2$, 4: $y = -x^2 - 1$

C2 a) The cost of making $b + 12$ bracelets, and it is a horizontal translation.
    b) The cost of making b bracelets plus 12 more dollars, and it is a vertical translation.
    c) Triple the cost of making b bracelets, and it is a vertical stretch.
    d) The cost of making $\frac{b}{2}$ bracelets, and it is a horizontal stretch.

C3 $y = 2(x - 3)^2 + 1$; a vertical stretch by a factor of 2 and a translation of 3 units right and 1 unit up

C4 a) H is repeated; J is transposed; K is repeated and transposed
    b) H is in retrograde; J is inverted; K is in retrograde and inverted
    c) H is inverted, repeated, and transposed; J is in retrograde inversion and repeated; K is in retrograde and transposed

1.4 Inverse of a Relation, pages 51 to 55

1. a) 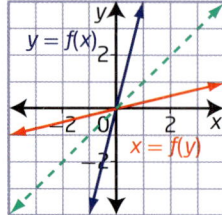   b)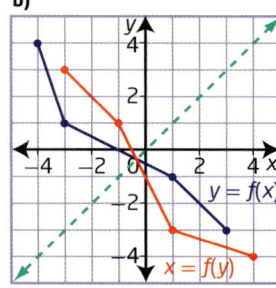

2. a)

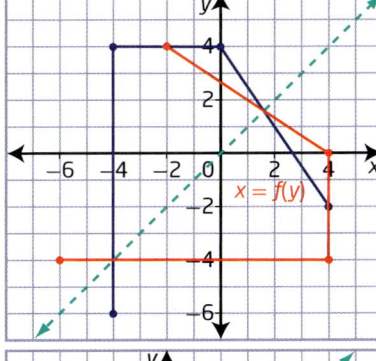

b)

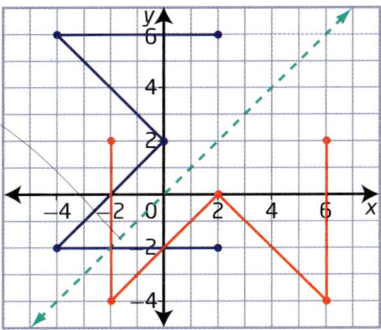

3. a) The graph is a function but the inverse will be a relation.
  b) The graph and its inverse are functions.
  c) The graph and its inverse are relations.

4. Examples:
  a) $\{x \mid x \geq 0, x \in R\}$ or $\{x \mid x \leq 0, x \in R\}$
  b) $\{x \mid x \geq -2, x \in R\}$ or $\{x \mid x \leq -2, x \in R\}$
  c) $\{x \mid x \geq 4, x \in R\}$ or $\{x \mid x \leq 4, x \in R\}$
  d) $\{x \mid x \geq -4, x \in R\}$ or $\{x \mid x \leq -4, x \in R\}$

5. a) $f^{-1}(x) = \frac{1}{7}x$ **b)** $f^{-1}(x) = -\frac{1}{3}(x-4)$
   c) $f^{-1}(x) = 3x - 4$ **d)** $f^{-1}(x) = 3x + 15$
   e) $f^{-1}(x) = -\frac{1}{2}(x-5)$ **f)** $f^{-1}(x) = 2x - 6$

6. a) E   **b)** C   **c)** B   **d)** A   **e)** D

7. a)

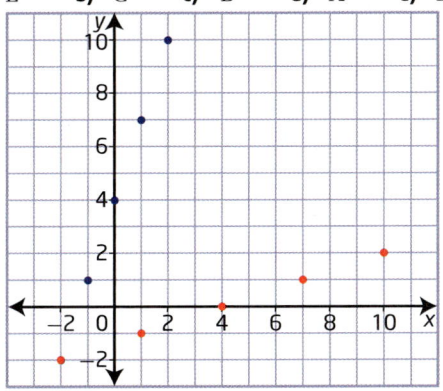

function: domain $\{-2, -1, 0, 1, 2\}$,
range $\{-2, 1, 4, 7, 10\}$
inverse: domain $\{-2, 1, 4, 7, 10\}$,
range $\{-2, -1, 0, 1, 2\}$

b)

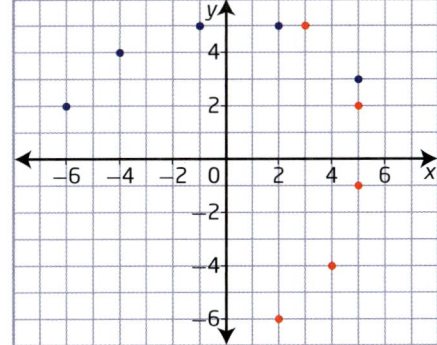

function: domain $\{-6, -4, -1, 2, 5\}$, range $\{2, 3, 4, 5\}$
inverse: domain $\{2, 3, 4, 5\}$, range $\{-6, -4, -1, 2, 5\}$

8. a)

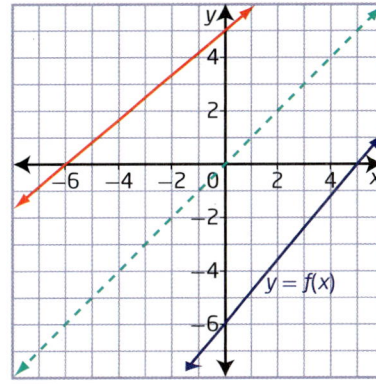

The inverse is a function; it passes the vertical line test.

b)

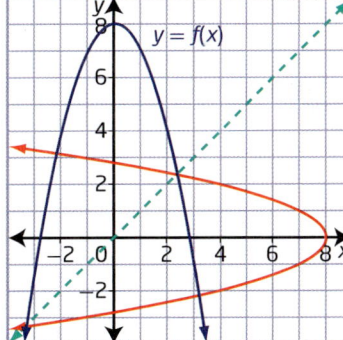

The inverse is not a function; it does not pass the vertical line test.

c)

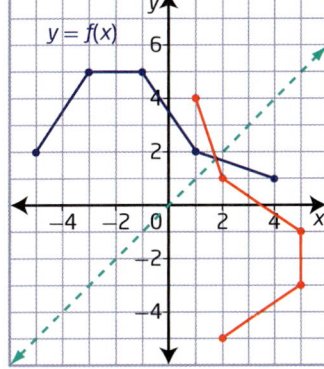

The inverse is not a function; it does not pass the vertical line test.

Answers • MHR **559**

9. a) $f^{-1}(x) = \dfrac{1}{3}(x - 2)$

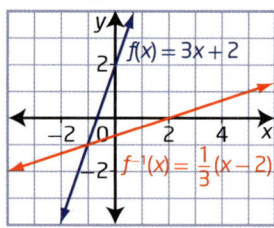

$f(x)$: domain $\{x \mid x \in R\}$, range $\{y \mid y \in R\}$
$f^{-1}(x)$: domain $\{x \mid x \in R\}$, range $\{y \mid y \in R\}$

b) $f^{-1}(x) = \dfrac{1}{2}(-x + 4)$

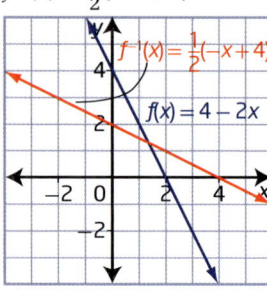

$f(x)$: domain $\{x \mid x \in R\}$, range $\{y \mid y \in R\}$
$f^{-1}(x)$: domain $\{x \mid x \in R\}$, range $\{y \mid y \in R\}$

c) $f^{-1}(x) = 2x + 12$

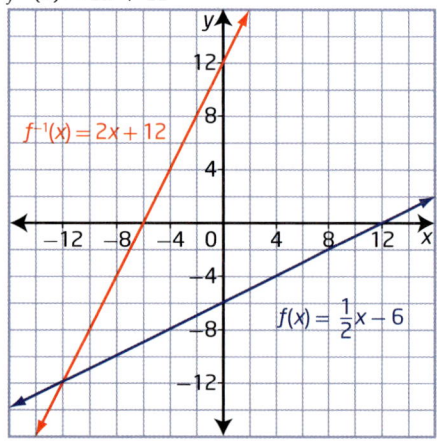

$f(x)$: domain $\{x \mid x \in R\}$, range $\{y \mid y \in R\}$
$f^{-1}(x)$: domain $\{x \mid x \in R\}$, range $\{y \mid y \in R\}$

d) $f^{-1}(x) = -\sqrt{x - 2}$

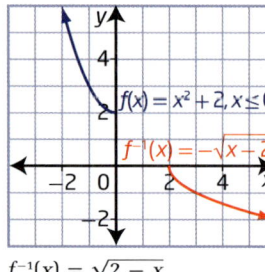

$f(x)$: domain $\{x \mid x \leq 0, x \in R\}$, range $\{y \mid y \geq 2, y \in R\}$
$f^{-1}(x)$: domain $\{x \mid x \geq 2, x \in R\}$, range $\{y \mid y \leq 0, y \in R\}$

e) $f^{-1}(x) = \sqrt{2 - x}$

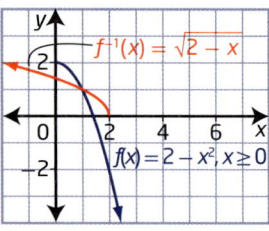

$f(x)$: domain $\{x \mid x \geq 0, x \in R\}$, range $\{y \mid y \leq 2, y \in R\}$
$f^{-1}(x)$: domain $\{x \mid x \leq 2, x \in R\}$, range $\{y \mid y \geq 0, y \in R\}$

10. a) i) $f(x) = (x + 4)^2 - 4$, inverse of $f(x) = \pm\sqrt{x + 4} - 4$

ii)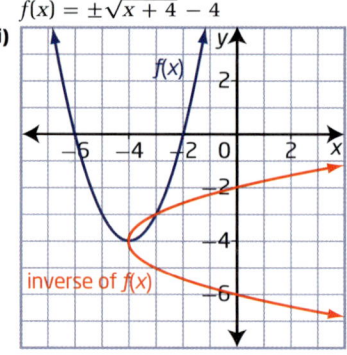

b) i) $y = (x - 2)^2 - 2$, $y = \pm\sqrt{x + 2} + 2$

ii)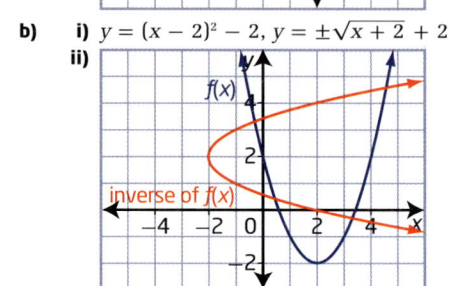

11. Yes, the graphs are reflections of each other in the line $y = x$.

12. a) $y = \pm\sqrt{x - 3}$ restricted domain $\{x \mid x \geq 0, x \in R\}$

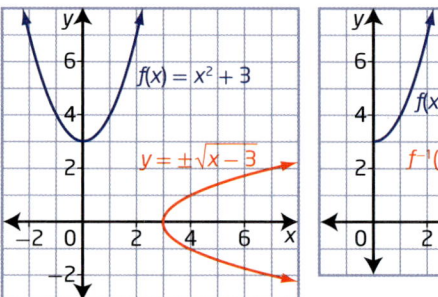 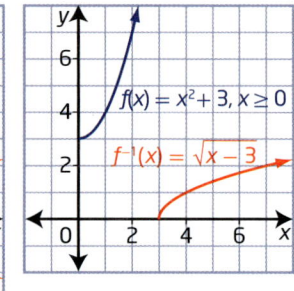

b) $y = \pm\sqrt{2x}$ restricted domain $\{x \mid x \geq 0, x \in R\}$

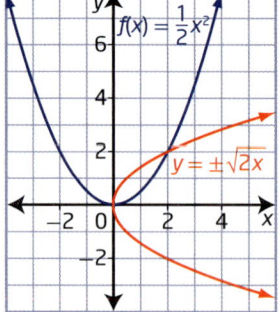 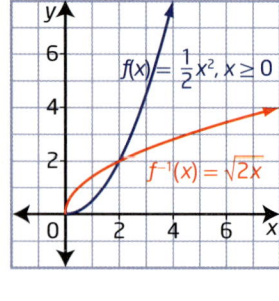

c) $y = \pm\sqrt{-\frac{1}{2}x}$ restricted domain $\{x \mid x \geq 0, x \in R\}$

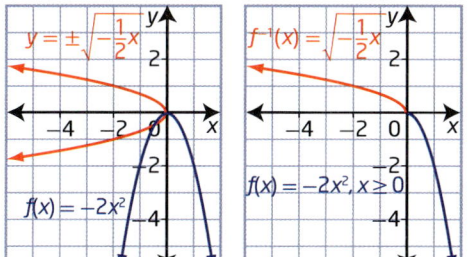

d) $y = \pm\sqrt{x} - 1$ restricted domain $\{x \mid x \geq -1, x \in R\}$

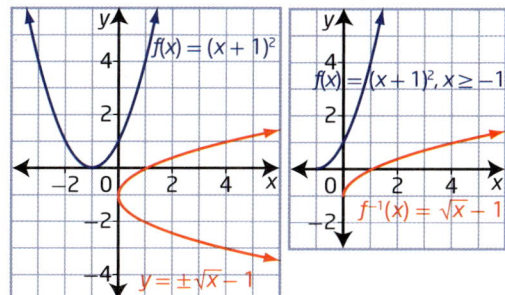

e) $y = \pm\sqrt{-x} + 3$ restricted domain $\{x \mid x \geq 3, x \in R\}$

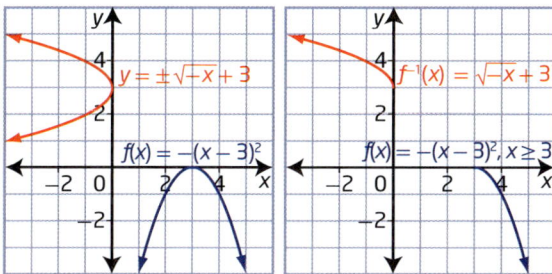

f) $y = \pm\sqrt{x+2} + 1$ restricted domain $\{x \mid x \geq 1, x \in R\}$

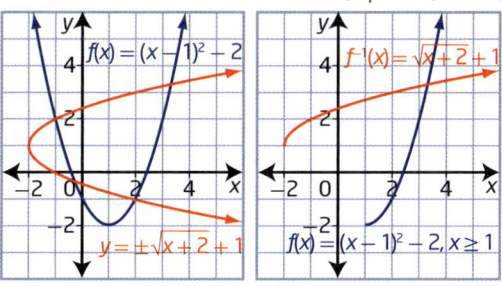

13. a) inverses   **b)** inverses   **c)** not inverses
   d) inverses   **e)** not inverses
14. Examples:
   a) $x \geq 0$ or $x \leq 0$ **b)** $x \geq 0$ or $x \leq 0$
   c) $x \geq 3$ or $x \leq 3$ **d)** $x \geq -2$ or $x \leq -2$
15. a) $\frac{3}{2}$ **b)** 0   **c)** $\frac{5}{2}$ **d)** $\frac{1}{2}$

16. a) approximately 32.22 °C
   b) $y = \frac{9}{5}x + 32$; x represents temperatures in degrees Celsius and y represents temperatures in degrees Fahrenheit
   c) 89.6 °F
   d) 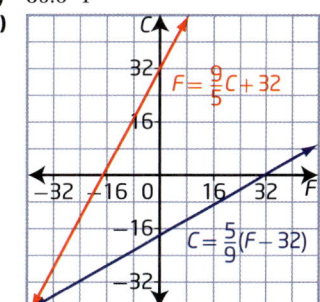 The temperature is the same in both scales (-40 °C $= -40$ °F).

17. a) male height = 171.02 cm, female height = 166.44 cm
   b) **i)** male femur = 52.75 cm
       ii) female femur = 49.04 cm
18. a) 5
   b) $y = 2.55x + 36.5$; y is finger circumference and x is ring size
   c) 51.8 mm, 54.35 mm, 59.45 mm
19. Examples:
   a) **i)** $3 \leq x \leq 6$ **ii)** $-2 \leq x \leq 3$

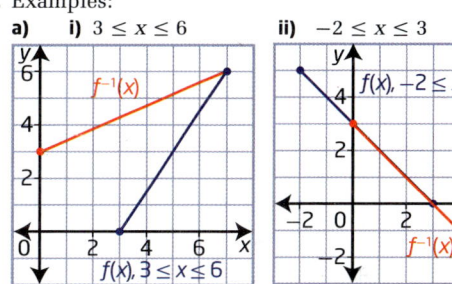

   b) **i)** $4 \leq x \leq 8$ **ii)** $-10 \leq x \leq -6$

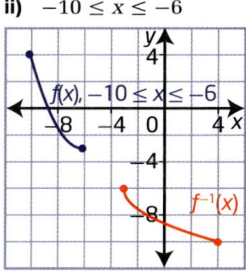

20. a) 17   **b)** $\sqrt{3}$ **c)** 10
21. a) (6, 10)   **b)** (8, 23)   **c)** ($-8, -9$)
C1 a) Subtract 12 and divide by 6.
   b) Add 1, take the positive and negative square root, subtract 3.
C2 a)   **b)** Example: The graph of the original linear function is perpendicular to $y = x$, thus after a reflection the graph of the inverse is the same.

   c) They are perpendicular to the line.

C3 Example: If the original function passes the vertical line test, then it is a function. If the original function passes the horizontal line test, then the inverse is a function.

C4 Step 1

$f(x)$: $(1, 2)$, $(4, 3)$, $(-8, -1)$, and $\left(a, \dfrac{a+5}{3}\right)$;

$g(x)$: $(2, 1)$, $(3, 4)$, $(-1, -8)$, and $\left(\dfrac{a+5}{3}, a\right)$

The output values for $g(x)$ are the same as the input values for $f(x)$.

Example: Since the functions are inverses of each other, giving one of them a value and then taking the inverse will always return the initial value. A good way to determine if functions are inverses is to see if this effect takes place.

Step 2 The order in which you apply the functions does not change the final result.

Step 4 The statement is saying that if you have a function that when given a outputs b and another that when given b outputs a, then the functions are inverses of each other.

Chapter 1 Review, pages 56 to 57

1. a) 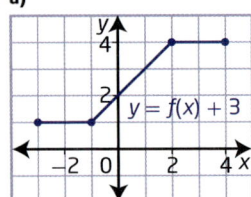 **b)**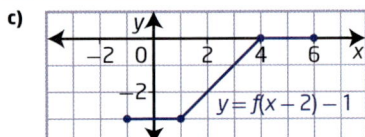

c)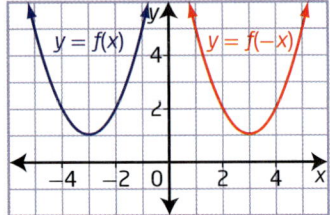

2. Translation of 4 units left and 5 units down:
$y + 5 = |x + 4|$

3. range $\{y \mid 2 \leq y \leq 9, y \in R\}$

4. No, it should be $(a + 5, b - 4)$.

5. a) x-axis, $(3, -5)$ **b)** y-axis, $(-3, 5)$

6. a)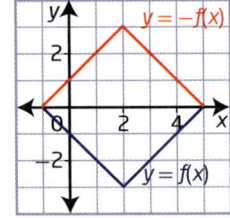

$f(-x)$: domain $\{x \mid x \in R\}$, range $\{y \mid y \geq 1, y \in R\}$
$(0, 10)$

b) $-f(x)$: domain $\{x \mid -1 \leq x \leq 5, x \in R\}$, range $\{y \mid 0 \leq y \leq 3, y \in R\}$
$(5, 0)$, $(-1, 0)$

7. a)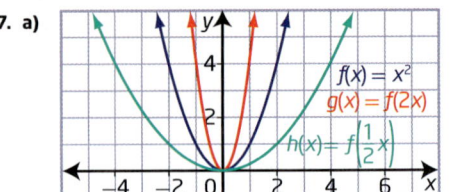

b) If the coefficient is greater than 1, then the function moves closer to the y-axis. The opposite is true for when the coefficient is between 0 and 1.

8. a) In this case, it could be either. It could be a vertical stretch by a factor of $\dfrac{1}{2}$ or a horizontal stretch by a factor of $\sqrt{2}$.

b) Example: $g(x) = \dfrac{1}{2}f(x)$

9. a) 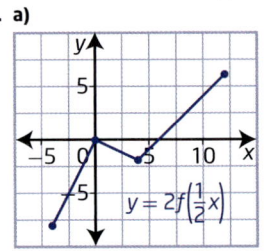 **b)**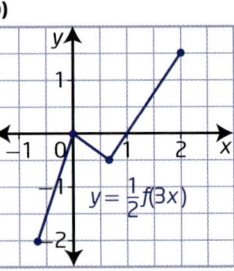

10. They are both horizontal stretches by a factor of $\dfrac{1}{4}$. The difference is in the horizontal translation, the first being 1 unit left and the second being $\dfrac{1}{4}$ unit left.

11. $g(x) = f(2(x - 5)) - 2$

12. a)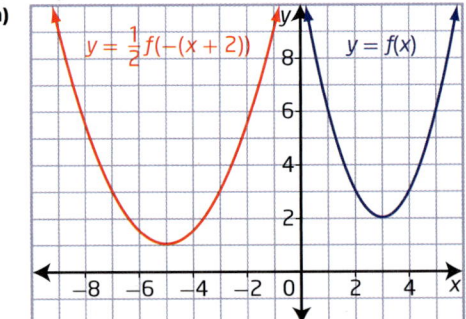

b) **c)**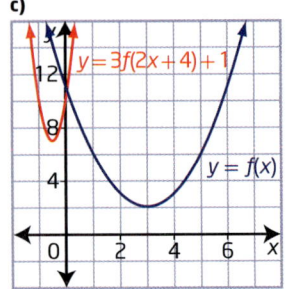

13. a)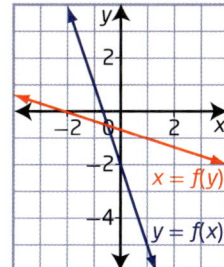

b) $y = x$, $\left(-\frac{1}{2}, -\frac{1}{2}\right)$
c) $f(x)$: domain $\{x \mid x \in R\}$, range $\{y \mid y \in R\}$
$f(y)$: domain $\{x \mid x \in R\}$, range $\{y \mid y \in R\}$

14.

$y = f(x)$		$y = f^{-1}(x)$	
x	y	x	y
-3	7	7	-3
2	4	4	2
10	-12	-12	10

15. a) 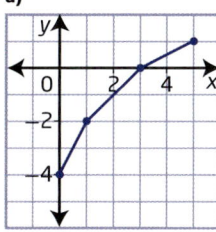 **b)**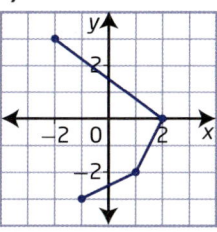

The relation and its inverse are functions. The relation is a function. The inverse is not a function.

16. $y = \sqrt{x-1} + 3$, restricted domain $\{x \mid x \geq 3, x \in R\}$
17. a) not inverses **b)** inverses

Chapter 1 Practice Test, pages 58 to 59

1. D **2.** D **3.** B **4.** B **5.** B **6.** C **7.** C
8. domain $\{x \mid -5 \leq x \leq 2, x \in R\}$
9.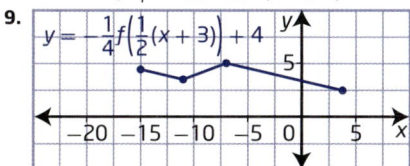

10. a)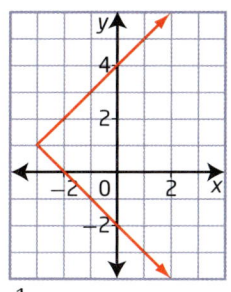

b) To transform it point by point, switch the position of the x- and the y-coordinate.
c) $(-1, -1)$

11. $y = \frac{1}{5}(x - 2)$
12. $y = 3f\left(-\frac{1}{2}(x-2)\right)$
13. a) It is a translation of 2 units left and 7 units down.
b) $g(x) = |x + 2| - 7$ **c)** $(-2, -7)$
d) No. Invariant points are points that remain unchanged after a transformation.
14. a) $f(x) = x^2$
b) $g(x) = \frac{1}{4}f(x)$; a vertical stretch by a factor of $\frac{1}{4}$
c) $g(x) = f\left(\frac{1}{2}x\right)$; a horizontal stretch by a factor of 2

d) $\frac{1}{4}f(x) = \frac{1}{4}x^2$; $f\left(\frac{1}{2}x\right) = \left(\frac{1}{2}x\right)^2 = \frac{1}{4}x^2$
15. a) Using the horizontal line test, if a horizontal line passes through the function more than once the inverse is not a function.
b) $y = \pm\sqrt{-x-5} - 3$
c) Example: restricted domain $\{x \mid x \geq -3, x \in R\}$

Chapter 2 Radical Functions

2.1 Radical Functions and Transformations, pages 72 to 77

1. a)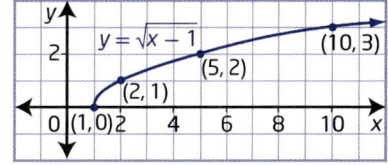

domain $\{x \mid x \geq 1, x \in R\}$, range $\{y \mid y \geq 0, y \in R\}$

b)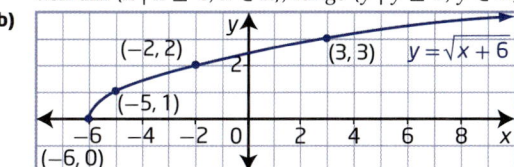

domain $\{x \mid x \geq -6, x \in R\}$, range $\{y \mid y \geq 0, y \in R\}$

c)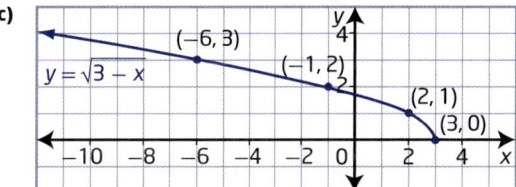

domain $\{x \mid x \leq 3, x \in R\}$, range $\{y \mid y \geq 0, y \in R\}$

d)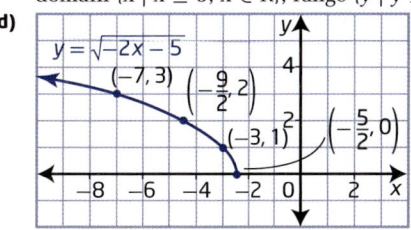

domain $\left\{x \mid x \leq -\frac{5}{2}, x \in R\right\}$, range $\{y \mid y \geq 0, y \in R\}$

2. a) $a = 7 \to$ vertical stretch by a factor of 7
$h = 9 \to$ horizontal translation 9 units right
domain $\{x \mid x \geq 9, x \in R\}$, range $\{y \mid y \geq 0, y \in R\}$
b) $b = -1 \to$ reflected in y-axis
$k = 8 \to$ vertical translation up 8 units
domain $\{x \mid x \leq 0, x \in R\}$, range $\{y \mid y \geq 8, y \in R\}$
c) $a = -1 \to$ reflected in x-axis
$b = \frac{1}{5} \to$ horizontal stretch factor of 5
domain $\{x \mid x \geq 0, x \in R\}$, range $\{y \mid y \leq 0, y \in R\}$
d) $a = \frac{1}{3} \to$ vertical stretch factor of $\frac{1}{3}$
$h = -6 \to$ horizontal translation 6 units left
$k = -4 \to$ vertical translation 4 units down
domain $\{x \mid x \geq -6, x \in R\}$,
range $\{y \mid y \geq -4, y \in R\}$
3. a) B **b)** A **c)** D **d)** C
4. a) $y = 4\sqrt{x+6}$ **b)** $y = \sqrt{8x} - 5$

Answers • MHR **563**

c) $y = \sqrt{-(x-4)} + 11$ or $y = \sqrt{-x+4} + 11$

d) $y = -0.25\sqrt{0.1x}$ or $y = -\frac{1}{4}\sqrt{\frac{1}{10}x}$

5. a) 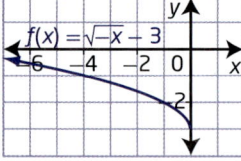 domain $\{x \mid x \leq 0, x \in R\}$, range $\{y \mid y \geq -3, y \in R\}$

b) 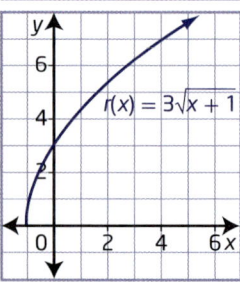 domain $\{x \mid x \geq -1, x \in R\}$, range $\{y \mid y \geq 0, y \in R\}$

c) 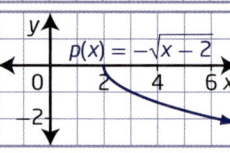 domain $\{x \mid x \geq 2, x \in R\}$, range $\{y \mid y \leq 0, y \in R\}$

d) 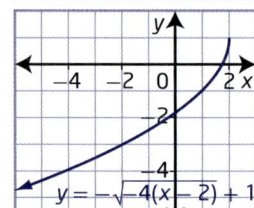 domain $\{x \mid x \leq 2, x \in R\}$, range $\{y \mid y \leq 1, y \in R\}$

e) 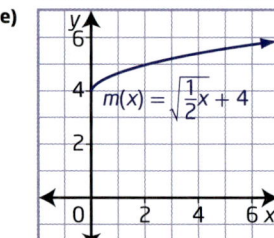 domain $\{x \mid x \geq 0, x \in R\}$, range $\{y \mid y \geq 4, y \in R\}$

f) 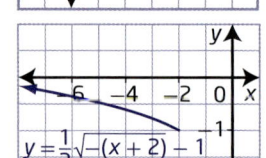 domain $\{x \mid x \leq -2, x \in R\}$ range $\{y \mid y \geq -1, y \in R\}$

6. a) $a = \frac{1}{4} \to$ vertical stretch factor of $\frac{1}{4}$
$b = 5 \to$ horizontal stretch factor of $\frac{1}{5}$

b) $y = \frac{\sqrt{5}}{4}\sqrt{x}$, $y = \sqrt{\frac{5}{16}x}$

c) $a = \frac{\sqrt{5}}{4} \to$ vertical stretch factor of $\frac{\sqrt{5}}{4}$
$b = \frac{5}{16} \to$ horizontal stretch factor of $\frac{16}{5}$

d)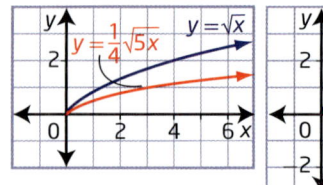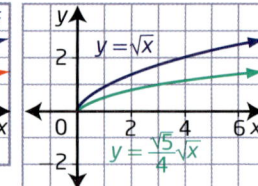

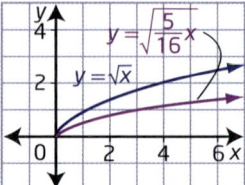 All graphs are the same.

7. a) $r(A) = \sqrt{\frac{A}{\pi}}$

b)

A	r
0	0
1	0.6
2	0.8
3	1.0
4	1.1

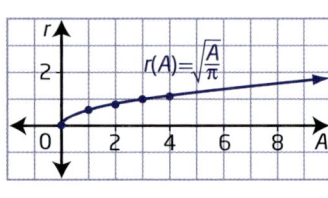

8. a) $b = 1.50 \to$ horizontal stretch factor of $\frac{1}{1.50}$ or $\frac{2}{3}$

b) $d \approx 1.22\sqrt{h}$ Example: I prefer the original function because the values are exact.

c) approximately 5.5 miles

9. a) domain $\{x \mid x \geq 0, x \in R\}$, range $\{y \mid y \geq -13, y \in R\}$

b) $h = 0 \to$ no horizontal translation
$k = 13 \to$ vertical translation down 13 units

10. a) $y = -\sqrt{x+3} + 4$ **b)** $y = \frac{1}{2}\sqrt{x+5} - 3$

c) $y = 2\sqrt{-(x-5)} - 1$ or $y = 2\sqrt{-x+5} - 1$

d) $y = -4\sqrt{-(x-4)} + 5$ or $y = -4\sqrt{-x+4} + 5$

11. Examples:
a) $y - 1 = \sqrt{x-6}$ or $y = \sqrt{x-6} + 1$
b) $y = -\sqrt{x+7} - 9$ **c)** $y = 2\sqrt{-x+4} - 3$
d) $y = -\sqrt{-(x+5)} + 8$

12. a) $a = 760 \to$ vertical stretch factor of 760
$k = 2000 \to$ vertical translation up 2000

b)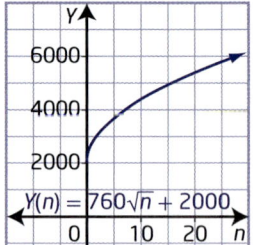

c) domain $\{n \mid n \geq 0, n \in R\}$ range $\{Y \mid Y \geq 2000, Y \in R\}$

d) The minimum yield is 2000 kg/hectare. Example: The domain and range imply that the more nitrogen added, the greater the yield without end. This is not realistic.

13. a) domain $\{d \mid -100 \leq d \leq 0, d \in R\}$
range $\{P \mid 0 \leq P \leq 20, P \in R\}$ The domain is negative indicating days remaining, and the maximum value of P is 20 million.

b) $a = -2 \to$ reflected in d-axis, vertical stretch factor of 2; $b = -1 \to$ reflected in P-axis; $k = 20 \to$ vertical translation up 20 units.

c)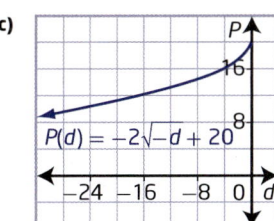

Since d is negative, then d represents the number of days remaining before release and the function has a maximum of 20 million pre-orders.

d) 9.05 million or 9 045 549 pre-orders.

14. a) Polling errors reduce as the election approaches.
b) $y = 0.49\sqrt{-x}$ There are no translations since the graph starts on the origin. The graph is reflected in the y-axis then $b = -1$. Develop the equation by using the point $(-150, 6)$ and substituting in the equation $y = a\sqrt{x}$, solving for a, then $a = 0.49$.
c) $a = 0.49 \rightarrow$ vertical stretch factor of 0.49
$b = -1 \rightarrow$ reflected in the y-axis

15. $y \approx 2.07\sqrt{-x}$

16. Examples
a) $y = -2\sqrt{x-2} + 5$ **b)** $y = \frac{2}{3}\sqrt{3-x} - 2$

17. a) China, India, and USA (The larger the country the more unfair the "one nation – one vote" system becomes.) Tuvalu, Nauru, Vatican City (The smaller the nation the more unfair the "one person – one vote" system becomes.)

b)

Nation	Percentage
China	18.6%
India	17.1%
US	4.5%
Canada	0.48%
Tuvalu	0.000 151%
Nauru	0.000 137%
Vatican City	0.000 014%

d)

Nation	Percentage
China	4.82%
India	4.62%
US	2.36%
Canada	0.77%
Tuvalu	0.014%
Nauru	0.013%
Vatican City	0.004%

c) $V(x) = \frac{1}{1000}\sqrt{x}$

e) The Penrose system gives larger nations votes based on population but also provides an opportunity for smaller nations to provide influence.

18. Answers will vary.

19. a)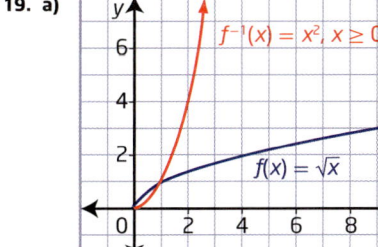

The positive domain of the inverse is the same as the range of the original function.

b)
i) $g^{-1}(x) = x^2 + 5, x \leq 0$
ii) $h^{-1}(x) = -(x-3)^2, x \geq 3$
iii) $j^{-1}(x) = \frac{1}{2}(x+6)^2 + \frac{7}{2}, x \geq -6$

20. Vertical stretch by a factor of $\frac{16}{25}$. Horizontal stretch by a factor of $\frac{7}{72}$. Reflect in both the x and y axes. Horizontal translation of 3 units left. Vertical translation of 4 units down.

C1 The parameters b and h affect the domain. For example, $y = \sqrt{x}$ has domain $x \geq 0$ but $y = \sqrt{2(x-3)}$ has domain $x \geq 3$. The parameters a and k affect the range. For example, $y = \sqrt{x}$ has range $y \geq 0$ but $y = \sqrt{x} - 4$ has range $y \geq -4$.

C2 Yes. For example, $y = \sqrt{9x}$ can be simplified to $y = 3\sqrt{x}$.

C3 The processes are similar because the parameters a, b, h, and k have the same effect on radical functions and quadratic functions. The processes are different because the base functions are different: one is the shape of a parabola and the other is the shape of half of a parabola.

C4 Step 1 $\sqrt{2}$; Step 2 $\sqrt{3}$
Step 4

Triangle Number, n	Length of Hypotenuse, L
First	$\sqrt{2} = 1.414...$
Second	$\sqrt{3} = 1.732...$
Third	$\sqrt{4} = 2$

Step 5 $L = \sqrt{n+1}$ Yes, the equation involves a horizontal translation of 1 unit left.

2.2 Square Root of a Function, pages 86 to 89

1.

$f(x)$	$\sqrt{f(x)}$
36	6
0.09	0.3
1	1
−9	undefined
2.56	1.6
0	0

2. a) $(4, 3.46)$ **b)** $(-2, 0.63)$ **c)** does not exist
d) $(0.09, 1)$ **e)** $(-5, 0)$ **f)** $(m, \sqrt{n})$

3. a) C **b)** D **c)** A **d)** B

4. a)

b) When $4 - x < 0$ then $\sqrt{4-x}$ is undefined; when $0 < 4 - x < 1$ then $\sqrt{4-x} > 4 - x$; when $4 - x > 1$ then $4 - x > \sqrt{4-x}$; $4 - x = \sqrt{4-x}$ when $y = 0$ and $y = 1$

c) The function $f(x) = \sqrt{4-x}$ is undefined when $4 - x < 0$, therefore the domain is $\{x \mid x \leq 4, x \in R\}$ whereas the function $f(x) = 4 - x$ has a domain of $\{x \mid x \in R\}$. Since $\sqrt{f(x)}$ is undefined when $f(x) < 0$, the range of $\sqrt{f(x)}$ is $\{f(x) \mid f(x) \geq 0, f(x) \in R\}$, whereas the range of $f(x) = 4 - x$ is $\{f(x) \mid f(x) \in R\}$.

5. a)

For $y = x - 2$, domain $\{x \mid x \in R\}$, range $\{y \mid y \in R\}$; for $y = \sqrt{x-2}$, domain $\{x \mid x \geq 2, x \in R\}$, range $\{y \mid y \geq 0, y \in R\}$.

The domains differ since $\sqrt{x-2}$ is undefined when $x < 2$. The range of $y = \sqrt{x-2}$ is $y \geq 0$, when $x - 2 \geq 0$.

b)

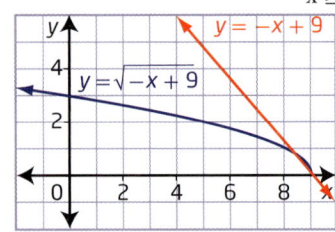

For $y = 2x + 6$, domain $\{x \mid x \in R\}$, range $\{y \mid y \in R\}$. For $y = \sqrt{2x + 6}$, domain $\{x \mid x \geq -3, x \in R\}$, range $\{y \mid y \geq 0, y \in R\}$. $y = \sqrt{2x + 6}$ is undefined when $2x + 6 < 0$, therefore $x \geq -3$ and $y \geq 0$.

c)

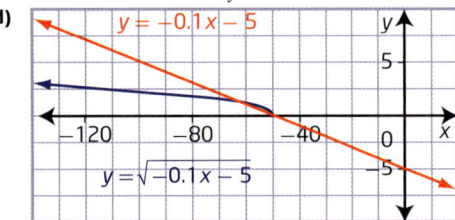

For $y = -x + 9$, domain $\{x \mid x \in R\}$, range $\{y \mid y \in R\}$; for $y = \sqrt{-x + 9}$, domain $\{x \mid x \leq 9, x \in R\}$, range $\{y \mid y \geq 0, y \in R\}$. $y = \sqrt{-x + 9}$ is undefined when $-x + 9 < 0$, therefore $x \leq 9$ and $y \geq 0$.

d)

For $y = -0.1x - 5$, domain $\{x \mid x \in R\}$, range $\{y \mid y \in R\}$; for $y = \sqrt{-0.1x - 5}$, domain $\{x \mid x \leq -50, x \in R\}$, range $\{y \mid y \geq 0, y \in R\}$. $y = \sqrt{-0.1x - 5}$ is undefined when $-0.1x - 5 < 0$, therefore $x \leq -50$ and $y \geq 0$.

6. a) For $y = x^2 - 9$, domain $\{x \mid x \in R\}$, range $\{y \mid y \geq -9, y \in R\}$.
For $y = \sqrt{x^2 - 9}$, domain $\{x \mid x \leq -3 \text{ and } x \geq 3, x \in R\}$, range $\{y \mid y \geq 0, y \in R\}$. $y = \sqrt{x^2 - 9}$ is undefined when $x^2 - 9 < 0$, therefore $x \leq -3$ and $x \geq 3$ and $y \geq 0$.

b) For $y = 2 - x^2$, domain $\{x \mid x \in R\}$, range $\{y \mid y \leq 2, y \in R\}$. For $y = \sqrt{2 - x^2}$, domain $\{x \mid -\sqrt{2} \leq x \leq \sqrt{2}, x \in R\}$, range $\{y \mid 0 \leq y \leq \sqrt{2}, y \in R\}$. $y = \sqrt{2 - x^2}$ is undefined when $2 - x^2 < 0$, therefore $x \leq \sqrt{2}$ and $x \geq -\sqrt{2}$ and $0 \leq y \leq \sqrt{2}$.

c) For $y = x^2 + 6$, domain $\{x \mid x \in R\}$, range $\{y \mid y \geq 6, y \in R\}$.
For $y = \sqrt{x^2 + 6}$, domain $\{x \mid x \in R\}$, range $\{y \mid y \geq \sqrt{6}, y \in R\}$. $y = \sqrt{x^2 + 6}$ is undefined when $x^2 + 6 < 0$, therefore $x \in R$ and $y \geq \sqrt{6}$.

d) For $y = 0.5x^2 + 3$, domain $\{x \mid x \in R\}$, range $\{y \mid y \geq 3, y \in R\}$.
For $y = \sqrt{0.5x^2 + 3}$, domain $\{x \mid x \in R\}$, range $\{y \mid y \geq \sqrt{3}, y \in R\}$. $y = \sqrt{0.5x^2 + 3}$ is undefined when $0.5x^2 + 3 < 0$, therefore $x \in R$ and $y \geq \sqrt{3}$.

7. a) Since $y = \sqrt{x^2 - 25}$ is undefined when $x^2 - 25 < 0$, the domain changes from $\{x \mid x \in R\}$ to $\{x \mid x \leq -5 \text{ and } x \geq 5, x \in R\}$ and the range changes from $\{y \mid y \geq -25, y \in R\}$ to $\{y \mid y \geq 0, y \in R\}$.

b) Since $y = \sqrt{x^2 + 3}$ is undefined when $x^2 + 3 < 0$, the range changes from $\{y \mid y \geq 3, y \in R\}$ to $\{y \mid y \geq \sqrt{3}, y \in R\}$.

c) Since $y = \sqrt{32 - 2x^2}$ is undefined when $32 - 2x^2 < 0$, the domain changes from $\{x \mid x \in R\}$ to $\{x \mid -4 \leq x \leq 4, x \in R\}$ and the range changes from $\{y \mid y \leq 32, y \in R\}$ to $\{y \mid 0 \leq y \leq \sqrt{32}, y \in R\}$ or $\{y \mid 0 \leq y \leq 4\sqrt{2}, y \in R\}$.

d) Since $y = \sqrt{5x^2 + 50}$ is undefined when $5x^2 + 50 < 0$, the range changes from $\{y \mid y \geq 50, y \in R\}$ to $\{y \mid y \geq \sqrt{50}, y \in R\}$ or $\{y \mid y \geq 5\sqrt{2}, y \in R\}$.

8. a)

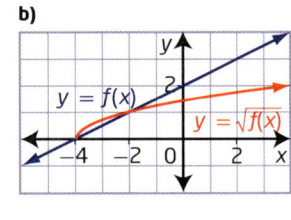

b)

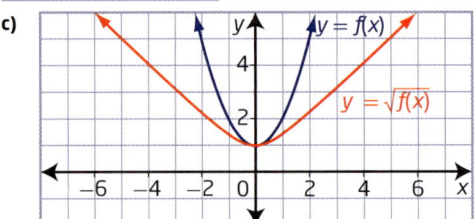

c)

9. a) and **b)**

i)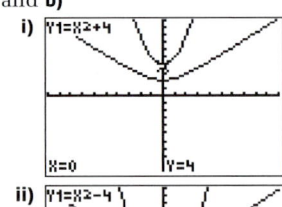

For $y = x^2 + 4$, domain $\{x \mid x \in R\}$, range $\{y \mid y \geq 4, y \in R\}$

ii)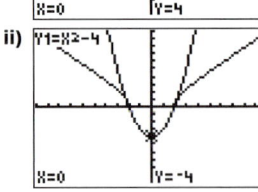

For $y = x^2 - 4$, domain $\{x \mid x \in R\}$, range $\{y \mid y \geq -4, y \in R\}$

iii)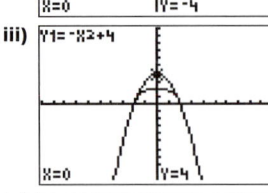

For $y = -x^2 + 4$, domain $\{x \mid x \in R\}$, range $\{y \mid y \leq 4, y \in R\}$

iv)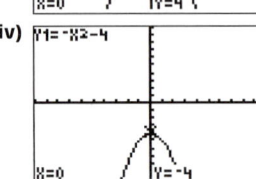

For $y = -x^2 - 4$, domain $\{x \mid x \in R\}$, range $\{y \mid y \leq -4, y \in R\}$.

c) The graph of $y = \sqrt{j(x)}$ does not exist because all of the points on the graph $y = j(x)$ are below the x-axis. Since all values of $j(x) < 0$, then $\sqrt{j(x)}$ is undefined and produces no graph in the real number system.

d) The domains of the square root of a function are the same as the domains of the function when the value of the function ≥ 0. The domains of the square root of a function do not exist when the value of the function < 0. The ranges of the square root of a function are the square root of the range of the original function, except when the value of the function < 0 then the range is undefined.

10. a) For $y = x^2 - 4$, domain $\{x \mid x \in R\}$, range $\{y \mid y \geq -4, y \in R\}$; for $y = \sqrt{x^2 - 4}$, domain $\{x \mid x \leq -2$ and $x \geq 2, x \in R\}$, range $\{y \mid y \geq 0, y \in R\}$.

b) The value of y in the interval $(-2, 2)$ is negative therefore the domain of $y = \sqrt{x^2 - 4}$ is undefined and has no values in the interval $(-2, 2)$.

11. a) 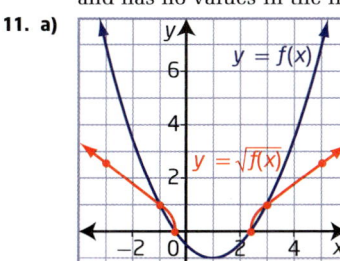 I sketched the graph by locating key points, including invariant points, and determining the image points on the graph of the square root of the function.

b) For $y = f(x)$, domain $\{x \mid x \in R\}$, range $\{y \mid y \geq -1, y \in R\}$; for $y = \sqrt{f(x)}$, domain $\{x \mid x \leq -0.4$ and $x \geq 2.4, x \in R\}$, range $\{y \mid y \geq 0, y \in R\}$

The domain of $y = \sqrt{f(x)}$, consists of all values in the domain of $f(x)$ for which $f(x) \geq 0$, and the range of $y = \sqrt{f(x)}$, consists of the square roots of all values in the range of $f(x)$ for which $f(x)$ is defined.

12. a) $d = \sqrt{h^2 + 12756h}$
b) domain $\{h \mid h \geq 0, h \in R\}$, range $\{d \mid d \geq 0, d \in R\}$
c) Find the point of intersection between the graph of the function and $h = 800$. The distance will be expressed as the d value of the ordered pair (h, d). In this case, d is approximately equal to 3293.
d) Yes, if h could be any real number then the domain is $\{h \mid h \leq -12\ 756$ or $h \geq 0, h \in R\}$ and the range would remain the same- since all square root values must be greater than or equal to 0.

13. a) No, since $\sqrt{a}$, $a < 0$ is undefined, then $y = \sqrt{f(x)}$ will be undefined when $f(x) < 0$, but $f(x)$ represents values of the range not the domain as Chris stated.
b) If the range consists of negative values, then you know that the graph represents $y = f(x)$ and not $y = \sqrt{f(x)}$.

14. a) $v = \sqrt{3.24 - h^2}$
b) domain $\{h \mid 0 \leq h \leq 1.8, h \in R\}$, range $\{v \mid 0 \leq v \leq 1.8, v \in R\}$ since both h and v represent distances.
c) approximately 1.61 m

15. Step 1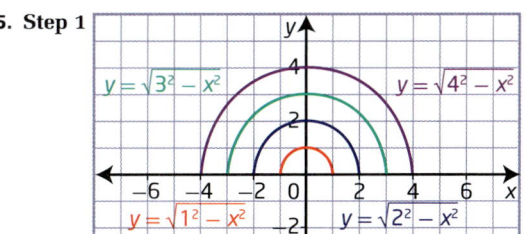

Step 2 The parameter a determines the minimum value of the domain $(-a)$ and the maximum value of the domain (a); therefore the domain is $\{x \mid -a \leq x \leq a, x \in R\}$. The parameter a also determines the maximum value of the range, where the minimum value of the range is 0; therefore the range is $\{y \mid 0 \leq y \leq a, y \in R\}$.

Step 3 Example: $y = \sqrt{3^2 - x^2}$ the reflection of the graph in the x-axis is the equation $y = -\sqrt{3^2 - x^2}$.

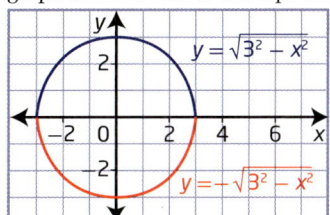 The graph forms a circle.

16. a) $(-27, 4\sqrt{3})$ b) $(-6, 12 - 2\sqrt{3})$
c) $(26, 6 - 4\sqrt{3})$

17. a)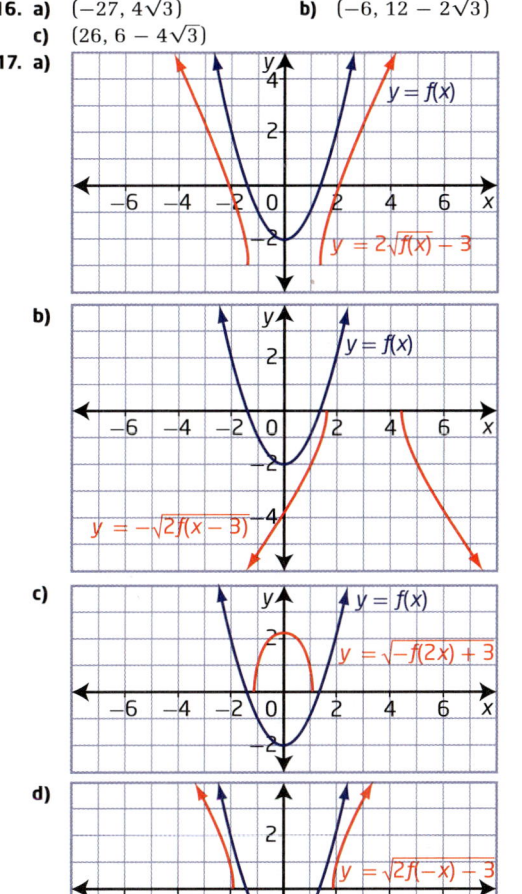
b)
c)
d)

18. Example: Sketch the graph in the following order:
1) $y = 2f(x)$ — Stretch vertically by a factor of 2.
2) $y = 2f(x - 3)$ — Translate horizontally 3 units right.
3) $y = \sqrt{2f(x - 3)}$ — Plot invariant points and sketch a smooth curve above the x-axis.
4) $y = -\sqrt{2f(x - 3)}$ — Reflect $y = \sqrt{2f(x - 3)}$ in the x-axis.

19. a) $r = \sqrt{\dfrac{A}{6\pi}}$ **b)** $r = \sqrt{\dfrac{A}{\pi(1 + \sqrt{37})}}$

C1 Example: Choose 4 to 5 key points on the graph of $y = f(x)$. Transform the points $(x, y) \to (x, \sqrt{y})$. Plot the new points and smooth out the graph. If you cannot get an idea of the general shape of the graph, choose more points to graph.

C2 The graph of $y = 16 - 4x$ is a linear function spanning from quadrant II to quadrant IV with an x-intercept of 4 and a y-intercept of 16. The graph of $y = \sqrt{16 - 4x}$ only exists when the graph of $y = 16 - 4x$ is on or above the x-axis. The y-intercept is at $\sqrt{16} = 4$ while the x-intercept stays the same. x-values for $x \leq 4$ are the same for both functions and the y-values for $y = \sqrt{16 - 4x}$ are the square root of y values for $y = 16 - 4x$.

C3 No, it is not possible, because the graph of $y = f(x)$ may exist when $y < 0$ but the graph of $y = \sqrt{f(x)}$ does not exist when $y < 0$.

C4 a)

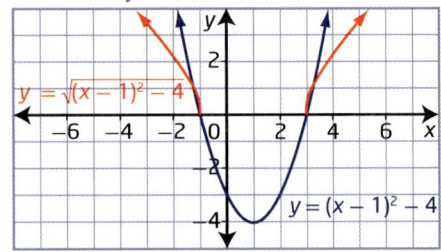

b) The graph of $y = (x - 1)^2 - 4$ is a quadratic function with a vertex of $(1, -4)$, y-intercept of -3, and x-intercepts of -1 and 3. It is above the x-axis when $x > 3$ and $x < -1$.
The graph of $y = \sqrt{(x - 1)^2 - 4}$ has the same x-intercepts but no y-intercept. The graph only exists when $x > 3$ and $x < -1$.

2.3 Solving Radical Equations Graphically, pages 96 to 98

1. a) B **b)** A **c)** D **d)** C

2. a) $x = 9$ **b)**

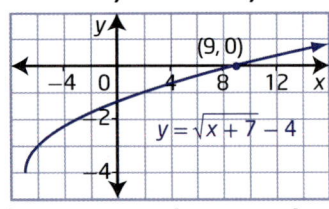

c) The roots of the equation are the same as the x-intercept on the graph.

3. a) 24.714

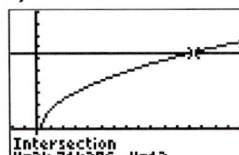

b) -117.273

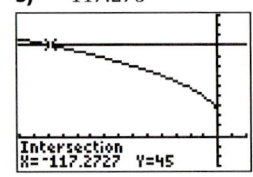

c) ± 4.796

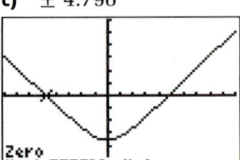

d) no solution

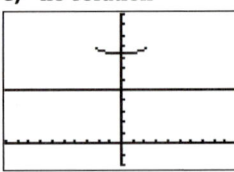

4. a) $x = 5.08\overline{3}$ **b)**

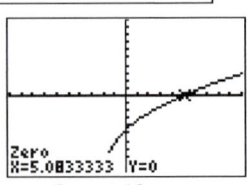

5. a) $x = 65$, $x \geq \dfrac{9}{2}$ **b)** $x = 3$, $x \leq 12$

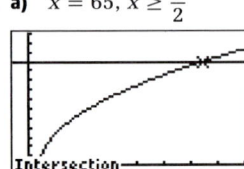 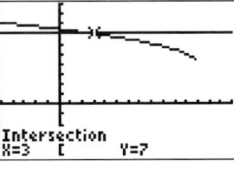

c) $x = -3.95$, $x \geq -6.4$ **d)** $x = -19.5$, $x \leq 12.5$

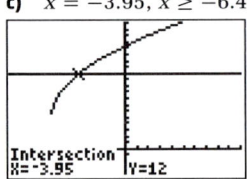 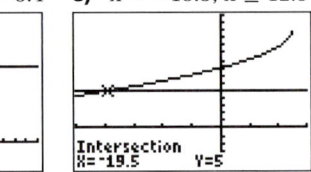

6. a) $x = \dfrac{7}{2}$, $x = -1$

b) $x = 8$, $x = -2$, $x \leq -\dfrac{\sqrt{14}}{2}$ or $x \geq \dfrac{\sqrt{14}}{2}$

c) $x = 1.8$, $x = -1$, $-\dfrac{\sqrt{13}}{2} \leq x \leq \dfrac{\sqrt{13}}{2}$

d) $x = 0$, $x = 2$, $\dfrac{-3\sqrt{2}}{2} \leq x \leq \dfrac{3\sqrt{2}}{2}$

7. a) $x \approx -2.725$, $x \leq 8$ **b)** no real roots, $x \geq 7$

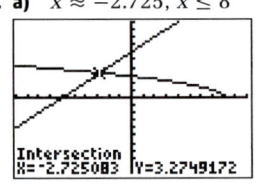 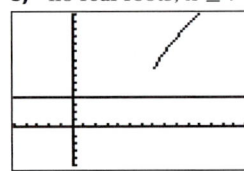

c) $x = 3$, $x \geq \dfrac{\sqrt{33}}{3}$ or $x \leq -\dfrac{\sqrt{33}}{3}$ **d)** $x = 2$, $x \geq 2$ or $x \leq -2$

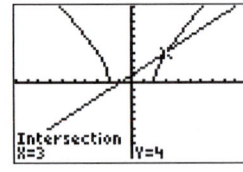

8. a) $a \approx 13.10$ **b)** $a \approx -2.25$

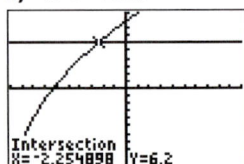

c) no solution
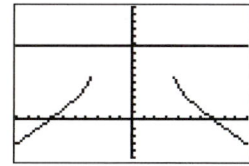

d) $a \approx -2.25, a \approx 15.65$
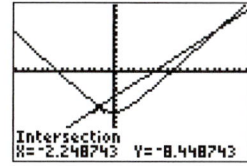 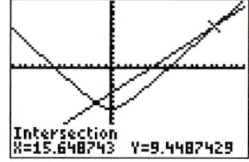

9. a) $6 + \sqrt{x+4} = 2$
$\sqrt{x+4} = -4$
$x + 4 = 16$
$x = 12$
Left Side $= 6 + \sqrt{12 + 4}$
$= 6 + \sqrt{16}$
$= 6 + 4$
$= 10$
Right Side $= 2$
Left Side $\neq$ Right Side
Since $10 \neq 2$, there is no solution.

b) Yes, if you isolate the radical expression like $\sqrt{x+4} = -4$, if the radical is equal to a negative value then there is no solution.

10. Greg $\rightarrow N(t) = 1.3\sqrt{t} + 4.2 = 1.3\sqrt{6} + 4.2$
≈ 7.38 million,
Yolanda $\rightarrow N(t) = 1.3\sqrt{t} + 4.2 = 1.3\sqrt{1.5} + 4.2$
≈ 5.79 million
Greg is correct, it will take more than 6 years for the entire population to be affected.

11. approximately 99 cm

12. a) Yes   **b)** 3000 kg

13. No, $\sqrt{x^2} = 9$ has two possible solutions ± 9, whereas $(\sqrt{x})^2 = 9$ has only one solution $+9$.

14. $x = \dfrac{3 + \sqrt{5}}{2}$

15. a) 5 m/s   **b)** 75.2 kg

16. $c = -2$ or 1

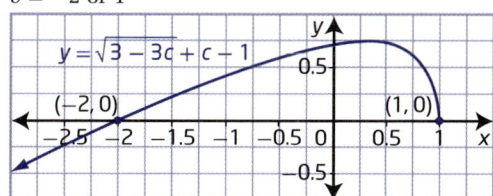

If the function $y = \sqrt{-3(x+c)} + c$ passes through the point $(0.25, 0.75)$, what is the value of c?

17. Lengths of sides are 55.3 cm, 60 cm, and 110.6 cm or 30.7 cm, 60 cm, and 61.4 cm.

C1 The x-intercepts of the graph of a function are the solutions to the corresponding equation. Example: A graph of the function $y = \sqrt{x-1} - 2$ would show that the x-intercept has a value of 5. The equation that corresponds to this function is $0 = \sqrt{x-1} - 2$ and the solution to the equation is 5.

C2 a) $s = \sqrt{9.8d}$ where s represents speed in metres per second and d represents depth in metres.

b) $s = \sqrt{9.8d}$
$s = \sqrt{(9.8 \text{ m/s}^2)(2500 \text{ m})}$
$s = \sqrt{24\,500 \text{ m}^2/\text{s}^2}$
$s \approx 156.5$ m/s

c) approximately 4081.6 m

d) Example: I prefer the algebraic method because it is faster and I do not have to adjust window settings.

C3 Radical equations only have a solution in the real number system if the graph of the corresponding function has an x-intercept. For example, $y = \sqrt{x} + 4$ has no real solutions because there is no x-intercept.

C4 Extraneous roots occur when solving equations algebraically. Extraneous roots of a radical equation may occur anytime an expression is squared. For example, $x^2 = 1$ has two possible solutions, $x = \pm 1$. You can identify extraneous roots by graphing and by substituting into the original equation.

Chapter 2 Review, pages 99 to 101

1. a)
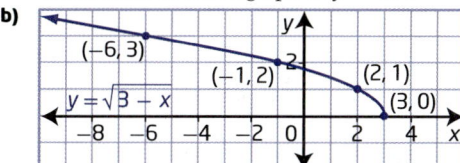
domain $\{x \mid x \geq 0, x \in R\}$
range $\{y \mid y \geq 0, y \in R\}$ All values in the table lie on the smooth curve graph of $y = \sqrt{x}$.

b)
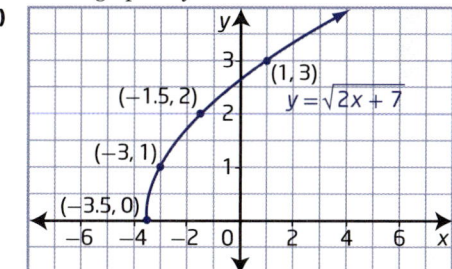
domain $\{x \mid x \leq 3, x \in R\}$
range $\{y \mid y \geq 0, y \in R\}$ All points in the table lie on the graph of $y = \sqrt{3 - x}$.

c)

domain $\{x \mid x \geq -3.5, x \in R\}$
range $\{y \mid y \geq 0, y \in R\}$ All points in the table lie on the graph of $y = \sqrt{2x + 7}$.

2. Use $y = a\sqrt{b(x - h)} + k$ to describe transformations.

a) $a = 5 \rightarrow$ vertical stretch factor of 5
$h = -20 \rightarrow$ horizontal translation left 20 units;
domain $\{x \mid x \geq -20, x \in R\}$; range $\{y \mid y \geq 0, y \in R\}$

b) $b = -2 \rightarrow$ horizontal stretch factor of $\dfrac{1}{2}$, then reflected on y-axis: $k = -8 \rightarrow$ vertical translation of 8 units down.
domain $\{x \mid x \leq 0, x \in R\}$; range $\{y \mid y \geq -8, y \in R\}$

c) $a = -1 \to$ reflect in x-axis
$b = \frac{1}{6} \to$ horizontal stretch factor of 6
$h = 11 \to$ horizontal translation right 11 units;
domain $\{x \mid x \geq 11, x \in R\}$, range $\{y \mid y \leq 0, y \in R\}$.

3. a) $y = \sqrt{\frac{1}{10}x} + 12$, domain $\{x \mid x \geq 0, x \in R\}$,
range $\{y \mid y \geq 12, y \in R\}$
b) $y = -2.5\sqrt{x+9}$
domain $\{x \mid x \geq -9, x \in R\}$, range $\{y \mid y \leq 0, y \in R\}$
c) $y = \frac{1}{20}\sqrt{-\frac{2}{5}(x-7)} - 3$,
domain $\{x \mid x \leq 7, x \in R\}$, range $\{y \mid y \geq -3, y \in R\}$

4. a) domain $\{x \mid x \geq 1, x \in R\}$, range $\{y \mid y \leq 2, y \in R\}$

b) domain $\{x \mid x \leq 0, x \in R\}$, range $\{y \mid y \geq -4, y \in R\}$

c)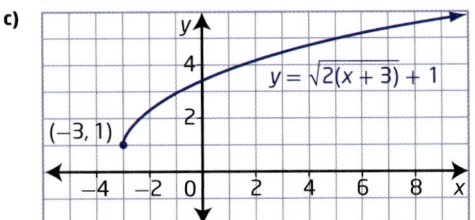
domain $\{x \mid x \geq -3, x \in R\}$, range $\{y \mid y \geq 1, y \in R\}$

5. The domain is affected by a horizontal translation of 4 units right and by no reflection on the y-axis. The domain will have values of x greater than or equal to 4, due to a translation of the graph 4 units right. The range is affected by vertical translation of 9 units up and a reflection on the x-axis. The range will be less than or equal to 9, because the graph has been moved up 9 units and reflected on the x-axis, therefore the range is less than or equal to 9, instead of greater than or equal to 9.

6. a) Given the general equation $y = a\sqrt{b(x-h)} + k$ to describe transformations, $a = 100$ indicates a vertical stretch by a factor of 100, $k = 500$ indicates a vertical translation up 500 units.
b)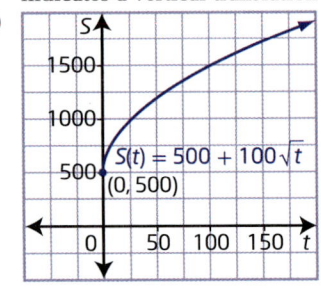
Since the minimum value of the graph is 500, the minimum estimated sales will be 500 units.

c) domain $\{t \mid t \geq 0, t \in R\}$ The domain means that time is positive in this situation.
range $\{S(t) \mid S(t) \geq 500, S(t) \in W\}$. The range means that the minimum sales are 500 units.
d) about 1274 units

7. a) $y = \sqrt{\frac{1}{4}(x+3)} + 2$ b) $y = -2\sqrt{x+4} + 3$
c) $y = 4\sqrt{-(x-6)} - 4$

8. a) For $y = x - 2$, domain $\{x \mid x \in R\}$,
range $\{y \mid y \in R\}$; for $y = \sqrt{x-2}$,
domain $\{x \mid x \geq 2, x \in R\}$,
range $\{y \mid y \geq 0, y \in R\}$. The domain changes because the square root function has restrictions. The range changes because the function only exists on or above the x-axis.
b) For $y = 10 - x$, domain $\{x \mid x \in R\}$,
range $\{y \mid y \in R\}$; for $y = \sqrt{10-x}$,
domain $\{x \mid x \leq 10, x \in R\}$,
range $\{y \mid y \geq 0, y \in R\}$ The domain changes because the square root function has restrictions. The range changes because the function only exists on or above the x-axis.
c) For $y = 4x + 11$, domain $\{x \mid x \in R\}$,
range $\{y \mid y \in R\}$; for $y = \sqrt{4x+11}$,
domain $\{x \mid x \geq -\frac{11}{4}, x \in R\}$,
range $\{y \mid y \geq 0, y \in R\}$. The domain changes because the square root function has restrictions. The range changes because the function only exists on or above the x-axis.

9. a) Plot invariant points at the intersection of the graph and lines $y = 0$ and $y = 1$. Plot any points $(x, \sqrt{y})$ where the value of y is a perfect square. Sketch a smooth curve through the invariant points and points satisfying $(x, \sqrt{y})$.
b) $y = \sqrt{f(x)}$ is positive when $f(x) > 0$,
$y = \sqrt{f(x)}$ does not exist when $f(x) < 0$.
$\sqrt{f(x)} > f(x)$ when $0 < f(x) < 1$ and
$f(x) > \sqrt{f(x)}$ when $f(x) > 1$
c) For $f(x)$: domain $\{x \mid x \subset R\}$,
range $\{y \mid y \in R\}$; for $\sqrt{f(x)}$,
domain $\{x \mid x \geq -6, x \in R\}$,
range $\{y \mid y \geq 0, y \in R\}$, since $\sqrt{f(x)}$ is undefined when $f(x) < 0$.

10. a) $y = 4 - x^2 \to$ domain $\{x \mid x \in R\}$,
range $\{y \mid y \leq 4, y \in R\}$ for $y = \sqrt{4-x^2} \to$
domain $\{x \mid -2 \leq x \leq 2, x \in R\}$,
range $\{y \mid 0 \leq y \leq 2, y \in R\}$,
since $4 - x^2 > 0$ only between -2 and 2 then the domain of $y = \sqrt{4 - x^2}$ is $-2 \leq x \leq 2$. In the domain of $-2 \leq x \leq 2$ the maximum value of $y = 4 - x^2$ is 4, so the maximum value of $y = \sqrt{4 - x^2}$ is $\sqrt{4} = 2$ then the range of the function $y = \sqrt{4 - x^2}$ will be $0 \leq y \leq 2$.

b) $y = 2x^2 + 24 \rightarrow$ domain $\{x \mid x \in R\}$, range $\{y \mid y \geq 24, y \in R\}$ for $y = \sqrt{2x^2 + 24} \rightarrow$ domain $\{x \mid x \in R\}$, range $\{y \mid y \geq \sqrt{24}, y \in R\}$. The domain does not change since the entire graph of $y = 2x^2 + 24$ is above the x-axis. The range changes since the entire graph moves up 24 units and the graph itself opens up, so the range becomes $y \geq \sqrt{24}$.

c) $y = x^2 - 6x \rightarrow$ domain $\{x \mid x \in R\}$, range $\{y \mid y \geq -9, y \in R\}$ for $y = \sqrt{x^2 - 6x} \rightarrow$ domain $\{x \mid x \leq 0$ or $x \geq 6, x \in R\}$, range $\{y \mid y \geq 0, y \in R\}$, since $x^2 - 6x < 0$ between 0 and 6, then the domain is undefined in the interval $(0, 6)$ and exists when $x \leq 0$ or $x \geq 6$. The range changes because the function only exists above the x-axis.

11. a) $h(d) = \sqrt{625 - d^2}$

b)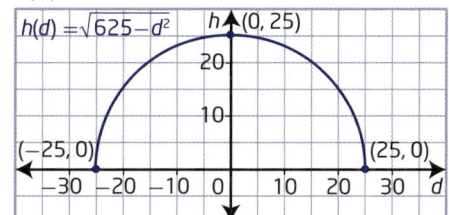

domain $\{d \mid -25 \leq d \leq 25, d \in R\}$
range $\{h \mid 0 \leq h \leq 25, h \in R\}$

c) In this situation, the values of h and d must be positive to express a positive distance. Therefore the domain changes to $\{d \mid 0 \leq d \leq 25, d \in R\}$. Since the range of the original function $h(d) = \sqrt{625 - d^2}$ is always positive then the range does not change.

12. a) 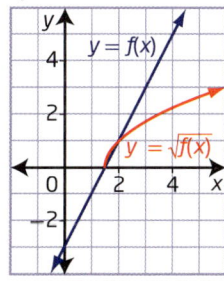 b)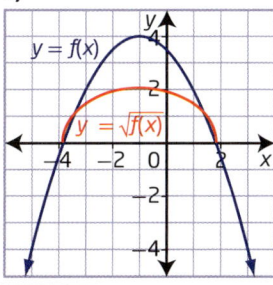

c)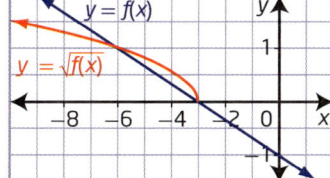

13. a) $x = 46$ b)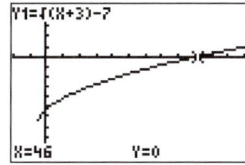

c) The root of the equation and the x value of the x-intercept are the same.

14. a) $x \approx 3.571$ 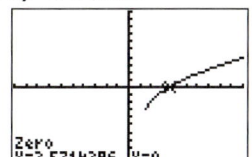 b) $x \approx -119.667$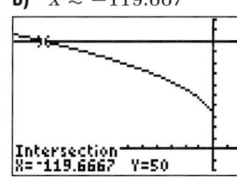

c) $x \approx -7.616$ and $x \approx 7.616$

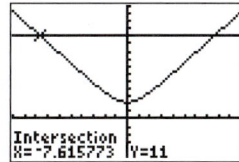

15. 4.13 m

16. a) $x = 13.4$ 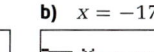 b) $x = -17$

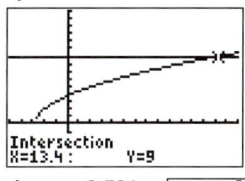 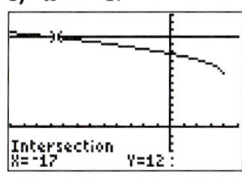

c) $x \approx 8.781$

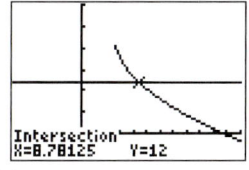

d) $x = -3$ and 1

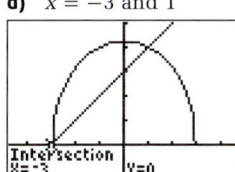 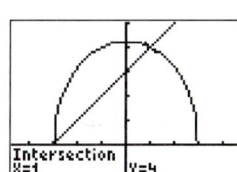

17. a) Jaime found two possible answers which are determined by solving a quadratic equation.
b) Carly found only one intersection at (5, 5) or x-intercept (5, 0) determined by possibly graphing.
c) Atid found an extraneous root of $x = 2$.

18. a) 130 m² b) 6 m

Chapter 2 Practice Test, pages 102 to 103

1. B **2.** A **3.** A **4.** C **5.** D **6.** B

7. $x \approx -16.62$

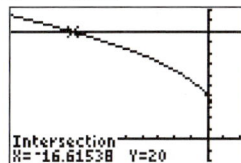

8. $y = 4\sqrt{x}$ or $y = \sqrt{16x}$

9. For $y = 7 - x \rightarrow$ domain $\{x \mid x \in R\}$, range $\{y \mid y \in R\}$. Since $y = \sqrt{7 - x}$ is the square root of the y-values for the function $y = 7 - x$, then the domain and ranges of $y = \sqrt{7 - x}$ will differ. Since $7 - x < 0$ when $x > 7$, then the domain of $y = \sqrt{7 - x}$ will be $\{x \mid x \leq 7, x \in R\}$ and since $\sqrt{7 - x}$ indicates positive values only, then the range of $y = \sqrt{7 - x}$ is $\{y \mid y \geq 0, y \in R\}$.

10. The domain of $y = f(x)$ is $\{x \mid x \in R\}$, and the range of $y = f(x)$ is $\{y \mid y \leq 8, y \in R\}$. The domain of $y = \sqrt{f(x)}$ is $\{x \mid -2 \leq x \leq 2, x \in R\}$ and the range of $y = \sqrt{f(x)}$ is $\{y \mid 0 \leq y \leq \sqrt{8}, y \in R\}$.

11.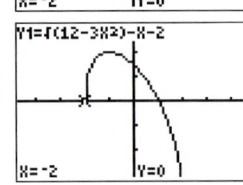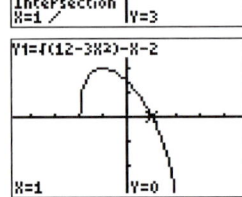

$x = -2, x = 1$

12. $4 + \sqrt{x + 1} = x$
$\sqrt{x + 1} = x - 4$
$x + 1 = (x - 4)^2$
$x + 1 = x^2 - 8x + 16$
$0 = x^2 - 9x + 15$
$x = \dfrac{-b \pm \sqrt{b^2 - 4ac}}{2a}$
$= \dfrac{-(-9) \pm \sqrt{(-9)^2 - 4(1)(15)}}{2(1)}$
≈ 2.2 or 6.8

By checking, 2.2 is an extraneous root, therefore $x \approx 6.8$.

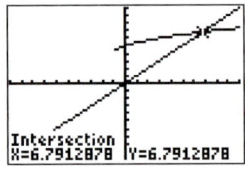

$x \approx 6.8$

13. a) Given the general equation $y = a\sqrt{b(x - h)} + k$ to describe transformations, $b = 255 \rightarrow$ indicating a horizontal stretch by a factor of $\dfrac{1}{255}$. To sketch the graph of $S = \sqrt{255d}$, graph the function $S = \sqrt{d}$ and apply a horizontal stretch of $\dfrac{1}{255}$, every point on the graph of $S = \sqrt{d}$ will become $\left(\dfrac{d}{255}, S\right)$.

b)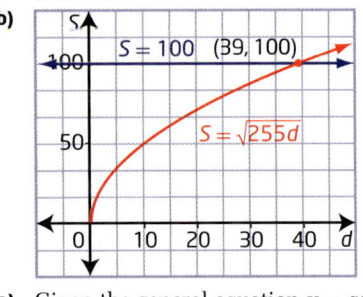

$d \approx 39$ m
The skid mark of the vehicle will be approximately 39 m.

14. a) Given the general equation $y = a\sqrt{b(x - h)} + k$ to describe transformations, $a = -1 \rightarrow$ reflection of the graph in the x-axis, $b = 2 \rightarrow$ horizontal stretch by a factor of $\dfrac{1}{2}$, $k = 3 \rightarrow$ vertical translation up 3 units.

b)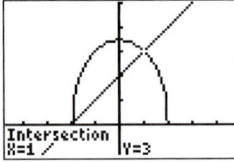

c) domain $\{x \mid x \geq 0, x \in R\}$, range $\{y \mid y \leq 3, y \in R\}$.
d) The domain remains the same because there was no horizontal translation or reflection on the y-axis. But since the graph was reflected on the x-axis and moved up 3 units and then the range becomes $y \leq 3$.
e) The equation $5 + \sqrt{2x} = 8$ can be rewritten as $0 = -\sqrt{2x} + 3$. Therefore the x-intercept of the graph $y = -\sqrt{2x} + 3$ is the solution of the equation $5 + \sqrt{2x} = 8$.

15.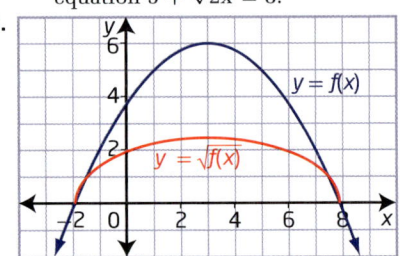

Step 1 Plot invariant points at the intersection of $y = f(x)$ and functions $y = 0$ and $y = 1$.
Step 2 Plot points at $\sqrt{\text{max value}}$ and $\sqrt{\text{perfect square value of } y = f(x)}$
Step 3 Join all points with a smooth curve, remember that the graph of $y = \sqrt{f(x)}$ is above the original graph for the interval $0 \leq y \leq 1$. Note that for the interval where $f(x) < 0$, the function $y = \sqrt{f(x)}$ is undefined and has no graph.

16. a) $y = (\sqrt{5})\sqrt{-(x - 5)}$
b) domain $\{x \mid 0 \leq x \leq 5, x \in R\}$, range $\{y \mid 0 \leq y \leq 5, y \in R\}$.
Domain: x cannot be negative nor greater than half the diameter of the base, or 5. Range: y cannot be negative nor greater than the height of the roof, or 5.
c) 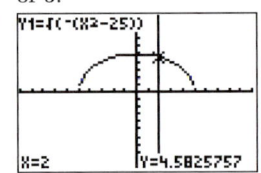 The height of the roof 2 m from the centre is about 4.58 m.

Chapter 3 Polynomial Functions

3.1 Characteristics of Polynomial Functions, pages 114 to 117

1. a) No, this is a square root function.
b) Yes, this is a polynomial function of degree 1.
c) No, this is an exponential function.
d) Yes, this is a polynomial function of degree 4.
e) No, this function has a variable with a negative exponent.
f) Yes, this is a polynomial function of degree 3.

2. a) degree 1, linear, −1, 3
   b) degree 2, quadratic, 9, 0
   c) degree 4, quartic, 3, 1
   d) degree 3, cubic, −3, 4
   e) degree 5, quintic, −2, 9
   f) degree 0, constant, 0, −6
3. a) odd degree, positive leading coefficient, 3 x-intercepts, domain $\{x \mid x \in \mathbb{R}\}$ and range $\{y \mid y \in \mathbb{R}\}$
   b) odd degree, positive leading coefficient, 5 x-intercepts, domain $\{x \mid x \in \mathbb{R}\}$ and range $\{y \mid y \in \mathbb{R}\}$
   c) even degree, negative leading coefficient, 3 x-intercepts, domain $\{x \mid x \in \mathbb{R}\}$ and range $\{y \mid y \leq 16.9, y \in \mathbb{R}\}$
   d) even degree, negative leading coefficient, 0 x-intercepts, domain $\{x \mid x \in \mathbb{R}\}$ and range $\{y \mid y \leq -3, y \in \mathbb{R}\}$
4. a) degree 2 with positive leading coefficient, parabola opens upward, maximum of 2 x-intercepts, y-intercept of −1
   b) degree 3 with negative leading coefficient, extends from quadrant II to IV, maximum of 3 x-intercept, y-intercept of 5
   c) degree 4 with negative leading coefficient, opens downward, maximum of 4 x-intercepts, y-intercept of 4
   d) degree 5 with positive leading coefficient, extends from quadrant III to I, maximum of 5 x-intercepts, y-intercept of 0
   e) degree 1 with negative leading coefficient, extends from quadrant II to IV, 1 x-intercept, y-intercept of 4
   f) degree 4 with positive leading coefficient, opens upward, maximum of 4 x-intercepts, y-intercept of 0
5. Example: Jake is right as long as the leading coefficient a is a positive integer. The simplest example would be a quadratic function with $a = 2$, $b = 2$, and $n = 2$.
6. a) degree 4
   b) The leading coefficient is 1 and the constant is −3000. The constant represents the initial cost.
   c) degree 4 with a positive leading coefficient, opens upward, 2 x-intercepts, y-intercept of −3000
   d) The domain is $\{x \mid x \geq 0, x \in \mathbb{R}\}$, since it is impossible to have negative snowboard sales.
   e) The positive x-intercept is the breakeven point.
   f) Let $x = 15$, then $P(x) = 62\ 625$.
7. a) cubic function
   b) The leading coefficient is −3 and the constant is 0.
   c)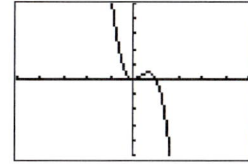
   d) The domain is $\{d \mid 0 \leq d \leq 1, d \in \mathbb{R}\}$ because you cannot give negative drug amounts and you must have positive reaction times.
8. a) For 1 ring, the total number of hexagons is given by $f(1) = 1$. For 2 rings, the total number of hexagons is given by $f(2) = 7$. For 3 rings, the total number of hexagons is given by $f(3) = 19$.
   b) 397 hexagons

9. a) End behaviour: the curve extends up in quadrants I and II; domain $\{t \mid t \in \mathbb{R}\}$; range $\{P \mid P \geq 10\ 071, P \in \mathbb{R}\}$; the range for the period $\{t \mid 0 \leq t \leq 20, t \in \mathbb{R}\}$ that the population model can be used is $\{P \mid 15\ 000 \leq P \leq 37\ 000, P \in \mathbb{R}\}$.
   t-intercepts: none; P-intercept: 15 000
   b) 15 000 people c) 18 000 people d) 18 years
10. a) 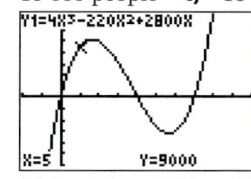 From the graph, the height of a single box must be greater than 0 and cannot be between 20 cm and 35 cm.
    b) $V(x) = 4x(x − 20)(x − 35)$. The factored form clearly shows the three possible x-intercepts.
11. a) The graphs in each pair are the same.
    Let n represent a whole number, then $2n$ represents an even whole number.
    $y = (-x)^{2n}$
    $y = (-1)^{2n} x^{2n}$
    $y = 1^n x^{2n}$
    $y = x^{2n}$
    b) The graphs in each pair are reflections of each other in the y-axis.
    Let n represent a whole number, then $2n + 1$ represents an odd whole number.
    $y = (-x)^{2n+1}$
    $y = (-1)^{2n+1} x^{2n+1}$
    $y = (-1)^{2n}(-1)^1 x^{2n+1}$
    $y = -(1)^n x^{2n+1}$
    $y = -x^{2n+1}$
    c) For even whole numbers, the graph of the functions are unchanged. For odd whole numbers, the graph of the functions are reflected in the y-axis.
12. a) vertical stretch by a factor of 3 and translation of 4 units right and 2 units up
    b) vertical stretch by a factor of 3 and translation of 4 units right and 2 units up
    c)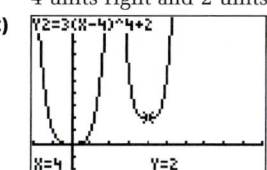
13. If there is only one root, $y = (x − a)^n$, then the function will only cross the x-axis once in the case of an odd-degree function and it will only touch the x-axis once if it is an even-degree function.
C1 Example: Odd degree: At least one x-intercept and up to a maximum of n x-intercepts, where n is the degree of the function. No maximum or minimum points. Domain is $\{x \mid x \in \mathbb{R}\}$ and range is $\{y \mid y \in \mathbb{R}\}$.
Even degree: From zero to a maximum of n x-intercepts, where n is the degree of the function. Domain is $\{x \mid x \in \mathbb{R}\}$ and the range depends on the maximum or minimum value of the function.
C2 a) Examples:
   i) $y = x^3$ ii) $y = x^2$
   iii) $y = -x^3$ iv) $y = -x^2$

b) Example: Parts i) and ii) have positive leading coefficients, while parts iii) and iv) have negative leading coefficients. Parts i) and iii) are odd-degree functions, while parts ii) and iv) are even-degree functions.

C3 Example: The line $y = x$ and polynomial functions with odd degree greater than one and positive leading coefficient extend from quadrant III to quadrant I. Both have no maximums or minimums. Both have the same domain and range. Odd degree polynomial functions have at least one x-intercept.

C4 Step 1

Function	Degree	End Behaviour
$y = x + 2$	1	extends from quadrant III to I
$y = -3x + 1$	1	extends from quadrant II to IV
$y = x^2 - 4$	2	opens upward
$y = -2x^2 - 2x + 4$	2	opens downward
$y = x^3 - 4x$	3	extends from quadrant III to I
$y = -x^3 + 3x - 2$	3	extends from quadrant II to IV
$y = 2x^3 + 16$	3	extends from quadrant III to I
$y = -x^3 - 4x$	3	extends from quadrant II to IV
$y = x^4 - 4x^2 + 5$	4	opens upward
$y = -x^4 + x^3 + 4x^2 - 4x$	4	opens downward
$y = x^4 + 2x^2 + 1$	4	opens upward
$y = x^5 - 2x^4 - 3x^3 + 5x^2 + 4x - 1$	5	extends from quadrant III to I
$y = x^5 - 1$	5	extends from quadrant III to I
$y = -x^5 + x^4 + 8x^3 + 8x^2 - 16x - 16$	5	extends from quadrant II to IV
$y = x(x + 1)^2(x + 4)^2$	5	extends from quadrant III to I

Step 2 The leading coefficient determines if it opens upward or downward; in the case of odd functions it determines if it is increasing or decreasing.
Step 3 Always have at least one minimum or maximum. Not all functions will have the same range. Either opens upward or downward.
Step 4. Always have the same domain and range. Either extends from quadrant III to I or from quadrant II to IV. No maximum or minimum.

3.2 Remainder Theorem, pages 124 to 125

1. a) $\dfrac{x^2 + 10x - 24}{x - 2} = x + 12$
  b) $x \neq 2$ **c)** $(x - 2)(x + 12)$
  d) Multiplying the statement in part c) yields $x^2 + 10x - 24$.
2. a) $\dfrac{3x^4 - 4x^3 - 6x^2 + 17x - 8}{x + 1}$
  $= 3x^3 - 7x^2 + x + 16 - \dfrac{24}{x + 1}$
  b) $x \neq -1$
  c) $(x + 1)(3x^3 - 7x^2 + x + 16) - 24$
  d) Expanding the statement in part c) yields $3x^4 - 4x^3 - 6x^2 + 17x - 8$.
3. a) $Q(x) = x^2 + 4x + 1$ **b)** $Q(x) = x^2 + 4x + 1$
  c) $Q(w) = 2w^2 - 3w + 4$ **d)** $Q(m) = 9m^2 + 3m + 6$
  e) $Q(t) = t^3 + 5t^2 - 8t + 7$
  f) $Q(y) = 2y^3 + 6y^2 + 15y + 45$

4. a) $Q(x) = x^2 - 3x + 12$ **b)** $Q(m) = m^3 + m + 14$
  c) $Q(x) = -x^3 + x^2 - x + 1$ **d)** $Q(s) = 2s^2 + 7s + 5$
  e) $Q(h) = h^2 - h$ **f)** $Q(x) = 2x^2 + 3x - 7$
5. a) $\dfrac{x^3 + 7x^2 - 3x + 4}{x + 2} = x^2 + 5x - 13 + \dfrac{30}{x + 2}, x \neq -2$
  b) $\dfrac{11t - 4t^4 - 7}{t - 3}$
  $= -4t^3 - 12t^2 - 36t - 97 - \dfrac{298}{t - 3}, t \neq 3$
  c) $\dfrac{x^3 + 3x^2 - 2x + 5}{x + 1} = x^2 + 2x - 4 + \dfrac{9}{x + 1}, x \neq -1$
  d) $\dfrac{4n^3 + 7n - 5}{n + 3} = 4n - 5 + \dfrac{10}{n + 3}, n \neq -3$
  e) $\dfrac{4n^3 - 15n + 2}{n - 3} = 4n^2 + 12n + 21 + \dfrac{65}{n - 3}, n \neq 3$
  f) $\dfrac{x^3 + 6x^2 - 4x + 1}{x + 2} = x^2 + 4x - 12 + \dfrac{25}{x + 2}, x \neq -2$
6. a) 16   **b)** 38   **c)** -23
  d) -67 **e)** -2 **f)** 8
7. a) 9   **b)** -40 **c)** 41   **d)** -4
8. a) -1 **b)** 3   **c)** 2   **d)** -1
9. 11
10. 4 and -2
11. a) $2x + 3$
  b) 9, it represents the rest of the width that cannot be simplified any more.
12. a) $2n + 2 + \dfrac{9}{n - 3}$ **b)** -2 and -0.5
13. a) $9\pi x^2 + 24\pi x + 16\pi$, represents the area of the base
  b) $\pi(3x + 4)^2(x + 3)$
  c) 10 cm $\leq r \leq$ 28 cm and $5 \leq h \leq 11$
14. $m = -\dfrac{11}{5}, n = \dfrac{59}{5}$
15. $a = -\dfrac{14}{3}, b = -\dfrac{2}{3}$
16. Divide using the binomial $x - \dfrac{3}{2}$.
17. Examples: **a)** $x^2 - 4x - 1$
  b) $x^3 + 3x^2 + 3x + 6$ **c)** $2x^4 + x^3 + x^2 + x$
C1 Example: The process is the same. Long division of polynomials results in a restriction.
C2 a) $(x - a)$ is a factor of $bx^2 + cx + d$.
  b) $d + ac + a^2b$
C3 a) 77   **b)** 77
  c) The remainder is the height of the cable at the given horizontal distance.

3.3 The Factor Theorem, pages 133 to 135

1. a) $x - 1$ **b)** $x + 3$ **c)** $x - 4$ **d)** $x - a$
2. a) Yes   **b)** No   **c)** No   **d)** Yes
  e) Yes   **f)** No
3. a) No   **b)** No   **c)** No   **d)** No
  e) Yes   **f)** No
4. a) $\pm 1, \pm 2, \pm 4, \pm 8$ **b)** $\pm 1, \pm 2, \pm 3, \pm 6, \pm 9, \pm 18$
  c) $\pm 1, \pm 2, \pm 3, \pm 4, \pm 6, \pm 8, \pm 12, \pm 24$
  d) $\pm 1, \pm 2, \pm 4$ **e)** $\pm 1, \pm 3, \pm 5, \pm 15$
  f) $\pm 1, \pm 2, \pm 4$
5. a) $(x - 1)(x - 2)(x - 3)$ **b)** $(x - 1)(x + 1)(x + 2)$
  c) $(v - 4)(v + 4)(v + 1)$
  d) $(x + 4)(x + 2)(x - 3)(x + 1)$
  e) $(k - 1)(k - 2)(k + 3)(k + 2)(k + 1)$

6. a) $(x + 3)(x - 2)(x - 3)$ **b)** $(t - 5)(t + 4)(t + 2)$
c) $(h - 5)(h^2 + 5h - 2)$ **d)** $x^5 + 8x^3 + 2x - 15$
e) $(q - 1)(q + 1)(q^2 + 2q + 3)$

7. a) $k = -2$ **b)** $k = 1, -7$
c) $k = -6$ **d)** $k = 6$

8. $h, h - 1,$ and $h - 1$

9. $l - 5$ and $l + 3$

10. $x - 2$ cm, $x + 4$ cm, and $x + 3$ cm

11. $x + 5$ and $x + 3$

12. a) $x - 5$ is a possible factor because it is the corresponding factor for $x = 5$. Since $f(5) = 0$, $x - 5$ is a factor of the polynomial function.
b) 2-ft sections would be weak by the same principle applied in part a).

13. $x + 3, x + 2,$ and $x + 1$

14. Synthetic division yields a remainder of $a + b + c + d + e$, which must equal 0 as given. Therefore, $x - 1$ is a possible divisor.

15. $m = -\frac{7}{10}, n = -\frac{51}{10}$

16. a) i) $(x - 1)(x^2 + x + 1)$ ii) $(x - 3)(x^2 + 3x + 9)$
iii) $(x + 1)(x^2 - x + 1)$ iv) $(x + 4)(x^2 - 4x + 16)$
b) $x + y, x^2 - xy + y^2$ **c)** $x - y, x^2 + xy + y^2$
d) $(x^2 + y^2)(x^4 - x^2y^2 + y^4)$

C1 Example: Looking at the x-intercepts of the graph, you can determine at least one binomial factor, $x - 2$ or $x + 2$. The factored form of the polynomial is $(x - 2)(x + 2)(x^2 + 1)$.

C2 Example: Using the integral zero theorem, you have both ±1 and ±5 as possible integer values. The x-intercepts of the graph of the corresponding function will also give the factors.

C3 Example: Start by using the integral zero theorem to check for a first possible integer value. Apply the factor theorem using the value found from the integral zero theorem. Use synthetic division to confirm that the remainder is 0 and determine the remaining factor. Repeat the process until all factors are found.

3.4 Equations and Graphs of Polynomial Functions, pages 147 to 152

1. a) $x = -3, 0, 4$ **b)** $x = -1, 3, 5$ **c)** $x = -2, 3$

2. a) $x = -2, -1$ **b)** $x = 1$ **c)** $x = -4, -2$

3. a) $(x + 3)(x + 2)(x - 1) = 0$, roots are $-3, -2$ and 1
b) $-(x + 4)(x - 1)(x - 3) = 0$, roots are $-4, 1$ and 3
c) $-(x + 4)^2(x - 1)(x - 3) = 0$, roots are $-4, 1$ and 3

4. a) i) $-4, -1,$ and 1
ii) positive for $-4 < x < -1$ and $x > 1$, negative for $x < -4$ and $-1 < x < 1$
iii) all three zeros are of multiplicity 1, the sign of the function changes
b) i) -1 and 4
ii) negative for all values of $x, x \neq -1, 4$
iii) both zeros are of multiplicity 2, the sign of the function does not change
c) i) -3 and 1
ii) positive for $x < -3$ and $x > 1$, negative for $-3 < x < 1$
iii) -3 (multiplicity 1) and 1 (multiplicity 3), at both the function changes sign but is flatter at $x = 1$
d) i) -1 and 3
ii) negative for $-1 < x < 3$ and $x > 3$, positive for $x < -1$

iii) -1 (multiplicity 3) and 3 (multiplicity 2), at $x = -1$ the function changes sign but not at $x = 3$

5. a) B   **b)** D   **c)** C   **d)** A

6. a) $a = 0.5$ vertical stretch by a factor of 0.5, $b = -3$ horizontal stretch by a factor of $\frac{1}{3}$ and a reflection in the y-axis, $h = 1$ translation of 1 unit right, $k = 4$ translation of 4 units up

b)

$y = x^3$	$y = (-3x)^3$	$y = 0.5(-3x)^3$	$y = 0.5(-3(x-1))^3 + 4$
$(-2, -8)$	$\left(\frac{2}{3}, -8\right)$	$\left(\frac{2}{3}, -4\right)$	$\left(\frac{5}{3}, 0\right)$
$(-1, -1)$	$\left(\frac{1}{3}, -1\right)$	$\left(\frac{1}{3}, -\frac{1}{2}\right)$	$\left(\frac{4}{3}, \frac{7}{2}\right)$
$(0, 0)$	$(0, 0)$	$(0, 0)$	$(1, 4)$
$(1, 1)$	$\left(-\frac{1}{3}, 1\right)$	$\left(-\frac{1}{3}, \frac{1}{2}\right)$	$\left(\frac{2}{3}, \frac{9}{2}\right)$
$(2, 8)$	$\left(-\frac{2}{3}, 8\right)$	$\left(-\frac{2}{3}, 4\right)$	$\left(\frac{1}{3}, 8\right)$

c)

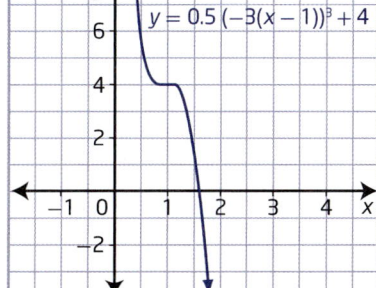

7. a) i) $-5, 0,$ and 9
ii) degree 3 from quadrant III to I
iii) $-5, 0,$ and 9 each of multiplicity 1
iv) 0
v) positive for $-5 < x < 0$ and $x > 9$, negative for $x < -5$ and $0 < x < 9$
b) i) $-9, 0$ and 9
ii) degree 4 opening upwards
iii) 0 (multiplicity 2), -9 and 9 each of multiplicity 1
iv) 0
v) positive for $x < -9$ and $x > 9$, negative for $-9 < x < 9, x \neq 0$
c) i) $-3, -1,$ and 1
ii) degree 3 from quadrant III to I
iii) $-3, -1,$ and 1 each of multiplicity 1
iv) -3
v) positive for $-3 < x < -1$ and $x > 1$, negative for $x < -3$ and $-1 < x < 1$
d) i) $-3, -2, 1,$ and 2
ii) degree 4 opening downwards
iii) $-3, -2, 1,$ and 2 each of multiplicity 1
iv) -12
v) positive for $-3 < x < -2$ and $1 < x < 2$, negative for $x < -3$ and $-2 < x < 1$ and $x > 2$

8. a) 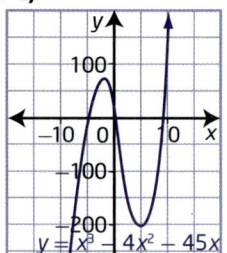 **b)**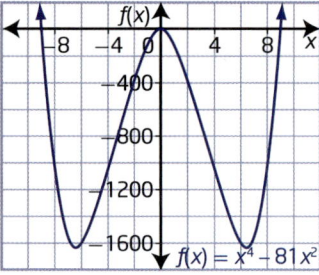
c) 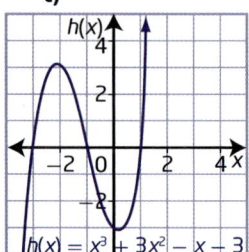 **d)**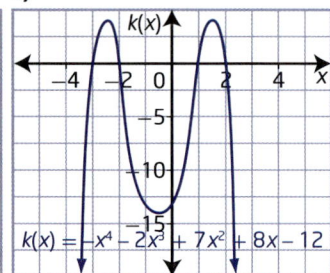

9. a) 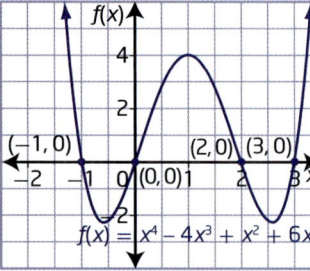 **b)**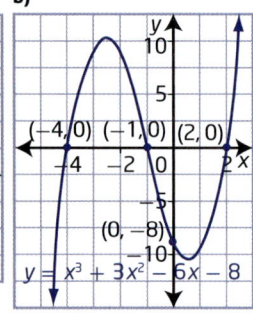
c) 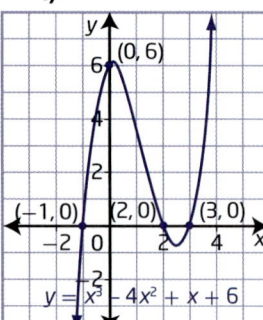 **d)**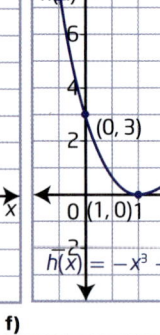
e) 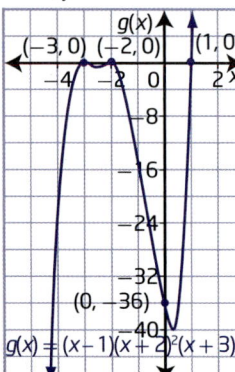 **f)**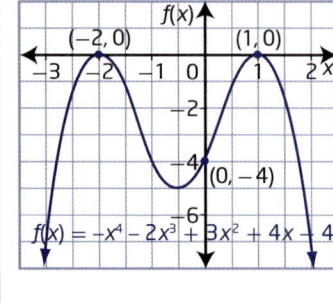

10. a) positive leading coefficient, x-intercepts: −2 and 3, positive for −2 < x < 3 and x > 3, negative for x < −2, $y = (x + 2)^3(x - 3)^2$
b) negative leading coefficient, x-intercepts: −4, −1, and 3, positive for x < −4 and −1 < x < 3, negative for −4 < x < −1 and x > 3, $y = -(x + 4)(x + 1)(x - 3)$
c) negative leading coefficient, x-intercepts: −2, −1, 2, and 3, positive for −2 < x < −1 and 2 < x < 3, negative for x < −2 and −1 < x < 2 and x > 3, $y = -(x + 2)(x + 1)(x - 2)(x - 3)$
d) positive leading coefficient, x-intercepts: −1, 1, and 3, positive for x < −1 and 1 < x < 3 and x > 3, negative for −1 < x < 1, $y = (x + 1)(x - 1)(x - 3)^2$

11. a) $a = 1$, $b = \frac{1}{2}$, $h = 2$, $k = -3$
b) Horizontal stretch by a factor of 2, translation of 2 units right, and translation of 3 units down
c) domain $\{x \mid x \in \mathbb{R}\}$, range $\{y \mid y \in \mathbb{R}\}$

12. 2 m by 21 m by 50 m
13. 5 ft
14. a) $y = (x + 3)^2(x - 2)$ **b)** $y = (x + 1)^3(x - 2)^2$

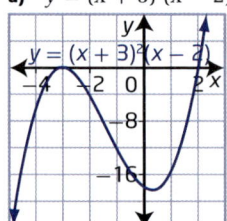 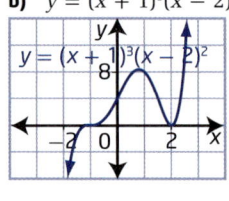

c) $y = -\frac{1}{6}(x + 2)^2(x - 3)^2$

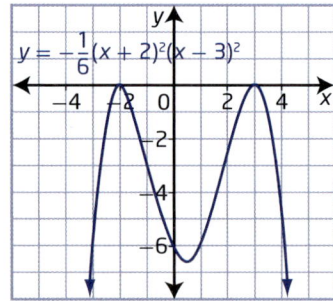

15. 4 cm by 2 cm by 8 cm
16. −7, −5, and −3
17. The side lengths of the two cubes are 2 m and 3 m.
18. a) $(x^2 - 12)^2 - x^2$ **b)** 5 in. by 5 in.
c) 13 in. by 13 in.
19. 4, 5, 6, and 7 or −7, −6, −5, and −4
20. $y = -\frac{1}{3}(x - \sqrt{3})(x + \sqrt{3})(x - 1)$
21. roots: −4.5, 8, and 2; $0 = (x + 4.5)(x - 8)(x - 2)$
22. a) translation of 2 units right
b)
c) $y = x^3 - x^2 = x^2(x - 1)$: 0 and 1, $y = (x - 2)^3 - (x - 2)^2 = (x - 2)^2(x - 3)$: 2 and 3

23. When $x \approx 0.65$, or when the sphere is at a depth of approximately 0.65 m.

C1 Example: It is easier to identify the roots.

C2 Example: A root of an equation is a solution of the equation. A zero of a function is a value of x for which $f(x) = 0$. An x-intercept of a graph is the x-coordinate of the point where a line or curve crosses or touches the x-axis. They all represent the same thing.

C3 Example: If the multiplicity of a zero is 1, the function changes sign. If the multiplicity of a zero is even, the function does not change sign. The shape of a graph close to a zero of $x = a$ (order n) is similar to the shape of the graph of a function with degree equal to n of the form $y = (x - a)^n$.

C4 Step 1 Set A

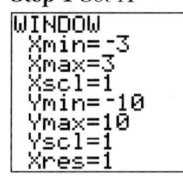 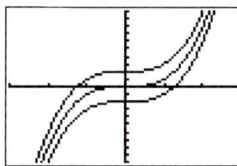

Set B

 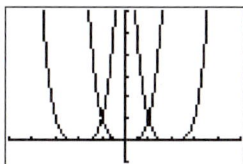

a) The graph of $y = x^3 + k$ is translated vertically k units compared to the graph of $y = x^3$.

b) The graph of $y = (x - h)^4$ is translated horizontally h units compared to the graph of $y = x^4$.

Step 2 h: horizontal translation; k: vertical translation

Step 3 Set C

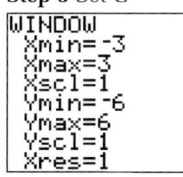 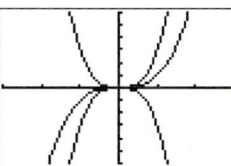

Set D

 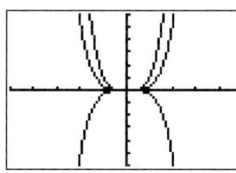

a) The graph of $y = ax^3$ is stretched vertically by a factor of $|a|$ relative to the graph of $y = x^3$. When a is negative, the graph is reflected in the x-axis.

b) When a is $-1 < a < 0$ or $0 < a < 1$, the graph of $y = ax^4$ is stretched vertically by a factor of $|a|$ relative to the graph of $y = x^4$. When a is negative, the graph is reflected in the x-axis.

Step 4 Set E

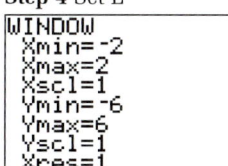 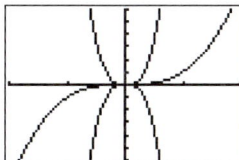

Set F

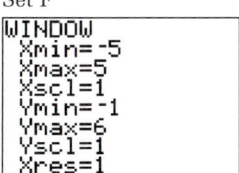 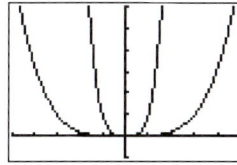

a) The graph of $y = (bx)^3$ is stretched horizontally by a factor of $\frac{1}{|b|}$ relative to the graph of $y = x^3$. When b is negative, the graph is reflected in the y-axis.

b) When b is $-1 < b < 0$ or $0 < b < 1$, the graph of $y = (bx)^4$ is stretched horizontally by a factor of $\frac{1}{|b|}$ relative to the graph of $y = x^4$. When b is negative, the graph is reflected in the y-axis.

Step 5 a: vertical stretch; reflection in the x-axis; b: horizontal stretch; reflection in the y-axis

Chapter 3 Review, pages 153 to 154

1. a) No, this is a square root function.
   b) Yes, this is a polynomial function of degree 4.
   c) Yes, this is a polynomial function of degree 3.
   d) Yes, this is a polynomial function of degree 1.

2. a) degree 4 with positive leading coefficient, opens upward, maximum of 4 x-intercepts, y-intercept of 0
   b) degree 3 with negative leading coefficient, extends from quadrant II to quadrant IV, maximum of 3 x-intercepts, y-intercept of 4
   c) degree 1 with positive leading coefficient, extends from quadrant III to quadrant I, 1 x-intercept, y-intercept of -2
   d) degree 2 with positive leading coefficient, opens upward, maximum of 2 x-intercepts, y-intercept of -4
   e) degree 5 with positive leading coefficient, extends from quadrant III to quadrant I, maximum of 5 x-intercepts, y-intercept of 1

3. a) quadratic function **b)** 9196 ft
   c) 25 s **d)** 26.81 s

4. a) 37, $\dfrac{x^3 + 9x^2 - 5x + 3}{x - 2}$
$= x^2 + 11x + 17 + \dfrac{37}{x - 2}, x \neq 2$

   b) 2, $\dfrac{2x^3 + x^2 - 2x + 1}{x + 1}$
$= 2x^2 - x - 1 + \dfrac{2}{x + 1}, x \neq -1$

   c) 9, $\dfrac{12x^3 + 13x^2 - 23x + 7}{x - 1}$
$= 12x^2 + 25x + 2 + \dfrac{9}{x - 1}, x \neq 1$

   d) 1, $\dfrac{-8x^4 - 4x + 10x^3 + 15}{x + 1}$
$= -8x^3 + 18x^2 - 18x + 14 + \dfrac{1}{x + 1}, x \neq -1$

5. a) -3 **b)** 166

6. -34

7. a) Yes, $P(1) = 0$. **b)** No, $P(-1) \neq 0$.
   c) Yes, $P(-4) = 0$. **d)** Yes, $P(4) = 0$.

8. a) $(x - 2)(x - 3)(x + 1)$ **b)** $-4(x - 2)(x + 2)(x + 1)$
   c) $(x - 1)(x - 2)(x - 3)(x + 2)$
   d) $(x + 3)(x - 1)^2(x - 2)^2$

9. a) $x + 3, 2x - 1$, and $x + 1$
   b) 4 m by 1 m by 2 m

10. $k = -2$

11. a) x-intercepts: -3, -1, and 2; degree 3 extending from quadrant III to quadrant I; -3, -1, and 2 each of multiplicity 1; y-intercept of -6; positive for $-3 < x < -1$ and $x > 2$, negative for $x < -3$ and $-1 < x < 2$

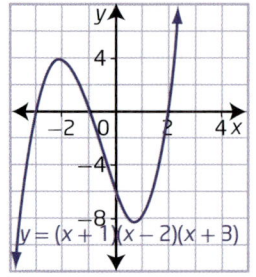

b) x-intercepts: -2 and 3; degree 3 extending from quadrant III to quadrant I; -2 (multiplicity 2) and 3 (multiplicity 1); y-intercept of -12; positive for $x > 3$, negative for $x < 3$, $x \neq -2$

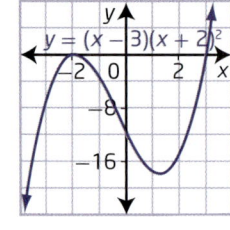

c) x-intercepts: -4, 0, and 4; degree 4 opening upwards; 0 (multiplicity 2), -4 and 4 each of multiplicity 1; y-intercept of 0; positive for $x < -4$ and $x > 4$, negative for $-4 < x < 4$, $x \neq 0$

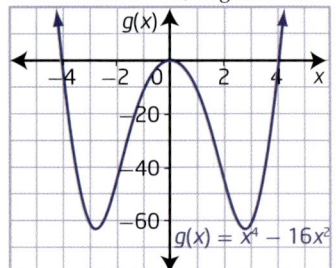

d) x-intercepts: -2, 0, and 2; degree 5 extending from quadrant II to quadrant IV; -2, 0, and 2 each of multiplicity 1; y-intercept of 0; positive for $x < -2$ and $0 < x < 2$, negative for $-2 < x < 0$ and $x > 2$

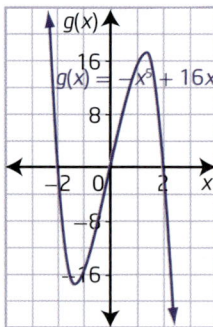

12. a) $a = 2$ vertical stretch by a factor of 2, $b = -4$ horizontal stretch by $\frac{1}{4}$ and reflection in the y-axis, $h = 1$ translation of 1 unit right, $k = 3$ translation of 3 units up

b)

Transformation	Parameter Value	Equation
horizontal stretch/ reflection in y-axis	-4	$y = (-4x)^3$
vertical stretch/ reflection in x-axis	2	$y = 2(-4x)^3$
translation right	1	$y = 2(-4(x-1))^3$
translation up	3	$y = 2(-4(x-1))^3 + 3$

c)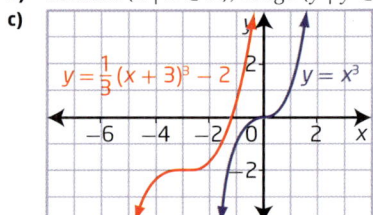

13. a) $y = (x+1)(x+3)^2$ **b)** $y = -(x+1)(x-2)^3$

14. a) Examples: $y = (x+2)(x+1)(x-3)^2$ and $y = -(x+2)(x+1)(x-3)^2$
b) $y = 2(x+2)(x+1)(x-3)^2$

15. a) $V = 2l^2(l-5)$ **b)** 8 cm by 3 cm by 16 cm

Chapter 3 Practice Test, pages 155 to 156

1. C   **2.** B   **3.** D   **4.** B   **5.** C
6. a) -4 and 3   **b)** -1 and 3
   c) -2, 2, and 5   **d)** -3 and 3
7. a) $P(x) = (x+2)(x+1)^2$
   b) $P(x) = (x-1)(x^2 - 12x - 12)$
   c) $P(x) = -x(x-3)^2$
   d) $P(x) = (x+1)(x^2 - 4x + 5)$
8. a) B   **b)** C   **c)** A
9. a) $V = x(20 - 2x)(18 - x)$
   b) 2 cm by 16 cm by 16 cm
10. a) $a = \frac{1}{3}$, vertical stretch by a factor of $\frac{1}{3}$; $b = 1$, no horizontal stretch; $h = -3$, translation of 3 units left; $k = -2$, translation of 2 units down
   b) domain $\{x \mid x \in \mathbb{R}\}$, range $\{y \mid y \in \mathbb{R}\}$
   c)

Cumulative Review, Chapters 1–3, pages 158 to 159

1. a)

b)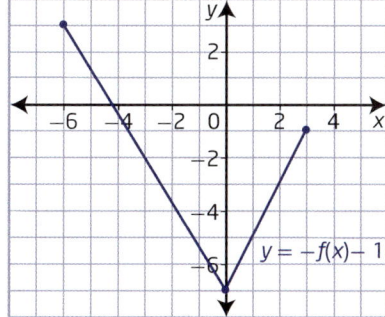

c) 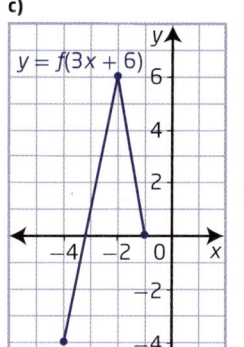   d)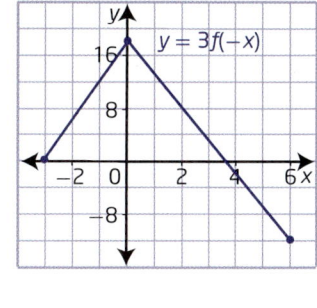

2. $y + 4 = f(x - 3)$
3. a) translation of 1 unit left and 5 units down
   b) vertical stretch by a factor of 3, reflection in the x-axis, and translation of 2 units right
   c) reflection in the y-axis and translation of 1 unit right and 3 units up
4. a) $(9, 10)$ b) $(6, -18)$ c) $(-2, 9)$
5. a) x-intercepts: $-\frac{4}{3}$ and 2, y-intercept: -3
   b) x-intercepts: -4 and 6, y-intercept: 6
6. a) Yes   b)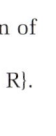
   c) Example: No; restrict domain of $y = |x| + 4$ to $\{x \mid x \geq 0, x \in R\}$.

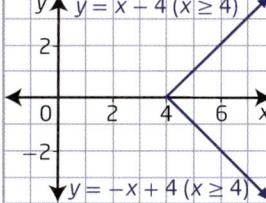

7. $g(x) = \sqrt{2(x + 2)} - 3$
8. $y = 2\sqrt{-(x + 1)}$

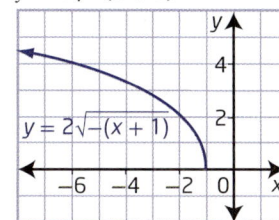

domain $\{x \mid x \leq -1, x \in R\}$, range $\{y \mid y \geq 0, y \in R\}$

9. a) $g(x) = \sqrt{9x}$ b) $g(x) = 3\sqrt{x}$
   c) $\sqrt{9x} = \sqrt{9}(\sqrt{x}) = 3\sqrt{x}$
10. a) The x-intercepts are invariant points for square roots of functions, since $\sqrt{0} = 0$.
    b) $f(x)$: domain $\{x \mid x \in R\}$, range $\{y \mid y \geq -1, y \in R\}$; $g(x)$: domain $\{x \mid x \leq -1$ or $x \geq 1, x \in R\}$, range $\{y \mid y \geq 0, y \in R\}$; The square root function has a restricted domain.

11. a) No, substituting -2.75 back into the equation does not satisfy the equation.
    b) Only one solution, $x = -2$.
12. a) 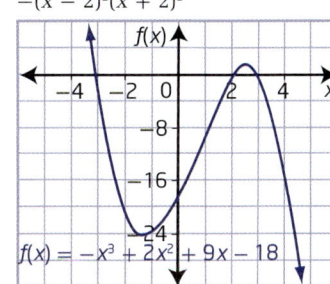   The x-intercept is 8.
    b) $x = 8$
    c) They are the same.

13. a) $\dfrac{x^4 + 3x + 4}{x + 1} = x^3 - x^2 + x + 2 + \dfrac{2}{x + 1}$; $P(-1) = 2$
    b) $\dfrac{x^3 + 5x^2 + x - 9}{x + 3} = x^2 + 2x - 5 + \dfrac{6}{x + 3}$; $P(-3) = 6$
14. $\pm 1, \pm 2, \pm 3, \pm 6$; $P(1) = 0$, $P(-1) = -16$, $P(2) = -4$, $P(-2) = 0$, $P(3) = 0$, $P(-3) = 96$, $P(6) = 600$, $P(-6) = 1764$
15. a) $(x + 5)(x - 1)(x - 4)$ b) $(x - 3)(x + 4)(x + 2)$
    c) $-(x - 2)^2(x + 2)^2$
16. a)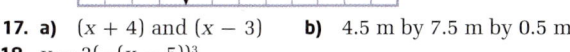

x-intercepts: $-3, 2$, and 3; y-intercept: -18

b)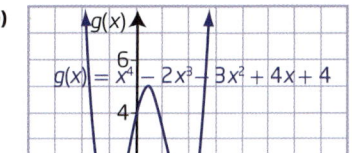

x-intercepts: -1 and 2, y-intercept: 4

17. a) $(x + 4)$ and $(x - 3)$ b) 4.5 m by 7.5 m by 0.5 m
18. $y = 3(-(x - 5))^3$

Unit 1 Test, pages 160 to 161

1. D   2. C   3. D   4. A   5. D   6. C   7. A
8. -13
9. $\{y \mid y \geq 8, y \in R\}$
10. $g(x) = |x + 2| + 3$
11. 5
12. a) 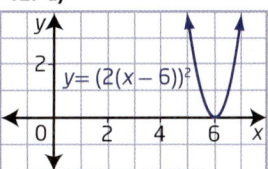   b)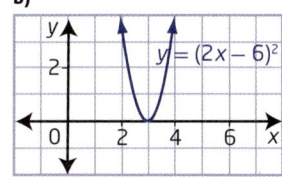

c) They both have the same shape but one of them is shifted right further.

13. a) 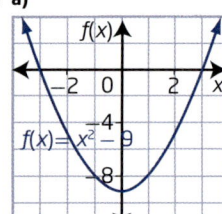 b) $y = \pm\sqrt{x+9}$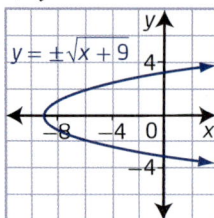

c) $y = \sqrt{x^2 - 9}$

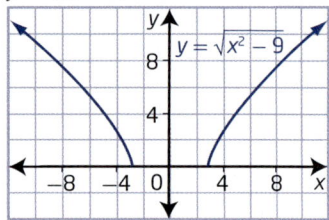

d) for part a): domain $\{x \mid x \in R\}$, range $\{y \mid y \geq -9, y \in R\}$; for part b): domain $\{x \mid x \geq -9, x \in R\}$, range $\{y \mid y \in R\}$; for part c): domain $\{x \mid x \leq -3 \text{ or } x \geq 3, x \in R\}$, range $\{y \mid y \geq 0, y \in R\}$

14. Quadrant II: reflection in the y-axis, $y = f(-x)$; quadrant III: reflection in the y-axis and then the x-axis, $y = -f(-x)$; quadrant IV: reflection in the x-axis, $y = -f(x)$

15. a) Mary should have subtracted 4 from both sides in step 1. She also incorrectly squared the expression on the right side in step 2. The correct solution follows:
    $2x = \sqrt{x+1} + 4$
    Step 1: $(2x - 4)^2 = (\sqrt{x+1})^2$
    Step 2: $4x^2 - 16x + 16 = x + 1$
    Step 3: $4x^2 - 17x + 15 = 0$
    Step 4: $(4x - 5)(x - 3) = 0$
    Step 5: $4x - 5 = 0$ or $x - 3 = 0$
    Step 6: $x = \frac{5}{4}$ $x = 3$
    Step 7: A check determines that $x = 3$ is the solution.

    b) Yes, the point of intersection of the two graphs will yield the possible solution, $x = 3$.

16. $c = -3$; $P(x) = (x + 3)(x + 2)(x - 1)^2$

17. a) $\pm 1, \pm 2, \pm 3, \pm 6$
    b) $P(x) = (x - 3)(x + 2)(x + 1)$
    c) x-intercepts: $-2, -1$ and 3; y-intercept: -6
    d) $-2 \leq x \leq -1$ and $x \geq 3$

Chapter 4 Trigonometry and the Unit Circle

4.1 Angles and Angle Measure, pages 175 to 179

1. a) clockwise   b) counterclockwise
   c) clockwise   d) counterclockwise

2. a) $30° = \frac{\pi}{6}$ 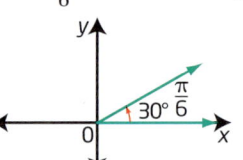 b) $45° = \frac{\pi}{4}$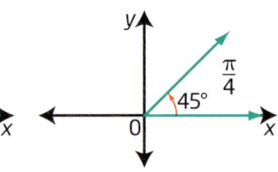

   c) $-330° = -\frac{11\pi}{6}$ 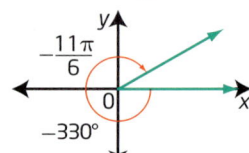 d) $520° = \frac{26\pi}{9}$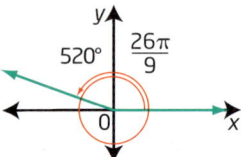

   e) $90° = \frac{\pi}{2}$ 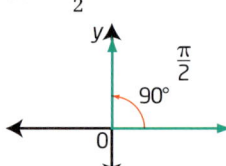 f) $21° = \frac{7\pi}{60}$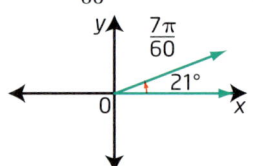

3. a) $\frac{\pi}{3}$ or 1.05 b) $\frac{5\pi}{6}$ or 2.62
   c) $-\frac{3\pi}{2}$ or -4.71 d) $\frac{2\pi}{5}$ or 1.26
   e) $-\frac{37\pi}{450}$ or -0.26 f) 3π or 9.42

4. a) $30°$ b) $120°$
   c) $-67.5°$ d) $-450°$
   e) $\frac{180°}{\pi}$ or $57.3°$ f) $\frac{495°}{\pi}$ or $157.6°$

5. a) $\frac{360°}{7}$ or $51.429°$ b) $\frac{1260°}{13}$ or $96.923°$
   c) $\frac{120°}{\pi}$ or $38.197°$ d) $\frac{3294°}{5\pi}$ or $209.703°$
   e) $\frac{-1105.2°}{\pi}$ or $-351.796°$ f) $\frac{-3600°}{\pi}$ or $-1145.916°$

6. a) quadrant I 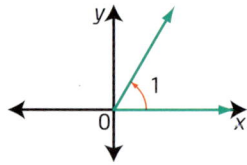 b) quadrant II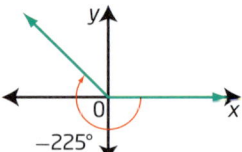

   c) quadrant II 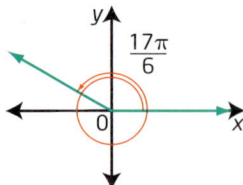 d) quadrant IV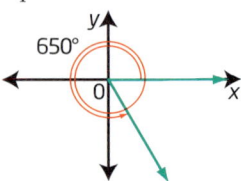

   e) quadrant III 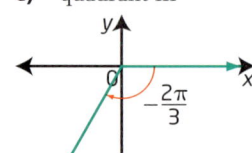 f) quadrant IV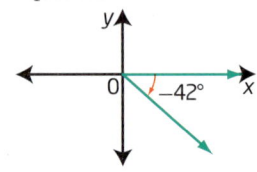

7. Examples:
   a) 432°, −288° **b)** $\frac{11\pi}{4}, -\frac{5\pi}{4}$
   c) 240°, −480° **d)** $\frac{7\pi}{2}, -\frac{\pi}{2}$
   e) 155°, −565° **f)** 1.5, −4.8

8. a) coterminal, $\frac{17\pi}{6} = \frac{5\pi}{6} + \frac{12\pi}{6} = \frac{5\pi}{6} + 2\pi$
   b) not coterminal   **c)** not coterminal
   d) coterminal, −493° = 227° − 2(360°)

9. a) 135° ± (360°)n, $n \in \mathbb{N}$ **b)** $-\frac{\pi}{2} \pm 2\pi n$, $n \in \mathbb{N}$
   c) −200° ± (360°)n, $n \in \mathbb{N}$ **d)** 10 ± 2πn, $n \in \mathbb{N}$

10. Example:

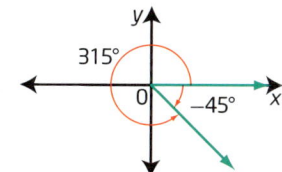

   −45° + 360° = 315°, −45° ± (360°)n, $n \in \mathbb{N}$

11. a) 425°   **b)** 320°
   c) −400°, 320°, 680°   **d)** $-\frac{5\pi}{4}$
   e) $-\frac{23\pi}{6}, \frac{\pi}{6}, \frac{13\pi}{6}$ **f)** $-\frac{5\pi}{3}, \frac{\pi}{3}$
   g) −3.9   **h)** −0.9, 5.4

12. a) 13.30 cm   **b)** 4.80 m
   c) 15.88 cm   **d)** 30.76 in.

13. a) 2.25 radians   **b)** 10.98 ft
   c) 3.82 cm   **d)** 17.10 m

14. a) $\frac{25\pi}{3}$ or 26.18 m
   b) $\frac{A_{\text{sector}}}{A_{\text{circle}}} = \frac{\text{sector angle}}{2\pi}$
   $A_{\text{sector}} = \frac{\pi r^2 \left(\frac{5\pi}{3}\right)}{2\pi}$
   $A_{\text{sector}} = \frac{5\pi(5)^2}{6}$
   $A_{\text{sector}} = \frac{125\pi}{6}$
   The area watered is approximately 65.45 m².
   c) 16π radians or 2880°

15. a) Examples: $\frac{\pi}{12}$ radians/h, 1 revolution per day, 15°/h
   b) $\frac{100\pi}{3}$ or 104.72 radians/s
   c) 54 000°/min

16. a) 2.36   **b)** 135.3°

17.

	Revolutions	Degrees	Radians
a)	1 rev	360°	2π
b)	0.75 rev	270°	$\frac{3\pi}{2}$ or 4.7
c)	0.4 rev	150°	$\frac{5\pi}{6}$
d)	−0.3 rev	−97.4°	−1.7
e)	−0.1 rev	−40°	$-\frac{2\pi}{9}$ or −0.7
f)	0.7 rev	252°	$\frac{7\pi}{5}$ or 4.4
g)	−3.25 rev	−1170°	$-\frac{13\pi}{2}$ or −20.4
h)	$\frac{23}{18}$ or 1.3 rev	460°	$\frac{23\pi}{9}$ or 8.0
i)	$-\frac{3}{16}$ or −0.2 rev	−67.5°	$-\frac{3\pi}{8}$

18. Jasmine is correct. Joran's answer includes the solution when $k = 0$, which is the reference angle 78°.

19. a) 55.6 grad
   b) Use a proportion: $\frac{\text{gradians}}{\text{degrees}} = \frac{400 \text{ grad}}{360°}$.
   So, measure in gradians = $\frac{10(\text{number of degrees})}{9}$.
   c) The gradian was developed to express a right angle as a metric measure. A right angle is equivalent to 100 grads.

20. a) (diagram: Yellowknife 62.45°, Crowsnest 49.63°, 12.82°, 6400 km)
   b) 1432.01 km
   c) Example: Bowden (51.93° N, 114.03° W) and Airdrie (51.29° N, 114.01° W) are 71.49 km apart.

21. a) 2221.4 m/min   **b)** 7404.7 radians/min
22. 8.5 km/h
23. 66 705.05 mph
24. a) 69.375° = 69° + 0.375(60′)
   = 69° 22.5′
   = 69° 22′ 30″
   b) i) 40° 52′ 30″   **ii)** 100° 7′ 33.6″
   iii) 14° 33′ 54″   **iv)** 80° 23′ 6″

25. a) 69° 22′ 30″ = 69°22.5′
   = 69° + $\left(\frac{22.5}{60}\right)°$
   = 69.375°
   b) i) 45.508°   **ii)** 72.263°
   iii) 105.671°   **iv)** 28.167°

26. $A_{\text{segment}} = \frac{1}{2}r^2(\theta - \sin \theta)$

27. a) 120°   **b)** 65°   **c)** Examples: 3:00 and 9:00
   d) 2   **e)** shortly after 4:05

C1 (diagram: $2\pi \approx 6.28$)
π is 180° and 2π is 360°. 2(3.14) = 6.282 which is more than 6. Therefore, 6 radians must be less than 360°.

C2 (diagram: circle with points O, A, B, radii r, arc of length 1)
1° is a very small angle, it is $\frac{1}{360}$ of one rotation. One radian is much larger than 1°; 1 radian is the angle whose arc is the same as the radius, it is nearly $\frac{1}{6}$ of one rotation.

C3 a) 40°; 140° ± (360°)n, $n \in \mathbb{N}$
   b) 0.72; 0.72 ± 2πn, $n \in \mathbb{N}$

C4 a)

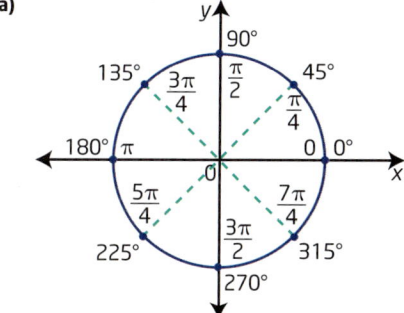

b)

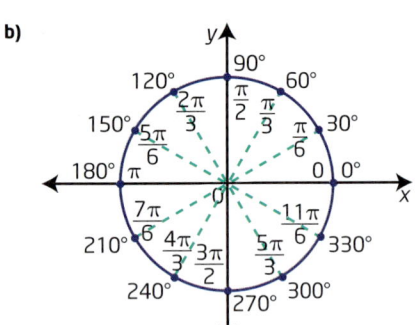

C5 a) $x = 3$ b) $y = x - 3$

4.2 The Unit Circle, pages 186 to 190

1. a) $x^2 + y^2 = 16$ b) $x^2 + y^2 = 9$
   c) $x^2 + y^2 = 144$ d) $x^2 + y^2 = 6.76$

2. a) No; $\left(-\frac{3}{4}\right)^2 + \left(\frac{1}{4}\right)^2 = \frac{5}{8} \neq 1$
   b) No; $\left(\frac{\sqrt{5}}{8}\right)^2 + \left(\frac{7}{8}\right)^2 = \frac{27}{32} \neq 1$
   c) Yes; $\left(-\frac{5}{13}\right)^2 + \left(\frac{12}{13}\right)^2 = 1$
   d) Yes; $\left(\frac{4}{5}\right)^2 + \left(-\frac{3}{5}\right)^2 = 1$
   e) Yes; $\left(-\frac{\sqrt{3}}{2}\right)^2 + \left(\frac{-1}{2}\right)^2 = 1$
   f) Yes; $\left(\frac{\sqrt{7}}{4}\right)^2 + \left(\frac{3}{4}\right)^2 = 1$

3. a) $y = \frac{\sqrt{15}}{4}$ b) $x = -\frac{\sqrt{5}}{3}$

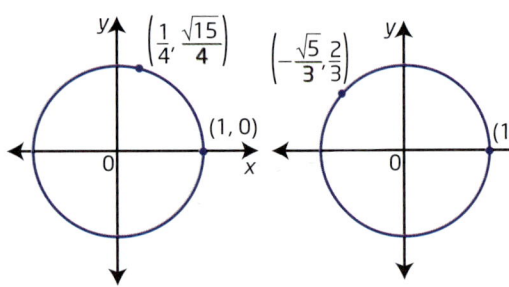

   c) $y = -\frac{\sqrt{15}}{8}$ d) $x = \frac{2\sqrt{6}}{7}$

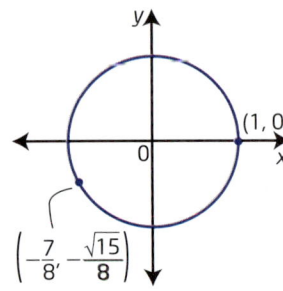 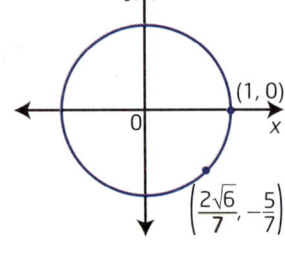

e) $x = -\frac{2\sqrt{2}}{3}$ f) $y = -\frac{5}{13}$

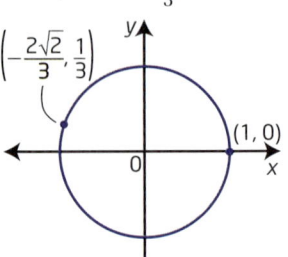 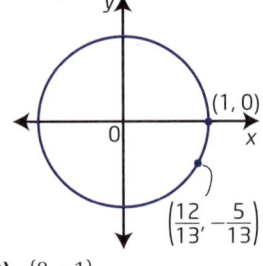

4. a) $(-1, 0)$ b) $(0, -1)$
   c) $\left(\frac{1}{2}, \frac{\sqrt{3}}{2}\right)$ d) $\left(\frac{\sqrt{3}}{2}, -\frac{1}{2}\right)$
   e) $\left(-\frac{\sqrt{2}}{2}, \frac{\sqrt{2}}{2}\right)$ f) $\left(\frac{\sqrt{2}}{2}, \frac{\sqrt{2}}{2}\right)$
   g) $(1, 0)$ h) $(0, 1)$
   i) $\left(-\frac{\sqrt{3}}{2}, \frac{1}{2}\right)$ j) $\left(-\frac{1}{2}, \frac{\sqrt{3}}{2}\right)$

5. a) $\frac{3\pi}{2}$ b) 0 c) $\frac{\pi}{4}$ d) $\frac{3\pi}{4}$
   e) $\frac{\pi}{3}$ f) $\frac{5\pi}{3}$ g) $\frac{5\pi}{6}$ h) $\frac{7\pi}{6}$
   i) $\frac{5\pi}{4}$ j) π

6. $\frac{5\pi}{6}$ and $-\frac{7\pi}{6}$

7. a)

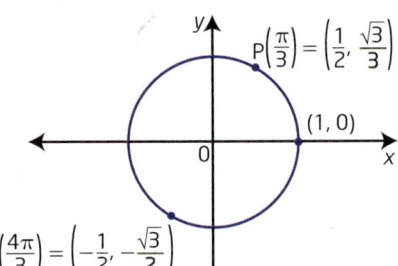

   If $\theta = \frac{\pi}{3}$ then $\theta + \pi = \frac{\pi}{3} + \pi$ or $\frac{4\pi}{3}$ since
   $P\left(\frac{\pi}{3}\right) = \left(\frac{1}{2}, \frac{\sqrt{3}}{2}\right)$ and $P\left(\frac{4\pi}{3}\right) = \left(-\frac{1}{2}, -\frac{\sqrt{3}}{2}\right)$

   b)

   $P\left(\frac{3\pi}{4}\right) = \left(-\frac{\sqrt{2}}{2}, \frac{\sqrt{2}}{2}\right)$

   $P\left(\frac{7\pi}{4}\right) = \left(\frac{\sqrt{2}}{2}, -\frac{\sqrt{2}}{2}\right)$

   If $\theta = \frac{3\pi}{4}$ then $\theta + \pi = \frac{3\pi}{4} + \pi$ or $\frac{7\pi}{4}$ since
   $P\left(\frac{3\pi}{4}\right) = \left(-\frac{\sqrt{2}}{2}, \frac{\sqrt{2}}{2}\right)$ and $P\left(\frac{7\pi}{4}\right) = \left(\frac{\sqrt{2}}{2}, -\frac{\sqrt{2}}{2}\right)$

8.

Point	$+\frac{1}{4}$ rotation	$-\frac{1}{4}$ rotation	Step 4: Description
$P(0)$ $= (1, 0)$	$P\left(\frac{\pi}{2}\right)$ $= (0, 1)$	$P\left(-\frac{\pi}{2}\right)$ $= (0, -1)$	x- and y-values change places and take signs of new quadrant
$P\left(\frac{\pi}{3}\right)$ $= \left(\frac{1}{2}, \frac{\sqrt{3}}{2}\right)$	$P\left(\frac{\pi}{3} + \frac{\pi}{2}\right)$ $= P\left(\frac{5\pi}{6}\right)$ $= \left(-\frac{\sqrt{3}}{2}, \frac{1}{2}\right)$	$P\left(\frac{\pi}{3} - \frac{\pi}{2}\right)$ $= P\left(-\frac{\pi}{6}\right)$ $= \left(\frac{\sqrt{3}}{2}, -\frac{1}{2}\right)$	x- and y-values change places and take signs of new quadrant
$P\left(\frac{5\pi}{3}\right)$ $= \left(\frac{1}{2}, -\frac{\sqrt{3}}{2}\right)$	$P\left(\frac{5\pi}{3} + \frac{\pi}{2}\right)$ $= P\left(\frac{\pi}{6}\right)$ $= \left(\frac{\sqrt{3}}{2}, \frac{1}{2}\right)$	$P\left(\frac{5\pi}{3} - \frac{\pi}{2}\right)$ $= P\left(\frac{7\pi}{6}\right)$ $= \left(-\frac{\sqrt{3}}{2}, -\frac{1}{2}\right)$	x- and y-values change places and take signs of new quadrant

Diagrams:
Steps 1–3

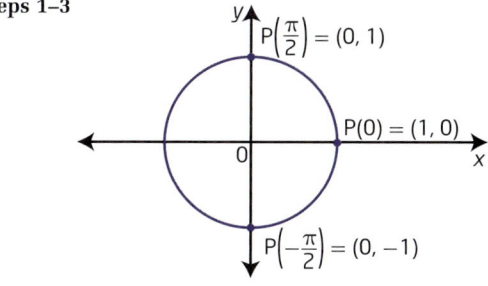

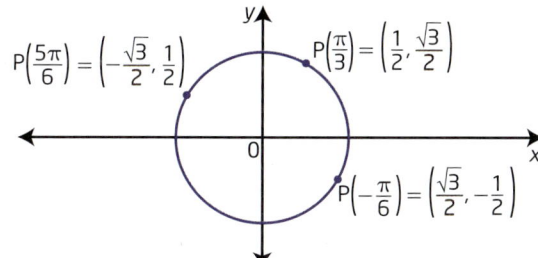

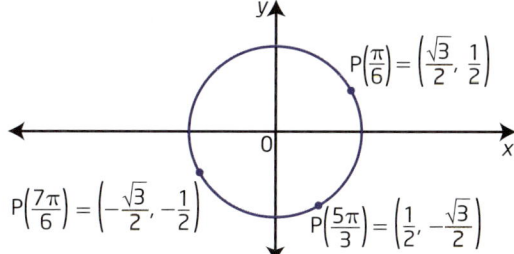

Step 4

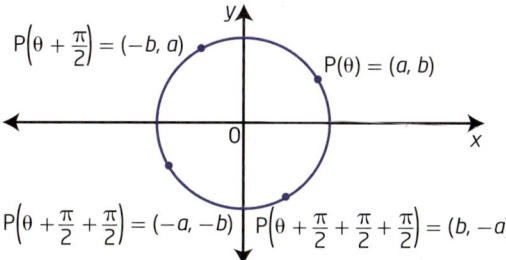

9. a) $x^2 + y^2 = 1$ b) $\left(\frac{\sqrt{5}}{3}, \frac{2}{3}\right)$
   c) $\theta + \frac{\pi}{2}$ d) quadrant IV
   e) maximum value is $+1$, minimum value is -1
10. a) Yes. In quadrant I the values of $\cos\theta$ decrease from 1 at $\theta = 0°$ to 0 at $\theta = 90°$, since the x-coordinate on the unit circle represents $\cos\theta$, in the first quadrant the values of x will range from 1 to 0.
    b) Substitute the values of x and y into the equation $x^2 + y^2 = 1$, Mya was not correct, the correct answer is $y = \sqrt{1 - (0.807)^2}$
    $= \sqrt{0.348\ 751}$
    $\approx 0.590\ 551$
    c) $x = 0.9664$
11. b) All denominators are 2.
    c) The numerators of the x-coordinates decrease from $\sqrt{3}, \sqrt{2}, \sqrt{1} = 1$, the numerators of the y-coordinates increase from $\sqrt{1}, \sqrt{2}, \sqrt{3}$. The x-coordinates are moving closer to the y-axis and therefore decrease in value, whereas the y-coordinates are moving further away from the x-axis and therefore increase in value.
    d) Since $x^2 + y^2 = 1$ then $x = \sqrt{1 - y^2}$ and $y = \sqrt{1 - x^2}$, all solutions involve taking square roots.
12. a) $-2\pi \leq \theta < 4\pi$ represents three rotations around the unit circle and includes three coterminal angles for each point on the unit circle.
    b) If $P(\theta) = \left(-\frac{1}{2}, \frac{\sqrt{3}}{2}\right)$, then $\theta = -\frac{4\pi}{3}$ when $-2\pi \leq \theta \leq 0$, $\theta = \frac{2\pi}{3}$ when $0 \leq \theta \leq 2\pi$, and $\theta = \frac{8\pi}{3}$ when $2\pi \leq \theta < 4\pi$.
    c) All these angles are coterminal since they are all 2π radians apart.
13. a)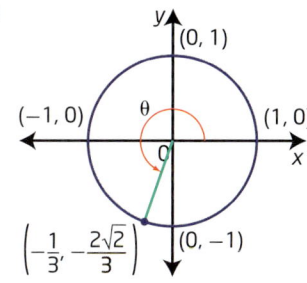

    This point represents the terminal point of an angular rotation on the unit circle.

    b) quadrant III   c) $P\left(\theta + \frac{\pi}{2}\right) = \left(\frac{2\sqrt{2}}{3}, -\frac{1}{3}\right)$
    d) $P\left(\theta - \frac{\pi}{2}\right) = \left(-\frac{2\sqrt{2}}{3}, \frac{1}{3}\right)$
14.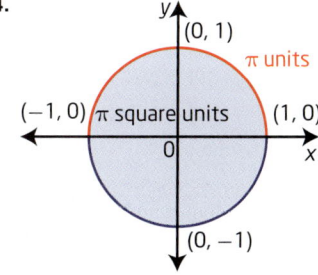

    π units is the perimeter of half of a unit circle since $a = r\theta = (1)\pi = \pi$ units. π square units is the area of a unit circle since $A = \pi r^2 = \pi(1)^2 = \pi$ square units.

15. a) B(−a, b), C(−a, −b), D(a, −b)
  b)   **i)** θ + π = C(−a, −b)   **ii)** θ − π = C(−a, −b)
       iii) −θ + π = B(−a, b)   **iv)** −θ − π = B(−a, b)
  c) They do not differ.

16. a) $\theta = \frac{5\pi}{4}$; $a = r\theta = (1)\left(\frac{5\pi}{4}\right) = \frac{5\pi}{4}$

  b) $P\left(\frac{13\pi}{2}\right)$ represents the ordered pair of the point where the terminal arm of the angle $\frac{13\pi}{2}$ intersects the unit circle. Since one rotation of the unit circle is 2π, then $\frac{13\pi}{2}$ represents three complete rotations with an extra $\frac{\pi}{2}$ or quarter rotation, therefore ending at point A.

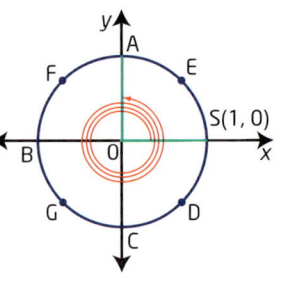

  c) Point $C = P\left(\frac{3\pi}{2}\right) \approx P(4.71)$ and point $D = P\left(\frac{7\pi}{4}\right) \approx P(5.50)$. Therefore P(5), lies between points C and D.

17. a) $\left(-\frac{1}{\sqrt{10}}, \frac{3}{\sqrt{10}}\right)$ and $\left(\frac{1}{\sqrt{10}}, -\frac{3}{\sqrt{10}}\right)$

  b)

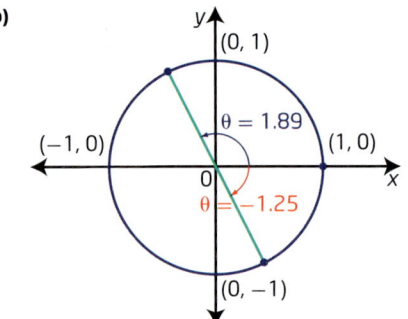

  θ represents the angle in standard position.

18. a) $\left(\frac{5}{\sqrt{29}}, \frac{2}{\sqrt{29}}\right)$ **b)** $\sqrt{29}$
  c) $x^2 + y^2 = 29$

19.

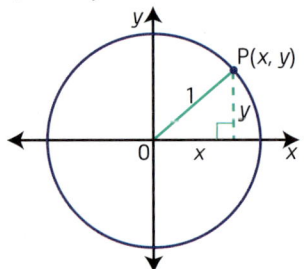

From the diagram: opposite side = y, adjacent side = x and hypotenuse = 1. Since $\sin \theta = \frac{\text{opposite}}{\text{hypotenuse}}$ then $\sin \theta = \frac{y}{1} = y$ or $y = \sin \theta$. Similarly, $\cos \theta = \frac{\text{adjacent}}{\text{hypotenuse}}$, so $\cos \theta = \frac{x}{1} = x$ or $x = \cos \theta$. Therefore any point on the unit circle can be represented by the coordinates $(\cos \theta, \sin \theta)$.

20. a) $\left(1, \frac{\pi}{4}\right)$ **b)** $\left(\frac{\sqrt{31}}{6}, 3.509\right)$
  c) $\left(2\sqrt{2}, \frac{\pi}{4}\right)$ **d)** (5, 5.640)

C1 a)

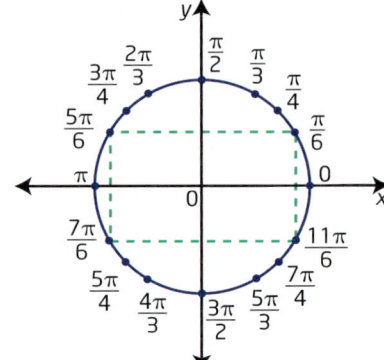

  b)

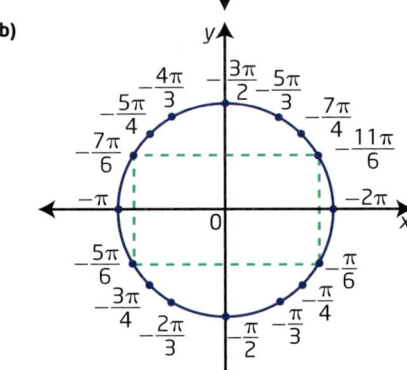

  c) $\left(\frac{\sqrt{3}}{2}, \frac{1}{2}\right), \left(-\frac{\sqrt{3}}{2}, \frac{1}{2}\right), \left(-\frac{\sqrt{3}}{2}, -\frac{1}{2}\right), \left(\frac{\sqrt{3}}{2}, -\frac{1}{2}\right)$

  d) Example: The circumference is divided into eighths by successive quarter rotations, each eighth of the circumference measures $\frac{\pi}{4}$. The exact coordinates of the points can be determined using the special right triangles $(1:1:\sqrt{2}$ and $1:\sqrt{3}:2)$ with signs adjusted according to the quadrant.

C2 a) $\frac{\pi}{5}$ **b)** $\frac{3\pi}{20}$

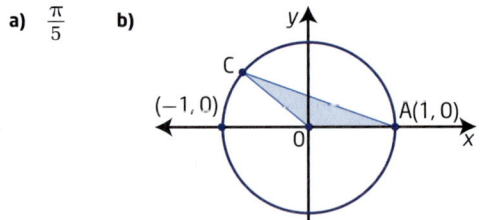

C3 a)

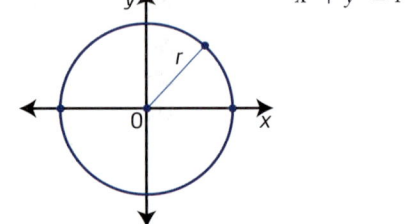

b) Compare with a quadratic function. When $y = x^2$ is translated so its vertex moves from (0, 0) to (h, k), its equation becomes $y = (x - h)^2 + k$. So, a reasonable conjecture for the circle centre (0, 0) moving its centre to (h, k) is $(x - h)^2 + (y - k)^2 = r^2$. Test some key points on the circle centre (0, 0) such as (r, 0). When the centre moves to (h, k) the test point moves to (r + h, k). Substitute into the left side of the equation.
$(r + h - h)^2 + (k - k)^2 = r^2 + 0 =$ right side.

C4 a) 21.5%   **b)** $\pi:4$

4.3 Trigonometric Ratios, pages 201 to 205

1. a) $\frac{\sqrt{2}}{2}$ **b)** $\frac{1}{\sqrt{3}}$ or $\frac{\sqrt{3}}{3}$ **c)** $-\frac{\sqrt{2}}{2}$
d) $\sqrt{3}$ **e)** -2 **f)** -2
g) undefined **h)** -1 **i)** $\frac{1}{\sqrt{3}}$ or $\frac{\sqrt{3}}{3}$
j) $\frac{\sqrt{3}}{2}$ **k)** $-\frac{\sqrt{3}}{2}$ **l)** $\sqrt{2}$

2. a) 0.68 **b)** -2.75 **c)** 1.04
d) -1.00 **e)** -0.96 **f)** 1.37
g) 0.78 **h)** 0.71 **i)** 0.53
j) -0.97 **k)** -3.44 **l)** undefined

3. a) I or IV **b)** II or IV **c)** III or IV
d) II **e)** II **f)** I

4. a) $\sin 250° = -\sin 70°$ **b)** $\tan 290° = -\tan 70°$
c) $\sec 135° = -\sec 45°$ **d)** $\cos 4 = -\cos(4 - \pi)$
e) $\csc 3 = \csc(\pi - 3)$ **f)** $\cot 4.95 = \cot(4.95 - \pi)$

5. a) 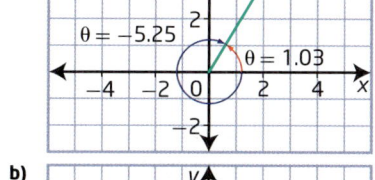   1.03, -5.25

b) 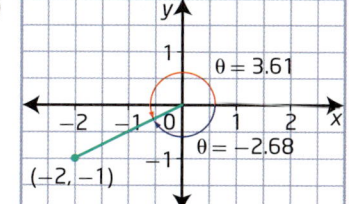   3.61, -2.68

c) 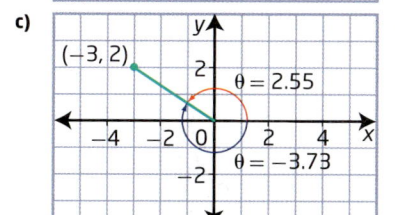   2.55, -3.73

d) 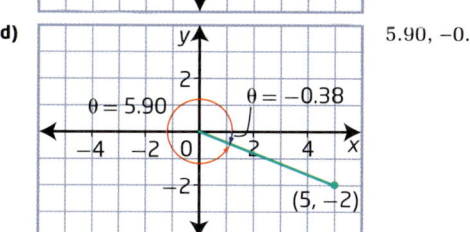   5.90, -0.38

6. a) positive **b)** negative **c)** negative
d) positive **e)** positive **f)** positive

7. a) $\sin^{-1} 0.2014 = 0.2$; an angle of 0.2 radians has a sine ratio of 0.2014
b) $\tan^{-1} 1.429 = 7$; an angle of 7 radians has a tangent ratio of 1.429
c) $\sec 450°$ is undefined; an angle of 450° has a secant ratio that is undefined
d) $\cot(-180°)$ is undefined; an angle of $-180°$ has a cotangent ratio that is undefined

8. a) $-\frac{4}{5}$ **b)** $-\frac{4}{3}$ **c)** -1.25

9. a) 1 **b)** 2 **c)** 1
d) -1 **e)** 1 **f)** 3

10. a) $\frac{7\pi}{6}, \frac{11\pi}{6}$ **b)** $-\frac{3\pi}{4}, \frac{\pi}{4}, \frac{5\pi}{4}$

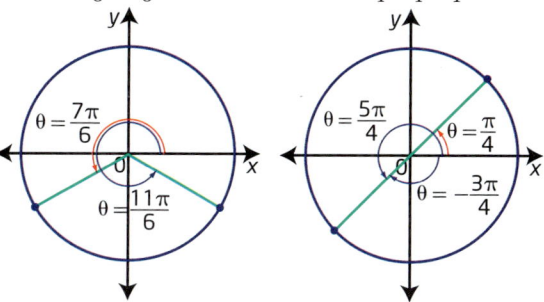

c) $-60°, 60°$ **d)** $-360°, -180°, 0°, 180°$

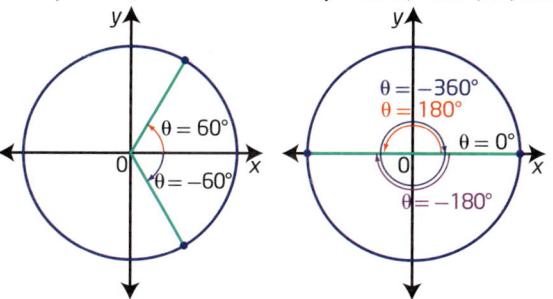

11. a) 1.14 or -1.14 **b)** -1.37 or 1.77

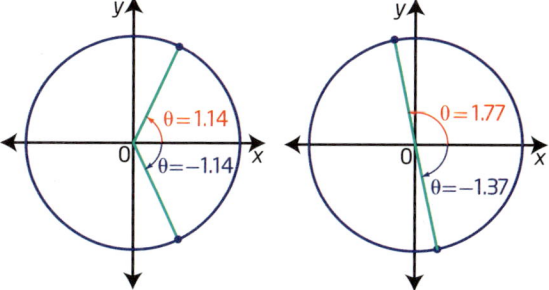

c) 11.85°, 168.15°, $-191.85°$, and $-348.15°$ **d)** 33.69°, 213.69° and $-146.31°$

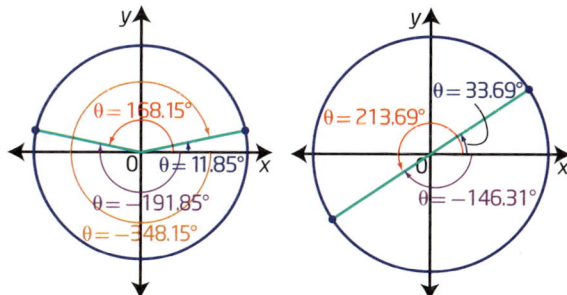

12. a) $\cos\theta = -\frac{4}{5}$, $\tan\theta = -\frac{3}{4}$, $\csc\theta = \frac{5}{3}$,
$\sec\theta = -\frac{5}{4}$, $\cot\theta = -\frac{4}{3}$

b) $\sin\theta = \pm\frac{1}{3}$, $\tan\theta = \pm\frac{\sqrt{2}}{4}$, $\csc\theta = \pm 3$,
$\sec\theta = -\frac{3\sqrt{2}}{4}$, $\cot\theta = \pm 2\sqrt{2}$

c) $\sin\theta = \pm\frac{2}{\sqrt{13}}$, $\cos\theta = \pm\frac{3}{\sqrt{13}}$,
$\csc\theta = \pm\frac{\sqrt{13}}{2}$, $\sec\theta = \pm\frac{\sqrt{13}}{3}$, $\cot\theta = \frac{3}{2}$

d) $\sin\theta = \pm\frac{\sqrt{39}}{4\sqrt{3}}$ or $\pm\frac{\sqrt{13}}{4}$, $\cos\theta = \frac{3}{4\sqrt{3}}$ or $\frac{\sqrt{3}}{4}$,
$\csc\theta = \pm\frac{4\sqrt{3}}{\sqrt{39}}$ or $\pm\frac{4\sqrt{13}}{13}$, $\tan\theta = \pm\frac{\sqrt{39}}{3}$,
$\cot\theta = \pm\frac{3}{\sqrt{39}}$ or $\pm\frac{\sqrt{39}}{13}$

13. Sketch the point and angle in standard position. Draw the reference triangle. Find the missing value of the hypotenuse by using the equation $x^2 + y^2 = r^2$. Use $\cos\theta = \frac{\text{adjacent}}{\text{hypotenuse}}$ to find the exact value.
Therefore, $\cos\theta = -\frac{2}{\sqrt{13}}$ or $-\frac{2\sqrt{13}}{13}$.

14. a) $\frac{4900°}{360°} = 13\frac{11}{18}$ revolutions counterclockwise

b) quadrant III **c)** 40°

d) $\sin 4900° = -0.643$, $\cos 4900° = -0.766$,
$\tan 4900° = 0.839$, $\csc 4900° = -1.556$,
$\sec 4900° = -1.305$, $\cot 4900° = 1.192$

15. a) 0.8; For an angle whose cosine is 0.6, think of a 3-4-5 right triangle, or in this case a 0.6-0.8-1 right triangle. The *x*-coordinate is the same as the cosine or 0.6, the sine is the *y*-coordinate which will be 0.8.

b) 0.8; Since $\cos^{-1} 0.6 = 90° - \sin^{-1} 0.6$ and $\sin^{-1} 0.6 = 90° - \cos^{-1} 0.6$, then $\cos(\sin^{-1} 0.6) = \sin(\cos^{-1} 0.6)$. Alternatively use similar reasoning as in part a) except the *x*- and *y*-coordinates are switched.

16. a) He is not correct. His calculator was in degree measure but the angle is expressed in radians.

b) Set calculator to radian mode and find the value of $\cos\left(\frac{40\pi}{7}\right)$. Since $\sec\theta = \frac{1}{\cos\theta}$, take the reciprocal of $\cos\left(\frac{40\pi}{7}\right)$ to get $\sec\left(\frac{40\pi}{7}\right) \approx 1.603\,875\,472$.

17. a) sin 4, sin 3, sin 1, sin 2

b) 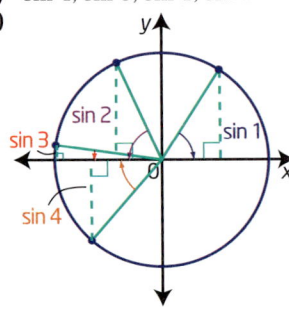 Sin 4 is in quadrant III and has a negative value, therefore it has the least value. Sin 3 is in quadrant II but has the smallest reference angle and is therefore the second smallest. Sin 1 has a smaller reference angle than sin 2.

c) cos 3, cos 4, cos 2, cos 1

18. a) 2 units

b)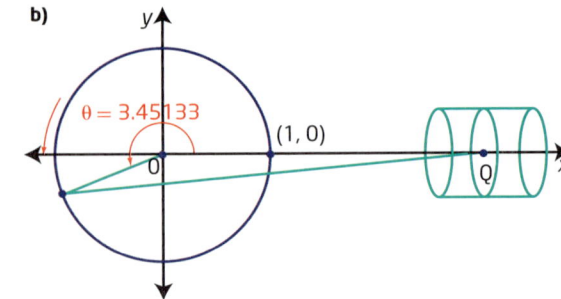

c) 0.46 units

19. a) 2.21, 8.50 **b)** −11.31°, 348.69°
c) −2.16, 4.12, 10.41

20.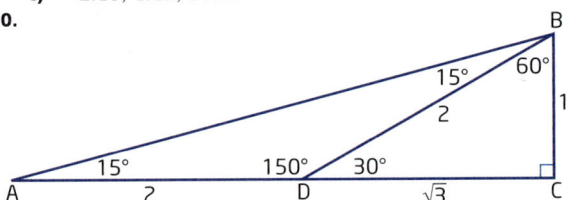

△BCD is a 30°-60°-90° triangle, so DC = $\sqrt{3}$ units and BD = 2 units. △ABD has two equal angles of 15°, so AD = BD = 2. Then
$\tan 15° = \frac{BC}{AC} = \frac{BC}{CD + DA} = \frac{1}{\sqrt{3} + 2}$.

21. Since $\cos\theta = \frac{\text{adjacent}}{\text{hypotenuse}} = \frac{2.5}{5.0} = \frac{1}{2}$ then $\theta = 60°$.
Since 60° is $\frac{2}{3}$ of 90° then the point is $\frac{1}{3}$ the distance on the arc from (0, 5) to (5, 0).

22. a)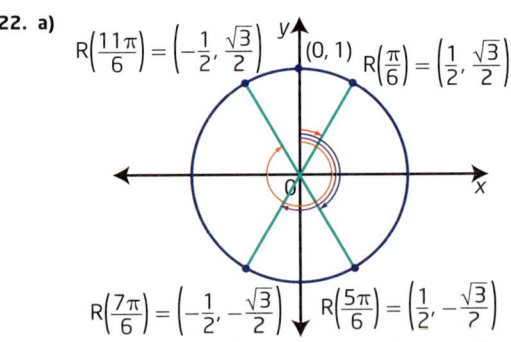

b) $R\left(\frac{\pi}{6}\right) = \left(\frac{1}{2}, \frac{\sqrt{3}}{2}\right)$ and $R\left(\frac{5\pi}{6}\right) = \left(\frac{1}{2}, -\frac{\sqrt{3}}{2}\right)$

c) $R\left(\frac{\pi}{6}\right) = P\left(\frac{\pi}{3}\right)$, $R\left(\frac{5\pi}{6}\right) = P\left(\frac{5\pi}{3}\right)$, $R\left(\frac{7\pi}{6}\right) = P\left(\frac{4\pi}{3}\right)$,
$R\left(\frac{11\pi}{6}\right) = P\left(\frac{2\pi}{3}\right)$, where R(θ) represents the new angle and P(θ) represents the conventional angle in standard position.

d) The new system is the same as bearings in navigation, except bearings are measured in degrees, not radians.

23. a) In △OBQ, $\cos\theta = \frac{OB}{OQ} = \frac{1}{OQ}$.
So, $\sec\theta = \frac{1}{\cos\theta} = OQ$.

b)

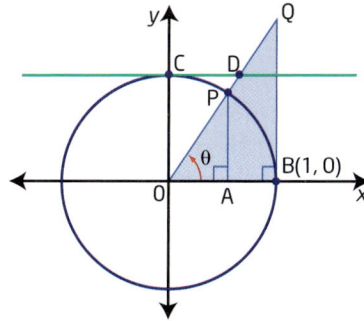

In △OCD, ∠ODC = θ (alternate angles). Then, sin θ = $\frac{OC}{OD}$ = $\frac{1}{OD}$. So, csc θ = $\frac{1}{\sin \theta}$ = OD. Similarly, cot θ = CD.

C1 a) Paula is correct. Examples: sin 0° = 0, sin 10° ≈ 0.1736, sin 25° ≈ 0.4226, sin 30° = 0.5, sin 45° ≈ 0.7071, sin 60° ≈ 0.8660, sin 90° = 1.
b) In quadrant II, sine decreases from sin 90° = 1 to sin 180° = 0. This happens because the *y*-value of points on the unit circle are decreasing toward the horizontal axis as the value of the angle moves from 90° to 180°.
c) Yes, the sine ratio increases in quadrant IV, from its minimum value of −1 at 270° up to 0 at 0°.

C2 When you draw its diagonals, the hexagon is composed of six equilateral triangles. On the diagram shown, each vertex will be 60° from the previous one. So, the coordinates, going in a positive direction from (1, 0) are $\left(\frac{1}{2}, \frac{\sqrt{3}}{2}\right)$, $\left(-\frac{1}{2}, \frac{\sqrt{3}}{2}\right)$, (−1, 0), $\left(-\frac{1}{2}, -\frac{\sqrt{3}}{2}\right)$, and $\left(\frac{1}{2}, -\frac{\sqrt{3}}{2}\right)$.

C3 a) slope$_{OP}$ = $\frac{\sin \theta}{\cos \theta}$ or tan θ
b) Yes, this formula applies in each quadrant. In quadrant II, sin θ is negative, which makes the slope negative, as expected. Similar reasoning applies in the other quadrants.
c) $y = \left(\frac{\sin \theta}{\cos \theta}\right)x$ or $y = (\tan \theta)x$
d) Any line whose slope is defined can be translated vertically by adding the value of the *y*-intercept *b*. The equation will be $y = \left(\frac{\sin \theta}{\cos \theta}\right)x + b$ or $y = (\tan \theta)x + b$.

C4 a) $\frac{4}{5}$ **b)** $\frac{3}{5}$ **c)** $\frac{5}{4}$ **d)** $-\frac{4}{5}$

4.4 Introduction to Trigonometric Equations, pages 211 to 214

1. a) two solutions; sin θ is positive in quadrants I and II
b) four solutions; cos θ is positive in quadrants I and IV, giving two solutions for each of the two complete rotations
c) three solutions; tan θ is negative in quadrants II and IV, and the angle rotates through these quadrants three times from −360° to 180°
d) two solutions; sec θ is positive in quadrants I and IV and the angle is in each quadrant once from −180° to 180°

2. a) θ = $\frac{\pi}{3}$ + 2πn, n ∈ I   **b)** θ = $\frac{5\pi}{3}$ + 2πn, n ∈ I
3. a) θ = $\frac{\pi}{6}, \frac{11\pi}{6}$ **b)** θ = 0°, 180°
c) θ = −135°, −45°, 45°, 135°, 225°, 315°
d) θ = $-\frac{3\pi}{4}, \frac{3\pi}{4}, \frac{5\pi}{4}$
4. a) θ = 1.35, 4.49   **b)** θ = 1.76, 4.52
c) θ = 1.14, 2.00   **d)** θ = 0.08, 3.22
e) 1.20 and 5.08   **f)** 3.83 and 5.59
5. a) θ = π   **b)** θ = $-\frac{\pi}{6}, \frac{5\pi}{6}, \frac{11\pi}{6}$
c) x = −315°, −225°, 45°, 135°
d) x = −150°, −30°
e) x = −45°, 135°, 315°
f) θ = $-\frac{5\pi}{6}, \frac{5\pi}{6}, \frac{7\pi}{6}, \frac{17\pi}{6}$
6. a) θ ∈ [−2π, 2π]   **b)** θ ∈ $\left[-\frac{\pi}{3}, \frac{7\pi}{3}\right]$
c) θ ∈ [0°, 270°]   **d)** 0 ≤ θ < π
e) 0° < θ < 450°   **f)** −2π < θ ≤ 4π
7. a) θ = 0, $\frac{\pi}{3}, \frac{5\pi}{3}$
b) θ = 63.435°, 243.435°, 135°, 315°
c) θ = 0, $\frac{\pi}{2}$, π
d) θ = −180°, −70.529°, 70.529°
8. Check for θ = 180°.
Left Side = 5(cos 180°)² = 5(−1)² = 5
Right Side = −4 cos 180° = −4(−1) = 4
Since Left Side ≠ Right Side, θ = 180° is not a solution.
Check for θ = 270°.
Left Side = 5(cos 270°)² = 5(0)² = 0
Right Side = −4 cos 270° = −4(0) = 0
Since Left Side = Right Side, θ = 270° is a solution.
9. a) They should not have divided both sides of the equation by sin θ. This will eliminate one of the possible solutions.
b)
$2 \sin^2 \theta = \sin \theta$
$2 \sin^2 \theta - \sin \theta = 0$
$\sin \theta (2 \sin \theta - 1) = 0$
$\sin \theta = 0$ and $2 \sin \theta - 1 = 0$
$\sin \theta = \frac{1}{2}$
θ = $\frac{\pi}{6}, \frac{5\pi}{6}$, π
10. Sin θ = 0 when θ = 0, π, and 2π but none of these values are in the interval (π, 2π).
11. Sin θ is only defined for the values −1 ≤ sin θ ≤ 1, and 2 is outside this range, so sin θ = 2 has no solution.
12. Yes, the general solutions are θ = $\frac{\pi}{3}$ + 2πn, n ∈ I and θ = $\frac{5\pi}{3}$ + 2πn, n ∈ I. Since there are an infinite number of integers, there will be an infinite number of solutions coterminal with $\frac{\pi}{3}$ and $\frac{5\pi}{3}$.
13. a) Helene can check her work by substituting π for θ in the original equation.
Left Side = 3(sin π)² − 2 sin π
= 3(0)² − 2(0)
= 0
= Right Side
b) θ = 0, 0.7297, 2.4119, π
14. 25.56°
15. a) June   **b)** December
c) Yes. Greatest sales of air conditioners be expected to happen before the hottest months (June) and the least sales before the coldest months (December).

16. The solution is correct as far as the statement "Sine is negative in quadrants II and III." Sine is actually negative in quadrants III and IV. Quadrant III solution is 180° + 41.8° = 221.8° and quadrant IV solution is 360° − 41.8° = 318.2°.

17. Examples: Tan 90° has no solution since division by 0 is undefined. sin θ = 2 does not have a solution. The range of y = sin θ is −1 ≤ y ≤ 1 and 2 is beyond this range.

18. sec θ = $-\frac{5}{3}$

19. **a)** 0 s, 3 s, 6 s, 9 s **b)** 1.5 s, 1.5 + 6n, n ∈ W
    c) 1.4 m below sea level

20. **a)** Substitute I = 0, then 0 = 4.3 sin 120πt
    0 = sin 120πt
    sin θ = 0 at θ = 0, π, 2π, …
    0 = 120πt → t = 0
    π = 120πt → t = $\frac{1}{120}$
    2π = 120πt → t = $\frac{1}{60}$
    Since the current must alternate from 0 to positive back to 0 and then negative back to 0, it will take $\frac{1}{60}$ s for one complete cycle or 60 cycles in one second.
    b) t = 0.004 167 + $\frac{1}{60}$n, n ∈ W seconds
    c) t = 0.0125 + $\frac{1}{60}$n, n ∈ W seconds
    d) 4.3 amps

21. x = $\frac{\pi}{3}, \frac{2\pi}{3}$

22. **a)** No. **b)** sin θ = $\frac{-1 + \sqrt{5}}{2}$ and $\frac{-1 - \sqrt{5}}{2}$
    c) 0.67, 2.48

23. **a)** The height of the trapezoid is 4 sin θ and its base is 4 + 2(4 cos θ). Use the formula for the area of a trapezoid:
    A = $\frac{\text{sum of parallel sides}}{2}$ × height
    A = $\left(\frac{4 + 4 + 8 \cos \theta}{2}\right)$(4 sin θ)
    A = 8(1 + cos θ)(2 sin θ)
    A = 16 sin θ(1 + cos θ)
    b) $\frac{\pi}{3}$
    c) Example: Graph y = 16 sin θ(1 + cos θ) and find the maximum for domain in the first quadrant.

C1 The principles involved are the same up to the point where you need to solve for a trigonometric ratio.

C2 a) Check if $x^2 + y^2 = 1$. Yes, A is on the unit circle.
b) cos θ = 0.385, tan θ = 2.400, csc θ = 1.083
c) 67.4°; this angle measure seems reasonable as shown on the diagram.

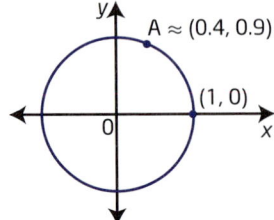

C3 a) Non-permissible values are values that the variable can never be because the expression is not defined in that case. For a rational expression, this occurs when the denominator is zero.
Example: $\frac{3}{x}, x \neq 0$

b) Example: tan $\frac{\pi}{2}$ **c)** $\frac{\pi}{2}, \frac{3\pi}{2}, \frac{5\pi}{2}, \frac{7\pi}{2}$
d) $\frac{\pi}{2} + \pi n, n \in I$

C4 a) 30°, 150°, 270°
b) Exact, because sin⁻¹(0.5) and sin⁻¹(−1) correspond to exact angle measures.
c) Example: Substitute θ = 30° in each side. Left side = 2 sin² 30° = 2(0.5)² = 0.5. Right side = 1 − sin 30° = 1 − 0.5 = 0.5. The value checks.

Chapter 4 Review, pages 215 to 217

1. **a)** quadrant II **b)** quadrant II
   c) quadrant III **d)** quadrant II

2. **a)** 450° **b)** $\frac{4\pi}{3}$

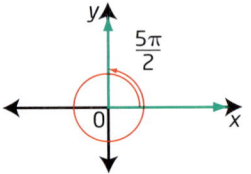 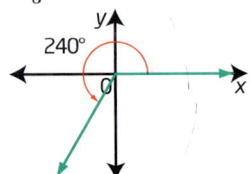

c) $-\frac{9\pi}{4}$ **d)** $-\frac{630°}{\pi}$

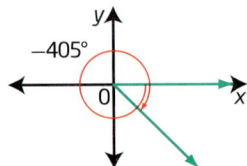 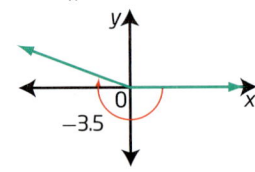

3. **a)** 0.35 **b)** −3.23 **c)** −100.27° **d)** 75°
4. **a)** 0.467 **b)** 40°

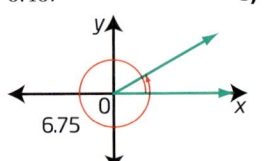 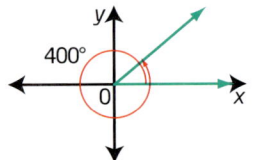

c) 3.28 **d)** 255°

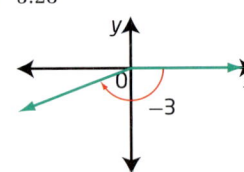 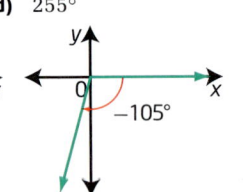

5. **a)** 250° ± (360°)n, n ∈ N **b)** $\frac{5\pi}{2}$ ± 2πn, n ∈ N
   c) −300° ± (360°)n, n ∈ N **d)** 6 ± 2πn, n ∈ N
6. **a)** 160 000π radians/minute **b)** 480 000°/s
7. **a)** $\left(\frac{-\sqrt{3}}{2}, \frac{1}{2}\right)$ **b)** $\left(-\frac{\sqrt{3}}{2}, -\frac{1}{2}\right)$ **c)** (0, 1)
   d) $\left(\frac{\sqrt{2}}{2}, \frac{\sqrt{2}}{2}\right)$ **e)** $\left(-\frac{1}{2}, \frac{\sqrt{3}}{2}\right)$ **f)** $\left(\frac{1}{2}, -\frac{\sqrt{3}}{2}\right)$

8. **a)** Reflect P$\left(\frac{\pi}{3}\right)$ = $\left(\frac{1}{2}, \frac{\sqrt{3}}{2}\right)$ in the y-axis to give
   P$\left(\frac{2\pi}{3}\right)$ = $\left(-\frac{1}{2}, \frac{\sqrt{3}}{2}\right)$; then reflect this point in the x-axis to give P$\left(\frac{4\pi}{3}\right)$ = $\left(-\frac{1}{2}, -\frac{\sqrt{3}}{2}\right)$. Reflect about the original point in the x-axis to give
   P$\left(\frac{5\pi}{3}\right)$ = $\left(\frac{1}{2}, -\frac{\sqrt{3}}{2}\right)$.
   b) $\left(-\frac{1}{3}, -\frac{2\sqrt{2}}{3}\right)$

c) quadrant IV; $P\left(\dfrac{5\pi}{6}\right)$ lies in quadrant II and $P\left(\dfrac{5\pi}{6} + \pi\right)$ is a half circle away, so it lies in quadrant IV. $\theta = \dfrac{11\pi}{6}$ $P\left(\dfrac{11\pi}{6}\right) = \left(\dfrac{\sqrt{3}}{2}, -\dfrac{1}{2}\right)$

9. a) $P\left(\dfrac{\pi}{2}\right)$ and $P\left(-\dfrac{3\pi}{2}\right)$ **b)** $P\left(\dfrac{11\pi}{6}\right)$ and $P\left(-\dfrac{\pi}{6}\right)$
c) $P\left(\dfrac{3\pi}{4}\right)$ and $P\left(-\dfrac{5\pi}{4}\right)$ **d)** $P\left(\dfrac{2\pi}{3}\right)$ and $P\left(-\dfrac{4\pi}{3}\right)$

10. a) $P(-150°)$ and $P(210°)$ **b)** $P(180°)$
c) $P(135°)$ **d)** $P(-60°)$ and $P(300°)$

11. a) $\theta = 318°$ or 5.55 **b)** IV
c) $\left(-\dfrac{\sqrt{5}}{3}, \dfrac{2}{3}\right)$
d) $\left(\dfrac{2}{3}, \dfrac{\sqrt{5}}{3}\right)$
e) $\left(-\dfrac{2}{3}, -\dfrac{\sqrt{5}}{3}\right)$

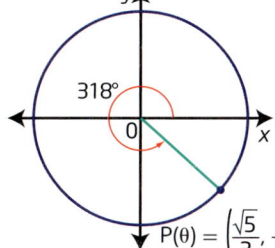

12. $\sin\theta = \dfrac{2\sqrt{2}}{3}$, $\tan\theta = 2\sqrt{2}$, $\sec\theta = 3$,
$\csc\theta = \dfrac{3}{2\sqrt{2}}$ or $\dfrac{3\sqrt{2}}{4}$, $\cot\theta = \dfrac{1}{2\sqrt{2}}$ or $\dfrac{\sqrt{2}}{4}$

13. a) 1 **b)** $-\dfrac{\sqrt{2}}{2}$ **c)** $\sqrt{3}$
d) $-\dfrac{2\sqrt{3}}{3}$ **e)** 0 **f)** $-\dfrac{2\sqrt{3}}{3}$

14. a) $\theta = -5.71, -3.71,$ **b)** $\theta = -96.14°, 83.86°,$
$0.57,$ and 2.57 $263.86°$

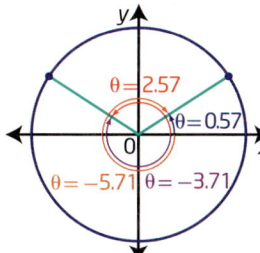 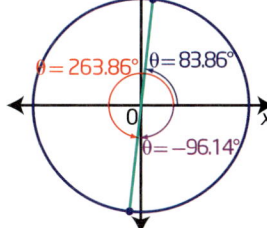

c) $\theta = -2.45, 2.45$ **d)** $\theta = -186.04°, 6.04°$

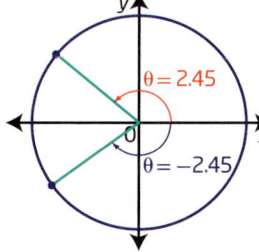 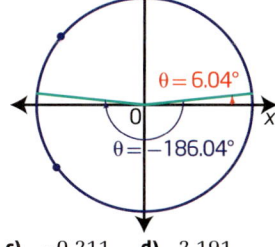

15. a) -0.966 **b)** -0.839 **c)** -0.211 **d)** 2.191
16. a) Example: $127°$

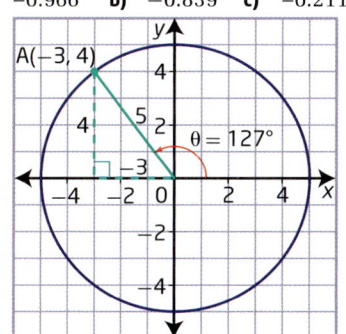

b) $\cos\theta = \dfrac{\text{adjacent}}{\text{hypotenuse}} = -\dfrac{3}{5}$ **c)** $-\dfrac{1}{12}$
d) $126.9°$ or 2.2

17. a) $\cos\theta(\cos\theta + 1)$ **b)** $(\sin\theta - 4)(\sin\theta + 1)$
c) $(\cot\theta + 3)(\cot\theta - 3)$ **d)** $(2\tan\theta - 5)(\tan\theta - 2)$

18. a) 2 is not a possible value for $\sin\theta$, $|\sin\theta| \leq 1$
b) $\tan 90° = \dfrac{\sin 90°}{\cos 90°} = \dfrac{1}{0}$, but division by 0 is undefined, so $\tan 90°$ has no solutions

19. a) 2 solutions **b)** 2 solutions
c) 1 solution **d)** 6 solutions

20. a) $\theta = 45°, 135°$ **b)** $\theta = \dfrac{2\pi}{3}, \dfrac{4\pi}{3}$
c) $\theta = -150°, 30°, 210°$ **d)** $\theta = -\dfrac{\pi}{4}, \dfrac{3\pi}{4}$

21. a) $\theta = \dfrac{\pi}{2}$
b) $\theta = 108.435°, 180°, 288.435°, 360°$
c) $\theta = 70.529°, 120°, 240°,$ and $289.471°$
d) $\theta = -\dfrac{2\pi}{3}, -\dfrac{\pi}{3}, \dfrac{\pi}{3}, \dfrac{2\pi}{3}$

22. Examples:
a) $0 \leq \theta < 2\pi$ **b)** $-2\pi \leq \theta < \dfrac{\pi}{2}$
c) $-720° \leq \theta < 0°$ **d)** $-270° \leq \theta < 450°$

23. a) $x = \dfrac{7\pi}{6} + 2\pi n, n \in I$ and $x = \dfrac{11\pi}{6} + 2\pi n, n \in I$
b) $x = 90° + (360°)n, n \in I$ and $x = (180°)n, n \in I$
c) $x = 120° + (360°)n, n \in I$ and
$x = 240° + (360°)n, n \in I$
d) $x = \dfrac{\pi}{4} + \pi n, n \in I$ and $x = \dfrac{\pi}{3} + \pi n, n \in I$

Chapter 4 Practice Test, pages 218 to 219

1. D **2.** C **3.** A **4.** B **5.** B
6. a) $4668.5°$ or 81.5
b) 92.6 Yes; a smaller tire requires more rotations to travel the same distance so it will experience greater tire wear.
7. a) $x^2 + y^2 = 1$
b) **i)** $y = \pm\dfrac{\sqrt{13}}{5}$

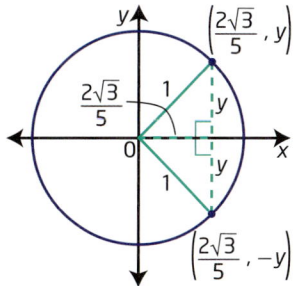

ii) $x = -\dfrac{3}{4}$

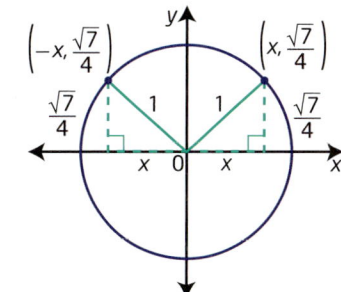

Answers • MHR **589**

c) In the expression $\sin \theta = \dfrac{\text{opposite}}{\text{hypotenuse}}$, substitute the *y*-value for the opposite side and 1 for the hypotenuse. Since $x^2 + y^2 = 1$ then $\cos^2 \theta + \sin^2 \theta = 1$. Substitute the value you determined for $\sin \theta$ into $\cos^2 \theta + \sin^2 \theta = 1$ and solve for $\cos \theta$.

8. a) Cosine is negative in quadrants II and III. Find the reference angle by subtracting π from the given angle in quadrant III. To find the solution in quadrant II, subtract the reference angle from π.
   b) Given each solution θ, add $2\pi n$, $n \in I$ to obtain each general solution $\theta + 2\pi n$, $n \in I$.

9. $\theta = \dfrac{3\pi}{4} + 2\pi n$, $n \in I$ or $\theta = \dfrac{5\pi}{4} + 2\pi n$, $n \in I$

10. Since $1° = \dfrac{\pi}{180}$, then $3° = \dfrac{3\pi}{180}$ or $\dfrac{\pi}{60}$.
    $3 = \dfrac{3(180°)}{\pi} \approx 172°$.

11. a) quadrant III b) $40°$
    c) $\sin(-500°) = -0.6$, $\cos(-500°) = -0.8$, $\tan(-500°) = 0.8$, $\csc(-500°) = -1.6$, $\sec(-500°) = -1.3$, $\cot(-500°) = 1.2$

12. a) $\dfrac{5\pi}{4}, -\dfrac{3\pi}{4}; \dfrac{5\pi}{4} \pm 2\pi n$, $n \in N$
    b) $145°, -215°, 145° \pm (360°)n$, $n \in N$

13. 7.7 km

14.
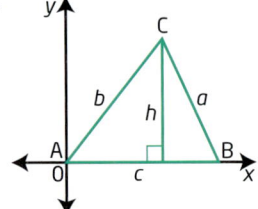

Given $A = \dfrac{1}{2}bh$, $b = $ side c, since $\sin \theta = \dfrac{\text{opposite}}{\text{hypotenuse}}$ then $\sin A = \dfrac{h}{b}$ or $h = b \sin A$ and $A = \dfrac{1}{2}bc \sin A$ or

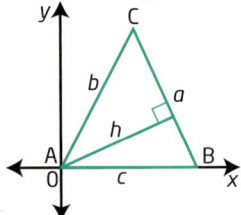

Given $A = \dfrac{1}{2}bh$, $b = $ side a, since $\sin \theta = \dfrac{\text{opposite}}{\text{hypotenuse}}$ then $\sin B = \dfrac{h}{c}$ or $h = c \sin B$, therefore $A = \dfrac{1}{2}ac \sin B$.

15. a) $\theta = -\dfrac{\pi}{4}, \dfrac{3\pi}{4}, \dfrac{7\pi}{4}, -2.21, 0.93, 4.07$
    b) 0.67, 2.48   c) 0, π, 2π, 4.47, 1.33

16. $\dfrac{28\pi}{3}$ m or 29.32 m

Chapter 5 Trigonometric Functions and Graphs

5.1 Graphing Sine and Cosine Functions, pages 233 to 237

1. a) $(0, 0), \left(\dfrac{\pi}{2}, 1\right), (\pi, 0), \left(\dfrac{3\pi}{2}, -1\right), (2\pi, 0)$
   b)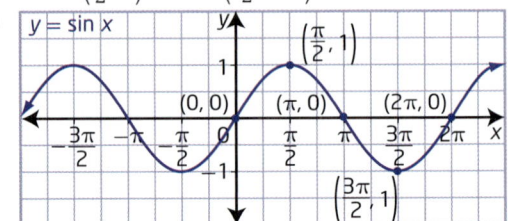
   c) *x*-intercepts: $-2\pi, -\pi, 0, \pi, 2\pi$
   d) *y*-intercept: 0
   e) The maximum value is 1, and the minimum value is -1.

2. a) $(0, 1), \left(\dfrac{\pi}{2}, 0\right), (\pi, -1), \left(\dfrac{3\pi}{2}, 0\right), (2\pi, 1)$
   b)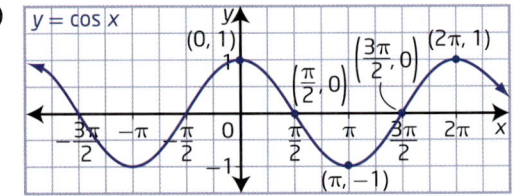
   c) *x*-intercepts: $-\dfrac{3\pi}{2}, -\dfrac{\pi}{2}, \dfrac{\pi}{2}, \dfrac{3\pi}{2}$
   d) *y*-intercept: 1
   e) The maximum value is 1, and the minimum value is -1.

3.
Property	$y = \sin x$	$y = \cos x$
maximum	1	1
minimum	-1	-1
amplitude	1	1
period	2π	2π
domain	$\{x \mid x \in R\}$	$\{x \mid x \in R\}$
range	$\{y \mid -1 \leq y \leq 1, y \in R\}$	$\{y \mid -1 \leq y \leq 1, y \in R\}$
y-intercept	0	1
x-intercepts	πn, $n \in I$	$\dfrac{\pi}{2} + \pi n$, $n \in I$

4. a) 2   b) $\dfrac{1}{2}$

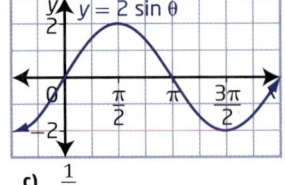 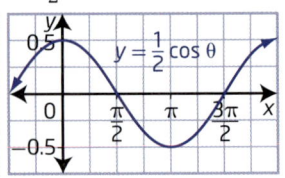

c) $\dfrac{1}{3}$ d) 6

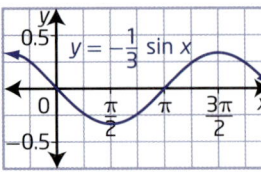 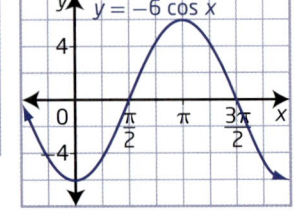

590 MHR • Answers

5. a) $\frac{\pi}{2}$ or 90°

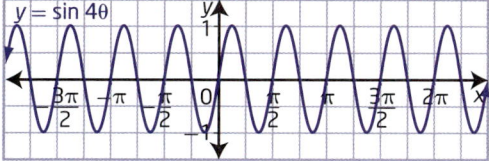

b) 6π or 1080°

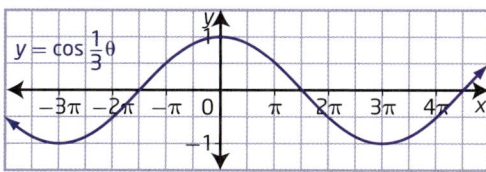

c) 3π or 540°   **d)** $\frac{\pi}{3}$ or 60°

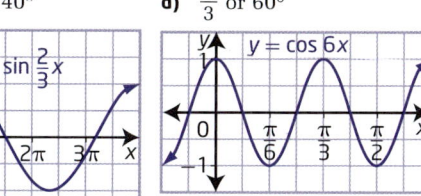

6. a) A   **b)** D   **c)** C   **d)** B

7. a) Amplitude is 3; stretched vertically by a factor of 3 about the x-axis.
b) Amplitude is 5; stretched vertically by a factor of 5 about the x-axis and reflected in the x-axis.
c) Amplitude is 0.15; stretched vertically by a factor of 0.15 about the x-axis.
d) Amplitude is $\frac{2}{3}$; stretched vertically by a factor of $\frac{2}{3}$ about the x-axis and reflected in the x-axis.

8. a) Period is 180°; stretched horizontally by a factor of $\frac{1}{2}$ about the y-axis.
b) Period is 120°; stretched horizontally by a factor of $\frac{1}{3}$ about the y-axis and reflected in the y-axis.
c) Period is 1440°; stretched horizontally by a factor of 4 about the y-axis.
d) Period is 540°; stretched horizontally by a factor of $\frac{3}{2}$ about the y-axis.

9. a) Amplitude is 2; period is 360° or 2π.
b) Amplitude is 4; period is 180° or π.
c) Amplitude is $\frac{5}{3}$; period is 540° or 3π.
d) Amplitude is 3; period is 720° or 4π.

10. a) Graph A: Amplitude is 2 and period is 4π. Graph B: Amplitude is 0.5 and period is π.
b) Graph A: $y = 2 \sin \frac{1}{2}x$; Graph B: $y = 0.5 \cos 2x$
c) Graph A starts at 0, so the sine function is the obvious choice. Graph B starts at 1, so the cosine function is the obvious choice.

11. a)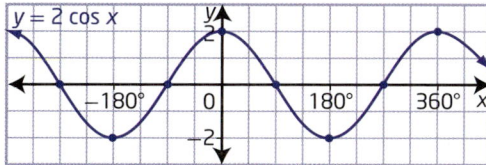

Property	Points on the Graph of $y = 2 \cos x$
maximum	(−360°, 2), (0°, 2), (360°, 2)
minimum	(−180°, −2), (180°, −2)
x-intercepts	(−270°, 0), (−90°, 0), (90°, 0), (270°, 0)
y-intercept	(0, 2)
period	360°
range	$\{y \mid -2 \leq y \leq 2, y \in R\}$

b)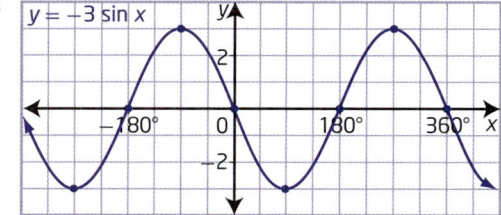

Property	Points on the Graph of $y = -3 \sin x$
maximum	(−90°, 3), (270°, 3)
minimum	(−270°, −3), (90°, −3)
x-intercepts	(−360°, 0), (−180°, 0), (0°, 0), (180°, 0), (360°, 0)
y-intercept	(0, 0)
period	360°
range	$\{y \mid -3 \leq y \leq 3, y \in R\}$

c)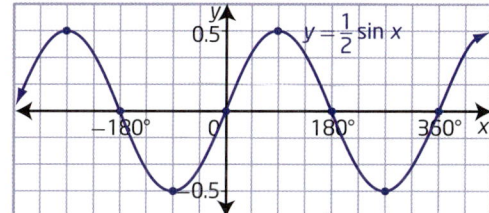

Property	Points on the Graph of $y = \frac{1}{2} \sin x$
maximum	(−270°, 0.5), (90°, 0.5)
minimum	(−90°, −0.5), (270°, −0.5)
x-intercepts	(−360°, 0), (−180°, 0), (0°, 0), (180°, 0), (360°, 0)
y-intercept	(0, 0)
period	360°
range	$\{y \mid -0.5 \leq y \leq 0.5, y \in R\}$

d)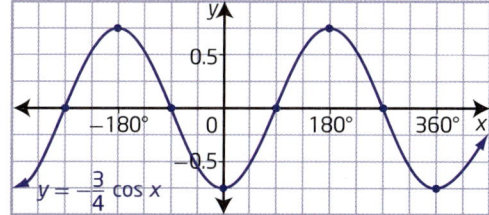

Property	Points on the Graph of $y = -\frac{3}{4} \cos x$
maximum	(−180°, 0.75), (180°, 0.75)
minimum	(−360°, −0.75), (0°, −0.75), (360°, −0.75)
x-intercepts	(−270°, 0), (−90°, 0), (90°, 0), (270°, 0)
y-intercept	(0, −0.75)
period	360°
range	$\{y \mid -0.75 \leq y \leq 0.75, y \in R\}$

12. a) $B(\frac{\pi}{4}, 3)$, $C(\frac{\pi}{2}, 0)$, $D(\frac{3\pi}{4}, -3)$, $E(\pi, 0)$
b) $C(\frac{\pi}{2}, 0)$, $D(\pi, -2)$, $E(\frac{3\pi}{2}, 0)$, $F(2\pi, 2)$
c) $B(-3\pi, 1)$, $C(-2\pi, 0)$, $D(-\pi, -1)$, $E(0, 0)$

13.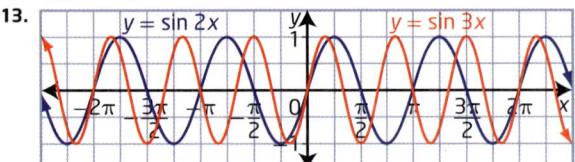

The amplitude, maximum, minimum, y-intercepts, domain, and range are the same for both graphs. The period and x-intercepts are different.

14. a) Amplitude is 5; period is $\frac{4\pi}{3}$.
b) Amplitude is 4; Period is $\frac{2\pi}{3}$.

15. a) Amplitude is 20 mm Hg; Period is 0.8 s.
b) 75 bpm

16. Answers may vary.

17. a)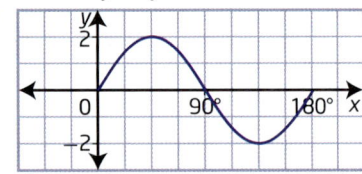

b)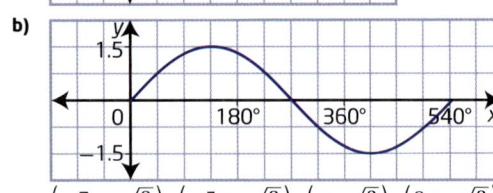

18. a) $\left(-\frac{7\pi}{4}, \frac{\sqrt{2}}{2}\right), \left(-\frac{5\pi}{4}, \frac{\sqrt{2}}{2}\right), \left(\frac{\pi}{4}, \frac{\sqrt{2}}{2}\right), \left(\frac{9\pi}{4}, \frac{\sqrt{2}}{2}\right)$;
Find the points of intersection of $y = \sin\theta$ and $y = \frac{\sqrt{2}}{2}$.

b) $\left(-\frac{11\pi}{6}, \frac{\sqrt{3}}{2}\right), \left(-\frac{\pi}{6}, \frac{\sqrt{3}}{2}\right), \left(\frac{11\pi}{6}, \frac{\sqrt{3}}{2}\right), \left(\frac{13\pi}{6}, \frac{\sqrt{3}}{2}\right)$;
Find the points of intersection of $y = \cos\theta$ and $y = \frac{\sqrt{3}}{2}$.

19.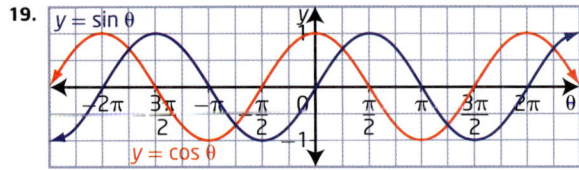

a) The graphs have the same maximum and minimum values, the same period, and the same domain and range.
b) The graphs have different x- and y-intercepts.
c) A horizontal translation could make them the same graph.

20. 12
21. a) $\frac{2\pi}{3}$ **b)** 12
22. 0.9
23. a) Example: The graph of $y = \sqrt{\sin x}$ will contain the portions of the graph of $y = \sin x$ that lie on or above the x-axis.
b)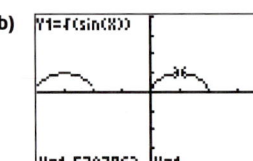

c) Example: The function $y = \sqrt{\sin x + 1}$ is defined for all values of x, while the function $y = \sqrt{\sin x}$ is not.

d)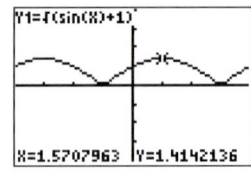

24. It is sinusoidal and the period is 2π.

C1 Step 5
a) The x-coordinate of each point on the unit circle represents $\cos\theta$. The y-coordinate of each point on the unit circle represents the $\sin\theta$.
b) The y-coordinates of the points on the sine graph are the same as the y-coordinates of the points on the unit circle. The y-coordinates of the points on the cosine graph are the same as the x-coordinates of the points on the unit circle.

C2 The constant is 1. The sum of the squares of the legs of each right triangle is equal to the radius of the unit circle, which is always 1.

C3 a) Cannot determine because the amplitude is not given.
b) $f(4) = 0$; given in the question.
c) $f(84) = 0$; the period is 40° so it returns to 0 every 40°.

C4 a) Sine and Cosine **b)** Sine and Cosine
c) Sine and Cosine **d)** Sine and Cosine
e) Sine **f)** Cosine **g)** Cosine **h)** Sine
i) Cosine **j)** Sine **k)** Cosine **l)** Sine
m) Sine **n)** Cosine

C5 a)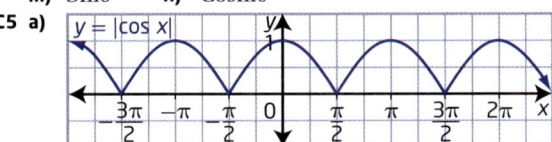

The parts of the graph below the x-axis have been reflected across the x-axis.

b)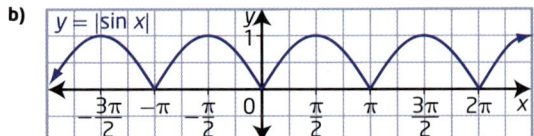

The parts of the graph below the x-axis have been reflected across the x-axis.

5.2 Transformations of Sinusoidal Functions, pages 250 to 255

1. a)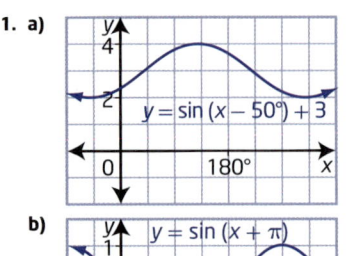

The phase shift is 50° right. The vertical displacement is 3 units up.

b)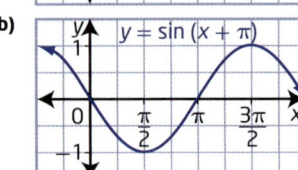

The phase shift is π units left. There is no vertical displacement.

592 MHR • Answers

c)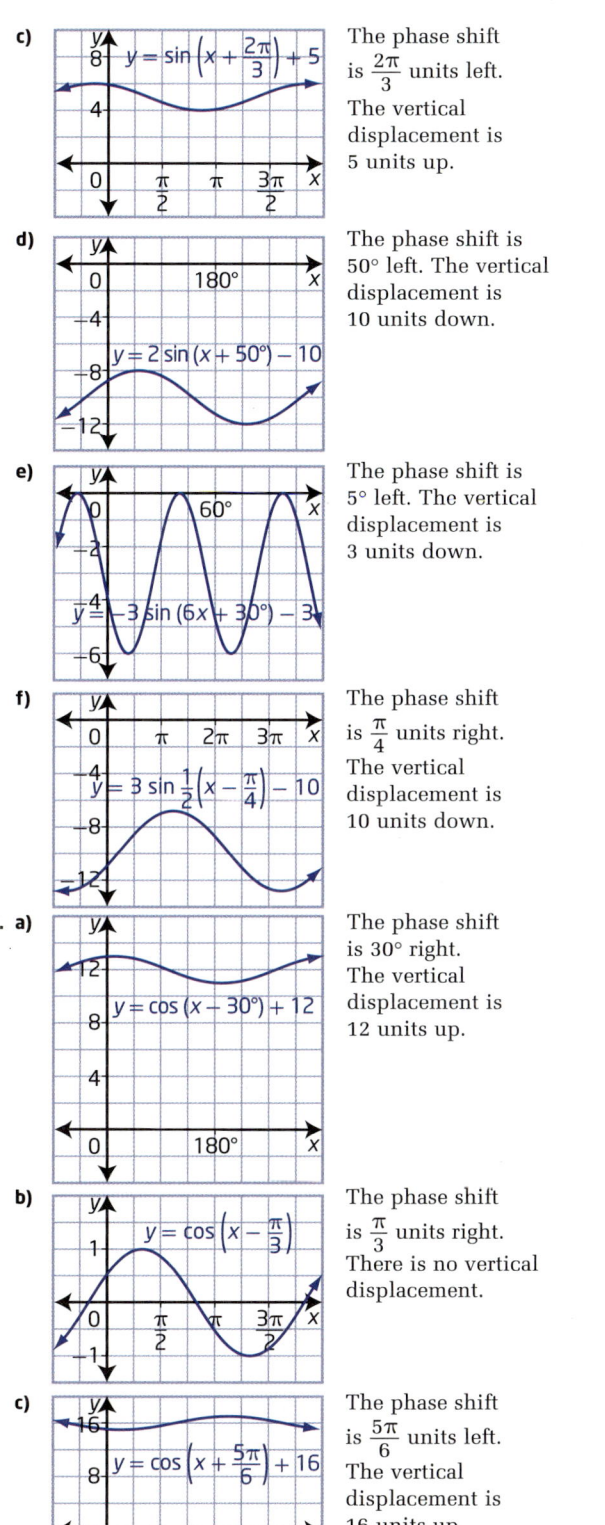
The phase shift is $\frac{2\pi}{3}$ units left. The vertical displacement is 5 units up.

d) The phase shift is 50° left. The vertical displacement is 10 units down.

e) The phase shift is 5° left. The vertical displacement is 3 units down.

f) The phase shift is $\frac{\pi}{4}$ units right. The vertical displacement is 10 units down.

2. a) The phase shift is 30° right. The vertical displacement is 12 units up.

b) The phase shift is $\frac{\pi}{3}$ units right. There is no vertical displacement.

c) The phase shift is $\frac{5\pi}{6}$ units left. The vertical displacement is 16 units up.

d)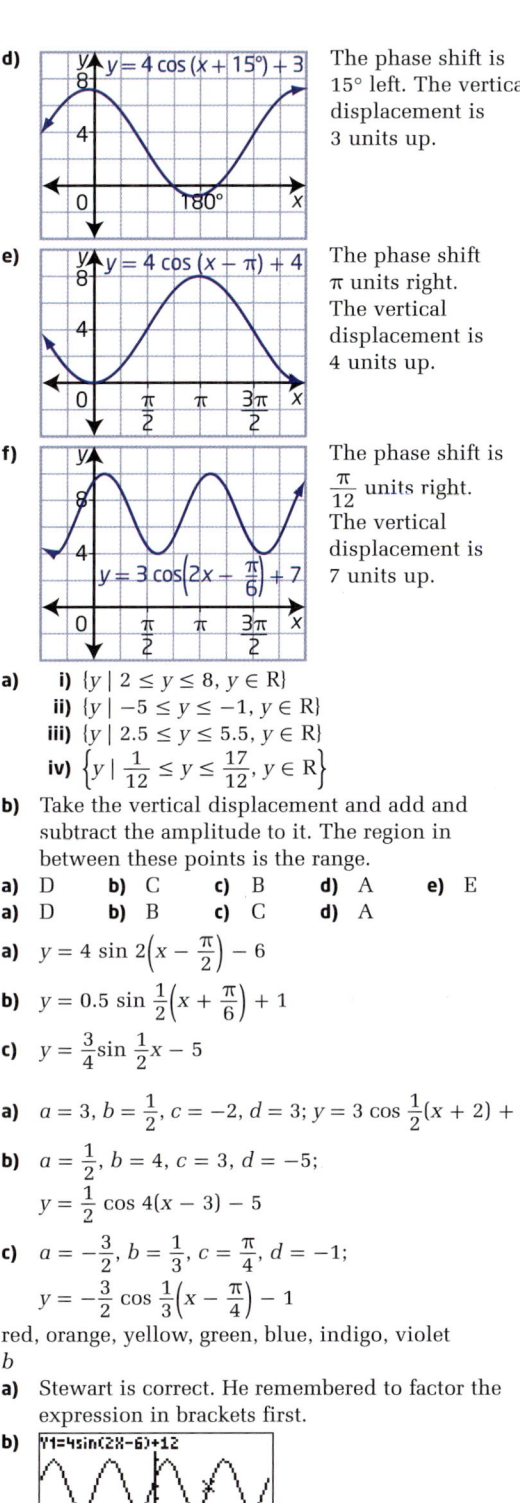
The phase shift is 15° left. The vertical displacement is 3 units up.

e) The phase shift is π units right. The vertical displacement is 4 units up.

f) The phase shift is $\frac{\pi}{12}$ units right. The vertical displacement is 7 units up.

3. a) i) $\{y \mid 2 \leq y \leq 8, y \in R\}$
   ii) $\{y \mid -5 \leq y \leq -1, y \in R\}$
   iii) $\{y \mid 2.5 \leq y \leq 5.5, y \in R\}$
   iv) $\left\{y \mid \frac{1}{12} \leq y \leq \frac{17}{12}, y \in R\right\}$

b) Take the vertical displacement and add and subtract the amplitude to it. The region in between these points is the range.

4. a) D b) C c) B d) A e) E
5. a) D b) B c) C d) A
6. a) $y = 4 \sin 2\left(x - \frac{\pi}{2}\right) - 6$

b) $y = 0.5 \sin \frac{1}{2}\left(x + \frac{\pi}{6}\right) + 1$

c) $y = \frac{3}{4} \sin \frac{1}{2}x - 5$

7. a) $a = 3, b = \frac{1}{2}, c = -2, d = 3; y = 3 \cos \frac{1}{2}(x + 2) + 3$

b) $a = \frac{1}{2}, b = 4, c = 3, d = -5;$
$y = \frac{1}{2} \cos 4(x - 3) - 5$

c) $a = -\frac{3}{2}, b = \frac{1}{3}, c = \frac{\pi}{4}, d = -1;$
$y = -\frac{3}{2} \cos \frac{1}{3}\left(x - \frac{\pi}{4}\right) - 1$

8. red, orange, yellow, green, blue, indigo, violet
9. b
10. a) Stewart is correct. He remembered to factor the expression in brackets first.

b)

11. a) $\{y \mid -1 \leq y \leq 5, y \in R\}$ b) $\{y \mid -6 \leq y \leq 0, y \in R\}$
c) $\{y \mid -13 \leq y \leq -7, y \in R\}$
d) $\{y \mid 5 \leq y \leq 11, y \in R\}$

12. a)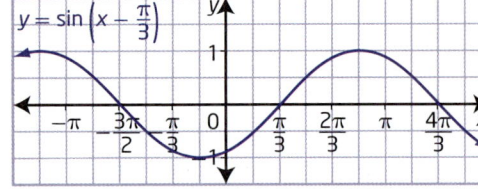

b)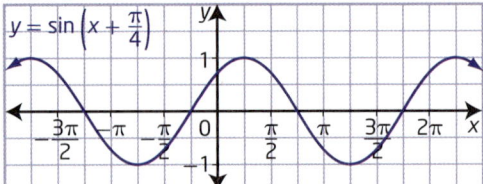

c)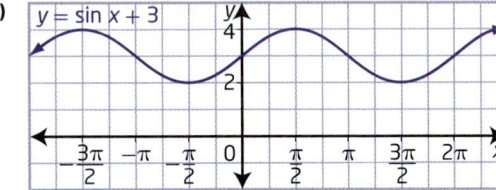

d)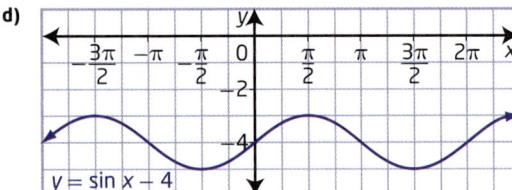

13. $a = 9$, $d = -4$

14. a) i) 3 ii) 2π
    iii) $\frac{\pi}{4}$ units right iv) none
    v) domain $\{x \mid x \in R\}$, range $\{y \mid -3 \leq y \leq 3, y \in R\}$
    vi) The maximum value of 3 occurs at $x = \frac{3\pi}{4}$.
    vii) The minimum value of -3 occurs at $x = \frac{7\pi}{4}$.

    b) i) 2 ii) 2π
    iii) $\frac{\pi}{2}$ units right iv) 2 units down
    v) domain $\{x \mid x \in R\}$, range $\{y \mid -4 \leq y \leq 0, y \in R\}$
    vi) The maximum value of 0 occurs at $x = \frac{\pi}{2}$.
    vii) The minimum value of -4 occurs at $x = \frac{3\pi}{2}$.

    c) i) 2 ii) π
    iii) $\frac{\pi}{4}$ units right iv) 1 unit up
    v) domain $\{x \mid x \in R\}$, range $\{y \mid -1 \leq y \leq 3, y \in R\}$
    vi) The maximum value of 3 occurs at
    $x = \frac{\pi}{2}$ and $x = \frac{3\pi}{2}$.
    vii) The minimum value of -1 occurs at
    $x = 0$, $x = \pi$, and $x = 2\pi$.

15. a) $y = 2 \sin x - 1$ b) $y = 3 \sin 2x + 1$
    c) $y = 2 \sin 4\left(x - \frac{\pi}{4}\right) + 2$

16. a) $y = 2 \cos 2\left(x - \frac{\pi}{4}\right) + 1$
    b) $y = 2 \cos \left(x + \frac{\pi}{2}\right) - 1$ c) $y = \cos(x - \pi) + 1$

17. a) 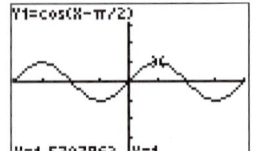 b) $y = \sin x$

    c) The graph of the cosine function shifted $\frac{\pi}{2}$ units right is equivalent to the graph of the sine function.

18. phase shift of $\frac{\pi}{2}$ units left

19. a) i) Phase shift is 30° right; period is 360°; x-intercepts are at 120° and 300°.
    ii) Maximums occur at (30°, 3) and (390°, 3); minimum occurs at (210°, -3).

    b) i) Phase shift is $\frac{\pi}{4}$ units right; period is π; x-intercepts are at $\frac{\pi}{2}$ and π.
    ii) Maximums occur at $\left(\frac{\pi}{4}, 3\right)$ and $\left(\frac{5\pi}{4}, 3\right)$; minimum occurs at $\left(\frac{3\pi}{4}, -3\right)$.

20. $y = 50 \cos \frac{\pi}{2640}(x - 9240) + 5050$

21. The graphs are equivalent.
    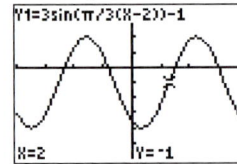 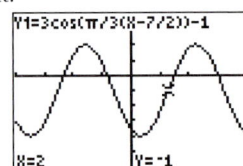

22. $y = 4 \sin 4(x + \pi)$

23. a) 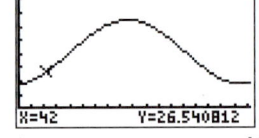 b) approximately 26.5°
    c) day 171 or June 21

24. a) 4 s b) 15 cycles per minute
    c)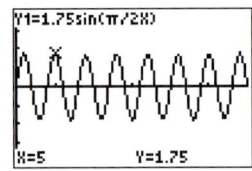

    d) The air flow velocity is 0 L/s. This corresponds to when the lungs are either completely full or completely empty.
    e) The air flow velocity is -1.237 L/s. This corresponds to part of a cycle when the lungs are blowing out air.

25. a) 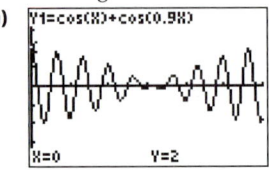 b) The amplitude is 2. The period is 20π.

26. a) i) 120° ii) $\frac{3\pi}{4}$ iii) π iv) $\frac{\pi}{4}$
    b) Example: When graphed, a cosine function is ahead of the graph of a sine function by 90°. So, adding 90° to the phase shift in part a) works.

27. a) $y = 3 \sin(x + \pi) + 2$ **b)** $y = 3 \sin 2\left(x - \frac{\pi}{2}\right) + 1$
  c) $y = 2 \sin\left(x + \frac{\pi}{2}\right) + 5$ **d)** $y = 5 \sin 3(x - 120°) - 1$
28. a) $P = \frac{2}{5} \cos \sqrt{\frac{9.8}{20}}\, t$

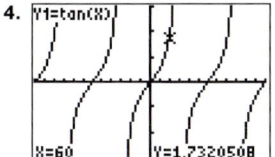

  b) approximately -0.20 radians or 3.9 cm along the arc to the left of the vertical
C1 a changes the amplitude, b changes the period, c changes the phase shift, d changes the vertical translation; Answers may vary.
C2 a) They are exactly same.
  b) This is because the sine of a negative number is the same as the negative sine of the number.
  c) They are mirror images reflected in the x-axis.
  d) It is correct.
C3 $\frac{5\pi}{4}$ square units
C4 a) $0 < b < 1$ **b)** $a > 1$
  c) Example: $c = 0, d = 0$ **d)** $d > a$
  e) Example: $c = -\frac{\pi}{2}, b = 1, d = 0$ **f)** $b = 3$

5.3 The Tangent Function, pages 262 to 265

1. a) 1, 45° **b)** -1.7, 120.5°
  c) -1.7, 300.5° **d)** 1, 225°
2. a) undefined **b)** -1 **c)** 1
  d) 0 **e)** 0 **f)** 1
3. No. The tangent function has no maximum or minimum, so there is no amplitude.
4. $-300°, -120°, 240°$

5. $\frac{\tan \theta}{\sin \theta} = \frac{1}{\cos \theta}$; $\tan \theta = \frac{\sin \theta}{\cos \theta}$
6. a) slope $= \frac{y}{x}$
  b) Since y is equal to $\sin \theta$ and x is equal to $\cos \theta$, then $\tan \theta = \frac{y}{x}$.
  c) slope $= \frac{\sin \theta}{\cos \theta}$ **d)** $\tan \theta = \frac{y}{x}$
7. a) $\tan \theta = \frac{y}{x}$ **b)** $\tan \theta = \frac{\sin \theta}{\cos \theta}$
  c) $\sin \theta$ and $\cos \theta$ are equal to y and x, respectively.
8. a)

θ	tan θ
89.5°	114.59
89.9°	572.96
89.999°	57 295.78
89.999 999°	57 295 779.51

  b) The value of tan θ increases to infinity.

  c)

θ	tan θ
90.5°	-114.59
90.01°	-5729.58
90.001°	$-57\,295.78$
90.000 001°	$-57\,295\,779.51$

  The value of tan θ approaches negative infinity.

9. a) $d = 5 \tan \frac{\pi}{30} t$ **b)**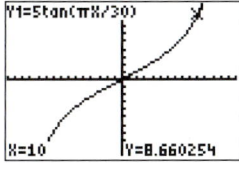
  c) 8.7 m
  d) At $t = 15$ s, the camera is pointing along a line parallel to the wall and is turning away from the wall.
10. a) $d = 500 \tan \pi t$ **b)**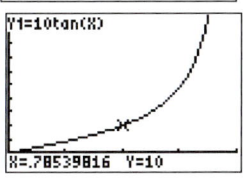
  c) The asymptote represents the moment when the ray of light shines along a line that is parallel to the shore.
11. $d = 10 \tan x$

12. a) a tangent function
  b) The slope would be undefined. It represents the place on the graph where the asymptote is.
13. Example:
  a) (4, 3) **b)** 0.75
  c) tan θ is the slope of the graph.
14. a) tan 0.5 ≈ 0.5463, power series ≈ 0.5463
  b) sin 0.5 ≈ 0.4794, power series ≈ 0.4794
  c) cos 0.5 ≈ 0.8776, power series ≈ 0.8776
C1 The domain of $y = \sin x$ and $y = \cos x$ is all real numbers. The tangent function is not defined at $x = \frac{\pi}{2} + n\pi, n \in I$. Thus, these numbers must be excluded from the domain of $y = \tan x$.
C2 a) 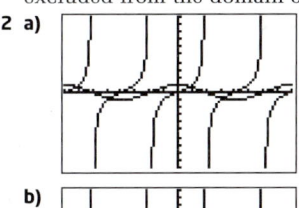 Example: The tangent function has asymptotes at the same x-values where zeros occur on the cosine function.

  b) 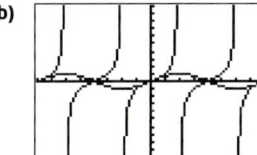 Example: The tangent function has zeros at the same x-values where zeros occur on the sine function.

C3 Example: A circular or periodic function repeats its values over a specific period. In the case of $y = \tan x$, the period is π. So, the equation $\tan(x + \pi) = \tan x$ is true for all x in the domain of tan x.

5.4 Equations and Graphs of Trigonometric Functions, pages 275 to 281

1. a) $x = 0, \pi, 2\pi$ **b)** $x = \pi n$ where n is an integer
  c) $x = 0, \frac{\pi}{3}, \frac{2\pi}{3}, \pi, \frac{4\pi}{3}, \frac{5\pi}{3}, 2\pi$
2. Examples:
  a) 1.25, 4.5
  b) $-3, -1.9, 0.1, 1.2, 3.2, 4.1, 6.3, 7.2$
3. Examples: $-50°, -10°, 130°, 170°, 310°, 350°$

4. a)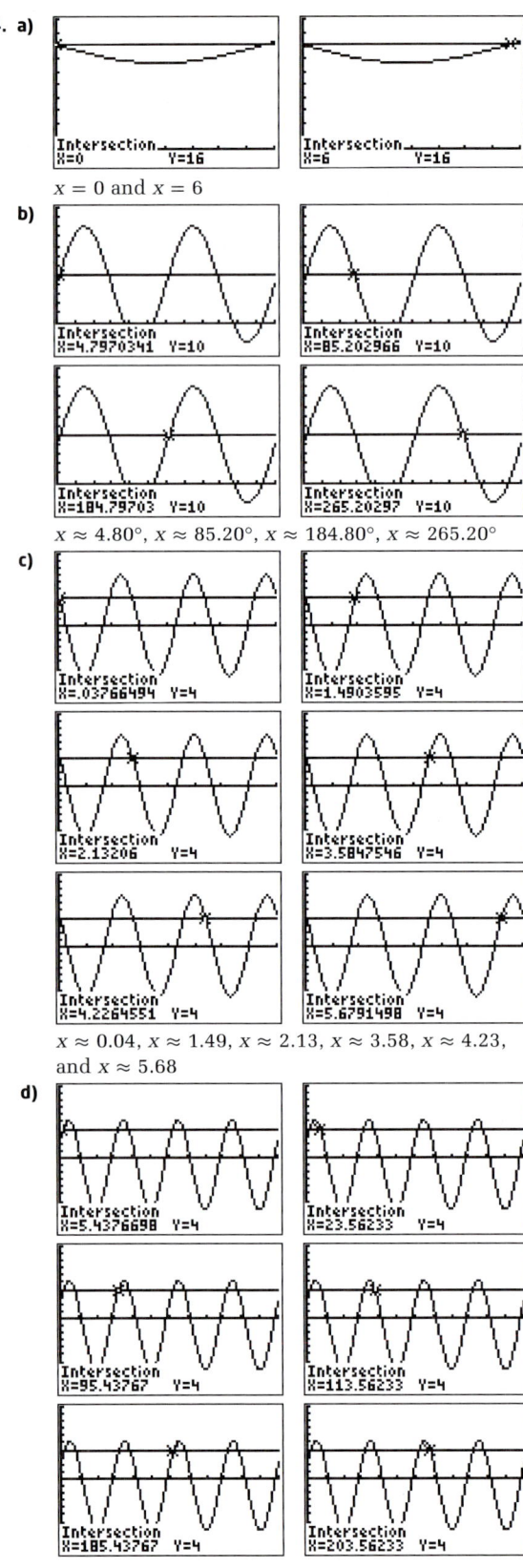

$x = 0$ and $x = 6$

b)

$x \approx 4.80°$, $x \approx 85.20°$, $x \approx 184.80°$, $x \approx 265.20°$

c)

$x \approx 0.04$, $x \approx 1.49$, $x \approx 2.13$, $x \approx 3.58$, $x \approx 4.23$, and $x \approx 5.68$

d)

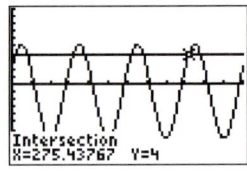 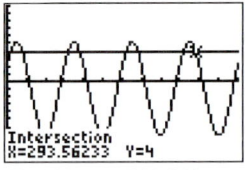

$x \approx 5.44°$, $x \approx 23.56°$, $x \approx 95.44°$, $x \approx 113.56°$, $x \approx 185.44°$, $x \approx 203.56°$, $x \approx 275.44°$, and $x \approx 293.56°$

5. a) $x \approx 1.33$
b) $x \approx 3.59°$ and $x \approx 86.41°$
c) $x \approx 1.91 + \pi n$ and $x \approx 3.09 + \pi n$, where n is an integer
d) $x \approx 4.50° + (8°)n$ and $x \approx 7.50° + (8°)n$, where n is an integer

6. a) domain $\{t \mid t \geq 0, t \in \mathbb{R}\}$, range $\{P \mid 2000 \leq P \leq 14\,000, P \in \mathbb{N}\}$
b) domain $\{t \mid t \geq 0, t \in \mathbb{R}\}$, range $\{h \mid 1 \leq h \leq 13, h \in \mathbb{R}\}$
c) domain $\{t \mid t \geq 0, t \in \mathbb{R}\}$, range $\{h \mid 6 \leq h \leq 18, h \in \mathbb{R}\}$
d) domain $\{t \mid t \geq 0, t \in \mathbb{R}\}$, range $\{h \mid 5 \leq h \leq 23, h \in \mathbb{R}\}$

7. $\frac{1}{200}$ s or 5 ms

8. a) Period is $100°$; sinusoidal axis is at $y = 15$; amplitude is 9.
b) Period is $\frac{4\pi}{3}$; sinusoidal axis is at $y = -6$; amplitude is 10.
c) Period is $\frac{1}{50}$ s or 20 ms; sinusoidal axis is at $y = 0$; amplitude is 10.

9. a) 28 m **b)** 0 min, 0.7 min, 1.4 min, …
c) 2 m **d)** 0.35 min, 1.05 min, 1.75 min, …
e) 0.18 min **f)** approximately 23.1 m

10. 78.5 cm

11. $V = 155 \sin 120\pi t$

12. a) $\frac{1}{14}$ days **b)** 102.9 min **c)** 14 revolutions

13. a)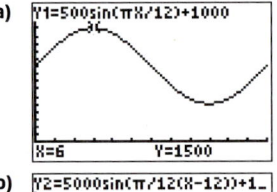

It takes approximately 15 months for the fox population to drop to 650.

b)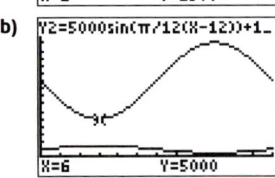

c)

	Arctic Fox	Lemming
Maximum Population	1500	15 000
Month	6	18
Minimum Population	500	5000
Month	18	6

d) Example: The maximum for the predator occurs at a minimum for the prey and vice versa. The predators population depends on the prey, so every time the lemming's population changes the arctic fox population changes in accordance.

14. a) 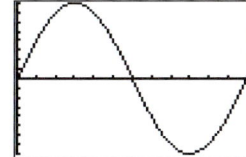   **b)** 35.1 cm
 c) 1 s

15. a) Maximum is 7.5 Sun widths; minimum is 1 Sun width.
 b) 24 h
 c) $y = -3.25 \sin \frac{\pi}{12}x + 4.25$, where x represents the time, in hours, and y represents the number of Sun widths

16. a) 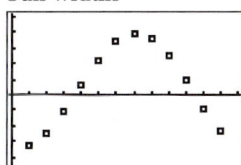   **b)** 1.6 °C

 c) $y = -18.1 \cos \frac{\pi}{6}(x - 1) + 1.6$, where x represents the time, in months, and y represents the average monthly temperature, in degrees Celsius, for Winnipeg, Manitoba
 d) 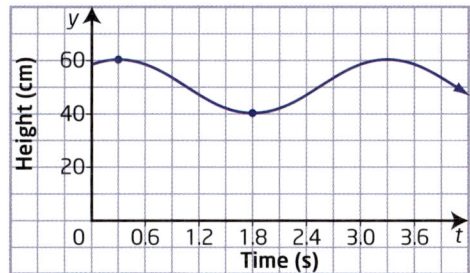   **e)** about 2.5 months

17. a) $T = -4.5 \cos \frac{\pi}{30}t + 38.5$ **b)** 36.25 °C

18. a)

 [Graph showing height (cm) vs time (s), with height ranging 20-60 cm over time 0-3.6 s]

 b) $y = 10 \sin \frac{2\pi}{3}(t + 0.45) + 50$, where t represents the time, in seconds, and y represents the height of the mass, in centimetres, above the floor
 c) 43.3 cm   **d)** 0.0847 s

19. a) $h = -10 \cos \frac{\pi}{30}t + 12$, where t represents the time, in seconds, and h represents the height of a passenger, in metres, above the ground
 b) 15.1 m
 c) approximately 21.1 s, 38.9 s

20. a) $h = 7 \sin \frac{2\pi}{5}(t + 1.75) + 15$ or
 $h = 7 \cos \frac{2\pi}{5}(t + 0.5) + 15$, where t represents the time, in seconds, and h represents the height of the tip of the blade, in metres, above the ground
 b) 20.66 m   **c)** 4.078 s

21. a) $y = -9.7 \cos \frac{\pi}{183}(t - 26) + 13.9$, where t represents the time, in days, and y represents the average daily maximum temperature, in degrees Celsius
 b) 18.6 °C   **c)** 88 days

22. a) $y = 15 \cos \frac{\pi}{20}t + 5$ **b)**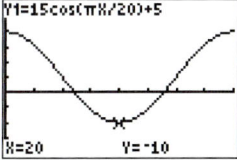
 c) approximately +9.6% of the total assets
 d) Example: No, because it fluctuates too much.

23. a) $y = 1.2 \sin \frac{\pi}{2}t$, where t represents the time, in seconds, and y represents the distance for a turn, in metres, from the midline
 b) $y = 1.2 \sin \frac{2\pi}{5}t$; The period increases.

C1 Examples:
 a) Use a sine function as a model when the curve or data begins at or near the intersection of the vertical axis and the sinusoidal axis.
 b) Use a cosine function as a model when the curve or data has a maximum or minimum near or at the vertical axis.

C2 Example:
 a)–b) The parameter b has the greatest influence on the graph of the function. It changes the period of the function. Parameters c and d change the location of the curve, but not the shape. Parameter a changes the maximum and minimum values.

C3 Examples:
 a) $y = -0.85 \sin \frac{2\pi}{5.2}x + 0.85$, where x represents the height of the door, in metres, and y represents the width of the door, in metres
 b)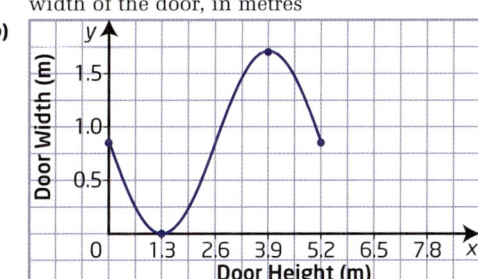

Chapter 5 Review, pages 282 to 285

1. a)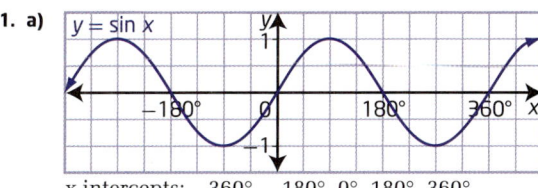
 x-intercepts: $-360°, -180°, 0°, 180°, 360°$
 b) y-intercept: 0
 c) domain $\{x \mid x \in R\}$, range $\{y \mid -1 \leq y \leq 1, y \in R\}$, period is 2π
 d) $y = 1$

2. a)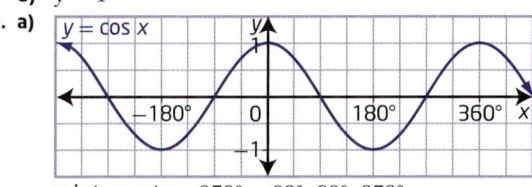
 x-intercepts: $-270°, -90°, 90°, 270°$
 b) y-intercept: 1

Answers • MHR **597**

c) domain $\{x \mid x \in R\}$,
range $\{y \mid -1 \leq y \leq 1, y \in R\}$, period is 2π
d) $y = 1$
3. a) A b) D c) B d) C
4. a) Amplitude is 3; period is π or 180°.
b) Amplitude is 4; period is 4π or 720°.
c) Amplitude is $\dfrac{1}{3}$; period is $\dfrac{12\pi}{5}$ or 432°.
d) Amplitude is 5; period is $\dfrac{4\pi}{3}$ or 240°.
5. a) Compared to the graph of $y = \sin x$, the graph of $y = \sin 2x$ completes two cycles in $0° \leq x \leq 360°$ and the graph of $y = 2 \sin x$ has an amplitude of 2.
b) Compared to the graph of $y = \sin x$, the graph of $y = -\sin x$ is reflected in the x-axis and the graph of $y = \sin (-x)$ is reflected in the y-axis. The graphs of $y = -\sin x$ and $y = \sin (-x)$ are the same.
c) Compared to the graph of $y = \cos x$, the graph of $y = -\cos x$ is reflected in the x-axis and the graph of $y = \cos (-x)$ is reflected in the y-axis. The graph of $y = \cos (-x)$ is the same as $y = \cos x$.
6. a) $y = 3 \cos 2x$ b) $y = 4 \cos \dfrac{12}{5}x$
c) $y = \dfrac{1}{2} \cos \dfrac{1}{2}x$ d) $y = \dfrac{3}{4} \cos 12x$
7. a) $y = 8 \sin 2x$ b) $y = 0.4 \sin 6x$
c) $y = \dfrac{3}{2} \sin \dfrac{1}{2}x$ d) $y = 2 \sin 3x$
8. a) Amplitude is 2; period is $\dfrac{2\pi}{3}$; phase shift is $\dfrac{\pi}{2}$ units right; vertical displacement is 8 units down

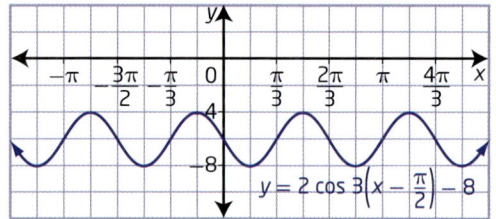

b) Amplitude is 1; period is 4π; phase shift is $\dfrac{\pi}{4}$ units right; vertical displacement is 3 units up

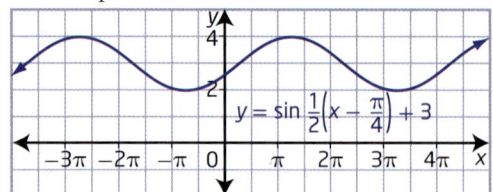

c) Amplitude is 4; period is 180°; phase shift is 30° right; vertical displacement is 7 units up

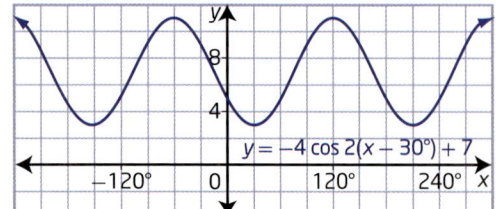

d) Amplitude is $\dfrac{1}{3}$; period is 1440°; phase shift is 60° right; vertical displacement is 1 unit down

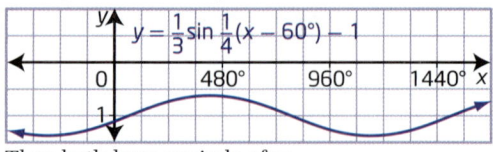

9. a) They both have periods of π.
b) $f(x)$ has a phase shift of $\dfrac{\pi}{2}$ units right; $g(x)$ has a phase shift of $\dfrac{\pi}{4}$ units right
c) π units right d) $\dfrac{\pi}{b}$ units right
10. a) $y = 3 \sin 2(x - 45°) + 1$, $y = -3 \cos 2x + 1$
b) $y = 2 \sin 2x - 1$, $y = 2 \cos 2(x - 45°) - 1$
c) $y = 2 \sin 2\left(x - \dfrac{\pi}{4}\right) - 1$, $y = -2 \cos 2x - 1$
d) $y = 3 \sin \dfrac{1}{2}\left(x - \dfrac{\pi}{2}\right) + 1$, $y = 3 \cos \dfrac{1}{2}\left(x - \dfrac{3\pi}{2}\right) + 1$
11. a) $y = 4 \sin 2\left(x - \dfrac{\pi}{3}\right) - 5$
b) $y = \dfrac{1}{2} \cos \dfrac{1}{2}\left(x + \dfrac{\pi}{6}\right) + 1$
c) $y = \dfrac{2}{3} \sin \dfrac{2}{3}x - 5$
12. a)

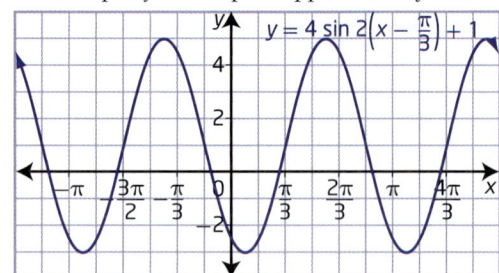

domain $\{x \mid x \in R\}$, range $\{y \mid 1 \leq y \leq 5, y \in R\}$, maximum value is 5, minimum value is 1, no x-intercepts, y-intercept of approximately 4.41

b)

domain $\{x \mid x \in R\}$, range $\{y \mid -3 \leq y \leq 5, y \in R\}$, maximum value is 5, minimum value is -3, x-intercepts: approximately $0.92 + n\pi$, $2.74 + n\pi$, $n \in I$, y-intercept: approximately -2.5

13. a) vertically stretched by a factor of 3 about the x-axis, horizontally stretched by a factor of $\dfrac{1}{2}$ about the y-axis, translated $\dfrac{\pi}{3}$ units right and 6 units up
b) vertically stretched by a factor of 2 about the x-axis, reflected in the x-axis, horizontally stretched by a factor of 2 about the y-axis, translated $\dfrac{\pi}{4}$ units left and 3 units down
c) vertically stretched by a factor of $\dfrac{3}{4}$ about the x-axis, horizontally stretched by a factor of $\dfrac{1}{2}$ about the y-axis, translated 30° right and 10 units up

d) reflected in the *x*-axis, horizontally stretched by a factor of $\frac{1}{2}$ about the *y*-axis, translated 45° left and 8 units down

14. **a)**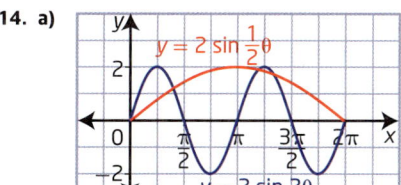

   b) Compared to the graph of $y = \sin \theta$, the graph of $y = 2 \sin 2\theta$ is vertically stretched by a factor of 2 about the *x*-axis and half the period. Compared to the graph of $y = \sin \theta$, the graph of $y = 2 \sin \frac{1}{2}\theta$ is vertically stretched by a factor of 2 about the *x*-axis and double the period.

15. **a)**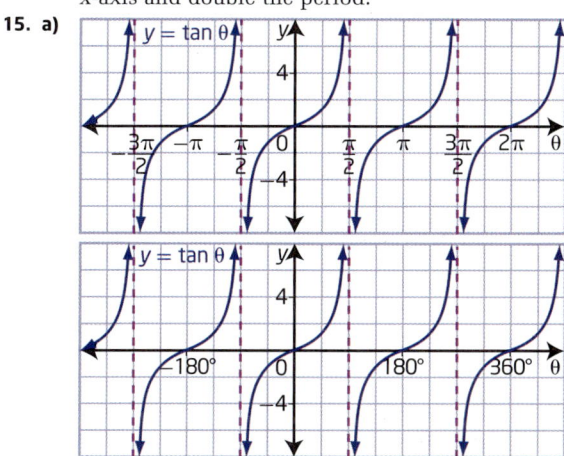

   b) **i)** domain $\{x \mid -2\pi \leq x \leq 2\pi, x \neq -\frac{3\pi}{2}, -\frac{\pi}{2}, \frac{\pi}{2}, \frac{3\pi}{2}, x \in R\}$ or $\{x \mid -360° \leq x \leq 360°, x \neq -270°, -90°, 90°, 270°, x \in R\}$
   ii) range $\{y \mid y \in R\}$ **iii)** *y*-intercept: 0
   iv) *x*-intercepts: $-2\pi, -\pi, 0, \pi, 2\pi$ or $-360°, -180°, 0°, 180°, 360°$
   v) asymptotes: $x = -\frac{3\pi}{2}, -\frac{\pi}{2}, \frac{\pi}{2}, \frac{3\pi}{2}$ or $x = -270°, -90°, 90°, 270°$

16. **a)** $\left(1, \frac{1}{\sqrt{3}}\right)$ **b)** $\tan \theta = \frac{\sin \theta}{\cos \theta}$
   c) As θ approaches 90°, $\tan \theta$ approaches infinity.
   d) $\tan 90°$ is not defined.

17. **a)** Since $\cos \theta$ is the denominator, when it is zero $\tan \theta$ becomes undefined.
   b) Since $\sin \theta$ is the numerator, when it is zero $\tan \theta$ becomes zero.

18. The shadow has no length which makes the slope infinite. This relates to the asymptotes on the graph of $y = \tan \theta$.

19. A vertical asymptote is an imaginary line that the graph comes very close to touching but in fact never does. If a trigonometric function is represented by a quotient, such as the tangent function, asymptotes generally occur at values for which the function is not defined; that is, when the function in the denominator is equal to zero.

20. **a)**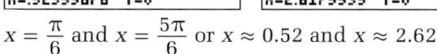
   $x = \frac{\pi}{6}$ and $x = \frac{5\pi}{6}$ or $x \approx 0.52$ and $x \approx 2.62$
   b)  no solution
   c)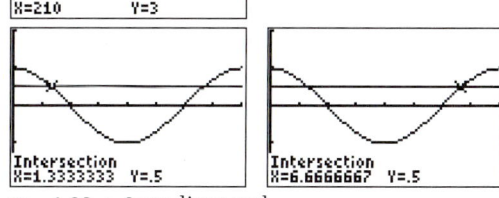
   $x \approx 1.33 + 8n$ radians and $x \approx 6.67 + 8n$ radians, where *n* is an integer
   d)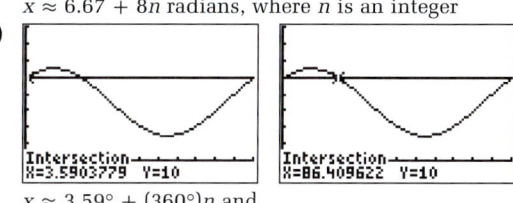
   $x \approx 3.59° + (360°)n$ and $x \approx 86.41° + (360°)n$, where *n* is an integer

21. **a)** 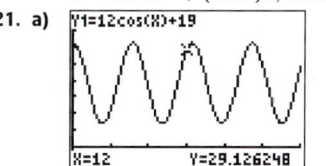   **b)** 9.4 h
   c) Example: A model for temperature variance is important for maintaining constant temperatures to preserve artifacts.

22. **a)** 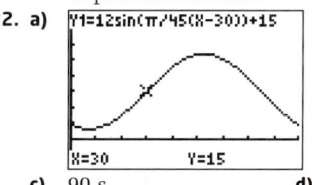   **b)** maximum height: 27 m, minimum height: 3 m
   c) 90 s   **d)** approximately 25.4 m

23. **a)** $L = -3.7 \cos \frac{2\pi}{365}(t + 10) + 12$
   b) approximately 12.8 h of daylight

24. **a)** approximately 53 sunspots
   b) around the year 2007
   c) around the year 2003

Chapter 5 Practice Test, pages 286 to 287

1. A   2. D   3. C   4. D   5. B   6. A   7. C   8. $\frac{\pi}{2}$
9. asymptotes: $x = \frac{\pi}{2} + n\pi, n \in I$,
   domain $\{x \mid x \neq \frac{\pi}{2} + n\pi, x \in R, n \in I\}$,
   range $\{y \mid y \in R\}$, period is π
10. Example: They have the same maximum and minimum values. Neither function has a horizontal or vertical translation.

11. Amplitude is 120; period is 0.0025 s or 2.5 ms.
12. The minimum depth of 2 m occurs at 0 h, 12 h, and 24 hour. The maximum depth of 8 m occurs at 6 h and 18 h.
13. a)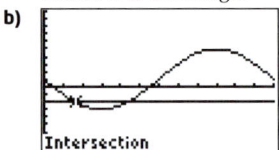
    $x = 1.5 + 6n$ radians and $x = 3.5 + 6n$ radians, where n is an integer
    b)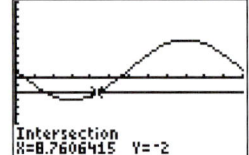
    $x \approx 3.24° + (24°)n$ and
    $x \approx 8.76° + (24°)n$, where n is an integer
14. Example: Graph II has half the period of graph I. Graph I represents a cosine curve with no phase shift. Graph II represents a sine curve with no phase shift. Graph I and II have the same amplitude and both graphs have no vertical translations.
15. a) $h = 0.1 \sin \pi t + 1$, where t represents the time, in seconds, and h represents the height of the mass, in metres, above the floor
    b)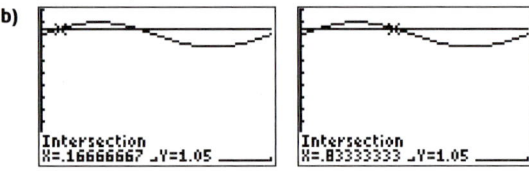
    approximately 0.17 s and 0.83 s
    c) $t = \frac{1}{6}$ or 0.1666... and $t = \frac{5}{6}$ or 0.8333
16. a) $y = 3 \sin 2\left(x - \frac{\pi}{4}\right) - 1$ b) $y = -3 \cos 2x - 1$
17. a) A, B b) A, B or C, D, E c) B

Chapter 6 Trigonometric Identities

6.1 Reciprocal, Quotient, and Pythagorean Identities, pages 296 to 298

1. a) $x \neq \pi n; n \in I$ b) $x \neq \left(\frac{\pi}{2}\right)n, n \in I$
   c) $x \neq \frac{\pi}{2} + 2\pi n$ and $x \neq \pi n, n \in I$
   d) $x \neq \frac{\pi}{2} + \pi n$ and $x \neq \pi + 2\pi n, n \in I$
2. Some identities will have non-permissible values because they involve trigonometric functions that have non-permissible values themselves or a function occurs in a denominator. For example, an identity involving sec θ has non-permissible values $\theta \neq 90° + 180°n$, where $n \in I$, because these are the non-permissible values for the function.
3. a) tan x b) sin x c) sin x
4. a) cot x b) csc x c) sec x
5. a) When substituted, both values satisfied the equation.
   b) $x \neq 0°, 90°, 180°, 270°$
6. a) $x \neq \pi + 2\pi n, n \in I$; $x \neq \frac{\pi}{2} + \pi n, n \in I$

b)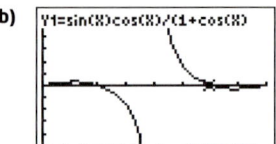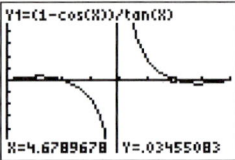
Yes, it appears to be an identity.
c) The equation is verified for $x = \frac{\pi}{4}$.
7. a) $\cos^2 \theta$ b) 0.75 c) 25%
8. a) All three values check when substituted.
b)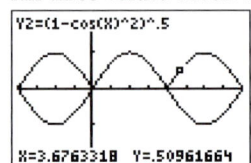
c) The equation is not an identity since taking the square then the square root removes the negative sign and sin x is negative from π to 2π.
9. a) $E = \frac{I \cos \theta}{R^2}$ b) $E = \frac{I \cot \theta}{R^2 \csc \theta}$
   $E = \frac{I\left(\dfrac{\cos \theta}{\sin \theta}\right)}{R^2\left(\dfrac{1}{\sin \theta}\right)}$
   $E = \left(\frac{I \cos \theta}{\sin \theta}\right)\left(\frac{\sin \theta}{R^2}\right)$
   $E = \frac{I \cos \theta}{R^2}$
10. $\cos x, x \neq 0, \frac{\pi}{2}, \pi, \frac{3\pi}{2}$
11. a) It appears to be equivalent to sec x.
    b) $x \neq \frac{\pi}{2} + \pi n, n \in I$
    c) $\dfrac{\csc^2 x - \cot^2 x}{\cos x} = \dfrac{\dfrac{1}{\sin^2 x} - \dfrac{\cos^2 x}{\sin^2 x}}{\cos x}$
    $= \dfrac{\dfrac{1 - \cos^2 x}{\sin^2 x}}{\cos x}$
    $= \dfrac{\dfrac{\sin^2 x}{\sin^2 x}}{\cos x}$
    $= \dfrac{1}{\cos x}$
    $= \sec x$
12. a) Yes, it could be an identity.
    b) $\dfrac{\cot x}{\sec x} + \sin x = \dfrac{\cos x}{\sin x} \div \dfrac{1}{\cos x} + \sin x$
    $= \dfrac{\cos^2 x}{\sin x} + \sin x$
    $= \dfrac{\cos^2 x + \sin^2 x}{\sin x}$
    $= \csc x$
13. a) $1 = 1$
    b) The left side $= 1$, but the right side is undefined.
    c) The chosen value is not permissible for the tan x function.
    d) The left side $= \dfrac{2}{\sqrt{2}}$, but the right side $= 2$.
    e) Giselle has found a permissible value for which the equation is not true, so they can conclude that it is not an identity.
14. 2
15. 7.89

16. $\dfrac{1}{1+\sin\theta} + \dfrac{1}{1-\sin\theta} = \dfrac{1-\sin\theta+1+\sin\theta}{(1-\sin\theta)(1+\sin\theta)}$
$= \dfrac{2}{(1-\sin^2\theta)}$
$= 2\sec^2\theta$

17. $m = \csc x$

C1 $\cot^2 x + 1$
$= \dfrac{\cos^2 x}{\sin^2 x} + \dfrac{\sin^2 x}{\sin^2 x}$
$= \dfrac{\cos^2 x + \sin^2 x}{\sin^2 x}$
$= \dfrac{1}{\sin^2 x}$
$= \csc^2 x$

C2 $\left(\dfrac{\sin\theta}{1+\cos\theta}\right)\left(\dfrac{1-\cos\theta}{1-\cos\theta}\right)$
$= \dfrac{\sin\theta - \sin\theta\cos\theta}{1-\cos^2\theta}$
$= \dfrac{\sin\theta - \sin\theta\cos\theta}{\sin^2\theta}$
$= \dfrac{1-\cos\theta}{\sin\theta}$

It helps to simplify by creating an opportunity to use the Pythagorean identity.

C3 Step 1

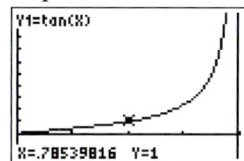 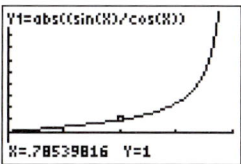

Yes, over this domain it is an identity.

Step 2

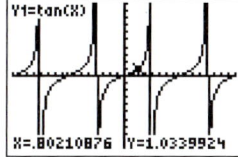 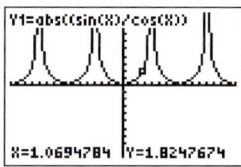

The equation is not an identity since the graphs of the two sides are not the same.

Step 3 Example: $y = \cot\theta$ and $y = \left|\dfrac{\cos\theta}{\sin\theta}\right|$ are identities over the domain $0 \leq \theta \leq \dfrac{\pi}{2}$ but not over the domain $-2\pi \leq \theta \leq 2\pi$.

Step 4 The weakness with this approach is that for some more complicated identities you may think it is an identity when really it is only an identity over that domain.

6.2 Sum, Difference, and Double-angle Identities, pages 306 to 308

1. a) $\cos 70°$ **b)** $\sin 35°$ **c)** $\cos 38°$
d) $\sin\dfrac{\pi}{4}$ **e)** $4\sin\dfrac{2\pi}{3}$

2. a) $\cos 60° = 0.5$ **b)** $\sin 45° = \dfrac{1}{\sqrt{2}}$ or $\dfrac{\sqrt{2}}{2}$
c) $\cos\dfrac{\pi}{3} = 0.5$ **d)** $\cos\dfrac{5\pi}{6} = -\dfrac{\sqrt{3}}{2}$

3. $\cos 2x = 1 - 2\sin^2 x$;
$1 - \cos 2x = 1 - 1 + 2\sin^2 x = 2\sin^2 x$

4. a) $\sin\dfrac{\pi}{2}$ **b)** $6\sin 48°$ **c)** $\tan 152°$ **d)** $\cos\dfrac{\pi}{3}$
e) $-\cos\dfrac{\pi}{6}$

5. a) $\sin\theta$ **b)** $\cos x$ **c)** $\cos\theta$ **d)** $\cos x$

6. Example: When $x = 60°$ and $y = 30°$, then left side $= 0.5$, but right side ≈ 0.366.

7. $\cos(90° - x) = \cos 90°\cos x + \sin 90°\sin x$
$= \sin x$

8. a) $\dfrac{\sqrt{3}-1}{2\sqrt{2}}$ or $\dfrac{\sqrt{6}-\sqrt{2}}{4}$ **b)** $\dfrac{-\sqrt{3}+1}{\sqrt{3}+1}$ or $\sqrt{3}-2$
c) $\dfrac{1+\sqrt{3}}{2\sqrt{2}}$ or $\dfrac{\sqrt{2}+\sqrt{6}}{4}$ **d)** $\dfrac{-\sqrt{3}-1}{2\sqrt{2}}$ or $\dfrac{-\sqrt{6}-\sqrt{2}}{4}$
e) $\sqrt{2}(1+\sqrt{3})$ **f)** $\dfrac{1-\sqrt{3}}{2\sqrt{2}}$ or $\dfrac{\sqrt{2}-\sqrt{6}}{4}$

9. a) $P = 1000\sin(x + 113.5°)$
b) i) 101.056 W/m² **ii)** 310.676 W/m²
iii) -50.593 W/m²
c) The answer in part iii) is negative which means that there is no sunlight reaching Igloolik. At latitude 66.5°, the power received is 0 W/m².

10. $-2\cos x$

11. a) $\dfrac{119}{169}$ **b)** $-\dfrac{120}{169}$ **c)** $-\dfrac{12}{13}$

12. a) Both sides are equal for this value.
b) Both sides are equal for this value.
c) $\tan 2x = \dfrac{2\tan x}{1-\tan^2 x}$
$= \dfrac{2\tan x}{1-\tan^2 x}\left(\dfrac{\cos^2 x}{\cos^2 x}\right)$
$= \dfrac{2\left(\dfrac{\sin x}{\cos x}\right)(\cos^2 x)}{\left(1-\dfrac{\sin^2 x}{\cos^2 x}\right)\cos^2 x}$
$= \dfrac{2\sin x\cos x}{\cos^2 x - \sin^2 x}$

13. a) $d = \dfrac{v_0^2 \sin 2\theta}{g}$ **b)** $45°$
c) It is easier after applying the double-angle identity since there is only one trigonometric function whose value has to be found.

14. $k - 1$

15. a) $\cos^4 x - \sin^4 x = (\cos^2 x - \sin^2 x)(\cos^2 x + \sin^2 x)$
$= \cos^2 x - \sin^2 x$
$= \cos 2x$
b) $\dfrac{\csc^2 x - 2}{\csc^2 x} = 1 - \dfrac{2}{\csc^2 x}$
$= 1 - 2\sin^2 x$
$= \cos 2x$

16. a) $\dfrac{1-\cos 2x}{2} = \dfrac{1-1+2\sin^2 x}{2} = \sin^2 x$
b) $\dfrac{4-8\sin^2 x}{2\sin x\cos x} = \dfrac{4\cos 2x}{\sin 2x} = \dfrac{4}{\tan 2x}$

17. $-\dfrac{2}{\sqrt{29}}$

18. $k = 3$

19. a) 0.9928, $-0.392\,82$ or $\dfrac{\pm 4\sqrt{3}+3}{10}$
b) 0.9500 or $\dfrac{\sqrt{5}+2\sqrt{3}}{6}$

20. a) $\dfrac{56}{65}$ **b)** $\dfrac{63}{65}$ **c)** $\dfrac{-7}{25}$ **d)** $\dfrac{24}{25}$

21. a) $\sin x$ **b)** $\tan x$

22. $\cos x = 2\cos^2\left(\dfrac{x}{2}\right) - 1$
$\dfrac{\cos x + 1}{2} = \cos^2\left(\dfrac{x}{2}\right)$
$\pm\sqrt{\dfrac{\cos x + 1}{2}} = \cos\dfrac{x}{2}$

23. a) **b)** $a = 5$, $c = 37°$
c) $y = 5\sin(x - 36.87°)$

24. $y = 3 \sin 2x - 3$

C1 a) i) $\dfrac{120}{169}$ or 0.7101   **ii)** $\dfrac{120}{169}$ or 0.7101

   b) Using identities is more straightforward.

C2 a)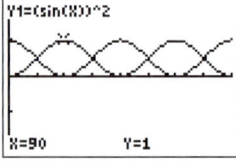

   b) To find the sine function from the graph, compare the amplitude and the period to that of a base sine curve. The alternative equation is $y = 3 \sin 2x$.

C3 a)

   b) 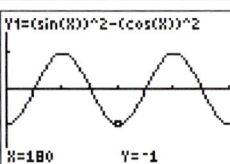 The graph will be the horizontal line $y = 1$.

   c) The resultant graph is a cosine function reflected over the x-axis and the period becomes π.

   d) $f(x) = -\cos 2x$. Using trigonometric identities,
$$\sin^2 x - \cos^2 x = 1 - \cos^2 x - \cos^2 x$$
$$= 1 - 2\cos^2 x$$
$$= -\cos 2x$$

6.3 Proving Identities, pages 314 to 315

1. a) $\sin x$ **b)** $\dfrac{\cos x + 1}{6}$

   c) $\dfrac{\sin x}{\cos x + 1}$ **d)** $\sec x - 4 \csc x$

2. a) $\cos x + \cos x \tan^2 x = \cos x + \dfrac{\sin^2 x}{\cos x}$
$$= \dfrac{\cos^2 x}{\cos x} + \dfrac{\sin^2 x}{\cos x}$$
$$= \dfrac{1}{\cos x}$$
$$= \sec x$$

   b) $\dfrac{\sin^2 x - \cos^2 x}{\sin x + \cos x} = \dfrac{(\sin x - \cos x)(\sin x + \cos x)}{\sin x + \cos x}$
$$= \sin x - \cos x$$

   c) $\dfrac{\sin x \cos x - \sin x}{\cos^2 x - 1} = \dfrac{\sin x \cos x - \sin x}{-\sin^2 x}$
$$= \dfrac{-\sin x(1 - \cos x)}{-\sin^2 x}$$
$$= \dfrac{1 - \cos x}{\sin x}$$

   d) $\dfrac{1 - \sin^2 x}{1 + 2\sin x - 3\sin^2 x} = \dfrac{(1 - \sin x)(1 + \sin x)}{(1 - \sin x)(1 + 3\sin x)}$
$$= \dfrac{1 + \sin x}{1 + 3\sin x}$$

3. a) $\dfrac{\sin x + 1}{\cos x}$ **b)** $\dfrac{-2 \tan x}{\cos x}$

   c) $\csc x$ **d)** $2 \cot^2 x$

4. a) $\dfrac{1}{\sin x} - \dfrac{\cos^2 x}{\sin x}$ **b)** $\sin x$

5. $\dfrac{\sin 2x}{2 \sin x} = \dfrac{2 \sin x \cos x}{2 \sin x} = \cos x, \; x \neq \pi n; \; n \in I$

6. $\cos x$

7. a) $\dfrac{\csc x}{2 \cos x} = \dfrac{1}{2 \sin x \cos x}$
$$= \dfrac{1}{\sin 2x}$$
$$= \csc 2x$$

   b) $\sin x + \cos x \cot x = \sin x + \dfrac{\cos^2 x}{\sin x}$
$$= \dfrac{1}{\sin x}$$
$$= \csc x$$

8. Hannah's choice takes fewer steps.

9. a) 42.3 m

   b) $\dfrac{v_o^2 \sin 2\theta}{g} = \dfrac{v_o^2 2 \sin \theta \cos \theta}{g}$
$$= \dfrac{2v_o^2 \sin^2 \theta \cos \theta}{g \sin \theta}$$
$$= \dfrac{2v_o^2 \sin^2 \theta}{g \tan \theta}$$
$$= \dfrac{2v_o^2 (1 - \cos^2 \theta)}{g \tan \theta}$$

10. a) Left Side
$$= \dfrac{\csc x}{2 \cos x}$$
$$= \dfrac{1}{2 \sin x \cos x}$$
$$= \dfrac{1}{\sin 2x}$$
$$= \csc 2x$$
$$= \text{Right Side}$$

   b) Left Side
$$= \dfrac{\sin x \cos x}{1 + \cos x}$$
$$= \dfrac{(\sin x \cos x)(1 - \cos x)}{(1 + \cos x)(1 - \cos x)}$$
$$= \dfrac{\sin x \cos x - \sin x \cos^2 x}{\sin^2 x}$$
$$= \dfrac{\cos x - \cos^2 x}{\sin x}$$
$$= \dfrac{1 - \cos x}{\tan x}$$
$$= \text{Right Side}$$

   c) Left Side $= \dfrac{\sin x + \tan x}{1 + \cos x}$
$$= \left(\dfrac{\sin x}{1} + \dfrac{\sin x}{\cos x}\right) \div (1 + \cos x)$$
$$= \left(\dfrac{\sin x \cos x + \sin x}{\cos x}\right) \times \dfrac{1}{1 + \cos x}$$
$$= \left(\dfrac{\sin x(1 + \cos x)}{\cos x}\right) \times \dfrac{1}{1 + \cos x}$$
$$= \dfrac{\sin x}{\cos x}$$

Right Side $= \dfrac{\sin 2x}{2 \cos^2 x}$
$$= \dfrac{2 \sin x \cos x}{2 \cos^2 x}$$
$$= \dfrac{\sin x}{\cos x}$$

Left Side = Right Side

11. a) Left Side $= \dfrac{\sin 2x}{\cos x} + \dfrac{\cos 2x}{\sin x}$
$$= \dfrac{2 \sin x \cos x}{\cos x} + \dfrac{1 - 2 \sin^2 x}{\sin x}$$
$$= 2 \sin x + \csc x - 2 \sin x$$
$$= \csc x$$
$$= \text{Right Side}$$

b) Left Side
$= \csc^2 x + \sec^2 x$
$= \dfrac{1}{\sin^2 x} + \dfrac{1}{\cos^2 x}$
$= \dfrac{\sin^2 x + \cos^2 x}{\sin^2 x \cos^2 x}$
$= \dfrac{1}{\sin^2 x \cos^2 x}$
$= \csc^2 x \sec^2 x$
$=$ Right Side

c) Left Side
$= \dfrac{\cot x - 1}{1 - \tan x}$
$= \dfrac{\dfrac{1 - \tan x}{\tan x}}{1 - \tan x}$
$= \dfrac{1 - \tan x}{\tan x(1 - \tan x)}$
$= \dfrac{1}{\tan x}$
$= \dfrac{\csc x}{\sec x}$
$=$ Right Side

12. a) Left Side $= \sin(90° + \theta)$
$= \sin 90° \cos \theta + \cos 90° \sin \theta$
$= \cos \theta$
Right Side $= \sin(90° - \theta)$
$= \sin 90° \cos \theta - \cos 90° \sin \theta$
$= \cos \theta$

b) Left Side $= \sin(2\pi - \theta)$
$= \sin(2\pi) \cos(\theta) - \cos(2\pi) \sin(\theta)$
$= -\sin \theta$
$=$ Right Side

13. Left Side $= 2 \cos x \cos y$
Right Side $= \cos(x + y) + \cos(x - y)$
$= \cos x \cos y - \sin x \sin y + \cos x \cos y + \sin x \sin y$
$= 2 \cos x \cos y$

14. a) 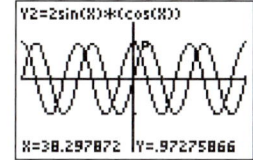 No, this is not an identity.

b) Replacing the variable with 0 is a counter example.

15. a) $x \neq \pi n; n \in I$
b) Left Side $= \dfrac{\sin 2x}{1 - \cos 2x}$
$= \dfrac{2 \sin x \cos x}{1 - 1 + 2 \sin^2 x}$
$= \dfrac{\cos x}{\sin x}$
$= \cot x$
$=$ Right Side

16. Right Side
$= \dfrac{\sin 4x - \sin 2x}{\cos 4x + \cos 2x}$
$= \dfrac{2 \sin 2x \cos 2x - 2 \sin x \cos x}{\cos 4x + 2 \cos^2 x - 1}$
$= \dfrac{2(2 \sin x \cos x)(2 \cos^2 x - 1) - 2 \sin x \cos x}{2 \cos^2 2x - 1 + 2 \cos^2 x - 1}$
$= \dfrac{(2 \sin x \cos x)(2(2 \cos^2 x - 1) - 1)}{2(2 \cos^2 x - 1)^2 + 2 \cos^2 x - 2}$
$= \dfrac{(2 \sin x \cos x)(4 \cos^2 x - 3)}{2(4 \cos^4 x - 4 \cos^2 x + 1) + 2 \cos^2 x - 2}$
$= \dfrac{(2 \sin x \cos x)(4 \cos^2 x - 3)}{8 \cos^4 x - 6 \cos^2 x}$
$= \dfrac{(2 \sin x \cos x)(4 \cos^2 x - 3)}{2 \cos^2 x(4 \cos^2 x - 3)}$
$= \dfrac{2 \sin x \cos x}{2 \cos^2 x}$
$= \tan x$
$=$ Left Side

17. Left Side $= \dfrac{\sin 2x}{1 - \cos 2x}$
$= \dfrac{\sin 2x}{1 - \cos 2x} \left(\dfrac{1 + \cos 2x}{1 + \cos 2x} \right)$
$= \dfrac{\sin 2x + \sin 2x \cos 2x}{1 - \cos^2 2x}$
$= \dfrac{\sin 2x + \sin 2x \cos 2x}{\sin^2 2x}$
$= \dfrac{1}{\sin 2x} + \dfrac{\cos 2x}{\sin 2x}$
$= \dfrac{1}{\sin 2x} + \dfrac{1 - 2 \sin^2 x}{\sin 2x}$
$= \dfrac{2}{\sin 2x} - \dfrac{2 \sin^2 x}{\sin 2x}$
$= 2 \csc 2x - \dfrac{2 \sin^2 x}{2 \sin x \cos x}$
$= 2 \csc 2x - \tan x$
$=$ Right Side

18. Left Side $= \dfrac{1 - \sin^2 x - 2 \cos x}{\cos^2 x - \cos x - 2}$
$= \dfrac{\cos^2 x - 2 \cos x}{\cos^2 x - \cos x - 2}$
$= \dfrac{\cos x(\cos x - 2)}{(\cos x - 2)(\cos x + 1)}$
$= \dfrac{\cos x}{\cos x + 1}$
$= \dfrac{\dfrac{\cos x}{\cos x}}{\dfrac{\cos x + 1}{\cos x}}$
$= \dfrac{1}{1 + \sec x}$
$=$ Right Side

19. a) $\sin \theta_t = \dfrac{n_1 \sin \theta_i}{n_2}$

b) Using $\sin^2 x + \cos^2 x = 1$, $\cos x = \sqrt{1 - \sin^2 x}$
Then, replace this in the equation.

c) Substitute $\sin \theta_t = \dfrac{n_1 \sin \theta_i}{n_2}$.

C1 Graphing gives a visual approximation, so some functions may look the same but actually are not. Verifying numerically is not enough since it may not hold for other values.

C2 Left Side $= \cos\left(\dfrac{\pi}{2} - x\right)$
$= \cos\left(\dfrac{\pi}{2}\right) \cos x + \sin\left(\dfrac{\pi}{2}\right) \sin x$
$= \sin x$
$=$ Right Side

C3 a) $\cos x \geq 0$, $\dfrac{\pi}{2} + 2\pi n < x < \dfrac{3\pi}{2} + 2\pi n, n \in I$

b) $x = 1$

c) $x = \pi$, $\cos x$ will give a negative answer and radical functions always give a positive answer, so the equation is not an identity.

d) An identity is always true whereas an equation is true for certain values or a restricted domain.

6.4 Solving Trigonometric Equations Using Identities, pages 320 to 321

1. a) $0, \dfrac{\pi}{4}, \pi, \dfrac{5\pi}{4}$ **b)** $0, \dfrac{\pi}{3}, \pi, \dfrac{5\pi}{3}$
c) $\dfrac{3\pi}{2}$ **d)** $\dfrac{\pi}{6}, \dfrac{5\pi}{6}, \dfrac{3\pi}{2}$
2. a) $0°, 120°, 240°$ **b)** $270°$
c) no solution **d)** $0°, 120°, 180°, 300°$

3. a) $2\sin^2 x + 3\sin x + 1 = 0$; $\frac{7\pi}{6}, \frac{3\pi}{2}, \frac{11\pi}{6}$
   b) $2\sin^2 x + 3\sin x + 1 = 0$; $\frac{7\pi}{6}, \frac{3\pi}{2}, \frac{11\pi}{6}$
   c) $\sin^2 x + 2\sin x - 3 = 0$, $\frac{\pi}{2}$
   d) $2 - \sin^2 x = 0$; no solution
4. $-150°, -30°, 30°, 150°$
5. 0.464, 2.034, 3.605, 5.176
6. There are two more solutions that Sanesh did not find since she divided by cos (x). The extra solutions are $x = 90° + 360°n$ and $x = 270° + 360°n$.
7. a) $\frac{\pi}{12}, \frac{5\pi}{12}, \frac{13\pi}{12}, \frac{17\pi}{12}$ b) $\frac{\pi}{12}, \frac{5\pi}{12}, \frac{13\pi}{12}, \frac{17\pi}{12}$
8. $x = \frac{\pi}{2} + \pi n$, $n \in I$
9. $x = \frac{\pi}{2} + 2\pi n$, $n \in I$
10. 7. Inspection of each factor shows that there are $2 + 1 + 4$ solutions, which gives a total of 7 solutions over the interval $0° < x \leq 360°$.
11. $\frac{\pi}{2}, \frac{4\pi}{3}, \frac{3\pi}{2}, \frac{5\pi}{3}$
12. $B = -3$, $C = -2$
13. Example: $\sin 2x - \sin 2x \cos^2 x = 0$; $x = \left(\frac{\pi}{2}\right)n$, $n \in I$
14. $x = \left(\frac{\pi}{2}\right)(2n+1)$, $n \in I$, $x = \frac{\pi}{6} + 2\pi n$, $n \in I$,
    $x = \frac{5\pi}{6} + 2\pi n$, $n \in I$
15. 12 solutions
16. $x = \pi + 2\pi n$, $n \in I$, $x = \pm 0.955\,32 + n\pi$, $n \in I$
17. $x = \frac{\pi}{4} + \pi n$, $n \in I$, $x = -\frac{\pi}{4} + \pi n$, $n \in I$
18. -1.8235, 1.8235
19. $x = 2\pi n$, $n \in I$, $x = \pm \frac{\pi}{3} + 2\pi n$, $n \in I$
20. 1 and -2
C1 a) $\cos 2x = 1 - 2\sin^2 x$ b) $(2\sin x - 1)(\sin x + 1)$
   c) $30°, 150°, 270°$ d)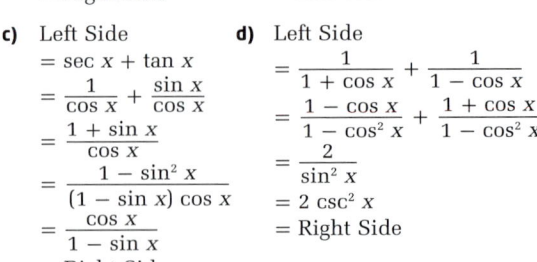

C2 a) You cannot factor the left side of the equation because there are no two integers whose product is -3 and whose sum is 1.
   b) $-0.7676, 0.4343$
   c) $64.26°, 140.14°, 219.86°, 295.74°, 424.26°, 500.14°, 579.86°, 655.74°$
C3 Example: $\sin 2x \cos x + \cos x = 0$; The reason this is not an identity is that it is not true for all replacement values of the variable. For example, if $x = 30°$, the two sides are not equal. The solutions are $90° + 180°n$, $n \in I$ and $135° + 180°n$, $n \in I$.

Chapter 6 Review, pages 322 to 323

1. a) $x \neq \frac{\pi}{2} + n\pi$, $n \in I$ b) $x \neq \left(\frac{\pi}{2}\right)n$, $n \in I$
   c) $x = \pm\frac{\pi}{3} + 2\pi n$, $n \in I$ d) $x \neq \frac{\pi}{2} + n\pi$, $n \in I$
2. a) $\cos x$ b) $\tan x$ c) $\tan x$ d) $\cos x$
3. a) 1 b) 1 c) 1
4. a) Both sides have the same value so the equation is true for those values.
   b) $x \neq 90°, 270°$

5. a) Example: $x = 0, 1$
   b)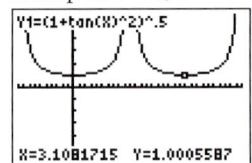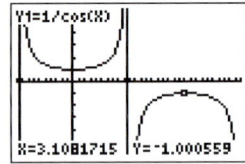
   c) The graphs are the same for part of the domain. Outside of this interval they are not the same.
6. a) $f(0) = 2$, $f\left(\frac{\pi}{6}\right) = 1 + \sqrt{3}$
   b) $\sin x + \cos x + \sin 2x + \cos 2x$
      $= \sin x + \cos x + 2\sin x \cos x + 1 - \sin^2 x$
   c) No, because you cannot write the first two terms as anything but the way they are.
   d) You cannot get a perfect saw tooth graph but the approximation gets closer as you increase the amount of iterations. Six terms give a reasonable approximation.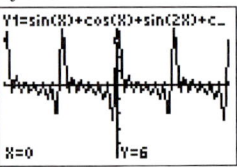
7. a) $\sin 90° = 1$ b) $\sin 30° = 0.5$
   c) $\cos \frac{\pi}{6} = \frac{\sqrt{3}}{2}$ d) $\cos \frac{\pi}{4} = \frac{1}{\sqrt{2}}$
8. a) $\frac{\sqrt{3}-1}{2\sqrt{2}}$ or $\frac{\sqrt{6}-\sqrt{2}}{4}$ b) $\frac{\sqrt{3}+1}{2\sqrt{2}}$ or $\frac{\sqrt{6}+\sqrt{2}}{4}$
   c) $\sqrt{3} - 2$ d) $\frac{\sqrt{3}+1}{2\sqrt{2}}$ or $\frac{\sqrt{6}+\sqrt{2}}{4}$
9. a) $\frac{7}{13\sqrt{2}}$ or $\frac{7\sqrt{2}}{26}$ b) $\frac{12 - 5\sqrt{3}}{26}$
   c) $-\frac{120}{169}$
10. $1 + \frac{1}{\sqrt{2}}$
11. $\tan x$
12. a) $\frac{\cos x}{\sin x - 1}$ or $\frac{-1 - \sin x}{\cos x}$
    b) $\tan^2 x \sin^2 x$
13. a) Left Side
       $= 1 + \cot^2 x$
       $= 1 + \frac{\cos^2 x}{\sin^2 x}$
       $= \frac{\sin^2 x + \cos^2 x}{\sin^2 x}$
       $= \frac{1}{\sin^2 x}$
       $= \csc^2 x$
       $=$ Right Side
    b) Right Side
       $= \csc 2x - \cot 2x$
       $= \frac{1}{\sin 2x} - \frac{\cos 2x}{\sin 2x}$
       $= \frac{1 - (2\cos^2 x - 1)}{2\sin x \cos x}$
       $= \frac{2\sin^2 x}{2\sin x \cos x}$
       $= \tan x$
       $=$ Left Side
    c) Left Side
       $= \sec x + \tan x$
       $= \frac{1}{\cos x} + \frac{\sin x}{\cos x}$
       $= \frac{1 + \sin x}{\cos x}$
       $= \frac{1 - \sin^2 x}{(1 - \sin x)\cos x}$
       $= \frac{\cos x}{1 - \sin x}$
       $=$ Right Side
    d) Left Side
       $= \frac{1}{1 + \cos x} + \frac{1}{1 - \cos x}$
       $= \frac{1 - \cos x}{1 - \cos^2 x} + \frac{1 + \cos x}{1 - \cos^2 x}$
       $= \frac{2}{\sin^2 x}$
       $= 2\csc^2 x$
       $=$ Right Side
14. a) It is true when $x = \frac{\pi}{4}$. The equation is not necessarily an identity. Sometimes equations can be true for a small domain of x.
    b) $x = \frac{\pi}{2} + n\pi$, $n \in I$

604 MHR • Answers

c) Left Side = $\sin 2x$
$= 2 \sin x \cos x$
$= \dfrac{2 \sin x \cos^2 x}{\cos x}$
$= \dfrac{2 \tan x}{\sec^2 x}$
$= \dfrac{2 \tan x}{1 + \tan^2 x}$
= Right Side

15. a) Left Side
$= \dfrac{\cos x + \cot x}{\sec x + \tan x}$
$= \dfrac{\cos x + \dfrac{\cos x}{\sin x}}{\dfrac{1}{\cos x} + \dfrac{\sin x}{\cos x}}$
$= \dfrac{\dfrac{\sin x \cos^2 x}{\sin x} + \dfrac{\cos^2 x}{\sin x}}{1 + \sin x}$
$= \dfrac{(\sin x + 1)\cos^2 x}{\dfrac{\sin x}{1 + \sin x}}$
$= \dfrac{\cos x \cos x}{\sin x}$
$= \cos x \cot x$
= Right Side

b) Left Side
$= \sec x + \tan x$
$= \dfrac{1}{\cos x} + \dfrac{\sin x}{\cos x}$
$= \dfrac{1 + \sin x}{\cos x}$
$= \dfrac{1 - \sin^2 x}{(1 - \sin x)\cos x}$
$= \dfrac{\cos x}{1 - \sin x}$
= Right Side

16. a) You can disprove it by trying a value of x or by graphing.
b) Substituting $x = 0$ makes the equation fail.

17. a) $x = 0, \dfrac{2\pi}{3}, \pi, \dfrac{4\pi}{3}$ **b)** $x = \dfrac{5\pi}{6}, \dfrac{11\pi}{6}$
c) $x = \dfrac{7\pi}{6}, \dfrac{11\pi}{6}$ **d)** $x = 0, \dfrac{\pi}{2}, \dfrac{3\pi}{2}$

18. a) $x = 15°, 75°, 195°, 255°$ **b)** $x = 90°, 270°$
c) $x = 30°, 150°, 270°$ **d)** $x = 0°, 180°$

19. $x = \pm\dfrac{\pi}{3} + n\pi, n \in I$

20. $\cos x = \pm\dfrac{4}{5}$

21. $x = -2\pi, -\pi, 0, \pi, 2\pi$

Chapter 6 Practice Test, page 324

1. A **2.** A **3.** D **4.** D **5.** A **6.** D

7. a) $\dfrac{1 - \sqrt{3}}{2\sqrt{2}}$ or $\dfrac{\sqrt{2} - \sqrt{6}}{4}$
b) $\dfrac{\sqrt{3} + 1}{2\sqrt{2}}$ or $\dfrac{\sqrt{6} + \sqrt{2}}{4}$

8. Left Side = $\cot \theta - \tan \theta$
$= \dfrac{1}{\tan \theta} - \tan \theta$
$= \dfrac{1 - \tan^2 \theta}{\tan \theta}$
$= 2\left(\dfrac{1 - \tan^2 \theta}{2 \tan \theta}\right)$
$= 2 \cot 2\theta$
= Right Side

$\theta = \left(\dfrac{\pi}{2}\right)n, n \in I$

9. Theo's Formula = $I_0 \cos^2 \theta$
$= I_0 - I_0 \sin^2 \theta$
$= I_0 - \dfrac{I_0}{\csc^2 \theta}$
= Sany's Formula

10. a) $A = \dfrac{2\pi}{3} + 2\pi n, n \in I, A = \dfrac{4\pi}{3} + 2\pi n, n \in I$
b) $B = \pi n, n \in I, B = \dfrac{\pi}{6} + 2\pi n, n \in I$,
$B = \dfrac{5\pi}{6} + 2\pi n, n \in I$
c) $\theta = \pi n, n \in I, \theta = \pm\dfrac{\pi}{3} + 2\pi n, n \in I$

11. $x = \dfrac{\pi}{2} + n\pi, n \in I$

12. $\dfrac{-4 - 3\sqrt{3}}{10}$

13. $x = \dfrac{\pi}{4}, \dfrac{5\pi}{4}$

14. $x = 0°, 90°, 270°$

15. a) Left Side = $\dfrac{\cot x}{\csc x - 1}$
$= \dfrac{\cot x(\csc x + 1)}{\csc^2 x - 1}$
$= \dfrac{\cot x(\csc x + 1)}{1 + \cot^2 x - 1}$
$= \dfrac{(\csc x + 1)}{\cot x}$
= Right Side

b) Left Side = $\sin(x + y)\sin(x - y)$
$= (\sin x \cos y + \sin y \cos x) \times$
$(\sin x \cos y - \sin y \cos x)$
$= \sin^2 x \cos^2 y - \sin^2 y \cos^2 x$
$= \sin^2 x(1 - \sin^2 y) - \sin^2 y(1 - \sin^2 x)$
$= \sin^2 x - \sin^2 y$
= Right Side

16. $x = \dfrac{\pi}{2} + 2\pi n, n \in I, x = \dfrac{\pi}{6} + 2\pi n, n \in I$,
$x = \dfrac{5\pi}{6} + 2\pi n, n \in I$

Cumulative Review, Chapters 4–6, pages 326 to 327

1. a) $\dfrac{7\pi}{3} \pm 2\pi n, n \in N$ **b)** $-100° \pm (360°)n, n \in N$

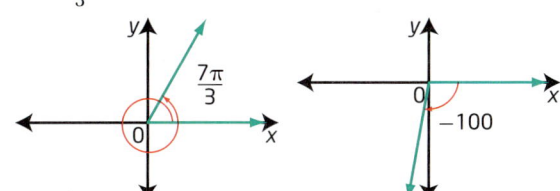

2. a) $229°$ **b)** $-300°$
3. a) $\dfrac{7\pi}{6}$ **b)** $-\dfrac{25\pi}{9}$
4. a) 13.1 ft **b)** 106.9 ft
5. a) $x^2 + y^2 = 25$ **b)** $x^2 + y^2 = 16$
6. a) quadrant III **b)** $-\dfrac{2\pi}{3}, \dfrac{4\pi}{3}$
c) $\left(\dfrac{\sqrt{3}}{2}, -\dfrac{1}{2}\right)$; when the given quadrant III angle is rotated through $\dfrac{\pi}{2}$, its terminal arm is in quadrant IV and its coordinates are switched and the signs adjusted.
d) $\left(\dfrac{1}{2}, \dfrac{\sqrt{3}}{2}\right)$; when the given quadrant III angle is rotated through $-\pi$, its terminal arm is in quadrant I and its coordinates are the same but the signs adjusted.

Answers • MHR **605**

7. a) $\left(\frac{1}{\sqrt{2}}, -\frac{1}{\sqrt{2}}\right), \left(\frac{1}{\sqrt{2}}, \frac{1}{\sqrt{2}}\right)$; the points have the same x-coordinates but opposite y-coordinates.

b) $\left(\frac{1}{\sqrt{2}}, -\frac{1}{\sqrt{2}}\right), \left(\frac{1}{\sqrt{2}}, \frac{1}{\sqrt{2}}\right)$; the points have the same x-coordinates but opposite y-coordinates.

8. a) $-\frac{\sqrt{3}}{2}$ **b)** $\frac{1}{2}$ **c)** $-\frac{1}{\sqrt{3}}$ or $-\frac{\sqrt{3}}{3}$
d) $\sqrt{2}$ **e)** undefined   **f)** $-\sqrt{3}$

9. a)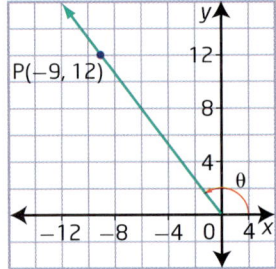

b) $\sin\theta = \frac{4}{5}, \cos\theta = -\frac{3}{5}, \tan\theta = -\frac{4}{3},$
$\csc\theta = \frac{5}{4}, \sec\theta = -\frac{5}{3}, \cot\theta = -\frac{3}{4}$

c) $\theta = 126.87° + (360°)n, n \in I$

10. a) $-\frac{5\pi}{6}, -\frac{\pi}{6}, \frac{7\pi}{6}, \frac{11\pi}{6}$ **b)** $-30°, 30°$
c) $\frac{3\pi}{4}, \frac{7\pi}{4}$

11. a) $\theta = \frac{3\pi}{4} + 2\pi n, n \in I; \frac{5\pi}{4} + 2\pi n, n \in I$
b) $\theta = \frac{\pi}{2} + 2\pi n, n \in I$ **c)** $\theta = \frac{\pi}{2} + \pi n, n \in I$

12. a) $\theta = 0, \frac{\pi}{4}, \pi, \frac{5\pi}{4}, 2\pi$ **b)** $\theta = \frac{2\pi}{3}, \frac{4\pi}{3}$

13. a) $\theta = 27°, 153°, 207°, 333°$
b) $\theta = 90°, 199°, 341°$

14. $y = 3\sin\frac{1}{2}\left(x + \frac{\pi}{4}\right)$

15. a) amplitude 3, period 180°, phase shift 0, vertical displacement 0

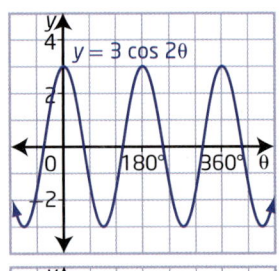

b) amplitude 2, period 120°, phase shift 20° left, vertical displacement 0

c) amplitude $\frac{1}{2}$, period 2π, phase shift π units left, vertical displacement 4 units down

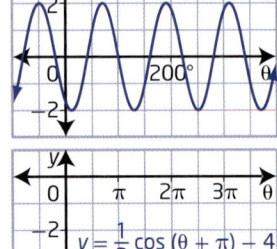

d) amplitude 1, period 4π, phase shift $\frac{\pi}{4}$ units right, vertical displacement 1 unit up

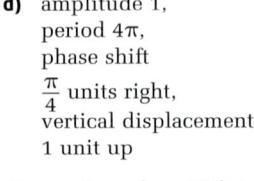 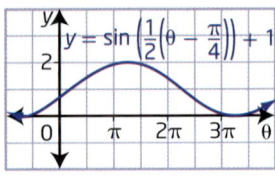

16. a) $y = 2\sin(x - 30°) + 3, y = 2\cos(x - 120°) + 3$
b) $y = \sin 2\left(x + \frac{\pi}{3}\right) - 1, y = \cos 2\left(x + \frac{\pi}{12}\right) - 1$

17. $y = 4\cos 1.2(x + 30°) - 3$

18. a) 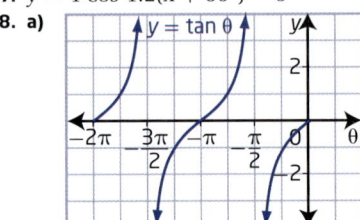   **b)** $x = -\frac{\pi}{2}, x = -\frac{3\pi}{2}$

19. a) $h(x) = -25\cos\frac{2\pi}{11}x + 26$ **b)** $x = 3.0$ min

20. a) $\theta \neq \frac{\pi}{2} + \pi n, n \in I, \tan^2\theta$
b) $x \neq \left(\frac{\pi}{2}\right)n, n \in I, \sec^2 x$

21. a) $-\frac{\sqrt{3} - 1}{2\sqrt{2}}$ or $-\frac{\sqrt{6} - \sqrt{2}}{4}$
b) $\frac{\sqrt{3} - 1}{2\sqrt{2}}$ or $\frac{\sqrt{6} - \sqrt{2}}{4}$

22. a) $\cos\frac{3\pi}{4} = -\frac{1}{\sqrt{2}}$ **b)** $\sin 90° = 1$
c) $\tan\frac{7\pi}{3} = \sqrt{3}$

23. a) Both sides have the same value for A = 30°.
b) Left Side $= \sin^2 A + \cos^2 A + \tan^2 A$
$= 1 + \tan^2 A$
$= \sec^2 A$
$=$ Right Side

24. a) It could be an identity as the graphs look the same.

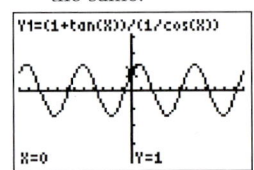 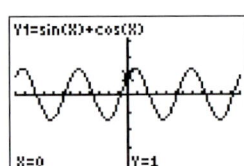

b) Left Side $= \frac{1 + \tan x}{\sec x}$
$= \frac{1}{\sec x} + \frac{\tan x}{\sec x}$
$= \cos x + \frac{\sin x}{\cos x} \div \frac{1}{\cos x}$
$= \cos x + \sin x$
$=$ Right Side

25. Right Side $= \frac{\cos 2\theta}{1 + \sin 2\theta}$
$= \frac{\cos^2\theta - \sin^2\theta}{\cos^2\theta + \sin^2\theta + 2\sin\theta\cos\theta}$
$= \frac{(\cos\theta - \sin\theta)(\cos\theta + \sin\theta)}{(\cos\theta + \sin\theta)(\cos\theta + \sin\theta)}$
$= \frac{\cos\theta - \sin\theta}{\cos\theta + \sin\theta}$
$=$ Left Side

26. a) $x = \frac{5\pi}{6} + \pi n, n \in I, x = \frac{\pi}{6} + \pi n, n \in I$

b) $x = \frac{\pi}{2} + \pi n$, $n \in I$, $x = \frac{7\pi}{6} + 2\pi n$, $n \in I$,
$x = \frac{11\pi}{6} + 2\pi n$, $n \in I$

27. a) This is an identity so all θ are a solution.
    b) Yes, because the left side can be simplified to 1.

Unit 2 Test, pages 328 to 329

1. B 2. D 3. C 4. C 5. B 6. D 7. C 8. A
9. $-\frac{\sqrt{3}}{2}$
10. $-\frac{2}{3}, \frac{2}{3}$
11. $\frac{7}{13\sqrt{2}}$ or $\frac{7\sqrt{2}}{26}$
12. 1.5, 85.9°
13. $-\frac{11\pi}{6}, -\frac{\pi}{6}, \frac{\pi}{6}, \frac{11\pi}{6}$
14. a)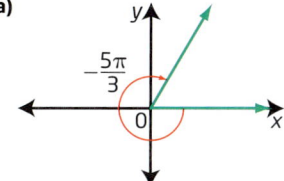
    b) −300°
    c) $-\frac{5\pi}{3} \pm 2\pi n$, $n \in N$
    d) No, following the equation above it is impossible to obtain $\frac{10\pi}{3}$.
15. $x = 0.412, 2.730, 4.712$
16. Sam is correct, there are four solutions in the given domain. Pat made an error when finding the square root. Pat forgot to solve for the positive and negative solutions.
17. a)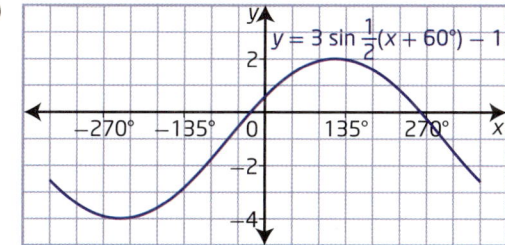
    b) $-4 \leq y \leq 2$
    c) amplitude 3, period 720°, phase shift 60° left, vertical displacement 1 unit down
    d) $x \approx -21°, 261°$
18. a)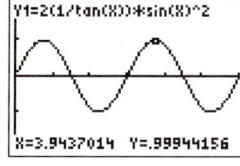
    b) $g(\theta) = \sin 2\theta$
    c) $f(\theta) = 2 \cot \theta \sin^2 \theta$
    $= \frac{2 \cos \theta \sin^2 \theta}{\sin \theta}$
    $= 2 \cos \theta \sin \theta$
    $= \sin 2\theta$
    $= g(\theta)$
19. a) It is true: both sides have the same value.
    b) $x \neq \frac{\pi n}{2}$, $n \in I$
    c) Left Side
    $= \tan x + \frac{1}{\tan x}$
    $= \frac{\tan^2 x + 1}{\tan x}$
    $= \frac{\sec^2 x}{\tan x}$
    $= \sec x \left(\frac{1}{\cos x}\right)\left(\frac{\cos x}{\sin x}\right)$
    $= \frac{\sec x}{\sin x}$
    = Right Side
20. a) 6.838 m   b) 12.37 h   c) 3.017 m

Chapter 7 Exponential Functions

7.1 Characteristics of Exponential Functions, pages 342 to 345

1. a) No, the variable is not the exponent.
   b) Yes, the base is greater than 0 and the variable is the exponent.
   c) No, the variable is not the exponent.
   d) Yes, the base is greater than 0 and the variable is the exponent.
2. a) $f(x) = 4^x$ b) $g(x) = \left(\frac{1}{4}\right)^x$
   c) $x = 0$, which is the y-intercept
3. a) B   b) C   c) A
4. a) $f(x) = 3^x$ b) $f(x) = \left(\frac{1}{5}\right)^x$
5. a) 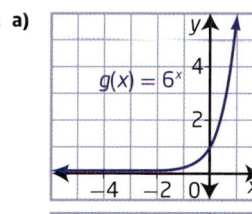 domain $\{x \mid x \in R\}$, range $\{y \mid y > 0, y \in R\}$, y-intercept 1, function increasing, horizontal asymptote $y = 0$
   b) domain $\{x \mid x \in R\}$, range $\{y \mid y > 0, y \in R\}$, y-intercept 1, function increasing, horizontal asymptote $y = 0$
   c) domain $\{x \mid x \in R\}$, range $\{y \mid y > 0, y \in R\}$, y-intercept 1, function decreasing, horizontal asymptote $y = 0$
   d) 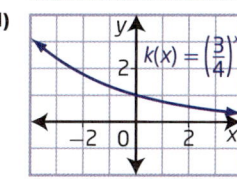 domain $\{x \mid x \in R\}$, range $\{y \mid y > 0, y \in R\}$, y-intercept 1, function decreasing, horizontal asymptote $y = 0$
6. a) $c > 1$; number of bacteria increases over time
   b) $0 < c < 1$; amount of actinium-225 decreases over time
   c) $0 < c < 1$; amount of light decreases with depth
   d) $c > 1$; number of insects increases over time
7. a) 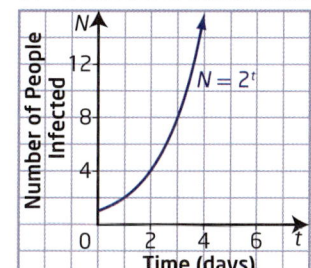 The function $N = 2^t$ is exponential since the base is greater than zero and the variable t is an exponent.
   b) i) 1 person   ii) 2 people
      iii) 16 people   iv) 1024 people

8. a) If the population increases by 10% each year, the population becomes 110% of the previous year's population. So, the growth rate is 110% or 1.1 written as a decimal.

b)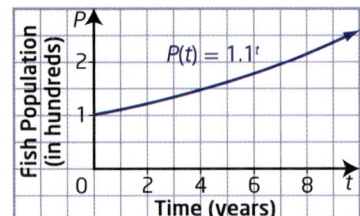

domain $\{t \mid t \geq 0, t \in R\}$ and range $\{P \mid P \geq 100, P \in R\}$

c) The base of the exponent would become 100% − 5% or 95%, written as 0.95 in decimal form.

d)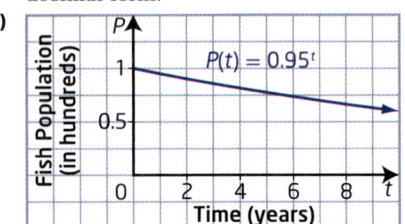

domain $\{t \mid t \geq 0, t \in R\}$ and range $\{P \mid 0 < P \leq 100, P \in R\}$

9. a) $L = 0.9^d$

b)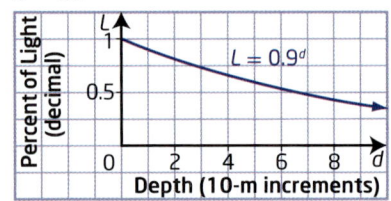

c) domain $\{d \mid d \geq 0, d \in R\}$ and range $\{L \mid 0 < L \leq 1, L \in R\}$

d) 76.8%

10. a) Let P represent the percent, as a decimal, of U-235 remaining. Let t represent time, in 700-million-year intervals. $P(t) = \left(\dfrac{1}{2}\right)^t$

b)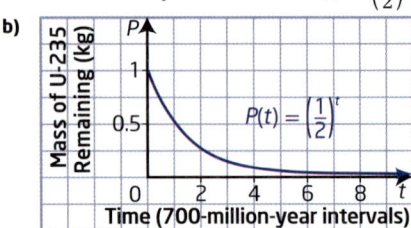

c) 2.1×10^9 years

d) No, the sample of U-235 will never decay to 0 kg, since the graph of $P(t) = \left(\dfrac{1}{2}\right)^t$ has a horizontal asymptote at $P = 0$.

11. a)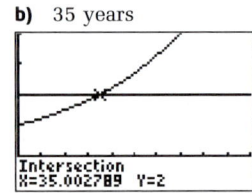
   b) 64 years
   c) No; since the amount invested triples, it does not matter what initial investment is made.
   d) graph: 40 years; rule of 72: 41 years

12. 19.9 years

13. a)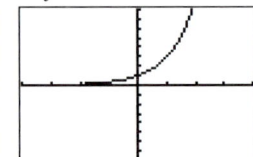

b) The x- and y-coordinates of any point and the domains and ranges are interchanged. The horizontal asymptote becomes a vertical asymptote.

c) $x = 5^y$

14. a) Another way to express $D = 2^{-\varphi}$ is as $D = \left(\dfrac{1}{2}\right)^\varphi$, which indicates a decreasing exponential function. Therefore, a negative value of φ represents a greater value of D.

b) The diameter of fine sand (0.125 mm) is $\dfrac{1}{256}$ the diameter of course gravel (32 mm).

15. a) 34.7 years   b) 35 years

c) The results are similar, but the continuous compounding function gives a shorter doubling period by approximately 0.3 years.

C1 a)

b)

Feature	$f(x) = 3x$	$g(x) = x^3$	$h(x) = 3^x$
domain	$\{x \mid x \in R\}$	$\{x \mid x \in R\}$	$\{x \mid x \in R\}$
range	$\{y \mid y \in R\}$	$\{y \mid y \in R\}$	$\{y \mid y > 0, y \in R\}$
intercepts	x-intercept 0, y-intercept 0	x-intercept 0, y-intercept 0	no x-intercept, y-intercept 1
equations of asymptotes	none	none	$y = 0$

c) Example: All three functions have the same domain, and each of their graphs has a y-intercept. The functions $f(x)$ and $g(x)$ have all key features in common.

d) Example: The function $h(x)$ is the only function with an asymptote, which restricts its range and results in no x-intercept.

C2 a)

x	$f(x)$
0	1
1	−2
2	4
3	−8
4	16
5	−32

b)

c) No, the points do not form a smooth curve. The locations of the points alternate between above the x-axis and below the x-axis.

d) The values are undefined because they result in the square root of a negative number.

$f(x) = (-2)^x$ $f(x) = (-2)^x$
$f\left(\dfrac{1}{2}\right) = (-2)^{\frac{1}{2}}$ $f\left(\dfrac{5}{2}\right) = (-2)^{\frac{5}{2}}$
$f\left(\dfrac{1}{2}\right) = \sqrt{-2}$ $f\left(\dfrac{5}{2}\right) = \sqrt{(-2)^5}$

e) Example: Exponential functions with positive bases result in smooth curves.

7.2 Transformations of Exponential Functions, pages 354 to 357

1. **a)** C   **b)** D   **c)** A   **d)** B
2. **a)** D   **b)** A   **c)** B   **d)** C
3. **a)** $a = 2$: vertical stretch by a factor of 2; $b = 1$: no horizontal stretch; $h = 0$: no horizontal translation; $k = -4$: vertical translation of 4 units down
   b) $a = 1$: no vertical stretch; $b = 1$: no horizontal stretch; $h = 2$: horizontal translation of 2 units right; $k = 3$: vertical translation of 3 units up
   c) $a = -4$: vertical stretch by a factor of 4 and a reflection in the x-axis; $b = 1$: no horizontal stretch; $h = -5$: horizontal translation of 5 units left; $k = 0$: no vertical translation
   d) $a = 1$: no vertical stretch; $b = 3$: horizontal stretch by a factor of $\dfrac{1}{3}$; $h = 1$: horizontal translation of 1 unit right; $k = 0$: no vertical translation
   e) $a = -\dfrac{1}{2}$: vertical stretch by a factor of $\dfrac{1}{2}$ and a reflection in the x-axis; $b = 2$: horizontal stretch by a factor of $\dfrac{1}{2}$; $h = 4$: horizontal translation of 4 units right; $k = 3$: vertical translation of 3 units up
   f) $a = -1$: reflection in the x-axis; $b = 2$: horizontal stretch by a factor of $\dfrac{1}{2}$; $h = 1$: horizontal translation of 1 unit right; $k = 0$: no vertical translation
   g) $a = 1.5$: vertical stretch by a factor of 1.5; $b = \dfrac{1}{2}$: horizontal stretch by a factor of 2; $h = 4$: horizontal translation of 4 units right; $k = -\dfrac{5}{2}$: vertical translation of $\dfrac{5}{2}$ units down
4. **a)** C: reflection in the x-axis, $a < 0$ and $0 < c < 1$, and vertical translation of 2 units up, $k = 2$
   b) A: horizontal translation of 1 unit right, $h = 1$, and vertical translation of 2 units down, $k = -2$
   c) D: reflection in the x-axis, $a < 0$ and $c > 1$, and vertical translation of 2 units up, $k = 2$
   d) B: horizontal translation of 2 units right, $h = 2$, and vertical translation of 1 unit up, $k = 1$
5. **a)** $a = \dfrac{1}{2}$: vertical stretch by a factor of $\dfrac{1}{2}$; $b = -1$: reflection in the y-axis; $h = 3$: horizontal translation of 3 units right 3; $k = 2$: vertical translation of 2 units up

   b)

$y = 4^x$	$y = 4^{-x}$	$y = \dfrac{1}{2}(4)^{-x}$	$y = \dfrac{1}{2}(4)^{-(x-3)} + 2$
$\left(-2, \dfrac{1}{16}\right)$	$\left(2, \dfrac{1}{16}\right)$	$\left(2, \dfrac{1}{32}\right)$	$\left(5, \dfrac{65}{32}\right)$
$\left(-1, \dfrac{1}{4}\right)$	$\left(1, \dfrac{1}{4}\right)$	$\left(1, \dfrac{1}{8}\right)$	$\left(4, \dfrac{17}{8}\right)$
$(0, 1)$	$(0, 1)$	$\left(0, \dfrac{1}{2}\right)$	$\left(3, \dfrac{5}{2}\right)$
$(1, 4)$	$(-1, 4)$	$(-1, 2)$	$(2, 4)$
$(2, 16)$	$(-2, 16)$	$(-2, 8)$	$(1, 10)$

c)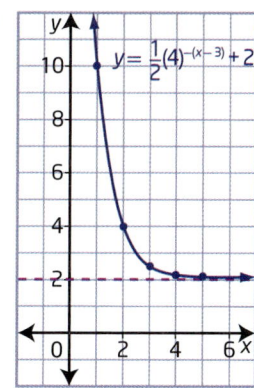

d) domain $\{x \mid x \in \mathbb{R}\}$, range $\{y \mid y > 2, y \in \mathbb{R}\}$, horizontal asymptote $y = 2$, y-intercept 34

6. **a) i), ii)** $a = 2$: vertical stretch by a factor of 2; $b = 1$: no horizontal stretch; $h = 0$: no horizontal translation; $k = 4$: vertical translation of 4 units up

   iii)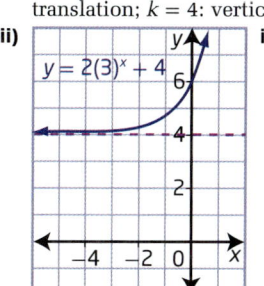

   iv) domain $\{x \mid x \in \mathbb{R}\}$, range $\{y \mid y > 4, y \in \mathbb{R}\}$, horizontal asymptote $y = 4$, y-intercept 6

   b) i), ii) $a = -1$: reflection in the x-axis; $b = 1$: no horizontal stretch; $h = 3$: horizontal translation of 3 units right; $k = 2$: vertical translation of 2 units up

   iii)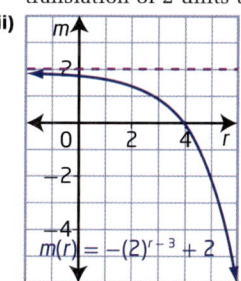

   iv) domain $\{r \mid r \in \mathbb{R}\}$, range $\{m \mid m < 2, m \in \mathbb{R}\}$, horizontal asymptote $m = 2$, m-intercept $\dfrac{15}{8}$, r-intercept 4

   c) i), ii) $a = \dfrac{1}{3}$: vertical stretch by a factor of $\dfrac{1}{3}$; $b = 1$: no horizontal stretch; $h = -1$: horizontal translation of 1 unit left; $k = 1$: vertical translation of 1 unit up

   iii)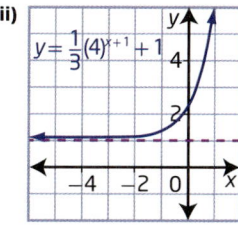

   iv) domain $\{x \mid x \in \mathbb{R}\}$, range $\{y \mid y > 1, y \in \mathbb{R}\}$, horizontal asymptote $y = 1$, y-intercept $\dfrac{7}{3}$

   d) i), ii) $a = -\dfrac{1}{2}$: vertical stretch by a factor of $\dfrac{1}{2}$ and a reflection in the x-axis; $b = \dfrac{1}{4}$: horizontal stretch by a factor of 4; $h = 0$: no horizontal translation; $k = -3$: vertical translation of 3 units down

iii)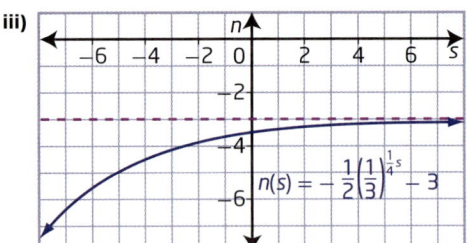

iv) domain $\{s \mid s \in \mathbb{R}\}$, range $\{n \mid n < -3, n \in \mathbb{R}\}$, horizontal asymptote $n = -3$, n-intercept $-\frac{7}{2}$

7. a) horizontal translation of 2 units right and vertical translation of 1 unit up; $y = \left(\frac{1}{2}\right)^{x-2} + 1$

   b) reflection in the x-axis, vertical stretch by a factor of 0.5, and horizontal translation of 3 units right; $y = -0.5(5)^{x-3}$

   c) reflection in the x-axis, horizontal stretch by a factor of $\frac{1}{3}$, and vertical translation of 1 unit up; $y = -\left(\frac{1}{4}\right)^{3x} + 1$

   d) vertical stretch by a factor of 2, reflection in the y-axis, horizontal stretch by a factor of 3, horizontal translation of 1 unit right, and vertical translation of 5 units down; $y = 2(4)^{-\frac{1}{3}(x-1)} - 5$

8. a) 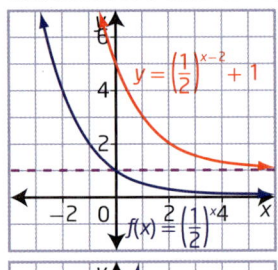 Map all points (x, y) on the graph of $f(x)$ to $(x + 2, y + 1)$.

   b) 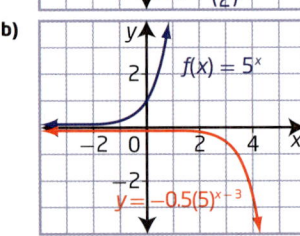 Map all points (x, y) on the graph of $f(x)$ to $(x + 3, -0.5y)$.

   c) 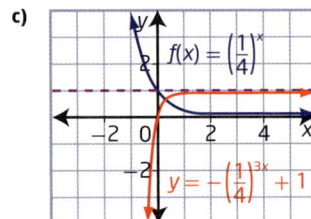 Map all points (x, y) on the graph of $f(x)$ to $\left(\frac{1}{3}x, -y + 1\right)$.

   d) 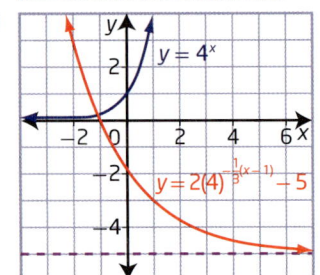 Map all points (x, y) on the graph of $f(x)$ to $(-3x + 1, 2y - 5)$.

9. a) 0.79 represents the 79% of the drug remaining in exponential decay after $\frac{1}{3}$ h.

   b)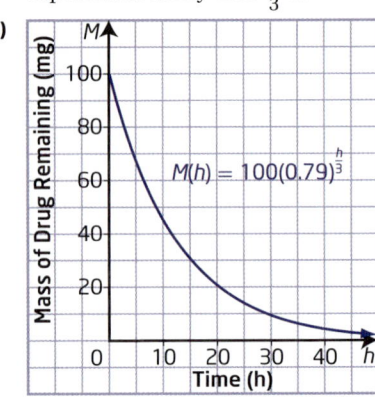

   c) The M-intercept represents the drug dose taken.

   d) domain $\{h \mid h \geq 0, h \in \mathbb{R}\}$, range $\{M \mid 0 < M \leq 100, M \in \mathbb{R}\}$

10. a) $a = 75$: vertical stretch by a factor of 75; $b = \frac{1}{5}$: horizontal stretch by a factor of 5; $h = 0$: no horizontal translation; $k = 20$: vertical translation of 20 units up

    b)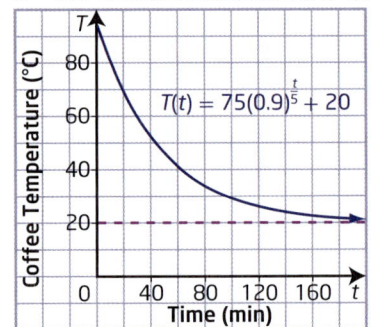

    c) 29.1 °C
    d) final temperature of the coffee

11. a) $P = 5000(1.2)^{\frac{1}{2}x}$

    b) $a = 5000$: vertical stretch by a factor of 5000; $b = \frac{1}{2}$: horizontal stretch by a factor of 2

    c) 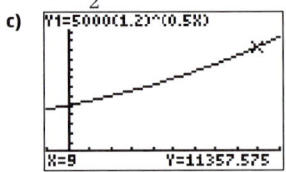 approximately 11 357 bacteria

12. a) $P = 100\left(\frac{1}{2}\right)^{\frac{t}{5730}}$

    b) 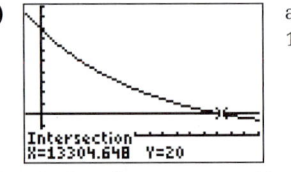 approximately 13 305 years old

13. a) 527.8 cm² b) 555 h

14. a) 1637 foxes

    b) Example: Disease or lack of food can change the rate of growth of the foxes. Exponential growth suggests that the population will grow without bound, and therefore the fox population will grow beyond the possible food sources, which is not good if not controlled.

C1 Example: The graph of an exponential function of the form $y = c^x$ has a horizontal asymptote at $y = 0$. Since $y \neq 0$, the graph cannot have an x-intercept.

C2 a) Example: For a function of the form $y = a(c)^{b(x-h)} + k$, the parameters a and k can affect the x-intercept. If $a > 0$ and $k < 0$ or $a < 0$ and $k > 0$, then the graph of the exponential function will have an x-intercept.

b) Example: For a function of the form $y = a(c)^{b(x-h)} + k$, the parameters a, h, and k can affect the y-intercept. The point $(0, y)$ on the graph of $y = c^x$ gets mapped to $(h, ay + k)$.

7.3 Solving Exponential Equations, pages 364 to 365

1. a) 2^{12} **b)** 2^9 **c)** 2^{-6} **d)** 2^4

2. a) 2^3 and 2^4 **b)** 3^{2x} and 3^3
c) $\left(\frac{1}{2}\right)^{2x}$ and $\left(\frac{1}{2}\right)^{2x-2}$ **d)** 2^{-3x+6} and 2^{4x}

3. a) 4^2 **b)** $4^{\frac{2}{3}}$ **c)** 4^3 **d)** 4^3

4. a) $x = 3$ **b)** $x = -2$ **c)** $w = 3$ **d)** $m = \frac{7}{4}$

5. a) $x = -3$ **b)** $x = -4$ **c)** $y = \frac{11}{4}$ **d)** $k = 9$

6. a) 10.2 **b)** 11.5 **c)** -2.8 **d)** 18.9

7. a) 58.71 **b)** -1.66 **c)** -5.38 **d)** -8
e) 2.71 **f)** 14.43 **g)** -3.24 **h)** -1.88

8. a)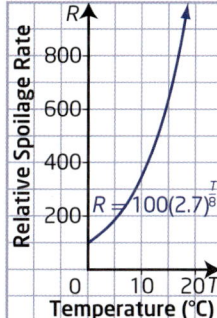
b) approximately 5.6 °C
c) approximately 643
d) approximately 13.0 °C

9. 3 h

10. 4 years

11. a) $A = 1000(1.02)^n$ **b)** \$1372.79 **c)** 9 years

12. a) $C = \left(\frac{1}{2}\right)^{\frac{t}{5.3}}$ **b)** $\frac{1}{32}$ of the original amount
c) 47.7 years

13. a) $A = 500(1.033)^n$ **b)** \$691.79
c) approximately 17 years

14. \$5796.65

15. a) i) $x > 2$ **ii)** $x > -\frac{3}{2}$

b) i)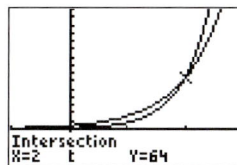
Since the graph of $y = 2^{3x}$ is greater than (above) the graph of $y = 4^{x+1}$ when $x > 2$, the solution is $x > 2$.

ii)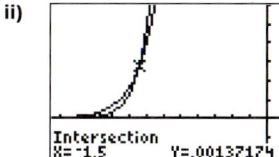
Since the graph of $y = 81^x$ is less than (below) the graph of $y = 27^{2x+1}$ when $x > -\frac{3}{2}$, the solution is $x > -\frac{3}{2}$.

c) Example: Solve the inequality $\left(\frac{1}{2}\right)^{x+3} > 2^{x-1}$.
Answer: $x < -1$

16. Yes. Rewrite the equation as $(4^x)^2 + 2(4^x) - 3 = 0$ and factor as $(4^x + 3)(4^x - 1) = 0$; $x = 0$

17. $(2^x)^x = \left(2^{\frac{5}{2}}\right)^{\frac{5}{2}} \approx 76.1$

18. 20 years

C1 a) You can express 16^2 with a base of 4 by writing 16 as 4^2 and simplifying.
$16^2 = (4^2)^2$
$16^2 = 4^4$

b) Example: You can express 16^2 with a base of 2 by writing 16 as 2^4 and simplifying.
$16^2 = (2^4)^2$
$16^2 = 2^8$

Or, you can express 16^2 with a base of $\frac{1}{4}$ by writing 16 as $\left(\frac{1}{4}\right)^{-2}$ and simplifying.
$16^2 = \left(\left(\frac{1}{4}\right)^{-2}\right)^2$
$16^2 = \left(\frac{1}{4}\right)^{-4}$

C2 a) $16^{2x} = 8^{x-3}$
$(2^4)^{2x} = (2^3)^{x-3}$
$2^{8x} = 2^{3x-9}$
$8x = 3x - 9$
$5x = -9$
$x = -\frac{9}{5}$

b) Step 1: Express the bases on both sides as powers of 2.
Step 2: Apply the power of a power law.
Step 3: Equate the exponents.
Step 4: Isolate the term containing x.
Step 5: Solve for x.

Chapter 7 Review, pages 366 to 367

1. a) B **b)** D **c)** A **d)** C

2. a)

x	y
-2	$11.\overline{1}$
-1	$3.\overline{3}$
0	1
1	0.3
2	0.09

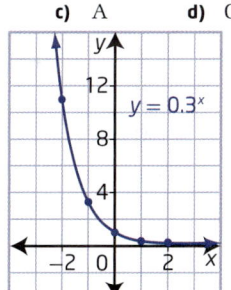

b) domain $\{x \mid x \in \mathbb{R}\}$, range $\{y \mid y > 0, y \in \mathbb{R}\}$, y-intercept 1, function decreasing, horizontal asymptote $y = 0$

3. $y = \left(\frac{1}{4}\right)^x$

4. a) Since the interest rate is 3.25% per year, each year the investment grows by a factor of 103.25%, which, written as a decimal, is 1.0325.
b) \$1.38 **c)** 21.7 years

5. a) $a = -2$: vertical stretch by a factor of 2 and reflection in the x-axis; $b = 3$: horizontal stretch by a factor of $\frac{1}{3}$; $h = 1$: horizontal translation of 1 unit right; $k = 2$: vertical translation of 2 units up

b)

Transformation	Parameter Value	Function Equation
horizontal stretch	$b = 3$	$y = 4^{3x}$
vertical stretch	$a = -2$	$y = -2(4)^x$
translation left/right	$h = 1$	$y = (4)^{x-1}$
translation up/down	$k = 2$	$y = 4^x + 2$

c)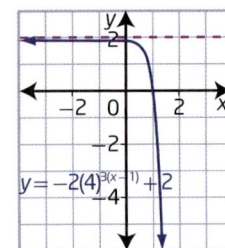

d) domain $\{x \mid x \in R\}$, range $\{y \mid y < 2, y \in R\}$, horizontal asymptote $y = 2$, y-intercept $\frac{63}{32}$, x-intercept 1

6. a) horizontal translation of 3 units right
   b) vertical translation of 4 units down
   c) reflection in the x-axis and a translation of 1 unit left and 2 units up

7. a) $y = 4(5)^{-2(x+4)} + 1$ b) $y = -3\left(\frac{1}{2}\right)^{4(x-2)} - 1$

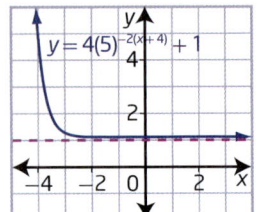   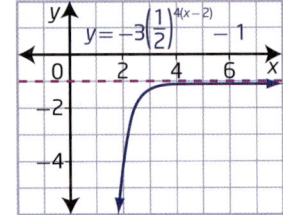

8. a) $a = 190$: vertical stretch by a factor of 190; $b = \frac{1}{10}$: horizontal stretch by a factor of 10

b)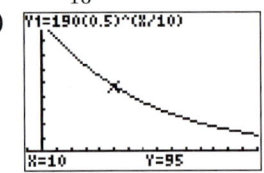

c) domain $\{t \mid t \geq 0, t \in R\}$, range $\{T \mid 0 < T \leq 190, T \in R\}$
d) approximately 31.1 h

9. a) 6^2 b) 6^{-2} c) 6^5
10. a) $x = -\frac{3}{2}$ b) $x = \frac{12}{11}$
11. a) $x \approx -4.30$ b) $x \approx -6.13$
12. a) $N = \left(\frac{1}{2}\right)^{\frac{t}{2.5}}$ b) $\frac{1}{16}$ c) 25 h

Chapter 7 Practice Test, pages 368 to 369

1. B   2. C   3. B   4. A   5. D
6. a) $y = 5^{x+3} + 2$ b) $y = -0.5(2)^{x-1} - 4$
7. a) 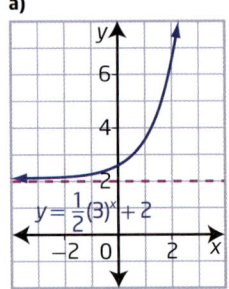   b)

c)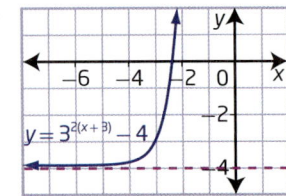

8. a) $a = 2$: vertical stretch by a factor of 2; $h = -3$: horizontal translation of 3 units left; $k = -4$: vertical translation of 4 units down

b)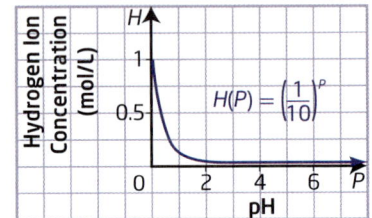

c) domain $\{x \mid x \in R\}$, range $\{y \mid y > -4, y \in R\}$, horizontal asymptote $y = -4$

9. a) $x = -4$ b) $x = 18$ c) $x = \frac{13}{8}$
10. a) $x \approx 9.7$ b) $x \approx 0.1$
11. a) 1.0277   b) $P = 100(1.0277)^t$
   c) domain $\{t \mid t \geq 0, t \in R\}$, range $\{P \mid P \geq 100, P \in R\}$
   d) approximately 8.2 years
12. a)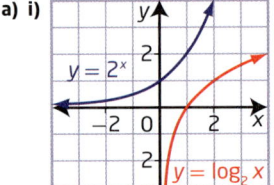

b) 1.0×10^{-7} [H$^+$]
c) 1.0×10^{-7} to 2.5×10^{-8} [H$^+$]
13. 4.5 years
14. 9.97 years

Chapter 8 Logarithmic Functions

8.1 Understanding Logarithms, pages 380 to 382

1. a) i)   ii) $y = \log_2 x$
      iii) domain $\{x \mid x > 0, x \in R\}$, range $\{y \mid y \in R\}$, x-intercept 1, no y-intercept, vertical asymptote $x = 0$

   b) i)   ii) $y = \log_{\frac{1}{3}} x$
      iii) domain $\{x \mid x > 0, x \in R\}$, range $\{y \mid y \in R\}$, x-intercept 1, no y-intercept, vertical asymptote $x = 0$

2. a) $\log_{12} 144 = 2$ b) $\log_8 2 = \frac{1}{3}$
   c) $\log_{10} 0.00001 = -5$ d) $\log_7 (y+3) = 2x$
3. a) $5^2 = 25$ b) $8^{\frac{2}{3}} = 4$
   c) $10^6 = 1\,000\,000$ d) $11^y = x + 3$
4. a) 3   b) 0   c) $\frac{1}{3}$ d) -3
5. $a = 4$; $b = 5$
6. a) $x > 1$ b) $0 < x < 1$ c) $x = 1$
   d) Example: $x = 9$
7. a) 0 raised to any non-zero power is 0.
   b) 1 raised to any power is 1.
   c) Exponential functions with a negative base are not continuous.

8. a) $y = \log_5 x$

 b)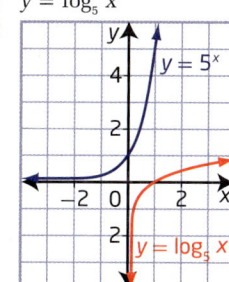
 domain $\{x \mid x > 0, x \in R\}$,
 range $\{y \mid y \in R\}$,
 x-intercept 1,
 no y-intercept,
 vertical asymptote $x = 0$

9. a) $g^{-1}(x) = \left(\dfrac{1}{4}\right)^x$

 b)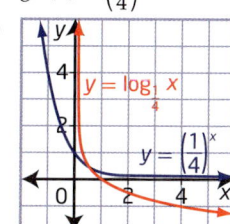
 domain $\{x \mid x \in R\}$,
 range $\{y \mid y > 0, y \in R\}$,
 no x-intercept,
 y-intercept 1,
 horizontal asymptote $y = 0$

10. They are reflections of each other in the line $y = x$.

11. a) They have the exact same shape.
 b) One of them is increasing and the other is decreasing.

12. a) 216 **b)** 81 **c)** 64 **d)** 8

13. a) 7 **b)** 6

14. a) 0 **b)** 1

15. -1

16. 16

17. a) $t = \log_{1.1} N$ **b)** 145 days

18. The larger asteroid had a relative risk that was 1479 times as dangerous.

19. 1000 times as great

20. 5

21. $m = 14, n = 13$

22. $4n$

23. $y = 3^{2^x}$

24. $n = 8; m = 3$

C1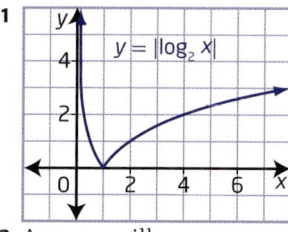
The function has the same general shape, but instead of decreasing, after $x = 1$ the function increases without limit.

C2 Answers will vary.

C3 Step 1: a) $e = 2.718\ 281\ 828$ **b)** 10^{10}
 Step 2: a) domain $\{x \mid x > 0, x \in R\}$, range $\{y \mid y \in R\}$,
 x-intercept 1, no y-intercept,
 vertical asymptote $x = 0$
 b) $y = \ln x$
 Step 3: a) $r = 2.41$
 b) i) $\theta = \dfrac{\ln r}{0.14}$ **ii)** $\theta = 17.75$

8.2 Transformations of Logarithmic Functions, pages 389 to 391

1. a) Translate 1 unit right and 6 units up.
 b) Reflect in the x-axis, stretch vertically about the x-axis by a factor of 4, and stretch horizontally about the y-axis by a factor of $\dfrac{1}{3}$.
 c) Reflect in the y-axis, stretch vertically about the x-axis by a factor of $\dfrac{1}{2}$, and translate 7 units up.

2. a)
 b) $y = 2\log_3(x + 3)$

3. a)
 b) $y = \log_2(-x) + 5$

4. a) **b)**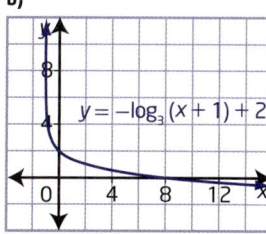
 c)

5. a) i) vertical asymptote $x = -3$
 ii) domain $\{x \mid x > -3, x \in R\}$, range $\{y \mid y \in R\}$
 iii) y-intercept -5 **iv)** x-intercept -2
 b) i) vertical asymptote $x = -9$
 ii) domain $\{x \mid x > -9, x \in R\}$, range $\{y \mid y \in R\}$
 iii) y-intercept 2 **iv)** x-intercept -8.75
 c) i) vertical asymptote $x = -3$
 ii) domain $\{x \mid x > -3, x \in R\}$, range $\{y \mid y \in R\}$
 iii) y-intercept -1.3 **iv)** x-intercept 22
 d) i) vertical asymptote $x = -1$
 ii) domain $\{x \mid x > -1, x \in R\}$, range $\{y \mid y \in R\}$
 iii) y-intercept -6 **iv)** x-intercept $-\dfrac{3}{4}$

6. **a)** $y = 5 \log x$ **b)** $y = \log_8 2x$
   c) $y = \frac{1}{3} \log_2 x$ **d)** $y = \log_4 \left(\frac{x}{2}\right)$
7. **a)** stretch horizontally about the y-axis by a factor of $\frac{1}{4}$; translate 5 units left and 6 units up
   b) stretch horizontally about the y-axis by a factor of 3; stretch vertically about the x-axis by a factor of 2; reflect in the y-axis; translate 1 unit right and 4 units down
8. **a)** $a = -1, b = 1, h = -6, k = 3; y = -\log_3 (x + 6) + 3$
   b) $a = 5, b = 3, h = 0, k = 0; y = 5 \log_3 3x$
   c) $a = 0.75, b = -0.25, h = 2, k = -5;$
   $y = \frac{3}{4} \log_3 \left(-\frac{1}{4}(x - 2)\right) - 5$
9. **a)** Reflect in the y-axis, stretch vertically about the x-axis by a factor of 5, stretch horizontally about the y-axis by a factor of $\frac{1}{4}$, and translate 3 units right and 2 units down.
   b) Reflect in the x-axis, reflect in the y-axis, stretch vertically about the x-axis by a factor of $\frac{1}{4}$, translate 6 units right and 1 unit up.
10. **a)** $y = \log_3 x - 6$ **b)** $y = \log_2 \left(\frac{x}{4}\right)$
11. Stretch vertically about the x-axis by a factor of 3 and translate 4 units right and 2 units down.
12. **a)** Stretch vertically about the x-axis by a factor of 0.67, stretch horizontally about the y-axis by a factor of $\frac{25}{9}$ or approximately 2.78, and translate 1.46 units up.
    b) 515 649 043 kWh
13. **a)** 0.8 μL **b)** 78 mmHg
14. **a)** 172 cm **b)** 40 kg
15. $a = \frac{1}{3}$
16. **a)** $y = -2 \log_5 x + 13$ **b)** $y = \log 2x$
17. $a = \frac{1}{2}, k = -8$

C1 $a = \frac{1}{4}, b = \frac{1}{3}, h = 4, k = -1;$
$g(x) = 0.25 \log_5 \left(\frac{1}{3}\right)(x - 4) - 1$

C2 a) $y = -\log_2 x, y = \log_2 (-x), y = 2^x$
b) Reflect in the x-axis, reflect in the y-axis, and reflect in the line $y = x$.

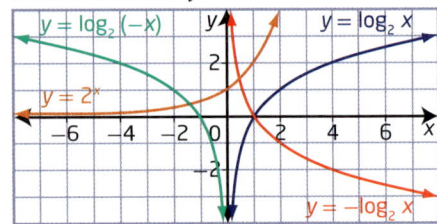

C3 a) $y = \frac{1}{2} \log_7 \frac{(x - 5)}{3} + \frac{1}{2}$ **b)** $y = 3^{\frac{x-8}{2}} + 1$
C4 Answers will vary.

8.3 Laws of Logarithms, pages 400 to 403

1. **a)** $\log_7 x + 3 \log_7 y + \frac{1}{2} \log_7 z$
   b) $8(\log_5 x + \log_5 y + \log_5 z)$
   c) $2 \log x - \log y - \frac{1}{3} \log z$
   d) $y = \log_3 x + \left(\frac{1}{2}\right)(\log_3 y - \log_3 z)$
2. **a)** 2 **b)** 3 **c)** 3.5 **d)** 3

3. **a)** $\log_9 \left(\frac{xz^4}{y}\right)$ **b)** $y = \log_3 \frac{\sqrt{x}}{y^2}$
   c) $\log_6 \left(\frac{x}{\sqrt[5]{xy^2}}\right)$ **d)** $\log \sqrt[3]{xy}$
4. **a)** 1.728 **b)** 1.44 **c)** 1.2
5. **a)** 27 **b)** 49
6. **a)** Stretch horizontally about the y-axis by a factor of $\frac{1}{8}$.
   b) Translate 3 units up.
7. **a)** False; the division must take place inside the logarithm.
   b) False; it must be a multiplication inside the logarithm.
   c) True
   d) False; the power must be inside the logarithm.
   e) True
8. **a)** $P - Q$ **b)** $P + Q$ **c)** $P + \frac{Q}{2}$ **d)** $2Q - 2P$
9. **a)** $6K$ **b)** $1 + K$ **c)** $2K + 2$ **d)** $\frac{K}{5} - 3$
10. **a)** $\frac{1}{2} \log_5 x, x > 0$ **b)** $\frac{2}{3} \log_{11} x, x > 0$
11. **a)** $\log_2 \left(\frac{x + 5}{3}\right), x < -5$ or $x > 5$
    b) $\log_7 \left(\frac{x + 4}{x + 2}\right), x < -4$ or $x > 4$
    c) $\log_8 \left(\frac{x + 3}{x - 2}\right), x > 2$
12. **a)** Left Side $= \log_c 48 - (\log_c 3 + \log_c 2)$
    $= \log_c 48 - \log_c 6$
    $= \log_c 8$
    $=$ Right Side
    b) Left Side $= 7 \log_c 4$
    $= 7 \log_c 2^2$
    $= 2(7) \log_c 2$
    $= 14 \log_c 2$
    $=$ Right Side
    c) Left Side $= \frac{1}{2}(\log_c 2 + \log_c 6)$
    $= \frac{1}{2}(\log_c 2 + \log_c 3 + \log_c 2)$
    $= \frac{1}{2}(2 \log_c 2) + \frac{1}{2} \log_c 3$
    $= \log_c 2 + \log_c \sqrt{3}$
    $=$ Right Side
    d) Left Side $= \log_c (5c)^2$
    $= 2 \log_c 5c$
    $= 2 (\log_c 5 + \log_c c)$
    $= 2 (\log_c 5 + 1)$
    $=$ Right Side
13. **a)** 70 dB **b)** approximately 1995 times as loud
    c) approximately 98 dB
14. Decibels must be changed to intensity to gauge loudness. The function that maps the change is not linear.
15. 3.2 V
16. **a)** 10^{-7} mol/L **b)** 12.6 times as acidic **c)** 3.4
17. 0.18 km/s
18. **a)** The graphs are the same for $x > 0$. However, the graph of $y = \log x^2$ has a second branch for $x < 0$, which is the reflection in the y-axis of the branch for $x > 0$.
    b) The domains are different. The function $y = \log x^2$ is defined for all values of x except 0, while the function $y = 2 \log x$ is defined only for $x > 0$.
    c) $x > 0$

19. a) $y = \log_c x$
$c^y = x$
$\log_d c^y = \log_d x$
$y \log_d c = \log_d x$
$y = \dfrac{\log_d x}{\log_d c}$

b) 3.2479
c) $\varphi = -\dfrac{\log D}{\log 2}$
d) 207.9 times larger

20. a) Left Side
$= \log_{q^3} p^3$
$= \dfrac{\log_q p^3}{\log_q q^3}$
$= \dfrac{3 \log_q p}{3 \log_q q}$
$= \dfrac{\log_q p}{1}$
$=$ Right Side

b) Left Side
$= \dfrac{1}{\log_p 2} - \dfrac{1}{\log_q 2}$
$= \dfrac{1}{\frac{\log_2 2}{\log_2 p}} - \dfrac{1}{\frac{\log_2 2}{\log_2 q}}$
$= \dfrac{\log_2 p}{\log_2 2} - \dfrac{\log_2 q}{\log_2 2}$
$= \dfrac{\log_2 p - \log_2 q}{\log_2 2}$
$= \log_2 \dfrac{p}{q}$
$=$ Right Side

c) Left Side
$= \dfrac{1}{\log_q p} + \dfrac{1}{\log_q p}$
$= \dfrac{1}{\frac{\log p}{\log q}} + \dfrac{1}{\frac{\log q}{\log p}}$
$= \dfrac{\log q}{\log p} + \dfrac{\log q}{\log p}$
$= \dfrac{2 \log q}{\log p}$

Right Side
$= \dfrac{1}{\log_{q^2} p}$
$= \dfrac{1}{\frac{\log p}{\log q^2}}$
$= \dfrac{\log q^2}{\log p}$
$= \dfrac{2 \log q}{\log p}$

Left Side $=$ Right Side

d) Left Side $= \log_{\frac{1}{q}} p$
$= \dfrac{\log_q p}{\log_q q^{-1}}$
$= -\log_q p$
$= \log_q \dfrac{1}{p}$
$=$ Right Side

C1 a) Stretch vertically about the x-axis by a factor of 3.
b) Stretch vertically about the x-axis by a factor of 5 and translate 2 units left.
c) Reflect in the x-axis.
d) Reflect in the x-axis, stretch vertically about the x-axis by a factor of $\frac{1}{2}$, and translate 6 units right.
C2 -1
C3 a) $\log 2$ **b)** $15 \log 2$
C4 Answers will vary.

8.4 Logarithmic and Exponential Equations, pages 412 to 415

1. a) 1000 **b)** 14 **c)** 3 **d)** 108
2. a) 1.61 **b)** 10.38 **c)** 4.13 **d)** 0.94
3. No, since $\log_3 (x - 8)$ and $\log_3 (x - 6)$ are not defined when $x = 5$.
4. a) $x = 0$ is extraneous.
b) Both roots are extraneous.
c) $x = -6$ is extraneous.
d) $x = 1$ is extraneous.
5. a) $x = 8$ **b)** $x = 25$ **c)** $x = 96$ **d)** $x = 9$

6. a) Rubina subtracted the contents of the log when she should have divided them. The solution should be
$\log_6 \left(\dfrac{2x + 1}{x - 1}\right) = \log_6 5$
$2x + 1 = 5(x - 1)$
$1 + 5 = 5x - 2x$
$6 = 3x$
$x = 2$

b) Ahmed incorrectly concluded that there was no solution. The solution is $x = 0$.
c) Jennifer incorrectly eliminated the log in the third line. The solution, from the third line on, should be
$x(x + 2) = 2^3$
$x^2 + 2x - 8 = 0$
$(x - 2)(x + 4) = 0$
So, $x = 2$ or $x = -4$.
Since $x > 0$, the solution is $x = 2$.

7. a) 0.65 **b)** -0.43 **c)** 81.37 **d)** 4.85
8. a) no solution ($x = -3$ not possible)
b) $x = 10$ **c)** $x = 4$ **d)** $x = 2$ **e)** $x = -8, 4$
9. a) about 2.64 pc **b)** about 8.61 light years
10. 64 kg
11. a) 10 000 **b)** 3.5%
c) approximately 20.1 years
12. a) 248 Earth years **b)** 228 million kilometres
13. a) 2 years **b)** 44 days **c)** 20.5 years
14. 30 years
15. approximately 9550 years
16. 8 days
17. 34.0 m
18. $x = 4.5, y = 0.5$
19. a) The first line is not true.
b) To go from line 4 to line 5, you are dividing by a negative quantity, so the inequality sign must change direction.
20. a) $x = 100$ **b)** $x = \dfrac{1}{100}, 100$ **c)** $x = 1, 100$
21. a) $x = 16$ **b)** $x = 9$
22. $x = -5, 2, 4$
C1 a) $\log 8 + \log 2^x = \log 512$
$x \log 2 = \log 512 - \log 8$
$x \log 2 = \log 64$
$x = 6$
b) She could have divided by 8 as the first step.
c) Answers will vary.
C2 12
C3 14
C4 a) $x = \dfrac{\pi}{4}, \dfrac{7\pi}{4}$ **b)** $x = \dfrac{\pi}{2}$
C5 Answers will vary.

Chapter 8 Review, pages 416 to 418

1. a)

b) i) domain $\{x \mid x > 0, x \in R\}$, range $\{y \mid y \in R\}$
ii) x-intercept 1
iii) no y-intercept
iv) vertical asymptote $x = 0$
c) $y = \log_{0.2} x$
2. $c = 4$
3. $2^4 = 16$ and $2^5 = 32$, so the answer must be between 4 and 5.

Answers • MHR **615**

4. a) 25 b) −2 c) 3.5 d) 16 e) 0.01
5. 40 times as great
6. a) 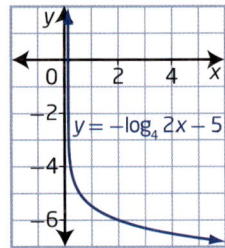 b) $a = -1, b = 2, c = 4, h = 0, k = -5$

7. $y = \log_2 4x$
8. a) Reflect in the x-axis, stretch horizontally about the y-axis by a factor of $\frac{1}{3}$, and translate 12 units right and 2 units up.
   b) Reflect in the y-axis, stretch vertically about the x-axis by a factor of $\frac{1}{4}$, and translate 6 units right and 7 units down.
9. a) $x = -8$
   b) domain $\{x \mid x > -8, x \in R\}$, range $\{y \mid y \in R\}$
   c) y-intercept 15   d) x-intercept -7.75
10. a) Transform by stretching the graph horizontally about the y-axis by a factor of 440 and stretching vertically about the x-axis by a factor of 12.
    b) 5 notes above   c) 698.46 Hz
11. a) $5 \log_5 x - \log_5 y - \frac{1}{3} \log_5 z$
    b) $\frac{1}{2}(\log x + 2 \log y - \log z)$
12. a) $\log \dfrac{xz^{\frac{2}{3}}}{y^3}$ b) $\log_7 \dfrac{x}{y^{\frac{1}{2}} z^{\frac{3}{2}}}$
13. a) $\log \sqrt{x}, x > 0$ b) $\log \dfrac{x-5}{x+5}, x < -5$ or $x > 5$
14. a) 2   b) 0.5
15. 6.3 times as acidic
16. 398 107 times as bright
17. 93 dB
18. a) 1.46   b) 4.03
19. a) 5   b) 10   c) $\dfrac{5}{3}$ d) $-4, 25$
20. 6.5 years
21. 35 kg
22. 2.5 h
23. a) 14 years   b) 25.75 years

Chapter 8 Practice Test, pages 419 to 420
1. D 2. A 3. B 4. A 5. C 6. B
7. a) $\dfrac{1}{81}$ b) 25 c) 5 d) 3 e) $\dfrac{13}{3}$
8. $m = 2.5, n = 0.5$
9. Example: Stretch vertically about the x-axis by a factor of 5, stretch horizontally about the y-axis by a factor of $\frac{1}{8}$, reflect in the x-axis, and translate 1 unit right.
10. a) $x = -5$
    b) domain $\{x \mid x > -5, x \in R\}$, range $\{y \mid y \in R\}$
    c) y-intercept 8   d) $-4\dfrac{124}{125}$
11. a) no solution   b) $x = 6$ c) $x = -2, 4$
12. a) 1.46   b) 21.09
13. 33 years
14. 875 times as great
15. She should not be worried: adding another refrigerator will only increase the decibels to 48 dB.
16. 4.8 h
17. 2029

Cumulative Review, Chapters 7–8, pages 422 to 423
1. a) 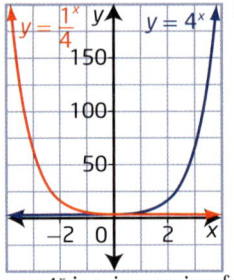 b) The two functions have the same domain, $x \in R$; the same range, $y > 0$; the same y-intercept, 1; and the same horizontal asymptote, $y = 0$.
   c) $y = 4^x$ is a increasing function: as x increases, the corresponding values of y also increase. $y = \dfrac{1}{4}^x$ is a decreasing function: as x increases, the corresponding values of y decrease.
2. a) B   b) D   c) A   d) C
3. a) 1000   b) 3 h   c) 256 000   d) 21 h
4. a) a vertical stretch by a factor of 2 about the x-axis, a horizontal translation of 4 units left, and a vertical translation of 1 unit up
   b) [graph of $g(x) = 2(3)^{x+4} + 1$]
   c) The domain remains the same: $x \in R$; the range changes from $y > 0$ to $y > 1$ due to the vertical translation; the equation of the horizontal asymptote changes from $y = 0$ to $y = 1$ due to the vertical translation; the y-intercept changes from 1 to 163 due to the vertical stretch and the vertical translation.
5. a) 2^{3x+6} and 2^{3x-15} or 8^{x+2} and 8^{x-5}
   b) 3^{12-3x} and 3^{-4x} or $\left(\dfrac{1}{3}\right)^{3x-12}$ and $\left(\dfrac{1}{3}\right)^{4x}$
6. a) -1 b) $\dfrac{1}{8}$
7. a) -0.72 b) 0.63
8. a) 39%   b) 3.7 s
9. a) $\log_3 y = x$ b) $\log_2 m = a + 1$
10. a) $x^4 = 3$ b) $a^b = x + 5$
11. a) -4 b) 4.5 c) -1 d) 49
12. a) 2 b) 32 c) $\dfrac{1}{125}$ d) $\dfrac{243}{32}$
13. a vertical stretch by a factor of $\dfrac{1}{3}$ about the x-axis, a horizontal stretch by a factor of $\dfrac{1}{2}$ about the y-axis, a horizontal translation of 4 units right and a vertical translation of 5 units up
14. a) $y = 3 \log (x + 5)$ b) $y = -\log 2x - 2$
15. a) 1.6×10^{-8} mol/L to 6.3×10^{-7} mol/L
    b) yes
16. a) $\log \dfrac{m^2}{\sqrt{n}p^3}, m > 0, n > 0, p > 0$
    b) $\log_a 3x^{\frac{13}{6}}, x > 0$ c) $\log (x + 1), x > 1$
    d) $\log_2 3^{2x}, x \in R$
17. In the last step, Zack incorrectly factored the quadratic equation; $x = -5$ and 13.
18. a) 0.53   b) 9   c) 3   d) 2
19. a) $E = 10^{10}$ J and $E = 10^{11.4}$ J
    b) approximately 25.1 times
20. 54.25 years

Unit 3 Test, pages 424 to 425

1. D 2. B 3. A 4. C 5. A 6. A 7. D
8. $y = -2\left(\dfrac{1}{4}\right)^{x-3}$
9. 3^{-1}
10. $(2, -2)$
11. 0.001
12. -2
13. a)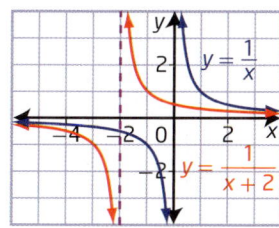
    b) domain $\{x \mid x \in R\}$, range $\{y \mid y > -2, y \in R\}$
    c) $x = -0.6$
14. a) -7 b) 2
15. a) domain $\{x \mid x > 2, x \in R\}$, range $\{y \mid y \in R\}$, asymptote $x = 2$
    b) $y = 10^{1-x} + 2$ c) 12
16. a) $\dfrac{1}{3}, 4$ b) 7
17. Giovanni multiplied the base by 2, which is not correct. The second line should be $3^x = 4$. Giovanni also incorrectly applied the quotient law of logarithms in the sixth line. This line should be deleted. This leads to the solution $x = 1.26$.
18. 5.0
19. a) $P(t) = 6(1.013^t)$, where t is the number of years since 2000
    b) year 2040
20. 12 deposits

Chapter 9 Rational Functions

9.1 Exploring Rational Functions Using Transformations, pages 442 to 445

1. a) Since the graph has a vertical asymptote at $x = -1$, it has been translated 1 unit left; $B(x) = \dfrac{2}{x+1}$.
   b) Since the graph has a horizontal asymptote at $y = -1$, it has been translated 1 unit down; $A(x) = \dfrac{2}{x} - 1$.
   c) Since the graph has a horizontal asymptote at $y = 1$, it has been translated 1 unit up; $D(x) = \dfrac{2}{x} + 1$.
   d) Since the graph has a vertical asymptote at $x = 1$, it has been translated 1 unit right; $C(x) = \dfrac{2}{x-1}$.
2. a) Base function $y = \dfrac{1}{x}$; vertical asymptote $x = -2$, horizontal asymptote $y = 0$

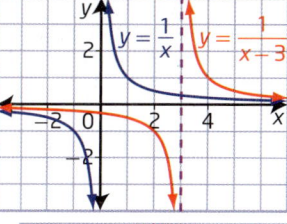

b) Base function $y = \dfrac{1}{x}$; vertical asymptote $x = 3$, horizontal asymptote $y = 0$

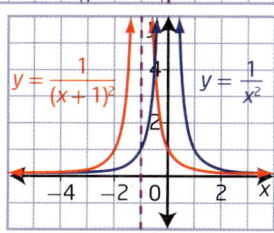

c) Base function $y = \dfrac{1}{x^2}$; vertical asymptote $x = -1$, horizontal asymptote $y = 0$

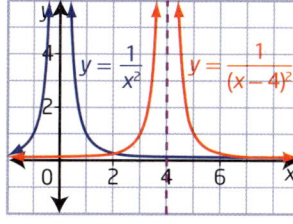

d) Base function $y = \dfrac{1}{x^2}$; vertical asymptote $x = 4$, horizontal asymptote $y = 0$

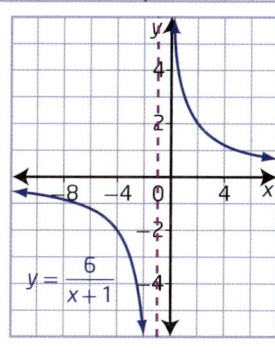

3. a) Apply a vertical stretch by a factor of 6, and then a translation of 1 unit left to the graph of $y = \dfrac{1}{x}$. domain $\{x \mid x \ne -1, x \in R\}$, range $\{y \mid y \ne 0, y \in R\}$, no x-intercept, y-intercept 6, horizontal asymptote $y = 0$, vertical asymptote $x = -1$

b) Apply a vertical stretch by a factor of 4, and then a translation of 1 unit up to the graph of $y = \dfrac{1}{x}$. domain $\{x \mid x \ne 0, x \in R\}$, range $\{y \mid y \ne 1, y \in R\}$, x-intercept -4, no y-intercept, horizontal asymptote $y = 1$, vertical asymptote $x = 0$

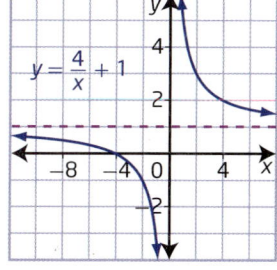

c) Apply a vertical stretch by a factor of 2, and then a translation of 4 units right and 5 units down to the graph of $y = \frac{1}{x}$.
domain $\{x \mid x \neq 4, x \in R\}$, range $\{y \mid y \neq -5, y \in R\}$, x-intercept 4.4, y-intercept −5.5, horizontal asymptote $y = -5$, vertical asymptote $x = 4$

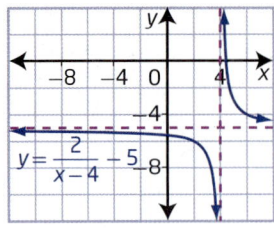

d) Apply a vertical stretch by a factor of 8 and a reflection in the x-axis, and then a translation of 2 units right and 3 units up to the graph of $y = \frac{1}{x}$.
domain $\{x \mid x \neq 2, x \in R\}$, range $\{y \mid y \neq 3, y \in R\}$, x-intercept $\frac{14}{3}$, y-intercept 7, horizontal asymptote $y = 3$, vertical asymptote $x = 2$

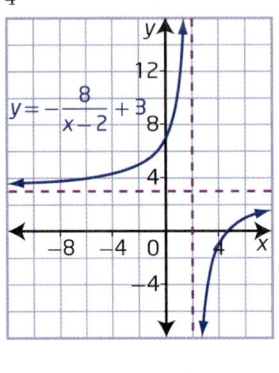

4. a) 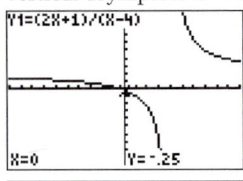 horizontal asymptote $y = 2$, vertical asymptote $x = 4$, x-intercept −0.5, y-intercept −0.25

b) horizontal asymptote $y = 3$, vertical asymptote $x = -1$, x-intercept 0.67, y-intercept −2

c) 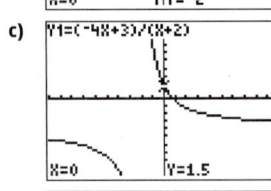 horizontal asymptote $y = -4$, vertical asymptote $x = -2$, x-intercept 0.75, y-intercept 1.5

d) horizontal asymptote $y = -6$, vertical asymptote $x = 5$, x-intercept 0.33, y-intercept −0.4

5. a) $y = \frac{12}{x} + 11$; horizontal asymptote $y = 11$, vertical asymptote $x = 0$, x-intercept −1.09, no y-intercept

b) $y = -\frac{8}{x+8} + 1$; horizontal asymptote $y = 1$, vertical asymptote $x = -8$, x-intercept $x = 0$, y-intercept $y = 0$

c) $y = \frac{4}{x+6} - 1$; horizontal asymptote $y = -1$, vertical asymptote $x = -6$, x-intercept −2, y-intercept −0.33

6.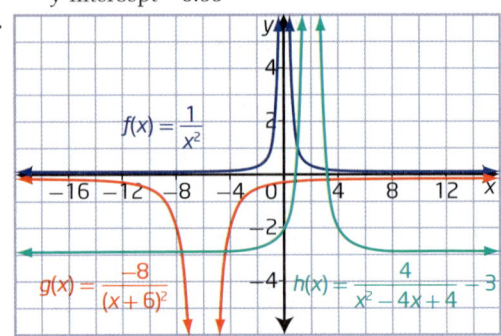

For $f(x) = \frac{1}{x^2}$:
- Non-permissible value: $x = 0$
- Behaviour near non-permissible value: As x approaches 0, $|y|$ becomes very large.
- End behaviour: As $|x|$ becomes very large, y approaches 0.
- Domain $\{x \mid x \neq 0, x \in R\}$, range $\{y \mid y > 0, y \in R\}$
- Asymptotes: $x = 0, y = 0$

For $g(x) = \frac{-8}{(x+6)^2}$:
- Non-permissible value: $x = -6$
- Behaviour near non-permissible value: As x approaches −6, $|y|$ becomes very large.
- End behaviour: As $|x|$ becomes very large, y approaches 0.
- Domain $\{x \mid x \neq -6, x \in R\}$, range $\{y \mid y < 0, y \in R\}$
- Asymptotes: $x = -6, y = 0$

For $h(x) = \frac{4}{x^2 - 4x + 4} - 3$:
- Non-permissible value: $x = 2$
- Behaviour near non-permissible value: As x approaches 2, $|y|$ becomes very large.
- End behaviour: As $|x|$ becomes very large, y approaches −3.
- Domain $\{x \mid x \neq 2, x \in R\}$, range $\{y \mid y > -3, y \in R\}$
- Asymptotes: $x = 2, y = -3$

Each function has a single non-permissible value, a vertical asymptote, and a horizontal asymptote. The domain of each function consists of all real numbers except for a single value. The range of each function consists of a restricted set of the real numbers. $|y|$ becomes very large for each function when the values of x approach the non-permissible value for the function.

7. a) $y = -\frac{4}{x}$ b) $y = \frac{1}{x+3}$
c) $y = \frac{8}{x-2} + 4$ d) $y = \frac{-4}{x-1} - 6$

8. a) $a = -15, k = 6$
b)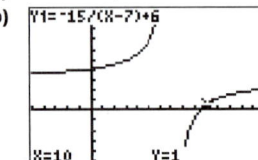

618 MHR • Answers

9. a) $y = \dfrac{1}{x-2} - 3$

   b)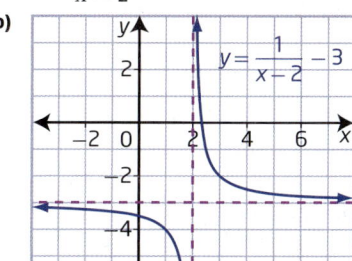

   domain $\{x \mid x \neq 2, x \in \mathbb{R}\}$, range $\{y \mid y \neq -3, y \in \mathbb{R}\}$

   c) No, there are many functions with different values of a for which the asymptotes are the same.

10. a) When factoring the 3 out of the numerator, Mira forgot to change the sign of the 21.

    $y = \dfrac{-3x + 21 - 21 + 2}{x - 7}$

    $y = \dfrac{-3(x - 7) - 19}{x - 7}$

    $y = \dfrac{-19}{x - 7} - 3$

    b) She could try sample points without technology. With technology, she could check if the asymptotes are the same.

11. a) $y = \dfrac{-2}{x + 2} + \dfrac{1}{2}$

    b)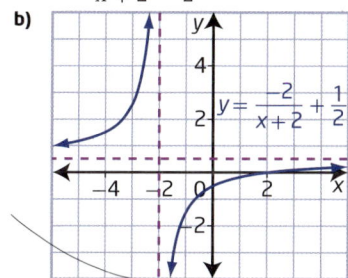

12. x-intercept $\dfrac{5}{3}$, y-intercept $-\dfrac{5}{3}$, horizontal asymptote $y = 1.5$, vertical asymptote $x = -1.5$

13. As p increases, N decreases, and vice versa. This shows that as the average price of a home increases, the number of buyers looking for a house decreases.

14. a) $l = \dfrac{24}{w}$

    b) As the width increases, the length decreases to maintain the same area.

15. a) $y = \dfrac{4000}{x}$

    b)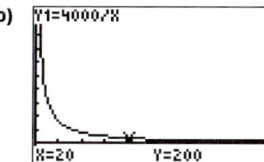

    c) If 4000 students contribute, they will only need to donate $1 each to reach their goal.

    d) $y = \dfrac{4000}{x} + 1000$; This amounts to a vertical translation of 1000 units up.

16. a) $y = \dfrac{100x + 500}{x}$, $y = \dfrac{60x + 800}{x}$

    b)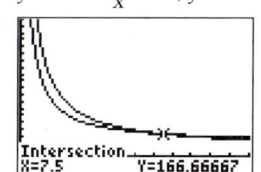

    c) The graph shows that the more years you run the machine, the less the average cost per year is. One of the machines is cheaper to run for a short amount of time, while the other is cheaper if you run it for a longer period of time.

    d) If Hanna wants to run the machine for more than 7.5 years, she should choose the second model. Otherwise, she is better off with the first one.

17. a) $I = \dfrac{12}{x + 15}$

    b) Domain $\{x \mid 0 \leq x \leq 100, x \in \mathbb{R}\}$; the graph does not have a vertical asymptote for this domain.

    c) 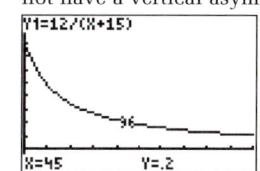 A setting of 45 Ω is needed for 0.2 A.

    d) In this case, there would be an asymptote at $x = 0$.

18. a) $y = \dfrac{4x + 20}{x}$, $y = \dfrac{5x + 10}{x}$

    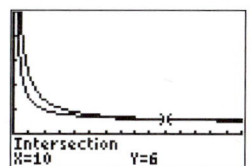

    b) The graph shows that for a longer rental the average price goes down.

    c) No. For rentals of less than 10 h, the second store is cheaper. For any rental over 10 h, the first store is cheaper.

19. a) $v = \dfrac{100t + 80}{t + 2}$

    b)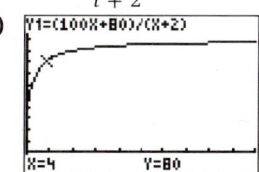

    c) Horizontal asymptote $y = 100$; the horizontal asymptote demonstrates that the average speed gets closer and closer to 100 km/h but never reaches it. Vertical asymptote $t = -2$; the vertical asymptote does not mean anything in this context, since time cannot be negative.

    d) 4 h after the construction zone

    e) Example: Showing the average speed is a good indication of your fuel economy.

20. $y = \dfrac{-4x - 4}{x - 6}$

21. a) $y = \dfrac{-x - 3}{x - 1}$ b) $y = \dfrac{5(x - 4)}{x - 6}$

22. 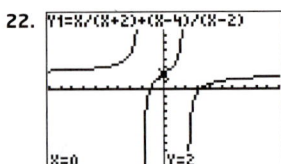 This rational function has two vertical asymptotes ($x = -2$ and $x = 2$) and appears to have a horizontal asymptote ($y = 2$) for values of x less than -2 and greater than 2.

C1 Answers may vary.

C2 a) Domain $\{p \mid 0 \leq p < 100, p \in R\}$; you can nearly eliminate 100% of emissions.

b) 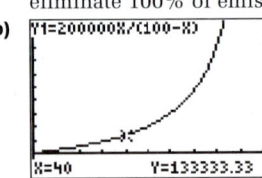 The shape of the graph indicates that as the percent of emissions eliminated increases, so does the cost.

c) It costs almost 6 times as much. This is not a linear function, so doubling the value of p does not correspond to a doubling of the value of C.

d) No it is not possible. There is a vertical asymptote at $p = 100$.

C3 Example: Both functions are vertically stretched by a factor of 2, and then translated 3 units right and 4 units up. In the case of the rational function, the values of the parameters h and k represent the locations of asymptotes. For the square root function, the point (h, k) gives the location of the endpoint of the graph.

9.2 Analysing Rational Functions, pages 451 to 456

1. a)

Characteristic	$y = \dfrac{x - 4}{x^2 - 6x + 8}$
Non-permissible value(s)	$x = 2, x = 4$
Feature exhibited at each non-permissible value	vertical asymptote, point of discontinuity
Behaviour near each non-permissible value	As x approaches 2, $|y|$ becomes very large. As x approaches 4, y approaches 0.5.
Domain	$\{x \mid x \neq 2, 4, x \in R\}$
Range	$\{y \mid y \neq 0, 0.5, y \in R\}$

b) There is an asymptote at $x = 2$ because 2 is a zero of the denominator only. There is a point of discontinuity at $(4, 0.5)$ because $x - 4$ is a factor of both the numerator and the denominator.

2. a)

x	y
-1.5	-4.5
-1.0	-4.0
-0.5	-3.5
0.5	-2.5
1.0	-2.0
1.5	-1.5

Since the function does not increase or decrease drastically as x approaches the non-permissible value, it must be a point of discontinuity.

b)

x	y
1.7	40.7
1.8	60.8
1.9	120.9
2.1	-118.9
2.2	-58.8
2.3	-38.7

Since the function changes sign at the non-permissible value and $|y|$ increases, it must be a vertical asymptote.

c)

x	y
-3.7	74.23
-3.8	120.6
-3.9	260.3
-4.1	-300.3
-4.2	-160.6
-4.3	-114.23

Since the function changes sign at the non-permissible value and $|y|$ increases, it must be a vertical asymptote.

d)

x	y
0.17	1.17
0.18	1.18
0.19	1.19
0.21	1.21
0.22	1.22
0.23	1.23

Since the function does not increase or decrease drastically as x approaches the non-permissible value, it must be a point of discontinuity.

3. a)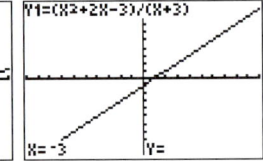

Both of the functions have a non-permissible value of -3. However, the graph of $f(x)$ has a vertical asymptote, while the graph of $g(x)$ has a point of discontinuity.

b) The graph of $f(x)$ has a vertical asymptote at $x = -3$ because $x + 3$ is a factor of the denominator only. The graph of $g(x)$ has a point of discontinuity at $(-3, -4)$ because $x + 3$ is a factor of both the numerator and the denominator.

4. a) Vertical asymptote $x = -5$; point of discontinuity $(-4, -4)$; x-intercept 0; y-intercept 0

b) Vertical asymptotes $x = \pm 1$; no points of discontinuity; x-intercepts $-0.5, 3$; y-intercept 3

c) Vertical asymptotes $x = -2, 4$; no points of discontinuity; x-intercepts $-4, 2$; y-intercept 1

d) Vertical asymptote $x = -1.5$; point of discontinuity $(1.5, -1.083)$; x-intercept -5; y-intercept -1.67

5. a) The graph of $A(x) = \dfrac{x(x + 2)}{x^2 + 4}$ has no vertical asymptotes or points of discontinuity and x-intercepts of 0 and -2; C.

b) The graph of $B(x) = \dfrac{x-2}{x(x-2)}$ has a vertical asymptote at $x = 0$, a point of discontinuity at $(2, 0.5)$, and no x-intercept; A.

c) The graph of $C(x) = \dfrac{x+2}{(x-2)(x+2)}$ has a vertical asymptote at $x = 2$, a point of discontinuity at $(-2, -0.25)$, and no x-intercept; D.

d) The graph of $D(x) = \dfrac{2x}{x(x+2)}$ has a vertical asymptote at $x = -2$, a point of discontinuity at $(0, 1)$, and no x-intercept; B.

6. a) Since the graph has vertical asymptotes at $x = 1$ and $x = 4$, the equation of the function has factors $x - 1$ and $x - 4$ in the denominator only; the x-intercepts of 2 and 3 mean that the factors $x - 2$ and $x - 3$ are in the numerator; C.

b) Since the graph has vertical asymptotes at $x = -1$ and $x = 2$, the equation of the function has factors $x + 1$ and $x - 2$ in the denominator only; the x-intercepts of 1 and 4 mean that the factors $x - 1$ and $x - 4$ are in the numerator; B.

c) Since the graph has vertical asymptotes at $x = -2$ and $x = 5$, the equation of the function has factors $x + 2$ and $x - 5$ in the denominator only; the x-intercepts of -4 and 3 mean that the factors $x + 4$ and $x - 3$ are in the numerator; D.

d) Since the graph has vertical asymptotes at $x = -5$ and $x = 4$, the equation of the function has factors $x + 5$ and $x - 4$ in the denominator only; the x-intercepts of -2 and 1 mean that the factors $x + 2$ and $x - 1$ are in the numerator; A.

7. a) $y = \dfrac{x^2 + 6x}{x^2 + 2x}$ b) $y = \dfrac{x^2 - 4x - 21}{x^2 + 2x - 3}$

8. a) $y = \dfrac{(x+10)(x-4)}{(x+5)(x-5)}$ b) $y = \dfrac{(2x+11)(x-8)}{(x+4)(2x+11)}$

   c) $y = \dfrac{(x+2)(x+1)}{(x-3)(x+2)}$ d) $y = \dfrac{x(4x+1)}{(x-3)(7x-6)}$

9. a) Example: The graphs will be different. Factoring the denominators shows that the graph of $f(x)$ will have two vertical asymptotes, no points of discontinuity, and an x-intercept, while the graph of $g(x)$ will have one vertical asymptote, one point of discontinuity, and no x-intercept.

b)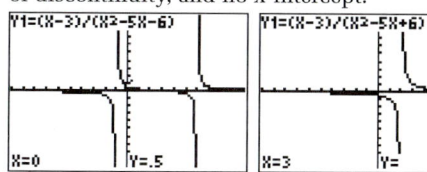

10. $y = -\dfrac{3(x-2)(x+3)}{(x-2)(x+3)}$

11. a) The function will have two vertical asymptotes at $x = -1$ and $x = 1$, no x-intercept, and a y-intercept of -2.

b)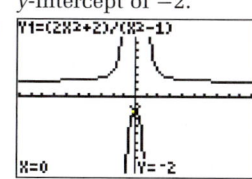

c) i) The graph will be a line at $y = 2$, but with points of discontinuity at $(-1, 2)$ and $(1, 2)$.
   ii) The graph will be a line at $y = 2$.

12. a) $t = \dfrac{500}{w + 250}$, $w \neq -250$

b)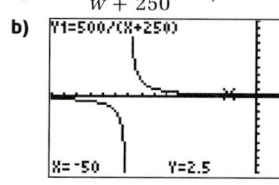

c) When the headwind reaches the speed of the aircraft, theoretically it will come to a standstill, so it will take an infinite amount of time for the aircraft to reach its destination.

d) Example: The realistic part of the graph would be in the range of normal wind speeds for whichever area the aircraft is in.

13. a) $t = \dfrac{4}{w + 4}$; $\{w \mid -4 < w \leq 4, w \in \mathbb{R}\}$

b)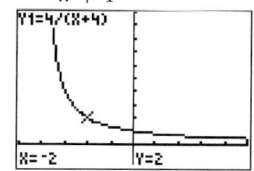

c) As the current increases against the kayakers, in other words as the current reaches -4 km/h, the time it takes them to paddle 4 km approaches infinity.

14. a) The non-permissible value will result in a vertical asymptote. It corresponds to a factor of the denominator only.

b) 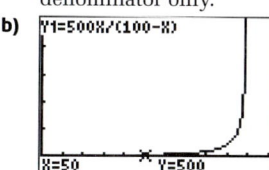   It is not possible to vaccinate 100% of the population.

c) Yes, the vaccination process will get harder after you have already reached the major urban centres. It will be much more costly to find every single person.

15. a) 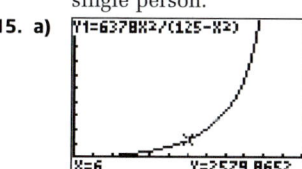   The only parts of the graph that are applicable are when $0 \leq x < \sqrt{125}$.

b) As the initial velocity increases, the maximum height also increases but at a greater rate.

c) The non-permissible value represents the vertical asymptote of the graph; this models the escape velocity since when the initial velocity reaches the escape velocity the object will leave Earth and never return.

16. $y = \dfrac{-(x+6)(x-2)}{2(x+2)(x-3)}$

17. a)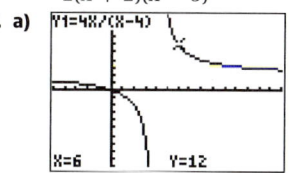

b) The image distance decreases while the object distance is still less than the focal length. The image distance starts to increase once the object distance is more than the focal length.
   c) The non-permissible value results in a vertical asymptote. As the object distance approaches the focal length, it gets harder to resolve the image.
18. a) Example: Functions $f(x)$ and $h(x)$ will have similar graphs since they are the same except for a point of discontinuity in the graph of $h(x)$.
   b) All three graphs have a vertical asymptote at $x = -b$, since $x + b$ is a factor of only the denominators. All three graphs will also have an x-intercept of $-a$, since $x + a$ is a factor of only the numerators.
19. The x-intercept is 3 and the vertical asymptote is at $x = \frac{3}{4}$.
20. $y = \frac{x^2 - 4x + 3}{2x^2 - 18x - 20}$
21. a) $y = \frac{(x + 4)(x - 2)(3x + 4)}{4(x + 4)(x - 2)}$
   b) $y = \frac{(x - 1)(x + 2)^2(x - 2)}{(x - 1)(x + 2)}$
22.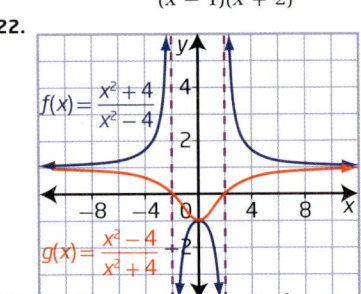
   They are reciprocals since when one of them approaches infinity the other approaches 0.
23. a) There are two vertical asymptotes at $x = \pm 2$.
   b) There is a point of discontinuity at $\left(5, \frac{65}{9}\right)$ and a vertical asymptote at $x = -4$.
C1 Examples:
   a) No. Some rational functions have no points of discontinuity or asymptotes.
   b) A rational function is a function that has a polynomial in the numerator and/or in the denominator.
C2 Example: True. It is possible to express a polynomial function as a rational function with a denominator of 1.
C3 Answers may vary.

9.3 Connecting Graphs and Rational Equations, pages 465 to 467

1. a) B   b) D   c) A   d) C
2. a) $x = -2, x = 1$
   b) $x = -2, x = 1$

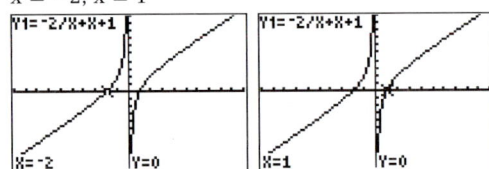

   c) The value of the function is 0 when the value of x is -2 or 1. The x-intercepts of the graph of the corresponding function are the same as the roots of the equation.
3. a) $x = -\frac{7}{4}$ b) $x = 4$ c) $x = \frac{3}{2}$ d) $x = -\frac{6}{5}$

4. a) $x = -8, x = 1$ b) $x = 0, x = 3$
   c) $x = 4$ d) $x = 1, x = \frac{5}{3}$
5. a) $x \approx -0.14, x \approx 3.64$ b) $x \approx -2.30, x \approx 0.80$
   c) $x \approx -2.41, x \approx 0.41$ d) $x \approx -5.74, x \approx -0.26$
6. a) $x = -\frac{2}{5}$ b) $x = 1$
   c) $x = -5$ d) $x = -\frac{1}{3}$
7. Example: Her approach is correct but there is a point of discontinuity at $(1, 4)$. Multiplying by $(x - 1)$ assumes that $x \neq 1$.
8. $x = -1, x = -\frac{2}{7}$
9. No solutions
10. 2.82 m
11. 20.6 h
12. 15 min
13. a) $y = \frac{0.5x + 2}{x + 28}$
   b) After she takes 32 shots, she will have a 30% shooting percentage.
14. a) 200.4 K   b) 209.3 K
15. a) $C(x) = \frac{0.01x + 10}{x + 200}$ b) 415 mL
16. $x \approx 1.48$
17. a) $x \leq -\frac{13}{4}$ or $x > 1$ b) $-8 \leq x < -6, 2 < x \leq 4$
C1 Example: No, this is incorrect. For example, $\frac{1}{x} = 0$ has no solution.
C2 Example: The extraneous root in the radical equation occurs because there is a restriction that the radicand be positive. This same principle of restricted domain is the reason why the rational equation has an extraneous root.
C3 Answers may vary.

Chapter 9 Review, pages 468 to 469

1. a) Apply a vertical stretch by a factor of 8, and then a translation of 1 unit right to the graph of $y = \frac{1}{x}$. domain $\{x \mid x \neq 1, x \in R\}$, range $\{y \mid y \neq 0, y \in R\}$, no x-intercept, y-intercept -8, horizontal asymptote $y = 0$, vertical asymptote $x = 1$
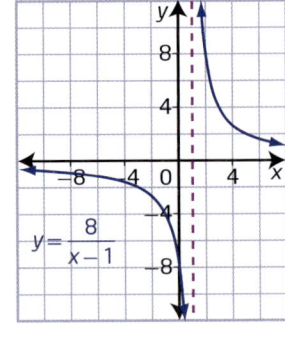
   b) Apply a vertical stretch by a factor of 3 and then a translation of 2 units up to the graph of $y = \frac{1}{x}$. domain $\{x \mid x \neq 0, x \in R\}$, range $\{y \mid y \neq 2, y \in R\}$, x-intercept -1.5, no y-intercept, horizontal asymptote $y = 2$, vertical asymptote $x = 0$
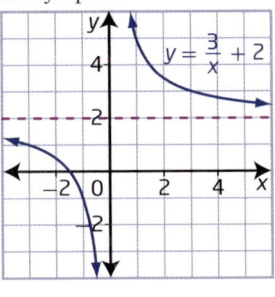

c) Apply a vertical stretch by a factor of 12 and a reflection in the x-axis, and then a translation of 4 units left and 5 units down to the graph of $y = \frac{1}{x}$.
domain $\{x \mid x \neq -4, x \in R\}$, range $\{y \mid y \neq -5, y \in R\}$, x-intercept -6.4, y-intercept -8, horizontal asymptote $y = -5$, vertical asymptote $x = -4$

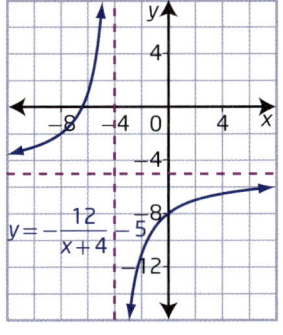

2. a) Horizontal asymptote $y = 1$, vertical asymptote $x = -2$, x-intercept 0, y-intercept 0

b) Horizontal asymptote $y = 2$, vertical asymptote $x = 1$, x-intercept -2.5, y-intercept -5

c) Horizontal asymptote $y = -5$, vertical asymptote $x = 6$, x-intercept -0.6, y-intercept 0.5

3.

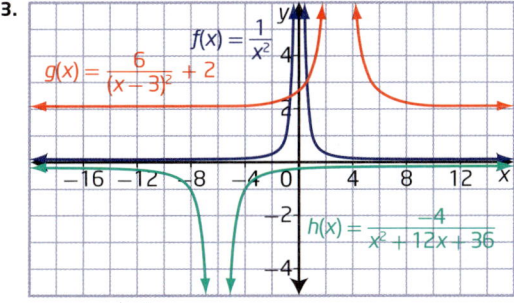

For $f(x) = \frac{1}{x^2}$:
- Non-permissible value: $x = 0$
- Behaviour near non-permissible value: As x approaches 0, $|y|$ becomes very large.
- End behaviour: As $|x|$ becomes very large, y approaches 0.
- Domain $\{x \mid x \neq 0, x \in R\}$, range $\{y \mid y > 0, y \in R\}$
- Asymptotes: $x = 0, y = 0$

For $g(x) = \frac{6}{(x-3)^2} + 2$:
- Non-permissible value: $x = 3$
- Behaviour near non-permissible value: As x approaches 3, $|y|$ becomes very large.
- End behaviour: As $|x|$ becomes very large, y approaches 2.
- Domain $\{x \mid x \neq 3, x \in R\}$, range $\{y \mid y > 2, y \in R\}$
- Asymptotes: $x = 3, y = 2$

For $h(x) = \frac{-4}{x^2 + 12x + 36}$:
- Non-permissible value: $x = -6$
- Behaviour near non-permissible value: As x approaches -6, $|y|$ becomes very large.
- End behaviour: As $|x|$ becomes very large, y approaches 0.
- Domain $\{x \mid x \neq -6, x \in R\}$, range $\{y \mid y < 0, y \in R\}$
- Asymptotes: $x = -6, y = 0$

Each function has a single non-permissible value, a vertical asymptote, and a horizontal asymptote. The domain of each function consist of all real numbers except for a single value. The range of each function is a restricted set of real numbers. $|y|$ becomes very large for each function when the values of x approach the non-permissible value for the function.

4. a) $y = \frac{35x + 500}{x}$

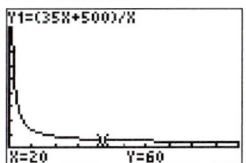

b) The more uniforms that are bought, the less expensive their average cost.

c) They will need to buy 100 uniforms.

5. a) 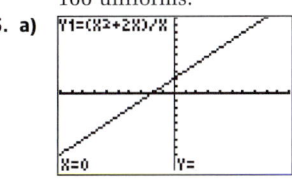 linear with a point of discontinuity at $(0, 2)$

b) 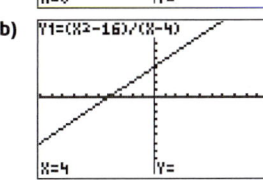 linear with a point of discontinuity at $(4, 8)$

c) 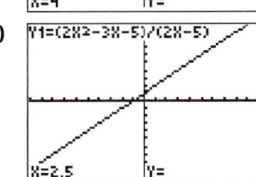 linear with a point of discontinuity at $(2.5, 3.5)$

6. The graph of $A(x) = \frac{x - 4}{(x - 4)(x - 1)}$ has a vertical asymptote at $x = 1$, a point of discontinuity at $\left(4, \frac{1}{3}\right)$, and no x-intercept; Graph 3.

The graph of $B(x) = \frac{(x + 4)(x + 1)}{x^2 + 1}$ has no vertical asymptotes or points of discontinuity and x-intercepts of -4 and -1; Graph 1.

The graph of $C(x) = \frac{x - 1}{(x - 2)(x + 2)}$ has vertical asymptotes at $x = \pm 2$, no points of discontinuity, and an x-intercept of 1; Graph 2.

7. a)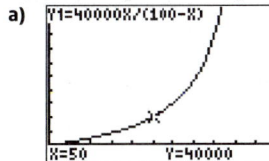

b) As the percent of the spill cleaned up approaches 100, the cost approaches infinity.

c) No, since there is a vertical asymptote at $p = 100$.

8. a) $x = 3, x = 6$
   b)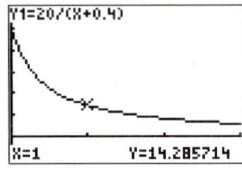
   c) The value of the function is 0 when the value of x is 3 or 6. The x-intercepts of the graph of the corresponding function are the same as the roots of the equation.
9. a) $x = -3, x = 11$ b) $x = 4, x = 6$
   c) $x = -1, x = 5$ d) $x = -2, x = 4.5$
10. a) $x \approx 2.71$ b) $x \approx -6.15, x \approx 3.54$
    c) $x \approx \pm 0.82$ d) $x \approx 2.67$
11. a) $\{d \mid -0.4 \le d \le 2.6, d \in R\}$
    b) As the distance along the lever increases, less mass can be lifted.
    c) The non-permissible value corresponds to the fulcrum point $(d = -0.4)$, which does
    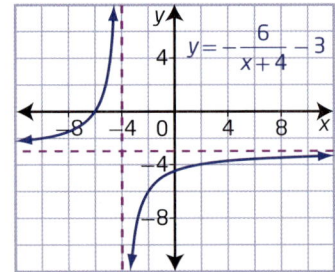
    not move when the lever is moved. As the mass gets closer to the fulcrum, it is possible to move a much heavier mass, but when the mass is on the fulcrum, it cannot be moved.
    d) 0.74 m

Chapter 9 Practice Test, pages 470 to 471

1. C   2. D   3. C   4. B   5. D   6. C   7. $x = -\dfrac{6}{5}$
8. a)

   [graph of $y = -\dfrac{6}{x+4} - 3$]

   b) domain $\{x \mid x \ne -4, x \in R\}$, range $\{y \mid y \ne -3, y \in R\}$, horizontal asymptote $y = -3$, vertical asymptote $x = -4$, x-intercept -6, y-intercept $-\dfrac{9}{2}$
9. $x \approx -2.47, x \approx -0.73$
10. a)

    [graph of $y = \dfrac{x^2 - 2x - 8}{x - 4}$]

    b) As x approaches 4, the function approaches 6.

11. vertical asymptote $x = 3$, point of discontinuity $\left(-4, \dfrac{9}{7}\right)$, x-intercept 0.5, y-intercept $\dfrac{1}{3}$
12. a) The graph of $A(x) = \dfrac{x(x - 9)}{x}$ has no vertical asymptote, a point of discontinuity at $(0, -9)$, and an x-intercept of 9; D.
    b) The graph of $B(x) = \dfrac{x^2}{(x - 3)(x + 3)}$ has vertical asymptotes at $x = \pm 3$, no points of discontinuity, and an x-intercept of 0; A.
    c) The graph of $C(x) = \dfrac{(x - 3)(x + 3)}{x^2}$ has a vertical asymptote at $x = 0$, no points of discontinuity, and x-intercepts of ± 3; B.
    d) The graph of $D(x) = \dfrac{x^2}{x(x - 9)}$ has a vertical asymptote at $x = 9$, a point of discontinuity at $(0, 0)$, and no x-intercept; C.
13.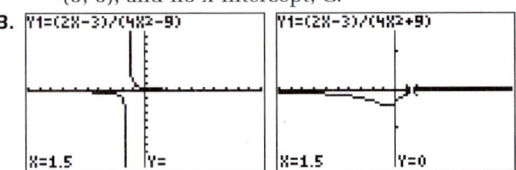
    The main difference is that the second function has no non-permissible values since the denominator cannot be factored.
14. a) $x = 3$; Alex forgot to take into account the restricted domain.
    b) Using graphical methods, it is easier to see true solutions.
15. a) $A = \dfrac{0.5x + 10}{x + 31}$ b) an additional 24 putts
16. a) $\{v \mid v > 4, v \in R\}$; speed must be positive and the function is undefined when $v = 4$.
    b) 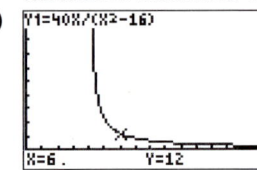 As the boat's speed increases, the total time for the round trip decreases.
    c) As the boat's speed approaches 4 km/h, the time it takes for a round trip approaches infinity. The water flows at 4 km/h. If the boat's speed is less, the boat will never make the return trip, which is why there is an asymptote at $x = 4$.
    d) approximately 27.25 km/h

Chapter 10 Function Operations

10.1 Sums and Differences of Functions, pages 483 to 487

1. a) $h(x) = |x - 3| + 4$ b) $h(x) = 2x - 3$
   c) $h(x) = 2x^2 + 3x + 2$ d) $h(x) = x^2 + 5x + 4$
2. a) $h(x) = 5x + 2$ b) $h(x) = -3x^2 - 4x + 9$
   c) $h(x) = -x^2 - 3x + 12$ d) $h(x) = \cos x - 4$
3. a) $h(x) = x^2 - 6x + 1; h(2) = -7$
   b) $m(x) = -x^2 - 6x + 1; m(1) = -6$
   c) $p(x) = x^2 + 6x - 1; p(1) = 6$
4. a) $y = 3x^2 + 2 + \sqrt{x + 4}$; domain $\{x \mid x \ge -4, x \in R\}$
   b) $y = 4x - 2 - \sqrt{x + 4}$; domain $\{x \mid x \ge -4, x \in R\}$
   c) $y = \sqrt{x + 4} - 4x + 2$; domain $\{x \mid x \ge -4, x \in R\}$
   d) $y = 3x^2 + 4x$; domain $\{x \mid x \in R\}$

5. a) domain $\{x \mid x \in \mathbb{R}\}$, range $\{y \mid y > 1, y \in \mathbb{R}\}$

b) domain $\{x \mid x \in \mathbb{R}\}$, range $\{y \mid y > -1, y \in \mathbb{R}\}$

c) domain $\{x \mid x \in \mathbb{R}\}$, range $\{y \mid y < 1, y \in \mathbb{R}\}$

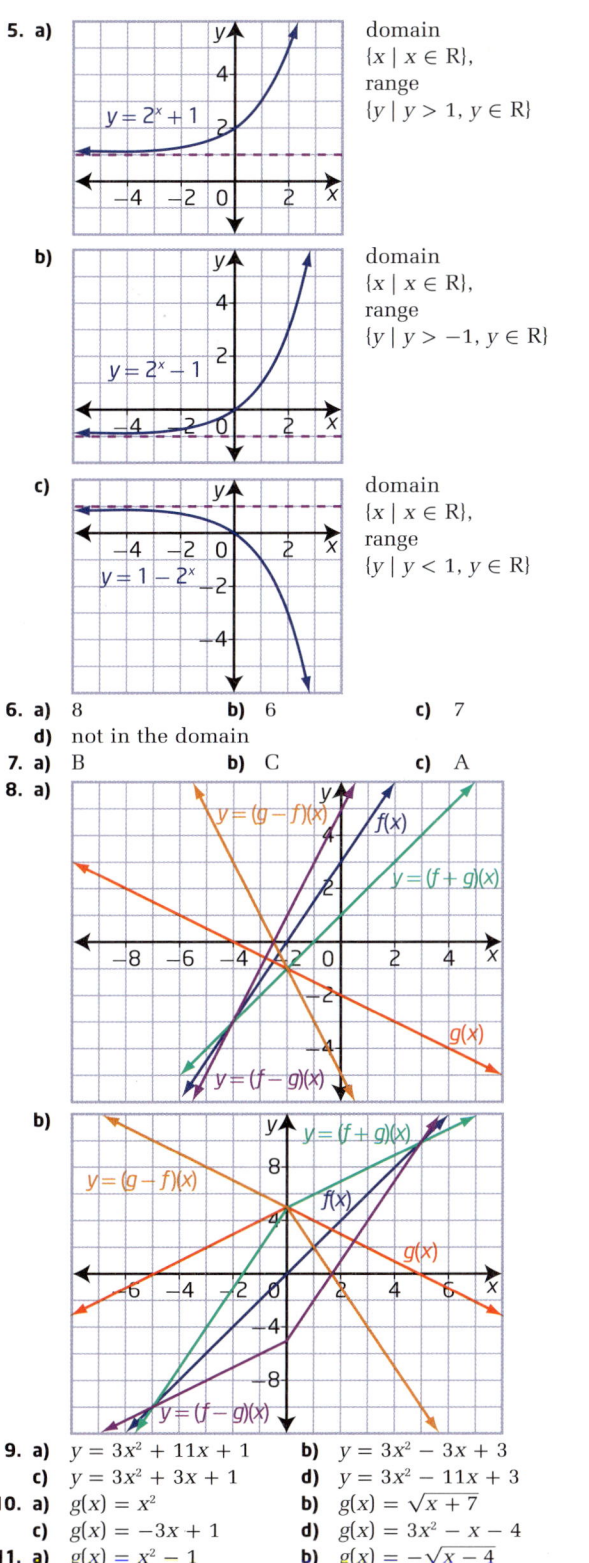

6. a) 8 **b)** 6 **c)** 7 **d)** not in the domain

7. a) B **b)** C **c)** A

8. a)

b)

9. a) $y = 3x^2 + 11x + 1$ **b)** $y = 3x^2 - 3x + 3$
c) $y = 3x^2 + 3x + 1$ **d)** $y = 3x^2 - 11x + 3$

10. a) $g(x) = x^2$ **b)** $g(x) = \sqrt{x+7}$
c) $g(x) = -3x + 1$ **d)** $g(x) = 3x^2 - x - 4$

11. a) $g(x) = x^2 - 1$ **b)** $g(x) = -\sqrt{x-4}$
c) $g(x) = 8x - 9$ **d)** $g(x) = 2x^2 - 11x - 6$

12. a)

b)

The points of intersection represent where the supply equals the demand. The intersection point in quadrant III should not be considered since the price cannot be negative. It represents the excess supply as a function of cost.

13. a) $C(n) = 1.25n + 135$, $R(n) = 3.5n$
b)
c) $(60, 210)$
d) $P(n) = 2.25n - 135$
e) $540

14. a)

b)

c) 4 cm

15. a)

b) The maxima and minima are located at the same x-coordinates. This will result in destructive interference.

c)

16. a)

b)

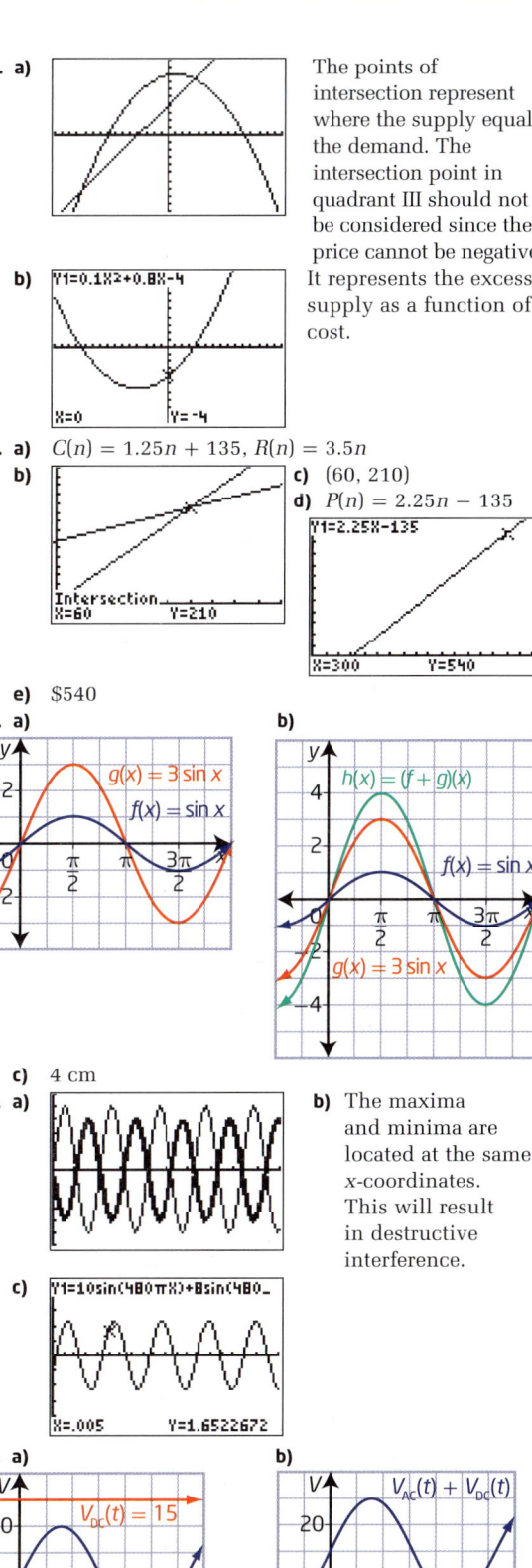

Answers • MHR **625**

c) domain $\{t \mid t \in R\}$, range $\{V \mid 5 \leq V \leq 25, V \in R\}$
d) i) 5 V ii) 25 V
17. $h(t) = 5t^2 - 20t - 20$
18. a)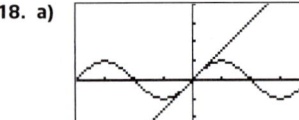

b) It will be a sinusoidal function on a diagonal according to $y = x$.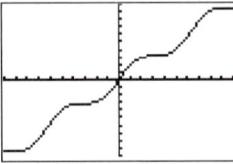

19. a) $d = 200 - t$
b) $h(t) = 200 - t + 0.75 \sin 1.26t$
c)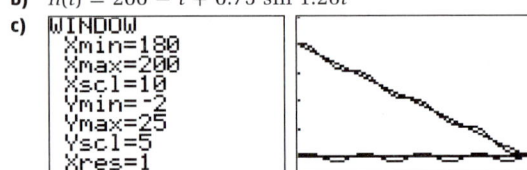

20. Example: Replace all x with $-x$ and then simplify. If the new function is equal to the original, then it is even. If it is the negative of the original, then it is odd. Answers may vary.
21. The graph shows the sum of an exponential function and a constant function.
22. a) $f(x)$: domain $\{x \mid x \in R\}$, range $\{y \mid y \geq -9, y \in R\}$;
$g(x)$: domain $\{x \mid x \neq 0, x \in R\}$, range $\{y \mid y \neq 0, y \in R\}$
b) $h(x) = x^2 - 9 + \dfrac{1}{x}$
c) Example: The domain and range of $f(x)$ are different from the domain and range of $h(x)$. The domain and range of $g(x)$ are the same as that of $h(x)$.

C1 a) Yes, addition is commutative.
b) No, subtraction is not commutative.
C2 a) $y_3 = x^3 + 4$
b) domain $\{x \mid x \in R\}$, range $\{y \mid y \in R\}$
C3 Example:
Step 1: 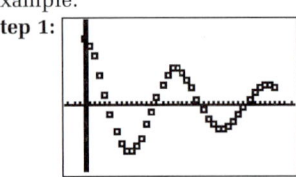 The graph exhibits sinusoidal features in its shape and the fact that it is periodic.

Step 2: The graph exhibits exponential features in that it is decreasing and approaching 0 with asymptote $y = 0$.
Step 3: $h = \cos 0.35t$
Step 4: $h = 100(0.5)^{0.05t}$
Step 5: $h = (100 \cos 0.35t)((0.5)^{0.05t})$
Step 6: 15.5 m

10.2 Products and Quotients of Functions, pages 496 to 498

1. a) $h(x) = x^2 - 49$, $k(x) = \dfrac{x+7}{x-7}$, $x \neq 7$
b) $h(x) = 6x^2 + 5x - 4$, $k(x) = \dfrac{2x-1}{3x+4}$, $x \neq -\dfrac{4}{3}$

c) $h(x) = (x+2)\sqrt{x+5}$, $k(x) = \dfrac{\sqrt{x+5}}{x+2}$, $x \geq -5$, $x \neq -2$
d) $h(x) = \sqrt{-x^2 + 7x - 6}$, $k(x) = \dfrac{\sqrt{x-1}}{\sqrt{6-x}}$, $1 \leq x < 6$

2. a) -3 b) 0 c) -1 d) 0
3. a)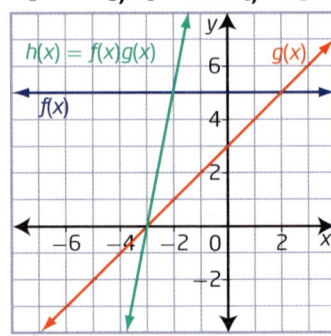

b)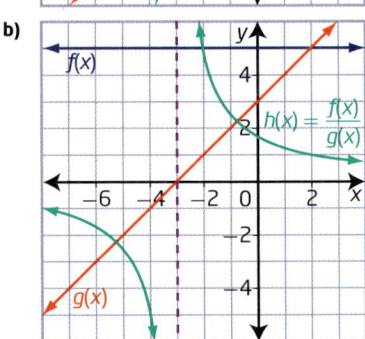

4. a) $h(x) = x^3 + 7x^2 + 16x + 12$
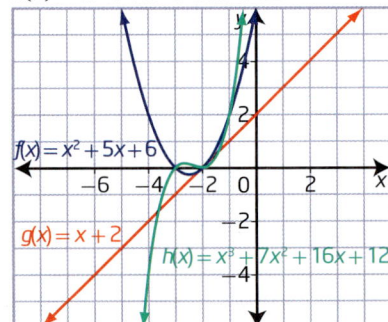
domain $\{x \mid x \in R\}$, range $\{y \mid y \in R\}$
b) $h(x) = x^3 - 3x^2 - 9x + 27$
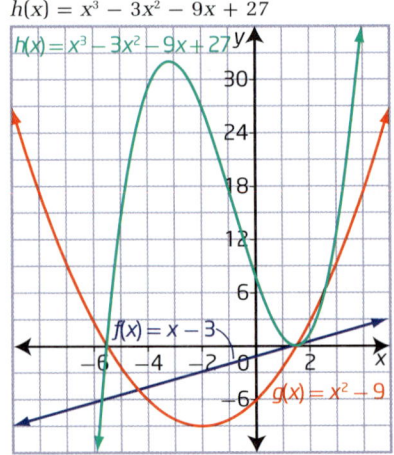
domain $\{x \mid x \in R\}$, range $\{y \mid y \in R\}$

c) $h(x) = \dfrac{1}{x^2 + x}$

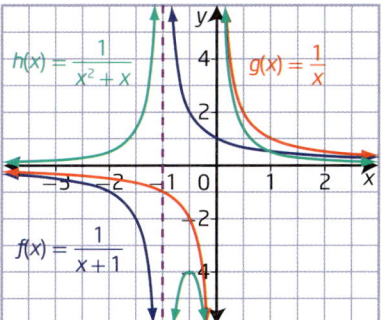

domain $\{x \mid x \neq 0, -1, x \in R\}$,
range $\{y \mid y \leq -4 \text{ or } y > 0, y \in R\}$

5. a) $h(x) = x + 3, x \neq -2$

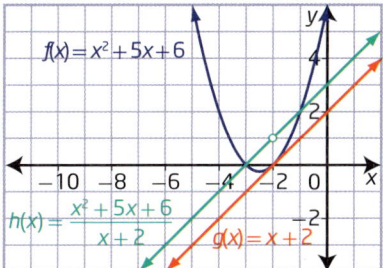

domain $\{x \mid x \neq -2, x \in R\}$,
range $\{y \mid y \neq 1, y \in R\}$

b) $h(x) = \dfrac{1}{x + 3}, x \neq \pm 3$

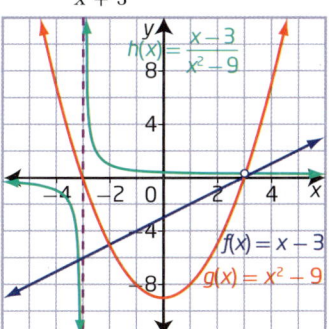

domain $\{x \mid x \neq \pm 3, x \in R\}$,
range $\left\{y \mid y \neq 0, \dfrac{1}{6}, y \in R\right\}$

c) $h(x) = \dfrac{x}{x + 1}, x \neq -1, 0$

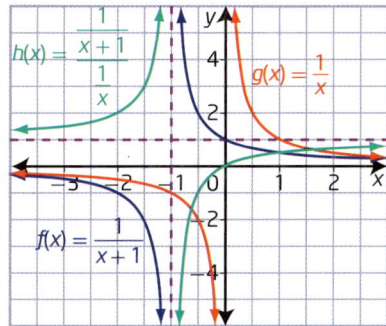

domain $\{x \mid x \neq -1, 0, x \in R\}$,
range $\{y \mid y \neq 0, 1, y \in R\}$

6. a) $y = x^3 + 3x^2 - 10x - 24$
b) $y = \dfrac{x^2 - x - 6}{x + 4}, x \neq -4$ **c)** $y = \dfrac{2x - 1}{x + 4}, x \neq -4$
d) $y = \dfrac{x^2 - x - 6}{x^2 + 8x + 16}, x \neq -4$

7. a) $g(x) = 3$ **b)** $g(x) = -x$
c) $g(x) = \sqrt{x}$ **d)** $g(x) = 5x - 6$

8. a) $g(x) = x + 7$ **b)** $g(x) = \sqrt{x + 6}$
c) $g(x) = 2$ **d)** $g(x) = 3x^2 + 26x - 9$

9. a) $f(x)$: domain $\{x \mid x \in R\}$, range $\{y \mid y \in R\}$
$g(x)$: domain $\{x \mid x \in R\}$, range $\{y \mid -1 \leq y \leq 1, y \in R\}$

b) 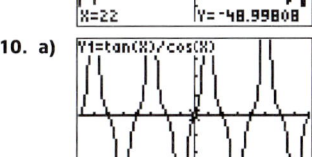 domain $\{x \mid x \in R\}$, range $\{y \mid y \in R\}$

10. a) 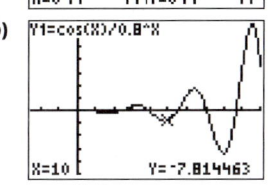 domain $\{x \mid x \neq (2n - 1)\dfrac{\pi}{2}, n \in I, x \in R\}$, range $\{y \mid y \in R\}$

b) 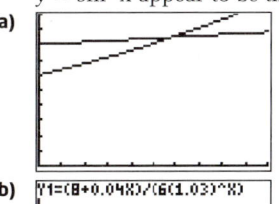 domain $\{x \mid x \in R\}$, range $\{y \mid y \in R\}$

11. a) $y = \dfrac{f(x)}{g(x)}$ **b)** $y = f(x)f(x)$
c) The graphs of $y = \dfrac{\sin x}{\cos x}$ and $y = \tan x$ appear to be the same. The graphs of $y = 1 - \cos^2 x$ and $y = \sin^2 x$ appear to be the same.

12. a) Both graphs are increasing over time. However, the graph of $P(t)$ increases more rapidly and overtakes the graph of $F(t)$.

b) Yes; negative values of t should not be considered.

c) $t = 0$
d) In approximately 11.6 years, there will be less than 1 unit of food per fish; determine the point of intersection for the graphs of $y = \dfrac{F(t)}{P(t)}$ and $y = 1$.

13. a)

b) domain $\{x \mid -6 \leq x \leq 6, x \in R\}$,
range $\{y \mid -5.8 \leq y \leq 5.8, y \in R\}$

c) 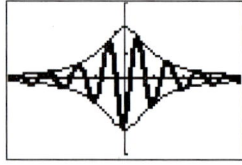 domain
$\{x \mid -6 \leq x \leq 6,$
$x \neq n\pi, n \in I, x \in R\}$,
range $\{y \mid y \in R\}$

d) The domain in part d) is restricted to $-6 < x < 6$ but has no non-permissible values. In part c), the domain is restricted to to $-6 \leq x \leq 6$ with non-permissible values. The ranges in parts c) and d) are the same..

14. a), b) $f(t) = A \sin kt$,
$g(t) = 0.4^{ct}$
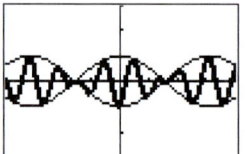

15. a) 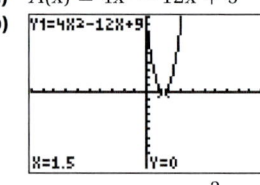 **b)** Yes

16. The price per tonne decreases.
17. $A = 4x\sqrt{r^2 - x^2}$
C1 Yes; multiplication is commutative. Examples may vary.
C2 Example: Multiplication generally increases the range and domain, although this is not always true. Quotients generally produce asymptotes and points of discontinuity, although this is not always true.
C3 a) $A(x) = 4x^2 - 12x + 9$
b) 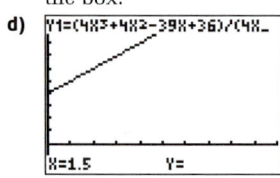 domain
$\{x \mid x \geq 1.5, x \in R\}$,
range
$\{A \mid A \geq 0, A \in R\}$

c) $h(x) = x + 4, x \neq \frac{3}{2}$; this represents the height of the box.
d) 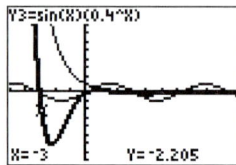 domain
$\{x \mid x > 1.5, x \in R\}$,
range
$\{h \mid h > 5.5, h \in R\}$

10.3 Composite Functions, pages 507 to 509

1. a) 3   **b)** 0   **c)** 2   **d)** -1
2. a) 2   **b)** 2   **c)** -4 **d)** -5
3. a) 10   **b)** -8 **c)** -2 **d)** 28
4. a) $f(g(a)) = 3a^2 + 1$ **b)** $g(f(a)) = 9a^2 + 24a + 15$
c) $f(g(x)) = 3x^2 + 1$ **d)** $g(f(x)) = 9x^2 + 24x + 15$
e) $f(f(x)) = 9x + 16$ **f)** $g(g(x)) = x^4 - 2x^2$

5. a) $f(g(x)) = x^4 + 2x^3 + 2x^2 + x$,
$g(f(x)) = x^4 + 2x^3 + 2x^2 + x$
b) $f(g(x)) = \sqrt{x^4 + 2}$, $g(f(x)) = x^2 + 2$
c) $f(g(x)) = x^2$, $g(f(x)) = x^2$

6. a)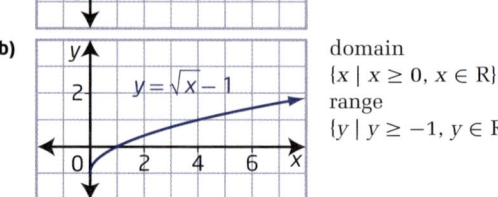
domain
$\{x \mid x \geq 1, x \in R\}$,
range
$\{y \mid y \geq 0, y \in R\}$

b) domain
$\{x \mid x \geq 0, x \in R\}$,
range
$\{y \mid y \geq -1, y \in R\}$

7. a) $g(x) = 2x - 5$ **b)** $g(x) = 5x + 1$
8. Christine is right. Ron forgot to replace all x's with the other function in the first step.
9. Yes. $k(j(x)) = j(k(x)) = x^6$; using the power law: $2(3) = 6$ and $3(2) = 6$.
10. No. $s(t(x)) = x^2 - 6x + 10$ and $t(s(x)) = x^2 - 2$.
11. a) $W(C(t)) = 3\sqrt{100 + 35t}$
b) domain $\{t \mid t \geq 0, t \in R\}$, range $\{W \mid W \geq 30, W \in W\}$
12. a) $s(p) = 0.75p$ **b)** $t(s) = 1.05s$
c) $t(s(p)) = 0.7875p$; $70.87
13. a) $g(d) = 0.06d$ **b)** $c(g) = 1.23g$
c) $c(g(d)) = 0.0738d$; $14.76
d) $d(c) = 13.55c$; 542 km
14. a) $3x^2 - 21$ **b)** $3x^2 - 7$
c) $3x^2 - 42x + 147$ **d)** $9x^2 - 42x + 49$
15. a) $h(\theta(t)) = 20 \sin \frac{\pi t}{15} + 22$
b)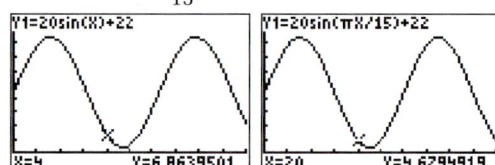

The period of the combined functions is much greater.
16. a) $C(P(t)) = 14.375(2)^{\frac{t}{10}} + 53.12$
b) approximately 17.1 years
17. a) $f(x) = 2x - 1, g(x) = x^2$
b) $f(x) = \frac{2}{3 - x}, g(x) = x^2$
c) $f(x) = |x|, g(x) = x^2 - 4x + 5$
18. a) $g(f(x)) = \frac{1 - x}{1 - 1 + x} = \frac{1 - x}{x} = \frac{1}{g(x)}$
b) $f(g(x)) = 1 - \frac{x}{1 - x} = \frac{1 - 2x}{1 - x} \neq \frac{1}{f(x)}$
No, they are not the same.
19. a) $m = \dfrac{m_0}{\sqrt{1 - \dfrac{t^6}{c^2}}}$ **b)** $\dfrac{2}{\sqrt{3}} m_0$

20. a) The functions $f(x) = 5x + 10$ and $g(x) = \frac{1}{5}x - 2$ are inverses of each other since $f(g(x)) = x$ and $g(f(x)) = x$.
b) The functions $f(x) = \frac{x - 1}{2}$ and $g(x) = 2x + 1$ are inverses of each other since $f(g(x)) = x$ and $g(f(x)) = x$.

c) The functions $f(x) = \sqrt[3]{x + 1}$ and $g(x) = x^3 - 1$ are inverses of each other since $f(g(x)) = x$ and $g(f(x)) = x$.

d) The functions $f(x) = 5^x$ and $g(x) = \log_5 x$ are inverses of each other since $f(g(x)) = x$ and $g(f(x)) = x$.

21. a) $\{x \mid x > 0, x \in R\}$ **b)** $f(g(x)) = \log (\sin x)$

c)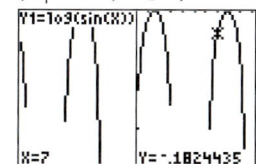

d) domain $\{x \mid 2n\pi < x < (2n + 1)\pi, n \in I, x \in R\}$, range $\{y \mid y \leq 0, y \in R\}$

22. $f(g(x)) = \dfrac{x + 2}{x + 3}$, $x \neq -3, -2, -1$

23. a)   **i)** $y = \dfrac{1}{1 - x}$, $x \neq 1$ **ii)** $y = -\dfrac{x}{1 - x}$, $x \neq 1$

   iii) $y = \dfrac{1}{x}$, $x \neq 0$ **iv)** $y = \dfrac{1}{x}$, $x \neq 0$

b) $f_2(f_3(x))$

C1 No. One is a composite function, $f(g(x))$, and the other is the product of functions, $(f \cdot g)(x)$. Examples may vary.

C2 a) Example: Since $f(1) = 5$ and $g(5) = 10$, $g(f(1)) = 10$.

b) Example: Since $f(3) = 7$ and $g(7) = 0$, $g(f(3)) = 0$.

C3 Yes, the functions are inverses of each other.

C4 Step 1: a) $f(x + h) = 2x + 2h + 3$

b) $\dfrac{f(x + h) - f(x)}{h} = 2$

Step 2: a) $f(x + h) = -3x - 3h - 5$

b) $\dfrac{f(x + h) - f(x)}{h} = -3$

Step 3: $\dfrac{f(x + h) - f(x)}{h} = \dfrac{3}{4}$; Each value is the slope of the linear function.

Chapter 10 Review, pages 510 to 511

1. a) 26   **b)** 1   **c)** -5 **d)** 13

2. a) i) $f(x) = x^2 + x - 2$
domain $\{x \mid x \in R\}$, range $\{y \mid y \in R\}$

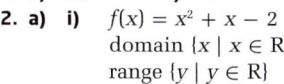

ii) $f(x) = x^2 - x - 6$
domain $\{x \mid x \in R\}$, range $\{y \mid y \in R\}$

iii) $f(x) = -x^2 + x + 6$
domain $\{x \mid x \in R\}$, range $\{y \mid y \in R\}$

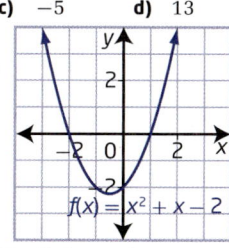

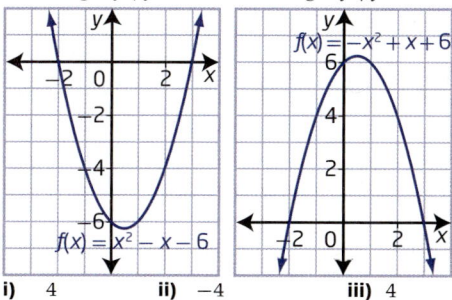

b) i) 4   **ii)** -4 **iii)** 4

3. a) $y = x^2 - 2x$

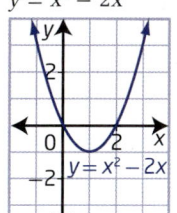

domain $\{x \mid x \in R\}$, range $\{y \mid y \geq -1, y \in R\}$

$y = x^2 + 2x - 6$

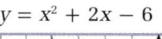
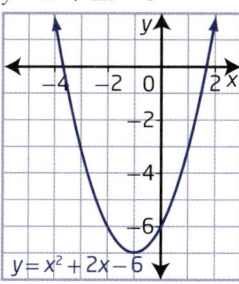

domain $\{x \mid x \in R\}$, range $\{y \mid y \geq -7, y \in R\}$

b) $y = \sqrt{x - 3} - x + 2$

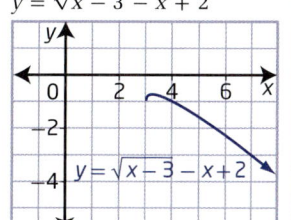

$y = \sqrt{x - 3} + x - 2$

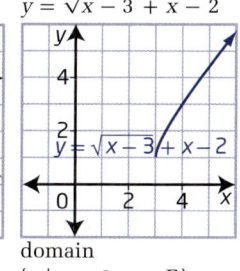

domain $\{x \mid x \geq 3, x \in R\}$, range $\{y \mid y \leq -0.75, y \in R\}$

domain $\{x \mid x \geq 3, x \in R\}$, range $\{y \mid y \geq 1, y \in R\}$

4. a) $y = \dfrac{1}{x - 1} + \sqrt{x}$; domain $\{x \mid x \geq 0, x \neq 1, x \in R\}$, range $\{y \mid y \leq -0.7886 \text{ or } y \geq 2.2287, y \in R\}$

b) $y = \dfrac{1}{x - 1} - \sqrt{x}$; domain $\{x \mid x \geq 0, x \neq 1, x \in R\}$, range $\{y \mid y \in R\}$

5. a) $P = 2x - 6$

b) The net change will continue to increase, going from a negative value to a positive value in year 3.

c) after year 3

6. a) $f(x) = x^3 + 2x^2 - 4x - 8$

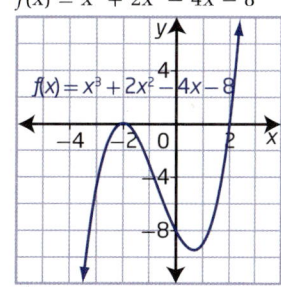

domain $\{x \mid x \in R\}$, range $\{y \mid y \in R\}$, no asymptotes

b) $f(x) = x - 2$, $x \neq -2$

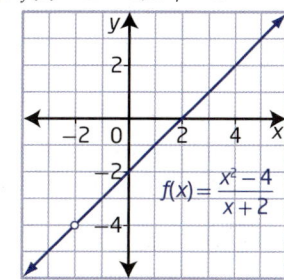

domain $\{x \mid x \neq -2, x \in R\}$, range $\{y \mid y \neq -4, y \in R\}$, no asymptotes

Answers • MHR **629**

c) $f(x) = \dfrac{1}{x-2}$, $x \neq -2, 2$

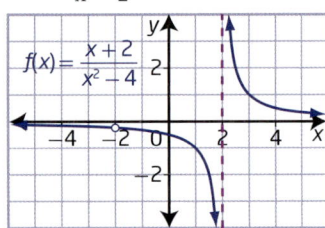

domain $\{x \mid x \neq -2, 2, x \in R\}$,
range $\left\{y \mid y \neq -\dfrac{1}{4}, 0, y \in R\right\}$, horizontal asymptote $y = 0$, vertical asymptote $x = 2$

7. a) 0   **b)** does not exist
c) does not exist

8. a) $f(x) = \dfrac{1}{x^3 + 4x^2 - 16x - 64}$, $x \neq \pm 4$
domain $\{x \mid x \neq -4, 4, x \in R\}$,
range $\{y \mid y \neq 0, y \in R\}$
b) $f(x) = x - 4$, $x \neq \pm 4$
domain $\{x \mid x \neq -4, 4, x \in R\}$,
range $\{y \mid y \neq -8, 0, y \in R\}$
c) $f(x) = \dfrac{1}{x-4}$, $x \neq \pm 4$
domain $\{x \mid x \neq -4, 4, x \in R\}$,
range $\left\{y \mid y \neq -\dfrac{1}{8}, 0, y \in R\right\}$

9. a) $y = -x^2 - 7x - 12$

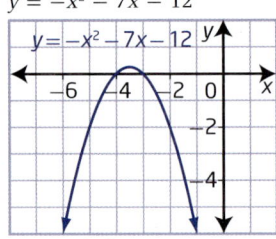

domain $\{x \mid x \in R\}$,
range $\{y \mid y \leq 0.25, y \in R\}$

$y = \dfrac{x+3}{-x-4}$, $x \neq -4$

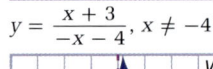

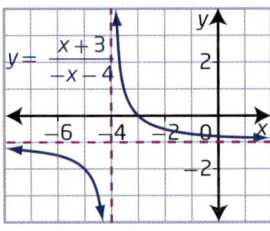

domain $\{x \mid x \neq -4, x \in R\}$,
range $\{y \mid y \neq -1, y \in R\}$

b) $y = x^3 + 14x^2 + 60x + 72$

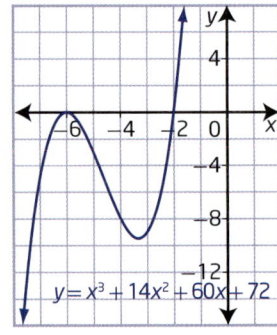

domain $\{x \mid x \in R\}$,
range $\{y \mid y \in R\}$

$y = x + 2$, $x \neq -6$

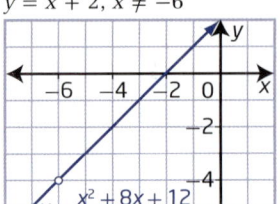

domain $\{x \mid x \neq -6, x \in R\}$,
range $\{y \mid y \neq -4, y \in R\}$

10. a) 1   **b)** 5
11. a) $y = \dfrac{32}{x^2}$; $x \neq 0$ **b)** $y = \dfrac{2}{x^2}$; $x \neq 0$
c) 0.5
12. a) $y = -\dfrac{2}{\sqrt{x}}$, $x > 0$
b) domain $\{x \mid x > 0, x \in R\}$, range $\{y \mid y < 0, y \in R\}$

13.

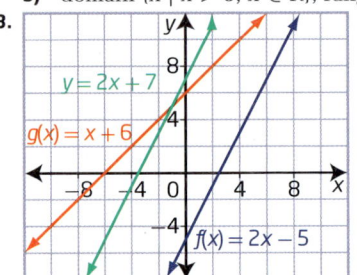

14. $T = 0.05t + 20$
15. a) $d(x) = 0.75x$; $c(x) = x - 10$
b) $c(d(x)) = 0.75x - 10$; this represents using the coupon after the discount.
c) $d(c(x)) = 0.75x - 7.5$; this represents applying the coupon before the discount.
d) Using the coupon after the discount results in a lower price of $290.

Chapter 10 Practice Test, pages 512 to 513

1. B   **2.** D   **3.** A   **4.** C   **5.** A
6. a) $h(x) = \sin x + 2x^2$ **b)** $h(x) = \sin x - 2x^2$
c) $h(x) = 2x^2 \sin x$ **d)** $h(x) = \dfrac{\sin x}{2x^2}$, $x \neq 0$

7.

	$g(x)$	$f(x)$	$(f+g)(x)$	$(f \circ g)(x)$
a)	$x - 8$	$\sqrt{x}$	$\sqrt{x} + x - 8$	$\sqrt{x - 8}$
b)	$x + 3$	$4x$	$5x + 3$	$4x + 12$
c)	x^2	$\sqrt{x - 4}$	$\sqrt{x - 4} + x^2$	$\sqrt{x^2 - 4}$
d)	$\dfrac{1}{x}$	$\dfrac{1}{x}$	$\dfrac{2}{x}$	x

8. $y = \dfrac{1}{2x^2 + 5x + 3}$, $x \neq -\dfrac{3}{2}, -1$
domain $\left\{x \mid x \neq -\dfrac{3}{2}, -1, x \in R\right\}$

9. a)

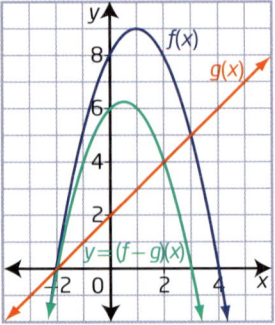

b)

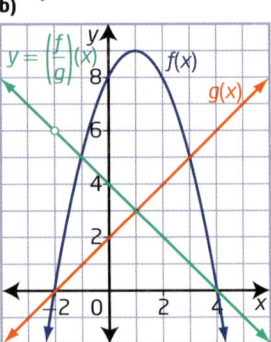

10. a) $y = |6 - x|$; domain $\{x \mid x \in R\}$, range $\{y \mid y \geq 0, y \in R\}$
    b) $y = 4^x + 1$; domain $\{x \mid x \in R\}$, range $\{y \mid y \geq 1, y \in R\}$
    c) $y = x^2$; domain $\{x \mid x \in R\}$, range $\{y \mid y \geq 0, y \in R\}$
11. a) $r(x) = x - 200$; $t(x) = 0.72x$
    b) $t(r(x)) = 0.72x - 144$; this represents applying federal taxes after deducting from her paycheque for her retirement.
    c) $1800   d) $1744
    e) The order changes the final amount. If you tax the income after subtracting $200, you are left with more money.
12. a)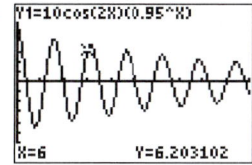
    b) The function $f(t) = 10 \cos 2t$ is responsible for the periodic motion. The function $g(t) = 0.95^t$ is responsible for the exponential decay of the amplitude.
13. a) $y = 2x^2 + 9x - 18$ b) $y = 2x^2 + 13x - 24$
    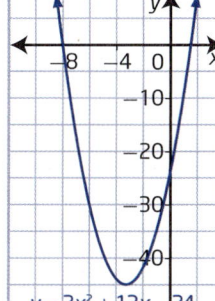
    c) $y = x + 7$, $x \neq \frac{3}{2}$ d) $y = 8x^2 - 2x - 36$
    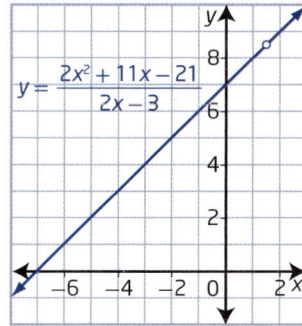 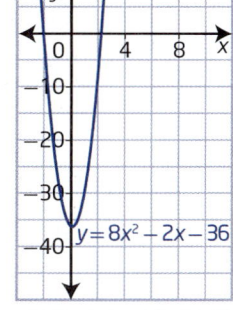
14. a) $A(t) = 2500\pi t^2$ b)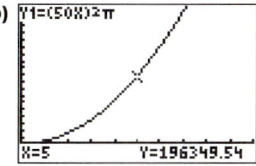
    c) approximately 196 350 cm^2
    d) Example: No. In 30 s, the radius would be 1500 cm. Most likely the circular ripples would no longer be visible on the surface of the water due to turbulence.

Chapter 11 Permutations, Combinations, and the Binomial Theorem

11.1 Permutations, pages 524 to 527

1. a)

Position 1	Position 2	Position 3
Jo	Amy	Mike
Jo	Mike	Amy
Amy	Jo	Mike
Amy	Mike	Jo
Mike	Jo	Amy
Mike	Amy	Jo

6 different arrangements

b)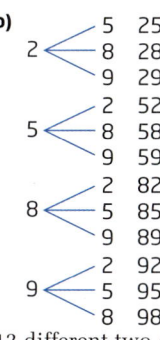

12 different two-digit numbers

c) Use abbreviations: Soup (So), Salad (Sa), Chili (Ci), Hamburger (H), Chicken (C), Fish (F), Ice Cream (I) and Fruit Salad (Fs). 16 different meals

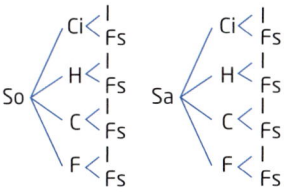

2. a) 56   b) 2520   c) 720   d) 4
3. Left Side $= 4! + 3!$ Right Side $= (4 + 3)!$
   $= 4(3!) + 3!$ $= 7!$
   $= 5(3!)$
   Left Side $\neq$ Right Side
4. a) $9! = (9)(8)(7)(6)(5)(4)(3)(2)(1)$
       $= 362\,880$
   b) $\dfrac{9!}{5!4!} = \dfrac{(9)(8)(7)(6)(5!)}{(5!)(4)(3)(2)(1)}$
       $= 126$
   c) $(5!)(3!) = (5)(4)(3)(2)(1)(3)(2)(1)$
       $= 720$
   d) $6(4!) = 6(4)(3)(2)(1)$
       $= 144$
   e) $\dfrac{102!}{100!2!} = \dfrac{(102)(101)(100!)}{100!(2)(1)}$
       $= (51)(101)$
       $= 5151$
   f) $7! - 5! = (7)(6)(5!) - 5!$
       $= 41(5!)$
       $= 4920$
5. a) 360   b) 420   c) 138 600
   d) 20   e) 20   f) 10 080
6. 24 ways
7. a) $n = 6$ b) $n = 11$ c) $r = 2$
   d) $n = 6$
8. a) 6   b) 35   c) 10
9. a) Case 1: first digit is 3 or 5; Case 2: first digit is 2 or 4
   b) Case 1: first letter is a B; Case 2: first letter is an E
10. a) 48   b) 240   c) 48
11. a) 5040   b) 2520   c) 1440   d) 576
12. 720 total arrangements; 288 arrangements begin and end with a consonant.

13. No. The organization has 25 300 members but there are only 18 000 arrangements that begin with a letter other than O followed by three different digits.
14. 20
15. $266\frac{2}{3}$ h
16. a) 5040   b) 1440   c) 3600
17. a) 3360   b) 360
18. a) AABBS   b) Example: TEETH
19. 3645 integers contain no 7s
20. a) 17 576 000
    b) Example: Yes, Canada will eventually exceed 17.5 million postal communities.
21. a) 10^{14}
    b) Yes, $10^{14} = 100\,000\,000\,000\,000$, which is 100 million million.
22. a) $r = 3$ b) $r = 7$ c) $n = 4$ d) $n = 42$
23. $_nP_n = \dfrac{n!}{(n-n)!} = \dfrac{n!}{0!}$ and $_nP_n = n!$, so $0! = 1$.
24. The number of items to be arranged is less than the number of items in each set of arrangements.
25. 63   26. 84   27. 737   28. 15   29. 10
30. Example: Use the numbers 1 to 9 to represent the different students.

Day 1	Day 2	Day 3	Day 4
1 2 3	1 4 7	1 4 9	1 6 8
4 5 6	2 5 8	2 6 7	2 4 9
7 8 9	3 6 9	3 5 8	3 5 7

31. 24 zeros; Determine how many factors of 5 there are in 100!. Each multiple of 5 has one factor of 5 except 25, 50, 75, and 100, which have two factors of 5. So, there are 24 factors of 5 in 100!. There are more than enough factors of 2 to match up with the 5s to make factors of 10, so there are 24 zeros.
32. a) EDACB or BCADE   b) 2
    c) None. Since F only knows A, then F must stand next to A. However, in both arrangements from part a), A must stand between C and D, but F does not know either C or D and therefore cannot stand next to either of them. Therefore, no possible arrangement satisfies the conditions.
C1 a) $_aP_b = \dfrac{a!}{(a-b)!}$ is the formula for calculating the number of ways that b objects can be selected from a group of a objects, if order is important; for example, if you have a group of 20 students and you want to choose a team of 3 arranged from tallest to shortest.
   b) $b \leq a$
C2 By the fundamental counting principle, if the n objects are distinct, they can be arranged in $n!$ ways. However, if a of the objects are the same and b of the remaining objects are the same, then the number of different arrangements is reduced to $\dfrac{n!}{a!b!}$ to eliminate duplicates.
C3 a) $\dfrac{(n+2)(n+1)n}{4}$ b) $\dfrac{7+20r}{r(r+1)}$
C5 a) 362 880   b) 5.559 763…   c) 6.559 763
   d) Example: The answer to part c) is 1 more than the answer to part b). This is because $10! = 10(9!)$ and $\log 10! = \log 10 + \log 9! = 1 + \log 9!$.

11.2 Combinations, pages 534 to 536

1. a) Combination, because the order that you shake hands is not important.
   b) Permutation, because the order of digits is important.
   c) Combination, since the order that the cars are purchased is not important.
   d) Combination, because the order that players are selected to ride in the van is not important.
2. $_5P_3$ is a permutation representing the number of ways of arranging 3 objects taken from a group of 5 objects. $_5C_3$ is a combination representing the number of ways of choosing any 3 objects from a group of 5 objects. $_5P_3 = 60$ and $_5C_3 = 10$.
3. a) $_6P_4 = 360$ b) $_7C_3 = 35$
   c) $_5C_2 = 10$ d) $_{10}C_7 = 120$
4. a) 210   b) 5040
5. a) AB, AC, AD, BC, BD, CD
   b) AB, BA, AC, CA, AD, DA, BC, CB, BD, DB, CD, DC
   c) The number of permutations is 2! times the number of combinations.
6. a) $n = 10$ b) $n = 7$ c) $n = 4$ d) $n = 5$
7. a) Case 1: one-digit numbers, Case 2: two-digit numbers, Case 3: three-digit numbers
   b) Cases of grouping the 4 members of the 5-member team from either grade: Case 1: four grade 12s, Case 2: three grade 12s and one grade 11, Case 3: two grade 12s and two grade 11s, Case 4: one grade 12 and three grade 11s, Case 5: four grade 11s
8. Left Side $= {}_{11}C_3$ Right Side $= {}_{11}C_8$
   $= \dfrac{11!}{(11-3)!3!}$ $= \dfrac{11!}{(11-8)!8!}$
   $= \dfrac{11!}{8!3!}$ $= \dfrac{11!}{3!8!}$
   Left Side = Right Side
9. a) $_5C_5 = 1$
   b) $_5C_0 = 1$; there is only one way to choose 5 objects from a group of 5 objects and only one way to choose 0 objects from a group of 5 objects.
10. a) 4   b) 10
11. a) 15   b) 22
12. Left Side
    $= {}_nC_{r-1} + {}_nC_r$
    $= \dfrac{n!}{(n-(r-1))!(r-1)!} + \dfrac{n!}{(n-r)!r!}$
    $= \dfrac{n!}{(n-r+1)!(r-1)!} + \dfrac{n!}{(n-r)!r!}$
    $= \dfrac{[n!(n-r)!r] + [n!(n-r+1)!(r-1)!]}{(n-r+1)!(r-1)!(n-r)!r!}$
    $= \dfrac{n!(n-r)!r(r-1)! + n!(n-r+1)(n-r)!(r-1)!}{(n-r+1)!(r-1)!(n-r)!r!}$
    $= \dfrac{n!(n-r)!(r-1)![r + (n-r+1)]}{(n-r+1)!(r-1)!(n-r)!r!}$
    $= \dfrac{n!(n-r)!(r-1)!(n+1)}{(n-r+1)(r-1)!(n-r)!r!}$
    $= \dfrac{n!(n+1)}{(n-r+1)!r!}$
    $= \dfrac{(n+1)!}{(n-r+1)!r!}$
    Right Side $= {}_{n+1}C_r$
    $= \dfrac{(n+1)!}{(n+1-r)!r!}$
    Left Side = Right Side
13. 20 different burgers; this is a combination because the order the ingredients is put on the burger is not important.

14. a) 210
    b) combination, because the order of toppings on a pizza is not important
15. a) Method 1: Use a diagram.
       Method 2: Use combinations.
       $_5C_2 = 10$, the same as the number of combinations of 5 people shaking hands.
    b) 10
    c) The number of triangles is given by $_{10}C_3 = \frac{10!}{(10-3)!3!} = \frac{10!}{7!3!}$. The number of lines is given by $_{10}C_2 = \frac{10!}{(10-2)!2!} = \frac{10!}{8!2!}$. The number of triangles is determined by the number of selections with choosing 3 points from 10 non-collinear points, whereas the number of lines is determined by the number of selections with choosing 2 points from the 10 non-collinear points.

16. Left Side $= {}_nC_r$
    $= \frac{n!}{(n-r)!r!}$
    Right Side $= {}_nC_{n-r}$
    $= \frac{n!}{(n-(n-r))!(n-r)!}$
    $= \frac{n!}{(n-n+r)!(n-r)!}$
    $= \frac{n!}{r!(n-r)!}$
    Left Side = Right Side
17. a) 125 970   b) 44 352   c) 1945
18. a) 2 598 960   b) 211 926   c) 388 700
19. a) 525   b) 576
20. a) $\frac{40!}{20!20!}$ b) 116 280
21. a) $\frac{52!}{39!13!} \times \frac{39!}{26!13!} \times \frac{26!}{13!13!} \times \frac{13!}{0!13!}$
    b) $\frac{52!}{13!13!13!13!} = \frac{52!}{(13!)^4}$ c) $5.364\ldots \times 10^{28}$
22. 90
23. a) 36   b) 1296
24. a) $_5C_2 = 10$, $10 \div 3 = 3$ Remainder 1. $_{15}C_6 = 5005$, and $5005 \div 3 = 1668$ Remainder 1.
    b) yes, remainder 3   c) 7; 0, 1, 2, 3, 4, 5, 6
    d) Example: First, I would try a few more cases to try to find a counterexample. Since the statement seems to be true, I would write a computer program to test many cases in an organized way.
C1 No. The order of the numbers matters, so a combination lock would be better called a permutations lock.
C2 a) $_aC_b = \frac{a!}{(a-b)!b!}$ is the formula for calculating the number of ways that b objects can be selected from a group of a objects, if order is not important; for example, if you have a group of 20 students and you want to choose a team of any 3 people.
    b) $a \geq b$ c) $b \geq 0$
C3 Example: Assuming that the rooms are the same and so any patient can be assigned to any of the six rooms, this is a combinations situation. Beth is correct.

C4 Step 1: Example:

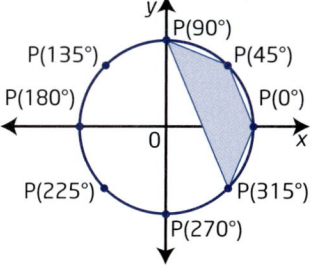

Step 2: Number of each type of quadrilateral:
Squares: 2
Rectangles: 4
Parallelograms: 0
Isosceles trapezoids: 24

Step 3: Example: In the case drawn in Step 1, because of the symmetry of the given points on the unit circle, many of the possible quadrilaterals are the same. In general, there will be $_8C_4$ or 70 possible quadrilaterals.

11.3 The Binomial Theorem, pages 542 to 545

1. a) 1 4 6 4 1   b) 1 8 28 56 70 56 28 8 1
   c) 1 11 55 165 330 462 462 330 165 55 11 1
2. a) $_2C_0\ _2C_1\ _2C_2$ b) $_4C_0\ _4C_1\ _4C_2\ _4C_3\ _4C_4$
   c) $_7C_0\ _7C_1\ _7C_2\ _7C_3\ _7C_4\ _7C_5\ _7C_6\ _7C_7$
3. a) $\frac{3!}{2!1!}$ b) $\frac{6!}{3!3!}$ c) $\frac{1!}{0!1!}$
4. a) 5   b) 8   c) $q+1$
5. a) $1x^2 + 2xy + 1y^2$ b) $1a^3 + 3a^2 + 3a + 1$
   c) $1 - 4p + 6p^2 - 4p^3 + 1p^4$
6. a) $1a^3 + 9a^2b + 27ab^2 + 27b^3$
   b) $243a^5 - 810a^4b + 1080a^3b^2 - 720a^2b^2 + 240ab^4 - 32b^5$
   c) $16x^4 - 160x^3 + 600x^2 - 1000x + 625$
7. a) $126a^4b^5$ b) $-540x^3y^3$ c) $192\,192t^6$
   d) $96x^2y^2$ e) $3072w^2$
8. All outside numbers of Pascal's triangle are 1's; the middle values are determined by adding the two numbers to the left and right in the row above.
9. a) 1, 2, 4, 8, 16
   b) 2^8 or 256
   c) 2^{n-1}, where n is the row number
10. a) The sum of the numbers on the handle equals the number on the blade of each hockey stick.
    b) No; the hockey stick handle must begin with 1 from the outside of the triangle and move diagonally down the triangle with each value being in a different row. The number of the blade must be diagonally below the last number on the handle of the hockey stick.
11. a) 13   b) $220x^9y^3$ c) $r = 6$, $_{12}C_6 = 924$
12. a) $(x+y)^4$ b) $(1-y)^5$
13. a) No. While $11^0 = 1$, $11^1 = 11$, $11^2 = 121$, $11^3 = 1331$, and $11^4 = 14\,641$, this pattern only works for the first five rows of Pascal's triangle.
    b) m represents the row number minus 1, $m \leq 4$.
14. a) $(x+y)^3 = x^3 + 3x^2y + 3xy^2 + y^3$,
       $(x-y)^3 = x^3 - 3x^2y + 3xy^2 - y^3$; the signs for the second and fourth terms are negative in the expansion of $(x-y)^3$
    b) $(x+y)^3 + (x-y)^3$
       $= x^3 + 3x^2y + 3xy^2 + y^3 + x^3 - 3x^2y + 3xy^2 - y^3$
       $= 2x^3 + 6xy^2$
       $= 2x(x^2 + 3y^2)$

c) $2y(3x^2 + y^2)$; the expansion of $(x + y)^3 - (x - y)^3$ has coefficients for x^2 and y^2 that are reversed from the expansion of $(x + y)^3 + (x - y)^3$, as well as the common factors $2x$ and $2y$ being reversed.

15. a) Case 1: no one attends, case 2: one person attends, case 3: two people attend, case 4: three people attend, case 5: four people attend, case 6: all five people attend
  b) 32 or 2^5
  c) The answer is the sum of the terms of the sixth row of Pascal's triangle.

16. a)
  H — H — H — HHH
        T — HHT
      T — H — HTH
        T — HTT
  T — H — H — THH
        T — THT
      T — H — TTH
        T — TTT

  b) HHH + HHT + HTH + HTT + THH + THT + TTH + TTT
  $= H^3 + 3H^2T + 3HT^2 + T^3$
  c) H^3 represents the first term of the expansion of $(H + T)^3$ and $3H^2T$ represents the second term of the expansion of $(H + T)^3$.

17. a) $\dfrac{a^3}{b^3} + 6\left(\dfrac{a^2}{b^2}\right) + 12\left(\dfrac{a}{b}\right) + 8$ or $\dfrac{a^3}{b^3} + \dfrac{6a^2}{b^2} + \dfrac{12a}{b} + 8$

  b) $\dfrac{a^4}{b^4} - 4\left(\dfrac{a^4}{b^3}\right) + 6\left(\dfrac{a^4}{b^2}\right) - 4\left(\dfrac{a^4}{b}\right) + a^4$
  $= a^4\left(\dfrac{1}{b^4} - \dfrac{4}{b^3} + \dfrac{6}{b^2} - \dfrac{4}{b} + 1\right)$

  c) $1 - 3x + \dfrac{15}{4}x^2 - \dfrac{5}{2}x^3 + \dfrac{15}{16}x^4 - \dfrac{3}{16}x^5 + \dfrac{1}{64}x^6$

  d) $16x^8 - 32x^5 + 24x^2 - 8x^{-1} + x^{-4}$

18. a) $5670a^4b^{12}$ **b)** the fourth term; it is $-120x^{11}$
19. a) 126 720 **b)** the fifth term; its value is 495
20. $m = 3y$
21. Examples:
  Step 1: The numerators start with the second value, 4, and decrease by ones, while the denominators start at 1 and increase by ones to 4.
  For the sixth row:
  $1 \times 5 = 5$, $5 \times \dfrac{4}{2} = 10$, $10 \times \dfrac{3}{3} = 10$, $10 \times \dfrac{2}{4} = 5$,
  $5 \times \dfrac{1}{5} = 1$.
  Step 2: The second element in the row is equal to the row number minus 1.
  Step 3: The first 2 terms in the 21st row are 1 and 20.
  $\times \dfrac{20}{1}; \times \dfrac{19}{2}, \times \dfrac{18}{3}$, and so on to $\times \dfrac{3}{18}, \times \dfrac{2}{19}, \times \dfrac{1}{20}$

22. a) Each entry is the sum of the two values in the row below and slightly to the left and the right.
  b) $\dfrac{1}{6}$ $\dfrac{1}{30}$ $\dfrac{1}{60}$ $\dfrac{1}{60}$ $\dfrac{1}{30}$ $\dfrac{1}{6}$
  $\dfrac{1}{7}$ $\dfrac{1}{42}$ $\dfrac{1}{105}$ $\dfrac{1}{140}$ $\dfrac{1}{105}$ $\dfrac{1}{42}$ $\dfrac{1}{7}$
  c) Examples: Outside values are the reciprocal of the row number. The product of two consecutive outside row values gives the value of the second term in the lower row.

23. Consider $a + b = x$ and $c = y$, and substitute in $(x + y)^3 = x^3 + 3x^2y + 3xy^2 + y^3$.
$(a + b + c)^3$
$= (a + b)^3 + 3(a + b)^2c + 3(a + b)c^2 + c^3$
$= a^3 + 3a^2b + 3ab^2 + b^3 + 3(a^2 + 2ab + b^2)c + 3ac^2 + 3bc^2 + c^3$
$= a^3 + 3a^2b + 3ab^2 + b^3 + 3a^2c + 6abc + 3b^2c + 3ac^2 + 3bc^2 + c^3$

24. a)

Diagram	Points	Line Segments	Triangles	Quadrilaterals	Pentagons	Hexagons
○	1					
○	2	1				
○	3	3	1			
○	4	6	4	1		
○	5	10	10	5	1	
○	6	15	20	15	6	1

  b) The numbers are values from row 1 to row 6 of Pascal's triangle with the exception of the first term.
  c) The numbers will be values from the 8th row of Pascal's triangle with the exception of the first term: 8 28 56 70 56 28 8 1.

25. a) 2.7083…
  b) The value of e becomes more precise for the 7th and 8th terms. The more terms used, the more accurate the approximation.
  c) Example: 2.718 281 828
  d) $15! = \left(\dfrac{15}{e}\right)^{15}\sqrt{2\pi(15)} \approx 1.300 \times 10^{12}$; on a calculator $15! \approx 1.3077 \times 10^{12}$
  e) Using the formula from part d),
  $50! = \left(\dfrac{50}{e}\right)^{50}\sqrt{2\pi(50)}$
  $\approx 3.036\ 344\ 594 \times 10^{64}$;
  using the formula from part e),
  $50! = \left(\dfrac{50}{e}\right)^{50}\sqrt{2\pi(50)}\left(1 + \dfrac{1}{12(50)}\right)$
  $\approx 3.041\ 405\ 168 \times 10^{64}$; using a calculator $50! = 3.041\ 409\ 32 \times 10^{64}$, so the formula in part e) seems to give a more accurate approximation.

C1 The coefficients of the terms in the expansion of $(x + y)^n$ are the same as the numbers in row $n + 1$ of Pascal's triangle. Examples: $(x + y)^2 = x^2 + 2xy + y^2$ and row 3 of Pascal's triangle is 1 2 1; $(x + y)^3 = x^3 + 3x^2y + 3xy^2 + y^3$ and row 4 of Pascal's triangle is 1 3 3 1.

C2 Examples:
   a) Permutation: In how many different ways can four different chocolate bars be given to two people? Combination: Steve has two Canadian quarters and two U.S. quarters in his pocket. In how many different ways can he draw out two coins? Binomial expansion: What is the coefficient of the middle term in the expansion of $(a + b)^4$?
   b) All three problems have the same answer, 6, but they answer different questions.

C3 Examples:
   a) For small values of n, it is easier to use Pascal's triangle, but for large values of n it is easier to use combinations to determine the coefficients in the expansion of $(a + b)^n$.
   b) If you have a large version of Pascal's triangle available, then that will immediately give a correct coefficient. If you have to work from scratch, both methods can be error prone.

C4 Answers will vary.

Chapter 11 Review, pages 546 to 547

1. a) 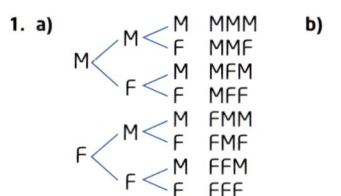   **b)** 3

2. a) 81   **b)** 32
3. a) 24   **b)** 360   **c)** 60   **d)** $\dfrac{12!}{2!3!2!}$
4. a) 48   **b)** 24   **c)** 72
5. a) 5040   **b)** 288   **c)** 144
6. a) 1 160 016   **b)** $8.513\,718\,8 \times 10^{11}$
   c) about 270 000 years
7. a) $\dfrac{n+1}{n-1}$ **b)** $\dfrac{x^2 + x + 1}{x}$
8. a) 210   **b)** 63
9. a) 120   **b)** 5040   **c)** 200   **d)** 163 800
10. a) 15
   b) amounts all in cents: 1, 5, 10, 25, 6, 11, 26, 15, 30, 35, 16, 31, 36, 40, 41
11. a) $n = 8$, $_8C_2 = 28$
   b) $n = 26$, $_{26}C_3 = 2600$ and $4(_{26}P_2) = 4(650) = 2600$
12. 2520
13. a) Example: Permutation: How many arrangements of the letters AAABB are possible? Combination: How many ways can you choose 3 students from a group of 5?
   b) Yes, $_5C_2 = \dfrac{5!}{(5-2)!2!} = \dfrac{5!}{3!2!}$ and $_5C_3 = \dfrac{5!}{(5-3)!3!} = \dfrac{5!}{2!3!}$.

14. a) 1 3 3 1
   b) 1 9 36 84 126 126 84 36 9 1
15. Examples: Multiplication: expand, collect like terms, and write the answer in descending order of the exponent of x.
$(x + y)^3 = (x + y)(x + y)(x + y)$
$= x^3 + 3x^2y + 3xy^2 + y^3$
Pascal's triangle: Coefficients are the terms from row $n + 1$ of Pascal's triangle. For $(x + y)^3$, row 4 is 1 3 3 1.
Combination: coefficients correspond to the combinations as shown:
$(x + y)^3 = {_3C_0}x^3y^0 + {_3C_1}x^2y^1 + {_3C_2}x^1y^2 + {_3C_3}x^0y^3$
16. a) $a^5 + 5a^4b + 10a^3b^2 + 10a^2b^3 + 5ab^4 + b^5$
   b) $x^3 - 9x^2 + 27x - 27$
   c) $16x^8 - 32x^4 + 24 - \dfrac{8}{x^4} + \dfrac{1}{x^8}$
17. a) $36a^7b^2$ **b)** $-192xy^5$ **c)** $-160x^3$
18. a)

					B
1	5	15	35	70	126
1	4	10	20	35	56
1	3	6	10	15	21
1	2	3	4	5	6
A	1	1	1	1	1

   b) Pascal's triangle values are shown with the top of the triangle at point A and the rows appearing up and right of point A.
   c) 126
   d) There are 4 identical moves up and 5 identical moves right, so the number of possible pathways is $\dfrac{9!}{4!5!} = 126$.
19. a) 45 moves
   b) 2 counters: 1 move; 3 counters: $1 + 2 = 3$ moves; 4 counters: $1 + 2 + 3 = 6$ moves; and so on up to 12 counters: $1 + 2 + 3 + \cdots + 10 + 11 = 66$ moves
   c) 300 moves

Chapter 11 Practice Test, page 548

1. C   **2.** D   **3.** C   **4.** B   **5.** A   **6.** C
7. a) 180
   b) AACBDB, ABCADB, ABCBDA, BACBDA, BACADB, BBCADA
8. No, n must be a whole number, so n cannot equal -8.
9. a) 10   **b)** $\dfrac{5!}{2!3!}\left(\dfrac{4!}{2!2!}\right) = 60$
10. 69
11. Permutations determine the number of arrangements of n items chosen r at a time, when order is important. For example, the number of arrangements of 5 people chosen 2 at a time to ride on a motorcycle is $_5P_2 = 20$. A combination determines the number of different selections of n objects chosen r at a time when order is not important. For example, the number of selections of 5 objects chosen 2 at a time, when order is not important, is $_5C_2 = 10$.
12. $672x^9$
13. a) 420   **b)** 120
14. a) $n = 6$ **b)** $n = 9$
15. $y^5 - 10y^2 + 40y^{-1} - 80y^{-4} + 80y^{-7} - 32y^{-10}$
16. a) 24   **b)** 36   **c)** 18

Cumulative Review, Chapters 9–11, pages 550 to 551

1. a) a vertical stretch by a factor of 2 about the x-axis and a translation of 1 unit right and 3 units up

b)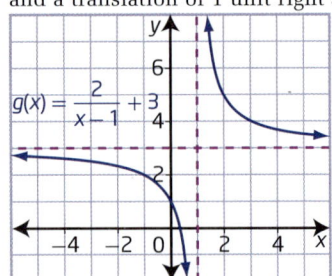

c) domain $\{x \mid x \neq 1, x \in R\}$,
range $\{y \mid y \neq 3, y \in R\}$, x-intercept $\frac{1}{3}$,
y-intercept 1, horizontal asymptote $y = 3$,
vertical asymptote $x = 1$

2. a)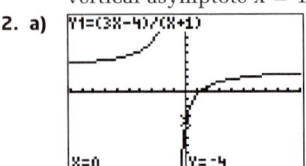

b) domain $\{x \mid x \neq -1, x \in R\}$,
range $\{y \mid y \neq 3, y \in R\}$, x-intercept $\frac{4}{3}$,
y-intercept -4, horizontal asymptote $y = 3$,
vertical asymptote $x = -1$

3. a) The graph of $y = \dfrac{x^2 - 3x}{x^2 - 9}$ has a vertical asymptote at $x = -3$, a point of discontinuity at $(3, 0.5)$, and an x-intercept of 0; C.

b) The graph of $y = \dfrac{x^2 - 1}{x + 1}$ has no vertical asymptote, a point of discontinuity at $(-1, -2)$, and an x-intercept of 1; A.

c) The graph of $y = \dfrac{x^2 + 4x + 3}{x^2 + 1}$ has no vertical asymptote, no point of discontinuity, and x-intercepts of -3 and -1; B.

4. a) 2   **b)** $-1, 9$ **c)** 0

5. a) $-0.71, 0.71$ **b)** $0.15, 5.52$

6. a) $h(x) = \sqrt{x + 2} + x - 2$, $k(x) = \sqrt{x + 2} - x + 2$

b)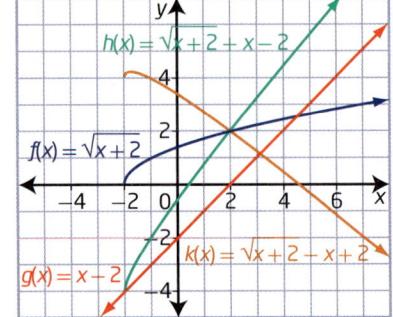

c) $f(x)$: domain $\{x \mid x \geq -2, x \in R\}$,
range $\{y \mid y \geq 0, y \in R\}$
$g(x)$: domain $\{x \mid x \in R\}$, range $\{y \mid y \in R\}$
$h(x)$: domain $\{x \mid x \geq -2, x \in R\}$,
range $\{y \mid y \geq -4, y \in R\}$
$k(x)$: domain $\{x \mid x \geq -2, x \in R\}$,
range $\{y \mid y \leq 4.25, y \in R\}$

7. a)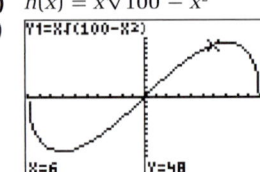

$f(x)$: domain $\{x \mid x \in R\}$, range $\{y \mid y \in R\}$
$g(x)$: domain $\{x \mid -10 \leq x \leq 10, x \in R\}$,
range $\{y \mid 0 \leq y \leq 10, y \in R\}$

b) $h(x) = x\sqrt{100 - x^2}$

c) domain $\{x \mid -10 \leq x \leq 10, x \in R\}$,
range $\{y \mid -50 \leq y \leq 50, y \in R\}$

8. a) $h(x) = \dfrac{x + 1}{x - 2}, x \neq -2, 2$; $k(x) = \dfrac{x - 2}{x + 1}, x \neq -2, -1$

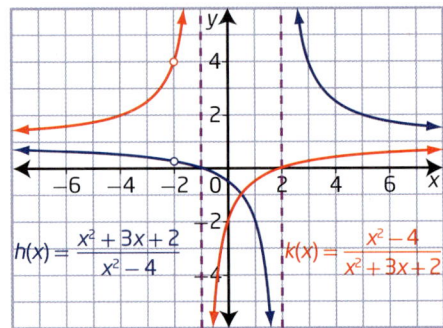

b) The two functions have different domains but the same range; $h(x)$: domain $\{x \mid x \neq -2, 2, x \in R\}$, range $\{y \mid y \neq 1, y \in R\}$, $k(x)$: domain $\{x \mid x \neq -2, -1, x \in R\}$, range $\{y \mid y \neq 1, y \in R\}$

9.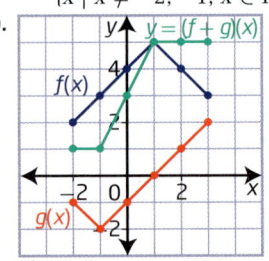

10. a) -3 **b)** $\dfrac{1}{2}$

11. a) $(f \circ g)(x) = (x - 3)^3$ and $(g \circ f)(x) = x^3 - 3$

b) [calculator screens: Y1=(X-3)^3 with X=3, Y=0; Y2=X^3-3 with X=0, Y=-3]

c) The graph of $(f \circ g)(x) = (x - 3)^3$ is a translation of 3 units right of the graph of $f(x)$. The graph of $(g \circ f)(x) = x^3 - 3$ is a translation of 3 units down of the graph of $f(x)$.

12. a) $f(g(x)) = x$; domain $\{x \mid x \in R\}$

b) $g(f(x)) = \csc x$; domain $\{x \mid x \neq \pi n, n \in I, x \in R\}$

c) $f(g(x)) = \dfrac{1}{x^2 - 1}$; domain $\{x \mid x \neq \pm 1, x \in R\}$

13. 96 meals
14. 480 ways
15. 55
16. 525 ways

17. a) 103 680 **b)** 725 760
18. a) 3 **b)** 6 **c)** 5
19. Examples: Pascal's triangle:
$(x + y)^4 = 1x^4y^0 + 4x^3y^1 + 6x^2y^2 + 4x^1y^3 + 1x^0y^4$;
the coefficients are values from the fifth row of Pascal's triangle.
$(x + y)^6 = 1x^6y^0 + 6x^5y^1 + 15x^4y^2 + 20x^3y^3 + 15x^2y^4 + 6x^1y^5 + 1x^0y^6$; the coefficients are values from the seventh row of Pascal's triangle.
Combinations: $(x + y)^4 = {}_4C_0x^4y^0 + {}_4C_1x^3y^1 + {}_4C_2x^2y^2 + {}_4C_3x^1y^3 + {}_4C_4x^0y^4$; the coefficients ${}_4C_0$, ${}_4C_1$, ${}_4C_2$, ${}_4C_3$, ${}_4C_4$ have the same values as in the fifth row of Pascal's triangle.
$(x + y)^6 = {}_6C_0x^6y^0 + {}_6C_1x^5y^1 + {}_6C_2x^4y^2 + {}_6C_3x^3y^3 + {}_6C_4x^2y^4 + {}_6C_5x^1y^5 + {}_6C_6x^0y^6$; the coefficients ${}_6C_0$, ${}_6C_1$, ${}_6C_2$, ${}_6C_3$, ${}_6C_4$, ${}_6C_5$, ${}_6C_6$ have the same values as the seventh row of Pascal's triangle.
20. a) $81x^4 - 540x^3 + 1350x^2 - 1500x + 625$
  b) $\dfrac{1}{x^5} - \dfrac{10}{x^3} + \dfrac{40}{x} - 80x + 80x^3 - 32x^5$
21. a) 250 **b)** -56
22. a) ${}_{25}C_4$ **b)** 26 **c)** ${}_{25}C_3 = {}_{24}C_2 + {}_{24}C_3$

Unit 4 Test, pages 552 to 553

1. D **2.** B **3.** A **4.** B **5.** B **6.** D **7.** C
8. $\left(3, \dfrac{1}{7}\right)$
9. 0, 3.73, 0.27 **10.** $600x^2y^4$ **11.** -1
12. a) vertical stretch by a factor of 2 and translation of 1 unit left and 3 units down
  b) $x = -1$ and $y = -3$
  c) as x approaches -1, $|y|$ becomes very large
13. a)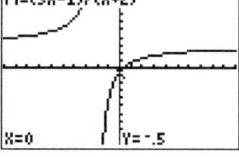
  b) domain $\{x \mid x \neq -2, x \in \mathbb{R}\}$, range $\{y \mid y \neq 3, y \in \mathbb{R}\}$, x-intercept $\dfrac{1}{3}$, y-intercept $-\dfrac{1}{2}$
  c) $x = \dfrac{1}{3}$
  d) The x-intercept of the graph of the function $y = \dfrac{3x - 1}{x + 2}$ is the root of the equation $0 = \dfrac{3x - 1}{x + 2}$.
14. a) The graph of $f(x) = \dfrac{x - 4}{(x + 2)(x - 4)}$ has a vertical asymptote at $x = -2$, a point of discontinuity at $\left(4, \dfrac{1}{6}\right)$, y-intercept of 0.5, and no x-intercept.
  b) The graph of $f(x) = \dfrac{(x + 3)(x - 2)}{(x + 3)(x - 1)}$ has a vertical asymptote at $x = 1$, a point of discontinuity at $(-3, 1.25)$, y-intercept of 2, and an x-intercept of 2.
  c) The graph of $f(x) = \dfrac{x(x - 5)}{(x - 3)(x + 1)}$ has vertical asymptotes at $x = -1$ and $x = 3$, no points of discontinuity, y-intercept of 0, and x-intercepts of 0 and 5.

15. a)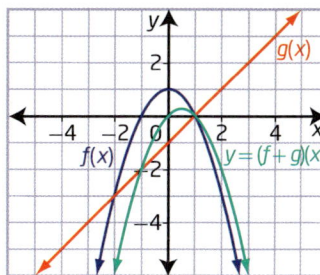
domain $\{x \mid x \in \mathbb{R}\}$, range $\{y \mid y \leq 0.25, y \in \mathbb{R}\}$
  b)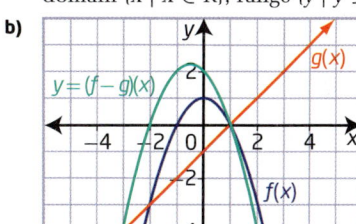
domain $\{x \mid x \in \mathbb{R}\}$, range $\{y \mid y \leq 2.25, y \in \mathbb{R}\}$
  c)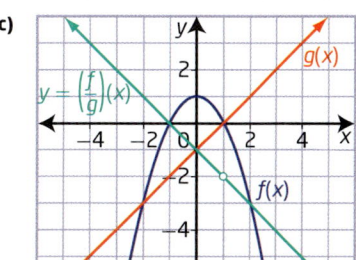
domain $\{x \mid x \neq 1, x \in \mathbb{R}\}$, range $\{y \mid y \neq -2, y \in \mathbb{R}\}$
  d)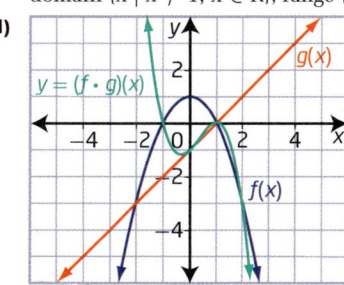
domain $\{x \mid x \in \mathbb{R}\}$, range $\{y \mid y \in \mathbb{R}\}$
16. a) $h(x) = x - 3 + \sqrt{x - 1}$; $x \geq 1$
  b) $h(x) = x - 3 - \sqrt{x - 1}$; $x \geq 1$
  c) $h(x) = \dfrac{x - 3}{\sqrt{x - 1}}$; $x > 1$
  d) $h(x) = (x - 3)\sqrt{x - 1}$; $x \geq 1$
17. a) 1 **b)** 1
  c) $f(g(x)) = x^2 - 3$ **d)** $g(f(x)) = |x^2 - 3|$
18. a) $f(x) = 2^x$ and $g(x) = 3x + 2$
  b) $f(x) = \sqrt{x}$ and $g(x) = \sin x + 2$
19. a) 21 **b)** 13 **c)** 10
20. a) 24 **b)** 232 more
  c) There are fewer ways. Because the letter C is repeated, half of the arrangements will be repeats.
21. a) 60 **b)** 81
22. 4, -4

Glossary

A

absolute value For a real number a, the absolute value is written as $|a|$ and is a positive number.

$$|a| = \begin{cases} a, \text{ if } a \geq 0 \\ -a, \text{ if } a < 0 \end{cases}$$

amplitude (of a sinusoidal function) The maximum vertical distance the graph of a sinusoidal function varies above and below the horizontal central axis of the curve.

angle in standard position The position of an angle when its initial arm is on the positive x-axis and its vertex is at the origin of a coordinate grid.

arithmetic series The terms of an arithmetic sequence expressed as a sum. This sum can be determined using the formula $S_n = \frac{n}{2}[2t_1 + (n-1)d]$ or $S_n = \frac{n}{2}(t_1 + t_n)$, where n is the number of terms, t_1 is the first term, d is the common difference, and t_n is the nth term.

asymptote A line whose distance from a given curve approaches zero.

B

binomial theorem Used to expand $(x + y)^n$, $n \in N$; each term has the form ${}_nC_k(x)^{n-k}(y)^k$, where $k + 1$ is the term number.

C

combination A selection of objects without regard to order.

> For example, all of the three-letter combinations of P, Q, R, and S are PQR, PQS, PRS, and QRS (arrangements such as PQR and RPQ are the same combination).

common logarithm A logarithm with base 10.

composite function The composition of $f(x)$ and $g(x)$ is defined as $f(g(x))$ and is formed when the equation of $g(x)$ is substituted into the equation of $f(x)$. $f(g(x))$ exists only for those x in the domain of g for which $g(x)$ is in the domain of f. $f(g(x))$ is read as "f of g of x" or "f at g of x" or "f composed with g."

$(f \circ g)(x)$ is another way to write $f(g(x))$.

cosecant ratio The reciprocal of the sine ratio, abbreviated csc. For $P(\theta) = (x, y)$ on the unit circle, $\csc \theta = \frac{1}{y}$.

If $\sin \theta = -\frac{\sqrt{3}}{2}$, then $\csc \theta = -\frac{2}{\sqrt{3}}$ or $-\frac{2\sqrt{3}}{3}$.

cosine ratio For $P(\theta) = (x, y)$ on the unit circle, $\cos \theta = \frac{x}{1} = x$.

cotangent ratio The reciprocal of the tangent ratio, abbreviated cot. For $P(\theta) = (x, y)$ on the unit circle, $\cot \theta = \frac{x}{y}$.

If $\tan \theta = 0$, then $\cot \theta$ is undefined.

coterminal angles Angles in standard position with the same terminal arms. These angles may be measured in degrees or radians.

For example, $\frac{\pi}{4}$ and $\frac{9\pi}{4}$ are coterminal angles, as are $40°$ and $-320°$.

D

domain The set of all possible values for the independent variable in a relation.

E

end behaviour The behaviour of the y-values of a function as $|x|$ becomes very large.

exponential decay A decreasing pattern of values that can be modelled by a function of the form $y = c^x$, where $0 < c < 1$.

exponential equation An equation that has a variable in an exponent.

exponential function A function of the form $y = c^x$, where c is a constant ($c > 0$) and x is a variable.

exponential growth An increasing pattern of values that can be modelled by a function of the form $y = c^x$, where $c > 1$.

extraneous root A number obtained in solving an equation that does not satisfy the initial restrictions on the variable.

F

factor theorem A polynomial in x, $P(x)$, has a factor $x - a$ if and only if $P(a) = 0$.

factorial For any positive integer n, the product of all of the positive integers up to and including n.

$4! = (4)(3)(2)(1)$
$0!$ is defined as 1.

function A relation in which each value of the independent variable is associated with exactly one value of the dependent variable. For every value in the domain, there is a unique value in the range.

fundamental counting principle If one task can be performed in a ways and a second task can be performed in b ways, then the two tasks can be performed in $a \times b$ ways.

> For example, a restaurant meal consists of one of two drink options, one of three entrees, and one of four desserts, so there are (2)(3)(4) or 24 possible meals.

G

general form An expression containing parameters that can be given specific values to generate any answer that satisfies the given information or situation; represents all possible cases.

H

half-life The length of time for an unstable element to spontaneously decay to one half its original mass.

horizontal asymptote Describes the behaviour of a graph when $|x|$ is very large. The line $y = b$ is a horizontal asymptote if the values of the function approach b when $|x|$ is very large.

horizontal line test A test used to determine if an inverse relation will be a function. If it is possible for a horizontal line to intersect the graph of a relation more than once, then the inverse of the relation is not a function.

I

image point The point that is the result of a transformation of a point on the original graph.

integral zero theorem If $x = a$ is an integral zero of a polynomial, $P(x)$, with integral coefficients, then a is a factor of the constant term of $P(x)$.

invariant point A point on a graph that remains unchanged after a transformation is applied to it. Any point on a curve that lies on the line of reflection is an invariant point.

inverse of a function If f is a function with domain A and range B, the inverse function, if it exists, is denoted by f^{-1} and has domain B and range A. f^{-1} maps y to x if and only if f maps x to y.

isosceles trapezoid A trapezoid in which the two non-parallel sides have equal length.

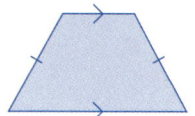

L

logarithm An exponent; in $x = c^y$, y is called the logarithm to base c of x.

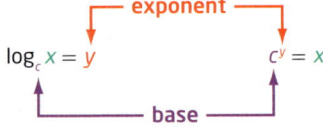

logarithmic equation An equation containing the logarithm of a variable.

logarithmic function A function of the form $y = \log_c x$, where $c > 0$ and $c \neq 1$, that is the inverse of the exponential function $y = c^x$.

M

mapping The relating of one set of points to another set of points so that each point in the original set corresponds to exactly one point in the image.

For example, the relationship between the coordinates of a set of points, (x, y), and the coordinates of a corresponding set of points, $(x, y + 3)$, is shown in mapping notation as $(x, y) \rightarrow (x, y + 3)$.

multiplicity (of a zero) The number of times a zero of a polynomial function occurs. The shape of the graph of a function close to a zero depends on its multiplicity.

N

non-permissible value Any value for a variable that makes an expression undefined. For rational expressions, any value that results in a denominator of zero.

In $\dfrac{x + 2}{x - 3}$, you must exclude the value for which $x - 3 = 0$, giving a non-permissible value of $x = 3$.

P

period The length of the interval of the domain over which a graph repeats itself. The horizontal length of one cycle on a periodic graph.

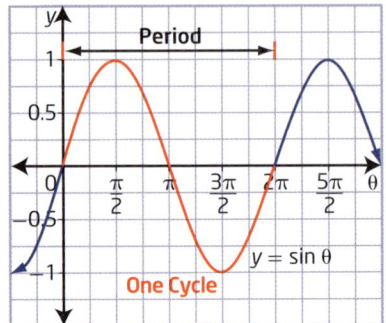

periodic function A function that repeats itself over regular intervals (cycles) of its domain.

permutation An ordered arrangement or sequence of all or part of a set.

For example, the possible permutations of the letters A, B, and C are ABC, ACB, BAC, BCA, CAB, and CBA.

phase shift The horizontal translation of the graph of a periodic function.

point of discontinuity A point, described by an ordered pair, at which the graph of a function is not continuous. Occurs in a graph of a rational function when its function can be simplified by dividing the numerator and denominator by a common factor that includes a variable. Results in a single point missing from the graph, which is represented using an open circle. Sometimes referred to as a "hole in the graph."

polynomial function A function of the form $f(x) = a_n x^n + a_{n-1} x^{n-1} + a_{n-2} x^{n-2} + \cdots + a_2 x^2 + a_1 x + a_0$, where n is a whole number, x is a variable, and the coefficients a_n to a_0 are real numbers.

For example, $f(x) = 2x - 1$, $f(x) = x^2 + x - 6$, and $y = x^3 + 2x^2 - 5x - 6$ are polynomial functions.

Q

quadrant On a Cartesian plane, the *x*-axis and the *y*-axis divide the plane into four quadrants.

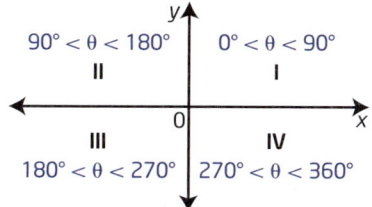

quadratic formula The formula $x = \dfrac{-b \pm \sqrt{b^2 - 4ac}}{2a}$ for determining the roots of a quadratic equation of the form $ax^2 + bx + c = 0$, $a \neq 0$.

R

radian One radian is the measure of the central angle subtended in a circle by an arc equal in length to the radius of the circle. $2\pi = 360° = 1$ full rotation (or revolution).

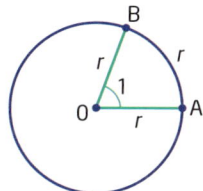

radical Consists of a root symbol, an index, and a radicand. It can be rational (for example, $\sqrt{4}$) or irrational (for example, $\sqrt{2}$).

radical equation An equation with radicals that have variables in the radicands.

radical function A function that involves a radical with a variable in the radicand.

For example, $y = \sqrt{3x}$ and $y = 4\sqrt[3]{5 + x}$ are radical functions.

range The set of all possible values for the dependent variable as the independent variable takes on all possible values of the domain.

rational equation An equation containing at least one rational expression.

Examples are $x = \dfrac{x-3}{x+1}$ and $\dfrac{x}{4} - \dfrac{7}{x} = 3$.

rational function A function that can be written in the form $f(x) = \dfrac{p(x)}{q(x)}$, where $p(x)$ and $q(x)$ are polynomial expressions and $q(x) \neq 0$.

Some examples are $y = \dfrac{20}{x}$, $C(n) = \dfrac{100 + 2n}{n}$, and $f(x) = \dfrac{3x^2 + 4}{x - 5}$.

reference angle The acute angle whose vertex is the origin and whose arms are the terminal arm of the angle and the *x*-axis. The reference angle is always a positive acute angle.

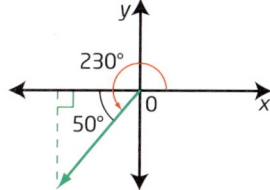

reflection A transformation where each point of the original graph has an image point resulting from a reflection in a line. A reflection may result in a change of orientation of a graph while preserving its shape.

remainder theorem When a polynomial in *x*, $P(x)$, is divided by $x - a$, the remainder is $P(a)$.

root(s) of an equation The solution(s) to an equation.

S

secant ratio The reciprocal of the cosine ratio, abbreviated sec. For $P(\theta) = (x, y)$ on the unit circle, $\sec \theta = \dfrac{1}{x}$.

If $\cos \theta = \dfrac{1}{2}$, then $\sec \theta = \dfrac{2}{1}$ or 2.

sine ratio For $P(\theta) = (x, y)$ on the unit circle, $\sin \theta = \dfrac{y}{1} = y$.

sinusoidal curve The name given to a curve that fluctuates back and forth like a sine graph. A curve that oscillates repeatedly up and down from a centre line.

square root of a function The function $y = \sqrt{f(x)}$ is the square root of the function $y = f(x)$. The function $y = \sqrt{f(x)}$ is only defined for $f(x) \geq 0$.

stretch A transformation in which the distance of each x-coordinate or y-coordinate from the line of reflection is multiplied by some scale factor. Scale factors between 0 and 1 result in the point moving closer to the line of reflection; scale factors greater than 1 result in the point moving farther away from the line of reflection.

synthetic division A method of performing polynomial long division involving a binomial divisor that uses only the coefficients of the terms and fewer calculations.

T

tangent ratio For $P(\theta) = (x, y)$ on the unit circle, $\tan \theta = \dfrac{y}{x}$.

transformation A change made to a figure or a relation such that the figure or the graph of the relation is shifted or changed in shape. Examples are translations, reflections, and stretches.

translation A slide transformation that results in a shift of the original figure without changing its shape. Vertical and horizontal translations are types of transformations with equations of the forms $y - k = f(x)$ and $y = f(x - h)$, respectively. A translated graph is congruent to the original graph.

trigonometric equation An equation involving trigonometric ratios.

trigonometric identity A trigonometric equation that is true for all permissible values of the variable in the expressions on both sides of the equation.

U

unit circle A circle with radius 1 unit. A circle of radius 1 unit with centre at the origin on the Cartesian plane is known as *the* unit circle.

V

vertical asymptote For reciprocal functions, vertical asymptotes occur at the non-permissible values of the function. The line $x = a$ is a vertical asymptote if the curve approaches the line more and more closely as x approaches a, and the values of the function increase or decrease without bound as x approaches a.

vertical displacement The vertical translation of the graph of a periodic function.

Z

zero(s) of a function The value(s) of x for which $f(x) = 0$. These values of x are related to the x-intercept(s) of the graph of a function $f(x)$.

Index

A

absolute magnitude, 413
amplitude (of a sinusoidal function), 225–227
angles and angle measure, 166–175
   approximate values, 197–200
   exact trigonometric values, 304–305
apparent magnitude, 413, 417
arc length of a circle, 173–174, 184
Archimedes' principle, 151
asymptotes, 447–448

B

binomial expansion, 539–540
binomial theorem, 540–541

C

career connections
   actuary, 515
   athletic therapist, 289
   chartered accountant (CA), 429
   chemist, 333
   computer engineer, 105
   engineer, 61
   forensic analysis investigator, 165
   geologist, 221
   laser research, 473
   physicist, 5
   radiologist, 371
cases, 522–523, 532
circular number lines, 180–181
combinations, 529–533
   with cases, 532
   fundamental counting principle, 530–533
common logarithms, 373
commutative operation, 480
composite functions, 500–506
continuous data, 341
cosecant ratio, 193, 196
cosine function, 196, 224
   graphing, 222–232
cosine tables, 225
cotangent ratio, 193, 196
coterminal angles, 170–172

D

degree, 268
   angles, 168–169, 198, 205
   of a polynomial, 106, 107
difference identities, 300
   simplification of expressions, 301
   tangent, 304
differences of functions, 476–482
discrete data, 341
domain
   in degrees, 198
   expression of, 21
   maximum values, 82
   minimum values, 82
   in radian measure, 198
   restriction, and inverse of a function, 48
double-angle identities, 301
   alternative forms, for cosine, 302
   proof of identity, 311
   simplification of expressions, 301, 302

E

Ehrenberg relation, 391
Euler's number, 382
even-degree polynomial function, 110, 111, 113
even function, 255, 487
even integers, 210
exponential equations, 404–415
   equality statements, 406
   exponential growth and decay, 411
   solving, 406–408
exponential functions
   application, 340–341
   base, 335, 360–363
   characteristics, 334–342
   continuous data, 341
   graph, 335, 336–339
   inverse, 372, 376–377
      see also logarithmic function
   modelling, 352–357
   sketch of transformed graph, 348–351
   solving, 358–363
   transformations, 346–354
   ways of expressing, 358–362

F

factor theorem, 127–128, 133
factorial, 518
factorial notation, 519–520
factoring
   factor theorem, 127–128, 133
   polynomials, 126–133
   trigonometric equations, 208–209, 210
   trigonometric identities, 317
Fourier analysis, 235
Fourier series, 322
Fresnel equations, 315
function
   notation, 7
   one-to-one function, 47
   periodic functions, 223
   radical functions, 62–77
   reflections, 16–31
   square root, 78–85
   stretches, 16–31
function operations
   combined function, 480–481
   composite functions, 500–506
   differences of functions, 476–482
   products of functions, 490–495
   quotients of functions, 490–495
   sums of functions, 476–482
fundamental counting principle, 517–518, 530–531

G

gain, 401
graphing
   combined function, 480–481
   end behaviour, 106
   transformed function, 34–35, 37–38
   reflections, 16–17
   stretches, 17–18
   translated, 8–9
Guilloché patterns, 299

H

Heron's formula, 98
hole (in a graph), 447–449
horizontal line test, 47
horizontal stretch, 20–27
horizontal translations, 6–15

Index • MHR **643**

I

image point, 10, 19
   prime, use of, 10
   square root of a function, 84, 85
integral zero theorem, 129–130, 133
interval notation, 21
invariant point, 20, 27, 84
inverse of a function, 44–55
inverse properties, 375
irrational numbers, 382

K

Kleiber's law, 418
Krumbein phi scale, 345, 402

L

laws of logarithms, 394–400
   power law, 394–395
   product law, 394
   quotient law, 394
laws of powers, 394
Leibniz triangle, 544
line of reflection, 18, 19, 20, 27
logarithmic equations, 404–412
logarithmic function, 373–389
logarithmic scales, 370, 399–400
logarithmic spirals, 370, 382
logarithms
   common logarithms, 373
   estimate of value of, 377
   laws of logarithms, 394–400
Lorentz transformations, 4

M

mapping, 7
mapping notation, 7, 66, 67
Moore's law, 346
multiplicity, 138

N

negative angles, 196
Newton's law of cooling, 356
non-rigid transformations, 22
number theory, 119

O

odd-degree polynomial function, 111, 113
odd function, 255
odd integers, 210
one-to-one function, 47
order of the zero or root, 138
order of transformations, 32–38

P

Pascal's triangle, 514, 537–538
Penrose method, 76
period, 223, 227–229
period of a pendulum, 76, 97
periodic functions, 223, 224–225
permutations, 519–524
phase shift, 240, 242
polynomial function
   characteristics, 106–113
   equations, 136–147
   even-degree, 110, 111, 113
   graphs, 106–107, 110–111, 136–147
   long division, 118–123
   modelling with, 145–146
   negative, 137, 140
   odd-degree polynomial function, 111, 113
   positive, 137, 140
   remainder for a factor of a polynomial, 126–127
   x-intercepts, 136–137
   zeros of, 127, 132, 136–137, 138
power law of logarithms, 394–395
product law of logarithms, 394
products of functions, 490–495
Pythagorean identity, 294–295, 317
Pythagorean theorem, 78, 182, 294

Q

quadratic functions
   honeycomb, hexagons in, 106
   inverse of a function, equation of, 50
quotient identities, 291
   with sine and cosine, 305
   substitution, 318
quotient law of logarithms, 394
quotients of functions, 490–495

R

radian, 167–169, 174, 184, 198, 205, 247, 269–270
radical equations, 90–96
   approximate solutions, 93–94
   graphical solutions, 90–96
   single function method, 93
   two function method, 93–94
radical functions, 62–77
   base radical function, 72
   changing parameters, 65
   domain, 63–64, 72
   graphing, 63–68
   inverse, 62
   range, 64, 72

range
   expression of, 21
   maximum values, 82
   minimum values, 82
rational equations
   approximate solutions, 460–462
   with extraneous root, 462–463
   relating roots and x-intercepts, 459–460
rational functions
   applying, 439–441
   comparison of, 437–438
   equations for, 449–450
   graphing, 432–438, 447–451
   with a hole, 447–449
reciprocal identities, 291, 319–320
reciprocal trigonometric ratios, 193–194
reference angle, 170, 194
reflection, 16–31
   combining reflections, 33
   graphing, 16–17
   line of reflection, 18, 19, 20, 27
   logarithmic function, 384–386
   order of transformations, 33
   rigid transformations, 22
   vs. translations, 18
remainder theorem, 123
root
   extraneous roots, 91, 92
   multiplicity, 138
   order of, 138
   polynomial function, 136–137
   radical equations, 91
   rational equations, 459–460, 462–463
rule of 72, 344

S

secant ratio, 193, 196
   see also trigonometric ratios
set notation, 21
simplification of expressions
   difference identities, 301
   double-angle identities, 301, 302
   sum identities, 301
   trigonometric identity, 293–294, 302–303
sine curve, 235
sine function, 196, 224
   difference identities, 300
   graphing, 222–232
   period, 227–229
   periodic functions, 223
   quotient identities, 305
   sine curve, 235
   sinusoidal curve, 223
   sum identities, 299–300

sine tables, 225
sinusoidal curve, 223
sinusoidal functions
   amplitude, 225–227
   graphing, 240–248
   period, 229
   transformations, 238–249
Snell's law of refraction, 212, 315
square root of a function, 78–85
   comparison of calculation of y values, 80
   comparison of function and its square root, 79, 80–81
   domain, 81–83
   graphing, 84–85
   range, 81–83
Square Root Spiral, 77
Stirling's formula, 544
stretch, 16–31
sum identities, 300
sums of functions, 476–482
synthetic division, 122

T

tangent function, 196, 256–262
   asymptotes, 259, 260
   difference identities, 300, 304
   graphing, 256–258, 259–260
   modelling a problem, 260–261
   slope of terminal arm, 257–258
   sum identities, 300
   tangent ratio, 258
   undefined, 260
Torricelli's law, 101
transformation
   amplitude of a sine function, 226
   combining transformations, 32–38
   equation of transformed function, 25–27
   equation of transformed function graph, 37–38
   exponential functions, 346–354
   general transformation model, 34
   logarithmic function, 383–389
   order of transformations, 32–38
   polynomial function, graphing, 143–144
   radical functions, 65–68
   rational functions, 434–435
   stretches, 20–27
   translations, 6–15
translated graph, 8–9
translation
   combining translations, 33

   equation of translated function, 10–12
   horizontal and vertical translations, 6–15
   logarithmic function, 385–387
   order of transformations, 33
   phase shift, 240, 242
   translated graph, 8–9
   vertical displacement, 240, 242
trigonometric equations, 206–211
   algebraic solution, 268, 270
   notation, 206, 207
   points of intersection, 269–270
   reciprocal identities, 319–320
   solving, 207–210, 268–270, 316–320
   square root principles, 209
   zeros of the function, 269
trigonometric functions
   amplitude (of a sinusoidal function), 225–227
   circular, 223
   equations, 266–274
   graphing sine and cosine functions, 222–232
   period, 223, 227–229
   periodicity, 266, 267
   sinusoidal functions, transformations of, 238–249
   solution of trigonometric equation, 268–270
   tangent function, 196, 256–262
trigonometric identity
   difference identities, 299–305
   double-angle identities, 299–305, 311
   exact trigonometric values for angles, 304–305
   proving identities, 309–313
   Pythagorean identity, 294–295, 317
   quotient identities, 291
   quotient identity substitution, 318
   reciprocal identities, 291, 319–320
   sum identities, 299–305
   verification vs. proof, 310–311
trigonometric ratios, 191–201
   for angles in unit circle, 193–194
   approximate values of angles, 197–200
   approximate values of trigonometric functions, 195–197
   cosecant ratio, 193, 196
   cotangent ratio, 193, 196
   exact values, 194–195

   negative angles, 196
   reciprocal trigonometric ratios, 193–194
   secant ratio, 193, 196
   and unit circle, 191–192, 193–194
trigonometry
   angles and angle measure, 166–175
   trigonometric equations, 206–211
Tsiolkovsky rocket equation, 402

U

unit circle, 180–186
   arc length, and angle measure in radians, 184
   coordinates for points of, 183
   equation of circle centred at origin, 182
   multiples of $\frac{\pi}{3}$, 184–185
   trigonometric functions, 223
   trigonometric ratios, 191–194

V

vertical displacement, 240, 242
vertical line test, 47
vertical stretch, 20–27
vertical translations, 6–15

W

Wheel of Theodorus, 77

X

x-intercepts, 9, 91
   polynomial function, 136–137
   rational equations, 459–460

Y

y-intercepts, 9
Yang Hui's triangle, 537

Z

zero
   integral zero theorem, 129–130, 133
   of multiplicity, 138
   order of, 138
   polynomiography, 137
   zero product property, 317
   zeros of the function, 269
   zeros of the polynomial function, 127, 132, 136–137, 138

Credits

Photo Credits

Page v Mervyn Rees/Alamy; **vi** top GIPhotoStock/Photo Researchers, Inc., Steven Foley/iStock, Sheila Terry/Photo Researchers, Inc., Taily/Shutterstock, NASA, bottom, top left clockwise images.com/Corbis, George Hall/Corbis, Pat Canova/All Canada Photos, bottom right Photo courtesy of INRS (Institut national de la recherche scientifique); **vii** florintt/iStock; **pp2–3** left clockwise Dmitry Naumov/iStock, PhotoDisc/Getty, NASA, Luis Carlos Torres/iStock, bottom right Photo courtesy of Simone McLeod; **pp4–5** top left clockwise mathieukor/iStock, Charles Shug/iStock, Ajayclicks/All Canada Photos, overlay Bill Ivy, bottom right Public Domain/wiki; **p6** Bill Ivy; **p14** top Tony Lilley/All Canada Photos, Bill Ivy; **p15** Twildlife/dreamstime; **p16** Robert Estall Photo Agency/All Canada Photos; **p30** left European Space Agency, Howard Sayer/All Canada Photos; **p32** imagebroker/All Canada Photos; **p42** left David Wall/All Canada Photos, Bracelet created by Kathy Anderson. Photo courtesy of Kathy Anderson and Diana Passmore; **p43** B. Lowry/IVY IMAGES; **p44** Masterfile; **pp60-61** top left clockwise P.A. Lawrence LLC/All Canada Photos, Mike Agliolo/Photo Researchers, Inc., Agnieszka Gaul/iStock, NASA, bottom right USGS; **p62** top Steven Allan/iStock, Science Source/Photo Researchers, Inc.; **p71** Jeff McIntosh/The Canadian Press; **p73** brenton west/All Canada Photos; **p74** Radius/All Canada Photos; **p78** J. DeVisser/IVY IMAGES; **p88** Sherman Hines/Masterfile; **p89** top David Tanaka, Dan Lee/Shutterstock; **p90** Dreamframer/iStock; **p95** Top Thrill Dragster Photo courtesy of Cedar Point Sandusky, Ohio; **p98** Saskia Zegwaard/ iStock; **p101** David Tanaka; **p103** David Tanaka; **pp104–105** left Creative Commons License, iStock, ilker canikligil/Shutterstock, james boulette/iStock, bottom right Rad3 Communications; **p106** florintt/iStock; **p115** left Christian Waldegger/iStock, Mark Rose/iStock; **p117** left 36clicks/iStock, Masterfile; **p118** David Tanaka; **p126** David Tanaka; **p131** faraways/iStock; **p134** left Jeff Greenberg/All Canada Photos, Walrus (c.1996) by Mikisiti Saila (Cape Dorset) Photo courtesy of Eric James Soltys/Spirit Wrestler Gallery (Vancouver); **p135** Library of Congress; **p136** top age fotostock/maXx Images.com, Canadian Aviation Hall of Fame. Used by permission of Rosella Bjornson; **p137** Courtesy of Dr. Bahman Kalantari; **p145** Paul Browne/Lone Pine Photo; **p150** left Chris Cheadle/All Canada Photos, B. Lowry/IVY IMAGES; **p151** artist unknown, Photo courtesy of WarkInuit; **p157** top Masterfile, Dan Lee/Shutterstock, David Tanaka, 36clicks/iStock, B. Lowry/IVY IMAGES; **pp162–163** top left clockwise GIPhotoStock/Photo Researchers, Inc., Steven Foley/iStock, Sheila Terry/Photo Researchers, Inc., Taily/Shutterstock, NASA; **pp164–165** left Dency Kane/Beat/Corbis, Courtesy of Suncor, talaj/iStock, Doug Berry/iStock, Dency Kane/Beat/Corbis, Espion/dreamstime, bottom right PhotoStock/Israel/All Canada Photos; **p166** top Schlegelmilch/Corbis, Photos courtesy of Yvonne Welz, The Horse's Hoof, Litchfield Park, Arizona; **p177** Photo courtesy of SkyTrek Adventure Park; **p178** Photo Courtesy of Arne Hodalic; **p180** Major Pix/All Canada Photos; **p189** Engraving from Mechanics Magazine published in London 1824; **p191** top mrfotos/iStock, Masterfile; **p204** Don Farrall/iStock; **p205** Art Resource, N. Y.; **p206** Edward S. Curtis Collection, Library of Congress (ref:3a47179u); **p213** Albert Lozano/iStock; **p215** Morris Mac Matzen/Reuters/Corbis; **p219** Fallsview/dreamstime; **pp220–221** Peter Haigh/All Canada Photos, bottom right mikeuk/iStock; **p222** Paul A.Souders/Corbis; **p223** Photo Researchers, Inc.; **p225** Sheila Terry/Science Photo Library; **p238** top left Lawrence Lawry/Photo Researchers, Inc., MasPix/GetStock, Keren Su/Corbis; **p253** imagebroker/All Canada Photos; **p256** Macduff Everton/Corbis; **p264** Fridmar Damm/Corbis; **p266** rotofrank/iStock; **p277** top left clockwise Canadian Space Agency, Tom McHugh/Photo Researchers, Inc., blickwinkel/Meyers/GetStock; **p278** Kennan Ward/Corbis; **p279** Bayne Stanley/The Canadian Press; **p280** Marc Muench/Corbis; **p281** top Photo by Dinesh Mehta Matharoo Associates, Chuck Rausin/iStock; **p285** Photos Canada; **pp288–289** left clockwise Sean Burges/Mundo Sport Images, J.A. Kraulis/All Canada Photos, Ivy Images, Chris Cheadle/All Canada Photos, Ivy Images, bottom right jabejon/iStock; **p290** top National Cancer Institute/Science Faction/Corbis, CCL/wiki; **p297** top left clockwise Visuals Unlimited/Corbis, M. Keller/IVY IMAGES, Tom Grill/Corbis; **p299** top Interfoto/All Canada Photos, Joel Blit/iStock; **p306** eyebex/iStock; **p308** Christopher Pasatieri/Reuters; **p309** Brian McEntire/iStock; **p314** Daniel Laflor/iStock; **p316** left Mike Bentley/iStock; eddie linssen/All Canada Photos; **p329** Mike Grandmaison/All Canada

Photos; **pp330–331** top left clockwise NASA, background Visual Communications/iStock, all insets 3D4Medical/Photo Researchers, Inc., David Tanaka, bottom right Baris Simsek/iStock; **pp332–333** top left clockwise Gustoimages/Photo Researchers, Inc., Ria Novosti/Science Photo Library, Philippe Psaila/Photo Researchers, Inc., Public Domain/wiki, bottom right Chip Henderson/Monsoon/Photolibrary/Corbis; **p343** Sebastian Kaulitzki/iStock; **p344** Radius Images/maXximages.com; **p345** Public Domain/wiki; **p346** top James King-Holmes/Photo Researchers, Inc., D-Wave Systems Inc.; **p356** BSIP/Photo Researchers, Inc.; **p358** David Tanaka; **p362** Lisa F.Young/Shutterstock; **p368** David Tanaka; **p370** left Science Source/Photo Researchers, Inc.; **pp370–371** background NASA, top left clockwise Nico Smit/iStock, Nicholas Homrich/iStock, Linda Bucklin/iStock, Slawomir Fajer/iStock, bottom right Mauro Fermariello/Photo Researchers, Inc.; **p372** Huntstock, Inc./All Canada Photos; **p378** David Nunuk/All Canada Photos; **p382** CCL/Chris73; **p383** Jom Barber/Shutterstock; **p388** WvdM/Shutterstock; **p389** jack thomas/Alamy; **p392** JMP Stock/Alamy, CCL/wiki; **p398** Petesaloutos/dreamstime; **p401** National Geographic Image Collection/All Canada Photos; **p402** Jack Pfaller/NASA; **p403** Stockbroker xtra/maXximages.com; **p404** David Tanaka; **p410** Mervyn Rees/Alamy; **p411** Paul Horsley/All Canada Photos; **p414** left Joe McDaniel/iStock, Leif Kullman/The Canadian Press; **p417** Blue Magic Photography/iStock; **p418** left The Edmonton Journal, Denis Pepin/iStock; **p421** left Marcel Pelletier/iStock, top right Stockbroker xtra/maXximages.com, Izabela Habur/iStock, Jeremy Hoare/All Canada Photos; **pp426–427** top left clockwise imagebroker/All Canada Photos, Lloyd Sutton/All Canada Photos, Aurora Photos/All Canada Photos, Public Domain/wiki, Jerry Woody from Edmonton Canada, bottom right "The Gateways" Stanley Park by Coast Salish artist Susan A. Point. Photo by Jon Bower/All Canada Photos; **pp428–429** top left clockwise Dave Reede/All Canada Photos, ekash/iStock, National Geographic Image Collection/All Canada Photos, bottom right Chad Johnston/Masterfile; **p430** Don Weixl/All Canada Photos; **p439** g_studio/iStock; **p441** Phil Hoffman/Lone Pine Photos; **p446** imagebroker/All Canada Photos; **p454** Chris Cheadle/All Canada Photos; **p456** Copyright SMART Technologies. All rights reserved; **p457** Jose Luis Pelaez, Inc./Corbis; **p463** Upper Cut Images/Alamy; **p466** Chris Ryan/Alamy; **p469** Photo courtesy of CEDA International Corporation; **pp472–473** top left clockwise images.com/Corbis, George Hall/Corbis, Pat Canova/All Canada Photos, bottom right Photo courtesy of INRS (Institut national de la recherche scientifique); **p474** Berenice Abbott/Photo Researchers, Inc.; **p486** top ray roper/iStock, David Allio/Icon/SMI/Corbis; **p488** John Woods/The Canadian Press; **p497** left Dirk Meissner/The Canadian Press, David Tanaka; **p498** Dennis MacDonald/All Canada Photos, **p499** Dougall Photography/iStock; **p505** CCL/wiki; **p508** Michael Doolittle/All Canada Photos; **pp514–515** Courtesy of the Bill Douglas Centre for the History of Cinema and Popular Culture, University of Exeter, bottom right Ocean/Corbis; **p516** David Tanaka; **p528** EPA/ZhouChao/Corbis; **p530** Adam Kazmierski/iStock; **p535** Courtesy of the artist, George Fagnan; **p536** David Tanaka; **p537** Public Domain/wiki; **p544** New York Public Library Picture Collection/Photo Researchers, Inc.; **p545** left clockwise CCL/Jlrodi, Photo courtesy of Brian Johnston, Photo courtesy of Jos Leys; **p549** left clockwise Copyright SMART Technologies. All rights reserved, Dennis MacDonald/All Canada Photos, Photo courtesy of Brian Johnston, Photo courtesy of Jos Leys

Technical Art

Brad Black, Tom Dart, Dominic Hamer, Kim Hutchinson, Brad Smith, and Adam Wood of First Folio Resource Group, Inc.

PROPERTY OF HARRY AINLAY HIGH SCHOOL

3 0059 00162 793 4